THE NEW TROUSER PRESS RECORD GUIDE

Third Edition

THE NEW TROUSER PRESS RECORD GUIDE

Third Edition

IRA A. ROBBINS, Editor

REGINA JOSKOW, Associate Editor

JIM GREEN and DAVID SHERIDAN, Contributing Editors

COLLIER BOOKS
Macmillan Publishing Company, New York

Collier Books
Macmillan Publishing Company
866 Third Avenue, New York, NY 10022
Collier Macmillan Canada, Inc.

Library of Congress Cataloging-in-Publication Data
The New Trouser Press record guide.
    1. Popular music—Discography. 2. Sound recordings—
Reviews. I. Robbins, Ira A.
ML156.4.P6N48   1989   789.9'13645   88-25821
ISBN 0-02-036370-2

Macmillan books are available at special discounts for bulk purchases
for sales promotions, premiums, fund-raising, or educational use.
For details, contact:

                    Special Sales Director
                    Macmillan Publishing Company
                    866 Third Avenue
                    New York, NY 10022

10 9 8 7 6 5 4 3 2 1

Printed in the United States of America

CONTENTS

PREFACE

This book originated in 1982 as an almost-successful attempt to review all of the significant albums with a direct connection to new wave music—records that either led to or resulted from the 1976-7 upheaval spearheaded by the Sex Pistols, Clash, Ramones, Television, Blondie, etc. ("New wave" later came to be used by some Americans as a designation for watered-down bands who managed a hip style but were presentable enough for radio. To many people, it remains a low-life alternative to the punk essence. In fact, "new wave" was originally used merely as a more general description of bands upsetting the norm in the late-'70s, with the punk designation reserved for a specific sound.)

The first edition, published by Scribners in 1983, was an outgrowth of *Trouser Press*, which regularly reviewed a lot of albums well outside the mainstream. We already had a firm sense of the kind of records the magazine would cover (adventurous, esoteric or grass-rootsy), and thus it was easy to map out the first book's contents along those lines (although we decided not to reprint existing reviews, but to do it all new, from a more current vantage point). As a result, the original book was fairly parochial in scope, essentially reviewing every American or imported rock album we could get hold of that had some connection—even plainly superficial or fraudulent—to a genre that was then fairly well circumscribed.

That first book was fine for what it was, but the ceaseless development and cross-fertilization of styles (not to mention the proliferation of independent label releases in every imaginable idiom) quickly made the focus seem unduly narrow and limited. By the time we got around to a second edition, times had changed. For one thing, *Trouser Press* had ceased publishing in early '84. For another, the music that had once been considered anti-commercial in this country was being given enormous exposure by MTV, where a colorful image and a good interview spiel were adequate antidotes for seemingly unpalatable (to the mass audience) music.

The second edition (Scribners, 1985) broadened the essential concept and abandoned the by-then-outmoded notion of new wave for a more general slice of the musical hemisphere, one that extrapolated stylistically (and genealogically) from the groups covered in the original book. This book was more far-reaching, but it lacked an easily definable aesthetic basis. (No better name suggested itself, so the book was published as *The New Trouser Press Record Guide.* We're still stuck for a new title, so that's where it still stands, four years later.)

A version of this book was first published in the United Kingdom in late 1987 as *The New Music Record & Tape Guide* (Omnibus). It updated and expanded on the 1985 edition, but deleted a lot of internationally obscure bands on American independent labels. In exchange, substantial coverage of reggae, rap, hardcore and African artists was added. That edition has never been distributed in the US.

By official nomenclature, then, this is the third edition. It builds on all of the preceding incarnations, increasing the coverage on every front. Most of what was excised from the British book has been restored, and a smattering of indie metal records (in some cases, a next step for hardcore bands) and new folk music has been added. The update is thorough through early (say April) 1988 and sketchy for a few months more (around July). For the first time, information on compact discs is included to catch up with the spread of that format through new and old albums.

Although there is certainly no unanimity of style guiding the selection process of what artists are included in this edition, there is still an essential standard that underlies the decision-making. Bands and artists that favor experimentation, innovation and self-expression—those who embrace music as something beyond its potential financial or ego-massaging rewards—are, for the most part, the ones who are included. Obviously there's a lot of personal bias in such appraisals, but I'm not going to apologize for that. Generally speaking, musicians who can't be said to have added anything original, fresh or exceptionally entertaining to the culture are ignored here. Money for music is one thing; music made for money is rarely worth critiquing. Readers will undoubtedly disagree with the selection presented here, but that's what makes a horse race. Future editions will, it is hoped, expand the scope even further, incorporating more exotic, international and experimental musics.

ACKNOWLEDGMENTS

First of all, I'd like to extend my gratitude to all the people whose kind and encouraging words convinced me that this book is useful enough to keep updating it as soon as I've forgotten how arduous a project it is. The feedback is enormously gratifying. Greatest thanks are also due to the contributors, all of whom generously did far more than was asked of them in a heartwarming spirit of dedication to the project, regardless of personal sacrifice. Jim Green especially knocked himself out. Art Black and Monica Dee, Bill Ashton, Andy Dunkley (Rockpool), Andrea 'Enthal, Jack Rabid, Wendy Harte and Michael Krumper also went beyond the call of duty in the interest of making this book as complete and accurate as it can be. I am also, as ever, grateful to my family for their support and assistance. Most of all, I'd like to express my deepest gratitude to Regina Joskow for her partnership in this enterprise. Without her work, support and encouragement, this edition would never have existed.

Other people who made an essential contribution of one sort or another: Nick Cucci and Michele Mena (Rough Trade), James Moreland (Leaving Trains), Brenda Kelly (Rough Trade), Randy Crittendon (DB), Nick DeBenedetto (Freuhauf), Lisa Fancher (Frontier), Arthur Levy (Columbia), Philip Turner (Collier), Adam Kaplan (What Goes On), Todd Bisson (Virgin), Tom Cording (Enigma), Howard Wuelfing Jr. (Jem), Sheri Hood (Thirsty Ear), Lisa Markowitz (Epic), Michael Whittaker, Jocelyn Loebl (Relativity), Scott Givens (Combat), Michael Meister (Texas), Geordie Gillespie (Celluloid), Peter Wright (Mute), Patrick Mathé (New Rose), Bruce at Au-go-go, Julianna Raeburn (Nettwerk), Steve Daly (Coyote), Pat Hoed (SST), Fiona Nichols (Flying Nun), Brad Klein (RAS), Joni Solomon (Chameleon), Carrie-Ann Svingen (Rykodisc), Maria Kleinman (Restless), Neil Cooper (ROIR), Greg Shaw (Bomp), Ron Bally (Midnight), Michael Schnapp (SPV), Cary Baker (IRS), Gary Strassburg (Alternative Tentacles), Abbie Kane, Ruth Schwartz (Mordam), Amy Gelman (Twin/Tone), Erik Lindgren, Lenny Sblendorio (Buy Our), Yvonne Garrett (Caroline), Curtis Taang!, Tracey Miller (Profile), Tom Timony (Ralph), Corey Rusk (Touch and Go), Brian Paulson (ESD), Pat Naylor (Blast First), Glenn Morrow, Langdon Faust, Lisa Hayes, Rich Punzi, Don Ireland. And Michael Pietsch for getting this thing going in the first place.

My apologies to those who kindly proffered vinyl by bands we failed to include— time simply ran out. Every effort will be made to get them in the next edition.

This book is dedicated to the fond memory of Joel Webber, a friend whose enthusiasm and dedication played a major role in aiding—in some cases, allowing—the music of many bands it covers to be heard. While working on this edition, many of the names elicited memories of Joel and it struck me just how widely his work and interests have been felt. This book is my inadequate way of gratefully acknowledging his contribution to music and my life.

Ira A. Robbins
New York City
2 August 1988

INTRODUCTION

The format is straightforward: entries are arranged purely alphabetically by the last name of individuals and the first word of group names, with no precedence given to acronyms, abbreviations, numerals, etc. Groups that have taken their collective name from an actual member (even a pseudonymous one) are alphabetized as if they were individuals; fabricated group names that don't refer to a person within the group are treated as band names. (For instance: Brinsley Schwarz is in "S" and Ike Yard is in "I.") Articles are ignored and omitted from headings unless integral to the name or part of a non-English name; bands that get to keep them are alphabetized by them (cf. A Flock of Seagulls) depending on editorial whim. This form of alphabetization is untraditional, but has proven appropriate and functional so far.

Groups that have gone under more than one name (including solo efforts and side-projects) are listed under all the recording names (and cross-referenced as such), but alphabetized under the most recent and/or significant. Every attempt has been made to make it easy and logical to find things quickly, but if an artist's listing isn't where you think it should be, keep looking.

Each heading includes complete album listings (US, UK or whatever else applies without being redundant) through spring 1988, with some listings as late as the fall of 1988. We've included as many EPs as could be uncovered and all of the compact disc information we could find. Some mid-'88 releases that we received too late to review are merely listed for reference without being discussed in the text. Discographies do not reflect deletions and only indicate cassette availability when vinyl does not exist.

In the interests of completeness, discographies occasionally include secondhand information—records we've seen listed in catalogues, reviewed in publications, mentioned in ads. Those records are, of course, not reviewed in this work, merely listed and mentioned in the text if there's reliable information regarding content (compilations, concerts, outtakes, etc.). However, release dates and exact titles of such records are sometimes impossible to determine. In the absence of a firm release date, a "c." indication precedes the year to acknowledge the possibility of error. Every effort was made to resolve such questions, but in some cases we were unable to do so. Any corrections brought to our attention will be incorporated into the next edition.

Albums that have been released on compact disc are noted with a bullet (●) at the end of the heading line. However, the ● indication does not mean that a domestic (US) CD exists or that the CD was issued by the record's original album label, merely that the title has been issued *somewhere* by someone in the format. We've completely sidestepped the question of differences between US, UK and European CD releases because consistently reliable information on that topic is difficult to come by. We've made every attempt to note differences between album and CD releases, although no doubt there are plenty we missed.

Labels are constantly finding old things to put out on CD. Therefore, that information is likely to become outdated very quickly: many records that are not designated as CD-available here may very well become available tomorrow, as there is no rhyme or reason to what's being recycled.

CD-only releases are indicated as [CD] prior to the label; no • follows such listings. In cases where one CD incorporates another listed piece of vinyl, both are marked • regardless of whether a compact disc was issued under that title: if it's on CD, it's on CD.

The heading style has been changed from previous editions. Rather than listing both US and UK label information, only one label is given. Records that have been issued in the US only cite the US label. UK releases are given as (nr/Label Name). Records that have not been released in the US or the UK note a country of origin before the label name: (Fr. New Rose) or (Aus. Au-go-go). Refer to the list of abbreviations for specifics. (An exception: Canadian releases sometimes take precedence over British, so a Canadian label may be indicated on a record that indeed has had a British release.)

The year given in headings is the earliest release date the album was originally issued, anywhere. This occasionally results in confusing anomalies. A record released in the UK in 1985 and in the US a year later will have the US company but the UK date. An effort has been made to treat lengthy gaps as reissues, but consistency in this department is lamentably low.

Reissues are noted by a second date (and new label information, for those records not reissued by the original label). Reissue information may be incomplete, since companies often fail to publicize the reactivation of catalogue material. CD releases of old records are not considered reissues and their release may be utterly unrelated to the original release date indicated.

The "[tape]" notation signifies a cassette-only release. The "EP" designation covers everything from a titled three-song 7-inch to a six-song mini-album, regardless of how a record is billed. There are a few exceptions. Albums with six or fewer long tracks that are clearly full-length LPs are considered as such; 7-inchers with eight or ten tracks are, by the same logic, not albums. Otherwise, anything with six or fewer tracks is an EP here; a 12-inch record with seven or more is an album. Tapes are always considered albums (and cassette singles are therefore excluded). CD singles are for the most part ignored.

Because many entries were updated by people other than the original reviewers, there are multiple bylines. (Bylines appear as lower-case initials at the end of each entry.) Refer to the list of contributors to decode names. Cross-references at the bottom of entries are intended mainly to provide direction to other related entries of interest that may not be obvious, but the text of an entry may also suggest artists worth investigating.

Political note: music critics often refer to "black music" and "white music" as if skin color determined the sound of music one is obliged to make. In the hopes of avoiding the patent racism inherent in such simpleminded generalizing, when those phrases are used here, they're in quotes to stress that a musical style, not a performer's race, is being addressed.

Comments, criticisms, corrections, quibbles, quarrels and kudos are gladly accepted. Please address all correspondence to:

The New Trouser Press Record Guide
c/o Collier Books
866 Third Avenue
New York, NY 10022

THE CONTRIBUTORS

ag	Altricia Gethers
bk	Bud Kliment
cpl	Charles P. Lamey
df	David Fricke
dgs	David Sheridan
ds	Dave Schulps
'e	Andrea 'Enthal
ep	Elizabeth Phillip
gf	Graham Flashner
hd	Harold DeMuir
iar	Ira Robbins
jg	Jim Green
jl	John Leland
jr	Jack Rabid
jw	John Walker
jy	Jon Young
kh	Kathy Haight
ks	Karen Schlosberg
mf	Mark Fleischmann
mp	Michael Pietsch
rg	Richard Gehr
rj	Regina Joskow
rnp	Robert Payes
sg	Steven Grant
si	Scott Isler
tr	Terry Rompers
wk	Wayne King

ABBREVIATIONS

●: also available on compact disc
[CD]: CD-only release
[tape]: cassette-only release
EP: maxi-single, extended-play
    single, mini-album (up to six
    songs)
nr: not released
c.: circa
Aus.: Australian
Bel.: Belgian
Can.: Canadian
Fr.: French
Ger.: German
Hol.: Dutch
Ice.: Icelandic
It.: Italian
Jam.: Jamaican
Jap.: Japanese
Nor.: Norwegian
NZ: New Zealand
Port.: Portuguese
Sp.: Spanish
Sw.: Swiss
UK: British
US: American
DIY: do-it-yourself
aka: also known as

A A A A A A A

ABC

The Lexicon of Love (Mercury) 1982 ●
Beauty Stab (Mercury) 1983 ●
How to Be a . . . Zillionaire! (Mercury)
  1985 ●
Alphabet City (Mercury) 1987 ●

ABC revolves around the talented but often misguided Martin Fry, whose detailed notions of style include, on the quartet's first album, setting his own Ferry/Bowiesque vocals in lustrous pop production (by Trevor Horn) laden with keyboards and strings, mostly to a supple techno-soul disco pulse. He succeeds admirably with "Poison Arrow" and "The Look of Love," but an entire album on the same subject—Fry is stuck in the lexicon's lack-of/loss-of love section—can be a strain. Taken in toto, the melodies seem like retreads, and his attempts at urbane metaphoric wit seem forced.

Fry unexpectedly converted ABC into a rock band for Beauty Stab, making guitar the main instrument on most tracks. Fielding the same core lineup as latter-day Roxy Music (vocals, guitar, sax) and, coincidentally (?), joined by the session bassist and drummer (Alan Spenner and Andy Newmark) used on Flesh + Blood, ABC offers a remarkable impression (discounting Fry's usual howler lyrics) of that band on "That Was Then and This Is Now." ABC makes additional overtures towards Roxyish guitar rock but with little aptitude in direction, identity or grace. Quotes from Bo Diddley, the Move and other rock icons abound, but ABC has no idea how to use them.

Fry and guitarist/keyboardist Mark White then took a long vacation, returning in '85 with Zillionaire!, a mixed bag of sarcasm ("So Hip It Hurts," "Vanity Kills," "How to Be a Millionaire") and sweetness ("Be Near Me") on which the prime new influence is American hip-hop. (Sugar Hill techno-rhythm vet Keith LeBlanc figures prominently on the record.)

ABC returned to its (adopted) roots on Alphabet City, an easygoing, confident modern soul record which draws from various contemporary genres but basks from start to finish in a soothing wash of strings, horns and heavenly background vocals. Fry and White have clearly matured, dropping the arch lyrical humor and self-conscious stylistic adventures to concentrate on painstaking pop craftsmanship. The clear highlight is "When Smokey Sings," a touching and slyly tributary ode to William Robinson, but the remainder of the record is also easily enjoyable. [jg/iar]

ACCELERATORS

Leave My Heart (Dolphin) 1983
The Accelerators (Profile) 1987 ●

One of numerous Southeastern bands nurtured in the Mitch Easter/Don Dixon pop bosom (both play on the quartet's first album; Dixon produced the first and two cuts on the second), North Carolina's Accelerators blend crisp, energetic, well-mannered rock with a little 'billy and some mild R&B to give Leave My Heart just enough grit and soul to make it both memorable and charming. Guitarist/songwriter Gerald Duncan sings pleasantly enough (although more spunk would be an asset); simplicity and restraint make Doug Welchel's drumming noticeably good.

There's even better-sounding guitar rock on The Accelerators' dozen uneven cuts, including a remake of the tuneful "Two Girls in Love" from **Leave My Heart**. Duncan and Welchel are the lineup's only holdovers; new lead guitarist Brad Rice adds excitement and extra vocals to strong, melodic numbers like "Radio," "(Why You) Hang Up on Me" and "Tears." Unfortunately, the band's lyrics are often simpleminded, and a fiery guitar solo can't salvage the ill-conceived funeral-speed cover of "Black Slacks." (A version of Alex Chilton's "The Letter" flies at a brisk clip, but gets them nowhere.) **The Accelerators** has its fine qualities, but still leaves plenty of room for improvement. [iar]

A CERTAIN RATIO

The Graveyard and the Ballroom [tape]
    (nr/Factory) 1979 + 1985
Do the Du EP (Factory) 1980
Blown Away EP (nr/Factory) 1980
To Each . . . (nr/Factory) 1981
Sextet (nr/Factory) 1981
I'd Like to See You Again (nr/Factory) 1982
The Old and the New (nr/Factory) 1985
Force (nr/Factory) 1986
Live in America (nr/Dojo) 1986

Hailing from Manchester and managed by Factory label head Tony Wilson, A Certain Ratio (ACR) use horns and other instruments to play a soulful brand of modern music that has proven significantly influential to many outfits.

The **Graveyard** cassette compiles '79 material—half studio work produced by Martin Hannett, the rest live from their hometown's famed Electric Ballroom. With the subsequent **Do the Du**, an exciting and original post-punk dance record that does ACR proud (check out "Shack Up" for the decay of modern social values), it seemed certain that ACR would quickly join Public Image in the vanguard of the New Rock Left. However, the studied tedium of the band's first full-length album, **To Each . . .** , snuffed the band's early promise, burying itself in dreary rhythms and astonishing self-indulgence. Leader Simon Topping—he of the free-form trumpet that stamped songs like "The Fox" (here on a subdued remake from **Do the Du**)—evidently believed that ACR would fill the gap left by Joy Division. Unfortunately, while Joy Division was at least lyrical in its despair, A Certain Ratio is merely monotonous. **Blown Away** is a three-song 12-inch of non-LP blasts of horns and rhythms.

ACR relocated their energy on **Sextet**, but didn't apply it in the right places. There's

no real focus to the discoid beats and wailing female vocals (Martha Tilson); ACR don't seem especially motivated by the music they're making.

I'd Like to See You Again suffers from Tilson's absence, and stumbles about, evincing self-consciousness and conservatism in place of the previously aggressive experimental attitude.

The Old and the New compilation was originally released with a bonus 45 of "Shack Up." The live album contains renditions of that song as well as such other ACR standards as "The Fox" and "Knife Slits Water." **Force** is an album of new material by this hardy outfit. [gf]

ACT

Too Late at 20 (Hannibal) 1981

Impeccable production gives singer/songwriter Nick Laird-Clowes' controlled passion and the band's tight, tasteful playing a clearly-deserved chance to be heard. Elvis Costello and Tom Petty appear to be the Act's major influences—there are also nods to the Byrds and Springsteen—but the quartet rises above derivation, giving such songs as "Touch and Go" and "The Long Island Sound" indelible emotional authenticity.
[mf]

See also *Dream Academy*.

ACTIFED

Dawn of a Legion EP (nr/Jungle) 1984

Produced by ex-Gen X-er Tony James, this four-song 12-inch pounds out powerful semi-bleak rock with dense guitar noise. Neither awesome nor awful, Actifed (perhaps the only band ever named after a brand of antihistamine) are muscular but undistinguished. [iar]

!ACTION PACT!

Mercury Theatre—on the Air! (nr/Fall Out)
    1983
Survival of the Fattest (nr/Fall Out) 1984

George Cheex—!Action Pact!'s female singer—sounds perenially outraged, terrified and amazed, all at once. She doesn't quite shriek, but comes damn close to it, which makes the four Londoners rather tiresome, especially as their music manages nowhere near the same level of aggression, holding rather to relatively tame medium-speed punk. Lyrics on **Mercury Theatre** are pointedly political, addressing royalty ("Blue Blood"), yellow journalism ("Currant Bun"), racism, etc. Aided by guest saxophone, "London Bouncers" resembles X-Ray Spex a bit; otherwise, these best intentions are barely listenable.

Survival of the Fattest (no one said this lot weren't clever) introduces a new member, Thistles (taking over bass from Dr. Phibes), joining George, Grimly Fiendish and Wild Planet in the lineup. Lyrics are slightly refined and subtler; likewise, the music offers more variety and better playing, but George's artless singing—despite flashes of adequacy—remains the group's undoing. [iar]

ADAM AND THE ANTS
Dirk Wears White Socks (nr/Do It) 1979
 (Epic) 1983
Kings of the Wild Frontier (Epic) 1980 ●
Prince Charming (Epic) 1981 ●
Antmusic EP (nr/Do It) 1982
ADAM ANT
Friend or Foe (Epic) 1982 ●
Strip (Epic) 1983 ●
Vive le Rock (Epic) 1985 ●
Hits (nr/CBS) 1986 ●

When Adam turned up with his Ants on the awful **Jubilee** movie soundtrack in 1978, you'd never have guessed he'd amount to anything. His two cuts were just ordinary meatgrinder punk, like much of the rest of the record. Nor was the ambitious **Dirk Wears White Socks** all that encouraging, despite the considerable effort Adam obviously expended on it. The LP's word-heavy tunes examine sexual excess ("Cleopatra"), bizarre visions ("Day I Met God"), alienation ("Digital Tenderness") and the like. Adam's dour, uncomfortable vocals find compatible backing from his band, which sounds nearly dead and far too slow. It's as if the nastiest portion of **Ziggy Stardust** had come to life full-blown. (After he'd made it big, Adam obtained the rights to the record, remixed and resequenced the tracks, added some early 45 sides and had it reissued with a new cover.)

Adam's old Ants subsequently left for the employ of Malcolm McLaren, transmuting (more or less) into Bow Wow Wow. In their place, Adam recruited drummer/producer Chris Hughes (aka Merrick) and guitarist Marco Pirroni, who proved to be a significant collaborator. A single from this transitional period ("Cartrouble" b/w

"Kick") was later included with three other early tracks on the **Antmusic** EP, issued after his breakthrough.

Adam found his groove with **Kings of the Wild Frontier**. Goodbye heaviness and failure, hello hit parade. Dressed in flamboyant pirate gear, Adam and his merry crew bounce through a delightful program of modern bubblegum with shrewd underpinnings. "Dog Eat Dog" uses the rampaging tribal drums Adam learned from McLaren. "Antmusic" shamelessly self-promotes (as do many of Adam's lyrics) to the accompaniment of an irresistible stop-start melody. The sourness of **Dirk** survives on **Kings**, but there's so much exuberant fun on the surface that it's hard not to have a good time.

Prince Charming is a letdown. Though "Stand and Deliver" offers more percussive entertainment à la "Dog Eat Dog," and the title track is florid melodrama, much of the LP seems forced, ill-tempered and silly. Adam hits bottom on "Ant Rap," an embarrassing rap tune filled with braggadocio.

After dumping the Ants (save Marco), Adam went solo and came up with his neatest LP yet. **Friend or Foe** has a surfeit of energy and plenty of variety. Adam and Marco touch on everything—soul, rockabilly and his usual weightless pop—with convincingly joyful results. Highlights include "Goody Two Shoes" (a spirited, cheeky self-defense) and the Doors' "Hello, I Love You." This may be junk, but it's classy junk.

After that triumph, time for another bad album? No problem! **Strip** is pathetic. Adam's attempt to grow up was recorded at Abba's state-of-the-art studio in Stockholm and features two cuts produced by Phil Collins. By taking a less sensational approach, Adam exposes the weakness of his melodies and the inherent silliness of his sleazoid attitudes. Best suited for emotionally stunted *Playboy* readers.

For the next outing, Adam pulled in his horns and, with the production suss of Tony Visconti, made a big-league pop album even a mother could endure. **Vive le Rock**'s title track is a perfect Electric Light Orchestra send-up; "Rip Down" likewise recalls Marc Bolan. Other songs ("Razor Keen," "Miss Thing") proffer Bolanesque lyrics but suffer from characterless backing. "Apollo 9," a wonderfully gimmicky single (an a cappella version is also included), proves that the old boy's still got it, whatever *it* may be. "Yabba yabba ding ding," indeed!

3

Monsieur Ant has not been singing much lately, instead concentrating his energies on an acting career. So far, his best role was in 1987's stylish *Slamdance*.   [jy/iar]

See also *Bow Wow Wow, Wide Boy Awake*.

KING SUNNY ADÉ AND HIS AFRICAN BEATS
Juju Music (Mango) 1982 ●
Synchro System (Mango) 1983
Aura (Island) 1984

Nigeria's King Sunny Adé came to prominence in Europe and the US in 1982, following a decade spent establishing himself as one of Africa's most prolific and successful pop artists. Almost unanimously embraced by critics (if not consumers) everywhere, he plays juju, a flowing, sonorous musical style which has its origins in the Yoruba people of Nigeria. Adé has made about four dozen albums; only three have so far been released in the US.

Adé's music is almost as formulaic as it is intoxicating. His songs are long (often filling an entire side on African releases) and contain some of the most irresistible grooves anywhere. As many as a half-dozen guitarists and an equal number of percussionists play simple figures to collectively weave an intricate web that serves as background for call-and-response vocals. Within this framework Adé, borrowing from many other cultures, adds his own touches. **Juju Music**, culled from several prior LPs, relies heavily on synthesizers, Hawaiian steel guitars and reggae dub techniques. It is the densest of the three: ghostlike guitars float through one another with near-vocal textures for perhaps as organic a sound as can be produced with electric instruments.

Synchro System is more melodically stripped-down. Percussion dominates, especially the bubbling sound of the talking drum, an African instrument of variable pitch. On **Aura**, Adé sets his pan-cultural sights even further, and the rhythm tracks are almost pure beatbox in style. The vocal harmonies in his work all have a distinctive Latin feel.

Adé has been tagged by many as the heir apparent to Bob Marley as preeminent Third World musical/cultural ambassador to the world. But even with all of Marley's well-earned popularity, he lacked the musicological instincts which enable Adé to incorporate such a wide range of idioms into a truly global pop style. (He and his band are said to listen mostly to country-western while touring the US.) Quite simply, Adé is one of the most captivating and important musical talents anywhere in the world today.   [dgs]

ADICTS
Lunch with the Adicts EP (nr/Dining Out) 1979
Songs of Praise (nr/Dwed Wecords) 1981 (nr/Fall Out) 1986
Sound of Music (nr/Razor) 1982
This Is Your Life (nr/Fall Out) 1985
Smart Alex (nr/Razor) 1985
Bar Room Bop (nr/Fall Out) 1985
Fifth Overture (nr/Fall Out) 1987

Although neither startling nor overly original, this Ipswich glam-punk quartet makes highly enjoyable records that owe more to the Ramones than anyone else. Their image may be lifted directly from *A Clockwork Orange*, but the music on **Songs of Praise** and **Sound of Music**—played hard'n' fast with vicious, thick rhythm guitar—is memorable, definitely teenage and, best of all, fun.

Following the group's 1984 signing (as the AD-X) to Sire, an Adicts retrospective was compiled from 1978–1980 demos, singles and radio sessions. **This Is Your Life** may be poorly annotated but the 15 tracks are musically entertaining. Many of the studio numbers sound like early Clash; the slightly rawer live-in-the-studio takes more resemble prototypical punkers like Chelsea or the Members. If you've never heard the Adicts, this odds-and-ends album is as good a place as any to introduce yourself.

[cpl/iar]

ADOLESCENTS
Adolescents (Frontier) 1981
Brats in Battalions (S.O.S.) 1987
Balboa Fun*Zone (XXX) 1988
RIKK AGNEW
All by Myself (Frontier) 1982

Adolescents is one of the better longplayers to come out of the early Southern California hardcore punk scene. The high-energy Orange County quintet (drawing some of its membership from Agent Orange and Social Distortion) had a crisp, metallic guitar sound and clear, comprehensible vocals. What distinguished their fierce, no-nonsense rock'n' roll was aggression that didn't go so fast to make the band a joke to nonbelievers.

Guitarist Rikk Agnew followed the band's dissolution with a nifty one-man solo album that may not be long on studio sophistication or clever lyrics, but does contain enjoyable punk and loud pop songs played with enough spunk and variety to prove that his budding abilities would not be restrained by any simple genre formula. (Agnew was later part of Christian Death in that awful band's not-so-terrible early days.)

The reformed Adolescents—led by Agnew and original bassist Steve Soto, cowriting the material and trading off lead vocals—issued a new album, **Brats in Battalions**, on their own label in 1987 and returned the following year with **Balboa Fun*Zone**, a lyrically provocative rock record of substantial merit. Agnew sings "Alone Against the World," a strongly cautionary tale about heroin addiction; Soto takes charge on "It's Tattoo Time," a paean to the epidermal art. Even an uncalled-for version of "Instant Karma" receives reverent, intelligent treatment. Topped off with crisp production of the quartet's thick guitar sound, the green-vinyl **Balboa** is an impressively mature record.　　　　　　　　　　　　　　[cpl/iar]

See also *Christian Death*.

ADRENALIN O.D.

Let's Barbeque with Adrenalin O.D. EP (Buy Our) 1983
The Wacky Hi-Jinks of . . . Adrenalin O.D. (Buy Our) 1984
Humungousfungusamongus (Buy Our) 1986
Cruisin' with Elvis in Bigfoot's U.F.O. (Buy Our) 1988

It's always nice to encounter punks with a sense of humor (not to mention last names). Although they got off to a slow start on **Let's Barbeque**—six songs on seven inches recorded in 15 minutes—these New Jerseyites have revealed increasing talent on vinyl and have earned a growing following as a result. The first record's sound is barrel-bottom, but the playing has a nice industrial buzz about it, and creative use of spoken and shouted vocals adds punctuation to the drone.

"Middle-aged Whore" on **Wacky Hi-Jinks** was, as noted on the back cover, "recorded in our underwear." Musically, however, they're no joke, a fact immediately apparent from "A.O.D. vs. Godzilla," the killer stun-guitar instrumental that leads off the album. Unfortunately, muddy production buries mediocre vocals (spewing funny, satiric lyrics) in fuzzy speedrock, leaving incisive numbers like "White Hassle" (alienation at the Castle) and the sketchy "Rock & Roll Gas Station" half of what they might have been.

The improved production of **Humungousfungusamongus**, which opens with another monster movie instrumental ("A.O.D. vs. Son of Godzilla"), allows the warp-speed quartet to vent their wits and expanding musical imagination with greater clarity than ever before. "Fishin' Musician," "Pope on a Rope," "Bugs" and "The Nice Song in the Key of D" put a full-frontal guitar assault to semi-clever lyrics. But A.O.D. has other ideas: "Masterpiece" gives punks their own version of the theme music from PBS's **Masterpiece Theatre** (composed in 1729 by J.J. Mouret!), while "Pizza-n-Beer" changes gears entirely for all-percussion instrumentation. Above-average hardcore for suburban smartasses.

Teaming up with guitarist/producer Daniel Rey (Shrapnel, Ramones, Manitoba's Wild Kingdom), A.O.D. then made an enormous musical leap into the punk-pop mainstream. A neat pre-LP 12-inch ("Theme from an Imaginary Midget Western" b/w "Coffin Cruiser" and Kiss' "Detroit Rock City") revealed the band's new direction—towards clear, medium-speed rock'n'roll—with conviction. Well-played and almost tuneful, the post-hardcore **Cruisin' with Elvis** contains "Theme" and other deadly potshots ("Something About . . . Amy Carter," "Bulemic Food Fight," "Flipside Unclassified") that thunder along with concise, well-recorded energy and the group's characteristic sense of whimsy.　　　　　　[iar]

A DROP IN THE GRAY

Certain Sculptures (Geffen) 1985

The good news about this California-based Scottish-American trio is that they're not as pretentious or as distant as their name. The bad news is they're close to it. Utterly without personality or purpose, the 11 slickly-produced tracks (with titles like "Heartache Feeds Heartache" and "Past Your Frame") blur into one another, with the smooth, modern sound of guitars and keyboards approximating an updated Moody Blues. Except for Dan Phillips' cloyingly over-emotional and gimmicky vocals, these sculptures are faultless to a fault.　　[iar]

ADVERTISING
Jingles (nr/EMI) 1978

Britain's Advertising was a clever young pop quartet with a penchant for quirky but catchy tunes, punny teenager lyrics and the color pink. They had a near brush with chart success via a 45 called "Lipstick" (included on **Jingles**); their failure to win a large following caused an early breakup. This album (produced separately by Andy Arthurs and Kenny Laguna) is chock-a-block with engaging numbers, cheery vocals and snappy, clean playing; the songs (written by guitarists Tot Taylor and Simon Boswell) are literate and charming. Highly recommended to pop fans. Since leaving Advertising, Tot Taylor has recorded under his own name, while Boswell became a producer and formed Live Wire, who made three swell albums.   [iar]

See also *Data, Tot Taylor.*

ADVERTS
Crossing the Red Sea with the Adverts
(nr/Bright) 1978 (nr/Butt) 1982
Cast of Thousands (nr/RCA) 1979
The Peel Sessions EP (nr/Strange Fruit) 1987

When the four Adverts (including female bassist Gaye Advert) debuted on a 1977 Stiff 45 with "One Chord Wonders," the young Londoners could barely play their instruments, but that didn't keep Tim Smith's song from being a witty commentary on earnest incompetence. By the time they re-recorded it for their first LP, the Adverts had acquired just enough proficiency to make a positive difference. In its own way, **Red Sea** is the equal of the first Sex Pistols or Clash LP, a hasty statement that captures an exciting time. Smith's tunes almost all offer a new wrinkle on issues of the day; when they fall into a rut, as in "Bored Teenagers," his breathy, urgent vocals compensate. It's too bad the album didn't include the ghoulishly funny "Gary Gilmore's Eyes," a wicked single about a blind person who receives a transplant from you-know-(but-may-not-remember)-who.

Oddly, **Cast of Thousands** is as feeble as **Red Sea** is vital. Fatigue and depression permeate the LP, suggesting that Smith's muse had made a hasty exit. One need only read the cover quote from 1 John 2:15 to get the picture: "Love not the world, neither the things that are in the world." Pretty punky, huh?

The Adverts' John Peel broadcast session EP was recorded in early 1977 and contains live-in-the-studio run-throughs of all the aforementioned songs plus two others. [jy]

See also *T.V. Smith's Explorers.*

A FLOCK OF SEAGULLS
Telecommunication EP (Jive) 1981
A Flock of Seagulls (Jive) 1982 ●
Listen (Jive) 1983
The Story of a Young Heart (Jive) 1984
Dream Come True (Jive) 1986
Greatest Hits (Jive) 1987 ●

Amid all the talented and adventurous bands of the second Liverpool explosion, A Flock of Seagulls was ironically the first to score a gold record in the US. Led by singer/keyboardist/guitarist Mike Score (he of the ludicrous hairdo) and including his brother Ali on drums, the quartet's first break came when Bill Nelson produced and released a single for them on his own Cocteau label; the 12-inch EP (somewhat different in the UK) includes the title track, also on their debut LP.

Telecommunication has a catchy tune or two, but it wasn't until AFOS entered the studio with producer Mike Howlett and cut **A Flock of Seagulls** that they developed any real style of their own. Relying on guitarist Paul Reynolds' U2-influenced textural wash, distended strains of synthesizer and some fancy studio maneuvers, the band's inadequacies (mainly dumb lyrics and limited conceptual range) fade into the background, overshadowed by listenable, danceable techno-rock that proved to have broad commercial appeal.

Faced with the challenge of following a hugely successful album, the Seagulls' second longplayer was recorded again with Howlett (except for one cut) and hits some real highs. They retreated from gimmicky sci-fi themes (despite the circuit-board cover photo) and found an affecting path in the lushly pretty, languid "Wishing (If I Had a Photograph of You)" and the understated "Nightmares," but fouled out on several boring tracks and "What Am I Supposed to Do," which starts off alright but winds up repeating the title endlessly as the song fades out. Score does the same thing on "(It's Not Me) Talking," but a propulsive synth-dance-beat and some neat sonic maneuvers keep it exciting.

Dispensing with Howlett, **The Story of a Young Heart** is decidedly inferior. The bland romantic ballads on the first side lack character, have tedious vocals and point up the group's finite songwriting skill. "The More You Live, the More You Love" comes closest to creative merit but is plodding and forgettable. The rockier songs on the flipside are marginally better, but can't carry the record on their own. The best effort is the formulaic "Suicide Day," which at least offers a catchy refrain and some emotional intensity. A vain attempt at artistic maturity and sophistication, the real story here is one of overambition at odds with realistic capabilities.

Reynolds left and AFOS made their next record as a trio (augmented by half a dozen different guitarists), with Mike Score producing. Although somewhat short on personality, the almost modestly appointed **Dream Come True** is reasonably listenable, a collection of simpleminded romantic numbers led by the single, "Heartbeat Like a Drum."

[iar]

AFRAID OF MICE

Afraid of Mice (nr/Charisma) 1982

This Liverpool quartet's sole LP is humorless Bowiesque dance-rock, produced by former Bowie collaborator Tony Visconti. Leader Philip Franz Jones, who wrote all but one of the songs, performs on sax, flute and keyboards in addition to providing mannered lead vocals. For all his versatility, Jones' songs are not particularly memorable; the dour, solipsistic views of life and romance he expresses, while fashionable, seem petty and witless. Sophomoric boredom.   [ds]

AFTER THE FIRE

Signs of Change (nr/Rapid) 1978
Laser Love (nr/CBS) 1979
80-F (nr/Epic) 1980
Batteries Not Included (nr/CBS) 1982
ATF (Epic) 1982
Der Kommissar (nr/CBS) 1982

This smart foursome from East London and Essex update traditional Anglo-rock values. Think of the sonic characteristics of Queen, Supertramp, Yes, 10cc and then (before you puke) imagine a composite that's too young, irreverent and modest to get bogged down in excessive soloing and flash for flash's sake, too full of beans to sit still for ponderous epics or pompous pronunciations. That's After the Fire.

Unfortunately, after perking up A&R ears with a do-it-yourself debut LP, the band

was shunted from one producer to another, despite chart action on its first UK CBS 45, "One Rule for You." **Laser Love** and **80-F** display a moderately talented, promising band trying its hand at a number of approaches (even '80s Ventures-cum-guitar'n' synth) with results never less—but rarely more—than decent.

By **Batteries Not Included**, though, the group's obvious melodic capabilities, effervescent playing and frequently tongue-in-cheek attitude were most profitably harnessed by Queen/Sparks producer Mack. Instruments mesh cleverly over a snappy drum line while the harmonies (even football shouts) nicely complete the picture on consistently strong songs.

The last two LPs are compilations. **ATF** stresses more commercial programming; **Der Kommissar** ranges further afield to better results, save the omission of "One Rule for You." Both contain the English-language version of Falco's "Der Kommissar," which was a hit for the group in 1983.   [jg]

AGENT ORANGE

Living in Darkness (Posh Boy) 1981 ●
Bitchin' Summer EP (Posh Boy) 1982
When You Least Expect It . . . EP (Enigma) 1984 + 1987 ●
This Is the Voice (Enigma) 1986 ●

Picture a band that combines the best elements of the Sex Pistols, the Ventures and early Blue Oyster Cult. Got that? Then you've got Agent Orange, a Fullerton, California trio whose style hybridizes surf-twang sounds, smart-metal chops and punky drive. Their debut album, **Living in Darkness**, is a short, concise collection of seven originals (like "Bloodstains") plus an appropriate memory-tweaker: the instrumental classic, "Miserlou." **Bitchin' Summer** further explores the band's enthusiasm for guitar instrumentals while retaining full burn potential.

The four songs on the 1984 EP display relative restraint, subordinating Mike Palm's guitar to a secondary role in favor of his echoed vocals on the pop "It's Up to Me and You." The two instrumentals are likewise less enflamed, although that doesn't stop "Out of Limits" from being great. A tepid cover of the Jefferson Airplane's "Somebody to Love," however, is a total mistake.

Established high enough in the skate-rock pantheon to rate an official band skateboard fans can purchase, Agent Orange issued **This Is the Voice**, a dynamic collection of high-energy vocal numbers that benefit greatly from Daniel Van Patten's crisp electric production. The echo on Palm's strong voice, the lush guitar roar and the stiff-backed power drumming collectively suggest a slight '60s/'80s mod influence, but this impressive outing has a sound all its own. The record steers clear of punk overdrive to stand as Agent Orange's finest and most popular-sounding release yet.   [rnp/iar]

AGE OF CHANCE
Crush Collision EP (Virgin) 1987
One Thousand Years of Trouble (Virgin) 1987 ●

Leeds' Age of Chance dresses up harsh British-beatbox-metal-pop with colorful, vaguely apocalyptic sloganeering. Despite all the shouting, the quartet's biggest problem is the lack of a cohesive identity to match their records' careening sonic stew. The six-track **Crush Collision** is generally shrill and undistinguished, but it does include a pretty decent cover of Prince's "Kiss" (as well as a really awful one of the Trammps' "Disco Inferno").

One Thousand Years of Trouble benefits from being more gimmicky and over-the-top, with *lots* more sampling; even so, an album's worth of this stuff is pretty grating. You'd be better off going no further than Side Two, song one: Age of Chance's insistent UK hit, "Who's Afraid of the Big Bad Noise?" Or skipping the whole thing.   [hd]

RIKK AGNEW
See *Adolescents, Christian Death.*

AGNOSTIC FRONT
Victim in Pain (RatCage) 1984 (Combat Core) 1986 ●
Cause for Alarm (Combat Core) 1986 ●
Liberty & Justice for . . . (Combat) 1987 ●

This pioneering skinhead outfit has been on the New York hardcore scene since the early '80s, debuting with an album of standard-issue punk—fast and blurry, but not absurdly so—with well-intentioned, if simpleminded, lyrics about unity, authority and justice. Roger Miret's an adequate run-of-the-mill shouter; like him, little about **Victim in Pain** is especially distinguished. (Remastering the LP for its 1986 reissue doesn't clear

things up that much; one CD contains both **Victim in Pain** and **Cause for Alarm**.)

Agnostic Front's demi-metal second album has relentless kick-drum sound and a pernicious right-wing outlook. Songs about Bernhard Goetz ("Shoot His Load") and racist resentment of welfare recipients ("Public Assistance") join the typical bonehead detritus about killing, war, youth and the failings of the public education system. The one random moment of lucidity is "Toxic Shock," a protest against dioxin pollution.

Drums and guitars fill up every nanosecond of **Liberty & Justice**, a dull onrushing storm of flailing limbs and incinerating transistors. Bottom heavy and routine to the max, the music is utterly disposable; Miret's vocals dissolve in an incomprehensible hysterical gurgle. Even worse: vague religious references portend troubled waters ahead.   [iar]

JANE AIRE AND THE BELVEDERES
Jane Aire and the Belvederes (nr/Virgin) 1979

Another talented singer from Akron, Ohio whose career really got started outside her homeland. Accompanied here by a sharp four-piece English band otherwise known as the Edge (no, not that Edge), Aire works confidently through a solid set of tunes that includes the oft-recorded "Breaking Down the Walls of Heartache," Pearl Harbor's "Driving," Holland/Dozier/Holland's "Come See About Me," plus some of producer Liam Sternberg's better original compositions.   [iar]

ALARM
The Alarm EP (IRS) 1983
Declaration (IRS) 1984 ●
Strength (IRS) 1985 ●
Eye of the Hurricane (IRS) 1987 ●

If these four young Welshmen weren't so studiedly intense, they might be able to drop the Clash/U2 pretensions and use their evident talent to make enjoyable records. Singer Mike Peters and bassist Eddie MacDonald write catchy, anthemic songs, but the tireless exhortations soon become tiring and, worse, ludicrous.

The Alarm compiles pre-LP UK singles: "The Stand," the first (but not last) pop song based on a Stephen King novel, "Marching On" and three more slices of roughed-up folk-rock. **Declaration** further exploits the

8

pose (and the big haircuts) with a batch of memorable tunes ("Sixty Eight Guns," "Blaze of Glory," "Where Were You Hiding When the Storm Broke?"), all smeared with Peters' melodramatic bawling. The Alarm's got an excess of passion; what they lack is the subtlety that keeps U2 from becoming histrionic.

Mike Howlett produced **Strength** and managed to rein in some of the Alarm's brassiness, slowing them down, focusing Peters' vocals and opening up the sound with dynamics and silence. Keyboards and stronger songs also contribute to the overall improvement, but it's still an Alarm LP. Highlights: the title track, which rips off Billy Idol to amusing effect, and "Spirit of '76," a Springsteenish crypto-ballad about the group's punk roots. Other tracks sound like old Gen X and Mott the Hoople. Weird, but encouraging.

U2's ascendancy to global domination did not pass unnoticed in the Alarm camp, and the dull and disappointing **Eye of the Hurricane** has its share of echoed guitars and sweeping vocal theatrics. (Although, to be fair, most of the songs have too little personality—of any sort—to warrant comparisons.) "Rain in the Summertime," an energetic dance-rocker with a catchy melody, is the album's standout; the oddest piece of inanity here is "Shelter," which mixes Pete Townshend's riff from "The Good's Gone" with lyrics lifted (in part) from various Stones songs. [iar]

ALBANIA
Are You All Mine (nr/Chiswick) 1981

Albania's strength was prolix, interesting lyrics about winning and losing at romance, delivered over multinational-styled rock with guitars, keyboards and saxophone providing the basic sound and K-Y McKay's songs and vocals adding personality. The album's sound stretches from polka to punk—like Deaf School and other demi-theatrical outfits—but it's really the words that made the band. [iar]

WILLIE ALEXANDER AND THE BOOM BOOM BAND
Willie Alexander and the Boom Boom Band (MCA) 1978
Meanwhile . . . Back in the States (MCA) 1979

WILLIE ALEXANDER AND THE CONFESSIONS
Autre Chose (Fr. New Rose) 1982
A Girl Like You (Fr. New Rose) 1982

WILLIE "LOCO" ALEXANDER
Solo Loco (Bomp) 1981
Taxi-Stand Diane EP (Fr. New Rose) 1984
Greatest Hits (nr/New Rose) 1985

WILLIE ALEXANDER
Tap Dancing on My Piano (Fr. New Rose) 1986
The Dragons Are Still Out (Fr. New Rose) 1988

Long-time Boston scene patriarch Alexander is an intriguing figure whose redoubtable three-decade résumé includes such groups as the Lost, Bagatelle, Grass Menagerie—even a stint in the post-Lou Reed Velvet Underground. With countless club gigs under his belt, Alexander's credentials are impressive; unfortunately, his inconsistent records aren't. (The appellation is a tribute to Latin pianist Joe Loco.)

Willie Alexander and the Boom Boom Band is dedicated to Jack Kerouac, and includes the tributary "Kerouac," which was a cult hit when it appeared as an independent single in 1975. The song's a heartfelt standout; the rest of the record is routine bar-band rubbish, wanting for both songs and style. **Meanwhile** follows the same path, but is noticeably better, thanks to Alexander's looser singing. For him, sloppiness is definitely an asset.

Willie left the Boom Boom Band behind for **Solo Loco**, relying instead on his own keyboards and percussion, with some outside guitar assistance. The record is a real departure, using occasional synthesizers to support extended, moody numbers that refer back to his earliest recorded work and a voice that seems at once weary and sanguine. The material is uneven; when it's good, the record shines brightly. (**Solo Loco** was originally released on French New Rose; the American version is slightly different.)

Autre Chose—two disques of live Willie—was recorded in France during a March/April 1982 tour with a new backing trio. The choice of material is eclectic, beginning with "Tennesse [sic] Waltz" performed a cappella and including all of his best (-known) songs, plus some new things.

The Confessions on **A Girl Like You** (recorded in an American studio but unreleased outside France) include a saxophonist, the same bassist and guitarist, but no drummer; Willie (a longtime drummer) picks up the sticks for this effort. Like a low-key version of a '70s Rolling Stones album, there's a little rock'n'roll, a blues number, lots of sex (including the painfully tacky cover image) and some good times. Probably as good as Alexander's going to get, **A Girl Like You** shows various sides of this mature—if limited—performer.

Continuing along his odd Boston-and-Paris path, Alexander recorded a spare album that excludes guitar and rock in favor of keyboards for a bluesy, late-night sound: **Tap Dancing on My Piano** has the loose, funky feel of old friends tinkering in the studio. Basically, Willie accompanies himself on piano with varying amounts of harmonica, sax and drums thrown in for accent. There's nothing here you would call arranged: even the busiest tracks sound like a first rehearsal. The boozy, seemingly extemporaneous "I'm So Lonesome I Could Cry" is a heartwarming highlight; the rest varies from Randy Newmanesque ("The Ballad of Boby Bear") to the bizarre ("Me & Stravinsky Now"). A modest and appealing slice of sincerity.

[iar]

ALIEN SEX FIEND

Who's Been Sleeping in My Brain (Relativity) 1983
Acid Bath (Relativity) 1984
Liquid Head in Tokyo (nr/Anagram) 1985
Maximum Security (nr/Anagram) 1985
I Walk the Line EP (nr/Flicknife) 1986
It (The Album) (nr/Anagram) 1986
"The Impossible Mission" Mini L.P. (PVC) 1987
Here Cum Germs (PVC) 1987
The First Alien Sex Fiend Compact Disc [CD] (nr/Anagram) c. 1987
All Our Yesterdays (nr/Anagram) 1988

Out of the Batcave came Alien Sex Fiend, in a rush of ugly noise. The quartet flails away with all their might and produce nothing of merit on their first album. The moronic slices of morbidity read like Cramps discards; the music never rises above sub-Dead Boys— a glum, muddy mix of identispeed drums, sporadic blurts of guitar and synth and wanky, over-stylized shout-singing. The net result is a headache with a beat and some comic book images that lack humor, drama or impact of any kind. Utterly awful.

Acid Bath doesn't deserve many kind words either, but smarter, sharper production turns the group's basic components into something almost sensual and then bakes on gimmicky effects to further help counteract the inherent miserableness. (The US LP contains an extra track and two alternate versions from the original British issue.)

Recorded as a trio, **Maximum Security** employs tedious electronic percussion, murky guitar noise and little else, making the lengthy tracks unbelievably boring. Thankfully not ear-splitting, it's still too loud to function effectively as a sleeping aid. The cassette of **It (The Album)** contains **Maximum Security** as a bonus.

Largely setting aside their noisy doom mongering for long and haphazardly organized synth meanderings (electronic dance percussion overlaid with bits of music, echoed vocals, tape tricks and sound effects), Nik (Wade) Fiend and his missus issued a pair of overlapping records, **Here Cum Germs** and **The Impossible Mission**. The former was recorded in one 1987 session and contains seven selections; the latter repeats two of those tracks ("The Impossible Mission" and a remix, plus the Crampsy guitar-rock of "My Brain Is in the Cupboard Above the Kitchen Sink," which quotes Alice Cooper), adding four more selections from two other 1986 studio visits. At this point, the band's semi-serious fooling around has ceased to offend and is actually on the verge of being goofy enough to be fun (on a conceptual if not musical basis).

Liquid Head is an unnecessary live album; **All Our Yesterdays** is a compilation of Alien Sex Fiend's first nine 45s. [iar]

ALL

See *Descendents*.

ALLEY CATS

Nightmare City (Time Coast) 1981
Escape from the Planet Earth (MCA) 1982

ZARKONS

Riders in the Long Black Parade (Enigma) 1985
Between the Idea and the Reality . . . Falls the Shadow (Atlantic) 1988 ●

The Alley Cats—Dianne Chai (bass/vocals), Randy Stodola (guitar/vocals) and John McCarthy (drums)—were an early (and longstanding) fixture on the Los Angeles punk scene, churning out loudhardsemifast rock with awful, predictable lyrics. The Alley

Cats' two LPs show some progress—i.e., **Nightmare City** is more samey and less imaginatively produced than **Escape from Planet Earth.** If Stodola's songs were any good, there might be more about these Cats to praise.

Chai and Stodola, joined by a female vocalist and a drummer, resurfaced later in the '80s as the Zarkons, a slick and vapid radio wannabe that is every bit as awful as the Alley Cats ever were, only geometrically more pretentious. Their second LP (title courtesy of T.S. Eliot) begins by ruining the Yardbirds' "Heart Full of Soul" with synth drums and a noxious sax solo and then proceeds to desecrate Dylan Thomas' work by setting one of his poems ("The Hunchback in the Park") to atrocious fake folk music. Beyond contempt.   [iar]

ALLEZ ALLEZ
African Queen (nr/Kamera) 1982
Promises (nr/Virgin) 1982

On **African Queen**, a Belgian sextet with Briton Sarah Osbourne's strong, sure alto voice out front produces lush discoid funk of no great consequence. On **Promises**, aside from more contrast between Osbourne and low-pitched male vocal backing, Allez Allez and their producer (Martyn Ware of Heaven 17) were unable to create anything more than pleasant dance music with unfortunately pretentious lyrics. The group may think this is subtle and elegant art, but the hard truth is that they offer little music to remember and a few phrases best forgotten (e.g., the stuff about "My name is culture . . . her name is the devil").   [jg]

GG ALLIN
Always Was, Is and Always Shall Be
     (Orange) 1980
No Rules EP (Orange) 1983
Live Fast, Die Fast EP (Black & Blue) 1984 +
     1987
Hated in the Nation [tape] (ROIR) 1987
Public Animal #1 EP (Black & Blue) 1987
You Give Love a Bad Name (Homestead)
     1987
Freaks, Faggots, Drunks and Junkies
     (Homestead) 1988

GG ALLIN AND THE SCUMFUCS
Eat My Fuc (Blood) 1984
Hard Candy Cock EP (Blood) 1984
I Wanna Fuck Your Brains Out EP (Blood)
     1985

GG ALLIN AND THE SCUMFUCS/ARTLESS
GG Allin and the Scumfucs/Artless (Ger.
     Starving Missile-Holy War) 1985

New Hampshire professional victim Allin is one of the lewdest, wildest, most sexist ravers of the Iggy/Detroit supercharge school, easily matching the Dead Boys (or, for that matter, Meatmen) at their most unrepentantly obnoxious. He also has more vicious slash'n'burn energy than the Dead Boys ever committed to vinyl, which may be why the sound quality on the 1980 album stinks. Not pretty, but a highly convincing genre exercise.

The relentless obscenity has continued unchecked. On the 1984 **Eat My Fuc** LP, co-produced by—get this—Dick Urine, Allin bawls, hurls foul sexual invective and generally acts like the all-around swell guy he is, conveying real gonzo enthusiasm for his chosen self-abusive work. The Scumfucs blaze along in medium-speed high-octane fashion.

Hated in the Nation is a cassette-only résumé of Allin's worst excesses, supported by various bands of bystanders (including the Scumfucs, one with ex-MC5 members and another with rock writer/Homestead label head Gerard Cosloy). Interrupted only by messages left on Allin's answering machine and abusive onstage patter, the tape is a nonstop juggernaut of puerile mania, demented concupiscence, *Hustler*-level humor and whatever other vileness punk rock's foul-mouthed reply to Morton Downey can throw up. It's hard to describe **Hated in the Nation** as entertainment, but there it is if you want (or need) to hear it.

In this calculated-to-enrage rock style, Allin is the uncontested federation champ. Actually, his lyrical repugnance is a real mistake—if the words—jeez, even the album titles are embarrassing!—weren't so vile, more people might be impressed by the remarkably powerful music.   [jg/iar]

STEVE ALMAAS
See *Beat Rodeo.*

MARC ALMOND
MARC AND THE MAMBAS
"Untitled" (nr/Some Bizzare) 1983
Torment and Toreros (nr/Some Bizzare) 1983

11

MARC ALMOND AND THE WILLING SINNERS

Vermin in Ermine (nr/Some Bizzare) 1984 ●
Tenderness Is a Weakness EP (nr/Some Bizzare) 1984
Stories of Johnny (nr/Some Bizzare) 1985

MARC ALMOND

Mother Fist . . . and Her Five Daughters (nr/Some Bizzare-Virgin) 1987
Singles 1984–1987 (nr/Some Bizzare-Virgin) 1987
The Last and Live (nr/Line) 1987 ●

Leaving the evident confines of Soft Cell behind—during, and subsequent to the dissolution of, his partnership with Dave Ball—singer Marc Almond assembled various associates to be the Mambas on his first two solo albums, both of them double-record sets. **"Untitled"** (an LP plus a three-song 12-inch) is a swell hodgepodge of originals, covers, collaborations and excesses, all sung in Almond's appealing but pitch-poor voice. With Ann Hogan and Matt (the The) Johnson as the main Mambas, Almond ventures into summery soul ("Angels"), ambient balladry ("Big Louise") and obvious source material (Lou Reed's "Caroline Says," Syd Barrett's "Terrapin," Jacques Brel's "If You Go Away"), covering a phenomenal variety of terrain. More an audio sketchbook than a coordinated album, **"Untitled"** is nonetheless a fine excursion outside the techno-pop corridors of Soft Cell.

Torment and Toreros, on the other hand, is a vile and pathetic attempt to ape '30s German cabaret decadence with mostly piano/orchestral backing and calculated-to-shock vulgar lyrics. A sleazy drag that elicits pity and disgust rather than any intended emotional response.

Almond's two subsequent albums with the Willing Sinners are far less offensive, and border on the amusing. He plays his gutter queen persona to the hilt, posing for the cover of **Vermin in Ermine** perched on a garbage can wearing a Liza Minelli spangled jacket and devil's horns. The songs typically reflect Almond's seamy, negativist taste ("Ugly Head," "Tenderness Is a Weakness," "Crime Sublime," "Shining Sinners," etc.), while the Sinners (and sidemen) provide theatrical, often sarcastically caricatured music to accompany his stylized singing. **Vermin** isn't that involving—the jolly presentation works against the grungy intent, leaving a sense of aimlessness rather than artistic ten-

sion. (The cassette has three extra cuts.)

Stories of Johnny is more on track, matching moody, sometimes pretty atmospherics with Almond's disconsolate (but brightening) outlook. The backing sporadically includes slick synthesizer maneuvers, bringing him full circle and proving once again just how important Soft Cell was to developing that instrument's place in pop music. The title track sounds more like a hit single than anything he's recorded since "Tainted Love" without resembling that tune's simple presentation; it's a full-scale Spectorized production number with excellent singing. All told, **Stories of Johnny** is Almond's most enjoyable, least posey or willfully perverse record yet.

The singles compilation offers a complete post-Soft Cell retrospective, including such British 45 tracks as "Stories of Johnny," "Tenderness Is a Weakness" and "This House Is Haunted." [iar]

ALPHAVILLE

Forever Young (Atlantic) 1984
Afternoons in Utopia (Atlantic) 1986

Obnoxious synthesizer rock from a German trio with English vocals making trite hit records for morons. Slickly polished and lyrically vapid ("Big in Japan," "The Jet Set"), Alphaville is at best inconsequential but more frequently overbearingly dumb. The title track of the first album comes within hailing range of a bewitchingly textured Ultravox-like sound; otherwise this insipid fare is utterly resistible. [iar]

ALTER BOYS

Soul Desire (Big Time) 1987 ●

Former Dictator Andy Shernoff may have produced the only LP by New York's Alter Boys, but the group's roots seem closer to two other great erstwhile Gotham bands—Television and the Velvet Underground. The group's two guitarists seem promising enough, but they often seem held back by the relatively stiff rhythm section. The band sounds most comfortable on their best (and most Television-like) number, "One Eye Only," and "Sweet Blossom Mary," which borrows its chorus from "Anarchy in the UK." Depressives may enjoy the more VU-oriented gloom and doom turf of numbers like "Mid-Winter Deathtrip" and "Dry-Out Center." [ds]

ALTERED IMAGES

Happy Birthday (Portrait) 1981
Pinky Blue (Portrait) 1982
Bite (Portrait) 1983
Collected Images (nr/Epic) 1984

Led by baby-voiced singer (and budding film actress) Claire Grogan, this twinky Scottish nuevo pop outfit hit high in the British singles charts with catchy, uncomplicated tunes like "Happy Birthday" and "Dead Pop Stars." Grogan's cutesy-poo vocals, however, are not universally appreciated, and many found the group more precious than charming. Four different producers are credited on the three original albums; they clearly wielded powerful influence on these impressionable youngsters.

The first LP, produced mainly by Banshees bassist Steve Severin, shows no signs of life, except on the Martin Rushent-produced title track. The songs drag along, refusing to make any instrumental impression, relying on the singing, which just isn't enough.

Fortuitously, Rushent produced all of **Pinky Blue**, revealing Altered Images to be a clever dance-pop force. With gleaming, bouncy sound, the songs jump out in classic hit single fashion—"See Those Eyes" and "I Could Be Happy" especially provide the joyous setting that Grogan's voice needs to succeed. (The cover of Neil Diamond's cloying "Song Sung Blue," however, should have been nixed.)

Bite, the band's final album before splitting, is something of a departure. From the mature-young-sophisticate photo of Grogan on the front cover to the lush disco sound—strings, chorus, sax, wah-wah guitar, the works—of "Bring Me Closer," the album foolishly attempts to haul Altered Images out of their adolescent innocence and make them a Scottish Blondie. **Bite** suffers from serious schizophrenia induced by the equal division of production responsibilities between Tony Visconti and Mike Chapman. Visconti's tracks are basically heartless dance numbers—Abba gone funky; Chapman's trespass into the same terrain, but "Change of Heart," "Another Lost Look" and the memorable "Don't Talk to Me About Love" are attractive pop tunes that retain some of the band's winsome charm. (The English cassette release has extra tracks and bonus remixes.) **Collected Images** is a posthumous compilation.   [iar]

See also *Hipsway*.

ALTERNATIVE TV

The Image Has Cracked (nr/Deptford Fun City) 1978
What You See . . . Is What You Are (nr/Deptford Fun City) 1978
Vibing Up the Senile Man (nr/Deptford Fun City) 1979
Live at the Rat Club '77 (nr/Crystal-Red) 1979
Action Time Vision (nr/Deptford Fun City) 1980
Strange Kicks (IRS) 1981
Peep Show (nr/Anagram) 1987

GOOD MISSIONARIES

Fire from Heaven (nr/Deptford Fun City) 1979

MARK PERRY

Snappy Turns (nr/Deptford Fun City) 1981

The hipness and success of London punk-explosion photocopy fanzine *Sniffin' Glue* was almost entirely due to the irreverent, pugnacious sincerity of its founder/sparkplug Mark P(erry). That Perry should form a band seemed a natural progression; that it was any good at all a surprise; that it maintained a stance utterly disdainful of compromise a small miracle. Unfortunately, this musical Diogenes had neither adequate vision nor foresight to avoid the pitfalls of Striving for Artistic Expression.

Live at the Rat Club '77 (an authorized bootleg) consists of messy-sounding live material taped before co-founder/guitarist Alex Fergusson split. (Temporarily replaced by the Police's then-road manager Kim Turner, Fergusson rejoined in time for **Strange Kicks**.) By **The Image Has Cracked**, Perry's urge to experiment was taking intriguing turns (e.g., a half-studio, half-live attempt at meaningful audience participation). Although the abstract stuff doesn't hold up so well, it's still an amazing document of a time and place. The straighter efforts are better: an early Buzzcocks/Clash sock is well-exercised on the band's rousing manifesto, "Action Time Vision." It's also why the compilation of the same name, including non-LP singles sides (through '79) on which Perry's righteously vented spleen is effectively displayed, works better than **Image** as entertainment if not artifact.

What You See . . . Is What You Are is also live, but shared half-and-half with tour partners Here & Now, a horrid hippie offshoot of Gong. Worse (even discounting the tinny sound) still, such disillusion had set in that Perry remade his song as "Action Time Lemon" in sheer disgust. While a move toward edge music could be seen coming—further spurred by Mick Linehan (later in the Lines) replacing Kim Turner—ATV here sounds aimless and desperate. **Vibing Up the Senile Man** was made by Perry and stalwart bassist Dennis Burns; while some of the lyrics are eloquently impassioned, Perry's tuneless vocals ride atop music that's up the pseudo-avant creek without a paddle.

Come 1981, Perry, Burns and the more pop-minded Fergusson reunited (adding a drummer and a keyboard player) for **Strange Kicks**, an album that's a different proposition altogether. The one-time quasi-nihilist says, "What the hey!" and rattles off smart, vernacular humor, easygoing if still reasonably cynical, thereby unifying ATV's snappy romp through an assortment of styles (ska, pop-punk, even electro-dance). Still, "There must be more to life than a heading in a record store."

Perry launched the Good Missionaries, unfortunately nothing special, during one period of ATV's dissolution. This band recalls Frank Zappa at his most self-indulgent; the music meanders without form or reason. Maybe creating this chaos was enjoyable for the people involved (including Henry Badowski), but that doesn't justify its release on record. Perry's subsequent solo outing belies its title by dishing up more of his semi-tortured recitation of what-a-bloody-world-it-is to the tune of . . . well, no recognizable tune at all.

ATV still had some life in it, evidently, as another incarnation surfaced in 1987 and issued **Peep Show**, an all-new album.

[cpl/jg]

See also *Henry Badowski, Psychic TV.*

DAVE ALVIN
Romeo's Escape (Epic) 1987 ●
VARIOUS ARTISTS
Border Radio (Enigma) 1987

Following his long tenure as the Blasters guitar-slinging songwriter, and a brief stay with X, Dave Alvin struck out on his own with the very fine **Romeo's Escape** LP (originally released in the UK as **Every Night About This Time**). In his first try as a lead singer, big Dave won't win any awards, but his hoarse vocals are more expressive than many technically superior vocalists. The contents are familiar roots rock and country,

ranging from scorching boogie ("New Tattoo") to the weary testimony of a union man ("Brother on the Line"). Other highlights include gritty versions of tunes first recorded by the Blasters ("Long White Cadillac") and X ("Fourth of July"). They're less polished here, and plenty persuasive.

The **Border Radio** soundtrack is a decent bunch of odds'n'ends featuring Alvin, Chris D., Green On Red and members of X and Los Lobos. Tony Kinman of Rank and File delivers a nicely lazy version of Dave's title track (which he does on his own LP), Alvin and Steve Berlin contribute ambient instrumentals and so forth. Mainly for completists.

[jy]

See also *Blasters, X.*

PHIL ALVIN
Un"Sung" Stories (Slash) 1986

Without his brother Dave's stirring songs, what on earth will Blasters frontman Phil Alvin sing? Not to worry, 'cause this traditional music buff assembles an enticing lineup of blues, jazz and gospel goodies on his solo debut. Good ol' Phil wraps his homey vocals around such venerable delights as Cab Calloway's "Minnie the Moocher" and "Brother, Can You Spare a Dime?" in this engaging tour of classic styles, making **Un-"Sung" Stories** a delightful history lesson. Sun Ra and the Arkestra even guest on three, nicely complementing Phil with their own loopy charm.

[jy]

See also *Blasters.*

AMBITIOUS LOVERS
See *Arto Lindsay.*

LAURIE ANDERSON ET AL
You're the Guy I Want to Share My Money With (Giorno Poetry Systems) 1981
LAURIE ANDERSON
Big Science (Warner Bros.) 1982 ●
Mister Heartbreak (Warner Bros.) 1984 ●
The United States Live (Warner Bros.) 1984
Home of the Brave (Warner Bros.) 1986 ●

Balanced on a high-wire above the designations "performance art" and "art pop," Laurie Anderson's **Big Science** is perhaps the most brilliant chunk of psychedelia since **Sgt. Pepper.** She combines singsong narrative (often electronically treated) with a strong musical base that evokes, yet postdates, traditional musical forms. **Big Science**, featuring the surprise hit single, "O Superman," is a most enjoyable work of genius. (Anderson had previously appeared on several compilation albums, the most prominent being **You're the Guy I Want to Share My Money With**, a two-record set also featuring John Giorno and patriarch William S. Burroughs.)

Anderson continues merging not-readily-identifiable morsels of '60s psychedelia and '70s progressivism into a blinding studio-perfect maelstrom of oddity on **Mister Heartbreak**, with the help of co-producers Bill Laswell, Roma Baran and Peter Gabriel (who sings on "his" cut). But this excellent record was overshadowed in the year of its release by the five-record (!) **United States Live**, a summation of the state of Anderson's bewildering but popular performance art. Anderson and crew perfomed **United States** whole in London, Zurich and New York, where the Brooklyn Academy of Music, which commissioned the last of its four parts, provided the site (in February 1983) for recording it. Perhaps better suited for videotape, it mixes spoken-word monologues, music and noise (in that order) with snippets of film, slides, lighting and other visual effects that are inevitably lost here. Anderson's impressionistic multimedia portrait of the USA makes a good case for her talents as standup comedian ("There are ten million stories in the naked city, but nobody can remember which is theirs"), yet reveals its miscellany of truths slowly and coolly. Although it's a little like having an artsy friend over who always talks *at,* rather than *to,* you, **United States Live** remains a definitive statement of what a clever artist can get away with—and that's a compliment.

Home of the Brave is the digitally-recorded soundtrack to Anderson's performance film. Joined by an all-star collection of players (Adrian Belew, David Van Tieghem, Nile Rodgers, Bill Laswell), Anderson proffers technically exquisite versions of familiar items as well as new compositions, all imbued with her usual blend of dadaist humor and bemused social criticism.   [jw/mf]

MARK ANDREWS AND THE GENTS
Big Boy (A&M) 1980

Keyboardist Andrews was Joe Jackson's bandmate in Arms & Legs during the latter's formative years in Portsmouth, England.

Funnily enough, shortly after Jackson's initial success, Andrews wound up on the same label, playing a not terribly dissimilar style of music. Unfortunately for him, he's not Jackson's equal as a singer or songwriter. Some may find that **Bad Boy** shares many attributes with **Look Sharp**, though others may wonder why Andrews bothered, since he offers nothing new, except a slow, reggae-tinged version of "Born to Be Wild."   [ds]

ANGELIC UPSTARTS
Teenage Warning (nr/Warner Bros.) 1979
We Gotta Get Out of This Place (nr/WEA) 1980
2,000,000 Voices (nr/EMI) 1981
Live (nr/EMI) 1981
Still from the Heart (nr/EMI) 1982
Reason Why? (nr/Anagram) 1983
Angel Dust (nr/Anagram) 1983
Last Tango in Moscow (nr/Picasso) 1985
Bootlegs and Rarities (nr/Dojo) 1986
Blood on the Terrace (nr/Link) c. 1986
Brighton Bomb (Chameleon) 1987

With the commanding Mensi (Tommy Mensforth) as singer and spokesperson, the Angelic Upstarts came down from Newcastle in 1977 and found a patron in Sham 69's Jimmy Pursey, who produced their first album. Partly responsible for the continued strength of '70s punk in England, it is to the Upstarts' credit that they have avoided the demagogic stupidity of other skinhead bands by maintaining a progressive attitude and speaking out against racism and fascism.

The Upstarts' early records are generally just for fans of loud, fast and not-too-intellectual thrash: similar and predictable in their accented electric rabble-rousing. **Reason Why?**, however, takes a major step forward, blending the Upstarts' social observation/protest lyrics with a controlled and melodic rock attack (broken on the title track with a reggae digression and on the unaccompanied folk ballad, "Geordies Wife") that is punky only in Mensi's unpolished bellow and the band's gang-shouted backing vocals. Otherwise, the guitars build an attractive base—like the Clash on **Give 'Em Enough Rope**—that is embellished by guest sax and keyboards. The songs are competent enough and the production, by guitarist Mond, captures it all with clarity and energy. A surprisingly good record for all rock tastes.

The (old) Clash comparison carries through on the equally listenable **Brighton**

Bomb, which actually contains a song addressed specifically to Strummer. "Joe Where Are You Now?" quotes assorted Clash tunes to make its point about punk traditionalism. As modern electric folksingers, the Upstarts' unprepossessing but palatable musical approach may be excused in consideration of the lyrics' good intentions: simplicity is in direct proportion to the sincerity. Two appropriate non-originals—"Soldier" and Eric Bogle's "Greenfields of France"—show a healthy broadening of scope and a fearless respect for folk music in all its many variants.

Angel Dust, subtitled "The Collected Highs 1978–1983," is a two-record compilation. [tr]

ANGRY SAMOANS

Inside My Brain EP (Bad Trip) 1981 (PVC) 1987
Back from Samoa (Bad Trip) 1982 (PVC) 1987
Yesterday Started Tomorrow EP (PVC) 1987
Gimme Samoa: 31 Garbage-Pit Hits [CD] (PVC) 1987

Hypothetically following in the Dictators tradition at first, this Los Angeles quintet led by an erstwhile rock critic plays self-conscious conceptual punk satire. Unfortunately, the Samoans aren't very funny. **Inside My Brain** does manage to spit out some snickering lyrics on "Get off the Air," a vituperative attack on dj Rodney Bingenheimer, but otherwise offers nothing to get excited about. The brief, well-played songs on **Back from Samoa** have brilliant titles ("My Old Man's a Fatso," "Tuna Taco," "They Saved Hitler's Cock," etc.), but the lyrics are rarely as clever.

Yesterday Started Tomorrow adds a half-dozen terse new items to the catalogue; neither the words nor the plain-issue rock tracks evince effort or imagination beyond the bare essentials. Hardly amateurish, this impersonal recording is adequate only in a technical sense.

The CD-only **Gimme Samoa** takes advantage of the laser format and consolidates the entire contents (31 tracks) of the three aforementioned records on one disc. [iar]

ANGST

Angst EP (Happy Squid) 1983 (SST) 1986
Lite Life (SST) 1985

Mending Wall (SST) 1986
Mystery Spot (SST) 1987

This decade-old Denver-to-San Francisco artpunk trio (brothers Joe Pope and Jon E. Risk, plus drummer Michael Hursey) serves up uncompromising, driving music in a number of directions on their debut EP. They get funky on "Pig," a heartwarmingly old-fashioned song about the law, drone on the junked-out "Another Day" and drive straight ahead on a would-be political anthem, "Die Fighting." Throughout, Angst manage to stay just one step ahead of their pretensions. Credit a sense of humor, exercised at the expense of some great Americans: "Neil Armstrong" is a goofy look at a space cadet; "Nancy" asks, chanting over a drum beat, "Does Nancy perform acts of oral copulation?"

The articulate lyrics on **Lite Life** again prove Angst's prowess for turning politically informed ideas into mature and witty tunes. Plain sound and no-frills arrangements underscore the preeminence of function over form. "I'm Glad I'm Not in Russia," delivered as dust bowl country-rock, is a fairly incisive comment on the cultural divisions between the superpowers; "This Gun's for You," skittish and busy dance-funk, mixes up several topics but stays sharp; personal emotional issues ("Friends," "Turn Away," "Never Going to Apologize") receive the same coldly objective analysis.

Stylistic variety also underpins **Mending Wall,** another dose of Angst's tense and rough-edged musical simplicity, enhanced this time with noticeably stronger vocal harmonies. The lyrics are less specific and more thoughtful; individual alienation, confusion and anomie are transformed into powerful, uniquely directed songs. A cover of Paul Simon's "Richard Cory," however, goes wrong, pruning the melody and bare-bonesing it into an ugly ghost of the original.

Angst took a calculated risk on **Mystery Spot,** engaging producer Vitus Mataré to help them flesh out and upgrade their sound. It almost worked. Multi-tracked guitars and dynamic arrangements bring the songs into near-pop focus, with unprecedented melody, sensitivity, structure and vocal appeal, but atrocious recording quality (and/or a heinously bungled mix) buries them in a flat, muddy swamp. Pope and Risk continue to reveal themselves in emotionally resonant songs—it's a shame their most ambitious effort was spoiled by a technicality. [jl/iar]

16

ANNABELLA

Fever (RCA) 1986 ●

Having recovered from her traumatic youth with Malcolm McLaren and Bow Wow Wow, Annabella's (no last name, please) first solo album is basically high-gloss rubbish, despite the efforts of six very different producers (including Slade's Jim Lea, John Robie and Zeus B. Held). It's not that Annabella can't sing, it's just that here she founders without purpose or personality. Even a cover of Alice Cooper's "School's Out" goes appallingly wrong.   [iar]

ADAM ANT

See *Adam and the Ants*.

ANTHRAX

Fistful of Metal (Megaforce) 1984 ●
Armed and Dangerous EP (Megaforce)
    1985 ●
Spreading the Disease (Megaforce
    Worldwide-Island) 1985 ●
Among the Living (Megaforce
    Worldwide-Island) 1987 ●
I'm the Man EP (Megaforce
    Worldwide-Island) 1987 ●

Disproving the conventional wisdom that New York bands were too cool to play heavy metal, Anthrax abandoned the hardcore scene early enough to get in on the ground floor of the underground movement that eventually spawned such estimable headbanging ensembles as Megadeth and Metallica. The quintet's debut, **Fistful of Metal**, is fast and furious, but not overbearingly so, holding to a near-rock sound punctuated by dizzying guitar solos. Singer Neil Turbin has a good strong voice but lets fly with stereotypical falsetto howls far too often for adult audio comfort.

Bassist Dan Lilker and Turbin were subsequently replaced. (The former went on to form Nuclear Assault.) The **Armed and Dangerous** mini-LP unveiled the new lineup on five unassuming cuts: a pair of studio previews for **Spreading the Disease**, two live renditions of songs from the previous LP and a reverent, hard-hitting version of the Sex Pistols' "God Save the Queen." The album that followed is, all things considered, much better, a scalding assault that reasserts the band's punk bearings with chunky chords, reasonable tempos and characteristic vocals.

The back cover of **Among the Living**, co-produced by Eddie Kramer, shows Anthrax looking relaxed in a New York subway station, wearing sneakers, jeans and leather jackets. The band's best record likewise avoids old-fashioned metal clichés, focusing instead on a bottom-heavy arena-scaled demi-hardcore approach that shifts tempos like crazy and has great gang-shouted lyrics. Besides "Caught in a Mosh," two songs based on Stephen King prose and one inspired by a British comic character, Anthrax trots out a bit of common Bronx street slang to humorous effect in "Efilnikufesin (N.F.L.)," while using the word "dissin" in "Indians." An entirely different sort of post-metal record that is uniquely New York.

Anthrax's merry cross-cultural adventure stretches even further afield on **I'm the Man**, a six-cut EP with three versions—"Censored," "Def Uncensored" and "Extremely Def Ill Uncensored"—of the hysterical Beasties-styled rap-rocking title track. The EP also contains live takes of "Caught in a Mosh" and "I Am the Law," plus a convincing remake of "Sabbath Bloody Sabbath." An expert mix of serious and silly that works on a bunch of different levels, **I'm the Man** clearly proves that this increasingly inventive and witty band refuses to be stuck in any musical compartment.   [iar]

ANTIETAM

Antietam (Homestead) 1985
Music from Elba (Homestead) 1986

Named after an 1862 Civil War battle, this politically-minded quartet from Kentucky (now resettled in New York) rushes madly through raucous neo-popland on its first album. Guitarist Tara Key's strident voice clashes with her three male bandmates' (everybody sings), obliterating intelligent lyrics and potentially nice melodies in the fray. Michael Weinert's clumsy drumming never finds the same beat as the others; occasional flashes of mellifluous invention (this is, after all, pop music) suggest what Antietam might accomplish if they spent some time practicing.

A new drummer, more coordinated playing and moderated tempos all make **Music from Elba** a big improvement, although the LP's appeal is still limited by discordant dual vocals—think of X's worst moments—and dull songwriting. Danna Pentes of Fetchin Bones guests on violin.   [iar]

ANTI-NOWHERE LEAGUE

Anti-Nowhere League EP (WXYZ) 1982
We Are . . . the League (WXYZ) 1982 (nr/ID)
1984
Live in Yugoslavia (nr/ID) 1983
Long Live the League (nr/ABC) 1985
The Perfect Crime (GWR-Profile) 1987

At first, it was awfully hard to take this cartoonish punk quartet seriously. The songwriting team of Animal (Nick Karmer) and Magoo penned irate diatribes aimed at what they call the "nowheres" of the world: straights, nine-to-fives, etc. Although one can't doubt them when they spit "I Hate . . . People," they do manage to inject a sense of humor on the first album, which can soften even the most potentially offensive song, such as the ragingly misogynist "Woman." And anyone who doubts their ingenuity should listen to the blazing (but surprisingly appropriate) treatment of Ralph McTell's folkie chestnut, "Streets of London." (That number also appears on the prior American EP, joined by two other tunes from the album and a bonus cut.)

The live album was indeed recorded in Tito-land, in April 1983, and features a full program of the band's repertoire, including "I Hate People," "Woman," "We Are the League," "Streets of London" and "Let's Break the Law." The Zagreb audience is surprisingly enthusiastic as the quartet puts on a no-holds-barred rock show, captured in trebly but adequately clear sound.

Four years later, the League has evidently decided to try a new approach—or two. Like an '80s rock jukebox gone out of control, tracks on **The Perfect Crime** imitate Big Country, the Stranglers, Alarm, Buzzcocks and others, with surprisingly good results. "(I Don't Believe) This Is My England," which actually doesn't sound like anybody, is a touchingly anthemic folk ballad that couldn't be further from punk. Overall, the album boasts reasonably sturdy melodies, intelligent and positive-minded political lyrics—a likable new chapter in this unlikely saga.

Long Live the League is a compilation of outtakes and remixes.   [ks/iar]

ANTI-PASTI

The Last Call (Shatter) 1981
Caution in the Wind (nr/Rondelet) 1982
Anti-Pasti (nr/Rondelet) 1983

These five young Britons pound out loud and angry punk with a message—against war, nuclear testing, espionage, the army, Thatcher and the like. The playing is solid and straightforward; the songs may be simple, but at least they're songs, not merely riffs. Their lyrics, though rudimentary, are better than some of the competition's.

The Last Call is too typical of the genre to merit any serious notice. **Caution in the Wind**, which borrows liberally from the Clash's early stylings, is a much better record, employing three-dimensional arrangements that expand on the band's subtler assets without losing any power. The third album is a compilation of singles.   [iar]

ANY THREE INITIALS

See *Flipper*.

ANY TROUBLE

Where Are All the Nice Girls? (Stiff) 1980
Live and Alive EP (Stiff) 1980
Wheels in Motion (Stiff) 1981
Any Trouble (EMI America) 1983
Wrong End of the Race (EMI America) 1984

CLIVE GREGSON

Strange Persuasions (nr/Demon) 1985

CLIVE GREGSON AND CHRISTINE COLLISTER

Home and Away (Cooking Vinyl-Flying Fish)
1987
Mischief (Rhino) 1988

Stiff Records had great commercial hopes for this Manchester quartet, led by balding, bespectacled singer/guitarist/pianist Clive Gregson, whose songs—mostly about the unhappy side of love—have always shown real talent. It unfortunately took the group a long time to escape their basic facelessness and locate a sound, a slow start that may be why Any Trouble ended without ever receiving the acclaim they deserved.

The first LP suffers from (reasonable) comparisons to early Elvis Costello, and shows Any Trouble to be a pub band five years after the end of that era, playing competent, melodic rock with no special character. Only "The Hurt" and the stunningly derivative "Second Choice" (a retread of "Less than Zero") leave any lasting impression beyond overall nice-guy swellness.

Live and Alive, recorded onstage in London, includes both aforementioned songs and a rendition of Bruce Springsteen's "Growing Up" (shades of Greg Kihn). The band shows a helpful increase in spunk and velocity, but still falls short of being exciting.

Wheels in Motion, produced by Mike Howlett (later a hitmaker for A Flock of Seagulls), evinces further improvement, adding impressive intricacy and dynamics to the arrangements. Gregson's growing confidence as a singer helps put across his pessimistic (but not cynical) lyrics on songs like "Trouble with Love," "Another Heartache" and the album's standout, "Walking in Chains." **Wheels in Motion** still isn't a record to make you stop in your tracks, but nonetheless a likable collection of intelligently written rock songs performed ably and without pretense.

Any Trouble, by a half-new lineup, is the band's first great album, a wonderful new blend of soul and pop strengthened by Gregson's sharpening melodic sense and lightening lyrical outlook. "Please Don't Stop," "Man of the Moment," "Northern Soul" and other tracks resemble a non-obnoxious Hall and Oates crossed with Costello and recorded in Motown; production by David Kershenbaum provides the sonic variety and sophistication previously lacking. Gregson's development into a powerful, sensitive singer is merely the icing on the cake.

The group inexplicably re-recorded three early (and not timeless) songs for **Wrong End of the Race**, adding a rousing cover of "Baby Now That I've Found You," and a bunch of new Gregson compositions. Featuring an illustrious cast of guests (Richard Thompson, Billy Bremner, Geoff Muldaur), the LP is less stylized than its remarkable predecessor, but bristles with renewed vigor and rich horn-and-vocal-filled arrangements. Without fanfare, that was the end of Any Trouble.

Gregson's first solo record, with minimal outside contributions on drums, horns and backing voices, is a one-man show that plainly lays out its author's heartbreak and pain. In "Summer Rain," the record's centerpiece, he questions the wisdom of a court decision which evidently cost him the custody of a son; elsewhere he limns love lost and mistakes made with self-critical resignation. Over simple music that is attractive and effective, Gregson sings with pride and dignity, making this a deeply moving document of sincere, honest emotions translated into song.

The folky **Home and Away**, recorded at a handful of acoustic 1986 gigs and chez Gregson, features vocalist Christine Collister, a guest on **Strange Persuasion** who, like Gregson, has toured and recorded with Richard Thompson. Her deep, strong voice blends nicely with his on a broad assortment of originals (Any Trouble material like "Northern Soul" and "All the Time in the World," as well as tunes from **Strange Persuasion**) and classics (Merle Haggard's "Mama Tried," Carl Perkins' "Matchbox," Larry Williams' "Slow Down") that is as warmly likable as it is unaffected. [iar]

APB
Something to Believe In (Link) 1985
Cure for the Blues (Link) 1986
Missing You Already (Link) 1987

A popular component of Scotland's neo-funk movement, Aberdeen's five-man APB found a friend in American college radio, where their records have been very well-received. **Something to Believe In** is a compilation of singles—some effectively claustrophobic and offbeat, others trite and obnoxious. **Cure for the Blues** is a fine album of new tunes (not all in the band's basic mold—"Part of the Deal" is light pop that resembles Aztec Camera). Iain Slater's pressure-funk bass and mildly adenoidal vocals drive the dance songs, leaving the rest of the band to play a subsidiary role. [iar]

A POPULAR HISTORY OF SIGNS
A Popular History of Signs EP (Wax Trax!) 1984
Comrades (nr/Jungle) 1985
Taste (nr/Jungle) 1987
England in the Rain EP (nr/Jungle) 1988

This quartet plays generally boring arty dance music that is variously chilly, funky, humorless and clever. Save for a few exceptions on Side Two, the poorly structured songs on **Comrades** typically work one groove for several minutes and then fade out with the vocals still going. Despite the nicely spare arrangements, provocative subject matter ("Lenin," for instance), crystalline production and flawless playing, this is mighty boring, suited only for utilitarian club play.

The eponymous American 12-inch consists of four tracks from pre-**Comrades** British singles that sound like bad O.M.D. Ministry's Al Jourgensen remixed "Ladder Jack" and "House" for the occasion, making them longer and heavier. [iar]

ARCADIA
See *Duran Duran.*

19

JOAN ARMATRADING

Whatever's for Us (nr/Cube) 1972 (A&M) 1973
Back to the Night (A&M) 1975
Joan Armatrading (A&M) 1976 ●
Show Some Emotion (A&M) 1977 ●
To the Limit (A&M) 1978
Steppin' Out (A&M) 1979
How Cruel EP (A&M) 1979
Me Myself I (A&M) 1980
Walk Under Ladders (A&M) 1981 ●
The Key (A&M) 1983 ●
Track Record (A&M) 1983 ●
Secret Secrets (A&M) 1985 ●
Sleight of Hand (A&M) 1986 ●
The Shouting Stage (A&M) 1988 ●

For over 15 years, singer/guitarist/song-writer Joan Armatrading—born in the West Indies and raised in Birmingham, England—has been making records of warm, emotionally resonant music that has earned her a devoted following on at least two continents. Despite brushes with chart stardom, Armatrading remains an independently-minded cult star whose remarkable and individual voice, regardless of her albums' assorted settings, never wavers. In recent years, newcomers like Suzanne Vega (the two share a label) and Tracy Chapman (the two seemingly share one voice) have found success holding to much the same folk-based traditions as Armatrading, underlining the latter's great creative achievements by following in her path.

Whatever's for Us, produced by Gus Dudgeon between Elton John albums, was a collaborative effort with lyricist Pam Nestor; on her own, with Dada/Vinegar Joe member Pete Gage at the helm, **Back to the Night** proved equally uncommercial. She then teamed up with Glyn Johns, who brought in ex-Fairport Convention backing musicians, for **Joan Armatrading**, an extraordinarily thoughtful and moving album that contains "Down to Zero" and "Love and Affection," two of her most enduring and powerful compositions.

The intimate, upbeat **Show Some Emotion** is warm and lovely, an unaffected, casual-sounding album of songs that, if not among her best, are more than presentable and occasionally captivating. Armatrading stuck with Johns for that LP as well as the subsequent **To the Limit** and **Steppin' Out**, taken from American live performances.

Me Myself I was produced by Richard Gottehrer and performed by a stellar cast of Anglo-American rock musicians (including Chris Spedding, Clarence Clemons, Danny Federici and three current members of David Letterman's band). Even in this all-electric setting, Armatrading and her songs hold up nicely. "Me Myself I" is brilliant, a chillingly beautiful declaration of independence with a memorable pop melody; the rest of the record explores the vagaries of love while it percolates with energy, grace and sensitivity.

Steve Lillywhite took the production reins for **Walk Under Ladders**, engaging a fascinating selection of players—XTC's Andy Partridge, King Crimsonites Tony Levin and Mel Collins, Sly and Robbie and Thomas Dolby. Although the stylized results shortchange Joan's personality a bit, successful numbers like "I Wanna Hold You" and "At the Hop" affirm her courageous desire to explore uncharted areas.

The Key is Armatrading's most commercially-geared record to date, a slick package that employs many of the same players as **Walk Under Ladders** to recapture the potent melodic pop elements of **Me Myself I**. "(I Love It When You) Call Me Names" is a spectacular should-have-been-a-hit single with spectacular multi-tracked harmonies and a hair-raising Adrian Belew guitar solo. "The Game of Love" has an Edge-like echoed guitar sound and a memorable chorus. Motels starmaker Val Garay produced the bristling "Drop the Pilot" (Lillywhite did all but one other track) with loud power chords and a stomping backbeat; although spoiled by ill-advised synths, "I Love My Baby" ends the record with a tender lullaby.

Track Record basically compiles popular songs from six prior records, but also includes a pair of previously non-LP items: "Frustration" and "Heaven."

Secret Secrets is Armatrading's admission of pain and suffering. In "Persona Grata" she announces, "I'm your whipping boy," adding "I'm in love with you" in a resigned, grim tone. "Love by You" and "Friends Not Lovers" mourn the end of a relationship with tragic depth. In "Strange," she realizes "I am not missing you"; other songs ("Moves," "One Night") allow more hope to shine through the tears. Pino Paladino's inimitable fretless bass provides the most notable instrumental characteristic; the sophisticated modern backing is otherwise a bit faceless. (Although "Moves" is a notable exception.)

Armatrading produced **Sleight of Hand,** using just a drummer, bassist and keyboardist (with a few minor guest contributions). She acquits herself well, both on guitar and behind the board, with songs that suggest more personal happiness and stability than **Secret Secrets**. Without falling into any easily identifiable musical department, **Sleight of Hand** has only fascinating sounds, able songwriting and the peerless performing talents of Ms. A to recommend it. Not bad.

[iar]

ARMOURY SHOW
Waiting for the Floods (EMI America) 1985
RICHARD JOBSON
The Ballad of Etiquette (nr/Cocteau) 1981

It's nice to see musicians with the courage of their convictions. After turning the Skids into a joke with his absurd pretensions, Richard Jobson pursued an effete career of poetry and preciousness, allying himself with assorted artsy types. Meanwhile, his onetime bandmate Stuart Adamson got on with Big Country, turning the Skids' anthemic Scottishness into a salable guitar-rock commodity. Jobbo ultimately abandoned his worthless posing and—with Russell Webb (ex-Skids), John McGeoch and John Doyle (both ex-Magazine)—formed the Armoury Show, whose resemblance to Big Country didn't escape notice. **Waiting for the Floods** is not a bad album, it's just a shame Jobson had to take such a long way 'round to get back to where he started.

Released the same year as the Skids ended, Jobson's first solo album, **The Ballad of Etiquette,** was a collaboration with Virginia Astley, John McGeoch and someone named Josephine. The LP, released on Bill Nelson's Cocteau label, consists of the would-be poet's recitations over lovely music, some of it adapted from pieces by Debussy and Britten. Piano, clarinet, flute, sax and guitar provide a much more enticing component than Jobson's unpleasantly accented readings. [iar]

KEVIN ARMSTRONG
See *Local Heroes SW9.*

ART & LANGUAGE
See *Red Crayola.*

ART BEARS
See *Henry Cow.*

ART OF NOISE
Into Battle with the Art of Noise EP
(ZTT-Island) 1983
(Who's Afraid of?) the Art of Noise!
(ZTT-Island) 1984
In Visible Silence (China-Chrysalis) 1986 ●
Re-works of Art of Noise (China-Chrysalis)
1986 ●
In No Sense? Nonsense! (China-Chrysalis)
1987 ●

Originally a pop producer's idea of nouveau hip-hop instrumentals, the Art of Noise—a brilliant meld of studio/tape wizardry, floor-shaking dance percussion and unabashedly adventurous audio experimentation—has turned into a hardy, self-sufficient organization with a distinctive creative outlook. The post-rock group began as a semi-anonymous studio band directed by Trevor Horn, who put out their records as an art statement on his Zang Tuum Tumb label between editing Frankie Goes to Hollywood remixes. **Into Battle** has the aptly-named "Beat Box," with choral vocals and crazy effects (including, repeatedly, a car starting) punctuating typically booming electronic drums. But it also has far lighter essays: "The Army Now," with cut-up Andrews Sisters-style vocals, and "Moments in Love," an obsequious, lush backing track (for Barry White, perhaps?) that goes nowhere for an unconscionably long time. Produced to some incomprehensible blueprint, bits from one track often turn up in the midst of another.

The full-length **Who's Afraid of?** album contains some of the same cuts, but most notably adds the brilliant "Close (to the Edit)," a furious and unforgettable march of highly organized rhythm, effects and jagged musical and vocal ejaculations. Elsewhere, spoken-word collages mingle with the disjointed assemblages to create newsreel-inflected dance music of enormous vitality and originality. Remarkable and significant, with an electronic language all its own.

Proving their autonomy, the heart of Art of Noise—Anne Dudley, J.J. Jeczalik and producer Gary Langan—split from Horn and ZTT in 1985. Forming a label (China), the group issued the "Legs" single, revealing a desire to invade the pop market by locating a functional compromise between it and them. A full new album, **In Visible Silence,**

21

followed several months later. Although no individual track is as gripping as "Close (to the Edit)," a semi-straight version of "Peter Gunn," with twang legend Duane Eddy playing the unforgettable guitar line, became a substantial international hit; the rest is typically intriguing, aggravating and entertaining.

A long 12-inch mix of "Peter Gunn," joined by two other previously issued 45s—"Legacy" (a drastic variation on "Legs") and "Paranoimia," recorded with the voice of Max Headroom breaking the usual vocal silence—comprise one side of **Re-Works**. The rest of the long mini-album documents Art of Noise live onstage in London, playing "Legs," "Paranoimia" and the ten-minute "Hammersmith to Tokyo and Back." The concert format has its obvious hazards for a painstaking group which is so reliant on the studio, but the results are more unsatisfying than disappointing. In any case, the ability to put this stuff over in front of an audience is noteworthy.

Shelving their pop ambitions, Art of Noise outfoxed themselves on **In No Sense? Nonsense!**, an overreaching undertaking that incorporates an orchestra, choir, horn section and guest rock musicians. The flaccid tracks are short on rhythmic power and wander all over the stylistic map with little logic or focus. Taken as a whole, this indeed makes no sense. The handful of numbers which indifferently plunder past adventures manage to be dull even when they resemble things that were exciting. Sonic quality is shortchanged by the technical considerations of recording so many musicians: abandoning modern high-tech claustrophobia for the inappropriately warm, open ambience of a cathedral ranks as a severe creative mistake. [iar]

ART ZOYD

Musique pour l'Odyssée (Fr. Atem) 1979
Generation sans Futur (Fr. Atem) 1980
Symphonie pour le Jour du Brûleront les Cités (Fr. Cryonic) 1981
Phase IV (nr/Recommended) 1982
Les Espaces Inquiets (Fr. Cryonic) 1984

THIERRY ZABOITZEFF

Prométhée (Fr. Cryonic) 1984

These French avant-gardists play both classical music and jazz, eschewing drums for a primary reliance on strings, horns and piano. Art Zoyd have released a number of albums on European labels. **Phase IV** is generally acknowledged to be one of their best,

a two-disc set of excellently recorded, unstructured blurts of evocative instrumental sound that ebb and flow in meter and volume and never stop resembling the unpleasant soundtrack to an unpleasant art film. **Les Espaces Inquiets** takes a more experimental tack but is essentially the same sort of affair, with polyrhythmic threads of various instruments weaving in and out of each other in seemingly formless hunks, all cut from one endless ramble.

Prométhée, a far simpler solo album from one of Zoyd's two string players, contains music from a theatrical production; it varies crazily from quietly soothing to ear-splittingly tense. [iar]

A'S

The A's (Arista) 1979
A Woman's Got the Power (Arista) 1981

One of the first bands on Philadelphia's new wave club scene to sign with a major label, the A's made their reputation through an energetic stage show which featured singer Richard Bush's Jerry Lewis-like antics. On the group's first album, Bush shows an equal aptitude for playing the comedian ("Teenage Jerk Off," an affectionately tongue-in-cheek nod to punk) and the straight man (the outstanding "After Last Night"). If anything, **The A's** resembles the Boomtown Rats' **Tonic for the Troops** in the way it combines wit, street savvy and relatively intricate hard-pop arrangements.

On **A Woman's Got the Power**, the group's sound and material changed drastically, and not for the better. The album is an exercise in misplaced bombast that would probably make Phil Spector cringe. Bush's occasional excesses are charming on the first outing, but here he consistently over-emotes, imbuing the songs with angst they don't really merit. While the big sound works well enough for the first couple of tracks (the soulful title tune and the pretty "Electricity"), the bluster then begins to grate; there isn't another listenable cut on the album. [ds]

STEPHEN ASHMAN

See *Zasu Pitts Memorial Orchestra*.

ASSOCIATES

The Affectionate Punch (nr/Fiction) 1980 + 1982
Fourth Drawer Down (nr/Situation 2) 1981 (nr/Beggars Banquet) 1982

Sulk (Sire) 1982
Perhaps (nr/Associates-WEA) 1985

The Associates—Billy MacKenzie (most words and all vocals, eventually everything) and Alan Rankine (most music and all instruments except drums)—once attempted brilliance; later they settled for playing at being clever. **The Affectionate Punch** boldly tried to stake a claim for some of the no-man's land between Bowie's theatrical, tuneful rock and Talking Heads' semi-abstract, intellectual dance approach, with a slight flavoring of the pair's native Scottish traditional music. Not fully mature, and sometimes almost burying its own best points, the band seemed a promise of riches to come.

Unfortunately, the duo veered off into a more art-conscious—at times willfully obscure—direction, with harsh musical textures often dominating the melodies. **Fourth Drawer Down**, a compilation of singles, gives the somewhat redeeming impression of determined experimentation that is, however, lessened by the exclusion of certain B-sides in favor of other, later tracks which reveal MacKenzie's growing preference for pose over accomplishment.

By **Sulk**, such talent as comes through seems strained under the weight of MacKenzie's self-consciousness. Rankine's emphasis on keyboards over guitar is symptomatic of the defection away from rock and toward a sort of neo-pop, but the melodies are hindered by tinny sound, arrangements that muddle rather than clarify, and vocal excesses that make Bowie's worst sound tame. The US edition subtracts three cuts, inserting instead a pair from **Fourth Drawer Down** and two subsequent singles. Net result: Associates (no article) are a shrill, non-synth Human League for emotional infants. The title's all too accurate—MacKenzie comes across as a callow, shallow poseur.

To write off **Perhaps** with a snide "perhaps not" would be a cheap shot, but more than generous. The article is back in the name, but Rankine's gone, which makes MacKenzie the entire band. He does have associates, including guitarist Steve Reid—who co-wrote half the songs—yet whether any given track was produced by Heaven 17's Martyn Ware, Martin Rushent or the team of Billy Mac and Dave Allen, it all sounds like Heaven 17 or the Human League—*with* synths, now—making undanceable dance music with a few ho-hum twists. The lyrics include strange, gratuitous, incomprehensible non sequiturs; the music is at best unin-volving, even if you listen for sheer sound and ignore the pose. The one all-around good track ("Waiting for the Loveboat"), at seven minutes, overstays its welcome by half. If you must, the cassette edition has extra tracks.

[jg]

See also *Paul Haig, Holger Hiller, Yello.*

VIRGINIA ASTLEY

From Gardens Where We Feel Secure
  (nr/Happy Valley-Rough Trade) 1983
Promise Nothing (Bel. Crépuscule) 1983
Hope in a Darkened Heart (Geffen) 1986

A classically trained pianist and flautist less known for her own work than for the illustrious company she keeps, Astley has played sessions for Siouxsie and the Banshees, Richard Jobson and Troy Tate, among others. Her father, Ted Astley, is an accomplished composer best known for television themes; her brother-in-law is Pete Townshend. (She plays piano on his "Slit Skirts.") However, Astley's own pastoral and tranquil records are markedly different from those of family and friends.

Evoking images of summer afternoons in the countryside, **From Gardens Where We Feel Secure** is, superficially at least, soothing sonic wallpaper. Except for a few syllables, it's entirely instrumental, consisting basically of piano, flute, clarinet and tape loops. Upon closer scrutiny, the tapes (animal sounds, church bells, etc.) build subliminal tension; there's more to Ms. Astley than initially meets the ear. **Promise Nothing** is a compilation, including cuts from **Gardens** and various singles. The orchestration on the earlier work is thicker—synthesizers, sax and percussion place the material more in the rock realm—but her choir-boy soprano keeps things from getting too raucous. Standouts: the irresistible "Love's a Lonely Place to Be" and "Arctic Death," as haunting as any John Cale effort. An impressive record from an intriguing artist.

In 1985, Astley signed to Elektra in the United Kingdom and released a pair of singles, neither of which broke any new musical ground for her. **Hope in a Darkened Heart**, her US debut, was mostly produced by Ryuichi Sakamoto, who adds more synths and drum machines. David Sylvian sings along on the opening "Some Small Hope." While it's still very pretty, there's more substance, as well. Most of the lyrics by this single mother (the baby's father left Astley during her pregnancy) are rather angry, made even more effective by the charm of her voice and the delicacy of the music. I shouldn't like to be the guy to whom "A Father" or "So Like Dorian" are directed. Remixes of earlier tracks, including "Love's a Lonely Place to Be" round out Side Two. She may never be prolific or commercially popular, but Virginia Astley is one of the most unique talents around these days.   [dgs]

See also *Armoury Show.*

ASWAD

Aswad (Mango) 1976
Hulet (nr/Grove) 1978 (nr/Grove-Island) 1979
Showcase (nr/Grove-Island) 1981
New Chapter (nr/CBS) 1981
Not Satisfied (Columbia) 1982
New Chapter of Dub (Mango) 1982
Live and Direct (Mango) 1983
Rebel Souls (Mango) 1984
To the Top (nr/Simba) 1986 •
Distant Thunder (Mango) 1988 •

Though they've never really caught on in the States, Aswad is one of Britain's best and most popular reggae bands. The trio's work is characterized by consistently excellent musicianship (Aswad's adjunct horn section is superlative) and a sound that is modern yet authentic. Their easygoing groove may resemble UB40's, but Aswad is thoroughly unique; after more than a decade, their continued growth and versatility are remarkable. Along with Linton Kwesi Johnson and Dennis Bovell, Aswad represents the flowering of British reggae. Their recording history, however, is disjointed and reflects shifts in personnel, musical direction and labels.

The first album (with "Back to Africa") is of mixed quality, but showcases the band's stylistic variety, featuring lovers rock, dub and Marley-inspired roots. **Hulet**, released two years later, is much better—assured and capable—but indecision about direction is clearly audible. Shortly after this release, bassist George Oban left; Tony Gad (Robinson), who had played keyboards in the group, took over on bass. A stint with British CBS yielded two albums, **New Chapter** and **Not Satisfied**, both rich with fine songs and performances, particularly the latter. **New Chapter of Dub**, while decent enough, is for fans only.

Rebel Souls has a genial consistency and includes significant covers of Toots Hibbert's "54-46" and Marvin Gaye's "Mercy Mercy Me." Quite rightly, Aswad were linking themselves to tradition as they geared up for the future.

The group's full yet rootsy sound continued on their next LP, **To The Top**, which featured the UK hit, "Bubbling." Strong and full of punch, the album is one of their best, with top-notch writing, singing and playing throughout. With the band operating at peak power, the record is probably their most representative studio effort, but curiously was never released in the US.

Distant Thunder, which is available domestically, marks a distinct change in direction. Feeling perhaps that they had pushed their old sound to its limit, the band experiments with funk and soul, as well as keyboards. The crossover-geared sound is more lightweight and was bound to alienate some fans. But while several of the new songs sound tentative, others (like the pop-soul single "Don't Turn Around") are engaging and credible, featuring the same musical craftsmanship that has always characterized Aswad's work.

To some extent, Aswad's strongest releases have been their singles. No proper greatest-hits package exists, but two albums fill the gap. **Showcase**—remixes of their most popular non-LP numbers, including "Rainbow Culture," "Warrior Charge" and "Babylon" (the title theme of a film which starred Aswad's Brinsley Forde)—is both stunning and welcome, a fine place for novices to start. In addition, **Live and Direct** compiles some of Aswad's best-loved songs and gives a hint of their live power. "Rockers Medley" stands out, but the whole LP is great.   [bk]

ATHLETICO SPIZZ 80
See *Spizz.*

ATLANTICS
Big City Rock (ABC) 1979

The only album by this talented Boston rock band with strong, melodic material and a slightly overdramatic vocalist was unfortunately issued on a label that was breathing its corporate last. Two standout songs—"When You're Young" and "One Last Night"—suggest abundant power pop promise, but weak production and a crucial lack of promotion kept these five neat guys a local phenomenon.
                [iar]

ATTRACTIONS
See *Elvis Costello.*

AU PAIRS

Playing with a Different Sex (nr/Human) 1981
Sense and Sensuality (nr/Kamera) 1982
Live in Berlin (nr/AKA) 1983

Although the quartet was evenly divided between the sexes, Au Pairs' trademarks were singer/guitarist Lesley Woods' husky vocals and her feminist themes. They favored stripped-down, generally tuneless dance-rock, perhaps the better to drive home ironic messages like "We're So Cool," "Set-Up" (both on the first album), "Sex Without Stress" and "Intact" (on **Sense and Sensuality**). A female viewpoint is, unfortunately, still novel for pop music; Woods is humorless and sometimes oozingly graphic, but usually thought-provoking in her romantic analyses. Au Pairs' few overtly political songs ("Armagh," "America") are less successful. [si]

AVANT GARAGE

Music (NZ Unsung Music) 1983

A jazzy-cum-classical nine-person ensemble with clarinets, cello, tuba and bassoon (in addition to guitar, bass and drums), New Zealand's determinedly oddball Avant Garage sounds like something Zappa might have done in his dada orchestral phase. The music is generally pleasant (despite occasional skewed digressions, as on the instrumental "Funky Cockroach"); it's the lyrics and vocals on songs like "Garage Sale" and "Mr Granite" that give this its modern, boundary-breaking character. Intelligent, esoteric and fascinating. [iar]

AVANT GARDENERS

Dig It (It. Appaloosa) 1980

It's unclear how this frivolous English wideboy new wave trio, known in the singular when originally signed to Virgin, ended up with an Italian album that mates all four tracks from a 1977 UK EP (like "Strange Gurl [sic] in Clothes" and "Bloodclat Boogie Baby") with a version of Roky Erickson's "Two Headed Dog," a porno pisstake called "Johnny Cash" and "Never Turn Your Back on a Silicon Chip," as well as other semi-inspired bits of doggerel. It's pretty funny—like Johnny Moped—and not badly played; an odd footnote to new wave's original explosion. [iar]

AVENGERS

Avengers EP (White Noise) 1978
Avengers (CD Presents) 1983 ●

PENELOPE HOUSTON

Birdboys (Subterranean) 1988

What allegedly began as an excuse for punk fashions became, briefly, the most powerful band in the San Francisco area; the Avengers' original EP was a minor classic at the time, indicating that they might have become America's best straight-ahead punk (*not* hardcore) band had they lasted. It boasts tight, memorable cuts instrumentally akin to Johnny Thunders and the Sex Pistols, though it's Penelope Houston's intoning words of some depth that makes the difference. Like X without any pretensions; too bad Steve Jones couldn't finish the production (the mix needed him).

The posthumous album reprises the entire contents of that EP, adding a stack of ace punk tunes recorded (with one subsequent exception) in 1977 and 1978. Houston clearly prefigures Chrissie Hynde as the archetypal indomitable rock'n'roll woman—her strength and aggression are what elevates these tracks from energetic but typical punk to remarkable personal statements. Whether anyone outside of San Francisco realized it at the time, the Avengers were a major national musical asset. (The CD and cassette versions contain two bonus cuts.)

After the Avengers folded in 1979, Houston worked with Alex Gibson and Howard Devoto. In 1986, her cleverly-named (journalists will get the reference) acoustic folk group, Dash Thirty Dash, issued a smart and melodic single, "Full of Wonder." She later released an entire album of acoustic folk, some of which was produced by the late Snakefinger. [jg/iar]

AZTEC CAMERA

High Land, Hard Rain (Sire) 1983 ●
Oblivious EP (Sire) 1984
Knife (Sire) 1984
Still on Fire EP (nr/WEA) 1984
Backwards and Forwards EP (Sire) 1985
Love (Sire) 1987 ●

Glaswegian's guitarist-singer-songwriter Roddy Frame is the creative force behind Aztec Camera, whose delicate pop conveys his poetic sensibility and rampant originality. **High Land, Hard Rain** is a magnificent debut, airy yet somehow lush, filled with lovely melodies and thoughtful, impressionistic lyrics. "Oblivious," "Walk Out to Winter" and "We Could Send Letters" are all memorable, distinguished by layered acoustic guitars, beautiful vocal arrangements and jazzy rhythms; "Down the Dip" displays Frame's playful side.

There are two **Oblivious** EPs. Both include the same remix of the title tune, but the US version has three British B-sides, while the earlier UK edition contains one B-side, an LP track and a live take.

Knife, produced by Dire Straits' Mark Knopfler, is a lot less ethereal, employing a stronger backbeat, sterner vocals and horns. Frame's lyrics continue to walk the line between profound and ludicrous but, for the most part, manage to stay within the realm of lucidity. His writing shows the influence of Elvis Costello and also incorporates a mild R&B feel. Typical of the record's approach, the lead-off track, "Still on Fire," faintly recalls the Jackson 5's "I Want You Back."

(That song's 12-inch release adds four live cuts.)

It's rare to encounter a marketing gimmick worthy of special mention, but the commercially-available **Backwards and Forwards** EP is brilliant. The folder covering the 10-inch record contains the band's complete discography and history, plus profiles and photos, all avoiding hype and sales pressure. The swell record offers four live tracks (only two encores from the aforementioned EP) plus the band's languid acoustic cover of Van Halen's "Jump."

Reduced to a titular shell for Frame's solo career, Aztec Camera returned to action three years later with **Love**, a heartfelt but colorless Philly soul record made with studio musicians and half a dozen producers. (Think of Boy George or Paul Young, with music by Steve Winwood.) Although Frame's singing and songwriting don't quite suit this musical style, his low-key charm and basic talent keep him from embarrassing himself.   [iar]

B B B B B B B B

BABY BUDDHA

See *Microwaves.*

WALLY BADAROU

Echoes (Island) 1985 ●
Chief Inspector EP (Island) 1986

Paris-born keyboardist Badarou is a veteran of Sly and Robbie's Compass Point All-Stars band and has played behind such luminaries as Grace Jones, Black Uhuru and M (on "Pop Muzik"). He's also done significant production and playing for Marianne Faithfull, Level 42 and others. Moving into soundtracks, he's most notably been featured on *Kiss of the Spider Woman* and *Countryman.*

Following a debut solo single ("Chief Inspector," a hard synth-funk instrumental) that topped British dance charts, Badarou's first album under his own name reveals Indian, African and jazz influences, but the best track remains that single. Glossy, versatile and forgettable. **Chief Inspector** contains remixes of five tracks, including the title tune and "Spider Woman." [bk]

BAD BRAINS

Bad Brains [tape] (ROIR) 1982
Bad Brains EP (nr/Alternative Tentacles) 1982
I and I Survive/Destroy Babylon EP
   (Important) 1982
Rock for Light (PVC) 1983 ●
I Against I (SST) 1986 ●

H.R.

Its About Luv (Olive Tree) 1985
Human Rights (SST) 1987

In their quest to become a crossover band, these black jazz-rock fusionists from Washington, DC (later based in New York)

turned to orthodox speedpunk and released the memorable 1980 super-fast single "Pay to Cum!" that established their mastery of that genre. Bad Brains' hardcore is a more distinctively modulated roar than most, but what really sets them apart are radically contrasting excursions into dub and rasta reggae. Hardcore's dogmatic streak makes it harder on chameleons than most rock subgenres; these guys almost get away with it.

On the cassette album (and the four-song **Bad Brains** EP excerpted from it), the quartet excels in both fields: loping, Jah-praising reggae and powerhouse slam-rock. The Ric Ocasek-produced **Rock for Light** includes newly-recorded versions of five songs from the tape and offers the same dualism, with subject matter covering everything from angry politics ("Riot Squad") to minor pop culturisms ("At the Movies"), stretching from rasta topics to "How Low Can a Punk Get" sociology. Throughout, Joseph I's (aka H.R.) reedy vocals set off the hardcore roar led by guitarist Dr. Know and sweetly color the reggae rumble. A fascinating and truly unique blend.

I Against I is a bracing all-rock explosion, a mature collection of well-written originals played at varying speeds with authority and enthusiasm. Dr. Know trots out varied effects, sounds and approaches; H.R. has likewise never sounded better. Shrugging off punk conventions, Bad Brains explore sophisticated and subtle terrain all their own. At its most explosive, the record crosses Van Halen with Black Flag; more restrained passages resemble an energized, younger Police. The quartet holds reggae rhythms to a bare minimum, although lyrics continue to reflect their religious and political convictions.

H.R. (Paul Hudson) has left and rejoined

the group several times, releasing a pair of solo albums along the way. The fascinating if indifferently recorded **Its About Luv** (on his own Olive Tree label) offers chaotic punk—class of '77 UK division—with anthemic melodies ("Let's Have a Revolution") on one side and upbeat Caribbean funk ("Who Loves You Girl?"), jazzy reggae ("Happy Birthday My Son") and a live rocker ("Free Our Mind") on the back. The high-tech **Human Rights**—featuring, among others, Oscar Brown Jr. and H.R.'s brother, Bad Brains drummer Earl Hudson—is a bizarre but captivating pastiche of reggae-based rock/pop, carefully arranged and delicately textured rock and funk, studio experimentation and other offbeat manifestations of H.R.'s Rastafarianism. Strange and intriguing. [mf/iar]

BAD MANNERS

Ska'n'B (nr/Magnet) 1980
Loonee Tunes! (nr/Magnet) 1980
Bad Manners (MCA) 1981
Gosh It's . . . (nr/Magnet) 1981
Forging Ahead (Portrait) 1982
The Height of Bad Manners (nr/Telstar) 1983
Klass (MCA) 1983
Mental Notes (Portrait) 1985

This rollicking nine-piece London neo-ska nonsense ensemble is fronted by a cartoon character vocalist dubbed Buster Bloodvessel, an immense bald hulk. The rest of the lineup—three horns, guitar, bass, drums, keyboards and harmonica (played, but of course, by Winston Bazoomies)—churns out smooth, tight bluebeat like early Madness or Specials, while embracing all manner of musical silliness for humorous effect. Bad Manners is strictly entertainment; their records, juvenile though they may sometimes be, consistently provide smile-inducing, good-natured, toe-tapping value in every groove.

Ska'n'B (the band's original musical self-description) has fewer originals than subsequent LPs; versions of "Monster Mash," "Scruffy Was a Huffy Chuffy Tug Boat," the "Magnificent Seven" theme and "Ne-Ne Na-Na Na-Na Nu-Nu" are ludicrous but engaging. Their first American escape, **Bad Manners**, draws tracks from **Ska'n'B** as well as **Loonee Tunes!**, released in the meantime. **Gosh It's** . . . squeezes in a frisky instrumental rearrangement of "Can Can" amid pleasing originals like "Gherkin" (giddily de-

scribed on the back cover as a "deeply moving tribute to Charles Aznavour") and "Ben E. Wriggle," plus some almost serious numbers that suggest insidious maturation.

Forging Ahead, the group's finest record, has a (thankfully) instrumental version of "Exodus," a cover of "My Boy (Girl) Lollipop" and an original called "Samson and Delilah (Biblical Version)." When released in the US two years later, a great subsequent single, "That'll Do Nicely," had been added.

With **Mental Notes**, B.M. pulls away from their original concept, managing to cover Todd Rundgren's "Bang the Drum All Day" without serious damage. Like Madness' transitional period (which came a lot earlier, careerwise), the bluebeat tempos remain, but they're under a slick coat of restraint, sophistication and—dare we say it—maturity. Bring back giddy stupidity!

A pair of compilations was issued in 1983. The American one has a truly disgusting pig-out cover and most of the band's best early tracks; the British release offers a different selection, with only six songs in common. [iar]

HENRY BADOWSKI

Life Is a Grand . . . (IRS) 1981

Badowski—who's played with Wreckless Eric, the Doomed and Good Missionaries—has a deep, pleasant, near-conversational voice that's almost always on key plus a dry and/or whimsical sense of humor. Henry plays virtually every note here (even drums and sax), often with simple eloquence, on songs about getting married and swimming with fish in the sea. Could you ask for more? [jg]

BAD RELIGION

How Could Hell Be Any Worse? (Epitaph) 1982
Into the Unknown (Epitaph) 1983
Back to the Known EP (Epitaph) 1984

On their first album, this California hardcore quartet adds such unexpected attributes as piano, dynamics and university-level lyrics to an otherwise routine sore-throat-vocals/maximum-overload-guitar sound. The well-recorded LP (engineered by future Concrete Blonde star Jim Mankey) meets the minimum daily requirement of loud and fast rock without sacrificing basic human intelligence in the process. **Into the Unknown**, a mini-album, is even better, a swirling blizzard of noisy but catchy psychedelia and paisley rock, with real songs and a sound that might be Nazz songs played by early Deep Purple. A masterpiece.

After that adventure, half the original lineup, joined by guitarist Greg Hetson on loan from the Circle Jerks and a guest bassist, recanted it on a one-sided 12-inch punk EP. **Back to the Known** banishes the stylish keyboard sound in favor of an unreconstructed guitar attack. Still, Greg Graffin's articulate vocals are way above average and the stun-volume chords don't swamp out the melodies or lyrics. Not bad at all.   [iar]

CHRIS BAILEY
See *Saints*.

BAILTER SPACE
See *Clean*.

JOE BAIZA AND THE UNIVERSAL CONGRESS OF
See *Saccharine Trust*.

BALAAM & THE ANGEL
The Greatest Story Ever Told (Virgin) 1986
Live Free or Die (Virgin) 1988 •

Despite their goth garb, Scotland's Morris brothers—singer/bassist Mark, guitarist Jim and drummer Des—are popsters at heart, a fact which they take pains to disguise on these unremarkable albums. **The Greatest Story Ever Told** does have some charm, but the melodies are too often buried in feeble attempts to whip up a vague air of menace. (Balaam are, after all, protégés of the Cult's Ian Astbury.) **Live Free or Die**, produced by former Cult boardman Steve Brown, is closer to Van Halen-styled AOR metal and is no worse (or better) than anything Bon Jovi's ever put on wax. (The CD adds two tracks.)   [hd]

BALANCING ACT
New Campfire Songs EP (Type A) 1986
   (Primitive Man) 1987 •
Three Squares and a Roof (Primitive Man) 1988 •

This semi-electric LA rock quartet is earnest enough on its Peter Case-produced debut EP, but with the exception of "Wonderful World Tonight," a likable and evocative update of the "Goin' Up the Country" ethos, none of these half dozen **New Campfire Songs** is likely to show up alongside "Blowin' in the Wind" at the next weenie roast. Give the Balancing Act credit for a unique blend of acoustic and electric elements, though. Also, they've got a melodica, and they know how to use it!

Three Squares and a Roof is a lot less precious and more interesting than its predecessor. The playing and production are better, the material vastly improved. Songs cover substantial lyrical territory, nearly all of it previously uncharted. Like 'em or not, the Balancing Act are originals. The CD contains both records.   [ds]

DAVE BALL
In Strict Tempo (nr/Some Bizzare) 1983

Without erstwhile Soft Cell partner Marc Almond supplying the sleaze, shy keyboard man Dave Ball is a cold-hearted bore. In **Strict Tempo**'s drab mood pieces strain for wry wit to leaven the pretentiousness but with little success and wind up just a jumble of undeveloped ideas. Genesis P-Orridge of Psychic TV warbles on two tracks.   [jy]

BALLISTIC KISSES
Total Access (nr/Don't Fall off the Mountain) 1982
Wet Moment (nr/Don't Fall off the Mountain) 1983

Pseudo-streetwise lyrics tend to distract attention from the solidly danceable, cleanly produced synth-dominated pop on this New York band's first album. When their political stance turns to political role-playing, though, the result is oversimplification that borders on insincerity. Little wonder, then, that vocalist/wordsmith Michael Parker strives to sing like Joe Strummer (cough, cough), though he sounds more comfortable in a Brian Eno mode.

Wet Moment is a tedious cross between the B-52's and Gang of Four: minimal melodies, propulsive rhythms and bleak vocals. It's easy to believe freaked-out tunes like "Emotional Ice" and "Everything Leaks," but how alienated do you really want to feel?   [mf/jy]

AFRIKA BAMBAATAA & THE JAZZY 5
"Jazzy Sensation" (Tommy Boy) 1981

AFRIKA BAMBAATAA & SOULSONIC FORCE
"Planet Rock" (Tommy Boy) 1982
"Looking for the Perfect Beat" (Tommy Boy) 1982
"Renegades of Funk" (Tommy Boy) 1983
Planet Rock—The Album (Tommy Boy) 1986

TIME ZONE
"The Wildstyle" (Celluloid) 1983
"World Destruction" (Celluloid) 1984

SHANGO
Shango Funk Theology (Celluloid) 1984 ●

AFRIKA BAMBAATAA & JAMES BROWN
"Unity" (Tommy Boy) 1984

AFRIKA BAMBAATAA AND FAMILY
"Funk You!" (Tommy Boy) 1985
Beware (The Funk Is Everywhere) (Tommy Boy) 1986
The Light (Capitol) 1988 ●

Bronx dj-turned-hip-hop-superstar Bambaataa not only created the record that thrust beatbox electro-funk into the '80s, he has made pioneering sides with numerous performers and established himself as a major figure in contemporary music. Working mainly in the 12-inch format, Bam's ascent began with a routine boast rap, "Jazzy Sensation," but got into gear with "Planet Rock," the Arthur Baker-produced (and co-written, with the band and John Robie) explosion of scratch cuts, electronic gimmickry, processed vocals and solid-state rhythms. (Both tracks were later compiled on the Tommy Boy label retrospective, **Greatest Beats**.) "Looking for the Perfect Beat" is even better, with Baker mostly soft-pedaling the monolithic pounding in favor of a skittish electronic metronome and tacking on fancier effects, vocals and mix tricks to create an ultra-busy urban symphony. The megarhythmic "Renegades of Funk" adds social/historical/political lyrics to the dance-floor dynamism and delivers a really bizarre blend of rap, synthesizers and oppressive electronic percussion.

As a precursor to a long-promised album (which ultimately included it), Bambaataa released "Funk You!," a corny rap idea stretched out over a 12-inch in four very different mixes, with borrowings from James Brown and Queen. When it finally appeared, **Beware** proved that the LP format presents no obstacle to the imposing Overseer: the record's variety and invention make it an exciting electro-beat vision of a freewheeling stylistic future. "Funk Jam Party" is exactly that; "Tension" sounds like Bowie comes to Harlem; "Rock America" incorporates howling electric guitars, a munchkin chorus and chintzy organ without ever losing the funk. Easily the highlight, and another amazing cross-cultural accomplishment by Bambaataa, is Bill Laswell's earthy, energized production of the MC5's "Kick Out the Jams." Awesome.

In a fascinating cross-generational culture mix, Bambaataa teamed with the Godfather of Soul to record "Unity," a positive political message released in six alternate versions (connected by studio patter) on one disc. Hitting a funky compromise between classic soul and modern hip-hop, the record works on a number of levels and is certainly a significant milestone in rap. Taking another startling detour, Bambaataa wrote and recorded "World Destruction" with Bill Laswell, sharing the vocals with John Lydon, jump-cutting the Englishman's no-wave keen into an intense, ominous funk-rock maelstrom for one of the most remarkable dance singles in recent memory.

Bambaataa also records as a member of Shango, a vocal trio that is supported by Material (for this purpose, Laswell and Michael Beinhorn). The album-length **Funk Theology** offers five sophisticated party creations that also feature guitarist Nicky Skopelitis. The originals get no heavier, lyrically, than "Let's Party Down"; a version of Sly Stone's "Thank You" is utterly appropriate. Good for dancing but a bit dull for listening.

Extending the Family to extraordinary lengths, **The Light** features UB40, Nona Hendryx, Boy George, George Clinton, Bootsy Collins, Yellowman and others. At times, the appealing and diverse pan-ethnic album involves Bam only tangentially—a brief rap on UB40's "Reckless" track, a couple of brief interjections on the Hendryx/George rendition of Curtis Mayfield's "Something He Can Feel." The only credit he takes on "Shout It Out" is as co-publisher of the composition. The individual tracks are fine, but the lack of focus leaves this plainly commercial effort more a various artists sampler than a cohesive Bambaataa creation.

Planet Rock—The Album is a compilation of the three classic 12-inch records with Soulsonic Force plus previously unreleased tracks featuring Melle Mel and Trouble Funk. [iar]

BAMBI SLAM

Is . . . EP (Product Inc.-Rough Trade) 1987

Admittedly inspired by the Jesus and Mary Chain, this Canadian-British quartet (guitar/bass/drums/cello!) takes a less claustrophobic and more rhythmic approach to noise-laden echo-pop than the Reids but still winds up sounding a lot like **Psychocandy** on this six-track American compilation of British singles. Although not prominent in the mix, the big fiddle adds a nice touch to songs like "La La La (It's Out of Hand)" and "Hit Me with Your Hairbrush." Redundant but amusing. [iar]

BANANARAMA

Deep Sea Skiving (London) 1983 ●
Bananarama (London) 1984 ●
True Confessions (London) 1986 ●
Wow! (London) 1987 ●

Keren Woodward, Sarah Dallin and Siobhan Fahey became a trio in London in 1979. They first gained notoriety singing with the Fun Boy Three, who later returned the favor by producing and backing them on their earliest singles. **Deep Sea Skiving** essentially compiles their first string of infectious 45s, encompassing a panoply of styles: percussive Afro-beat ("He Was Really Sayin' Somethin' "), girl-group soul ("Shy Boy"), '60s chart silliness ("Na Na Hey Hey Kiss Him Goodbye") and lush pop ("Cheers Then"). Additionally, **Deep Sea Skiving** offers Paul Weller's "Doctor Love," the charming and light "Hey Young London" and the morose "What a Shambles." An assortment of producers yields little uniformity of sound, but the ensemble vocals provide the crucial character regardless of setting.

For their first real album, Bananarama gave the ball to hitmakers Swain and Jolley (Spandau, Alison Moyet, Imagination) who, as is their custom, co-wrote the material. Over the lush, highly arranged backing, the ladies croon two wonderful singles—the evocatively tropical "Cruel Summer" (a hit, one year apart, in the UK and US) and "Robert De Niro's Waiting." Otherwise, the album deflects much of their engaging individuality and substitutes a vacuous sheen that's too functional and defeats their ingenuous image. **Bananarama** isn't bad—the vocals are charming in any case—but it is forgettable.

Although Swain and Jolley still held the reins for **True Confessions**, they lost their franchise to the up-and-coming Stock-Aitken-Waterman team, who placed two sides—including an irresistibly catchy disco remake of Shocking Blue's "Venus" that became Bananarama's first US chart-topper—on the LP. Overall, however, **True Confessions** is a limp outing that sculpts a refined, contemporary adult sound, evaporating the group's youthful vitality and charm in the process.

Capitalizing on their Moroder-based sequencer formula, Stock, Aitken and Waterman wrote, produced and programmed **Wow!**, a peppy synth-driven dance record that disguises Bananarama's vocal limitations in an overwhelming wash of electronic music simulation. The crass gimmickry and mock-Supremes arrangements of "I Heard a Rumour" and "I Can't Help It" are as predictable as the tunes are unshakable; the rest of the record resembles those tracks so closely that it might as well be remixes. Sure it's total trash, but what else does a car need to keep it running in the hot summer sun?

In early 1988, following **Wow!**'s enormous success, Fahey (now married to Dave Stewart of Eurythmics) left the band to pursue a solo career and was replaced by Jacquie O'Sullivan, formerly of the Shillelagh Sisters. [iar]

BAND APART

Band Apart EP (Bel. Crammed Discs) 1982
Marseille (Bel. Crammed Discs) 1983

Centered around expatriate Frenchman Medak Mader (guitars, synth) and one Jane Bliss Nodland (vocals, e-bow guitar), Band Apart make grimly impressive music: an intimidating bass'n'drums 4/4 laid down just faster than a stroll (but with vicious inexorability) and whining, gnashing guitars, plus scary vocals. One near-mesmerizing track of multiple guitar/synth washes on the EP is hampered only by the limits of recording and pressing quality.

Marseille is an interesting assortment; more thoughtful, arty, varied and uneven than the EP, but also less confrontational. The one out-and-out turkey is a go at Rodgers and Hart's "Lover" (!?!). Other than that, even its lesser tracks have a sort of bohemian charm. [jg]

BAND OF BLACKY RANCHETTE

See *Giant Sandworms.*

BAND OF SUSANS

Blessing and Curse EP (Trace Elements) 1986
Hope Against Hope (Furthur-Blast First) 1988 ●

Indeed there were, for a time, three Susans (Stenger, Tallman and Lyall) in this New York sextet. The four songs on the 12-inch **Blessing and Curse**, produced by (ex-Western Eyes) guitarist/songwriter/vocalist Robert Poss, locate an exciting niche between anti-music chaos and accessible rock by setting simple, repetitive chord patterns in motion and then slathering on layers of vocals and noisy guitar. Dense without being forbidding, "You Were an Optimist" and the speeding "Where Have All the Flowers Gone" (an original) clearly indicate the Susans' intriguing direction and skill.

Hope Against Hope (titled after a song picked off the EP; a second track was re-recorded here) is an improvement on all fronts, revealing a bracingly loud—but never actually strident—band that seemingly can't put enough guitar electricity on vinyl to satisfy itself. Besides the benefit of Poss' febrile production, his songs are better formed, with chord progressions that actually resolve. (In a touching show of pop cognizance, "I the Jury" quotes the Stones' "Last Time.") Anchored by a solidly plain rhythm section, the storm of strings continues to rage unabated, making **Hope Against Hope** something of a rockier American response to **Psychocandy**. The CD adds two tracks from the debut EP: "Where Have All the Flowers Gone" and "Sometimes."

Two Susans left following the LP's recording in mid-'87; the 1988 lineup is a five-piece. [iar]

BANGLES

Bangles EP (Faulty Products) 1982 (IRS) 1982
All Over the Place (Columbia) 1984 ●
Different Light (Columbia) 1986 ●

These four young women from Los Angeles—originally known as the Bangs—display an odd collection of influences on their five-track debut EP, neatly produced by Craig Leon. The swell harmonies on several cuts come straight from the Mamas and the Papas, while the music alternates between evoking **Rubber Soul** and energetic, bantam-weight Yardbirds-styled garage rock. The playing's fine and the vocals are great—the songs just aren't up to snuff.

The Bangles' young career was temporarily derailed when Faulty Products went out of business and an original member left to join Blood on the Saddle. (In retrospect not a very wise move.) No matter. Come 1984, the Bangles swung back into action, armed with a new bassist, a contract with a more reliable record company, the best American power-pop producer money can buy (David Kahne) and a passel of brilliant new songs—mostly guitarist Vicki Peterson's, but also Kimberley Rew's "Going Down to Liverpool," which indirectly led to *his* group, Katrina and the Waves, finally securing an American deal. **All Over the Place** has everything a pop album needs: exceptional harmony vocals, catchy, memorable and intelligent tunes and a full dose of rock'n'roll guitar energy. Unlike the Go-Go's, who never fully clarified their lyrical stance, the Bangles offer an adult play-fair-or-take-a-hike independence that is a lot more contemporary than their joyously evocative sound. The best cuts other than "Liverpool"—"Hero Takes a Fall," "Tell Me" and "James"—feature Susanna Hoffs' alluring vocals and are unassailable gems; the worst tracks only fall short of that by a smidge. Simply wonderful.

Prince became a fan, and gave the Bangles a song, "Manic Monday" (written pseudonymously by "Christopher"), for **Different Light**. Despite trivial lyrics, it became a gigantic hit single, establishing the quartet's stardom, but causing many to overlook the LP's finer points: Jules Shear's "If She Knew What She Wants," Alex Chilton's classic "September Gurls" and bassist Michael Steele's harrowing "Following." Maybe not as consistently top-notch as **All Over the Place**, it's still an enjoyable (and often memorable) sophomore showing. These women know how to sing! [iar]

See also *Blood on the Saddle.*

LESTER BANGS AND THE DELINQUENTS

Jook Savages on the Brazos (Live Wire) 1981

LESTER BANGS AND BIRDLAND

Birdland (Add On) 1986

No aspiring rock writer who came of age in the golden era of rock criticism could fail to be aware of the late Lester Bangs, though few have ever matched his brave, hilarious, autobiographical wit. The **Jook Savages** LP—which recalls Richard Hell's offhanded, blues-inflected punk raunch—is like Bangs himself: just when you write it off for hopeless slovenliness, it kicks in with a rakish charm. (Attentiveness and volume can ameliorate the dry sound.)

Bangs died in Manhattan in April 1982. **Birdland**, an album on which he had collaborated (writing and playing) with Mickey Leigh of the Rattlers, was released posthumously four years later. [mf]

BARNES & BARNES

Voobaha (Rhino) 1980
Fish Heads: Barnes and Barnes Greatest Hits
    EP (Rhino) 1981
Spazchow (Rhino) 1981
Soak It Up EP (Boulevard-CBS) 1983
Amazing Adult Fantasy (Rhino) 1984
Sicks (Rhino) 1987
Zabagabee: The Best of Barnes & Barnes
    (Rhino) 1988 ●

Art and Artie Barnes (one of whom had a highly public former life as Billy Mumy, child actor) are a sick pair of perverts you would not want to know personally. At your party, they would stage disgusting practical jokes; they would tell obscene lies to your parents just to get a laugh. Both **Voobaha** and **Spazchow** offer heavy doses of dark-hued novelty music that chews up modern culture and spits it back, producing an equal number of chuckles and shudders. The first features the underground hit "Fish Heads" plus "Boogie Woogie Amputee" and "Party in My Pants." On **Spazchow** you get "Spooky Lady on Death Avenue," "Swallow My Love" and a merciless dissection of (the group) America's "I Need You."

In what clearly was the only possible response, two members of America provided backing vocals on the pair's next effort, **Soak It Up**, a relatively restrained five-song EP. (The earlier retrospective EP is a fish head-shaped picture disc.)

Amazing Adult Fantasy offers further proof that age is softening the Barnes boys. Not only does Steve Perry of Journey sing on the utterly presentable "Don't You Wanna Go to the Moon," but the pair makes a vain stab at commercial accessibility with "I Don't Remember Tomorrow" and other wimpolinos. **Sick**, however, returns them to the disgustatorium, with such garbage pail

tunes as "Pizza Face," "Pussy Whipped" and "Sit on My Lap and Call Me Daddy."

Zabagabee contains many of the pair's finest and most essential moments, including "Fish Heads," "Party in My Pants," "Boogie Woogie Amputee," "Pizza Face" and a fine reading of "What's New Pussycat?" produced by kindred weirdo Bob Casale. Lovers of absurdist, sleazy humor should consider Barnes & Barnes highly recommended. All others should proceed with extreme caution. [jy/iar]

See also *Wild Man Fischer.*

RICHARD BARONE

See *Bongos.*

BARRACUDAS

Drop Out with the Barracudas (Voxx)
    1981 ●
Mean Time (Fr. Closer) 1982
House of Kicks EP (nr/Flicknife) 1983
Live 1983 (Fr. Coyote) 1983
Endeavor to Persevere (Fr. Closer) 1984
I Wish It Could Be 1965 Again (Fr. GMG)
    1986

JEREMY GLUCK WITH NIKKI SUDDEN & ROWLAND S. HOWARD

I Knew Buffalo Bill (nr/Flicknife) 1987
Burning Skulls Rise EP (nr/Flicknife) 1988

Despite a cheerfully self-deprecating stance, Britain's Barracudas offer quite an enjoyable sentimental journey through assorted American traditions on **Drop Out**. Some tunes plunge headlong into dense, ringing folk-rock—see "We're Living in Violent Times" or "I Saw My Death in a Dream Last Night" for an update of the Byrds on a gloomy day. Surf tunes like "Summer Fun" and "His Last Summer" strive a little too hard for laughs to overcome fundamental flimsiness, but are fun and can't be faulted on attitude. (The UK and US versions of the LP differ by a track.)

After losing drummer Nicky Turner to the nascent Lords of the New Church, a new Barracudas lineup put together the more R&B-geared **Mean Time**. Their recording career since has taken a few unpredictable turns. **House of Kicks** is a four-song 12-inch. The live album, packaged and recorded so amateurishly as to resemble a bootleg, finds them an older and far less innocent-sounding quintet, playing blues and rock cover tunes like "Seven and Seven Is," "You're Gonna Miss Me" and "Fortunate Son."

The Barracudas seem to have ceased. Erstwhile vocalist Gluck's musically unrelated solo LP is a collaborative effort with Nikki Sudden and Epic Soundtracks (both ex-Swell Maps), Rowland S. Howard (Birthday Party, etc.) and Gun Club leader Jeffrey Lee Pierce (on guitar). Various permutations of that gang play Gluck/Sudden compositions in simple recordings that have a nice, casual feel and little selfconsciousness. Stylistic variety—from acoustic guitars ("Gone Free," the nicest tune here) to near-noise (the last portion of the epic "All My Secrets")—keeps **Buffalo Bill** interesting, but Gluck's artless voice doesn't really suit the material. Intriguing but unsatisfying.

The same troops reunited the following year for another go-round, this time producing a 12-inch EP. [jy/iar]

SYD BARRETT
The Madcap Laughs (nr/Harvest) 1970 ●
Barrett (nr/Harvest) 1970 ●
The Madcap Laughs/Barrett (Harvest) 1974
The Peel Sessions EP (nr/Strange Fruit)
    1988 ●

One of rock's legendary living dead casualties, guitarist/songwriter Syd Barrett formed Pink Floyd in 1965 and made it one of the first art-school bands to abandon blues for druggified psychedelia. Syd fell out of Pink Floyd after a debut album that put the band on the verge of major international success; having grown erratic, withdrawn and unpredictable, he pretty much retired in 1968, and has since lived a private, reclusive existence—except for making two solo records in 1970. Barrett has influenced many bands and remains an enduring rock icon for the chronically dislocated. Twenty years later, his unselfconscious looniness continues to set a framework in which artists can explore updated acid-rock with little more than an acoustic guitar. The Television Personalities have sung about him, Robyn Hitchcock, Anthony More and others have been compared to him, and numerous art, psychedelic and neo-mod bands have invoked his name, recorded his songs and acknowledged his impact. Tormented but unquestionably brilliant, Barrett left a musical legacy which is wholly contained on Floyd's first LP and these two discs, which were originally issued separately but subsequently repackaged as a double album.

The Madcap Laughs sounds as though it was a difficult record to make. Having dragged Syd into a studio, ex-bandmates David Gilmour and Roger Waters had to get him organized enough to produce tracks that could be released. False starts and between-take discussions included on the record make it obvious this was no easy task. Still, the songs are wonderful, and Syd's delicate but clumsy singing lends charm to the effort, which alternates between one-man performances and subtly-played group efforts.

Barrett features an all-star trio of Gilmour, Richard Wright (Floyd's keyboardist) and Humble Pie drummer Jerry Shirley; Gilmour and Wright produced. This more consistent-sounding record—relatively confident and upbeat—offers Barrett's idiosyncratic view of life in songs like "Waving My Arms in the Air" and "Effervescing Elephant." Confusion and anger lurk just below the surface of misleadingly chipper bits of Carnaby Street flower-power music. [iar]

WILD WILLY BARRETT
See *John Otway.*

BASEMENT 5
1965–1980 (Antilles) 1981
In Dub (nr/Island) 1981

Basement 5 came out of Island Record's London art department playing a blend of reggae and synth-pop under the production auspices of Martin Hannett. **1965–1980** waffles between both forms, never quite achieving the hoped-for marriage, but does sport a number of light ditties with heavy political overtones. The contrast between roots and futurism gives Basement 5 a fascinating, if ephemeral flavor. Even more interesting is **In Dub**, a paean to Hannett's control-booth genius, which naturally features dub versions of some material from the first LP. Bassist Leo Williams later surfaced in Big Audio Dynamite. [sg]

See also *Big Audio Dynamite.*

TONI BASIL
Word of Mouth (Chrysalis) 1981
Toni Basil (Chrysalis) 1983

This veteran choreographer-turned-video director-and actress (she had a role in *Easy Rider* and continues to work in films 20 years later) skipped America for England, where she briefly became a glamourpuss pop star with the Chinn/Chapman-penned "Mickey," a simpleminded bit of new wave bubblegum that was an enormous hit in the States a year later. Unfortunately, the rest of her first album is disjointed, touching on more synth-dance rock and Pat Benatar-level mundanity, plus a trio of Devo songs on which Ms. B. is backed by the Akronites themselves. (The American release has two track substitutions and different artwork.) Basil is clever, likable and sings well enough, but the album has a disconcerting lack of cohesion and believability.

Except for the hyperactive "Over My Head," Basil's follow-up is a drag, filled with banal, clichéd rock and none of the inspired lunacy or even personality that made **Word of Mouth** spottily diverting.   [iar]

JIM BASNIGHT
See *Moberlys.*

MARTYN BATES
See *Eyeless in Gaza.*

BATFISH BOYS
Head (Twilight) 1986
Lurve: Some Kinda Flashback (Twilight) 1987

Formed by former March Violet lead singer Simon Denbigh, England's Batfish Boys play hard, guitar-driven rock with psychedelic blues overtones, not unlike the Godfathers. They display plenty of panache, but their material has an all-too-familiar ring to it; they're like a warmup band that's interesting enough to keep your attention for about 15 minutes. The compilation of British singles issued as **Lurve** features a much cleaner sound than the rather muddy **Head,** but its song titles ("Swamp Liquor," "Lootenant Lush," "Detroit Chrome Mountain") are at least sillier, and the guitar riffs get a bit more metallic. Neither offensive nor intriguing.   [dgs]

STIV BATORS
Disconnected (Bomp) 1980 ●
The Church and the New Creatures (Fr. Lolita) 1983

So what does a typecast Dead Boy do when his band breaks up? He moves to Los Angeles, hires local musicians and cuts a tremendous album of melodic rock tunes. Play-

ing down his outrageous side, Bators' first solo record maintains an Iggy-like persona while replacing chaotic garage-punk with thoughtful music that owes power pop a sizable debt. Originals like "Evil Boy" and "The Last Year" mask their dark messages with pretty tunes; a great cover of the punk classic "I Had Too Much to Dream Last Night" clarifies Bators' roots and caps off the album nicely.

The French LP contains all of **Disconnected**, adding three sides from a pair of Bomp singles and one other cut. In 1987, Bators released a 12-inch ("Have Love Will Travel" b/w a sharp swipe at the Moody Blues' "Story in Your Eyes") on Bomp, with musical assistance from various co-conspirators. In another recent endeavor, Stiv sings with Jeff Conolly on a Lyres song, issued as a 12-inch and included on that band's 1988 LP.   [iar]
See also *Lords of the New Church, Wanderers.*

BAUHAUS
Bela Lugosi's Dead EP (nr/Small Wonder) 1979 ●
In the Flat Field (nr/4AD) 1980 ●
Mask (nr/Beggars Banquet) 1981 ●
The Sky's Gone Out (A&M) 1982 ●
Press the Eject and Give Me the Tape (nr/Beggars Banquet) 1982 ●
Ziggy Stardust EP (nr/Beggars Banquet) 1982
Burning from the Inside (A&M) 1983 ●
The Singles 1981–1983 EP (nr/Beggars Banquet) 1983
4.A.D. EP (nr/4AD) 1983
1979–1983 (nr/Beggars Banquet) 1985 ●

DAVID J
Etiquette of Violence (nr/Situation 2) 1983 ●
Crocodile Tears and the Velvet Cosh (nr/Glass) 1985 ●
Blue Moods Turning Tail (nr/Glass) 1985 ●
David J on Glass (nr/Glass) 1987 ●

At one time the leading proponents of gloomy angst-rock, Bauhaus combined guitars and electronics into a bleak backdrop for Peter Murphy's tortured vocals. Adding theatrical makeup, poseur lyrics and a nearly hidden but stubborn pop streak, Bauhaus was both popular (in the UK) and influential. Their biggest shortcoming was a complete lack of irony; while promoting a somber image of deep seriousness, the band was an utter joke, a laughably pretentious attempt to be something way beyond its realistic ken.

Bauhaus' self-produced debut, **In the Flat Field**, is a dense, disjointed patchwork of sounds and uncertain feelings, supported by a pressured, incessant beat. Delving deep into the dark side of the human psyche with chilling results, Bauhaus conjures up unsettling images of a world given over to death and decay. **Mask** attempts an exploration of styles, incorporating airs of heavy metal, funk brass and Tangerine Dreamlike electronics into their work. Though still weighty, the lyrics make occasional intentional stabs at humor and show an increasingly romantic nature.

The Sky's Gone Out opens with a lively, bright version of Brian Eno's "Third Uncle," signaling a more upbeat period for Bauhaus, offsetting the ongoing themes of damnation and destruction. Good production opens up the sound considerably as Bauhaus draws even closer to the heavy metal frontier. In a flash of ambition, the album includes a three-part mini-opera, "The Three Shadows."

Press the Eject and Give Me the Tape, a live LP recorded in London and Liverpool, was first included as a bonus second disc in UK copies of **The Sky's Gone Out**, then re-issued as a separate album.

In their role as a singles band, Bauhaus' late '82 release of a copycat live-in-the-studio version of "Ziggy Stardust" (joined on the 12-inch by "Third Uncle," a bizarre, funny original consisting of Faustian film dialogue over cool instrumental backing, and a live recording of "Waiting for the Man," with guest vocalist Nico) supported their self-image as descendants of early '70s glam-rockers. (They had released a single of T. Rex's "Telegram Sam" in 1980.) A strange artistic dichotomy, to be sure.

The final Bauhaus album, **Burning from the Inside**, took them further into new realms of dark-spirited, mildly abrasive rock, with pounding drums, booming bass, buzzing guitars and some of the most ludicrous wanky lyrics you're ever likely to encounter. The nicest track is "King Volcano," an instrumental with skimpy chanting. Still, many took Bauhaus very seriously, and certainly a lot of bands have followed them into the solemn, pretentious depths of goth rock.

The Singles EP consolidates six A-sides, including "Ziggy Stardust," "Kick in the Eye" and "Lagartija Nick." **4.A.D.** compiles several 1980 singles, including "Telegram Sam," "Dark Entries" and a rare version of John Cale's "Rosegarden Funeral of Sores."

Bauhaus split up in late 1983; several of the members stuck together to form Tones on Tail and then Love and Rockets. Peter Murphy teamed with ex-Japan bassist Mick Karn to form Dalis Car and then went solo. Bassist David J(ay) recorded as a solo, joined the Jazz Butcher and then reunited with two of his bandmates in Love and Rockets.

Many of Bauhaus' CDs have extra tracks.

[sg/iar]

See also *Dalis Car, Jazz Butcher, Love and Rockets, Tones on Tail.*

BEARS

The Bears (Primitive Man) 1987 ●
Rise and Shine (Primitive Man) 1988 ●

What would Adrian Belew's catalogue of eccentric guitar noises sound like in the context of a traditional pop-rock band like, say, the Beatles, Hollies, Squeeze or XTC? When Belew hooked up with his pre-Crimson bar buddies the Raisins to form the Bears he seemingly set out to answer just that question. And what a revelation these two wonderful records are! Challenging, muscular, tuneful, idiosyncratic and accessible, **The Bears** (replete with group cover portrait by *Mad* magazine's inimitable Mort Drucker) is a superlative record. Everyone contributes and it all works—songs, playing, vocals and production. The only catch (if there is any): it's too pop for weirdo purists, too weird for pop purists. You figure out why it didn't sell mega-records.

Rise and Shine is nearly as good. While a bit more adventurous in song structure and playing, it also contains the occasional heavy-handed lyric (especially when bassist Rob Nyswonger writes alone) and one or two fewer memorable songs than **The Bears**. You'd be foolish to pass up either of these, though—get 'em while you can. As a bonus, the CD adds remixed versions of two songs ("Man Behind the Curtain" and "Figure It Out") that were on **The Bears**. [ds]

BEASTIE BOYS

Polly Wog Stew EP (Rat Cage) 1982 + 1988
Rock Hard EP (Def Jam) 1984
Licensed to Ill (Def Jam-Columbia) 1986 ●

New York's Beastie Boys began as a hardcore band in 1979; they broke up, re-formed, cut a 7-inch EP (**Polly Wog Stew**, containing such punk creations as "Egg Raid on Mojo" and "Transit Cop"; the record was reissued as a 12-inch import, with added tracks, in 1988) and then headed for the big time as a hip-hop band. Their 1983 single, "Cookie Puss," combined a tremendous beat pulsing with rock energy and sharp mix tricks with puerile spoken-word jive, including crank telephone calls. Ridiculous but undeniably funny and danceable, the 12-inch includes a bogus reggae song ("Beastie Revolution") that mugs Musical Youth and the entire Rasta culture.

In 1984, Ad-Rock, MCA and Mike D became a credible (later, incredibly successful) rap band with the release of the "Rock Hard" 12-inch. Unmistakably white and middle class, their '70s rock heritage leads producer Rick Rubin to toss in hunks of guitar—AC/DC riffs pop up in "Rock Hard" and "Party's Gettin' Rough," shards of Led Zeppelin fill "Beastie Groove." The Beasties then appeared in the film *Krush Groove,* for which they cut "She's on It," a fun, dumb stomper with a great guitar hook and obnoxious couplets like "She'd get down on her knees/If we'd only say *please.*" The Beasties had reached the heights of offensiveness and were squinting upwards.

The release of **Licensed to Ill** caught the guardians of popular culture napping. Within months, the album and its attendant 45s were skyrocketing towards astronomical sales levels as kids of all colors in countless countries rapped and danced to such intentionally moronic celebrations of self-indulgent stupidity and trash culture as "Fight for Your Right (To Party)," "No Sleep Till Brooklyn," "Brass Monkey," "Time to Get Ill" and the absurdly catchy "Girls." Rubin's brilliant stew of dodgy bits lifted from records by the Stones, Led Zep, Clash and dozens more still unidentified, combined with the whining nasal roar of the three stooges' inventive sexist drivel somehow hit that perfect beat, and made the Beasties international stars, dragging controversy, anger and damage reports in their wake. The next chapter has yet to be written. [iar/dgs]

BEAT

The Beat (Columbia) 1979
To Beat or Not to Beat EP (Passport) 1983

PAUL COLLINS' BEAT

The Kids Are the Same (CBS) 1982

Paul Collins, once a third of SF-to-LA's fabled Nerves (the other two were Peter Case, later of the Plimsouls, and tunesmith-to-the-stars Jack Lee), writes songs calling to

mind the early Hollies (except grittier and American) and a more down-to-earth, less poetic Byrds. Though never scaling the heights of either band, **The Beat** (issued prior to the name conflict with the English Beat) is simple, satisfying power pop, all meat and no filler. If anything, though, it's a little too no-frills, with unimaginative production; the lack of idiosyncrasy and variation gives it a monotonous feel.

This problem was remedied somewhat on the Beat's second album, which is quite a bit heavier. Although they seem to run out of steam—and songs—halfway through, they show a high degree of musical volatility up to that point.

Collins refurbished the Beat's lineup for the 1983 EP. The new combo includes ex-Patti Smith Group drummer Jay Dee Daugherty and guitarist Jimmy Ripp, both of whom have played on Tom Verlaine LPs. Although the band smokes and the songs are stylistically varied, this glorified demo surprisingly failed to get Collins a new major-label deal. [jg]

(ENGLISH) BEAT

I Just Can't Stop It (Sire) 1980 (IRS) 1983 ●
Wha'ppen? (Sire) 1981 (IRS) 1983
Special Beat Service (IRS) 1982 ●
What Is Beat? (IRS) 1983 ●

Although lumped in with the 2-Tone crowd upon emerging in 1979, the Beat (known in America as the English Beat) proved far more versatile and broadly talented than most of their skanking contemporaries. True, **I Just Can't Stop It** has its share of ska-influenced upbeats—a delightful reworking of "Tears of a Clown" (on the US release only) and patois-tinged toasting ("Rough Rider") from Ranking Roger—but the Birmingham band's furious drive and pumping bass ("Two Swords," "Click Click," "Twist & Crawl") relate more to the rock tradition. A recording of Andy Williams' warm-bath "Can't Get Used to Losing You" is a nice gesture, regardless of the outcome. (The US release also includes another track not on the original British album.)

By **Wha'ppen?**, the Beat had mellowed out, preferring midtempo grooves drawn from various Third World cultures. Loping music, playful combinations of voices (Roger and lead singer/guitarist Dave Wakeling) and Saxa's effervescent sax almost obscure the songs' depressing views of personal and social troubles ("Drowning," "All Out to Get You," "Cheated").

Special Beat Service is the band's slickest offering. The polished music generates more light than heat, but lyrics—dwelling more on romantic than political problems—depict believably complex scenarios. Ranking Roger's lighthearted showcases are now isolated from the group's main concerns, but the Beat here remains a fine band committed to pan-cultural understanding.

The **What Is Beat?** farewell compilation is actually three different records. The 14-track English album is a straight greatest hits collection of their most memorable work; early copies (and the cassette) added a bonus disc's worth of eight extended remixes. Although there's a lot of overlap in material, the American release is altogether different—single sides, two live renditions, a couple of remixes, etc. Collect 'em all!

Following the Beat's much-lamented dissolution, Ranking Roger and Dave Wakeling stuck together a while to form General Public while David Steele and Andy Cox assembled Fine Young Cannibals. [si/iar]

See also *Fine Young Cannibals, General Public.*

but falls flat on its bum, anyway—even as guitarist Buddy Blue's energetic slide work threatens to save the day. A wry Blue original called "Gun Sale at the Church" offers faint breath in the mirror, but otherwise this one's ready for burial.

Guitarist/singer Joey Harris (who already had a neat 1983 major-label album with a former band, the Speedsters, under his belt) replaced Blue on **The Pursuit of Happiness**, a commercially-minded record that meanders further from the simple glories of **The New West**. Echoes of Springsteen, Jeff Lynne and John Cougar Mellencamp don't exactly improve the originality quotient, but Harris' witty songwriting—gossiping about cow-pokers in "Texas" and expressing religious skepticism in "God Is Here Tonight"—does. Covers of Tom Waits and Johnny Cash are beneficial; guest pianist Nicky Hopkins does his bit with typical (but long-missing) aplomb.

Genealogical aside: singer/drummer Country Dick Montana was at one time the drummer in California's beat-revivalist Crawdaddys. [iar]

BEAT FARMERS
Tales of the New West (Rhino) 1985 •
Glad'n'Greasy EP (nr/Demon) 1986
Van Go (Curb-MCA) 1986
The Pursuit of Happiness (Curb-MCA)
1987 •

You can tell a lot about musicians by the company they keep. On **Tales of the New West**, produced by Steve Berlin, this San Diego quartet gets vocal assistance from Peter Case (ex-Plimsouls), Chip and Tony Kinman (Rank and File) and Sid Griffin (Long Ryders). The Farmers do the '50s-cum-'80s neo-country-rock stomp with enthusiasm, economy and not a hint of phoniness or selfconsciousness. The mock-cowboy nonsense of "California Kid" (disregarding its atypical resemblance to the Bonzo Dog Band) proves they're not sensitive about the genre; post-punk roots even show on a cover of Lou Reed's "There She Goes Again." An honest album from an honest band. During a month-long British tour, the Farmers cut their second record, the six-song **Glad'n' Greasy** EP, produced by Bob Andrews (ex-Rumour) and Colin Fairley.

Neil Young's "Powderfinger" (the sole holdover from the EP) is one of the few highlights of **Van Go**, a halfbaked, halfhearted outing that doesn't step in anything odious

BEAT HAPPENING
Beat Happening (K) 1986
Jamboree (K-Rough Trade) 1988

BEAT HAPPENING/SCREAMING TREES
Beat Happening/Screaming Trees EP
(K-Homestead) 1988

Overweening ambition is such a common component of contemporary music that it's nice to find a young band that truly doesn't give a shit. Consider Beat Happening, a talented trio of minimalists from Olympia, Washington. They write swell songs and sing them accompanied only by shoddy shards of electric guitar and rudimentary drum(s). Bret, Heather and Calvin sound like the Shaggs' smarter cousins on **Jamboree**, a fresh breeze of seemingly unrehearsed one-take serious nonsense that is remorselessly amateurish but—except for "The This Many Boyfriends Club," which was cut live without melody—thoroughly, legitimately enjoyable.

The four songs on the joint EP with members of another Northwest band (this record melds the two otherwise autonomous bodies without detailing individual contributions) suggest that someone in Olympia's been listening to **Disraeli Gears** a lot. (The wah-wah and mock-Ginger Baker drumming is a dead giveaway.) "Polly Pereguin" and "Tales of Brave Aphrodite," a loopy confessional, are roughly-cut electric pop with definite '60s ambience. Like groovy, man!

Beat Happening has released numerous tapes and records of themselves and other artists on their own K label. [iar]

BEAT NIGS
The Beat Nigs (Insight-Alternative Tentacles) 1988

This remarkable San Francisco quintet explodes in a tight and danceable riot of industrial percussion, vocals and tape manipulations on their debut album. According to an enclosed booklet ("Aural Instruction Manual"), the word "nig" is defined as "a positive acronym . . . [it] has taken on a universal meaning in describing all oppressed people who have actively taken a stand against those who perpetuate ethnic notions and discriminate on the basis of them." Assailing "Television" (the medium, not the band), poverty and hunger ("Burritos"), the "CIA" and South Africa ("Control"), the Beat Nigs cross Devo, Test Dept. and the Dead Kennedys in a brilliant, original coincidence of extremist musical ideas and radical politics. [iar]

BEATNIKS
See *Yukihiro Takahashi.*

BEAT RODEO
Staying Out Late with Beat Rodeo (IRS) 1985
Home in the Heart of the Beat (IRS) 1986 ●

STEVE ALMAAS
Beat Rodeo EP (Coyote) 1982

CRACKERS
Sir Crackers! EP (Twin/Tone) 1980

Following the breakup of the Suicide Commandos (in which he played bass), Minneapolis' Steve Almaas turned to guitar and formed the Crackers (not the New Mexico band with the same name). Unfortunately, the trio's EP is of little consequence except to vaguely indicate the direction he'd pursue: rough-hewn melodic rock. **Sir Crackers!** threatens to take off, but just fizzles.

After working with the Bongos, Almaas and boss Bongo Richard Barone headed down to North Carolina to visit Mitch Easter at his Drive-In Studio. The three of them whipped up the **Beat Rodeo** EP, finally showing Almaas off to great advantage. If Marshall Crenshaw's treatment of the Buddy Holly legacy irks you for being wrapped in candy floss, this charming, rocking disc should be right up your alley—swell tunes, Almaas' straight-as-an-arrow vocals and Easter's clear production that adds no sugar but lets the natural sweetness shine through.

Almaas almost immediately formed a quartet named for the EP but not including any previous bandmates. **Staying Out Late** (originally issued in Germany in 1984) shows a country bent implicit in its name (but absent from the EP) and integrates it (country-ish guitar sound, even a dash of fiddle) rather well into the already established pop-rock context. The problem is that they master the form with little memorable content and insufficient élan. They almost rock out on "Without You," but shortcircuit the power by overloading the arrangement. Also, lyrical tension is never conveyed by Almaas' vocals, which run the emotional gamut from A(miable) to B(oringly benign).

Staying Out Late was produced by Don Dixon (with two tracks by Richard Gottehrer). Whether resulting from the switch to Scott Litt or simply the educational benefit of past mistakes, **Home in the Heart of the Beat** is a definite improvement. The band tends to play more to its strengths and avoid (or compensate for) its weaknesses. The country-ness is now a feel rather than a form, and as such suits them far better; the songs are more mature and less awkward. The record's title may be a tad pretentious, but in several ways Beat Rodeo really *is* more at home—with themselves, at any rate. Solid, enjoyable fare.
[jg]

JEAN BEAUVOIR
Drums Along the Mohawk (Columbia) 1986 ●
Jacknifed (Columbia) 1988 ●

This onetime Plasmatic and, more recently, producer and Little Steven sideman did almost everything on his first solo album—writing, playing, producing, arranging, etc. Side One of **Drums Along the Mohawk** (the reference is tonsorial) owes a huge debt to Prince (see the "Little Red Corvette" chapter), but the mainstream rock LP makes chameleonic room for other soundalikes: "Rockin' in the Street" favors Eddy Grant, while most of "This Is Our House" could be Foreigner with better vocals. And darned if that ain't Tom Petty singing "Drive You Home." Welcome to the wax museum . . .

Recorded in New York, Paris, Stockholm and elsewhere, **Jacknifed** lets a few musicians share in the fun. Beauvoir thankfully downplays the stylistic clone action (although the Prince influence is far from gone), but forgets to replace it with anything sufficiently original or substantial. His lyrics—clever and provocative—are the best aspect of this highly accomplished and salable album which is neither diverting nor memorable.   [iar]

BEFOUR THREE O'CLOCK
See *Three O'Clock*.

ADRIAN BELEW
Lone Rhino (Island) 1982
Twang Bar King (Island) 1983
Desire Caught by the Tail (Island) 1986

Having served with David Bowie, Talking Heads, the Tom Tom Club and—most notably and recently—King Crimson, guitarist Belew echoes famous associates on his first solo LP without staking out any turf to call his own. The Kentucky native employs pre-stardom friends from Midwestern bands rather than big names, serving up a varied program of calculated weirdness, straight rock and semi-funk. Mildly charming and rather unfocused, the tenuous unifying thread is his David Byrne-influenced voice.

On his second outing, Belew shows much more self-assurance in putting over the same ingredients—an assurance that spills over into self-indulgence long before the album is over. But this record does underscore his contributions to King Crimson: the distinctive vocabulary of extramusical noises, the personality and especially the humor, which is in abundant evidence here. When it all works, it works incredibly well.

Before forming the Bears, Belew issued a one-man instrumental record, **Desire Caught by the Tail**. The simply-overdubbed guitars and percussion have a casual home-studio air but no discernible direction. Unlike his (ex?)-bandmate's obsessively controlled Frippertronics, these excursions, while occasionally evocative, hold scant listener appeal.
                                    [jy/mf/iar]
See also *Bears*.

BELFEGORE
Belfegore (Elektra) 1984

An American bassist, a Canadian drummer and a German guitarist comprise this unique crypto-metal band, a strange incident of subversive musical activity. **Belfegore** was produced by Conny Plank, best known for his Ultravox and D.A.F. work; their first video was directed by Zbigniew Rybczynski right after his landmark Art of Noise clip. Musically dark and energetic, Belfegore avoids the clichés of metal for a somber intelligence that has common ground with everyone from Motorhead to Joy Division. Fascinating.   [iar]

BELLE STARS
The Belle Stars (Stiff-Warner Bros.) 1983

Offering a self-contained, funkier alternative to early Bananarama, London's seven-woman Belle Stars played and sang neo-soul and dance-rock. At their most glamorous (the excellent "Sign of the Times") they resemble that era's ABC, but with added spunk and less chrome. Much of the material is, however, much plainer. Far more enjoyable than the band's originals on the sole LP are covers of "Iko Iko," "Mockingbird," "Needle in a Haystack" and "The Clapping Song," which provoke a good time largely through the band's own evident enjoyment.
                                    [iar]

BOND BERGLAND
See *Saqqara Dogs*.

BERLIN
Pleasure Victim (MAO-Enigma) 1982 (Geffen) 1983 ●
Love Life (Geffen) 1984 ●
Count Three & Pray (Geffen) 1986 ●

Los Angeles-based Berlin (has there ever been a Berlin band named Los Angeles?) had been active for several years—an almost totally different lineup issued a 1980 single on IRS—before bursting onto the national scene. The impressively slick **Pleasure Victim** is a seven-song mini-album which commercializes routine synth-rock with singer Terri Nunn's audio pornography. The record's most blatant (and hence, popular) track, "Sex (I'm a . . .)," is tasteless and offensive, with crude lyrics and ridiculous moaning. There are two likably atmospheric tunes ("Masquerade" and "The Metro"); otherwise this ranges from bland to inept.

Berlin serves up more singles-bar smarm on **Love Life**, which makes a bid for respectability as a techno-dance band. Unfortunately, leader John Crawford is too shallow a songwriter; at best, Berlin can only manage a polished Mike Howlett-produced noise (Giorgio Moroder did a pair of tracks as well) to glamorize a vapid and depressing view of sex. Pathetic.

Nunn, Crawford and Rob Brill brought only vocals, bass and drums to the party for **Count Three & Pray**. With unannotated guitar work by Ted Nugent, Dave Gilmour and Elliot Easton, plus a heap of other session players, Berlin made what thankfully proved to be their last record. (The band ended its miserable existence in 1987, perhaps to make way for Pretty Poison). While Brill's "Like Flames" is an adequate song with a catchy singalong chorus, Crawford's "Sex Me, Talk Me" is straight from the stunted rut of his attitudes about copulation. Originally cowritten and produced by Moroder for the soundtrack of *Top Gun*, "Take My Breath Away" is a terrible, characterless ballad that somehow became a forgettable hit single.

[iar]

BERLIN BLONDES
Berlin Blondes (nr/Odeon-EMI) 1980

Their name notwithstanding, this band hailed from Glasgow and played undistinguished, danceable hybrid synth/bass/drums clichés, occasionally adding colorful Sparks-like vocals for character. Mike Thorne produced the album with skill, allowing the music to be heard loud and clear. Too bad there isn't much reason you'd want to.

[iar]

CINDY LEE BERRYHILL
Who's Gonna Save the World? (Rhino) 1987

Cindy Lee is an endearing flake who at times may remind you of a folky Patti Smith or a female Jonathan Richman in his Modern Lovers days. Like them, she's no great singer or musician, but her songs—mostly about such middle-class adolescent/post-adolescent life crises as alienation, drug addiction and suicide—not only ring true, but do so without lapsing into cliché or self-pity. There's also an ironic sense of humor at work, best seen in "Damn, Wish I Was a Man," a catalogue of reasons for penis envy that contains such gems as "Wish I was a man, I'd be sexy with a belly like Jack Nicholson." [ds]

BETHNAL
Dangerous Times (nr/Vertigo) 1978
Crash Landing (nr/Vertigo) 1978

On the strength of live performances during 1976, this multi-ethnic London band (named after Bethnal Green) was considered one of the most promising new groups in Britain. Admittedly different from the pack, lead singer George Csapo played keyboards and violin—instruments not then in vogue among new wavers. Unfortunately, Bethnal was never able to properly translate its hard-driving mid-period-Who-influenced sound to vinyl. They came closest on **Dangerous Times**, but were thwarted by Kenny Laguna's thin, pop-oriented production which highlights the band's material and vocals (both spotty) over its superior musicianship and energy; covers of "Baba O'Reilly" [sic] and "We Gotta Get Out of This Place," while interesting choices, add nothing to the originals.

Crash Landing, produced by Phil Chapman and Pete Townshend's brother-in-law, Jon Astley, moves Bethnal into glossy, empty-headed arena-style terrain that effectively alienated the band's supporters and failed to interest a new audience. [ds]

B-52's
The B-52's (Warner Bros.) 1979 ●
Wild Planet (Warner Bros.) 1980
Party Mix EP (Warner Bros.) 1981
Mesopotamia EP (Warner Bros.) 1982
Whammy! (Warner Bros.) 1983
Bouncing off the Satellites (Warner Bros.) 1986 ●

FRED SCHNEIDER AND THE SHAKE SOCIETY
Fred Schneider and the Shake Society (Warner Bros.) 1984

Just when new wave seemed to be bottoming out, along came Athens, Georgia's B-52's to rev it back up again, with distinctive junk-store '60s visuals (the two women in the band sport bouffant wigs—"B-52's" in Southern regional slang) and stark, highly danceable songs with appropriately surreal kitsch lyrics. The B-52's' wacky sense of humor made their self-titled first album a sleeper that was certified (US) gold in 1986. Now a cult classic, it contains such cornerstones of the repertoire as "52 Girls," "Dance This Mess Around," "6060-842" and the ever-popular "Rock Lobster."

The B-52's have been wondering what to do for an encore ever since. The eagerly awaited **Wild Planet** has its inspired moments: "Private Idaho" and "Devil in My Car" mesh a firm beat with dark and/or silly sentiments. "Give Me Back My Man" takes a new direction—a serious (!) showcase for Cindy Wilson's Patsy Cline-influenced singing. (Vocalist Fred Schneider is usually up front for comic relief.) But too much of the album, with its short length and recycled ideas, comes across as a pale imitation of its predecessor.

Apparently the band felt the same way, and stayed away from the recording studio for the next year and a half. **Party Mix**, issued in the interim, takes three songs from each of the two LPs and—through the miracle of tape loops, overdubs and other studio tomfoolery—inflates them to nearly 30 minutes playing time. The result is functional for discos but antithetical to the B-52's' minimalist precepts.

The band was next "officially" heard from with another mini-LP, **Mesopotamia**, salvaged from sessions produced by Talking Head David Byrne. Whether under Byrne's humorless influence or not—he plays on the record and engages a couple of Heads-family percussionists to help out—the B-52's get serious with dire results. "Loveland" and "Deep Sleep" sacrifice élan for slickness—not a fair trade. "Cake" and the title cut (one of only two Schneider vocals) come off as selfconscious parodies of the old, carefree B-52's. Only "Throw That Beat in the Garbage Can" taps the zany reservoir that made the group popular in the first place.

After the curious abortion of **Mesopotamia, Whammy!** came as a reassuring return to form, or perhaps formula. On some cuts ("Whammy Kiss," "Trism," "Butterbean"), the band goes through the by-now-well-worn motions. Elsewhere ("Big Bird," "Queen of Las Vegas"), horns—introduced on **Mesopotamia**—and intriguing narratives show the B-52's are only on semi-automatic pilot. Drummer Keith Strickland and guitarist Ricky Wilson (Cindy's brother) play all the instruments save horns; the sound is more electronic than funky-human.

Schneider's solo project hardly discouraged fears about the state of the B-52's. (Kate Pierson helps Fred out with vocals.) The *pro tem* Shake Society is a fine stopgap for the parent band's looniness. Schneider's lyrics continue to dwell on campy sci-fi

("This Planet's a Mess," "Orbit") and campy fantasy ("Summer in Hell," "Boonga"), with campy sex ("Monster," "It's Time to Kiss") thrown in for good measure (and a bit of controversy).

Tragically, Ricky Wilson died of cancer in October 1985, shortly after the recording sessions for **Bouncing off the Satellites**. Produced by British popmeister Tony Mansfield (who also plays Fairlight on every track) and with Schneider hardly in evidence, the bittersweet record was eventually completed and released in late 1986. The first side is entirely delightful, filled with such classic B-52 silliness as "Wig," "Detour Thru Your Mind" and "Girl from Ipanema Goes to Greenland," but the flip is overly smooth, limp and uninspired. Typifying the record's structural oddness, Schneider is the only band member on the lengthy "Juicy Jungle," co-written and largely played by one John Coté.

The band's future—indeed, its existence—remains unsettled.   [si/iar]

JELLO BIAFRA
See *Dead Kennedys, Witch Trials.*

BIFF BANG POW!
Pass the Paintbrush, Honey.. (nr/Creation)
   1985 ●
Love's Going Out of Fashion EP (nr/Creation)
   1986
The Girl Who Runs the Beat Hotel
   (nr/Creation) 1987 ●
Oblivion (Creation-Relativity) 1987
Love Is Forever (Creation-Relativity) 1988 ●

Besides doing his part to influence the sound of new British music by founding and running the influential Creation label, Glaswegian Alan McGee leads this hip neo-pop quartet, which he formed in London. Fans of the band for which both company and band are named, however, may be put off to find little evidence of the Creation's peerless '60s art-rock here.

Psychedelia and nostalgia inform Biff Bang Pow!'s records but, often as not, the wiry guitar pop sounds like a compromise between Josef K, Orange Juice and Haircut One Hundred. Although they would seem spiritually in synch with the Television Personalities or Times, Biff Bang Pow! don't share those groups' winsome charm or demonstrative cultural resonance.

The cover photo of **Pass the Paintbrush** shows a set of Vox gear that would do any revivalist band proud. The first side offers little such personality; noisy interludes of non-chromatic harmonica provide the most noticeable component of the short ditties. Side B has the real goods, containing the rushing Kinksy "Colin Dobbins" and the outstanding "A Day out with Jeremy Chester," a lengthy acid-rock trip loaded with wild feedback and exciting guitar crashes. The **Paintbrush** CD also contains the band's next album, **The Girl Who Runs the Beat Hotel**.

Poorly produced with thin, shrill sound, **The Girl Who Runs the Beat Hotel** reveals much stronger, more attractive songwriting. "Someone Stole My Wheels" and "The Happiest Girl in the World" are convincing period pieces colored in, respectively, with prominent organ and female vocals; "Five Minutes in the Life of Greenwood Goulding" uses crazy backwards guitars. Strangely, McGee's vocals suggest Robert Smith on "Love's Going Out of Fashion" and Lloyd Cole on "He Don't Need That Girl." The melodies and varied arrangements are stylishly appropriate, but the botched mix prevents them from being fully appreciated. The 12-inch of "Love's Going Out of Fashion" avoids that sonic pothole and includes three atmospheric non-LP tracks.

Almost all of the remaining sharp edges have been eliminated from **Oblivion**, a handsomely polished effort with brilliant vocals and sparkling guitar uplifting the finely-constructed songs. Still, it's heartwarming to hear "A Girl Called Destruction" devolve into a noisy old-fashioned raveup; "I See the Sun" contrasts acoustic strumming with massive distortion on the solo. If Paul Weller had grown up listening to the Hollies as much as the Who, the Jam might have made an album like **Oblivion**; fortunately, Biff Bang Pow! did.

Side One of **Love Is Forever** mixes electric and acoustic guitars (played by McGee and Richard Green) with pretty harmonica to yield music akin to the Bluebells' sprightly folk-rock (but not songs of that group's caliber). The other side—all-electric and at times loud!—is bracing but largely unfathomable, despite the inclusion of such delicacies as "She Went Away to Love." While remnants of **Oblivion**'s appeal and clarity are evident, **Love Is Forever** is comparatively dull and uninspiring. [iar]

BIG AUDIO DYNAMITE

This Is Big Audio Dynamite (Columbia) 1985 ●
No. 10, Upping St. (Columbia) 1986 ●
Tighten Up Vol. '88 (Columbia) 1988 ●

The rote replay of the non-Clash's **Cut the Crap** only underscores the accomplishment of Mick Jones' band with filmmaker Don Letts. Joe Strummer attempted to purify the Clash by purging Jones, but wound up liberating the guitarist's muse and (for a while) misplacing his own. B.A.D.—which also includes ex-Basement 5 bassist Leo Williams in the uncommon lineup—takes off from various things the Clash had tried on **Sandinista!** and **Combat Rock**, but goes much further with audio vérité, sonic effects and beatbox funk. The adventurous band's recordings are creatively ambitious crazy quilts of half-baked songs with fascinating lyrics, slathered over with shards of film dialogue and news reports. Although flimsy and gimmicky on first exposure, the meandering dance grooves on **This Is Big Audio Dynamite** (especially "E=MC2" and "The Bottom Line") prove far more alluring and resilient with repeated exposure. Jones' monochromatic vocals can be a negative factor in spots, but they're generally adequate to the task, and occasionally perfectly suited.

In a truly startling development, Strummer wound up co-producing (and co-writing half of) B.A.D.'s second album with Jones. Appraising the nature of his contribution or understanding the pair's ongoing synergy is impossible, but finding this uniquely conceived pan-cultural record fascinating is easy. Similar to the first album, but improved by greater studio mastery and better writing, **No. 10, Upping St.** deconstructs modern culture and politics in a wild soup of sounds and lyrics. "C'mon Every Beatbox" quotes Jeff Beck and Eddie Cochran over a powerful groove with ricocheting drumbeats; the shuffling "Beyond the Pale" and the attractively melodic "V. Thirteen" (reprised in an instrumental version as "The Big V.") are the closest things to Clash songs since **Combat Rock**. "Dial a Hitman" starts as a song but winds up as a musical bed for a crazy phone call. A unique, danceable hybrid of art and life. [iar]

See also *Jah Wobble*.

BIG BALLS AND THE GREAT WHITE IDIOT

Foolish Guys (Ger. Strand) 1978

With some guidance by ex-Grapefruit George Alexander (né Alec Young, as in the family that gave us the Easybeats and AC/DC), the three Grund brothers play high-spirited punk in the style of the day (Pistols, Ramones, et al.). It's charming by dint of amusingly awkward attempts to translate their idea of punky aggro into English ("Hell So Neat," "Hang Yourself from an Apple Tree") and general goofiness.   [jg]

BIG BLACK

Lungs EP (Ruthless) 1983
Bulldozer EP (Ruthless-Fever) 1984
Racer-X EP (Homestead) 1984
Atomizer (Homestead) 1986 ●
The Hammer Party (Homestead) 1986
Headache EP (Touch and Go) 1987
Sound of Impact (nr/Walls Have Ears) 1987
The Rich Man's 8-Track Tape [CD]
   (Homestead) 1987
Songs About Fucking (Touch and Go)
   1987 ●

"The only good policeman is a dead one/ The only good laws aren't enforced/I've never hung a darkie but I've fed one/I've never seen an Indian on a horse." With these gentle words, acerbic Chicago fanzine writer Steve Albini began his extremely serious adventures in the rock'n'roll skin trade. For a while, Albini assembled makeshift lineups from other bands (Big Black subsequently stabilized a lineup of its own); regardless of who, they make music that's grating, angular, humorless and very intelligent—sort of a cross between Gang of Four, PiL and the Great Crusades (not a band). Albini's self-righteousness sometimes causes him to be as much unaccommodating as uncompromising, but his bile is generally well-directed, and he's immune to corruption, except from within. All these records are challenging and rewarding.

Lungs is at once the most homegrown and overwrought Big Black release. Over a skeletal art-funk background, Albini creates bleak, tough images of recessioned industrial America. While "I Can Be Killed" is almost laughable for its delusionary self-importance, "Steelworker" is intensely muscular. **Bulldozer** goes for a chunkier sound and more violent imagery. The recording quality and playing are more sophisticated, making it less

alluring than the spartan **Lungs**. "Cables" is about voyeurs at a slaughterhouse; "The Pigeon Kill" is about poisoning birds; "Seth" is about a dog trained to attack black people. Overambitious, but sincere and scary. (A limited number of copies of **Bulldozer** were packaged in a sheet metal sleeve, with the band's name etched in acid.)

Racer-X is less obsessively cranky than the first two records (a positive development). The basic elements remain: one-riff industrial funk grooves, coarse vocals, jagged guitar. But this EP fills out the sound without sacrificing any of its amateur appeal. The musicians, while skilled technicians all, keep the sound raw. And if Albini is still something of a cartoon curmudgeon in his boasts about being "The Ugly American," he at least includes a James Brown cover and a tribute to Speed Racer's cooler brother. Not as idiosyncratically brilliant as **Lungs**, but fine stuff nonetheless.

Atomizer comes thundering out of the starting gate like a wounded rhino, charging around madly with awesome, claustrophobic rock power. Albini leads his troupe through such angry slices of niho-philosophy, depravity and arson as "Big Money," "Stinking Drunk," "Fists of Love," "Jordan, Minnesota," "Kerosene" and "Bazooka Joe" (for which the liner notes note "part of the drum track is an M1 carbine being fired in a field exercise by a guy named Joe"). A magnificently rugged record.

As its sticker prudently warns, **Headache** is nowhere near as good as **Atomizer**. With the exception of the slow-to-fast chugger "Ready Men," nothing approaches the same level of excellence. Although **Headache** is the weakest Big Black LP or EP, it will forever be remembered for its original (fortunately?) limited edition sleeve: the most gruesome, disgusting photo imaginable, an accident victim's head so grotesque the record had to be sold with a covering black jacket.

Sound of Impact is a rather mysterious, extraordinarily limited edition live LP. Big Black's name appears nowhere on the sleeve or spine; many are unaware of the record's existence. Recorded live in Muncie, Indiana and Minneapolis, it includes early versions with different lyrics of later material, and is as jarring and unrelenting as their concerts were.

The CD-only **Rich Man's 8-Track** (ha-ha) is a 16-track compilation containing all of **Atomizer**, plus cuts from **Headache** and **Hammer Party**.

As Big Black was splitting up, they released their finest work—a second actual LP, **Songs About Fucking**. As if to go out kicking, screaming, howling and biting, it's their most raging, abrasive, pulverizing record, with only an excellent and ironic guitar take of Kraftwerk's "The Model" providing any relief. Albini's screeched vocals are so low in the mix they're just another instrument. Obsessing as usual on the excessive and bizzare side of human life, his stories remain mini horror movies set to the punishing, scathing guitar attack. Lyrically and aurally like **Atomizer**, it's liable to alter your perceptions. A final blowout from a seemingly exhaustive force; Albini (besides getting busy a bunch of times as a record producer) has already formed a new band called Rapeman. [jl/iar/jr]

BIG BOYS

Where's My Towel (Wasted Talent) 1981
Fun Fun Fun EP (Moment) 1982
Lullabies Help the Brain Grow (Moment) 1983
No Matter How Long the Line Is at the Cafeteria, There's Always a Seat! (Enigma) 1984

BIG BOYS/DICKS

Big Boys & the Dicks Recorded Live at Raul's Club (Rat Race) 1980

Austin's best punk band was drawn together by its members' shared love of skateboarding. Turned out the thrashers had a thing for funk as well, and so the Big Boys escaped the confines of hardcore by syncopating some of their speedrock. A lot of their stuff is still straight hardcore—very good hardcore—but the funk is what makes them noteworthy, a high power James Brown-styled groove at ten times the tempo. But even with the punk connection intact, once the jam starts moving, the horns don't sound out of place. **Fun Fun Fun** presents the Big Boys' vision rather crudely; **Lullabies** brings sturdy (if not spectacular) songwriting together with muscular playing and good recording quality. And it even adds a third wrinkle: "Sound on Sound," a slow, spacy underground pop song that drones over a background of radio noise. [jl]

BIG COUNTRY

The Crossing (Mercury) 1983 ●
Wonderland EP (Mercury) 1984

Steeltown (Mercury) 1984 ●
The Seer (Mercury) 1986 ●

Guitarist Stuart Adamson—the unsung hero and sound shaper of the Skids—survived that once-wonderful band's miserable end to form a down-to-earth rock quartet unhampered (at the outset, anyway) by grandiose artistic pretensions. Rounded out by guitarist Bruce Watson and the ace rhythm section of Tony Butler and Mark Brzezicki (who have also played, individually and collectively, on records by Pete Townshend, the Pretenders, Roger Daltrey and others), Big Country quickly jumped into the vanguard of resurgent guitar-hero bands.

Retaining some of the Skids' pseudo-Scottish six-string-bagpipe effects, **The Crossing**, brilliantly produced by Steve Lillywhite, offers rousing anthems ("In a Big Country," "Inwards" and "Fields of Fire," its riff cleverly lifted from "The Guns of Navarone") and moving romantic ballads ("The Storm," "Chance") that neatly intertwine Celtic folk traditions with blazing guitar riffs. (The UK tape edition has extra tracks.) The **Wonderland** EP consists of four songs, including an early B-side and the uplifting, catchy title track, one of the band's best efforts.

Steeltown breaks no new ground and is basically a formulaic reprise, but the band is so unique, passionate and skilled at what they do that you don't really mind. Best selections: "East of Eden," "Where the Rose Is Sown" (a virtual rewrite of "In a Big Country," itself not all that different from "Fields of Fire") and "Just a Shadow."

Well-crafted, with melancholy lyrics and a guest vocal appearance by Kate Bush on the title track, **The Seer** holds close to the band's by-now-standard sound, with no loss in appeal. Even if they don't vary much in content or style, Big Country's records offer an original and invigorating brand of modern rock'n'roll with deep cultural resonance. [iar]

BIG PIG

Bonk (A&M) 1988 ●

From the cruel metaphor of the opening "Iron Lung" to the weary conclusion of "Devil's Song," **Bonk** is one angry record. Although technically an Australian group, Big Pig began in London around 1985, and hatred of Margaret Thatcher's England seems to fuel the bittersweet material. Lead

45

singer Sherine has a dark alto that complements the songs' often depressing tone. But vocals aren't the half of Big Pig. The instrumentation is keyboards, harmonica and drums—lots of drums, played by three out of seven members. The trundling, tribal rhythms give the songs the effect of steamrollers extinguishing their protagonists' burned-out lives. Sparse musical textures, including group chants and that anomalous bluesy harmonica, help make **Bonk** compelling listening. Big Pig's obviously got attitude to burn, and who couldn't use a healthy blast of protest? [si]

BIG STAR
See *Alex Chilton.*

BIG YOUTH
Screaming Target (nr/Trojan) 1973
Dreadlocks Dread (nr/Klik) 1975 (nr/Front Line) 1978 (nr/Virgin) 1983
Natty Cultural Dread (nr/Trojan) 1976
Hit the Road Jack (nr/Trojan) 1976
Isaiah, First Prophet of Old (nr/Front Line) 1978
Everyday Skank—The Best of Big Youth (nr/Trojan) 1980
Some Great Big Youth (Heartbeat) 1981
The Chanting Dread inna Fine Style (Heartbeat) 1983
Live at Reggae Sunsplash (Sunsplash) 1984
A Luta Continua (Heartbeat) 1985 ●
Manifestation (Heartbeat) 1988 ●

His front teeth inlaid with red, green and gold gems, Big Youth is probably the best-known and most popular of all reggae djs, with a career that's been going strong for more than 15 years. Born Manley Buchanan in Jamaica, he began toasting in the early '70s, after working as a cabbie and a mechanic. His success was quick: records like "The Killer" and "S.90 Skank" (named after a motorcycle) scaled the charts with ease, demonstrating his power and versatility. Many years and albums later he remains a major reggae presence, an influence on an entire generation of toasters. (He's credited with coining the term "natty dread.") If U-Roy laid the foundation, Big Youth made it happen—he gave toasting style as well as something to say.

Eccentric and startling, all of Big Youth's early records sounded radical when they first appeared, and have held up marvelously

well. Featuring instrumental tracks from songs by Dennis Brown, Gregory Isaacs and others, **Screaming Target** boasts two versions of the wild title cut, along with "The Killer" and "Solomon a Gunday." **Natty Cultural Dread** features the amazing "Every Nigger Is a Star" and "Jim Squashy," which invokes John Coltrane. **Hit the Road Jack** has several loopy covers of American soul hits, including Marvin Gaye's "What's Going On," the Ray Charles song of the title and Teddy Pendergrass' "Wake Up Everybody." You've never heard these songs this way—offbeat and wonderful. Although all of the Trojan releases are worth owning, **Everyday Skank** is an invaluable compilation of LP tracks and early singles.

Dreadlocks Dread (reissued by Virgin in the **Crucial Cuts** series) features "Marcus Garvey Dread" (a toast of the Burning Spear classic), "Train to Rhodesia" and "House of Dread Locks." The LP marks Big Youth's development as a composer, and his increased reliance on Rasta subject matter. Side Two has a couple of filler instrumentals, but the record is widely considered his best.

Isaiah continues the evolution heard on **Dreadlocks Dread**. He does more singing (or sing-jaying, as it's called) than toasting and originals outnumber covers. The groove is steady and appealing. Big Youth's recent releases, available mostly on Heartbeat, are also marked by their able consistency. All four listed boast a variety of styles, tough and relevant protest lyrics and rootsy playing. Not as wild as his early sides, these records are nonetheless some of the best contemporary reggae—authentic and uncorrupted, personal and moving. He's mellowed a bit with age—parts of **Manifestation** are downright sluggish—but Big Youth remains as formidable an artist as ever.

Rounding out the canon, **Live at Reggae Sunsplash** (from a 1982 festival) proves he hasn't lost his ability to work a crowd, and provides a decent document of one of his better shows. [bk]

BIJOU
Danse avec Moi (Fr. Philips) 1977
OK Carole (Fr. Philips) 1978
Pas Dormir (Fr. Philips) 1979
En Public (Fr. Philips) 1980
Jamais Domptés (Fr. Philips) 1981
Bijou Bop (Fr. Philips) 1981

Bijou was billed on the shrink wrap of its debut LP as France's top punk band. Considering how mild and derivative of basic rock'n'roll moves they are—there are musical quotes all over the LP—this says little for the Gallic sense of rock in revolt. Bijou plays with no frills and few surprises; kind of poppy here (especially the earlier stuff), more boogieoid there, a token "arty" touch or bit of '60s nostalgia, a modest rockabilly orientation (**Bijou Bop**), and so on. Very few tracks (aside from the live **En Public**) are as long as four minutes, with most barely reaching three.

What makes the trio likable is their almost naive enthusiasm, which is supported by confident playing ability that strengthened with each album. Bijou loves what they're doing and don't want to change it, only to hone it; even cutting **Pas Dormir** in LA under the supervision of Sparks' Ron and Russell Mael made little difference, except to underline the melodies. The lyrics (for those conversant *en français*) range from corny and jokey (especially the first LP) to flippantly snotty and angry-young-rocker, with an increasing degree of wit. **Jamais Domptés** is their best overall show of strength.   [jg]

BIRDSONGS OF THE MESOZOIC

Birdsongs of the Mesozoic EP (Ace of Hearts) 1983
Magnetic Flip (Ace of Hearts) 1984
Beat of the Mesozoic EP (Ace of Hearts) 1986
Sonic Geology [CD] (Rykodisc) 1987

BIRDSONGS OF THE MESOZOIC—ERIK LINDGREN—PINK INC.

Soundtracks (Arf Arf) 1987

ERIK LINDGREN

Polar Yet Tropical (Arf Arf) 1987

Launched in 1980 as a one-off experimental keyboard collaboration between two former Boston bandmates—Mission of Burma guitarist Roger Miller and producer/synthesist Erik Lindgren—the all-instrumental Birdsongs of the Mesozoic expanded to a real band with the addition of keyboardist Rick Scott and another Burmite, tape manipulator-turned-guitarist Martin Swope. The group (which now describes itself as "the world's hardest rocking chamber music quartet") remained a part-time sideline until Miller developed tinnitus and decided to continue his musical career at a lower volume, thus forcing an end to Burma. Often compared to new minimalist composers like Philip Glass and Terry Riley—who do a lot with a little—Birdsongs seem to be doing a lot with more. And probably going right over the heads of many old Burma fans in the process.

Their debut finds Birdsongs taking quite a different tack from Burma's impassioned, chaotic noise-on-the-brink, with six instrumentals ranging from the achingly pretty romance of "The Orange Ocean" to juxtaposed chords played as much against as with each other. **Magnetic Flip** improves substantially on the first record's flat production, allowing the band's whole idea and execution to become bolder and more aggressive. The opening of "Shiny Golden Snakes" is pure rock power chording, while the variations on Stravinsky's "The Rite of Spring" pile one thundering dissonance over another and the austere keyboard repetition starting off "Ptoccata" does recall Glass. (The loopy rendition of "Theme from Rocky and Bullwinkle" proves that the band's highbrow inclinations are only one facet of its personality.)

The five songs on **Beat of the Mesozoic** take a generally less radical approach, allowing beauty to be a prime directive. Still, "Scenes from a . . . " layers taped voices and bells over the soothing piano cant; the title piece employs numerous types of sonic effects. The tense "Lost in the B-Zone" is the most unsettling track, a complex conflation of synthesizer lines going off in a half-dozen directions, with syncopated electronic percussion tripping over itself in the background. The CD-only **Sonic Geology** retrospective draws large portions from those three records, adding two new items to complete this rewarding 72-minute package.

Side One of **Soundtracks** consists of the Birdsongs' improvised 1986 score for Michael Burlingame's independent film, **To a Random**. With Lindgren on synth, Miller on piano, Scott on Farfisa and Swope on guitar, the quietly anxious piece lacks some of the group's offbeat studio invention but maintains the usual standards of taste and musicianship. The rest of the album contains a witty Lindgren suite entitled "The Last 68 Million Years Summed Up in Less Than 13 Minutes" and "Flames in Trains," his varied 1984 collaboration with two female vocalists.

Recorded sporadically between 1975 and 1987, Lindgren's **Polar Yet Tropical** contains an entire side of '60s (loosely defined) covers. Showing moderate wit and maximum reverent enthusiasm—these are mid-tech garage renditions rather than smugly modern reinterpretations—he confronts such classics as "I Wanna Be Your Dog," "Iron Man" and "In-a-Gadda-da-Vida," armed with sophisticated keyboard instruments and occasional assistance by his bandmates. ("Out of Limits" is, in fact, played by Birdsongs.) The original keyboard instrumentals—colored by guest horns, reeds, strings, etc.—on the other side show Lindgren's diverse compositional skills. [ep/iar]

BIRTHDAY PARTY

The Birthday Party (Aus. Missing Link) 1980
Prayers on Fire (Thermidor) 1981
Drunk on the Pope's Blood EP (nr/4AD) 1982
Junkyard (nr/4AD) 1982
The Bad Seed EP (nr/4AD) 1983
The Birthday Party EP (nr/4AD) 1983
Mutiny! EP (nr/Mute) 1983
It's Still Living (Aus. Missing Link) 1985
A Collection . . . (Aus. Missing Link) 1985
(Suite Beat) 1986 ●
The Peel Sessions EP (nr/Strange Fruit) 1987

BOYS NEXT DOOR

Door Door (Aus. Mushroom) 1979
Hee Haw EP (Aus. Missing Link) 1979 + 1983

This intensely challenging and influential Australian band put everything it had into the pursuit of making inhospitable and unyielding records. With partial comparisons possible to such noisy free-formists as the Fall, Pere Ubu and Public Image Ltd., the Birthday Party's unique sensibility sprang from singer Nick Cave (who wrote most of the lyrics) and guitarist Rowland Howard, who took care of a good chunk of the songwriting.

Before relocating from Melbourne to London, the Birthday Party released several Australian-only records, the first two under their original name, the Boys Next Door. **Door Door** is surprisingly normal-sounding aggressive rock with traditional song structures and musical values. Cave's vocals invest the album with an ominous undercurrent, but the overall ambience hardly suggests the insanity that lay ahead.

That insanity began with their next release, **The Birthday Party** (the label credits the band under both monikers). Whatever their name, though, serious derangement was setting in fast. Cave's vocals and Howard's newly developed wall of feedback make **Door Door** sound inhibited; each track here is un-

settling. The LP's opening kick, "Mr. Clarinet," presents an ultra-distorted organ sitting atop a stiff, martial goose-step beat. The second side is even more crazed: "The Friend Catcher" (relentless and hypnotic) and "Happy Birthday" both contain some of the most frenzied guitar work ever captured on vinyl.

After moving to the UK, the Birthday Party recorded and released their first international LP, **Prayers on Fire**, a raging vinyl beast filled with agonized howling, braying Cave vocals flung against a backdrop of violently attacked guitars and no-wave horn noise. Drums and bass alone toe the line of established patterns; everything else ignores the song at hand and goes flat out in competition with Cave's literate invective.

The **Drunk on the Pope's Blood** EP followed, coupling one side of live Birthday Party with a side of live Lydia Lunch (who later formed the Immaculate Consumptives with Cave and worked with Howard others in the axis). Recorded in London at the end of 1981, the disc is honestly described on the jacket as "16 minutes of sheer hell!" Drawing two of its four songs from **Prayers on Fire**, Cave and his ensemble growl and shriek through the slow pieces with stunning gruesomeness—incomprehensibility aside, no one else has ever suffered with a more effective sonic display than is caught in these grooves. **Junkyard** has less energy to the sound, but still manages to lift blood pressure with such assaults as "Dead Joe," "Big-Jesus-Trash-Can" and "6-inch Gold Blade."

Four BP EPs were released in 1983 (one a reissue of a disc recorded four years earlier as the Boys Next Door), the same year the band broke up. The first was **The Bad Seed**, four concise cuts of incredible visceral impact. Whether on the slow psycho-blues of "Deep in the Woods" or the frenzied blur of "Sonny's Burning," it leaves the listener helpless and enthralled. **The Birthday Party** EP and **Hee Haw** both contain material from **The Birthday Party** album, along with assorted singles and previously unreleased tracks.

The posthumous **Mutiny!** was released at the correct time: it wouldn't have been easy to follow. Like **The Bad Seed**, it mixes two furious numbers with a pair of funereal dirges. "Jennifer's Veil," a harrowing lament, is perhaps the band's finest song ever. Neither John Cale nor Alfred Hitchcock was ever this scary.

It's Still Living was released in Australia

two years later. Recorded in Melbourne in 1982, it offers spirited performances of material from **Prayers on Fire** and **Junkyard** and, although decried by the band, is recommended for fans. **The Peel Sessions** EP was recorded for radio broadcast in London in April 1981. **A Collection . . .** (also known as **The Best and the Rarest**) takes its tracks from **Junkyard, Hee Haw, Prayers on Fire** and some singles, adding a few alternate versions and other rarities. For completists only. The American CD is somewhat different.

Bassist Tracy Pew died in 1986 of complications arising from his epilepsy. [iar/dgs]

See also *Nick Cave and the Bad Seeds, Crime and the City Solution, KaS Product, Lydia Lunch, Nikki Sudden, These Immortal Souls.*

BISHOPS

See *Count Bishops.*

BITING TONGUES

Don't Heal (nr/Situation 2) 1981
Libreville (nr/Paragon) 1983
Feverhouse (nr/Factory) 1985

On **Don't Heal** a fellow named Capalula delivers monotonic spoken-word vocals over a no-wavish backing of sax (squealing, of course), guitar (noise, of course) and rhythm section (altered funk, of course)—none particularly distinguished. A pretender to the throne once occupied by Joy Division's late Ian Curtis (also from Manchester), Capalula seems to have acquired Curtis' psychic stomachache, but lacks the dark depths of black feeling that made Curtis unique.   [mf]

BIZARROS/RUBBER CITY REBELS

From Akron (Clone) 1977

BIZARROS

Bizarros (Mercury) 1979

Although not generally well known like other Ohio rockers (Devo, Chrissie Hynde, Pere Ubu), the Bizarros did make a contribution, both through their records and singer Nick Nicholis' Clone label, which released vinyl by the Waitresses, Human Switchboard and others. A classic case of bridesmaiding, the Bizarros' career was more influential than popular.

Playing serious, intense, sometimes hypnotic rock with poetically inclined verbiage and pre-Gang of Four jabbing guitars, Bizarros music is less pleasant than affecting. The

two-band **From Akron** sampler shared with the Rubber City Rebels is raw and not enjoyable. By the time of their own album, however, the Bizarros had developed considerable polish which they use to good advantage without compromising their original character.   [iar]

BLACK

Wonderful Life (A&M) 1987 ●
Black (nr/WEA) 1987

Liverpool's Colin Vearncombe adopted the name Black in the hopes of becoming another pre-fab British singing sensation, a gambit which evidently paid off when the song after which the album was subsequently titled became a hit single there. He's got a pleasant, slightly husky voice with little character, no clue about phrasing and little songwriting talent. The tunes, produced with a capable studio band, all go on too long and lean towards lyrical clichés in lieu of ideas. Not hideous, but rather clumsy. The **Black** mini-album is a prior label's cash-in release of pre-fame recordings (mostly singles) dating from 1984.   [iar]

BLACKBEARD

See *Dennis Bovell.*

BLACK FLAG

Jealous Again EP (SST) 1980 ●
Damaged (SST) 1981 ●
Everything Went Black (SST) 1983 + 1984 ●
The First Four Years [tape] (SST) 1984 ●
My War (SST) 1984 ●
Family Man (SST) 1984 ●
Slip It In (SST) 1984 ●
Live '84 [tape] (SST) 1984
Loose Nut (SST) 1985 ●
The Process of Weeding Out EP (SST) 1985 ●
In My Head (SST) 1985 ●
Who's Got the 10 1/2? (SST) 1986 ●
Wasted . . . Again (SST) 1987 ●

Black Flag was, for all intents and purposes, America's first hardcore band. They emerged from Southern California to gain international prominence, touring enough to become a major attraction in virtually every city where a scene existed and undoubtedly inspiring others to get in the game. Via the band's still-thriving SST label, Black Flag played an essential role in the development and popularization of American punk. Through countless revolving-door personnel changes—which spawned numerous outfits along the way—Black Flag persevered until 1986, finally dissolving after locating and exploring the zone where punk and heavy metal intersect and overlap.

Jealous Again, five brief tracks by an early lineup on a 12-inch 45, is a convincing but restrained primal punk roar; the ghost of the Sex Pistols comes floating through the brazen blare of guitars and vocals. **Damaged** features a superior cast (with Washington, DC singer Henry Rollins and stun guitarist Dez Cadena joining) and includes the culture classic "TV Party," as well as other goofy paeans to dissipated suburban life ("Six Pack," "Thirsty and Miserable") and the ultimo American punk anthem, "Rise Above." Rollins' hoarse shout grates, but the barely-contained rock energy and tongue-in-cheek lyrics make **Damaged** a great rock'n'roll LP that isn't beholden to any clichéd genre. (The **Damaged** CD also contains the contents of **Jealous Again**.)

In the midst of a horrible legal dispute with Unicorn Records, the group found itself enjoined from using the Black Flag name and logo on any new records, and resorted to releasing the double-album outtakes-and-more career retrospective, **Everything Went Black**, with only a listing of band members on the cover for identification. (It was later reissued with all the proper nomenclature.) The tracks, which date from 1978 to 1981, feature various lineups attacking a motley collection of songs. ("Police Story," "Gimmie Gimmie Gimmie," "Damaged" and "Depression" all get done twice.) Collectors note: the European edition is very different. As a developmental Black Flag sampler, **Everything Went Black** is both illuminating and entertaining, but the real treat is Side Four, "Crass Commercialism," a hysterically funny collection of crazed radio spots for Flag gigs, most with music, that say a lot about the cultural milieu in which the band existed. **The First Four Years** is a tape-only (subsequently CD but never LP) reissue compilation of early releases, including the "Six Pack" maxi-single and **Jealous Again**.

Following the resolution of their litigation (Unicorn helpfully went bankrupt), a new and prolific Black Flag—Rollins, guitarist Greg Ginn, ex-Descendents drummer Bill Stevenson and (briefly) bassist Dale Nixon—drifted vaguely towards metal on **My War**, a mediocre album with some interminably long songs. (One plodding side has a grand total of three!) There *are* some good punk tunes ("I Love You") but elsewhere, a heavy-bottomed, labored sound and appallingly bad guitar solos cross the line from sarcasm into sheer awfulness. Rollins' vocals are the same as ever, which makes the bad tracks even stranger.

Kira took over on bass for **Slip It In**. With far clearer sound on the eight tracks, the LP further blurs the line between moronic punk and moronic metal. Songs are mostly built on trite riffs repeated endlessly (check any Black Sabbath record for elaboration). The rude lyrics of the title song are performed complete with enthusiastic sex noises for anyone who fails to grasp the point and/or be offended by it. Other songs are less tasteless but little more interesting. **Family Man** dissects Black Flag: half-and-half Henry Rollins reading his poetry and group instrumentals without him.

The cassette-only **Live '84** puts the band's recent creative output and selected oldies onstage for an hour of wanton loud fun. Black Flag concerts were typically an utter mess, which suits the songs perfectly, making this chaotic explosion naturally one of their best releases.

In 1985, Black Flag continued their torrid pace, releasing three new records: **Loose Nut**, **In My Head** and **The Process of Weeding Out**. The last-named is a Henryless instrumental EP: four lengthy improvs displaying unexpected technical prowess (especially Kira on "Your Last Affront") and a new side to the band. There's a certain nostalgia factor for those who remember Canned Heat or Ten Years After in the old days, but on its own merits, little here would entice you into multiple listenings. The other two records feature the complete Rollins-Ginn-Kira-Stevenson lineup and are fairly similar: nine songs each of varied but mostly medium-tempo guitar rock that keeps a safe distance from metal, hardcore *and* sleazemongering. **Loose Nut** has clean sound, Rollins' brutally self-hating "This Is Good" and lyrics on the inner sleeve—the best Black Flag LP of 1985. (The **In My Head** cassette contains three bonus tracks.)

With new drummer Anthony Martinez, Black Flag recorded **Who's Got the 10 1/2?** in Portland, Oregon on 23 August 1985. Besides a great cover photo of the band's actual tour calendar that says more about the rock'n'roll life than any half-dozen magazine articles, the album features hot versions of 1984/1985 material, plus a genuine oldie, "Gimmie Gimmie Gimmie." (The cassette and CD adds 24 more minutes of fun.)

The posthumous **Wasted . . . Again** neatly recapitulates Black Flag's high career points with a dozen essential tracks, from "Wasted" to "Drinking and Driving." Everything you'd want in a single disc is included, and brief annotation adds the veneer of history.
[iar]

See also *D.C.3, Dos, Gone, Minutemen, October Faction, Henry Rollins, SWA, Tom Troccoli's Dog, Würm.*

BLACK RANDY AND THE METROSQUAD

Pass the dust, I think I'm Bowie.
(Dangerhouse) 1980

John (Black Randy) Morris writes and sings the lyrics of these wild and funny pieces of sharp social commentary; the five-man Metrosquad provides twisted, dissonant rock and funk to set them in the proper chaotic ambience. Like a punkified Mothers of Invention, there's a definite method behind this inspired madness, but you'll be laughing (or squirming during the vulgar numbers) too hard to notice. Sample lyrics: "Marlon [Brando] took his Learjet to the Indian nation/They thought he was Led Zeppelin on a rock vacation." Or, from "I Slept in an Arcade": "There was a dog in 24B/Working undercover for the LAPD/I took his paw and he winked at me/He said "I'm man's best friend and I'm off at 3'." More titles: "I Wanna Be a Nark," "Sperm Bank Baby," "Idi Amin." Dirty, rude, politically uncool—but funny!

Trivia note: Black Randy and the Metrosquad make a brief and bizarre appearance in a great 1981 film, *Ladies and Gentlemen, the Fabulous Stains.* [iar]

BLACK UHURU

Love Crisis (nr/Third World) 1977
Showcase (Heartbeat) 1979 (nr/Butt) 1980
Sinsemilla (Mango) 1980
Black Sounds of Freedom (Shanachie) 1981
Red (Mango) 1981
Black Uhuru (nr/Virgin) 1981
Guess Who's Coming to Dinner (Heartbeat) 1981 ●
Tear It Up—Live (Mango) 1982

Chill Out (Mango) 1982
The Dub Factor (Mango) 1983
Anthem (Mango) 1983
Reggae Greats (Mango) 1985 ●
Brutal (RAS) 1986 ●
Brutal Dub (RAS) 1986
Positive (RAS) 1987 ●
The Positive Dub (RAS) 1988 [tape] (ROIR) 1988

The leading second generation reggae vocal group, Black Uhuru was formed in Jamaica in 1974 by Duckie Simpson; after a couple of false starts, he enlisted Michael Rose, whose quivery voice makes him sound like a Rasta cantor, and recorded **Love Crisis**—competent but hardly distinctive (although the best track, "I Love King Selassie," survived to become a live staple). (**Black Sounds of Freedom** is a remix of the same album.) After American expatriate Puma Jones joined to add haunting high harmony, Black Uhuru joined forces with Sly and Robbie; their riddims pushed the singing along with the force of a tank.

Showcase, a compilation of their early singles ("Abortion," "General Penitentiary," "Guess Who's Coming to Dinner," etc.), is an unqualified classic. It was reissued by Heartbeat in 1981 as **Guess Who's Coming to Dinner**.

Sinsemilla firmly established Uhuru as an album act. The record delivers a level of consistency only Bob Marley himself had achieved. Their breakthrough, however, came with **Red**. From the first track, "The Youth of Eglington," listeners—even those not particularly interested in reggae—had a compelling reason to discover Black Uhuru.

The band spent considerable time on the road. A live album (**Tear It Up**) recycles a lot of the material from **Showcase** and is only a so-so approximation of their in-concert excitement. But **Chill Out**, the next studio effort, is great. Rose had moved to New York and takes on the city in the title cut; "Darkness," "Emotional Slaughter" and others reveal a departure from Rasta subject matter. The American-only **Dub Factor** is a ferocious dub disc, more of which can be found on Sly and Robbie's **Raiders of the Lost Dub**.

The release of **Anthem** was troubled. The original issue was remixed and revised for America; that version was subsequently re-released in Europe. In any case, it's a spotty record, despite a couple of killer tracks ("Party Next Door" and Steve Van Zandt's "Solidarity"). Sly and Robbie's synthetics are more pronounced, perhaps to compensate for the weak material and convictionless performances. (Ironically, it won a Grammy award in the US.) A decent hit collection in the **Reggae Greats** series followed. Then Michael Rose left, hypothetically to go solo, although nothing of his has since been issued.

On **Brutal**, Black Uhuru unveiled their new lead singer, Junior Reid, who displays an awkward tendency to mimic Rose. Sly and Robbie still provide backup; Arthur Baker is among the producers. While the Reid/Simpson songs attempt a number of different styles, not all are successful. (A companion dub LP, featuring mixes by Baker, Scientist and Steven Stanley is also available.)

Dissension continued. Puma Jones left the lineup and was replaced by Olafunke, a Jamaican-born soundalike. Released after her departure, the aptly-named **Positive** nevertheless shows the reconstituted group moving forward. The LP finds Reid coming into his own as a vocalist, and features a few songs that are striking and original (Simpson's apocalyptic "Fire City," for example). Sly and Robbie continue to be the featured musicians, but producer Steven Stanley offers flourishes and variations from their familiar martial drums and bass lines. In short, there are still echoes of the old Black Uhuru on **Positive**, but a new band identity and sound are slowly emerging. An OK dub version of the LP has also been released, first as a limited-pressing LP, then on cassette.   [bk]

See also *Sly Dunbar and Robbie Shakespeare.*

RUBÉN BLADES Y SEIS DEL SOLAR

Greatest Hits (Musica Latina Int'l) 1983
Buscando America (Elektra) 1984 ●
Escenas (Elektra) 1985
Agua de Luna (Elektra) 1986

RUBÉN BLADES

Nothing but the Truth (Elektra) 1988 ●
Antecedentes (Elektra) 1988 ●

VARIOUS ARTISTS

Crossover Dreams (Elektra) 1986

Rubén Blades is the first major salsa perfomer to integrate rock aesthetics into his music. After a successful stint with Willie Colón, Blades went solo, rocketing to the top of salsa charts with songs that avoided the music's clichés in favor of topical narratives and carefully-crafted imagery. The best of these, including the classic gangster tale of "Pedro Navaja," are found on **Greatest Hits**.

In 1984, after releasing numerous albums on various other labels, Blades signed two contracts with Elektra, one for Spanish-language recordings, the other for English-language ones. **Buscando America** stands as the finest of his major-label recordings to date. Blades' band, Seis del Solar (Tenement Six), includes four percussionists and two electric keyboardists, instead of salsa's traditional horn section. Blades sings frank songs about abortion, Latin America's political disappeared and the banality of evil.

Blades is also a screen actor. His first starring role was in **Crossover Dreams**, which charted the rise and fall of a *salsero* who denies his roots in search of American chart success. The soundtrack includes two pop tunes by Blades, plus a healthy selection of salsa classics performed by some of the field's finest players.

Escenas finds Blades making first steps toward the sort of crossover (he calls it "convergence") acceptability he so obviously desires. Joe Jackson and Linda Ronstadt make guest appearances, but except for "Muévete," things don't sizzle quite so much as before. Some of Blades' songs on **Agua de Luna** were inspired by Gabriel García Márquez short stories, with limited success. An audacious experiment, but the results tend to be tepid.

Without his usual band, Blades collaborated with Elvis Costello, Lou Reed and Sting on **Nothing but the Truth**, his first all-English album. Recorded with studio journeymen, the music ranges from hard-core salsa to mainstream rock to political doo-wop. The tunes co-written by Costello hold up the best, but that's to be expected. As if to atone for an apparent sell-out (sorry, I mean "crossover"), Blades quickly followed it up with another Spanish-language album with Seis del Solar, the rootsy **Antecedentes**.
                                           [rg]

See also *Sting.*

BLAM BLAM BLAM

Blam Blam Blam EP (NZ Propeller) 1980 + 1982
Luxury Length (NZ Propeller) 1982
The Blam Blam Blam Story (NZ Propeller) 1984

Reckoned by some to be New Zealand's top local group, Blam Blam Blam share a bit of their genealogy with the Swingers. An intriguing and somewhat strange trio, they have a sure-handed, full but uncluttered approach and oblique melodies, with a lot of indigenous references, as in "There Is No Depression in New Zealand," a Top 20 hit there, and included on a revised second edition of the EP. Guitars may chime like bells or whine sweetly like violins; drums aptly support muscular bass work; the vocals are a bit dry but deliver a pinch of tartness when needed. Not wildly spectacular, but definitely stimulating.   [jg]

BLANCMANGE
Happy Families (Island) 1982
Mange Tout (London-Sire) 1984
Believe You Me (London-Sire) 1985

One of the more individual and original synth-based duos, Stephen Luscombe and Neil Arthur mix dominant percussion with bizarre, often exotic seasonings to create tracks with abundant personality and enormous dance potential. There is one major and general drawback: Arthur has a rough, unpleasant singing voice which becomes riddled with melodrama when he gets excited.

On **Happy Families**, Blancmange offer typically eccentric concepts—"God's Kitchen," "Living on the Ceiling"—in varied settings that fall into two general styles: (1) Loud, rhythmic and derivative of Talking Heads. These tunes, especially "Feel Me," suffer from extreme monochromatic tediousness. (2) Delicate and reserved. "I've Seen the Word" and others are quite lovely, resembling the spare grace of mid-period Orchestral Manoeuvres in the Dark.

Mange Tout (a brilliant bilingual pun that raises my estimation of the band a few notches) is simultaneously a bit sillier and grander overall, using more horns, woodwinds and strings than before. Largely neglecting option 2 but not sounding much like the Heads either, Blancmange opt to let the beat send the message, while thankfully maintaining better song quality and, thus, less boredom. The four major tracks—"Don't Tell Me," "My Baby," "Blind Vision" and "That's Love That It Is"—all offer different levels of melodiousness (most pretty high) with Arthur's vocals, though improved, still an occasional stumbling block in the way of enjoyment.

Believe You Me is an ambitious undertaking, recorded in seven different studios

with four producers and zillions of guest musicians. The results are hardly as inconsistent as they might have been, and, in fact, the restrained album is quite agreeable, reasonably free of the overzealousness, busyness and absurdity that diminished some of their prior work. The songs aren't consistently wonderful, but simplicity and understatement make inquisitive tracks like "Don't You Love It All" (with flugelhorn played by Hugh Masekela), "What's Your Problem?" and "Why Don't They Leave Things Alone?" pleasant, if not immediately memorable.   [iar]

BLASTERS
American Music (Rollin' Rock) 1980
The Blasters (Slash-Warner Bros.) 1981
Over There: Live at the Venue, London EP
    (Slash-Warner Bros.) 1982
Non Fiction (Slash-Warner Bros.) 1983
Hard Line (Slash-Warner Bros.) 1985

They say everything old becomes new again, and California's Blasters proved it in 1981 by jumping into the national spotlight with an utterly familiar brew of blues, rockabilly and rock'n'roll. Detractors might call them little more than an updated Canned Heat—as if anything were wrong with that—but such criticism ignores their strengths: tight ensemble work, swingin' original tunes in the classic mold and Phil Alvin's ageless, confident vocals.

American Music appeared on an independent rockabilly revival label, which is probably one reason it didn't reach a larger audience. The band already had total control of R&B and rock conventions, fusing them into a supple, flowing style. Although there's not quite as much sting here as later on, Dave Alvin's guitar work displays plenty of spirit. Oldies like "Buzz Buzz Buzz" and "I Wish You Would" (Billy Boy Arnold via the Yardbirds) mingle with catchy new tunes like "Marie, Marie," later a big UK hit for Shakin' Stevens.

The Blasters established the quintet nationwide. Originally released on LA independent Slash, it did so well that the label was able to strike a licensing/distribution deal with Warner Bros. No wonder: it smokes. The band is tighter than a drum, and Dave Alvin's songs—including "No Other Girl," a re-recorded "Marie, Marie" and "Border Radio"—have a joyous, irresistible momentum. R&B legend Lee Allen guests on sax.

Highlighted by a crackling hot sound, the live London EP serves as a good introduction to the Blasters, but offers no new wrinkles. Definitely suitable for parties, though.

Any lingering suspicions that the Blasters were just an oldies band at heart were surely dispelled by the fine **Non Fiction**. Dave Alvin's essay on real life, the LP presents a series of well-crafted vignettes reminiscent of Robbie Robertson's work with the Band. Songs like "One More Dance" and "Fool's Paradise" depict the trials and tribulations of the little people, while "Long White Cadillac" laments Hank Williams. The playing on the self-produced record is smoother and not as quaint as before.

A shade less stirring than **Non Fiction**, **Hard Line** reprises that LP's formula, but also includes a blatant stab at commercialism. Although "Colored Lights," penned for the Blasters by John Cougar Mellencamp, isn't bad, other songs are more heartfelt. Highlights include "Trouble Bound" and "Help You Dream," both featuring the Jordanaires (of Elvis Presley fame for you young'uns).

In 1986, Dave Alvin left to join X, briefly replacing Billy Zoom who had quit to form his own band; Alvin soon moved on to launch his own solo career. His replacement in the Blasters was a guitarist known as Hollywood Fats (Michael Mann), who tragically died a few months later. Ironically, Zoom later joined the Blasters, who have been less active since Phil Alvin began attending graduate school.   [jy]
See also *Dave Alvin, Phil Alvin, X.*

BLEACHED BLACK
Wrist Slashing Romance EP (RiJiD) 1985
Bleached Black (Relativity) 1986 ●

Ignore the misleading name: New Haven, Connecticut's Bleached Black offer up a unique brand of keen-edged power/punk pop. Hard and driving, yet sublimely melodic, the trio intermingles unusual influences (Buzzcocks and R.E.M., to name two), enhanced by the dual vocal attack of guitarist Stevo and bassist Greg Prior.

The indie-land debut, **Wrist Slashing Romance**, suffers as a result of poor recording. However, what it lacks in production it makes up for with first-class songs. "Prey for Me," "I Can't Be Happy" and the raging instrumental "Chainsmoking with Nigel" are absolutely outstanding.

With crisp sound (production by Lou Gi-

ordano) and abundant tunefulness, **Bleached Black** is an excellent full-length debut. "I Was in Your Life," "Chelsea" and "Circuitry Spiders" typify the band's characteristic mix of energetic drive, alluring harmony vocals and modulated guitar roar. Bleached Black are honing a viable audio personality and seem able to write well enough to make even better records than this.   [ag]

PETER BLEGVAD
See *John Greaves.*

BLESSED VIRGINS
Blessed Virgins (Fr. Epic) 1982

After playing this French band's record, you know the joke in their moniker is funnier (and more joyful) than you thought. Youth really is on their side. Of course, the forms—a pinch of revved-up blues, a dash of chugging punk, a whole lotta high-energy rock'n' roll—aren't new, and the songs won't change the world, despite a passel of catchy riffs. (The lyrics are in slangy French, but seem smart enough.) What makes this album a blessing is that the Virgins make it all sound new and fresh, including a reworded (in French!) "Summertime Blues"! Vibrant, free of pose—if anything can keep rock'n'roll eternally young, this is a snapshot of it.
[jg]

BLIND IDIOT GOD
Blind Idiot God (SST) 1987

Refusing to compromise their chops with some cut-rate rock vocalist, this young instrumental trio (originally from St. Louis but now living in Brooklyn) constructs a huge, brash sound influenced (consciously or not) by Blue Cheer, Jimi Hendrix, the Velvet Underground, the Meters (Blind Idiot God covers the Crescent City funk geniuses' "More Time"), the Sex Pistols, Glenn Branca and Jamaican dub (their first LP concludes with a trio of dubwise treats). Simultaneously leaning towards heavy metal (with less ego) and reggae (with more voltage), these demonic decibel gluttons are having the time of their lives in hammer-of-the-gods territory.
[rg]

BLONDIE
Blondie (Private Stock) 1976 (Chrysalis) 1977 ●
Plastic Letters (Chrysalis) 1977 ●

Parallel Lines (Chrysalis) 1978 ●
Eat to the Beat (Chrysalis) 1979 ●
Autoamerican (Chrysalis) 1980 ●
The Best of Blondie (Chrysalis) 1981 ●
The Hunter (Chrysalis) 1982

JIMMY DESTRI
Heart on a Wall (Chrysalis) 1982

DEBBIE HARRY
KooKoo (Chrysalis) 1981
Rockbird (Geffen) 1986 ●

That Blondie may be remembered as perhaps the best singles band to emerge from the new wave—in fact, a world-class hitmaking powerhouse—is extraordinary for those who recall the group's humble genesis and occasionally appalling early efforts. Even after the New Yorkers had secured a recording contract, few—even supporters—expected that they could ever surpass the commercial level of, say, Lou Reed—i.e., a moderate fluke hit single, perhaps a charting album, but mainly cult status. How could the torpid, immovable, generally disgusting commercial music establishment of the day somehow reverse itself and open up to *Blondie*? Like the rest of the us they were part of, it seemed they'd always be on the outside looking in.

Yet the core members (Jimmy Destri and Clem Burke, as well as Debbie Harry and Chris Stein) always had a vision that anything was possible. So what if they weren't slick studio musicians? They'd still be able to put the sounds in their heads on plastic, sounds that weren't just "Pure Pop for Now People" but pure pop for hit radio, yet in the most sincere, uncynical and popularly resonating tradition. So they engaged in inspired—positively subversive—musical "pilferage" and synthesis in ways few others have consistently sustained. Through all of that, Blondie maintained a distinctive group identity. (Until the last album, anyway.)

Some of their dabblings weren't successful, but if Blondie could be called a bunch of dilettantes, it's only fair to note that many others wet their musical toes in the same exotic waters only after Blondie set the precedent. Moreover, Blondie largely pursued their commercial and artistic goals in nonconformist fashion, often to the dismay of their record company and even some of their fans.

Blondie effervesces with exuberance which, at points, extends the band's reach beyond its grasp. Still, it's a guileless classic, and arguably the group's best album. They create a series of charming musical Franken-

stein monsters—stitched together from salsa, funk, Broadway pop and thrill-flick soundtracks—in addition to their more typical girl group/surf/Anglo hybrids, as on "X Offender," the debut single included here. Any lapses in expertise are counterbalanced by the sense of ebullient abandon, as captured by producer Richard Gottehrer.

Plastic Letters reflects not only professional seasoning and closer work with Gottehrer, but also the turmoil of changes in personnel, management and record label. The result—fuller, tighter and more authoritatively rocking—includes the band's first two UK hits, "(I'm Always Touched by Your) Presence, Dear" (written by, and recorded as a sort of tribute to, departed bassist Gary Valentine) and "Denis" (a revamp of the 1963 Randy & the Rainbows oldie). There's also a brooding feel to many of the tracks, the hard, riffy stuff and the thoughtful experimentation ("Cautious Lip") alike. More conservative than **Blondie**, and less exciting.

By **Parallel Lines**, the new lineup had already jelled, and producer Mike Chapman (looking to repeat the massive success he enjoyed during the early '70s English glitter-pop days) took over the console, imposing his exacting, disciplined approach. The band seem totally in control of every musical form they take on, from zombie metal to popability, from quasi-avant spaciness to the hitbound electro-disco flirtation, "Heart of Glass" (originally demoed as "The Disco Song"). Compared to Gottehrer's first-take spontaneity, some of the LP might seem a tad clinical, but it's easily good enough to be considered America's answer to Nick Lowe's first solo LP.

Eat to the Beat, surprisingly, proved less artistically and commercially successful than an album that recapitulates a soaring band's strong points should have been, but it does have some of the best sheer rock'n'roll the group ever produced. **Autoamerican** goes in precisely the opposite direction; breaking out of a stylistic cul-de-sac, Blondie jumped out in a number of new directions again: cocktail jazz, Eurodrama, country (sort of) and rap. An "A" for effort, but Blondie's most uneven album, ranging from obvious boo-boos to the hits "Tide Is High" and "Rapture."

Within two years after that ambitious LP, the "successful rock band collapses under its own weight" syndrome had apparently set in. **The Hunter** sounds as though their excitement about musical recombination had simply degenerated into a polished but sterile capability of manipulating a wide variety of stylistic devices. Bereft of things to say, or ways to say nothing with style and grace, the LP is aimless, elephantine—its largely impenetrable pretentiousness not that far removed from dinosaurs like Jefferson Starship or Yes. The following mega-tour was staged with the suspicion, if not outright knowledge, that it would be their last go-round together.

The Best of Blondie should really be called **The Singles Album**, since that's exclusively what's on it and what limits the view it gives of the group. It doesn't include the spiffy version they did of Johnny Cash's "Ring of Fire" on the soundtrack of the movie *Roadie,* but it does have three special remixes and the otherwise non-LP hit, "Call Me" (from the Richard Gere film, *American Gigolo*). The US and UK editions differ according to Blondie's chart strengths in those markets.

Keyboardist Destri's solo outing, produced by Lou Reed/Pink Floyd cohort Michael Kamen, takes traditional pop values and updates them with decidedly Bowiesque leanings. He'd already proved himself a creative and occasionally inspired musician and songwriter in the group context; here, he proves solid, if not exemplary, in those capacities, but his lack of vocal ability or even identity is a definite drag on the proceedings.

KooKoo, Debbie Harry's collaboration with Nile Rodgers and Bernard Edwards of Chic (with a little help from Chris Stein), finds her out of her depth. Trying to insert herself into their musical format, she strains for vocal personae (serious romantic and quasi-politically streetwise) to which she is unsuited. About a third of the record is moderately successful infectious funk-pop. For all of its shortcomings, however, the then-controversial pairing with the pre-crossover Chicmen still stands as an example of the adventurous and prescient trailblazing that had typified Harry and Stein within Blondie.

The couple lost the next few years to Stein's extended and debilitating illness, although Harry did contribute a song to the 1985 *Krush Groove* soundtrack and pursue the other side of her career, acting. Regrettably, **Rockbird,** Harry's first attempt at a real comeback, is nearly a cipher. Although nicely enough produced (by J. Geils Band keyboardist/songwriter Seth Justman) and starting off well with the bouncy "I Want

You" ("got you on my mind and it's mind over manners"), the album makes little overall impression. There isn't much in the way of catchy tunes; the lyrics are surprisingly flat. "Secret Life" is particularly annoying for announcing a revelation but saying nothing at all. The only song that most recalls Blondie's lovable playfulness is "French Kissin'," but Harry didn't have a hand in writing it.   [jg/iar]

See also *Chequered Past.*

ALPHA BLONDY

Apartheid Is Nazism (Shanachie) 1987
Jerusalem (Shanachie) 1988

Since the death of Bob Marley, numerous Third World performers have been proposed as his successor, likely to assume his dominant role in reggae. Ziggy Marley has been one obvious choice; Alpha Blondy is another, more unusual, candidate. For starters, Blondy is African; he performs reggae in French, English, Hebrew, Arabic and other African languages. Rather than Rasta and Jah, he sings about the Middle East and South Africa, on records which he writes, produces and arranges himself. He's enormously popular in Europe and Africa, where he tours frequently. Because of his global success, Blondy has come to signify the internationalization of reggae as a music and phenomenon—the true world beat.

Both of Blondy's LPs available in America are genuinely exciting, and shouldn't be missed. If **Jerusalem** has the slight edge, it's because the Wailers play behind him (strengthening the comparison to Marley) and they always sound so good. On **Apartheid Is Nazism,** he's supported by members of his touring group, the Solar System Band, who are less distinctive but just as tight. Combining roots rhythms and exotic foreign lyrics, the music is at once familiar and strange, but its depth of feeling never falters, and needs no translation. Delightfully haunting—this is reggae and then some.   [bk]

BLOOD ON THE SADDLE

Blood on the Saddle (New Alliance) 1984
Poisoned Love (Chameleon) 1986
Fresh Blood (Chameleon) 1987

These California cow-punks are less concerned with revering C&W icons than trashing them at a furious pace: their country is Hank Williams OD-ing in the back of his car;

their western, that of spaghetti flicks. On their first album, ragged harmonies, yodelled vocals and the slap of stand-up bass lend authenticity, making the record a rodeo where even the horses are doing speed. One of three lead singers in the band, ex-Bangle Annette Zalinskas, vocalizes on the best songs, including "Do You Want to Dance?" and "(I Wish I Was a) Single Girl (Again)," where she sounds like a real down-home country singer trying to stay straight while her band, out of control, beats her to the finish. [ep]

BLOTTO

Hello! My Name Is Blotto. What's Yours? EP
  (Blotto) 1980
Across and Down EP (Blotto) 1980
Combo Akimbo (Blotto) 1982
I Wanna Be a Lifeguard (Performance) 1987

Albany, New York's whimsical comic-pop sextet made their biggest splash with the silly summer song, "I Wanna Be a Lifeguard," included on the first EP. All three original records have witty observations and skillfully played parodic music, but Blotto reached its peak on the pre-*Spinal Tap* brainbanger, "(I'm Turning into a Heavy) Metal Head," from **Combo Akimbo**.

I Wanna Be a Lifeguard is a fair career summary, putting the best items from both EPs and **Combo Akimbo** on one easy-to-use record, with a bonus flexi-disc of "I Wanna Be a Lifeguard" (live) and a studio cut.

[iar]

KURTIS BLOW

Kurtis Blow (Mercury) 1980
Deuce (Mercury) 1981
Tough (Mercury) 1982
Party Time? (Mercury) 1983
Ego Trip (Mercury) 1984
America (Mercury) 1985
Kingdom Blow (Mercury) 1986 ●
Back by Popular Demand (Mercury) 1988 ●

One of the earliest and most enduring stars of rap, New York's Kurtis Blow consistently makes solid records with workable grooves and lyrics that alternately address topics of social and socializing interest. In doing so, Blow has become something of a modern black culture maven, singing the praises of Harlem ("One-Two-Five (Main Street, Harlem, USA)" on **Party Time?**), waxing eloquent about hoops ("Basketball" on **Ego Trip**) and competing with "The Mes-

sage" in discussing the urban challenge ("Tough" on the LP of the same name, "Street Rock" on **Kingdom Blow**). All of the records are state-of-the-art in an almost mainstream vein; *Ego Trip* makes a concerted effort to get hipper by having Run—DMC do a guest rap on "8 Million Stories." (**Kingdom** tops that in the cameo stakes: the first voice you hear belongs to Bob Dylan.)

Taking a turn towards patriotism in the title cut of **America**, Blow (who also produced) shows off his dichotomous musical goals. In the same song he uses aggressive electronic percussion and mixing techniques to mimic the Bambaataa/Lydon Time Zone sound (with Art of Noise effects) *and* sings like Kool and the Gang. The rest of the album is passable but only the catchy and soulful strut of "If I Ruled the World" is worth remembering. (And "Super Sperm" is well worth forgetting.)

Kingdom Blow not only has Dylan and a homely but sincere paean to "The Bronx," but George Clinton and "Zip-a-Dee-Doo-Dah" to boot. Kurtis is nothing if not open-minded and adventurous. The eight long cuts—some more compelling than others—throw in just about everything (TV lifts, Donald Duck, party sounds, Emulator gimmickry, etc.) except the London Philharmonic. Maybe next time . . . [iar]

BLOW MONKEYS

Limping for a Generation (nr/RCA) 1984 ●
Forbidden Fruit EP (RCA) 1985
Animal Magic (RCA) 1986 ●
She Was Only a Grocer's Daughter (RCA)
  1987 ●

Moving in to fill the vapid-soul vacancy left by Culture Club during that band's terminal creative drought, the Blow Monkeys whipped up "Digging Your Scene," a disturbingly familiar-sounding bit of fluff, for their second album. While the absurdly-named Dr. Robert manages a passable imitation of George's vocals and songwriting, his subordinates are no match for the Clubbers, and the rest of **Animal Magic** is equally redundant and stupid. The title track is an appalling T. Rex knock-off; "Sweet Murder" attempts to rewrite Talking Heads' "I Zimbra." The album's most consistent feature is its pathetic lack of originality.

As an introduction to America, **Forbidden Fruit** mixes "Atomic Lullaby" and the Smithsy "Wild Flower" from **Limping** with

57

four foretastes of **Animal Magic**. The only items of note are a pair of crazed Eek-a-Mouse dub mixes that largely obscure the songs.

The uncontrollably egotistical Dr. Robert sorted out his stylistic desires in time for **She Was Only a Grocer's Daughter**, which consistently focuses on a danceable pop-soul format that crosses Culture Club's basic ideas with lush ABC-like production, including enough strings and backing vocals—the credits list a dozen session singers—to fill a stadium. If the band can't hack it instrumentally on their own, a studio full of players are on hand to help. The trivial songs at least sound fine; the peerless Curtis Mayfield provides a huge, if undeserved, credibility boost by duetting on the appropriately derivative (of him) "The Day After You." The album title is an effete slap at Margaret Thatcher; the CD adds two extra tracks. [iar]

BLUE AEROPLANES

Bop Art (nr/Abstract) 1984
Action Painting and Other Original Works EP (nr/Fire) 1985
Lover and Confidante and Other Stories (nr/Fire) 1986
Tolerance (nr/Fire) 1986
Spitting Out Miracles (Restless) 1987

Aided by numerous friends, this eccentric Bristol quintet often has as many as a dozen people playing on its records; the diversity of ideas shows in the rich sound. Referents such as the Velvets, Fall, Pere Ubu, Feelies and others ricochet from all sides, topped off by Gerard Langley's poetic lyrics.

From the hard funk of "Pinkies Hit the Union" to the sonic landscape of "Owls," **Bop Art** has something for everyone. Along with a barrage of guitars, bass and percussion, the instrumentation includes saxes, bagpipes and several 16th century guitar ancestors. The band is such an effective ensemble that, even with all the masterful variety, the LP manages a logical progression.

The **Action Painting** EP builds some nice Velvets-cum-early Cabaret Voltaire drones; **Lover and Confidante**, another four cuts, is a trailer for **Tolerance**. Not quite as kaleidoscopic as **Bop Art**, **Tolerance** trades much of the oddness and idiosyncracy of previous work for some psychedelic touches, adding just enough characteristic embellishment to prevent deep identification with the paisley bandwagon.

By the time of their first American release, **Spitting Out Miracles**, the Blue Aeroplanes were up to an eight-piece (if you count the dancer and the guy who contributes tapes and records), with an equal number of guests (including Michelle Shocked on mandolin). Amazingly, with all those ingredients, it often manages to sound like a singer-songwriter album; the musicianship is so controlled and artistic that the focus stays on Langley's beat-influenced wordplay and Dylanesque delivery. And on "Bury Your Love Like Treasure," the artistes rock out fine and everybody gets home happy. The Blue Aeroplanes' entire catalogue is highly recommended. [dgs]

BLUE ANGEL

Blue Angel (Polydor) 1980 + 1984

As crass trash goes, you could certainly do worse than New York City's Blue Angel. Their painfully obvious mixture of '50s hokum, '60s girl-group theatrics and '70s detachment might have been more noteworthy if Blondie hadn't issued their own, more original version a few years earlier. The singer warbles and trills skillfully, but without much charm. The album was reissued in 1984, after said warbler, Cyndi Lauper, topped the charts with a song called "Girls Just Want to Have Fun." [jy]

See also *Cyndi Lauper*.

BLUEBELLS

The Bluebells EP (Sire) 1983
Sisters (Sire) 1984

Although they've been recording since 1982, the rustic pure-pop Bluebells haven't made anything near their full impact yet. For one thing, they've concentrated far more on making singles than albums; additionally, they seem to change producers every time they go in the studio, and have had some lineup shuffles as well. But even if their output hasn't exactly been enormous—they've only got one LP—no matter. Guitarist and ex-fanzine publisher Robert Hodgens (aka Bobby Bluebell) writes instantly memorable classics and sings 'em in a likably plain voice, making every track count. The five-song EP and the album have three songs in common (a moving folk classic, "The Patriot's Game," the beautiful "Cath" and—re-recorded for the LP—"Everybody's Somebody's Fool"), all of them winners. **Sisters** also has "I'm Falling (Down Again)" and six others, all subtly shaded with country fiddles and mandolins, ringing guitars, a light bouncy beat and choruses that you'll be humming all the way home. Utterly wonderful.

[iar]

BLUE HIPPOS

Blue Hippos (Twin/Tone) 1987
Forty Forty (Twin/Tone) 1988

On the seven-song **Blue Hippos**, this Twin Cities trio, led by singer/guitarist Paul Osby (former leader of Otto's Chemical Lounge), wavers between garage and tentative funk, with competent but unexceptional results. **Forty Forty** sounds more confident, and shows a somewhat greater mastery of funk dynamics, but the band still lacks the musical and/or lyrical bite that would give its R&B appropriations more authority. [hd]

BLUE IN HEAVEN

All the Gods' Men (Island) 1985
Explicit Music (Island) 1986

Although this young Irish quartet debuted on 45 with a fiery guitar anthem ("Julie Cries"), a poor choice of producer (sometimes gothic master Martin Hannett) for their first album turned them into bass-heavy doom mongers. A remix of the single on **All the Gods' Men** tells the whole sordid tale. A little light does shine through in "Sometimes," "Big Beat" and "In Your Eyes," but Hannett's lush atmospherics detract rather than complement the effect.

The second record (titled **Head** in the UK) was co-produced by Island Records chief Chris Blackwell, Eric Thorngren and Blue in Heaven to far more appealing effect. Guitars power the mostly melodic songs along without overly coloring them; Shane O'Neill's vocals provide the band's dominant character. Amidst the attractive pop, Shane's avowed Iggy fixation comes through on the grungy "Be Your Man" (which also mentions a familiar canine variation). [ag/iar]

BLUE NILE

A Walk Across the Rooftops (Virgin-A&M) 1984

This unique Scottish trio has considerable creative depth, building atmosphere with lots of empty space and well-controlled conflicting musical maneuvers. The title track mixes strings, horns, drum and bass with a meandering, disjunct vocal for something like a blend of Robert Wyatt, Joni Mitchell and John Cale. Although the LP defies easy acceptance, at its most accessible point ("Stay," which actually has a chorus and more of a verse melody than the others), it's quite appealing. [iar]

BLUE ORCHIDS

The Greatest Hit (Money Mountain)
  (nr/Rough Trade) 1982
Agents of Change EP (nr/Rough Trade) 1982
The Peel Sessions EP (nr/Strange Fruit) 1988

This Manchester quartet included two early members of the Fall and used organ as its main instrument, but at times it sounds as if Una Baines is playing a different song from the rest of the band. There are many overlapping layers in the deceptively simple sound of **The Greatest Hit**: the long organ washes are interrupted by guitars lurching to the fore. Bass and drums keep the steady beat, but the others don't necessarily fall in line behind them. Vocals are half-sung, half-spoken and full of poetic pretense, but it's the mesmerizing music that captures the listener in bright swirling folds. While **The Greatest Hit** can be simply tagged as neo-psychedelia, that doesn't cover the full scope of this fascinating band's music.

The EP, packaged in a printed plastic shopping bag, offers four very nice subsequent tracks that are at once subtler and more conservatively structured, sounding like nothing so much as the pretty side of early Velvet Underground. [iar]

BLUE RONDO A LA TURK

The Heavens Are Crying (nr/Diable
  Noir-Virgin) 1981
Chewing the Fat (nr/Diable Noir-Virgin) 1982

BLUE RONDO

Bees Knees and Chickens Elbows (nr/Virgin)
  1984

It shows you how far and fast new wave traveled: five years earlier, Chris Sullivan might have been screaming lyrics in a punk band; in 1980, he could have been skanking in front of some neo-ska bunch. But in 1982, he was singing in a quasi-salsa/cool-jazz group wanting, in his words, to bring back show biz. **Chewing the Fat** uses a number of big name producers (Langer and Winstanley, Godley and Creme, Mike Chapman), and the multi-ethnic London-based ten-piece turns in solid performances. But why bother settling for imitations when you can get the originals? (Sullivan did paint an attractive neo-Cubist album cover, though.) [jg]

BLURT

In Berlin (Ruby) 1981
Blurt (nr/Red Flame) 1982
Bullets for You (nr/Divine) 1984
Friday the 12th (PVC) 1985
Poppycock (nr/Tocblock) 1986
Smoke Time (Moving Target) 1988 ●

Blurt's formula is simple and unvarying: Ted Milton alternately (over)blows alto sax and shouts hoarsely, all against Pete Creese's minimal guitar licks and brother Jake Milton's steady drumbeat. You either love it or press "reject" after 30 seconds.

Ted Milton was known as a poet before taking up sax, but his vocals, rampant with echo and distortion, are largely incoherent. Instead, Blurt operates on a more visceral wavelength. The pulsing drums and steady ostinatos anchor free-form sax squeals and (from what can be discerned) lyrical flights of fancy. The more variegated and upbeat In Berlin has an edge over Blurt. This band is really sayin' something.

Blurt returned after a two-year absence with Bullets for You. Recorded live in a wine cellar, it's not quite as manic as the first two albums, displaying instead a well-controlled, tight little noise. The overall sound—especially vocals—is clearer than before; this new precision shows Ted Milton's lyrics as ugly, satirical views of politics and death, but then one wouldn't expect moon-June-party stuff from this bunch. As usual, the band plays with considerable heart—the guitar and drum interplay on tracks like "Sugar-Coated" and "Enemy Ears" makes it easy to miss the fact that they don't use bass.

Friday the 12th is a ten-track live album recorded in Belgium. Ted Milton has also recorded solo albums; Blurt has also continued to issue records. [si/dgs]

BMOVIE

Forever Running (Sire) 1985
The Peel Sessions EP (nr/Strange Fruit) 1988

"Nowhere Girl," this trio's best-known effort, is a lame (although catchy enough) pop song employing a '60s sound somewhere near the Left Banke's. The rest of Forever

Running attempts a collection of other styles, but proves neither as memorable nor as clever. (And the lyrics are embarrassingly pseudo-intellectual as well.) [iar]

BODEANS

Love & Hope & Sex & Dreams (Slash-Warner Bros.) 1986 ●
Outside Looking In (Slash-Reprise) 1987 ●

Despite the unappetizing roots-rock-saviours hype, Waukesha, Wisconsin's BoDeans (not to be confused with Britain's Bodines) are "new music" by default, simply because the rock mainstream at which they aim their earnest, plain-spoken tunes no longer exists. (If it ever did.) And while a lack of pretension is the BoDeans' principal charm, it's also their biggest liability, as the band rarely strives for much more than competent tunefulness.

Love & Hope & Sex & Dreams—on which all four members bear the surname BoDean—is an agreeably modest debut, thanks to T-Bone Burnett's homey production and the downright bizarre interplay of singers Sammy Llanas and Kurt Neumann (the band's only concession to eccentricity). But even at this early stage, the material is alarmingly thin, with memorable singles like "Fadeaway," "She's a Runaway" and "Angels" contrasting obvious filler.

Depending upon your reference points, Outside Looking In—on which the BoDeans lose a drummer but regain their real names—either suffers or benefits from Talking Head (and fellow Wisconsinite) Jerry Harrison's radio-ready production, which smooths out most of the rough edges and leaves the band sounding suspiciously like everybody else. Still, the combo's natural grit shines through the gloss on "Only Love," "What It Feels Like" and a few others. It's significant that Outside Looking In's most appealing and memorable numbers are a trio of self-produced four-track demos included on the CD and cassette. [hd]

BOLLOCK BROTHERS

The Last Supper (nr/Charly) 1983
Never Mind the Bollocks 1983 (nr/Charly) 1983
Live Performances (nr/Charly) 1983
'77 '78 '79 (nr/Konexion) 1985
The 4 Horsemen of the Apocalypse (nr/Charly) 1985 ●

The Prophecies of Nostradamus (Blue Turtle)
1987 ●

Under the enthusiastic (mis)guidance of singer Jock McDonald, the semi-serious Bollock Brothers will try anything once, and make an art out of prole wideboy absurdity. Over the years, they've wavered unpredictably between conceptual brilliance and total creative failure. **The Last Supper**, a double studio album, has "Horror Movies," a corny Munsterized dance theme, and a swipe at political criticism ("The Act Becomes Real," with regard to Reagan), plus lots more, all characterized by inept singing and ept playing.

The conceptually bizarre **Never Mind the Bollocks 1983** parodically reprises the entire contents (and cover design) of the Sex Pistols' 1977 album. Rather than merely attempting to mimic the Pistols, however, the Bollock Bros. simply borrow the material in toto, adding a few lyrics of their own, and employ synthesizers to convert most of the tunes into a sub-New Order update with McDonald's blandly artless vocals serving in lieu of Rotten's sneering bile. Not exactly a piece of timeless musical history, but an amusing novelty record made just a bit weirder by the guest vocal appearance of Michael Fagin (a headcase once arrested for sneaking into Buckingham Palace) on "God Save the Queen" and "Pretty Vacant." Fagin also appears on one side of the "official bootleg" **Live Performances**, a two-record collection of various concert appearances which reprises the band's catalogue, including a set of Pistols tunes. Ridiculous.

The 4 Horsemen employs three of the least likely songwriters you'd ever expect to find sharing one album—McDonald, the late Alex Harvey and Vangelis—yet this well-produced studio job isn't as bizarre as that might indicate. Jock still can't sing worth a damn, although his dumb B-movie lyrics remain as crazed and offbeat as ever; combined with the conservative rock backing, it makes for a regrettably tepid and laborious album.

Each side of **The Prophecies of Nostradamus** leads off with a typically devolved and irreverent cover version (Steppenwolf's "Magic Carpet Ride" and Led Zeppelin's "Heartbreaker"). Berlin's "Sex (I'm a . . .)" (mysteriously retitled "God Created Woman") is also featured, complete with a brief interpolation of "Satisfaction." Despite a few good originals, McDonald's cloying metaphysics on the title track and proselytic

religious numbers like "Ceremony" and "The Beast Is Calling" degrade the music, appealingly played by a proficent five-person European band. (But what are we to make of Genevieve French's credit for "backing vocals & special entertainment"?)   [iar]

BOLSHOI
Giants EP (IRS) 1986 ●
Friends (IRS) 1986 ●
Lindy's Party (Beggars Banquet-RCA) 1987 ●

Sounding like a cross between U2 and the Cult, this Leeds trio isn't exactly good (vocalist Trevor Tanner ain't got what it takes), but they're not dead in the water, either. **Giants**, a six-track mini-album, has only some promising ideas and intriguing production qualities to recommend it. With the arrival of keyboardist Paul Clark, the quartet turned out **Friends**, more of a glossy guitar-and-synth dance record, colored by sporadic echoes of Big Country, a crisp drum sound and self-important vocalist Tanner's alternately Antlike/Bonoesque overtones. (The American **Friends** CD incorporates the contents of **Giants**; the UK tape and CD merely add a bonus track.)

The self-production on **Lindy's Party**, however, locates a workably thick equilibrium between guitar and keyboards and sticks with it, allowing Tanner to be his usual semi-listenable self on ten new slices of threadbare lyrical pretension. Less specifically derivative than the previous records, **Lindy's Party** should have been the Bolshoi's debut.   [iar]

BONEDADDYS
A-Koo-De-A! (Chameleon) 1988

Uplifting Afrobeat, uptight contemporary funk and sizzling rock'n'roll collide with delightful results on the merry gumbo of the Bonedaddys' first LP. The large interracial outfit takes a knowledgeable approach to exotica (confidently covering two Manu Dibango songs) and a witty pen to localism. "Zouk Attack," co-written by Bonedaddy guitarist Paul Lacques and ex-Motels/Burning Sensations leader Tim McGovern, critiques the trendy club scene; "Dumpster Girl," penned by singer Kevin Williams, is a twisted love song. Other LA bands—like the Red Hot Chili Peppers and Oingo Boingo—have confronted the challenge of rampant cross-culturalization and large-ensemble organization, but the Bonedaddys have established a musical nationality all their own.

[iar]

BONE ORCHARD

Jack (nr/Jungle) 1984
Princess Epilepsy EP (nr/Jungle) 1985
Penthouse Poultry (nr/Vax) 1985

The artwork on this Brighton quintet's debut LP employs the same scratchy/violent style as Batcave bands like Specimen and Alien Sex Fiend; the music on **Jack** is similarly gloomy and intense, but generally less clichéd and more engaging. Credit singer Chrissy McGee (an original, intelligent lyricist—check the story-like "Five Days in the Neighbourhood" for details), whose deep, deadpan voice sounds a little like Siouxsie's, and the use of four guest musicians augmenting the guitar-based lineup with piano, strings and sax. Bone Orchard's other strength is a sense of dynamics—they can thunder oppressively or drop back for contrast. **Jack** may not be an overly pleasant disc, but it is a well-crafted one with several nice touches. [iar]

BONGOS

Time and the River (nr/Fetish) 1982
Drums Along the Hudson (PVC) 1982
Numbers with Wings EP (RCA) 1983
Beat Hotel (RCA) 1985

RICHARD BARONE/JAMES MASTRO

Nuts and Bolts (Passport) 1983

RICHARD BARONE

Cool Blue Halo (Passport) 1987 •

Led by enthusiastic guitarist/singer Richard Barone, this Hoboken, New Jersey pop band makes no effort to conceal its roots. On **Drums Along the Hudson** (an expanded version of the **Time and the River** mini-album, itself a compilation of singles), mixed among original songs, is a breathy cover of T. Rex's "Mambo Sun"; elsewhere, Barone spins out streamlined Byrds guitar licks and maintains a brisk pace (à la Sparks) throughout. Tuneful originals like "In the Congo" and "Video Eyes" may trade a certain amount of substance for guaranteed immediate appeal, but there's no better musical equivalent of whipped cream anywhere.

The Bongos subsequently expanded from a trio with the full-time addition of guitarist James Mastro. In an offbeat variation on the solo record concept, Barone and Mastro dropped down to North Carolina to record **Nuts and Bolts** in collaboration with Mitch Easter. Each Bongo takes a side to showcase his own writing and singing, while helping the other out as well. Barone's results are bland and resemble unfinished band demos or outtakes, with dull sound matching uninspired material; Mastro takes a more idiosyncratic approach, using the opportunity to express some individuality and clearly delineate his contribution to the Bongos.

Recording for the first time as a quartet, the Bongos cut five new songs for **Numbers with Wings**, produced by Richard Gottehrer. "Barbarella" and the title track are prime, filled with swell harmonies, driving acoustic guitars and subtle structural tricks; the rest is adequate but dispensable.

Beat Hotel, produced by John Jansen (Lou Reed, Television), is the most rocking Bongos record to date, a sparkling explosion of guitar pop. "Space Jungle" has a nagging hook and a full-blown arrangement; "Apache Dancing" is similarly ambitious in a different vein; "Come Back to Me" and "A Story (Written in the Sky)" hark back to the band's simpler days; "Totem Pole" sounds a bit like the dB's except for the overblown big-band finale. Given the best audio treatment of their career, the Bongos prove their mettle, simultaneously exposing their main inadequacy: inconsistent songwriting.

Recorded live onstage at New York's Bottom Line, **Cool Blue Halo** trades the Bongos' big pop for airy chamber music, as Barone leads a scaled-down attack flanked by a cellist, acoustic guitarist and a percussionist-pianist-vibraphonist. This gentler approach shows off his romanticism to good effect, especially on such well-chosen covers as the Beatles' "Cry Baby Cry" and Bowie's "The Man Who Sold the World," not to mention Bongos classics ("The Bulrushes" and "Numbers with Wings"). A perfect three a.m. record, though it sounds a tad precious in broad daylight. [jy/iar]

See also *Beat Rodeo*.

BONZO GOES TO WASHINGTON

See *Jerry Harrison*.

BOOK OF LOVE

Book of Love (I Square-Sire) 1986
Lullaby (I Square-Sire) 1988 •

Produced by Ivan Ivan for his custom label, this New York art-school quartet's first album is a clever synthesis of catchy electro-pop minimalism and dance-driven rhythmatics. Susan Ottaviano's breathy, almost spoken vocals on atmospheric tunes like "Boy" and "Happy Day" neatly offset the simple, spacious arrangements; others aren't quite as memorable. A little like Trio without the irony, or Dominatrix cleaned up for mass appeal, **Book of Love** is an alluring if insignificant way to while away time in clubland. (Special note to aficionados of esoteric cover versions: the LP contains Liliput's "Diematrosen.") [iar]

BOOKS
Expertise (nr/Logo) 1980

Singer/synthesist/songsmith Stephen Betts uses the middle initials "F.X.," and quirky electronic effects are predictably rife on this well-produced (by Colin Thurston) batch of hollow numbers that have substantially more flash than substance. The band plays well in a vaguely modern way, but with none of the originality or talent that characterizes Thurston's success story, Duran Duran. Betts sings like a right poseur, and his songs don't even steal enough from others to resemble anything in particular. Intensely second-rate. [iar]

BOOM CRASH OPERA
Boom Crash Opera (Warner Bros.) 1987 ●

Melbourne's Boom Crash Opera play heavy drum-driven dance-oriented rock much in the manner of their countrymen INXS, but without much individuality or ingenuity to recommend them. [ds]

BOOMTOWN RATS
The Boomtown Rats (Mercury) 1977
A Tonic for the Troops (Columbia) 1978
The Fine Art of Surfacing (Columbia) 1979 ●
Mondo Bongo (Columbia) 1981
Rat Tracks EP (Can. Vertigo) 1981
V Deep (Columbia) 1982 ●
The Boomtown Rats EP (Columbia) 1982
Ratrospective EP (Columbia) 1983
In the Long Grass (Columbia) 1985
Greatest Hits (Columbia) 1987 ●
BOB GELDOF
Deep in the Heart of Nowhere (Atlantic) 1986 ●

Like Madness and the Jam, the Rats generally matched considerable Anglo-European success with American obscurity. De-spite a string of intelligent, irresistible pop singles and intricate, skillful, unpredictable albums filled with assorted musical styles and sounds, with the exception of the morbid ballad, "I Don't Like Mondays," the Rats never sold many records in the US. While their albums are not all equally excellent—two are self-indulgent and hard to like—the band's commitment to quality and growth, plus singer/songwriter Bob Geldof's magnetic personality, help elevate even lesser efforts to listenability, and much of their work is downright brilliant.

The six future Rats left the unemployment lines in Dublin to enter the rock sweepstakes and had become a going concern on Irish concert stages by the time new wave came along. While the resulting upsurge in record-industry openness toward young, energetic bands undoubtedly helped them get a contract, it was clear from the start that the Rats were a different breed, musically. Produced in Germany by Mutt Lange, the first album is more tradition-minded than punky, but there's no mistaking the verve and independence, which tied the Rats solidly to the less accomplished, more enraged outfits. From the Springsteenish "Joey's on the Street Again" to the Dr. Feelgoody "Never Bite the Hand that Feeds" to a Mott the Hoople-styled ballad, "I Can Make It If You Can," and the album's sarcastic standout, "Looking After No. 1," the ambience is hip, but the rock is fairly routine. Geldof's incisive lyrics and the entire band's credible musicianship invest the stylistically diverse selections with character, making this a top-notch, timeless record.

Assumptions about the Rats' musical intent were dispelled with **A Tonic for the Troops**. Taking giant steps forward in invention and sophistication, Geldof turned from a junior rock singer into a skilled vocalist with a recognizable style; the band likewise exhibited new-found intricacy and multifaceted versatility, thanks in large part to Johnnie Fingers' keyboard cleverness and Mutt Lange's layered production. **Troops** is not a total departure—"Rat Trap" picks up precisely where "Joey" left off, and "She's So Modern" merely improves on "Mary of the Fourth Form"—but "Me and Howard Hughes," "Like Clockwork" and "Living in an Island" display development on all fronts: writing, singing, performing, arranging. (The American version deletes "Can't Stop" and "Watch Out for the Normal People" in favor of two tracks retrieved from the first LP, which had sunk without a trace upon its release by the Rats' previous label.)

The Rats took another big leap on **The Fine Art of Surfacing,** but with less rewarding results. Substandard songs get unenthusiastic treatment, and an overwhelming sense of self-importance only highlights the ennui, despite impressive technical aptitude and obviously strengthened confidence and stylistic reach. The record does contain the powerful "I Don't Like Mondays" and a few other standouts—"Someone's Looking at You," which is clumsy but melodic and charming, and "When the Night Comes," a showstopper with ace Geldof lyrics and a swell arrangement that uses Latin-flavored acoustic guitar for color—but otherwise **Surfacing** is a slick drag.

On first listen, **Mondo Bongo** is even more outlandish, but a little application reveals a number of great tracks in a percussion-laden Afro-Carib style, delivered up in gonzo fashion by co-producer Tony Visconti. "Up All Night," "The Elephants Graveyard" and "Don't Talk to Me" are rollicking good fun, but "Mood Mambo" takes the genre detour too literally, and a totally unnecessary rewrite of an old Rolling Stones tune ("Under Their Thumb . . . Is Under My Thumb") adds to the record's shortcomings. Neither a triumph nor a disaster, **Mondo Bongo** is a halfbaked but entertaining digression. The Canadian-only **Rat Tracks** has a live cut, a remix of "Up All Night" and several otherwise UK-only obscurities; five tracks in all.

Total confusion as to the band's direction and frustration at the disinterest shown by the American audience may have been the reasons why Columbia tried to avoid releasing **V Deep,** opting instead for a 12-inch condensation of it. (The company eventually came around and issued the entire LP, including the EP's contents.) Although heavily stylized and partially overproduced, **V Deep** (so named as the band's fifth LP and their first as a quintet following the departure of guitarist Gerry Cott, who then released a couple of solo singles) contains some of the Rats' strangest songs, but also some of their most evocative and moving efforts. Geldof is at his driven best, and the band keeps pace in a number of styles (including an encore of **Mondo Bongo**'s sound and a Dennis Bovell dub mix of one track) that don't neatly hang together, but paint the group in a most fascinating light. Controversial perhaps, but

thoughtful and intriguing—a fine album to be savored repeatedly.

After **V Deep,** the Rats dropped out for several years, prompting the US issue of **Ratrospective,** a mini-album containing "I Don't Like Mondays," "Up All Night," "Rat Trap" and three other familiar cuts. In late 1984, Geldof surfaced as the co-instigator of Band Aid, an all-star 45 fundraiser for Africa that inspired a wave of similar ventures throughout the music world. The band returned to action in early 1985 with a new single, followed several months later by an entire new album, **In the Long Grass,** which had actually been recorded in 1983 but initially rejected by their label and ultimately held from release until early 1985. (The inner sleeve thanks people "For making an unbearable year tolerable . . . ") The Rats look miserable and spent on the cover; the lyrics are unremittingly bitter, defiant and angry. Matching the verbal onslaught, the music is as dense and rugged as any they have ever made, yet uplifting in their refusal to buckle under whatever pressures they had to face. An extraordinarily powerful record. (In an ironic final bit of tampering, Columbia inexplicably forced the Rats to rewrite the lyrics of "Dave," a song on the UK LP, resulting in an entirely different vocal and title: "Rain.")

Later that year, Geldof organized the massive Live Aid charity concert/telecast and was mooted for Nobel Prize consideration, but it hardly aided the Rats, who met 1986 without an American label and decided to call it quits. Acknowledging the group's demise and taking fair (and dignified) advantage of the attention Geldof had earned, Columbia attempted to convert some of that notoriety into record sales, expanding **Ratrospective** by four tracks and calling it **Greatest Hits,** a fair compilation improved by Arthur Levy's enthusiastic liner notes.

In mid-1986, after enormous efforts on behalf of others, Geldof took a few steps in his own behalf, writing an autobiography (*Is That It?*) and signing a solo record deal. **Deep in the Heart of Nowhere** is best heard on CD or cassette (the one-disc vinyl version has three fewer tracks and truncates others), bears the onerous marks of Rupert Hine's tritely commercial overproduction but also contains some swell tunes and affecting lyrics. The outstanding "Pulled Apart by Horses" (amazingly omitted from the vinyl version) and "This Is the World Calling" both resemble Rat tracks and allude to recent experiences; "In the Pouring Rain" could easily have come from **Surfacing**. The record contains some true wretchedness (like the melodramatically recited "The Beat of the Night") that will confirm skeptics' worst fears about Geldof's ego, but this is by no means a bad showing. Musical supporters here include Dave Stewart (who was originally scheduled to produce), Annie Lennox, Midge Ure, Brian Setzer, Eric Clapton and Alison Moyet.   [iar]

DUKE BOOTEE
Bust Me Out (Mercury) 1984

Duke Bootee (Edward Fletcher) is one of the unsung heroes of rap. As a member of the Sugar Hill label's crack house band, he wrote the tune, "chorus" and half the raps for "The Message." Although that groundbreaking single came out under the name Grandmaster Flash and the Furious Five, the raps belong to Bootee and Melle Mel. The two paired up less successfully (and more formulaically) on "Message II" and "New York, New York," before Bootee rediscovered the urban claustrophobia groove on the title track of his solo LP. The album boasts aggressive playing and production from his old Sugar Hill friends, and the rap side (as opposed to the song side) smokes.   [jl]

BOOTHILL FOOT-TAPPERS
Get Your Feet Out of My Shoes EP (nr/Go! Discs) 1984
Ain't That Far from Boothill (nr/Mercury) 1985

In yet another installment of "Musical Styles Traverse the Ocean," these seven rustic English lads and lassies play a charming and catchy version of old-timey folk (banjo, fiddle, guitar, washboard, accordion) on the wonderful title track of their five-song 12-inch. But it doesn't stop there: they also essay a soulful choral arrangement of Curtis Mayfield's "People Get Ready" and a rousing assault on Margaret Thatcher called "True Blues." The only duff item is the rushed, tuneless "Milk Train."

Unfortunately, the album makes a crime of eclecticism: the band dabbles in everything from ska to country-western, connecting emotionally with none of it. Flat, insipid production (mostly by Dick Cuthell) matches the performances' lack of spunk; the net re-

sult is a record without depth or charm. Even a new version of "Get Your Feet Out of My Shoes" sounds tedious and contrived. What a shame. The Boothill Foot-Tappers disbanded at the end of 1985.   [iar]

BOUNTY HUNTERS
See *Nikki Sudden.*

DENNIS BOVELL
Brain Damage (nr/Fontana-Phonogram) 1981
BLACKBEARD
Strictly Dub Wize (nr/Tempus) 1978
    (nr/Ballistic-UA) 1978
I Wah Dub (nr/More Cut-EMI) 1980
DENNIS BOVELL AND THE DUB BAND
Audio Active (Moving Target) 1986 ●
WINSTON EDWARDS & BLACKBEARD
Dub Conference/Winston Edwards & Blackbeard at 10 Downing Street (Fr. Celluloid) c. 1975

Guitarist Dennis "Blackbeard" Bovell has long been a reggae musician and producer of high standing. (He co-founded Matumbi, defunct for several years now but still remembered as one of England's first and best self-contained reggae bands; try their **Point of View** LP on EMI America.) Bovell also happened to have been a school chum of white jazz-pop keyboardist Nick Straker and hit musician/producer Tony Mansfield (New Musik, Captain Sensible, etc.), with whom he maintained contact; such eclectic musical connections have enabled him to bring a fresh perspective to the production of early new wave bands like the Slits and the Pop Group.

This same eclecticism informs his dub LPs in conceptual outlook and willingness to take chances beyond the usual electronic overkill. (Regrettably, billing aside, he merely engineered the **Dub Conference** LP— Edwards produced it—which is pleasant but quite ordinary.) Bovell creates strong instrumentals that are mainly written and arranged for dub; the catchy melody lines are dissected but not disintegrated.

Strictly Dub Wize (mostly performed by Bovell, with some help from Matumbi and others) exhibits cleverness and humor by the bagful (one track even bases itself on "Surrey with the Fringe On Top"!). **I Wah Dub** carries Bovell's creation of aurally pungent tracks infused with musical witticisms from merely excellent to brilliant. Aside from some drumming, the odd piano part here or melodica toot there, Bovell plays everything.

Brain Damage and **Audio Active** are also both consistently enjoyable, though less spectacular: neither uses much dub at all. The former adds a mixed bag of boogie-woogie, rock'n'roll and R&B to the reggae, and Bovell's homely but good-humored vocals adorn several tracks. (A bonus dub LP—all new tracks, similar to **I Wah Dub**, though not as engrossing—is included.) Good lightweight groove music, ideal for summer.

The later record—a band effort, including Straker and Matumbi's horn duo—is mostly vocal and almost all reggae. Surprisingly, the instrumental and dub tracks are less interesting than the vocal tunes; Bovell's songwriting has grown and his singing's matured. If Eddy Grant stuck to reggae for most of an LP it might sound like this. Durably likable, it goes by too darn fast—all ten tracks are between three and four minutes long. [jg]

DAVID BOWIE

The Man Who Sold the World (Mercury) 1971 ●
Hunky Dory (RCA) 1971 ●
The Rise and Fall of Ziggy Stardust and the Spiders from Mars (RCA) 1972 ●
Aladdin Sane (RCA) 1973 ●
Pin-Ups (RCA) 1973 ●
Diamond Dogs (RCA) 1974 ●
Young Americans (RCA) 1975 ●
Station to Station (RCA) 1976 ●
Low (RCA) 1977 ●
"Heroes" (RCA) 1977 ●
Lodger (RCA) 1979 ●
Scary Monsters (RCA) 1980 ●
Let's Dance (EMI America) 1983 ●
Tonight (EMI America) 1984 ●
Never Let Me Down (EMI America) 1987 ●

Throughout his lengthy career, David Bowie has worked in many widely disparate musical areas, and virtually all of them have proven enormously influential, even if sometimes it's taken years for the rest of the rock world to catch up with him. Nonetheless, the mercurial star continues to shift gears, styles and fashions almost as often as shirts and, by example, helps keep pop and rock developing and changing. Unfortunately, long after he's abandoned some excessive dalliance or an-

other, his camp followers trundle on, missing the ephemeral and transitory essence of Bowie's work. Even if only as the source of unreproachably hip songs to cover, Bowie has played an essential role in glam-rock, new wave, post-punk, neo-soul, dance music, etc.

Although he actually began recording in the late '60s, we join the Bowie show in progress at the dawn of the last decade, when he dropped some of his more theatrical Anthony Newley affectations and got down to rock'n'roll cases. (The discography above omits compilations, reissues, repackages, soundtracks, EPs, spoken-word records and live albums, of which there are more than a few.)

The Man Who Sold the World begins Bowie's affair with guitar-heavy rock'n'roll, courtesy Mick Ronson. Tony Visconti's compressed production gives the album an utterly synthetic audio quality; few records this simply played sound as studio-created. In retrospect, the grim futurist imagery of "Saviour Machine," "The Supermen" and "Running Gun Blues" seems far more prescient than the thrilling but unadventurous band's music. Still, a shockingly strong debut for the electrified Bowie.

Hunky Dory was a detour of sorts, briefly returning a seemingly innocent Bowie to his hippie/folkie/cabaret days for the catchy "Changes" and the obnoxiously precious "Kooks," plus such atypically direct tributes as "Song for Bob Dylan" and "Andy Warhol." But the album also contains the redemptive "Life on Mars," "Queen Bitch" and "Oh! You Pretty Things," all essential cornerstones in the burgeoning glam/sci-fi/decadence world Bowie was assembling.

Bowie began his fey alien role-playing in earnest on **Ziggy Stardust**, an unquestionably classic rock'n'roll album. He introduces this new persona via the pseudo-biographical title track; otherwise, songs paint a weird portrait of an androgynous (but sexy) world ahead. Armed with supercharged guitar rock and truly artistic production (Bowie and Ken Scott) and mixing rock'n'roll stardom imagery with a more general *Clockwork Orange* outlook, the peerless set of songs (including "Suffragette City," "Hang on to Yourself," "Rock'n'Roll Suicide" and "Moonage Daydream") outline some of the concerns that have underpinned a lot of rock songwriting in the '70s and '80s.

Having peaked so gloriously with a character that could not last indefinitely, Bowie adjusted Ziggy a bit on **Aladdin Sane** and came up with a weird set of tunes—some tremendous, some minor—and a distant, unpleasant left-field studio sound. "Panic in Detroit," "Watch That Man," "The Jean Genie" and "Drive-In Saturday" are some of his greatest songs, painting bleak pictures of detached existences with cinematic strokes and killer riffs. Rather than singing about apocalypse, Bowie captures the barren feel of a dead world, and feeds it into the music. **Aladdin Sane** is also notable for allowing a serious crooner side to re-emerge—as on "Time"—a foreshadow of future developments. That said, it must be noted that Bowie's revisionist cover of "Let's Spend the Night Together" is utterly misguided.

In a surprisingly guileless gesture, Bowie filled his next album exclusively with his versions of songs by mid-'60s English bands. Although not easily related creatively to Bowie's contemporaneous originals, **Pin-Ups** is a wonderful, loving tribute that just happens to contain (almost all) ace renditions of great and, at the time in America at least, largely unknown songs. Perhaps recognizing that his own records are destined to become more obscure to future generations, by recording these classics Bowie generated interest in his forebears, giving the bands he chose (Pretty Things, Pink Floyd, Them, Mojos, Merseys, Kinks, Yardbirds, Easybeats and Who) much-deserved cachet in the new rock world.

Bowie then jettisoned his band and drafted a new bunch of sidemen to further his trendily somber vision of a doomed future on **Diamond Dogs**. Although the LP contains one of Bowie's most incredible and concise songs—"Rebel Rebel," perfectly describing his followers and their role in the new society—it also has an overblown and underdeveloped concept that falls under the wheels of mammoth pomposity. In retrospect, it's not so bad, but does suffer significantly from audio clumsiness and strident, seemingly unfinished sound.

Dropping one set of gimmicky costumes and British players, Bowie made **Young Americans**, an album mainly of phony (but pleasant) Philadelphia-styled soul/rock mixed with other oddities, like his truly awful collaboration with John Lennon, "Fame." It took five years for the British new wave, finally bereft of their own new ideas, to ape Bowie and start absorbing black American idioms into their work.

Following that brief infatuation, Bowie launched an experimental phase that directly influenced far more bands, especially the "new romantics" and arty minimalists. **Station to Station** is a strangely impersonal mixture of chilly show ballads, techno-pop and whatever was passing for disco that year. The album features the hit "Golden Years," but also the experimental and challenging "TVC15." It also marked the beginning of Bowie's distancing himself from his former rock-idol role.

That trend was formally instigated with **Low**, on which Bowie arranged to co-opt the modernistic sensibility of Brian Eno (his collaborator on three consecutive studio LPs) and present a selection of tracks that are not so much songs as word-paintings or, in many cases, simply mood pieces. From the grandiosity of **Young Americans** to the sketchy minimalist slices here, Bowie took heart from intellectual, bare-bones rock bands like Wire and, in turn, helped legitimize and promote such spartan stylings.

The follow-up to **Low**, **"Heroes"** has slightly fleshier production, though nearly one full side is comprised of whizzing synthesizers and amorphous textural noodling. Robert Fripp contributes lead guitar, and his presence adds a bit of sinew to the overall sound, something lacking in the less-forceful **Low**. The album leans heavily on chilly, European affectations (with a large debt owed to Kraftwerk), but also has room for a genuine pop single, the atmospheric title track.

Lodger, the third installment of the Bowie-Eno trilogy, finds Bowie drifting back into a solid song-oriented context. Though much of the material seems to be stream-of-consciousness, there are a couple of pure poppers, such as "D.J." and "Boys Keep Swinging," that recall a more commercial time. Also of interest is Bowie's version of "Sister Moonlight," rewritten as "Red Money."

Scary Monsters is Bowie's most consistent LP since the pre-**Low** period, a culmination of the styles that had been showcased individually on previous discs. The tone is up-front, a confrontation with the real world of alienation Bowie always ascribed to his fictional settings. **Scary Monsters** contains two Bowie standards: "Ashes to Ashes" and "Fashion."

Having tired of years of acclaim and only sporadic and middling glimmers of the kind of success that usually befits a superstar (although Bob Dylan could teach him a few lessons about humility in that area), Bowie changed labels and made **Let's Dance**, a calculated effort (with the production assistance of Nile Rodgers) to get in step with the sound of today, rather than tomorrow or yesterday, Bowie's far more common habitats. Not surprisingly, as it usually happens, Bowie succeeds at whatever he sets his mind to, and the record was a worldwide smasheroonee. "Let's Dance," "Modern Love" and "China Girl" may not be the Thin White Duke's finest creations, but they do hit a solid compromise between art and commerce, and don't harm his reputation nearly as much as expand his audience (and bank balance).

Several years later, Bowie regained the rights to his back catalogue and attempted to arrange for his entire *oeuvre* to be reissued by his new label. The plan backfired, and now all of the RCA albums—on vinyl, tape and CD—are currently out of print.

After a mega-tour to consolidate the album's huge success, Bowie banged out a quickie, **Tonight**, which has all the earmarks of being a casual, smug cookie-cutter job geared for the charts. (What other recording challenges are left for Bowie? He's tried self-indulgent art and jugular commercialism, scoring just what he wanted on both fronts.) In its losing defense, the album does include a duet with Tina Turner and a remarkably swell pop hit, "Jazzin' for Blue Jean," that recalls far earlier times in his career.

The styleless **Never Let Me Down** was released to general indifference and critical derision. Although this casual loud-rock outing—Peter Frampton and Carlos Alomar share guitar responsibilities with D.B.— seems on first blush to be slapdash and slight, the first side is actually quite good, offering provocative pop-culture lyrics delivered with first-take enthusiasm and carefree backing. "Day-In Day-Out" is silly but charming in its way; the verses' catchy ticktock pop on "Beat of Your Drum" makes it resemble a Cars song; the Lennonish title track is equally weird and likable. Bowie has rarely sounded so unconcerned and relaxed. The inferior second side starts off with the subsequent tour's fantasyland nonsense theme song, "Glass Spider," and ends with Iggy's "Bang Bang," a cute digression in keeping with the record's flip attitude.

There's utterly no point in trying to predict Bowie's future. He's really done it all and still somehow remains in touch and in charge. The safest assumption? Whatever he does, it won't be boring.   [jw/iar]

See also *Iggy Pop, Lou Reed.*

BOW WOW WOW

Your Cassette Pet [tape] (nr/EMI) 1980
See Jungle! See Jungle! Go Join Your Gang Yeah! City All Over, Go Ape Crazy (RCA) 1981
The Last of the Mohicans EP (RCA) 1982
I Want Candy (RCA) 1982
Twelve Original Recordings (Harvest) 1982
When the Going Gets Tough the Tough Get Going (RCA) 1983

Bow Wow Wow may have been easily dismissed by some as rock entrepreneur Malcolm McLaren's creation, but the band deserved better. (McLaren and Bow Wow Wow parted company in 1982.) Combining musicians lured away from Adam and the Ants (with whom McLaren had briefly worked) and 15-year-old singer Annabella Lwin, the ever-provocative McLaren formed the band, launching their career via a 45, "C-30, C-60, C-90 Go," which espoused the virtues of home taping at a time when the band's record company (and virtually all others) were beginning to bitterly oppose it. True to McLaren's precepts (although it should be noted that tapes at that time were not as commonly copied as discs), **Your Cassette Pet** is a tape-only collection of eight songs. Except for "I Want My Baby on Mars" and a painful rendition of "Fools Rush In," the material is marked by Annabella's breathless ranting and incessant drumming "borrowed" from the African Burundi tribe. The results are cheerful if smarmy.

The first full-length album, **See Jungle! See Jungle!**, isn't as wound up as **Cassette Pet**, but does show artistic growth. By downplaying the leering football chants, Bow Wow Wow is able to investigate subtler lyrics and rhythms. And fueled by drummer Dave Barbarossa, they pack quite a wallop.

Last of the Mohicans is a four-song EP whose producer (Kenny Laguna of Joan Jett fame) and lead-off track (the Strangeloves' "I Want Candy") were chosen presumably for their American commercial potential. If nothing else, the sound is cleaner than before.

The discographical plot thickens with **I Want Candy**, released in two distinctly different versions. The American LP is comprised of the **Mohicans** EP, four tracks from **See Jungle!** (three of them remixed) and two "new" cuts. The UK album of the same title makes **Your Cassette Pet** available on vinyl, except for "Louis Quatorze." It also includes a few British single sides and the US-only EP, with its re-recorded "Louis Quatorze." Got that?

Not to be outdone, EMI's American affiliate issued **Twelve Original Recordings**. This is essentially the British **I Want Candy** LP minus several tracks. Pay your money and take your choice.

The all-new **When the Going Gets Tough** was recorded free of McLaren's machinations. On this, their final album, Bow Wow Wow delivered much the same musical barrage as before without any propagandistic pretense. The band subsequently ejected Annabella (who launched a solo career in 1985) and regrouped as the Chiefs of Relief. [si]

See also *Annabella, Chiefs of Relief.*

THE BOX

The Box EP (nr/Go! Discs) 1983
Secrets Out (nr/Go! Discs) 1983
Great Moments in Big Slam (nr/Go! Discs) 1984
Muscle In EP (nr/Doublevision) 1985
Muscle Out (nr/Rough Trade) 1985

One of the few bands capable of effectively combining the spontaneity and musicianship of jazz with the urgency and rough-edged sound of rock, the Box are a five-piece spin-off from British industrial funksters Clock DVA. Comparisons to Captain Beefheart, Gang of Four, the Minutemen and Ornette Coleman are all appropriate; execution is first-rate (especially by ex-Clocks Paul Widger on guitar and saxophonist Charlie Collins), their material frantic.

The eponymous debut EP contains five manic cuts, setting instruments on wild collision courses behind Peter Hope's vocals. **Secrets Out** improves on that formula by injecting unexpected subtleties and an underlying murkiness that give even more impact to the hyperactive guitar/sax counterpoint. A solid, frenzied album guaranteed to keep any listener on his/her toes.

Great Moments in Big Slam, however, is quite a letdown. The pace is slower and the band really doesn't get a chance to cut loose, but that's not the problem so much as the heavy-handed percussion and grossly exaggerated vocals which dominate the production. After releasing the **Muscle In** EP, the Box announced a trial separation to pursue other projects. The posthumous **Muscle Out** was recorded live at the Leadmill in the Box's hometown, Sheffield. [dgs]

BOY GEORGE
See *Culture Club.*

BOYS
The Boys (nr/NEMS) 1977
Alternative Chartbusters (nr/NEMS) 1978
To Hell with the Boys (nr/Safari) 1979
Boys Only (nr/Safari) 1981
YOBS
The Christmas Album (nr/Safari) 1979

Too unseriously pop-minded for the punks but too punky for the power-poppers, well received nearly everywhere in Europe except their homeland (England), beset with label woes in the UK and name confusion in the US, the star-crossed Boys were perennially in the wrong place at the wrong time.

Norwegian expatriate Casino Steel (the band's keyboard player and co-writer of much of their first three albums) was already a veteran of this sort of thing, having been a member of the Hollywood Brats, a London glitter band like the New York Dolls but with better musicianship. The Brats' self-titled album, recorded in '73, came out at the time in Scandinavia, was bootlegged in the US as **Grown Up Wrong** two years later, and finally appeared in 1980 on UK Cherry Red.

The first Boys album is an inconsistent (if promising) melange of Steel's Bratisms, standard punkarama and the stirrings of a Beatle (and other pop) influence. **Alternative Chartbusters**, though, presents infectiously rocking tunes played with irreverent elan, featuring Duncan "Kid" Reid's engagingly adolescent readings of the mostly humorous lyrics (often, as on **To Hell with the Boys**, playing the punk schlemiel), culminating in a pair of classic pop-punk singles, "Brickfield Nights" and "First Time." The third album (recorded in the tiny Norwegian town of the punny title) delivers more of the same, but with slicker and fuller sound—organ in addition to piano, more dual guitars—and more variety.

Sadly, reverses (among them, Steel's deportation) took their toll, and the Boys, as a quartet, made a fourth album that sounds flatter than stale soda tastes. Perhaps they knew they were recording their swan song.

Under the pseudonym of the Yobs, the

Boys, early in their career, recorded an LP of Yuletide favorites, plus their own holiday compositions, in various variations on pop-punk, sometimes just cute, but mostly skipping irreverence and heading straight for sheer tastelessness, e.g., "Silent Night" by Nazi-punks and "Twelve Days of Christmas" translated by "Oi" brigands into locker-room scatology. Subsequently, Boys guitarist Honest John Plain cut an LP, **New Guitars in Town**, with Lurker Pete Stride, supported by other members of both bands, who had formed an alliance of sorts. [jg]

See also *Lurkers*.

BOYS NEXT DOOR
See *Birthday Party*.

BPEOPLE
See *Alex Gibson*.

BILLY BRAGG

Life's a Riot with Spy vs. Spy (nr/Utility) 1983 (nr/Utility-Go! Discs) 1983
Brewing Up with Billy Bragg (CD Presents) 1984
Between the Wars EP (nr/Go! Discs) 1985
Life's a Riot Etc (CD Presents) 1985
"Days Like These" (nr/Go! Discs) 1985
Talking with the Taxman About Poetry (Go! Discs-Elektra) 1986 ●
Back to Basics (Go! Discs-Elektra) 1987 ●
The Peel Sessions EP (nr/Strange Fruit) 1987
Help Save the Youth of America EP (Go! Discs-Elektra) 1988 ●

Bard of the '80s, Billy Bragg is a rough-hewn modern troubadour playing a solitary electric guitar and singing his pithy compositions in a gruff voice. Although his tools are utterly simple, Bragg is capable of enormous strength and depth in his writing and performing, spinning off touching, warm love songs as well as trenchant social satire and socialist political commentary.

On the seven tracks of **Life's a Riot** (recorded originally as songwriting demos), Bragg waxes tender ("The Milkman of Human Kindness"), bitter ("A New England") and sarcastic ("The Busy Girl Buys Beauty"), keeping things blunt and one-take spartan, making it an ultimate no-frills pop record. Combining the wordplay wit and strong emotions of Elvis Costello with the grumpy melodic charm of Paul Weller, it's a small, articulate masterpiece.

Brewing Up, a relatively ambitious full-length undertaking with a tiny bit of organ and trumpet (not to mention—gasp!—over-dubbed guitars and vocals), finds Bragg retaining all of his rugged pop appeal while sharpening his pen. The songs focus on romance, offering nervous but perceptive angles on love and lust ("Love Gets Dangerous," "The Saturday Boy," "A Lover Sings"). He also shreds Fleet Street journalism with "It Says Here."

Bragg then turned his attentions to another traditional subject for angry young men with guitars: politics. He's done countless benefit concerts, played in Communist countries and, via Red Wedge, the musicians' organization he helped found, campaigned for the Labour Party. **Between the Wars**, an extraordinarily powerful 7-inch EP, is Bragg at his finest, singing of England's peacetime recessions ("Between the Wars"), chronicling a 17th century rebellion ("World Turned Upside Down") and reviving the 1940s union classic, "Which Side Are You On."

"Days Like These," a subsequent three-song single, shows Bragg's deepening commitment to socialist political activities. This latter-day Woody Guthrie belts out sincere (if occasionally awkward) constructs like "I see no shame in putting my name to socialism's cause/Nor to seek some more relevance than spotlight and applause."

Talking with the Taxman About Poetry ("the difficult third album") is a great leap forward, the deft application of understated instrumental accompaniment on some of Bragg's best-ever songs. "Levi Stubbs' Tears" tells chillingly of a tragic couple, colored with a touch of flugelhorn, trumpet and percussion; "Ideology" consciously paraphrases Dylan ("Chimes of Freedom") for a scathing look at Britain's old-boy buddy club; rinky-tink piano provides the setting for "Honey, I'm a Big Boy Now," a sharp-eyed appraisal of marital failure; "Help Save the Youth of America" is a powerful—and not ill-considered—indictment from abroad. The only wrong step is a cover of the Count Bishops' tuneless "Train Train," which abruptly interrupts the flow of Side One.

Subtitled "live and dubious," the 1988 EP, issued to coincide with an American tour, contains four live recordings (including the title track, captured in Moscow, complete with translated intro), "There Is Power in a Union," done bluegrass style with accompaniment by the Pattersons, an alternate studio version of "Days Like These" and a leaf-let promoting voter registration and electoral responsibility. **Life's a Riot Etc** is a handy American-only release that combines all of the first mini-album with **Between the Wars** for a Bragg then-and-now extravaganza, complete with lyric sheet. **Back to Basics** goes that effort one better by putting **Life's a Riot**, **Between the Wars** and **Brewing Up** on two discs, billed as "the first 21 songs from the roots of urbane folk music." **The Peel Sessions** EP was recorded live in July 1983 for broadcast on British radio and contains renditions of "A New England," "Love Gets Dangerous," John Cale's "Fear" and two others.   [iar]

BRIAN BRAIN
See *Brian Brain.*

BRAINS
The Brains (Mercury) 1980
Electronic Eden (Mercury) 1981
Dancing Under Streetlights EP (Landslide) 1982

The Brains' story is typical of many inde-pendent bands who signed to not-so-swift big labels. Led by lanky Tom Gray, this Atlanta-based quartet first garnered widespread at-tention with a striking homemade single, "Money Changes Everything." The Brains subsequently recorded two LPs for Mercury, but neither sold a speck. Following a divorce by mutual consent, the group returned, poorer and wiser, to the independent label scene.

On both albums, producer Steve Lilly-white concocts a thick, heavy sound that sub-jugates Gray's synthesizers and Rick Price's aggressive guitars to the tunes themselves. And for good reason: Gray's songs are tart accounts of love and confusion perfectly suited to his dry, sardonic voice. The Brains offer a rougher and less glib variant of the Cars' ironic sensibility, which is probably why they never achieved widespread popu-larity. Gray and crew unsettle rather than divert.

The Brains includes a re-recording of the cynical "Money Changes Everything" and "Gold Dust Kids," a pithy, unsentimental portrait of decadence. **Electronic Eden** fea-tures the bitter romanticism of "Heart in the Street," covered (badly) by Manfred Mann and "Collision," a humorously tasteless look at a brain-damaged car-crash survivor.

The four-song EP is more of the same intense longing and hidden passion. If the Brains sound a bit weary, chalk it up to the record biz blues. **Dancing Under Streetlights** isn't the best starting point, but it's a worthy continuation. The Brains have since dis-banded. (As an undoubtedly lucrative foot-note, Cyndi Lauper covered "Money Changes Everything" on her first LP.) [jy]

GLENN BRANCA
Lesson No.1 (99) 1980
The Ascension (99) 1981
Symphony No.1 (Tonal Plexus) [tape] (ROIR) 1983
Symphony No.3/Gloria (Neutral) 1983
GLENN BRANCA/JOHN GIORNO
Who You Staring At? (Giorno Poetry Systems) 1982

Many artists have had their music de-scribed as a wall of sound, but few have de-served it as much as New York composer/ guitarist Glenn Branca. One of the first to realize that a classical-rock fusion need not be technique-crazed keyboardists soloing away to the accompaniment of rehashed Brahms or Stravinsky, Branca writes music of orchestral richness that retains—intact— all of rock's danger, urgency and impact.

With his roots in the downtown no-wave movement of the late '70s, Branca's **Lesson No.1** was the first release on the influential local label, 99 Records. Slow, repetitive har-monic changes and hidden sub-motifs invite comparisons to minimalists like Philip Glass, but Branca's music is more dissonant, primi-tive and—above all—loud.

The Ascension is the closest he's ever come to an out-and-out rock album. Atop pulverizing bass/drum combinations, Branca and three other guitarists build a thick, lay-ered mass of shifting textures, sometimes all on one chord, sometimes in a dense cacoph-ony of six-string clusters. Suffice to say, it packs quite a wallop. Branca's side of the joint disc with poet John Giorno is music commissioned for Twyla Tharp's dance, *Bad Smells.* Most of it is much like **The Ascen-sion**, except for very brief sections of quiet.

Only two of Branca's five symphonies have been recorded and released commer-cially so far, and it is in this format that he is most effective. Played by large ensembles, the pieces incorporate a plethora of instru-ments of his own design (primarily dulcimer-like things strung with steel wire and ham-mered with mallets) in addition to guitars, horns and a battery of percussion. He builds intense drones and ear-shattering crescendos while exploring the sonic possibilities of large tonal clusters and the resultant overtones. **Symphony No.1** alternates between one relentless, thundering chord and primal rhythmic pounding. As instrumental layers build, overtones clash to produce melodies of their own, and can even trick the listener into hearing instruments that aren't there. **Symphony No.3** adds homemade keyboards, giving an orchestral and almost Oriental sound to the piece—delicacy amidst the thunder. Both recordings are hindered in that it is impossible to capture the full effect of his live performances, where the volume generally runs around wake-the-dead level. [dgs]

See also *Hugo Largo*.

BRANDOS

Honor Among Thieves (Relativity) 1987 ●

Well-groomed quartet mines all the right influences and comes up with dramatic, workmanlike melodic rock, with occasional flashes of moral and political conscience. Though too much of the band's material lacks real distinction, **Honor Among Thieves** (produced by singer/guitarist Dave Kincaid) is a generally impressive debut, with Kincaid's sharp, twangy vocals calling up visions of Orbison and Fogerty and the band's pneumatic, radio-ready snap marking them as a natural for mainstream success.

The Brandos' knack for big, classically-styled pop comes in handy on the grandiose "Hard Luck Runner" and the anti-war hit "Gettysburg," as well as a memorable lonely ballad, "In My Dreams," and a credible cover of Creedence's "Walking on the Water." In the wake of **Honor Among Thieves**' surprise popularity, the Brandos signed with Geffen. [hd]

BRAVE COMBO

Music for Squares (Four Dots) 1981
World Dance Music (Four Dots) 1984
No Sad Faces (Four Dots) 1984
People Are Strange EP (Rogue) 1986
Musical Varieties [CD] (Rounder) 1987
Polkatharsis (Rounder) 1987 ●

Formed by Denton, Texas homeboy Carl Finch in 1979, Brave Combo are witty and wise purveyors (and perverters) of polkas and musics of many nations. A highly successful tour of local mental institutions honed their chops, and each record reveals an ever-more-adventurous and itinerant package of sounds. By exploring and exploiting the least hip music on god's green earth—the polka—Finch and Co. demonstrate that everything most people know about pop music is wrong.

The aptly titled debut album, **Music for Squares,** finds them grinding out polka, cha-cha, twist, waltz and tango standards and originals with rockish energy. On **World Dance Music** they began to take rock standards, such as the Doors' "People Are Strange," and twist them into weird ethnic shapes (such as the Romanian hora). You'll hear an African-ska version of a Perez Prado hit, as well as the usual assortment of *cumbias, norteñas, schottisches* and, of course, polkas. "If we missed your part of the world," suggests the cover, "please check future releases."

The live **No Sad Faces** contains an unforgettable "In-a-Gadda-da-Vida," a cha-cha version of "O Holy Night," a ska take on "Little Bit of Soul" and much more. The CD-only **Musical Varieties** compilation is an excellently-produced and generous introduction to the band which sets the stage for **Polkatharsis,** the Combo's brave return to its roots. They play hardball with 11 polkas—from "Happy Wanderer" to "Who Stole the Kishka"—on this all-trad collection, adding a couple of sweet waltzes and a *schottische.* [rg]

BREAKFAST CLUB

Breakfast Club (MCA) 1987 ●

The Breakfast Club's notability comes from the quartet's drummer, Stephen Bray, who helped write and produce several hits for Madonna (including "True Blue" and "Into the Groove") and can be considered one of the chief architects of her hit sound. (Actually, Madonna played drums in an early incarnation of the band around 1979 and helped bring college friend Bray in after she quit.) As might be expected, that sound—soft funk basslines under bubbling synthesizer counterpoint—is featured prominently on this debut, but to less satisfying ends. The group's limitations expose the formula's, and vice versa: despite five different producers, all of the songs on **Breakfast Club** sound pretty much the same. There's no vocal personality to distinguish them. (Singer Dan Gilroy sounds vaguely like Elvis Costello.) Still, the one exception, "Right on Track," about a dancing fool trying to capture a girl's attention and her heart, is so giddily persuasive that it seems just a matter of time before the group finds its own formula for success.

[bk]

BREAKING CIRCUS
The Very Long Fuse (Homestead) 1985
The Ice Machine (Homestead) 1987
Smokers' Paradise EP (Homestead) 1987

Breaking Circus began as a vehicle for Steve Björklund, veteran of the '80–'83 Chicago punk explosion (as a member of the seminal Strike Under and, later, Terminal Beach). The eight-song 45 rpm **Very Long Fuse** is terse, post-punk vitriol set to a banging dance-beat drum machine. "The Imperial Clawmasters' Theme" and "Precision" are sharp, jagged and guitar-powered, unique for such dancefloor bop. (The closest stylistic reference is Three Johns, whose songs Breaking Circus have played live.)

Björklund then relocated seven hours away in Minneapolis and put together a more stable band-type environment, borrowing the rhythm section of Rifle Sport when that group isn't working. **The Ice Machine** contains, as the title suggests, sinister and methodical blows like "Song of the South," "Ancient Axes" and "Took a Hammering." Trading fire for poisoned darts, **Ice Machine** gets under the skin with repeated listenings.

Smokers' Paradise offers much the same fare (complete with another imposing hammer adorning the cover), only better. The instrumental title track adds smoky, ghostly acoustic and tiptoeing piano, a walk through a haunted graveyard; the trademark sabertoothed guitars on "Eat Lead" and "Three Cool Cats" (not the 1959 Coasters hit) are an equally hair-raising experience. A consistent, innovative, heavy, eerie pleasure.   [jr]

BILLY BREMNER
Bash! (nr/Arista) 1984

Erstwhile Rockpile guitarist Bremner is far more talented than his low profile would indicate; insecurities have hampered him considerably. In many ways, **Bash!** is the Dave Edmunds album Edmunds never made (and more consistent than anything Dave's done since **Repeat When Necessary**, which included three Bremner songs). Billy's a bit poppier and a better, more prolific songwriter than his former bandmate.

Ex-Records drummer Will Birch produced and supplied the lyrics on **Bash!**, which also benefits from previously-unrecorded donations (one each) from Elvis Costello (brilliant!) and Difford/Tilbrook (they should have finished writing it first). The album doesn't contain Bremner's Stiff 45, "When Laughter Turns to Tears," but still delivers the goods track after track.

Bremner now lives in Los Angeles and plays with local talents, including Rosie Flores.   [jg]

BRIAN BRAIN
Unexpected Noises (nr/Secret) 1980
Fun with Music! EP (Plaid) 1985
Time Flies When You're Having Toast
   (Moving Target) 1987 ●

Although Brain—or, more accurately, Martin Atkins—was the drummer in Public Image for a time, his subsequent solo career has taken a much less dour direction. So while **Unexpected Noises**—mostly his own work—is of little consequence, at least it attempts to be anarchic and funny rather than anarchic and glum. Biggest problem here is the poor production, which leaves the sound muddled and flat.

Five years later, Atkins emerged from a period of inactivity and returned to the concert circuit and vinyl world in Brian Brain (the Group), an outfit including original Go-Go's bassist Margot Olavarria. **Fun with Music!** is a four-song 12-inch recorded in New York. Brain's body may be in America (the cut-up tribal chant of "U.S.A." is a jaundiced cultural appraisal) but his brain is on clean living: two numbers pitch anti-drug-use messages. Interestingly, the ex-PiLer does a song called "Happy?" two years before the album of that name.

The subsequent album (which sounds a bit like a modernized cross between Captain Sensible and John Otway) reprises a pair of songs from the EP and adds eight more, all recorded with Olavarria, guitarist Geoff Smyth and others. The rhythm-heavy hip-hop/massed-drums tracks—with jungle ambience, found sounds and other sonic ephemera keeping things appropriately offbeat—are a bit short on melody, but not concept or wit. Atkins isn't a great singer, but he has a lively mind and an absurdist outlook that guarantees mental stimulation even when the music drags.   [iar]

BRIAN T. AND PLAN 9

See *Plan 9*.

BETTE BRIGHT AND THE ILLUMINATIONS

Rhythm Breaks the Ice (nr/Korova) 1981

Criminally underused in Deaf School, Bette Bright blossomed into an exciting performer on this solo effort, thanks partly to the help of clever friends. **Rhythm Breaks the Ice** was produced by fellow DS graduate Clive Langer and his partner, Alan Winstanley, the team behind Madness' phenomenal success. (Bright intertwined the family trees by marrying that band's singer, Graham McPherson, in 1981.) Here they balanced studio smarts with the need to emphasize Bright's plaintive tones, and came up with a canny modern-day variation on Phil Spector. The full, smooth sound has a kaleidoscopic quality, continually shifting to highlight the key element in the arrangement—guitar, marimba or whatever—and providing Bright with a perfect launching pad for her soaring style. [jy]

BRILLIANT

Kiss the Lips of Life (Atlantic) 1986

YOUTH & BEN WATKINS

The Empty Quarter (nr/Illuminated) 1984

Three years after opting out of Killing Joke, dreadlocked bassist Youth teamed up with former Hitmen vocalist Ben Watkins (now also versed in keyboards, drums and guitar) to record **The Empty Quarter**, the soundtrack to a play. Forceful and musically intelligent, with layers of disembodied sound lunging and pulsing in and out, it's a striking collection of dramatic, largely electronic instrumentals that bear some of Youth's former band's fury, mixed with subtlety and artsiness. Surprising.

Equally unexpected is the sound of the trio Youth subsequently formed with vocalist June Montana (ex-Dream Academy backing singer) and guitarist/keyboardist Jimi Cauty (who formerly played with Zodiac Mindwarp and was a leading album/poster designer in the '70s). The Stock-Aitken-Waterman team produced the dismal **Kiss the Lips of Life**, revealing the cynical Brilliant to be into high-tech dance-rock and neo-soul that could just as easily be by the Thompson Twins, Swing Out Sister or Bananarama.

And what this bunch does to James Brown's "It's a Man's Man's Man's World" is sad. [iar]

BRILLIANT CORNERS

Growing Up Absurd (nr/SS20) 1985
Fruit Machine EP (nr/SS20) 1986
What's in a Word (nr/SS20) 1986
Somebody Up There Likes Me (nr/McQueen) 1988 •

Bristol's Brilliant Corners are capable of the most joyous of pop sounds—bright, ringing guitars skipping through a mix of peppy drums, tight bass, trumpet and piano. By the same token, these Britons are also capable of the most depressing of lyrics. Like Morrissey, singer/songwriter Davey Woodward has curious preoccupations—with death and dying and lost and unrequited loves. The Brilliant Corners' music is beyond reproach, but Woodward is one miserable boy.

Growing Up Absurd, while not as striking as it might have been, sets the course for the quintet's releases—bouncy pop with the unusual novelty of a trumpeter as a full member of the five-piece. The **Fruit Machine** EP sparkles, thanks to much needed invention: piercing guitar lines, nimble trumpeting and keyboards make "Meet Me on Tuesdays" and "Jim's Room" the best of these four tracks. Highly recommended.

The band continued their expansion on **What's in a Word**, which adds strings and female backing vocals. The band's greatest songs are here: "Laugh I Could've Cried," "A Very Easy Death" and "Egotistical Me." The delightful "Boy and a Cloud" suggests that Davey may not be as miserable as we think he is.

Somebody Up There Likes Me shows the Brilliant Corners at their most accomplished; musically *and* lyrically, they are unnervingly precise. A dozen ardent testimonials on life and love in the '80s—"She's Dead," "Never a Young Girl" and "With a Kiss" are a far cry from the trite pop ditties we've come to expect from this kind of musical backing. It's rare to find such soul-baring honesty in pop music. [ag]

BRITISH ELECTRIC FOUNDATION

Music for Stowaways [tape] (nr/Virgin) 1981
Music for Listening To EP (Can. Virgin) 1981
Music of Quality and Distinction, Volume 1 (nr/Virgin) 1982

In search of more meaningful dance music, Martyn Ware and Ian Craig Marsh abandoned the just-about-to-be-enormous Human League in 1980 to form the more experimental (musically and structurally) British Electric Foundation. The core members—Marsh, Ware and singer Glenn Gregory—also work as Heaven 17, a "division" of B.E.F. Confused? While Heaven 17 is geared for dance funk'n'soul, B.E.F. for a while pursued one-off concept projects with a variety of other people.

Music for Stowaways—released only on tape—consists of moody instrumentals, ranging from funk-rock to icy Germanic synthgarde to electro-bop and sound experiments. Much of it was reissued on a Canadian EP, **Music for Listening To**, which also includes an extra track, "A Baby Called Billy."

Music of Quality and Distinction, B.E.F.'s first venture into pop experimentation, brings in a number of interesting people (including Tina Turner, Gary Glitter, Sandie Shaw and John Foxx) to perform cover versions of well-known and not-so-well-known oldies, from "These Boots Are Made for Walking" and "Wichita Lineman" to David Bowie's "Secret Life of Arabia" and Lou Reed's "Perfect Day." Older songs hold up better under this treatment than new ones but, overall, choices of singers and musicians are on the mark. Despite any social implications (or lack thereof), a good time.   [sg]

See also *Heaven 17.*

DAVE BROCK

See *Hawkwind.*

BROKEN BONES!

Decapitated (nr/Fall Out) 1983
Dem Bones (nr/Fall Out) 1984
Live at the 100 Club (nr/Subversive Sounds) 1985
Bone Crusher (Combat Core) 1986
F.O.A.D. (Combat Core) 1987

This quartet (originally comprising Bones, Baz, Oddy and Nobby) may not be good spellers, but they certainly have a clear idea which end of a guitar to bash at. Playing at maximum stun volume, the band's lack of literacy seems no obstacle to their creating blunt protest songs with clear and indomitable rock power on **Dem Bones**. A very British center ground between parochial punk (BB generally play too slow) and modern metal (but more topical and fiery), Broken Bones could be the modern answer to the MC5. Or just another would-be Black Sabbath.

By the time of the half-studio/half-live **F.O.A.D.** (suffice to say three of the initials stand for "off and die"), Tezz had taken over bass chores from Oddy and the band had grown older and louder, finding a niche in the pre-dinosaur echelon of indie metal. The seven studio tracks sound pretty routine—all muddy bottom and squalling guitars—while the boiling nine-song speed-metal/Oi! live side (London, 1986) is treblier but equally indistinct.   [iar]

BRONSKI BEAT

The Age of Consent (London-MCA) 1984 ●
Hundreds & Thousands (London-MCA) 1985 ●
Truth Dare and Double Dare (London-MCA) 1986 ●

Playing only electronic instruments and singing unequivocal gay lyrics in an astonishing, somewhat grating falsetto, this English trio burst full-blown onto the scene. Jimmy Somerville (who left the band in early 1985 and formed the Communards) has a piercing voice which he can modulate for greater appeal (as on "Junk"); the band plays a powerful and unique breed of techno-dance, with room for such digressions as George and Ira Gershwin's "It Ain't Necessarily So" and Giorgio Moroder-for-Donna Summer's "I Feel Love." Far more blunt and sexy (the cover image and sleeve notes are similarly plain-spoken) than Tom Robinson's old records, the Bronskis are a highly original entity, drawing on a wide variety of sources to create an invigorating, courageous and memorable album of modern dance music.

The **Hundreds & Thousands** album offers six lengthy remixes of songs including **Consent**'s "Why," "Smalltown Boy," "Junk" and "Heat Wave." Horns have been added, and all the tunes extended to the six-minute-plus range; the cassette and CD contain two bonus 12-inch mixes.

Replacing Somerville with a far less distinctive singer, Bronski Beat released **Truth Dare and Double Dare**, a peppy collection of adequate tracks that notably lack a strong vocal presence.   [iar]

JAMES BROWN

See *Afrika Bambaataa.*

JULIE BROWN

Goddess in Progress EP (Rhino) 1984
Trapped in the Body of a White Girl (Sire)
1987 ●

Versatile comedy vocalist Brown offers five hysterical slices of modern culturecide on **Goddess in Progress**: "I Like 'Em Big and Stupid," "The Homecoming Queen's Got a Gun," "Will I Make It Through the Eighties," "Cause I'm a Blonde" and "Earth Girls Are Easy." Bouncily entertaining music, Brown's astute, wacky lyrics and her astute delivery make this more fun than a long trip to the mall.

An attempt to turn Brown into a Madonna/Lauper-style star (1950s version) by downplaying the humor and wrapping her in witless synthesizer dance-pop fails miserably on **Trapped in the Body of a White Girl**. Except for the title track and inferior remakes of "Big and Stupid" and "Homecoming Queen," the humorlessness of this turgid major-label boo-boo buries Brown's talent.   [iar]

BRYGADA KRYZYS

Brygada Kryzys (Polish Tonpress) 1982
Brygada Kryzys (nr/Fresh) 1982

This semi-underground (and I don't mean that figuratively) Polish quartet is not exactly in the mainstream of world punk rock, but does play a slightly-toned-down version of high-octane guitar (and sax) raunch that compares favorably to bands from Bauhaus to the Sex Pistols. While not breaking any new creative ground, Brygada Kryzys is a fascinating and credible example of stylistic transliteration from one culture to a rather different one.   [iar]

BUCKWHEAT ZYDECO

On a Night Like This (Island) 1987 ●

For an untraditional introduction to zydeco—the indigenous Anglo-French Louisiana stew of accordion, cajun fiddle music, gritty black R&B, Chicago blues and other influences—try **On a Night Like This**, the major-label debut (ninth album overall) by Grammy-nominated Buckwheat Zydeco and the Ils Sont Partis Band, led by accordion-toting singer Stanley "Buckwheat" Dural. Following in the footsteps of Clifton Chenier and commercially eclipsing Queen Ida, Rockin' Sidney, Chenier and other superior practitioners of the art, Buckwheat throws down an enjoyable but commercially compromised sound that covers Chenier ("Hot Tamale Baby"), Booker T. ("Time Is Tight"), the Blasters ("Marie Marie") and Bob Dylan (the title tune) with too much studio polish and a horn section that cuts into the invincible sweaty truth of the form. Dural's originals (like "Ma 'Tit Fille") are fine, but he doesn't exactly exert himself on this night.

[iar]

HAROLD BUDD/BRIAN ENO

See *Cocteau Twins, Brian Eno*.

BUGGLES

The Age of Plastic (Island) 1980
Adventures in Modern Recording (Carrere)
1982

After "Video Killed the Radio Star" changed the course of electro-pop forever, it was straight downhill for the Buggles as a group. The two members, however, proved a lot more durable on their own: Geoffrey Downes went on to enormous success with Yes and Asia; Trevor Horn became a hit record producer (for ABC and Malcolm McLaren) before founding ZTT Records and guiding Frankie Goes to Hollywood into the record books.

The Age of Plastic was a disappointment to fans of the Buggles' cogent 45s, while **Adventures** amounted to little more than a self-explanatory post-mortem. Both albums are technically stunning, reasonably catchy and crashingly hollow.   [iar]

See also *Art of Noise, Frankie Goes to Hollywood, Bruce Woolley*.

BUNNYDRUMS

Feathers Web EP (Funk Dungeon Music) 1983
PKD (Red) 1983
Holy Moly (Fundamental Music) 1984

This commanding, arty Philadelphia quartet uses guitars to play a sinewy, challenging brand of rhythmic snake-rock (think Shriekback) with almost-abrasive vocals. On **Feathers Web** (dedicated to the memory of science fiction author Philip K. Dick), they roar through an affecting slithery instrumental ("Crawl") and a trio of draggy dirges unsalvaged by interesting sonic effects. **PKD** adds five new and mostly improved tracks to a reprise of the EP's contents, showcasing the band on pieces that crackle with electricity and evince growing control of their intense sound. Best new item: "Ugh," a mega-funky instrumental with squalling sax.

Holy Moly integrates a variety of different approaches, from a cover of the Stooges' "T.V. Eye" to dense drones where instruments flow in and out of the mix. Overall, **Holy Moly** uncovers more dynamics and audio coloration, making it an intriguing record by a skilled, occasionally visionary band.

[iar]

BUREAU
See *Dexy's Midnight Runners.*

RICHARD JAMES BURGESS
See *Landscape.*

PATRICK BURKE
See *Parasites of the Western World.*

J.J. BURNEL
See *Stranglers.*

T-BONE BURNETT
Truth Decay (Takoma) 1980 ●
Trap Door EP (Warner Bros.) 1982
Proof Through the Night (Warner Bros.) 1983
Behind the Trap Door EP (nr/Demon) 1984
T Bone Burnett (Dot-MCA) 1986 ●
The Talking Animals (Columbia) 1988 ●

Singer, songwriter, ace producer (Los Lobos, Marshall Crenshaw, etc.), Christian, moralist and pal of Elvis Costello, T(-)Bone Burnett has been a steadily growing influence on the music scene since the late '70s. Whether his inconsistent records leave any lasting mark or not, he's likely to make his presence felt in some role for a long time to come.

Burnett debuted on disc as a member of the Alpha Band, part of the extended family surrounding Bob Dylan during his mid-'70s Rolling Thunder period. Following the three Alpha Band LPs, he went solo on what remains his best full-length album, **Truth Decay**. The loose rockabilly and blues grooves offer a sympathetic backdrop for Burnett's sweet (countryish) 'n' sour (Dylanish) vocals, as he delivers romantic laments and scathing commentaries on the sorry state of contemporary life. His moral essays generally don't grate ("Madison Avenue" being an exception), thanks to the sheer musicality of the sounds.

The **Trap Door** EP is even better, with the gleaming folk-rock of "Hold on Tight" and "I Wish You Could Have Seen Her Dance" making an exhilarating tonic for troubled souls. And the sly, sarcastic "Diamonds Are a Girl's Best Friend" gets his point across perfectly.

Guess the boy's head got turned by too many good reviews and famous fans, 'cause everything since has been tainted by a smug self-righteousness. **Proof Through the Night** boasts a stellar supporting cast, including Ry Cooder, Richard Thompson and Pete Townshend. However, the big arrangements and epic pretensions grow tiresome, especially his attempts to encapsulate an era in "The Sixties," "Hefner and Disney," et al. Burnett's got some valid points, but who made him judge and jury?

While **Behind the Trap Door** may be a sequel to his successful EP, it plays more like outtakes. A waste. Far better is **T Bone Burnett**, a sparse, largely acoustic country LP that marks his first outing without a hyphen. Songs tend to be more personal than preachy, with the standard "Poison Love" and "Oh No Darling" among the highlights. (The CD adds three bonus Burnetts.)

The Talking Animals is a return to the mainstream attempts of the Warner discs, and features creative input by such kindred souls as Bono and Tonio K. Some of the songs rock tougher than anything he's done before (see "The Monkey Dance" and "You Could Look It Up"); others succeed only in scaling new heights of pretension. Sung in four languages, "Images" could be a Brecht castoff, while "The Strange Case of Frank Cash and the Morning Paper" is a tedious five-minute spoken-word tale. Skip instead to "The Killer Moon," a mid-period Beatles soundalike, and the aptly titled "Relentless." All in all, worth hearing, though one wishes this talented jerk weren't so impressed with himself. [jy]

KATE BUSH
The Kick Inside (Harvest) 1978 ●
Lionheart (EMI America) 1978 ●
Live on Stage EP (nr/EMI) 1979
Never for Ever (EMI America) 1980 ●
The Dreaming (EMI America) 1982 ●
Kate Bush EP (EMI America) 1983

Hounds of Love (EMI America) 1985 ●
The Whole Story (EMI America) 1986 ●

Falling somewhere between Joni Mitchell, Laura Nyro, Peter Gabriel and Laurie Anderson, Kate Bush's literate, masterful, enchanting records have won her enormous popularity, even if she can be overbearingly coy and preciously self-indulgent. Bush is a huge pop star in Great Britain; America has never canonized her commercially, although a large cult does exist. Over the years, she has become increasingly ambitious, turning what might have been a career dominated by others into an singleminded pursuit of her own muse. The young piano-playing singer on **The Kick Inside** bloomed into a fully autonomous artist.

The Kick Inside is dominated by Bush's startling falsetto and such imaginative songs as "Them Heavy People," "Wuthering Heights" and "Kite." Top-notch sessionmen and Andrew Powell's sparkling production provide a rich setting for the songs. The record's huge popularity didn't seem to faze Bush, who returned before the end of the same year with another well-crafted album, **Lionheart**. More subtle, jazz-inflected arrangements keep it less immediate, but the cinema-minded "Hammer Horror" and theater-minded "Wow," as well as the fondly nationalistic "Oh England My Lionheart," make it memorable.

Bush's next release was a 7-inch EP wisely reproducing four songs from the first two albums in a concert setting. She then arranged and co-produced **Never for Ever**, which yielded three singles ("Babooshka," "Breathing" and "Army Dreamers") and provided further evidence of her compositional depth. Songs about dead rock stars ("Blow Away"), a murder ("The Wedding List") and a tribute to the "Violin" are among her strangest lyrical concerns. A credit line thanking Richard Burgess and John Walters for "bringing in the Fairlight" gains significance in hindsight, given how integral the sampling device subsequently became to her music-making.

Self-produced, **The Dreaming** offers Bush's first truly rock-oriented work, tinted with strong rhythms and clever Fairlight sounds. Almost free of her little-girl voice, Bush is by this record a highly skilled, controlled singer with abundant drama and personality on which to draw. The Peter Gabriel resemblance—in terms of what can be done artfully within the song form—is obvious, still, it's all Kate Bush and perhaps her first really extraordinary album.

Hounds of Love divides into separately titled halves. The "Hounds of Love" contains one of Bush's most impressive songs, "Running Up That Hill (A Deal with God)," plus other similarly complex and enticing creations; "The Ninth Wave" offers an overextended side-long contemplation on drowning—impressive, but not really enjoyable.

Kate Bush is an American mini-album: one track from the UK live EP plus a pair of cuts from **The Dreaming** and one each from the two preceding LPs. **The Whole Story** is a fine career compilation (not in chronological order) of a dozen singles, from "Wuthering Heights" (with the vocals redone) to 1986's energetic "Experiment IV." [tr]

BUSH TETRAS
Rituals EP (Stiff) 1981
Wild Things [tape] (ROIR) 1983

Arising from the New York post-rock scene, the Bush Tetras attempted a synthesis of African sensibilities (as perceived by white Americans) with the modern dance to form a global tribal music. The 12-inch **Rituals** (produced by then-Clash drummer Topper Headon) sets songs against a funk/reggae beat with horns and punchy guitar work tossed in liberally. "Can't Be Funky" and its doppelgänger, "Funky Version," are the most explicitly Third World tunes, while "Cowboys in Africa" rushes along with punk intensity and "Rituals" employs a threnody pace.

The **Wild Things** cassette is a concert recording compiled from late 1982 performances in and around New York. The band is in fine, ferocious form, and Cynthia Sley spits and scowls her vocals as if the songs really meant something. The material reprises most of the Tetras' slim recorded repertoire, plus a couple of appropriately savage covers.
[sg/iar]

BUTTHOLE SURFERS
Butthole Surfers (Alternative Tentacles) 1983
Live PCPPEP (Alternative Tentacles) 1984
Psychic . . . Powerless . . . Another Man's
    Sac (Touch and Go) 1985 ●
Cream Corn from the Socket of Davis EP
    (Touch and Go) 1985 ●
Rembrandt Pussyhorse (Touch and Go)
    1986 ●

Locust Abortion Technician (Touch and Go)
  1987 ●
Hairway to Steven (Touch and Go) 1988 ●

There are few experiences in this life that leave one feeling as sullied as a spin through the grooves of a Butthole Surfers record. Unlike so many nouveau scuzzbos, Austin's Buttholes don't descend into the depths of squalor to make a point about the human condition—they just like it down there. Splotches of guitar noise and tortured screams are these enigmatic Texans' bread and butter. When the noise revs up really fast, it sounds almost like hardcore, but this band relies more on filth than speed or power. The Butties inflict and exorcise pain like other people eat potato chips, and whatever debts they owe to Flipper and PiL would probably be forgotten if they'd just go away. There's clearly no one like 'em.

The debut mini-LP (for some obscure reason, aka **Brown Reason to Live**) poses its threat to the social order through a varied thrash-to-Beefheart-blues attack and an inspired/inspiring set of lyrics. "The Shah Sleeps in Lee Harvey's Grave" is the obvious anthem while, on "Suicide," singer Gibby Haynes leaves aside political matters for an intensely personal statement: "I'm not fucking kidding man, it hurts!" On the other hand, "Hey Hey" is almost subdued, Feelies-style material—extremism sometimes takes the oddest forms, don't it?

The seven-song **Live PCPPEP** offers denser and dirtier treatments of some of the first record's non-hits. The biggest improvement is the new brother and sister standup drumming team. **Another Man's Sac** (originally pressed on clear vinyl) shows an addled creative sensibility—you were expecting them to develop into Hall and Oates? The faint-at-heart may not survive this assault, but then they probably don't deserve to.

The 12-inch **Cream Corn** EP hauls more sediment and sludge up from the gutter and onto the turntable, hitting its high point with "Moving to Florida," a cloying ear nuzzle imparted over Crampsian dirtabilly. (The CD of **Another Man's Sac** and the cassette of **Rembrandt Pussyhorse** both include the EP's four songs as a bonus.) Mixing deranged blues, metal-punk and an overriding sense of anarchy, these loonies don't make guitars scream, they make 'em vomit and choke on it.

Rembrandt Pussyhorse takes a gonzo psychedelic approach that is (dare it be said)

downright arty in its bizarre sonic experimentation. With some of the bowel-grinding dregs toned down, piano, organ, violin and a plethora of guitar techniques make the album a real diversion. Of special note is a cover of the Guess Who's "American Woman," which, in the Butties' bloody hands, sports a huge drum sound and metallic guitar, with tinny, atonal voices—imagine Nile Rodgers producing the Residents.

Locust Abortion Technician—which typically offers absolutely no information about the parties responsible—ebbs and flows like organic waste, an unpredictable flux of noise, movie score politeness, grating grunge-rock, fake folk, chirping birds, voices, tape manipulations and words, done at various recording speeds. "Sweat Loaf" launches the record with silence, speaking and then manic rock gusto; "22 Going on 23" ends it with grinding radio vérité.

With an incredible cover and numerous nods to the '60s, **Hairway to Steven** is as varied as it is entertaining: the program includes acoustic guitars competing with bowling alley sounds, half-speed vocals mixed (shades of "Third Stone from the Sun") with Hendrixy guitar psychedelia, live (maybe) cowbunk storytelling, straightforward (well . . .) melodic songsmithery and flat-out audio hysteria. Love 'em or hate 'em, reactionary times demand more inspirational rebels like the Buttholes.   [jl/tr]

BUZZARDS
Jellied Eels to Record Deals (nr/Chrysalis)
  1979

Although the Buzzards (originally the Leyton Buzzards) appeared on the surface to be another London-area group of punk/reggae dilettantes, closer examination revealed them to be a subversive vehicle for satiric songwriters Geoff Deane (vocals) and David Jaymes (bass). Comprising all their recorded output, this 17-track retrospective is jammed with lively (if heavy-handed) potshots at everything from Pink Floyd ("No Dry Ice or Flying Pigs") to modern mores ("Disco Romeo") to punk itself ("We Make a Noise"). And be sure not to miss "Saturday Night Beneath the Plastic Palm Trees." The tone throughout is cheerfully abusive; it's appropriate that two (Monty) Pythons get thanked on the cover.

Underscoring the band's undiscovered assets, Deane and Jaymes went on to major commercial stardom playing dance music as Modern Romance. [jy]

See also *Modern Romance.*

BUZZCOCKS

Spiral Scratch EP (nr/New Hormones) 1977 + 1981
Another Music in a Different Kitchen (nr/UA) 1977
Love Bites (nr/UA) 1978
Singles Going Steady (IRS) 1979 ●
A Different Kind of Tension (IRS) 1980
Parts One, Two, Three EP (IRS) 1984
The Peel Sessions EP (nr/Strange Fruit) 1987
Total Pop 1977–1980 (Ger. Weird Systems) 1987 ●
Lest We Forget [tape] (ROIR) 1988

Inspired by the Sex Pistols, Howard Devoto and Pete Shelley formed the Buzzcocks in Manchester in 1975, specializing in high-energy, staccato delivery of stripped-down pop songs. With John Maher (drums) and Steve Diggle (bass), the Buzzcocks released **Spiral Scratch**, one of the earliest new wave EPs and a pioneering independent label release. Though ragged and rudimentary, the 7-inch features the frantic, minimalistic pop stylings that would characterize the group's work and, with songs like "Breakdown" and "Boredom," remains the most exciting version of the band on record.

Devoto departed shortly thereafter to form Magazine, and Steve Garvey joined, taking over bass while Shelley switched to vocals (in addition to guitar) and Diggle to lead guitar. **Another Music in a Different Kitchen** expands on the stark three-minute pop song and themes of confusion, alienation and betrayal, adding a new emphasis on harmony and humor and a growing coordination of the players in contrast to the earlier inspired chaos.

Love Bites demonstrates both the Buzzcocks' perfection of their particular brand of pop and their disillusionment with its restrictions. Producer Martin Rushent clarifies the elements of the sound even further, and Shelley's songwriting reaches its peak, but the strongest numbers—"Ever Fallen in Love" and "Just Lust"—are essentially singles as opposed to album tracks, underscoring a problem that plagued the band.

A Different Kind of Tension makes tentative maneuvers into the new, as the Buzzcocks attempt to throw off the yoke of pop music. This schizophrenic album features some of Shelley's finest songs, notably "You Say You Don't Love Me" and "I Believe." Diggle provides some of the material, and the band reaches a zenith of effortless craft. The aptly named **Tension** marked the end of the Buzzcocks, with Shelley pursuing a fascinating solo career and the others working in a number of outfits, including the Teardrops and Flag of Convenience.

Singles Going Steady is a compilation of stunning, classic singles, proving conclusively that the Buzzcocks *were* a singles band, and a great one at that. From the teen angst of the Devoto/Shelley "Orgasm Addict" to the 20th century malaise of "Something's Gone Wrong Again," the songs are across-the-board great, and the album is a non-stop hit parade. **Parts One, Two, Three**—another compilation of sorts—reprises a conceptual trio of singles released in 1980: "Are Everything" and "What Do You Know?" are prime; the other four cuts are less essential.

Total Pop, an offbeat German collection, draws from **Singles Going Steady, One, Two, Three, Love Bites** and **Tension**, adding the band's two live tracks ("Breakdown" and "Love Battery") from **The Roxy London WC2**, a classic 1977 scene document. (The CD and cassette have three bonus cuts.)

The **Peel Sessions** EP only contains three songs: "Fast Cars," "Moving Away from the Pulsebeat" and "What Do I Get." The long-delayed **Lest We Forget** is a fine-sounding live compilation tape recorded at—with one Mancunian exception—various US gigs in 1979 and 1980. [sg/iar]

See also *Howard Devoto, Flag of Convenience, Magazine, Pete Shelley, Teardrops.*

DAVID BYRNE AND BRIAN ENO
My Life in the Bush of Ghosts (Sire) 1980 ●
DAVID BYRNE
Songs from the Broadway Production of "The Catherine Wheel" (Sire) 1981 ●
Music for *The Knee Plays* (ECM) 1985
DAVID BYRNE ET AL
Sounds from True Stories (Sire) 1986
RYUICHI SAKAMOTO, DAVID BYRNE AND CONG SU
The Last Emperor (Virgin Movie Music) 1988 ●

As a Talking Head, David Byrne—guitarist, songwriter, singer—has long shown an inquisitive, intelligent interest in unusual applications of pop music. His solo musical work (Byrne also creates in video and film) revolves around transfiguring pop through the infusion of alien elements or by injecting it into foreign situations. **My Life in the Bush of Ghosts**, a continuation of his (and the band's) collaboration with Eno, blends found vocal tapes with electronic music centering around Third World (notably African) rhythms to interesting effect and uneven results.

Byrne created the music on **The Catherine Wheel** for a dance production by the renowned Twyla Tharp. Listeners can get either a selection of tracks on the album, or the complete score on the cassette version. The pace and instrumentation on the poppier material bears a strong resemblance to Talking Heads' work of the **Remain in Light** period, with volatile rhythms and jazz inflections, while other songs are more experimental, drawing heavily on Eno's ambient and tape-editing techniques.

Byrne next forayed into theatrical music by writing and producing the dixieland-inflected horn score for **The Knee Plays**, a section of director/avant-garde opera conceptualist Robert Wilson's unperformed-in-toto stage work **The Civil Wars** that actually was presented. Inspired by the Dirty Dozen Brass Band, Byrne created angular pieces that remove the swing from ragtime, turning New Orleans jazz into engaging machine music over which he occasionally recites lyrics.

Although Talking Heads released an album of songs to coincide with *True Stories,* a soundtrack record of incidental music for the film was also issued. Byrne produced and wrote the majority of **Sounds from True Stories** (subtitled "Music for Activities Freaks"), earning his star billing while performing on just two tracks. The rest of the musical cast—Kronos Quartet, Carl Finch, Steve Jordan, Terry Allen, the Heads, Prairie Prince and others—plays his (and their) instrumentals in a panoply of styles, from country to polka to electronics to jazz.

Working individually on separate segments of it, Sakamoto, Byrne and Cong Su shared a Golden Globe award and an Oscar for the score of Bernardo Bertolucci's *The Last Emperor.* Byrne's segment—15 instrumental minutes on Side Two—avoids trite Oriental clichés while managing to adequately evoke the cultural locale with gongs, strings and woodwinds. Lovely.   [sg/iar]

C C C C C C C

CABARET VOLTAIRE
Extended Play EP (nr/Rough Trade) 1978
"Mix-Up" (nr/Rough Trade) 1979
Live at the YMCA 27-10-79 (nr/Rough Trade) 1980
Three Mantras EP (nr/Rough Trade) 1980
Voice of America (Rough Trade) 1980
1974–1976 tape (nr/Industrial) 1980
3 Crépuscule Tracks (Rough Trade) 1981
Red Mecca (Rough Trade) 1981
Live at the Lyceum [tape] (nr/Rough Trade) 1981
2 X 45 (nr/Rough Trade) 1982
Hai! Live in Japan (Rough Trade) 1982
The Crackdown (nr/Some Bizzare-Virgin) 1983
Johnny YesNo (nr/Doublevision) 1983
Micro-Phonies (nr/Some Bizzare-Virgin) 1984
Drinking Gasoline (Caroline) 1985
The Arm of the Lord (Caroline) 1985 ●
The Drain Train EP (Caroline) 1986
The Golden Moments of Cabaret Voltaire [CD] (nr/Rough Trade) 1987
Code (EMI Manhattan) 1987 ●
Eight Crépuscule Tracks (Giant) 1988 ●

PRESSURE COMPANY
Live in Sheffield 19 Jan 82 (nr/Paradox) 1982

RICHARD H. KIRK
Disposable Half-Truths [tape] (nr/Industrial) 1980
Time High Fiction (nr/Doublevision) 1984
Ugly Spirit (nr/Rough Trade) 1986
Black Jesus Voice (nr/Rough Trade) 1986

PETER HOPE & RICHARD KIRK
Hoodoo Talk (Native-Wax Trax) 1988

STEPHEN MALLINDER
Pow-Wow EP (nr/Fetish) 1982
Pow-Wow Plus EP (nr/Doublevision) 1985

The prolific Cabaret Voltaire is one of the most energetic, progressive and dissonant forces in modern music. Working primarily in the electronic form, specializing in found sounds and tape manipulations, Cabaret Voltaire has relentlessly pushed at the outer edges of style, shedding an early primitivism for a subsequent accessibility that plays on the (almost) familiar. Coming from the industrial city of Sheffield, they have spent years attempting to make a music that reflects their experience and perceptions.

Extended Play virtually launched both Cabaret Voltaire and the Rough Trade label (it was the label's third single), and highlights the Cabs' main features: unpredictable sounds and eerie, disembodied vocals manipulated over a very physical beat. It is particularly notable for a distorted cover version of Lou Reed's "Here She Comes Now."

The more professionally produced **"Mix-Up"** has better coordinated use of electronics, increasing the bizarre intensity of the sound. Bass, guitar and flute are evident (but deformed) in the mix, and Cabaret Voltaire makes visible use of other people's material, as with the Seeds' "No Escape."

Live at the YMCA (as well as the later **Live at the Lyceum** tape) dispels any notions of Cabaret Voltaire as a sterile studio group. Wisely, they don't seek to precisely duplicate their recorded sound, but convert it into outré-populist dance music that is almost improvisational in nature. Though the live recordings are more fragmented than their studio counterparts, they compensate for that in energy.

Three Mantras is Cabaret Voltaire's first explicit venture into non-Western musical forms. The Arabic material used is successfully developed into a chant, and then its structure is applied to a new work. It also features a shift in Cabaret Voltaire's technique, with musical demands taking precedence over production, to strange and beautiful effect.

Voice of America is an uneven release, combining older material with much more assured newer work, such as the political "The Voice of America/Damage Is Done," which uses found tape and sparse electronics to juxtapose the repressive and libertarian aspects of American life. The new material shows much greater focus and cleaner production than the older, with the mantra technique rising in place of the former chaotic electro-noise.

For completists and/or fanatics, **1974–1976** is a series of curious and intriguing false starts and experiments from the band's earliest days.

3 Crépuscule Tracks shows the band in transition between their found-vocals/art-noise period and a commitment to dance-floor electronics. "Sluggin' fer Jesus (Part One)" is a masterful combination of the two, as a right-wing TV preacher demands large cash contributions over a powerful, trance-inducing synth beat.

On **Red Mecca**, Cabaret Voltaire tighten the focus to produce an album more coherent than its predecessors, underscored by a reworking of Henry Mancini's score for Orson Welles' *Touch of Evil.* As their music reaches a new level of maturity and polish in both production and performance, Cabaret Voltaire focus and extend their film noir theme through all the material, making this an odd, deceptively accessible record.

Two 12-inch EPs packaged as an album, **2 X 45** picks up the trends begun on **Red Mecca** and compresses them into a new form. Also interesting is the move away from obvious electronics and manipulations to a more naturalistic sound, with emphasis on acoustic instruments like saxophone and clarinet. This is the closest the group has come to making a rock'n'roll album.

Like earlier live albums, **Hai! Live in Japan** marks time, playing with the band's recent development, funky in nature and far more coherent than **Live in Sheffield**. The latter was a one-off show to raise funds for the Polish Solidarity union, and was released under the Pressure Company name for contractual reasons. Disordered and trenchant, it is a reminder that the band is still capable of electrifying cacophony.

In 1983, Cabaret Voltaire signed with that noted asylum for eccentrics, Some Bizzare (here in consort with Virgin), a move criticized by some as a sell-out. The resulting LP, **The Crackdown**, is perhaps the most left-field record ever accused of commercial compromise. Sticking mostly to a funk format, the songs are more structured than those on **2 X 45**, and the band displays a plethora of high-tech but dark electronic textures. Probably the strongest of their many albums.

Johnny YesNo is a soundtrack to Peter Care's film about a junkie. Released on the band's own Doublevision label, it was recorded in 1981, prior to co-founder Chris Watson's departure. Like most soundtracks, it's not designed for careful listening, consisting primarily of eerie electronic noodling. **Micro-Phonies** is similar to **The Crackdown**, except the sound is a bit sparser and decidedly more rhythm-conscious. Much of the material would be very much at home coming from a beatbox, particularly "Sensoria" and "James Brown," the 12-inch remixes of which are both highly recommended.

Drinking Gasoline is a double 12-inch (running over 30 minutes) recorded primarily as a video soundtrack. The four numbers are entirely interchangeable, the sort of hard electro-funk found on previous LPs. Fans will enjoy it, but the Cabs seem stuck in a rut, an unsurprising problem after so many releases. **The Arm of the Lord** (reissued on CD as **The Covenant, The Sword and the Arm of the Lord**) proves that no band could be so productive without a few tricks up its sleeve. Titled after an American neo-Nazi religious zealot organization, the record crossbreeds trademark electro-rhythm attack with odd breaks, varied tempos, the return of eerie found voices, unpolished production and harsh dissonance. "I Want You" and "Motion Rotation" actually have catchy melodies—a first for the band!

The Drain Train is a two-disc 12-inch, consisting mostly of three (not vastly different) versions of a track quite similar to other recent material. The other two tracks don't do much groundbreaking, either. **Code**'s allowance of outside assistance (Bill Nelson on guitar and Adrian Sherwood as co-producer) makes for some interesting but rather subtle touches, as they reach for crystal-clear, state-of-the-art sound. But the material is a stylistic reprise of **The Arm of the Lord**: tempos are varied quite a bit, but each track has the same feel. Artsy British industrialists or computerized hip-hoppers?

Definitely the latter in recent releases, but those nostalgic for the Cabs' white noise and distortion period will appreciate **The Golden Moments of Cabaret Voltaire** (and agree with the title) and **Eight Crépuscule Tracks**. The first is a CD-only release of material from the band's Rough (Trade) days; there's nothing more recent than **2 X 45**, and most of it is earlier than that. The juxtaposition inherent in digital reproduction of primitive music makes it a very interesting collection. **Eight Crépuscule Tracks** draws from the same approximate time frame, taking the original **3 Crépuscule Tracks** and adding some singles and a previously unreleased cover of "The Theme from Shaft," which sounds as if it was recorded around the time of **Voice of America**.

The two remaining members of Cab Volt maintain low individual profiles, but have each done solo work, especially interesting as it allows identification of who brings what to the band. Stephen Mallinder's **Pow-Wow** mini-album is dominated by muscular bass and drum combinations, tapes and his husky voice. On his own, he seems to prefer electronically-treated acoustic instruments rather than synthesizers. **Pow-Wow Plus** repackages that record with the addition of 1981's "Temperature Drop" single. Richard Kirk's **Time High Fiction** is a one-man double album recorded over a three-year period; it's richer in texture (mostly electronic) and less rhythmic than his partner's work. The two-side-long "Dead Relatives" is even more dissonant than anything the two have done together.

Kirk released a pair of solo LP's in 1986: **Black Jesus Voice** and **Ugly Spirit**. (Both were released on a single cassette under the title of the former.) **Black Jesus Voice** is not a drastic departure from Cabaret Voltaire; rhythmically similar but with slightly harsher sounds. Most of the vocals are from tapes rather than sung by Kirk himself. **Ugly Spirit** changes gears completely, however, and takes a sound-sculpture approach with often very effective results.   [sg/dgs]

JOHN CALE

Vintage Violence (Columbia) 1969
Church of Anthrax (Columbia) 1971
The Academy in Peril (Reprise) 1972
Paris 1919 (Reprise) 1973

Fear (Island) 1974 ●
Slow Dazzle (Island) 1975 ●
Helen of Troy (nr/Island) 1975
Animal Justice EP (nr/Illegal) 1977
Guts (Island) 1977
Sabotage/Live (Spy) 1979
Honi Soit (A&M) 1981
Music for a New Society (ZE-Passport) 1982
Caribbean Sunset (ZE-Island) 1984
John Cale Comes Alive (ZE-Island) 1984
Artificial Intelligence (Beggars Banquet-PVC) 1985

KEVIN AYERS/JOHN CALE/ENO/NICO

June 1, 1974 (Island) 1974

John Cale's musical career since leaving the Velvet Underground—after two albums on which his viola-scraping and genuine musical training played a pivotal role—has been diverse and unpredictable, exploring both classical/avant-garde "serious" music as well as more shoot-from-the-hip rough rock. Throughout, the inscrutable Welshman has surrounded himself with able and distinguished cohorts, and has produced some music of real challenge and quality.

His first solo efforts after the Velvets were effectively collaborations: **Vintage Violence**, with low-key backing by a New York rock group, Grinderswitch; **Church of Anthrax**, with avant-garde titan Terry Riley; **Academy in Peril**, with the Royal Philharmonic Orchestra. Also in much the same vein, Cale made **Paris 1919** with backing by members of Little Feat. It wasn't until he signed to Island that his music became weird and abrasive, signifying a partial return to the chaos of his Velvet days.

His first such release was as a member of the **June 1, 1974** project, a one-off concert documented on an LP and featuring Kevin Ayers, Brian Eno and Nico as well as Cale, Robert Wyatt and others. It's a wonderful album, with Cale taking a vocal on "Heartbreak Hotel" and elsewhere contributing viola and piano.

Cale emerged into pre-new wave weirdness with **Fear**, an aggressively wild record made with assistance from the likes of Eno and Roxy Musician Phil Manzanera. Clean production only heightens the anxiety inherent in Cale's voice and created by the skittering, modified guitar sounds. "Fear Is a Man's Best Friend" and "Gun" build a claustrophobically intense aura; quieter efforts like "Ship of Fools" only slightly diminish the queasiness level. A brilliant record full of neat surprises and great, unsettling songs.

Slow Dazzle adds Chris Spedding to the lineup and pursues some curious pathways: "Heartbreak Hotel," recast as a haunted-house dirge; "Mr. Wilson," an homage to the Beach Boys' Brian; "The Jeweller," a recitation reminiscent of the Velvets' "The Gift." More restrained, but no less entrancing than **Fear**.

Helen of Troy, featuring Phil Collins as well as Spedding and Eno (but not Manzanera), is a gripping, morbid collection of songs, including Jonathan Richman's "Pablo Picasso," powered by Cale's commanding vocals and whining slide guitars, and "Leaving It All Up to You" which has a reference to Sharon Tate that caused it to be removed from the album when first issued; it was subsequently replaced. A dark and pained album.

The **Animal Justice** EP—three cuts on a 12-inch disc—features what remained of a touring band after half had quit in protest of a legendary onstage chicken-chopping incident. The EP's leadoff track ("Chicken Shit") concerns that brouhaha; the other songs are a pointless version of Chuck Berry's "Memphis" and a stunning Cale original, "Hedda Gabler." **Guts** is an excellent collection of tracks from the three preceding LPs and is very highly recommended.

Sabotage, recorded onstage at New York's CBGB in June 1979, presents almost all new material. The sound's just passable, and the album never jells. **Honi Soit** used an outside producer (Mike Thorne) for a change and a totally new band as well; some tracks are good, but it's not on a par with Cale's best. With **Music for a New Society**, Cale retreated from nakedly aggressive music and turned to a more orchestrated style that owes something to his early pre-punk efforts, like **Paris 1919**. Cale's lyrics, however, have rarely been as grim or violent as they are here. The arrangements prominently feature keyboards and the music effectively matches the darkly moody subject matter.

Caribbean Sunset is Cale's least interesting album to date. Even if his puzzlingly muddy self-production hadn't stifled everything but his jagged-edged vocals, the songs themselves are too flimsy to support his words or passion.

Perhaps realizing this, Cale released **Caribbean Sunset** back-to-back with another LP showcasing his in-concert strengths with the same band. Though he self-defeatingly begins *and* ends **Comes Alive** with half-assed studio efforts, the disappointment ends there and the virtuosity begins. Forming the live core of the album are gripping versions of vintage material like "Fear" and "Leaving It All Up to You"; a death-rattling "Heartbreak Hotel" performed solo at the electric piano; a bouncily tongue-in-cheek "Waiting for the Man" as a tip of the hat to Lou Reed, now that he can be taken seriously again; and a couple of **Sabotage Live** songs minus the overly metallic sound that made them almost unlistenable on that LP. Cale should record *all* his material this way: live and with a solid band.

Artificial Intelligence has the solid band, a trio of James Young, Graham Dowdall and David Young. It also has Cale co-writing lyrics with journalist Ratso Sloman, whose Dylan fixation comes through clearly on the articulately verbose "Everytime the Dogs Bark" and other songs. Elsewhere, a mild island lilt suggests a well-read Jimmy Buffett. Moody and contained, but energetic and occasionally stimulating, **A.I.** is a reasonable if unspectacular addition to Cale's extensive catalogue.   [iar/mf]

ROBERT CALVERT
See *Hawkwind*.

STAN CAMPBELL
See *Specials*.

CAMPER VAN BEETHOVEN
Telephone Free Landslide Victory
   (Independent Project) 1985 ●
Take The Skinheads Bowling EP
   (Pitch-A-Tent-Rough Trade) 1986
Camper Van Beethoven II & III
   (Pitch-A-Tent-Rough Trade) 1986 ●
Camper Van Beethoven (Pitch-A-Tent-Rough
   Trade) 1986 ●
Vampire Can Mating Oven EP
   (Pitch-A-Tent-Rough Trade) 1987 ●
Our Beloved Revolutionary Sweetheart
   (Virgin) 1988 ●

MONKS OF DOOM
Soundtrack to the Film: "Breakfast on the
   Beach of Deception" (Pitch-A-Tent-Rough
   Trade) 1988
Because they understand why middle-Eastern ethnic music isn't really all *that* dif-

ferent from rock'n'roll, and because they realize that the underground is no less stupid and petty than the mainstream, playfully eclectic post-hippie California surrealists Camper Van Beethoven are the sort of band whose mere existence validates the very concept of pop music. Unselfconciously absorbing inspiration from any musical style that strikes their fancy, and adding leader David Lowery's dizzy absurdist lyrics, Santa Cruz's Campers make records that suggest what the Grateful Dead might sound like if they had a sense of humor and knew how to write pop songs.

The band has gradually downplayed the giddy shifts in style that distinguished their early LP's, gradually integrating their disparate influences into a more cohesive individual voice. Still, the Camper catalogue is a remarkably consistent one, showcasing a remarkable aesthetic that seemed to emerge fully-developed on **Telephone Free Landslide Victory**.

In addition to the underground in-jokes "Take the Skinheads Bowling" and "Where the Hell is Bill?," **Telephone** includes a woozy cover of Black Flag's "Wasted" and self-explanatory instrumentals like "Border Ska," "Yanqui Go Home," "Balalaika Gap" and "Mao Reminisces About His Days in Southern China." The 20-track **II & III** features lots of country references and a hoedown version of Sonic Youth's "I Love Her All the Time," plus the raga-pop "Circles," the phony anti-rock protest anthem "No More Bullshit," and the delightful "ZZ Top Goes to Egypt."

Camper Van Beethoven shows a more integrated band style and an emerging political consciousness on "Good Guys and Bad Guys" and "Joe Stalin's Cadillac"; there's also a respectful cover of Pink Floyd's "Interstellar Overdrive" and "Une Fois," the most impressive Indian-cajun fusion in recent memory.

Judging by **Our Beloved Revolutionary Sweetheart**, Camper Van Beethoven's move to the majors doesn't seem to have had much of an effect on the combo's inconoclasm, though Dennis Herring's production is more ambitious than on the band's indepedent releases. Highlights include the catchy "Never Go Back," the goofily metaphoric "Devil Song," the Zep-like "Waka" and a cover of "O Death," borrowed from '60s kindred spirits Kaleidoscope.

Take the Skinheads Bowling pairs that

college-radio hit with five non-LP tracks of varying length. The six-song **Vampire Can Mating Oven** collects some enjoyable odds and ends, including a jolly remake of Ringo Starr's "Photograph." (A 1987 CD combines **Camper Van Beethoven** and **Vampire Can Mating Oven**.)

The mostly-instrumental **Monks of Doom** LP is a side project featuring three Campers—guitarist Greg Lisher, bassist Victor Krummenacher and drummer Chris Pedersen—and guitarist David Immerglück playing mildly psychedelic improvisational guitar rock, with occasional forays into jazzy ethnicity. [hd]

See also *Eugene Chadbourne*.

CAN
Monster Movie (nr/UA) 1969
Soundtracks (nr/UA) 1970
Tago Mago (nr/UA) 1971
Ege Bamyasi (UA) 1972
Future Days (UA) 1973
Limited Edition (nr/UA) 1974
Soon Over Babaluma (UA) 1974
Landed (nr/Virgin) 1975
Unlimited Edition (nr/Caroline) 1976
Flow Motion (nr/Virgin) 1976
Opener (nr/Sunset) 1976
Saw Delight (Harvest) 1977
Out of Reach (Peters Int'l) 1978
Cannibalism (nr/UA) 1978
Can (nr/Laser) 1979
Incandescence (nr/Virgin) 1981
Delay 1968 (Ger. Spoon) 1982
Prehistoric Future—June, 1968 [tape] (Fr. Tago Mago) 1984

HOLGER CZUKAY
Movies (nr/EMI) 1980
On the Way to the Peak of Normal (nr/EMI) 1982
Der Osten Ist Rot (nr/Virgin) 1984
Rome Remains Rome (nr/Virgin) 1987

HOLGER CZUKAY/ROLF DAMMERS
Canaxis (Ger. Spoon) 1982

IRMIN SCHMIDT
Filmmusik Vol. II (Ger. Spoon) 1982

A German group that arose during the psychedelic movement of 1968 from jazz, avant-garde and rock sources, Can (essentially Holger Czukay, Irmin Schmidt, Jaki Liebezeit, Michael Karoli) developed (and perfected) electronic collage in rock music and actively absorbed a number of musical traditions into their eclectic work. In addition to providing an example of individualistic behavior remote from commercial music, Can's output influenced a number of more modern figures, including Pete Shelley and John Lydon, while Can's Holger Czukay has worked with musicians as disparate as Eurythmics and Jah Wobble.

Monster Movie and **Soundtracks** are interesting but forgettable excursions into psychedelia, the latter compiling actual film work the band had done, but **Tago Mago** features a full-blown burst into electronic collage and tape effects, continued on **Ege Bamyasi**, which has reverberations in music as late as Public Image's **Metal Box**. These new techniques are pared down and subdued in the minimalistic **Future Days** and **Soon Over Babaluma**, but make a reappearance in superior form on the darkly perverse **Landed**.

Limited Edition, meanwhile, exposed Can's fascination with non-Western musics by unveiling several pieces in the Ethnological Forgery Series, more of which appear on **Unlimited Edition, Flow Motion** and **Can**. The inclusion of Rosko Gee and Reebop Kwaku Baah in the group gave a Jamaican voodoo flair to **Saw Delight** that prefigured the reggae absorption of the Clash, the Police and other groups.

Relative popular success with "I Want More" from **Flow Motion** strained the group to the point where they opted to break up, but Holger Czukay continues his tape collage experiments on the excellent **Movies** and **On the Way to the Peak of Normal**, the latter with Jah Wobble guesting. Similarly, **Der Osten Ist Rot (The East Is Red)**, with Liebezeit and Conny Plank helping out, takes a lighthearted and often amusing tack, splicing found tapes to fairly straightforward songs that run the gamut from cabaret crooning to demented instrumentals. A wonderfully foolish excursion with serious undercurrents of political satire.

The guest sidemen on Czukay's winningly loopy **Rome Remains Rome** include Liebezeit and Karoli, making it virtually a Can reunion record, as well as Wobble and his associate, Olli Morland. Playing everything from guitar to french horn to radio, Czukay takes his usual jaundiced view, deflating musical convention ("Hey Baba Reebop" puts a hysterical electro twist on bigband swing) as he experiments with sounds, including a lot of vocals (some in English,

many sung by a chameleonlike female chorus) this time.

Opener and **Cannibalism** both anthologize work from 1968 to 1973, with the latter featuring several songs in re-edited versions. **Delay 1968** features heretofore-unreleased work by the original group—including highly inappropriate singer Malcolm Mooney—from 1968/69. **Incandescence** (enough with the corny puns already!) is also a compilation.

Canaxis—dating from 1969 (when it was released in a tiny private pressing)—consists of two long pieces of environmental mood music incorporating various ethnic components. Schmidt's album contains excerpts from his music for films; on the whole, unobtrusive audio wallpaper.   [sg/iar]
See also *Jah Wobble.*

CAPTAIN BEEFHEART AND THE MAGIC BAND

Safe as Milk (Kama Sutra) 1967 (Buddah) 1970
Dropout Boogie (nr/Buddah) 1967
Strictly Personal (Blue Thumb) 1968
Trout Mask Replica (Straight) 1969 (Reprise) 1970
Lick My Decals Off Baby (Straight) 1970 (Reprise) 1970
Mirror Man (Buddah) 1970 + 1974 (nr/Demon) 1986
The Spotlight Kid (Reprise) 1972
Clear Spot (Reprise) 1972
Unconditionally Guaranteed (Mercury) 1974
Bluejeans and Moonbeams (Mercury) 1974
The Captain Beefheart File (nr/Pye) 1977
Shiny Beast (Bat Chain Puller) (Warner Bros.) 1978
Doc at the Radar Station (Virgin) 1980
Ice Cream for Crow (Virgin-Epic) 1982
The Legendary A&M Sessions EP (A&M) 1984

CAPTAIN BEEFHEART WITH FRANK ZAPPA AND THE MOTHERS

Bongo Fury (Discreet) 1975
Possessor of a five-octave vocal range, fluent on saxophone and harmonica, intuitively musical enough to compose for, play (after a fashion) and even teach other instruments so as to enable sidemen to function in his rarefied musical world, Captain Beefheart (alias Don Van Vliet) is one of rock's genuine geniuses. He's also an accomplished poet, sculptor and painter. Starting with a mixture

of blues and rock, Beefheart has dismembered and reassembled rhythms, song structure, harmony and tonality, adding in quantities of free jazz—all without getting academic, flashy or selfconsciously pompous about it.

Beefheart's awesome yet idiosyncratic (as well as groundbreaking) talent has deeply influenced bands like Devo, Pere Ubu, the Residents, Public Image and others, each in a different way. Bridging the worlds of freeform jazz and modern rock, Beefheart has demolished conventions and paved the way for much of rock's recent adventurousness.

Awarded a two-single A&M contract as the grand prize in a Vox battle of the bands, Beefheart—from Southern California's Mojave Desert—made the first a regional hit with a footstomping version of Bo Diddley's "Diddy Wah Diddy," but A&M judged his album demos too unsettling to keep him on the roster. (Nearly 20 years later, the two original 45s, plus one hitherto unissued track, were packaged as **The Legendary A&M Sessions**; the producer, who also wrote one song, was David Gates, founder-to-be of pap-rockers Bread.)

Another label gave him a shot and, with 19-year-old guitar wiz Ry Cooder, Beefheart spewed out **Safe as Milk**, which cannily redefined what white boys could do with the blues, not to mention rock'n'roll. Although Buddah released it, the label—then best known as the purveyors of the bubblegum sounds of the 1910 Fruitgum Co. et al.—evidently wasn't thrilled about it. Cooder departed just in time to force the cancellation of an appearance at the fabled Monterey Pop Festival.

Beefheart got another record deal with a hip, maverick independent label and recorded **Strictly Personal**, an even punchier and more irreverent version of what he'd essayed on **Safe as Milk**. But the LP was remixed while he was away on a European tour; Beefheart was understandably disgusted by the results. At this remove, however, the silly effects added without his consent merely date the record a bit; looking past that, it's virtually the equal of its more celebrated predecessor.

Beefheart may have felt like his third strike had been thrown while he wasn't looking, but along came childhood friend and former (albeit briefly) bandmate Frank Zappa, who'd wangled a custom label deal that allowed him to offer Beefheart complete cre-

ative control. What popped out was **Trout Mask Replica**, generally regarded as his first masterpiece. The minimalist rock blossomed, mated at times with free jazz. (Between cuts, he can faintly be heard telling visitors that he calls it "bush music.") The lyrics (and straight-up poetry) received, and warranted, increasing prominence. **Decals** was a consolidation of artistic gains that suffers only in comparison to **Trout Mask**. Both attracted enough attention that Buddah brought out **Mirror Man**, an LP consisting of four extended live tracks that was derided as a subpar exploitation move. Regardless, it's damn good stuff, and didn't do much exploiting, either: all three albums were commercial stiffs. (Two songs from **Mirror Man** were later re-recorded for **Strictly Personal**.)

The Spotlight Kid reverted to a simpler, bluesier sound (à la the first two LPs), though sonically enriched by the Captain's subsequent explorations. Further changes and commercial pressures resulted in **Clear Spot**, which sported a more stylized, heavy-rock style (varied by an excellent, if uncharacteristic, Memphis-style soul number).

On the other hand, **Unconditionally Guaranteed** and **Bluejeans and Moonbeams** are even more simplified, sometimes to the point of inanity, and the musicians on the records don't seem to have a clue about Beefheart or his music. (The second—allegedly outtakes from the first—is actually better.) He made some money for a change and won new European fans, but some of the faithful felt he'd sold out.

Beefheart cut an album called **Bat Chain Puller** for Virgin, but legal problems prevented its release. With a new band that included ex-Mothers of Invention trombonist Bruce Fowler, he signed to Warners and released **Shiny Beast**, which incorporated much of the material first cut for **Bat Chain Puller** (and therefore used that name as a subtitle). It's a progression from **Decals**, as if the intervening albums had never happened, and stands as one of his best. The words are more direct than on **Decals**; the music smoother and more orchestral.

He then proceeded to top himself with **Doc at the Radar Station**. A minor shift in the band had toughened the sound, and the LP combined his continuing refinement with a touch of **Clear Spot**'s hard-nosed attack.

Beefheart went still further with **Ice Cream for Crow**, the height of his career's most sustained upward creative swing, despite (because of?) a near-total lineup turn-over right after the recording of **Doc. Crow** is Beefheart at his most distinctively and beautifully melodic, his most frightening and his most danceable. And it's apparently his musical swan song. The painter/sculptor has made the sad but understandable decision that visual, not audio, art is his best means of support—a depressing comment on the record business and our culture.

As some music progresses further into—and past—the outer frontiers of convention, the great bulk of it sloshes down the toilet. But Captain Beefheart's trailblazing efforts seem ever more impressive and precious. In 1988, Britain's Imaginary Records saluted him by assembling performances of his material by various groups—including XTC and Sonic Youth—into an album, **Fast'n'Bulbous: A Tribute to Captain Beefheart.**   [jg]
See also *Robert Williams.*

CAPTAIN SENSIBLE

Women and Captains First (nr/A&M) 1982
The Power of Love (nr/A&M) 1983
A Day in the Life of . . . Captain Sensible
  (A&M) 1984
One Christmas Catalogue EP (nr/A&M) 1984
Sensible Singles (nr/A&M) 1984

When not playing guitar and keyboards in the Damned, this good Captain (Ray Burns to his parents) makes lighthearted hit records with producer Tony Mansfield. His two best weird'n'wonderful chart-toppers—the joke-rapping "Wot" and "Happy Talk" (from the musical *South Pacific,* no less)—are included on **Women and Captains First,** alongside other equally ridiculous concepts ranging from country-western to cabaret. Aided and abetted by such divergent talents as Robyn Hitchcock and female vocal trio Dolly Mixture, Sensible's homely singing is invariably ingratiating (if not always on key).

His second album, **The Power of Love,** is less varied and novelty-filled, but nonetheless contains a few subtler gems: "It's Hard to Believe I'm Not" and "Secrets," both co-written with Hitchcock, "Stop the World" and "The Power of Love," all distinguished by Sensible's engaging wideboy vocals and silly/serious lyrics.

In a vain attempt to introduce Sensible to America, **A Day in the Life** compiles tracks from both English albums (plus a previously non-LP single) and has most of what you would want to hear by the lad. But you should also be aware of the seasonal EP, **One Christmas Catalogue,** which came complete with a plastic Santa beard and, amidst three great originals, Sensible's puzzling *nearly* straight version of Frankie Goes to Hollywood's "Relax." For completists, there's also **Sensible Singles,** a 13-cut collection that largely overlaps the albums.   [iar]

BELINDA CARLISLE

Belinda (IRS) 1986 ●
Heaven on Earth (MCA) 1987 ●

Following the breakup of the Go-Go's, Belinda Carlisle stuck with guitarist Charlotte Caffey and recorded a mixed-up solo album whose stylish cover shows the newly glamorized singer striking a stylish Cyd Charisse pose. Inside **Belinda** however, the mock-girl groupisms, misbegotten Motown take-offs and lush quasi-Ronstadt rock are easy on the ears but utterly lacking in conviction or charm. Carlisle's voice was never the Go-Go's' strongest feature; with training, her skills have improved over the years, but she still isn't very appealing. Dull material and unimaginative production adds little to her first bid for acceptance as an adult artist.

Following an embarrassing legal gaffe that freed her to sign with a different label, Carlisle's handlers hit the commercial motherlode on her second LP, an absurd but stylistically focused big-budget studio concoction that turned her into a huge, meaningless star. Hit rock-pop production numbers like "I Get Weak" and "Heaven Is a Place on Earth" mingle with such bizarrities as a lame cover of Cream's "I Feel Free." Carlisle's limited voice is obvious on some songs; producer-mastermind Rick Nowels' slim repertoire of ideas (mainly loud electric guitars thrown against synthesized strings and heavenly backing chorus) is also a problem. The album's only hint of wit? Carlisle's credit for air guitar.   [iar]

CARMEL

Carmel EP (nr/Red Flame) 1982
The Drum Is Everything (Warner Bros.) 1984
The Falling (nr/London) 1986

Brassy belter Carmel McCourt and her two-man band (drummer Gerry Darby and stand-up bassist Jimmy Paris), plus various organists, singers, drummers and hornmen, make the Mike Thorne-produced **The Drum Is Everything** a joyous and raucous outing that has a bit in common with nouveau jazz-pop crooners like Sade, but is far more adventurous and ambitious in scope. "More, More, More" and "Willow Weep for Me" are inspiring, near-gospel outbursts of enthusiasm; "Tracks of My Tears" (no, not that one) and "Stormy Weather" (yes, that one) show a bluesier, more reserved side that isn't as appealing in this setting. Carmel doesn't modulate all that well—for her, singing is a full-blooded pastime with no room for pussyfooting—and tends to overpower the more subtly played songs. [iar]

CARPETTES
Cream of the Youth EP (nr/Small Wonder) 1978
Frustration Paradise (nr/Beggars Banquet) 1979
Fight Amongst Yourselves (nr/Beggars Banquet) 1980

This trio may have personified modest, no-frills rock'n'roll, almost singlehandedly defining the area just above mediocrity. The competent Carpettes played with goodly speed and made occasional forays into reggae territory, but the closest musical analogue is probably early Kiss—with brighter tunes replacing the show-biz snarl, and without the dumb macho/sleazoid pose.

Following a ragged 7-inch EP, the Carpettes made two albums in the same style, despite very different producers—Bob Sargeant (the Beat, early Fall, Haircut One Hundred) and Colin Thurston (Duran Duran, Thompson Twins, Magazine). Sargeant's **Frustration Paradise** has the edge for containing more of those songs you'll be surprised to find yourself remembering. [jg]

PAUL CARRACK
Nightbird (nr/Vertigo) 1980
Suburban Voodoo (Epic) 1982 [acd]
One Good Reason (Chrysalis) 1987 [acd]

One of rock's more circuitous success stories: Carrack was the lead-singing keyboardist in Ace, a pub-rock outfit of the era before "pub-rock" became a rock press sub-genre—strictly background music for soaking up suds. Ace hadn't the faintest idea what to do when Carrack's catchy (if banal) "How Long" became an international hit in 1975, and proved it with three LPs of boring laid-backism. Carrack hung on through Ace's dissolution and his all-too-pat first solo LP, **Nightbird**. He got a real boost, though, when

Squeeze hired him to replace Jools Holland. It was only for the **East Side Story** album—just one Carrack lead vocal, but that's on "Tempted," one of Squeeze's most popular numbers. The song became a Carrack calling card, too.

That LP also brought him into contact with the Elvis Costello/Nick Lowe axis (EC produced the Squeeze LP, Lowe had produced Elvis, both were managed by Jake Riviera). Carrack and Lowe then formed Noise to Go, a Rockpilish arrangement in which the two alternated top billing. No surprise, then, that **Suburban Voodoo** sounds like the souled-up flipside of **Nick the Knife**—if anything, it's better. Yet it succeeds because of Lowe's production and composing presence, which complements Carrack's excellent voice with the kind of pop smarts that bring out his best.

Carrack next found employment with Mike & the Mechanics (Mike Rutherford's extra-Genesis sideline), and wound up singing (strangely anonymous sounding) lead on that group's big hit, "Silent Running." This exposure got Carrack a touring-band job with Roger Waters.

Next came **One Good Reason**. Half of it's decent-to-good, and the rest is mediocre-to-poor. Produced by former Hall & Oates overseer Christopher Neil, it's got more radio-music slickness than Carrack's had in years, but at the cost of some identity. (Although you can clearly tell Carrack's to blame for the demolition of "When You Walk in the Room.") It did yield a genuine not-bad pop hit ("Don't Shed a Tear"). Fourteen years after "How Long," he looms as a contender for commercial credibility. [jg]

JOE "KING" CARRASCO AND EL MOLINO
Joe "King" Carrasco and El Molino (Lisa) 1978

JOE "KING" CARRASCO AND THE CROWNS
Joe "King" Carrasco and the Crowns (Hannibal) 1980
Party Safari EP (Hannibal) 1981
Synapse Gap (Mundo Total) (MCA) 1982
Party Weekend (MCA) 1983
Tales from the Crypt [tape] (ROIR) 1984
Bordertown (nr/Big Beat) 1984 ●
Viva San Antone EP (nr/Big Beat) 1985

JOE KING CARRASCO Y LAS CORONAS

Bandido Rock (Rounder) 1987 ●

Austin's Joe "King" Carrasco grew up in the Lone Star state under the spell of Tex-Mex border music. El Molino, his first band, straddled this tradition (with horns and marimba) and rock (with Doug Sahm's keyboard player, Augie Meyers, and songs like "Rock Esta Noche"). El Molino's only album is pleasant enough, but sounds pale compared to what followed.

Whether influenced by new wave or reverting to more adolescent taste, Carrasco traded in El Molino for the Crowns. This no-nonsense backing trio, dominated by Kris Cummings' cheesy organ, is built for speed. The Crowns' debut album touches on rockabilly ("One More Time"), polka ("Federales") and border influences ("Buena," "Caca de Vaca"). Their forte, though, is performing "96 Tears" under a variety of thin guises, all of them delightful ("Let's Get Pretty," "Betty's World," you name it). The tempos are revved-up punk, the feeling, Southwestern *mestizo*. (The Stiff LP has two numbers not on the American album, but Hannibal's release has three songs not on the English version, and a funnier cover as well.)

Party Safari is a four-song EP further displaying Carrasco's cultural dementia; the Crowns' next album, **Synapse Gap**, finds them only slightly more subdued. Besides re-recording two of **Party Safari**'s songs, Carrasco dabbles in reggae rhythms and somehow got Michael Jackson (!) to sing along on "Don't Let a Woman (Make a Fool Out of You)."

In a last-ditch effort to sell out (well, to sell a few records at least), Carrasco made **Party Weekend**, a non-stop heap o' fun. Richard Gottehrer produced it, and tunes like "Let's Go" and "Burnin' It Down" (not to mention a spiffy remake of "Buena") perfectly crystallize all of the group's strengths. Murderously infectious and upbeat—attitudinally the Southwest's answer to the Ramones—**Party Weekend** seemed perfectly designed to introduce the world to Carrasco's abundant talent and charm. But it didn't take off, and so Carrasco unceremoniously returned from his safari in the majors.

Joe's next release was the tape-only **Tales from the Crypt**, a marvelous set of demos from 1979 with embryonic (read: raw and exciting) versions of many of Carrasco's best tunes, from "Let's Get Pretty" to "Caca de Vaca" to "Federales." Although not intended as such, it's an ideal introduction to a world of boundless spirit and infectious fun.

By **Bordertown**, Carrasco's act is getting kind of, er, familiar: too many of the songs employ not only the same chords and melody, but a lot of 'em stick to the same Spanglicized rhyming patterns. Adding to the fatigue is a new-found political sensibility, yielding well-intentioned bores like "Who Buys the Guns" and "Current Events (Are Making Sense)." If you haven't been following the Carrasco saga for long, **Bordertown** is as good as any of his prior records; however, those with a complete collection will likely live happier without it.

Bandido Rock finds the increasingly politicized Carrasco (note retitled band) mouthing sentiments like "Juarez and Zapata/Stood for love of the people." Just a glance at the album's song list—including "Fuera Yanqui" and "Hey Gringo 'No Pasaran' "—confirms suspicions of monomania. Too bad, because the band, now mostly accordion-led, still sounds fine. But with only three out of ten songs in a *yanqui* 4/4, **Bandido Rock** is strictly for the musically converted, and/or anyone ready to follow Joe into Nicaragua.   [si]

CARS

The Cars (Elektra) 1978 ●
Candy-O (Elektra) 1979 ●
Panorama (Elektra) 1980 ●
Shake It Up (Elektra) 1981 ●
Heartbeat City (Elektra) 1984 ●
Greatest Hits (Elektra) 1985 ●
Door to Door (Elektra) 1987 ●

RIC OCASEK
Beatitude (Geffen) 1982
This Side of Paradise (Geffen) 1986 ●

GREG HAWKES
Niagara Falls (Passport) 1983

ELLIOT EASTON
Change No Change (Elektra) 1985

BEN ORR
The Lace (Elektra) 1986 ●

For an example of shifting perceptions, consider the Cars. When their debut LP appeared in 1978, the Boston-based quintet was tagged as a prime commercial *and* critical prospect of the emerging post-punk phenomenon called new wave. In other words, they were cool and potentially popular. Then, presto! Upon release of an album, the Cars became an immediate smash and entered the ranks of platinum-sellers, where they remained. Quickly, they lost all artistic credibility among critics, despite their remarkable consistency on disc.

The Cars have changed little since that first record established the ground rules. On their debut, singer/songwriter Ric Ocasek pursues the trail of ironic, sometimes wistful romanticism blazed by David Bowie and especially Bryan Ferry. "Good Times Roll," "My Best Friend's Girl" and other tunes contradict blithe surfaces with nervous undercurrents. As sparely produced by Roy Thomas Baker, virtually interchangeable lead singers Ocasek and bassist Ben Orr ride a slick, pulsing current generated by Elliot Easton's skittish guitar, Greg Hawkes' poised synths and ex-Modern Lover David Robinson's booming drums. Here, and on subsequent albums, the alluring glibness serves as a gateway to underlying emotional anguish.

Candy-O's main flaw is that it offers the same accomplished style. Emotions are more directly expressed on the title track and the frankly sentimental "It's All I Can Do," but the polish remains. "Let's Go" and "Dangerous Type" express a muted ambivalence that allows the Cars to continue pleasing superficial listeners. **Panorama** tampers with the formula slightly, though not enough to jeopardize the band's enormous popularity. Many tunes are murkier and less immediate, giving greater play to the creeping desperation that permeates Ocasek's writing. More unsettling, though still highly listenable.

Shake It Up is the Cars' lightest album so far. The title track comes the closest they've gotten to a conventional good-time tune, and others are less haunting than you might like Ocasek's songs to be. Highlight: the feverish, blatantly Roxyesque "This Could Be Love." Then the Cars took a group vacation.

For his first solo album, Ocasek enlisted Hawkes, handpicked musicians from various semi-underground bands (Bad Brains, New Models, Ministry, etc.) and created a moody collection of stimulating but only semi-commercial new songs. **Beatitude** bears an unavoidable resemblance to the Cars' sound, but the prevalence of synthesizer over guitar and an avoidance of choppy, driving rhythms make it different enough. While several Cars tracks have worked similar languid terrain ("Since You're Gone" on **Shake It Up** and

"You Wear Those Eyes" on **Panorama** are two), Ocasek's solo approach is subtler and texturally richer; his lyrics here are also exemplary. Best track: "Jimmy Jimmy," a sympathetic portrait of a troubled teen.

Niagara Falls confirms keyboardist Hawkes' role in shaping the Cars' instrumental sound, but it's mighty dull fare all the same. Take away the band's lyrics, vocals and tension and you get this sort of muzak.

After that dalliance, the Cars reconvened for **Heartbeat City**, a more substantial LP than **Shake It Up** and the band's most commercially potent record to date. The disc yielded no less than three major hits: the dreamy "Drive," the ebullient "You Might Think" and "Magic," which might best be described as the Cars meet the Electric Light Orchestra. The lyrics are Ocasek's usual neurotic doodlings, though he shows more compassion for his "lost generation" characters than before.

Buoyed by that album's stellar performance, the Cars took another solo break. Easton's **Change No Change** is a minor work to be sure, but a surprisingly good record nonetheless. A more immediate and electric record than the band would ever dare make, it contains some pithy harmonies, some snarling boogie and even a Costello soundalike. Irrepressible Jules Shear co-wrote all the tunes.

Joined by co-producer/drummer Chris Hughes, Ocasek drafted another set of famous friends (including most of his bandmates, guitarists Steve Stevens, Tom Verlaine and G.E. Smith) to help him imitate the Cars some more on **This Side of Paradise**. The man's stylistic consistency is indeed amazing. Orr's tepid record is also Cars-like, but with a lighter, more vocal-oriented feel and a warmly non-mechanical pop approach. That's not to say the songs—co-written by Orr and Diane Grey Page—are any good, but **The Lace** is nice and harmless.

Once more into the breach: **Door to Door**, which Ocasek wrote and produced, is cosmically irrelevant but likable. (Audiences were evidently more convinced of the former and let it become the first Cars album to fall short of selling a million copies.) Ocasek has never before allowed this much noisy guitar rock to corrupt the chilly tension of the Cars' formula; the overenthusiastic intrusion on the group's familiar sound is noticeable but not unpleasant. As of mid-1988, the general consensus is that the Cars have called it quits and disbanded.   [jy/iar]

CARSICKNESS

Shooting Above the Garbage (tmi) 1981
Sharpen Up for Duty (tmi) 1982

This intriguing Pittsburgh band's lineup includes two keyboardists (one doubling on guitar, the other on violin) and a saxophone player, in addition to a singer/guitarist, bassist and drummer. The ability to arrange their music in a number of directions makes Carsickness a complex force; only Joe Sopa's dramatic vocals maintain any stylistic consistency from track to track. Without being identifiably derivative, Carsickness draws bits from modern jazz, new romanticism, rock-funk and other sources, using flexible rhythmic intensities and thoughtful lyrics to drive the songs. Troublesome, yet impressive and invigorating.   [iar]

CHRIS CARTER

See *Chris and Cosey.*

PETER CASE

See *Plimsouls.*

CASINO MUSIC

Jungle Love (nr/ZE-Island) 1979

Blondie's Chris Stein produced this French quartet's album in New York; Island Records chief Chris Blackwell mixed the tapes in the Bahamas and released the LP in England—all for no audible reason. While the cool ambience of relaxed disco (complete with a female vocal trio and Cristina guesting on one track) may be soothing to tired dancers, the music is too bland to avoid instant forgettability, despite the suave French vocals.   [iar]

CATHEADS

Hubba (Restless) 1987 ●
Submarine (Restless) 1988 ●

If anything, this San Francisco quartet suffers from an excess of talent: three members write, all four sing. Understandably, **Hubba** is all over the place stylewise, from the agreeably noisy post-folk-rock of "Hangin' Around" to the stately romanticism of "Final Letter" to the mock-country of "Saved by the Bottle" to the playful hippie-punk of "Golden Gate Park." Most of it's quite good, but the jarring lack of focus makes the album an unnecessarily distracting listen.

The winsome **Submarine**, on the other hand, wisely concentrates on the band's strengths, sticking to more melodic material and allowing drummer Melanie Clarin (who also plays with Donner Party) to sing more. As a result, **Submarine** (co-produced by Dave Lowery of Camper Van Beethoven) consistently captures the haunting melody of **Hubba**'s best moments (as on "Postcard" and "Sister Tabitha") without ditching the goofy humor ("Jiggy Sawdust/Gumshoe") or the melodic rock edge ("Upside Down," "Apologize"). Meow.   [hd]

CATHEDRAL OF TEARS

See *True Sounds of Liberty.*

NICK CAVE

From Her to Eternity (nr/Mute) 1984
The Firstborn Is Dead (Mute-Homestead) 1985
Tupelo EP (Homestead) 1985

NICK CAVE & THE BAD SEEDS

Kicking Against the Pricks (Homestead) 1986 ●
Your Funeral . . . My Trial (Mute-Homestead) 1986 ●

ANITA LANE

Dirty Sings EP (nr/Mute) 1988

Following the Birthday Party's self-destruction, singer/lyricist Nick Cave formed the Bad Seeds as a new vehicle for his foreboding visions of love and death. As well as his passionate bellowing fit in with his former mates' wall of noise, **From Her to Eternity** sounds like the record he always wanted to make. The Bad Seeds—an all-star unit including ex-Magazine bassist Barry Adamson, ex-Birthday Party drummer Mick Harvey and guitarist Blixa Bargeld on loan from Einstürzende Neubauten—provide a sparse twisted-blues setting that gives Cave plenty of room for his vocal pyrotechnics. The guitars are bizarre but subdued, bass and drums slow and deliberate; rudimentary piano fills the gaps. While the album relies less on shock effects than any the Birthday Party ever made, the explosive parts are resultingly much more effective. The title track, "A Box for Black Paul" and a chilling rendition of Leonard Cohen's "Avalanche" stand up to anything Cave did with the Birthday Party. (A contemporaneous single of "In the Ghetto" is also highly recommended.)

The Firstborn Is Dead takes Cave's fixations on the blues and Elvis Presley one step further, this time with somewhat mixed results. A resident of London and Berlin, the Melbourne native leaves himself open to accusations of romanticizing a culture he's never known, but this doesn't sound like a man singing out of ignorance. Slow-moving and perhaps as self-indulgent as it is heartfelt, **The Firstborn** is a mature work which may at first disappoint those awaiting another "Big-Jesus-Trash-Can," but the patient listener will find Cave's emotional range intact, albeit in a subtler setting. The American **Tupelo** EP takes the album's opening track as its title and adds "In the Ghetto," "The Moon Is in the Gutter" and a drastically different version of the old Birthday Party live staple, "The Six Strings That Drew Blood."

Kicking Against the Pricks is an all-covers LP on which Cave really makes his mark as a song stylist. He performs passionate takes of blues standards ("Muddy Water," "I'm Gonna Kill That Woman"), gospel ("Jesus Met the Woman at the Well"), '60s classics ("Hey Joe," "All Tomorrow's Parties") and surprisingly enough, "By the Time I Get to Phoenix." His voice has never sounded stronger, and no musical style among those selected is beyond his grasp. Some interpretations are faithful to originals, others (especially "All Tomorrow's Parties") are completely unique, and the album's success owes as much to the work of the Bad Seeds as it does to Cave's talents; this is the most integrated record they've ever done. Thomas Wydler is now the drummer, with Harvey back to jack-of-all-trades; Tracy Pew, the late Birthday Party bassist, makes his final recorded appearance on "Hey Joe." An almost flawless album.

Your Funeral . . . My Trial is an eight-song double-45 disc LP. The format enhances the production, which is the clearest and most up-front of any Cave release. That in turn augments the melodicism and increased energy level of the music. **Your Funeral** also stands as Cave's best lyrical effort (with the notable exception of the blunt "Hard on for Love"); he takes the persona of old Nick the storyteller, and the images are haunting.

Anita Lane's claim to fame is that she's Nick Cave's girlfriend and has supplied him with occasional lyrics for solo and Birthday Party records. (Her picture is on the back cover of **From Her to Eternity**, making it appear she was then a Bad Seed.) For those who need to know more than that, **Dirty Sings** is a four-song EP with spoken, groaned and badly-sung Lydia Lunch-like vocals

above slow-moving but interestingly arranged backing (anonymous musicians, but Cave's Bad Seeds are readily identifiable and receive songwriting credits). Amazingly enough, she covers Chic's "Lost in Music," but the track here called "I'm a Believer" is not the Monkees'. Dark without being too gloomy or morbid, Lane does have an intriguing presence on vinyl. Not a bad little record.   [dgs]

See also *die Haut, Lydia Lunch.*

CELIBATE RIFLES

But Jacques, the Fish? EP (Aus. no label) 1982
Sideroxylon (Aus. Hot) 1983
The Celibate Rifles (Aus. Hot) 1984
Quintessentially Yours (What Goes On) 1985
The Turgid Miasma of Existence (Hot-Rough Trade) 1986
Mina Mina Mina (What Goes On) 1986
Kiss Kiss Bang Bang (What Goes On) 1987
Roman Beach Party (What Goes On) 1987
Dancing Barefoot EP (What Goes On) 1988

EASTERN DARK

Long Live the New Flesh! EP (What Goes On) 1986

DAMIEN LOVELOCK

It's A Wig, Wig, Wig, Wig World (Aus. Hot-Survival) 1988

The antithesis of a sex pistol is a celibate rifle but Sydney, Australia's Celibate Rifles are anything but the opposite of loud, snotty and fast. A fusion between Detroit-style straight-ahead hardrock and Ramones pop, steeped in Stooges and Radio Birdman milk, the Rifles began as a party-time band, racing through deliberately silly and simple Ramonesque lyrics ("What about the kids? Get a baby sitter . . . and some kitty litter") with three fast/loud chords. But unlike the Ramones, the Rifles insert loud, sinewy guitar solos between the slash'n'burn verses; on tracks like **Jacques'** "24 Hours," warped and warbly guitar effects.

By **Sideroxylon**, the Rifles had dropped most of early punk's stripped-down economy for the heavy guitar sound that would follow them through the rest of their career. Although they're essentially a metal band, we're talking the guitar excursions of Jimi Hendrix, not the theatrical excesses of Kiss. (An obvious Hendrix reference pops up in the middle of **Sideroxylon's** "God Squad.")

Three of the four tracks from **Jacques** and five of **Sideroxylon's** 11 were later issued in the US and UK as **Quintessentially Yours**.

Mina Mina Mina is also a compilation, featuring four more **Sideroxylon** selections and all but "Electric Snake River" from **The Celibate Rifles** (aka **Les Fusiles Célibataires**).

Turgid Miasma (whose title is said to have been taken from a Hari Krishna pamphlet) sums up the band's past without reissuing any material and takes them in new directions (some of which they've never again tried). Split almost evenly between early-style fast, poppy rockers, metallic guitar-excursions and a new style which melds everything from piano through zither and glockenspiel into their mix, **Miasma** is anything but turgid. Lead vocalist Damien Lovelock adds a sinisterly effective soft deadpan to his singing repertoire—a deep, dark grumble which meshes into the guitar texture in "No Sign" and stands out in contrast with the bright chugga chords at the opening of "Conflict of Instinct." **Miasma** is one of their most interesting LPs.

Lest their new-found studio prowess convince fans they had a secret craving to become sons of Steely Dan, their next release, **Kiss Kiss Bang Bang**, is a straight-ahead live album recorded at New York's CBGB. Most of the material comes from **Celibate Rifles** and **Miasma**, with covers of the Only Ones' "City of Fun" and Radio Birdman's "Burn My Eye." No keyboards. No soft thinky-feely moments. Just party-hearty rock'n'roll.

Roman Beach Party and **Dancing Barefoot** take the band in an even harder direction, back to the metallic '70s music they first admired. On "The More Things Change" and "Junk" (from the **Barefoot** EP), loud twists of feedback meet fuzzy scuzzy chords that are deep and dark—heavy as molasses and powered by 200 proof adrenalin. "Dancing Barefoot" itself couples twisted solos with Patti Smith's lyrics about heroin for an acid-hard '60s revivalist version of the song.

Bassist James Darroch left the Rifles and formed a trio called the Eastern Dark, in which he played guitar and sang. The band's five-song EP, released after Darroch was killed in a 1986 automobile accident, has plenty of noisy electric excitement, but his songwriting isn't quite strong enough to make the band special. Mixing acoustics and electrics in a Woodentopsy rush, "I Don't Need the Reasons" comes the closest.

Lovelock is backed on his first solo album by colleagues from the Rifles and the Church. ['e/iar]

EXENE CERVENKA
See *X.*

EUGENE CHADBOURNE
There'll Be No Tears Tonight (Parachute) 1980
The President: He Is Insane (Iridescence) 1985
Country Music of Southeastern Australia (RRRecords) 1986
Country Protest (Fundamental Music) 1986
Corpses of Foreign Wars (Fundamental Music) 1987
LSD C&W (Fundamental Music) 1987
Kill Eugene Chadbourne (Placebo) 1987

EUGENE CHADBOURNE WITH EVAN JOHNS AND THE H-BOMBS
Vermin of the Blues (Fundamental Music) 1987

EUGENE CHADBOURNE WITH CAMPER VAN BEETHOVEN
Camper Van Chadbourne (Fundamental Music) 1987 ●

On his compulsive own, the guitarist and leader of the late, lamented Shockabilly has spewed forth a ceaseless stream of records and cassettes (the latter on his own Parachute label) that easily represent the oddest version of country and folk music ever. While the noted lefty's guitar playing is looser than clams, it harbors wildly unique energy. The North Carolinian is also the master of several different voices, some of them deceptively sincere. Harsh, funny, irritating and packed with ideas, Chadbourne often suggests a politically correct Frank Zappa.

There'll Be No Tears Tonight lovingly takes on 13 country-western standards. Eugene acts out his "free improvised country & western bebop" with several game free-music experts on everything from Carl Perkins' "Honey Don't" to Merle Haggard's "Swingin' Doors." The results are hilarious and touching.

The President contains Chadbourne's own politically charged ditties, many in a Phil Ochs-ish bag. His targets include Jerry Falwell, Women Against Pornography and his arch-nemesis, Senator Jesse Helms.

Country Music of Southeastern Australia mixes ten country standards and ten originals, played free-form style with such noted noise mongers as Rik Rue, John Rose, and David Moss. **Country Protest** features the quintessential Chadbourne cover-version collage, "Medley in C." He's joined by Lenny Kaye on steel guitar and the Red Clay Ramblers for 11:25 of everything from "Imagine" to "TV Party" to "Dang Me" to "The Shah Sleeps in Lee Harvey's Grave."

Corpses of Foreign Wars is an all-protest vehicle featuring Violent Femmes Victor DeLorenzo and Brian Ritchie; highlights include a wonderful Phil Ochs medley and originals that range from verbal assaults on despicable neighbors to the "KKKremlin." Somehow, it all fits together.

Chadbourne cleaned out his closet, using the two-record **LSD C&W** as the merry receptacle. Much of the material here—including a Beatles medley, "In a Sentimental Mood," a Roger Miller medley and other free-jazz, blues and rock faves—derives from mid-'80s sessions featuring former Shockabilly members Kramer and David Licht, plus John Zorn, Tom Cora, Toshinori Condo and many others. It also includes some of EC's finest originals sung solo. **LSD C&W** is the most of EC on vinyl, and possibly the best.

Chadbourne goes it alone on **Kill Eugene Chadbourne** (the complete title of which is **Dear Eugene What You Did Was Not Very Nice So I Am Going to Kill . . .**), although a nutty old lady on the radio and a few appreciative audiences (for the tracks recorded live) do put in guest appearances. Covers on this mostly acoustic outing include "8 Miles High," "Purple Haze," "Oh Yoko," "Lucifer Sam," "Ramblin' Man" and the *Pee-wee's Playhouse* theme, which got a rewrite and became the topical "Ollie's Playhouse."

Two successful collaborations round out the Chadbourne vinyl oeuvre. Top-notch Austin stompers Evan Johns and the H-Bombs provide authentic rock'n'roll accompaniment on **Vermin of the Blues**, which covers ground from Count Basie to the Count Five, along with his usual amusing rants.

Eugene almost comes off as a father-figure on **Camper Van Chadbourne**, although he easily out-eccentrics the Santa Cruz eclecticians. Check out their Zappa medley, the long-inevitable cover of Pink Floyd's "Careful with That Axe, Eugene," Tim Hardin's "Reason to Believe," Joe South's "Games People Play" and Chadbourne's own witty 'n'wise originals. [rg]

CHALICE
Up Till Now (RAS) 1987

Jamaica's Chalice has a big, full reggae sound (much like Third World) and a reputation for fiery live performances. Happily, that enthusiasm translates to the sextet's studio work, as demonstrated by their first US release, **Up Till Now**, a 1981-'87 hits compilation. The group has a strong pop streak, and the rootsy, simply-produced LP is rich in melodies and hooks. Best of all, it's uptempo from start to finish, which makes it perfect dance party fare. [bk]

CHAMELEONS (UK)
Script of the Bridge (MCA) 1983 ●
What Does Anything Mean? Basically? (nr/Statik) 1985 ●
Strange Times (Geffen) 1986

THE SUN AND THE MOON
The Sun and the Moon (Geffen) 1988 ●

Somehow, this stylish British pop quartet managed to bring something of their own to such much-traveled terrain, making songs like the melodic "Up the Down Escalator" and the far denser "Don't Fall" moody and memorable. Bassist Mark Burgess recalls Psychedelic Fur Richard Butler's world-weariness in his singing; the band's playing is, however, generally lighter in tone and simpler in design than that band's. **Script of the Bridge** isn't a great album, but it has very appealing moments. (US and UK editions differ.)

What Does Anything Mean? Basically? is even better, with much stronger production underscoring both the ghostly atmospherics of the icy church keyboards and delay-ridden guitars, and the band's direct power. More than just songs, the Chameleons build meticulous puzzles, forests of sound with heartfelt melodies. "Intrigue in Tangiers" and "On the Beach" show the muscle beneath the beauty, while "Perfume Garden" and "One Flesh" spring with such fresh life they're instantly enveloping.

Strange Times was produced by Dave Allen (Sisters of Mercy, Cure), who adds a dark edge to the normally bright sound. The dreamy undercurrents add a luster to the three epic tracks, "Caution," with its odd 6/8 time swing, "Soul in Isolation," an emotional piece of knowing loneliness, and "Swamp Thing," a delicious, building mini-masterpiece. "Time" and "In Answer" are aggressive, no-holds barred post-punk rockers that such sound architects as these are supposed to be neither capable of or inclined towards, and they add a breathless whoosh to the proceedings. (Some US copies come with a not-to-be-missed six-song bonus 12-inch disc including covers of the Beatles' "Tomorrow Never Knows" and Bowie's "John, I'm Only Dancing.")

The Chameleons' body of work is strongly recommended. After the group split up in February 1988, Burgess and drummer John Lever joined with a pair of guitarists to form a new quartet, the Sun and the Moon, which debuted in mid-'88 with an eponymous album that sounds a lot like the Chameleons. [iar/jr]

JAMES CHANCE
Theme from Grutzi Elvis FP (7F) 1979
JAMES CHANCE AND THE CONTORTIONS
Live aux Bains Douches (Fr. Invisible) 1980
Live in New York [tape] (ROIR) 1981
VARIOUS ARTISTS
No New York (Antilles) 1978
CONTORTIONS
Buy (ZE-Arista) 1979
JAMES WHITE AND THE BLACKS
Off White (ZE-Buddah) 1979
Sax Maniac (Animal) 1982
JAMES WHITE AND THE CONTORTIONS
Second Chance (ZE-PVC) 1980
JAMES WHITE
Flaming Demonics (nr/ZE-Island) 1983

Arriving from Milwaukee with a saxophone on his knee, James (Siegfried) Chance/White/Black quickly became the linchpin of the budding New York no wave movement, appearing in Teenage Jesus and the Jerks with Lydia Lunch. More than any of his contemporaries, Chance turned harsh, abrasive music into an art form, and at one time or another almost everyone of any importance on the New York art music scene was in the Contortions.

No New York, produced by Brian Eno and shared by three other bands, features Chance and the Contortions at their most cacophonous, shattering the limits of taste and anti-commerciality with a mixture of punk and jazz. Recommended in all its jangle. Buy lacks the jagged edge of the No New York material, but expands the Contortions into a first-class, no-holds barred act, with every note and vocal oozing out Chance's deranged contempt for man and society with passionately cold renditions of normally pleasant dance music, epitomized by his then-anthem, "Contort Yourself."

Theme from Grutzi Elvis separates Chance's haranguing, bitter vocals from what turns out to be unusual if colorful music. Notably, Chance sings a subdued, oddly touching version of "That's When Your Heartaches Begin."

The very rare Live aux Bains Douches features Chance and the Contortions live in Paris, but the more readily available Live in New York demonstrates that there is real emotion energizing Chance's savage, solipsistic music.

Off White is a set of funky, demented disco tunes performed with the help of New York luminaries George Scott, Jody Harris, Don Christensen and Pat Place. Though milder and more accessible than White's Chance-work, Off White plays freely with his attempts at sexual ennui ("Stained Sheets") and racial ambiguity ("Almost Black") and features a wonderfully weird and erotic version of Irving Berlin's "(Tropical) Heat Wave." Recommended. After White/Chance left the label, ZE compiled material from Off White and Buy to make Second Chance.

Sax Maniac, which he produced, proved that several years' absence hadn't harmed White at all, and that he is a wonderful, inventive sax player. Similar in all respects except personnel to Off White, Sax Maniac (complete with a cover of "That Old Black Magic") is a fevered masterpiece of white funk. [sg]

See also False Prophets, Jody Harris.

SHEILA CHANDRA
Out on My Own (nr/Indipop) 1984
Quiet! (nr/Indipop) 1984
Nada Brahma (nr/Indipop) 1985
The Struggle (nr/Indipop) 1985

It's hard to figure out why Sheila Chandra's post-Monsoon solo career, also masterminded by Steve Coe and Martin Smith, is less compelling than her former band's one stunning album. The blend of Indian instrumentation with standard Anglo-pop maneuvers keeps the music from being mistaken for anyone but Chandra, and all are utterly listenable, with some fine moments scattered throughout, but none are as hypnotic or memorable as Third Eye. [iar]

CHANNEL THREE
CH3 EP (Posh Boy) 1981
Fear of Life (Posh Boy) 1982

I've Got a Gun (nr/No Future) 1982
After the Lights Go Out (Posh Boy) 1983
Airborne EP (Enigma) 1984
Last Time I Drank (Enigma) 1985

Channel Three (aka CH3) hailed from Cerritos, one of numerous Southern California suburban hardcore bands signed to pioneering and influential local label Posh Boy. An aggressive, speedy mixture of Black Flag and early Ramones, the **CH3 EP** and **Fear of Life** album are fairly typical genre fare, and not very inspired at that. The quartet's lyrics predictably concern school, girls and the angst of growing up middle-class, making CH3 of potential interest only to the least discerning element of hardcore fandom.

The one-take-live-in-the-studio feel of **After the Lights Go Out** benefits from crisp, balanced sound and charged-up performances. Singer/guitarist Mike Magrann's wordy originals are routine enough that a burning version of the Stones' "Stupid Girl" is easily the record's highlight.

The trio on **Airborne** is far more proficient and creatively developed than any prior CH3 lineup; the songs—written by Magrann with ex-Stepmother Jay Lansford (who likely has a lot to do with the band's improvement)—are strong aggro-folk of some note. [iar]

CHANT
Three Sheets to the Wind (Safety Net) 1985

Florida's four-man Chant plays energetic and sparkling Southern folk-pop with a strong R.E.M. influence on their first album. The peppy tempo and flat-picked guitars of "All Behind Me" make that band's overwhelming impact evident from the very start; Walter Czachowski's husky (but articulate) singing furthers the comparison. But the loose-limbed guitar jam of " . . . For You," the striking country feel of "Heaven Assumes" and a spectacular cover of a classic late-'60s obscuro, "Little Black Egg" by Florida's Nightcrawlers, help give **Three Sheets** a legitimacy all its own. [iar]

TRACY CHAPMAN
Tracy Chapman (Elektra) 1988 ●

Unquestionably the most impressive new solo artist of 1988, Chapman is a young singer/songwriter whose powerful lyrics and extraordinary voice—which does, in fact, strongly resemble Joan Armatrading's—give her debut album the impact of a rock

wrapped in cotton. Tasteful electric backing and simple, clear production allows the uncomplicated songs to be the record's focus, and what a sharp image they draw! "Fast Car" addresses obstacles to escaping urban poverty; "Behind the Wall" paints a chilling picture of domestic violence; "Talkin' Bout a Revolution" has the uplifting symmetry of a classic folk anthem. Songs about romance ("Baby Can I Hold You," "For My Lover," "For You") leaven the anger but not the intensity. Despite the utter familiarity of **Tracy Chapman**'s sound, its creator's voice is truly unique. [iar]

CHARGED G.B.H.
See *G.B.H.*

CHEAP TRICK
Cheap Trick (Epic) 1977 ●
In Color (Epic) 1977 ●
Heaven Tonight (Epic) 1978 ●
At Budokan (Epic) 1979 ●
Dream Police (Epic) 1979 ●
Found All the Parts EP (Epic) 1980
All Shook Up (Epic) 1980
One on One (Epic) 1982 ●
Next Position Please (Epic) 1983
Standing on the Edge (Epic) 1985 ●
The Doctor (Epic) 1986 ●
Lap of Luxury (Epic) 1988 ●

At a time when heavy metal had lost its menace and was fading into side-show stupidity, Rockford, Illinois' Cheap Trick blew out of the Midwest, where they had long been dominating clubs and bars, and set about proving that commercial rock writ large enough for football fields could also be witty, casual and sarcastic. Rick Nielsen stood the guitar hero stereotype on its head, wringing out glorious garbage with a goofy look that echoed the punk ethos by refusing to take any pose seriously. Although the quartet went wrong by buying into the expectations raised by large-scale success, Trick's early records and live performances influenced a generation of future bands growing up American in the late '70s. Many of today's heartland ex-punks (Replacements, Soul Asylum, Pontiac Brothers, Redd Kross, etc.—even Big Black went to the trouble of covering "He's a Whore" on a 1987 single) took something from them. Cheap Trick provided an American alternative archetype at a time when big-league success was almost a guarantee of total timidity and tedium and the opposite was just as true.

In proving that a certain dose of commercial savvy was cool, Cheap Trick discovered that too much could be a deadly. By failing to keep up with what they had launched, they wound up nearly as dinosaurish and irrelevant as the stiffs they had originally displaced.

Drawing primary inspiration from the Move and Beatles, Cheap Trick synthesized a loud and brilliant rock powerdrive and backed it up with shows that, while formulaic and gimmicky in the extreme, had all the punch and spirited good humor that older, tired arena bands lacked. **Cheap Trick** is an absolute stunner, an immediately recognizable onslaught of Tom Petersson's 8 and 12-string basses, Nielsen's guitar overachiever theatrics, Robin Zander's nuclear assault voice and Bun E. Carlos' Watts-like steady drumming. Well-honed songs explode under Jack Douglas' all-electric production. "Taxman" turns the Beatles upside down with a twist; "He's a Whore" rocks with a ragingly melodic chorus; "The Ballad of TV Violence (I'm Not the Only Boy)" displays a healthy nasty streak by concerning Chicago mass murderer Richard Speck (albeit in the vaguest terms); "Oh Candy" laments a depressed male friend's suicide. One of the world's all-time greatest albums. (But don't put too much faith in the fabricated biographical liner notes by future superstar novelist Eric Van Lustbader.)

In Color (And in Black and White), produced by Tom Werman (who went on to score metal with Ted Nugent, Mötley Crüe and Poison) is another spectacular record which reduces the buzzy guitar raunch in favor of a cleaner, more clearly pop-oriented sound. Trick maintained its anti-establishment coolness by including "Downed," an undisguised paean to barbiturates, and offering the bitchy "You're All Talk." Meanwhile, the LP contained the band's first hit single: the twinky "I Want You to Want Me."

Heaven Tonight hit a new pinnacle with the brilliant "Surrender" and a new low with the gimmicky "On the Radio." In between, the LP covers the Move ("California Man"), conveys the ambience of depressant use in song ("Heaven Tonight") and paraphrases arena rock in the leering "Stiff Competition."

As a result of burgeoning Asian popularity, the band's Japanese label recorded a pair of April '78 Tokyo shows and released a live album, **At Budokan**. The concert version of "I Want You to Want Me" caught American radio programmers' attention and they jumped on the record—especially a dynamic rendition of Fats Domino's "Ain't That a Shame"—forcing its domestic release the following year and providing the group's first hit album.

Dream Police (also available on picture disc) continues the dedication to diversity. The wimpy ballad "Voices" and the paranoid mega-produced title track are pure pop; "Gonna Raise Hell," meanwhile, builds a rock disco groove with a powerful bass riff and overlays melodramatic vocals about the massacre at Jonestown, fading out with Zander's anguished shrieks. "I Know What I Want" is quintessential three-chord rock with a delightfully goofy Petersson vocal; the magnificent "Need Your Love" starts out slow and restrained, but builds to an intense boogie-based climax that closes the LP—and the essential segment of Cheap Trick's career.

As if to celebrate that juncture, a four-song 10-inch EP (later repackaged as a 12-inch) was released with a previously-unissued track from each year, 1976–1979. "Take Me I'm Yours" is a worthwhile studio number; "Daytripper," ostensibly recorded live, lets the group display its affection (if not reverence) for the Beatles.

The George Martin-produced **All Shook Up** is a bewildering array of production tricks, inferior material, halfbaked experiments and self-conscious mimicry of the Faces and the Rolling Stones. A few songs ("Baby Loves to Rock," "Can't Stop It but I'm Gonna Try") do withstand the overall botch, but the LP—Petersson's last—remains best unheard. **One on One**, produced by Roy Thomas Baker, is more realistic in its aspirations but suffers from second-rate material. Only the lascivious "She's Tight" and the obligatory ballad ("If You Want My Love") make strong impressions in this lackluster outing. New bassist Jon Brant adds nothing to the group's sound.

Nielsen had played with post-Rundgren remnants of Nazz around 1970, so the choice of Todd as the producer of the refreshing **Next Position Please** was a circle closer of sorts. (Given Cheap Trick's evident studio uncertainty the LP could have been titled **Next Producer Please**.) Returning somewhat to the straight rock-pop of **In Color**, but with

Rundgren's unique imprint, songs like "Borderline," "I Can't Take It," "Won't Take No for an Answer" and Rundgren's contribution, the stunning "Heaven's Falling," make it a welcome return (almost) to form. On the downside, the LP also contains an atrocious self-produced version of the Motors' "Dancing the Night Away" inserted at the label's unfortunate insistence. The cassette adds "You Talk Too Much" and the slide-guitar blues festival, "Don't Make Our Love a Crime."

The next two LPs find Cheap Trick flailing about with skimpy ideas, no self-confidence and little enthusiasm. Reuniting with Jack Douglas for **Standing on the Edge** yielded a likable rote ballad ("Tonight It's You"), a charged riff-rocker ("She's Got Motion") and one good pop tune ("This Time Around"), all co-written with professional song doctor Mark Radice, who also plays the LP's keyboards. **The Doctor,** produced by metal-man Tony Platt (who mixed **Standing on the Edge**) is loud and abrasive, with the barest of worthy tunes ("Rearview Mirror Romance," "The Doctor," "Good Girls Go to Heaven") and almost no trace of lyrical personality.

Petersson rejoined the group in time for **Lap of Luxury,** Cheap Trick's creative nadir and commercial renaissance. Produced by the bombastic Richie Zito, with songs from all sorts of hacks (Nielsen only co-wrote four; Petersson and Zander collaborated on two others), the album gets off to a great start with "Let Go" but runs straight downhill from there. The version of "Don't Be Cruel" is a nice touch, but not a great achievement; "Wrong Side of Love" indicates they can still rev up the engines. Despite the promise of the original lineup and the sales figures, this album is running on empty. [iar]

CHELSEA

Chelsea (nr/Step Forward) 1979
Alternative Hits (nr/Step Forward) 1980
No Escape (IRS) 1980
Evacuate (IRS) 1982
Just for the Record (nr/Step Forward) 1985
Original Sinners (nr/Communique) 1985

Dismissed by more than a few as a bad joke, the never-say-die Chelsea was one of the few original punk groups to forge a unique sound *and* survive. Their distinctiveness stems from the grunt'n'groan vocals of Gene October, the guiding force and only constant

member through numerous lineup changes.

Even in the early days, Chelsea didn't pursue the buzzsaw punk stereotype, instead favoring a less-fevered, sometimes lumbering intensity, suggestive of an ignorant, lower-class background. **Chelsea** does offer plenty of thrills, however. James Stevenson's guitar enlivens slashing rockers like "I'm on Fire," and October constantly seems about to burst from the pressure. On the cover of Jimmy Cliff's exquisite "Many Rivers to Cross," he renders a vivid portrayal of someone suffering extreme pain who can't articulate it properly. It's poignant.

Alternative Hits (aka **No Escape**) consists largely of tracks originally (and better) heard on singles. Collected on an album, these songs betray the band's lack of versatility. But at least it includes Chelsea's electrifying debut 45, "Right to Work."

Evacuate brings Gene October about as far into the modern age as he can go. The bull-in-a-china-shop approach is toned down somewhat in a bid for relative respectability. Somehow, it just doesn't seem right.   [iy]

CHEQUERED PAST

Chequered Past (EMI America) 1984

Although listening to this run-of-the-mill Bad Company arena rock may not, a glance at the credits indicates why Chequered Past was one of the most depressing groups/albums of recent years. Clem Burke and Nigel Harrison (both ex-Blondie) and Steve Jones (ex-Pistols) formed three-fifths of the band, proving conclusively that even talented new wavers, no matter how idealistic and rebellious, were merely a few years away from becoming just as bogus as the musicians they originally served to dethrone. Disgusting.

[iar]

CHESTERFIELD KINGS

Here Are the Chesterfield Kings (Mirror) 1983
stop! (Mirror) 1985 + 1987
Don't Open Til Doomsday (Mirror) 1987

Unless you check the copyright date, you'll swear that this upstate New York band with pudding bowl haircuts and Beatle boots existed two decades back. The Kings' faithful re-creation of '60s guitar rock and garage punk (the first album's material is strictly covers, most of it so esoteric that only a fanatic record collector would find more than one or two tunes familiar) is so spot-on that it's impossible to discern from the real thing. In their chosen idiom, the group's records are as consistent and reliable as early Ramones.

The Kings' staggeringly true alternatation of Merseybeat and sneery trash remains uncompromised on **stop!**; surprisingly, the high proportion of originals scarcely diminishes the lifelike effect. (Two extra songs were added when Mirror remastered **stop!** for its 1987 reissue.)

The shag haircuts on the cover of **Don't Open Til Doomsday** should be fair warning that the quintet has loosened the stylistic strings. Leavening the slavish fundamentalism with a little modern sonic character, they hit on something comparable to late-'70s Flamin Groovies. As a concession to the less obscure-minded, the waning proportion of non-originals draws on T-Bone Burnett and Ray Davies. The album is enthusiastically played and cleanly recorded, but once a band has painted itself up such a stylistic tree, musical development may mean a straight path down. (Esoterica note: "They were never born/they were thrown out of hell" is inscribed in the run-off groove.)   [iar]

CHIEFS OF RELIEF

Chiefs of Relief (Sire) 1988

Bow Wow Wow guitarist Matthew Ashman (now also a vocalist) formed the Chiefs of Relief as the post-Annabella version of that band, but it took a few years before anything came of it. By that time, he had teamed with ex-Pistols/Professionals drummer Paul Cook and, joined by a bassist and keyboard player, begun playing a pop-safe hybrid of rap, beatbox funk and loud rock. At times resembling a tamer Big Audio Dynamite (a bit too closely), the Chiefs are nonetheless an agreeable dance-powered outfit that draws on the varied experiences of its creative team to kick their songs into fun gear. Richard Gottehrer's production accommodates the assorted directions handily, making **Chiefs of Relief** an easy pill to swallow.   [iar]

THE CHILLS

The Lost EP (NZ Flying Nun) 1985
    (Homestead) 1988 ●
Kaleidoscope World (nr/Creation) 1986
House with 100 Rooms (nr/Flying Nun) 1987
Brave Words (NZ Flying Nun) 1987
    (Homestead) 1988 ●

New Zealand's Chills make white-bread music; lightweight, non-controversial pop.

But they do it with such fresh-scrubbed integrity that it's hard not to like them. Guitars may twinkle like harps and jangle over angelically whispery vocals but somehow the love songs are never gooey. Gooey bands do not write lines like "Oh god this white ward stinks, sterilized stench of sticky death, sniveling relatives at the feet of another moist corpse, but that corpse is Jayne and Jayne can't die" (from **Brave Words'** "16 Heart-Throbs"). Soppy sentimentalists aren't honest enough to admit "I'd like to say how I love you but it's all been said in other songs" as Martin Phillipps (the only Chill who has been with the band through ten lineups since its 1981 inception) does on the same album's "Night of Chill Blue."

The Chills write mostly love songs. They love women, rain, the Otago Peninsula at the southern tip of New Zealand's southern island and their leather jackets. They even love to be hurt because out of hurt comes growth. They love cool, clean production with sparkling high notes, keeping just enough homestyle dustiness to avoid slickness. At times, their music seems like a low-budget answer to the Moody Blues. Other times they sound like they just stepped out of a renaissance market square with folky acoustic guitars and delicate drums.   ['e]

ALEX CHILTON

Singer Not the Song EP (Ork) 1977
Like Flies on Sherbert (Peabody) 1980 (Ger. Line) 1981
Bach's Bottom (Ger. Line) 1981 ●
Live in London (nr/Aura) 1982 ●
Feudalist Tarts EP (Big Time) 1985
Document (nr/Aura) 1985
The Lost Decade (Fr. Fan Club) 1986
Stuff [CD] (Fr. New Rose) 1987
High Priest (Big Time) 1987 ●

BIG STAR

#1 Record (Ardent) 1972
Radio City (Ardent) 1974
#1 Record/Radio City (nr/Stax-EMI) 1977
    [CD] (nr/Big Beat) 1987
3rd (PVC) 1978 ●
Sister Lovers (PVC) 1985 ●

A seemingly unlikely figure for a new wave progenitor, Memphis-born ex-Box Tops singer Chilton nonetheless exerted tremendous influence on many groups via his unconventional early '70s recordings with Big Star. **#1 Record** is the most cohesive of Big Star's three LPs, if not the best. Recorded in 1972, when its Beatlesque four-part harmonies, early Byrds/Kinks guitar sound and crisp, tight, live-sounding production were decidedly out of vogue, it signals an early rejection of then-dominant bloated "progressive" rock, which had already fallen victim to the giant ego-tripping of not-so-giant talents.

Whereas **#1 Record** is a collaborative effort in every sense of the word (Chilton co-wrote and shares lead vocals with the talented Chris Bell; all four members sing), **Radio City** is more a showcase for Chilton's increasingly quirky talents. Bell had left the group (he died in a 1978 car crash), and Chilton, whose gruff tenor epitomized the Top 40 sound of the Box Tops, sings at the very top of his range, straining at times to reach high notes of his own songs. The well-organized production values of **#1 Record** give way to a more emotional and spontaneous sound, a middle ground between Lennon's **Plastic Ono Band** and early Sun records. If the material on **Radio City** is spotty, it's never uninteresting, and the best songs—"September Gurls" and "Back of a Car"—are as good as any rock'n'roll produced in the first half of the '70s. (Note: the joint CD of **#1 Record/ Radio City** deletes two tracks from the earlier LP.)

Recorded in 1974 but unreleased until 1978, by which time Big Star had broken up, **3rd** (reissued much later under its original title, **Sister Lovers**) is almost a Chilton solo album: Alex, drummer Jody Stephens and a host of Memphis friends and sessioneers (Jim Dickinson and Steve Cropper among them) comprise the band. It's an eclectic mix, alternately depressing and uplifting, ugly and beautiful. Though a bit of a pastiche, it's quite often brilliant, if strangely so. (The American LP contains a larger and better track selection than the British.)

Between the release of **Radio City** and **3rd**, Chilton had recorded an album's worth of material in a series of stormy sessions in Memphis with rock critic/musician Jon Tiven producing. Chilton was reportedly so out of it during the recording that Tiven ended up playing all the guitar. The results of the sessions were released in 1977 on an Ork Records EP. **Singer Not the Song** includes versions of the Stones song of the title and a 59-second "Summertime Blues," plus a couple of decent Chilton co-compositions that might have sounded better under other circumstances. In 1981, the EP's contents plus more material from the same wild sessions

(including five more minutes of "Summertime Blues") were released in Germany as **Bach's Bottom**. Only the really faithful will want to know.

Despite leading bands in New York and Memphis between 1975 and 1980, the years when he was rediscovered and lionized by critics and musicians alike, Chilton has no extant studio recordings from that period. Live shows did serve to increase his reputation as an erratic and eccentric performer, and 1980's **Like Flies on Sherbert** painfully confirms the degradation of a once-major talent. The LP sounds like a bunch of drunken louts running amok in a studio with no producer to restrain or guide them. Sadly, some potentially good Chilton material is trampled to death in the process, as well as some covers. In short, it stinks. (The 1980 British edition on Aura apparently utilized the wrong master tapes; the original mix from the tiny Peabody release, most widely available on a German Line issue, is far superior.)

Live in London captures a 1981 performance at Dingwalls on what is, for Chilton, a fairly good night. Backed by the Soft Boys rhythm section (Matthew Seligman and Morris Windsor) and Vibrator Knox on guitar, Chilton runs through material from all three Big Star LPs and **Like Flies on Sherbert**. Although characteristically sloppy and erratic, the album has moments that indicate there may be life in the old boy yet. As such, it's his best solo LP to date.

After a long period spent drying out and laying low in New Orleans and Memphis, a revived Chilton returned to active duty in late 1984, touring with a new pair of sidemen and recording his first new studio release in many years. **Feudalist Tarts** is a delight, six sides marked by control, easy confidence and entertaining variety. Chilton even sounds like he's enjoying the work for a change. Among Alex's originals are a humorously raunchy blues, "Lost My Job," and the absurdist jivey "Stuff" (with horns); covers include a slow, lazy take on "B-A-B-Y" (remember Rachel Sweet's version?) and a funky slide from the Slim Harpo songbook. The EP is a bit insubstantial, but most encouraging and a fine slice of Chilton.

Document is a 1985 compilation covering both Big Star and solo tracks; **The Lost Decade** packages one disc of Chilton's solo work as a performer with one as producer of various obscure records. **Stuff** is an amazing French CD-only collection that contains all of **Feudalist Tarts**, the three songs on the 1986 "No Sex" 12-inch and seven more solo items, including "Bangkok" and Sky Saxon's "Can't Seem to Make You Mine," both reclaimed from a 1978 single.

Having influenced scores of garage rockers from the Replacements (who, of course, wrote a song about him) on down, Chilton can be forgiven for calling his next album **High Preist**. The record consists of Alex tackling virtually every type of song you can imagine him playing (and some you wouldn't, like "Volaré") from the Memphis soul of his Box Tops days to Brill Building pop to Jimmy Reed-style blues to gospel to Big Star to a twisted version of the Bill Justis instrumental "Raunchy," all lovingly delivered in a casual live-or-near-live garage style. What it lacks in polish, it more than makes up in charm, verve and just plain ol' soul. This could be what rock'n'roll is all about. The CD adds nine tracks.   [ds/iar]

See also *Panther Burns*.

CHINA CRISIS

Difficult Shapes & Passive Rhythms, Some
    People Think It's Fun to Entertain
    (nr/Virgin) 1982 (Virgin) 1987 ●
Working with Fire and Steel EP (Warner
    Bros.) 1983
Working with Fire and Steel Possible Pop
    Songs Volume Two (Warner Bros.) 1983
Flaunt the Imperfection (Virgin-Warner Bros.)
    1985
What Price Paradise (Virgin-A&M) 1986 ●

The weird title of the first album by this Liverpool group—essentially a duo of Gary Daly (words, keyboards, vocals) and Eddie Lundon (guitar and music), plus Dave the percussionist—does convey a sense of what China Crisis is about. The rhythms—R&B, funk, reggae, Afro-gypsy, bossa nova—are so gently, modestly, melodiously proffered that it goes down *too* smoothly. Then you notice that the dreamily-enunciated sentiments interface the political and the personal, with hopeful dreams and admissions of self-doubt and inner struggle. The cohesive feel is maintained despite four different producers; China Crisis' sturdy intellectual backbone emerges often enough to avoid wimpiness.

Working with Fire and Steel has just as much going for it. A sax and/or oboe (!) appears on all but two tracks, with more horns on occasion plus even strings (real and synth). Mike Howlett's production, plus a new drummer and a permanent bassist, help them attain a bit more sonic snap; the lyrics are less tortured, if just as thoughtfully, melancholically personal. The EP of the same name unites two versions of the title track with a pair of pretty, wistful instrumentals originally released as British 45 B-sides.)

Flaunt the Imperfection was produced by Steely Dan's Walter Becker but, while displaying a bit of Dan influence (see "The Highest High" and "Black Man Ray," both memorable pieces of modern art-pop), it's far more obviously a refinement of the band's own style. The lyrical art seems so artless, the musical airiness so effortless; like the first album, it's almost too subtle for its own good. (I said almost.)

By **What Price Paradise**, Daly had handed the keyboards over to a fifth band member, but that had no audible, directly traceable influence compared to the switch to the production team of Clive Langer and Alan Winstanley. The sound has more edge to it, yet is somehow less delicate, less distinctive than on previous albums. In fact, the vocals (lead and backing) on one track are so different that the group is nearly unrecognizable. Still, it pretty much is China Crisis; if the songs occasionally seem more conventionally written, they're still attractive, even almost (gulp) commercial. What'll they think of next?   [jg]

CHOIR INVISIBLE

Choir Invisible (Frontier) 1981
Sea to Shining Sea EP (PVC) 1984

FLYBOYS

The Flyboys EP (Frontier) 1980

Drummer Danny Benair, onetime mainstay of LA's Quick and currently in the Three O'Clock, was—between those two outfits—one-fourth of Choir Invisible, known as the Flyboys when they released the trebly EP which was Frontier's first record. The band bears some resemblance to early U2 on **Choir Invisible**—credit the guitar work by Thames Sinclair (great name)—but singer John Curry's melodramatic voice doesn't put the songs across convincingly. There's variety and depth, but also some problems that need to be resolved.

Adding a keyboard player and switching drummers, Choir Invisible made the much-improved six-song **Sea to Shining Sea**, adopting a lush à la mode dance-synth style that sounds veddy British. Feigning the same mid-Atlantic accent (but pruned of its excesses), Curry's voice better suits this material, although he's still not a great singer. Sinclair's textures keep the midtempo tunes from dragging too much; he *is* a great guitar player. "I Walked Away," with its surprising Association-like harmonies, is the disc's best offering. There's nothing essential here, but it's more amusing than records by many likeminded outfits, and there are certainly enough of them. [iar]

CHORDS
So Far Away (nr/Polydor) 1980
No One's Listening Anymore (nr/Unicorn) 1988

It is impossible to describe the Chords without referring to the Jam's early albums. In essence a copy of a copy, these four earnest young Englishmen weren't half bad, merely redundant. **So Far Away** manages one truly great song ("Maybe Tomorrow") that out-Jams Paul Weller's power pop concoctions and two properly reverent oldies ("She Said, She Said" and "Hold On, I'm Coming"); otherwise, the LP belongs in the dustbin. The talent was there to some measure; a chronic lack of individuality prevented singer/guitarist Chris Pope from achieving anything lasting. [iar]

CHRIS AND COSEY
Heartbeat (nr/Rough Trade) 1981
Trance (nr/Rough Trade) 1982
Flow Motion (nr/Integrated Circuits) 1982
Songs of Love and Lust (nr/Rough Trade) 1984
European Rendezvous (nr/Doublevision) 1984
Techno Primitiv (nr/Rough Trade) 1985
Take Five EP (Can. Nettwerk) 1986
Exotika (Can. Nettwerk) 1987 •
Action (nr/Licensed) 1987

CREATIVE TECHNOLOGY INSTITUTE
Elemental 7—The Original Soundtrack (nr/Doublevision) 1984

CHRIS CARTER
Mondo Beat (nr/Conspiracy Int'l) 1986

Rising from the corpse of Throbbing Gristle, Chris Carter and Cosey Fanni Tutti (aka the Creative Technology Institute) infuse their electronic mantras with the beat of the factory to create a desolate industrial vision. Much of the work on **Heartbeat** follows solidly in Throbbing Gristle's footsteps, with found voices playing over pulsating synthesizer sounds, while the remainder strives towards lightweight Kraftwerkian metal pop. (The cassette has extra tracks.)

Trance's songs unfold more slowly and deliberately, only reaching their final rock forms after passing through stages that frequently bear an uncanny resemblance to Gregorian chant warped into the future. As the title suggests, the mood is dark and contemplative; within the inventive and apparently emotionless electronics lie deep wells of terror and claustrophobia. Worth looking into.

Songs of Love and Lust has a distinctively icy sound, with precise, percussive synths not very far to the left of Depeche Mode. Cosey's cold, distant voice, paying only passing attention to intonation at times, fits in perfectly amidst the machines. The problem is the songs—they're highly repetitive and go nowhere. (Five of the LP's nine tracks exceed five minutes.) Considering the pair's background, this record takes few chances.

CTI's **Elemental 7**, the soundtrack to a long-form video, consists primarily of tempoless washes of synthesizers, bordering on '70s-style space rock. Not very listenable as an album. **European Rendezvous** is a live set recorded throughout the continent in 1983. **Techno Primitiv** is interchangeable with **Songs of Love and Lust**, dominated by unchallenging, mechanical electro-pop. Tempos and textures vary, but each track has an air of familiarity. One could possibly find some interest if the production were at least good, but the album has a really dead sound to it.

Still without a US record deal, Chris and Cosey signed with the hippest label north of the border, Nettwerk, and released **Take Five** in 1986. It begins with "October Love Song," which is worthy of the Human League; the four other tracks fall between that approach and previous work. The production is at least much improved (two numbers are remixes of early material).

The liner notes on **Exotika** explain, "Today we have tremendously diverse kinds of music," but the grooves contain very little to demonstrate that these two are actually aware of that fact; each (lengthy) cut is an electro-Eurodisco variation on the same theme, introduced long ago. Again, the sound is nice, but other bands have done (and overdone) this same stuff much better. Chris and Cosey are just about up to the point of being permanently dismissable.   [sg/dgs]

CHRIS D.
See *Divine Horsemen, Flesh Eaters.*

CHRISTIAN DEATH
Only Theatre of Pain (Frontier) 1982 ●
Death Wish EP (Bemisbrain) 1983
Catastrophe Ballet (Fr. L'Invitation au Suicide) 1984 ●
Ashes (Nostradamus) 1985
The Decomposition of Violets [tape] (ROIR) 1985
The Wind Kissed Pictures EP (Nostradamus-Chameleon) 1985
Atrocities (Ger. Normal) 1986 ●
Jesus Christ Proudly Presents Christian Death (Ger. Normal) 1987
The Scriptures (Ger. Normal) 1987 ●
An Official Anthology of ''Live'' Bootlegs (nr/Nostradamus) 1987
Past and Present [CD] (It. Viva) 1988
Church of No Return (nr/Jungle) 1988

Formed originally in Los Angeles as a theatrical shock-horror outgrowth of the punk scene (guitarist Rikk Agnew was a recent refugee from the Adolescents), Christian Death has survived and grown into a multinational organization with a vast catalogue of pretentious gothic records.

The first album is hampered by singer Rozz Williams' ghastly voice, but the loud/not-too-fast music is appropriately doomy'n' gloomy, with inventive arrangements and clear sound to capture the mood in full B-movie fidelity. The lyrics irreverently address horror topics and religion: they're overwrought and dumb (the backwards masking of "Mysterium Iniquitatis" being a clever exception) but easy to overlook in the wash of inspired rock noise.

Fronting an entirely different lineup on the stylish-looking **Ashes**, Williams has evidently learned to temper his harsh voice by burying it low in the mix. Unfortunately, keyboardist Gitane DeMone also sings, creating a bit of internal controversy over which key any given song employs. The ponderous Bauhausian music, which sets it solid foundation on David Glass' drumming, is more mature and sophisticated; lyrics (some in German) drop religion for vague evocations of medieval debauchery and evil. The

contemporaneous live tape of that same lineup onstage in Hollywood is loud and enthusiastic but suffers greatly from the blatant overuse of synthesizer effects and terribly recorded vocals.

With guitarist Valor taking over the vocals and songwriting, Christian Death became a trio on **The Wind Kissed Pictures**. Occasionally colored with gusty vampire movie ambient effects, the clear, open music—no gloomsters left in this group—makes the would-be decadence of "Believers of the Unpure" and the title track easier to endure, if not actually enjoy. Valor's singing, alone and mixed with DeMone's, is also something of an improvement, although his lyrics are actually worse than his predecessor's. The Italian CD-only **Past and Present** combines **The Wind Kissed Pictures** with three later recordings.

Valor continues to distinguish himself as a pompous prat on **Atrocities**, the trio's dark-hearted return to the somber cesspool of slow-paced grimness. "Herein contained are the emotional remains of millions," his liner notes to the impenetrable concept album exclaim, but I rather doubt that's true.

Raging ego and unchecked ambition allow Valor to attempt a laughable comparative history of religion on **The Scriptures**, subtitled "A Translation of World Beliefs by Valor." After the LP begins with a fundamentalist preacher, V. goes on to crib lyrics from the Bible and sing with a straight face of Huns, horsemen and Ma'gog, pontificating in a most truly offensive manner. The trio also manages to include their cover of a Jimi Hendrix song ("1983") and play the relatively incidental (but agreeable) rock music with a bit of outside assistance. The original pressing included a bonus single of "Jezebel's Tribulation" and "Wraeththu."

Although the story begs credulity, Christian Death claims to have assembled **An Official Anthology** by collecting and culling the prodigious number of illicit concert recordings made of them between 1981 and 1986. Shows from London, Amsterdam and Los Angeles are included.   [iar]

CHRISTIANS
The Christians (Island) 1987 ●

Brothers Garry and Russell Christian and ex-Yachts helmsman Henry Priestman (who left It's Immaterial to join them) comprise the core of this Liverpool group. Sonically, their debut is a treat: airy harmonies float angelically above and around Priestman's crisp keyboards and percolating percussion while Garry sings with restrained soul about life in a (depressed) Northern town. Still, the messages of songs like "Forgotten Town," "When the Fingers Point," "Hooverville" and "Ideal World" are almost undermined by the prettiness and pop sparkle of it all, as if, in an effort not to overstate the case, they've muted the passion the songs require. With a few more memorable melodies and a bit more punch, **The Christians** might have been something special.   [ds]

CHRISTMAS
In Excelsior Dayglo (Big Time) 1986

The kooky Boston trio eulogizes Pee-wee Herman, "Fish Eye Sandwiches," "Tommy the Truck" and "Pumpkinhead" on their first album, an enjoyable folk-rock escape into wry absurdity that owes an emotional debt to Redd Kross. Drummer Liz Cox and guitarist Michael Cudahy alternate appealing lead vocals over simple well-played music that is far from skeletal. Christmas comes up a bit short on identifiable personality here, but considerable wit and native ability almost make up for that.   [iar]

CHROME
The Visitation (Siren) 1977
Alien Soundtracks (Siren) 1978
Half Machine Lip Moves (Siren) 1979
Read Only Memory EP (Siren) 1979
Red Exposure (Siren) 1980
Inworlds (Siren) 1981
Blood on the Moon (Siren) 1981
3rd from the Sun (Siren) 1982
No Humans Allowed (Siren) 1982
Chrome Box (Subterranean) 1982
Raining Milk (Fr. Mosquito) 1983
Chronicles (Ger. Dossier) c. 1984
Into the Eyes of the Zombie King (Ger. Dossier) 1984 ●
The Lyon Concert (Ger. Dossier) 1985 ●
Another World (Ger. Dossier) 1986 ●
Dreaming in Sequence (Ger. Dossier) 1987

DAMON EDGE
Alliance (Fr. New Rose) 1985 ●
The Wind Is Talking (Fr. New Rose) 1985
Grand Visions (Fr. New Rose) 1986
The Surreal Rock (Ger. Dossier) 1987

DAMON EDGE AND CHROME
Eternity (Ger. Dossier) 1986

HELIOS CREED
X-Rated Fairy Tales (Subterranean) 1985
Superior Catholic Finger (Subterranean) 1988

Under the innocuous name of Chrome, two San Franciscans—Damon Edge and Helios Creed—created an awesome (some would say awful) series of LPs that explore a dark state of mind only hinted at by '60s psychedelia. Their dense, chaotic science-fiction epics are vivid vinyl nightmares—a thick blend of mechanical noises, filtered, twisted voices and fantastic, bizarre lyrics—that flesh out a frightening world both absorbing and repellent. Though conventional song structures are preserved to the point where tracks can be distinguished, Chrome's strength is its ability to create sounds of horrible beauty that transcend discrete musical units. If Chrome isn't as conceptually out there as other contemporary noisemongers, their sonic intensity is still something to behold.

Apart from refinements, Edge and Creed have stuck to the same uniquely nerve-shattering style—metal-drone-punk—throughout their time together. The utterly feckless are recommended to begin with the **Chrome Box**, a limited-edition set of six albums, including two that are otherwise unreleased.

Following Chrome's dissolution in 1983, Creed and Edge each launched solo careers. Guitarist Creed's first album finds him leading a noisy quartet that drops the science-fiction content but retains Chrome's sonic density and mild dissonance. Kind of low-rent and faintly cheesy, **X-Rated Fairy Tales** has to contend with Creed's ponderous singing and the superficial synthesized chaos; occasionally the LP wins. **Superior Catholic Finger** is much better, an inspired collage of found sounds, noise, tape manipulation and overdriven punky assault, played by a trio lineup that leans towards guitar, keyboards and drums. (The diminution of vocals is duly noted and appreciated.) Gonzo and gripping.

One CD, issued by German Dossier, contains both **Into the Eyes of the Zombie King** and Edge's first solo undertaking, **Alliance**.   [jy/iar]

CHRON GEN
Chronic Generation (nr/Secret) 1982
Apocalypse Live Tour (nr/Chaos) 1984
Nowhere to Run EP (nr/Picasso) 1984

Top-notch British punk-core, rippling with strength and clarity. Played at reasonable speed with a generally high level of comprehensibility, **Chronic Generation** offers songs about the expected subjects (drugs, rock'n'roll, kids, fighting) that take a mature stance against mindless violence and substance abuse. Perhaps a little tame for true thrash aficionados, Chron Gen has much greater potential for growth than most of their punk contemporaries.   [iar]

CH3
See *Channel 3*.

CHURCH
Of Skins and Heart (Aus. Parlophone) 1981
  (Arista) 1988 ●
The Church (Capitol) 1982 (nr/Carrere) 1985
Temperature Drop in Downtown Winterland
  EP (nr/Carrere) 1982
The Blurred Crusade (nr/Carrere) 1982
  (Arista) 1988 ●
Sing-Songs EP (Aus. Parlophone) 1982
The Unguarded Moment EP (nr/Carrere) 1982
Seance (nr/Carrere) 1983 + 1985 (Arista)
  1988 ●
Persia EP (Aus. Parlophone) 1983
Remote Luxury EP (Aus. Parlophone) 1984
Remote Luxury (Warner Bros.) 1984 (Arista)
  1988 ●
Heyday (Warner Bros.) 1986 (Arista) 1988 ●
Starfish (Arista) 1988 ●

STEVE KILBEY
Unearthed (Enigma) 1987 ●
Earthed (Rykodisc) 1988 ●
The Slow Crack (Aus. Red Eye) 1988

PETER KOPPES
Manchild and Myth (Rykodisc) 1988 ●

MARTY WILLSON-PIPER
In Reflection (Aus. Chase) 1987
Art Attack (Rykodisc) 1988 ●

Of all the comparisons this Australian foursome's music may conjure up, the most helpful is perhaps that the Church is to the Beatles (musically) and early Bowie (lyrically and vocally) what Dire Straits is to Bob Dylan, c. '65–'66. Such a simplification is less unfair than you'd think; Marty Willson-Piper explores the guitar territory first mapped out by George Harrison and John Lennon but in greater detail and with a more practiced hand, while bassist Steve Kilbey chants/talks/sings articulate lyrics with a world-weary melancholy, like early Bowie, but drier and more forceful.

The Church, consisting of most of the first Australian LP plus the best of a subsequent double-45 release, has much to offer in its gorgeous guitar soundscapes and evocative verbal imagery, but **The Blurred Crusade** displays dangerous tendencies toward confessional windiness amid melodies stretched too thin. **Seance** never found its way to America, but the Sydney band finally got a proper shot with **Remote Luxury**, a combination of the two preceding Australian EPs. The attractive, often Byrdslike album of shimmering folk-rock is hampered a bit by Kilbey's overly oblique lyrics.

Heyday, seemingly recorded as an album for a change, is really good; well-produced, straightforward guitar pop housed in an ironically paisleyfied cover. Although titles like "Tristesse" and "Myrrh" suggest otherwise, Kilbey's lyrics are more tangible (albeit in an engagingly vague manner) than usual. The melodies are stronger and catchier than any since the first album.

The production of **Starfish** (by LA session guitarists Waddy Wachtel and Danny Kortchmar) may have something to do with its shortcomings. At first blush, the album seems pleasant but unfulfilling; after a while, I was able to get past any lack of zip in the grooves and discover them to be the Church's most consistent, engrossing, memorable tunes yet. Even Kilbey's off-the-wall lyrics seem to be better integrated, more cohesive and more evocative. Willson-Piper's unexpected but delightful '60s Anglo-pop-rock concoction ("Spark") is a bonus.

Following **Starfish**'s enormous Stateside success, Arista reissued all of the group's albums and made them available on compact disc.

Kilbey's **Unearthed** (originally issued in Australia in 1986) is a mixed bag, an assortment of songs (some solid if short on polish, others insignificant) interlarded with some brief, generally forgettable instrumentals. **Earthed** goes all the other members' solo LPs one better: the Church's prime lyricist concentrates on purely instrumental ideas, many of which would fall beyond the band's purview even with lyrics. The worst of it sounds like intros in search of actual songs. The good stuff ranges from a sonic montage, to a pleasant, gently rocking ditty, to a queer but fetching little waltz. (A 76-page booklet of poetry meant to complement the music accompanies some copies.)

The eight songs (all with vocals) on **The**

Slow Crack have a full, produced sound. In fact, "Fireman" leads it off with a sort of Phil Spector-gone-folk-rock feel (synth strings, sax, the works). Regrettably, the rest of the record is static and melodically undistinguished; even Kilbey can't make sense of some of the silly pseudo-poetic lines he spouts.

The songs on both of Willson-Piper's solo albums are mostly softish folk-pop—virtually no real rock—with sparse instrumentation, sometimes no bass or drums. In Reflection seems like (justifiably) unused demos, while Art Attack appears to be a finished product outside the band's context. Like most of In Reflection, some of Art Attack has a cottony airheadedness, but it's easily the more varied and stimulating disc. As Willson-Piper sings ("On the Tip of My Tongue"), he's just offering whatever odd ideas he had for anyone who may be interested; over-indulgent but intriguing. There's a lilting paean to Stockholm (once in English and again later in Swedish), and an unaccompanied rant with some electronic voice processing (once forwards and once backwards). "You Whisper" is like Peter Frampton imitating Elvis Costello gone psychedelic ("Your marzipan skin in a crystal stare/ Your chocolate box of fears"). "Word" is eight-and-a-half minutes of one-syllable words listed to a melody vaguely reminiscent of Pachelbel's "Canon". Is it a cleverly created mood, willful obscurity or just plain twaddle? "Evil Queen of England" offers nifty lyrical bile accompanied only by an acoustic bass. (The US cassette and CD include 6 tracks from In Reflection.)

Guitarist Peter Koppes' solo work has a strike against it straightaway: he can barely carry a tune. Covering it up (surrounding him with other voices and burying him in the mix) isn't hard, but his monotone mumble doesn't cut through anyway, but that doesn't do much for the vocal melodies or lyrics. To top it off, he lacks dynamism in arrangement and production. There are precisely three good tracks on the album—two stylistically routine but better than the rest, the third a totally atypical moody Eurosynth instrumental. (The US CD and cassette editions include the OK material on his 1987 3-track EP, When Reason Forbids.)

These non-Church projects are more genuinely solo than most (with only the smallest of contributions from wives, girlfriends, brothers, etc.). The results may be best left to completists but, if you must, Art Attack and Earthed (each would make a swell EP) are clearly the best places to start. Following their initial US release on CD, Ryko Analogue brought the three 1988 solos out on vinyl as well.   [jg]

CICCONE YOUTH
See *Sonic Youth.*

CINECYDE
I Left My Heart in Detroit City (Tremor) 1982

Detroit has been the site of several musical generations of punk; Cinecyde was active on the local scene there for several years beginning in the late '70s, gigging and releasing records on their own label. This album unleashes enough raw power to stun, but a superior sense of song structure and skilled musicianship keep it above the reaches of simple hardcore or heavy metal.   [iar]

CIRCLE JERKS
Group Sex (Frontier) 1980 ●
Wild in the Streets (Faulty Products) 1982
     (Frontier) 1988 ●
Golden Shower of Hits (LAX) 1983 ●
Wönderful (Combat Core) 1985 ●
VI (Relativity) 1987 ●

Singer Keith Morris left Black Flag after appearing on that group's debut single ("Nervous Breakdown") and formed this popular and durable LA slam band with ex-Redd Kross guitarist Greg Hetson. First immortalized on celluloid in *The Decline of Western Civilization* hardcore documentary, the Circle Jerks' vinyl success (via the film soundtrack and their own releases) came later. Typically crude and undisciplined, despite occasional offbeat choices of material (Wild in the Streets contains a hyper remake of Jackie DeShannon's "Put a Little Love in Your Heart"), these Jerks have managed to become a live success; their shows generate some of the most intense slam-dancing and stage-diving on the face of the earth. (In 1988, Frontier remixed and reissued Wild in the Streets, appending Group Sex to the CD.)

With a joyously tasteless urinal cover photo, Golden Shower of Hits offers a new batch of tuneless kinetic guitar rock, built around the titular centerpiece ("Jerks on 45"), which dismembers a number of well-known wimp classics (including "Along

Comes Mary," "Afternoon Delight," "Having My Baby" and "Love Will Keep Us Together") in a medley that's unfortunately funnier in concept than execution.

Joined by a new rhythm section, Morris and Hetson cut **Wönderful**, a tepid self-produced imitation of a punk record by a band that, while bearing a passing resemblance to the Dictators, sounds old, tired and bored. Amazingly, the identical lineup is also responsible for **VI**, a far better high-burn collection (it *really* sounds like the Dictators) that gets off to a great start with "Beat Me Senseless" and continues from there, going so far as to strip down and speed up Creedence's "Fortunate Son" for a fun cover. After eight years, the self-aware Circle Jerks have a sharp focus; the charged-up enthusiasm is tempered by a sense of musical responsibility. Some of the songs suck but, in general, **VI** is cogent, powerful and thoughtful—punk the old-fashioned way. [rnp/iar]

CIRCUIT II
Can't Tempt Fate (Elektra) 1985

With Arthur Baker producing, this interracial Detroit trio plays a different combination of rock and funk, avoiding all the contemporary stereotypes to forge a blend quite their own. The balance shifts from song to song, electronically syncopated beats sharing the grooves with rock-inflected guitar; overlaid tape effects (edits by the Latin Rascals) color some of the tracks a hip-hop hue. A solidly played, interesting record. [iar]

CIRCUS MORT
Circus Mort EP (Labor) 1981

These New Yorkers—led by future Swans founder/guitarist Michael Gira—sound like they want to back you into a corner and harangue you into a screaming fit. They're not some punks on a rampage, though—this is amphetaminized dance music with a faint European tinge and cool, discreet keyboards. As a hectoring vocalist, Gira is, under the circumstances, quite articulate. I'll be good—honest! [jg]

GARY CLAIL'S TACKHEAD SOUND SYSTEM
See *Adrian Sherwood.*

CLAN OF XYMOX
The Clan of Xymox (Relativity) 1985
Medusa (nr/4AD) 1986 ●

Despite competent musicianship and complexity, this Dutch quartet's gothic dance gloom is more imitative than distinctive. On their Anglo-American debut, the right components are present but the record is disappointingly lacking in personality. Despite three alternating vocalists (deeply anguished to breathlessly fragile), jutting electric and acoustic guitars, sinewy bass and a wealth of synths, Clan of Xymox can't seem to make anything out of the ordinary happen, and only three songs approach memorability. What would have made a commendable EP flounders as an album.

Medusa wallows even deeper in the bland Eurodisco gloom of the dismal debut album. "Michelle," a bouncy psychedelic pop tune, offers the only relief. Obviously out of place on this depressing LP, that song would serve as an excellent starting point for Xymox's future endeavors. [ag]

JOHN COOPER CLARKE
Où Est la Maison de Fromage? (nr/Rabid) 1978
Disguise in Love (nr/CBS) 1978
Walking Back to Happiness EP (nr/Epic) 1979
Snap, Crackle [&] Bop (nr/Epic) 1980
Me and My Big Mouth (nr/Epic) 1981
Zip Style Method (nr/Epic) 1982

The first acknowledged new wave poet, Manchester's John Cooper Clarke created a genre all on his own, reciting trenchant, often hilarious poetry in a thickly accented, adenoidal voice; a deviant British precursor of rap. Looking like **Blonde on Blonde**-era Dylan (but skinnier) and suggesting a mindset lifted from Jack Kerouac or Lenny Bruce, Clarke exists with one foot in literature and the other in rock music, using both but succumbing wholly to neither. On most of his recordings, musical backing is provided by a nebulous organization known as the Invisible Girls, which—besides a nucleus of keyboardist Steve Hopkins and producer Martin Hannett—has included such name-brand players as Pete Shelley and Bill Nelson. When combined on vinyl, the two forces—Clarke as satiric commentator and the Invisible Girls as musical adventurers—make for a unique listening experience.

Où Est la Maison de Fromage?, released

on a Manchester independent label, is a sloppy, ragged, (almost) unaccompanied, poorly-recorded but enthralling hodge-podge—demos, rehearsals and recitations—of pieces that wound up on later albums. Clarke's major-league debut, **Disguise in Love**, contains such classic inventions as "(I Married a) Monster from Outer Space," "Psycle Sluts 1 & 2" and "I Don't Want to Be Nice." The collaboration between words and music works splendidly, although it should be noted that Clarke's approach doesn't vary on two tracks performed a cappella. The music leans heavily to electronics, but varies the sound with guitar and weird noises.

Walking Back to Happiness is a live recording released as a 10-inch EP on clear vinyl. For over 20 minutes, Clarke goes one-on-all against a generally appreciative but partially hostile audience, reciting, jousting, cracking deadly one-liners, dealing with hecklers and being captivating with scathing, funny numbers like "Majorca" (an attack on tourists) and "Twat." As a bonus, the EP closes with a studio track called "Gimmix."

Snap, Crackle [&] Bop matches impressive packaging (the front cover is a photo of a sports coat with working pocket containing a lyric book) with awesomely powerful songs like "Beasley Street," recalling nothing so much as Dylan's "Desolation Row." And while "Conditional Discharge" is a cheap pun about venereal disease, the notable "Thirty Six Hours" is his most songlike effort to date. On it, the Invisible Girls' backing matches the bard's intensity dram for dram, creating dense waves of electronics and electrics that fit the words perfectly.

Me and My Big Mouth collects Clarke's greatest non-hits, drawing equally from the three previous records, and suffices as an ideal introduction and overview.

Zip Style Method, still JCC's most recent release, finds him in a more upbeat humor, and includes a pair of love songs amidst the remorseless satire. The Invisible Girls are at their best, working in a number of idioms. More than any of the other albums, this seems to be a cooperative venture—more organically entwined than autonomous—between poet and players. That's a major development, because it makes Clarke's words stand out less, but convey more. There aren't any bad tracks; although the intensity level isn't up there with "Beasley Street," songs like "Midnight Shift," "The Day the World Stood Still" and "Night People" present dif-

ferent, entertaining sides to Clarke's musical persona. Clarke has continued to perform as a poet, but regrettably has not recorded anything of late.   [iar]

See also *Pauline Murray and the Invisible Girls*.

CLASH

The Clash (nr/CBS) 1977 ●
Give 'Em Enough Rope (Epic) 1978 ●
The Clash (Epic) 1979 ●
London Calling (Epic) 1979 ●
Black Market Clash (Epic) 1980
Sandinista! (Epic) 1980 ●
Combat Rock (Epic) 1982 ●
Cut the Crap (Epic) 1985 ●
The Story of the Clash Volume 1 (Epic) 1988 ●

TOPPER HEADON

Waking Up (nr/Mercury) 1986

That the Clash survived as long as they did and, in fact, proved commercially viable in both the UK and US is a clear testament to rugged integrity and a stubborn refusal to buckle despite enormous adversity, much of it self-induced. The Clash were formed to fall apart, but it took better than seven years for the Joe Strummer-Mick Jones bustup to finally take place.

If any rock band ever insisted on doing it their way, the Clash takes first-place honors, despite the price their nonconformity exacted. Nonetheless (or as a result), they became enormously popular, even in America, where their Top 20 chart success stands as redemptive proof of an indomitable spirit. The Clash received no small amount of criticism over the years: damned for their integrity (or lack thereof); assailed for absorbing black musical styles; attacked for injecting politics into their songs; blamed for changing; blamed for not changing; ridiculed for having ideals; branded sell-outs, hypocrites, rockists, opportunists and worse. Through it all, the Clash consistently proved equal to the task of confounding everyone that ever followed or dealt with them, offering contradictory and inconsistent statements in classic Bob Dylan obfuscatory oratory and generally failing to act in their own self-interest.

With continuous chaos and controversy swirling around them, the Clash still managed to make some of the most brilliant, absorbing, potent and staggering rock'n'roll of all time. Alone save for Elvis Costello and the Sex Pistols, Joe Strummer, Mick Jones and Paul Simonon (plus various drummers) stand as new wave's original and most significant trendsetters; like Costello, the original Clash never made an album that isn't worth owning.

The Clash, 1977's finest LP bar none, was not issued in the US until 1979, and then in radically altered form, adding subsequent single sides and deleting four original tracks, making it paradoxically fragmentary but stronger. In the album's original form, the 14 songs explode in a scathing frenzy of venom and sardonic humor, ranging in subject from unemployment ("Career Opportunities") to the underground music scene ("Garageland") to cultural imperialism ("I'm So Bored with the U.S.A.") to rebellion ("White Riot," "London's Burning," "Hate and War"). Strummer's incomprehensible bellow exudes focused rage, while Jones' flaming guitar work both sets and supersedes the style for countless derivators who followed. Since the original album lacks a lyric sheet (the US label couldn't resist adding one), the exact words were—as is appropriate—undiscernible, but there's no missing the power of the music. A full disc of classics, including the Clash's first stab at reggae, a brilliant rendition of Junior Murvin's "Police and Thieves." (The American LP also included a bonus 45 with two odd numbers recorded a few years later: "Groovy Times" and "Gates of the West.")

The pairing of the fiercely English and (then) anti-commercial Clash with American big-shot producer Sandy Pearlman (Blue Oyster Cult, but also the Dictators) proved controversial but fruitful on **Give 'Em Enough Rope**. By exchanging the band's garageland raunch for heavily overlaid (but crystal-clear) guitars and drums, Pearlman delivered a supercharged rock sound and Strummer and Jones came up with some of their best songs—"Safe European Home," "Tommy Gun," "English Civil War," "Stay Free" and "All the Young Punks." The band's new-found studio sophistication did nothing to blunt their power—quite the opposite, especially in terms of Topper Headon's crisp, authoritative drumming—and their defiant confidence to mix in more liberal amounts of sensitivity and cleverness add to the album's appeal. Jones' vocal on "Stay Free" casts him as the tenderhearted member of the band but, as a guitarist, his work throughout goes against punk's early egalitarian precepts, proudly standing up as a genuine guitar hero for the new age.

London Calling established the Clash's major-league stature, regardless of commercial considerations. The two records, produced by the legendary (and now late) Guy Stevens (Mott the Hoople), stretch over an enormously expanded musical landscape with few weak tracks. Unlike most double albums, **London Calling** needs all four sides to say its piece; while not especially coherent or conceptual, the tracks share a maturity of vision and a consistency of character. Whichever way the band turns, the record bears their unique stamp—from the anti-nuclear throb of the title track to the updated blues oldie, "Brand New Cadillac," to the bebop of "Jimmy Jazz" and the anthemic "Rudie Can't Fail." And that's just the first side! Some of the other stunners are "Death or Glory," "Koka Kola," "Lost in the Supermarket" (Jones' spotlight), "Guns of Brixton" (a powerful reggae rumble featuring Simonon), "Spanish Bombs," "The Right Profile" (about actor Montgomery Clift—how's that for a change of pace?) and "Working for the Clampdown," collectively proof positive that the Clash would not be limited by anyone's expectations. A masterwork.

The Clash's many singles contained as much exciting music as their albums, and a lot of non-LP tracks were issued along the way. Since very few of their early 45s were even released in the US, Epic assembled an odds-and-ends collection, **Black Market Clash**—nine tracks on a 10-inch platter, subsequently reissued as 12-inch. Tracks appended to the US release of the first album were left off here; the two records collectively fill in the non-LP gaps through 1980. Essential items like "Capital Radio One," "Armagideon Time," "The Prisoner" and "City of the Dead" join interesting but less exciting things like versions of "Time Is Tight" and "Pressure Drop." **Black Market Clash** is a worthwhile and entertaining record, not a collection of inferior scraps.

Whatever self-restraint the Clash might once have had evaporated on **Sandinista!**, six sprawling sides of wildly varied styles and, to put it mildly, uneven quality. There are proper songs, kiddie renditions, guest artists coming and going, utter self-indulgent rubbish—you name it, it found its way onto vinyl here, with neither rhyme, rhythm nor evidence of editing. While it may be nice to give the Clash high marks for iconoclasm, much of **Sandinista!** is indefensible, burying one album's worth of sheer excellence in a towering heap of endurance-defying nonsense.

In fairness, the guff doesn't diminish the

LP's greatness, it just makes the gems harder to find. Kudos for Side One ("The Magnificent Seven," "Hitsville U.K.," "Ivan Meets G.I. Joe," "Something About England") and Side Four (Eddy Grant's ace oldie "Police on My Back," "The Call Up," "Washington Bullets") and a few other things. The wide stylistic swath is hypothetically interesting though not musically rewarding; a better-focused album would have been much more powerful and politically meaningful, as the enormous catalogue of social and international concerns dilutes each's effectiveness. If pared down to a single LP (as many fans probably did on tape), **Sandinista!** would have been truly worthy of the Clash.

Returning to a manageable one-disc format, **Combat Rock** found the Clash taking a new musical detour, absorbing and regurgitating American rap and funk with more conviction than ever before (**Sandinista!** contained a few test runs) and also becoming arty enough to invite poet Allen Ginsberg to appear on the record. A bizarre collection of material that seems to be diverging at a blinding rate, the dozen tracks proved extremely popular, yielding two bona fide US chart hits (the simple "Should I Stay or Should I Go?" and the danceable "Rock the Casbah"). Despite slick production possibilities (ace studio hand Glyn Johns "mixed"), the Clash sound more ragged than ever, getting dolled up only for the dance numbers like "Overpowered by Funk," which features a guest rap by Futura 2000. A perplexing but partially entertaining set of sounds from the world's most unpredictable rock band.

Although it wasn't well known at the time, the Clash had split into two musical camps. With commercial success tugging on one side, abiding fascination for "black music" on the other, and problematic idealism presenting a genuine challenge up the middle, the Clash finally rended, with Strummer and Simonon unexpectedly booting Jones out of the band. Joined by three young players, the remaining pair later toured and recorded **Cut the Crap**, ostensibly a Clash album. With one notable exception (a movingly mournful anthem, "This Is England"), **Crap** is just that, a painfully tired and hopelessly inept attempt to catch up with an elusive, fading legend. Strummer and manager Bernard Rhodes co-wrote the songs (a dead giveaway of major creative problems right there), but they needn't have bothered: Sham 69 outtakes would've been preferable to these prosaic, forgettable shouters. "We Are the Clash," indeed. Shortly after the album appeared, the lineup dissolved. Jones played with General Public in the studio during that band's formative months, and unveiled his new group, Big Audio Dynamite, to great critical acclaim, in late 1985. (The story doesn't quite end there: Strummer wound up taking a significant role in B.A.D.'s second album.)

Eleven years after the Clash's debut and five since their demise, a two-record compilation was released, thankfully forgetting **Crap** had ever happened. The running order is far from chronological; still, the 28-song selection, despite some notable omissions, conveys the band's diversity and depth. The only rarity is the 1977 London tube interview portion of "Capital Radio One," originally released on a giveaway flexi-disc. Overall, the remastered sound quality is fairly clear and hot, even on the old stuff; liner notes by one Albert Transom (probably Strummer) may shed little light for neophytes, but are amusing enough. Suggestions for **Volume 2**: "Hate and War," "I'm So Bored with the U.S.A.," "The Prisoner," "Jail Guitar Doors," "All the Young Punks" and "Hitsville U.K."

Topper Headon, who vanished from the Clash and the music business soon after the release of **Combat Rock**, reportedly because of drug problems (Terry Chimes—"Tory Crimes" of the first LP—replaced him for live work), launched a solo career in 1986 with **Waking Up**. Ambitious and plucky but surprisingly underwhelming, this horn-soul album is so humble his drums aren't even mixed high enough. Despite an impressive talent roster (including ex-Blockhead and frequent Clash collaborator Mickey Gallagher and ex-Beck guitarist Bobby Tench), Headon's songs are amateurish, and the arrangements routine and uninvolving; even another version of Booker T's can't-miss "Time Is Tight" doesn't hit a nerve. (Chimes went on to form the Cherry Bombz with former members of Hanoi Rocks and Toto Coelo.) [iar]

See also *Big Audio Dynamite, Mikey Dread, Ellen Foley, Ian Hunter, 101ers, Joe Strummer.*

CLASSIX NOUVEAUX

Night People (nr/Liberty) 1981
Classix Nouveaux (Liberty) 1981

La Vérité (nr/Liberty) 1982
Secret (nr/Liberty) 1983

This quartet of poseurs, led by singer/multi-instrumentalist Sal Solo (whose totally bald pate and permanently serious expression make him resemble a constipated Yul Brynner), uses both synthesizers and regular rock tools (guitar, bass, drums, sax) to turn out talented if shallow dance rock that's utterly pretentious but not unattractive.

Night People (retitled **Classix Nouveaux** in the US) actually includes a couple of enjoyable tracks ("Guilty" stands out) that are straightforward and melodic enough to be recognizable as songs; the remainder of the record consists of windy instrumentals and foolish sci-fi tales. Their second effort, **La Vérité**, goes over the top, being far too intricate and overblown. Turn down the volume and the music serves as subtle ambient noise.

Produced by Alex Sadkin and employing guest musicians to add horns and other embellishments, **Secret** takes a more aggressive and rhythmic attack, aiming straight for the dance-floor with loud, energetic numbers like "All Around the World" and "No Other Way." They still find room to include refined and textured creations (à la Japan) and even an engaging pop song, "Forever and a Day." Although Solo's singing remains the band's least enticing feature, the impressive variety and sophistication makes **Secret** the band's best album, one well worth repeated playings.

Sal Solo has most recently fashioned a career in keeping with his surname.   [iar]

CLEAN
Boodle Boodle Boodle EP (NZ Flying Nun) 1981
Great Sounds EP (NZ Flying Nun) 1982
Oddities [tape] (NZ Flying Nun) 1983
Live Dead Clean EP (NZ Flying Nun) 1986
Compilation (Aus. Au-go-go) 1986
     (Homestead) 1988 ●

GREAT UNWASHED
Clean Out of Our Minds (NZ Flying Nun) 1983
Singles (NZ Flying Nun) 1983

BAILTER SPACE
Nelsh (NZ Flying Nun) 1987

If all Flying Nun bands sound alike to you, don't feel bad: they're supposed to. Peter Gutteridge, for instance, began with the Clean, helped form the Chills, returned to join the Great Unwashed, then spent some

time in the Alpaca Brothers and the Puddle. Clean drummer Hamish Kilgour continued on to the Great Unwashed and then formed Bailter Space where he was joined by the formerly Unwashed Ross Humphries. Hamish also has a guitar-playing brother named David who was with him in the Clean and involved in the Chills. The Clean's **Boodle Boodle Boodle** EP was produced by Tall Dwarf Chris Knox, adding legitimacy to the sonic similarity between the two bands. The list goes on. Figuring it all out is like dissecting a family tree where every other band-member is a Siamese twin. But if you could put all the information together to make some semblance of sense, you'd find the Clean somehow at the center of the whole story.

"Tally Ho!," a 1981 single, was Flying Nun's first release. A fuzz-encrusted do-it-yourself slice of rough pop with deliberately unmelodic, sing-songy male vocals and scratchy lead guitar, it jangles through dramatic pace changes before ending in sparse applause. Sales funded a follow-up EP, the equally poppy **Boodle Boodle Boodle**, which was meticulously recorded on Knox's home tape recorder. Those and other early tracks are assembled on **Compilation**, where the percussively hard-strummed acoustic guitar of "Billy Two" meets the hesitantly squirmy soft psychedelia of "Point That Thing Somewhere Else" (slow-paced single-stroke drum beat and sitaresque '60s guitar lines). A thoroughly enjoyable and lighthearted festival of pop fuzz, it ranges from the silliness of a Donald Duck guest appearance through artful backward-tracking.

What it doesn't do is show how great the band was live. **Live Dead Clean** does. From the melodically scratchy guitar dips of "Happy Birthday John" (which Hamish Kilgour describes as being "about time passing, people dying and nuclear bombs going off") through the powerfully Western-tinged "Attack of the Teddy Bears," it's a high-energy (though sometimes low-fi) excursion into pleasantly scraped pop guitar.

The Clean didn't last long. Their whole recording career was over within 18 months. But the split was amicable and, since the two founding Kilgours were still brothers, they formed a new Clean (jokingly named the Great Unwashed in response to numerous cleanliness puns that always cropped up when the band was reviewed). The Unwashed had (pun unintentional) a cleaner sound than the original band but still made vigorously vibrant rock with poppy chords, avant twists, fragile vocals and infectious warmth.

Bailter Space combines simple vocal styles with low-budget (but always clear) production, crisp drumming, tambourine pounding, rusty-gate guitar and not-quite perky keyboards to give **Nelsh** the shimmery, mildly avant-garde rough pop that characterizes Flying Nun records.   ['e]

JOHNNY CLEGG & SAVUKA
See *Juluka.*

CLIMIE FISHER
See *Naked Eyes.*

CLOCK DVA
White Souls in Black Suits [tape]
(nr/Industrial) 1980
Thirst (nr/Fetish) 1981 (nr/Doublevision) 1985
Advantage (nr/Polydor) 1983
Breakdown EP (Relativity) 1983

Appearing in 1980 and allied with industrial bands like Throbbing Gristle and Cabaret Voltaire, Sheffield's Clock DVA aped the sound of British white soul groups of the day on **White Souls in Black Suits**, though the mock-soul energy is strangely vitiated by urban metal noise that distorts the songs around the edges. Eerie but captivating, with a punchy beat. (Although available in England only on cassette, **White Souls** *was* released on disc in Italy.)

On **Thirst**, the band maintained an interest in dance music, but abandoned soul pretensions for electro-noise, and the album is a playground of startling, unearthly machine chants. **Advantage** is their strongest, most powerful LP, a funky concoction of intense dance-powered bass/drums drive with splatters of feedback, angst-ridden vocals by mainman Adi Newton, tape interruptions and dollops of white-noise sax and trumpet. The band also digresses into devolved be-bop. Released as a British single from **Advantage**, "Breakdown" was also issued on an American EP, joined by an extended version, another great LP cut and a mesmerizing take on the Velvet Underground's "Black Angel's Death Song."

Clock DVA's often-shifting lineup provided members for the Box, Siouxsie and the Banshees, and even Gun Club. After Clock DVA broke up, Newtown formed the Anti-Group, whose first single was produced by Cabaret Voltaire.   [sg/iar]
See also *Box.*

CLUSTER
See *Brian Eno.*

COCKNEY REJECTS
Greatest Hits Vol. 1 (nr/EMI) 1980
Greatest Hits Vol. 2 (nr/EMI) 1980
Greatest Hits Vol. 3 (nr/EMI) 1981
The Power and the Glory (nr/EMI) 1981
The Wild Ones (nr/a.k.a.) 1982
We Are the Firm (nr/Dojo) 1986

These London skinheads were discovered in the early days of British post-Pistols punk by Sham 69 leader Jimmy Pursey, who co-produced their first album. The Rejects gained immortality of a sort on **Vol. 2** by coining a name for the UK punk resurgence with the chant "Oi Oi Oi." **Vol. 3** (reasonably subtitled **Live and Loud**) was recorded in a studio with a vociferous audience of fans adding background vocals to the band's fast rock'n'roll noise.

While retaining the aggressiveness and spunk, **The Power and the Glory** took a big chance by trying such experimental ventures as acoustic guitar, melodies, musicianship and semi-tasteful artwork. The album contains impressive moments, especially noteworthy given the Rejects' prior blitzkrieg approach. Not stunning, but their best effort, and an LP of interest not solely to punk aficionados.

Having gotten "art" out of their systems (and switching labels), the Rejects' next move (subsequently not such an uncommon gambit for punk bands) was a heavy metal album. Produced by UFO bassist Pete Way, **The Wild Ones** is unfortunately terrible; although the distance from teen punk sludge to adult metal sludge is not very far, this lot was much better suited for numbers like "Greatest Cockney Rip-off."   [iar]

COCONUTS
See *Kid Creole and the Coconuts.*

COCTEAU TWINS
Garlands (nr/4AD) 1982 ●
Lullabies EP (nr/4AD) 1982
Head Over Heels (nr/4AD) 1983 ●

Sunburst and Snowblind EP (nr/4AD)
    1983 •
Pearly-Dewdrops' Drop EP (nr/4AD) 1984
Treasure (nr/4AD) 1984 •
Aikea-Guinea EP (nr/4AD) 1985
Treasure/Aikea-Guinea (Can. Vertigo) 1985
The Pink Opaque (4AD-Relativity) 1985 •
Tiny Dynamine EP (nr/4AD) 1985
Echoes in a Shallow Bay EP (nr/4AD) 1985
Tiny Dynamine/Echoes in a Shallow Bay
    (Can. Vertigo) 1985 •
Victorialand (nr/4AD) 1986 •
Love's Easy Tears EP (4AD-Relativity) 1986

HAROLD BUDD/ELIZABETH FRASER/ROBIN GUTHRIE/SIMON RAYMONDE

The Moon and the Melodies (4AD-Relativity)
1986 •

The Cocteau Twins are actually a Scottish trio who, on their first album, add a borrowed drum synthesizer to vocals, bass and heavily treated guitar, producing atmospheric dirges with rich textures and little structure. Elizabeth Fraser's vocals are essentially tuneless, and the backing goes nowhere, but it's all artily agreeable enough for those with the patience to wade through the murk and mire.

Head Over Heels shows marked improvement, both in terms of songwriting technique and vocal performances. "Sugar Hiccup" (a different version of which appears on **Sunburst and Snowblind**) exhibits a stronger melodic sense, and Fraser's voice soars on songs like "In the Gold Dust Rush" and "Musette and Drums." The record also offers more varied tempos: the rather Bansheelike "In Our Angelhood" rocks more than anything previous by the Cocteaus.

Sunburst and Snowblind is a strong four-song EP, well-honed for those who'd rather meet the Cocteau Twins in smaller doses. Delicate, precious yet accessible, the instrumental backing is a little thinner and the vocals more confident. **Head Over Heels** and **Sunburst and Snowblind** were issued together on CD and cassette.

Pearly-Dewdrops' Drop strips down the sound a little further; "The Spangle Maker" and the title track even forego much of the reverb that permeates their records. By this point, the Cocteau Twins had become ubiquitous figures in the alternative record charts and a major live attraction as well. **Treasure** stands as their finest hour. It contains no black and white sounds—just intriguing shades of gray—immersing the listener in a full range of emotions, with Fraser's now-powerful voice alternately full of sorrow, joy, calm and fury. The production is meticulously detailed; increased use of keyboards and drums provides a wider range of tone colors. All ten diverse tracks work well; "Persephone" and "Ivo" are particularly noteworthy.

Since **Treasure**, the Cocteaus have been running a little short on new ideas. In 1985, they released three four-song EPs. **Aikea-Guinea** could pass as outtakes from previous albums, while **Tiny Dynamine** and **Echoes in a Shallow Bay** are virtually identical, not only in cover art but in sound. On **Victorialand**, an album issued the following year, almost all the instrumental backing is psychedelic-tinged treated acoustic guitar. While that opens things up and gives Fraser's voice more room, the material again recalls earlier records. All of these recent works, if heard individually, are pleasant, effective mood music; taken as a whole, however, they're all cut from the same cloth.

The Moon and the Melodies (not credited as a Cocteau Twins record in name) enlists pianist/minimalist composer/Eno collaborator Harold Budd and gives him equal billing. Let's just say that the results don't exactly kick butt; the band's remaining redeeming feature, Fraser's voice, sounds noticeably uninspired on the (only) three tracks on which she appears. Firmly entrenched in the dangerous realm of New Age mush, those familiar with the band's recent work will know what this one sounds like before the needle hits the record (or before the laser beam hits the CD). Highly recommended for anyone who purchased crystals for the Harmonic Convergence.

Love's Easy Tears is four tracks of déjà vu. **The Pink Opaque**, a career-spanning compilation, was originally issued as a British CD; the vinyl version became the band's first American release. The Cocteau Twins have recorded some of the '80s most rewarding records; here's hoping they have some more tricks up their sleeves. [dgs]

See also *This Mortal Coil.*

CODE BLUE

Code Blue (Warner Bros.) 1980
True Story (Index-Enigma) 1982

LA-based Code Blue may be best remembered for the fact that its first album was released encased in a blue plastic bag; the group, which actually had talent, fell victim to the post-Knack backlash against Angelino power pop. The brainchild of original Motels guitarist Dean Chamberlain, Code Blue came together after the first version of the Motels disbanded in 1977, with drummer Randall Marsh and bassist Gary Tibbs (Vibrators, Roxy Music) completing the lineup. Despite three good musicians, some decent material and lofty artistic aspirations, the combination of the Knack-lash and the lack of any really killer tracks doomed the LP to prompt oblivion.   [ds]

COIL

Scatology (nr/Some Bizzare) 1986
Horse Rotorvator (Some Bizzare-Relativity) 1987 ●
The Anal Staircase EP (Some Bizzare-Relativity) 1987
Gold is the Metal (nr/Threshold House) 1988

Upon the demise of Throbbing Gristle, Peter Christopherson teamed up with Genesis P-Orridge and other assorted oddballs to form Psychic TV. It must be hard to work with P-Orridge forever, as Christopherson left PTV to start up Coil with John Balance and Stephen Thrower. Playing a wide variety of styles with very interesting arrangements and pan-cultural borrowings, Coil's weirdness manifests itself in a totally different way from that of its predecessors. An AIDS-era cover of "Tainted Love," done as a funeral dirge, is perhaps in questionable taste, but shows just one level at which this band operates.

Horse Rotorvator (which contains two of The Anal Staircase's three cuts) is a mélange of electronic tone poems of varying textures and styles, from haunting drones to detective-movie jazz (complete with a Clint Ruin horn section) to quasi-Middle Eastern/African modalities. Rather than falling into the trap of making an academic exercise of the whole thing though, Coil breathes life into the proceedings with spoken/sung vocals mixed up front and all sorts of acoustic instruments interjected among the electronics. A strong album that could have been a disaster if done incorrectly.   [dgs]

LLOYD COLE AND THE COMMOTIONS

Rattlesnakes (Geffen) 1984 ●
Easy Pieces (Geffen) 1985 ●

Mainstream (nr/Polydor) 1987 (Capitol) 1988 ●

Bursting with promise as both singer and writer on his first LP, Scotland's Lloyd Cole puts the post-beatnik lyrical outlook of a young Bob Dylan to textured backing. Rattlesnakes' strength lies in Cole's well-constructed folk-rock tunes and casually emotive vocals; the four Commotions make a tight, talented unit capable of subtlety and power in many voices. Cole's prose occasionally overreaches (but never by much); lyrics that hit their mark do so sharply. Those hypersensitive to creeping Dylanitis will find Rattlesnakes a bit hard to accept; open-minded adventurers will be immediately engrossed.

Easy Pieces, smoothly produced by Langer/Winstanley, succumbs to hazards threatened on the first LP. While the solid band remains unprepossessing, Cole's vocals are overly stylized; quoting Bolan and the Beatles, his lyrics veer towards meaningless self-importance. Given that it's not strikingly different from Rattlesnakes, Easy Pieces makes you wonder why you liked the band in the first place. (The CD has three extra tracks.)

Cole regained his footing and momentum on Mainstream: factoring in maturity and experience (his and the band's), it actually winds up a better album than the first. Subtly cast and deftly played arrangements that range from Aztec Camera airiness to fleshed-out light rock keep songs like "Sean Penn Blues" and "Mister Malcontent" from drifting into ponderousness; Cole's affecting singing is likewise finely wrought. "Hey Rusty," an ace song about an old friendship that builds tension slowly, and the shimmering "From the Hip" are highlights of this welcome return.   [iar]

WANDA COLEMAN
See X.

HENRIETTA COLLINS AND THE WIFEBEATING CHILDHATERS
See Henry Rollins.

PAUL COLLINS' BEAT
See Beat.

COLOR ME GONE

See *Marti Jones.*

COLOURBOX

Colourbox EP (nr/4AD) 1984 ●
Colourbox (nr/4AD) 1985 ●

Although this London trio's music is not particularly avant-garde, the group does fit in with the uncompromising 4AD family due to their steadfast determination to totally redefine a musical style. Instrumentalists Martyn and brother Steven Young, along with vocalist Lorita Grahame, take soul places it's never been—and is unlikely to go again.

The eponymous EP—three hours of sessions edited down to a half-hour of hip-hop/scratch and reggae/dub experiments, with a graphic depiction of horses mating on the cover—largely earned its negative reception. The LP, however, is a vast improvement, an eclectic display that embraces the entire realm of dance music: reggae, vibrant industrial dance, hard'n'heavy funk, '50s R&B. Screeching guitar on the almost-metal "Maniac" segues into the highlight, a sparkling remake of the Supremes' "You Keep Me Hanging On." (Footnote: the cassette of **Colourbox** is double-length, adding an LP's worth of remixes; some copies of the LP have the same on a bonus disc.)

Other than the occasional one-off single, Colourbox remained unexpectedly dormant following the release of the LP. However, Steven and Martyn did achieve notoriety in 1987 due to their involvement with M/A/R/R/S (the "S" for Steven and the "M" for Martyn), the band behind the influential club smash "Pump Up the Volume." [ag]

COLOUR FIELD

Virgins and Philistines (Chrysalis) 1985
The Colour Field EP (Chrysalis) 1986
Deception (Chrysalis) 1987 ●

Vocalist Terry Hall's post-Fun Boy Three band started out slowly, with just an eponymous single in 1984, but the trio's first album a year later was well worth the wait. **Virgins and Philistines** kicks off brilliantly with the mock-"96 Tears" organ intro to "Can't Get Enough of You Baby," itself a fine imitation of Georgie Fame-era beat music. The music mixes metaphors, from stripped-down Fun Boys rock to samba, folk and jazzy '60s R&B; Hall's sharp tongue and the band's intelligent creativity make each

track different. Of special note: a shimmering acoustic version of the Roches' "Hammond Song" and "Pushing Up Daisies," a vicious condemnation of celebrity. Drama, beauty, ideas and energy make **Virgins and Philistines** provocative, stylish and memorable.

The EP—featuring an expanded four-piece lineup—contains a pair of live cuts ("Pushing Up Daisies" and "Yours Sincerely") plus four excellent new tracks, including the memorable "Faint Hearts," an almost psychedelic folk tune, and "Things Could Be Beautiful," a soulful rocker.

Hall is the only person pictured on the disappointing **Deception**, a subdued and mechanical-sounding LP that employs a guest drum programmer, a keyboard player and Tears for Fears guitarist Roland Orzabal. Producer Richard Gottehrer misplaces the resonant stylistic variety and energy that previously typified the group, leaving pale jazzy support—occasionally resembling a less constipated Dream Academy—for Hall's characteristically wispy singing. The material ("Badlands," "Confession," Boyce/Hart's "She") isn't bad, but the facile arrangements leave Hall barking up the wrong tree. [iar]

COMATEENS

Comateens (Cachalot) 1981
Pictures on a String (Virgin-Mercury) 1983
Deal with It (Virgin-Mercury) 1984

This New York trio played a bouncy brand of dance rock rooted in chintzy '60s Farfisa organ pop and spooky horror-movie soundtrack music. The group first gained recognition in 1979 with a homemade single that featured a stripped-down version of Bowie's "TVC 15," which they re-recorded for their first LP. After a number of personnel changes, the lineup solidified at Lyn Byrd (keyboards), Oliver North (guitar, not international subterfuge), Nic North (bass) and synthetic drums. **Comateens** is a delightful distillation of the aforementioned influences, with neat contrasts between the thin-sounding synth fills and the chunky, rhythmic guitar. There's also a three-track 12-inch—on the same label—of the hypnotic "Ghosts," the pure pop "Late Night City" and the theme for TV's *Munsters,* which pretty much sums up the Comateens' music.

Signed to a major label, the Comateens made **Pictures on a String**, which diverges into rock quirkiness and danceable commercialism, pushing a powerful disco beat on

"Get Off My Case," "Cinnamon" and other numbers. The rock-oriented material, especially the Beatlesque "Comateens," with its awesome fuzz-blizzard guitar solo, and a weird overdrive cover of the oldie "Uptown," are more intriguing; the dance tracks don't really go anywhere.

With a guest drummer and veteran hit-maker Pete Solley producing, **Deal with It** sublimates the big beat into various styles, much the way Blondie often did. Rather than base tunes on rhythms, these songs explore widely differing pop modes, welded to strong, emphasized drum tracks, resulting in a fascinating mix full of unexpected, delightful juxtapositions. This is the album that finally and fully realizes the Comateens' hybridizing potential. [ds/iar]

COMMUNARDS

Communards (London-MCA) 1986 ●
Red (London-MCA) 1987 ●

When Glaswegian falsetto vocalist Jimmy Somerville split from Bronski Beat in 1985 and formed the Communards with classically-trained pianist Richard Coles, many assumed this group would take an even more determined political stance than the Bronskis' gay activism. Indeed, the pair participates in the Socialist Red Wedge movement but, graphics aside, you'd never know it from their records.

The first track on **Communards** is an hysterical hi-energy remake of "Don't Leave Me This Way," the 1977 Thelma Houston hit; the remainder mixes boring dance music with overly precious arrangements (strings, horns and the orchestral kitchen sink in spots) of songs that occasionally lean towards light opera. Except for those whose homophobia intrudes, the lyrics about sex and romance are merely tired and trivial. Worse, the group's best asset is squandered: Somerville's inimitable voice is totally unsuited for this half-baked material.

Endorsing disco's ongoing commercial viability, the duo did a version of "Never Can Say Goodbye" (following Gloria Gaynor's interpretation, not the Jacksons) on **Red**. Stephen Hague's keyboard-oriented Euro-dance production (half of the record; Jimmy and Richard did the rest) better suits the much improved material, trimming the rococo excess for a slicker, more appealing sound. This thoughtful, melodic album is as likable as the first is cloying.

Discographical curios: by the end of 1987, the group had issued 34 discrete singles and EPs (counting remixes, repackages and alternate formats). The **Communards** CD adds a song and a remix. [iar]

COMSAT ANGELS

Red Planet EP (nr/Junta) 1979
Waiting for a Miracle (nr/Polydor) 1980
Sleep No More (nr/Polydor) 1981
Comsat Angels EP (nr/Polydor) 1981
Fiction (nr/Polydor) 1982
Land (Jive) 1983
Independence Day EP (nr/Jive) 1984
Enz (nr/Polydor) 1984
7 Day Weekend (Jive) 1985
Chasing Shadows (Island) 1987 ●

Like Joy Division and the Cure, Sheffield's Comsat Angels have mastered the art of atmospherics; only nominally involved in rock'n'roll at the outset, they were actually interested in creating haunting mood music. Firm beats play against melancholy melodies and hushed vocals to create the impression you're spying on someone's inner turmoil, an approach which is morosely fascinating on **Waiting for a Miracle** (hailed in one UK paper as "the greatest debut LP of all time," it remains a stunning masterwork) and tunes like "Total War" and "Independence Day" (both included live on the 1984 EP).

Sleep No More, morose yet oddly beautiful, is a hotbed of tension, frayed edges, shattered nerves and spilled coffee. Too somber for some, its tone too dark and scary for others; given a chance, it's a fascinating, underrated and often misunderstood work, ambitious as opposed to accommodating or immediately accessible.

Fiction is a full-fledged recovery, with an unsettling sense of tension underlying Stephen Fellows' dejected vocals and guitar on "Ju-Ju Money" and "Zinger." However, even this success raises questions about how much longer the band could prosper working in such a seemingly uncommercial style.

They did attempt to expand, trying their hand in the synth-pop market, a radical departure. Switching labels and getting American release for the first time, the Comsat Angels ran into name problems and had to be billed as the C.S. Angels for the US. **Land**, produced by Mike Howlett, fails i1580 effort to cast them as a variant on A Flock of Seagulls, but does contain a number of upbeat, memorable tunes that resemble a poppier, less serious Simple Minds. The first side especially is one of the genre's finest hours (well, quarter-hours).

The subsequent EP takes two good songs off the LP and adds three early tracks; **Enz** is a compilation of pre-Jive releases.

The liner notes on the back cover of **7 Day Weekend** are downright sad ("We had a stretch of good luck, which rapidly turned into bad . . . "); the music fortunately is more self-assured and dignified. Produced variously by Mtume, Chris Tsangarides and Mike Howlett, there is scant sonic continuity, but that causes overall little damage.

Dissatisfied with their musical progress, the Comsats retrenched, once again switching labels (Island signed them on the advice of singer Robert Palmer, who claims they're his favorite band), and totally abandoning their four-year synth-pop experiment. **Chasing Shadows** thus picks up where **Fiction** left off (in fact, the group has called it their fourth LP), with the return of thudding drums, booming bass and echo guitar, while mixing in some of the poppier melodies of the better tracks on **Land** and **7 Day Weekend**. If not nearly as impressive as the early LPs, it's still a strong record with a few choice cuts, the best being "Under the Influence." [jy/jr]

CONCRETE BLONDE
Concrete Blonde (IRS) 1986 ●
DREAM 6
Dream 6 EP (Happy Hermit) 1983
EARLE MANKEY
Real World EP (Happy Hermit) 1985

The original guitarist and bassist in Half-nelson-cum-Sparks were the Mankey brothers, Earle and Jim. When the Maels left for England without them, the former quickly became a well-known producer on the LA scene and beyond. It took Jim a lot longer to re-enter the spotlight, but Concrete Blonde proved, at least commercially, worth the wait.

Jim's collaboration with singer/bassist Johnette Napolitano began in Dream 6, whose six-song 12-inch EP, co-produced by Earle, is an intriguing, unassuming minor item. Using the same organizational chart as the Police, Dream 6 here draws on various styles, offering little personality besides the vocals, which are plain but pleasant.

Replacing drummer Michael Murphy with Harry Rushakoff, Dream 6 became Concrete Blonde, signed to IRS and released a terrible album that sounds like half-finished demos no one with ears would give a second listen. Napolitano's untrained voice is remarkably unattractive (especially when she tries too hard to ape Chrissie Hynde); the guitar playing imitates everyone from Mark Knopfler to Andy Summers on duff songs that thrust along with neither focus nor flair. Even George Harrison's "Beware of Darkness" is left for dead in a pointless cover version.

Between studio stints with Dream 6 and Concrete Blonde, Earle—who launched his solo career with a nifty 1978 single ("Mau Mau" b/w "Crazy") and an overlapping 1981 EP—issued the six-song **Real World**. Johnette N. "designed" the cover (the art is an adorable primitive portrait of the artist by his son) and, along with brother Jim, "yells" on one track. "Bigger Than Life" has tongue-in-cheek Nick Lowe charm and harmonies Brian Wilson might enjoy; otherwise **Real World** passes by quickly and uneventfully.

[iar]

CONFLICT
Live at Centro Iberico EP (nr/Xntrix) 1982
It's Time to See Who's Who (nr/Corpus Christi) 1983
Increase the Pressure (nr/Mortarhate) 1984
From Protest to Resistance (nr/Mortarhate) 1985
The Ungovernable Force (nr/Mortarhate) 1986
Turning Rebellion into Money (Mortarhate-Rough Trade) 1987
Only Stupid Bastards Help EMI (nr/Mortarhate) 1988

I'm not sure what to think about the music of a band that informs me that "three members are vegetarians" and then tattles on the one—Paco—who isn't. The sleeve of the second album by these Crass-family anarchists also notes that the band "still wear articles of leather" but they've gotten down to "just boots," which "they will continue to wear until they are useless" but "will not buy more." I certainly respect people with a highly developed and self-disciplined political consciousness, but I can't shake the feeling that a record album should do more than announce how deep the musicians' commitment runs. In the rock world, only the young and the gullible expect their favorite bands to abide by any lofty personal standards.

119

All that aside, Conflict is a pretty good punk band, powered with fire and intelligence. The first album has incredibly ornate artwork and songs about media, Vietnam, vegetarianism (Smiths fans should note Conflict's "Meat Means Murder" here) and other proto-anarchist issues. **Increase the Pressure** is a more proletarian production with black and white artwork; the LP itself is half-studio (dynamic) and half-live (raucous). This time out, the prominent issue illustrated on the graphics is Save the Seals; songs attack cruise missles, the music press, the police, etc. with undiminished zeal and venom.

The double-live **Turning Rebellion into Money** was recorded in April 1987 at a London show; the back cover enumerates the progressive organizations sharing—as per the title's promise—the proceeds. The sleeve lists nine members of Conflict who appear here and seven more who don't, making them easily the world's biggest punk-rock musical collective. The 32 artless punk tunes, a veritable best-of-Conflict collection, bark out with righteous guitar-and-sax rage at every topic imaginable, from specific events to assorted socio-economic-political issues.   [iar]

CONNELLS
Darker Days (Black Park) 1986 (Black
  Park-TVT) 1987
Boylan Heights (TVT) 1987 ●

This North Carolina combo, led by guitarist Michael Connell and his bassist brother David, possess a fragile, vaguely Celtic melodic sense that nicely complements the introspective lyrics, making for music that combines the best impulses of Southern guitar jangle and the sensitive singer-songwriter tradition.

Darker Days broods a bit too intently, and suffers from Doug MacMillan's awkward, affected vocals. The band sounds too inexperienced to properly execute their sophisticated songwriting and arranging ideas, but enough obvious talent shines through to make the album a standout in the new-Southern-pop sweepstakes.

The Mitch Easter-produced **Boylan Heights** is altogether more graceful, as the band has matured into a distinctive enough unit to do justice to Michael's yearning collegiate considerations of love, war and alienation. MacMillan's vocals are likewise considerably more effective, lending emotional authority to swirling folk-rockers like

"Scotty's Lament" and "Try," as well as fragile spectres like "Pawns" and "Choose a Side."   [hd]

CONTORTIONS
See *James Chance.*

CONTRACTIONS
Something Broke (Trotter) 1984

Now sadly disbanded, San Francisco's Contractions (originally from Austin, Texas) were a marvelous, criminally underrated female trio with great material (all three wrote and sang), solid playing and a unique earthy sound somewhere to the left of pop. Although the album could have been sequenced and mastered better, its ten numbers are varied, original, engaging and memorable. Unlike almost all other bands composed exclusively of women, the Contractions totally downplay gender issues—they're neither overtly feminist, sex-image-oriented or self-conscious, finding the ideal out by simply being an excellent rock band. (Also of interest: the album was produced by one of very few women in the field, Lisa Wexler.) [iar]

COOLIES
dig..? (DB) 1986
Doug (DB) 1988 ●

These Georgia jokesters made an underground splash with **dig..?,** a collection of goofy Simon and Garfunkel covers (plus a version of Paul Anka's "Having My Baby"). Great concept for a frat-party set; the psychedelic-funk "Scarborough Fair" and surf-instrumental "Mrs. Robinson" would have made chuckleworthy B-sides, but the idea of devoting an entire LP to such tomfoolery is a product of the same sort of thinking that produced **Having Fun with Elvis on Stage.**

Amazingly, the Coolies followed the one-joke **dig..?** with the brilliant **Doug,** a trenchant "rock opera" about a skinhead who murders a transvestite short-order cook, gets rich by publishing his victim's recipes, falls into paranoia and substance abuse and ends up in the gutter. The sad tale is related through ingenious knockoffs of the Who ("Cook Book"), John Lennon ("Poverty"), the Replacements ("Coke Light Ice"), rap ("Pussy Cook") and metal ("The Last Supper"), and in a comic book—not included with the cassette or CD, alas—designed by

Jack Logan, of *Pete Buck Comics* fame. A quantum leap from its predecessor's one-dimensional silliness, **Doug** is a work of demented genius. [hd]

JULIAN COPE
World Shut Your Mouth (nr/Mercury) 1984 •
Fried (nr/Mercury) 1984 •
Julian Cope EP (Island) 1986 •
Saint Julian (Island) 1987 •

Welsh-born Liverpool legend (now resettled in a British town called Tamworth) Julian Cope called a halt to The Teardrop Explodes during 1983 sessions for their third album and decided it was time to set off on a solo career instead. Aided by the Teardrops' drummer and a guitarist, Cope took the songs he'd written for the band and finished them as **World Shut Your Mouth** (which does not contain the song of that title), a highly inventive take on '60s psychedelia. Mainly blending weird sounds with charming pop, his acceptably inelegant voice and period organ playing add substantial personality to the non-nostalgic venture. The humorous and sensitive lyrics may be a touch *too* sensitive in spots, but Cope's openness and fanciful streak undercut any semblance of pretentiousness.

The title and sleeve photos (he's pictured hiding under a huge tortoise shell) of **Fried** suggest Cope's mental state at the time. This flaky collection is energetic and less stylized than the first; rocking forthrightness, intuitive musicianship and a strong backing quartet keep it from drifting away on disoriented meanderings like "Bill Drummond Said," "Laughing Boy" and "O King of Chaos." A fine, disturbing and bewildering document of a man on the edge.

The confident stomp of "World Shut Your Mouth," a brilliant 1986 British hit first issued in the US on the waters-testing **Julian Cope** EP and the following year included as the centerpiece of the triumphant **Saint Julian** album, proudly announced Cope's full recovery and return to action. The rip-roaring EP adds two originals and brilliant covers of Pere Ubu ("Non Alignment Pact") and the 13th Floor Elevators ("She's Got Levitation"). **Saint Julian**, produced by Ed Stasium, proceeds from there, a loud and melodic collection of uniformly delectable tunes that reflect Cope's idiosyncratic personality and imagination. [iar]

STEWART COPELAND
Rumble Fish (A&M) 1983
The Rhythmatist (A&M) 1985 •
The Equalizer & Other Cliff Hangers (No Speak-IRS) 1988 •

KLARK KENT
Music Madness from the Kinetic Kid (IRS) 1980

Though possessing competence on all the necessary instruments, not to mention a homely yet winning boy-next-doorish voice, Police drummer Stewart Copeland—in a one-off guise as Welsh looney Klark Kent—turns in less a do-it-yourself showcase than a mildly amusing show of self-indulgence, pressed on 10 inches of green vinyl in a K-shaped jacket, no less! There are plums to be found in the tongue-in-cheek pop-punk of "Don't Care" and a clever Zappaesque instrumental, "Kinetic Ritual," but the other six tracks are merely variations on those two styles.

Three years later, with the Police nearing an end, Copeland launched a career in film and TV soundtracks by writing, producing and playing (except horns and strings) the music for Francis Coppola's *Rumble Fish.* The atmospheric instrumentals downplay drums; some are strongly enough structured that they could support lyrics. "Don't Box Me In," an actual song co-written and vocalized by ex-Wall of Voodooer Stan Ridgway, is easily the album's highlight.

Copeland's second solo record is the soundtrack to an African safari video. Described on the sleeve as "a curious blend of musical snatches from Tanzania, Kenya, Burundi, Zaire, the Congo and Buckinghamshire," **The Rhythmatist** is variously a rock album with Africanisms layered on and a rock interpretation (or imitation) thereof. The blurry line between what is genuine and what Copeland has made of whole Anglo-American cloth is disturbing, to say the least, and there's obviously real African music where this dubious rock star contraption came from. Still, the invigorating record sounds lovely, especially thanks to his collaborator, vocalist Ray Lema.

Copeland's latest one-man-orchestra instrumental release collects music done for television's *The Equalizer,* along with unrelated but harmonious new compositions. Favoring keyboards (seemingly piano and organ; the sketchy credits indicate reliance on a Fairlight synthesizer) and strong rhythms, Copeland's technically impressive work here occasionally recalls some of Keith Emerson's lighter crypto-classical moments.

[jg/iar]

HUGH CORNWELL
See *Stranglers*.

CORTINAS
True Romances (nr/CBS) 1978

The Cortinas' pounding, belligerent independent singles ("Fascist Dictator," "Defiant Pose") offered no clue that they'd cut such a mild-mannered album for a major label, on which the few confrontational gestures sound forced. **True Romances** reveals the Cortinas as simple rock'n'rollers with a taste for primitive, good-time R&B/pop-rock and endearingly yobbish vocals (e.g., "Heartache" and the jolly "Ask Mr. Waverly"—remember *The Man from U.N.C.L.E.*?). Nonetheless, halfway through, the record decays into bland forgettability. [jg]

ELVIS COSTELLO
My Aim Is True (Columbia) 1977 ●

ELVIS COSTELLO AND THE ATTRACTIONS
This Year's Model (Columbia) 1978 ●
Armed Forces (Columbia) 1979 ●
Get Happy!! (Columbia) 1980 ●
Taking Liberties (Columbia) 1980 ●
Ten Bloody Marys & Ten How's Your Fathers
   (nr/F-Beat) 1980 (nr/Imp) 1984 ●
Trust (Columbia) 1981 ●
Almost Blue (Columbia) 1981 ●
Imperial Bedroom (Columbia) 1982 ●
Punch the Clock (Columbia) 1983 ●
Goodbye Cruel World (Columbia) 1984 ●
The Best of Elvis Costello and the Attractions
   Vol. 1 (Columbia) 1985 ●
Elvis Costello EP (nr/Stiff) 1985
Blood & Chocolate (Columbia) 1986 ●

THE COSTELLO SHOW
King of America (Columbia) 1986 ●

VARIOUS ARTISTS
Out of Our Idiot (nr/Demon) 1987 ●

ATTRACTIONS
Mad About the Wrong Boy (nr/F-Beat) 1980
   (nr/Demon) 1984

Elvis Costello has become the King Kong of contemporary music, looming so large over everything that admirers and detractors alike feel compelled to take note of his most trivial actions. A remarkable performer with a cutting voice, he's charted a consistently interesting course in an intensely productive decade-plus and shows no sign of fatigue. He's arguably the most significant individual creative voice to emerge in rock'n'roll since Bob Dylan, and definitely one of music's most unforgettable characters.

My Aim Is True quickly established Elvis as an angry young man armed with cleverly worded insults and taut melodies. Although the backing (by American band Clover, *sans* future star Huey Lewis, the group's harmonica player) lacks his intensity, the bespectacled one's passion comes through full force. Many of the songs are already standards: "Watching the Detectives," a sizzling, disorienting excursion into reggae (not included on the original UK version of the LP); "Alison," a searing ballad later ineptly covered by Linda Ronstadt, and "Less Than Zero," Elvis' first single and a wry attack on one of his preferred targets, fascism. The overall effect is that of an updated Buddy Holly, neurotic and tormented by sexual insecurity. For more information, consult "Miracle Man" and "No Dancing."

This Year's Model improves significantly on Costello's stunning debut by winding the music uncomfortably tight. Elvis gained confidence from the addition of an outstanding permanent backing band: Bruce Thomas on bass, Pete Thomas (no relation) on drums and Steve Nieve, whose piano and organ, rather than Elvis' guitar, generally fill in melodies. The album finds Costello's anger and insecurity grown harsh and nasty. The surging "No Action," "Pump It Up" (something of a rewrite on Dylan's "Subterranean Homesick Blues") and "Lipstick Vogue" fairly bristle with ingeniously stated, hard-rocking vitriol. "Radio Radio" (not on the UK edition) became Costello's unofficial theme song, a daring and snotty attack on the powers that rule the airwaves.

Costello avoids sneering himself into a dead end on **Armed Forces**, with the help of producer Nick Lowe. The prettier, less demanding and more varied sound still allows him freedom of expression. The lyrically potent "Oliver's Army" borrows from Abba's pop lushness; "Accidents Will Happen" mixes a beautiful melody with a driving arrangement; Lowe's "(What's So Funny 'Bout) Peace, Love and Understanding" offers an unironic, unexpected and agitated plea for tolerance. **Armed Forces** was the "nicest" of Costello's first three LPs.

Get Happy!! marks the beginning of Elvis' concerted stylistic fiddling and his first serious attempt to shift the emphasis to the music and away from the overpowering persona. The watchword here is simplicity, with 20 short songs and borrowings from such soul greats as Booker T & the M.G.'s and Sam and Dave, whose "I Can't Stand Up for Falling Down" gets disheveled but earnest treatment. Other highlights include "Motel Matches," an early flirtation with Nashville country; the moving "King Horse" and a rip snorting version of the Merseybeats' "I Stand Accused." By lessening the intensity somewhat, Elvis comes up with a most personable LP.

Reflecting Costello's prolific nature, **Taking Liberties** collects an amazing 20 previously non-LP odds and ends in wildly divergent styles. (The UK counterpart, **Ten Bloody Marys & Ten How's Your Fathers**, is altogether different, thanks to the willful creation of alternate international releases. Originally issued only on cassette, it appeared on vinyl four years later.) Despite a few dull entries, there's plenty of remarkable stuff. The classic "My Funny Valentine" is a harbinger of **Imperial Bedroom**; "Talking in the Dark" gaily recalls "Penny Lane"; "Stranger in the House," dating from the period of **This Year's Model**, masterfully reflects his growing obsession with country music. Chaotic and marvelous.

Trust exhibits new self-confidence, blending some of the polish of **Armed Forces** with the straightforward delivery of **This Year's Model**. Though few tracks stand out individually, the LP packs a powerful, coherent punch. "Clubland" is an impassioned lament while "Lovers Walk" overlays a Bo Diddley-ish motif with Latin piano and heaps of anxiety. On the fierce "From a Whisper to a Scream," Costello engages in a spirited dialogue with Squeeze's Glenn Tilbrook, reaffirming his presence in the real world.

Elvis was bound to goof eventually, and **Almost Blue** is a real stinker. This album of country cover versions, recorded in Nashville with veteran producer Billy Sherill (Tammy Wynette, George Jones, just about everyone else), is surprisingly clumsy in light of Costello's previously demonstrated ability to come up with fine originals in the same genre. Curiously, he succumbs to the urge to oversing instead of finesse the vocals, a mistake

his obvious model, the late Gram Parsons, never made.

Imperial Bedroom is a resounding return to form, and indicates Costello's interest in becoming a classic tunesmith in the Tin Pan Alley tradition instead of just a venerated rocker. This is certainly his most subdued LP, with songs such as "Beyond Belief," "Kid About It" and "Town Cryer" more suitable to a cocktail lounge torch singer than a garage band. How time flies.

Punch the Clock is yet another tour de force. Produced by Madness architects Clive Langer and Alan Winstanley, the disc continues in the pop vein of **Imperial Bedroom**, but with considerably more attention paid to mixing up styles and textures. Hence you get politically motivated ballads like the brooding "Pills and Soap" and the ethereal, desperately angry "Shipbuilding," as well as swaggering rave-ups ("The World and His Wife"), classic Costello angst ("Charm School") and much more. Best of all is the lilting "Everyday I Write the Book," a winning tune worthy of being sung by Aretha Franklin (and the closest Costello's come to a US hit single).

By contrast, **Goodbye Cruel World** seems awkward and forced. The playing's overly baroque, the melodies mild and too much of Costello's edge is sublimated by the Langer/Winstanley cushion of sound. However, "Sour Milk-Cow Blues" has a cranky charm and "Peace in Our Time" brilliantly captures the chilling madness of nuclear politics. Otherwise, Costello sounds like he needs a vacation.

Perhaps **The Best Of** LP did the trick. Or maybe it was the decision to shelve the Attractions temporarily. Then again, maybe his burgeoning romance with (soon-to-be-ex-) Pogue bassist Cait O'Riordan was the reason. In any case, the extraordinary **King of America**—billed as the Costello Show and recorded with co-producer T-Bone Burnett and a bunch of top American sessioneers, including Elvis P's old sidemen—returned him to masterful top form. MacManus (as he then wished to be known) banged together 15 intelligent, mature creations in a variety of idioms, many recalling styles he had already tried and abandoned (C&W, R&B, nightclub sophistication) and some (folk, blues) not so familiar. The sound often recalls the Band in its unique blending of country and urban traditions; elsewhere, it's latter-day Elvis Presley, played by his own musicians. As articulate and clear-headed as he's ever been, Mac-Manus dissects several major themes—the British perception of America, alcoholism, his own stardom—each from more than one vantage point. Not only do all these forays work individually, the songs fit together with surprising ease. In addition, he's never sung better, with such subtlety and control. A career highlight.

Released by the end of the same calendar year, **Blood & Chocolate** brought the Attractions back into the picture, joined on a few tunes by guest vocalist O'Riordan. (More nomenclatural absurdity: while the name Elvis Costello appears on the front cover, the composer of all but one track is MacManus and the vocalist/guitarist is named Napoleon Dynamite.) Although the LP has no characteristic sound, overall theme or discernible organizational logic, the individual songs are quietly excellent—simply-played gems performed with restrained enthusiasm, if little color. Eschewing any new stylistic statement, Elvis the unnameable ambles back into personal commentary with subdued eloquence. A bit underwhelming at first, but substantial nonetheless.

The 1987 **Out of Our Idiot** crypto-compilation serves up a brace of B-sides and side projects employing enough different monikers to justify the record's "various artists" billing. Besides assorted Elvis Costello organizations, the hodgepodge of good-to-incredible tracks are by such artists as Napoleon Dynamite & the Royal Guard, the Emotional Toothpaste and the Coward Brothers. There are alternate versions of "Blue Chair" and "American Without Tears," plus collaborations with Jimmy Cliff and Nick Lowe. The CD adds a genuine EC & the Attractions outtake—"Little Goody Two Shoes," from 1982—as well as cuts by the MacManus Gang (from the *Straight to Hell* soundtrack) and the Imposter. The 1985 Stiff EP consists of four early sides, all previously available. The British TV-label (like K-Tel) equivalent to **The Best of Elvis Costello and the Attractions Vol. 1** is entitled **The Best of Elvis—The Man** and contains four additional cuts.

On their own, the Attractions sound more like Nick Lowe than their boss. The 16 snappily-executed ditties on **Mad About the Wrong Boy** feature bright, breezy surfaces and very little depth, which isn't so bad in light of the cheerful atmosphere. The title cut, "La-La-La-La-La Loved You" and others offer agreeably washed-out harmonies reminiscent of UK flower-power pop of the late-'60s. Decent. [jy/iar]

See also *Steve Nieve, Twist.*

JOSIE COTTON

Convertible Music (Elektra) 1982
From the Hip (Elektra) 1984

Josie Cotton's debut album, with the exception of one dumbly offensive number ("Johnny, Are You Queer?"), is really good '60s-derived '80s California pop, powered by a subtly solid band and spiced up with exactly enough atmospheric organ. Cotton has a strong, expressive voice that suits the material (mostly hers, some written by producers Bobby and Larson Paine) just fine, especially on the bouncy "He Could Be the One" and a cover of the 1962 Exciters' hit, "Tell Him."

Cotton offers another sophisticated come-hither look on the cover of **From the Hip**; the music is pretty much a repeat engagement of the first LP as well, although not as creatively successful. "Jimmy Loves Maryann" leads off the record and is its best number; elsewhere, intrusive rock moves muddy the pop clarity, although not enough to be fatal. Cotton has a great voice, but she's totally subservient to production and songwriting; here, with fewer of her own songs and a baring of increased commercial intentions, she gets a second-rate assist. [iar]

COUCH FLAMBEAU

Curiosity Rocks [tape] (no label) 1982
Mammal Insect Marriage (Ludwig Van Ear) 1983
The Day the Music Died (It's Only a Record) 1985
Rock with Your Sock On [tape] (It's Only a Record) 1987
Models EP (It's Only a Record) 1987

If education is a dangerous thing, these Wisconsin smartboys have been in school far too long for public safety. Armed with Jay Tiller's rapier wit, dadaist visions, squawky voice and ear-busting guitar work, the group records hysterically funny exercises in eminently enjoyable noise-to-go.

The lyrics of **Mammal Insect Marriage**'s opening track, "ADM 12," immediately make it clear you've checked into a real hellhouse of collegiate weasel weirdness: "I saw a car accident near the zoo. There were mangled bodies all over. I felt sick, but I found a finger. I still have it in my freezer." Recorded in seven fun-filled hours, **Mammal Insect Marriage** has 13 additional warped and funny B-movie haikus. Brilliant and extraordinary.

The tape-only reissue entitled **Rock with Your Sock On** contains the entire contents of **Curiosity Rocks** and **Mammal Insect Marriage**. The former contains sketchy versions of the latter's "ADM 12" and "I Don't Want to Be an Eddie," as well as "Mobile Home," "Satan's School for Girls" and "Curtains for You," all of which surfaced again on Couch's third album.

The Day the Music Died gets off to a slow start with the instrumental title track, but revs into high gear with "We'll Go Through the Windshield Together," a romantic tale of vehicular homicide (complete with sound effects) told from the victim's perspective. Other highlights include the pessimistic "Life's Rough," a feedback-filled mantra ("You Hate It, It Hates You") and bassist Neil Socol's "Curtains for You," in which the protagonist makes a major educational discovery: "I hate Shakespeare/He's too hard to read/I wish he were dead/Oh, he is?"

Done as a duo (Tiller doubles on real and electronic drums), the five songs on the **Models** EP go easy on the radical sounds, laying the pointed cultural sarcasm of "Models," "White Boy Blues" and "Vipers" over relatively easygoing music that paradoxically undercuts the lyrics by failing to match their absurdity. The one exception is "Song with a Message," a wimpy dance groove underlying a random series of messages left on Socol's answering machine.   [iar]

COUNT

I'm a Star (Fr. Flamingo) 1979
Love & Flame (Fr. New Rose) 1982
The Intuition Element (VAR Int'l) 1984

The Count—Joseph A. Viglione—has been a visible and important fixture on the local Boston scene ever since the mid-'70s. Besides recording and performing his own material, he's published fanzines, promoted concerts, produced other bands and operated the Varulven label. Oddly enough, his first two albums have never been issued outside France.

I'm a Star owes quite a bit to the influence of the Velvet Underground and, like Lou Reed, the Count knows how to make the most of a voice with a limited range. The tracks—many previously issued in the US on singles and EPs—are appealing because of their simple, romantic outlook on life. **Love & Flame** finds the Count in a more mainstream new wave format. At times, he tries too hard as a vocalist, and parts are overarranged, but it's still a generally listenable record.

The Intuition Element, dynamically produced by veteran Jimmy Miller, is a highly charged near-metal rock album filled with blistering guitar solos (credit Fudge Keegan), thundering drums and more of the Count's individualistic songs. A lot heavier than usual, but above average (except for some awkward vocals and lyrics) as such things go.   [cpl/iar]

COUNT BISHOPS

Speedball EP (nr/Chiswick) 1975
Good Gear (Fr. Dynamite) 1977
The Count Bishops (nr/Chiswick) 1977

BISHOPS

Bishops Live (nr/Chiswick) 1978
Cross Cuts (nr/Chiswick) 1979

Although they never attained major popularity, hits or even a US release, the Bishops played a small but important role in the development of British punk. First, they provided a stylistic and chronological link between the raw R&B revivalism of Dr. Feelgood and early demi-punk flailings of Eddie and the Hot Rods. Second, their four-cut 7-inch **Speedball** EP was the debut release by the first independent new wave label in England, Chiswick, preceding Stiff by a matter of months.

The group's only recording with American (Brooklyn, no less) singer Mike Spencer (replaced by the gravel-throated Dave Tice soon after, for reasons that are audibly obvious), **Speedball** clearly defines the group's style. Combining rock-a-boogie rave-ups of mid-'60s style material with mid-'70s chops and energy, the Bishops re-cover the same R&B and rock'n'roll songs favored by the first wave of British beat groups (Stones, Yardbirds, Kinks) and American punks (Standells, Strangeloves). The idea was obviously to recapture the rawness and spontaneity of that period, and although the concept is both limited and doomed almost by definition, **Good Gear** (probably drawn from live-in-the-studio demos) is so raunchy and spirited that it succeeds, even if it is essentially a copy of a copy.

Trouble set in with their first *real* album, **The Count Bishops**. How do you convey a style that works best after a few beers and really offers nothing new to vinyl? Even with two solid guitarists and a fine rhythm section, the Bishops never were quite able to resolve the problem. Though it sounds nasty as hell on **Bishops Live** (available as both a 12-inch and 10-inch LP), Tice's growl is hard to take over two sides of a recording made in the rarefied atmosphere of the studio. And where most bands use cover versions to fill space, the filler here is the Bishops' self-penned stuff. With rare exception, their originals are sub-Status Quo boogie, which just about destroys most of **Cross Cuts**. Following the death of guitarist Zenon de Fleur in an auto accident just prior to the release of **Cross Cuts**, the Bishops called it a day.   [ds]

WAYNE COUNTY AND THE ELECTRIC CHAIRS

The Electric Chairs (nr/Safari) 1978
Storm the Gates of Heaven (nr/Safari) 1979
Things Your Mother Never Told You (nr/Safari) 1979
The Best of Jayne/Wayne County and the Electric Chairs (nr/Safari) 1982

JAYNE COUNTY

Rock 'n' Roll Resurrection (nr/Safari) 1981

Transsexual County was a (male) fixture on the budding New York club scene in the early '70s, stretching the limits of vulgarity and outrage on stages alongside the New York Dolls, et al. After writing and recording the theme song for Max's Kansas City, County migrated to England, just as the London punk scene was getting underway. Having been commercially unappreciated at home, County found a sympathetic British label and recorded a series of albums, none of which were ever released Stateside.

High camp posturing and foul-mouthed (but not unfunny) lyrics form the basis of County's work. Along with a skillful trio playing routine rock, County sings (with more enthusiasm than talent) touching ballads ("Eddie and Sheena," a minor hit single recounting a love story between a Ted and a punk), catty putdowns ("Bad in Bed") and narcissistic scene celebrations ("Max's Kansas City") on the first album.

Storm the Gates of Heaven has a great cover, was pressed on sickly-colored lavender vinyl and showcases two new guitarists hired to replace one left behind. The songs are less contrived and more interesting; the beginnings of a band sound can be discerned. All in all, a vast improvement that even includes a smoking version of "I Had Too Much to Dream Last Night." Flying Lizard David Cunningham produced the subsequent **Things Your Mother Never Told You** with the same lineup, but came up with a flat-sounding, dull LP.

A New Year's Eve gig in Toronto yielded the live **Rock'n'Roll Resurrection**. Fronting a largely new band, Jayne (following the surgery) belts out a shambling selection of non-hits, including such gutter faves as "Cream in My Jeans" and "F . . . Off." Pretty dire. A nicely packaged best-of collection (pressed on white vinyl) brought together everything you'd ever want to hear by Wayne or Jayne.

[iar]

COWBOYS INTERNATIONAL

The Original Sin (Virgin) 1979

KEN LOCKIE

The Impossible (nr/Virgin) 1981

Ken Lockie, an early cog in the vague Clash/Pistols axis that revolved around guitarist Keith Levene and eventually led to the creation of Public Image Ltd., *was* for a time Cowboys International, specializing in deceptively chipper numbers about fear and loathing and love betrayed. **The Original Sin** is a cornucopia of clever and well-tooled high-tech pop songs, every one of them a should-have-been hit. Lockie's vocals provide a human counterpoint to the crisp metallic happenings in the instrumental work, aided by a musical team that includes drummer Terry Chimes as well as a guest turn by Levene.

The Impossible is less successful, due mostly to stiff production by Steve Hillage. Lockie's accompaniment is once again impressive—Magazine's John Doyle and John McGeoch, Nash the Slash, Steve Shears (then of Ultravox), among others—and his songs still have a guileless punch when they aren't buried under the slick production. The whole thing never quite meshes, but all the parts are there to be enjoyed if you have the patience.

Lockie, like Levene, subsequently relocated to New York, where he participated in numerous other musical projects.   [sg]

See also *Dominatrix*.

CRACKERS

See *Beat Rodeo*.

CRAMPS

Gravest Hits EP (Illegal) 1979
Songs the Lord Taught Us (Illegal) 1980
Psychedelic Jungle (IRS) 1981
Off the Bone (nr/Illegal) 1983
Smell of Female EP (Enigma) 1983 ●
Bad Music for Bad People (IRS) 1984 ●
A Date with Elvis (nr/Big Beat) 1986 ●

Predating and never quite participating in the early '80s rockabilly revival, the Cramps used that genre's primal sound as a jumping-off point for their own weird pastiche of rock'n'roll, psychedelia and a monster movie/junk food/swamp-creature aesthetic. The band had its roots in Cleveland but was actually formed in New York; they crashed the 12-inch barrier with **Gravest Hits**, reissuing two 1977 self-released 45s plus a fifth track from the same time, all produced by Alex Chilton.

Like a seance or voodoo session, the Cramps' music needs time to work its spell, and so the albums make a better introduction. **Songs the Lord Taught Us** is a delirious invocation to the demons behind rock'n'roll. Besides horror-comic originals like "TV Set," "The Mad Daddy" and "Zombie Dance," the band overhauls classics like "Tear It Up" and "Strychnine" to emphasize their Dionysian inheritance. A minimal approach—no bass, rudimentary drumming, Lux Interior's monotonous vocals—underlines the music's incantatory power. As a result of slower tempos, **Psychedelic Jungle** is not quite as intense; still, it contains prime Cramps psychobilly ("Voodoo Idol," "Can't Find My Mind") as well as related phenomena ("The Crusher," "Rockin' Bones").

On **Smell of Female**, a six-song live EP recorded at New York's Peppermint Lounge, the group's maniacal sense of humor comes through loud and clear on well-recorded mung like "Thee Most Exalted Potentate of Love" and "I Ain't Nuthin' but a Gorehound."

Amid rotating guitarists and disputes with their record label, the Cramps then temporarily submerged. IRS issued **Bad Music for Bad People**, a kiss-off collection of singles sides (both LP and non-LP) and other obscure gems, like the hilariously offensive "She Said." Meanwhile, the Cramps' foreign cult following was temporarily sated by **Off the Bone**, a 15-track compilation including all of **Gravest Hits** and the contents of **Bad Music for Bad People**, with two earlier album cuts replacing the latter's "TV Set" (originally from **Songs the Lord Taught Us**) and "Uranium Rock."

The Cramps returned to the living dead in late '85 with a wonderfully smarmy single ("Can Your Pussy Do the Dog?"), followed by an all-new sex-crazed studio album, **A Date with Elvis**. A bit more professional and less stylized than usual, but as happily crazed as ever, **Elvis** contemplates such Interior designs as "What's Inside a Girl?," "(Hot Pool of) Womanneed" and "The Hot Pearl Snatch." Visually and musically, the Cramps are the Addams Family of rock.   [si/iar]

CRASS

The Feeding of the Five Thousand, The Second Sitting (nr/Crass) 1978
Stations of the Crass (nr/Crass) 1980
Penis Envy (Crass) 1981
Christ—The Album (nr/Crass) 1982
Yes Sir, I Will (nr/Crass) 1983
Best Before 1984 (nr/Crass) 1986

PENNY RIMBAUD & EVE LIBERTINE

Acts of Love (nr/Crass) 1985

Lords of English punk's extreme left, the Essex-based Crass don't just sing about anarchy in the UK—they *do* something about it. Formed in 1977 as a band much in the Sex Pistols/Sham 69 image, they soon evolved into an anarchist commune, several record labels and an information service. Crass espouse all the proper causes—anti-war, anti-nuclear, feminism, flushing out hypocrisy in organized religion—with blood-curdling vehemence on their own records and on the numerous singles and albums by likeminded bands they've released (or inspired). The group has found itself embroiled in legal battles with various government agencies, but in an era largely typified by apathy, Crass stand as a successful model of dead-serious political commitment in rock.

The Feeding of the Five Thousand is a reissue of the group's debut EP on Small Wonder. Fitting 18 songs on a 12-inch 45, it is typical of Crass' shock tactics: The first cut is a sneering recitation of "Asylum," an irreverent dismissal of Christ as anybody's lord over droning guitar feedback. The rest is mostly raw faster/louder punk spiked with protest demagoguery, four-letter words and harsh cockney ranting.

Stations of the Crass is even harder going—three studio sides and a live side containing a full 17 songs. Almost in spite of the oppressive, relentless punk bluster, Crass often write anthemic songs (like the ironic "Banned from the Roxy" and "Do They Owe Us a Living?" from **Five Thousand**), but over the course of this album (all of the studio material was cut in one day!), they blur into white noise. "White Punks on Hope" forcefully summarizes their scorn of punk as fashion and the Sham 69 parody, "Hurry Up Garry," is a wicked snipe at the music press.

Better production and more expansive arrangements distinguish **Penis Envy**. Drawing an ugly parallel between rampant sexism and man's rape of nature and society, the album bounces vibrantly from the strident bash of the ironic rape fantasy "Bata Motel" to the LP's unsettling church-organ coda.

Christ—The Album is quintessential Crass. A boxed two-record studio and live set, it comes with a 28-page booklet packed with emotional small print about the revolution and one man who died for it. Musically, it builds on the daring of **Penis Envy**, even including a mock string arrangement in "Reality Whitewash," without tempering the band's brute punk rage. The severity of their sound and their belligerent politics can be predictable, even petulant, but **Christ—The Album** and the other records prove that Crass at least have the courage and strength of their convictions.

Yes Sir, I Will is Crass' response to the Falklands' War, a series of musical speeches covering the conflict and indicting Prime Minister Thatcher for the deaths. Although most of the backing is typically abrasive, a couple of passages are quite beautiful.

The **Best Before 1984** singles compilation begins with "Do They Owe Us a Living (1977)" and runs up through the same song in a 1984 version: 20 songs in all.   [df]

CRAWDADDYS

Crawdaddy Express (Voxx) 1979
Still Steamin' (Ger. Line) 1980
Here 'Tis (Voxx) 1987

This San Diego band delivers a 1979 record straight from 1964. Taking their name from the London R&B club where the Stones and Yardbirds started out, the Crawdaddys copy those and other appropriate period groups, like the Pretty Things and Downliners Sect. Unfortunately, their lame renditions of various blues obscurities and originals from the same mold make **Crawdaddy Express** a well-intentioned tribute to the genre, little more than nostalgia-mongering. **Here 'Tis** is a posthumous collection with unreleased items.

Country Dick Montana of the Beat Farmers was the Crawdaddys drummer at some point subsequent to **Express**.   [wk]
See also *Beat Farmers.*

ROBERT CRAY BAND

Who's Been Talkin' (Tomato) 1980 (Atlantic) 1987 ●
Bad Influence (HighTone) 1983 ●
False Accusations (HighTone) 1985 ●
Strong Persuader (HighTone-Mercury) 1986 ●

The most acclaimed new American blues artist in years, Robert Cray comes from Georgia by way of Washington. After leading bands for over a decade, the young singer/guitarist got a commercial break by appearing as a bassist in *Animal House.* Cray is a smooth singer—his phrasing recalls Otis Redding and Al Green—and a deft Stratocaster slinger, mixing jazzy leads with driving raunch. He has an enlightened way with songs about traditional blues concerns that carefully sidesteps 12-bar convention for more soul/R&B-based constructs of the sort B.B. King found commercially rewarding in the late '60s.

Cray's now-obscure first album was generally overlooked upon its release; critics and fans on both sides of the Atlantic discovered him only upon the release of **Bad Influence**. Both it and **False Accusations** rely on familiar-sounding originals, with a supple quartet providing appropriate support. (Around the same time, Cray played and sang on **Showdown**, a joint album with Albert Collins and Johnny Copeland.)

Strong Persuader is Cray's graduation into the big leagues—no mean feat for a blues performer in the 1980s, no matter how pop-oriented he may be—and he makes the most of it, spinning his intimate tales of romance gone wrong (and, on "Fantasized," right) with confidence and charm. The Memphis Horns provide delicate seasoning; Cray's thoughtful solos are tasteful and to the point.   [iar]

CRAZY BACKWARDS ALPHABET

See *Henry Kaiser.*

CREATIVE TECHNOLOGY INSTITUTE

See *Chris and Cosey.*

CREATURES

Wild Things EP (nr/Polydor) 1981
Feast (nr/Wonderland-Polydor) 1983

Soon after the Banshees released their **Juju** album, Siouxsie Sioux and drummer Budgie, under the sobriquet Creatures, collaborated on a five-song double-45 of voice-and-percussion pieces, including a nasty reworking of the Troggs classic, "Wild Thing." The full-length **Feast,** however, is a dilettantish excursion into the only previously untested flavor-of-the-month: Hawaiian. The instrumentation incorporates marimba, while an ethnic choir adds bogus authenticity to the messy proceedings. Even worse, the lyrics are bad acid visions written by people evidently unfamiliar with their subject matter. The Creatures did make one great 1983 single, "Right Now," which is fortunately (for it) not on the LP. [rnp/dgs]

HELIOS CREED

See *Chrome.*

CREEPERS

See *Marc Riley with the Creepers.*

MARSHALL CRENSHAW

Marshall Crenshaw (Warner Bros.) 1982
Field Day (Warner Bros.) 1983
Our Town EP (nr/Warner Bros.) 1984
Downtown (Warner Bros.) 1985
The Distance Between EP (nr/Warner Bros.) 1986
Mary Jean & 9 Others (Warner Bros.) 1987 •

Detroit native Crenshaw spent some time in a road company of *Beatlemania* before moving himself (and drummer brother Robert) to New York, where he became an original critical fave, following a local indie 12-inch with a major-label recording contract. Notwithstanding the Buddy Holly comparisons (not diminished when Crenshaw portrayed Holly in *La Bamba*), his main strength lies in a bland, scrubbed pop presence—the first album sounds like an audio test for studio sound quality. Clean, crisp, neat and simple, free of frills and pretense, what makes **Marshall Crenshaw** great are the songs—"Someday, Someway," "She Can't Dance," "Cynical Girl," "Brand New Lover"—sparkling, tuneful gems that are instantly memorable and steadily enjoyable.

Field Day, rather bombastically overproduced by Steve Lillywhite, has a walloping drum sound, lots of sonic holes and a few of Crenshaw's best songs. Although not an artistic success in toto, joyous numbers like "Whenever You're on My Mind," "All I Know Right Now" and "Our Town" mine Crenshaw's shuffle-pop resources effectively and salvage it from disaster. A clumsy piece of studio madness, it didn't help Crenshaw's career much. Mindful of the criticism the record engendered, "Our Town" and two other tracks from it were given a simplifying remix by John Luongo, attached to a live oldie ("Little Sister") and issued as an impressive second-chance 12-inch in the UK.

With production assistance by T-Bone Burnett and a large bunch of savvy sidemen in place of his usual band, Crenshaw filled **Downtown** with extraordinarily memorable and intelligent pop songs in a number of musical veins. Easily the finest, most mature of his first three albums, **Downtown** swings with easy confidence through heartbreakers ("The Distance Between," "Like a Vague Memory"), lovemakers ("Yvonne," "Terrifying Love"), country laments and blues struts. It also features Ben Vaughn's hauntingly wistful "I'm Sorry (But So Is Brenda Lee)."

Continuing on his onward and upward path, Crenshaw returned to the small-combo format, cutting the brilliant, often beautiful **Mary Jean** with two sidemen—his drummer brother and longtime Joe Jackson associate, bassist Graham Maby. Don Dixon's simple but full production sparkles, with just the right echo on the snare and spring in the strings. Guest crooners (including Tom Teeley and Marti Jones) pitch in to enrich well-crafted tunes—"Wild Abandon," "Mary Jean," a thoughtfully reflective Crenshaw/Dixon composition, "Calling Out for Love (at Crying Time)," Peter Case's atmospheric (and metaphoric) ode to the guitar, "Steel Strings"—with an uplifting spirit that wordlessly conveys both the ecstasy and misery of romance. [iar]

CRIME AND THE CITY SOLUTION

The Dangling Man EP (nr/Mute) 1985
Just South of Heaven EP (nr/Mute) 1985
Room of Lights (nr/Mute) 1986 ●
Shine (nr/Mute) 1988 ●

Growing out of the Birthday Party's debris, this oddly-named outfit was formed by guitarist Rowland S. Howard and drummer Mick Harvey (also one of Nick Cave's Bad Seeds). Howard's brother Harry plays bass and Simon Bonney (another Australian) does the singing. On the second EP, former Swell Map Epic Soundtracks took over on drums, allowing Harvey to reclaim his original BP role as multi-instrumentalist.

The Dangling Man is a four-track disc that picks up where the Party ended—a slow, stripped-down, blues-flavored horror show. (Considering that Cave did much the same on his first solo recordings, one wonders if the band didn't break up out of boredom rather than any musical differences.) None of the songs really take off, but it does show promise.

Just South of Heaven is cleaner and more powerful: all six tracks work well. Howard's guitar is as strong as ever, but piano and organ figure just as prominently. A hauntingly beautiful record by a well-integrated band.

Room of Lights, their first full-length LP, features a noticeably heavier and thicker sound. With the predominance of slow tempos, Bonney's somewhat unattractive voice and the (perhaps overly) serious lyrics, supplied mostly by Bronwyn Adams, apparently Bonney's girlfriend, the disc becomes laborious to endure in one sitting. It's well done, but one would hope that by this point the band would have developed further—these eight songs are just variations on themes introduced on prior releases.

Following **Room of Lights**, Soundtracks and the Howards split to form These Immortal Souls, leaving Bonney, Harvey and Adams, who also plays violin. Three more musicians were recruited before **Shine** was recorded in Berlin. With Bonney and Adams taking control (her violin is prominent throughout), it works well with quite a few surprises. The overall tone is much lighter and livelier; "Fray So Slow" could almost be old Simple Minds. Several other tracks move along nicely and melodically. Listeners who thought Howard had been the band's major creative force will be caught off-guard by this impressive disc. [dgs]

CRISTINA

Cristina (ZE-Buddah) 1980
Sleep It Off (ZE-Mercury) 1984

August Darnell wrote five and produced all of the six long rhythmic romps on Cristina Monet's first album, but her impassive, inelegant singing ankles them, leaving it a botched mess of colliding styles and sensibilities. At its best, in "Mama Mia," Darnell effectively buries her in an active mix.

Sleep It Off, produced by Don Was, plays up the satirical possibilities of Cristina's pre-Madonna ultra-bitch pose (?), having her coolly pronounce witty songs (all her own lyrics) like "Don't Mutilate My Mink" and "What's a Girl to Do?" over richly executed multi-styled backing tracks. The musicians—the unofficial Friends of ZE/Was—include erstwhile Knackman Doug Feiger, James Chance, Barry Reynolds, Howie Wyeth and the two Was Bros. Cristina's deadpan voice perfectly suits this setting and the record is excellent, from the disconcertingly sadistic cover, until the last strummed guitar chord of "He Dines Out on Death" gives way to a brief snippet of restaurant noise. [iar]

CRO-MAGS

The Age of Quarrel (Rock Hotel-Profile) 1986 ●

These New York hardcore kings claimed for a while to be Hare Krishna devotees, but they sure don't jangle finger cymbals or chant religious mantras on **The Age of Quarrel**, a blazing slice of state-of-the-art punk aggro. Vocalist John Joseph (co-lyricist with bassist/head-Mag Harley Flanagan) roars through philosophically humanist (don't laugh!) lyrics about peace, trust, independence and justice as the band keeps up the mid-speed speaker shredding with two guitarists doing their best to update Ritchie Blackmore's throaty Deep Purple sound. Drummer Mackie regulates the tempo enough to ensure an adequate proportion of mosh parts (generally at the beginning of songs rather than the middle), but often (and unnervingly) sounds like he's playing an entirely different song from his bandmates. [iar]

CROOKS

Just Released (nr/Blueprint) 1980

Following the Jam came an onslaught of mod/pop bands boasting great songs and not a shred of individual character. The Crooks, in fact, were a significantly superior outfit with better songs, less derivative stylization and more overall inventiveness than their skinny-tie competitors. A shame really—if there hadn't been such a glut, the Crooks would have stood out and might have been noticed. [iar]

CROSSFIRE CHOIR
Crossfire Choir (Passport) 1986 ●

A major American label signed this up-from-Florida New Jersey quartet but never released their album; after being dropped, tracks recorded in England with producer Steve Lillywhite were retrieved and issued (along with three subsequent items) on this belated debut. Although the group had built a reputation for punky outrageousness in New York-area clubs, this is far more familiar fare: urgent pop/rock with keyboards and a hint of possibile pomposity. The music isn't bad, but guitarist J Pounders sings in a grating dramatic warble and the songs aren't especially memorable. [iar]

CROWDED HOUSE
Crowded House (Capitol) 1986 ●
Temple of Low Men (Capitol) 1988 ●

Songwriter/singer/guitarist Neil Finn's post-Split Enz group follows the trend—reflected in that band's later albums—toward simplification. As a trio, with occasional added keyboards (on disc by Finn and producer Mitchell Froom, onstage by ex-Enzman Eddie Rayner, who co-wrote one of the first LP's songs), the sound is a bit thin, but ultimately the songs do come across. The melodious mix of tunes about dreams and nightmares, aching for love and the aching love causes, and so forth is affecting and enjoyable well beyond expectations of its lightweight, modest surface. (The LP proved to be an extremely slow but substantial commercial success.)

A second LP, again produced by Froom, was released in mid-'88. Miscellaneous notes: bassist Nick Seymour painted the first LP's cover, and drummer Paul Hester's brother leads Hunters and Collectors. [jg]

CRUCIFUCKS
The Crucifucks (Alternative Tentacles) 1985
Wisconsin (Alternative Tentacles) 1987

In pursuit of the ultimately offensive band name, these confrontational Michigan-

ders were so successful that their first album incorporates actual spoken-word comments and run-ins with the law over it. Unfortunately, little else about the record is amusing: rudimentary slow-to-mid-speed punk with a truly obnoxious singer and songs like "Hinckley Had a Vision," "Cops for Fertilizer" and "Go Bankrupt and Die."

Eulogizing the cheese state (where it was recorded) on their second LP, the Crucifucks unveil a surprising bit of wit and musical development. The unnamed vocalist still sounds like Pete Shelley's tuneless nerd cousin, but intelligent, politically correct lyrics ("Laws Against Laughing," "The Savior") and well-recorded electric and acoustic guitar raunch ("Concession Stand," "Pig in a Blanket") make **Wisconsin** commendable to, say, fans of the Dead Kennedys. [iar]

CRUMBSUCKERS
Life of Dreams (Combat Core) 1986
Beast on My Back (Combat) 1988 ●

Life of Dreams is second-rate New York (Long Island) hardcore with a metal crossover edge: the Crumbsuckers have the essential audio elements (speed, volume, chops, croaked vocals) but nothing much on their minds. The LP has one oddity—a discussion of the 1984 Presidential campaign in "Super Tuesday"—but otherwise offers such routine middle-class contemplations as "Live to Work" and "Bullshit Society."

Beast on My Back (aka **B.O.M.B.**) turns the Crumbsuckers on their head, stylistically speaking. This time out, armed with a new flight-of-the-bumblebee lead guitarist and high-def production (Randy Burns, remixed by Genya Ravan), they're a speedmetal band with some recalcitrant 'core tendencies. The nine long songs (none under three minutes; two over five) have mosh parts and shouted vocals, but don't all rely on breakneck downstrumming or double-bass foot-pedaling. More impressive than listenable, **B.O.M.B.** is an exhausting ride to nowhere. [iar]

CRUZADOS
Cruzados (Arista) 1985 ●
After Dark (Arista) 1987 ●

Despite the quartet's impressive nonmainstream pedigree—Tito Larriva and Chalo Quintana were in the Plugz, Steven Hufsteter has been involved with various Kim Fowley-related ventures, including the Quick—**Cruzados** is a rather familiar-sounding melodic rock album with few distinguishing characteristics and no evident Southwest influences. Perhaps it's the fault of producer Rodney Mills, veteran of countless .38 Special albums. Or maybe the work these guys did on film scores or backing Bob Dylan on TV made them too slick. In any case, **Cruzados** is nothing to get excited about.

Smelling chart possibilities in the post-Mellencamp world of simple heartland rock, the Cruzados replaced Hufsteter and augmented Mills with four more producers (including Waddy Wachtel) for their second LP. With guest appearances by everyone from the late Paul Butterfield to Pat Benatar and Don Henley, **After Dark** is a plain but solid effort. (Except for Larriva's "Time for Waiting," which sounds nauseatingly like the Eagles.) What the Cruzados lack in personality, they make up for with craftsmanship and sincerity; if **After Dark** isn't the Del-Lords, it's at least a viable alternative to the likes of Bob Seger and Tom Petty. [iar]

CRYSTAL FUTURES
The Truth (Strange Fruit) 1983

One David Elbee is behind this disc, all done on the Fairlight synthesizer and dedicated to Screaming Lord Sutch, Kamahl (international piano version of Mantovani) and Plastic Bertrand. When it's not too busy parodying one thing or another (including itself), **The Truth** delivers striking, Residents-like passages. [jg]

CUBAN HEELS
Work Our Way to Heaven (nr/Cuba
   Libre-Virgin) 1981

These four young Glaswegians make impressive ragged pop noise in a style that recalls both XTC and the Skids. Despite a somber back cover pic, this is infectious, quirky music; witty and wily. [iar]

CUCUMBERS
Fresh Cucumbers EP (Fake Doom) 1983
Who Betrays Me . . . and Other Happier
   Songs (Fake Doom) 1985
The Cucumbers (Profile) 1987 ●

Charming, original pop from Hoboken, New Jersey. Guitarist Deena Shoshkes' lead vocal on "My Boyfriend" is Brenda Lee magic set to a dB's-like tune; elsewhere, the blend includes more edgy guitar work (fea-

turing Jon Fried) and less fizzy charm. The other three songs on **Fresh** sacrifice some catchiness while adding complexity, but all are likable.

The half-new quartet's **Who Betrays Me** is a full album of peppy melodies, thoughtful lyrics, semi-intricate guitar-based arrangements and appealing harmonies by Shoshkes and Fried. The spare "Everything Goes" blends a sultry melody and a fine dual vocal; "Desperation" sounds like an update on the Everly Brothers; "Walking and Talking" mixes and matches rhythms for a kicky B-52's effect; "Want to Talk" grafts on a mild Latin feel for a danceable slice of summer. A consistent and likable first album.

Recorded in London with a new bassist in the lineup, **The Cucumbers** leads off with a new version of "My Boyfriend" and then fails to deliver anything else equal to it. Overall, the fancier production (by the same guy who did the previous records) reduces the group's amateurish appeal and obscures its quirky personality; smoothed out and spruced up, the entirely presentable songs blur together. There are some acute lyrics, however: "My Town" is a clever ode to 'Boken, while "Shower" makes an interesting observation about men, women and water temperatures. [iar]

CUDDLY TOYS
Guillotine Theatre (nr/Fresh) 1981
Trials and Crosses (nr/Fresh) 1982

As an early punk band, these morons called themselves the Raped; changing to Cuddly Toys, they also dyed their hair, dressed in androgynous threads and began playing Bowie-style glam-rock. Despite an auspicious debut 45 ("Madman," a curiosity piece—the only song co-written by Bowie and Marc Bolan), their first album is merely a pathetic attempt to clone **Ziggy Stardust**; lacking anything original or clever to add, it's a total flop. **Trials and Crosses**, by a revamped lineup (retaining only singer Sean Purcell), tries to be more modern by adding '80s rhythms and keyboards, but comes up similarly devoid of creativity and substance. [iar]

CULT
Dreamtime (nr/Beggars Banquet) 1984
Love (Beggars Banquet-Sire) 1985 ●
Revolution EP (nr/Beggars Banquet) 1985
Electric (Beggars Banquet-Sire) 1987 ●

SOUTHERN DEATH CULT

The Southern Death Cult (nr/Beggars
  Banquet) 1983

DEATH CULT

Brothers Grimm EP (nr/Situation 2) 1983

Less is more . . . or the saga of a British
band whose fame grew as its name shrunk.
As our story begins, the Southern Death Cult
(from northern England) has just broken up
without releasing an album; various sessions
and live takes were, however, compiled for a
posthumous LP. As such, **The Southern
Death Cult** paints an inconsistent picture of
ominous and dense doom-punks with a serious power supply and few original ideas. The
songs aren't much to brag about—drum-
dominated drones at various tempos—and
the performances, given their mongrel origins, are too muddy to really judge the band.
Pass on this one.

Singer Ian Astbury subsequently formed
Death Cult, which released two 12-inch singles, including the four-song **Brothers
Grimm**. The following year, with its name
reduced to just the Cult, the quartet finally
got around to releasing a proper album.
Dreamtime, an extremely well-produced and
intense outing, reveals Astbury's true intentions: hip heavy metal. Domineering drums
blend with Billy Duffy's layered lead guitar
figures and Astbury's drama-drenched vocals
on pseudo-poetic songs that oddly connect
with the Doors and other bands of the first
psychedelic era. Impressive in its clear-
headed strength and attractive for its electric
sound, **Dreamtime** is, like a lot of metal, exciting but empty and not a little stupid.

The well-produced **Love** also chugs along
enthusiastically, awash in Duffy's guitars and
Astbury's sweeping vocals. The material—
except for the atmospherically powerful and
catchy "She Sells Sanctuary"—is pretty naff,
with simple chord riffs providing a loud bed
for draggy melodies and too much pointless
riffing. (A lot of the drive and precision is due
to drummer Mark Brzezicki, on loan from
Big Country.) The invocation of '60s hard-
rock and grunge-punk bands is subtle enough
not to be obnoxious, but the Cult's relevance
to modern times remains marginal at best. A
subsequent EP adds non-LP tracks to **Love**'s
"Revolution" (not the Beatles tune).

In these high concept times, it made perfect sense for the braindead all-style Cult to
hook up with a grand poobah of '70s revisionism: Rick Rubin, Def Jam titan and production svengali behind numerous rap and
metal acts, including the Beastie Boys and
Slayer. On **Electric**, Rubin outfitted the Cult
with a gargantuan drum sound and a frenetic
guitar maelstrom, partially succeeding in
having them mimic his favorite rock'n'roll
band, AC/DC (although Astbury's vocals
occasionally favor Leslie West on steroids
and the opening guitar on "Love Removal
Machine" replicates the Stones' "Start Me
Up"). As sensually gratifying as it is cornball
retro-moronic, **Electric** has one of history's
worst versions of "Born to Be Wild." Not
surprisingly, the first track, "Wild Flower,"
is virtually a rewrite of "She Sells Sanctuary." [iar]

CULTURE

Two Sevens Clash (Lightning) 1978
  (Shanachie) 1987
Baldhead Bridge (nr/Magnum Force) 1978
Africa Stand Alone (nr/April) 1978
Harder Than the Rest (nr/Front Line) 1978
Cumbolo (nr/Front Line) 1978
International Herb (nr/Front Line) 1979
Culture in Culture (nr/Joe Gibbs) 1981
Vital Selection (Virgin Int'l) 1981
Lion Rock (Heartbeat) 1982
Culture at Work (Shanachie) 1986
The Peel Sessions EP (nr/Strange Fruit) 1987

A Jamaican vocal trio with a string of fine
albums to its credit, Culture is nevertheless
most closely identified with their debut LP,
Two Sevens Clash. And rightly so: the song,
first released in 1977, is a reggae classic, a
perfect marriage of Rasta ideology and musicianship. The music on the LP is smokey and
mysterious—the keyboards are mixed way
up front—but also rhythmically dynamic,
with Sly Dunbar turning in some of his best
work. But the center is lead singer Joseph
Hill's high, wavering voice. In song after
song, he conveys his own distinctive blend of
conviction and dread. The title cut, about
apocalypse in 1977, struck a chord in punk
England and was a hit there at the time. Reissued a decade later, the album is every bit
as consistent and compelling. [bk]

SMILEY CULTURE

"Cockney Translation" (nr/Fashion) 1984
"Police Officer" (nr/Fashion) 1984
The Complete Smiley Culture (nr/Fashion)
  1986

A recent arrival on the British reggae
scene, toaster Smiley Culture is a fresh, smart

comic who scored a left-field hit with "Cockney Translation," a bright and funny number comparing cockney with West Indian slang. The follow-up, "Police Officer," which pokes fun at the local constabulary, also topped the pop charts for weeks.

Smiley Culture's records speak directly to and for Britain's black people. "Cockney Translation" jokes about the confusing dialects that exist side-to-side in London but makes a point about how separate the groups that use them really are. Similarly, "Police Officer" is about racist treatment. Smiley gets off easy in the song when he's recognized, but the suggestion remains that not all blacks enjoy the same protection. (The two singles were recently repackaged as a single showcase EP with a couple of extended remixes thrown in for good measure.)   [bk]

CULTURE CLUB

Kissing to Be Clever (Virgin-Epic) 1982 ●
Colour by Numbers (Virgin-Epic) 1983 ●
Waking Up with the House on Fire
  (Virgin-Epic) 1984 ●
From Luxury to Heartache (Virgin-Epic)
  1986 ●
This Time—The First Four Years (Virgin-Epic)
  1987 ●

BOY GEORGE

Sold (Virgin) 1987 ●

For a time England's biggest pop sensation, ludicrously heralded (in the States by people oblivious to the music of the past decade or two) as leaders of a second British Invasion, Culture Club capitalized on Boy George's outrageous nightlife cross-dressing and aimed-to-shock intelligent interviews to slip their mushy mainstream soul-pop into respectable homes the world over. Phenomenology aside, the foursome never sounded anywhere near as bizarre as they originally appeared; regarding their albums in coldly critical terms reveals them to be nice but meaningless: sophisticated fodder, insidiously memorable and utterly disposable.

Kissing to Be Clever has such Club standards as "Do You Really Want to Hurt Me," a warm reggae pulse supporting the catchy melody, and "I'll Tumble 4 Ya," a boppy, upbeat dance number. Spurred by the American success of the former as a single, the US label switched the LP's track order to highlight it, and later reissued it with a subsequent 45, "Time (Clock of the Heart)," appended.

Dropping the silly "white boy" crypto-sociology that threads through the first album, **Colour by Numbers** gets right to the business at hand, which is the creation of irresistible pop hits in a variety of molds. And in that regard, the album is a real success, containing as it does the mildly folk-rock-psychedelicized "Karma Chameleon" and "Church of the Poison Mind," as well as the more soul-oriented "Miss Me Blind" and "Black Money." Easily the best of the four albums, **Colour by Numbers** prominently features singer Helen Terry, who provides a powerful foil to George's smooth crooning.

Riding high on stardom, Culture Club blew their rock credibility and career momentum totally with the ultra-dull **Waking Up with the House on Fire**. George's voice is fine and the band—drummer Jon Moss, guitarist/keyboardist Roy Hay and bassist Mikey Craig—plays with maximum slickness and sophistication, but the songs is irredeemably awful. From the torpid velveeta of "Mistake No. 3" (apt title, that) to the juvenile stupidity of "The War Song" ("War is stupid . . . ") and the inane stop-start mess of "Hello Goodbye," there's no material equal to the early singles. With misguided intentions of achieving political relevance *and* added middle-of-the-road acceptance, this sophomore album is an unmitigated disaster.

At that point, it seemed likely that the Club was on the verge of splitting up, and the lengthy delay in producing a new album only fueled pessimistic speculation about the group's future. Nonetheless, they managed to deliver **From Luxury to Heartache**, which isn't awful at all. Culture Club's new problem is their irrelevance: lacking controversy, a style to call their own or truly catchy songs, the album offers nothing to hold onto, just a bunch of well-produced (Arif Mardin and Lew Hahn) mild soul/funk MOR disposables. Given that Culture Club had never really changed musically, **From Luxury to Heartache** underscores the inexplicability of their original reception: it was ever thus.

Billed as "Twelve Worldwide Hits," **This Time—The First Four Years** consolidates all the essential 45s, plus "Love Is Love" from the *Electric Dreams* soundtrack. Despite occasionally brittle sound and the obligatory inclusion of dimwitted later material, "Karma Chameleon," "I'll Tumble 4 Ya," "Church of the Poison Mind," "Do You Really Want to Hurt Me" and "Time (Clock of the Heart)" just about covers Culture Club's basics for all but the most devoted aficionados. (The CD adds two cuts.)

Following the band's dissolution with public bouts of drug addiction and well-reported tabloid scandals, George resumed his life and his post-Culture Club career with the wretched **Sold**. Away from his bandmates, George and producer Stewart Levine whipped up a forgettable, overblown concoction that is dead on arrival. Indicative of George's total creative bewilderment, the album's dubious high point is an absurd reggae-ized version of Bread's "Everything I Own."

Jon Moss attempted to launch a new band, Heartbeat UK, in 1987, releasing a debut single called "Jump to It."   [iar]

See also *Edge, London, Mood*.

DAVID CUNNINGHAM

See *Flying Lizards*.

CURE

Three Imaginary Boys (nr/Fiction) 1979
Boys Don't Cry (PVC) 1980 (Elektra) 1987 ●
Seventeen Seconds (nr/Fiction) 1980 (Elektra)
    1987 ●
Faith (nr/Fiction) 1981 (Elektra) 1987 ●
Carnage Visors [tape] (nr/Fiction) 1981
. . . Happily Ever After (Fiction-A&M) 1981
Pornography (Fiction-A&M) 1982 ●
The Walk EP (Fiction-Sire) 1983
Japanese Whispers: The Singles (Fiction-Sire)
    1983 ●
The Top (Fiction-Sire) 1984 ●
Concert/The Cure Live (nr/Fiction) 1984 ●
The Head on the Door (Elektra) 1985 ●
Quadpus EP (Elektra) 1986
Standing on a Beach: The Singles (Elektra)
    1986 ●
Kiss Me Kiss Me Kiss Me (Elektra) 1987 ●
The Peel Sessions EP (nr/Strange Fruit)
    1988 ●

Though catapulted to some early success with the pop hit "Boys Don't Cry," the Cure—led by obsessive singer/guitarist Robert Smith, originally with Michael Dempsey on bass (replaced after one LP by Simon Gallup) and Laurence (Lol) Tolhurst on drums—originally (and to some extent continues to) specialized in the presentation of a gloomy, nihilistic world view.

Three Imaginary Boys (released in America—and later England—as **Boys Don't Cry**, with several songs replaced by singles) shows the Cure to be masters of the three-minute form, and includes some amaz-

ingly terse and effective musical dissertations on loneliness ("10:15 Saturday Night"), war and hatred ("Killing an Arab," "Fire in Cairo"), the precariousness of urban life ("Subway Song") and trendiness ("Jumping Someone Else's Train"). An intelligent, unique halfway point between Gang of Four and the Jam.

Seventeen Seconds moved the Cure further into terra incognita, away from the pop song and into the angst epic. Some songs ("Play for Today," "In Your House") still offer a fading element of hope, but the title track, "The Final Sound" and "A Forest" all take a turn toward disconsolateness.

Faith shows the arrival of despair as an element of style. Sacrificing any pretense of fun, the music is strengthened by an impassioned but sedated mood, its themes as powerful and defiant as any in recent music. (**Carnage Visors**, which appears only as a bonus on the UK cassette version of **Faith**, is the instrumental soundtrack of a short film, and provides even stronger reasons for locking up the razorblades while listening.)

The sarcastically titled **Happily Ever After** combines **Seventeen Seconds** and **Faith** whole into a double album for American release.

Pornography seems to be the climax of Smith's obsessions, by now coalesced into resigned paranoia; the music firmly establishes the group as superior if idiosyncratic. As usual, the true star here is the phobic, morbid atmosphere. Recommended, but not for the suicide-prone.

With Smith temporarily splitting his time between Siouxsie and the Banshees and his own band (which by this point had essentially become a core duo with Tolhurst), a far different Cure emerged. The playful "Let's Go to Bed" heralded a new era of stylistic innovation and sporadic whimsy, played out on a series of singles beginning in late 1982. **The Walk EP**—four songs of New Orderish synth-based music that's more solemn than miserable—was also issued in the US with the earlier "Let's Go to Bed" and its flipside added. A compilation of recent 45s, **Japanese Whispers**, then appeared in both countries, reprising the entire American EP plus a subsequent bit of jazzy froth, "The Lovecats," and its similar B-side, "Speak My Language."

Having almost fully exercised their dalliance with light relief, Smith and Tolhurst, joined by a drummer and sax player, recorded an all-new album, **The Top**, which basically returns them to more familiar corners of gloomy self-indulgence. Except for "The Caterpillar," which is upbeat and likable pop, the record is not among their best, and disjointed excursions into psychedelia, heavy rock and dance rhythms only punctuate its shortcomings.

Over the course of the following two years, the Cure issued a lot of music, although only one new studio album was among the onslaught of "product." The UK-only live record is most notable in its cassette version, which adds a bonus album's worth of outtakes and esoterica under the name **The Cure Anomalies 1977–1984**. Ditto the fine career-long (13) singles compilation, **Standing on a Beach**: the CD adds four tracks, the tape a dozen B-sides. (In a bizarre development, the LP's inclusion of "Killing an Arab" created an enormous tumult when an American pro-Arab organization, ignoring that the song dates from 1979, took its title from a famous Albert Camus novel and in no way advocates violence to Arabs, launched a political campaign against the band.)

With "In Between Days," **The Head on the Door** opens sounding exactly like New Order. By the second song, of course, Smith's fickle idiom dabbling returns the band—here a revamped quintet, with Simon Gallup back in the fold—to an entirely different world, via the mildly oriental "Kyoto Song," and follows in flamenco style with "The Blood." Toeing a line here between pop and sullenness keeps the Cure from achieving maximal creative impact, but it's an altogether listenable album that is sporadically ("Push" and "Close to Me," for example) as eclectically brilliant as can be. The **Quadpus EP** joins two B-sides—including the bizarre "A Man Inside My Mouth"—to "Close to Me" and "A Night Like This" from the album.

Doubtless encouraged by growing international stardom, the Cure released an ambitious and challenging double-album, **Kiss Me Kiss Me Kiss Me**. Sporting a dense and dynamic arena-scaled rock sound and adding such odd touches as wah-wah guitar, sitar, strings and horns, the organically coherent album surges with gloomy power but also percolates with occasional bits of charming low-key pop. Smith's resolutely miserable, ironic lyrical visions ("The Kiss," "Shiver and Shake," "How Beautiful You Are . . . ") infuse even some of the musically lighter songs, although a few (including "Catch," "The Perfect Girl," "Hey You!!!" and "Why

Can't I Be You?") do offer giddy love sentiments.

The Peel Sessions EP contains early renditions of "Killing an Arab," "10:15 Saturday Night," "Fire in Cairo" and "Boys Don't Cry," recorded in 1978 for a BBC broadcast.

[sg/iar]

See also *Glove, Siouxsie and the Banshees.*

CURIOSITY KILLED THE CAT
Keep Your Distance (Mercury) 1987 ●

The fickle finger of British chart-pop has elevated many unlikely but worthwhile bands to stardom, but of late has seen fit to anoint this sort of mainstream twaddle. The London quartet (originally known as the Twilight Children) plays highly-produced (mostly by Stewart Levine, although one track was actually—if imperceptibly—done by and with Sly and Robbie!) mechanized mild soul-pop like Boz Scaggs used to do with no discernible personality. But singer Ben Volpelière-Pierrot does wear a beret, so that explains everything, doesn't it? The CD adds four. [iar]

CURTISS A
Courtesy (Twin/Tone) 1980
Damage Is Done (Twin/Tone) 1983
A Scarlet Letter (Twin/Tone) 1988

SPOOKS
1980–1990 EP (Twin/Tone) 1978

Curt Almsted is a talented songwriter with a great sense of humor, an adequate if colorless voice and apparent connections with every other local Minneapolis musician (except maybe Prince), many of whom played on his first album. The tracks are energetic rockers in a niche between Marshall Crenshaw, Bruce Springsteen and George Thorogood, but much rawer and less predictable.

Damage Is Done is a more mature record that draws further on sources like primal soul to stretch Almsted's expanding skills (most notably as a singer, now showing signs of Van Morrison and Willy DeVille as well) and better display 11 well-drawn, heartfelt songs. The production is generally quite sympathetic, but the drums sound like distant cardboard boxes, and that significantly cuts the album's impact. There's still something missing—maybe a grander setting—that keeps Almsted a minor-leaguer, but he certainly has the wherewithal to move on up.

Almsted then went through a bad patch, losing longtime sideman Bob Dunlap to the Replacements, suffering a death in the family and ultimately winding up in jail on a battery charge involving an ex-girlfriend. Piling up years of bitterness over a number of women, Almsted spews out the pain on **A Scarlet Letter**, with NRBQ guitarist Al Anderson producing and heading up the backing band. Nakedly emotional missives like "I Wanna Make You Happy," "Starting to Cry," "I Can't Call Mary Anymore" and the brilliantly titled "(I Feel Just Like George Jones When IIe Was a) IIeel to Tammy" get soulful treatment from Almsted's impassioned voice, which has really come to resemble DeVille's. Easily Curtiss A's best record, **A Scarlet Letter**—unironically dedicated to Ike Turner—avoids hysteria for deep feelings that translate into resonant roots rock.

Almsted's early band, Spooks, debuted in '78 with a 7-inch EP of weird, punkish rock'n'roll (including "Scum of the Earth," a tribute to Travis Bickle) that bears little resemblance (but not none) to his subsequent work.   [iar]

ANDRE CYMONE

Livin' in the New Wave (Columbia) 1982
Survivin' in the 80's (Columbia) 1983
AC (Columbia) 1985 ●

An early member of Prince's touring ensemble, Cymone did his own "look ma, no band" musical crossover LP in 1982. Less horny and inspired than his former employer's contemporaneous approach, Cymone is nonetheless a strong contender in his own right and seems exhilarated (note the title of his first album) by the possibilities inherent in the same area of musical commingling.

Although **Survivin' in the 80's** still shows a lot of Prince's influence (especially image-wise—check the costumed male/female black/white band photo on the cover), Cymone is working more typical dance-floor terrain than the Purple One, with processed vocals and mild scratch production adjusting the slow funk grooves of numbers like "Make Me Wanna Dance" and "Body Thang." Slick and functional, but no creative biggie.

Back on his own in the studio, Cymone created **AC** with only skimpy outside assistance. Prince wrote and co-produced one easily recognizable track ("The Dance Electric") that also features backing vocals by Lisa and Wendy of the Revolution; he allowed others to add a few jots of percussion and vocals as well. Otherwise, Cymone remains perfectly capable—like his ex-boss—of working easily and independently in a number of styles, from languid reflection ("Pretty Wild Girl") to pretty balladry ("Sweet Sensuality") to kinetic dance music ("Book of Love," "Satisfaction").   [jg/iar]

CYNICS

Blue Train Station (Get Hip-Skyclad) 1986
Twelve Flights Up (Get Hip-Skyclad) 1988

Neo-garage-psychedelia from a Pittsburgh quintet weaned on "the punk explosions of '66 and '77." Standouts in an overworked genre, the Cynics achieve a quintessential evocation of their ancestors' glorious sound on **Blue Train Station** and **Twelve Flights Up**. Gregg Kostelich's guitars buzz with primal distortion as Michael Kastelic blurts out the lyrics in a sneery whine from somewhere deep within the sonic blur. Grungier than a seedy bar and more energetic than a class of hyperkinetic toddlers, the Cynics pack both albums (mostly originals, but some obscurities as well) with sure-footed atmosphere and excitement.   [iar]

HOLGER CZUKAY

See *Can, David Sylvian, Jah Wobble.*

D D D D D D D

DA
Time Will Be Kind EP (Autumn) 1982

Da was an early and important fixture on the Chicago hardcore scene, although the trio was musically removed from punk. Spare guitar, bass and drums create a cold, tense background for Lorna Donley's introspective lyrics, which she delivers with surety and strength, occasionally set in pretty melodies. Not a pleasant record, but one with conviction and a definite style on the way to being impressive. [iar]

DALE
See *Missing Persons.*

DALEK I
Compass Kum'Pas (nr/Back Door) 1980
Dalek I Love You (nr/Korova) 1983

Following several different lineups during 1977 and 1978, Dalek I Love You's name was shortened to Dalek I and the band reduced to a duo by the time their first album was recorded. Alan Gill and Dave Hughes (the former was subsequently guitarist in The Teardrop Explodes; the latter, drummer on OMD's first album) play a multitude of synths, guitars and percussion instruments on **Compass Kum'Pas,** an LP that should have been subtitled **Yet Another Green World,** what with its unabashedly Eno-esque soundscapes (not to mention a reading of "You Really Got Me" that owes its existence to Eno's **801 Live** arrangement). Still, any group that can segue the dirgelike "A Suicide" into a bouncy, poppy ditty like "The Kiss" is quirky enough to warrant investigation; also, as an exercise in stereo recordmaking, **Compass Kum'Pas** is a gem. A reformed Dalek I made a second album in 1983. [ds]

DALIS CAR
The Waking Hour (nr/Paradox-Beggars Banquet) 1984 ●

PETER MURPHY
Should the World Fail to Fall Apart (nr/Beggars Banquet) 1986
Love Hysteria (Beggars Banquet-RCA) 1988 ●

Peter Murphy (ex-Bauhaus) and Mick Karn (ex-Japan) plus a less illustrious drummer comprise Dalis Car, mixing Japan's sensuous sound with Bauhaus' obsequious lyrical constructs. As a mellifluous noise, **The Waking Hour** is fine if a bit heavy on the bass; dig any deeper, however, and what you get is a hollow attempt to create art without any redeeming artistry.

Murphy's subsequent solo career isn't much better. On **Love Hysteria,** his first post-Bauhaus effort issued in America, he walks a better-lit path than his gloomy band ever did. The intrinsic melodrama of Murphy's baritone benefits from the contrast with brittle, airy music that continues his dual fixation with Bowie (**Lodger**-era) and Japan. (Although the commercial moments resemble the dreaded Fixx.) Unfortunately, Murphy's chronically pompous pseudo-babble lyrics, coupled with horrible production (the bottom is as notably absent as D.B. Cooper), limits the appeal of **Love Hysteria** to late-'70s nostalgists and implacable Bauhaus fanatics. [iar]

ROLF DAMMERS
See *Can.*

138

DAMNED

Damned Damned Damned (nr/Stiff) 1977
(nr/Demon) 1986 ●
Music for Pleasure (nr/Stiff) 1977 (nr/Demon)
1986 ●
Machine Gun Etiquette (nr/Chiswick) 1979 ●
Black Album (IRS) 1980 ●
Friday the 13th EP (nr/NEMS) 1981
Best of the Damned (nr/Chiswick) 1981 ●
Strawberries (nr/Bronze) 1982 ●
Live at Shepperton 1980 (nr/Big Beat) 1982
Live in Newcastle (nr/Damned) 1983
Damned EP (nr/Stiff) 1985
Damned but Not Forgotten (nr/Dojo) 1985 ●
Is It a Dream? EP (nr/MCA) 1985
Phantasmagoria (MCA) 1985 ●
Damned Damned Damned/Music for Pleasure
(nr/Stiff) 1986
The Captain's Birthday Party (nr/Stiff) 1986
The Peel Sessions EP (nr/Strange Fruit)
1986 ●
The Peel Sessions EP (nr/Strange Fruit) 1986
Not the Captain's Birthday Party?
(nr/Demon) 1986
Anything (MCA) 1986 ●
Mindless, Directionless, Energy. Live at the
Lyceum 1981 (ID-Revolver) 1987 ●
The Light at the End of the Tunnel (MCA)
1987 ●
The Long Lost Weekend: Best of
Volume 1 1/2 (nr/Big Beat) 1988

NAZ NOMAD & THE NIGHTMARES

Give Daddy the Knife Cindy (nr/Big Beat)
1984

Holding the distinction of being the very first British punk band to issue an album (Stiff's first LP) as well as the first to tour America, the Damned hold a special position, historically if not always musically. Over an exceedingly checkered multi-label career—breakups, reformations, side projects, farewell gigs, a spell as the Doomed, vast popularity, near obscurity—the Damned have consistently managed to shatter expectations and defy the odds, wreaking havoc and nonchalantly tweaking convention. But getting a cogent critical perspective on their large recorded oeuvre is as elusive as attempting to read the label on a spinning 45.

Damned Damned Damned was a major groundbreaker, a stripped-down punk album of high-speed songs filled with raunchy guitar rock and equally aggressive sentiments. With Nick Lowe producing, the Damned trounced such traditional recording values as musical precision and studio-quality sound. Unfailingly energetic and vital, it's the only Damned album to feature the original lineup of Dave Vanian (vocals), Brian James (guitar), the exceptionally skillful Rat Scabies (drums) and Captain Sensible (bass). Just to heighten the bratty iconoclasm, early copies of the sleeve "goofed," and the back cover pictured rivals Eddie and the Hot Rods in lieu of the Damned.

Surprisingly enough, the second Damned opus was produced by Nick Mason of Pink Floyd. With added guitarist Lu (Edmonds), and no definite direction, the attack sounds blunted, and there aren't as many great songs as on the first. Despite its great cover, **Music for Pleasure** doesn't live up to the title. (Stiff reissued both LPs as a mail-order-only double in 1986.)

The Damned broke up and reformed several times before cutting **Machine Gun Etiquette** with a new lineup. Sensible had traded bass for guitar, Lu had departed (to join a number of bands including, most recently, Public Image) and ex-Saints bassist Algy Ward had joined. Despite the tumult, the band is totally revitalized and on top of things—more mature, but no less crazy—tearing through great numbers like "Love Song," "I Just Can't Be Happy Today" (both UK hits) and the anthemic "Noise Noise Noise." A great record by a band many had already counted out.

With a new bassist (ex-Hot Rod Paul Gray) in the lineup, the **Black Album**—a two-record set in the UK, one disc in America—takes off in a totally different direction, displaying unexpected character traits. The first two sides (the entire US release) are packed with melodic rock verging on power pop, using acoustic guitar, vocal harmonies, mellotron and synthesizers, as well as other seemingly inconceivable components. "Wait for the Blackout" and "Dr. Jekyll and Mr. Hyde" indicate how far the debonair Damned had traveled; other tracks prove that they had not abandoned the roar'n'roll with which they began. But the last two sides are dead weird: one is a single composition, strung together by church organ, that doesn't work; the other a live best-of that's impressive but half-baked. (**Live Shepperton 1980** comes from the same gig, but runs for two sides, not one, offering such bonuses as "Neat Neat Neat" and "Help.")

Mindless, Directionless, Energy was recorded in London (1981) with the Scabies-

Sensible-Vanian-Gray lineup and boasts crummy sound and an indifferent set of songs. "Smash It Up," "Love Song" and "I Feel Alright" are fair inclusions that receive exciting performances, but a terrible rendition of Sweet's "Ballroom Blitz" (dedicated to Lady Di and sung with a chorus of "great big tits") and other duff items make this dodgy record worth burying, not buying. (The CD adds a blistering "New Rose.") Yet another live album, **Not the Captain's Birthday Party?**, documents an earlier era, capturing the original band at work in late 1977. The two EPs of live-in-the-studio material recorded for broadcast by John Peel of the BBC date from December 1976 and May 1977; the latter is also available on CD.

A winning collection of great and diverse music, **Best of the Damned** consolidates the standout tracks from all the albums that preceded it, plus a couple of welcome non-LP sides to balance the bill. Stiff's 1985 **Damned** EP reissues five early cuts.

Strawberries, despite a humorous porcine cover shot, is a gormless, old-sounding affair that drags itself along with neither bite nor character, a few good songs notwithstanding. Short of truly terrible, it's merely forgettable.

Phantasmagoria is mainly Vanian's show. His imposing singing on graveyard items like "Grimly Fiendish" and "Sanctum Sanctorum" provides the character the songs themselves lack. Jon Kelly's production (complete with horror film effects and phantom-of-the-opera organ) is adequate, but the Damned no longer has a unique sound outside of Vanian, so it's fairly academic. (The LP was also issued in the UK with a bonus blue vinyl 12-inch of the subsequent "Eloise," a drippy Paul Ryan song which became a hit there.) An EP of the album's "Is It a Dream" adds four live tracks.

Released pseudonymously by Naz Nomad & the Nightmares, **Give Daddy the Knife Cindy** is the Damned's imaginary '60s psychedelic film soundtrack, filled with covers of such classics as "I Had Too Much to Dream (Last Night)," "Kicks," "Nobody but Me," Kim Fowley's "The Trip," plus a pair of originals. The material is great, but the unembellished studio performances are merely functional. A nice thought anyway.

Stability—the Damned's current lineup of Vanian, Rat, Welsh guitarist/keyboardist

Roman Jugg (who joined in 1981) and bassist Bryn Merrick has gone unchanged since 1984—has evidently had a negative effect on the band's creativity. **Anything** boasts a neat version of Love's "Alone Again Or," but otherwise falls well short of achieving anything memorable. Despite the Damned's proven ability to alternately rock gothic and play nice, there's no audible point to the music; it's hard to imagine who would find this LP pleasurable.

The Light at the End of the Tunnel is a haphazardly sequenced two-record decade-spanning compilation with a dandy family tree by that British national treasure, Pete Frame. The unassailable 27-cut selection includes hits, album cuts, non-LP mixes, B-sides (like "Help" from '77) and other rarities, but what possible illogic guided the track order? ("New Rose," "Neat Neat Neat," "I Feel Alright" and "I Feel the Pain" are all on different sides!)

The Long Lost Weekend puts a number of odds and ends on one compilation: **Friday the 13th**, B-sides, four cuts from **Strawberries**, even a joint recording with Motorhead: 15 tracks in all. [iar]

See also *Captain Sensible, Lords of the New Church.*

DANCE

Dance for Your Dinner EP (GoGo) 1980
In Lust (nr/Statik) 1981
Soul Force (nr/Statik) 1982

Dance for Your Dinner introduced a promising New York funk outfit heavy on rhythmic interplay, fronted by the seductive Eugenie Diserio, who veers cuts like "She Likes to Beat" closer to Donna Summer than authentic funk. Helped on drums by Material's Fred Maher, the four songs live up to the band's intricate intentions.

In Lust finds the Dance stiff and stifled in the studio; the band never stretches out its bass lines and there's not really enough material to fill an album. Diserio's softcore eroticism, so appealing on the EP, is held in check.

Soul Force has a similar lack of inspiration. Except for a stirring cover of Stevie Wonder's "Do Yourself a Favor," the album never hits a groove, though not for lack of effort. Diserio is the sexiest she's been, and the production is uncluttered, but the Dance has yet to record anything memorable.

[gf]

DANCING HOODS

12 Jealous Roses (Relativity) 1985
Hallelujah Anyway (Relativity) 1988 •

Formed on Long Island, birthplace of the Stray Cats and Billy Joel, Dancing Hoods (following a self-released eponymous EP) debuted with familiar-sounding heartland rock on **12 Jealous Roses**, a confident and likable collection of tuneful originals. Guitarist Bob Bortnick (with the others adding valid contributions) pens simple rockers about the usual topics and sings them in a melodic cut-to-the-chase style that isn't all that dissimilar to, say, the Del-Lords. A flat-footed cover of the Left Banke's pure-pop harmony classic "She May Call You Up Tonight" only serves to demarcate the quartet's vocal limitations.

Leaving singing/songwriting bassist Eric Williams behind, the Hoods relocated to Los Angeles, dropped their stylistic affectation and took a shot at heavy rotation with **Hallelujah Anyway**, an unambitious mainstream rock record produced by John Cougar Mellencamp associate Greg Edward. Although the songs aren't nearly as fresh or memorable as those on the first LP, the arrangements (newly colored by guest keyboards) make better use of them. Enjoy the Hoods' rudimentary debut and leave this one to radio programmers in satin jackets.   [iar]

DANNY & DUSTY

The Lost Weekend (A&M) 1985

This one-off studio bender assembles the cream of LA's cowpunk society for a batch of rowdy tunes about drinkin', lovin', gamblin' and losin'. The cast: Dan Stuart and Chris Cacavas of Green on Red, Steve Wynn and Dennis Duck of Dream Syndicate and most of the Long Ryders. Produced by Paul Cutler, **The Lost Weekend** offers a saucy good time, short on significance, but long on ambience and spirit. For reference, a version of Dylan's "Knockin' on Heaven's Door" typifies the tenor of Wynn/Stuart's collaborative songwriting.   [iar]

DANSE SOCIETY

Seduction EP (nr/Society) 1982
Heaven Is Waiting (Arista) 1984
Heaven Again (Arista) 1985
International (nr/Society) 1986
The Peel Sessions EP (nr/Strange Fruit) 1988

Arty and willfully obscure, Danse Society occasionally mixes almost-straightforward rock into dense dance rhythms, yielding a good song now and again. **Seduction** is a longwinded six-song effort with busy Bauhaus-strength mud supporting sporadic vocals and gimmicky sound effects. Tuneless and tedious. The first album contains additional plodding nonsense, but at least boasts the abrasive but catchy dance-rock of the title track and a weirdly modernized reading of the Stones' already spacey "2000 Light Years from Home." Danse Society subsequently metamorphosed into just Society and continued issuing records—to little notice—on their own Society label.   [iar]

TERENCE TRENT D'ARBY

Introducing the Hardline According to
  Terence Trent D'Arby (Columbia) 1987 •

Once he topped the US charts with "Wishing Well," the press was full of talk about hype, but hit or not, expatriate American Terence Trent D'Arby is an outstanding soul singer. Versatile, too, with the ability to produce a compelling gospel wail ("If You All Get to Heaven"), a funky shout ("Dance Little Sister") or a sultry romantic come-on ("Sign Your Name"). Confident down to his toenails, D'Arby inspires favorable comparisons to such luminaries as Al Green, Sam Cooke and Smokey Robinson, and he rocks out, to boot. (Fans of more obscure British rock may recognize the Roger Chapman influence on "If You Let Me Stay.") Should be interesting watching him develop.   [jy]

DARK DAY

See *DNA*.

DAS DAMEN

Das Damen EP (Ecstatic Peace) 1986 (SST)
  1986
Jupiter Eye (SST) 1987
Triskaidekaphobe (SST) 1988

Like many other young bands in the '80s, longhaired New York quartet Das Damen cavalierly crosses decades of musical influences to inbreed contemporary whateverism with '60s acid rock, '70s arena metal and '80s post-punk. The quartet relies on loud guitars, unrestrained energy and their college educations to produce music that has fire and intelligence, if not always impact.

The group's debut EP, released originally on a label run by Thurston Moore of Sonic

Youth but quickly reissued by SST, offers six badly mixed long songs that are noisy but fun. Roaring guitar chords, above-average vocals, solid drumming and an invaluable sense of dynamics balance the unfocused sonic wash and formless songwriting.

The dodgy sound quality on **Jupiter Eye** is similarly haphazard, but the album reveals enlarged stylistic ambition and sophistication. Hard-driving instrumental sections are enthralling, with the shambling electrified chaos of live improvisation; the poorly-recorded vocals are effective additions only some of the time. "Girl with the Hair" and "Name Your Poison" balance the two sides just right; the mild-mannered "Do" offers a most appealing low-key antidote. **Jupiter Eye** contains all the ingredients for excellence, but Das Damen is still fitting the pieces together. (A good producer wouldn't hurt.)

The well-rehearsed organization and clear, balanced audio fidelity of **Triskaidekaphobe** removes some of the rampant wildness in favor of moves towards syncopated hard-rocking power and disarmingly melodic tunes. "Bug" and "Candy Korn" are virtually pop songs (albeit with feedback); "Spider Birds" crosses Lynyrd Skynyrd with Cheap Trick; "Reverse into Tomorrow" updates sprightly power-pop with augmented chords and a knee-twisting time shift; "Pendant" takes a driving and textured Hüsker Dü approach and cuts it up with an unexpectedly delicate bridge. Although this impressive album diverges out of focus, it seems likely that Das Damen's growing bag of tricks will eventually yield a completely satisfying record. [iar]

DASH RIP ROCK
Dash Rip Rock (688) 1987

Taking their name from a character on *The Beverly Hillbillies* (Elly May's movie star paramour), this New Orleans trio puts a bloodboiling adrenaline rush under a pepper pot of rhythm & blues, old-time rock'n'roll and tradition-minded country. Guitarist/singer Bill Davis is a talented powerhouse; bassist Ned Hickel and drummer Fred LeBlanc keep the music at a constant boil; all three write. Dash is the kind of rough-and-ready band you imagine tearing up a roadhouse somewhere in dreams of highway adventures; **Dash Rip Rock** has a few flaws but bears the unmistakable imprint of a significant find. This new old-fashioned band is just waiting to burst into the big time. [iar]

DATA
Elegant Machinery (Sire) 1985

The unpredictable career of Georg Kajanus (once leader of the silly but entertaining Sailor) continues on a bizarre path with this appealing electro-pop duo. Joined by a femme singer named Frankie, with ex-Sailormate Henry Marsh and ex-Advertising man Simon Boswell providing added keyboards, Kajanus spins out technically facile but emotional numbers with enough formulaic pop sensibility to make them all could-have-been hit singles. [iar]

See also *Peter Godwin*.

DAVID & SYLVAIN
See *New York Dolls*.

MARTHA DAVIS
See *Motels*.

DAWGS
My Town (Star-Rhythm) 1982
On the Road to You (Fr. New Rose) 1983

These Boston bar rockers play ingenuous '60s Stones-styled original rock'n'roll tunes with choogling guitars and vocal panache on **My Town**. Produced by ex-Brownsville Station leader Cub Koda, the sound is muddy and the energy level only about half of what it might be, but a refreshing lack of pose and nostalgia-mongering redeems the project. On the Road to You reprises two of those tracks (which sound far better—must have been the mastering), adds three produced atmospherically by Elliot Easton and five more; the audio results are far crisper and the playing significantly hotter. [iar]

DANIELLE DAX
Pop-Eyes (nr/Initial) 1983 (nr/Awesome) 1985
Jesus Egg That Wept (nr/Awesome) 1984 + 1985
Inky Bloaters (nr/Awesome) 1987 ●
The Janice Long Session (nr/Nighttracks-Strange Fruit) 1988

LEMON KITTENS
Spoonfed and Writhing EP (nr/Step Forward) 1979
We Buy a Hammer For Daddy (nr/United Dairies) 1980
Cake Beast EP (nr/United Dairies) 1981

Those That Bite the Hand That Feeds Them Sooner or Later Must Meet the Big Dentist (nr/Illuminated) 1981

Danielle Dax, Our Lady of the Arabic dance slink, has a voice like vanilla yogurt: cool, high and honey-sweet with a tartly mysterious stylistic flavor that keeps her work from sounding the slightest bit mainstream. From the old Hebrew inscription of her Awesome Records logo (apparently gibberish) through the lyrics on **Inky Bloaters** (where "Big Hollow Man" reaps the wages of his materialistic hypocrisy), there's an underlying current of Biblical mysticism embedded in her work and an infectiously droney middle-Easternness to many of her melodies.

An eclectic collision between arty and rootsy, Dax's work ranges from the almost scientifically crisp and clinical " . . . In Wooden Brackets" (which she recorded while still a member of the Lemon Kittens) where backward instrumental tracks meet warbling pseudo-Chinese vocal chirps, to the mutant blues/gospel of "Evil-Honky Stomp" (from **Jesus Egg That Wept**) in which a moaning, off-kilter saxophone evokes images of Mississippi riverboats as she sings of branding slaves with all the sweetness of a Scarlett O'Hara wafting down a staircase.

The bright bop and twinkle of "Here Come the Harvest Buns" (included on both **Jesus Egg** and **Pop-Eyes**) bounces with perky electronic keyboard percussion, triangle and bottle plinks, disguising its dark message to cheating spouses: "Spin we go with a hi-de-ho, with a knee in the place where the hero roamed." The sweeter she sounds, the more sinister her ideas. (The reissued version of **Jesus Egg** contains an additional track.)

Dax has a million sounds and at least two million visions to cram onto vinyl. Those visions were originally explored with the help of collaborator Karl Blake, who shared vocals, writing, performing and production duties in the fecund Lemon Kittens. (He appears as a guest musician on **Jesus Egg**'s "Ostrich"). Around 1984, she began to work with guitarist/keyboardist David Knight; he appears on some of **Jesus Egg**'s tracks. Dax later brought in guitarist Ian Sturgess, who also plays everything from jaw harp to harmonica in the band. .

The positively brilliant **Inky Bloaters** finds the trio merrily plundering the sounds of the '60s (as well as ancient slinky Middle-Easternisms) with mock-sitars, giddy fuzz guitars and a by-the-numbers songbook that helps recall everyone from Mungo Jerry ("Inky Bloaters") to T. Rex ("Big Hollow Man"). "Flashback," "Sleep Has No Property" and the spacey "Brimstone in a Barren Land" are just three of the enticing potions Dax delivers in this remarkably inventive stylistic distillation of the Woodstock generation.

The Janice Long Session EP consists of four songs recorded live in the studio at the end of 1985.   ['e/iar]

MORRIS DAY

Color of Success (Warner Bros.) 1985 ●
Daydreaming (Warner Bros.) 1987 ●

Morris Day's relationship with Prince is the stuff of *Dynasty* or *Dallas*—a longstanding friendship marred by rivalry, jealousy, public one-upsmanship and other professional feuding. Prince raised Day to stardom by helping his band, the Time (Prince associates but not a puppet outfit), and later casting Morris in a starring role as his musical archenemy in *Purple Rain*. Soon after that, the Time collapsed and Day went solo, issuing an album with a thinly-veiled title and a mock radio announcement on the first track explaining his situation and promising great things ahead. Color of Success has less of Day's personality than the final Time LP, pointing him in a rather familiar-sounding pop-soul direction. Things get ridiculous when Morris introduces a new dance, "The Oak Tree," in a seemingly endless display of self-amusement; on stronger footing, he rocks steady with "Love Sign" and waxes smoothly romantic on "Don't Wait for Me."

Morris allowed his wildy successful former bandmates Jimmy Jam and Terry Lewis to co-write and produce a pair of songs on **Daydreaming**, turning them into a Time reunion with guest appearances by Jerome Benton, Jellybean Johnson and Jesse Johnson. Overall, the material is dire, a mix of dull ballads (including the macho bullshit of "A Man's Pride") and unexciting dance movers; even the Jam/Lewis efforts fail to connect. Although it lacks conviction, Day's smooth singing is appealing enough; the painfully obvious lack of substantial material is **Daydreaming**'s undoing.   [iar]

DB'S

Stands for Decibels (nr/Albion) 1981 (IRS) 1988 ●

143

Repercussion (nr/Albion) 1982 (IRS) 1988 ●
Like This (Bearsville) 1984 (Rhino) 1988 ●
The Sound of Music (IRS) 1987 ●

WILL RIGBY

Sidekick Phenomenon (Egon) 1985

It's difficult to understand why the dB's' first two albums—both well-conceived and accessible—were not released in the band's own country. On the first, the four New York-based North Carolina refugees draw inspiration from '60s pop psychedelia and quote freely from sources such as the Beatles, Move, Nazz and even the Beau Brummels. However, Peter Holsapple and Chris Stamey, the group's two singer-guitarist-songwriters, each have too individual a style to merely parrot, and nearly every song has some new twist, whether through production effects (few pop records are as consistently aurally interesting as this without resorting to gimmickry), or an unusual instrumental or lyrical approach. **Stands for Decibels** is not a happy record—often as not the songs are about deteriorating relationships—but the playing is so exuberant that it's uplifting.

Repercussion adds a number of flourishes to the group's style. Producer Scott Litt achieves a fuller, more modern overall sound; instrumentation on many of the tracks is denser than anything on its predecessor. The Rumour Brass makes an appearance on "Living a Lie." In addition, drummer Will Rigby—one of a mere handful of current rock drummers with a sound of his own beyond mere beat-keeping—is brought more to the fore on numbers like "Ask for Jill" and "In Spain." Depending on one's preferences in production style, **Repercussion** can be seen either as a great advance from **Decibels** or as a glossing-up of the group's sound.

Just as the dB's *finally* signed to an American label, Chris Stamey left for a solo career. With a little instrumental realignment, they recorded **Like This** as a trio, adding a new bassist afterwards. Although the reliance on Holsapple's songwriting cuts down on the band's eccentricities, their unpretentious intelligence, wit and ineffable pop smarts make it a wonderful album with no weak spots or inadequate songs. Dropping much of the British influence in favor of an Americanized, countryfied air, tunes like "Love Is for Lovers," "Lonely Is (As Lonely Does)" and "White Train" carry the banner of romance disappointed in memorable settings. An instantly lovable gem.

Unfortunately, Bearsville Records dis-solved shortly after the release of **Like This**, again leaving the group label-less. (**Like This** was subsequently picked up by Rhino, who also gave it its first CD release, and included two extra tracks, including an extended remix of the excellent "A Spy in the House of Love.") By the time IRS finally signed the band, the lineup had returned to a quartet, with the addition of New Orleans bassist Jeff Beninato.

The Sound of Music finds them continuing in the style of **Like This**, with similarly fine results. The country elements that began to surface on **Like This** continue on tracks like "Bonneville," complete with fiddles and mandolins, "Never Before and Never Again," a brilliant Holsapple duet with Syd Straw, and "Looked at the Sun Too Long," which could easily be mistaken for a Gram Parsons tune. There's still plenty of great pop, too, and the group gets heavy on "Any Old Thing." Gene Holder subsequently left to join the Wygals, leaving the dB's a trio for the second time.

IRS is scheduled to reissue (on LP and CD) the band's first two albums before the end of 1988, which means the dB's' entire superb output will finally be available domestically.

Drummer Rigby's solo record is a loopy laugh, a ramshackle one-man-band collection of country covers and likewise originals on which his kit is often the most prominent item in the mix. The singing is informal but engaging (as are his skills on piano, guitar, harmonica and other instruments); Holsapple's occasional contributions don't interrupt the casualness of this delightfully unselfconscious romp. [ds/iar]

See also *Kimberley Rew, Sneakers, Chris Stamey.*

D.C.3

This Is the Dream (SST) 1985
The Good Hex (SST) 1986
You're Only as Blind as Your Mind Can Be (SST) 1986

Erstwhile Black Flag guitarist Dez Cadena's current band (a trio for one LP, a quartet since) makes albums, to quote him, "in the style of the records that used to excite us when we were young." Unfortunately, what he remembers fondly is Deep Purple and Humble Pie, and the first two albums resemble various '60s and '70s nightmares, from Blue Oyster Cult to Black Sabbath. There's actually some fine music and an amusing undercurrent to both, although the subtle satirical value may be missed by those too young (or too old).

With the dated influences toned down, leaving a state of pleasantly mild nostalgia, the third LP turns up the lyrical power. As Cadena's liner notes note, "I ended up hurting someone who is very close to me. This album is about life without that person." With singleminded dedication, selections like "Baby, You Know Where I Live," "Party for One," "I Ain't Got You," "Lost Someone" and "Talkin' to the Mirror" verbalize his anguished cry with an intensity the upbeat music lacks.   [iar]

DEAD BOYS
Young Loud and Snotty (Sire) 1977
We Have Come for Your Children (Sire) 1978
Night of the Living Dead Boys (Bomp)
    1981 ●

Although originally from Cleveland, the Dead Boys made their international reputation in New York starting in early '77 by outpunking everyone else on the Bowery circuit. Having absorbed what had already happened in England (the Sex Pistols, Damned) and America (the Stooges), the Dead Boys took it a dozen steps further, uncovering new levels of violence, nihilism, masochism and vulgarity. Their two studio albums have aged well and now undoubtedly serve as guideposts to younger fans and players.

Young Loud and Snotty, one of the earliest punk albums released on a US label, benefits from the production skill of Genya Ravan, who made it loud and raw—an onslaught of sizzling guitars and Stiv Bators' sneering whine. Classic tracks include tasteless originals like "Sonic Reducer," "All This and More" and "Caught with the Meat in Your Mouth," as well as a dynamic rendition of the Syndicate of Sound's prototypical "Hey Little Girl."

We Have Come for Your Children, produced by Felix Pappalardi, has inferior sound, but equally strong playing. The material suffers from second-LP drought and an onset of self-parodic punk typecasting, leading to such dumb tunes as "Flame Thrower Love," the topical "Son of Sam" and "(I Don't Wanna Be No) Catholic Boy." The record's best track is the reflective "Ain't It Fun," co-written by guitarist Cheetah Chrome and the late Cleveland legend, Peter Laughner.

Night of the Living Dead Boys was re-corded live at CBGB in New York in 1979, and captures the end of the band, flailing through their best numbers in ultimate ragged-but-right fashion. Although the mix is trebly and muddled (a rare combination), this is still a punk documentary of some merit.

The Dead Boys—Bators, Chrome, Johnny Blitz and Jeff Magnum—reformed in 1987 and issued a single, "All the Way Down (Poison Lady)." Following the Dead Boys and assorted solo efforts, Stiv (the "s" on his surname comes and goes) recorded a 1988 single with the Lyres   [tr]

See also *Stiv Bators, Lords of the New Church, Lyres, Wanderers.*

DEAD CAN DANCE
Dead Can Dance (nr/4AD) 1984 ●
Garden of the Arcane Delights EP (nr/4AD)
    1984
Spleen and Ideal (nr/4AD) 1985 ●
Within the Realm of a Dying Sun (nr/4AD)
    1987 ●

Mesmerizing if a bit laborious, Australian quintet Dead Can Dance spin slow webs of drum-driven but mostly shapeless guitar music, with chanting, singing and howling by the two (male and female) singers: possibly of interest to undiscriminating fans of moody psychedelia and/or the Cocteau Twins. The more intriguing four-song **Garden of the Arcane Delights** EP has crisper production than the album, although roughly the same musical stylings.

By the time **Spleen and Ideal** was released, DCD were down to a duo of vocalists Brendan Perry and Lisa Gerrard. Some of the guitars have given way to ethereal keyboards, with tympani, cellos and trombones blended in; much of the LP sounds as though it belongs in a cathedral rather than a concert hall. The songs are more structured than before, but things do get a bit precious, and the first three, hymnalesque cuts are pretty tough to sit through. The music gets meatier as it progresses, though, and the end result is a record of haunting and solemn beauty.

With song titles such as "Xavier" and "Dawn of the Iconoclast," and credits to people contributing things like bass trombone, oboe and military snare, there's no way that **Within the Realm of a Dying Sun** (and how about that title?) could be quite as boring as it sounds. (Comes close at times, mind you.) Many will find it an all-too-precious '70s-style classical rock throwback, which it basically is; if this pair fancy themselves creators of some sort of "serious" modern classical music, they'll have to come up with things a little more harmonically interesting and texturally varied than this. Rock fans who really think that they're broadening their musical horizons by listening to Dead Can Dance should check out their local symphony orchestra schedules and go for the real stuff—this was done better a hundred years ago.

[dgs]

See also *This Mortal Coil*.

DEAD FINGERS TALK

Storm the Reality Studios (nr/Pye) 1978

Dead Fingers Talk, although never very well known, was an important band ahead of its time. Tom Robinson, for one, reportedly took heart from BoBo Phoenix's frank discussions of gay life on this record before taking the militantly gay stance that first won him recognition. On this lone album, DFT play with a gritty recklessness reminiscent of the early Velvet Underground, a resemblance heightened by Mick Ronson's audio vérité production. (Forget overdubs!) Singer/songwriter Phoenix's tunes don't mince words: "Nobody Loves You When You're Old and Gay" is simultaneously cutting and hilarious, while "Fight Our Way Out of Here" mixes desperation and anger. Elsewhere, he offers optimistic tunes just to show he's well rounded, but these too have a harsh intensity. Not to be missed, if you can find it.   [jy]

DEAD KENNEDYS

Fresh Fruit for Rotting Vegetables (IRS) 1980 ●

In God We Trust, Inc. EP (Alternative Tentacles) 1981

Plastic Surgery Disasters (Alternative Tentacles) 1982

Frankenchrist (Alternative Tentacles) 1985 ●

Bedtime for Democracy (Alternative Tentacles) 1986 ●

Give Me Convenience or Give Me Death (Alternative Tentacles) 1987 ●

KLAUS FLOURIDE

Cha Cha Cha with Mr. Flouride (Alternative Tentacles) 1985

JELLO BIAFRA

No More Cocoons (Alternative Tentacles) 1987

It took a while, but in the Dead Kennedys, America finally produced a powerful, self-righteously moral band to match the fury of the Sex Pistols. Led by audacious and inimitable singer Jello Biafra (who once stood—and received a substantial number of votes—for mayor in San Francisco, the band's base), the DKs combine blunt and sardonic discussions of touchy issues with crushing, high-speed guitar and drums. Generally acknowledged as prime pioneers of American hardcore, the Kennedys have been influential, not only by setting a style, sensibility and commendable standards, but with their productive Alternative Tentacles label and active support for grassroots rock activity. Biafra's legal confrontation over the poster included in **Frankenchrist** effectively ended the band, but left a powerful anti-censorship legacy for others to uphold.

Despite a few weak songs, **Fresh Fruit** is explosive and gripping (also controversial—a borrowed photo used on the back cover led to some funny but unpleasant legal trouble). Jello's political sarcasm erupts on "Kill the Poor" and "California über Alles," offering a funny but chilling condemnation of then-governor Jerry Brown and "zen fascists" in the latter. "Holiday in Cambodia" echoes the Pistols' "Holidays in the Sun" and became a DKs standard. In typically unsubtle broadside fashion, Jello nails another popular target with "Let's Lynch the Landlord."

In God We Trust, Inc. offers additional valid statements about the religious right, but the music is stripped of dynamics and reduced to routine hyperactive punk. Scrap the record and keep the lyric sheet.

Plastic Surgery Disasters, with a gruesome mock-*E.T.* cover, enlarges the musical blend to include more three-dimensionality while retaining the Kennedys' typical rock energy. Songs like "Terminal Preppie," "Winnebago Warrior," "Trust Your Mechanic" and "Well Paid Scientist" mix humor and activism for pointed and intelligent observations on social absurdity.

The DKs stopped recording for several years while the members worked on outside projects. Bassist Klaus Flouride was the busiest boy, producing other bands for release on Alternative Tentacles and recording his own one-man seven-song mini-album, **Cha Cha Cha with Mr. Flouride**. Displaying not the slightest trace of political consciousness, Klaus lets down his hair on a straight rock'n' billy (with a guest drummer and pianist) love ode, "My Linda." Elsewhere, he laments a serious social problem, "Dead Prairie Dogs," and takes an amusing cowboy ride with "Ghost Riders." The simple music—mostly guitars and cheap-sounding electronics—is lighthearted and goofy, showing more spirit than originality, but cute nonetheless. (And the cover is great.)

In early 1985, the band hit the hard road again with **Frankenchrist**, which generally repeats the psycho-punk of **Plastic Surgery Disasters**. There are some bad tracks that have forced, awkward lyrics, but the LP does contain two of the DKs' finest moments: "MTV Get off the Air" and "Stars and Stripes of Corruption," one of the most powerful political statements ever committed to vinyl. Instead of just bellyaching about problems (a common habit of politico-punks), Biafra offers possibilities for constructive change, demonstrating real American patriotism as opposed to jingoistic commie-bashing.

Bedtime for Democracy—21 strong cuts and an eight-page clip-art newspaper—ended the Kennedys' recording career on a high note. A full-tilt platform of targets, including working poverty, Reagan, toxic waste, macho attitudes, conformity and more, are decimated with energetic, well-played music and Biafra's uniquely quivery voice. The Kennedys' knowing cover of "Take This Job and Shove It" is also good for a chuckle.

In mid-'86, Biafra and others were charged by California authorities with "distribution of harmful matter to minors"—i.e., a reproduction of H.R. Giger's *Landscape #20,* which was included in **Frankenchrist**. More than a year later, the case—which might have led to a jail term—ended in a mistrial. The charges were dismissed but the Kennedys had had it.

The final chapter in the saga was **Give Me Convenience or Give Me Death**, a posthumous career recap, which contains 15 examples of the DKs' best work (hits, live performances and obscurities), a two-song flexi-disc ("Buzzbomb from Pasadena" and "Night of the Living Rednecks"—both added to the cassette and CD editions) and a newsprint art/lyric book. Essential for fans.

Biafra continued to ply his missionary trade with **No More Cocoons**, four sides of political satire recorded at college appearances, radio interviews, readings and instores. Spoken-word is definitely Biafra's ideal medium, and this is as sharp, funny and informative as any DKs record. Biafra applies his acerbic wit, endless wealth of outrage, abundant intelligence and dramatic skills to a variety of concerns, making the record highly worthwhile and grimly amusing. Those old enough to remember Lenny Bruce or even Mort Sahl in his prime may consider this a topical comedy record in the grand tradition; younger listeners are likely to hear it as a chilling reintroduction to what the DKs' songs were saying all along.

[jy/dgs/iar]

See also *Witch Trials.*

DEADLY HUME

Basement Tapes EP (Aus. Bulb) 1985
Me, Grandma, Iliko and Hilarian (Aus. Phantom) 1987
Lonely Mr. Happy (Aus. Phantom) 1988

The Deadly Hume take their name from the Hume Highway, a dangerous and desolate stretch of roadway between Melbourne and their hometown, Sydney. The band's sound derives from the clash and grind of urban Australia and the swampy darkness of American blues. On tracks like "Fine Line" (from **Me, Grandma, Iliko and Hilarian**), the rhythm-sticks-from-hell percussion clatter and sawing basslines could almost make the music pass for a lost outtake from **Fireman's Curse**-era Hunters and Collectors (Hume lead vocalist Greg Perano was in H&C at the time) while the swampy fuzz guitar and squealing chords of "My Head Feels Like It's Been Hit by a Train" drag the band through an intense and slithery Amer-Aussie version of '80s blues-rock. They use everything from a cappella spiritual choruses to acoustic guitar on their records.

The Nick Cave-esque "48 Coffees" intersperses shouts of "I'm nervous nervous nervous" with striptease-brash horns and mumbled stream-of-caffeine vocals, capturing the wiped-out frazzle anyone who's overdosed on java will recognize. "Trains Kept Shunting" (on **Grandma**) pounds with a soft, insistent drum pulse as what sounds like a box filled with sand shuffles and guitars peal out sheets of braking feedback and hard and clear chimes. Like impressionist painters working in sound instead of oils, Hume have the marvelous ability to make more than pop songs. They make art without a stuffy aftertaste. No desert island should be without a Hume record. ['e]

DEAD MILKMEN

Big Lizard in My Back Yard (Fever-Enigma) 1985 ●
Eat Your Paisley! (Fever-Restless) 1986 ●
Bucky Fellini (Enigma) 1987 ●

Instant Club Hit (You'll Dance to Anything)
  EP (Enigma) 1987 •

Philadelphia has been the subject of many jokes, but the mildly punky Milkmen, a homegrown insult machine with a snotty attitude and a grasp of modern society's cultural monstrosities, bring their own whoopie cushion to the party. On a lightweight foundation of plain, unfancy rock music, the Milkmen don't focus on individual victims so much as unleash their bratty irreverence in scattershot volleys.

The reckless insults and putdowns on **Big Lizard in My Back Yard** connect most memorably on 'Bitchin Camaro," a catchy cocktail-jazz/hardcore hybrid that makes light of AIDS while it satirizes teenagers, the Doors and sports car owners. Otherwise, the record's sense of humor is stupid and only spottily amusing.

Eat Your Paisley! makes less of an effort to be funny or offensive, and manages to convey the satire better by painting bizarre B-movie tales like "Moron," "Beach Party Vietnam" and "The Thing That Only Eats Hippies." The group's wacky observations of stereotypes and artifacts are vague but astute; the music is expendable but never less than politely presentable.

Often tasteless, **Bucky Fellini** is a relatively expansive effort, with guest musicians, improved songwriting and such dementedly parodic cultural concepts as "Nitro Burning Funny Cars," "Going to Graceland," "(Theme from) Blood Orgy of the Atomic Fern" and "Instant Club Hit (You'll Dance to Anything)." Rodney Anonymous is a self-assured if unmusical vocalist; Joe Jack Talcum leads the guitar-based band through the artless tunes with easygoing aplomb. The **Instant Club Hit** EP offers three mixes of that vindictively funny number (including the all-percussion "Boner Beats"), plus tracks that were bonuses on the CDs of the first two albums and the previously unreleased "Ask Me to Dance." [iar]

DEAD OR ALIVE

Dead or Alive EP (nr/Black Eyes-Rough Trade) 1982
Sophisticated Boom Boom (Epic) 1984 •
"Youthquake" (Epic) 1985 •
Mad, Bad, and Dangerous to Know. (Epic) 1987 •
Rip It Up (Epic) 1988 •

Pete Burns, Dead or Alive's cross-dressing poseur/leader/singer can claim historical credit in the second Liverpool explosion—he was in a brief but seminal band with Julian Cope and Pete (Wah!) Wylie—before founding Nightmares in Wax, the developmental predecessor to Dead or Alive. The early EP finds him searching for meaning and truth while attempting to appropriate Jim Morrison's vocal style; it's murky, to say the least.

Sophisticated Boom Boom includes a totally horrible and gratuitous remake of KC and the Sunshine Band's "That's the Way (I Like It)"—and that's as good as the album gets. Burns sings as if his atavistic urges ("What I Want," "You Make Me Wanna," "I'd Do Anything") were the stuff of Shakespearean drama; the backing is slickly competent dance-rock bereft of any personality. (Of possible interest to fact fans: future Sister of Mercy and Mission founder Wayne Hussey was a onetime Dead or Alive member and co-wrote much of this album's material.)

Burns' bunch subsequently issued a couple of better 45s, including "You Spin Me Round (Like a Record)," that cut a lot of the crap and substituted a kinetic, catchy pop sensibility. Produced by the shallow but successful Stock, Aitken and Waterman team, **"Youthquake"** contains "You Spin Me Round," as well as the equally appealing "Lover Come Back to Me" and a few others that show how much fun Dead or Alive can be. On the other hand, the record has its bad patches, proving the impossibility of pinning down DorA to any steady style or quality level.

Mad, Bad, and Dangerous to Know. employs the same hitmaking mechanics to conjure up a consistent—*extremely* consistent—synthesized pop-dance groove which is easy to grasp and hard to hold. That the pulsing sequencer patterns on the nine lengthy soundalikes vary little may be seen as either a functional advantage or a mark of limited creative effort. "Brand New Lover" is giddily hummable for the first three or four minutes but then gets dead boring; the rest of this shoddy effort isn't as catchy. [jg/iar]

See also *Mission (UK), Sisters of Mercy.*

DEAF SCHOOL

2nd Honeymoon (Warner Bros.) 1976
Don't Stop the World (Warner Bros.) 1977
English Boys/Working Girls (Warner Bros.) 1978

A sprawling nine-piece (later eight), Liverpool's Deaf School seemed like an ideal candidate for success in the quiet pre-punk doldrums of 1976. Visually, the group had more than enough going for it to guarantee a high profile in the British press. The cast included pasty-faced guitarist Clive Langer, who sported wire-rims and wrote most of the melodies; the Rev. Max Ripple, a keyboardist done up like a parson; and no less than *three* lead vocalists: mustachioed Enrico Cadillac, a Bryan Ferry disciple; Bette Bright, who suggested a somewhat frumpy torch singer; and the suave, acid-voiced Eric Shark, who sang as Humphrey Bogart might have.

Despite its slick, full sound, **2nd Honeymoon** has the clear markings of a first effort. The band cleverly mixes the melodrama of Roxy Music with the music hall vivacity of middle-period Kinks, but many of the songs are bloated and their intent unclear. As on later LPs, crooner Cadillac takes the lion's share of the vocals, making tales of modern desperation ("What a Way to End It All") and lost love ("Room Service") into intriguing, if incomplete, exercises in style.

Deaf School came into its own on **Don't Stop the World**, trimming the excesses of **2nd Honeymoon** and adding impressive new elements. While Cadillac continues to warble romantically, Shark belts out a vicious rocker ("Capaldi's Cafe") and Bright shines in a rare solo spot, the after-hours ballad, "Operator." (The two LPs were issued in the US as a double-pack in 1977.)

Although **English Boys/Working Girls** offers more of the same, it's the product of a band running out of steam. In a return to the clutter of their debut, Deaf School favors theatrics over substance; acounts of modern violence like "Ronny Zamora (My Friend Ron)" and "English Boys (With Guns)" are more exploitation than insight.

Deaf School's alumni remained busy after the band folded, making it—in retrospect—a startling fount of promise. Enrico Cadillac formed the Original Mirrors under his civilian name, Steve Allen, and recorded two albums. Bassist Steve "Average" Lindsey founded the Planets and did the same. Bette Bright cut a delightful solo record, produced by Clive Langer, who, with his partner Alan Winstanley, earned additional production credits (not to mention scads of money, no doubt) with Madness, Elvis Costello and Dexys Midnight Runners. Langer also formed a band and released records.   [jy]

See also *Bette Bright, Clive Langer and the Boxes, Original Mirrors.*

DEATH COMET CREW
See *Dominatrix.*

DEATH CULT
See *Cult.*

DEFENESTRATION
Defenestration (Green Iguana) 1986
Dali Does Windows (Relativity) 1987

Cheap Trick must have passed through Norman, Oklahoma on the day this brilliantly-named quartet was born, for evidence of that band's influence crops up more than once on **Dali Does Windows**, a promising rock/pop record undermined by banal lyrics and Tyson Todd Meade's unpleasantly hoarse and occasionally sharp vocals. Randy Burns' production brings out the best in Todd Walker's rich guitar work, and captures all the punch the rhythm section can muster. Traces of PiL, Gen X, Dylan and the Who also color the songs, leaving the glimmers of originality to fend for themselves. Keep passing those windows, guys. (The band's first record is an independent-label seven-song mini-album.)   [iar]

CARMAIG DE FOREST
I Shall Be Released (Good Foot) 1987
CARMAIG DE FOREST + BAND
6 Live Cuts EP (Fr. New Rose) 1988

Undoubtedly the rockingest singer/songwriter ever to rely on ukulele, San Francisco's Carmaig de Forest emerges on his debut album (produced with creative electric ferocity by Alex Chilton) as a strong, independent voice with plenty on his mind. Following in the tradition of John Hiatt and Billy Bragg, de Forest is a brilliant folk-based tunesmith who synthesizes rock and other influences into a characteristically wry style. Chilton surrounds his (Lou) Reedy singing and polite ukework with a simple, effective band that deftly realizes such sharp-tongued originals as "Big Business," "Hey Judas" and "Crack's No Worse Than the Fascist Threat" at assorted energy levels. **I Shall Be Released** occasionally resembles the Violent Femmes; throughout, it exudes confidence, righteous political anger and enormous originality.

The French live EP was recorded at a pair of October 1987 San Francisco gigs with a bassist, drummer and guitarist. The material includes two album tracks, a thrilling cover of "You Can't Always Get What You Want" and three previously unwaxed tunes, one of them quite good. [iar]

DEFUNKT

Defunkt (Hannibal) 1980
Thermonuclear Sweat (Hannibal) 1982
In America (Antilles/New Directions-Island) 1988 ●

Led by singing trombonist Joe Bowie, the seven-man Defunkt peddles black funk with dry bounce. Originally formed as James Chance's horn section, Defunkt also had ties with the world of avant-garde jazz, putting it in a unique and culturally resonant position. **Defunkt** isn't a revolutionary breakout, but does include the super-catchy (if obtusely titled) "Blues," which was extremely popular at the time around New York. **Thermonuclear Sweat**, named for a track from the first LP, is sweeter-sounding and jazzier, smoothed out by Joe Boyd's sage production.

Following a two-year stint spent living in the Caribbean, Bowie returned to New York and formed a new six-piece incarnation of the band which debuted on vinyl in mid-'88.
[jw/iar]

DEL AMITRI

Del Amitri (Chrysalis) 1985

This Glasgow quartet fell victim to excessive hype before the release of its debut album. Many who went overboard praising the group on the strength of two singles and a few live performances unjustly criticized the LP—ten quirky, country-flavored tracks, drenched in crystalline Rickenbacker guitar and Hugh Jones' spare production—for being too traditionalist. Although admittedly a conventional construct, few play this style with as much heart as Del Amitri. These boys love what they do, and you can hear (and feel) it in such rollicking songs as "Crows in the Wheatfield" and "Sticks and Stones Girl." [ag]

DEL-BYZANTEENS

Del-Byzanteens EP (nr/Don't Fall off the Mountain) 1981
Lies to Live By (nr/Don't Fall off the Mountain) 1982

Up from the murky pit of New York's art-punk scene came the Del-Byzanteens, a band with stylistic threads running back through Television and the Velvet Underground and the ability to give their dark, urgent arrangements a cinematic pan. An unsettling cover of the Supremes' "My World Is Empty (Without You)" on the three-track EP is a slice of jungle paranoia with voodoo percussion, ominous group vocals that sound like a satanic mass and a guitar quotation from *Perry Mason*.

The group's inventive resources are spread a little thin, though, on **Lies to Live By**. The quirky B-52's guitarisms and hyper-disco thump of "Draft Riot" and dour facelessness (Joy Division variety) of the title track dull the impact of both "War," a clever union of funk-punk drive with protest lyrics from Caribbean calypso records, and the gray soul of the old Jaynettes' shuffle, "Sally Go Round the Roses." Both "Lies to Live By" and a new version of "Girl's Imagination" (from the EP) were used by German filmmaker Wim Wenders in his movie *The State of Things*. [df]

DEL FUEGOS

The Longest Day (Slash) 1984
Boston, Mass. (Slash-Warner Bros.) 1985 ●
Stand Up (Slash-Warner Bros.) 1987 ●

A solid album, **The Longest Day** is bursting with high-energy beat'n'billy-inflected guitar rock. The songs are memorable without pandering; the playing is simple but never simpleminded. From the quivering "Nervous and Shakey" (which opens the LP) to the ominous hipshake, "Call My Name," which ends it, this is a full, therapeutic dose of mature, unaffected rock'n'roll from the '50s and '60s built strictly in and for the '80s.

The Boston band's second LP has atrocious art direction and is a hair more selfconscious than the first. In light of the popularity of "working class" rock (or at least Springsteen and Mellencamp), **Boston, Mass.** sounds like it was designed to please a wide audience, although it actually recalls the old Animals more than anything else. On the other hand, the Del Fuegos can't be accused of making any radical readjustment, and no one expects them to abandon a style simply because it's become the radio vogue.

The stupid fold-out back cover gimmick of **Stand Up** should serve as a warning: this messy indulgence has guest appearances (by Tom Petty, James Burton and others) instead of worthwhile songs or any intrinsic personality. Dan Zanes' voice is largely shot; the spunky band of music-crazy street kids has turned into a grizzled bunch of oldtimers who run through this tired assortment of horned-out grit-rockers like a third-rate beer commercial. [iar]

GABI DELGADO

See *Deutsche Amerikanische Freundschaft.*

DEL-LORDS

Frontier Days (Enigma-EMI America) 1984
Johnny Comes Marching Home (EMI America) 1986
Based on a True Story (Enigma) 1988 ●

Musical pioneers at the East Coast's westernmost boundaries, New York City's Del-Lords stand in the forefront of back-to-the-roots countryfied urban rock'n'roll, eschewing any particular stylistic imitation to enthusiastically bang out well-written tunes of hard times and true love. With guitarist Scott Kempner (once "Top Ten" of the Dictators) penning the material but occasionally relinquishing lead vocals to guitarist Eric Ambel, the Del-Lords embrace rock's basic components with such skill and verve that they outshine most everyone else on the scene. The best tracks on **Frontier Days**—"Burning in the Flame of Love," "Feel Like Going Home" and a cover of Alfred Reed's "How Can a Poor Man Stand Such Times and Live"—are true-blue and brilliant.

The songs on **Johnny Comes Marching Home**—produced by Pat Benatar's husband, Neil Geraldo, with no ill effects—are better and the playing is even more confident and enthusiastic. Lyrical topics stretch from the sunny optimism of "Heaven" to the misery of "Love Lies Dying," with stops along the way for a kidnapped victim of terrorism ("Against My Will"), a love letter to a real-life '60s radio dj ("Saint Jake") and a veteran's wistful view of militarism ("Soldier's Home"). The music runs from a greasy Link Wray instrumental to a wittily disguised rewrite of "If I Had a Hammer." Not trendy, twangy, corny or selfconscious, the Del-Lords simply play the old-fashioned way, with a sharp ear for melody and choruses that don't evaporate after a few listens. Considering that the group's roots are essentially a quarter-century old, they sure make it sound fresh and young.

Although Geraldo's commercially-minded production work on **Based on a True Story** loses sight of the Del-Lords' essence—leaving them sounding in spots ("Judas Kiss," for instance) like a bland bar band straining to cop a chart hit—it's generally another proud blast from the Bronx heartland. "We don't follow fashion," writes Kempner (in "The Cool and the Crazy"), "Who needs it when you got style?" Oddly, the band's intrinsic savoir faire is less apparent than ever before, perhaps a casualty of too many guest stars. Mojo Nixon's participation in "River of Justice" adds helpful absurdity to the proceedings, but when a multi-tracked Syd Straw and others sing the chorus, it's hard to remember exactly whose record this is. On the other hand, at least "Whole Lotta Nothin' Goin' On," "Cheyenne" and the 12-bar "A Lover's Prayer" prove that the Del-Lords are still firmly in charge. [iar]

DELTA 5

See the Whirl (nr/Pre) 1981

Their name sounds like a 1920s jug band, but Delta 5's album displays up-to-the-minute beat consciousness welded to songs of emotional discontent. Double female vocals in pronounced British accents are backed by whomping rhythm (two guitars, two basses) and occasional splashes of musical color (brass, keyboards, pedal steel guitar). Semi-cryptic lyrics, full of striking images, are worth the strain needed to pull them out of the seething mass. Jagged music for jagged times. [si]

DEPECHE MODE

Speak & Spell (Mute-Sire) 1981 ●
See You EP (Mute-Sire) 1982
A Broken Frame (Mute-Sire) 1982 ●
Construction Time Again (Mute-Sire) 1983 ●
Everything Counts EP (nr/Mute) 1983
Get the Balance Right! EP (Mute-Sire) 1983
People Are People (Mute-Sire) 1984 ●
Some Great Reward (Mute-Sire) 1984 ●
The Singles '81–'85 (nr/Mute) 1985 ●
Catching Up with Depeche Mode (Mute-Sire) 1985 ●
Black Celebration (Mute-Sire) 1986 ●
Music for the Masses (Mute-Sire) 1987 ●
Never Let Me Down Again EP [CD] (nr/Mute) 1987

Born in England's new romantic movement, Basildon's Depeche Mode immediately proved capable of making flawlessly captivating electro-pop tunes with simple formulae. What set them apart was reliance on synthesizers for the entirety of their sound, offering post-modernistic gloss to comfortably familiar (but new) material. Over the years, the increasingly successful group has grown pompous and gloomy, embracing heavier and denser sounds, but they've never abandoned the singles format or lost their appeal to teenage girls.

Not coincidentally, the best songs on **Speak and Spell** were the hits: "New Life," "Dreaming of Me" and the smash "Just Can't Get Enough." Oblivious to innovation or deep thinking, the album is simply a good collection of modern dance tunes.

Despite the dire predictions that followed songwriter Vince Clarke's departure to form Yazoo, Depeche Mode pressed on, essentially unhampered, as a trio to make **A Broken Frame**, which has similar virtues, tempered with some deviation from course. The vocals are stronger, and while funk forms the rhythmic base of "My Secret Garden," a Japanese tinge is given to "Monument" and "Satellite" centers around a ska beat. The rest of the album varies to a small degree from the dancemania of earlier work without abandoning it—a characteristic midpoint between experimenting and playing it safe.

Expanding back to a quartet, with Martin Gore continuing as the main songwriter, **Construction Time Again** exposes a mature outlook, dropping the simplistic pop tunes for a more intellectual, challenging approach. The transition is not altogether smooth. "Everything Counts" offers a bitter denunciation of the (presumably music) business world and "Shame" is a heartfelt confrontation with responsibility. Other tunes ("Pipeline," "More Than a Party") are less probing, although the former has interestingly industrialized music and chanted vocals. Both the English **Everything Counts** EP and the American **Get the Balance Right!** maxi-single have live cuts in addition to remixes of the title tracks. (The **Construction Time** CD adds a bonus cut as well.)

Although the reasons for its assembly are unclear, **People Are People** is a compilation of post-Clarke tunes, drawing five of its tracks from the two preceding albums and the rest from singles. Not a cohesive album, it does contain prime material blending synth-rock with real-life and industrial noises to make truly modern pop music for the new age.

Some Great Reward is Depeche Mode's best record, containing everything from the bitter religious doubt of "Blasphemous Rumours" to the societal/sexual role-playing of "Master and Servant" and the egalitarian "People Are People." Seamlessly incorporating unsettling concrète sounds—like synthesized factory din and clanking chains—into the music, the group achieves a masterful music/life mix few of the same mind have approached.

As Depeche Mode's international stature grew to awesome proportions, two compilation albums—**The Singles** and **Catching Up**—were released in 1985. The former, issued in the UK, is a fine collection of 13 familiar 45 sides; the cassette and CD add two more cuts. The American release has most of the same tracks (excluding those already compiled on **People Are People**), but includes "Fly on the Windscreen" (which also turns up on **Black Celebration**) and "Flexible." Complicated enough?

Depeche Mode has tackled many different lyrical concerns in the past, but never have they done such a consistently downcast record as **Black Celebration**. Except for intermittent bouts of romanticism and a bluntly political protest ("New Dress"), the songs are filled with doubt, disgust and depression, an attitude their dirgelike, minor-chord constructions reinforce. The big problem is that the tunes mostly sound like each other; shards of the same melody turn up repeatedly. There's a certain demented power to this work, but it's not one of their more appealing or accomplished albums.

Music for the Masses is marginally brighter in temperament, but shows the band running low on creative juice. Unambitious, bland and forgettable, the album displays Gore's emotional anxieties, David Gahan's vocal limitations and little else. The tense "Behind the Wheel" and "Never Let Me Down Again" are the only powerful songs here, and they both have dumb lyrics and skimpy, underdeveloped melodies. "Pimpf," a turgid piece of operatic nonsense, ends the album on a most unpromising note. The CD has four bonus tracks.   [sg/iar]

See also *Erasure, Yazoo.*

DEPRESSIONS
The Depressions (nr/Barn) 1978

DP'S
If You Know What I Mean (nr/Barn) 1978

In their first incarnation, this quartet was an awful fake-punk band. To the group's credit, the playing on their first LP isn't strictly inept, but the material is utterly detestable (a concept of punk as misogyny so ugly it would offend Mötley Crüe) and the pose so transparent that you have to hate them. Perhaps the embarrassment of this record caused the band's name change shortly after its release.

Switching from pseudo-punk to pseudo-power pop, the Depressions became the DP's and made a second record which is not nearly as offensive as their first. They still can't write a memorable song and the playing never surpasses adequate, but at least nil-content is innocuous compared to their earlier cretinous outlook.   [ds]

DESCENDENTS
Fat EP (New Alliance) 1981
Milo Goes to College (New Alliance) 1982
    (SST) 1988 •
Bonus Fat (New Alliance) 1985 (SST) 1988 •
I Don't Want to Grow Up (New Alliance)
    1985 (SST) 1988 •
Enjoy! (New Alliance-Restless) 1986 (SST)
    1988 •
All (SST) 1987 •
Liveage! (SST) 1987 •

ALL
Allroy Sez . . . . (Cruz) 1987 •

LA's Descendents did their growing up in public, releasing a lot of records in an on-again/off-again career. Debuting on a likable 1979 single as a young power-pop trio, the Descendents didn't return to vinyl until 1981, when a quartet lineup issued the smart, fast and punky 7-inch **Fat EP**: six fleeting (total time 5:52) Black Flag-like culture statements like "Wienerschnitzel," "I Like Food" and "My Dad Sucks." (Both of those early records were reissued on the 12-inch **Bonus Fat** in 1985.)

When singer Milo Aukerman left to study biochemistry in San Diego, the group pressed on and issued **Milo Goes to College**, a promising hardcore album with a few dumb bummers amidst the fun. Then drummer Bill Stevenson left to join Black Flag, and the Descendents evaporated for a while.

When they got back together in 1985, Milo, Stevenson, bassist Tony Lombardo and ex-SWA guitarist Ray Cooper (taking founder Frank Navetta's place) recorded **I Don't Want to Grow Up**, an excellent and surefooted punk album that knowingly uses the hyperkinetic musical idiom as a disguise for intelligent, sarcastic songwriting with melodies (a few border on power pop) and substantial lyrics that drift around the edge of obnoxiousness without entirely giving in to it.

Enjoy! features a new bassist and proves that even talented bands with positive attitudes are not immune to gratuitous vulgarity and base stupidity. The title song is a childish paean to farting, complete with audio vérité effects; two others reveal a juvenile attitude towards women. On the other hand, a peppy version of Brian Wilson's "Wendy" is spectacular; most of the originals—including the satirical hardcore of "Hiirtin' Crüe," the Anglo-popping "Get the Time" and the surly noise of the seven-minutes-plus "Days Are Blood"—are at least near-excellent, reflecting the band's loping musical strides. (Curious art note: the titles listed on the back cover have virtually nothing in common with the record's contents.)

The disappointing **All** starts with what must be the shortest song of all time: the 1-second title track. A new guitarist and bassist join Milo and Stevenson for a raunchier guitar-rock excursion (excepting the almost acoustic "Impressions") that downplays the band's melodic side. "Clean Sheets" and "Pep Talk" have solid tunes and invigorating performances, but "Van," "Coolidge," "Iceman," the high-concept "All-ogistics" and lengthy "Schizophrenia" are basically loud and witless, substituting routine guitar work for character.

Before vanishing forever, the Descendents released a live album, recorded in 1987 at First Avenue in Minneapolis. The 18 rushed songs (more on the cassette and CD) on **Liveage!** draw from the band's entire repertoire in a noisy, frenzied attack that's both fun and exciting.

The Descendents—with Dave Smalley (ex-Dag Nasty) taking over for Milo—then transmuted into All, an (inexplicable)concept quartet that puts a melodic spin and a goofy lyrical twist on punky, clear guitar rock. At the LP's silliest, the always-tasteful All sings a Dickiesish ode to "Alfredo's," a crummy Mexican fast food joint, in the hopes of getting free food. "Just Perfect," "#10 (Wet)" and "Hooidge" have killer hooks and a beach-blanket sound energized by unexpected 'core-derived moves. At once summarizing and surpassing the Descendents, All offers a spunky, electric post-punk alternative for those who miss Generation X and despise Billy Idol. Totally excellent.   [iar]

See also *Last*.

DESPERATE BICYCLES
Remorse Code (nr/Refill) 1979

Along with the far more heralded Soft Boys, this post-punk Chocolate Watch band predated the neo-psychedelic movement by several years with an LP of ten pop gems. The interplay of agile bass and near-perfect guitar on **Remorse Code** helps kick things along, and songs like "Sarcasm" and "It's Somebody's Birthday Today" are utter classics. Sly humor is exhibited with silly tape and sound effects, not to mention the guitarist's savvy pseudonym: Dan Electro.   [dgs]

JIMMY DESTRI
See *Blondie.*

DESTROY ALL MONSTERS
See *New Order.*

DEUTSCHE AMERIKANISCHE FREUNDSCHAFT
Ein Produkt der D.A.F. (Ger. Warning-Atatak) 1979
Die Kleinen und die Bosen (nr/Mute) 1980
Alles Ist Gut (nr/Virgin) 1981
Gold und Liebe (nr/Virgin) 1981
Für Immer (nr/Virgin) 1982
GABI DELGADO
Mistress (nr/Virgin) 1983
ROBERT GÖRL
Night Full of Tension (Elektra) 1984

Originating as Düsseldorf art-punk cacophony cultists in the holdout hippie culture of late 1970's Germany, D.A.F.—originally a group, but known generally as the duo of instrumentalist Robert Görl and singer Gabi Delgado-Lopez—broke away to find success in Europe as a synthesizer-and-dance band.

Ein Produkt der D.A.F. is an apocalyptic eruption of sound announcing the end of the German Republic, with shrieking, colliding overdubbed synths and guitars. The electrometal is simultaneously repellant and compelling. **Die Kleinen und die Bosen**, D.A.F.'s first international release, modifies the electronic chaos with an eye towards the modern dance. Material is more polished, with anarchic synthesizer work slowly integrating a solid, defined beat.

Alles Ist Gut abandons D.A.F.'s Faustian tendencies for cerebral dance music, pol-

ished to a metallic shine by producer Conny Plank. Typical funk rhythms are replaced by industrial pulses (trains, etc.); some vocal experimentation casts the band onto shrewd pop turf, despite decidedly libidinous lyrics. **Gold und Liebe** perfects the advances of **Alles Ist Gut**, emphasizing the punchy use of drum-box and de-emphasizing other instruments, creating a robot void that eerily strands the guttural vocals.

D.A.F.'s final album, **Für Immer**, breaks the pattern, with a variety of styles from funk to rock'n'roll to distorted metal drone before returning to a dance blowout for the final track. While it's all interesting, none of these excursions are displayed long enough to be truly impressive. The inner spaces of earlier work are filled by a range of instruments, including very gentle bells. Like all of D.A.F.'s LPs, it is sung in German.

Delgado and Görl dissolved their partnership to pursue solo careers (although they did reunite in 1985). For his first album, Gabi enlisted some top names in modern German music—Conny Plank and Jaki Liebezeit among them—to make slick but expendable disco, topped off with obsequious lyrics, mostly about sex.

Görl's flat singing (mostly in English) on **Night Full of Tension** leaves a lot to be desired. The fact that he wrote all of D.A.F.'s music doesn't appreciably aid these dull lumps of spare, rhythmic, go-nowhere electronics. The LP's only notable success is "Darling Don't Leave Me," an angst-ridden duet with Annie Lennox (who appears on several other tracks as well) that bears an unpleasant air of sado-masochism.   [sg/iar]

DEVIANTS
See *Mick Farren.*

WILLY DEVILLE
See *Mink DeVille.*

DEVO
Q: Are We Not Men? A. We Are Devo (Warner Bros.) 1978 ●
Be Stiff EP (nr/Stiff) 1979
Duty Now for the Future (Warner Bros.) 1979
Freedom of Choice (Warner Bros.) 1980 ●
Devo Live EP (Warner Bros.) 1981
New Traditionalists (Warner Bros.) 1981
Oh No! It's Devo (Warner Bros.) 1982
Shout (Warner Bros.) 1984

E-Z Listening Disc [CD] (Rykodisc) 1987
Total Devo (Restless) 1988 ●

From their first independent 45, Akron, Ohio's Devo has been one of the current era's most entertaining bands. Their records, short films/videos and live appearances are planned carefully to propagate a cynically offbeat view of humanity. Indeed, music sometimes seems like only one component of Devo's highly developed media mix.

The quintet's first album is the most concentrated presentation of the band's nebulous "devolutionary" theories. "Jocko Homo," "Mongoloid" and "Shrivel Up" employ a cold, assembly-line jerkiness to drive home their defeatist attitudes. The same nervous energy fuels more emotional messages like "Uncontrollable Urge," "Gut Feeling," "Sloppy (I Saw My Baby Gettin')" and a hilarious version of the Rolling Stones' "Satisfaction."

Be Stiff collects Devo's two indie 45s—four tunes that had been re-recorded for **Are We Not Men?**—and their third single, done for Stiff.

The second full-length album, **Duty Now for the Future**, doesn't score as many bullseyes as the first, but includes two Devo anthems of malaise, "Blockhead" and "S.I.B. (Swelling Itching Brain)." Amid disturbing signs of portentousness, Devo turns their bemused eyes to the mating ritual on "Strange Pursuit," "Triumph of the Will" and "Pink Pussycat."

Freedom of Choice is the band's most evocative pairing of words and music. Setting aside metaphysical foofaraw, they contrast choppy keyboard licks ("Girl U Want," "It's Not Right," "Snowball") and ironic but unalienated perceptions ("Gates of Steel," "Planet Earth," "Freedom of Choice"). Their tolerance was rewarded with a subversive hit single from the LP, "Whip It."

Milking the success of "Whip It," **Devo Live** is thoroughly redundant. Five of the six songs, including you-know-what and an instrumental version of "Freedom of Choice," are from the preceding LP; only "Be Stiff" is new to album buyers. Hardly a jamming band, Devo live sounds just like Devo in the studio, except maybe sloppier.

Devo's been soft-pedaling their philosophy (on record, at least) since **Freedom of Choice**'s breakthrough. Musically they're still held back by a stunted sense of melody, although the dance-rock movement created a favorable climate for a rhythmic orientation and probably led to Devo's increasing emphasis on a whomping beat.

New Traditionalists has a couple of attention-getting songs ("Going Under," "Beautiful World"). Most of it, though, is laissez-faire techno-dance stuff, less-than-compelling lyrics set to a metronomic 4/4 beat. The same can be said of **Oh No! It's Devo**; **Shout**'s only memorable contribution is a version of the Jimi Hendrix oldie, "Are You Experienced?" Songwriters Mark Mothersbaugh and Gerald Casale are evidently going through a dry spell of drought proportions, substituting clichés for the razor-sharp observations that used to keep Devo listenable as well as danceable. Has Devo succumbed to its own devolution?

Little was heard from the group proper after **Shout**, although Casale and the Mothersbaughs remained active, writing and performing music for films and television (including *Pee-wee's Playhouse*) and producing outside projects. Their Los Angeles (where the group relocated in the early '80s) recording studio has also been busy. But prior to 1988's **Total Devo**, the band's lone "new" release was the mistitled **E-Z Listening Disc**, an hour-plus CD containing the group's smugly straightfaced (and barely recognizable) schlocky instrumental remakes of 19 of their songs, originally heard on a pair of mail-order-only **E-Z Listening** cassettes. Is this the final stage of devolution?

The most notable aspect of **Total Devo** (besides the replacement of drummer Alan Myers by ex-Gleaming Spire David Kendrick) is its simultaneous four-format release: LP, tape, CD and digital audio tape (DAT). Otherwise, it's little more than a timid and bland imitation of the countless bands Devo originally inspired.

Of possible interest to fans (or anti-fans) is **KROQ-FM Devotees Album**, a 1979 compilation of goofball cover versions, parodies and tributes, released by Rhino.   [si/iar]

HOWARD DEVOTO
Jerky Versions of the Dream (IRS) 1983
LUXURIA
Unanswerable Lust (Beggars Banquet-RCA)
      1988 ●

Following influential and estimable careers with the Buzzcocks and Magazine, singer/writer Devoto continued his quest for independence as a solo artist. Using Dave Formula and Barry Adamson from Maga-

155

zine, as well as other players, Devoto offers his idiosyncratic worldview and original musical outlook on ten tunes that range from funky ("Topless," "Way Out of Shape") to ethereal ("Rainy Season") to playful ("I Admire You") and beyond. Full appreciation of the album requires a bit of forbearance and effort, but few artists make music that is as careful and intelligent as Devoto's.

Five years on, Devoto's next project— Luxuria, a duo with a man simply named Noko—leads him deep into the waters of overbearing pretension. His lyrics quote Proust, spout *français,* mention Rimbaud and announce such impenetrable silliness as "I am the street where you live." Even when the music—an unfocused mix of acoustic delicacy and walloping techno-dance crud— takes hold, it's swamped by Devoto's melodramatic quaver. [iar]

DEXY'S MIDNIGHT RUNNERS
Searching for the Young Soul Rebels (EMI America) 1980
Don't Stand Me Down (Mercury) 1985 ●

KEVIN ROWLAND AND DEXYS MIDNIGHT RUNNERS
Too-Rye-Ay (Mercury) 1982 ●
Geno (nr/EMI) 1983 + 1986

BUREAU
The Bureau (Atlantic) 1981

KEVIN ROWLAND
The Wanderer (nr/Mercury) 1988

Although changing Dexy's from a nouveau American-soul band to an ethnic Irish folk group may make singer/mastermind Kevin Rowland seem a tad fickle, his singleminded devotion to a chosen direction gives the Birmingham group's first two albums a powerful sense of care and dedication that many infinitely more consistent musicians never achieve.

Searching for the Young Soul Rebels, recorded by the original eight-man lineup, boldly challenged the direction new wave had taken music in 1979 and '80, long before soul music and horns became trendy. Taking inspiration from soul men like Sam & Dave and Geno Washington, onetime punk singer Rowland anted up a batch of emotionally powerful songs that work equally well as heartfelt tributes and modern creations. Despite the enormous amount of image-building that surrounded it, **Searching** is a fine, expressive album with no bad tracks.

Following a violent disagreement with Rowland, five bandmembers split off at the end of 1980 and formed the Bureau, augmenting their talents with a singer and a guitarist. While they recorded an LP of their own, Rowland began building his second version of Dexys.

Too-Rye-Ay, overalls and country instruments notwithstanding, is not as radically different at its core from **Searching** as it might first appear. Fronting a totally new band (including Seb Shelton, former Secret Affair drummer), plus a two-piece fiddle section and a vocal trio, Rowland retains some of the earlier throaty horn work to make a few tracks (one a spot-on cover of Van Morrison's "Jackie Wilson Said") sound a lot like the first LP. Elsewhere, fiddles, banjos, accordion and tin whistle take over to make jolly, rollicking jug band fare—the enormous worldwide hit "Come On Eileen" and "The Celtic Soulbrothers," for instance. Other songs mix metaphors and become something more indescribable. Although a truly weird smorgasbord, the clever melodies and arrangements keep it consistently entertaining.

Dexys' only album release in either 1983 or 1984 was **Geno**, a worthwhile compilation of early singles (A- and B-sides) assembled by the band's former label.

To everyone's discredit, the band didn't evaporate then and there: **Don't Stand Me Down** (forever to be recalled, if at all, as the "accountants" album due to yet another image change, this time into conservative pinstripes) is a torpid snore that denies entertainment on every level. With titles like "Knowledge of Beauty" and "Reminisce Part Two," the seven lengthy songs with absurd lyrics aim for a literate Van Morrison-like looseness, but end up just falling asleep or apart. Never mind the Dexys. [iar]

DIAGRAM BROTHERS
Some Marvels of Modern Science (nr/New Hormones) 1981

Something like XTC (but lacking their musical smarts or stellar wit), the Diagram Bros.—of the Manchester art-noise family encircling New Hormones—play dissonant weirdness with lyrics about current events. While the poorly-produced music only hints at talent hidden behind the anti-music self-indulgence, it's actually the four-sheet insert, containing detailed fold/cut/paste directions for assembly into a portfolio about the record, that indicates the presence of real cleverness. [iar]

MANU DIBANGO

Electric Africa (Celluloid) 1985 ●
Afrijazzy (Urban) 1987

Manu Dibango is the foremost international practitioner of Cameroon's traditional *makossa* rhythm. He's played variations on it—along with the jazz and R&B he often prefers—since the mid-'50s, achieving world notoriety in 1972 with the hit single, "Soul Makossa." Dibango's albums have been released fairly consistently in America and England ever since.

Vocal chants and choppy saxophone make an unlikely foil for producer/technophile Bill Laswell's revved-up keyboards and drum machines; the resultant LP, **Electric Africa** (featuring keyboardists Herbie Hancock and Bernie Worrell) is neither as soulful or as interesting as those involved probably hoped it would be. [rg]

DICE

Broken Rules (Fr. CBS) 1980
The Dice (Fr. CBS) 1982

This French quartet comes off insouciant, snotty and clever on **Broken Rules**. Maybe a touch too careful, enough to undercut the urgency that would have made more than a few of the songs memorable. By **The Dice**, the band consisted of the two prime movers (keyboardist Pascal Stive and singer J.M. Devlin) plus three backing vocalists (their soundman, manager and lyricist) and a few session players. While Elaine Rowen may have added to the band's image, her lyrics rework every old rock chestnut in the book; the cleaned-up music, while shiny and "new," is nothing more than a polished lemon without an engine. [jg]

DICKIES

The Incredible Shrinking Dickies (A&M) 1979
Dawn of the Dickies (A&M) 1979
Stukas Over Disneyland (PVC) 1983
We Aren't the World! [tape] (ROIR) 1986
Killer Klowns EP (Enigma) 1988 ●
Second Coming (Enigma) 1988 ●

For some reason, the lovable Dickies—a *Mad* magazine-flavored punk self-parody—never endeared themselves to as large an international cult as the Ramones have. Perhaps this West Coast mob of zanies is too unserious and knowing of their own idiocy, while their New York counterparts may well be playing it straight. (That's cooler, apparently).

The Incredible Shrinking Dickies is a burst of generic hyperactive punk, California style, c. 1979. Giddy good humor dominates, in blithe contrast to the surly conviction of more earnest bands. Seven of the 13 tracks clock in at under two minutes (each, not all told), and everything sounds the same, from covers of "Eve of Destruction," the Monkees' "She" and Black Sabbath's "Paranoid" to originals like "Mental Ward" and "Rondo (The Midget's Revenge)." Disposably nice.

On **Dawn of the Dickies**, the title of which, like that of its predecessor, alludes to a junk-movie classic, something wonderful happens: the Dickies get genuinely good. By slowing down the tempo a half step and coming up with strong melodies, guitarist Stan Lee and crew manage to reel off one maniacally catchy gem after another. The pop-culture slant is the same as before, as "Manny, Moe and Jack" and "Attack of the Mole Men" aptly demonstrate, and the mood is equally flippant, but this is a record with staying power.

After a prolonged absence, the boys next popped back into view with a frisky eight-song mini-album. Half of **Stukas Over Disneyland** dates from 1980, including a delightfully garbled version of Led Zeppelin's "Communication Breakdown." Of the others (cut around 1983), the highlight is "Pretty Please Me," a power-pop pearl. Not a work of demented genius like **Dawn**, but damn good fun.

More oddities and endities can be found on the cassette-only **We Aren't the World!**, 21 doses of live Dickiedom (many of them covers) done between 1978 and 1985, plus the raw 1977 four-song demo that, according to Lisa Fancher's belligerent liner notes, got them signed to A&M. Although the recording quality is as varied as the locales, this just might be **Dark Side of the Moon** for fans of chaotic smartassitude.

The Dickies signed to Enigma in 1988 and returned to nationwide action with an EP and a new album. [jy/iar]

DICKS/BIG BOYS

Recorded Live at Raul's Club (Rat Race) 1980

DICKS

Kill from the Heart (SST) 1983
These People (Alternative Tentacles) 1984

Kill from the Heart presents polemic Texas punk made bizarre and worthwhile by dint of singer Gary, a big ol' boy with a commanding voice that rises above the semi-competent blues-based rock his three bandmates crank out. (It may sound ridiculous, but these guys could be Canned Heat's suncrazed nephews.) Although the album's right-on titles ("Pigs Run Wild," "Bourgeois Fascist Pig," "No Nazi's Friend") are neither surprising nor especially thought-provoking, the Dicks are still a cool-sounding band.   [iar]

DICTATORS

Dictators Go Girl Crazy (Epic) 1975
Manifest Destiny (Asylum) 1977
Bloodbrothers (Asylum) 1978
Fuck 'Em if They Can't Take a Joke [tape]
   (ROIR) 1981

Considering that the Dictators' first album came out in 1975, scads of credit is due these hearty pre-punk New Yorkers for being there first. The idea of melding junk culture—wrestling, fast food, television, beer, cars, scandal sheets—with loud/hard/fast rock'n'roll has been subsequently adopted and adapted by dozens of bands, from Black Flag to Cyndi Lauper to the Beastie Boys, who revel in the same indulgent mentality. All four of the Dictators' albums (including the posthumous live tape) are great and, although wavering wildly in terms of style and track-to-track consistency, serve as memorable cornerstones for much of what followed. Protégés of genius music journalist Richard Meltzer, the Dictators helped translate a lot of intellectual fandom's crazed hypothetical theorizing about rock'n'roll's possibilities into wretchedly wonderful reality.

The Dictators were originally a quartet: former rockwriter/*Teenage Wasteland Gazette* publisher Adny Shernoff (vocals/bass), monster guitarist Ross the Boss, Scott "Top Ten" Kempner (rhythm guitar) and Stu-Boy King (drums). On their first LP, crazy-roadie-turned-crazy-singer Handsome Dick Manitoba was photographed in wrestling regalia for the cover, guested on some of the tracks and was listed in the credits as "secret weapon." The album itself is a wickedly funny, brilliantly played if hopelessly naive masterpiece of smartass rock'n'roll. An absolute classic that was utterly ignored at the time.

Immediately after the release of **Dictators Go Girl Crazy**, King took a hike and various troubles beset the band, resulting in a two-year delay before a follow-up was issued. By then, Manitoba had become the full-time vo-calist, drummer/singer Ritchie Teeter had come on board and bassist Mark "The Animal" Mendoza had joined, allowing Shernoff to switch from bass to keyboards. Although the sonic quality was mortally damaged in the original mastering, **Manifest Destiny** comes across with another helping of brilliant songs like "Science Gone Too Far," "Sleepin' with the TV On" and a stunning rip through the Stooges' seminal "Search and Destroy." The musical approach is less tongue-in-cheek and sounds nearly adult, but any band fronted by Handsome Dick Manitoba could hardly be prey to rock-star pretension.

Falling in with novelist Richard Price, the Dics' third album, **Bloodbrothers**, made some concessions, hoping for mass appeal in a last-ditch attempt to turn the band into a commercially viable proposition. Mendoza had already left for greener metal pastures (specifically Twisted Sister, with whom he became a huge star on several continents in 1984); the five-man lineup sent Shernoff back on bass. Despite the halfhearted sell-out attempt, the record has its share of great tracks—a tribute to Meltzer ("Borneo Jimmy"), a seamy tale of teenage prostitution ("Minnesota Strip") and an electric statement of purpose ("Faster and Louder"). A blinding cover of the Flamin Groovies' "Slow Death" closes the album, and put a lid on the Dics' studio days as well. They were soon without a label, and fell apart several months later.

A few reunion gigs played around the New York area in late 1980 and early '81 resulted in the album-length live cassette, which finds the band in fine form, playing old and new material as well as they ever did, and with Manitoba doing a riotous bravado star turn as singer, ringleader and MC. The Dictators played a tenth anniversary reunion concert in New York in January 1986 and another show the following year. By that point, Top Ten had formed the Del-Lords; Manitoba and Shernoff have continued working together in Manitoba's Wild Kingdom.
                                                      [iar]

See also *Del-Lords, Shakin' Street.*

DIDJITS

Fizzjob (Bam Bam) 1986
Hey Judester (Touch and Go) 1988

This Champaign, Illinois trio lays intentionally odd lyrics ("Under the Christmas

Fish," "Plate in My Head," "Stumpo Knee Grinder") over sharply-played fierce and fast guitar rock for a noisy good time on **Hey Judester**. Guitarist/pianist Rick Sims' voice varies from controlled singing (the surly "Dad") to a surging shout (on "Max Wedge") to an impressive freakout shriek (as on a manic Little Richard cover); the thick, loud music keeps pace. Well-produced by Iain Burgess and the band.   [iar]

DIED PRETTY

Died Pretty EP (nr/What Goes On) 1985
Next to Nothing EP (What Goes On) 1985
Free Dirt (What Goes On) 1986
Pre-Deity (Aus. Citadel) 1988

There aren't many bands whose names convey their sound as accurately as Sydney, Australia's Died Pretty. The coupling of dark and hard-hewn guitar chords with light and lilting jangles make the quintet's records both delicately pretty and devastatingly loud, though not at the same time. That contrast and the interplay between scream and shiver is what gives Died Pretty its appeal. One moment Ronald S. Peno is screeching like he's tried on Robert Plant's too-tight pants, the next he's got the voice of Jim Morrison calling from the grave. The band likewise essays both the cat-mating squeals of post-Hendrix guitar with sinister horns and crashing cymbals *and* a delicate church organ picking out a lovingly melody as their voices meld into a vanilla smooth background chorus.

The **Died Pretty** 12-inch is a compilation of their first two 45s, "Out of the Unknown" and "Mirror Blues." The four-song **Next to Nothing**, Died Pretty's debut US release, it should be noted, does not contain the song of that name—it's on **Free Dirt**. The highly recommended album—which contains glimmers of the '60s, Dylan, Gram Parsons, folk-rock and neo-psychedelic—has such guest contributions as mandolin, violin, pedal steel and sax, magnifying the band's own essential variety.   ['e/iar]

DIE KREUZEN

Cows and Beer EP (Version Sound) 1982
Die Kreuzen (Touch and Go) 1984
October File (Touch and Go) 1985
Century Days (Touch and Go) 1988 ●

Milwaukee's Die Kreuzen is simultaneously one of the most thrilling and conservative exponents of American hardcore.

While many quality thrash bands have escaped the genre's brutally circumscribed conventions by delving into metal, psychedelia, funk or bohemianism, this quartet plays punk strictly by the book. **Cows and Beer**, a six-song 7-inch debut (all of which is reprised on **Die Kreuzen**), contains such numbers as "Hate Me," "Pain" and "In School." The brief songs, although well-played, are as musically familiar as the titles.

On the first LP, armed with an antagonistic attitude and a predilection for velocity, the band burns through 21 explosive songs (riffs, really) that are interchangeable but not redundant. The primary ingredient, hyperkinetic energy, remains constant throughout **Die Kreuzen**, but the riffs are all different and uncommonly well-articulated. As loud and fast as these guys are, their playing remains crisp. (Dan Kubinski's vocals, however, are utterly unintelligible.)

October File pushes the envelope a bit, diverting the thrash energy into slower, more conceptual outpourings. (It's still loud, raunchy rock, but few of the 14 songs can be characterized as hardcore.) While the band's focus is being redefined by Kubinski's impassioned shrieking (metal . . . that's the word for you, son), the others—especially guitarist Brian Egeness and bassist Keith Brammer—seem to have different musical directions in mind. Now that they've escaped the realm of orthodox hardcore, it's time for this capable outfit to find a new singer and figure out where they're headed.   [jl/iar]

DIFFORD & TILBROOK

See *Squeeze.*

DIF JUZ

Huremics EP (nr/4AD) 1981 ●
Vibrating Air EP (nr/4AD) 1981 ●
Who Says So EP (nr/Red Flame) 1983
Extractions (nr/4AD) 1985 ●
Out of the Trees (nr/4AD) 1986

The cover of **Huremics** offers no information on the band whatsoever; the disc consists of four mood-setting improvisational guitar/drums/bass instrumentals. **Vibrating Air** maintains the enigmatic graphic pose and style, featuring four new diminutive atmospherics. While not exactly captivating fare, these slight records are actually quite nice. I wonder if anyone's ever thought of using these records for scratch mixes, or as backing tracks for unwritten songs.

The Cocteau Twins help out on Dif Juz's first full-length LP, **Extractions**: Robin Guthrie produced, Liz Fraser became the first vocalist on a Dif Juz record. With the addition of prominent keyboards and sax, it's not as atmospheric as prior work, shooting instead for a big, echoey sound, not unlike Simple Minds. As an instrumental band, Dif Juz must be vigilant not to fall into the nice-sound-few-ideas trap. They get by on **Extractions**, but just barely. [iar/dgs]

DILS

Live! (Iloki-XXX) 1988

That the Dils' first LP or EP (and first 12-inch) would come out seven years after the group called it quits should serve as a reminder how comparatively small and ineffectual the independent record scene of the late-'70s was. Although the now-legendary Dils were one of the best and largest-drawing West Coast punk groups of the original '77–'80 punk explosion, they released only three 7-inch singles during four years of existence.

The trio played primal-scream, 90-second, maximum punk ditties with fiery politics (they were almost alone in '77 Los Angeles on that score); Army brat brothers Chip and Tony Kinman topped them off with near-Everlyesque harmonies. John Silvers, the longest-running of four drummers who served with the pair over the years, makes his vinyl debut on **Live!**. As a result, even the half that's familiar from the singles sounds tighter and more powerful. Culled from two cassette recordings, the sound is hotter than most bootlegs, and is helped by the parade of neo-classics: "I Hate the Rich," "Class War" and an incredibly improved (slowed down to a more powerful pace) "You're Not Blank." (Fans will also recognize "The Sound of the Rain," a Dils' single the Kinmans re-recorded for the second Rank and File LP.) Rarely do historical documents seem so timely or so current. [jr]

See also *Rank and File.*

DINOSAUR

Dinosaur (Homestead) 1985

DINOSAUR JR.

You're Living All Over Me (SST) 1987 ●

Modern masters of high-decibel manipulation, this Amherst, Massachusetts power trio once had difficulty playing more than a single gig in any one club because of their ear-damaging attack. Prior to forming Dinosaur, guitarist J Mascis and bassist Lou Barlow played together in Deep Wound (heard twice on the 1984 Conflict compilation **Bands That Could Be God**), while drummer Murph served time on All White Jury.

Dinosaur finds the group sounding like ten different bands on as many songs. Mascis, also the primary singer and songwriter, employs an array of electronic devices to squeeze a myriad of variations from harmonic structures, utilizing a variety of tones from loud to louder to loudest. Meat Puppets, Neil Young and Sonic Youth comparisons are inevitable, but Dinosaur's raucous individuality is beyond dispute.

The band further reduced their already minimal pop factor on **You're Living All Over Me**, forging an even more blistering gestalt. At times, Dinosaur Jr. sound like three or four different bands within the same song (particularly "The Lung"). Sonic Youth member Lee Ranaldo warbles along on "Little Fury Things" (the 12-inch of which includes a parodic cover of Peter Frampton's "Show Me the Way," as does the album's CD.) **You're Living All Over Me** also includes a self-indulgent experiment in noise, "Poledo."

Shortly after the album's release, SST was informed through legal channels that a group of San Francisco Summer of Love veterans were already tongue-in-cheekishly calling themselves the Dinosaurs, and resented the Amherst lads' imposition. To avoid a "hassle," Dinosaur politely added "Jr." to their moniker after the record's initial appearance. [rg]

DIODES

The Diodes (Can. Columbia) 1977
Released (Can. Epic) 1979
Action-Reaction (Can. Orient) 1979
Survivors (Can. Fringe) 1982

This Toronto quartet got on the map with an inoffensive cover of the Cyrkle's hit, "Red Rubber Ball," but never made much of an international impression afterward. Their albums—three studio forays and one assemblage of unreleased odds and ends—prove the Diodes to be a competent but mundane rock group with faint punky instincts. Too mild-mannered to be aggressive but too energized to be wholly bland, the Diodes stuck close to the conservative rail, which keeps their albums from being very interesting.

The **Diodes** bears the marks of a first-time band anxious not to offend anyone. **Released**, which reprises "Red Rubber Ball" from the first album, contains the band's best work—melodic power pop, including a fine original, "Tired of Waking Up Tired." Unfortunately, the Diodes don't sustain that cut's vitality, and some of the other material here drags tediously.

Action-Reaction is the final album by the original lineup; the band subsequently replaced its bassist and drummer and relocated to England. A collection of previously unreleased tracks—outtakes, demos and a live version of the Stones' "Play with Fire"—was issued in 1982, named after its leadoff song, "Survivors." [iar]

DIRTY LOOKS

Dirty Looks (Stiff-Epic) 1980
Turn It Up (nr/Stiff) 1981

If you can get past the flat, brittle production on **Dirty Looks** (try cranking it up loud), you'll find this Staten Island, New York trio playing power pop with a vengeance. Chief assets: good melodic instincts coupled with tight, lean drive, like an adolescent Cheap Trick gone new wave. Moodily ranging through taut reggae ("Disappearing"), crazed quasi-rockabilly ("Drop That Tan"), even an emotionally masochistic ballad ("Lie to Me"), they may seem to let their depression run away with them, but when Dirty Looks soar, you might even be convinced that "rock'n'roll is still the best drug" (from the memorable "Let Go").

What a shock, then, to hear the trio descend into mediocrity on their second LP, despite production by Motor Nick Garvey. Halfbaked, full of misguided ideas and sputtering when it should smoke, **Turn It Up** slithers all too slickly. [jg]

DISLOCATION DANCE

Slip That Disc! (nr/New Hormones) 1981
Music Music Music (nr/New Hormones) 1981
Midnight Shift (nr/Rough Trade) 1984

At the time of its inception, dance-oriented rock was a good idea that quickly turned formulaic and mundane. But the irreverent genre-busting of Dislocation Dance, a skillful Manchester outfit, almost single-handedly redeems early DOR.

Slip That Disc!, an eight-song 12-inch, couches its peppy rhythms and schematic trumpet and guitar parts in kitchen-clean production. Only the cover of Lennon/McCartney's "We Can Work It Out" (which renders the hopeful outlook of the original dark and doubtful) and "Clarinetsource" (subversive dub with neurotic processed clarinet sounds) hints at DisDance's promise.

The **Music Music Music** LP fulfills the promise and then some, with busier, more stylized production and an eclectic brew of pop, funk and jazz. One of the many highlights is "Take a Chance (On Romance)," setting the demented '40s swing of the tune against the wistful "sadness that just won't go away" of the lyrics. Dislocation Dance's whimsical humor makes modern "dislocation" easier to take, and its use of varying jazz styles in a rock context is the widest and most effective since the Bonzo Dog Band held sway. [mf]

DISNEYLAND AFTER DARK

Call of the Wild (Danish Mega) 1986

The best thing about this perky Danish crew—who meld American cowboy-Western sounds with modern video rock choruses and brassy white soul horns—is their name. But their music is good-natured and their exaggerated forays into such American institutions as the Marlboro Man, long-haul trucking, and cinema can be hilarious if you're in the right mood, especially when they try to deadpan a Southern drawl with Danish accents. ['e]

DISTRACTIONS

Nobody's Perfect (nr/Island) 1980

Decades from now, rock historians will scratch their heads in bewilderment that the Distractions' one fine album didn't ensure the quintet a longer lifespan. A lot of records belong to a specific time, but **Nobody's Perfect** continues to measure up as an ace slab of educated pop rock, right in tune with the ground rules laid down by Blondie, Squeeze and others of that ilk. Part of the problem may be that **Nobody's Perfect** is too weighty to be passed off as a simple diversion. The band's eclecticism draws on everything from Chuck Berry to Phil Spector to psychedelia—often within the same song—and the vocals tend to be more somber than carefree. "Boys Cry" comes on like a Ronettes tune but delivers none of the upbeat emotional release seasoned pop listeners are trained to

expect. Regardless, **Nobody's Perfect** very
nearly is.   [jy]

DIVINE HORSEMEN

Time Stands Still (Enigma) 1984
Devil's River (SST) 1986
Middle of the Night (SST) 1986
Snake Handler (SST) 1987 ●
Handful of Sand EP (SST) 1988

Following his work with the Flesh Eaters, California's Chris D(esjardins) formed the Divine Horsemen, who debuted on the mostly-acoustic **Time Stands Still**. Without an electric band churning away steadily behind him, he's more appallingly effective than ever. The attractive, understated music belies such sentiments as "Past All Dishonor" and "Hell's Belle"; the all-star supporting cast includes Blasters, Gun Clubbers, an X and Texacala Jones of the Horseheads.

A no-star electric lineup made the similarly low-key and driven **Devil's River**, a record which, like its predecessor, leaves the major responsibility for conveying fear and loathing to the lyrics, here geared to Western/cowboy topics. Chris shares the vocals with Julie C(hristensen), who adds an X-like harmony to the proceedings. A dusty road, to be sure, but a fascinating one.

Predominately recorded in and around the same sessions as **Devil's River**, the oddly-compiled and countryfied **Middle of the Night** features the same crew, with John Doe and D.J. Bonebrake of X guesting on two of the eight cuts. Chris and Julie perform most of the vocals as a relatively mellifluous duo, making this the Horsemen's most attractive album. The title tune is a sweet lullabye; there are also alternate recordings of two previously-issued Chris D. efforts, an acoustic version of David Allen Coe's country classic "Field of Stone" and two other covers: a slow but accurate "Gimmie Shelter" and the Cramps' "Voodoo Idol."

Guitarist Peter Andrus replaced two departing members on **Snake Handler**, bringing the Horsemen into the light with a trimmed-down, tightened-up rock sound. Comparisons to X at this point are more than fair, although these joint vocals are far more divine than that band's. The lyrics don't bear a lot of scrutiny—they may be poetic, but aren't about much of anything. (The harrowing escape-from-heroin saga, "Fire Kiss" is a significant exception.) Chris' grip on the gritty fear-film idiom is intact, but lines like

"Fire is my home/and if you let me die alone/the fire will eat my bones" or "I been waiting for someone like you since I was just 13 years old" don't pack any punch.
[jy/iar]

DIVINYLS

Monkey Grip EP (Aus. WEA) 1982
Desperate (Chrysalis) 1983
What a Life! (Chrysalis) 1985
Temperamental (Chrysalis) 1988 ●

Sydney, Australia's Divinyls couple Christina Amphlett's unusual vocal mannerisms with the band's rowdy pop sound—kind of like AC/DC meets the Pretenders, with a soupçon of Lene Lovich and a few subtle, unexpected chord-progression shifts. The thick textures of guitars and keyboards pack a marvelous rock'n'roll punch; the downside is the band's occasional flirtation with arena rock clichés. Amphlett appeared in the movie *Monkey Grip,* for which the group recorded the six songs contained on the EP; some were redone for **Desperate**. The LP's standouts include "Only You" (all the above comparisons applicable in one song, and it works!) and the goofily lovable "Science Fiction." Even the weakest songs get by on sheer gusto. The Easybeats' "I'll Make You Happy" is given a hard-rock update, as Amphlett blithely assumes the song's assertive role which had, after all, been written for a man.

Intentionally or not, all three producers (Mark Opitz, Mike Chapman, Gary Langan) of **What a Life!** appear to have been determined to sell the group to US radio by polishing away their idiosyncracies (dousing the spark in the songs too, if there was any). The result comes awfully close to Anybandism. The worst offender is "Pleasure and Pain," the only track produced and co-written by Mike Chapman, which veers toward the territory of his onetime protégé, Pat Benatar.

That's why it's all the more surprising that Chapman not only produced **Temperamental**, he also allowed the quirky, rough-edged charm shown on **Desperate** to come through. There are some nifty little touches, like clever usage of backing choruses as aural coloring. Divinyls is now reduced to the songwriting team of Amphlett and lead guitarist Mark McEntee, but the hired hands on bass and drums provide a superbly compatible loose-limbed wallop. The title track is the killer; the others are also generally strong right off the bat. The Syndicate of Sound's

"Hey Little Girl" gets an impressive re-reading: the original is definitive, but Amphlett's rare ability to make the tune hers (as "Hey Little Boy") is an entertaining angle.   [jg]

DON DIXON
Most of the Girls Like to Dance but Only
    Some of the Boys Like To (Enigma)
    1985 ●
Praying Mantis EP (nr/Demon) 1986
Romeo at Juilliard (Enigma) 1987 ●

Before his name started showing up as a producer on albums by R.E.M., the Smithereens, Let's Active and many others, Don Dixon spent 14 years as bassist/singer/songwriter in a hot North Carolina band called Arrogance. On the 14-song solo debut from this jack-of-all-musical-trades, Dixon offers an uneven but engaging patchwork of singles and demos from his personal archives—some from the Arrogance days, others done at home on his 4-track and one recorded at Mitch's Drive-In Studio. The tracks span five years (and nearly as many studios), displaying Dixon's affection for '60s pop and R&B. Sometimes cynical, sometimes whimsical, his views of love and lust are delivered with a soulman's vocal passion. The wonderfully oddball images of kissing insects and claw action in "Praying Mantis" make it an instant gem. Mitch Easter contributes lead guitar to a cover of Nick Lowe's "Skin Deep." Although the album has some forgettable items, it leaves you anxious to hear what Dixon might do when he takes the time to record a fully developed LP.

The original British version of the album has a few different tracks, song annotation and different artwork. The four-song UK EP packages the title song with another album track and two more from the Arrogance library, including a sweat-drenched live version of Percy Sledge's "When a Man Loves a Woman," which also appears on the US album.

The all newly recorded **Romeo at Juilliard** fulfills the first album's promise in spades. Aided by a few guests (mainly drummers, but also Easter, Marti Jones and guitarist Jamie Hoover), Dixon rocks confidently in a country/pure pop/Atlantic soul /R&B style that equally suggests the gritty side of John Hiatt and the gloss of Nick Lowe. Expressing deep bitterness at a former loved one, his songs are well-written and brilliantly executed; each arrangement varies the approach without straying far from the LP's overall sound. Dixon's voice is wonderfully rich and emotional; that he's distinguished himself as a producer and not a singer/songwriter (yet) hardly seems believable from the evidence here. "Borrowed Time," "Your Sister Told Me" and "Swallowing Pride" are pained outpourings that channel the man's soul right into your speakers. (There are bonus tracks on the CD.)   [kh/iar]
See also *Marti Jones*.

DMZ
DMZ EP (Bomp) 1977
DMZ (Sire) 1978
Relics (Voxx) 1981
DMZ!! Live!! 1978!! (Crypt) 1986
Live!! 1978!! EP (Pryct) 1986

One of Boston's primary punk bands, DMZ was led by the maniacal Mono Mann (aka Jeff Conolly, now the leader of the Lyres), an organist/singer whose '60s roots (British and American garage punk, psychedelia) and Iggy Pop fixation formed the basis for the group's influential stylings. Their first album, produced by Flo and Eddie, has bad sound, sloppy playing and little character, despite the rave-up playing and general enthusiasm.

On the other hand, **Relics**—released four years after being recorded on a 4-track by Craig Leon—has the intensity and cutting sonic attack to effectively recreate the weird sounds of Mann's idols. Anyone that can do justice to a Roky Erickson number (as in the 13th Floor Elevators' "You're Gonna Miss Me") is alright by me. Four of **Relics'** cuts had first appeared on the cool 1977 7-inch; the other five had not previously been released.

Two 1986 releases from the same June 1978 club date capture DMZ live. One is a full-length LP, the other a 7-inch that contains four tracks, including "You're Gonna Miss Me" and "Can't Do That."   [iar]
See also *Lyres*.

DNA
A Taste of DNA EP (American Clavé) 1980
VARIOUS ARTISTS
No New York (Antilles) 1978
The Fruit of the Original Sin (Bel. Crépuscule)
    1981
DARK DAY
Exterminating Angel (Lust/Unlust) 1980
Dark Day EP (Lust/Unlust) 1981

Window (Plexus) 1983
Beyond the Pale [tape] (Nigh Eve) 1985

This controversial noise trio was a fixture on the New York scene for several years, initially tagged as part of the avant-garde no-wave wing of the city's punk movement. Despite a minuscule recorded output, DNA was a major presence of startling originality.

DNA's genius and power were immediately evident when the group entered four cuts on the **No New York** compilation album. Arto Lindsay—once described as James Brown trapped in Don Knotts' body—pits scratch-slash-kill guitar against Robin Crutchfield's sinister Suicidal electric piano and contributes two vocals showing his unique (if unintelligible) singing style in embryonic form. On "Not Moving," Lindsay's playing approximates Syd Barrett with an amphetamine edge.

It was on **A Taste of DNA** that the band matured. Six pithy, polished statements show Kabuki-painted drummer Ikue Mori coming into her own as a tight, tireless master of shifting asymmetrical rhythm; Lindsay drawls, yells, yelps, gulps, burbles and gurgles his way to left-field legend. Replacing Crutchfield's monolithic riffing is the sensitive, painterly bass of Tim Wright. This is no formless anarchic blare—each piece is a painstakingly crafted kernel of ideas organized with fearless unorthodoxy.

The three live performances ("Taking Kid to School," "Cop Buys a Donut," "Delivering the Goods") on **The Fruit of the Original Sin** compilation are a poor epitaph. They suffer from crummy sound quality—one shifts from stereo to mono right in mid-song!—and bizarre editing, though Wright's bass solo on "Delivering the Goods" is typically exquisite.

For the last encore of its final performance, DNA did Led Zeppelin's "Whole Lotta Love," fittingly capping an iconoclastic career with the utterly unexpected.

Keyboardist Robin Crutchfield formed Dark Day as a trio after his departure from DNA; **Exterminating Angel** uses machine-like riffs as the foundation for moody, Teutonic music. By the release of **Dark Day**, he had jettisoned his backing band, shifting the music into the twilight of ambient Eno or Dome. Never a complete original, Crutchfield manages to get extra mileage out of styles he borrows.   [mf/rnp]

See also *Golden Palominos, Arto Lindsay, Lounge Lizards.*

D.O.A.

Triumph of the Ignoroids EP (Can. Friend's) 1979
Something Better Change (Can. Friend's) 1980
Hardcore 81 (Can. Friend's) 1981
War on 45 EP (Alternative Tentacles) 1982
Bloodied but Unbowed (CD Presents) 1984
Don't Turn Yer Back (on Desperate Times) EP (Alternative Tentacles) 1985
Let's Wreck the Party (Alternative Tentacles) 1985
True (North) Strong & Free (Rock Hotel-Profile) 1987

Vancouver's premier punk outfit has never abandoned its righteous yet hedonistic spirit, as embodied by founding guitarist/vocalist/songwriter Joey Shithead (Keighley). After early personnel shifts, the lineup stabilized and the other members eventually began complementing Keighley's singing and songwriting with their own.

Triumph of the Ignoroids is raw and live, like stripped-down Dead Boys; **Something Better Change** is tighter, with more anthemic material fleshed out by two guitarists; **Hardcore 81** is faster and looser. **War on 45** sounds like a keyboardless Stranglers and includes a humorous (and highly charged) reworking of Edwin Starr's "War" ("good god y'all!!") that predates and obliterates Springsteen's. Although D.O.A. isn't above confusing scatology with rebellion (e.g., the "Let's Fuck" rewrite of Chris Montez's 1962 hit), this is mainly above-average punk. (The UK version of **War on 45** substitutes two tracks from **Something Better Change**.)

Subtitled "The Damage to Date: 1978–1983," **Bloodied but Unbowed** is a 19-track career recap (remixed and remastered) which convincingly confirms D.O.A.'s hard-won status as Canada's top punks, a raging behemoth of tightly organized high-compression rock aggression and four-letter-word titles. Incredible, intense and essential.

Don't Turn Yer Back is a ten-minute, four-song 12-inch cut in 1984 for a John Peel radio session. Dedicated to striking miners, it's more angry and political than ever. **Let's Wreck the Party** includes two of those tracks, but is overall more lighthearted. The clear, professional sound and occasional slowed tempos may turn off hardcore fanatics, but it's a cutting and witty record nonetheless.

True (North) boasts similar sonic variations and maturity—sheesh, these guys are almost growing up! (I said almost.) Topics include Canada's inferiority complex ("51st State"), an equation of Ramboid jingoism with nascent fascism ("Nazi Training Camp"), their gonzo work/play ethic (note the version of Bachman-Turner Overdrive's "Takin' Care of Business" with the lead riff played on guitar plus trumpet!) and a long-standing commitment to freedom. (Some royalties from the song "Ready to Explode" go to South Africa's outlawed African National Congress.) Weird angle: "Bullet Catcher," the grim tale of a woman cop who died in a hail of bullets; D.O.A.'s song is critical but sympathetic. [jg/dgs]

See also *Randy Rampage*.

DOCTOR & THE MEDICS

Doctor & the Medics (nr/Illegal) 1985
Spirit in the Sky EP (nr/Illegal) 1985
Laughing at the Pieces (IRS) 1986 ●
I Keep Thinking It's Tuesday (IRS) 1988 ●

If you're going to be a one-joke band, you'd better make it a doozy. England's absurd glam-psychedelic Doctor & the Medics chose to record a carefully unreconstructed version of the greatest god-rock bubblegum hit of all time, Norman Greenbaum's "Spirit in the Sky," and let the wave of '60s nostalgia do the rest. Defying all reason, it proved to be a brilliant commercial gambit, catapulting this ridiculously dressed trifle of a band into the charts on two continents. The quintet's otherwise self-penned first album has little else to recommend it, although Craig Leon's production (XTC's Andy Partridge takes easily audible credit for one song) and attractively musical vocal interplay between the Doctor (Clive Jackson) and Medics Wendi West and Colette Appleby keeps it listenable.

The America edition of the second LP contains the group's spot-on re-creation of Abba's spectacular "Waterloo," with saxual contributions by living legend Roy Wood. [iar]

DR. FEELGOOD

Down by the Jetty (nr/UA) 1975 (nr/Fame) 1982 (nr/Edsel) 1984
Malpractice (Columbia) 1975
Stupidity (nr/UA) 1976 (nr/Liberty) 1985
Sneakin' Suspicion (Columbia/UA) 1977
Be Seeing You (nr/UA) 1977
Private Practice (nr/UA) 1978

As It Happens (nr/UA) 1979
Let It Roll (nr/UA) 1979
A Case of the Shakes (Stiff America) 1980 (nr/Edsel) 1986
On the Job (nr/Liberty) 1981
Casebook (nr/Liberty) 1981
Fast Women and Slow Horses (nr/Chiswick) 1982
Doctors Orders (nr/Demon) 1984
Mad Man Blues EP (nr/ID) 1985

To suggest that all of Dr. Feelgood's records sound alike would be less than generous; there are, however, groups that have explored varying modes of musical expression with greater diligence. Yet, the band has been utterly true to its original aims; few contemporary groups can challenge this veteran outfit when it comes to playing basic, energetic R&B. Over the course of more than a dozen albums in a decade (comprising studio LPs, live sets and compilations), the Feelgoods'—or, more precisely, singer/harmonicat Lee Brilleaux, for it is he who has kept the group going through various lineups—dedication to preserving the gritty spirit of groups like the early Rolling Stones has scarcely wavered.

Regardless of inventiveness (or lack thereof), Dr. Feelgood deserves a place of respect in modern music annals by being the commercially successful leader of English pub-rock at its zenith, drawing huge crowds into small clubs all over Europe in the mid-'70s. By playing grassroots music that pleased not only critics but fans in large numbers, the Canvey Island quartet helped set the stage for the transitional—younger, more rock-oriented—Eddie and the Hot Rods, as well as the more radical punk outburst that followed *them*. Without Dr. Feelgood, there would have been fewer venues for these populist groups to play, less likelihood of a successful indie label scene (Stiff's founding was financed, in part, by Brilleaux) and a much smaller audience receptive to groups without dry ice and laser beams.

The original Dr. Feelgood lineup—Brilleaux, singer and shock-guitarist extraordinaire Wilko Johnson, drummer "The Big Figure" and bassman John Sparks—made four albums together. Johnson left the band in 1977; Sparks and the Figure in 1982. Mixing Johnson's original tunes with a hefty selection of classics from the catalogues of Chuck Berry, Willie Dixon, Rufus Thomas, Leiber and Stoller, Sonny Boy Williamson and Muddy Waters, the first three studio albums had the same R&B/primal rock/blues character as the original Stones. The band's fanatic devotion to the past led them to release the first album only in mono! While **Down by the Jetty** has a certain amateurish charm, **Malpractice** has a stronger, more confident sound, and includes better material, like "Back in the Night," "Riot in Cell Block #9" and "You Shouldn't Call the Doctor (If You Can't Pay the Bills)." Johnson's playing—a frantic, choppy, rhythm/lead style adapted from Mick Green and John Lee Hooker mixed with a spasmodic, Devoesque stage presence—and Brilleaux's hoarse singing may sound a bit out-of-date, but there's no mistaking the energy and honesty they bring to their work.

The live **Stupidity**, although an effective representation, suffers from its similarity to their studio work and lack of the exciting visual factor that made their early gigs so great.

Sneakin' Suspicion is the last LP to feature Johnson; although he appears on the whole thing, a disagreement over musical purity led to a split during the recording. In fact, it's equally good as **Malpractice**, with strong originals ("Walking on the Edge," in particular) and nifty covers ("Nothin' Shakin' (But the Leaves on the Trees)," "Lights Out"). The next Dr. Feelgood album, **Be Seeing You** (title and graphics borrowed from *The Prisoner* TV series), features new six-stringer John Mayo—a strong player with his own sound, but not an even swap for the inimitable Johnson—and Nick Lowe as producer. The change in guitarists is obvious; the band's overall style, however, survives nearly intact, and some of the tracks are good enough to carry the day.

Private Practice, a studio LP produced by Richard Gottehrer, has nothing on the ball, and is played too slow to avoid tedium. **As It Happens**, another live outing, is a *real* stiff, drawing its material almost totally from **Private Practice** and **Be Seeing You**. Completing this naff trilogy is **Let It Roll**, an inconsistent (not worthless) collection produced by blues veteran Mike Vernon.

Proving that they could still cut it, Dr. F. reunited with Lowe for **A Case of the Shakes**, a revitalized treat that brings the group up-to-date (relatively speaking) and in line with the likes of Rockpile, giving their traditionalist approach a more modern setting. Mayo's playing is great and the songs are surprisingly impressive and enjoyable.

On the Job is a needless concert rehash with all but one number drawn from the two preceding albums. **Casebook** is a compilation containing enough of the Feelgoods' best to make it worthwhile. **Fast Women and Slow Horses**, produced by Vic Maile, is the last LP to feature the original Figure/Sparks rhythm section. The follow-up, **Doctors Orders**, puts the Feelgoods—Brilleaux, guitarist Gordon Russell, bassist Phil Mitchell and drummer Kevin Morris—back in league with producer Mike Vernon for a program that includes Eddie Cochran's "My Way" and Muddy Waters' "I Can't Be Satisfied."

Sticking it out for another release, that lineup tears through six blues covers on the down-and-dirty **Mad Man Blues**. Brilleaux and the others sound just great, and the readings of Elmore James' "Dust My Broom," Willie Dixon's "My Babe" and John Lee Hooker's title growl are unfussy and packed with power. Not since the glory days of Canned Heat and Paul Butterfield has white blues sounded this wonderful and unselfconscious. [iar]

See also *Solid Senders*.

DOCTORS CHILDREN

Rose Cottage EP (nr/Upright) 1986
King Buffalo EP (nr/Upright) 1987
King Buffalo (Down There-Restless) 1987

Combining two UK-only mini-albums into a full American longplayer, this British quartet shows off leader Paul Smith's clever songwriting and artless singing on **King Buffalo**, as John Leckie's production does justice (but little more) to arrangements which lean towards the hard-pop guitar sound of Robyn Hitchcock and the Egyptians. Matthew Woodman's Hammond organ adds the only notable sonic element to these competent but rarely ear-catching tracks. For what it's worth, the earlier, less-polished recordings on Side 2 put more bite and backbone into the playing and thus leave a stronger impression. [iar]

DOCTORS' MOB

Headache Machine (Wrestler) 1985
Sophomore Slump (Relativity) 1987

The debut album by this gutsy power pop quartet from Austin, Texas shows abundant promise with melodies, roughly ringing guitars, electricity and a certain nascent stylistic flair. But **Sophomore Slump**, produced to order by Tommy Erdelyi, is definitely the record to get by these guys. Singer/guitarist Steve Collier's writing shows marked improvement; the band rushes at his songs with youthful eagerness and the self-confidence of seasoned roadhogs. Crossing an attractive Athens influence, a hint of folk and a dusty Southwestern truth those California cowboys would dearly love to borrow, Doctors' Mob may be onto something big.   [iar]

DOCTORS OF MADNESS

Late Night Movies, All Night Brainstorms
  (UA) 1976
Figments of Emancipation (UA) 1976
Sons of Survival (nr/Polydor) 1978
Revisionism 1975–1978 (nr/Polydor) 1981

This odd excuse for a rock group was essentially the warped musical vision of Kid (Richard) Strange, as realized in posh, over-the-top pretentious style by a manager who spent scads of money in an unsuccessful attempt to make them the Next Big (Ultra-Outrageous) Thing. Although the blue hair, silly theatrical gear and transparent glam pose were awfully out-of-step with the younger and faster safety-pinned hordes who stole their thunder, the Doctors did possess a unique style, thanks in large part to Urban Blitz's (no kidding) eerie violin work, an unlikely instrument in a band hoping to be perceived as Bowie's post-Ziggy disciples.

Late Night Movies (released in the US only as a double-record set with **Figments of Emancipation**) is the wildest and freshest of the group's three albums, going all out to be—or at least seem—weird and exciting. It's hard to take seriously, but there is something worth hearing in terms of the creepy ambience, substantial songs and subtle musical shadings. **Songs of Survival** and **Figments** refine the approach but lack the gonzo originality of the first record. **Revisionism** is an adequate career summary.

After a stint that saw Dave Vanian (on furlough during one of the Damned's collapses) a member, public response—a mixture of apathy and ridicule—proved terminal, and Strange embarked on a solo career. Whatever the verdict on the Doctors of Madness while they were in business, the fact that the new romantics later shouldered the same foolish mantle of narcissism, ludicrous costumes and stage names—an aberration also adopted by American nouveau-glam-metal

bands like Mötley Crüe—proves that this band was indeed ahead of its time.   [iar]

See also *Richard Strange.*

DOGMATICS

Everybody Does It (Homestead) 1986

These four young Bostonians are dirtbags and proud of it. A prior 45 contained their reverent version of an Eddie Cochran tune; on the brief eight-song mini-LP they tear up Dion's "Teenager in Love" with wicked glee, rewriting the lyrics to suit a less innocent lifestyle. Elsewhere, guitarist Jerry Lehane shows a talent for penning tuneful hard-rock power-chord originals like "Cry Myself to Sleep," "Everything Went Bad" and "Drinking by the Pool." Simple but effective.
[iar]

DOGS

Different (Fr. Phonogram) 1979
Walking Shadows (Fr. Phonogram) 1980
Too Much Class for the Neighborhood
  (nr/Epic) 1982
Legendary Lovers (Fr. Epic) 1983
Shout (Fr. Epic) 1985

There have been several American bands with the same name; this combo from Normandy, however, is one of the French new wave's minor legends. Their '77–'78 indie maxi-singles displayed a quartet made of tougher, rawer but more authoritative fiber than more commercially successful Gallic neo-rockers like Bijou and Telephone. As a trio, they chopped out a pair of punchy LPs, the second with more savvy and polish than the first.

Once again a two-guitar quartet, the Dogs cut a third LP with ex-heavy metal engineer Tony Platt producing, and consequently achieved the cutting yet resonant guitar sound they deserve. They're like an amped-up, French-accented, late-'70s Flamin Groovies (see "Death Lane") but not nearly as wimpy, and influenced more by the early Stones (e.g., the "Last Time" chord cops—with Byrds/Leaves vocals—on "Wanderin' Robin"). Following another studio LP, the Dogs issued a ten-song live album, **Shout.**   [jg]

THOMAS DOLBY

The Golden Age of Wireless (Capitol)
  1982 ●
Blinded by Science EP (Capitol) 1983

The Flat Earth (Capitol) 1984 ●
Music from the Film Gothic (Virgin) 1987
VARIOUS ARTISTS
Howard the Duck (MCA) 1986
THOMAS DOLBY AND THE LOST TOY PEOPLE
Aliens Ate My Buick (EMI Manhattan) 1988 ●

After years of session work and part-time employment with Lene Lovich, Bruce Woolley & the Camera Club, the early Thompson Twins, Foreigner and Joan Armatrading, Thomas Dolby revitalized a largely moribund and redundant synth-pop scene with his own recordings. **The Golden Age of Wireless** avoids the usual error, and gives the songs prominence over the instruments. Besides demonstrating an unfailing flair for sharp, snappy compositions, Dolby shows himself unusually capable of getting warm, touching feeling out of his synthesizers and his voice, creating an evocative sound that magnificently straddles nostalgia and futurism.

Although the album contains some really lovely tunes, like "Radio Silence" and "Europa and the Pirate Twins," Dolby followed it with an execrable moron-funk single, "She Blinded Me with Science" (evidently written about his archeologist father), which mystically made him a huge star. After the album was reissued with that song added on, a five-track mini-album appeared, combining it again with three LP tracks and another lovely new song, "One of Our Submarines." *That* was subsequently appended to the album for its third American variation.

On the side, Dolby worked on various projects, including a couple of tracks released by Whodini before getting around to making a whole new record of his own. **The Flat Earth** contains nothing really memorable, but does feature nicely restrained pieces of inviting atmospheric charm (including "The Flat Earth," "Screen Kiss" and others). Unfortunately, **The Flat Earth** is polluted by the utterly appalling, strident "Hyperactive!"

Dolby then put his own pop career on hold and worked on film soundtracks and other people's projects. He collaborated with Ryuichi Sakamoto on an EP, played on Belinda Carlisle's **Heaven on Earth** and co-produced and played on albums by George Clinton (**Some of My Best Jokes Are Friends**), Joni Mitchell (**Dog Eat Dog**) and Prefab Sprout (**Steve McQueen** and **From**

Langley Park to Memphis). In cinemaland, Dolby wrote, performed and produced five unexceptional new rock songs for George Lucas' misbegotten mega-flop *Howard the Duck,* filling one side of the soundtrack album. (The rest is John Barry's instrumental score.) For Ken Russell's equally atrocious *Gothic,* Dolby composed and performed (on Fairlight) appropriately menacing and dramatic accompaniment, actually using a real orchestra on five of the brief selections.

Aliens Ate My Buick, the long-awaited follow-up to **The Flat Earth**, suggests that the now-LA-based musical artist may be a little out of touch with the real world. The obnoxiously overcrowded '40s swing of "The Key to Her Ferrari" is only the most obvious self-important gaffe here; other lengthy tracks like "Airhead" and "Hot Sauce" are production-driven dance-rock creations with smarmy lyrics. "My Brain Is Like a Sieve" touches on reggae to no avail; "The Ability to Swing" announces Dolby's shortcomings in the music noir area; "Budapest by Blimp" is as annoying as the title suggests.

[sg/iar]

See also *Lene Lovich, Prefab Sprout, Ryuichi Sakamoto, Bruce Woolley and the Camera Club.*

DOLL BY DOLL
Remember (nr/Automatic) 1979
Gypsy Blood (nr/Automatic) 1979
Doll by Doll (MCA) 1981
Grand Passion (nr/Magnet) 1982

The one constant on these four albums is singer/guitarist/songwriter Jackie Leven, who started out the leader of a quartet and wound up its only member. On the first three records, his presence is so commanding—thanks to a deep, rich, expressive voice that leaps into falsetto or descends to an ominous whisper as the moment dictates—that everyone around him takes a back seat. The last album followed a total upheaval that left the band nothing more than Leven solo.

An impressive but flawed debut, **Remember** needlessly limits Doll by Doll's obvious rock strength. Although some tracks go flat out, the group's folk roots place the song before the performance, occasionally blunting the excitement. Still, it's a sophisticated work that serves mainly to introduce Leven's startling voice.

After some personnel changes, a reconstituted Doll by Doll made the fine **Gypsy**

Blood. With all restraint lifted and the emotional intensity turned up high, tunes like "Human Face" and "Teenage Lightning" are simply magnificent—crystal clear, intricately arranged and full of rock fire. Leven's voice and poetic lyrics invest the record with drama and grandeur. A bit overblown to be sure, but a real stunner nonetheless.

Long delayed by contractual problems, **Doll by Doll** suffers from creeping relaxation. The flame burns less brightly; although songs are strong and affecting, the reach isn't as expansive, and the results not as attention-grabbing.

In partnership with newcomer Helen Turner, Leven made **Grand Passion** using studio sidemen, attempting something in a different vein. Unfortunately, the experiment—whatever it may have been—failed. Turner's singing is like bad Nico and the songs are filled with pretentious and obnoxious lyrics. Musically adequate but totally unappealing. [iar]

DOME

Dome (nr/Dome-Rough Trade) 1980
3R4 (nr/4AD) 1980
Dome 2 (nr/Dome-Rough Trade) 1981
Dome 3 (nr/Dome-Rough Trade) 1981
MZUI/Waterloo Gallery (nr/Cherry Red) 1982
Will You Speak This Word (Nor. Uniton) 1983
8 Time [CD] (nr/4AD) 1988

DUET EMMO

Or So It Seems (nr/Mute) 1983

BRUCE GILBERT

This Way (nr/Mute) 1984
The Shivering Man (nr/Mute) 1986

HE SAID

Hail (nr/Mute) 1986

During Wire's lengthy hiatus (starting in 1980), bassist Graham Lewis and guitarist B.C. (Bruce) Gilbert continued their partnership—often under the name Dome—to explore the outer reaches of studio technique and synthetic sound, sidestepping Wire's arcane hitmaking tendencies and the more classical aspirations of former bandmate Colin Newman.

Dome abandons conventional song form for a hodgepodge of treated instruments and voices, with lurching mechanical noises infrequently keeping a vague beat. Melodies fragment under studio manipulation. Eerie. **3R4**

moves into the ambient drone music pioneered by Brian Eno, and its four tracks achieve an almost symphonic effect. **Dome 2** continues the ambient/minimalist experimentation of the first two albums, painting audio expressions of modern ennui, but **Dome 3** breaks stride, lifting the beats of other cultures and mixing them with abstracted bits of psychedelia and disembodied noises.

The 71-minute **8 Time** CD combines the contents of **3R4** with two singles released around the time under the name Cupol.

MZUI/Waterloo Gallery, done in conjunction with Russell Mills, makes extensive use of found noises and self-made instruments. Microphones placed around a London art gallery collected intentional and unintentional sounds from inside and out. The arhythmic result isn't music *per se,* but a curious examination of the relationship between environment and sound.

Will You Speak This Word, released by experimental Norwegian label Uniton, combines some of **Dome 3**'s ethnic borrowings with the repetitive minimalism of earlier works. The suite-like "To Speak" takes up all of one side; it begins with quasi-Arabic violin and random, atonal sax, moving into an acoustic guitar/sax/pseudo-African drum drone with slowly shifting textures before ending with extraterrestrial electronics. An interesting and well-composed piece. The other side's six tracks mix primal drum rhythms with light touches of art-noise generated on a variety of instruments, building intriguing trances. A progressive album in the truest sense of the term.

Duet Emmo was a one-off project by Gilbert, Lewis and Mute Records chief Daniel Miller (the Duet Emmo name is an anagram of Dome and Mute). The resultant LP, **Or So It Seems,** fluctuates between atonal, electronic sound collages and stiff, monotonous synth-funk reminiscent of D.A.F., with no track ever getting off the ground. Fun studio noodling no doubt, but little here of lasting import.

The year of Wire's reformation, 1986, saw the release of more new records outside of the group: Gilbert's second solo album and a first record by He Said, Lewis' flexible studio project. **Hail** includes contributions by Gilbert, co-producer/programmer John Fryer and Eno, among others. The well-organized music—essentially effects-laden electro-beat with ethereal vocals—never quite finds its stylistic voice, although individual passages are impressive enough.

Much more in line with Dome's experimental approach, **The Shivering Man** is a meandering instrumental collection of spare sonic doodles. Employing the kind of electronic production devices that often enliven adventurous modern music, the only component missing from **The Shivering Man** is the music itself. [sg/dgs/tr]

DOMINATRIX

The Dominatrix Sleeps Tonight EP (UpRoar) 1984

DEATH COMET CREW

At the Marble Bar EP (nr/Beggars Banquet) 1984

Charming and catchy, Dominatrix's one New York club hit consists of passionless dada femme recitation over light atmospheric music by Stuart Arbright (ex-Ike Yard) and Ken Lockie (ex-Cowboys International) with scratch mix effects by Ivan Ivan and Lockie. The 12-inch offers two full-scale versions plus two additional remixes ("Chants" and "Beat Me").

Collaborating again with Lockie as co-producer and joined by a few other musicians, Arbright became the Death Comet Crew for a 12-inch electro-funk exercise that's not as exceptional as Dominatrix, but still amusing and offbeat. "At the Marble Bar" offers a varied collection of percussion sounds; "Exterior St." has rap vocals by Rammellzee; "Funky Dream" is an amusingly reductionist cut-up edit of the word "funky." [iar]

DOS

Dos (New Alliance) 1986

Dos, meaning of course two, consists of bassists Mike Watt (of the late Minutemen, now with fIREHOSE) and Kira Roessler (ex-Black Flag). Since Kira has also composed for fIREHOSE, several of the short compositions comprising this charming album hint at that fine trio's signature sound. A dose of **Dos** entails little more (and nothing less) than two basses sniffing around one another like curious animals, making it an atmospheric, playful, even loving pleasure to hear. The partnership was further cemented when the pair married. [rg]

DOTS

The Return of the Dots (Ger. Rebel) 1985
I Can See You (Ger. Rebel) 1986
The Dots Live in West-Germany/15 Songs, 15 Stories (Ger. Rebel) 1986

This longstanding on-off secret of the NY scene has been able to pack clubs in certain Eastern US cities and in Germany (not to mention Holland and Yugoslavia), but can barely get a booking in their hometown. Such topsy-turvyness is part and parcel of Dotsongs, underlined by an unclassifiable grab-bag approach.

After a very brief stint in a precursor to the Ramones, guitarist and chief songwriter Rick Garcia founded the Dots in 1978 with singer Jimmi Quidd; early guitarists (Garcia began on bass) included the late Alison East. With a rhythm section, the lineup jelled when Garcia became sole guitarist. Most of **The Return of the Dots** had been cut as demos, over six years before a German record mogul heard the stuff completely by chance and decided to put it out. This phase of the band was punk energy, a heavy dose of Anglo-pop (especially early Who and Move), *The Honeymooners* and *Huckleberry Hound*. The musical styles are sort of jumbled, as are song topics (intra-office romance, marrying a monkey, a "Legend" in his own mind, etc.), yet it all somehow hangs together, partly through Quidd's high, reedy vocals. Plain and simple, it's a lot of fun.

The early Dots' high-speed battiness helped inspire some fans at a Washington, DC gig; next thing, Quidd found himself producing "Pay to Cum!," the landmark debut 45 by the Bad Brains. He also produced an EP for the Undead (led by an ex-Misfit). Then came **Return**, followed quickly by the other two LPs. Unfortunately, what makes the live album so fine is what makes the second studio LP unnecesary. The live LP has three fab reworkings (of the Beatles, the Count Five and Maxine Nightingale!), five new songs and seven numbers from previous Dots discs. Six of those are from **I Can See You.**

On the live LP, the nucleus of Quidd, Garcia and bassist Leigh Sioris was joined by Nat Seeley on drums (replacing Jeff Formosa, who was on **I Can See You**) and guitarist Al Maddy (ex-Nitecaps). The two guitars work together well, and the album's sound is full and punchy—in fact, better than the studio LP. Anyway, it's as much fun as

Return; where else can you find out why some people go to hell ("Hard Times"), what to do with a drunken sailor ("I Won't Cry 'Cause You Want Me To") or where "exceptionality" went ("Crime of Passion"). Dottiness may be an acquired taste (especially for New Yorkers), but it's quite savory in its own odd way. Meanwhile, Garcia's worked in the studio with ex-Roxy Music drummer Paul Thompson and on European TV with Mink DeVille; Quidd's produced a clutch of LPs for German bands.   [tr]

DOWNY MILDEW

Downy Mildew EP (Texas Hotel) 1986
Broomtree (Texas Hotel) 1987
Mincing Steps (Texas Hotel) 1988 ●

Those who like R.E.M. and 10,000 Maniacs, and rush out to get everything new on the English label 4AD, will find the shimmering acoustic and electric guitars and gauzy ambience of Southern California's Downy Mildew as refreshing as a cool sprinkle on a hot summer night. The first EP contains four songs written by the quartet's two singing guitarists, Charlie Baldonado and Jenny Homer, and introduces the band's two early sides: peppy folk-pop (he) and moodier rock balladry (she).

Broomtree is more accomplished, adding keyboards, autoharp, violin and dissonantly bowed cello to the acoustic guitars and buffered drums. Unfortunately, the slowed-down tempos and improved production reveals a faint resemblance to **Dark Side of the Moon**; a mild and dry jazzy side comes through as well. The alternation of lead vocals creates a certain tension, but the band's unassailable delicacy and taste provide enough stylistic unification to hold the album together.

Downy Mildew's increasingly refined escape from Planet Rock continues on **Mincing Steps**, a shimmering collection that reflects the group's transition into a distinguished chamber quartet. Touching on some of the ways '60s rock bands introduced baroque classical elements into their sound, Downy Mildew hit the right blend of energy and eclecticism about half the time. When it clicks, the record is a rare treat.   ['e/iar]

DP'S

See *Depressions.*

DRAGONS

Parfums de la Revolution (Fr. Blitzkrieg) 1982

A piece of punk exotica: three underground musicians from mainland China recorded in secret by a visiting Frenchman. (Done, thankfully, before the brief 1985 tour there by Wham!) Using only vocals, electric guitar, rudimentary drums and Chinese violin, the trio attempts "Anarchy in the UK" and "Get off My Cloud" with truly bizarre results; the remaining seven tracks are originals in a more traditional Oriental vein. A fascinating transliteration of rock from a country not generally considered in terms of modern music.   [iar]

DRAMATIS

For Future Reference (nr/Rocket) 1981

Gary Numan's post-Tubeway Army backing group gone solo, Dramatis tries a little of everything—mock symphonics, electro-disco, mainstream pop—in a vain effort to accomplish something on their own. Predictably, the only track worth a toss is the one on which former employer Numan sings, adding his deadpan signature to an otherwise faceless outfit.   [iar]

MIKEY DREAD

Dread at the Controls (nr/Trojan) 1979
World War III (nr/Dread at the Controls) 1980
Beyond World War III (Heartbeat) 1981
S.W.A.L.K. (Heartbeat) 1982
Pave the Way (Heartbeat) 1984
Pave the Way (Parts 1 & 2) (nr/DEP Int'l) 1985

Jamaican disc jockey Michael Campbell changed his name, moved to England and made it as a recording artist. **Dread at the Controls** (the name of his radio show and, later, record label) is a modest debut, but **World War III** is an out-and-out sonic adventure. Mixed up (and down) by Scientist, the LP features Dread's dance-hall-style toasting, beefed up with ultra-heavy production and sonic effects. The album tied into punk rockers' enthusiastic acceptance of both reggae's outlook and its techniques; Dread was thus considered a new wave reggae artist, a link he affirmed when he recorded (on **Sandinista!** and singles) and toured with the Clash. (**Beyond** is a slightly revised American edition.)

Unfortunately, none of his later releases

are as impressive as **WWIII**. **S.W.A.L.K.** is a halfhearted imitation filled with unconvincing lovers rock made worse by Dread's nasal singing. **Pave the Way (Parts 1 & 2)** is just as inconsistent. Although it offers stylistic variety, Dread's capable production and Paul Simonon on background vocals, the LP's best tracks are chant-down cuts like "Roots and Culture," the theme of a UK children's show. The two-LP British version is impressive at least for its ambition; the prior American single record seems spare in comparison.

[bk]

DREAM ACADEMY

The Dream Academy (Warner Bros.) 1985 ●
Remembrance Days (Reprise) 1987 ●

In a shocking success story, Dream Academy's easy-listening, generally dull pop found its way to the top of America's record charts in 1985. "Life in a Northern Town," the atmospheric Association-like '60s novelty tune (acoustic guitars, chanted vocals, cellos, tympani), is pleasant, pretentious and shallow, and nothing else on the first LP comes close to being as catchy or characteristic. Nick Laird-Clowes, who once led an act called the Act, is at best a bland vocalist; his partners (Gilbert Gabriel, keyboards; Kate St. John, woodwinds, horns) are equally inadequate to his transparent Thompson Twins fantasies. The LP employs many guest musicians; David Gilmour co-produced most of the tracks.

A riot of credits on **Remembrance Days** acknowledges production work by Hugh Padgham, Lindsey Buckingham and others. It's another airy record—stunningly clean, precise, sophisticated and of absolutely no significance. Dream Academy has thankfully abandoned the nostalgia gimmick, but Laird-Clowes' songs are still trifles, with clumsy lyrics that smack more of education than imagination. [iar]

See also *Brilliant*.

DREAM 6

See *Concrete Blonde*.

DREAMS SO REAL

Father's House (Coyote-Twin/Tone) 1986

This tuneful Athens trio, produced by Peter Buck, uses a bit of piano and close vocal harmonies—the Kingston Trio and Buffalo Springfield come to mind—to differentiate itself from That Other Local Band. Indeed, Dreams So Real's light, airy pop sound—although guitarist Barry Marler does favor Buck—doesn't really suggest an R.E.M. influence at all. (Close your ears when "Capitol Mall" comes on.) In any case, **Father's House** is too mild to truly matter: while the summery ambience is pleasant enough, the songs are insubstantial and many of the performances rush along in an overeager blur.

In 1987, Dreams So Real signed with Arista. [iar]

DREAM SYNDICATE

The Dream Syndicate EP (Down There) 1982
    (Enigma) 1984
The Days of Wine and Roses (Ruby) 1982
Tell Me When It's Over EP (nr/Rough Trade)
    1983
Medicine Show (A&M) 1984
This Is Not the New Dream Syndicate Album
    . . . Live! EP (A&M) 1984
Out of the Grey (Big Time) 1986 ●
50 in a 25 Zone EP (Big Time) 1987 ●
Ghost Stories (Enigma) 1988 ●

Dream Syndicate was one of the first bands from the Los Angeles psychedelic revival (misleadingly known as the paisley underground) to reach a national audience. While many of the movement's bands plumbed the Byrds/Buffalo Springfield or Pink Floyd archives for inspiration, Dream Syndicate's weird, obsessive lyrics, relentless noise maelstroms—mixed with eerie/pretty otherworldly dirges and ballads—and singer Steve Wynn's nasal rasping and ranting recalled the Velvet Underground, though (of course) they steadfastly denied that to be their intent. With driving, feedback-drenched guitars and stream-of-consciousness lyrical spume, **The Days of Wine and Roses**, rawly produced by Chris D. (Flesh Eaters/Divine Horsemen), appealed to sensitive English major college radio programmers too young to shoot up to the Velvets the first time around. (The UK-only **Tell Me When It's Over** EP contains five live cuts in addition to the title track, drawn from the album.)

Following the departure of bassist Kendra Smith, the band signed to A&M and recorded a second album, produced by metal guru Sandy Pearlman. Wynn's songs remain driven and obsessive, but he seems more inclined to ape Mick Jagger than Lou Reed this time. Also, guitarist Karl Precoda cuts back on the feedback and the entire album has more of a traditional rock'n'roll feel. Early fans cried sell-out, but with eight-minute jam/raps like "John Coltrane Stereo Blues" included, that accusation doesn't hold much water. Nine-and-a-half minutes of that song also appear on **This Is Not the New Dream Syndicate Album . . . Live!**, a dismal document recorded live in Chicago during the national tour that followed **Medicine Show**.

After guitarist/producer Paul B. Cutler (ex-45 Grave) replaced Precoda, a revitalized Dream Syndicate released **Out of the Grey**, nine rugged rock-cowboy songs characterized by Wynn's worn but hopeful vocals and Cutler's obsessive distorto-guitar madness. Proceeding from Neil Young's Crazy Horse period, songs like "Forest for the Trees," "Now I Ride Alone," "Slide Away" and "50 in a 25 Zone" (also released on a 12-inch with a bare-bones remix and three added tracks, including a maudlin version of "The Lonely Bull") hum with enough coarse energy and stylistic insouciance to cover their compositional deficiencies. (The **Out of the Grey** CD contains the EP's extra tracks.)   [ep/iar]

See also *Danny & Dusty, Opal.*

DREDD FOOLE AND THE DIN

See *(Dredd) Foole.*

DRONES

Further Temptations (nr/Valer) 1977

Featuring the effervescent Gus Gangrene on guitar, this Manchester quartet sounds like all of the other early punk bands reveling in the flush of enthusiasm that swept them along into careers that only the creative or crass survived. This album shows a few signs of life, but is generally a fairly uninspired and poorly produced example of the genre.   [iar]

DRONGOS

The Drongos (Proteus) 1984
Small Miracles (Proteus) 1985

A folky rock-pop quartet originally from New Zealand, the Drongos' eponymous debut (recorded in different sessions between 1981 and 1983) consists of unassuming songs about nebulous topics—nicely energized but a bit dull to make any serious impact. A few show melodic flair, and enthusiastic guitar

strumming doesn't hurt the effort. **Small Miracles** was recorded live one day in September 1984 at four locations on the streets of New York, providing a unique audio experience. Although they've got a lot of pluck (not to mention guts), the Drongos are too plain to attract notice, especially in such a jaded town as New York, where pedestrians have seen (and heard) just about everything.
[tr]

DROOGS

Heads Examined EP (Plug-n-Socket) 1983
Stone Cold World (Plug-n-Socket) 1984 (PVC) 1987
Anthology (Ger. Music Maniac) 1987
Kingdom Day (PVC) 1987 ●

On their first EP, LA's Droogs play bluesy garage rock and variously resemble the early Stones (thanks mostly to the harmonica wailing in "99 Steps"), the Yardbirds and the Seeds; a faithful cover of "Born to Be Wild" is both obligatory and superfluous. The first album, well-produced by Earle Mankey, sets a more ambitious course, relying on period-evocative psychedelic originals and mixing in different instrumental flavors and textures, while never straying far from recognizable clichés. The quartet deftly avoids genre slavishness but, a few notable exceptions (the solid title track, for instance) aside, still seems a few quarts shy of being exciting on their own recorded merits.

With the lineup intact and Mankey again manning the board, **Kingdom Day** drops the nostalgia shtick and mixes electric (kudos to Roger Clay) and acoustic guitars to good effect while keeping the focus on Ric Albin's growly vocals. Dynamic arrangements and enthusiastic, inspired playing make up for material that isn't all inherently memorable. The band's shorter songs work best, roughing up R&B and boogie stylings into modern rock, but the one non-original—"Call off Your Dogs," written by Jeffrey Lee Pierce and Peter Case—is the record's high point. This hot date proves the Droogs need no longer long to sound like anyone else.

Anthology is a German compilation of the Droogs' many self-released singles.
[iar]

DUBSET

Flesh Made Word (Elektra) 1984

Nigel Holland, bassist/writer/guitarist/ singer, waxes ultra-funky on this collection of energetic dance grooves, recorded with various musicians. If not for his upper-class-twit accent on pronouncements like "Promiscuity is boring and dangerous . . ." this would be a highly satisfying dance record.

[iar]

DUB SYNDICATE

See *Adrian Sherwood.*

DUCKS DELUXE

Ducks Deluxe (RCA) 1974
Taxi to the Terminal Zone (nr/RCA) 1975
Don't Mind Rockin' Tonite (RCA) 1978
Last Night of a Pub Rock Band (nr/Blue Moon) 1981

Heard in the cold light of the '80s, England's pub-rockin' Ducks Deluxe sound rather inconsequential (if amiable). Back in the dark ages of 1974, however, they were manna from heaven. Along with Brinsley Schwarz and Dr. Feelgood, the Ducks championed a much-needed return to basics by playing in traditional American styles diametrically opposed to the glitter and art trends then in vogue. And that paved the way for punk.

The Ducks' first (and best) LP captures the ultimate pub-rock band in all its glory—great for dancing and drinking, not critical analysis. Bursting with boisterous pride and spirit, the quartet careens through covers of songs by Eddie Cochran and the Stones, plus "originals" that borrow heavily from Chuck Berry, Lou Reed's "Sweet Jane," Otis Redding and so on. Three of the four sing: Nick Garvey is the rough-hewn romantic and Martin Belmont the awkward crooner, but it's Sean Tyla's growling boogie that sets the tempo.

Taking its title from a line in Chuck Berry's "Promised Land," **Taxi to the Terminal Zone** beats the sophomore jinx but also exposes the band's limitations. Many of the tracks are simply rewrites of songs from the first LP, which themselves were hardly groundbreakers. A cover of the Flamin Groovies' "Teenage Head" is inspired, however. The album benefits from Dave Edmunds' production and from the addition of keyboardist Andy McMaster, who contributes the surprisingly poppy "Love's Melody," foreshadowing the work he and Garvey would pursue in one of the Ducks' many subsequent outgrowths, the Motors.

In 1978, RCA sensed that the Ducks could be tied to the growth of new wave, and released **Don't Mind Rockin' Tonight**, a collection titled after one of the standout boogie tracks on the first album. A must for the band's fans, as it contains some previously non-LP B-sides; expendable for everyone else.

Last Night of a Pub Rock Band—that is, July 1, 1975—is so abysmally recorded that even aficionados should skip it. [jy]

See also *Nick Garvey, Motors, Graham Parker, Rumour, Sean Tyla.*

DUET EMMO

See *Dome.*

DUFFO

Duffo (nr/Beggars Banquet) 1979
The Disappearing Boy (nr/PVK) 1980
Bob the Birdman (nr/PVK) 1981

Australian oddball Duffo—a wan-looking androgynous waif—relocated to the UK before finding a record company that would sign him. A good move, since he proved to be a witty writer/singer (if a bit smutty at times), poking impish fun at the music industry and other targets. His eponymous first album, which bears the legend "Maybe god's a genius too!," has hints of the Bonzos, Bowie (in his guise as Anthony Newley), Tubes and Kinks. Duffo sings well and invests the entire disc with a self-deprecating sense of absurdity. A facile backing quartet follows him neatly into a variety of musical styles to support the diverse songs. [iar]

STEPHEN "TIN TIN" DUFFY

The Ups and Downs (nr/10-Virgin) 1985

STEPHEN DUFFY

Because We Love You (nr/10-Virgin) 1986

If awards were handed out for foresight, Stephen Duffy would not likely be considered for one. At the turn of the decade, he parted company with a trendy young new romantic band, saying they were just too reliant on synthesizers for his taste. Never mind that his own subsequent work has included plenty of electronics; the band he left was Duran Duran.

It took a little while, but Duffy did eventually get his own career off the ground. Using the ludicrous nom de rock Tin Tin, he had big international dance hits with "Kiss

Me" and "Hold Me," both annoying, stereotypical synth-pop ditties. The former was re-released several times and (two years later) included on **The Ups and Downs**, his long-delayed solo debut. (Duffy has not released an album in the US, although several singles have appeared.)

Because We Love You drops the Tin Tin tag and much of the electronic orchestration, replacing the latter with generic pop/rock/soul from the Wham!/Spandau school. With such ingenious titles as "I Love You," "Love Station" and "Unkiss That Kiss," almost every track is a predictable mélange of horns and standard bass/drums patterns, topped with Duffy's wimpy, emotionless voice. He can write good hooks, but neither of these albums offers anything you haven't been hearing more than enough of already.

[dgs]

DUKES OF STRATOSPHEAR
See *XTC*.

DUMPTRUCK
D Is for Dumptruck (Incas) 1983 (Big Time) 1985
Positively Dumptruck (Big Time) 1986 ●
For the Country (Big Time) 1987 ●

An interesting partnership from Massachusetts: Kirk Swan and Seth Tiven each sing, write and play guitar and bass on **D Is for Dumptruck**, with only a drummer for company. The dozen songs fall somewhere between Joy Division and the dB's—too bleak and intense to be happily engaging, yet rooted in a jagged pop melodicism. Insecure, downcast lyrics support the pair's darker side; occasionally chipper guitar bits elevate the mood. Although some tracks are disorientingly dense and chilly, Dumptruck can be a most entertaining and stimulating proposition. (The reissue is identical save for the back cover.)

Joined by a full two-man rhythm section and producer Don Dixon on keyboards, Tiven and Swan firmly pushed **Positively** towards the Chris Stamey facet of their personality, playing rugged guitar pop with the same intelligence but more melodicism. Although Swan and Tiven write separately, their musical styles meld together without seams. The strained, mildly anguished vocals definitely suggest the onetime dB's leader, but the busy drumming, swirling guitars and

raggedly Byrdsish harmonies ensure that Dumptruck's sound is their own. A powerful, thoughtful record that puts depth and ballast into an often lightweight and superficial genre.

Swan is absent from the third album, replaced by another singing guitarist; the lineup sports a new bassist as well. In a vain bid for commercial acceptance (Big Time having pacted with RCA for distribution and marketing), **For the Country** was produced in Wales by Hugh Jones. Dumptruck sounds stronger than ever: Tiven, now the sole writer, sings his dejected lyrics with a surprisingly determined edge, as a wall of strummed guitars and a loudly echoing backbeat surge behind him. He's certainly not a happy fellow: the irony of "Carefree," disgust of "Friends," anxiety and resignation of the delicately haunting "Dead Weight" are merely the tip of his melancholy iceberg. Involving and unsettling.

[iar]

SLY DUNBAR AND ROBBIE SHAKESPEARE
Sly and Robbie Present Taxi (Mango) 1981
The Sixties, Seventies + Eighties=Taxi (Mango) 1981
Raiders of the Lost Dub (Mango) 1981
Crucial Reggae Driven by Sly & Robbie (Mango) 1982
A Dub Encounter (Mango) 1985
Language Barrier (Island) 1985 ●
Rhythm Killers (Island) 1987 ●
The Summit (RAS) 1988 ●

TAXI GANG FEATURING SLY AND ROBBIE
The Sting (Moving Target-Celluloid) 1986 ●
Taxi Connection Live in London (Mango) 1986
Taxi Fare (Heartbeat) 1986 ●

SLY DUNBAR
Simple Sly Man (nr/Front Line) 1976
Sly, Wicked and Slick (nr/Front Line) 1977
Sly-go-ville (Mango) 1982

The cornerstone of contemporary roots, this nonpareil rhythm section has probably played on more reggae records than anyone else. Musical partners for many years beginning in various Jamaican studio bands, in the late '70s the pair founded Taxi, a production company and label that worked with many top Jamaican vocalists, including Black Uhuru. The Taxi sound was characterized by Robbie's clean, monolithic bass lines and

Sly's tasteful use of syndrums, decorating the reggae backbeat with state-of-the-art zing. The team went on to produce and play with such non-reggae artists as Grace Jones, Joan Armatrading and Ian Dury. Their trademark high-tech style has become familiar (some say tired), but Sly and Robbie's modern treatments have been a significant factor in reggae's development and popularity.

Many of their own albums are surprisingly unexciting. Sly's solo records sound like dry runs, uneventful groove collections (**Sly-go-ville** does have one Delroy Wilson vocal). **Sixties, Seventies + Eighties** is not much better. Their reworkings of past and present hits (including "El Pussy Cat Ska") demonstrate why they don't sing more often. Worse still is **The Sting**, a collection of uninspired dance tracks and reggeaized versions of "Peter Gunn," "The Entertainer" and "The Good, the Bad and the Ugly," each more dreadful than the last. Their most consistently listenable instrumental LP is probably **The Summit**, where the duo (joined by a piano player) pump out a variety of straightforward yet highly textured rhythms.

Two other releases that bear their names are actually departures, experiments in crossover. **Language Barrier**, a superstar fusion jam produced by Bill Laswell, features everyone from Afrika Bambaataa to Bob Dylan; danceable enough, but utterly unrelated to reggae. **Rhythm Killers** is the same idea, but more successful. Featuring covers of the Ohio Players' "Fire" and the Pointer Sisters' "Yes We Can Can," the LP is an unbroken song cycle, a seamless series of rap, funk, rock and reggae grooves. Again produced by Laswell, the session features Bootsy Collins, Henry Threadgill and many others. It's heavy-bottomed from start to finish, and interesting to boot.

In general, Sly and Robbie are most enjoyable on the various Taxi compilations, which also feature vocals. **Crucial Reggae**, which has the Mighty Diamonds' original "Pass the Kouchie," is not quite as good as **Sly and Robbie Present Taxi**, but both are fine introductions to the duo's playing and the Taxi roster of singers. (The British and American editions of the latter differ slightly.) Similarly, **A Dub Encounter** (released in the **Reggae Greats** series) and **Raiders of the Lost Dub** are remix collections of backing tracks originally done for Black Uhuru, Burning Spear and others. Both are supersonic headcharges that shouldn't be missed.

Less crucial are **Taxi Fare**, a largely instrumental collection of B-sides, and **Taxi Connection Live In London**. The concert LP, featuring songs by Ini Kamoze, Yellowman and Half Pint, conveys the drama and full sound of the live show (an all-star revue), but the performances are uneven.   [bk]

KEVIN DUNN AND THE REGIMENT OF WOMEN
The Judgement of Paris (DB) 1981
KEVIN DUNN
C'est toujours la même guitare. EP (Press) 1984
Tanzfeld (Press) 1986

The Judgement of Paris is a striking modern-music pop album by this onetime member of Atlanta's great pioneering independent band, the Fans. In reality a solo album, with lots of synths and guitars, Dunn mixes technical flash with semi-demented musical ideas, camouflaging nutty lyrics in engaging melodies and closing out the proceedings with an instrumental "Somewhere Over the Rainbow," complete with devolving rhythms.

Dunn's next release, a six-song EP, is far more ambitious but less adventurous, using guitar (adjusted with effects and varied playing styles) as a textural device to create fascinating, highly arranged clever avant-pop songs. (The cassette has two extra tracks, including one re-recorded from **Paris**.)

Tanzfeld is simply brilliant, a collection of adroit pop tunes wrapped with perceptive, informed lyrics. Besides such inspired originals as "Nam," "Giovenezza" (also on the first LP) and "Clear Title," there are wickedly satirical covers of "Burning Love," "Louie Louie" and other classics. Great!   [iar]

DURAN DURAN
Duran Duran (Harvest) 1981 (Capitol) 1983 ●
Rio (Harvest) 1982 ●
Carnival EP (Harvest) 1982 ●
Seven and the Ragged Tiger (Capitol) 1983 ●
Arena (Capitol) 1984 ●
Notorious (Capitol) 1986 ●
ARCADIA
So Red the Rose (Capitol) 1985
ANDY TAYLOR
Thunder (MCA) 1987 ●

Although conceived as a mix of the Sex Pistols and Chic, Birmingham's Duran

Duran was in fact launched as another pretty-boy-new-romantic-haircut-clothes-synth-pop-dance ensemble. Duran Duran surprisingly became an unimaginably popular teen sensation, drawing young fans into the seemingly unlikely world of techno-dance music. Taking cues (sound and image) from early Roxy Music and using simple electronics to flavor the lush but powerful rock sound, Duran Duran crossbred pop craft with a strong visual consciousness (using videos as a major strategic tool) to create records that are at once high-sheen disco and semi-inventive rock, even if that's not how the band and their fans view it.

Duran Duran introduced the dance attack, given a remarkable sonic setting by producer Colin Thurston. Tracks like "Planet Earth," "Girls on Film" and "Is There Anyone Out There," take the attributes of '70s disco—preeminent beat, repetition and studio gimmickry—and meld them to a variant on post-Ultravox rock to create something fairly original (at the time, at least). The elongated strains of synthesizer and syncopated tempos cover a multitude of creative shortcomings, but it's still an extraordinary album filled with now-classic songs.

Rio fulfills the band's potential, displaying stronger songwriting and far more intricate arrangements. The music's clearly danceable, but brilliantly listenable as well. Singer Simon Le Bon handles tantalizing melodies and obtuse lyrics with blithe confidence (if not profound ability), while honestly proficient musicianship by the other four defines each song's character differently. There isn't anything less than good, and "Rio," "Last Chance on the Stairway" and "New Religion" are downright astonishing in their melodic excellence. Thanks to a remix that features prominent female moaning (and an exotic video), "Hungry Like the Wolf" caught American radio programmers' attention, and lofted the band high into the charts, where they long remained a well-appointed fixture.

Quick to recognize their essential role as a dance band with rising commercial appeal, Duran's US label released a package of four remixes ("Hungry Like the Wolf," "Girls on Film," "Hold Back the Rain" and "My Own Way") as **Carnival**.

Parting ways with Thurston, Duran attempted to expand their musical horizons beyond the lush ambience of **Rio** and developed a herky-jerky rhythmic style aimed at creating catchy singles in a variety of modes.

Unfortunately, this led them to make the utterly detestable **Seven and the Ragged Tiger**, a sorry collection of half-baked melodies, meaningless lyrics (their earlier work may not have been poetry but it at least *sounded* clever) and over-active studio foolishness. Basically, the songs ain't no damn good. And even a passable item like "The Reflex" gets twisted with exaggerated, comical vocals; "Union of the Snake" sounds only half-written. The only truly noteworthy song, "New Moon on Monday," actually sounds like an outtake from **Rio**. Still, the album proved extremely successful among the audience who cheered the video monitors, not the band, during the tour that followed it.

Arena, the audio documentary of a mammoth coast-to-coast American trek, features surprisingly good playing (but extremely bad singing) on nine hits; additionally, the package (and I do mean package) includes a studio cut, "The Wild Boys," produced by Nile Rodgers, which resembles a possible theme song for *Lord of the Flies*. This album is irrelevant to anyone over the age of 15.

Duran Duran spent the next two years split into two camps. Taylor and Taylor (Andy and John) formed Power Station, while Simon, Nick and Roger stuck together, dubbing their sub-group Arcadia. Not surprisingly, with the artistic troublemakers out of the picture, Arcadia's **So Red the Rose** (produced by the late Alex Sadkin and featuring guest spots by Sting, Herbie Hancock, David Van Tieghem, David Gilmour, Andy Mackay and others) is virtually an old-fashioned Duran Duran album. Not an especially good one, mind you, but it does sound a lot more like **Rio** than **Seven and the Ragged Tiger** does.

Although they had a number one single in mid-'85 with the theme song for a James Bond film ("A View to a Kill"), the group never quite reformed after that. Roger left in 1986; Andy stayed long enough to play on four tracks on the next album before splitting for a solo career. That left Simon, Nick and John Taylor to carry the tattered but marketable banner, supported on **Notorious** by producer/guitarist Nile Rodgers (talk about realizing one's career ambitions), Missing Person guitarist Warren Cuccurullo and session drummer Steve Ferrone. A lack of material, a surplus of horns and the overall sterile pop/funk precision leave Duran resembling a dull, toned-down Power Station with no songs. The title track isn't entirely horrible, but that's not much to hang an album on.

(That same year, John Taylor wrote and recorded a big-selling solo single, "I Do What I Do," for the film *9 1/2 Weeks.*)

Andy Taylor's solo career got off to a bizarre start in mid-'86 when he scored a minor hit single with "Take It Easy," a song for the *American Anthem* soundtrack. Unlike anything else in his past work, the song unnervingly resembles the Bellamy Brothers' 1976 easy-listening smash, "Let Your Love Flow."

Although his name appears alone on the cover of **Thunder**, ex-Pistol Steve Jones cowrote, co-produced and played half the guitar on it. Impressionable Durannies must have plotzed upon hearing their beloved fashion plate roaring through demi-metal rock songs. Pathetic stabs at incorporating echoes of Duran and Power Station aside, the pair's power chords (and even some of the solos) ring loud and true, giving the louder songs conviction, if not artistic merit.   [iar]

See also *Power Station.*

DURUTTI COLUMN

The Return of the Durutti Column (nr/Factory) 1979
LC (nr/Factory) 1981
Another Setting (nr/Factory) 1982
Live at the Venue, London (nr/VU) 1983
Amigos in Portugal (Portuguese Fundacio Atlantica) 1984
Without Mercy (nr/Factory) 1984
Say What You Mean Mean What You Say EP (nr/Factory) 1985
Domo Arigato [CD] (nr/Factory) 1985
Circuses and Bread (Bel. Factory Benelux) 1985
Valuable Passages (Factory-Relativity) 1986
Live at the Bottom Line New York [tape] (ROIR) 1987
The Guitar and Other Machines (Venture-Virgin) 1988 ●

Unlike Blondie, Durutti Column is not a group. Guitarist Vini Reilly essentially comprises Durutti Column, although he has used other musicians in the studio and tours with other players. Of late, Reilly has been branching out, backing Morrissey on his solo record and working on an assortment of projects.

Producer Martin Hannett deserves equal credit on **The Return of the Durutti Column**, a perversely-titled debut of evocative guitar instrumentals, many multi-tracked and accented with environmental, synthetic and studio-created percussive effects. Occasionally reminiscent of Mike Oldfield's **Tubular Bells** and some of the Frippertronics recordings, Reilly pretty much creates his own style—a gentle, uncluttered amalgam of acoustic and electric guitar textures.

Hannett is absent from **LC**, Bruce Mitchell plays drums in spots and Reilly, regrettably, "sings" on a couple of the tracks, all of which makes it the lesser of Reilly's first two works, although the instrumentals still provide pleasant listening.

Continuing to experiment with various approaches, Reilly incoporated a cor anglais (English horn) player on **Another Setting**; **Without Mercy** employs an entire studio group, including Blaine Reininger of Tuxedomoon. While hardly raucous, Reilly moved further away from his ambient roots on **Say What You Mean**: deep, heavy electronic (or treated) percussion is annoyingly high in the mix on most of the six tracks. The record's highlight, "Silence," starts out sparsely, with electronic piano and marimba, and builds nicely with the addition of drums, trumpet, slide guitar and Reilly's much-improved voice. Although his vinyl output is perhaps more prolific than his creativity, Reilly is capable of producing rewarding music.

Domo Arigato is a live album released only on compact disc. **Valuable Passages** is a nicely compiled sampler of Durutti Column through the ages, including tracks from all of the prior studio efforts, an unreleased item and selections from singles and elsewhere. A perfect introduction to Reilly's soothing atmospherics.

The live-in-New York cassette finds Reilly, backed by drummer/xylophonist Mitchell and John Metcalfe (viola), playing piano and treated guitar on a career-spanning program of polite instrumentals that suffers from an inordinate amount of tape hiss, but otherwise shows that this stuff can be performed without incident in front of an audience.

Some of the new material presented at that late-'86 show wound up being recorded for **The Guitar and Other Machines**, which also relies on Mitchell and Metcalfe (plus others to a lesser degree) for studio support. The 11 pieces (three with guest vocals) are as sonically adventurous as anything Reilly has previously attempted. While remaining inside the group's traditional parameters, this ambitious record increases his emotional reach.   [ds/dgs/iar]

IAN DURY

New Boots and Panties!! (Stiff) 1977
   (nr/Demon) 1986 ●
Lord Upminster (Polydor) 1981

IAN DURY AND THE BLOCKHEADS

Do It Yourself (Stiff-Epic) 1979
Laughter (Stiff-Epic) 1980
Jukebox Dury (Stiff-America) 1981
Greatest Hits (nr/Fame) 1982
Sex & Drugs & Rock & Roll (nr/Demon)
   1986 ●

IAN DURY AND THE MUSIC STUDENTS

4000 Weeks' Holiday (nr/Polydor) 1984

Stunted in growth, crippled by polio and unrepentantly cockney, Ian Dury is one of rock's most memorable (and certainly lovable) figures. Hardly a newcomer in 1977—having been around with Kilburn and the High Roads—Dury came into his own with **New Boots and Panties!!**, an album whose energy almost defies it to stay on the turntable. With his motley but talented backing band, the Blockheads, Dury trounces merrily through outrageous odes like "Plaistow Patricia," "Billericay Dickie," "Blockheads" and the anthemic "Sex & Drugs & Rock & Roll" (not on the original UK LP, but added to the American edition and later to the British as well). But a more sensitive side emerges lyrically on "Sweet Gene Vincent," "My Old Man" and "If I Was with a Woman" and musically on "Wake Up and Make Love with Me."

Dury and the Blockheads' disco leanings came to the fore on the dazzling **Do It Yourself**. The band's rich interweaving behind Dury's playfully obscure vocals may have meant sensory overload for some, and the more sophisticated music (compared to **New Boots'** often raucous blare) must have turned away the punk cadres. With hindsight, though, **Do It Yourself** can be heard as a trailblazing fusion of dance musics, in both upbeat ("Sink My Boats," "Dance of the Screamers") and relaxed ("Inbetweenies," "Lullaby for Francies") modes.

Blockhead musical director Chaz Jankel left after **Do It Yourself**, but the band carried on with thinner textures and ex-Feelgood guitarist Wilko Johnson. (Jankel subsequently pursued a dull solo career as a pianist/singer.) **Laughter** is an uneasy and uneven mix of whimsical concepts like "Yes & No (Paula)," "Dance of the Crackpots" and "Over the Points," as well as less-inspired funk-rock like "(Take Your Elbow Out of the Soup You're Sitting on the Chicken)" and "Sueperman's Big Sister."

Dury next abandoned Stiff and scuttled the Blockheads, but reunited with Jankel for **Lord Upminster**, recorded in the Bahamas with reggae rhythm kingpins Robbie Shakespeare (bass) and Sly Dunbar (drums). After the Blockheads' joyful noise, **Lord Upminster**'s funk sounds ascetic. (Keyboard player Tyrone Downie is the only other musician.) Disappointingly, Dury scales down his writing for the occasion, approaching minimalist levels on "Wait (For Me)" and "Trust (Is a Must)." Aside from the notoriously frank "Spasticus (Autisticus)," the record amounts to a creative holding pattern.

It took Dury three years to bang out another record, this time with a mostly unfamiliar set of sidemen working under the ironic Music Students moniker. The homemade-look cover of **4000 Weeks' Holiday** belies the slickly-produced soul tracks inside; only Dury's homey speak-singing connects the songs to a non-mainstream aesthetic. Lyrically conservative as well, Dury waxes romantic ("You're My Inspiration"), treacly ("Friends"), political ("Ban the Bomb"), noirish ("The Man with No Face") and whimsical ("Take Me to the Cleaners").

Dury seems to work best outside the album format. "Hit Me with Your Rhythm Stick" was hastily added to **Do It Yourself** as a bonus 45; "Reasons to Be Cheerful (Part 3)" fell between **Do It Yourself** and **Laughter**. Although it could be ungenerously interpreted merely as Stiff's last chance to cash in, **Juke Box Dury** is also the best and most consistent Dury LP. Besides the two hits just mentioned, it has other fine 45 sides ("What a Waste," "Razzle in My Pocket," "Common as Muck") and a few choice album cuts. Dury's humanism comes through loud and clear, and the record is programmed swell.

[si/iar]

E E E E E E E E E

EARTHLING

Dance (Jap. King) 1981

This Japanese trio, led—believe it or not—by John (no last name) on vocals and guitar and Yoko (Fujiwara) on bass, toured both American coasts in 1981. Despite its title, the album is less influenced by current trends in terpsichore than by the group of performers that participated in the famous **June 1, 1974** concert/LP—Kevin Ayers, John Cale and pre-ambient Eno—with a healthy dollop of Roxy Music thrown in as well. The third Earthling, Jin Haijima, plays keyboards and synths à la Eno; there's even Andy Mackay-like sax on a couple of songs. Cale's influence is felt in the prevalent droning intensity; John's voice occasionally bears a striking resemblance to Ayers'. A strangely evocative combination.   [ds]

EASTERHOUSE

In Our Own Hands EP (nr/London) 1985
Inspiration EP (nr/Rough Trade) 1986
Contenders (Rough Trade-Columbia) 1986 ●

This Manchester quintet, led by argumentative brothers Andy and Ivor Perry (vocals/lyrics and guitar, respectively) turned strident leftist rhetoric into cathartic music, before predictably dissolving amidst internal ideological conflicts. It's a shame Easterhouse's end came so soon, though, as the band seemed well on its way towards perfecting a brand of explicitly political rock that compromised neither message nor music.

The four-track **In Our Own Hands** is a commanding debut, bursting with musical energy and topical fervor. **Inspiration** examines the troubles in Northern Ireland with convincing passion, while giving Ivor a convincing framework for his spidery guitar lines. Two **Inspiration** numbers—the title song and "Nineteen Sixty Nine"—later showed up on the band's sole longplayer.

Contenders, Easterhouse's abortive shot at the Stateside bigtime, almost makes good on the band's lofty goals. Their lyrical concerns are compelling and clear without falling prey to sloganeering or anthem-mongering. The music is both melodic and muscular, lending authority to Andy's regret-tinged broadsides. Songs like "Out on Your Own," "To Live Like This" and "Cargo of Souls" vilify various institutional targets (including England's liberal Labour Party) without losing sight of the human cost of governmental oppression.

Ruminations upon the contradictions inherent in a revolutionary Communist band's affiliation with America's largest record label proved moot when Easterhouse fell apart not long after **Contenders'** US release. Andy kept the Easterhouse name and announced his intention to recruit a new lineup, but has thus far been silent. Ivor, meanwhile, formed the Cradle with Easterhouse drummer Gary Rostock and Smiths/Aztec Camera guitarist Craig Gannon.   [hd]

EASTERN BLOC

Wall to Wall EP (Chetnick) 1986
Eastern Bloc (Paradox-Passport) 1987 ●

These three New York scene veterans—bassist Ivan Kral, guitarist Mark Sidgwick and drummer Frankie LaRocka—have individually backed the likes of Patti Smith, Iggy Pop, David Johansen, Holly Vincent, Tim Scott and John Waite. Their own band's album, while not exactly a groundbreaker, is a thoroughly respectable melodic rock collection that reflects the years they've spent in the trenches. Sidwgick has a pleasant if limited voice; his guitar playing is appropriately fiery and flexible; the rhythm section is dextrous and inventive. A Pink Floyd-speed version of Kral's estimable 1979 Smith collaboration, "Dancing Barefoot," is odd enough to work; the Sidgwick/Kral originals could use smarter lyrics, but don't want for hooks or commercial craft. [iar]

EASTERN DARK
See *Celibate Rifles*.

ELLIOT EASTON
See *Cars*.

EATER
The Album (nr/The Label) 1977
Get Yer Yo Yo's Out EP (nr/The Label) 1978
The History of Eater Vol. One (nr/De Lorean) 1985

One of Britain's primordial punk bands, Eater boasted a drummer too young to legally enter the clubs where they played, good taste in selecting songs to record ("Sweet Jane," "Queen Bitch," "Waiting for the Man," a rejuvenated adaptation of an Alice Cooper song: "Fifteen") but little else. Primeval hardcore. [tr]

EBN-OZN
Feeling Cavalier (Elektra) 1984

Ozn (Rosen) is the mannered vocalist; Ebn (Liben) the Fairlight synthesist. Together with some guest stars the pair makes highly-arranged modern yuppie rock with a few adventurous concepts: "TV Guide" is a massed-vocal exercise in dada that's pretty funny; the dramatic film-score sound of "Bag Lady (I Wonder)" contrasts powerfully with the sensitive lyrics about street people. The pair's best-known tune, "AEIOU (Sometimes Y)," takes a pushy David Lee Roth macho pose about "this incredible looking Swedish girl" and goes on too long, but the sound and chorus are great; an interposed spoken-word bridge concerning global language shows a bit of intelligence and adds excitement. Elsewhere, Ebn-Ozn turn out tepid ballads, dance rock, fake salsa ("Video D.J."), funk and even do a pointless update of "Rockin' Robin." Weird. [iar]

ECHO AND THE BUNNYMEN
Crocodiles (Sire) 1980 ●
Shine So Hard EP (nr/Korova) 1981
Heaven Up Here (Korova-Sire) 1981 ●
Porcupine (Korova-Sire) 1983 ●
Echo and the Bunnymen EP (Korova-Sire) 1983
Never Stop EP (nr/Korova) 1983
Ocean Rain (Korova-Sire) 1984 ●
Songs to Learn & Sing (Korova-Sire) 1985 ●
Echo & the Bunnymen (Sire) 1987 ●
Bedbugs & Ballyhoo EP (Sire) 1988

WILL SERGEANT
Themes for Grind (nr/92 Satisfied Customers) 1982

This vanguard foursome—at the start (1978) a trio plus Echo the drum machine—emerged from Liverpool's new wave renaissance with a debut album stunning in its starkness and power. Unlike also-rans with the same idea, Ian McCulloch's specter-of-Jim Morrison vocals are no mere pilferage; where Morrison would have ordered you on your knees, Mac does it himself, alternately writhing in resistance or slumped in resignation to the agonies of a whole other decade. On **Crocodiles**, the scratchy, yet ringing, guitar and unhurriedly relentless, pounding drums set the sonic scene for McCulloch's sometimes ambivalently delivered existential crises. (The US release adds a subsequent single track.)

Shine So Hard is actually part of the soundtrack to a half-hour film (same title) of a specially-staged concert (admittedly a logistic and musical disappointment), and mostly serves to preview the upcoming LP in lackluster fashion. But in its own right, the gloom engulfing **Heaven Up Here** seems to have smothered the band's cogency, with McCulloch less a fist-shaker than a whiner. The old potency is still audible at times (mainly on Side One) but, like McCulloch, the guitars sound fragile, even brittle; overall, it's a dreamy, depressed and depressing effort.

Echo's third LP is a far more enthralling proposition, an invigorating collection of bizarre, challenging songs given surprising but fitting color by the addition of violinst Shankar's offbeat wailings. Sweeping creations like "The Cutter" and "The Back of Love" are tremendously exciting; the rest of **Porcupine**, if not as consistently memorable, captures the band's unique essence with grace

181

and style. New-found efficiency dispatches past self-indulgent inaccessibility.

The even-better **Ocean Rain** exchanges Shankar's unique contribution for more routine string accompaniment, but offers an amazing skein of great songwriting. "Silver," "Crystal Days," "Seven Seas" and "The Killing Moon" all achieve the ideal marriage of pop with drama, using McCulloch's strong vocal presence and Will Sergeant's varied and textural guitar work to imbue the songs with majesty and subtlety.

Songs to Learn & Sing, a welcome career retrospective, adds a fine new tune ("Bring on the Dancing Horses") and one obscurity to nine more familiar items, concisely recapitulating the band's first five years. The eponymous EP is a 12-inch released after **Porcupine**, containing the album's two best tracks, two other studio cuts plus a live version of "Do It Clean"; The British-only **Never Stop** EP is similar, with some overlap.

In 1986, drummer Pete DeFreitas briefly left Echo (ex-Haircut One Hundred member Blair Cunningham took his place) but was back in the lineup in time for **Echo & the Bunnymen**, a solid and mature album which gains momentum as it plays. Produced by the talented Laurie Latham, engaging, reflective songs like "Lips Like Sugar," "Lost and Found," "New Direction" and "All in Your Mind" show the Bunnymen's ongoing refinement and consistent quality; the band acknowledges its debt to the Doors by prominently featuring Ray Manzarek, one of several guest keyboardists the record employs, on the distinctly reminiscent "Bedbugs and Ballyhoo." That track (in its LP version and an elongated remix) was subsequently issued as one side of an EP, the neat flipside of which offers three live covers: "Paint It Black," the Velvet Underground's "Run, Run, Run" and Television's "Friction." (Echo also recorded a version of the Doors' "People Are Strange" for the soundtrack of *The Lost Boys*.)

Sergeant's 1982 instrumental solo album is a weird, experimental effort.   [jg/iar]

EDDIE AND THE HOT RODS

Live at the Marquee EP (nr/Island) 1976
Teenage Depression (Island) 1976
Life on the Line (Island) 1977
Thriller (nr/Island) 1979

Fish 'n' Chips (EMI America) 1980
One Story Town (nr/Waterfront) 1985

It may be difficult to hear now, but London's Eddie and the Hot Rods played a crucial role in the birth of new wave. If the Rods hadn't been out there, playing wild and fast rock'n'roll in the clubs at a time when superstar pomposity was the currency of pop music, bands like the Sex Pistols would never have had the opportunity to join, intensify and broaden that rebellious spirit into a national—and international—musical upheaval.

Today, **Teenage Depression** sounds like a fairly tame set of R&B-influenced simple rock tunes, like early Flamin Groovies or Dave Edmunds, but at the time of its release had major impact on the British music scene. The title track (a hit single there) is the record's finest moment. (The American album replaced two soul covers with four tracks that had appeared on the live EP.)

For **Life on the Line**, the Rods expanded to a five-piece with the addition of ex-Kursaal Flyer Graeme Douglas. It was a wise move, as Douglas gave the band a smart kick in the pop direction, best exemplified on the wonderful "Do Anything You Wanna Do," which he co-wrote. Overall, a strong album (thanks to good songs and enthusiastic playing) that stands up much better than its predecessor.

By the time of **Thriller** (is Michael Jackson a fan?), the Hot Rods were a thing of the past, culturally speaking. They hadn't been able to keep pace with the changes, rendered redundant by the bands they had inspired. The album reeks with bitterness; although competent, it has neither the freshness of **Life on the Line** nor anything substantial to replace it. As a sign of the band's "maturity," Linda McCartney sang some backup parts.

With Al Kooper producing, a revised lineup (without Douglas or bassist Paul Gray) turned out an unnecessary fourth album that is best forgotten. **One Story Town** is a live LP.   [iar]

See also *Damned, Inmates*.

EDGE

Square One (nr/Hurricane) 1980

The Edge (the group, not the U2 mainstay) came about when guitarist Lu Edmonds and drummer Jon Moss (formerly of punk slouches London) left a brief and unrecorded incarnation of the Damned in 1978. With the addition of keyboardist Gavin Povey (who had played with Lew Lewis) and bassist Glyn Havard (whose long career has included stints with the Yachts and, er, Jade Warrior), the Edge fell together. They played behind Jane Aire as the Belvederes on her one LP and also appeared, nearly intact, on Kirsty MacColl's first album. Subsequent to the Edge, Lu has worked in a number of bands, including Shriekback, the Spizzles and Public Image Ltd., while Jon Moss went on to temporary fame and fortune in Culture Club.

Oh yeah—about the music. Never quite blending into any particular style, the Edge's eclectic, melodic rock has flashes of the Jam, Boomtown Rats, Deep Purple, Police and Stranglers—all united by the satirical outlook of amusing lyrics. [iar]

DAMON EDGE

See *Chrome.*

THE EDGE

See *U2, Jah Wobble.*

EDITH NYLON

Edith Nylon (Fr. CBS) 1979
Quatre Essaies Philosophique EP (Fr. CBS) 1980
Johnny Johnny (Fr. CBS) 1981
Echo, Bravo (Fr. Chiswick) 1982

This French band went from a singleminded obsession with machines and bio-robotics on their first album, in a style toning down Gary Numanisms to suit a somewhat high-tech Blondiesque approach, to an everything-but-the-kitchen-sink mélange on **Echo, Bravo** (an LP plus a 12-inch EP), incorporating all sorts of English and American influences along the way. As with Blondie, the name refers not to the female lead singer (Mylène Khaski) but the group itself; also like Blondie, the lineup expanded (from a quintet to a keyboards-plus-two-guitars sextet) while the founder members retained control of production as well as songwriting.

There's plenty of zip and charm to the CBS recordings. (**Echo, Bravo** is the most entertaining.) Khaski's French lyrics display moderate intelligence, and they're complemented by lighter-hearted humor as well as a mix-and-match stylistic grab-bag blending dance rock, '60s pop and bits that call to mind everyone from the Pretenders to Adam

and the Ants. Sure, it's a stew, but more often than not they come out sounding like nobody so much as themselves, and that on some pretty fair numbers. A smart producer could have worked wonders with 'em. [jg]

DAVE EDMUNDS

Rockpile (MAM) 1971
Subtle as a Flying Mallet (RCA) 1975
Get It (Swan Song) 1977
Tracks on Wax 4 (Swan Song) 1978
Repeat When Necessary (Swan Song) 1979
Twangin . . . (Swan Song) 1981
The Best of Dave Edmunds (Swan Song) 1981
D.E. 7th (Columbia) 1982
Information (Columbia) 1983
Riff Raff (Columbia) 1984

DAVE EDMUNDS BAND LIVE

I Hear You Rockin' (Columbia) 1987 ●

VARIOUS ARTISTS

Stardust (Arista) 1974
Porky's Revenge (Columbia) 1985

Can traditional rock'n'roll survive in the modern world? As long as Dave Edmunds is around, the answer will be yes. A rousing singer, superlative guitarist and wizard producer, Edmunds has preserved the simplicity and directness of '50s rock without ever sounding like a slavish revivalist. Along the way, he's also performed tricks with country music and even Phil Spector's elaborate constructions. Edmunds has had his ups and downs on record, but the one thing he's never been is pretentious.

Dave prefaced his solo career with two LPs as the leader of manic blues-psychedelic trio Love Sculpture. Those days are well documented on numerous compilations, the best being a two-disc French set, **Dave Edmunds, Rocker**.

Rockpile was recorded because Edmunds needed to make an LP to capitalize on his worldwide smash single, a one-man remake of Gale Storm's 1955 hit "I Hear You Knockin'." This LP established the boundaries of the first phase of his solo career: a Chuck Berry tune, a Willie Dixon blues, a country stomp (by Neil Young, no less) and so on. **Rockpile** is a mishmash in terms of recording dates—one track was cut in 1966—and creation, with Edmunds playing almost all the instruments himself. No matter—it rocks like crazy.

Of the 40 cuts on the two-LP soundtrack/

compilation for the David Essex film *Stardust*, seven are fine covers of oldies by Edmunds. A point to note here: six of those tracks are credited to the Stray Cats—years in advance of Brian Setzer's group.

By 1975, the unprolific Edmunds had a few more UK hits and enough other odds and ends to assemble another LP; unfortunately **Subtle as a Flying Mallet** doesn't hold together. The Everly Brothers' "Leave My Woman Alone" and a few other individual tracks work, but this is otherwise a largely lifeless record. The intricate one-man Spector homages ("Maybe," "Baby I Love You," etc.) are pretty but strained. Two tracks recorded live with Brinsley Schwarz point to the end of Edmunds' hibernation in the studio.

Get It lets air into the musty, old room of Edmunds' musical mind. Dave still laid down a lot of the tracks unaided, but also utilized the services of members of the Rumour and the defunct Brinsleys, forming a significant partnership with the latter's Nick Lowe. Highlights of this bright-sounding LP include Lowe's Chuck Berry rewrite, "I Knew the Bride," and the Lowe/Edmunds salute to the Everly Brothers, "Here Comes the Weekend."

Tracks on Wax 4 hardens and intensifies the attack, fully freeing Edmunds from the negative aspects of his nostalgic leanings. Give credit for that to the formation of Rockpile, a hard-working band composed of Edmunds, Lowe on bass, guitarist Billy Bremner and drummer Terry Williams; over the following few years, Rockpile recorded both Lowe and Edmunds solo albums, then cut one under the group name before splintering. On **Tracks on Wax 4**, they drive Dave to new heights of rock'n'roll glory.

Perhaps his best effort, **Repeat When Necessary** follows the course set by **Tracks on Wax**, with a bit of country sweetening. Standouts: Elvis Costello's "Girls Talk," "Queen of Hearts" (later a hit for the wretched Juice Newton) and the sultry "Black Lagoon."

Following the acrimonious breakup of Rockpile, Edmunds rushed out **Twangin . . .**, a resounding disappointment. Despite the presence of a few pearls, this is clearly an inferior patchwork. Outtakes deserve to remain outtakes. The return to the claustrophobic one-man-band sound of his early days is particularly disheartening.

The Best of Dave Edmunds, 13 tracks from the four Swan Song LPs, makes no chronological sense, but offers an impressive musical overview.

D.E. 7th marks a return to form. With a hot new supporting cast, Edmunds boogies like a happy man again. A new Springsteen song, "From Small Things (Big Things One Day Come)," and a rip-roaring version of NRBQ's "Me and the Boys" lead the parade.

Information and **Riff Raff** comprise Edmunds' Jeff Lynne period; a disastrous attempt to concoct slick, salable contemporary product. Though both albums have some good moments (generally those on which Lynne didn't collaborate), they're largely characterized by a glib, crass sensibility.

The **Porky's Revenge** soundtrack is, believe it or not, a fine platter. In addition to some sharp cuts of his own, Edmunds produced tracks by Jeff Beck, George Harrison (a new Dylan song) and Clarence Clemons. Boogie one more time!

Edmunds' artistic productivity may have dipped in the mid-'80s, but his career as a producer has stayed hot all decade. He guided the latter-day Stray Cats to the top of the charts and fulfilled a longstanding ambition of working with the Everly Brothers by producing their 1984 comeback album. In 1987, he produced a country album for Canada's k.d. lang.

The unprepossessing but delectable **I Hear You Rockin'** was recorded live in London, New York and New Jersey with veteran pub-rock pianist Geraint Watkins, guitarist Mickey Gee, bassist John David and drummer/engineer Dave Charles. Edmunds touches all the obvious bases with little fanfare (save some intrusive synthesizer), reprising the better half of his Swan Song compilation while adding "I Hear You Knocking," "Information," "Paralyzed," "Slipping Away" and a fine reading of Dion's "The Wanderer." [jy/iar]

WINSTON EDWARDS

See *Dennis Bovell.*

EEK-A-MOUSE

Wa-Do-Dem (Shanachie) 1982
Skidip! (Shanachie) 1982
Assassinator (RAS) 1983
The Mouse and the Man (Shanachie) 1983
Mouseketeer (Shanachie) 1984
King and I (RAS) 1985

Mouse-a-Mania [CD] (RAS) 1988
Eek-a-Nomics (RAS) 1988 ●

Probably the biggest new solo reggae star of the '80s, Eek-a-Mouse (Ripton Joseph Hylton) has no trouble keeping a high profile. Not only is he six-foot-six, his distinctive voice is easily recognized. He sings with a nasal twang (like a higher-pitched version of Michael Rose), but punctuates his vocals with all sorts of syllabic thrusts, like reggae's answer to scat. The effect is melodic, but also percussive—it keeps the groove moving forward. Eek's success is also attributable to the high quality of his records. He works primarily with Roots Radics, a popular Jamaican session band that's played behind Gregory Isaacs and countless others. With Eek, however, the chemistry is unique—they seem to play better with him—and the power of their collaboration helps keep his albums consistent and special.

Above all, Eek is funny, a comic as well as social critic. **Wa-Do-Dem**, a smart debut, features the hit single of the same name. ("Wa do dem stare? Because she's too short and he's too tall.") **Skidip!** also has its share of hits ("Modelling Queen" and "You Na Love Reggae Music"), though the second side is a little thin. **Assassinator** is steady and strong, but boasts no outstanding tracks.

The Mouse and the Man and **Mouseketeer** are his best albums—assured and versatile. The first includes the epic tale of Eek's meeting with Mickey Mouse, "Modelling King" (a followup to his earlier hit) and a curious ditty called "Hitler." **Mouseketeer** features "Star, Daily News or Gleaner," a song about anorexia and, for all who wondered, "How I Got Me Name." Not to be missed.

Eek's reign continues on his latest, but he's stretching out a bit. Working with a number of musicians besides Roots Radics, the instrumentation on **King and I** is fuller (and includes some synthesizer), but it's hardly a drastic departure from his successful formula. [bk]

EFFIGIES

Haunted Town EP (Autumn) 1981
We're Da Machine EP (Ruthless-Enigma) 1983
The Effigies EP (Ruthless-Enigma) 1984
For Ever Grounded (Ruthless-Enigma) 1984

Fly on a Wire (Fever-Enigma) 1985
Ink (Fever-Restless) 1986

The Effigies were the first band from Chicago's bald'n'booted brigade to gain any out-of-town recognition, and rightfully so. The quartet's five-song debut EP (later reissued with an extra track as **The Effigies** EP) showcased their bold, taut, spare punk attack on real songs about adult concerns, with prophetic (for punk) metal guitar lacing through their best material, including the anthemic "Mob Clash."

Although flat production obscured the disc's strong points, the Effigies fuzzed up the guitar (simultaneously experimenting with acoustic) and moved it to the fore on **We're Da Machine**. The best songs on **For Ever Grounded**—a lyrically and rhythmically more diverse (even adding dance beats) LP—wail with the urgency of a siren at night. Earl Letiecq's guitar screeches like whitewalls on sodden pavement—the raw nerve that keeps the Effigies' sound permanently on edge. Though sometimes seen as humorless and uncharismatic in comparison with other bands, the Effigies are solid and reliable.

Before recording their second album, **Fly on a Wire**, the Effigies replaced Letiecq with Robert O'Connor; by the powerful **Ink**, he was co-writing all of the band's material with singer John Kezdy. Removed from contemporaneous local trends, the quartet continues to play invigorating non-commercial rock with a punky edge, an uncomplicated guitar band walking a tightrope between metal and hardcore without sacrificing electricity or impact. [ep/iar]

MAX EIDER
See *Jazz Butcher*.

E*I*E*I*O
Land of Opportunity (Frontier) 1986
That Love Thang (Frontier) 1988 ●

Wisconsin's E*I*E*I*O is an "American Music" band in the tradition of Creedence Clearwater Revival and the Blasters. Like those two bands, their sound is an amalgam of rock'n'roll, rockabilly, country, blues and folk. They've also got a strong singer with an unmistakably individual voice in Steve Summers, two good songwriters (Summers and bassist Richard Szeluga) and a pair of shit-hot guitarists (one of whom was in Off Broadway at the turn of the decade) and harmony vocalists who can sing like Byrds.

185

The uniformly excellent material on **Land of Opportunity** (co-produced by Steve Berlin) ranges from flat-out ravers ("Tear It Down," "Go West Young Man" "The Middle of November") to songs about the ups and downs of the road ("White Lines, Blue Skies, Black Top" "Me and Jesus Christ"), country life ("Blue Mountaintop") and, of course, love ("This Time," "Hello Heartache," "Get Back to Arkansas," "Every Word True"). The music's emotional intensity and physical excitement make this an essential record. (The cassette adds "Stars Are Out and the Moon Is High" and "No Father in the Family.")

With guitarist Mike Hoffman gone to form Semi-Twang, the group uses **That Love Thang** to expand its sound further, adding a propulsive R&B-type horn section (on the wonderful "Hey, Cecelie" and the title track) and strings (for the LP's ambitious closer "Brother Michael"). While the songs here are a bit less involving than on **Land of Opportunity**, this is another fine record. (The cassette and CD append "Can't Stay Here.") [ds]

8 EYED SPY
Live [tape] (ROIR) 1981
8 Eyed Spy (nr/Fetish) 1981
LYDIA LUNCH
Hysterie (nr/Widowspeak) 1986 (CD Presents) 1986

Perhaps the acme of New York no-wave groups, 8 Eyed Spy collected the talents of Lydia Lunch, drummer Jim Sclavunos, ace bassist George Scott, sax and guitar player Pat Irwin and guitarist Michael Paumgarden. Considerably less shrill than other similarly conceived groups, 8 Eyed Spy was nonetheless dominated by Lunch's confrontational vocals and lyrics and Irwin's insistent quasi-jazz sax. On **Live**, it becomes apparent that Lunch's style is mutilated blues (especially on the Beefheart-inspired opener, "Diddy Wah Diddy") and that Sclavunos and Scott's flawless rhythm/bass collaboration is the band's axis. The blend of influences (jazz/blues/rock) creates exciting music that is beyond description.

8 Eyed Spy reproduces much of the material from the cassette and is split into a live side and a studio side. While the former (which includes a hilarious version of "White Rabbit") shows the same gifted chaos apparent on **Live**, the latter proves 8 Eyed Spy capable of considerable restraint and polish.

While the tone of the studio work implies an increasing reliance on jazz, the drumming rivets it to danceable rock. There is the hint of an impending breakthrough in these recordings; unfortunately, the band dissolved in the wake of George Scott's death.

Lydia's **Hysterie** compilation contains an entire side of previously-released 8 Eyed Spy, including live and studio tracks, all from 1980. [sg]

See also *Lydia Lunch, Raybeats.*

801
See *Phil Manzanera.*

EINSTÜRZENDE NEUBAUTEN
Kollaps (Ger. Zick Zack) 1982
Drawings of Patient O.T. (nr/Some Bizzare) 1983 (ZE-PVC) 1985
80–83 Strategies Against Architecture (nr/Mute) 1984 (Homestead) 1986
2 X 4 [tape] (ROIR) 1984
1/2 Mensch (Some Bizzare-Rough Trade) 1985 ●
Fuenf auf der Nach Oben Offenen Richterskla (Some Bizzare-Relativity) 1987 ●

Words such as "noisy," "raw," "primitive" and "radical" have been used to describe many a band, but few have earned these labels more than Berlin conceptual anti-artists Einstürzende Neubauten (Collapsing New Buildings). Their instrumentation includes power tools and large metal objects beaten with hammers, pipes, wrenches and axes. What traditional musical implements they use receive similar treatment; Blixa Bargeld supplies pained vocals and guitar often blurred to the point of white noise. Their live shows are even more daring, and many a club owner has stopped performances and/or barred them from returning after watching a stage practically demolished under Neubauten's creative supervision.

Having built a reputation in the German avant-garde underground, the band released **Kollaps** in 1982, combining guitar and bass drones with a barrage of metallic pounding, both rhythmic and random. Topped off with tortured howls (and titles like "Hear with Pain"), it is one of the most shocking visions ever committed to vinyl. Not recommended for dancing or romantic interludes.

Neubauten soon became the darlings of the UK press. In 1983, they signed to Some Bizzare and released **Drawings of Patient**

O.T. While no more melodic than **Kollaps**, the production is less primeval and the band shows a wider degree of textural variety. At times the sound is rather stripped down, and a few of the cuts are actually songs. (The title track *even has a chord progression!*) Two years later, the record was released in the US, adding four non-LP items on a bonus EP.

Strategies Against Architecture is a compilation of five tracks from **Kollaps**, an early single and some brilliant previously-unreleased works, three of them live. The itemization of instrumentation is amusing, including as it does an air conditioning duct, smashing glass, an amplified spring and a bridge. For more live material, try the cassette-only **2 X 4**, an admirable attempt to capture the mood of Neubauten on stage, recorded throughout Europe between 1980 and 1983. Like **Drawings**, it leaves more space in the sound, which makes the shock effects that much more shocking. "Armenisch Bitter" is, by their standards, a ballad, with plaintive sax warbling along with Bargeld's voice in a quasi-Middle Eastern style.

1/2 Mensch (aka **Halber Mensch** and **Half Man**) is the band's strongest record yet, displaying a wide range of creative compositional technique. Putting some of the junkyard orchestration aside, the title track is a cappella, sounding like some avant-garde opera; "Letztes Biest (am Himmel)" uses quiet bass harmonics as its only pitched instrument. Add such things as grand piano, inside-out dance beats and Neubauten's characteristic thunder, and **Halber Mensch** is truly remarkable.

The lads temporarily broke up in 1986, then reformed to record **Fuenf auf der Nach Oben Offenen Richterskala (Five on the Open-Ended Richter Scale)**, the most low-key LP they've ever done. Vocals, often almost at a whisper, are frequently predominant. A whole plethora of instruments (or whatever) are plunked, strummed and smashed way down in the mix, almost as though Neubaten was trying not to wake up the old lady next door. Quite a contrast to much of their previous work: **Fuenf**'s quiet intensity leaves one waiting for a noisy counterpoint which never comes. [dgs]
See also *Nick Cave.*

ELECTRIC CHAIRS

See *Wayne County and the Electric Chairs.*

ELECTRIC GUITARS
Electric Guitars EP (nr/Stiff) 1982

Yes, this septet of girls and boys from Bristol have all the chic moves: bi-sex vocals, fashionably funky beat, arty/clever lyrics and they even use electric guitars! (In between lots of percussion and some synth.) "Beat Me Hollow," or is it "Beat Me, I'm Hollow"? [jg]

DANNY ELFMAN
See *Oingo Boingo.*

ELVIS BROTHERS
Movin' Up (Portrait) 1983
Adventure Time (Portrait) 1985

This trio from Champaign, Illinois has roots in many local bands of that area (some credible, others cringeable); together, they play a marvelous (and deceptively simple) concoction of slicked-up rockabilly, stripped-down Cheap Trick-tinged melodic rock'n' roll and pristine pure pop that boasts superbly articulated energy, occasionally goofy lyrics and enough hooks to catch a school of minnows. **Movin' Up** traverses a panoply of mildly bent styles, from mock-Stray Cats ("Fire in the City") to Dave Edmunds-ish rock'n'roll ("Hey Tina") to Anglo-pop ("Hidden in a Heartbeat") to countryfied rock ("Santa Fe") and much more. Sure they futz around a lot (especially onstage), but their silliness never interferes with the serious task—playing catchy pop with maximum gusto. It may not mean a lot, but the album is truly mega-fun.

Adrian Belew produced **Adventure Time**, but didn't do too much damage to the E-Bros.' essentially lighthearted spirit. There are a couple of socially responsible messages about gun control and insanity in the modern world but, by and large, the Elvises go about their business with typical happy-go-lucky aplomb. From the high-powered rock of "Burnin' Desire" and "Somebody Call the Police" to the beauty of "Crosswinds" and "Akiko Shinoda," they effortlessly toss off tune after tune of infectious should-be-hits. [iar]

EMBARRASSMENT
The Embarrassment EP (Cynykyl) 1981
Death Travels West (Fresh Sounds) 1983
Retrospective [tape] (Fresh Sounds) 1984

The Embarrassment LP (Time to Develop)
1987

Before they broke up in 1983, these four guys from Wichita, Kansas could rock furiously, with less brittle/more melodious guitar than the Scottish nouveau pop bands (like Orange Juice and Josef K) to whom they were occasionally compared. While John Nichols' vocals weren't incredible (Bill Goffrier's guitar work nearly was), the Embarrassment did convey a promising array of nuances, from wistfulness to sarcasm, and an inquisitive, adventurous way with arrangements. The lyrics vary in quality, but "Don't Choose the Wrong Song" and "Elizabeth Montgomery's Face" show budding verbal pithiness and "Wellsville" a laconic melodic strength. Best of all, most of the eponymous debut EP's five songs grow on you with each listen.

The ambitious **Death Travels West** is essentially a historical concept album—on several levels—about a voyage. The melodic songs benefit from hot performances; while getting the thematic point requires some effort and attention, the charged, raw-edged pop is immediately likable, showing the Embarrassment's facility for creating memorable tunes.

The **Retrospective** tape is even more impressive, a posthumous collection of otherwise unissued studio recordings from 1979 to 1983, plus a side of live performances (originals and neat covers) from '82/'83. It's a treasure trove that shows the Embos in command of a wide stylistic range—from catchy pop to gutsy punk—and in possession of broad-based songwriting talent. The best of many fine songs is "Woods of Love," a mesmerizing slice of anti-imperialism played with Feeliesque folksy pop-psychedelia, recorded onstage in Lawrence.

One side of **The Embarrassment LP**, an unexpected 1987 arrival, repeats the EP; the remainder, from a 1983 live-in-the-studio session, are previously unreleased recordings, except for the insidious version of "Age of Five" that was included on **Retrospective**. Full-bodied, confident one-take performances of "Woods of Love," "Picture Women" and the pulsing "Rhythm Line" make the Embos' demise soon after this date all the more regrettable. [jg/iar]

EMBRACE

See *Minor Threat*.

EMPIRE

Empire (nr/Dinosaur) 1981

During their tenure in Generation X, guitarist Bob "Derwood" Andrews and drummer Mark Laff regularly suffered charges of being heavy metal musicians in disguise. In the foreground of Empire, they do indeed play with a metallic lack of subtlety, but the results aren't nearly as explosive as you might expect. Attempting their version of pop music, Andrews and Laff slow down the tempo to a pace that renders **Empire** labored and drab. [jy]

See also *Westworld*.

ENGLISH BEAT

See *(English) Beat*.

BRIAN ENO

Here Come the Warm Jets (Island) 1973 (EG) 1982 ●
Taking Tiger Mountain (By Strategy) (Island) 1974 (EG) 1982 ●
Another Green World (Island) 1975 (EG) 1982 ●
Discreet Music (Antilles) 1975 (EG) 1982 (EG) 1982 ●
Before and After Science (Island) 1978 (EG) 1982 ●
Music for Films (Antilles) 1978 (EG) 1982 ●
Music for Airports (Ambient) 1979 (EG) 1982 ●
On Land (EG) 1982 ●
Music for Films Volume 2 (EG) 1983
Working Backwards 1983–1973 (EG) 1984
Thursday Afternoon [CD] (EG) 1985
More Blank Than Frank (EG) 1986 ●

KEVIN AYERS/JOHN CALE/ENO/NICO

June 1, 1974 (Island) 1974

ENO WITH MOEBIUS AND ROEDELIUS

After the Heat (Ger. Sky) 1979

JON HASSELL/BRIAN ENO

Fourth World Vol. 1: Possible Musics (EG) 1980

HAROLD BUDD/BRIAN ENO

The Plateaux of Mirror (EG) 1980 ●
The Pearl (EG) 1984 ●

CLUSTER & BRIAN ENO

Cluster and Eno (Ger. Sky) 1978
Old Land (Relativity) 1985 ●

188

BRIAN ENO WITH DANIEL LANOIS & ROGER ENO

Apollo Atmospheres & Soundtracks (EG) 1983 ●

ROGER ENO & BRIAN ENO

Voices (EG) 1985

From his original role as electronics dabbler and art-rocker with the fledgling Roxy Music in the early 1970s, Brian Eno has become the epitome of the independent artist—articulate, intelligent, serious and intent on following his own impulses. He has progressed from a tight, wry pop music into more difficult forms, incorporating aspects of many different disciplines. As well as a solo artist, Eno has collaborated with many people; he became a major force in the emerging music of the '80s as producer of such adventurers as Ultravox, Talking Heads, New York no-wave bands, Devo, U2 and others.

Here Come the Warm Jets, Eno's first foray as a solo artist, featured sharply crafted, cerebral pop songs that put equal emphasis on quirky music and chatty, surrealistic lyrics—an endearing novelty record that no one else could have made.

Taking Tiger Mountain (By Strategy) saw Eno flirting with Chinese communism and dream psychology as grist for his lyric mill. The tone of the music is darker overall than on the first album; though Eno was already beginning to show a mistrust of pop forms, the songs here are filled with humor and joy and his continuing taste for experimentation.

By **Another Green World**, Eno was enhancing his work with crystal-clear production. Much of the album features beautiful, fragile instrumentals, leaving the manic rock tone of the first two albums behind. Electronics play a greater role, and Eno all but abandons standard pop forms for a less-formulaic sound that presages his future ambient work. Highly recommended.

Discreet Music (as well as his two collaborations with Robert Fripp) was first devised while Eno was recovering from an auto accident, and it marks his experimental break from pop forms, using classical structures as the basis for tape loops and manipulations. The result is striking and haunting, filled with beauty and apprehension, paralleling the minimalist music being made by Steve Reich and Philip Glass. Recommended.

Before and After Science was the apex of Eno's pop work, a collection of ten lyrical songs that ranged from bouncy, eccentric pop ("King's Lead Hat") to wistfully pastoral songs ("Spider and I," "Through Hollow Lands") that smack of vast distances. The pivotal work of Eno's career, it sees him spanning whole musical worlds, but from this point on, his involvement with pop music was relegated to production work.

Music for Films introduced Eno's subsequent focus, and consists of fragments done over the years as possible soundtracks for imaginary movies. (Eno's work has since appeared on several actual soundtracks.) Totally instrumental, the album features a return, with greater sophistication, to the work of **Discreet Music**—a conscious attempt to imply subtle moods and settings through electronically manipulated sound.

Ambient music, which goes directly against Western tradition by not demanding explicit attention from the listener, was introduced on **Music for Airports**, a stark but hypnotic collection of sounds especially composed for airport sound systems to inure passengers to flying and death. Whether successful (or even ever used) in that setting or not, the album's spare and delicate sounds open up the meditative possibilities of music.

Through numerous collaborations (with 801, Ayers/Cale/Nico, Bowie, Cluster, Jon Hassell, Talking Heads, etc.) Eno has dabbled in and influenced various strains of popular music, from fusion rock to electro-pop. **The Plateaux of Mirror**, with Harold Budd, found Eno expanding his ambient work to multi-dimensional proportions, while **My Life in the Bush of Ghosts**, with David Byrne, allowed him to indulge his fascination with African and other Third World rhythms, with the latter made more intriguing through the mixture of these rhythms and found speech and music tapes. **Possible Musics** is an exploration of different areas of ethno-musicology with experimental Canadian trumpeter Jon Hassell. Eno also continues to work occasionally with one of his earliest collaborators, Cluster. **Old Land** (another German Sky release, this one licensed for America) surprisingly has some vocals on it.

By **On Land**, Eno had polished his ambient music into a dense, evocative representation of terra incognita. Though sometimes obscure and always devoid of lyrics, the work shows Eno at his most expressive, with sound paintings that exist somewhere between ancient mantra and avant-garde. Highly recommended.

Invited to do the music for a film about the Apollo space missions, Eno used all of his inspiration about the grandeur and mystery of man's walking on the moon to create **Apollo Atmospheres & Soundtracks**, recorded in conjunction with his brother Roger and longtime collaborator, Daniel Lanois (also known for his solo production work with Martha and the Muffins and others). Avoiding any sensationalistic (or even typical space/rocketry) sounds, it's another hauntingly poetic collection of ambient pieces, written and played variously by all three musicians.

Working Backwards 1983–1973 is the ultimate Eno collection—an 11-disc boxed set containing all of his solo albums through **Music for Films Volume II**, plus an otherwise unavailable album of **Rarities**, featuring such items as "Seven Deadly Finns" and "The Lion Sleeps Tonight." Issued to coincide with the publication of the *More Dark Than Shark* book, the one-LP **More Blank Than Frank** is a more modest and idiosyncratic compilation—ten of the artist's own faves from his first four solo records (excluding **Discreet Music**) with careful annotation. (The cassette adds two tracks.)

Eno's most recent new—and, as has long been customary, entirely instrumental—material is contained on **Thursday Afternoon**, a 61-minute piece (logically enough issued only on CD) created to accompany a VHS cassette of "video paintings" by Christine Alicino. The soothing spaciousness of the soundtrack ambience belies its compositional sophistication, as explained in the liner notes.

Discographical footnote: these albums have been reissued, unchanged, numerous times due to label rearrangements in both England and America. [sg/iar]

See also *David Bowie, David Byrne, Fripp & Eno, Phil Manzanera, Talking Heads.*

EPIDEMICS
Shankar/Caroline (ECM) 1986

Indian violinst Shankar—star of Echo and the Bunnymen's "The Cutter" and notable records by Peter Gabriel, Talking Heads, etc.—takes a break from sessions and jazz to try his hand at leading a crypto-rock group on this exciting, offbeat experiment. The Epidemics' record tends to drone, but in a pleasant, Monsoonish sort of way, with bouncy synthesized percussion driving Shankar's weedy vocals and unique violin sound, which

neatly contrast Percy Jones' agile bass work. The songs are simple and their construction familiar, but artificial-sounding production and uncommon arrangements park the album well outside the pop mainstream.
[iar]

EQUATORS
Hot (Stiff America) 1981

The Equators' well-integrated (no pun intended) hybrid of ska, reggae and rock (check the rhythm section), produced by then-Rumour member Bob Andrews, is musically if not lyrically similar to much of the output of the 2-Tone bands from the same era. This all-black quintet leaves out the heavy messages and aims for the feet, making **Hot** refreshingly unpretentious—danceable as well as listenable. [ds]

ERASURE
Wonderland. (Mute-Sire) 1986 ●
The Circus (Mute-Sire) 1987 ●
The Two Ring Circus (Mute-Sire) 1987 ●
The Innocents (Mute-Sire-Reprise) 1988 ●

Vince Clarke's post-Yazoo band is a duo with Andy Bell, a melodramatically tremulous singer who bears a creepy vocal resemblance to Alison Moyet. Clarke's backing tracks on **Wonderland.** likewise sound like Yazoo songs (bizarre, considering that Bell co-wrote most of them), which is a mixed sin. On one hand, it's disconcerting; on the other, Yazoo was a fine band, and Clarke's more than welcome to keep up the good work, regardless of who with. The best tracks ("Heavenly Action" and "Oh l'Amour") are instantly memorable pop confections. (The CD adds two tracks.)

Erasure's second album was released twice: the original one-disc **The Circus** and, later, a double 12-inch set of remixes and re-recordings. (The latter version's CD has seven extra tracks.) Although the basic LP's material is mostly cut from the same synth-dance mold as the first record, the arrangements here are richer, more intricate and inventive. Unfortunately, Bell's flat delivery of the pessimistic and strife-ridden-romance lyrics makes them unaffecting and whiny; he even delivers the plainly lascivious "Sexuality" and "Sometimes" with a sickening lack of enthusiasm. This is the sort of misery that deserves to be left alone.

The Two Ring Circus—an abridged set of

songs with a revamped running order and a side of orchestral versions—is a significantly better record. Elongated remixes open up the instrumentation and downplay the vocals; gimcracks and mute breaks increase both listenability and dancefloor utility. The powerful "Hideaway," a sweepingly melodic number about a young person coming out of the closet, gets the most-improved award. Three songs (one recalled from Erasure's first LP) that eschew synthesizers for strings, pianos, horns and tympani not only indicate healthy stylistic catholicism, they coax Bell into far more emotive performances.

Stephen Hague produced **The Innocents**, an OMD-like collection of textured dance-pop. Well-fashioned melodies and clever arrangements render the nebulous romantic lyrics superfluous; the less attention you give Erasure the better they sound.   [iar]

ERIC B. & RAKIM
Paid in Full (4th & Broadway) 1987
Follow the Leader (Uni) 1988

Queens homeslice Eric B. (Barrier) is the dj and Long Islander Rakim (William Griffin) is the rapper; as the latter sings in "I Ain't No Joke," "I hold the microphone like a grudge/Eric B. hold the record so the needle don't budge." Beginning with a brilliant summer 1986 single—"Eric B. Is President"—on an obscure Harlem label, Eric B. and Rakim proved themselves if not the hardest, certainly the most technically intricate—both musically and lyrically—rap duo around. Their follow-up single, "Paid in Full," inspired more than 30 (!) different mixes; the standout was British duo Coldcut's "Seven Minutes of Madness" remix, which introduced Yemenite singer Ofra Haza to the international pop audience through the miracle of sampling. (Eric B. and Rakim themselves pioneered the musical appropriation of James Brown in their mixes, initiating an almost obligatory hip-hop homage to the Godfather of Soul.)

Paid in Full is a spectacular debut LP that includes new mixes of "Eric B. Is President" and its flipside, "My Melody." Rakim's lyrics focus on the duo's prodigious talents and celebrate the joy of money, with the accumulation of wealth's material accoutrements seemingly serving as an artistic end in itself. But with fabulous beats like Rakim's, Christmas carols would sound magnificent.   [rg]

ROKY ERICKSON AND THE ALIENS
Roky Erickson and the Aliens (nr/CBS) 1980
The Evil One (415) 1981 (Restless) 1987 ●
I Think of Demons (nr/Edsel) 1987

ROKY ERICKSON
Clear Night for Love EP (Fr. New Rose) 1985
   (nr/Fundamental Music) 1988
Don't Slander Me (Pink Dust) 1986 ●
Gremlins Have Pictures (Pink Dust) 1986
The Holiday Inn Tapes (Fr. Fan Club) 1987
Openers (nr/Five Hours Back) 1988

ROKY ERICKSON AND THE EXPLOSIVES
Casting the Runes (nr/Five Hours Back) 1987

Roky Erickson established his reputation as a raving looney two decades ago as lead singer of Texas' infamous psychedelic 13th Floor Elevators. On his 1980 UK LP, he plays that role to the hilt, singing such offbeat gems as "I Walked with a Zombie" and "Creature with the Atom Brain" in a tremulous voice that insists he's telling the truth—or at least believes he is. Former Creedence Clearwater bassist Stu Cook turned in an excellent production job, bringing the hard electric guitars into a sharp focus that underscores Roky's excitable state. Erickson and band seem less unstable than the drug-crazed Elevators (best remembered for "You're Gonna Miss Me"), but just barely.

Ditto for **The Evil One**, which takes five tracks from the UK release (overlooking the awesome "Two-Headed Dog") and adds five more, including the ghastly "Bloody Hammer." Which LP is better? They're both wonderfully ominous and frightening—splatter-film soundtracks done with real rock'n'roll conviction.

The five songs on **Clear Night**, recorded in Texas with a rudimentary quartet, begin on a note of relative restraint. "You Don't Love Me Yet" is acoustic folk; the title track recalls Creedence's rag-tag balladry. Side Two is a bit wilder, culminating in "Don't Slander Me," an angrily defensive accusatory diatribe. (It does, however, contain "Starry Eyes," which can only be described as Roky's Buddy Holly tribute.)

Erickson re-recorded (maybe not, in one instance) three songs from **Clear Night** for his subsequent full-length LP, cut with a five-man band that includes ex-Jefferson Airplane/Hot Tuna bassist Jack Casady *and* an electric autoharp player. Even without intentionally grisly put-ons, **Don't Slander Me** is typically gripping, although the inclusion of two Holly-inspired poptunes makes for a bizarre contrast to "Burn the Flames," a tune originally done for the *Return of the Living Dead* soundtrack.

Jeez, the way Erickson records have been proliferating lately, you'd think the guy was a platinum-seller or something. Anyway, **Gremlins Have Pictures** is an interesting if erratic hodgepodge of tracks ranging from 1975 to 1982, solo and with three different groups (the Explosives, the Aliens and Blieb Alien). Some thrilling, some shoddy, all loony. **The Holiday Inn Tapes** is simply an atrocity, one guy on an acoustic guitar fooling around aimlessly in '86, coming off pathetic. Even hardcore fans shouldn't bother.

Casting the Runes, however, mates Roky's twisted worldview with a hard, crunching band. Recorded on various Texas stages circa '79, it unleashes menacing renditions of such grisly Erickson classics as "Don't Shake Me Lucifer" and "Bloody Hammer," plus a weird version of the oldie "I Love How You Love Me." Highly recommended, especially to fans of **The Evil One**.   [jy/iar]

ERNEST ANYWAY AND THE MIGHTY SQUIRRELS
See *Young Fresh Fellows.*

ESG
ESG EP (99) 1981
ESG Says Dance to the Beat of Moody EP (99) 1982
Come Away with ESG (99) 1983

Who would have imagined that four sisters and a pal from the South Bronx would emerge as one of the most dynamic bands that New York could offer at the top of the '80s? (Or that they would pop up again in 1987 and start making new records?) Mixing a solid combination of dub, chant and beat, ESG—simply drums, bass and vocals—virtually stole the cosmic show with their first release, a six-song EP with a live side and a phenomenal studio side recorded under the hand of British producer Martin Hannett.

Their second EP, produced by 99 Records head Ed Bahlman, is not quite as crisp as the debut, but no less enjoyable, a brilliant synthesis of rhythm and restraint. To say the following album stayed in a similar vein and improved little over live shows of the same material would be to damn a fine record with faint praise. ESG offers bouncy funk instead of funk pretensions and elegant simplicity in place of mere primitivism.   [jw/mf]

ESSENTIAL LOGIC
Essential Logic EP (nr/Virgin) 1979
Beat Rhythm News (nr/Rough Trade) 1979

LORA LOGIC
Pedigree Charm (nr/Rough Trade) 1982

Essential Logic quickly outlived its usefulness as a vehicle for Lora Logic, once a member of X-Ray Spex, and a most distinctive talent. The original lineup—featured on the band's self-titled debut EP—includes two guitars, two saxes (including Logic herself) and a clunky rhythm section; a loose but comfortable ensemble. Logic's songwriting had yet to bloom, though her vocal style was already developing.

She was still loopy but lovable on **Beat Rhythm News**, but her singing had become highly stylized with a distinct edge. A tighter rhythm guitarist replaced the uninspired duo of the EP, and Essential Logic soared. The music's vivacity is occasionally undercut by tinny production and a tendency to ramble, and Lora's growth as a writer and performer warranted more versatile backing. The next Logical step: a solo career.

Logic continued to evolve on her first solo outing. Her voice—much better produced—had a slightly softer, jazzy inflection, and her eclectic writing assumed a poppy sheen. Even hitherto impenetrable lyrics revealed a translucent clarity in spots. Businesslike dance rhythms and fewer straying sax excursions took additional steps toward accessibility. **Pedigree Charm** is a delight.

Abandoning rock'n'roll, Logic—along with former bandmate Poly Styrene—wound up becoming a Hare Krishna devotee and playing in a (religious) cult band.   [mf]

EURYTHMICS
In the Garden (nr/RCA) 1981 ●
Sweet Dreams (Are Made of This) (RCA) 1983 ●
Touch (RCA) 1983 ●
Touch Dance (RCA) 1984 ●
1984 (For the Love of Big Brother) (RCA) 1984 ●
Be Yourself Tonight (RCA) 1985 ●
Revenge (RCA) 1986 ●
Savage (RCA) 1987 ●

Fresh from the unlamented ruins of the Tourists, Annie Lennox and Dave Stewart formed Eurythmics, at first to pursue their love affair with Germanic experimental/electronic music and attempt a translation of it into a peculiarly British form. Their first album (as yet unreleased in the US) features a wide variety of musicians—Blondie drummer Clem Burke, Can's Holger Czukay and Jaki Liebezeit, composer Karlheinz Stockhausen's son Marcus—and is filled with lyrical love songs and gently strident social anthems ("Your Time Will Come," "All the Young People of Today"). Empowering it all are Lennox's captivating, flexible but strong vocals and a commitment and humor that turn potentially pretentious material into unaffected, poetic work.

From such humble, non-mainstream beginnings was a new chart-topping, trend-setting group created. **Sweet Dreams (Are Made of This)**—thanks mostly to the horrible, monotonic dirge-song of the same name—took off, and lofted the pair into world prominence, a success they maintained on **Touch** by proving themselves capable of enormous stylistic and instrumental variety, as well as exceptional songwriting. From lovely ("Here Comes the Rain Again") to jaunty ("Right by Your Side") to dramatic ("Who's That Girl?") and driving ("The First Cut"), **Touch** is an excellent record filled with invention and chicly styled nouveau pop. To take advantage of sudden global stardom, an album of remixes (four songs with vocals, three of them also presented as instrumentals) by Jellybean Benitez and Francois Kevorkian was issued as **Touch Dance**.

The **1984** album—as the result of a contretemps with the film's director, not exactly the soundtrack but "music derived from Eurythmics' original score"—finds the pair moving further into rhythmic experimentation, as on the crazed cut-up stylings of "Sexcrime" and "Doubleplusgood." A strange but affecting record, although clearly not one intended to be taken as a normal chapter in the group's development.

The hard-edged, relatively low-tech **Be Yourself Tonight** marks a real change in the duo's thinking. Exciting, catchy soul-rock ("Would I Lie to You?"), insipid, aggravating soul-rock ("I Love You Like a Ball and Chain"), two swell duets ("Adrian," with Elvis Costello; "Sisters Are Doin' It for Themselves," with Aretha Franklin), plus five more tracks all have an underlying stylistic consistency. That's a new twist for Eurythmics, but one they seem capable of handling. Retooling into an '80s Motown factory might seem a little selfconscious, but they carry it off with aplomb and even a bit of heart.

Taking an unexpected but worthwhile hell-hath-no-fury detour, the breakup of Lennox's marriage yielded the vituperative lyrics of the blunt and aptly-titled **Revenge**. "To run away from you/was all that I could do," from "Thorn in My Side," is only the tip of the impassioned album's iceberg; other songs ("A Little of You," "The Last Time," "Missionary Man") turn a scornful postmortem into deeply felt cries that reverberate in Lennox's remarkable vocal cords. There are draggy spots that overdo the musical sentiment but, by and large, one of the pair's best records.

No such luck on the following year's **Savage**, a shoddy mess of scant merit. Where **Revenge** made fine use of a small, crack collection of studio hands to flesh out the material in a variety of luxurious idioms, **Savage** relies on a bed of chilly soundalike computer programs and absurdly multi-tracked vocal gimmicks. (Discounting Stewart's guitar work and the all-acoustic "I Need You," only "Wide Eyed Girl" sounds as if human beings played on it. Both add crowd noises, perhaps to underscore the point.) The wooden material has static rhythms, a shortage of melodies and entirely too few hooks; the mostly miserable lyrics suggest continental sophistication and thoughtful emotional reflection but fizzle in a hurried blur of triviality, obscurity and seeming creative apathy.

[sg/iar]

See also *Robert Görl, Ramones, Feargal Sharkey.*

EVERYTHING BUT THE GIRL

Eden (nr/Blanco y Negro) 1984
Everything but the Girl (Blanco y Negro-Sire) 1984
Love Not Money (Blanco y Negro-Sire) 1985
Baby, the Stars Shine Bright (Blanco y Negro-Sire) 1986 ●
Idlewild (Blanco y Negro-Sire) 1988 ●

TRACEY THORN

A Distant Shore (nr/Cherry Red) 1982 + 1985 ●

BEN WATT

North Marine Drive (nr/Cherry Red) 1983 ●

Ben Watt (guitar/keyboards/vocals/songs) and Tracey Thorn (vocals/guitar/songs) have been (individually) and presently are (collectively as Everything but the Girl)—prominent innovators in England's back-to-jazz pop movement. The popularity of artists like Sade and Swing Out Sister is due in large part to the pair's counter-current efforts, helping to lay the critical groundwork for acceptance of this lovely but thoroughly un-rock style.

While also a member of an all-female trio, the Marine Girls, Thorn cut **A Distant Shore**, a brief album of nostalgic singer/songwriter modernism with little more than an acoustic guitar for accompaniment. Her somewhat monotonous delivery hampers the effort, but including the Velvet Underground's utterly appropriate "Femme Fatale" helps considerably.

Watt had recorded on his own as well as in conjunction with Robert Wyatt; **North Marine Drive** is alluring and airy—light, melodic songs given syncopated, quasi-Latin rhythms, played simply and sung sweetly and beguilingly. (The CD appends **Summer into Winter**, a collaboration with Wyatt.)

Everything but the Girl's debut album, **Eden** (released later the same year in the US as **Everything but the Girl**), is a charming, fragile record delicately filled with winsome songs that drift in and out of neo-jazz-pop stylings but are never less than appealing and attractive. Showing enormous growth as a vocalist, Thorn makes the songs memorable even when the music is too low-key to stand out on its own. With harmonies that recall such wonders of the '60s as the Association, superbly understated pop creations prove Everything but the Girl to be an exceptional, unconventional band.

Love Not Money carries the pair away from jazz and into a pure pop approach that is far more accessible and immediately appealing. The album leads off with the utterly alluring "When All's Well" and continues with further literate considerations of growing up and getting along, including "Ugly Little Dreams," which is dedicated to doomed actress Frances Farmer. The US edition adds "Heaven Help Me" and a version of Chrissie Hynde's "Kid."

The cover of **Baby, the Stars Shine Bright** notes that it was "arranged for orchestra by Ben Watt." Indeed, other than his guitar playing, a prominent rhythm section and a pianist/organist, the musical backing consists of strings, horns and a choir. Fortunately, Thorn's rich voice and the pair's soaringly melodic songs carry it off without losing momentum. The music is neither sappy nor dull; the orchestra's role is supportive without shirking center stage. Like classic Dionne Warwick sides, rock'n'roll's energy and excitement is channeled into subtle sophistication that brings the music to life in vivid colors. Pointedly topical lyrics on "Sugar Finney" (for Marilyn Monroe) and "Little Hitler" don't undercut the songs' delicate beauty; other standouts are "Don't Leave Me Behind," "Fighting Talk" and "Cross My Heart."

Taking a turn toward self-contained simplicity, Watt and Thorn recorded the plain and folky **Idlewild** with only a small set of sidemen adding keyboards, bass and horns. (Oddly, there's no percussion credit of any sort; Watt breaks tradition by sharing in the lead vocals.) Thorn's lyrics have never been this introspective or revealing; the plainly articulated longings and autobiographical expositions resonate through "Oxford Street," "Blue Moon Rose," "Apron Strings" and "Shadow on a Harvest Moon" like a rainy day. With understated, superficially mild-on-arrival music, this is an achingly sad record, filled with quiet grief and deep disappointments.   [iar]

See also *Grab Grab the Haddock.*

EXPLOITED

Punks Not Dead (nr/Exploited-Secret) 1981
On Stage (nr/Exploited) 1981
Troops of Tomorrow (nr/Secret) 1982
Let's Start a War . . . Said Maggie One Day (Combat) 1983 ●
Horror Epics (Combat) 1985 ●
Live at the White House (Combat Core) 1985
Totally Exploited (nr/Blashadabee-Dojo) 1986 ●
Jesus Is Dead EP (Combat Core) 1986
Death Before Dishonour (Rough Justice-Combat) 1987 ●

Led by outspoken spike-haired shouter Wattie Buchan, Edinburgh's Exploited are one of the United Kingdom's most successful and enduring political thrash bands. Musically harsher, darker and cruder than their '77 forefathers, these gruff yobbos vent unrestrained and bottomless anger against their enemies—the army, warmongers, Margaret Thatcher (pictured on one album cover, cited in the title of another and the subject of assorted songs) and other symbols of government authority. As mainstream-uncommercial as the Exploited are, a huge hardcore audience—in the UK and increasingly in the US—have made Wattie and an ever-shifting set of accomplices respected genre stars.

Although hampered by muffled sound, **Punks Not Dead** is full of angry, gritty anthems of pain and frustration, including "I Believe in Anarchy," "Blown to Bits" and "Royalty." **On Stage** repeats much of the same material but is strictly for fans, as the bootleg-level sound quality is further diminished by the clear-vinyl pressing.

Troops of Tomorrow has a crisp, clean guitar sound, and the lyrics are a bit easier to understand, but the improved production doesn't mean the Exploited has gotten slick—the rough and tumble assault is still wild-eyed and unstoppable. The title song was written by the Vibrators; "Sid Vicious Was Innocent" is one of the record's more interesting arguments.

An entirely new lineup—Karl, Wully and Billy—joins Wattie for **Let's Start a War**. The production backslides into the murk a bit, but the band's fervor is undiminished and Wattie's singing is, if such a thing is possible, rawer and less melodic. A variety of tempos offers hope for a brighter future, but there's really nothing new going on here.

The Dracula cover and title of **Horror Epics** suggests a flirtation with the Damned's old turf, but the title track veers more towards Black Sabbath, with the rhythm guitars displaced by Willie's thundering drum attack and moaning lead guitar figures; echo on Wattie's vocals furthers the comparison to mid-'70s metal. Several other songs are variants on that style; the whole outing benefits from Wattie's growing production prowess. The lengthy numbers are standard Exploited issue, but a tiny hint of experimentalism is creeping into the stylistic complacency. The best tune—and certainly one of the band's catchiest ever—is "Maggie," which repeatedly calls the Prime Minister a bad name.

Live at the White House was recorded in Washington, DC in April 1985 and features a selection of the Exploited's most popular tunes. After a compilation LP came a 12-inch, **Jesus Is Dead**. Handling the production solo, Wattie captures another new lineup with clarity and venom. (Willie's drumming is again a highlight; Nig's spectacular guitar playing is a welcome addition.) For the first time, the Exploited's instruments are clearly articulated and separated in the mix; what a difference real dynamics and what sound like well-rehearsed arrangements make. A solid, fiery punk record with powerful lyrics about a drug bust, televangelism and "Politicians."

Willie and Nig also dominate the fuzzier sound on **Death Before Dishonour**, in which a slashing metal edge shows the Exploited waffling between forms. Although the music is essentially indistinguishable from any in the band's past, little bits of unexpected business (a fake Reagan speech on "Power Struggle," a brief drum solo and offstage insult on "Police Informer," the female chorus on "Sexual Favours") break up the monotony from time to time. [cpl/iar]

EXPLORERS
The Explorers (nr/Virgin) 1985

On their own, post-Roxy Musicians Phil Manzanera and Andy Mackay—joined by singer James Wraith and a collection of familiar session cohorts—make polite, sophisticated pop music with no edge. Superficially not too different from the music Roxy was making towards the end, the LP is pretty undistinguished, lacking memorable songs and Ferry's unique touch. (Wraith's obvious attempt at imitation on "Venus De Milo" is in questionable taste.) Not bad, just not what you'd hope for from people this talented. [iar]

EXPOSURE
Wild! (nr/Statik) 1984

Heavy, tightly-packed modern rock from an interracial English quintet who resemble a high-density version of U2. Differently put, if the Animals had changed with the times, they might sound like this: passionate, gruff vocals (with leavening harmonies); muscular rhythms with lots of power; multi-layered, danceable guitar-based music and nebulous positive protest lyrics about the state of the world. **Wild!** is an invigorating record—urgent and exciting—that, excepting a few romantic ballads, never lets up the pressure. If you're not out of breath after two sides, you'd better get a checkup. [iar]

EXPRESSION
The Expression (Oz-A&M) 1984

This Australian synth'n'guitar quintet is an MTV-generation hybrid that bears a pass-

195

ing resemblance to several bands—Men Without Hats, Talk Talk, Psychedelic Furs (largely because of vocal stylings). The lyrics are clumsy and in spots pretentious, but the music has a variety of modes (maybe too many) and is well-played. Nothing worth recommending, but nothing horrible either. [iar]

EXPRESSOS

Promises and Ties . . . (nr/WEA) 1981

Proving that Los Angeles isn't the only town that grows '60s-styled female pop singers these days, England's Expressos offer a dozen sparkling tunes full of ringing guitars and heartfelt crooning in a nearly forgotten mold. (Nancy Sinatra and Stone Poneys-era Linda Ronstadt provide reasonable comparisons.) The Expressos—one woman and three men—have the advantage of great songwriting ability and make each wonderful track count. [iar]

EXTRABALLE

Extraballe EP (Fr. Carrere) 1979
Sales Romances (Fr. CBS) 1980
Extraballe (Fr. CBS) 1981

On their self-titled EP, Extraballe—whose drummer at the time was Michel Peyronel, brother of Heavy Metal Kids/UFO keyboardist Danny—offered high-speed refried punk-a-boogie with hot axework and little else. Thereafter, the band became nothing more than a name owned by vocalist John Ickx, who wrote the songs. Just about on key, Ickx's French speak-singing covers most typical punk subjects (sex, violence, power, movies) plus a couple of less-likely topics for a young Frenchman. There's potent high-energy accompaniment with lots of organ and guitar vying for domination of the serviceable tunes. (The temporary band for **Sales Romances** included one-time Be-Bop Deluxe *batteur* Simon Fox; Blockhead Davey Payne blew some sax.) Ickx formed a different band for the **Extraballe** album; pity he couldn't update the sound more. [jg]

EYELESS IN GAZA

Photographs as Memories (nr/Cherry Red) 1981
Caught in Flux (nr/Cherry Red) 1981
Pale Hands I Loved So Well (Nor. Uniton) 1982
Drumming the Beating Heart (nr/Cherry Red) 1982
Rust Red September (nr/Cherry Red) 1983
Back from the Rains (nr/Cherry Red) 1986
Kodak Ghosts Run Amok (nr/Cherry Red) 1987

MARTYN BATES

Letters Written (nr/Cherry Red) 1982

Named for Aldous Huxley's ode to pacifist integrity, Eyeless in Gaza consists of Martyn Bates and Peter Becker, both credited with voice and instrumentation on the first album, a better-than-decent stab at hook-filled spareness. The tasteful music is marred only occasionally by overly anguished vocals. **Caught in Flux** has a more delicate flavor at first, then rapidly devolves into humpbacked squalor. This one-and-a-half-disc (LP/EP) set shows a hint of progress, with the vocals held in tighter rein. Caught in flux, indeed.

Pale Hands, released only in Norway, is fairly dissolute—a meandering, largely improvisational attempt to make music out of aimless doodles. **Drumming the Beating Heart** (also included in its entirety on the cassette of **Back from the Rains**) has the duo streamlining their sound to good effect, relying on church organ leads and spontaneous rhythm approaches. If the vocals could be relieved of their melodrama, these boys might have something here.

Back from the Rains has charming, Aztec Camera-like beat-pop sound; Bates' vocals aren't quite up to it, but the duo (aided by a drummer and a female backing singer) shows a real facility for shimmering studio arrangements. Just shy of being commercial, this is nonetheless a delight.

Kodak Ghosts Run Amok, a 1980–86 career-spanning singles (and more) compilation, chronicles Eyeless in Gaza's development from idiosyncratic home-brew experimentation through ragged melodicism to full-blown pop. This is really for fans; newcomers are instead recommended to the later, easier-to-like albums. (The double-play cassette appends **Caught in Flux**.) [jw/iar]

F F F F F F F F F

FACE TO FACE

Face to Face (Epic) 1984
Confrontation (Epic) 1985
One Big Day (Mercury) 1988 ●

Depending on where you put your needle down on their first record, this Boston quintet is either a fascinating blend of hip-hop and rock'n'roll or a noxious pre-fab MTV creation. Four producers—including Arthur Baker and Jimmy Iovine—worked on the album, yielding both the annoying hit single "10-9-8" and a gripping piece of political consciousness, "Under the Gun," on which Baker (who produced both tracks) drum-programs and scratch-mixes the band into a new realm that is both exciting and original. (A subsequent 12-inch further elaborates on "Under the Gun"—15 minutes' worth—with two remixes.)

Confrontation was mostly co-produced by Baker and Ed Stasium. Except for the increasing number of ballads, the band rocks enthusiastically, leaning into the rhythmic material. Singer Laurie Sargent remains a strong presence, but the routine presentation and sound make this **Confrontation** too radio-ready to really matter.

Anton Fier produced the band's third album, **One Big Day**.   [iar]

FAD GADGET

Fireside Favourites (nr/Mute) 1980
Incontinent (nr/Mute) 1981
Under the Flag (nr/Mute) 1982
Gag (nr/Mute) 1984

FRANK TOVEY

Snakes & Ladders (Mute-Sire) 1986 ●
The Fad Gadget Singles (Mute-Sire) 1987 ●
Civilian (Restless) 1988 ●

The enigmatic Fad Gadget (Frank Tovey) is a creative and unpredictable writer, singer and performer whose records all differ considerably from each other; he's an acquired taste with little consistency. After an eerie second 45 ("Ricky's Hand," on which Mute head Daniel Miller plays synthesizer and Fad contributes a "Black and Decker V8 double speed electric drill"—hey ma, can I get one of those, please, huh?), his first album sounds awfully like pre-fame Human League. Except for the title track, which bounces along cheerfully, the basic approach is to mix dour vocals, heavy, repetitive bass lines, solid drums and odd noises. Tacky tunes like "Coitus Interruptus" only cheapen the proceedings.

Incontinent, which pursues the grubbier side of Fad Gadgetry, employs more instrumental variety and better production. Forgetting tripe like "Swallow It" and the charming title tune, some of this is interesting enough, but none is really involving; overall, the self-indulgent album rambles incoherently.

Showing a quantum leap in maturity (lyrically and musically), **Under the Flag** joins pristine production quality with a no-nonsense synth drive that could pass for dance music, and shows absorption of a mild soul influence. (Then-labelmate Alison Moyet sings on a few tracks and even adds saxophone to one.) The funky approach gives Fad a direct and accessible sound, but that's not necessarily an accomplishment—it's hard to avoid the feeling that he's slumming in such relatively commercial seas.

By the time of his first American release, Tovey had retired his alter-ego. (A promo sticker on **Snakes & Ladders** lamely inquires, "Did you know that this guy used to be Fad Gadget?") The lively dance-rock—solid beats, strong synth lines, spurious electronic noises and occasional guitar solos and funk

197

bass—alternately suggests recent Wire and Human League, but could hardly be accused of imitating anyone. Tovey's sense of humor makes "Collapsing New People" (lifted from the British-only **Gag**) a satiric treat; "Luxury" and the poetic but dull "Small World" display an unexpectedly serious and mature side.

The Fad Gadget Singles offers 11 peeks at Tovey's past, from his overlong and rudimentary 1979 debut ("Back to Nature" b/w "The Box") and "Ricky's Hand" to 1984's "Collapsing New People." Most of these tracks are available on albums, and none are particularly essential, but new fans may find it an agreeable means to sample and catch up on his import-only releases.

Civilian returns Tovey to an adventurous land wherein percussion and electronic soundmakers triggered by percussion take the lead. Interestingly, the mix doesn't underscore the album's devotion to (non-dance-oriented) rhythm, allowing vocals and the scanty melody instruments a fair chance to compete. Nonetheless, this is a radical record which, if not for Tovey's firm grip on song structure and intelligent lyrics, might have turned into an endurance test. As is, **Civilian** poses its intriguing challenge without discouraging participation.   [iar]

See also *Boyd Rice.*

JAD FAIR
See *Half Japanese.*

MARIANNE FAITHFULL
Broken English (Island) 1979 ●
Dangerous Acquaintances (Island) 1981
A Childs Adventure (Island) 1983
Strange Weather (Island) 1987 ●

MARK ISHAM/MARIANNE FAITHFULL
Trouble in Mind (Island Visual Arts) 1986

Resuming her recording career after a gap of several years, erstwhile '60s pop singer Marianne Faithfull presents a whole new persona on these intensely individual and powerful albums. Armed with a life-roughened voice filled with suffering and rage, and backed by brilliantly original electro-rock, she grapples with mostly political subjects on **Broken English** and even includes a fascinating interpretation of John Lennon's "Working Class Hero." For **Dangerous Acquaintances**, Faithfull takes a more resigned

outlook, and sings of relationships and the passage of time with strength and depth.

Although the music on it is less exemplary, **A Childs Adventure** continues her harrowing voyage. Other than the political commentary of "Ireland," the songs concentrate on personal struggles, with only a glimmer of hope ("Ashes in My Hand") emerging from the otherwise bleak appraisal.

Despite co-billing with composer/horn player Mark Isham, Faithfull merely sings two songs on the **Trouble in Mind** soundtrack album. The cool jazz of the title track for Alan Rudolph's 1986 film offers a foretaste of the direction she took on her next record, **Strange Weather**. Cast as a sophisticated chanteuse (the echoes of Dietrich and Lotte Lenya are duly noted in Terry Southern's liner notes), Faithfull confronts a far-ranging program (blues, swing, folk, Tin Pan Alley) with delicate accompaniment by Lou Reed's sidemen (Fernando Saunders, Robert Quine and J.T. Lewis) as well as Mac Rebbenack, strings and a horn section. An old spiritual ("Sign of Judgment") connects beautifully with Faithfull's emotional conviction; two tunes from the early '30s—"Boulevard of Broken Dreams" and the schmoozy "Penthouse Serenade"—are also rich and wonderful. On the downside, a new version of "As Tears Go By" is mainly academic and her reading of Bob Dylan's "I'll Keep It with Mine" is simply horrible.   [iar]

FAITH GLOBAL
The Same Mistakes (nr/Survival) 1983

Although Faith Global features original Ultravox guitarist Stevie Shears, he shares control with singer/co-writer Jason Guy, a bored-sounding Ferry/Bowie dud. The music hasn't got much character either, relying on Shears' guitar, piano and synthesizer work to color the plodding creations. He shows signs of incipient creativity amidst the tedium (and the faster the tune, the less deadly the effect), but never quite enough to focus the songs or relieve the pervasive monotony.   [iar]

FALCO
Einzelhaft (A&M) 1982
Junge Roemer (A&M) 1984
3 (A&M) 1986 ●
Emotional (Sire) 1986 ●

Falco (Johann Hoelcel) is something of a hero in his native Austria; although he sings (in a random pastiche of accented English and German) like an arch, continental smoothie, his shtick is slick but thematically simpleminded chart fare, fashionably automated (lots of synth, computerized drums with roto-tom and cymbal overdubs) and syncopated. The best parts of **Einzelhaft** (co-produced with his songwriting partner, keyboardist Robert Ponger) are tedious rock; the tracks that have earned him international visibility ("Der Kommissar," a US hit when badly covered in English by After the Fire; "Maschine Brennt") are repulsive pseudo-funk with obnoxiously patronizing attempts at urban Afro-American lingo, accents and music, sung in a constipated gurgle as appealing as hearing someone vomiting in an alley.

On **Junge Roemer**, Ponger's generally lighter touch—leaning towards Philly soul in tone if not content—cuts a lot of the crap to expose a boring collection of tepidly delivered songs that drift dully from the speakers into the ozone without leaving a trace.

Lest anyone be lulled into imagining Falco on his way to Eurovision politesse, his third LP is one of history's most grotesque musical monstrosities. With two new collaborators replacing Ponger, Fal' essays a cultural outreach program with such garishly overproduced, overlong thumpers as "Vienna Calling" (7:40) and "Rock Me Amadeus" (8:20). Each repeats a cloying riff or chorus endlessly while all manner of gimmicky mix tricks (spoken word, scratching, dub echo, sound effects, etc.) attempt to obscure Falco's regurgo blather. Think of an endless loop of Queen's "We Will Rock You" with less melody and you'll get an idea of what a nightmare this is. To cap things off in maximally tasteless fashion, he debases Dylan's "It's All Over Now, Baby Blue" as a sneery lounge singer, complete with spoken asides. What a jerk! (For masochists, **3**—brilliantly mastered, incidentally—runs over 50 minutes.)

Falco seems a bit of a manipulated wimp on **Emotional**, a record to which he contributed some of the lyrics and none of the music. Producers Rob and Ferdi Bolland are in complete control, writing and playing almost everything except guitars and sax. The (mis-)concept album ranges from ABC-like slick soul to psychopathic shrieking; Falco is as awful as ever, babbling the verbose bilingual lyrics with auto-pilot enthusiasm and the assistance of mega-tracked female back-

ing vocals. The wildly bombastic production and pervasive low-brow mentality here cries out for Jim Steinman to produce Falco's next record. [jg/iar]

TAV FALCO'S PANTHER BURNS
See *Panther Burns.*

FALL
Live at the Witch Trials (Step Forward-IRS) 1979
Dragnet (nr/Step Forward) 1979
Live Totale's Turns (It's Now or Never) (nr/Rough Trade) 1980
Grotesque (After the Gramme) (Rough Trade) 1980
Early Years 77–79 (Faulty Products) 1981
Slates EP (Rough Trade) 1981
Live in London, 1980 [tape] (nr/Chaos) 1982
Hex Enduction Hour (nr/Kamera) 1982
Room to Live (nr/Kamera) 1982
A Part of America Therein, 1981 (Cottage) 1982
Perverted by Language (nr/Rough Trade) 1983
Fall in a Hole (NZ Flying Nun) 1983
Wonderful and Frightening World of the Fall (Beggars Banquet-PVC) 1984 ●
Call for Escape Route EP (nr/Beggars Banquet) 1984
Hip Priest and Kamerads (nr/Situation 2) 1985 ●
This Nation's Saving Grace (Beggars Banquet-PVC) 1985
The Fall EP (PVC) 1986
Bend Sinister (nr/Beggars Banquet) 1986 ●
The Domesday Pay-Off Triad—Plus! (Big Time) 1987
The Peel Sessions EP (nr/Strange Fruit) 1987
In Palace of Swords Reversed (Cog Sinister-Rough Trade) 1987 ●
The Frenz Experiment (Big Time) 1988 ●

Since forming in Manchester in 1977, the Fall has been a major cult favorite in numerous corners of the globe, despite few commercial efforts and uncompromising artistic integrity. Their fans are rabid, and their influence on likeminded conceptual noise-makers—in England, the US, Iceland, New Zealand and elsewhere—can't be overstated. Led by acid-tongued poet Mark E. Smith, whose lyrics and vocals provide the Fall's most distinguishing features, the band has created a huge body of unpleasant, challenging, inaccessible anti-rock that occasionally proves to be very moving. From humble experimental beginnings, the Fall have continued to explore and grow stronger over the course of more than ten prolific years, earning a place of real respect in left-wing musical circles. Whether you enjoy the sounds or not, the Fall have made a difference in the sound of modern music, and that counts.

After releasing some singles and contributing two tracks to the watershed Manchester compilation, **Short Circuit/Live at the Electric Circus,** the Fall recorded and mixed their debut LP, **Live at the Witch Trials,** in an economical two-day studio session with producer Bob Sargeant, who did nothing (audible) to soften their dissonant but well-organized rock noise. At once leaning toward punk's directness and charging headlong into poetic pretension, Smith and company (bass, drums, electric piano, guitar) drip sincerity on tracks like "Rebellious Jukebox" and "Crap Rap 2/Like to Blow," occasionally sounding "normal" amidst the tempest. **Dragnet** followed with a rougher-edged sound as well as a new lineup. (The Fall are a biographical nightmare.) The first album to feature Craig Scanlon's trademark scratchy, dissonant guitar (which has played a major role in the band's noise ever since), **Dragnet** is not one of the Fall's best efforts, but contains at least two of their classic numbers, "Spectre vs. Rector" and "A Figure Walks."

By the time of their first live album, **Totale's Turns**—recorded in late '79 and early '80—the Fall had consolidated a more commanding style, although it's no easier on the aurals. Jagged, largely recitative and nearly oblivious to musical convention, Smith's witty repartee carries the show—he sounds a bit like the Stranglers' Hugh Cornwell, only *less* melodious. The band lurches and grunts along noisily; 43 minutes of this is a bit much for non-fanatics.

Grotesque removes the Fall even further from the world of easy listening. The songs are mostly one-or-two-chord jams played too slowly to be hardcore, but structured similarly. Smith grafts on socio-political lyrics that would be more interesting on paper than accompanied by this one-take-live-in-the-studio atonality.

All of the Fall's pre-LP singles (featuring a lineup with keyboardist Una Baines and guitarist Martin Bramah, who went on together to form the Blue Orchids) are on one side of **Early Years**; the other collects later 7-inch efforts. One imagines that Public

Image listened to the 1977 vintage "Repetition" a couple of times before mapping out their first LP.

The 10-inch **Slates** has six tracks with substantially better production than the Fall's preceding ventures; evidence of much greater studio effort abounds. While still not quite Abba-smooth, several numbers, especially "Fit and Working Again" and "Leave the Capitol," are as close to enjoyable, routine (ahem) rock as the Fall have come. A solid record of greater potential appeal than just to cultists.

Part of **Hex Enduction Hour** was recorded in Iceland, a nation where the Fall's music is widely influential. An expanded lineup with two drummers greatly affects the sound, making it large and more rhythm-conscious. Despite a tendency to lumber along at a slow, methodical pace (a common hazard with multiple drummers), some of the tracks are an interesting departure. **Room to Live** features a sparser, less rhythmic sound than **Hex Enduction Hour,** occasionally returning to **Grotesque**'s flirtation with raw rockabilly. Smith is in top lyrical form, with pungent, satirical views of British life: "Marquis Cha Cha" offers biting commentary on the Falklands War.

Around this time, two live Fall discs emerged. **A Part of America Therein** was taped at a half-dozen gigs along a US tour. The sound quality varies considerably from track to track, but the performances are uniformly strong, particularly the epic "N.W.R.A." Even better, though, is **Fall in a Hole,** a two-disc authorized bootleg released only in New Zealand. Recording quality, execution and song selection (mostly from **Hex** and **Room to Live**) are superb but, suffice to say, it's not a common sight in record stores.

The **Live in London, 1980** cassette was recorded in front of a none-too-enthusiastic audience at Acklam Hall; it's of dubious legal origin, listing neither songwriting nor publishing credits. Drawing mostly from **Grotesque** and **Slates**, it warrants mention due to sharp performances (except for "Prole Art Threat," which falls apart) and very good sound quality.

Their next studio LP, **Perverted by Language,** marked a brief return to Rough Trade. On the first Fall record with Smith's American wife Brix as co-guitarist, they chug away with more conviction than ever, particularly on the relentless "Smile" and "Eat Y'self Fitter." Hindsight now shows it to be priming the audience for what was to follow: **The Wonderful and Frightening World of the Fall,** perhaps their finest work to date, produced by John Leckie. Strengthened by Brix's songwriting and gutsy guitar, the Fall are able to beckon a variety of styles with panache. All nine tracks (11 on the American release, which adds "C.R.E.E.P." and "No Bulbs," the latter from the subsequent EP, **Call for Escape Route)** jump out, highlighted by the fierce "Lay of the Land," "Elves" and the almost Syd Barrett-like "Disney's Dream Debased."

Hip Priest and Kamerads is a compilation of the band's releases on the Kamera label. Except for a live version of "Mere Pseud Mag Ed.," there's nothing otherwise unavailable, but it does offer a good introduction for the uninitiated. The tape has extra tracks.

With what at this point seems like an embarrassment of riches, the Fall unleashed **This Nation's Saving Grace.** Tracks like the (gasp!) synthesized and danceable "L.A." and the contemporaneous 45, "Cruiser's Creek," show that the Fall is not completely averse to commercial potential, but it's really just another new type of ammunition added to the arsenal. "Bombast" builds a guitar din that would make Sonic Youth jealous, while "Paintwork" and "I Am Damo Suzuki" (a song about Can's onetime lead singer) are two of the strangest things they've ever done. The tape adds tracks, and the US release substitutes "Cruiser's Creek" for "Barmy," which subsequently turned up on the eponymous American EP, alongside four other 45 cuts, like an unlikely cover of Gene Vincent's "Rollin' Dany."

Named for a novel by Vladimir Nabakov, **Bend Sinister** is a rather gloomy, dark sounding record; minor keys and Joy Division-like guitar riffing dominate tracks like "US '80s-'90s" and "Gross Chapel—British Grenadiers." But then in the middle of all that is "Shoulder Pads," probably the poppiest, most upbeat song they've ever done. Multi-instrumentalist Simon Rogers has become the Fall's chief sound-shaper, providing all kinds of odd synths and guitar fills and embellishments. **Domesday Pay-Off,** the equivalent US release, switches song order a bit and substitutes singles from the same approximate period, such as "Hey! Luciani" and their cover of R. Dean Taylor's "Ghost in My House." The four-song **Peel Sessions** disc (from November 1978) predates their debut album; two of the numbers are on that

LP, the other two are otherwise unreleased. A must for fans.

In Palace of Swords Reversed is a compilation of Rough Trade singles, flipsides and LP tracks from 1980 to 1983, released on Smith's own label, which he founded to release Fall compilations and records by artists with the Smith seal of approval. **The Frenz Experiment** is an unusual LP—almost a Smith solo—with more low-key backing than usual, and more willfully obscure lyrics than ever, particularly on "Athlete Cured" and the very odd "Oswald Defence Lawyer." Rogers, no longer a full-time band member, produced it with the most detailed sound of any Fall record. Adding to their growing reputation as an able and imaginative cover band, **Frenz** includes a version of the Kinks' "Victoria."

Recent Fall side projects have also established them in other fields. Smith expanded the idea from the "Hey! Luciani" 45 into a play which ran in London. They have also provided Michael Clarke's experimental dance company with much of the music they use, including songs that Rogers has arranged for full orchestra. Brix has her own band, the Adult Net, which has recorded several singles (including a great rendition of "Incense and Peppermints") and has at time included ex-Smiths Mike Joyce and Andy Rourke, as well as Rogers and current Fall keyboardist Marcia Schofield.

Fall CDs usually add a few concurrent singles and B-sides; their US LPs usually add the A-side of a single not on the British LP. For instance, "Hit the North" shows up on the UK CD (along with four other bonus cuts) and US LP of **Frenz.** (The UK **Frenz** cassette has one bonus less.) **Bend Sinister** adds "Living Too Late" and "Auto-Tech Pilot" on the CD; both of those, plus "Town and Country Hobgoblins," are on the UK cassette.

The Fall is requisite listening for anyone interested in a challenging, uncompromising band that refuses to stand still or follow any trends not of its own creation.   [iar/dgs]

See also *Blue Orchids, Marc Riley with the Creepers.*

FALSE PROPHETS

False Prophets (Alternative Tentacles) 1986
Implosion (Alternative Tentacles) 1987

Don't be thrown by the irreverent religious imagery on **False Prophets:** after they get through "Invokation" and "Seven

Deadly Sins," this punk-rocking New York five-piece trains its obviously educated intelligence on more traditional hardcore themes like war, authority, violence and rebellion. The Prophets mediate the punk onslaught with dynamics and tempos that don't all run on overdrive, but there's nothing remarkable about their debut.

Implosion, produced by living legend Giorgio Gomelsky, is light years better, breaking uncharted ground on three selections with the fourth-dimensional addition of a horn section led by James White. What a concept! Speedcore takes a back seat as False Prophets reveal their expansive and temperate rock imagination, testing varied rough waters with conviction and wild-eyed enthusiasm. Not great, but getting there.   [iar]

FAMILY FODDER

Monkey Banana Kitchen (nr/Fresh) 1980
All Styles 2 x 33 (nr/Jungle) 1983

These records are bizarre works of multifaceted genius from a strange musical collective. Let me try and elaborate: **Monkey Banana Kitchen**, listing 15 first-name-only musicians and produced by "The People in Control," begins with a choral piece and then slowly drifts into a lengthy dub workout; when that ends, a female voice sings a chipper pop song with weedy organ and a verse in French. After that, things begin to get odd . . .

Every track on **Monkey Banana Kitchen** is an adventure—there is absolutely no consistency. The often dada results run from likable to heinous. Remarkable and great fun, it's a record that will keep you on the edge of your seat.

All Styles, its cover adorned simply by a peace sign, is hypothetically just what the title suggests: two discs (15 discrete songs in all) that give new meaning to the word "variety." Pre-pigeonholed for ease of reviewing, Family Fodder (here a quartet) ostensibly essay folk, classical, soul, punk, easy listening, Euro-pop, opera, jazz, country-western and more, adapting existing material as well as writing their own. In point of fact, these styles, charming and rewarding as they may be, are not very disparate at all, undoubtedly due to self-definition/delusion and the limitations of 4-track at-home recordings. They are, however, consistently enjoyable and infused with invention, cleverness, talent and a totally open outlook that discards nothing without first having an enthusiastic go at it.   [iar]

FAMILY FUN

See *Space Negros.*

FARMER'S BOYS

Get Out and Walk (nr/EMI) 1983
With These Hands (nr/EMI) 1985

If you'd heard their early singles without paying much attention, you might have thought this quartet to be just another Anglo-dance-rock group: the usual rhythms (drum machine), the usual keyboards, the usual sort of a vocalist. One of the 45s (quite good, actually) even sounds like a cross between ABC and Dexys. But what's different? There's no overwrought melodrama, *that's* what—no posing. Stylistically, the sound just provides a jumping-off point for their catchy, distinctive songs; cleverly arranged, succinctly produced. They don't overdo a thing, so you can really relate to the tales of botched romance, self-doubt, even drinking too much after a long day's work. The Farmer's Boys get the points across engagingly, without taking themselves too seriously. The second album is more stylistically diverse than the first—leading off with a Shadows (!) tune about going out in the countryside (!!), done up in a marginally retooled version of '60s pop-rock somewhere between Spanky and Our Gang, the Turtles and the Grass Roots! (That track is one of four produced by Bruce Woolley; horns grace several others.)

The Farmer's Boys are a gas: four normal-looking guys from Norwich making consistently good, durable music. No brilliance here—they haven't got the killer instinct—but these two albums provide solace for sore (or cynical but openminded) ears with cut after cut of enjoyable tunes. Suggestion for trendies and art-lovers: get out and walk.
[jg]

MICK FARREN

Vampires Stole My Lunch Money (nr/Logo) 1978

DEVIANTS

Human Garbage (nr/Psycho) 1984

MICK FARREN & WAYNE KRAMER

Who Shot You Dutch? EP (Spectre) 1987

Mick Farren—journalist, novelist, vocalist, founding member of the (Social) Deviants and Pink Fairies, Motorhead songwriter, etc.—ventured into solo recording work several times in the '70s. On **Vampires**, with musical assistance from Wilko Johnson, Chrissie Hynde, Larry Wallis and others, he dishes out a harrowingly honest collection of songs about drinking, dissolution, depression, self-destruction and desperation. About as powerful as rock gets, this nakedly painful LP is most definitely not recommended to sissies, born-again Christians or prohibitionists.

After relocating to New York several years later, Farren pursued a number of musical endeavors with ex-MC5 guitarist Wayne Kramer. In February 1984, joined by ex-Fairies Larry Wallis and Duncan Sanderson and a drummer, the pair did a loose-limbed gig (billed as the Deviants) at London's Dingwalls, recorded and released as **Human Garbage**. The material mixes selections from **Vampires** ("I Want a Drink" and Frank Zappa's "Trouble Coming Every Day"), Kramer's solo work ("Ramblin' Rose"), Wallis ("Police Car") and similarly casual items like "Screwed Up," "Takin' L.S.D." and "Outrageous Contagious." No points for tightness or tuning, but a neat artifact nonetheless.

Three songs from *The Last Words of Dutch Schultz,* an "R&B musical" based on death-bed ramblings of the prohibition-era gangster written and performed by Farren and Kramer, comprise the 1987 12-inch. The powerful title track (sung by Kramer and produced by Don Was) is clever funk-rock rendered giggly by a disco chorus repeating the phrase throughout the number; the others are more theatrical and modestly appealing.   [iar]

FARTZ

World Full of Hate . . . (Alternative
    Tentacles) 1982

Seattle's delicately named Fartz are an intensely political hardcore band with a positive outlook and vocalist (Blaine Fart; the drummer's called Loud) whose sore-throat shriek rivals Wendy O. Williams' feral growl for sheer unpleasantness. The album—16 soundalikes at 45 rpm—is otherwise fairly routine and need be sought after only by fans of totally unlistenable singers. Get that boy some lozenges, quick!   [iar]

FASHION

Product Perfect (IRS) 1979
Fabrique (Arista) 1982
Twilight of Idols (Epic) 1984

Fashion emerged from Manchester during that city's great rock explosion of 1978-9 with a facility for clever pop that cannibalized aspects of reggae, punk and electro-pop and converted them into a mode that scarcely resembled the parent forms. **Product Perfect** verges on being cheerless, but Fashion infuses it with such good humor and imaginative effects that it seems a wry parody of everything from Madness to Joy Division. Lyrics and tunes are at first unmemorable, but subtle hooks become apparent after several listenings.

Fabrique finds the group, expanded from a trio to a quartet, in a more serious mood, exchanging jokey pop for fierce, funky dance music, including the striking "Move On." Curiously, the songs have immediate impact (in comparison to those on the first LP) but lack the staying power of their earlier work. Nevertheless, the playing is precise and energetic, with more distinct lyrics sung better than ever.

Despite a third label and another personnel change, the same musical style prevails on much of **Twilight of Idols**: muscular dance-rock with the emphasis on solid rhythms and rich vocals rather than gimmicky effects or stylish textures. The exceptional tunes (like the delicate instrumental title track) hold down the energy and get sensitive, at times nearing a Pink Floyd (!) sound. On the hotter numbers, wild guitar (Alan Darby, also the writer of nearly all the material) and slick production gambits (by Zeus B. Held) provide the character the songs themselves lack.   [sg/iar]

FAT BOYS

Fat Boys (Sutra) 1984
The Fat Boys Are Back! (Sutra) 1985
Big & Beautiful (Sutra) 1986
Crushin' (Tin Pan Apple-Polydor) 1987 ●
The Best Part of the Fat Boys (Sutra)
    1987 ●
Coming Back Hard Again (Tin Pan
    Apple-Polydor) 1988 ●

In a medium like rap, it helps to have a gimmick, and this trio from Brooklyn—originally known as the Disco 3—have several. While most rappers brag about what great lovers they are, Prince Markie Dee, Buff and Kool Rock-ski brag about what great eaters they are. In this, their claim to originality is undisputed. Gimmick number two is Buff the Human Beat Box (not to be confused with Doug E. Fresh, the self-proclaimed "Original

Human Beat Box"), who uses lips, cheeks and tongue to create a surprisingly varied array of rhythmic noises. The group's raps are also gimmicky, while the well-produced (most often Kurtis Blow) backing tracks employ full-scale instrumentation and stretch the form into such musical regions as reggae and rock. If the Fat Boys aren't the most talented crew in the business, they're at least consistently good fun.

The multifarious mountains have already been featured in two movies: *Krush Groove,* which recounts the legend of their formation and discovery, and the slapstick comedy *Disorderlies,* for which they covered the Fab boys' "Baby You're a Rich Man." (Another cover in the repertoire is James Brown's "Sex Machine.") Their latest gambit is cutting amusing novelty records with such co-conspirators as Chubby Checker ("The Twist") and the Beach Boys ("Wipeout"). The latter is included on **Crushin'**, a mild but winning collection of mainstream rap cuts with wide appeal, boundless entertainment spirit and unfailing good humor.

The Best Part of the Fat Boys is indeed that, as it compiles tracks from the first three albums and has everything you'd ever need to hear by them: "The Fat Boys Are Back," "All You Can Eat," "Hard Core Reggae," "Sex Machine," etc.   [jl/iar]

See also *Force M.D.'s.*

FEAR

The Record (Slash) 1982
More Beer (Restless) 1985

Fear was an early standout on the Los Angeles hardcore scene but quickly grew beyond its boundaries. Skilled, varied, instrumentally confident and inventive, Fear invests **The Record** with searing rock'n'roll and a wild-eyed sense of humor that seems somehow wholesomely good-natured. Lee Ving (who has also pursued a busy and successful acting career) sings like a drunk baseball fan bellowing in the bleachers, roaring like a lout, but completely intelligible, which allows funny—if disturbingly nasty with regard to women and homosexuals—lyrics to rise above the well-ordered din. Guitarist Philo Cramer tosses instrumental cleverness into the material, making Fear something of a cross between the Dictators and Dickies.

More Beer seems unnecessary, but is as loud, fast and viciously sarcastic as ever. The sporadic inter-song patter is more amusing

than the actual tunes themselves (which are in fact pretty stupid), but there's something pathetically wonderful about Fear, like a dog that you don't really like but keep around anyway because he's so faithful and predictable. (The best Fear on record remains **The Decline of Western Civilization** soundtrack LP, where Ving raises audience baiting to a sidesplitting art and a bandmate coins a new usage for a traditional colloquialism.)   [iar]

FEARLESS IRANIANS FROM HELL

Fearless Iranians from Hell EP (Boner) 1986
Die for Allah (Boner) 1987

While some punk bands include such current world affairs as Iran's Moslem fanaticism in their topical onslaught, only this powerful San Antonio hardcore outfit can lay claim to an actual Iranian (along with two former Butthole Surfers) in its lineup. The 7-inch EP boasts such topical tone poems as "Blow Up the Embassy"; the full-length album (the cover of which represents Ayatollah Khomeini) boasts such blistering speed tunes as "Life Inside Iran," "Iranians on Bikes," "Die for Allah" and "Chant," which is recited in Farsi.   [iar]

FEEDTIME

Feedtime (Aus. Aberrant) 1985
Shovel (Rough Trade) 1988
Cooper S (Rough Trade) 1988

They say that all of rock came from the blues. It's not true, but at least Feedtime's music does. Their sound is dark and dank and dense and devastatingly simple. "Ha Ha," the first track on their first album, pulses with deepness—an ultra-grumbling guitar sawing in repetitive circles like the mating call of a didgeridoo, with vocals that are pure low-frequency growl. The grumbled "I've got a Pontiac/gasoline/Pontiac/gasoline" of "Fastbuck" evokes images of Big Black's "Kerosene" with high-intensity drumming and hard, repeating chords. Most of all, Feedtime's music is descended from pre-hardcore punk. The result is a fast and loud journey down Tylenol territories, tempered with an urge to experiment and fuse mismatched genres with each other. Blues meets punk meets metal meets mantra. Everything is shaken down until it pounds. Even an air of shimmery progressive folk crops up in the vocals of "All Down." Listening to Feedtime's first album is like sand-blasting your ear canals. It may be painful for those accustomed to pop soundalikes, but it's worth the agony.

If your tweeters were blown by the last record you listened to, no problem. You won't miss them at all until you get to **Shovel**, where the same pounding sense of repetition slams guitar chords at your face but adds a touch of country warp and twang on the title cut and a crisp forefront drumbeat to the band's repertoire. Like Pere Ubu or Suicide or any number of bands that people didn't know how to appreciate in their time, Feedtime are originals, making music that is totally compiled from familiar bits but given enough of a twist to make it the band's own.

Cooper S is entirely composed of cover versions. ['e]

FEELIES

Crazy Rhythms (Stiff) 1980 (Ger. Line) 1986 ●
The Good Earth (Coyote-Twin/Tone) 1986 ●
No One Knows EP (Coyote-Twin/Tone) 1986
Only Life (Coyote-A&M) 1988 ●

TRYPES

The Explorers Hold EP (Coyote) 1984

YUNG WU

Shore Leave (Coyote-Twin/Tone) 1987

These New Jerseyites are the stuff of legend and cults. Led by guitarists Glenn Mercer and Bill Million (and originally featuring future avant-star drummer Andy Fisher, aka Anton Fier), the Feelies dressed like nerdy preppies and paid only passing attention to the conventional demands of rock'n'roll. Even during the original band's period of highest visibility, for example, live dates in New York tended to be infrequent and often fell on holidays.

Crazy Rhythms is far more unequivocal than the group's performances. Mercer and Million draw inspiration from the Byrds, Television and the Velvet Underground, emphasizing the interplay of their electric guitars above all else. The rigid vocals and lyrics take a back seat to the pure textures of the driving rockers and more avant-garde drones. Despite its distinct bloodlessness, **Crazy Rhythms** exudes a principled charm.

In the years that followed, the Feelies laid low, but never disbanded, recording and performing around the New York/New Jersey area in various guises and permutations: the Trypes, Willies and Yung Wu. The three bands sound different, although they all play

some Feelies songs and share a fascination with layered guitars, drones and the music of Brian Eno and the Velvet Underground.

The seven-person Trypes are the quietest, most introspective of the bunch, and **The Explorers Hold** is a placid, constantly shifting landscape of sounds. The four songs emphasize coloration, not beat; yet, for all its subdued calm, there's an explosive tension bubbling underneath the music. The muted guitars threaten—but never give way to—riotous mayhem. Only on the cover of George Harrison's "Love You To" do drummer Stan Demeski's hyperkinetic tom-tom patterns come to the fore, making the Trypes a loud psychedelic folk band. The quieter songs, complete with woodwinds and keyboards, are hauntingly beautiful.

In the mid-'80s, Million and Mercer reactivated the Feelies as a full-time band, with Demeski in place of Fier, Brenda Sauter taking over bass from Keith Clayton and the addition of percussionist Dave Weckerman. The Feelies finally released a second album, co-produced by Pete Buck, in 1986. **The Good Earth** approaches folk music with its light, airy feel, but intensity and obsession lurk near the intricately-woven surfaces; slashing lead guitars occasionally pierce the effectively atmospheric tapestry. Million and Mercer display their taut control even as they're strumming away madly in rapturous acceleration; the quiet sections are extraordinarily beautiful. When their voices join for spirited harmonies, you know it was worth the wait. The four-song **No One Knows** is a neat 12-inch sampler joining "The High Road" and "Slipping (Into Something)" from the LP with wonderful covers of the Beatles' "She Said, She Said" and Neil Young's "Sedan Delivery."

Dave Weckerman is the enthusiastically informal lead vocalist and songwriter in Yung Wu—the Feelies augmented by Trypes keyboard-player John Baumgartner. **Shore Leave** leans towards acoustic guitars and simplified drumming for a rustic sound that exchanges the Feelies' neurotic suburban intensity for a countrified gentleness. Influence-revealing covers of the Stones ("Child of the Moon"), Neil Young ("Powderfinger") and Eno ("Big Day") are intriguing but a bit on the plain side.

Film fans may be aware that the high school reunion scenes in Jonathan Demme's *Something Wild* show the Feelies (credited as the Willies) performing shards of five songs, including "I'm a Believer," "Crazy Rhythms" and "Fame," with tentative Bowiesque lead vocals by Weckerman.

[jy/jl/iar]

See also *Lounge Lizards.*

JOHN FELICE AND THE LOWDOWNS
See *Real Kids.*

FELT
Crumbling the Antiseptic Beauty (nr/Cherry Red) 1981 ●
The Splendour of Fear (nr/Cherry Red) 1984 ●
The Strange Idols Pattern and Other Short Stories (nr/Cherry Red) 1984
Ignite the Seven Cannons (nr/Cherry Red) 1985
Let the Snakes Crinkle Their Heads to Death (nr/Creation) 1986
Forever Breathes the Lonely Word (nr/Creation) 1986 ●
Rain of Crystal Spires EP (nr/Creation) 1986
Poem of the River EP (Creation-Relativity) 1987 ●
The Final Resting of the Ark EP (nr/Creation) 1987
Gold Mine Trash (PVC) 1987 ●
The Pictorial Jackson Review (Creation-Relativity) 1988
Train Above the City (Creation-Relativity) 1988

Aided by a second guitarist, a rhythm section and little more, Felt mainstay Lawrence (that's it—just Lawrence) has spent his career paying homage to Tom Verlaine without ever attempting to play his music. On **Crumbling the Antiseptic Beauty**, Felt patterns itself after Television's guitar interplay, with occasional understated vocals that cross Verlaine and Lou Reed. The instrumental passages are the true high points here, as the guitarists are both melodic and sympathetic to each other. Odd, derivative but exciting and evidently ambitious.

By **The Strange Idols Pattern**, Lawrence and his three associates have refined the approach into a strikingly attractive sound: clear guitar notes sparkle from every direction in a jewel-like blend that recalls Television without quite imitating it. A nylon-string flamenco piece ("Crucifix Heaven") demonstrates diverse stylistic faculties; the virtuosity of lead guitarist Maurice Dee-

bank—listen to his solo on "Whirlpool Vision of Shame"—is also quite impressive.

Gold Mine Trash is a fascinating developmental chronicle of Felt's Cherry Red years: singles, album tracks and a pair of previously unreleased 1984 demos that are swell. The LP ends on a pivotal note: "Primitive Painters," an obsessive 1985 British indie-chart hit with guest vocals by Cocteau Twin Liz Fraser which incorporates swirling organ for an entirely new effect.

Felt's Creation-label debut, **Let the Snakes Crinkle Their Heads to Death**, is a brief instrumental album by a stable new lineup (Lawrence, keyboardist Martin Duffy, bassist Marco Thomas and stalwart drummer Gary Ainge) that notably lacks a second guitarist. Ten perky cuts ("Lawrence's songs coloured in by Martin") rush by in under 19 minutes; it's a pleasant collection but not a Felt milestone. Although one or two of the simple pieces hold to the group's prior sound, most don't; organ takes a prominent role and there's little of the familiar instrumental blend.

Vocals and another guitarist make a welcome return on **Forever Breathes the Lonely Word**, a finely-wrought album with Dylanesque characteristics on which Lawrence sings exactly like Verlaine, adding a nifty Lou Reed imitation on "September Lady" and "Grey Streets." Lyrically, he's in top form, expressing religious doubt in "All the People I Like Are Those That Are Dead" and questioning a lover's faithfulness in "Gather Up Your Wings and Fly." Duffy's percolating Hammond organ (no clichéd sounds of the '60s) adds a wonderful component to these songs, especially "Down but Not Yet Out," giving them all new-found energy and texture. Unlike anything else in the group's catalogue, **Forever Breathes the Lonely Word** is easily Felt's best record. The worthy **Rain of Crystal Spires** 12-inch matches a pair of LP tracks with two quick B-sides.

After that, Felt produced a couple of radically different EPs. The six-song **Poem of the River**, mainly produced by Mayo Thompson, makes good use of both organ and piano, turning down the shimmering guitars for a rich instrumental blend that touches on the Smiths and Aztec Camera. **The Final Resting of the Ark**, produced by Cocteau Twin Robin Guthrie, is spare and largely acoustic, a forgettably minor outing that has two simple songs with vocals, an unaccompanied Duffy piano piece and two other instrumentals.

With Thomas moving over to lead guitar and a new bassist in the fold, Felt recorded the schizophrenic **Pictorial Jackson Review** "quickly on eight-track." Two of Duffy's jazzy instrumental contemplations (introduced on the preceding EP) fill one side, leaving eight concise Lawrence songs to huddle together on the other side. Resembling a stripped-down version of **Forever Breathes**, those numbers make Lawrence's Lou Reed fixation abundantly evident: most (not counting the precisely Dylanesque "How Spook Got Her Man" and "Don't Die on My Doorstep," which splices Bob and Lou together) suggest the early Velvet Underground's lighter, melodic side.

Alternate format complications: a 1987 CD released by German Rough Trade unites **Poem of the River** and **Forever Breathes the Lonely Word**; a 1986 UK Cherry Red CD and cassette joins **Crumbling the Antiseptic Beauty** and **The Splendour of Fear**; the **Strange Idols Pattern** cassette also includes **Ignite the Seven Cannons**.   [cpl/iar]

BRYAN FERRY

These Foolish Things (Atlantic) 1973 ●
Another Time, Another Place (Atlantic) 1974
Let's Stick Together (Atlantic) 1976
In Your Mind (Atlantic) 1977
The Bride Stripped Bare (Atlantic) 1978
Boys and Girls (Warner Bros.) 1985 ●
Windswept EP (nr/EG-Polydor) 1985
Bête Noire (EG-Reprise) 1987 ●

BRYAN FERRY/ROXY MUSIC

Street Life (nr/EG) 1986 ●

Braving waves of contemptuous reviews at first, the voice of Roxy Music began his irregular solo career as an aside, allowing it to become his primary work as Roxy Music faded out of existence in the early '80s. Although hardly the groundbreaking titan he once was, Ferry has had far-reaching stylistic influence over much of pop music. Disingenuous claims of total self-invention notwithstanding, many nouveau poseurs have let Ferry point the way for them to "be themselves."

A shocking break from Roxy Music's hip glam-rock, **These Foolish Things** quickly established the difference between the group's utter originality and Ferry's suave solo interpretations. (For a number of obvious reasons this gap closed over the years to the point of near-indistinguishability.) With a backing group that included then-Roxy drummer Paul Thompson as well as future Roxyite Eddie Jobson, Ferry croons his way through such surprising '60s selections as Bob Dylan's "A Hard Rain's A-Gonna Fall," the Beatles' "You Won't See Me" and the Stones' "Sympathy for the Devil." Even 15 years later, this warped '70s jukebox is weird but wonderful. **Another Time, Another Place** reprised the exercise, drawing on various epochs for material like "The 'In' Crowd," "You Are My Sunshine," "It Ain't Me Babe" and "Smoke Gets in Your Eyes." Only the title song is a Ferry original.

For **Let's Stick Together**, Ferry reached into the vaults and selected five Roxy Music songs (four from the band's first LP) and did something with them: recut the vocals, presented alternate versions or simply re-edited/ re-mixed the tracks. Some of these sound fine, but a funked-up "Re-Make/Re-Model" is too revisionist for words. The record is fleshed out with a new brace of neat covers, including the wonderful title track, "Shame Shame Shame" and the Everly Brothers' "Price of Love." It's a strange assemblage with some jarring contrasts; still, **Let's Stick Together** has more great tracks than any of Ferry's other solo records.

In Your Mind, produced during a period of Roxy inactivity, is Ferry's first "normal" solo album—all of the material is new and original—but, bereft of a gimmick and lacking the involvement of his usual collaborators, falls short of Ferry's best work. Despite a few good tunes ("This Is Tomorrow," "Tokyo Joe"), the bland sound allows little of Ferry's brilliance to shine through, and the writing is not up to snuff. Easily ignored.

Inspired by his broken romance with Jerry Hall, the future mother of Mick Jagger's children and a onetime Roxy LP cover model, **The Bride Stripped Bare**—loosely named after a surrealist painting by Marcel Duchamp—is Ferry at his most emotionally translucent. The hybrid approach—half new originals, half appropriate revivals—and backing by a new coterie of session pros (including Waddy Wachtel, Neil Hubbard and Alan Spenner) make it radically different in both construction and sound. Some of the tracks are intensely gripping ("Sign of the Times," Lou Reed's "What Goes On"); others are subtler and less rewarding. A mixed success.

After Roxy Music finally ceased to exist,

Ferry's solo career took on new significance. Unfortunately, the music he now makes is not far from end-time Roxy Music: perfectionist studio technique and seamless production of songs that are at best bland and frequently lifeless. Despite its extraordinarily sleek veneer, **Boys and Girls** (dedicated to Ferry's late father) is so short on tunes that several of the numbers rely on fatiguing one-note vamps to carry them along. Exceptional lyrics might allow one to overlook such inadequacy, but there's nothing much happening on that front, either. It's impossible to dislike the album with any enthusiasm—considerable care, thought and effort obviously went into its creation—still, the lack of even a trace of extremism or subversiveness is unforgivable.

The similarly restrained **Bête Noire** confirms that palatable adult music *is* Ferry's future. That wonderful voice has become the only important ingredient; what he's singing doesn't seem so important anymore. But this record's better melodic development and a wider variety of danceable tempos than on **Boys and Girls** are palpable signs of life; the involvement of ex-Smiths guitarist Johnny Marr as a player and the co-writer of one near-exciting song ("The Right Stuff") is another positive touch. All things considered, "Limbo," "Kiss and Tell" and "Day for Night" are coolly inviting and likable enough, given the diminished expectations one now brings to Bryan Ferry albums.

Street Life is a two-record career retrospective: 20 songs drawn from Roxy Music as well as solo releases, stretching from 1972's "Virginia Plain" to **Boys and Girls**' "Slave to Love." [iar]

FETCHIN BONES

Cabin Flounder (DB) 1985
Bad Pumpkin (DB-Capitol) 1986
Galaxy 500 (Capitol) 1987

SKEETERS

Wine, Women and Walleye (DB) 1988

Like the sublimely seedy roadside joints of America's rural South—where you can shoot pool, buy fishing worms and have your lawnmower repaired all in the same room—Fetchin Bones are dedicated to the sort of unexpected variety that somehow seems to work. On their debut album, the North Carolina quintet peddles an exciting mix of revved-up rock, country twang, folk, blues and swing, driving it all home with unre-

strained energy and unpolished charm. The crazed quaver in singer Hope Nicholls' voice (a rougher, more manic version of Lone Justice's Maria McKee) provides the heart of the Bones' sound; three (of 11) songs without her lead vocals are the album's weakest cuts. Producer Don Dixon admirably translates the group's wild-eyed persona to vinyl, but this is a band that must be seen live for a full grasp of their eclectic frenzy. Delightfully different graduates of the R.E.M.-inspired school of Southern pop.

Although docked a few fun points for the lack of focus, **Bad Pumpkin** basically stays the course, with equally direct Dixon production, rough-hewn playing, strong original songs and more inspired warbling by Nicholls. Gary White's spicy guitar work and bassist Danna Pentes' violin contributions provide a lot of the instrumental flavor; Marc Mueller keeps things moving along at a brisk pace with lickety-split country drumming.

The self-assured spunk of **Galaxy 500** is immediately evident; a lineup shift (Mueller and White are gone, replaced by Clay Richardson and Errol Stewart) also contributes to the clear and feverish dynamo. The Bones' control is clearly demonstrated by the juxtaposition of the wild'n'funky "Sammy" with the sweeping prettiness of "Steamwhistle." Alternating between a guttural growl, a delicate folk sensibility (faintly like Natalie Merchant's) and a half-dozen other voices, Nicholls is a commanding vocalist; the songs rise and fall strictly on her sing-so.

Answering the unasked question, Mueller and White formed the Skeeters, a trio with bassist Marco Heeter, and issued **Wine, Women and Walleye**, a charmingly ragged rock/pop/folk-rock record produced by Tim Lee. White's Neil Young-ish guitar solos spiff up intriguing material with a smartass streak that surfaces in tunes like "Slummin" and "Center of the Western Hemisphere." There's even a raving surf-twang instrumental number called "Porno Rock." Neat. [kh/iar]

FETUS PRODUCTIONS

Fetalmania EP (NZ Flying Nun) 1982

A weird blend of scratchy guitar, prominent percussion, disquieting noises and disembodied vocals—the Residents go to a disco, or Tuxedomoon takes a trip Down Under. There's enough melody and structure to make up for the obnoxious imagery and self-conscious strangeness, and the songs gallop along nicely. Very obscure.   [iar]

FIENDS
We've Come for Your Beer (Bemisbrain) 1984
Gynecölögy (PVC) 1987

Give this Los Angeles trio five points for title and ten more for the zombie movie-still cover of their debut album. The 12 punky party tunes (six each on the "Funny Side" and "Scary Side") aren't bad, either—gabbagabba rock silliness like "John Belushi," "Die Bob [Hope] Die" and "Riot in the Men's Room." Sloppy, sarcastic, cloddish and wild, the Fiends are the kind of kids high school teachers describe as having "attitude problems." All right!

Unfortunately, the hard-rocking production (John Doe and Randy Burns) on Gynecölögy is the album's best feature: guitarist Scott T. Morrow's sore-throat screaming otherwise makes listening something of a chore. The undistinguished music and puerile, smarmy lyrics like "Hugh G. Erection" and "Col. Lingus" further bury this tripe.
                                                            [iar]

54-40
Selection EP (Can. Mo-Da-Mu) 1982
Set the Fire (Can. Mo-Da-Mu) 1984
54-40 (Reprise) 1986
Show Me (Warner Bros.) 1987 ●

Vancouver's 54-40 take their name from an obscure bit of US history—"Fifty-four forty or fight" was the presidential campaign slogan of James K. Polk who promised to go to war with Canada if the northwestern US/Canadian border was not set at 54 degrees, 40 minutes, which would have made Canada primarily a nation of ice cubes and polar bears.

The edgy Selection, though now dated-sounding, is their strongest work—low budget production, warm squiggly guitar lines and funk undercurrents. There's a folky sense of shimmer, coupling acoustic and electric instruments and a twitchy feel that bounces and bobs and nearly yodels (on "Jamming with Lawrence"). The moody vocals, crisply muted drumming and scratchy guitar bubbles make "Yanks" nearly jump off the disc out of nervous energy, while the funk-infused "He's Got" couples post-Joy Division vocals with horns and dark guitars.

By 1984's Set the Fire, 54-40's formerly personality-filled drumming had evolved into the same rhythm box-inspired dance beat that every MTV-wannabe band uses. The horns trade their anxious edge for a homogenized white soul background sound; though the group still uses guitar, the feeling behind their music is synthetic. No quirks. No edges. No fire.

You can hear traces of how the band evolved from the early '80s gloom movement and what they might have become on their third release's best songs. The lonely and majestic "Me Island" seethes with echo and attempts to build into the kind of tense energy ball the band achieved on Selection. The cacophony section of "Holy Cow" screams with vitality, but the rest of the song is mired in dreary darkness. Side One is so bland that it barely qualifies as rock music. You can regularly find this third album in the 25-cent bin at used stores.

Which is probably where Show Me will end up. Brightly engineered with full-scale production, it has sparklingly loud and clear high notes and a thickly full sound. But there's precious little excitement underneath the commercial surface. The two rocking songs sound exactly like Human Frailty-era Hunters & Collectors; the ballads are patented 1987 nu musik wallpaper. All it needs is a blue stripe across the cover and it could be sold with the other plain-wrap generic items in the supermarket. A real waste. ['e]

FIGURES ON A BEACH
Swimming EP (Metro-America) 1983
Standing on Ceremony (I Square-Sire) 1987

From the astonishing Rene Magritte-tribute cover photograph to the sparkling music and sound on Swimming's four long songs, this Michigan quartet doesn't skimp or compromise in any regard. Figures on a Beach play complex, serious (but not dour) poetic compositions with intricate instrumental and vocal arrangements that rely mainly on guitars, drums and keyboards. Anthony Kaczynski has a strong, capable voice just on the edge of melodrama; multi-tracking gives him startling creative range. Hard to classify, you might think of this remarkable, unpredictable band as an American (not Americanized) Simple Minds. Don Was produced the Figures' 1984 dance single, "Breathless."

The full-length major-label debut finds the group, expanded to a quintet and relocated to Boston, holding to much the same art-dance rock sound. Confident flashes of Simple Minds, Duran Duran, Depeche Mode, Ultravox and their offspring may have been novel and intriguing on a 1983 indie record, those same stylistic attributes make for a quaint, not compelling, album four years later, when post-disco techno-rock is largely a relic. These guys are obviously skilled and facile, but they totally missed the boat.   [iar]

FINE YOUNG CANNIBALS
Fine Young Cannibals (IRS) 1985 ●

Factionalism led to the disbandment of the Beat; when the two mainmen formed General Public, the others looked set to fade from sight. But the group formed by guitarist Andy Cox and bassist David Steele, joined by fine young vocalist Roland Gift, has proven a most worthwhile venture. **Fine Young Cannibals** approaches modern R&B and soul from a number of fresh rock perspectives, but it's really Gift's classically Motownish, richly emotional vocals that ignite originals like "Johnny Come Back" and "Don't Ask Me to Choose," as well as a rousing cover of Elvis Presley's "Suspicious Minds."

Since the band's first album, their work has concentrated on film. Gift played a prominent dramatic part in 1987's *Sammy and Rosie Get Laid;* the entire band contributed an annoying misinterpretation of the Buzzcocks' "Ever Fallen in Love" to the *Something Wild* soundtrack.

In Gift's absence, Steele and Cox whipped up a high-tech danceable side project called 2 Men a Drum Machine and a Trumpet, releasing a 1988 IRS 12-inch, "Tired of Getting Pushed Around."   [iar]

FINGERPRINTZ
The Very Dab (Virgin Int'l) 1979
Distinguishing Marks (Virgin) 1980
Beat Noir (Stiff) 1981

It's difficult to categorize Fingerprintz, which may explain why this now-defunct group never garnered a large following. The primitively-recorded first album occupies a dark, throbbing zone of bobbing pop and wry-to-bizarre lyrics ("Punchy Judy," "Beam Me Up Scotty"). Leader/guitarist Jimme O'Neill's Scottish accent and offbeat songwriting combine to chilling effect on the crime-obsessed narratives "Fingerprince" and "Wet Job"; the former's music also sug-

gests a valid response to reggae/dub influence.

The considerably slicker **Distinguishing Marks**, in contrast, is pure pop in extremis—musically, anyway. The songs hum like a finely-tuned motor, with producer Nick Garvey removing any rough sonic edges. Only the relentlessly perverse lyrics betray a refusal to play by the book; O'Neill's disjointed visions are inspired by pulp fiction, police blotters and hospital charts. A catchy collection that all sounds like hit single material.

Beat Noir took yet another 180-degree turn, away from pop and toward a rock/funk fusion. Finally in synch with the times, Fingerprintz delivered a stunning, idiosyncratic package of heavy bass lines, winsome melodies and O'Neill's thematic fetishes (paranoia, frustration). The album was kinky enough to catch on in rock clubs, but too peculiar to reach a broader audience. (The US version deletes two songs.) Drenched in atmosphere, it remains a compelling work.

O'Neill subsequently co-wrote, co-produced and played on an excellent album (**Sob Stories**) by singer Jacqui Brookes. Drummer Bogdan Wiczling worked on that record as well, and later toured and recorded with Adam Ant.   [si]

See also *Silencers.*

TIM FINN
See *Split Enz.*

FIRE ENGINES
Lubricate Your Living Room (nr/Pop: Aural) 1980
Aufgeladen und Bereit für Action und Spass (Fast America) 1981

Fire Engines were the most manic of the new Scottish pop crop that surfaced around 1979: primal rock'n'roll drawing more on raw passion (via guitar din and repetitive noise) than melody or captivating structures. The quartet offers no traditional hooks, just six-string fire and aggressively unpleasant vocals. The two enigmatic albums have a lot of overlap: the American release with the German title adds two of the band's catchier numbers, namely the punk-country-flavored "Candyskin" (with ridiculously anomalous strings) and "Everythings Roses." It also replaces the tedious "Lubricate Your Living Room Pt. 2" with the more exciting "Meat Whiplash." Using electric guitars without regard to typical pop traditions, the abrasive but ruggedly handsome Fire Engines—kind of a blend of the Contortions and early Television—will poke and scratch their way into your heart if you let them. [gf/iar]

FIREHOSE

Ragin', Full-On (SST) 1986 •
if'n (SST) 1987 •

Born out of tragedy, fIREHOSE began after the death of Minutemen frontman D. Boon in a car crash. Knowing there was no way to recapture Boon's burly bluster, bassist Mike Watt and drummer George Hurley didn't try to find someone to fill those iconoclastic shoes. Instead, they recruited another kind of dude entirely in the person of ed fROMOHIO (aka Ed Crawford). A more restrained presence than the raucous Boon, not to mention a prettier singer, Ed settled right into the driver's seat on **Ragin', Full-On**. This bracing LP jumps all over the map, from edgy rockers ("Choose Any Memory") to absorbing mood pieces ("The Candle and the Flame") to acoustic reveries ("This . . . "). First note to last, there's a prickly, intangible integrity to the band that the restless Boon would have admired.

On **if'n**, the Hosers are more self-assured, more articulate and just as freewheeling. Ed really steps out on the propulsive "Anger," an unnerving portrayal of rage, and "For the Singer of REM," a devastating parody of that overrated band. Watt gets his turn at the mic, too, delivering an amusingly disjointed rap (he calls it a spiel) on "Me & You, Remembering." Unpredictable and unpretentious, fIREHOSE has the exciting aura of a group in constant evolution, willing to follow the muse in any direction whatsoever. First class. [jy]

See also *Dos, Sonic Youth*.

FIRETONES

See *Rubber City Rebels*.

FIRMAMENT AND THE ELEMENTS

See *Bruce Woolley*.

WILD MAN FISCHER

An Evening with Wild Man Fischer (Bizarre) 1969
Wildmania (Rhino) 1977

Pronounced Normal (Rhino) 1981
Nothing Scary (Rhino) 1984

One of the true wackos of our time, Los Angeles crypto-singer Wild Man (Larry) Fischer has been around forever. Originally discovered, signed and produced by Frank Zappa in the late '60s, he resurfaces periodically through the auspices of Dr. Demento and Rhino Records, for whom he first began recording in 1975, with a blatantly commercial single, "Go to Rhino Records." Utterly uninhibited and basically incapable of carrying a tune, Fischer recorded some of **Wildmania** in the left field (ahem) stands of Dodger Stadium; largely unaccompanied, he moans such dadaist attempts at musical expression as "My Name Is Larry" (twice) and generally performs in truly sad fashion. **Pronounced Normal** is much better, an entertaining and funny program of music and "skits" that ranges from a lovely (if atonal) guitar-assisted version of Brian Wilson's "In My Room" to a solo vocal rendition of "Fish Heads," composed (as is much of the material) by Barnes & Barnes, the disciples who also produced it.

They did the same (and more) for **Nothing Scary**, an assemblage of three years' worth of odds and ends. The LP contains 34 separate items (e.g., "Outside the Hospital," "Larry in Las Vegas," "Oh God, Please Send Me a Kid"), with Fischer's vocals recorded, besides in a studio, "on location in a park, in a tunnel, and over the telephone." [iar]

FISCHER-Z

Word Salad (UA) 1979
Going Deaf for a Living (UA) 1980
Red Skies over Paradise (nr/Liberty) 1981

JOHN WATTS

One More Twist (nr/EMI) 1982
The Iceberg Model (nr/EMI) 1983

An often excellent but widely ignored outfit, Fischer-Z was primarily a vehicle for John Watts, a singer/guitarist/songwriter whose intense vocals and semi-neurotic outlook provided its character. A flair for intricate but accessible arrangements and novel subject matter made Fischer-Z both easy to like and hard to dismiss.

Word Salad, produced by Mike Howlett and recorded as a quartet, displays Watts in the process of searching out an ego, still sharing songwriting credits and vocal chores with the others. It's an impressive debut album, full of great songs, fine musicianship and stylistic variety, all colored by Watts' reedy voice.

With the same personnel and producer, **Going Deaf for a Living** went for a sparer sound, downplaying the keyboards in favor of Cars-like simplicity, best exemplified on "So Long." An odd direction for a second record, but the band's attributes remained unchanged, and it's as good as the first.

Red Skies over Paradise is a solo album waiting for someone to inform the other members of the group. Watts co-produced, played the keyboards and allowed his songwriting to become entirely self-indulgent. With a serious baritone replacing the plaintive tenor (it's always a bad sign when singers change their voices) and no-nonsense message lyrics, there's a lot wrong with this disappointing album, despite four or five good numbers.

As a predictable next move, Watts went solo. The material on **One More Twist** is a bit forced and clearly less interesting than his earlier songwriting, with only a Tom Robinson-sounding single, "One Voice," showing any real signs of life. [iar]

FISHBONE

Fishbone EP (Columbia) 1985
In Your Face (Columbia) 1986
It's a Wonderful Life (Gonna Have a Good Time) EP (Columbia) 1987

One of America's brightest young hopes, this rowdy six-piece from LA specializes in ska with overtones of go-go, funk and rock. (Imagine George Clinton producing the first Beat LP.) Their sense of humor is surpassed only by the six tracks' non-stop hyperkinetic energy. Whether the lyrics are socially relevant ("Party at Ground Zero," "Another Generation") or just plain silly ("Ugly"), the vim and vigor level is maintained. If you can sit still throughout this, you're probably dead.

In Your Face has an "EXPLICIT LYRICS—PARENTAL ADVISORY" warning on the back, but it should serve as more of a warning to fans. With David Kahne's inappropriately slick production, the band has mellowed out considerably for their debut longplayer. Nothing wrong with trying a new direction, but several cuts here are just MOR soul-rock, and that's simply not what this bunch is cut out for. The lyrics are nowhere, too—the promising title "Post Cold War Politics" is an instrumental. Back to the drawing board.

The all-new Xmas EP, also produced by Kahne, puts a casual ho-ho-ho twist on everyone's favorite time of year. The title tune is actually the least interesting of the four gratuitous charmers; the soulful disenchantment of "Slick Nick, You Devil You" ("Spilling Jack Daniels all over the drapes/ Tattoos on his arms and knees/I never thought Santa Claus would be such a sleaze") and the funked-out "Just Call Me Scrooge" are the real winners. A welcome gift to cheer up any celebration. [dgs/iar]

MORGAN FISHER
See *Hybrid Kids.*

PATRIK FITZGERALD

Grubby Stories (nr/Small Wonder-Polydor) 1979 (nr/Red Flame) c. 1983
Gifts and Telegrams (nr/Red Flame) 1982
Drifting Towards Violence (nr/Red Flame) 1983
Tunisian Twist (nr/Red Flame) 1984

London punk folk singer Fitzgerald first attracted attention with his 1977 single, "Safety Pin Stuck in My Heart." After a few years and a few more 45s, he delivered the aptly titled **Grubby Stories** LP. Some tracks use just acoustic guitar and vocals, while others employ a full backing band that features the bassist from Penetration, the Buzzcocks' drummer and producer Peter Wilson on guitar and keyboards. The music is pretty mundane—Fitzgerald's strength is his angry/ sad/pathetic/strange lyrics, not lasting melodies—but the singing and unique attitude expressed make **Grubby Stories** a slight treasure for occasional enjoyment. The similarity to pre-rock Bowie is striking, although probably unintentional. [iar]

FIXX

Shuttered Room (MCA) 1982 ●
Reach the Beach (MCA) 1983 ●
Phantoms (MCA) 1984 ●
Walkabout (MCA) 1986 ●
React (MCA) 1987 ●

Although they sound like a dozen other pretentious synth-heavy atmospheric English dance bands, the vile Fixx, aided immeasurably by producer Rupert Hine's ability to sculpt their mundane songs and uncover marginal tense appeal, have managed to become enormously successful, regularly drawing a couple of hits from each album. **Shuttered Room** offers "Red Skies" and "Stand or Fall"; **Reach the Beach** contains "One Thing Leads to Another" and "Saved by Zero"; **Phantoms** has "Are We Ourselves?" Showing remarkable consistency, they are all equally unpleasant and trivial.

React, a "greatest hits live" package, contains performances, recorded at two late-1986 Canadian shows, of every one of those songs, plus three especially wretched new studio cuts. [iar]

FLAG OF CONVENIENCE
Life on the Telephone EP (PVC) 1982
Should I Ever Go Deaf EP (nr/MCM) 1987

F.O.C.
Northwest Skyline (nr/MCM) 1987
War on the Wireless Set (MCM) 1988
Back From Exile EP (nr/MCM) 1988

When Pete Shelley disbanded Buzzcocks in March 1981, guitarist Steve Diggle and drummer John Maher formed Flag of Convenience. Diggle had played the Dave Davies role in the group—writing and singing his two or three songs per LP, getting an occasional A-side, and improving all the while—so it was logical for him to carry on the Buzzcocks' frantic, ambitious pop as Shelley opted for techno-blip dance music. Sadly, they've been laboring in obscurity until recently, releasing but four singles between 1981 and '86.

Life on the Telephone, a US 12-inch with two versions of the title track and a pair of other songs, is immediately agreeable; the clever parts come into focus after a while. The US-only **War on the Wireless Set**, which compiles outtakes from '81–'86 (plus one previously released 45, "New House"), is just the kind of hardhitting, ballsy material you'd anticipate considering the people involved. "Heartbreak Story" is a particularly good find, with a martial beat and "Peter Gunn" guitar line. The real killer is "Back of My Mind," one of two tracks here recorded by three-quarters of the Buzzcocks (sans Shelley) for that band's fourth LP, which was scrapped when the band broke up. "Back of My Mind" proves again (as "Harmony in My Head" and "Airwaves Dream" had during the Buzzcocks' existence) that Diggle was coming into his creative own as a match for Shelley.

Maher quit around '86, but Diggle carries on under the abbreviated F.O.C. name,

releasing **Northwest Skyline** as his first real album. (Maher sits in on three songs.) Though seemingly more cheaply recorded than **War on the Wireless Set**, Diggle himself sounds more committed and more convincing, especially on social-issue lyrics (concerning, for instance, racial prejudice and northern England's chronic unemployment). Diggle has clearly emerged as the group's musical leader and his guitar dominates each track. Both "Northwest Skyline" and "Pictures in My Mind" (with Maher's easily identifiable buzzsaw rolls) are especially impressive.

All four songs on **Should I Ever Go Deaf** later turned up on **Northwest Skyline**, rendering its purchase unnecessary. [jr]

FLAMING LIPS
The Flaming Lips (Lovely Sorts of Death)
    1985 (Pink Dust) 1987 ●
Hear It Is (Pink Dust) 1986 ●
Oh My Gawd!!! . . . the Flaming Lips
    (Restless) 1987 ●

The Flaming Lips play around with the same sort of cartoon-psychedelia imagery used by lots of similarly-inclined combos, but these disenfranchised Oklahomans possess wit and ingenuity most of the acid-addled competition lacks. From its uniquely disgusting front cover to the brilliant alienation anthem "My Own Planet," **The Flaming Lips** shows considerably more promise than just about anything else in the college-radio underground's drooling-garage-thrash brigade.

Hear It Is fulfills some of that promise. While affectionately borrowing riffs here and there, the Lips (now a trio, with singer Mark Coyne gone and his brother Wayne taking over vocals) show real originality, balancing the rockin' grunge of "With You" and "Jesus Shootin' Heroin" with softer acoustic passages. One CD collects the contents of the first two records, adding a version of "Summertime Blues" that's considerably closer to Blue Cheer than Eddie Cochran.

The inventively self-produced **Oh My Gawd!!!** is a surprisingly mature and confident work, with more consistent material and performances. Alienation anthems ("Everything's Explodin' "), unselfconsciously anachronistic Pink Floydisms ("One Million Billionth of a Millisecond on a Sunday Morning") and moments of genuine sensitivity ("Love Yer Brain"), allow **Oh My Gawd!!!** to transcend the Lips' wacky-cult-

213

band image, marking them as one of the American heartland's brightest—if least likely—new hopes. [hd]

FLAMIN GROOVIES

Sneakers EP (Snazz) 1968 (Hol. Skydog) 1975
Supersnazz (Epic) 1969 (nr/Edsel) 1986
Flamingo (Kama Sutra) 1970
Teenage Head (Kama Sutra) 1971
This Is the Flamin Groovies (Ger. Kama Sutra-Metronome) 1975
Flamingo/Teenage Head (nr/Buddah) 1975
Shake Some Action (Sire) 1976 ●
Still Shakin (Buddah) 1976
Flamin' Groovies Now (Sire) 1978
Jumpin' in the Night (Sire) 1979
Flamin' Groovies '68 (Fr. Eva) 1983
Flamin' Groovies '70 (Fr. Eva) 1983
Bucketful of Brains (Voxx) 1983
Slow Death, Live! (Fr. Lolita) 1983
The Gold Star Tapes (Fr. Skydog) 1984
Live at the Whisky A Go-Go '79 (Fr. Lolita) 1985
Roadhouse (nr/Edsel) 1986
One Night Stand (nr/ABC) 1987

Starting out in San Francisco as early as 1965 (predating the Grateful Dead), the Flamin Groovies have always been out of step with the rock world. Ten years before anyone knew about bands releasing their own independent records, the Groovies issued a 10-inch mini-album, **Sneakers**; in the '70s, when that same do-it-yourself spirit was inspiring countless innovative bands to try and challenge the old boundaries, they retreated to make albums of beat group nostalgia, wearing period clothes and refusing to acknowledge that times had indeed changed.

Always more cult-popular and influential than commercially successful, the Groovies—led by irascible but talented guitarist/singer Cyril Jordan and (until 1972) singer/guitarist Roy A. Loney—have always embodied the rebellious, youthful spirit that fueled punk, but have held tenuously to their musical roots—'50s American rock'n'roll and '60s British pop. In effect, they have provided inspiration for countless bands (how many covers of "Slow Death" can you name?), and are legendary for good reason.

The Groovies' recording career, generally more exciting on hit-and-run singles than in a sustained album situation, began with the competent amateurism of **Sneakers**—Loney originals played with great energy and a

slight psychedelic undercurrent—and continued on their major-label debut, **Supersnazz**, which encompasses a variety of disparate styles and is more ambitious than impressive. **Flamingo** and **Teenage Head** (years later, the former was reissued as **This Is the Flamin Groovies** in Germany; a repackage of both LPs appeared in France and the UK as **Collectors Items**) are the band's strongest pre-nostalgia efforts, taking advantage of improved skills and equipment to make loud, brash records in sharp contrast to the era's prevailing bland music.

After moving to England and hooking up with Dave Edmunds as their producer, the reconstituted Groovies cut **Shake Some Action**, which features their finest pop creation, the title track, an apocalyptic Byrds-like classic. **Still Shakin** was rushed out by their old label (Buddah and Kama Sutra being related) as a last chance to cash in, combining tracks from **Flamingo** and **Teenage Head** with a 1971 live-in-the-studio side. **Now** and **Jumpin' in the Night** further explore Jordan's fixation with the past, mixing '60s standards with new soundalike originals. While this Groovies era is flawed and not immune to being awful at times, each of the three Sire albums does contain catchy, melodic pop tunes given careful, faithful and enthusiastic treatment.

The Groovies didn't issue any new recordings between 1979 and 1987, leading to suspicions that the band had ceased to exist. During that period, however, ongoing European (especially French) interest prompted the release of numerous reissues, compilations and vintage concert material. **Slow Death, Live!** and its equivalent American release, **Bucketful of Brains**, date from a 1971 Fillmore West show; **Roadhouse** is a British repackage combining tracks from the two Kama Sutra albums.

Although a modest return by any measure, Cyril, bassist George Alexander and three new bandmates did record a new album in 1986: **One Night Stand**, done in a single day (two, if you count mixdown) in an Australian (!) studio, sounds live and contains shaggy roadhouse renditions of classic originals ("Shake Some Action," "Slow Death," "Teenage Head") as well as Paul Revere and the Raiders' "Kicks," the Who's "Call Me Lightning" and other covers. Hardly a record to cherish, but a reassuring audible reminder that the band lives on—and that Jordan's heart is still in it. [iar]

See also *Kingsnakes, Roy Loney and the Phantom Movers.*

FLESH EATERS

No Questions Asked (Upsetter) 1980
A Minute to Pray, a Second to Die (Ruby) 1981
Forever Came Today (Ruby) 1982
A Hard Road to Follow (Upsetter) 1983
Greatest Hits—Destroyed by Fire (SST) 1986

Young poets on the East Coast were originally attracted to punk by its simplicity, directness and malleability. Most prominently, Patti Smith and Richard Hell found that crudely-executed rock'n'roll provided the perfect backdrop for their verbal barrages. Though less celebrated, California's Chris Desjardins made equally ambitious records with a constantly changing set of Flesh Eaters. Singing in a style akin to Hell's delirious hysterics, Chris D. (as he calls himself) turns morbid, sensational subjects like murder, vampirism and necrophilia into diverting entertainment through relentlessly intense lyrics. And though their demented tone will drive off most listeners, his albums bear hearing.

Cramming 14 tracks into 25 minutes, **No Questions Asked** uses the simplest punk structures to illustrate such overbearing tales as "Cry Baby Killer" (the name comes from an early Jack Nicholson film), "Suicide Saddle" and "Dynamite Hemorrhage." A formative effort.

By comparison, **A Minute to Pray** is like seeing Technicolor after a grimy home movie. Partial credit goes to a stellar band that includes the Blasters' Dave Alvin and X's John Doe and D.J. Bonebrake, but primarily it's due to Chris D.'s increased flamboyance. He roars instead of snarling, and his tunes are lively and varied horror-movie stuff. Highlights: "Digging My Grave," "See You in the Boneyard" and "Divine Horseman." For fans of carnival fun houses.

Forever Came Today reverts to a spot about midway between the first two LPs, but it's still riveting. The rudimentary quality of the band matters little when Chris tears into epics of sweaty desperation like "The Wedding Dice" and "Drag My Name in the Mud." **A Hard Road to Follow** features a revamped lineup and is the closest Chris D. has come to a conventional attack. With the group offering its own warped approximation of hard rock, he chews through a fetid batch

of tunes that includes "Life's a Dirty Rat" and the Sam and Dave classic, "I Take What I Want."

After Desjardins turned his attentions to a new band called the Divine Horseman, a Flesh Eaters' best-of record was compiled. It not only contains relevant tracks from all of the albums, but adds a compilation-LP rarity, an alternate version of "Impossible Crime" and the previously unissued "Hard Road to Follow" and "Lake of Burning Fire." [jy]

See also *Divine Horsemen.*

FLESH FOR LULU

Flesh for Lulu (nr/Polydor) 1984
Blue Sisters Swing EP (nr/Hybrid-Statik) 1985
Big Fun City (Caroline) 1985
Long Live the New Flesh (Beggars Banquet-Hughes-Capitol) 1987 ●

The ready adaptability of this Brixton quartet enabled them to rise from the ashes of London's ill-fated Batcave scene—a curious association to begin with, since these mascaraed, leather-clad poseurs are more closely related to old-fashioned rock than gothic grave-robbing. With undisguised superstar aspirations, they signed to Polydor and released two excellent singles ("Restless" and "Subterraneans"). The self-titled album that followed, despite the inclusion of both songs, sinks into the mire, an overlong, overproduced '80s punk take on the Rolling Stones (check the cover of "Jigsaw Puzzle"), making it a commodity not in great current demand.

Retreating to the world of independent labels, Flesh for Lulu released the controversial (some deemed the cover art sacrilegious) **Blue Sisters Swing** EP. An unexpected and most impressive change of course, the five tracks rock with verve and abandon, sometimes approaching heavy metal. Best song title: "I May Have Said You're Beautiful, but You Know I'm Just a Liar."

Big Fun City marks yet another transformation. Though sticking to rock, traces of other musical styles enter the mix: funk, country-western, punk-pop. Still a bunch of vain poseurs, their musical changes don't follow any fashion trends.

Forever the chameleons, Flesh for Lulu did another about-face on their third album, **Long Live the New Flesh**. This time it's quite clear in which direction the band's course is set—toward popular American acceptance.

"I Go Crazy," Flesh for Lulu's contribution to the soundtrack of the film *Some Kind of Wonderful,* generated a lot of radio airplay; the entire LP is similarly tailor-made for American radio. "I Go Crazy" (left off the British edition) and "Siamese Twist" are as adventurous as this record gets; the remainder is homogeneous AOR synth/guitar rock. Although a far cry from **Blue Sisters Swing**, one can assume—considering the band's track record—that this is just another phase they're going through.   [ag]

FLESHTONES

Up-Front EP (IRS) 1980
Roman Gods (IRS) 1981
Blast Off [tape] (ROIR) 1982
Hexbreaker! (IRS) 1983
Speed Connection (Fr. IRS) 1985
Speed Connection II (IRS) 1985
Fleshtones vs. Reality (Emergo) 1987 ●

FULL TIME MEN

Fast Is My Name EP (Coyote) 1985
Your Face My Fist (Coyote-Twin/Tone) 1988

PETER ZAREMBA'S LOVE
DELEGATION

Spread the Word (Moving Target) 1986

VARIOUS ARTISTS

Time Bomb! The Big Bang Theory (Skyclad) 1988

New York's Fleshtones are caught in the common contradiction of selfconsciously seeking to re-create the unselfconsciousness of '60s rock'n'roll, pre-**Sgt. Pepper** and pre-psychedelia. In other words, they've put a lot of thought and effort into becoming a mindless party band. Although the Fleshtones only occasionally fully capture their high spirits in the studio, the payoff is swell when they do.

Up-Front's five-song menu includes a fake surf instrumental and a jumped-up account of the Stones' "Play with Fire." Frontman Peter Zaremba's humorously tough approach comes through loud and clear, but the recording's cleanness borders on aridity.

The Fleshtones take a big leap forward on **Roman Gods** by adding new personality and passion to the beat, as witnessed by "I've Gotta Change My Life" and "Let's See the Sun." However, the album's standout underlines the progress remaining to be made elsewhere: "The World Has Changed" crackles like vintage Yardbirds, making ill-advised ventures such as the cover of Lee Dorsey's "Ride Your Pony" seem all the more unfortunate.

Blast Off dates from abortive 1978 sessions for Red Star Records and succeeds beautifully on its own limited terms. It's raw, noisy and incomplete-sounding—just right for keeping debauchery ongoing, though unsuitable for careful listening.

Hexbreaker! is the Fleshtones' finest record so far, an exuberant collection of memorable numbers made even better by brilliant playing and spot-on production by Richard Mazda. "Right Side of a Good Thing," with its hysterical falsetto chorus; "New Scene," a pulsing fuzz-guitar punk rave-up; and the shingaling title tune all roll with soul and frolic in the sounds of the '60s without ever losing a grip on the band's own identity. An ultimate '80s garage-rock classic.

The only way to live up to that achievement was to do it live, smearing as much sweat and personality on the vinyl as possible. It took two attempts: the first **Speed Connection** was issued in France but deemed inferior to the second, which was recorded at a different 1985 Paris show and released in the US and UK. Although technically casual, **Speed Connection II** is a stupendous, old-fashioned warts'n'all concert record, with all the chaos and frantic rock panache the Fleshtones possess. Especially potent is their brilliantly-titled "Kingsmen Like Medley," as well as "Return to the Haunted House" and "Wind Out," the latter featuring guest guitar by Pete Buck of R.E.M.

Buck also collaborated on Fleshtone axeman Keith Streng's Full Time Men first record, a pleasant but unchallenging trio of slightly retro-minded countryish pop tunes that would have benefited from a more confident vocalist than Streng. Streng released a full Full Time Men album in 1988.

Undeterred by the outside world's lack of interest, the lads continue to pursue party nirvana on a new label with **Fleshtones vs. Reality**. Typically, the results vary, though the high points are sublime: the snarling prehistoric Kinks guitars of "Way Up Here," the raise-the-dead soul fervor of "Whatever Makes You Happy," a swift remake of "Treat Her Like a Lady" and so on. The strain that comes from making what ought to be mass appeal pop-rock without financial success is reflected in the LP title, n'est-ce pas?

Despite relentless good humor, Zaremba's Love Delegation LP (with Streng, a

216

horn section and such guest vocalizers as Barrence Whitfield) illustrates the dangers of unchecked '60s camp revivalism—it sounds more disposable than dynamic. "Turn Me on Again" and Aretha's "Save Me" burn real good, but fluff like "Shama Lama Bing Bang" and a pseudo-heavy remake of "Some Velvet Morning" (ugh) best capture the dippy spirit of the unnecessary **Spread the Word**.

Time Bomb, ostensibly a various artists compilation, features variously permutated side projects by Fleshtones and their pals, along with non-LP tracks from the band proper. Love Delegation, Full Time Men, Action Combo, Cryin' Out Loud, Mad Violets and Wild Hyenas all toss in OK cuts, but the disc really catches fire on Action Dogs' sizzling "I Can't Get Through to You," starring Peter Case, and the mothergroup's "I Was a Teenage Zombie," from the film of the same name. Not great, but fun.   [jy/iar]

FLIPPER
Album—Generic Flipper (Subterranean) 1982
Blow'n Chunks [tape] (ROIR) 1984
Gone Fishin' (Subterranean) 1984
Public Flipper Limited Live 1980–1985
   (Subterranean) 1986
Sex Bomb Baby! (Subterranean) 1988
ANY THREE INITIALS
Ruins of America (Subterranean) 1988

Like a 45 slowed down to sub-LP pace, San Francisco's Flipper delivers a flawless impression of a downed-out hardcore band. The harsh music lumbers and creaks, oozing feedback all the way, while the singer (bassist Will Shatter or bassist—yes, that's right—Bruce Lose) moans and shouts painfully. Flipper could be your car on the verge of a total breakdown or your worst hangover nightmare amped up to brain-splitting volume. And yet, for all the intentional sloppiness and gratuitous noise, not to mention the superficial shock of **Album** tunes like "Life Is Cheap" and "Shed No Tears," Flipper can be uplifting. Underneath the tumult you'll find compassion, idealism and hope, best represented by "Life" ("the only thing worth living for"). That kind of moral statement takes courage.

Blow'n Chunks is a primo live tape of the band onstage in New York, November 1983. Playing all the hits that made them a legend—like "Love Canal" and "Ha Ha Ha"—as well as previewing some songs that made it onto the next LP, the quartet drones along

like a factory shutting down for the weekend, a stunning roar of guitar noise and bass pounding that is simply the ultimate loud rock'n'roll imaginable. A real classic album, and the ideal floor-clearer for any club.

Flipper's second studio album, **Gone Fishin'**, makes an ambitious effort to add unexpected sonic components to the din. With vocals taking a clearly predominant role, oddities like clavinet, sax, piano and even open spaces (!?!?) lurk around, while newly sophisticated rhythms (as on the consti/syncopated "First the Heart") and a relatively restrained mix make Flipper resemble a "normal" band at times. If all you want from Flipper is a visceral thrill, try the live tape; if you want to understand their creative mind, **Gone Fishin'** is the ideal synthesis of sickness and health.

Perhaps sensing that stages held the key to truest Flipperhood, the band's next release was the two-record career-spanning concert compilation, **Public Flipper Limited**. (The PiL parody here is revenge for that group's apparent appropriation of Flipper's generic labelling concept for their 1986 **Album**.) Wrapped in a foldout poster-cum-"Flipper on Tour" game, the LP offers a fine selection of tracks, from "Love Canal" to "Sex Bomb" to "Life" to "Flipper Blues." (Locales include San Francisco, New York, Toronto, Washington, DC and Los Angeles.) The obnoxious onstage patter only adds to the mind-boggling raucous entertainment.

Shatter's death in December 1987 (from a heroin overdose) ended Flipper's on-again-off-again existence once and for all, but didn't stanch the vinyl flow. The **Sex Bomb Baby!** compilation unites all of Flipper's singles (six sides) and tracks from sampler albums, going as far back as the group's 1979 recorded debut on Subterranean's first release, the **SF Underground** collection. The cassette adds three live tracks from the 1980 **Live at Target** compilation; limited quantities of the album contain Bruce Lose's solo single as a bonus.

Any Three Initials, a Shatter side project, was recorded in 1986. Joined by three local musicians (two from the band Bad Posture), Shatter is the lyricist and singer on A3I's **Ruins of America**, a varied album of country music, dirge-rock, PiL-esque anti-pop and other related styles, with subject matter as diverse as meteoric conditions and humanist philosophy. When the going gets rough, the ghost of Flipper rises from the platter; other tracks might be by anybody *but* that group.

Shatter and Flipper drummer Steve De-Pace were in a pre-Flipper band called Negative Trend, which released several EPs, including one (**We Don't Play, We Riot**, recorded in 1978) on Subterranean.

[jy/iar]

FLOAT UP CP

Kill Me in the Morning (Upside) 1985

Float Up CP's album lacks the diversity of the band's predecessor, Rip Rig + Panic. The material is straightforward funk/soul/jazz, with the rough edges left intact in just the right places. The real star is Neneh Cherry (daughter of avant-jazz trumpeter Don Cherry) who sings up a storm, even when the sexual metaphors ("Chemically Wet," "Joy's Address") get a bit trite. The band chugs along behind her with energy and panache, but there's nothing unique or catchy enough on **Kill Me in the Morning** to make a lasting impression. [dgs]

ROSIE FLORES

See *Screamin' Sirens!*.

KLAUS FLOURIDE

See *Dead Kennedys*.

FLOWERS

See *Icehouse*.

FLOY JOY

Into the Hot (nr/Virgin) 1984

Following his dance-music muse, Don Was produced this English trio's debut LP, giving it a full-blown wash of horns, synthesized strings and other high-tech keys to commercial success. Carroll Thompson has a swell, big voice; her two compatriots—the brothers Ward (with assistance from illustrious guests, including Yogi Horton and Monsieur Was)—churn out the music they wrote with ease and style. On a contextual note, however, the band's kicky name and kitsch artwork aside, it's hard to discern how this differs from a hundred other mainstream/radio-minded records by talented black singers. [iar]

FLUX OF PINK INDIANS

Strive to Survive Causing Least Suffering
Possible (nr/Spiderleg) 1982 (nr/One
Little Indian) 1987

The Fucking Cunts Treat Us Like Pricks
(nr/Spiderleg) 1984 (nr/One Little Indian)
1987

FLUX

The Uncarved Block (nr/One Little Indian)
1986 ●

Instead of the near-illiterate (and proud of it) hedonistic roughneckism of some hardcore outfits, this quartet (originally on a Crass-affiliated label) is one of the semi-intellectual, fiercely political bands who use punk-style rock as a medium for their strong leftist and/or anarchist views. Also similarly, Flux's packaging standards are impressive—the first LP boasts a twelve-page graphics-packed booklet enclosed in a dignified gatefold jacket.

The band has a good deal of punchy precision to its crisp drumming and distorto-chord guitar. The catch is that it's all sort of military, as in the way the tuneless vocals resemble the bark of a drill instructor. Like the graphics, these "melodies" and lyrics (not to mention the politics) are all black and white, and aside from the sterility inherent in preaching to the converted, Flux's monochromatic asceticism is ultimately quite numbing. [jg]

FLYBOYS

See *Choir Invisible*.

FLYING COLOR

Flying Color (Grifter-Frontier) 1987

Though hardly revivalist, the first LP by this Bay Area quartet abounds with unrepentant Beatlephilia, with generous servings of ringing choruses, exquisite guitar splashes and endearingly ragged harmonies. Sweetly stunning sensitive-but-not-wimpy pop-rock items like "Dear Friend" and "One Saturday" stand out, but Flying Color is equally adept with rock songs ("I'm Your Shadow," "Believe Believe"). Unfortunately, guitarist Richard Chase—author and singer of the memorably melancholic "It Doesn't Matter" and "Bring Back the Rain"—jumped ship shortly after this album was finished. Here's hoping his departure won't keep Flying Color from fulfilling the promise of this debut. [hd]

FLYING LIZARDS

The Flying Lizards (Virgin) 1979
Fourth Wall (nr/Virgin) 1981
Top Ten (nr/Statik) 1984

DAVID CUNNINGHAM

Grey Scale (nr/Piano) 1980

Led by pianist David Cunningham, the Flying Lizards started as (and largely continued to be) a novelty group that took classic rock songs and reduced them to parody with neo-Kraftwerk synthesizer minimalism and robotic deadpan vocal readings (as epitomized on the eponymous debut album by "Summertime Blues" and "Money"). The serious work shows Cunningham leaning toward the arty high-tech drone of Tangerine Dream, though, and that suffers from comparison with the inspired lunacy of the comedy turns.

Fourth Wall attempts to evolve a happy medium, with helpers including New Yorkers Pat Palladin and Peter Gordon and new-jazz artist Steve Beresford. Cunningham moves uneasily between electro-pop and trance music (as in Steve Reich and Philip Glass). Well-produced and interesting as individual songs, but it fails to jell as an album.

He attempts strictly serious music on **Grey Scale**, improvising on the piano by allowing the course of the music to be altered by random outside events. Though the technique derives from John Cage, the result falls closer to Reich and Terry Riley.

Following a long layoff, the Lizards returned in 1984 with **Top Ten**, another wacky album of demented rock'n'roll revisionism, this time assaulting the songwriting of Little Richard, Jimi Hendrix, James Brown, Leonard Cohen, Larry Williams and others. Purists and musical conservatives will find this impossible; keep an open mind and forget about the originals, and you'll be amazed at Cunningham's arcane wit and inventive dissection/reconstruction skill. Play this loud at your next party and watch the fun start!

[sg/iar]

FLYIN' SPIDERZ

The Flyin' Spiderz (Hol. EMI) 1977
Let It Crawl (Hol. Bovema Negram) 1978

These four erratic Dutchmen, led by rhythm guitarist/singer/songwriter Guus Boers, put forth solid, Stonesy punk just a hair better than a hundred others of like mind, threatening to turn derivation to their advantage but never quite succeeding. Neither album shows more than fleeting signs of excitement, and neither has better than perfunctory production.

Boers' declamatory vocals are often let down by his banal lyrics (the best are complaints about cramped housing and nosy groupies), but how frustrating it all is when out of the blue they turn around and serve up a track like **Let It Crawl**'s "Paper Girl," which sounds for all the world like an outtake from **Between the Buttons** or **Flowers**. Sigh. [jg]

FLYS

Waikiki Beach Refugees (nr/EMI) 1978
Own (nr/EMI) 1979

Although they neither dressed the part nor were tied down by its musical clichés, Coventry's Flys (not to be confused with a subsequent Boston outfit) used the feel of mod-era bands like the Who and Creation as a jumping-off point for the highly individual songs of guitarist/singer Neil O'Connor. **Waikiki Beach Refugees** is one of those minor masterpieces that passed unnoticed, probably because it preceded the full-scale mod revival (by months). Nevertheless, the songs are beautifully contructed, O'Connor's jangling 12-string meshing with Rob Freeman's power chords to create a brilliant metallic sound. The best songs—"We Don't Mind the Rave," "Don't Moonlight on Me" and "I Don't Know"—express both the bravado and confusion of adolescence with a rare eye for detail.

Own is, by contrast, rather bland. The songs, co-written by O'Connor and Freeman, lack the urgency of those on the first album. Not bad, mind you, but a letdown from the expectations the previous outing engendered.

[ds]

FOETUS
YOU'VE GOT FOETUS ON YOUR BREATH

Deaf (nr/Self Immolation) 1981
Ache (nr/Self Immolation) 1982

SCRAPING FOETUS OFF THE WHEEL

Hole (Self Immolation-ZE-PVC) 1984
Nail (Self Immolation-Some
  Bizzare-Homestead) 1985 ●
Ramrod (nr/Some Bizzare) 1987

FOETUS ALL-NUDE REVIEW

Bedrock EP (Self Immolation-Some
  Bizzare-Relativity) 1987

WISEBLOOD

Dirtdish (K.422-Some Bizzare-Relativity) 1987
Yank 'em Crank 'em Don't Stick Around to
  Thank 'em [tape] (nr/K.422-Some Bizzare)
  1987

FOETUS INTERRUPTUS

Thaw (nr/Self Immolation-Some Bizzare) 1988

Thank goodness for rock'n'roll—otherwise, what excuse would there be for people like Jim Thirlwell (aka Clint Ruin, aka Frank Want, aka Scraping Foetus off the Wheel, aka Foetus Over Frisco, aka Phillip and His Foetus Vibrations, aka You've Got Foetus on Your Breath, aka Foetus Art of Terrorism, etc.)? Although undeniably talented, it's virtually impossible to pin down just what the Anglo-Australian (now a New Yorker) does; suffice to say his projects are all characterized by violence, rudeness, irreverence, abrasion, unpredictability and an incredible grasp of music-making's never-ending possibilities to disturb.

The only thing to do with **Hole** is jump in and pray you survive. The LP (the US edition of which adds a retrospective bonus disc of previous issue) has a little of everything: industrial cacophony ("Clothes Hoist"), high political drama ("I'll Meet You in Poland, Baby"), spare crypto-blues ("Sick-Man"), demented surf music ("Satan Place"), something sick built on a swing beat ("Water Torture"), the *Batman* theme and lots more. Played at a confusion level that makes Christmas Eve at K-Mart seem placid, the cadences would make Test Dept. proud and the lyrics might upset Frank Zappa. Simply put, you've never heard *anything* like this before.

Nail is another delicious voyage into Foetus' crazed imagination. From the soundtrack-styled opening ("Theme from Pigdom Come"), through a generally cinematized concept collection of high-octane rants—sort of Birthday Party with a sense of humor meets latter-day Pink Floyd—Foetus goes about his usual business, layering sound on sound, insult on injury. An apparently nonexistent instrumental entitled "!" is the LP's definitive existential high point, but such vehement audio orgies as "The Throne of Agony" and the '40s-jazzy "Descent into the Inferno" provide plenty of clever lyrical competition.

The title track of **Bedrock** (most assuredly not about Fred and Wilma's hometown) fills one side of the EP and plays at 45 rpm; the four crunching rants on the back run at 33. "Diabolus Musica" and "Shut" are really one slow-starting instrumental that revs up to noise concrète (complete with machine guns, metallic clangs and animal noises) strong enough to peel layers off a boulder at a hundred paces; meanwhile, the vituperative and deliciously vulgar "Bedrock" (and its alternate take, "Bedrock Strip") is a guttural Tom Waits-like swing rap sneered over acoustic bass and bongos. One version adds horns and a backing chorus; both feature an industrial-strength rusty-door guitar solo.

Wiseblood is a duo of Clint Ruin and ex-Swan Roli Mosimann, assisted on **Dirtdish** by Robert Quine, Hahn Rowe (of Hugo Largo), Norman Westberg and Phoebe Legere. While the pair shares music writing chores, thereby diluting Foetus' awesome power, leaving Ruin in charge of words and vocals ensures that the familiar growled litany of sexually-charged insanity will be as damaging to the psyche as ever. (What does "The Fudge Punch" suggest to you?) So if the LP lacks a full load of explosive Foetus audio dynamite, there's more than enough ugliness and venom here to obliterate a roomful of hoodlums.

Yank 'em Crank 'em is the cassette-only soundtrack to a live Wiseblood video. [iar]

ELLEN FOLEY

Spirit of St. Louis (Cleveland Int'l) 1981

Ellen Foley made other solo albums after gaining fame in the performing company of Meat Loaf, but this one is very different. It was produced by "my boyfriend"—in this case and at this point Mick Jones of the Clash—and features his band in toto plus its musical associates (Tymon Dogg, Mickey Gallagher, etc.) as her accompaniment. Additionally, half the songs are new (and otherwise unissued) Strummer/Jones compositions; three others are Dogg's. Coming right after the loose, throwaway feel of **Sandinista!**, Jones did an about-face and created precious arty backing that strains Foley's vocal talent beyond endurance. Her interpretive abilities disappear under the weight of such screamingly pretentious tripe as "The Death of the Psychoanalyst of Salvador Dali." (*What* books were those boys reading?) A bizarre Clash footnote. [wk/iar]

FONTANA MIX

The Noise Spiral (nr/Compact Organization) 1984

An eccentric but musically responsible duo (mainly Michael Atavar) which blends the sensibility of Eno's early work (among many other stylistic avenues) with bizarre near-dada subjects/lyrics. Fontana Mix use synths and guitars to produce oddly-embroidered songs that are neither too weird for normals nor overly mundane for those who demand fringeness. (The band bills the LP as "nine chill splinters of unreality.") Mostly whimsical, occasionally serious, **The Noise Spiral** offers charming moments, witty turns and amazing treats. Fascinating and entertaining. [iar]

DREDD FOOLE AND THE DIN
Eat My Dust Cleanse My Soul [tape]
    (Religious) 1984 (Homestead) 1985
Take. off Your Skin (PVC) 1987

Pseudonymous singer Dredd Foole (Dan Ireton) was a longtime friend and musical associate of the late Mission of Burma; the Bostonian borrowed that group, redubbed it the Din and had it back him on an early 45. Volcano Suns—a Burma offshoot—fulfilled the same role on **Eat My Dust**, originally released on cassette but reissued on vinyl. Recorded live to two-track and including covers of the Doors' "People Are Strange," the Animals' "I'm Crying" and Iggy's "I Got a Right," the LP reveals Foole to be a tuneless bellower; his wobbly marble-mouthisms fit strangely with the skillfully-played demi-punk garage music. Enthusiasm may not be a problem, but melody sure is.

Take off Your Skin, which uses the same Din (Peter Prescott, Jon Williams and Jeff Weigand of Volcano Suns, plus guitarist Kenny Chambers), manages to make something more listenable out of Ireton's devolved oral emissions. By noising up the music and harnessing a more controlled singing style, the LP hits a workable—almost Crampsian—equilibrium that's plug ugly but bracing in its forceful post-punk courage. [iar]

FOOLS
Sold Out (EMI America) 1980
Heavy Mental (EMI America) 1981
World Dance Party (PVC) 1985
Wake Up . . . It's Alive!!! (PVC) 1988 ●

After an auspiciously flip debut—"Psycho Chicken," the hysterical barnyard parody of Talking Heads' "Psycho Killer"—Boston's Fools proved to be neither funny (intentionally or otherwise) nor musically enthralling on either **Sold Out** or **Heavy Men-**

tal, despite the best efforts of accomplished producers (Pete Solley and Vini Poncia, respectively). After several years of national-scene silence, the Fools returned with **World Dance Party** in 1985, sporting a half-new lineup and a bit of sunny cowpoke vapidity called "Life Sucks . . . Then You Die."

The club-rocking live album, recorded in Boston in early 1987 by the same humorless but competent quartet, includes terrible versions of "Mack the Knife" and "The Sound [sic] of Silence" along with equally enthralling originals, almost none drawn from prior albums. [iar]

FOOLS FACE
Here to Observe (Bar-Co) 1979
Tell America (Talk) 1981
Public Places (Talk) 1983
The Red Tape [tape] (Fools Face) 1984

Hailing from Springfield, Missouri, this raucous bunch combined the rough-and-tumble appeal of an ace bar band with diverse pop songwriting talent. Everyone in the quintet except the drummer wrote *and* sang, with roots from the Stones and Beatles to soft pop, Little Richard, Led Zeppelin and Bowie.

Here to Observe is an irrepressible low-budget debut that shows how a band can get and hold a listener's attention (by expending nonstop energy). **Tell America** finds Fools Face overdue for major-label exposure, with enthusiasm now matched by sophisticated melodies, rich harmonies and razor-sharp musicianship. Highlights include "American Guilt" and "L5," a science-fiction fantasy.

Public Places is more of the same: a slick and sophisticated major-league-quality album of flawless high-voltage melodic rock still on the band's own label. Reduced to a quartet, the so-called **Red Tape** is an untitled cassette-only album issued just to fans, containing eight excellent new songs with a more aggressive rock sound underneath the same attractive pop melodicism. In late 1984, Fools Face relocated to Los Angeles and later disbanded. [jy/iar]

FOR AGAINST
Echelons (Independent Project) 1987

For Against are one of the best new bands America has produced in the last two or three years, a secret the US new music public has yet to discover. The problem is that they hail from the unlikely mecca of Lincoln, Nebraska, and neither a brilliant 1985 debut "Autocrat" single nor a 1987 tour to support **Echelons** has changed that.

A trio obviously influenced by the UK post-Joy Division sound, For Against add their own distinct ripple. Singer Jeffrey Runnings' frantic bass and Greg Hill's charging drums are unusual for such atmospheric music. Yet all through **Echelons**, the echoed sound of guitarist Harry Dingman arouses—incendiary shards of guitar sparks, a berserk fireworks show, careening like a thousand power drills. Pin it to the non-stop rhythm section and Runnings' boyishly sweet catchy pop voice, and For Against are a waterfall of sound. When the tempo slows down, they draw you in like a hypnotist, as on the tantalizing six-minute closer, "Broke My Back." Such textural sound, vision and might is not to be missed. [jr]

FORCE M.D.'S

Love Letters (Tommy Boy) 1984
Chillin' (Tommy Boy) 1985 ●
Touch and Go (Tommy Boy) 1987 ●

This stylish clean-cut quintet from Staten Island, New York sets classic black vocal-group harmonies to a streetwise hip-hop beat. They rap occasionally, but even with the old Sugar Hill rhythm section providing backing on **Love Letters**, they're too sugary to throw down with much authority; their strength is an ability to wrap five fresh voices around a romantic ballad. On tracks like "Tears," "Let Me Love You" and "Forgive Me Girl," the infectious hooks and falsetto crooning defeat all critical cynicism. Elsewhere, the battle isn't so one-sided. Less cloying but also a little less talented than New Edition, the Force M.D.'s have tamed the beat-box without yet establishing an entirely credible identity or a consistent sound.

Chillin', the first record to be distributed by Warner Bros. under a deal with Tommy Boy, made the Force M.D.'s a major commercial entity, and with good reason. From the ridiculous rap of "Force M.D.'s Meet the Fat Boys" (partially sung to the melody of "Gilligan's Island" and guest-starring the tubby three) to the catchy, falsetto-over-scratch-beats title track, the versatile M.D.'s mix credible urban savvy with enough smooth showbiz to please hard beatboys and mature soul fans alike. "Tender Love," a hit single from the Jimmy Jam/Terry Lewis hit

factory is spectacularly heart-rending; "One Plus One" and "Uh Oh!" are perfectly charming New Edition-styled pop with a bigger drum sound; "Walking on Air" might be mistaken for an O'Jays standard. (Anti-sexism footnote: the album was produced, arranged and mixed by a woman, talented T-Boy house producer Robin Halpin.)

Aided by a different production squad on each track, a more mature and sophisticated four-man Force M.D.'s slides completely into a smooth romantic Philly soul groove on **Touch and Go**. Silly gimmicks are nowhere to be found; all but the final vestiges of hip-hop have been erased in favor of slow-tempo easy-listening mainstream acceptability. Tinged with a hint of Prince, the delicate falsettos and close harmony arrangements work with the polite, melodic backing for a lightweight delight. [jl/iar]

FORGOTTEN REBELS

This Ain't Hollywood . . . (Can. Star) 1983
In Love with the System (Can. Star) 1984
The Pride and the Disgrace (Can. Other
     People's Music) 1985
Surfin' on Heroin (Restless) 1988

CHRIS HOUSTON WITH THE SEX MACHINE

Hate Filled Man (Can. Caucasian) 1986

Ridiculous but fun, these Ontario glam punks lead off their first LP with a buzz-saw version of Gary Glitter's "Hello Hello" and then blast a perfect merseybeat melody into the Ramonized present. Elsewhere, they cover "Eve of Destruction," go "Surfin' on Heroin" and vent their frustration about the balance of rock trade in "England Keep Yer Stars." Throughout, singer Mickey DeSadist fights off an overactive echo chamber as the other three Rebels pound out efficient wall-of-guitar punk.

The second LP finds the revamped Rebels in a much more aggressive mood, cursing a lot and resembling Sham 69 on shoutalong choruses like "Bomb the Boats and Feed the Fish" and the title track. In spots, DeSadist affects an outdated Johnny Rotten voice; the subject matter is similarly well-trod: "Rich and Bored," "Elvis Is Dead," "The Punks Are Alright" (rewriting the Who's "Kids Are Alright"). Also, the playing is fancier, with dynamics and arrangements that often resemble early Clash. It's a weird mixture: pop-punk/straight punk. Not very inventive, but a highly enjoyable throwback.

A new gang of Rebels (DeSadist and guitarist Mike Mirabella are still in attendance) cropped up in 1988 with an American album containing all-new recordings of previously-released songs. **Surfin' on Heroin** retreads "Bomb the Boats," "Elvis Is Dead," "I'm in Love with the System" and others, adding a couple of topical new compositions (like "A.I.D.S.") for good measure. The vibrant, loud punk-rock sound recalls the Dead Boys or Generation X; low-brow/high-energy songwriting that crosses the Monkees with the Ramones gives the Rebels a solid basis for their polite blow-torch assault. If a total lack of originality can be excused, **Surfin' on Heroin** is a big fun date. But who played the organ?

Bassist Chris Houston—who went under the name Pogo Aù Go Go on **In Love with the System**—put his own version of "Surfin' on Heroin" on **Hate Filled Man**, a solo outing following his departure from the Rebels. [iar]

45 GRAVE
Sleep in Safety (Enigma) 1983
Autopsy (Restless) 1987 ●

Acknowledged kings of the California ghoul-rock school, LA's 45 Grave take a gloomy approach far less interesting than the flip swamp stylings of East Coast creatures like the Cramps. Playing with punky venom and a slick metallic sound, the fearsome fivesome was led by Phoenix-bred guitarist Paul Cutler, who has become a well-regarded record producer and left to join Dream Syndicate in 1986. The songs on **Sleep in Safety** have titles like "Evil" and "Violent Love" and sound like junior Black Sabbath/Kiss with a female singer and no mindless devotion to guitar solos. Why this is appealing to young people I do not know. [iar]

See also *Dream Syndicate, Thelonious Monster.*

4-SKINS
The Good, the Bad & the 4-Skins (nr/Secret) 1982
A Fistful of 4-Skins (nr/Syndicate) 1983
From Chaos to 1984 (nr/Syndicate) 1984

There hasn't been a recorded concert as powerful as Side Two of **The Good, the Bad & the 4-Skins** since the MC5's immortal **Kick Out the Jams**. This smokes! One of the leading Oi!/hardcore bands, the 4-Skins play

with impressive force and anger. The studio side is more structured and therefore less intense, but it's still several notches above most of the Skins' contemporaries. [cpl]

KIM FOWLEY
Sunset Boulevard (PVC) 1978
Snake Document Masquerade (1980–1989) (Antilles) 1979

Kim Fowley is less important for what he's done than what he gets away with. Once described as "the king of rock'n'roll pimps," Fowley is a master manipulator of artists and creator—as writer/producer/entrepreneur—of hit records that are both crassly commercial and smugly subversive. Fowley first scored big in 1960 with the million-selling "Alley Oop," by the Hollywood Argyles. His career in the '70s involved orchestrating the careers of the Runaways, Quick, Orchids and Venus and the Razorblades; in more recent years he has successfully infiltrated the MOR world, working with Helen Reddy and Steel Breeze. In Fowley's defense, he *was* the first person to record Jonathan Richman and the Modern Lovers.

Fowley periodically used to convince record companies to issue his own solo records. Over a dozen albums—ranging from psychedelic organ instrumentals to passable glitter pop—have been released since 1967, although he has refrained from making a new one for some time. **Sunset Boulevard**, like many of his records, is consumed with Hollywood pop decadence. Fowley's minimal singing talent—more like dry sing-speak dripping with cynicism—doesn't stop him from essaying a long Springsteenish piano ballad called "Black Camels of Lavender Hill" or copying the Music Explosion in his own song "Control."

Snake Document Masquerade (does that sound like a Captain Beefheart title or what?) is his twisted idea of a new wave concept album, a vision of '80s pop apocalypse that gets by on sheer audacity. Musically, it's a limp mélange of disco, reggae, punk-funk and electronic meditations distinguished by the spacey rap "1985: Physical Lies" (modeled on his own 1966 acid-rap hit, "The Trip") and robot sex fantasy "1988: Searchin' for a Human in Tight Blue Jeans."

There's plenty more where that came from: the paisley gimmickry of his 1967 LP debut, **Love Is Alive and Well**, **Outrageous** (1967; cheap Steppenwolf imitations) and the punkier **Animal God of the Streets** (1979). His **International Heroes** (1973) features the near-hit single of the same title, a clever variation on "All the Young Dudes." [df]

See also *Quick, Runaways, Venus and the Razorblades.*

BRUCE FOXTON

Touch Sensitive (Arista) 1984

Although he was one-third of an ultra-successful band, Foxton had to relaunch his career virtually from ground zero after Paul Weller bagged the Jam in 1982. Surprisingly, the bassist's first solo album is quite good, and happily free of any attempt to recapture the sound which made him a star. With a four-man band and a bunch of guests, Foxton sings and plays ten original tunes in a number of styles, from busy dance-rock to wistful big-production pop. Throughout, he adapts his bluff voice as best he can; ingenuous earnestness is a strong suit. The lyrics regularly mention loss, individual responsibility and uncertainty—it's obvious the Jam's end was a traumatic experience—but **Touch Sensitive** is a promising new beginning for a sincere, talented performer. [iar]

JOHN FOXX

Metamatic (nr/Metal Beat-Virgin) 1980
John Foxx (Can. Virgin) 1981
The Garden (nr/Metal Beat-Virgin) 1981
The Golden Section (nr/Metal Beat-Virgin) 1983
In Mysterious Ways (nr/Metal Beat-Virgin) 1985

After three albums as lead vocalist, John Foxx left Ultravox to pursue a solo career. A prime factor in the group's original sound, Foxx was, by extension, a major influence on the new romantic movement that followed in its wake. Fortunately, both Ultravox and Foxx solo continued to make music of quality and distinction.

Metamatic is Foxx's first venture alone into the world of synthesizers, Ultravox's subsequent instrument of choice. In emulation of his own work and Conny Plank's production on Ultravox's **Systems of Romance**, Foxx finds the perfect counterpart for his themes of alienation and dislocation in sterile, minimalist electronic sounds. His vocals are oddly distant, like echoes, but the record has an honesty and directness that are quite affecting. (**John Foxx** is a Canadian compila-

tion that rearranges a number of songs from **Metamatic**.)

The Garden is a lush, thick paean to Foxx's catholicism and the mysticism that has always lurked beneath his austere urbanity. Pastoral in tone, the album flourishes under a denser sound, replete with acoustic instruments that offset the onslaught of synthesizers. Foxx's themes remain the same, which is good, and his songwriting and flair for imagery reach new peaks on masterpieces like "Europe After the Rain" and "Walk Away," which provide melancholic views of familiar, mysterious worlds.

Co-produced by Foxx and the seemingly ubiquitous Zeus B. Held, **The Golden Section** has a bizarrely Beatlesque sound on several tracks, mildly resembling the Fab Four's later takes on psychedelia. Foxx is his usual enigmatic, inventive self, spinning moody creations that neatly sidestep synthesizer clichés; the only flaw is in his dramatic vocals. Previously released as a single, "Endlessly" is the album's clear standout, a magnificent multi-level pop creation that parallels Foxx's former group's development while clearly displaying a character all his own. The cassette version has six extra tracks. [sg/iar]

FRANK CHICKENS

We Are Frank Chickens (nr/Kaz) 1984
The Best of Frank Chickens [CD] (nr/Kaz) 1987
Get Chickenized (nr/Flying Lecords) 1987

Frank Chickens are a pair of Japanese women (Kazuko Hohki, Kazumi Taguchi) who are both proud of and amused by their country's diverse cultural contributions to the world. On one hand, the debut album pays tribute to Ninja warriors and emotional Enka ballads, but they also sing with mock reverence on "Mothra," named for a classic low-budget monster movie. Lyrics and liner notes are both hilarious and/or absurd (see "Shellfish Bamboo"). Musically mixing synth-pop (created in the main by the writing/production team of Steve Beresford and David Toop) with funk and jazz, the Chickens also incorporate Japanese musical traditions along the way. Guest musicians include Annie Whitehead and Lol Coxhill. Very entertaining.

Taguchi became an ex-Chicken and was replaced by Atsuko Kamura prior to the sophomore **Get Chickenized** LP. Lyrics are even more preposterously campy than before, this time dealing mostly with observations of, and experiences with, Western culture. "Yellow Toast" concerns being a hip but exploited flavor-of-the-month in England: "You think we are full of Zen/But we prefer lots of yen/We are stupid little Japs/And you are splendid English chaps." Other tracks are not as bitter and sarcastic as that, instead addressing subjects ranging from nonsensical Japanese lessons to female wrestling. The 15-track CD-only **Best of Frank Chickens** is perhaps a little premature, drawing from the debut LP and early 45s. [dgs]

FRANKIE GOES TO HOLLYWOOD

Welcome to the Pleasuredome (ZTT-Island) 1984 ●
Liverpool (ZTT-Island) 1986 ●

In one of rock history's most spectacular hype jobs (certainly the greatest since McLaren first perpetrated the Pistols swindle), Frankie Goes to Hollywood—a minor outfit with its origins in the watershed '70s Liverpool scene—became a highly controversial and enormously successful band in 1984, thanks to the combined talents of producer Trevor Horn and critic-turned-propagandist Paul Morley, via their ZTT label. The blatant homoerotica of "Relax" got Frankie banned on English radio while the leather-bar setting of its accompanying video earned them similar turndowns on television. "Two Tribes," an inchoate condemnation of the superpowers for the nuclear threat, complete with thundering dancebeat, continued the band's phenomenal, if inexplicable, rise. Having reached dizzying heights via what seemed like dozens of remixes of the two songs, all that remained for the icon of a million clever T-shirts was to record an album. And (thanks to the uncredited musical skills of former Ian Dury sidemen, it was later revealed) make one—or, more precisely, two—they did.

Welcome to the Pleasuredome has four sides of the Frankies in all their artificial/superficial glory. From the hits (the two pre-LP singles plus "War" and "Welcome to the Pleasuredome") to the pits ("Ferry Cross the Mersey," "Do You Know the Way to San Jose," "The Power of Love"), Frankie say, "We may not be able to do it ourselves, but when you care enough you get the very best to cover for us." A brilliant load of bullshit, served with as much panache—marketing and musical—as the 1980s can muster.

It proved increasingly difficult for the pseudo-group to even appear to work together harmoniously, and the prospects of a second album seemed, for a time, remote. Nonetheless, **Liverpool** was eventually cobbled together and issued: eight long songs that mimic the sound but possess none of the Oz-like glory that was Frankie.

With the golden goose laying nothing but plastic, the group's reason for continuing to exist disappeared and singer Holly Johnson moved to go solo, leading to an altogether embarrassing court dispute over contracts and the like. [iar]

FREIHEIT

See *Munchener Freiheit.*

FRENCH, FRITH, KAISER, THOMPSON

See *Henry Kaiser.*

FREUR

Doot—Doot (Epic) 1983
Get Us Out of Here (nr/CBS) 1985

UNDERWORLD

Underneath the Radar (Sire) 1988 ●

An insular and intentionally remote British art-pop band, Freur was originally identified only by an unpronounceable squiggle in lieu of a name. The gimmicky hubbub quickly subsided, leaving it clear that **Doot—Doot** contained only one truly memorable track—the title song, four magnificent minutes of lilting, haunting synthesizer ambience with quirky vocals and choral backing.

The quintet faded from sight after a second Freur album met with even less response, but four-fifths of it stayed together and returned in 1988 as the Underworld, an enigmatic but more commercially-geared organization. Rupert Hine's production of **Underneath the Radar** gave it a sturdy dance backbone and the familiar sound of late-'80s British techno-beat. (Think of Heaven 17 leaning towards the Thompson Twins.) A shade above average—although Karl Hyde's vocals here aren't very appealing—with more ideas and invention than one ordinarily expects, but still nothing to compare with the participants' one extraordinary item. [iar]

ROBERT FRIPP

Exposure (EG-Polydor) 1979 (Editions EG) 1985 ●

God Save the Queen/Under Heavy Manners
(EG-Polydor) 1980
Let the Power Fall (Editions EG) 1981 ●
The League of Gentlemen (EG-Polydor) 1981
+ 1985
Network EP (nr/EG) 1985

ROBERT FRIPP/THE LEAGUE OF GENTLEMEN
God Save the King (Editions EG) 1985 ●

ROBERT FRIPP AND THE LEAGUE OF CRAFTY GUITARISTS
Robert Fripp & the League of Crafty
Guitarists Live! (Editions EG) 1986 ●

TOYAH & FRIPP
The Lady or the Tiger (Editions EG) 1986

In the last half of a seven-year hiatus between King Crimsons, Robert Fripp—self-styled thinking-man's musician and guitarist's guitarist—played axeman/producer to the stars (David Bowie, Peter Gabriel, Blondie, Talking Heads, Brian Eno, Hall and Oates, the Roches) and contemporaneously cut a series of solo LPs reflecting his then-current obsessions.

The loosely autobiographical **Exposure** is the closest Fripp has come to a pop effort, with guest vocals by Gabriel, Daryl Hall, Peter Hammill and Terre Roche. Interlarded with tape-loop guitar episodes and enigmatic spoken-word communiqués from several sources, the record manages to overcome the self-referential preciousness inherent in such an enterprise—but just barely.

God Save the Queen/Under Heavy Manners offers two concepts for the price of one; both, unfortunately, are flops. The first half gets "Frippertronics" off to a bad start with a suite of samey, lackluster performances. It was Eno who showed Fripp this two-tape-recorder strategy that allows accumulation of rich textures. In performance, Fripp would build towering edifices of looped guitar sound and then spin stunning lead solos over them. The loops remained on tape; the solos didn't, thus the best parts of the concerts that produced **God Save the Queen** never made it onto the record. **Under Heavy Manners**, Fripp's first stab at "discotronics" (his version of dance-oriented rock) sounds less austere than impoverished, despite a memorable David Byrne vocal.

The next pair of LPs, continuing Fripp's self-appointed "Drive to 1981," gamely picked up the pieces. **Let the Power Fall** continues the Frippertronics methodology of **God Save the Queen**; although both were recorded during the same 1979 tour, this album's loops provide a far greater wealth of sounds, moods and ideas—Fripp's editing skills evidently having improved with time. However, several bootlegs documenting Frippertronics with the leads intact remain definitive, as much as Fripp may detest them.

Harnessing himself and keyboardist Barry Andrews (ex-XTC) to an adequate rhythm section (that included future Gang of Four bassist Sara Lee), Fripp's League of Gentlemen band/tour/LP firmly established Fripp's dance-rock territory. A typical League cut took a simple medium-to-fast backbeat over which Fripp and Andrews locked horns, with melodic development emerging slowly, surely, subtly. On the tour, Fripp played marvelous leads; on the LP, they are replaced by spoken-word in-jokes. **God Save the King** is a revised, remixed, remastered single-disc distillation of **Under Heavy Manners/God Save the Queen** and **The League of Gentlemen** albums.

In the mid-'80s, Fripp founded a guitar school in West Virginia and set about teaching the instrument to disciples in most extraordinary fashion. The all-acoustic League of Crafty Guitarists (as his students are dubbed) album, conceived as an educational challenge and recorded in concert at George Washington University, features 17 players performing pastoral Fripp instrumentals with delicacy and quiet appeal. (The LP does contain one lengthy and alluring Frippertronics piece for good electric measure.)

Another school project provided the basis for **The Lady or the Tiger**, wherein Fripp's missus, singer/actress Toyah Willcox, recites Frank R. Stockton's 1882 story (and its sequel, "The Discourager of Hesitancy") over a mild bed of inconspicuous guitar textures composed by Fripp and performed by him and the League of Crafty Guitarists.

[mf/iar]

See also *Shriekback.*

FRIPP & ENO
(No Pussyfooting) (Antilles) 1973 (EG)
1981 ●
Evening Star (Antilles) 1975 (EG) 1981 ●

These two early collaborations between Fripp and ex-Roxy Music muckraker Brian Eno are excursions into effete electronics, with Fripp simply playing his guitar through Eno's synthesizers/tape recorders. The resulting montage of loosely structured sound on the first album is pleasant and recalls the work of Terry Riley. **Evening Star** breaks no new ground; it is more a re-exploration of similar terrain.

While both records are available on individual compact discs, there is a double-cassette release of both. [jw]

FRIPP + SUMMERS

I Advance Masked (A&M) 1982
Bewitched (A&M) 1984 ●

What did Fripp and Policeman Andy Summers do on their summer vacations? Using a wide harmonic palette, they recorded **I Advance Masked**, a duet LP whose primary mood is tranquility, although Fripp the soloist ultimately reveals himself in ecstatic flights of fancy.

As the sequel proved, however, Andy Summers is no Brian Eno. Given another brief reprieve from producing those lighter-than-air guitar textures for the Police, he thickens the mix with electronic muck, leaving little solo space for himself or Fripp, who co-wrote only half the material on **Bewitched**; the rest is Summers' alone. Maybe they were too busy toying with the synth-pop trappings that dominate the record to bother playing much guitar. [mf]

FRED FRITH

Gravity (Ralph) 1980
Speechless (Ralph) 1981
Live in Japan (Jap. Recommended) 1982
Cheap at Half the Price (Ralph) 1983
The Technology of Tears (SST) 1988

If Fred Frith were remembered only for being the guitarist in Henry Cow he would be just another shadowy figure in the history of art-rock. Instead he has pursued a unique and influential solo career in the '80s that has made its mark on leading avant-gardists worldwide. Frith's sessioneering and collaborative work has figured prominently on records by Material, the Golden Palominos, Brian Eno, John Zorn and others. Massacre, his trio with the Material rhythm section, produced an unforgettably powerful record. His duo, Skeleton Crew, beguiled audiences all over the world. He has played and recorded effectively with Voice of America, compiled three early records of avant-guitar playing (**Guitar Solos 1, 2** and **3**) and recorded duet LPs and live tapes of varying

quality with Cow drummer Chris Cutler, saxophonist Lol Coxhill, guitarist Henry Kaiser and others.

But Frith's most engaging work has been for Ralph, the Residents' label. Structurally, the records resemble Henry Cow's early album in that they, like Frith himself, tend not to stay in one place long enough to try the attention span of neophytes. As such they are perfect vehicles for corrupting straitlaced rock'n'rollers into this world of joyful noise, which can include anything from polytonal polyrhytherama to Eastern European folk tunes to a taped snippet by New York's 13th Street Puerto Rico Summertime Band.

Gravity was recorded with members of several bands, the most substantial contributions coming from Sweden's Zamla and the Maryland-based Muffins (not Martha's). Frith's bass, guitar and violin are prominent, yet merged into a whole that is stronger than its dovetailed parts, all held together by ingenuity and force of will. Yes, "Dancing in the Streets" is a cover of you-know-what.

Speechless continues the process with a greater emphasis on reeds that should give Henry Cow fans a strong sense of déjà vu— yet Cow never did anything this strong. Many of Frith's melodies are influenced by the same strain of European folk music that inspired Bela Bartok. Helping out are Etron Fou Leloublan on one side and Massacre on the other. (Some of the latter's material has turned up, rearranged, on Massacre's album and during Skeleton Crew gigs.) Endlessly fascinating, this is Frith's best solo record.

Cheap at Half the Price marks not one departure but several. For the first time on a solo album, Frith sings. The songs are edgy whimsy squeezed out in a weird high-pitched tone, except "Same Old Me," whose rough lyrics emerge in a tape-slowed drawl over angry riffing. Much of the record, especially instrumental tracks, suffers from an experiment in recording "at home on a 4-track."

For those ready to graduate from the prog-rock safety of the Ralph platters to something harder and weirder, there's **Live in Japan**, which captures Frith's "guitars on the table" approach, concentrating not on standard instruments but on homemade ones that are plucked, raked, abraded and assaulted with a variety of objects. The two discs can be bought separately or together in a black corrugated box containing booklets in English and Japanese. A must for noise fans. [mf]

See also *Golden Palominos, Henry Cow, Henry Kaiser, Massacre, Material, Skeleton Crew.*

FULL FORCE

Full Force (Columbia) 1985 ●
Full Force Get Busy 1 Time! (Columbia) 1986 ●
Guess Who's Comin' to the Crib? (Columbia) 1987 ●

The six members of Brooklyn's Full Force—three brothers and three others—write, play, sing and produce themselves as well as other artists. In a very short time, boundless energy and a positive outlook have turned Paul Anthony, Bowlegged Lou, B-Fine and their three associates into a remarkably successful full-service hit machine and one of the most influential organizations in "black music."

Full Force first found fame by creating and performing the music for U.T.F.O.'s "Roxanne, Roxanne" rap smash. Then they did the same for Lisa Lisa and Cult Jam, yielding huge hits in "I Wonder if I Take You Home," "Head to Toe" and "Lost in Emotion." Their own debut album ties things up in a neat package, with "United," a track that features U.T.F.O., Lisa Lisa with Cult Jam and the Real Roxanne with Howie Tee. It also includes an answer to their own (rhetorical) song, "Girl if You Take Me Home." **Full Force** is nothing but genuine urban contemporary music, a vibrant mix of rap, rhythm, soul and rock.

Get Busy 1 Time! shows the same stylistic dexterity. Whether they're juicing up a mellow soul tune ("Temporary Love Thing," "Body Heavenly") with restrained beatbox percussion, harmonizing over a busy Howie Tee scratch track ("Never Had Another Lover," "So Much"), or showing their affection for Sly Stone ("Old Flames Never Die"), Full Force does right by their own music, abosrbing and processing various influences into a unique collection of dance sounds. Lisa Lisa makes a cameo.

In a strangely-directed crossover bid, the cover of **Guess Who's Comin' to the Crib?** shows a white suburban family freaking out over the Full Force record in the hands of their sunglass-sporting little girl. Musically, the band is on an energy rush, busying up the tracks with synth horns, complex vocal arrangements and all sorts of percussion action. Downplaying the ballads for a funkier street-wise rhythm sound, Full Force employs dialogue, slang, sound effects and turntable tricks to enliven the dance-ready cuts and provide surprises at every sonic turn. An entertaining record that, cover aside, isn't especially geared to appeal across color (or format: check out "Black Radio") lines.

[tr/iar]

See also *U.T.F.O.*

FULL TIME MEN

See *Fleshtones.*

FUN BOY THREE

The Fun Boy Three (Chrysalis) 1982
Waiting (Chrysalis) 1983
The Best of Fun Boy Three (nr/Chrysalis) 1985 ●

It came as quite a surprise when, at the height of the Specials' popularity, the group's vocalists (Terry Hall and Neville Staples) and rhythm guitarist (Lynval Golding) broke away to form their own self-contained group, making an offbeat LP that spawned two UK hit singles and took a large step toward injecting African influences into the new pop music vocabulary. On that first album, the Fun Boys' imaginative use of various conventional and exotic instruments—though the emphasis is on vocals and percussion—is countered by a pervasively dark, pessimistic feel, more so on the US edition, which places most of the brooding stuff on Side Two. Dick Cuthell (horns) and vocal trio Bananarama, whom the Fun Boys backed in return, occasionally brighten the proceedings.

Waiting, produced by David Byrne, follows that somber avenue much further, using assorted jazzy styles in minor keys to express cynicism in "The More I See (the Less I Believe)," tell a harrowing tale of molestation on "Well Fancy That!" and explode the mythical side of young romance on "The Tunnel of Love." The centerpiece of the album, however, is "Our Lips Are Sealed"—the Go-Go's' hit co-written by Hall and Jane Wiedlin—given a dramatically different reading here, slowed to dirge speed and laden with heavy atmosphere and a resigned feel, yet somehow played with a preternatural lightness. A remarkable track on a phenomenally powerful album.

The ever-restless and unsatisfied Hall subsequently left the band to form another trio, the Colour Field, a move which prompted Chrysalis to issue a Fun Boys compilation. [jg/iar]

See also *Colour Field*.

FUNKAPOLITAN
Funkapolitan (Pavillion) 1982

The name says it all: these eight multi-ethnic Britons play modern rhythmic dance music that doesn't skimp on melody, lyrics or invention. Produced by August (Kid Creole) Darnell, the eight long cuts on **Funkapolitan** bear some resemblance to other likeminded neo-soul/funk machines like ABC. Funkapolitan's unique listenability stems from myriad percussion instruments and no horns—synthesizers and varied vocals add subtle shading to otherwise straight thump-thump-thump numbers. [iar]

F.U.'S
Kill for Christ (X-Claim) 1982
My America (X-Claim) 1983
Do We Really Want to Hurt You?
  (Gasatanka) 1984
STRAW DOGS
Straw Dogs EP (Restless) 1986
We Are Not Amused (Restless) 1986

These Bostonians don't have a lot to say musically—as hardcore bands go, they're well above average but don't challenge the genre's boundaries. However, their lyrics put them in a better class. Notwithstanding some dumbo numbers on **Do We Really Want to Hurt You?** (the quartet's third album), guitarist Steve Grimes waxes verbose and semi-eloquent on "Rock the Nation" (defending punk-band life), "Young, Fast Iranians" (decrying religious fanaticism) and the title track (critiquing pop fads).

Adding lead guitarist Steve Martin to the lineup, the F.U.'s transmuted into the metalesque Straw Dogs, releasing a strong five-song debut (containing a remake of "Young, Fast Iranians" as well as a blistering version of Queen's "Tie Your Mother Down") on the day before 17-year-old drummer Chris "Bones" Jones was killed in a car crash. As it happened, he had finished recording basic tracks for the **We Are Not Amused** album, which was released, dedicated to his memory. Leaning harder towards metal, the Straw Dogs drop the offbeat lyrics for banalities like "Under the Hammer" and "Carnival in Hell," punctuating the well-produced riff-rockers with speedy guitar solos. [iar]

FUZZBOX
See *We've Got a Fuzzbox and We're Gonna Use It*.

FUZZTONES
Leave Your Mind at Home (Midnight) 1984
Lysergic Emanations (nr/ABC) 1984 (Pink Dust) 1985
SCREAMIN' JAY HAWKINS AND THE FUZZTONES
Live EP (Midnight) 1985

New York's garage-rocking Fuzztones—Rudi Protrudi, Deb O'Nair and three lesser-named cohorts—do their wild Crampabilly thing on **Leave Your Mind at Home**, seven numbers recorded live. The sound approaches bootleg quality, but that hardly matters—the shrieks and demented guitar solos here don't exactly call out for laser-level fidelity. Rave-up enthusiasm is all that counts, and that's exactly what the record delivers.

Lysergic Emanations is a fabulous studio LP, released originally in the UK and then, a year later, with new graveyard cover art (by Protrudi) and two different tracks, in the States. The sound is pure '60s garage punk—the Seeds, Chocolate Watch Band, Yardbirds, Animals, ? and the Mysterians, Standells, Shadows of Knight—produced clearly but without any excessive slickness. Absolutely first-rate—as good as the Lyres.

In fine early '60s rock'n'blues tradition, the live EP consists of the Fuzztones backing up veteran grandmaster Screamin' Jay Hawkins on four of his classic songs, including "I Put a Spell on You" and "Constipation Blues." [iar]

G G G G G G G

PETER GABRIEL

Peter Gabriel (Atco) 1977 ●
Peter Gabriel (Atlantic) 1978 ●
Peter Gabriel (Mercury) 1980 ●
Peter Gabriel (Geffen) 1982 ●
Plays Live (Geffen) 1983 ●
Music from the Film *Birdy* (Geffen) 1985 ●
So (Geffen) 1986 ●

As the lead vocalist in the estimable first version of Genesis, Peter Gabriel was the grand old man of the theatrical/commercial wing of the mildly-progressive art-rock movement. He abandoned that position in 1975 for a solo career, and has successfully positioned himself as the prototypically individualistic musician. His work is marked by dark humor, mature intelligence, strong compositional skill and excellent, often innovative use of rhythm and electronics. Like unnumbered issues of a magazine, his first four albums are titled only with his name. (The fourth **Peter Gabriel** was issued as **Security** by his American label, a move he did not endorse.)

The symphonic pretensions of the first **Peter Gabriel** power a dramatic perception of personal and global apocalypse. Produced by Bob Ezrin, and featuring the playing of Robert Fripp, Tony Levin, Steve Hunter and the London Symphony Orchestra, the album's dark rock songs ("Solsbury Hill," "Modern Love") on Side One are paired with disturbing visions of armageddon ("Slowburn," "Here Comes the Flood") on Side Two, delivered in a wall of sound that fills in every musical corner. Recommended.

In contrast, the second **Peter Gabriel**, produced by Fripp, employs the spare and uncluttered sound popularized by the punk movement. (Although you would hardly mistake this for a punk album, Gabriel does neatly display his cognizance and support of what was going on with the song "D.I.Y.") The new method showed Gabriel condensing his songs into tight units linked by themes of paranoia. Freed from the onus of art-rock, Gabriel presents his most obsessive and personal compositions (e.g., "On the Air," "Perspective"), packets of insight that are misleadingly restrained.

Gabriel returned to a fuller sound on his third—and best-known—album, emphasizing striking electronics developed over unusual rhythms and delivered with seeming desperation. The ballads of social violence and urban fear—including "I Don't Remember" and "Family Snapshot"—feature lyrics and intricate music finally blended (under producer Steve Lillywhite's direction) into perfectly integrated high pop. "Biko," a haunting political anthem about a South African martyr, and the internationalist "Games Without Frontiers" reveal Gabriel's deepening commitment to global issues and social action.

The fourth **Peter Gabriel** refines this, drawing further on exotic rhythms (from Africa, the Orient and native Americans) with a musique concrète technique made possible by the Fairlight synthesizer, which allows unlimited manipulation of recorded sounds. Gabriel delivers his examinations of fear and disaster with an oddly paradoxical new emphasis on hope and restraint, displaying his usual fine craft and quality. "Shock the Monkey," "I Have the Touch" and "Kiss of Life" are among the best things he's ever done, combining all of his strengths—lyrical, melodic, structural and experimental—into bracingly original pop music with a solid footing.

Peter Gabriel numbers three and four were also issued in Germany (the third in

Canada as well) as **Ein Deutsches Album** with Gabriel singing all the lyrics in German.

Three live tracks, recorded in 1979 and 1980, appear on the second edition of the **Bristol Recorder**, a combination album/magazine issued by a small English label in 1981, a forerunner of Gabriel's full-length live album. The two-disc **Plays Live** was recorded in America in 1982 (although some acknowledged "cheating" was later done) and features a good cross-section of his solo work, relying most heavily on the two most recent records. The four-piece band includes Tony Levin and Larry Fast.

Gabriel's recent career, like that of former bandmate Phil Collins, has involved a lot of appearances on film soundtracks. For the movie *Birdy,* however, he singlehandedly created the entire score, writing new material as well as adapting instrumental tracks from previous recordings. (And carefully explaining that on the back cover, lest there be any misapprehension.) Although it's uncommon to hear sustained instrumental work from someone so known for vocal music, the score is audibly identifiable, and provides a fascinating glimpse into his adaptational thinking. A strongly affecting work, and a major challenge vanquished admirably with style and character.

The announcement that Gabriel would end a four-year gap in new studio albums, led to a lot of understandable curiosity about **So.** No need to worry: the ever-deft artist made another adventurous, varied and striking record, with atypically self-reflective lyrics, some of them clearly demarcating a past-present-future boundary. (The cover portrait also suggests an attitudinal change of some sort.) Gabriel's characteristically sophisticated music touches on funk ("Sledgehammer"), lightly gospel-inflected balladry ("Don't Give Up," with prominent vocals by Kate Bush), folk ("In Your Eyes," with vocal backing by Jim Kerr and others) and catchy dance-rock ("Big Time," featuring Stewart Copeland on drums). The record's commercial sound and resultant big-time success led to complaints that Gabriel had compromised himself artistically, but, on its own merits, the record doesn't support such carping.

[sg/iar]

DIAMANDA GALAS

The Litanies of Satan (Y) 1982
Diamanda Galas (Metalanguage) 1984
The Divine Punishment (nr/Mute) 1986 ●

Saint of the Pit (nr/Mute) 1986 ●
You Must Be Certain of the Devil (Restless) 1988 ●

Desperate times lead to desperate actions. The three thematically-tied albums on Mute comprise "the plague mass" (**Masque of the Red Death**), a strident but striking response to AIDS by radical Southern California art vocalist Galas, sparked by her brother's 1986 death from the disease. **The Divine Punishment** is a collection of somehow appropriate Old Testament quotes delivered—in everything from a glass-breaking soprano to an urgent whisper to a depraved shriek to a wicked multi-voiced regurgo rumble—over droning synthesizer music with jarring sonic effects. The more operatic **Saint of the Pit** sets French decadent poetry (by Baudelaire, Nerval and Corbière) to wild vocal excursions, accompanied by keyboards that vary from subtle atmospherics to melodramatic horror-movie organ. Galas' astonishingly varied singing styles and the hypnotic effect of the record's three claustrophobic, obsessive pieces makes **Saint of the Pit** a powerful document of suffering.

Completing the trilogy on a conceptual high note, Galas fills **You Must Be Certain of the Devil** with lyrically specific (mostly) original songs, played with backing musicians. The record gets off to a bracing start with a unique a cappella interpretation of "Swing Low Sweet Chariot" and continues in an unassuming electro-rock vein as Galas warbles, sometimes singing counterpoint with herself in multi-track arrangements, using voice as both a percussion and melodic instrument. The audio intimacy here exaggerates emotional intensity beyond legal limits.

The Divine Punishment and **Saint of the Pit** are contained on one CD.   [iar]

GAME THEORY

Blaze of Glory (Rational) 1982
Pointed Accounts of People You Know EP (Rational) 1983
Distortion EP (Rational) 1984
Dead Center (Fr. Lolita) 1984
Real Nighttime (Rational-Enigma) 1985
The Big Shot Chronicles (Rational-Enigma) 1986
Lolita Nation (Rational-Enigma) 1987 ●
Two Steps from the Middle Ages (Rational-Enigma) 1988 ●

Game Theory is a clean, mildly psychedelic pop quartet from northern California, which means their departures from conventional meat-and-potatoes reality are more quirky than trippy. Like most over-educated popsters, they tend toward wimpiness—at which times the arcane lyrics don't help—but the hip catchiness of the songs mostly keeps them out of trouble.

Pointed Accounts is schizy. The first side is light; guitarist Scott Miller's songs are slightly off-kilter, with cryptic lines ("She likes metal and glass exact"—huh?), but the hooks make them go down smoothly. Bassist Fred Juhos carries things farther out on the second side with two tunes, including "I Wanna Get Hit by a Car." Juhos' vision is darker and somewhat more intriguing, but he isn't the tunesmith Miller is.

Distortion, co-produced by Michael Quercio of the Three O'Clock, is fuller, if not as fresh as the debut. With the more baroque sound, Miller's fey falsetto and fragile melodies sound too precious. The EP is pleasant listening, and the good ideas are still there, but it doesn't draw you in. A French label compiled a full Game Theory album, **Dead Center**, from both EPs, adding three extra items.

Real Nighttime, the band's first real album, was produced by Mitch Easter, with Quercio and others helping out. Miller wrote all the songs, except for a cover of Alex Chilton's Big Star-era "You Can't Have Me." Understandably, the wispy vocal sound crosses the Three O'Clock with Let's Active, but the music is tougher and more unpredictable than either influence. Whiny melodica, jagged guitar lines, ominous percussion and noisy sound effects lace through the arrangements, creating an odd but often productive tension. By consciously undercutting power-pop convention, Game Theory steers **Real Nighttime** into uncharted terrain that, for the most part, gives them something to sing about.

Sticking with Easter and paraphrasing John Cheever, **The Big Shot Chronicles** lights the afterburners for aggressively electric pop, louder and more powerful than anything in Game Theory's past. Miller's new lineup without Juhos doesn't fool around, keeping the arrangements relatively unadorned; unfortunately, his fly-away singing (self-described here as a "miserable whine") can sound silly competing with stacks of highly amplified rock; restrained songs that lean towards acoustic guitars (e.g., "Erica's World," "Where You Going Northern") provide a more conducive setting. With a swell organ hook, the catchy "Crash into

June" hits just the right balance and is hummably memorable.

The ambitious and occasionally bizarre two-disc **Lolita Nation** adds synthesizers and assorted crazy noises to an inconsistent set of songs—delivered in unpredictable lengths—and immerses them (especially on Side Three) in tape experimentation, spoken-word bridges and other audio ephemera. This new lineup—a resourcefully vocal quintet, here assisted by longtime friends of the band—provides variegated support that works wonders some of the time and falls flat in spots. Guitarist Donnette Thayer sings commendable lead on a few tunes, but isn't the strong counterpoint to Miller that would prevent the onset of listening fatigue. [jl/iar]

GANG GREEN
Drunk and Disorderly, Boston MA EP (Deluxe) 1986
Another Wasted Night (Taang!) 1986 ●
P.M.R.C. Sucks 12" EP (Taang!) 1987
You Got It (Roadracer-MCA) 1987 ●

VARIOUS ARTISTS
This Is Boston Not L.A. (Modern Method) 1982

Led by singer/guitarist Chris Doherty, Boston's greatest contribution to the skate-punk genre began as a faster'n'louder hardcore trio, with seven sketchy smears (e.g., "Snob," "Kill a Commie" and "Rabies"), averaging under a minute each, included on a local scene compilation. Lineup changes and a handful of singles and EPs followed, then **Another Wasted Night**. Cogent power and a notable melodic sense marks the quartet as a superior breed of punk. Doherty's Lemmy-like shriek is a fiendish attribute, as is Chuck Stilphen's occasional blitzkrieg solos. "Skate to Hell" is a rallying cry for skateboarders; the other originals are convincing thrash. The decision to cut a slow but incompetently irreverent cover of 'til Tuesday's "Voices Carry" (complete with synthesizer riff) probably had more to do with local band politics than musical taste, but it's a good giggle. Both the cassette and CD add bonus tracks.

The green-vinyl **P.M.R.C.** EP—which features a priceless cover photo of Doherty and Aimee Mann together—contains two versions of "Voices Carry," plus "Skate Hate" and "Protect & Serve."

You Got It finds an overhauled four-piece lineup again celebrating Budweiser and boards with ace playing and a stringent midtempo punk sound. (Kudos to lead guitarist Fritz Ericson.) The anthemic "We'll Give It to You" and "Born to Rock" are blistering statements (skatements?) of teen party solidarity; "L.D.S.B." ("let's drink some beer") typifies the band's commitment to hedonistic irresponsibility. [iar]

GANG OF FOUR

Damaged Goods EP (nr/Fast Product) 1978
Entertainment! (Warner Bros.) 1979
Gang of Four EP (Warner Bros.) 1980
Solid Gold (Warner Bros.) 1981
Another Day/Another Dollar EP (Warner Bros.) 1982
Songs of the Free (Warner Bros.) 1982
Hard (Warner Bros.) 1983
At the Palace (nr/Phonogram) 1984
The Peel Sessions EP (nr/Strange Fruit) 1986

If the Clash were the urban guerillas of rock'n'roll, Leeds' Gang of Four were its revolutionary theoreticians. The band's bracing funk-rock gained its edge from lyrics that dissect capitalist society with the cool precision of a surgeon's scalpel.

The Gang saw interpersonal relationships—"romance," if you must—as politics in microcosm, a view that gives **Entertainment!** its distinctive tartness. Jon King declaims brittle sentiments with the self-righteous air of someone who couldn't get to first base with his girlfriend the previous evening. The basic backing trio churns up a brutal, nearly unembellished accompaniment on this challenging album debut.

Solid Gold delves further into a quicksand of discontent. More choppy rhythms and pared-down arrangements drive home cries of despair like "Paralysed," "Cheeseburger" and "What We All Want." Not the sort of thing to pack discos, but as compelling as a steamroller.

Songs of the Free is a more upbeat dance of death. With Dave Allen gone, new bassist Sara Lee (fresh out of Fripp's League of Gentlemen) and Joy Yates' backing vocals relieve the gloom of "We Live as We Dream, Alone" and (with typical irony) contribute to the dance-floor success of the anti-militaristic "I Love a Man in Uniform." King's impassioned delivery, the songs' on-target attacks on society's ills and the band's musical wallop make **Songs of the Free** one of the most stirring, innovative "rock" albums you can find.

Unfortunately, the Gang's next outing

exposed an aesthetic about-face of Stalinesque proportions. Inappropriately co-produced by Ron and Howard Albert, **Hard** shifts from a political to a personal frame of reference; King drones lyrics against dirge-like music. It might be symbolic of disillusionment. It's certainly a sorry end to the group's career. Drummer Hugo Burnham left months prior to **Hard**'s release (there is no drummer credited on the LP); the Gang pressed on for a bit and then disbanded.

At the Palace (Hollywood's, that is) is a post-mortem souvenir of the Gang's final tour. With Steve Goulding replacing Burnham (who briefly sat in with ABC before joining Illustrated Man, later becoming Shriekback's manager), the album listlessly rehashes better days. Farewell, comrades!

To relieve between-album tension, the band's US label twice released 12-inch EPs consolidating British singles. **Gang of Four** contains one cut from their 1978 **Damaged Goods** debut EP, a non-LP flipside and both sides of the then-current "Outside the Trains Don't Run on Time" 45 (both later re-recorded for **Solid Gold**). **Another Day/Another Dollar** contains the "To Hell with Poverty" single, another non-LP flip, "History's Bunk!"—all required listening for fans—and two live versions of **Solid Gold** songs showing Gang of Four's prime-time concert intensity. **The Peel Sessions** was recorded in January 1979 and contains live-in-the-studio renditions of "I Found That Essence Rare," "At Home He's a Tourist" and others.

In 1988, guitarist Andy Gill released a solo single and created the music for a Derek Jarman film. [si]

See also *Illustrated Man, Shriekback.*

NICK GARVEY

Blue Skies (nr/Virgin) 1982

This ex-Motors/Ducks Deluxe guitarist/bassist/producer has a versatile voice (clear tenor, hoarse baritone, agile falsetto), but is even more adroit at the mixing console, able to whip up tuneful, ringing Spector/Springsteen pop melodrama—even make lush, spacious pop-rock out of the riff from "Willie and the Hand Jive." He also throws a curve or two, like the clever, 10cc-ish "(Think) Tough" or the semi-parodic Squeeze-cum-Bowie of "Skin." But even the support by members of the Motors/Tyla/Bram Tchaikovsky axis and his own genuine likability can't save this record when Garvey descends into schlocky, banal romanticism. [jg]

GAS

Emotional Warfare (nr/Polydor) 1982
From the Cradle to the Grave (nr/Good
  Vibrations) 1983

Frequently compared to Elvis Costello, and sometimes even to Graham Parker and the Clash, the Gas were more of the punk-pop-mod school of outfits like the Jam, Chords, TV21 and the Moondogs. **Emotional Warfare**, a ripping pop LP, shows off the trio with a sharp attack and some of the busiest pop this side of the Buzzcocks. "Definitely Is a Lie" and "Losing my Patience" are the kind of aural pummels one never expects from music so catchy; likewise, sheer vitality masked the incredibly bitter lyrics of singer Donnie Burke, a remarkably intelligent yet disillusioned and terminally unsatisfied front man. Imagine a man who'd been left in the lurch by a thousand women and you'd still have trouble imagining Burke's bleak anger. A young Costello seems content in comparison. **Emotional Warfare** indeed! But just try and stop playing it.

The title track of **From the Cradle to the Grave** (which sets the theme for the LP) predates the Godfathers' **Birth, School, Work, Death** by four years, stating almost exactly the same pessimistic outlook on UK existence. While the battering ram of Burke's rage and utter despair continues, here it's married to a more likely somber sound, with pretty piano, light tempos and atmospheric guitar. This soundtrack for a tear-gushing unhappy movie of an unhappy life was ignored by their older fans who preferred their fast and loud origins, and avoided by the post-punk doom and gloom school. The LP faded without much fanfare, as did the band soon thereafter. [jr]

GAYE BYKERS ON ACID

Everythang's Groovy EP (nr/In Tape) 1986
Nosedive Karma EP (nr/In Tape) 1987
Drill Your Own Hole (PFX-Caroline) 1987

Crazy times and the enormous reach of rock'n'roll have made the challenge of turning conscious weirdness into a commercial property increasingly difficult, one that few neophytes are equal to. The dirty, ugly Bykers, a post-pop-culture Leicester quartet, cross leather-clad Mad Max apocalyptics with late-'60s London people's-band values to forge a forward-looking/backward-thinking image that is worthless but evidently salable, at least in England. It is illustrative to note that the band's last album, **Drill Your Own Hole**, was produced with maximum gimmickry by Alex Fergusson (ATV/PTV) and includes a song by hippiedom's legendary Edgar Broughton Band. The intentionally chaotic noisy guitar rock (dressed up in wah wah and moronic solos) with inflamed vocals is spottily ear-catching but basically horrible. Next contestant, please . . . [iar]

G.B.H.

Midnight Madness and Beyond . . . (Combat
  Core) 1986 ●
Oh No It's G.B.H. Again! EP (Combat Core)
  1986
No Need to Panic! (Combat) 1987 ●

CHARGED G.B.H.

Leather, Bristles, Studs and Acne EP (nr/Clay)
  1981
Leather Bristles, No Survivors and Sick Boys
  . . . (Clay-Combat) 1982 ●
City Baby Attacked by Rats (nr/Clay) 1982
  (Clay-Combat) 1987 ●
City Baby's Revenge (Relativity) 1983
The Clay Years 1981 to 84 (Clay-Combat)
  1986 ●

First appearing in 1980, Birmingham's Charged G.B.H. (Grievous Bodily Harm—the "Charged" was appended to prevent confusion with a British metal band of the same name but later dropped) quickly joined the top ranks of England's second-generation buzzsaw punk firmament. **Leather Bristles, No Survivors and Sick Boys** compiles the similarly-titled 1981 EP and two subsequent releases in a bracing storm of morbid speedcore. Ignore the dismal lyrics and enjoy the sweeping, trebly adrenaline rush. **City Baby Attacked by Rats** is another onslaught that throws off sparks on dubious numbers like "Slut" and "The Prayer of a Realist." Enraged if not especially enlightened, the quartet tears through the record with chops and electrical venom.

The photos on **City Baby's Revenge** show singer Colin Abrahall and guitarist Jock Blyth sporting extraordinary hair-like extremities; the record is, conversely, marginally more restrained and less garishly violent than before. "Christianised Cannibals," "Vietnamese Blues," "Diplomatic Immunity" and other songs display a refined and more intelligent political punk sensibility, along with a slightly slower and easier-to-grasp sound. A blazing Stooges cover ("I Feel Alright") adds to the fun; on the downside, "Womb with a View" is an anti-feminist diatribe.

When G.B.H. left their original UK label, they also left behind the first part of their name. Clay issued a compilation—tracks drawn from EPs, singles and the two original albums, plus a strong pair of previously unreleased items, "Children of Dust" and "Do What You Do"—which fairly condenses the band's primal punk catalogue.

Taking a sidestep on **Midnight Madness**, G.B.H. replaced the shrill top with a thundering bottom and mixed speedmetal rhythms in with the breakneck hardcore tempos. It's still essentially a punk record, and a pretty good one at that, although it's disconcerting to see them writing songs about New York's Iroquois Hotel, horror movies and international touring. The inclusion of "Limpwristed" shows that egalitarian humanist sensibilities are still undeveloped.

The speaker-busting **Oh No EP** is one of the most explosive rock records ever, a blistering quartet of tunes that are easily among G.B.H.'s best. The unexpectedly melodic "Malice in Wonderland" is a revelation that pairs the old sound of Generation X and the Pistols with Megadeth production. Wow!

G.B.H. got themselves a new drummer with twin bass pedals and turned into metalheads on **No Need to Panic!** Echo on the vocals and blurry guitar over an overeager rhythm section typify the sonic approach; sporadic spoken bits, sound effects and TV bites don't add as much as the band might imagine. Another reason not to be cheerful: the dull and unfocused lyrics.   [iar]

GEILE TIERE
Geile Tiere (Ger. GeeBeeDee) 1981

To underscore the meaning of their name ("wild animals"), this self-billed "electronic sex band" put a photo of one horse mounting another on the LP cover. That aside, there's nothing erotic or even vulgar (in a sexual sense) about this German duo's music or bilingual lyrics. The vocals are heavily emphasized, processed through a harmonizer to add or subtract Mickey Mouse and/or Darth Vader timbres, but Geile Tiere's staple tactic of repetition removes meaning from words like "sex" and "love." Luciano Castelli and ex-Nina Hagenite Salome (an androgynous male) fill the rest of their soundscapes with scratchy guitar and bleepy synth in terse phrases with the beat supplied by a rhythm

box. Not only is it unencouraging as dance music, Geile Tiere goes nowhere with no flair.   [jg]

BOB GELDOF
See *Boomtown Rats.*

GENE LOVES JEZEBEL
Promise (nr/Situation Two) 1983 ●
Bruises EP (Can. Beggars Banquet-Vertigo) 1983
Immigrant (Relativity) 1985 ●
Desire EP (Relativity) 1985
Discover (Beggars Banquet-Geffen) 1986 ●
The House of Dolls (Beggars Banquet-Geffen) 1987 ●

On most of **Promise**, Welsh twins Jay and Michael Aston generate a powerful, dense sound that falls somewhere between U2, Adam Ant and Public Image: thickly textured guitars coloring a driving beat under aggressively impassioned, generally tuneless vocals that occasionally lapse into YokOno-esque wailing. The songs have a decidedly sexual air, but it's the sheer din—roughly-produced but convincing—that makes **Promise** worth repeated listenings. Numbers that don't go for maximum impact peddle a sensitive, spacious attractiveness that suggests considerable range and skill. (**Bruises** is a six-song précis of the album.)

On the enjoyable, atmospheric **Immigrant**, intelligently produced by John Leckie, the Jezebels (acknowledging a five-piece lineup) resemble a pop-sensitized version of Bauhaus, a gritty U2 or a smacked-out Duran Duran. "Always a Flame" is aggrodance rock with a walloping beat and a real melody; "Shame" has similar attributes, plus a catchy refrain. The US edition of the LP appends "Bruises," a solid number which brings all of the band's U2 tendencies to the fore. ("Worth Waiting For" is equally Bonoesque.) The **Desire** 12-inch combines two mixes of that song with three album tracks for a dose of Gene Loves Jezebel's best side.

"Desire" also appears on **Discover**, the band's first American major-label release (a development reflecting their burgeoning haircut-based popularity on college radio and in alternative media). Otherwise, the album wavers from obnoxious (the Lotte Lenya-meets-Bauhaus sound of "Heartache," the annoying push of "Sweetest Thing") to melodious ("Kick" and "A White Horse," which suggest a mild New Order influence). Throughout, Michael Aston warbles miserably in an unmusical voice which blends the worst excesses of Siouxsie and Bono; it hardly matters how well Gary Lyons' production renders the instrumentation as long as the vocal mic stays on. (The British tape configuration adds eight live tracks recorded in Nottingham in early 1986. Original pressings of the UK album included a bonus disc—**Glad to Be Alive**—of the same performance.) A transparent effort to commercialize the Jezebels made **The House of Dolls** their most listenable—that's not to say likable—record yet. Excepting a pair of songs ("The Motion of Love" and "Suspicion") handled by Jimmy Iovine, the LP was produced by Peter Walsh (Simple Minds, China Crisis, Peter Gabriel's live LP), who multitracks Aston's vocals (without completely eliminating his need to yelp and wail unexpectedly) and surrounds them in loud but clearly articulated arena-ready tuneful guitar rock, leaving the impresssion that GLJ is on the verge of discovering a most unpleasant hybrid of Van Halen, U2 and a billy goat.

[iar]

GENERAL PUBLIC
. . . All the Rage (IRS) 1984 ●
Hand to Mouth (IRS) 1986 ●
RANKING ROGER
Radical Departure (IRS) 1988 ●
DAVE WAKELING
The Happiest Man in the World (IRS) 1988

After terminating the wonderful Beat, leader Dave Wakeling and color commentator Ranking Roger stuck together to form General Public, later involving several other 2-Tone veterans. It's hard to hear why the Beat had to die for General Public to live, but evidently the pair felt they needed to leave some people and other career baggage behind. Although an unequal trade, General Public upheld the commitment to excellence that hallmarked the Beat.

Ex-Clashman Mick Jones plays guest guitar on the first LP (although just where on this democratic undertaking eludes my ears); such other luminaries as Aswad's brass section and Gary Barnacle also add bits. For their part, Wakeling and Roger craft passionate pop, packed with clever tempo shifts, in several styles: a happy Motown bounce ("Tenderness" and the romantic "Never You Done That"), textured drama ("General

Public," the political "Burning Bright") and a bluebeat kick ("Where's the Line"). On the negative side, GP engage in annoying verbal play on "Hot You're Cool" and "As a Matter of Fact." Some tracks go on too long and a few of the arrangements are overly busy, but those are small quibbles. **All the Rage** is a rich, mature album filled with intelligence and invention from a band fairly bursting with talent.

The second and final installment in the GP saga was **Hand to Mouth**, a milder and less striking record. The well-rehearsed lineup of six (augmented by ex-Beatman Saxa, Gaspar Lawal and others) exudes an air of relaxed precision on an easygoing pop program that shows little evidence of creative exertion. Although hardly exceptional, "Too Much of Nothing" is the album's best track; "Faults and All" and "Murder," with snappy horn charts, echo the first record but don't build on it. All in all, the music goes down smoothly enough, but without making a lasting impression.

In 1988, with General Public and their long partnership at an end, Ranking Roger and Wakeling each began solo careers. On **Radical Departure**, which he co-produced with Colin Fairley, Roger is supported by a new quartet which includes ex-Specials bassist Horace Panter.

[iar]

GENERATION X
Generation X (Chrysalis) 1978 ●
Valley of the Dolls (Chrysalis) 1979 ●
Kiss Me Deadly (Chrysalis) 1981 ●
Dancing with Myself EP (nr/Chrysalis) 1981
The Best of Generation X (nr/Chrysalis) 1985

Appearing on the London punk scene shortly after the Sex Pistols, Generation X was an extraordinary but ill-fated outfit that issued five tremendous singles, one classic album and some real dross. It also launched the mega-career of Billy Idol and the ditzy Sigue Sigue Sputnik, developments one must weigh when considering the band's historical significance.

With Idol as the band's voice and image and guitarist Bob "Derwood" Andrews providing its rock power, Generation X broke a lot of punk conventions, and were ultimately ostracized by their peers for refusing to be (or even feign being, as many others did) anti-commercial. Their breakup can be viewed as a parallel to the dispersal of the original punk spirit, although Billy Idol's phoenixlike ascent to world chart domination is equally indicative of the subsequent salability of that ethos.

Following a tremendous string of 45s ("Your Generation," "Wild Youth," "Ready Steady Go," all included on the US—not the UK—version of the first LP) that crossbred punk insolence with kitschy '60s pop culture to produce catchy, roaring anthems for disaffected youth, Generation X's debut album bore out their promise—not a bum track in the bunch. A commercial streak didn't preclude a punky outlook or closeness to their audience, while the songs don't threaten the established order, they do retain a cocky irreverence that made Generation X more than a latter-day Mott the Hoople. **Generation X**, regardless of the reputational damage Billy Idol may have subsequently caused, is a classic record.

Valley of the Dolls, produced by Ian Hunter, pales in comparison. Two or three numbers recall the sonic magnificence of the early singles, but the surrounding tracks leave much to be desired. A typical sophomore-record material shortage.

Kiss Me Deadly, recorded after Idol and bassist Tony James (co-writer with Idol of the band's songs) had sacked Andrews and drummer Mark Laff, is a shoddy affair, containing only the wonderful "Dancing with Myself" (later recut by Idol) to recommend it. Their moniker truncated to Gen X, Idol and James employed once and future Clash drummer Terry Chimes and a trio of guitar stars—Steve Jones, John McGeoch and Chelsea's James Stevenson—but the spirit was gone from the music, and the LP is merely a pale shadow of the band's early glories. [iar]

See *Empire, Billy Idol, Sigue Sigue Sputnik, Westworld*.

GEORGIA SATELLITES

Keep the Faith EP (nr/Making Waves) 1985
Georgia Satellites (Elektra) 1986 ●
Open All Night (Elektra) 1988 ●

These Southern boys have a fatal weakness for Rod Stewart's Faces and mid-period Stones, presumably not a real shrewd business approach in the synthetic '80s. At least that's what you'd think after hearing their spirited yet undistinguished EP, which features a plodding early version of "Keep Your Hands to Yourself" and a meatgrinder cover of George Jones' "The Race Is On."

The boys take off with their self-titled debut LP, which yields a bonanza of beer-breath boogie. In addition to the surprise chart hit "Keep Your Hands to Yourself," hot spots include the Chuck Berryish "Red Light" and the plaintive folk-rock of "Golden Light." But "Can't Stand the Pain," a yowling rocker reminiscent of **Exile on Main Street**, epitomizes this LP: greasy, groovy and right on target. Curiously, the only weak spot here is a cover of Stewart's "Every Picture Tells a Story."

Following the platinum success of **Georgia Satellites**, the quartet took a while getting a second album into the stores, but finally issued **Open All Night** in mid-1988.

[jy]

GERMS

(GI) (Slash) 1979
What We Do Is Secret (Slash) 1981
Germicide-Live at the Whisky [tape] (ROIR) 1982
Let the Circle Be Unbroken (Gasatanka) 1985
Lion's Share (Aus. Ghost o'Darb) 1985
Rock n' Rule (XES) 1986

In retrospect, it's easy to dismiss the Germs as the epitome of LA's early identipunk scene. Singer Darby Crash (real name Paul Beahm) was a barking spikey-haired brat, an alarming combination of Johnny Rotten's snarling vocal ferocity and Sid Vicious' self-destructive cool. Three years after the band's first live performance (at the Whisky in 1977), Crash died of a drug overdose, reportedly self-inflicted in morbid tribute to Vicious' own fatal OD in 1979.

Germicide, a cassette release of that first show (originally issued as a limited-edition bootleg LP), reinforces that notion. The tape is a raw documentary of spirited incompetence, with Crash ranting through "Sex Boy" and the rather prophetic "Suicide Madness" in a cynical bawl. Behind him, the band plods along with all the cheer of a migraine. A good third of the tape consists of Crash trading obscene insults with the crowd. Also of note: a tortuous disembowelment of the Archies' "Sugar Sugar."

After that, **(GI)** is a revelation, a kinetic outburst of brute punk force. Two years of tightening and a new drummer turned the Germs into a manic punk locomotive, speeding along with Damned intensity in spite of tinny production by Joan Jett. Aside from the overlong live "Shut Down," the songs go by in a breathless rush, fueled by Pat Smear's staccato fuzz guitar and Crash's sometimes confused but often potent punk protest imagery. A key album in the development of American hardcore.

What We Do Is Secret, a posthumous bow to Darby, packages what's left of the Germs' recorded legacy on a 12-inch mini-album. The material includes a 1977 stab at Chuck Berry's "Round and Round" with X drummer D.J. Bonebrake, an outtake from **(GI)** and live tracks recorded in late 1980, shortly before his death. **Lion's Share** is an Australian fan club compilation containing live cuts and assorted rarities.

Recorded under battle conditions by Geza X on a four-track, the fair-sounding **Rock n' Rule** documents a motley but amusing 1979 Christmas party at the Whisky—the noise of flying bottles crashing onstage only adds to the grimy charm. **Let the Circle Be Unbroken** is another document of the band's chaotic concert existence. [df/iar]

GET SMART!

Action Reaction (Fever) 1984
Swimming with Sharks (Fever-Restless) 1986

Born in Kansas and based in Chicago, Get Smart! plays simple, eager rock that rushes along busily, yet remains refreshingly distinct. Warm pop melodicism competes with punky bluntness and jagged noise tendencies on **Action Reaction**, creating a variety of stylistic voices within the plainly constructed guitar-bass-drums framework; harmony vocals add to the appeal.

Swimming with Sharks finds Get Smart! progressing along nicely. The trio speedily works its multifarious way through ten songs in various idioms, offering sketchy poetic lyrics along the way. They're still rough around the edges—drummer Frank Loose gets stuck in patterns that limit songs' appeal—and neither bassist Lisa Wertman nor guitarist Marc Koch is that great a singer, but workable ideas and cool sounds bubble up regularly enough to make **Swimming with Sharks** a safe and rewarding experience. [iar]

GIANT SANDWORMS

Will Wallow and Roam After the Ruin EP
  (Boneless) 1980

GIANT SAND

Valley of Rain (Enigma) 1985
Ballad of a Thin Line Man (nr/Zippo) 1986
Storm (What Goes On) 1988

BAND OF BLACKY RANCHETTE

Heartland (nr/Zippo) 1985

Howe Gelb, the guitarist/singer/pianist, moved from Pennsylvania to Tucson, Arizona in the late '70s and formed the Giant Sandworms, a quartet preserved on a white-vinyl 7-inch EP: five nifty songs of off-kilter electro-rock that owes rudimentary debts to Roxy Music, Devo and XTC.

Five years later, only Gelb and three syllables of his band's name remain. Bassist Scott Garber and two drummers (playing on different cuts) join him on **Valley of Rain**, a brash outpouring of dusty Southwestern rock. Gelb's enthusiastic vocals and the charging, well-written music set this apart from other bands of the region (and those from LA who fancy themselves cultural expatriates) who mix cowboys into their music. Green on Red's Chris Cacavas adds piano to one song.

The next Giant Sand incarnation resulted from the departure of one drummer and the arrival of Paula Jean Brown (vocals/guitar), who had served a short tenure (taking Jane Wiedlin's spot) in the Go-Go's. **Ballad of a Thin Line Man** moves in acoustic circles, adding equal parts of country and bracing Neil Youngesque electricity. Gelb and Brown harmonize richly; his writing—songs about real life with an uncommon outlook—just keeps getting better. Guests on the LP include Falling James (Leaving Trains), who co-wrote and sings "Last Legs," a smokey piano ballad with an atmospheric '30s feel. A peppy cover of Johnny Thunders' "You Can't Put Your Arms Around a Memory" speeds up the song and adds piano, but keeps its basic sound intact with mangy singing and noisily-strummed guitar.

Storm is the best Giant Sand record yet. Brown moved over to bass, Garber left and Neil Harry joined to play almost imperceptible pedal steel. (Interestingly, drummer Tom Larkins has maintained concurrent membership in both Giant Sand and Naked Prey since around 1986.) Crisp production plays up Gelb's guitarings, which sound remarkably like Neil Young at his grungiest; at times, his vocals hit an unnerving Lou Reed plateau. The band is in fine and sophisticated form, mixing up styles with aplomb. Burgh-oriented songs like "Town with Little or No Pity," "Bigger Than That" and "Town Where No Town Belongs" (which opens on the same riff as Cheap Trick's "She's Tight") demonstrate abundant talent and wit, especially in the lyrics department. A distinctive and invigorating album.

The Band of Blacky Ranchette is Gelb's parallel country-western outfit in which he indulges his passion for Hank Williams and Merle Haggard. [iar]

ALEX GIBSON
Passionnel EP (Faulty Products) 1981
Suburbia (Enigma) 1984

BPEOPLE
BPeople (Faulty Products) 1981
Petrified Conditions 1979–1981 (Restless) 1986

PASSIONNEL
The Apostle EP (Enigma) 1984
Our Promise (Enigma) 1985

Alex Gibson (vocals, guitar, main songwriter) led LA's BPeople for several years around the turn of the decade. Beginning as the Little Cripples, the quartet turned into BPeople after singer Michael Gira left for New York (forming Circus Mort and then the Swans). The eponymous 1981 eight-song mini-album consists of dark, moody music somewhere between Joy Division and Soft Cell, neither as jarring or desperately distorted as the former, nor as pervasively pop as the latter. On the positive side, there's smart use of sax and organ, but at times the music seems to be pulling in different directions, and poetic license should not be granted for lyrics like "We, they, it, that" (an actual line!).

Petrified Conditions—a full album of original recordings (some, but not all, previously issued on BPeople and other vinyl) remixed in 1984-5 by Gibson and Paul B. Cutler—is a more convincing introduction to BPeople's artsy sophistication. The sonic and stylistic variety is impressive, and Gibson's songwriting displays structural abilities far beyond the punk club milieu in which the band existed. A worthwhile archaeological find.

After BPeople collapsed, Gibson wrote, singlehandedly performed and produced Passionnel, an excellent four-song 12-inch of wide-screen rock, made grandiose with tympani and long strains of synthesizer that lurk prominently in the near-background. Very English in sound—like Simple Minds or Ultravox—but not particularly derivative, Passionnel is a remarkable achievement for an

individual, and a frighteningly good piece of theater in itself.

Not content with the confusion level his career had engendered up to that point, Gibson's next move was to create a band called Passionnel. The Apostle (including a surprisingly straight cover of the Beatles' "Glass Onion") offers rhythmic rock of varying intensity, from even-handed ("Make Like You Like It") to intense sheets of dense sound ("Everything Golden"), over which Gibson spills emotional, semi-tuneful vocals. Occasionally chaotic to the point of unpleasantness, elsewhere delicate and pretty, The Apostle is striking, but not always for the right reasons.

Gibson scored Penelope Spheeris' punk film, Suburbia, the results of which occupy one side of the soundtrack album. Performed with only Passionnel's drummer joining him, the music consists of brief, aggressive rock instrumentals that rely on drums for drive and sharp-edged guitar for flavor. Several pieces sound as if they might have been edited from a long jam session (hard to imagine given the size of the band); other portions create a somber, relaxed mood with synthesizer and piano.

Released under the Passionnel moniker, Our Promise pairs the contents of The Apostle on one side with five new tracks. Well-crafted, cleanly produced and varied (within Gibson's limited musical field), the songs make some impact but leave only a faint impression. [jg/iar]

BRUCE GILBERT
See Dome, Wire.

GINA X PERFORMANCE
Nice Mover (nr/EMI) 1979
X-traordinaire (nr/EMI) 1980

GINA X
Yinglish (nr/Statik) 1984

Gina X is beautiful Teutonic singer Gina Kikoine with backing by a German synths-and-drums trio (adding guitar for the second album) that plays technically impressive smooth (but dull) dance-rock. On Nice Mover and X-traordinaire, Kikoine's expressionless voice isn't exactly pleasant; her lyrics are in English (and occasionaly French), but that doesn't help the lifeless songs any. Boring!

With Kikoine opting for solo billing,

Yinglish continues her association with producer/keyboard player/co-writer Zeus B. Held (Dead or Alive, Fashion) and guitarist Dierk Hill; otherwise the cast is new. She sings nonsensical poseur lyrics variously in English, French and German; a cover of the Beatles' "Drive My Car" and a Serge Gainsbourg song offer some connection to the known world. The music displays an awareness of Yello and dance music developments like scratch mixing, while expanding the palette to include subtler forms. Gina'n'Zeus are reaching for a fey artiness that just isn't worth finding. Kikoine's vocal skills are improved, but sometimes misdirected; the album has its moments, but a lot of tedious patches as well. [iar]

JOHN GIORNO

See *Laurie Anderson, Glenn Branca.*

MICHAEL GIRA

See *Circus Mort, Alex Gibson, Lydia Lunch, Swans.*

GIRLS AT OUR BEST!

Pleasure (nr/Happy Birthday) 1981
The Peel Sessions EP (nr/Strange Fruit) 1987

Judy Evans is the only female Girl at Our Best! but her untrained trilling is the band's most distinctive element. The male musicians play pep-charged tunes about narcissistic youth; unflagging chord changes and witty lyrics prevent portentousness. A good romp.

The Peel Sessions EP, which was recorded in early 1981, contains versions of four tunes. [si]

GIST

Embrace the Herd (nr/Rough Trade) 1983

This record marks the return of Stuart and Phil Moxham, the Welsh brothers who comprised two-thirds of the Young Marble Giants. (Actually, the gist of the Gist is Stuart, although he receives assistance here from Phil on three tracks and other friends on several more.) **Embrace the Herd** is an unassuming (early era) Enoesque album of fragile pop songs and delicate-but-weird instrumentals; slight but special. [iar]

PHILIP GLASS

Music in Twelve Parts Parts 1 & 2
(nr/Caroline) 1974

North Star (Virgin) 1977
Einstein on the Beach (nr/Tomato) 1979 (CBS Masterworks) 1984
Glassworks (CBS) 1982
Koyaanisqatsi (Antilles) 1982 ●
The Photographer (CBS) 1983
Mishima (Nonesuch) 1985 ●
Satyagraha (CBS Masterworks) 1985
Songs from Liquid Days (FM) 1986
Dancepieces (CBS Masterworks) 1987 ●
Powaqqatsi (Nonesuch) 1988 ●

Though primarily renowned as a composer of experimental music, onetime taxi driver and plumber Philip Glass entered the rock domain via his production work with Polyrock and others. Furthering the connection, his compositional ideas and methods have been adopted by various progressive-thinking groups, especially in New York. With his increasing employment as a film scorer, Glass may be nearing mass popularity.

Music in Twelve Parts (not his first record) exemplifies Glass' basic style: near-mantric repetition of rhythms of different rates, looping and overlapping in ever-changing harmonic patterns. The minimalist method reduces musical composition to atomic components of rhythm and counterpoint. **North Star** polishes the technique, applying it to shorter pieces that sound uncannily like works of electronic music. **Einstein on the Beach**, an opera with libretto by Robert Wilson, is Glass' longest sustained example of minimalist technique to date. The work uses familiar music for its starting point, stripping it of its history and filtering it to yield new and unfamiliar meanings.

Glassworks is an attempt, following his work with Polyrock, to cross over into the pop market. Unlike most other Glass works, the source of rhythm is a steady beat (like dance music) and instruments—specifically horns and keyboards—are identifiable in themselves, whereas previously they would have been rendered anonymous.

Delving into a different aspect of the pop world, Glass wrote **The Photographer**, a music/theater piece chronicling the life of pioneering photographer Eadweard Muybridge, which was staged in Europe. Glass co-produced the record and contributes organ; an orchestra and chorus plays the three-act piece which, in performance, includes dance and projections.

The first of Glass' film music albums, **Koyaanisqatsi** is an hypnotic score for a bizarre dialogueless travelogue/documentary. In addition to his normal reliance on woodwinds and keyboards, Glass uses a large brass section and massed vocals to evoke a mood that is unusually dark and somber; parts could be a *Star Trek* soundtrack. **Mishima** accompanies a Paul Schrader film biography of the noted Japanese author. **Powaqqatsi** is his soundtrack to the **Koyaanisqatsi** sequel.

One of the most ambitious efforts in a generally ambitious career, **Satyagraha** is a three-disc boxed set (with complete libretto and background notes) recording of an opera about Gandhi commissioned by the city of Rotterdam. First performed in 1980, the album was digitally recorded—with overdubbing, an uncommon gambit for an orchestral/choral piece—in a New York studio.

Songs from Liquid Days, ostensibly an experimental effort in the pop song form, consists of six lengthy tracks, co-written with Paul Simon, Suzanne Vega, Laurie Anderson or David Byrne and sung by a guest vocalist (Linda Ronstadt, the Roches, Bernard Fowler, etc.). Most of the music is very much in Glass' recent mode (rolling, keyboard-driven mood pieces, like burbling streams) over which pretentious "art" lyrics sound quite ludicrous. "Open the Kingdom," on the other hand, takes the same compositional direction, but builds it up to awesome proportions with a large brass section and Douglas Perry's operatic vocals; "Forgetting" resembles (is?) a tiresome piece of draggy musical theater. The nicest track is "Freezing," which uses the Roche sisters' unique harmonies to fine effect.   [sg/iar]

See also *Polyrock*.

GLAXO BABIES

Nine Minutes to the Disco (nr/Heartbeat) 1980
Put Me on the Guest List (nr/Heartbeat) 1980

This Bristol quintet begs comparison to the Residents, as their first album uses all manner of noises to intrigue, confound, aggravate and entertain. Except for three song-like tracks that actually resemble rock music, **Nine Minutes to the Disco** consists mainly of formless sonic experiments, piling up seemingly unrelated sounds into an electronic jungle full of disjointed voices. Somehow, there's a pleasing quality to these random adventures; low-budget ambient insanity.

The second album actually consists of earlier recordings—essentially a compilation of previously unreleased studio efforts dating from 1978-9. There is a lot of variety, from disarmingly fragile pop to lightweight Public Image maunderings, with glimpses of Pere Ubu, Modern Lovers, Television and even the Cramps filling the spaces in between. As musical sketches for a group in progress, the tracks offer an interesting pastiche; taken as a proper album, what it lacks in consistency it makes up in unpredictability.   [iar]

See also *Transmitters*.

GLEAMING SPIRES

Songs of the Spires (Posh Boy) 1981
Life Out on the Lawn EP (Posh Boy) 1982
Walk on Well Lighted Streets (Posh Boy-PVC) 1983
Funk for Children EP (Vodka) 1984
Welcoming a New Ice Age (Tabb) 1985

Californians Les Bohem (bass/vocals) and David Kendrick (drums) lead a dual existence as members of Gleaming Spires and as the rhythm section (since 1981) of Sparks. Both were in Los Angeles punk band Bates Motel; their subsequent work together has taken two divergent paths. The first Spires album is full of catchy, synthesizer-strewn silliness ("Are You Ready for the Sex Girls?," "How to Get Girls Through Hypnotism"), while **Life Out on the Lawn** is more arty and serious, allowing electric guitar and wailing sax to routinize the sound, if not their bizarre outlook. While a somber cover of "Somewhere" (from *West Side Story*) demonstrates a continuing flair for incongruity, this approach is far less entertaining or original than their jollier early work.

As of **Walk on Well Lighted Streets**, the Spires became a quartet through the addition of Jim Goodwin and Bob Haag, both of whom had already played with the band. The stylistic influence of their employers in Sparks, Ron and Russell Mael, is beginning to show; the Spires seem to have located a workable mid-point between silly and serious. The lyrics are more bizarre than ever, while the music manages to be simultaneously catchy and quirky, throbbing with drive but punctuated with oddball effects and gimmicky production by Stephen Hague. Best tune: "A Christian Girl's Problems."

Gleaming Spires' "Party EP," **Funk for Children** (which includes an Abba song!), consists of four tracks on one side and extended versions of two on the flip. The title tune incorporates a children's chorus and "party" percussion for novelty effect, but is otherwise boring. Two numbers are essentially bubblegum rock-pop—robust and catchy, similar to the Spires' early efforts. The program is rounded out with a Zappa soundalike, "Brain Button." Unfortunately, the remix side features the wrong two songs.

Welcoming a New Ice Age isn't as funny as other Spires' endeavors, but its uncanny resemblance to contemporaneous Sparks records makes one wonder when Russell's voice is going to appear and push Bohem aside. Another credible record in this overlooked outfit's impressive catalogue. [iar]

See also *Devo, Sparks*.

GLOVE
Blue Sunshine (nr/Wonderland-Polydor) 1983

The band is named after the villain in *Yellow Submarine,* the record after a variety of LSD. The cover is filled with photos of '60s memorabilia. This one-off project by Banshee bassist Steve Severin and Cure leader Robert Smith (at the time also the Banshees guitarist) sounds much like their own bands crossed with the Beatles, circa 1967. The ten pseudo-psychedelic ditties show neither participant in top form, although the single "Like an Animal" (with Siouxsie-like guest vocalist Landray) and "Mr. Alphapbet Says" do stand out. Not a band to make a career of, but good harmless fun. [dgs]

JEREMY GLUCK WITH NIKKI SUDDEN AND ROWLAND S. HOWARD
See *Barracudas.*

GO-BETWEENS
Send Me a Lullaby (nr/Rough Trade) 1981
Very Quick on the Eye—Brisbane, 1981
  (Aus. Man Made) 1982
Before Hollywood (nr/Rough Trade) 1983
Springhill Fair (nr/Sire) 1984
Metals and Shells (PVC) 1985
Liberty Belle and the Black Diamond Express
  (Big Time) 1986 ●
Tallulah (Big Time) 1987 ●

One of the most critically respected and cultily adored neo-pop bands to emerge from Australia, the Go-Betweens began as a Dylan-inflected duo but had expanded to a more original-sounding trio by the time **Send Me a Lullaby** was recorded. With shades of Television and the Cure, the cool but not chilly LP offers a charming view that isn't overly pop—no slick gimmickry here—and songs that are more fascinating lyrically than melodically. Remarkably, the band's jagged, slightly coarse guitar sound has little trouble accommodating occasional intrusive blurts of blank sax noise. **Very Quick on the Eye** is a collection of outtakes and demos, some of which made it onto **Lullaby**.

Before Hollywood is a major improvement—more tunefulness, stronger harmonies, less stridency—suggesting R.E.M. and Aztec Camera a bit. The Go-Betweens, however, are clearly not just like anybody. Outstanding tracks: "Two Steps Step Out," "Dusty in Here" and the utterly wonderful, airy "Cattle and Cane." A marvelous, invigorating record.

Four Go-Betweens recorded the more mellifluous **Springhill Fair** in France, making it so smooth and well-ordered that it verges on commercialism. They still make genteel pop music, but color it with guest keyboards, strings, horns and even (gasp!) synthesizer. Fortunately, the Go-Betweens write such musically pleasant, lyrically fascinating and intelligent songs that even creeping complexity and slickness can't seriously damage their appeal.

Liberty Belle leaves a few more rough edges intact than its predecessor. The songwriting is again sharp and the sound nicely augmented with light touches of strings, vibes, bassoon, accordion and Tracey Thorn's backing vocals—all without even approaching over-production. (The CD adds two numbers.) Crafty and astute without ever condescending, we could use a few more pop bands like the Go-Betweens. **Metals and Shells** is a get-acquainted compilation for America, where the band has yet to break much ground.

Hate to say it, but **Tallulah** sounds like an attempt to become an essential yuppie acquisition. There's isn't anything very different going on, it's just so much more slick and professional sounding than ever before. Now a five-piece, they've incorporated a violinist/oboist (!) who adds relatively little, since they have often thrown in a few odd-instrument sidemen. Songwriters Grant McLennan and Robert Forster are not in top form at all, especially obvious on "The House That Jack Kerouac Built," a song that ought to be a lot

242

livelier and possess sharper lyrics if such a venerated name is going to be invoked. They *will* do better next time. [iar/dgs]

VIC GODARD & THE SUBWAY SECT

What's the Matter Boy? (nr/Oddball-MCA) 1980 + 1982
Songs for Sale (nr/London) 1982
A Retrospective (1977–81) (nr/Rough Trade) 1984

VIC GODARD

T.R.O.U.B.L.E. (Upside) 1986

Although the Subway Sect shared stages with the Clash, Sex Pistols and Buzzcocks as far back as 1976, the group's debut vinyl was a 1978 single; their first longplayer didn't follow until two years later. (In fact, the group did record an album in '78 for Clash manager Bernard Rhodes, but it was never released. As a result, Bristol-born singer-songwriter-arranger Vic Godard broke up the band and original drummer Mark Laff joined Generation X.)

By 1980, the Sect had reformed at least once. Several of these early hard guitar-pop incarnations are chronicled on **A Retrospective**, which consists of two singles and a radio broadcast from '78, a cut from that lost LP plus a 1981 45 side. The evidence is plain that the early Subway Sect had incorporated a strong Buzzcocks influence (plus flashes of Lou Reed and Television) and that Godard was a talented musician slowly fashioning an identity.

By the time of the first album, the Sect had again been revamped and was serving merely as a backing band for Godard, who had developed into a skillful vocalist with a budding predilection for folky, low-key, non-aggressive—hell, non-rock!—music. Considering the band's background, **What's the Matter Boy?** is a surprising belated debut. The cover is terrible and Rhodes' production is totally flat, but the charming songs' upbeat freshness and originality (start with "Enclave") compensates for the flimsy presentation.

The Subway Sect (prior to transmuting the following year into JoBoxers) may share titular credit with Vic on **Songs for Sale**—a collection of homages to (and one cover of) his idol, Cole Porter—but Godard is entirely in charge. Abandoning rock'n'roll completely, **Songs for Sale** is a wonderful record

of concise pop creations delivered in a cool, suave voice. Proving himself a masterful tunesmith and crooner, Godard manages to update 1930s/40s Tin Pan Alley without resorting to mimickry or selfconsciousness. As produced by Alex Sadkin, the memorable, sturdy tunes sound of the period without being corny. Sure it's a pose, but Godard is evidently sincere in his nostalgic affection, and he makes the music his own with real panache.

Finally emerging as an admitted solo artist, Vic made **T.R.O.U.B.L.E.**, a brasher, more ambitious and almost equally winning swing record with one Porter tune and 11 lively Godard originals. Dance rhythms of the '40s subtly seasoned with horns and a spot of accordion energize the giddy romance of songs like "The Devil's in League with You," "Caribbean Blue" and "Stop That Girl." "Out of Touch," a snazzy guitar instrumental that could have come from a '60s spy flick, is an intriguing change of pace.

[iar]

See also *JoBoxers*.

GODFATHERS

Hit by Hit (Link) 1986
Birth, School, Work, Death (Epic) 1987 ●

Remember Dr. Feelgood? How 'bout Eddie and the Hot Rods? If the white-hot pre-punk R&B/rock'n'roll of those two bands means anything to you, chances are you'll love the Godfathers—formed by brothers Peter and Chris Coyne from the ashes of the loopy Syd Presley Experience—to death. Not coincidentally, Vic Maile, the producer who worked with both the Feelgoods and the Hot Rods in their prime, is at the helm for these two LPs filled with songs of working-class angst in a Britain where, as Peter sings in "The Strangest Boy," "my future's past, already gone and been." Indeed it's the worst-case scenario of the Pistols' "no future in England's dream," played out in a landscape of poverty, drugs and desperation. Unlike the punks of yore, though, the Godfathers remain motivated, if only by sexual and material desires and a stubborn sense of self-preservation. Punk meets mod at the bottom of the social barrel.

For a debut, **Hit by Hit** presents a band already sporting a remarkably clear vision. Titles like "I Want Everything," "This Damn Nation," "I Want You" and "I'm Unsatisfied"—replete with explosive riffing and

243

angry vocals—tell you nearly all you need to know about what the Godfathers see as their lot in Maggie Thatcher's England. A strong cover of John Lennon's "Cold Turkey" and a version of Rolf Harris' "Sun Arise" that makes Alice Cooper's sound sickly round out an essential record.

If anything, **Birth, School, Work, Death** is even tougher and more focused. The dynamic title track and "Cause I Said So" are the high points of a record that seethes with an anger and aggression that seems to have all but gone out of non-hardcore British post-punk rock. Bravo, lads.   [ds]

PETER GODWIN

Images of Heaven EP (Polydor) 1982
Correspondence (Polydor) 1983

Once a member of the group Metro, Godwin turned into a synth-rocker and cut some pleasant tracks as a solo artist. Three of the EP tracks (singles in the UK) were produced by budding techno-sound designer Georg Kajanus (once of Sailor); the remaining entry by Midge Ure (still of Ultravox), whose then-bandmate, drummer Warren Cann, helps out. The one outstanding track is the title tune, which resembles Ultravox or Simple Minds.

Correspondence continues Godwin's association with Kajanus and imports a batch of keyboard players and guitarists for more well-crafted, occasionally memorable, adult synth-rock.   [iar]

GO-GO'S

Beauty and the Beat (IRS) 1981 •
Vacation (IRS) 1982 •
Talk Show (IRS) 1984 •

The enormous commercial success of **Beauty and the Beat** in America was not only a welcome breakthrough for new music, but proof that an all-female band could make it big without a man pulling the strings and without resorting to an image grounded in male fantasy, be it sex kitten or tough leatherette. The album mixes honest pop with healthy infusions of rock'n'roll and, besides containing two bona fide hit singles ("We Got the Beat" and "Our Lips Are Sealed"), provides a refreshingly different point of view on some familiar themes ("Lust to Love," "Skidmarks on My Heart").

Vacation, if not as exuberant or confident as its predecessor, is at least more ambitious.

The band sounds distinctive and skillful, but the songs generally fall short of the standards set by **Beauty and the Beat**, a not-uncommon sophomore album hazard. The exceptions, however, are delightful: "I Think It's Me," the bubbly, modernized girl-group sound of "This Old Feeling" and the crisp, wistful title track.

Following a horrible series of unforeseen maladies and delays, the Go-Go's finally released their third album, exchanging the wise punk-pop production hand of Richard Gottehrer for a more challenging experience with Martin Rushent. **Talk Show** attempted a major revamp, turning up the rock energy on all fronts: Gina Schock's drumming received new prominence in the mix while guitars blazed with added bite. As on the preceding two LPs, the material includes a few great singles ("Turn to You," "Head Over Heels" and "Yes or No," the last co-written by guitarist Jane Wiedlin with Ron and Russell Mael), plus a lot of forgettable filler. With three albums to consider, the first remains the most impressive.

Jane Wiedlin subsequently left for a solo career. The Go-Go's pressed on for a while, but disbanded in May 1985 without recording again. Joined by Charlotte Caffey, Belinda Carlisle made her first solo album in 1986 but hit it big the following year on her second attempt. Drummer Gina Schock took a few years off after the breakup and then launched her own band, the House of Schock.   [ks/iar]

See also *Belinda Carlisle, House of Schock, Jane Wiedlin*.

GOLDEN PALOMINOS

The Golden Palominos (OAO-Celluloid) 1983 •
Visions of Excess (Celluloid) 1985 •
Blast of Silence (Celluloid) 1986 •

The Golden Palominos—an above-average avant-funk album—would have been a milestone if it had sounded anything like the Palominos' New York gigs. At one memorable show, the lineup included bandleader Anton Fier (drums), David Moss (drums/noise), Arto Lindsay (guitar/vocals), John Zorn (reeds), Bill Laswell (bass) and Jamaaladeen Tacuma (bass). The double rhythm section packed a wallop in unison, but more often the players broke off into intense and fascinating duets and trios.

On the first record, the Palominos add

(Mark Miller, Fred Frith, Nicky Skopelitis) and subtract (most often Tacuma and Moss) players while preserving the basic material, tossing in a couple of new things ("Hot Seat," a song mostly by Miller, and "Cookout," a Fier percussion piece). Those who knew the magic of the Palominos' noise/funk synthesis firsthand will regret Fier's decision to go for the trendier Material sound in his co-production with Laswell. Still, when Lindsay rakes his untuned guitar and lets out a trademark yelp, or Zorn lowers some fragment of a clarinet underwater and gurgles with weird ferocity, you know you're hearing a trace—just a trace—of the real thing.

The second phase of Fier's Palomino experiment took an entirely different direction, converting a loose caravan of talent into an unstable side-group which performs and records in countless permutations and combinations. **Visions of Excess** is a brilliant neo-pop album of tuneful, lyrical songs featuring such luminaries as Michael Stipe, John Lydon, Richard Thompson, Jack Bruce, Chris Stamey and Jody Harris. As producer, drummer and co-writer of the songs, Fier is on stylistically unprecedented ground career-wise, but his control and taste are impeccable. A version of Moby Grape's "Omaha" sung by Stipe is a truly incisive piece of '80s psychedelia (with a crazed Stamey breakdown solo) that sounds like a pop hit; "(Kind of) True" and "Buenos Aires," both starring talented Hoboken singer Syd Straw, are equally memorable. Lydon's "The Animal Speaks" is, well, what you might expect from him. The LP closes with an Arto Lindsay extravaganza, "Only One Party," just so no one should forget where this project is coming from. Essentially a recap of 1985's semi-underground stars and sounds, **Visions of Excess** is one disc everyone should own.

Blast of Silence continues the Palominos' unique existence, employing many of the same people as **Excess** (but notably not Stipe or Lydon), while extending the musical family to incorporate Peter Blegvad, Don Dixon, T-Bone Burnett and other meta-stars. The Palominos' previous rotating ensemble work raised expectations of the unexpected, but this essentially ordinary album breaks that promise to repeat the structure but not the extraordinary content of its predecessor. Except for Straw singing Peter Holsapple's "Diamond," the material isn't especially interesting (two Lowell George songs?), the performances are downright ordinary and

the darkening outlines of a repeatable formula discourage faith in the future of Fier's creative vision and energy.   [mf/iar]

GONE
"Let's Get Real, Real Gone for a Change" (SST) 1986 ●
Gone II—But Never Too Gone! (SST) 1986

Black Flag guitarist Greg Ginn has pursued numerous side projects in recent years. Gone is an instrumental power trio that could use a vocalist as well as more organized power; the first album (named after an Elvis Presley remark) meanders aimlessly like a badly-run rehearsal session.

The song-things on **Gone II** (cover artwork by Ginn) are more coherent and tolerable, but still fall short of confirming the value of the band's existence. Riffs with solos make good interludes, but 16 unengaging pieces in a row do not a good time make. Is the world ready for heavy metal wallpaper? Still, give Andrew Weiss well-earned credit for bitchen bass work.   [iar]

See also *Henry Rollins*.

GONE FISHIN'
See *Windbreakers*.

GOOD MISSIONARIES
See *Alternative TV*.

PETER GORDON
Innocent (FM-CBS) 1986
Brooklyn (FM-CBS) 1987 ●
Otello—Falso Movimento [tape] (ROIR) 1987

Besides releasing and collaborating on numerous avant-garde records released by adventurous new music labels, New York hornman/synthesist/composer Peter Gordon—formerly the leader of the downtown post-punk art-fusion Love of Life Orchestra—has made solo albums for the CBS megalith. With the assistance of assorted East Coast luminaries, Gordon demonstrates a grasp of both the mainstream and the fringe on the mostly instrumental **Innocent**. Including one old LOLO recording ("Diamond Lane"), the carefully structured tracks allow the sensual, rhythmically rich sounds to be an audio end in themselves. Esoteric, but easy to enjoy.

Gordon evidently found a trans-river relocation inspirational: **Brooklyn**, recorded with a similar collection of underground celebrities, celebrates the borough in title, picture and song. Unfortunately, the funky "Brooklyn" is merely an obnoxious and juvenile iteration of neighborhood names. In general, Gordon's stabs at vocal song structure reveal a trivial lyricist and an unappealing singer, leaving the pleasant instrumental pieces—nothing too obscure this time—to carry the album, which they really don't.

Music Gordon composed in 1983 for an experimental Italian production of the Verdi opera is contained on the cassette-only **Otello**. Drawing bits from the original score and incorporating actual recordings of traditional performances, he created a distinctly offbeat modern electronic interpolation.

[tr]

ROBERT GORDON

Robert Gordon with Link Wray (Private Stock) 1977
Fresh Fish Special (Private Stock) 1978
Rock Billy Boogie (RCA) 1979
Bad Boy (RCA) 1980
Are You Gonna Be the One (RCA) 1981
Too Fast to Live, Too Young to Die (RCA) 1982

Singer Robert Gordon made one of the sharpest *volte-faces* in musical memory when he left New York pseudo-punkers Tuff Darts to reappear as a freeze-dried '50s rocker, complete with sideburns, pompadour, a songbook of Sun Records oldies and authentic guitar icon Link Wray in tow.

Superficial trappings aside, Gordon's strongest asset is his magnificent voice—a clear, clean baritone rarely heard in pop music of any stripe. His debut album, **Robert Gordon with Link Wray**, is suffused with rockabilly material (songs from Carl Perkins, Gene Vincent, Billy Lee Riley and Eddie Cochran), but the accompaniment by the Wildcats is more contemporary, with Wray contributing sizzling guitar licks.

Fresh Fish Special (named after Elvis Presley's haircut in *Jailhouse Rock*—typical homage) is more of the same, with barely more sophisticated tunes. The odd track here is Bruce Springsteen's "Fire," which was a hit for the Pointer Sisters. Nevertheless, its inclusion proved Gordon didn't need to rely exclusively on nostalgia.

Besides the addition of echo, **Rock Billy Boogie**'s distinction is the replacement of Wray with nimble guitarist Chris Spedding. On **Bad Boy**, Gordon seems to be evolving

from the '50s into the '60s via schlockier songs (Roy Orbison's "Uptown," Kris Jensen's "Torture").

Gordon's time-traveling into the present continues on **Are You Gonna Be the One**, his most accessible album for those who don't worship at the House of Butchwax. Despite his '50s fixation, Gordon best puts across those songs without a 25-year-old aroma.

Too Fast to Live, Too Young to Die is a compilation of tracks from all the preceding albums except **Bad Boy**, plus a live version of "Black Slacks" and previously unreleased recordings of two Marshall Crenshaw songs.

[si]

GORILLAS

Message to the World (nr/Raw) 1978

In the beginning, it seemed as if the only new wave/punk bands to get noticed were politically-minded, like the Pistols or Clash. That was tough luck for the (Hammersmith) Gorillas, an underrated London trio whose first few singles—especially "Gatecrasher" and "She's My Girl"—were tight, mod-inspired rockers. Jesse Hector's strained vocals recalled the best of Steve Marriott, while the rhythm section rocked with the fire of the Who. The Gorillas' lone album isn't as strong as prior 45s suggested, and a few of the tracks (such as an ill-advised version of Hendrix's "Foxy Lady") are dismal, but **Message**, for the most part, is upbeat and enjoyable.

[cpl]

ROBERT GÖRL

See *Deutsche Amerikanische Freundschaft.*

ERIC GOULDEN

See *Wreckless Eric.*

HUW GOWER

Guitarophilia EP (X-Disque) 1984

Gower was a guitarist—not a major songwriter—in the pure-pop Records; he later played with David Johansen. This solo EP is pretty much in the vein of the former: well-crafted, unprepossessing rock-pop, but without the Records' often-cloying preciousness. An earnest enough performer, Gower is a limited songwriter and not much of a singer; the EP's best track is a fascinating cover of Graeme Douglas' brilliant "Do Anything

You Wanna Do," recorded originally by Eddie and the Hot Rods. [iar]

GRAB GRAB THE HADDOCK

Three Songs by Grab Grab the Haddock EP
(nr/Cherry Red) 1984
Four More Songs by Grab Grab the
Haddock EP (nr/Cherry Red) 1985

A daft name if ever there was one, this terminally cute London quartet is a spinoff from the defunct Marine Girls. Unlike former bandmate Tracey Thorn (now in Everything but the Girl), Alice Fox and her crew still hawk the chaotic tunelessness that made the Marine Girls so insufferable.

The first EP has a sparse, almost minimalist feel; even the use of atypical pop instrumentation (maracas, conga drum, cello) does little to alleviate the disjointed clatter. Fox's childlike caterwauling further adds to the annoyance. **Four More** is a slight improvement—clear melodies and a near-logical organization level enhance the tracks. Guitarist/songwriter Lester Noel takes over vocal chores on "Last Fond Goodbye," a bright pop song that provides the 12-inch's only worthwhile interlude. [ag]

GRANDMASTER FLASH AND THE FURIOUS FIVE

The Message (Sugar Hill) 1982
Greatest Messages (Sugar Hill) 1983
On the Strength (Elektra) 1988 ●

GRANDMASTER MELLE MEL AND THE FURIOUS FIVE

Work Party (Sugar Hill) 1984
Stepping Off (Sugar Hill) 1985

GRANDMASTER FLASH

They Said It Couldn't Be Done (Elektra) 1985
The Source (Elektra) 1986
Ba-Dop-Boom-Bang (Elektra) 1987 ●

Although they were not rap's first stars, Grandmaster Flash's galvanizing 1982 hit "The Message" was the record that demonstrated the form's potential for socio-political commentary and, preceding Run—DMC, initially served to convey rap's urban excitement to an audience outside of urban blacks. Unfortunately, most of Flash's early raps were of the let's-party-and-tell-our-zodiac-signs variety, with absolutely no consciousness, political or otherwise—good for dancing, but not very stimulating. (Despite his star billing, dj Flash is not the rapper; lead

vocals are by Melle Mel, Rahiem and others. Adding to the credit-where-due confusion, most of the crew's early songwriting and performing was done in large part by Sugar Hill studio pros.)

Greatest Messages splits the difference between hard-edged social realism and mindless partytime, from "Freedom" (their first hit) and "Flash to the Beat" to "Survival (Message II)" and "New York, New York" (which was actually the follow-up to "The Message"). What the LP doesn't include is the brilliant 1983 anti-cocaine song, "White Lines (Don't Don't Do It)," the music for which, incidentally, copies a prior Liquid Liquid instrumental. (The **Greatest Messages** cassette has two bonus tracks.)

Following a bitter legal dispute over contracts and ownership of the name, the band split in two: most of the members remained with Grandmaster Flash (Joseph Saddler), dropped the "Furious Five" appellation and signed to Elektra; Melle Mel, who also got to wear the Grandmaster crown, recruited a mostly-new Furious Five and stuck with Sugar Hill. The former's **They Said It Couldn't Be Done** is a strained effort to diversify and make up for lost time and momentum. There's a rapped-up version of Fats Waller's "The Joint Is Jumpin'," a Run—DMC imitation unoriginally entitled "Rock the House" and two soulful all-singing tunes. Only "Sign of the Times" dips into topicality, employing a sound reminiscent of "White Lines."

The Source, which travels a number of awfully familiar verbal and musical roads, makes a regular point of arguing Flash's significance and supremacy. "Fastest Man Alive," the audio vérité "Street Scene," the hackneyed music-rap marriage of "Style (Peter Gunn Theme)" and the pretend-live "Freelance" make more personal introductions and absurd claims than a convention of used car salesmen. As a routine party record, it fulfills all the minimal obligations; as proof of Flash's creativity and ability to grow with the times, it's a sad example of commercial wheel-spinning.

The word funky gets an aromatically literal interpretation in **Ba-Dop-Boom-Bang**'s "Underarms," an amazingly tasteless put-down about bad smells. Otherwise, the LP avoids **The Source**'s hype to concentrate on praising women ("Them Jeans"), cars ("Big Black Caddy"), parties ("House That Rocked") and self-reliance ("Get Yours").

Interpolations of other people's music, including a lamely belated cover of Queen's "We Will Rock You" with other stuff stitched in, don't prevent **Ba-Dop-Boom-Bang** from being run-of-the-mill.

When members of Grandmaster Flash and the Furious Five—specifically Mele-Mel (new spelling), Scorpio and Cowboy—reunited, the result was **On the Strength**, either faction's best outing in years. The record gets off to a killer start with the streetwise "Gold"; the side ends with "King," a moving gospel-tinged tribute to MLK. (The intervening tracks are routine bragging, with only Flash's deadly turntable work on "Yo Baby" for diversion.) Side Two's bizarre highlight is a rock-rap cover of "Magic Carpet Ride" (shades of "Walk This Way"). Mr. Steppenwolf himself, John Kay, sings it; Flash's gang raps on the chorus and adds a few sections that I don't recall from the 20-year-old original. [iar]

EDDY GRANT

Message Man (nr/Ice) 1977
Walking on Sunshine (Epic) 1979
Love in Exile (nr/Ice) 1980
My Turn to Love You (Epic) 1980
Live at Notting Hill (nr/Ice) 1981 + 1984
Can't Get Enough (nr/Ice) 1981 + 1983
Killer on the Rampage (Ice-Portrait) 1982 ●
Going for Broke (Ice-Portrait) 1984 ●
All the Hits (nr/K-Tel) 1984
Born Tuff (Ice-Portrait) 1986 ●
File Under Rock (Capitol) 1988 ●

Three expatriate Caribbeans plus two Englishmen equalled the Equals, whose blend of pop-rock, psychedelia, blues, R&B and, of course, a slight Carib accent yielded a wildly diverse and uneven batch of singles and albums in the late '60s. Despite their problems, they amassed a few Top 10 hits, including the oft-revived (most recently by Grant himself) "Baby Come Back," a smash on both sides of the Atlantic in 1968. Several of their other hits now sound like utter tripe, but "Black Sin Blue Eyed Boys" and the LP track "Police on My Back" (covered by the Clash) show just how talented they could be.

The group provided a musical (and music-business) education for its guitarist/chief songwriter/leader (but not lead singer) Eddy Grant, who eventually left to go solo and set up his own record company, Ice. He plays almost everything on his studio albums, except sometimes bass and/or drums, plus horns (when he doesn't use synthesizer instead).

Message Man was a dodgy start, yet Grant immediately began forging his own reggae style ("Jamaican Child") and continued the interracial/cultural theme begun with the Equals ("Cockney Black").

Walking on Sunshine shows his potential in full flower: "Living on the Frontline" is a superb electronic-reggae single, and its remarkable extension into "The Frontline Symphony" on the LP is a lengthy tour de force that features a mock-classical vocal section. The title track and "Say I Love You" (a monster hit in Nigeria) add extra value to an LP already well worth owning.

Love in Exile showcases Grant working in various soul styles (like the Teddy Pendergrass-ish semi-funk of the title track), albeit with his own oddly-inflected vocals. "Preaching Genocide" is the one exception, a long mutant calypsoid political chant, but all in all it's only musical water-treading, and inferior. **My Turn to Love You** is the same record with an alternate title and graphics.

The live album is an excellent display of both Grant's talent as a performer and his best solo songs up to that point. It also makes available about half the otherwise rare songs from **Message Man**. Despite the usual live record drawbacks—it needn't have been a double—its best is mighty good.

Can't Get Enough is Grant's "I'm a love man" album, but it's great for what it is, as the catchy numbers take full advantage of Grant's genre-bending and blending. (The reissue adds a nifty instrumental, "Time Warp," that was originally available as the B-side of "Electric Avenue.")

The rock-oriented **Killer on the Rampage** is Grant's most consistent album to date, as well as his biggest commercial success in the US. "Electric Avenue" (the most rock-based track, save for some muscular guitar playing here and there) may prove to be an anthem of classic stature, and cuts like the title track and "I Don't Wanna Dance" demonstrate how Grant's songwriting has matured.

The proof that it was no fluke is that both **Going for Broke** and **Born Tuff**, though lacking high points as great as "Electric Avenue," are otherwise very nearly as good (and as varied). The former includes the theme song of the hit film *Romancing the Stone* (all but a smidge of which was inexplicably removed from the film itself in the final cut); the latter (on which Grant performs nearly every note) has a superb title track that's like a more confident companion to "Living on the Front Line." **Born Tuff** may be a bit stronger, but if you want more Grant after **Killer**, you'll want both. [jg]

GRAPES OF WRATH
The Grapes of Wrath EP (Can. Nettwerk) 1984
September Bowl of Green (Can. Nettwerk) 1985 (Capitol) 1986
Treehouse (Capitol) 1987

This Vancouver trio plays muscular pop that alternately resembles Southeastern bands like Let's Active and West Coast folk-rockers like Translator. The impressive four-song EP is a little short on personality but locates a viable commercial midpoint between the radio and the road. Guitarist Kevin Kane is a skilled player and a fair vocalist; drummer Chris Hooper proves his enthusiasm by overplaying.

September Bowl of Green retrieves one fine song ("Misunderstanding," which Chris Stamey might have written) from the EP, but the album's Canadian and American editions include different versions of it and another swell tune, "Love Comes Around." The former employs the originals, while the US substitutes similar but inferior productions and mixes by Red Rider major-domo Tom Cochrane. While the Canadian cassette adds bonus tracks, the US LP release deletes a harmonious rendition of the Beatles' "If I Needed Someone."

Cochrane produced all of **Treehouse**, giving Grapes of Wrath a crisp, clear sound, filled with airy guitar picking, subdued if busy drumming and delectable multi-voice arrangements. Neither novel nor progressive, **Treehouse** is simply flawless electric pop music written and played with skill and taste. [iar]

GRAPHIC
People in Glass EP (Dolphin) 1984
TREVA SPONTAINE
S'il Vous Plait (Moonlight) 1982

People in Glass is melodic North Carolina rock, produced by Don Dixon and characterized by Ms. Spontaine's earthy, passionate vocals, with energetic and able support by Graphic's three other members. Complex, only mildly adventurous, but untrendily up-to-date and exciting in a clear-headed, unassuming manner.

The earlier Spontaine solo recording, also produced by Don Dixon, has Mitch Easter playing on it. The seven songs include a plucky countrified cover of "I'm into Something Good," the Goffin/King number that was a 1964 smash for Herman's Hermits; a winning, horn-filled "Girl Don't Come" (Sandie Shaw, same year); also a Beatles song, a strong reading of the Chris Stamey-penned title track and a Dixon/Spontaine collaboration. [iar]

GRAVEDIGGER V
All Black and Hairy (Voxx) 1984
The Mirror Cracked (Voxx) 1986

This now-defunct California band played groovy, authentic-sounding (credit producer/label owner Greg Shaw) garage punk with convincing '60s clumsiness and sincerity. Any band that covers a song (the first album's title track) by Screamin' Lord Sutch is already a few rungs up the cool ladder; the Gravediggers further add to the fun with a singer who fairly approximates the legendary T.S. Bonniwell and perfectly evocative arrangements and licks. If **All Black and Hairy** were 20 years old, it would now be a collectors' item. [iar]

GREAT PLAINS
The Mark, Don & Mel E.P. (New Age) 1983
Born in a Barn (Homestead) 1984
Great Plains Naked at the Buy, Sell, and Trade (Homestead) 1985
Sum Things Up (Homestead) 1988

The Midwest not only provides a home to this casually intellectual Columbus, Ohio quintet, it also informs their post-collegiate cultural outlook. Following the eight-song **Mark, Don & Mel** mini-album (a giddily rudimentary introduction to the band's non-caloric pop), the offhandedly XTC-styled folk-rock of **Born in a Barn** supports witty lyrics about "Lincoln Logs" (ol' Abe's face appears all over the crypto-religious cover), "Rutherford B. Hayes" and the "Columbus Dispatch." Singer/guitarist Ron House's tentative voice lends unavoidable humility to the simply-conceived but eminently likable tunes.

Great Plains Naked at the Buy, Sell, and Trade is even better, a wonderfully topical romp that knowingly tweaks the underground rock culture ("Letter to a Fanzine"), the king of music television ("Dick Clark") and themselves ("Real Bad," "Origin of My Silly Grin"). Silly but never unserious, Great Plains is a breath of fresh air in the non-mainstream rock scene. Excellent.   [iar]

GREAT UNWASHED
See *Clean.*

JOHN GREAVES
Accident (Europa) 1982
JOHN GREAVES & PETER BLEGVAD
Kew Rhone (nr/Virgin) 1977
LODGE
Smell of a Friend (Antilles New Directions) 1988 ●

Greaves—who has played bass with such neo-progressives as Henry Cow, National Health and Robert Wyatt—encompasses a wide variety of sounds and moods on his first solo venture. Some of the instrumentation recalls Henry Cow, and Greaves employs the Cow principle: if a particular sound doesn't pull you in, the one on the next cut might, and all the songs are distinct unto themselves, even on first listening. Greaves' singing, however, is too flat and unemotive to sustain interest.

Greaves (music, keyboards) and ex-Slapp Happy member Peter Blegvad (lyrics, guitars) essay a jazzy theatricality on **Kew Rhone**, a stunning joint endeavor with singer Lisa Herman. Featuring a large cast of new music sidepeople, including Carla Bley and Michael Mantler, the album is consistently lyrical and lovely, incredibly precise and enduringly intelligent.

Greaves' latest project is a band called the Lodge, which features two Blegvads (Peter and his brother Kristoffer on vocals) and, on **Smell of a Friend**, Anton Fier on drums. Herman also guests.   [mf/iar]

GREEN
EP (Gang Green) 1984
Green (Gang Green) 1986
Elaine MacKenzie (Pravda) 1988

Drawing inspiration from the Kinks, Prince, Small Faces and Motown, Chicago's Green revolves around singer/guitarist Jeff Lescher, an ace songwriter with a stirring pop-rock voice, ear-pinning scream and a scarifying gospelly falsetto. On the debut EP (four songs, seven inches) the trio overcomes rudimentary production values to skirt nostalgia and introduce Lescher's mix of '60s Anglo-melodicism ("Gotta Getta Record Out," "Better Way"), punky rock ("I'm Not Going Down (Anymore)") and soul ("I Don't Wanna Say No"). Amateurish but inspired.

Re-recorded versions of those songs join ten new ones on **Green**, another inadequately-produced but patently brilliant collection of weirdly derivative originals played with spirit and innate power. Occasionally pedestrian lyrics (as on "Big in Japan") don't interfere with the amazing rugged pop tunes, a unique and energetic pairing of merseybeat and punk. "She's Not a Little Girl" seemingly takes its chorus straight out of the Hollies songbook; "Technology" employs a catchy Bolanesque bop; "For You" and "Curry Your Favor" are ballads that display a tender, sensitive side; "I Play the Records" introduces the group's Prince influence; "She, Probably" is achingly beautiful. An independent album that easily surpasses much of the mainstream competition.

Elaine MacKenzie (neat cover painting by Lescher) unveils Green's new rhythm section. Bassist Ken Kurson composed and delivers a pair of bilious demi-punk tunes, supplying albumwide backing vox as well; otherwise, the writing and singing is all by Lescher. Courageous ballads about screwed-up romance (including the haunting "She Was My Girl") coexist with Kinksy nostalgia ("Saturday Afternoon," complete with subtle French horn accompaniment), a Prince-inflected falsetto raveup ("My Love's on Fire") and the two-speed "I Can't Seem to Get It Through My Head," which somehow nails the Association to the Miracles. Endearingly corny puns and silly concepts demean songs like "Youth in Asia" and "Radio Caroline" but the group's overwhelming spirit and conviction handily saves the day.   [iar]

D. GREENFIELD/J.J. BURNEL
See *Stranglers.*

GREEN ON RED
Green on Red (Down There) 1982 (Enigma) 1984
Gravity Talks (Slash) 1983
Gas Food Lodging (Enigma) 1985 + 1987 ●
No Free Lunch (Mercury) 1985

The Killer Inside Me (Mercury) 1987
Here Come the Snakes (Red
    Rhino-Fundamental Music) 1988 ●

Many of California's psychedelic revival bands originally drew on spacey/chaotic sources like the Velvet Underground, Pink Floyd or classic trance-inducers like the Serpent Power. But Green on Red's early records alternately recall the fuzzified raunch of the Electric Prunes and Seeds and the merry flower power of the Strawberry Alarm Clock. Filling the tracks of its seven-song debut with buzzing guitars, droning organ and pretty melodies, the quartet delivers transcendental lyrics in a monotonic stupor that precisely suggests total pharmaceutical oblivion. Good studio sound helps convey the sincere nostalgia.

Gravity Talks has a simplified, and in one spot Dylanized, feel. (The title track uses chipper organ and reeling vocals to evoke "Most Likely You Go Your Way and I'll Go Mine.") Elsewhere, Green on Red largely abandons its previous style in favor of unembellished rock and folk-rock. At the LP's relative weirdest, Chris Cacavas' organ-playing sounds like several genres from the '60s, but only mildly; **Gravity Talks** never becomes as intentionally mannered as its predecessor. Unfortunately, Dan Stuart's not much of a singer and his songwriting could likewise be stronger.

Gas Food Lodging introduces guitarist Chuck Prophet IV to the lineup and adopts a full-scale countrified sound, a mangy cowpoke hybrid somewhere between **Pat Garrett**-era Dylan and old Neil Young. Stuart's boozy singing suits the sloppy playing and demi-melodies; the band's comfortable enthusiasm covers a lot of the record's flaws. (Original US copies were pressed on green vinyl; the CD adds a track.)

On the strength of **No Free Lunch**, a country-rock major-label debut, it's difficult to imagine that Green on Red was ever remotely connected to psychedelia. At its most believable, the mini-album includes a cover of Willie Nelson's "Funny How Time Slips Away." Otherwise, the band tries far too hard to fit the boots of hard-drinkin', populist-minded Amuhricuhns for the contents to be taken seriously. The music is adequate (for a loose, amateurish C&W bar band), but the fake accents and predictable lyrical imagery turn this would-be sincerity into a pretentious muddle.

With drummer Keith Mitchell, fresh from work with David Roback and Kendra Smith, joining the lineup, the freeway cowboys oddly add gospelly backup singers (shades of the Blackberries with Humble Pie) to the country-blues-rock mélange on **The Killer Inside Me**, roughly produced by Jim Dickinson. Stuart's raspy whine, which has come to resemble Alice Cooper's voice at times, announces itself as the record's only consistent focal point; alternately overblown and ragtag arrangements don't help selfconscious tunes like "Clarkesville" and "No Man's Land" stand on their own minor merits. [iar]

See also *Danny & Dusty, Naked Prey*.

CLIVE GREGSON
See *Any Trouble*.

GROUP
I Hear I See I Learn (Jive) 1984

Articulate lyrics and strong mainstream rock make this English trio's album a big improvement over their Thomas Dolby-produced introductory 12-inch, which consisted of three versions—25 minutes' worth!—of one terrible song, thankfully not reprised here. **I Hear I See I Learn** is a little short on personality—despite slick production, the songs are essentially banged out with little fanfare—but has a good overall sound and singer/guitarist Ian Martin's provocative lyrics to recommend it. [iar]

GRUPPO SPORTIVO
10 Mistakes (nr/Epic) 1978
Back to '78 (nr/Epic) 1978
Mistakes (Sire) 1979
Copy Copy (Can. Attic) 1980
Pop! Goes the Brain (Can. Attic) 1981

Holland's Gruppo Sportivo specialized in combining familiar rock riffs with outrageous humor, making it a group to be laughed with more than a band to be heard. **Mistakes** is an American compilation, including a bonus six-song EP, of the band's first two albums. Cannibalizing the pop music world (in both form and lyric) for laughs, this gruppo romps blissfully across the prostrate forms of Eric Clapton, the Shangri-Las, Beatles and Wings (among others), elevating mere parody to the level of satire. They have the musical ability to pull it off, and wind up sonically somewhere between Abba and early Squeeze.

Copy Copy falters as the lyrics take precedence over the music, despite an emphasis on dance beats and good vocal support from Bette Bright. Fortunately, their satire strikes firmly—at radio, the Westernization of Japan, airport dogs, etc.—and the words' savage precision somewhat compensates for the meandering, frequently nonexistent tunes.

Pop! Goes the Brain rediscovers melody, and leader Hans Vandenburg drops his Dutch accent for a pseudo-English voice that sounds disturbingly like Nick Lowe. A greater role for synthesizer and its attendant rhythmic noises corresponds to lighter satire, and an incursion of serious numbers. [sg]

GUADALCANAL DIARY
Walking in the Shadow of the Big Man (DB)
   1984 (Elektra) 1985 ●
Jamboree (Elektra) 1986
2 x 4 (Elektra) 1987 ●

The first album by this talented Athens, Georgia quartet, produced by Don Dixon, is too diverse for its own good. **Walking in the Shadow of the Big Man** mostly offers attractive, harmony-laden folk-rock. But then there's "Watusi Rodeo," with wiseacre lyrics, energetic Bongosish music and surf guitar, the country-punkish "Ghosts on the Road" and the Everlys/Edmunds-styled "Pillow Talk." The band write great songs; their delivery in spots resembles R.E.M. without the unique vocal style. Elsewhere, they get heavier, letting drummer John Poe fire things up with a ferocious rhythmic attack. Individual tracks are excellent, but the stylistic inconsistency *is* disconcerting.

While somewhat less idiosyncratic, the flashier **Jamboree** is no better for it: when the record doesn't sound disturbingly like R.E.M., it's blandly insubstantial. Rodney Mills (Cruzados, .38 Special) produced most of the tracks; Steve Nye (Japan, XTC, Bryan Ferry) did the rest, displaying marginally more imagination. "Michael Rockefeller" and "Country Club Gun" display lyrical acuity, and "Please Stop Me" has a pungent country-western feel, but the inconsistent record never ignites, haunted by an audible lack of enthusiasm.

Dixon returned to produce the much-improved **2 x 4**, which gets off to a brilliant start with "Litany (Life Goes On)." Big, lively sound and rich, multi-tracked vocals significantly reduce the R.E.M. comparisons; attention paid to melodies and arrangements

contribute to listenability and durability. "Lips of Steel" recalls the Beatles' psychedelia; "Say Please" and "Let the Big Wheel Roll" are vigorous rockers; "3 AM," dedicated to "alcoholics everywhere, recovered and otherwise," is heartfelt and touching. A few inadvisable detours remain—f'rinstance the clichéd and maudlin "Little Birds" (is that Greg Lake singing?) and "Things Fall Apart," which may be an intentional Jethro Tull parody—but **2 x 4** is, overall, the best Guadalcanal Diary album so far. [iar]

GUN CLUB
Fire of Love (Ruby) 1981 ●
Miami (Animal) 1982
Sex Beat 81 (Fr. Lolita) 1983
Death Party EP (nr/Animal) 1983
The Birth the Death the Ghost (nr/ABC) 1984
The Las Vegas Story (Animal) 1984
Two Sides of the Beast (nr/Dojo) 1985
Dance Kalinda Ballroom: Live in Pandora's
   Box (nr/Dojo) 1986
Mother Juno (Fundamental) 1987 ●
Death Party [CD] (Fr. Revenge) 1988

JEFFREY LEE PIERCE
Flamingo EP (nr/Statik) 1985
Wildweed (nr/Statik) 1985

Jeffrey Lee Pierce pulled together a band in LA around his obsession with the blues. But being unseasoned, young, middle-class, white and barely able to play guitar didn't mean he had to be to the blues what the Cramps are to rockabilly. For Pierce, the blues is a highly personal medium through which he can (and does) broadcast/exorcise inner demons.

Fire of Love is bona fide mutant blues, with Pierce using the musical structures and lyrical imagery for his own ends. Exciting, intense—even cathartic—and badly (if appropriately) recorded, with a dash of punk leavening, this also has homey and effective touches like bits of violin and slide guitar. **Miami** expands to include a little folk, country and pop-rock without diluting the strength one whit, not even via harmony vocalizing (by a pseudonymous Debbie Harry, for one). Producer and Animal magnate Chris Stein does procure a clearer sound, although bringing Pierce's generally strong Jim Morrison-styled vocals to the front of the mix does focus attention on his disconcerting tendency to hit notes sharp.

The next couple of turbulent years yielded little of value. The lineup of the first two albums is documented live on the poorly recorded, indifferently performed **Sex Beat 81** LP; the somewhat better live album on ABC features a later lineup, with pre-**Fire of Love** guitarist Kid Congo Powers back in the Club following his stint with the Cramps. There's an overlap of five songs; **The Birth** also has several otherwise unreleased numbers. **Death Party** dates from Pierce's sojourn in New York with a pick-up edition of Gun Club that includes a Bush Tetra and a member of Panther Burns; it's a lackluster episode that can be forgotten at no great loss.

By **The Las Vegas Story**, the band was properly reconstituted (notwithstanding a switch of bassists). Even with the realigned sound and some guest guitar from Blaster Dave Alvin, it's an uneven album. Evidently intended as a snapshot-mosaic portrait of America, with Pierce attempting to carve himself a Morrison/John Fogerty niche, it simply doesn't wash. That's not to say it's bad—just too unfocused and ineffectual for its ambitious goal. (The issue is further confused by opening Side Two with Pharaoh Sanders' "Master Plan" and following it with "My Man Is Gone Now," from *Porgy and Bess*.) Finally, it's instrumentally too sloppy/punky for the Middle America saga it aspires to be.

Wildweed is another matter altogether. Although typically erratic and idiosyncratic, it's also Pierce's best, most fully-formed work since **Fire of Love**. Produced by Craig Leon in London, it's crisply played by a good little band, and Pierce helps himself surprisingly well on lead guitar. All nine songs are strong; if at times the lyrics seem offhand, the music backs it up. He has apparently become a consistently worthwhile songwriter; one can only hope that he gets a chance to develop even further. (There's also a bonus 45 which features silliness like a drunken Pierce reciting a strange poem as if he plans to become William S. Burroughs.)

Jeffrey Lee then reformed the Gun Club with Powers and a dandy new rhythm section. Produced by Robin Guthrie (of the Cocteau Twins) in Berlin, **Mother Juno** is one of the band's best LPs yet. "The Breaking Hands" (a single which resembles some

of **Wildweed**), is relatively ornate; the rest takes a no-frills approach, sometimes more hard-rock than usual but entirely suited to Pierce's typically grim visions. The album cover painting captures the mood: through a car windshield (with a pair of dice *and* a plastic Jesus) we see a forlorn couple driving through the desert, a booze bottle on its side on the seat between them. The man's face is grim; the woman's got her eyes covered, but can't help peeking.   [jg]

MICHAEL GUTHRIE BAND
Direct Hits (Ear) 1981
MICHAEL GUTHRIE
Banned in America EP (Ear) 1982

Along with brother Herb on drums and bassist Ritchie McNally, singing guitarist/songwriter Michael Guthrie of Charlottesville, Virginia, works up a mighty sweat playing tuneful rockers on these two self-released records. A veteran (but unheralded) trio—which subsequently took the truth-in-advertising name Guitars and Drums—with scads of talent, the basic commodity here is high-octane power pop. Not the wimpy Angloid variety, but full-blooded American rock'n'roll with memorable melodies and catchy choruses.

Direct Hits contains a bunch of great numbers delivered with unpretentious but effective production. **Banned in America**—seven more originals—is more ambitious if not quite as enthralling. Echoes of early Cheap Trick are evident, and some songs shift away from pop toward more direct rock'n'roll; still, an impressive outing from a band deserving of the fame and fortune confidently hoped for in the leadoff track, "Big Time."   [iar]

GYROS
The Gyros EP (Fake Doom) 1984

Cool, unmannered rockabilly and R&B from a New York area quintet. The Gyros have two real gone guitarists and a soulful singer; the EP's five originals show a lot of spunk and not a little polish, eschewing heavy ambience for simple enjoyability.

[iar]

H H H H H H H

NINA HAGEN

Nina Hagen Band (nr/CBS) 1979
Unbehagen (nr/CBS) 1980
Nina Hagen Band EP (Columbia) 1980
Nunsexmonkrock (Columbia) 1982
Fearless (Columbia) 1983
Nina Hagen in Ekstasy (Columbia) 1985

Although born in East Berlin, one-of-a-kind singer/songwriter Nina Hagen is restricted by no national boundaries, working and living in Germany, England and America. Her approach to singing is consistently bizarre—on her albums she runs the gamut from quirky sing-song (à la Lene Lovich, whose "Lucky Number" gets a translation/transmutation on **Unbehagen**) to an anguished howl (much of **Nunsexmonkrock**) that sounds like Marianne Faithfull's contemporary work. Throughout, Hagen projects amazing intensity as well as a consistent and total lack of selfconsciousness in both delivery and subject matter. Whether despised by the unimaginative or hailed as a genius, Nina Hagen is a truly radical talent.

Nina Hagen Band, her first LP, is relatively restrained; all-German vocals mask the subject matter for non-linguists. (Although "TV Glotzer" is an adaptation of the Tubes' "White Punks on Dope.") A serviceable rock trio provides generic rock'n'roll backing which she easily upstages, even without dipping far into her seemingly bottomless bag of vocal tricks.

Unbehagen is light years better. The band (expanded to a much-improved quartet who later recorded on their own as Spliff) offers convincing, precise modern rock with neat keyboard work, while Hagen's out-of-control persona takes center stage to sing, scream, growl, whisper and wail her way through nine gripping tales of decadence. Listening to **Unbehagen** is like stumbling into a monster's lair—feelings of revulsion and transfixion mingle to make this true rock-at-the-edge art.

The American EP is a 10-inch with a pair of songs from each of the first two albums, including the aforementioned cover versions.

Hagen recorded **Nunsexmonkrock** in New York with a band that includes Chris Spedding. To describe it as wild hardly suffices—the drugs-sex-religion-politics-mystical imagery that spills out is nearly incomprehensible in its bag-lady introspection, but the music and singing combine into an aural bed of nails that carries stunning impact. It almost doesn't matter that Hagen sticks to English; what counts is the phenomenal vocal drama. Her range seems limitless, and the countless characters she plays make this fascinating.

Conceptually outdoing herself again, Hagen enlisted Giorgio Moroder and Keith Forsey to produce **Fearless** in California; unlike most of their projects, however, the artist emerges as the dominant force. The album finds her in a dance frame of mind, singing about club life ("New York New York"), enlisting the Red Hot Chili Peppers for a rap number ("What It Is"), doing the funky Hare Krishna ("I Love Paul") and generally acting the warped disco queen while her Felix the Cat bag of voices stretches from operatic to munchkin, Grace Jones to Mr T. It's not clear whether this alliance with naked commercialism was expected to deliver a hit record; fans know that Hagen's rampant individuality almost precludes mass comprehension, let alone full-scale popularity. Nonetheless, **Fearless**—which bears out its title—is hypnotic and hilarious. One of her best records.

Reflecting Hagen's continuing fascination with Los Angeles, **Ekstasy** pursues a similar set of mental and musical notions. "Universal Radio" and "Gods of Aquarius" are straightforward (well . . .) and catchy dance rock with (why not?) metaphysical lyrics. "Russian Reggae" and "1985 Ekstasy Drive" are Hagenized metal; her "Lord's Prayer" adds new meaning to the word sacrilegious. But then, for different reasons, so do her versions of the Sex Pistols' "My Way" (take that, Sid Vicious!) and Norman Greenbaum's "Spirit in the Sky." More joy from the planet Nina! [iar]

PAUL HAIG

Rhythm of Life (nr/Crépuscule-Island) 1983
Paul Haig EP (Crépuscule-Island) 1984
Swing in '82 (nr/Crépuscule-Island) 1985
The Warp of Pure Fun (nr/Crépuscule-Island)
    1985

For his first album following the dissolution of Scotland's Josef K, singer-guitarist-keyboardist Paul Haig enlisted some impressive sidemen—including Anton Fier, Tom Bailey and Bernie Worrell—and got Alex Sadkin to produce. A mostly pleasant but unexceptional and uneven record, the synth-driven tracks on **Rhythm of Life** variously resemble lighter-hearted versions of New Order and the Human League. Haig demonstrates a danceable solution that doesn't bang on your head; some of the numbers, however, do drag along tunelessly, replacing invention with mere repetition and nuance with clumsiness. The subsequent American EP offers five-ninths of the album (a wise condensation) as remixed by an obscure New York club dj. By leaving off a couple of dogs, it's a better way to meet Mr. Haig (musically speaking).

The **Warp of Pure Fun** teams him with ex-Associate Alan Rankine for a slicker, more adventurous and entertaining excursion. Haig's not much of a singer—a little dramatic and gruff for the dance-poppish material—but the nimble arrangements and some resilient melodies cover such deficiencies. "The Only Truth" crosses New Order with the Thompson Twins and, like "Love & War," features Bernard Sumner on guitar; "Heaven Help You Now" injects a bit of folk into synth-rock. A triumph of style over substance, but a likable record with some fine moments. [iar]

HAIRCUT ONE HUNDRED

Pelican West (Arista) 1982
Paint and Paint (nr/Polydor) 1983

NICK HEYWARD

North of a Miracle (Arista) 1983
Postcards from Home (nr/Arista) 1987

One of 1982's brightest new modern chart groups, these six energetic young Londoners created a crisp mixture of melodic pop and Afro-American and Latin rhythms, seasoned with horns and an occasional dash of jazz. Haircut's funk-oriented songs tend to be a bit samey (and placing three of them— "Favourite Shirts," "Lemon Firebrigade" and "Marine Boy"—together on the American version of **Pelican West** doesn't help); their pop songs are arguably more successful. "Love Plus One" and "Fantastic Day" are delightful, near-perfect confections with hooks that will snare even the tone deaf; "Snow Girl" and "Surprise Me Again" run a close second. Following the departure of leader/singer Nick Heyward for a solo career, Haircut proved their resourcefulness by returning with a credible second album, **Paint and Paint**.

On his own, Heyward continues the band's lightweight, ultra-commercial pop style with a few even-milder digressions. (**North of a Miracle**'s "Whistle Down the Wind" sounds remarkably like the Association.) His pristinely-produced solo debut is filled with layered vocals and peppy music played by a large collection of studio hands (including Steve Nieve!), given a slick veneer by co-producer Geoff Emerick. Obnoxiously, awesomely pleasant, **North of a Miracle** is everything a disposable pop record should be. [ks/iar]

HALF JAPANESE

Calling All Girls EP (50 Skidillion Watts)
    1977
1/2 Gentlemen/Not Beasts (nr/Armageddon)
    1980
Loud (nr/Armageddon) 1981
Horrible EP (Press) 1983
Our Solar System (Iridescence) 1984
Sing No Evil (Iridescence) 1984
Music to Strip By (50 Skidillion Watts) 1987

JAD FAIR

The Zombies of Mora Tau EP
    (nr/Armageddon) 1980 (Press) 1982
Everyone Knew . . . but Me (Press) 1982 +
    1985

Monarchs (Iridescence) 1984
Best Wishes (Iridescence) 1987

Maryland (by way of San Francisco) genius Jad Fair, America's preeminent idiot savant of revealingly amateurish rock, has led Half Japanese for over a decade, building a large and faithful following for his uniquely honest and unselfconscious approach to musicmaking. Originally comprising Jad and his brother David, 1/2 Jap's early records were noisy and slapdash; untuned guitars and an uncertain backup band providing minimalist settings from art rock to pre-punk. The Fairs recorded **Calling All Girls** alone, cramming nine neurotic songs ("Shy Around Girls," "Dream Date," "The Worst I'd Ever Do") onto a crude and unsettling 7-inch.

Heavy on the percussion and making no claims to melody, **1/2 Gentlemen/Not Beasts** is a three-record boxed set that combines elementary musicianship and electronics with tuneless vocals bursting with angst and ennui. Nods to Devo, the Ramones and Iggy Pop (whose "Fun Time" gets crushed) indicate that the atonal, jagged results are no accident. Many favorite punk tunes are "covered" with surprising results.

Loud expands the music's range, with help from six-part accompaniment, including horns, more guitar and almost-avant-garde drumming. The tendency toward jazz doesn't strip Half Japanese of their atavistic charm or chaotic raucousness. **Loud** includes a dirgelike rendition of Jim Morrison's "The Spy."

Horrible, the pair's first release after a long vinyl silence, is a five-song 12-inch obsessed with ghouls and horror movies. "Thing with a Hook" matches the tale of a one-handed insane man-beast "pulling heads off boy/girlfriends down in lover's lane" with truly distressing music; other tracks are about "Vampire" and "Rosemary's Baby." Where the Cramps do this type of cinematic craziness for fun, Half Japanese sound genuinely tormented.

Music to Strip By, produced (and played on) by New York hipster Kramer (ex-Shockabilly—which makes him an associate of the truly likeminded Eugene Chadbourne) and pressed on clear red vinyl, is a relatively sophisticated and appealing outing by a seemingly almost-rehearsed full-fledged band. Working without his brother, Jad is comfortably in control, singing typically strange lyrics in a typically artless voice. "Stripping for Cash" reflects a recent news item; "My Sor-

did Past" and the countrified "Ouija Board Summons Satan" scan like what they probably are—lifts from a supermarket tabloid. "Sex at Your Parents' House" would be funnier if it weren't being sung—with apparent conviction—by an adult. Versions of "La Bamba," Fats Domino's "Blue Monday" and Willie Dixon's "Hidden Charms" add to the stability of this eminently likable 22-song album.

Jad's solo records are even weirder than his band's, but it's impossible to compare them with any critical surety. **Everyone Knew . . . but Me** contains 29 sessions (mostly originals about girls, but two James Brown covers as well) of him whining and vocalizing (singing isn't exactly the word for it), accompanying himself on what sound like pots, pans and guitar. Emerging amidst all the painful primitivism, however, is touching naïveté and defenselessness, a pitiful lack of social abilities/success that makes Fair seem something of a tortured, not merely torturing, artist.

The one-man **Best Wishes**, recorded between 1982 and 1985, is a collection of 42 brief instrumentals, all titled either "O.K." or "A.O.K." Listenable? Yes—in brief spurts, as long as you don't pay too close attention and keep the volume down. Creatively significant? Er, no.   [sg/iar]

See also *Maureen Tucker.*

HALF MAN HALF BISCUIT

Back in the D.H.S.S. (nr/Probe Plus) 1985
The Trumpton Riots EP (nr/Probe Plus) 1986
Back Again in the D.H.S.S. (nr/Probe Plus) 1987

This entertaining Liverpool quintet emerged from total obscurity to become a dominant British indie chart regular in the first half of 1986. Playing low-key garage-punk singalong ditties (imagine a cross between Mark Riley and Jonathan Richman), the Biscuits like to name names—titles on **Back in the D.H.S.S.** include "Fuckin' 'ell, It's Fred Titmus," "The Len Ganley Stance" and "99% of Gargoyles Look Like Bob Todd." Throughout, they remain completely unassuming, and exhibit a dry, sarcastic wit. (As if a band with such a name would likely be dead serious.) One of the best debuts in recent years.

The Trumpton Riots EP is a little heavier—with raw drive and distorted synths, the snarling title cut and "Architecture, Morality, Ted and Alice" are both reminiscent of the early Stranglers. Side Two lightens up with the more hilarious "1966 and All That." Fans should look for the edition which adds a fifth track, "All I Want for Christmas Is a Dukla Prague Away Kit," the best soccer song since the Fall's "Kicker Conspiracy."

Half Man Half Biscuit called it quits in 1987, hence the title of their second album, **Back Again in the D.H.S.S.** (Department of Health and Social Services—where Britons get their unemployment checks). Some of the **Trumpton Riots** cuts are reprised, as is the penchant for titles with real-life stars ("Rod Hull Is Alive—Why?" and "The Bastard Son of Dean Friedman"). The band is a bit tighter this go-around, and has cleaner (but hardly what you'd call glossy) production. The record's highlight is "Dickie Davis Eyes," which contains the inspirational verse, "And all those people who you romantically like to still believe are alive are dead/So I'll wipe the snot on the arm of your chair/as you put another Roger Dean poster on the wall." No folks, it doesn't get any better than this.
[dgs]

HAMBI AND THE DANCE
Heartache (nr/Virgin) 1982

Liverpool's Hambi and the Dance attempted an interesting combination of synthesized art-rock and traditional rock'n'roll, with mixed results. When singer/songwriter Hambi Harambolous draws on influences ranging from Phil Spector and the Searchers to the Roxy/Bowie/Ultravox school, the record can be very impressive ("Living in a Heartache," "Madelaine"). He is less successful, however, when trying arty synthesized rock that sounds like Ultravox outtakes.
[ks]

HAPPY HATE ME NOTS
Scrap EP (Aus. Waterfront) 1987
Out (Rough Trade) 1988

"We work hard because miracles are not around," sings Christian Houllemare over Mick Searson's incessant drumbeat as two guitars intertwine and interact; one a warm box filled with enough fuzz to choke the lint screen on your dryer, the other dripping shimmering droplets of clear, clean shine in "This Is the Wrong World." Even if you hate commercial pop, it's hard to hate the Happy

Hate Me Nots. The six spunky songs about love and introspection on **Scrap**, their first non-single release, are so fresh and filled with buoyant energy that even the most dedicated pop-hater has to smile. This is utterly commercial in every sense of the word, full of hooks and lines to catch your ears and sink any trace of a frown. Depending on the cut, their vocal style is somewhere between the brighter side of Hüsker Dü and the harmonics of Youth Brigade. They use a horn (on "Go Away") and a piano (on "Blue Afternoon") and real verses with choral refrains on just about every track. The US version (retitled **Out**) adds two singles.
['e]

PEARL HARBOR AND THE EXPLOSIONS
Pearl Harbor and the Explosions (Warner Bros.) 1980
PEARL HARBOUR
Don't Follow Me, I'm Lost Too (Warner Bros.) 1981
Pearls Galore (Island) 1984

Pearl Harbor and the Explosions came out of San Francisco's early new wave scene, but their lone album consists of bouncy little pop tunes suitable for FM radio: watered-down soul and funk overtones topped off by Pearl E. Gates' theatrical vocal posturings. Danceably forgettable.

Harbour (dropping Gates and adopting the British spelling) hit her stride as a solo artist on **Don't Follow Me, I'm Lost Too**, a headlong plunge into rockabilly and similarly ancient styles. Smothered by producer Mickey Gallagher in waves of flutter echo, Pearl wails like a demon, obviously happy to have a sympathetic setting. "Fujiyama Mama" and "At the Dentist" rock wildly with old-fashioned panache; "Heaven Is Gonna Be Empty" takes a more countrified, though equally quaint, approach. This one's a memorable instant party.

A belated follow-up produced by Richard Gottehrer employs 20 musicians—from Ellie Greenwich to Chris Spedding to Masa Hiro Kajiura—for more fun in the old world. Harbour starts off by covering that 1963 Rocky Fellers chestnut, "Killer Joe," and then launches into a program of girl-group soundalikes that quiver with melodic conviction and shake with appropriate, cliché-free backing. Sounding uncannily like Kirsty MacColl in spots, **Pearls Galore** is a winning collection of tunes by a talented, adaptable vocalist who should be far better known than she is.

[jy/iar]

CHARLIE HARPER

See *U.K. Subs.*

JODY HARRIS
It Happened One Night (Press) 1982
JODY HARRIS AND ROBERT QUINE
Escape (Lust/Unlust) 1981

Jody Harris has worked with such New York luminaries as the Raybeats and James White and the Blacks, but remains one of the most underrated guitarists on the scene. His schizophrenic solo album proves him to be an accomplished composer as well, turning his talents toward straight pop ("It Happened One Night"), rockabilly ("I'm After Hours Again"), blues ("You Better Read This Before You Sign") and various forms of jazz, from be-bop to Stephane Grappelli. Harris amply proves that old forms can be given new life, especially with his exquisite, modernistic guitar work.

Along with Robert Quine (Richard Hell's Voidoids, later of Lou Reed's band) Harris made the beautiful **Escape**, which drifts through a plethora of styles—Frippist drone tunes, jazz, country swing—and proves that these two consistently surprising guitarists are even more surprising than suspected. Though hardly rock, **Escape** has a vitality and joy missing in most music today, and so much fun it's sexy. Highly recommended.

[sg]

JERRY HARRISON
The Red and the Black (Sire) 1981
Casual Gods (Sire) 1987 ●
BONZO GOES TO WASHINGTON
5 Minutes EP (Sleeping Bag) 1984

All of the Talking Heads have participated in extracurricular musical activities, and guitarist/keyboardist Harrison is no different—only less successful. Lacking a hit single (like the Tom Tom Club) or a Broadway production (Byrne), few got to hear the fruits of Harrison's efforts during the band's 1981 sabbatical. On **The Red and the Black** he continues to explore the pan-ethnic, cross-rhythmic music of **Remain in Light**, not a surprise, since many of the auxiliary Heads

(like Adrian Belew, Bernie Worrell and Nona Hendryx) also appear on Harrison's record. The results are fairly funky, albeit in a relaxed, slow-motion way.

Harrison's brief next solo outing hit a hip-hop groove, as he teamed with bassist Bootsy Collins for the "5 Minutes" 12-inch, a found-sound dance record (in three mixes) which uses Reagan's notorious "we begin bombing . . . " on-mic extemporization.

His second album, **Casual Gods**, also leads with its chin: the cover and inner sleeve photos show hordes of poor contemporary Brazilians working under horrendous conditions as goldminers. The music, however, is slick rock-funk with lyrics that are serious but not radical. Harrison, who's not a bad singer, doesn't write songs so much as techno grooves with sketchy melodies; his accomplished cohorts play with chops but little feeling.

[rnp/iar]

DEBBIE HARRY
See *Blondie.*

DIE HAUT
Schnelles Leben (Ger. Monogam) 1982
DIE HAUT WITH NICK CAVE
Burnin' the Ice (nr/Illuminated) 1983

Rising out of Berlin's post-punk bleakness, die Haut ("the skin") is a largely instrumental quartet with Beefheartian and psychedelic overtones but possessing a disciplined ferocity that gives them a strikingly Germanic sound. **Schnelles Leben** is a seven-song, 18-minute disc which utilizes terse bass and drum rhythms topped with scratchy guitar work, rarely settling into a tonal center. Five of the tracks are vocal-less and tend to lack development and textural variety. Not so much produced as simply recorded, in many places vocals are conspicuous by their absence.

Die Haut enlisted the services of Birthday Party singer Nick Cave for **Burnin' the Ice** and even gave him co-billing. Cave supplies all vocals and lyrics (for four of the seven cuts), generating an effect of leader and backing band. Much of the manic double-guitar work on **Schnelles Leben** turns into psychedelic droning behind Cave's bellowing, but at least the songwriting and production show improvement. Die Haut is a promising band that needs to locate a personality (not to mention a singer) of its own. [dgs]

See also *Lydia Lunch.*

GREG HAWKES

See *Cars*.

HAWKWIND

Hawkwind (UA) 1970 (nr/Sunset) 1975
In Search of Space (UA) 1971
Doremi Fasol Latido (UA) 1972
Space Ritual Live (UA) 1973
Hall of the Mountain Grill (UA) 1974
Warrior at the Edge of Time (UA) 1975
Road Hawks (UA) 1976
Astounding Sounds, Amazing Music
   (nr/Charisma) 1976
Masters of the Universe (nr/UA) 1977
   (nr/Fame) 1982
Quark Strangeness and Charm (Sire) 1977
P.X.R.5 (nr/Charisma) 1979
Live 1979 (nr/Bronze) 1980
Repeat Performance (nr/Charisma) 1980
Levitation (nr/Bronze) 1980
Sonic Attack (nr/RCA) 1981
Church of Hawkwind (nr/RCA) 1982
Choose Your Masques (nr/RCA) 1982
Friends and Relations, Volume 1 (nr/Flicknife)
   1982
[EP] (nr/Flicknife) 1984
Friends and Relations, Volume 2 (nr/Flicknife)
   1984
Friends and Relations, Volume 3 (nr/Flicknife)
   1985
Independent Days, Volume 1 (nr/Flicknife)
   1985
The Chronicle of the Black Sword
   (nr/Flicknife) 1985 ●
Independent Days, Volume 2 (nr/Flicknife)
   1986
Angels of Death (nr/RCA) 1986
Out & Intake (nr/Flicknife) 1987
British Tribal Music (nr/Start) 1987
Live Chronicles (GWR-Profile) 1988

VARIOUS ARTISTS

Greasy Truckers Party (nr/UA) 1972
Glastonbury Fayre (nr/Revelation) 1972

HAWKLORDS

25 Years On (nr/Charisma) 1978 + 1982

HAWKWIND ZOO

EP (nr/Flicknife) 1981

DAVE BROCK

Earthed to the Ground (nr/Flicknife) 1984

ROBERT CALVERT

Captain Lockheed and the Starfighters
   (nr/UA) 1974
Lucky Leif and the Long Ships (nr/UA) 1975
   (nr/BGO) 1987

STEVE SWINDELLS

Fresh Blood (Atco) 1980

Hawkwind's influence has been extensive, if often indirect and, when acknowledged at all, done so grudgingly. The group's faults (most notably a chronic tendency towards excess) have generally been over-criticized to the exclusion of its virtues: that gargantuan and impenetrable pre-metal/hardcore drone, those great riffs, that inexorable drive to destinations unknown. Unfashionable in Britain for most of its existence and almost unknown in the US, Hawkwind has often been judged offensive merely for existing. If that isn't pure punk . . .

Through a checkered, nearly *20-year* history, Hawkwind has been ruled either by a dictator under the guise of near-anarchy or by a purported leader with no control at all. Whichever it be, Dave Brock has been the lineup's only constant through 40 or so personnel changes. A busker who did a stint in the Dharma Blues Band (preserved on anthologies of early British blues), he formed Group X—which became Hawkwind Zoo and then Hawkwind—in 1969. Since then, Brock has written and sung the great majority of the material and played most of the guitar, not to mention a fair amount of synthesizer.

Hawkwind's first album is an unexciting hodgepodge of street folk/blues, riff-rock and electronics, with Nik Turner's sax and flute thrown in. The LP's indulgent improvisations fit in with the band's "rebellious hippie" image, as evidenced by their early drug busts and indefatigable benefit-playing, which initially got them positive attention in the "alternative culture" media. Stacia, a voluptuous semi-nude dancer who joined up in 1971, also drew attention to the group, and probably had some influence on it; she eventually got a full vote in Hawkwind affairs.

Despite its intricate, attractive unfolding sleeve (designed by Barney Bubbles), **In Search of Space** is pretty lukewarm; the sole song of canonical note here is "Master of the Universe." Most important, though, the aforementioned musical elements, along with a more explicit science-fiction orientation, can now be heard as a stylistic blend, integrating Turner, electronics gremlin Dik Mik and newly added synthesizer player Del Dettmar. Some of the electro-noise/saxoid drone bears a strange resemblance to subsequent mid-song blasts by early Roxy Music, whose own electronics specialist Eno had resided, like Dik Mik, in Ladbroke Grove. Hmm . . .

Doremi Fasol Latido is Hawkwind's first strong album. The band's intensity was lifted a notch or two by the manic hyper-drive of new bassist and occasional guitarist Ian "Lemmy" Kilmister, who had played in '60s beat group the Rockin' Vicars and horrible drummerless psychedelicians Sam Gopal. Also, Robert Calvert, who'd drifted into the group's periphery, began to shape its mythology, writing and declaiming some of its lyrics, just as Turner's own writing was starting to emerge.

Earlier the same year, Hawkwind had played at a London benefit concert for the Greasy Truckers, an alternative music organization. The subsequent double live album included a full side of Hawkwind but, more significantly, an *outtake* from it, the queerly poppy space-chug "Silver Machine," was released as a single and became a huge UK hit. (It didn't appear on LP until years later.) That success financed the tour chronicled on **Space Ritual Live**. The double LP includes versions of "Master of the Universe" and two-thirds of **Doremi**'s songs (although two had chunks cut out "because they were too long"); the new material included Calvert and Brock's synth-embroidered recitations of scary scenarios (e.g., the armageddon classic "Sonic Attack") penned by Calvert and their new buddy, noted sci-fi author Michael Moorcock. The LP is solid to super, and not as longwinded as might have been expected.

Dik Mik departed before **Hall of the Mountain Grill** and was replaced by violin-wielding keyboardist Simon House; Calvert left to do his solo albums. By **Warrior at the Edge of Time**, Dettmar had gone too, and Alan Powell picked up the slack for injured drummer Simon King, subsequently playing alongside him. House added formal musical knowledge and skill for a fuller, often more melodious brew. The actual sound of the discs was also clearer, which lent overall crispness, but also pointed up the anarchy of the droning rave-ups.

Hall of the Mountain Grill's highlights include the rampaging "Psychedlic Warlords (Disappear in Smoke)" and Lemmy's bleak "Lost Johnny" (co-written by Mick Farren). **Warrior at the Edge of Time** has four tracks co-written by Moorcock, who makes a murky, overly echoed thespian debut on two of them. It also sports Brock's own rocking

pseudo-mythology ("Magnu") and a quiet, thoughtful tune ("The Demented Man"), as well as "Kings of Speed," released as a single. The latter's B-side was "Motorhead"; Lemmy took that name for the band he formed after being sacked from Hawkwind following a 1974 on-tour Canadian drug bust.

By that point, Hawkwind had achieved all it ever would, in terms of trailblazing; from there on, it's all been refinements, variations, even regurgitations. This isn't to say none of the subsequent albums are any good, just not particularly original, moving in a more normal direction. They switched UK labels, from UA to Charisma, at which point UA decided to do some summing up. **Road Hawks** is a fine retrospective, and includes "Silver Machine"; **Masters of the Universe** is a strong secondary collection.

Astounding Sounds noticeably backed off from the heaviness of the Lemmy era. His replacement, Paul Rudolph (ex-Pink Fairies), had lots of zip, just no overkill. Meanwhile, Calvert had returned, more fully part of the band than ever. Almost every cut is quite good but too long by half, except for the single "Kerb Crawler," which is sharp and to the point. More internal problems: Turner was going over the top onstage and was asked to leave, while Rudolph and Powell, allegedly engaging in power play tactics, got the raw boot.

So next came—what else?—one of Hawkwind's best, and poppiest, albums. **Quark Strangeness and Charm** features tuff tracks like "Hassan I Sahba" (clever mating of Hawkwind's patented drone with Middle Eastern music) and the delightfully rollicking (!) title tune.

P.X.R.5's back cover suggests it's Hawkwind's penultimate LP, but it wasn't. It appears to be some gems'n'junk cut in '77 and '78 as the band teetered on the brink of extinction (on two tracks Brock plays everything but drums). Three otherwise unreleased live tracks, too.

After House left to join Bowie's tour band, the group did fall apart, but soon reassembled as the Hawklords (renamed for legal reasons): Brock and Calvert, plus songwriting bassist Harvey Bainbridge, keyboardist Steve Swindells (ex-String Driven Thing and Pilot) and drummer Martin Griffin. Fliply futuristic in lyrical slant, and more succinct and "modern" in sonic approach (heralded in bits of **P.X.R.5**), the Hawklords made immediately likable though lightweight music.

The alternate name became no longer necessary, and the band signed to Bronze. (**Repeat Performance** is a good distillation of their Charisma era, although it omits "Hassan I Sahba.") Following the live album, Swindells left to make his own solo LP, later becoming a hotshot club dj. He was replaced by Tim Blake (ex-Gong); the new drummer—surprise—was Ginger Baker. None of this could compensate for Calvert's departure; **Levitation** is bland and tame, its main grit supplied by newly returned guitarist Huw Lloyd-Langton, who'd left Hawkwind (to join Luther Grosvenor in Widowmaker) after cutting the very first album *a decade earlier!*

Griffin returned to replace Baker, and Bainbridge and Brock took up the keyboard slack for the departed Blake, as the band moved over to RCA. Hard, heavy, humorless but often grimly evocative, these three albums are aptly summarized on the generous (54 minutes plus) **Angels of Death** compilation. Following that, Hawkwind went into limbo, with a vast amount of previously unreleased material eventually flowing from the Flicknife label and helping stir up demand for the real thing.

When it came, it was with Bainbridge on keys only, Allan Davey on bass and Danny Thompson (ex-Pentangle!?!) on drums. With Moorcock's help (but not actual participation), **The Chronicle of the Black Sword** adapted his popular Elric sword-and-sorcery sagas. Even better is **Live Chronicles** (from the '85 tour), which includes versions of most of that record, numbers from the RCA years and even "Magnu" and "Master of the Universe." Hawkwind could still smash'n'slash.

The Flicknife catalogue started modestly in '81 with a good little 17-minute EP (credited to Hawkwind Zoo), containing an alternate version of "Hurry Sundown" (from **Hawkwind**), a live "Kings of Speed" and the early (and surprisingly erotic) "Sweet Mistress of Pain." More EPs followed, some with newly recorded material (e.g, "Night of the Hawks," with Lemmy); they were later collected onto two volumes of **Independent Days**. There's also a three-disc series of **Hawkwind Friends and Relations**, i.e., outtakes, alternate takes, demos, other bands, etc. **Out and Intake** is basically the most recent lineup (half with the previous rhythm section) doing an odd combination of new songs and old, even ones most of the personnel didn't originally play on (e.g., "Ejection," from a Calvert solo LP). Two tracks feature returning alumnus Nik Turner. **British Tribal Music** is- a fine retrospective with tracks from several different eras of the group's career.

In the solo album department, there's Brock's batch of demos, **Earthed to the Ground**, "recorded at home while waiting for Hawkwind to get going again." The writing and playing are pretty thin, although the odd number like "Green Finned Demon" suggests it would've been worth an EP.

Calvert's **Captain Lockheed** is a deluxe concept album dramatizing the true story of an airplane disastrously modified into an unstable, unsafe machine (aka the Widow Maker). Ambitiously outfitted: Rudolph, Lemmy, King, Dettmar, Turner, Brock, plus Eno (!) and—reading dialogue, yet—Viv Stanshall and Jim Capaldi, all overseen by Roy Thomas Baker. Despite some decent tracks, the talk segments are just plain awkward, and make it impossible for the songs to sustain a flow.

Another Calvert concept album, **Lucky Leif** argues that the Vikings really discovered America. Is this trip necessary? Some of it's just plain silly. Produced by Eno, music dominated by Rudolph, with House and Turner along for the ride. Other participants: Winkie Brian Turrington, Roxy bassist Sal Maida and Moorcock on banjo.

The best of the solos is Swindells' **Fresh Blood**. It's just him (producing, too), with Lloyd-Langton, King and ex-Van Der Graaf Generator bassist Nic Potter. It sounds like Thin Lizzy meets Graham Parker with a rocket up his ass. Narsty. Roger Daltrey sang Swindells' "Bitter and Twisted" in the soundtrack of his film, *McVicar*.

The mid-'70s lineup with Lemmy surfaced as protagonists (the Hawklords, led by "Baron Brock") of a trilogy of sci-fi novels by Moorcock and Michael Butterworth. Calvert died in mid-1988.   [jg]

See also *Inner City Unit, Motorhead.*

BONNIE HAYES WITH THE WILD COMBO
Good Clean Fun (Slash) 1982
Brave New Girl (Bondage) 1984

BONNIE HAYES
Bonnie Hayes (Chrysalis) 1987 ●

Originally known around San Francisco as the Punts, singer Bonnie Hayes and her backing trio take the grossly overused pure pop formula and actually manage to turn it interesting again on **Good Clean Fun**. She follows in the tradition of early Blondie and the Go-Go's by making bright, simple melodies hop and skip incessantly. Hayes and crew avoid the monotony that sometimes plagues their counterparts by downplaying the preciousness and incorporating a wide variety of influences, including jazz and R&B.

Hayes' 1987 major-label album employs a larger backing band and a brand-name producer (Stewart Levine), but nothing can stop the vim and infectious enthusiasm of this adorable one-woman pop dynamo. Hayes writes mature songs about romance from a gingerly hopeful, self-reliant standpoint and performs them with pristine, airy simplicity that at one point ("The Real Thing") precisely resembles Todd Rundgren at his most joyfully upbeat. Trivia: Bonnie's brother Chris plays with Huey Lewis. [jy/iar]

HAYSI FANTAYZEE
Battle Hymns for Children Singing (RCA) 1983

Battle Hymns is one of the most intentionally annoying records of all time. This now-defunct London trio—singing characters Jeremiah Healy and Kate Garner plus string-puller Paul Caplin—spew out juvenile nonsense lyrics attached to bouncy rock, gussied up with gimmicky production to make it reach maximum quirky obnoxiousness. A few tracks (like the McLarenesque square-dance rocker "Shiny Shiny," and the Bow Wow Wow-like "More Money") are fine for *very* occasional listening, but enduring this entire album in one sitting is like having painful dentistry performed by an overbearing three-year-old. Garner has since made solo records. [iar]

ROBERT HAZARD
Robert Hazard EP (RCA) 1982
Wing of Fire (RCA) 1984

Hazard was a popular figure on the Philadelphia scene before signing a big record contract. His debut EP delivers one great wriggly-rock track ("Escalator of Life"), three so-so numbers and a powerful but irrelevant update of Bob Dylan's "Blowin' in the Wind." Although talented, Hazard hasn't got much individual character—traces

of Bowie, Cars, Petty, Springsteen and others abound.

Cyndi Lauper assured Hazard of a comfortable retirement by recording "Girls Just Want to Have Fun," which he wrote in 1979. Although that high-water mark achievement makes the commercial failure of **Wing of Fire** largely academic, it is a passable album, kind of Tom Petty-meets-Willy DeVille (horns, modern outlook, drama, melody). The songs go on too long (or at least seem to) and David Kershenbaum's production could be a lot more exciting but, all in all, a solid effort from a reasonably talented guy. [iar]

TOPPER HEADON
See *Clash.*

HEARTBREAKERS
L.A.M.F. (nr/Track) 1977
Live at Max's Kansas City (Max's Kansas City) 1979
D.T.K.—Live at the Speakeasy (nr/Jungle) 1982

JOHNNY THUNDERS & THE HEARTBREAKERS
L.A.M.F. Revisited (nr/Jungle) 1984
D.T.K L.A.M.F. Revisited [tape] (nr/Jungle) 1984 ●
Live at the Lyceum Ballroom 1984 (nr/ABC) 1984

The New York club circuit's first supergroup, the early (around 1975) Heartbreakers consisted of ex-NY Dolls Johnny Thunders and Jerry Nolan, ex-Television bassist Richard Hell and previously unknown guitarist Walter Lure. After Hell quit to go solo and was replaced by Billy Rath, the band moved to England and recorded a technically disappointing debut LP, **L.A.M.F.**, for Track Records. The irony of that label's name was not lost on Heartbreakers fans, who suspected that the group's move to Britain was motivated primarily by the UK's heroin-maintenance program. So feeble was the album's mix that drummer Jerry Nolan actually quit over it, though the material itself shows the band to be masters of the stripped-down, souped-up arrangement later copied by many punk groups.

The Heartbreakers subsequently returned to New York, where they performed an endless succession of "farewell" gigs with various pickup drummers, most often Ty Styx. One of these shows was recorded for the **Live at Max's** LP, an ultimate party record—loud and sloppy with lots of dirty talk—and probably the best official document of any local band of the era.

In 1982, a 1977 London performance was sprung from the vaults and released as **D.T.K.—Live at the Speakeasy.** Recorded with Nolan, it presents the darker side of the ambience that pervades the **Live at Max's** set, if only because the band has a more secure drummer. Clearly the Johnny Thunders show, it exposes some incredibly sloppy playing, self-righteous audience baiting and a few devolved lyrics (like his reworking of "Can't Keep My Eyes on You" into "Can't keep my cock in you.")

Another live release—this one from a March '84 show at London's Lyceum—turned up a few years later, showing how far the Heartbreakers had come and how little they had changed. The program is a full-fledged Thunders retrospective: the Dolls' "Personality Crisis," the Heartbreakers' "Born To(o) Lo(o)se," "So Alone" from his solo career and a couple of classics (like "Pipeline" and "Do You Love Me?") from his youth. And there's more! The show is hot and reasonably coherent, with fine singing by JT and Lure; clear production (Thunders, assisted by Tony James) helps immeasurably.

Remixed to fix the miserable original sound, **L.A.M.F.** got a much-improved second life when it was reissued as **L.A.M.F. Revisited.** Jungle also created a double-play cassette under the name **D.T.K L.A.M.F.,** slapping the '77 live LP on the reverse side for maximum punk pleasure. [jw/iar]

See also *Richard Hell, Johnny Thunders, Sid Vicious.*

HEAVEN 17

Penthouse and Pavement (nr/B.E.F.-Virgin) 1981
Heaven 17 (nr/Arista) 1982
The Luxury Gap (Virgin-Arista) 1983 ●
How Men Are (Virgin-Arista) 1984
Endless [tape] (nr/Virgin) 1986 ●
Pleasure One (Virgin) 1986 ●

After disproving all accusations of synthesizers as limited vehicles of expression, the British Electric Foundation retreated to produce an LP with dance-troupe-turned-recording-group Hot Gossip and let themselves—in their alter-ego as the trio Heaven 17—get on with **Penthouse and Pavement.** Lyrically, the album ranges from silly to exciting; musically, it's an almost flawless blend

of funk and electronics. The American **Heaven 17** release combines six **Penthouse and Pavement** cuts with three new tracks. Two of those—the top-notch pop soul of "Let Me Go" and "Who Will Stop the Rain"—surfaced on **The Luxury Gap,** although they were replaced by a new pair on the American version of the LP. Common to both, "Crushed by the Wheels of Industry," "Temptation" and "We Live So Fast" (even if the last song's refrain of "motion" sounds *exactly* like "bullshit") are stellar examples of Heaven 17's chartbound craftsmanship: catchy, toe-tapping dance-pop with horns, guitars and an orchestra providing musical depth behind Ian Craig Marsh and Martyn Ware's synthesizers. Glenn Gregory's gruff vocals don't immediately sound mellifluous, but they suit the material and ambience perfectly.

With B.E.F. (the Concept) receding into the background for want of activity, Heaven 17 made their third album, graced with another awful cover painting. **How Men Are** features an expanding cast of musicians and concomitant sprawl—"And That's No Lie" runs over ten tedious minutes! The LP has a few lively cuts—"This Is Mine" and "Sunset Now" in particular—but is otherwise overblown, indulgent and excessive.

Pleasure One, recorded in various studios over a 17-month (hmmm . . .) span, uses scads of guest musicians and vocalists to flesh out an accessible collection of upbeat dance numbers held to almost reasonable song lengths. (Interestingly, at this juncture, the stylistic gap between Heaven 17 and the Human League, from which it sprang, has never been narrower.) "Contenders," "Trouble" and "Free" are the strongest tracks.

Endless is a poshly packaged, limited-edition, career-spanning retrospective that was released only on tape and CD. Besides such essentials as "(We Don't Need This) Fascist Groove Thang," "Crushed by the Wheels of Industry," "Let Me Go" and "We Live So Fast," the collection includes "Heaven 17 Megamix" and new versions of "Let's All Make a Bomb" and "Song with No Name." [sg/iar]

See also *British Electric Foundation.*

RICHARD HELL AND THE VOIDOIDS

Richard Hell EP (Ork) 1976
Blank Generation (Sire) 1977

Richard Hell/Neon Boys EP (Shake) 1980
Destiny Street (Red Star) 1982 (nr/ID) 1988
RICHARD HELL
R.I.P. [tape] (ROIR) 1984

Richard Hell embodied punk with his fierce poetic nihilism. He founded the prehistoric Neon Boys with Tom Verlaine in 1971; several years later, they changed its name to Television. Malcolm McLaren used Hell's mode of dress as the prototype for punk style.

Employing the double guitar threat of Ivan Julian and Robert Quine (later a Lou Reed sideman) and drummer Marc Bell (a former member of the horrifying Dust who departed to become Marky Ramone for several years), Hell formed the Voidoids, whose unwavering individualism kept the group out of the big time while producing a demanding and impressive corpus of work. "I was saying let me out of here before I was even born," opens Hell's masterpiece, "(I Belong to the) Blank Generation," on the 7-inch **Richard Hell** EP. (It also includes "Another World" and "You Gotta Lose.") The line sums up Hell's attitude, expanded and perfected on **Blank Generation**. It combines manic William Burroughs-influenced poetry and raw-edged music for the best rock presentation of nihilism and existential angst ever. Hell's voice, fluctuating from groan to shriek, is more impassioned and expressive than a legion of Top 40 singers.

After a gap of three years (issuing only a single produced by Nick Lowe during brief management by Jake Riviera), the 7-inch **Richard Hell/Neon Boys** was released, featuring grimly touching songs by the modern Voidoids on one side and old demos by the Neon Boys on the other.

Destiny Street shows a more contemplative Hell, with even sharper imagery and guitar work (again courtesy of the stunning and underrated Robert Quine) and expressively painted poetry. Ruthless yet touchingly romantic, Richard Hell may be rock's last real visionary.

R.I.P. is a résumé of Hell's post-Television decade, from his 1975 days with the Heartbreakers through 1984 sessions in New Orleans. It is inevitably his least polished and most inconsistent work, which may be why it sums up his style so well. Neither as mannered as his first LP nor as professional as his second, this collection showcases his most uninhibited singing on retreads, live takes and previously unissued material. Although the liner notes (signed with the artist's real name—Lester Meyers) describe the tape as Richard Hell's swan song, he nonetheless pressed on, unveiling a new band in New York a few months after its release.

[sg/mf]

See also *Heartbreakers, Robert Quine, Ramones.*

NONA HENDRYX
Nona (RCA) 1983
The Art of Defense (RCA) 1984
The Heat (RCA) 1985
Female Trouble (EMI America) 1987 ●

Following a mainstream hard-rock solo album in the '70s, ex-Labelle singer Hendryx has upped her hipness quotient considerably this decade. **Nona**, co-produced by Material (Bill Laswell and Michael Beinhorn), features an all-star cast, incorporating members of Talking Heads and the Go-Go's, as well as Laurie Anderson, Nile Rodgers, Jamaaladeen Tacuma and Sly Dunbar. The dance-funk is, unfortunately, more stimulating on paper than disc; Hendryx is a powerful singer and there are some slick production moves, but the tunes (with the exception of the memorable "Keep It Confidential") are too shapeless to be gripping.

On **The Art of Defense**, again teamed with Material (as well as much of the preceding LP's cast, plus Afrika Bambaataa and Eddie Martinez), Hendryx sings seven long songs about passion with passion, obliterating any possible emotional impact with numbing one-note, one-beat repetition. Technically excellent and funky as hell, the album is also boring beyond words.

Produced in large part by Bernard Edwards and Arthur Baker, **The Heat** is a lot better. The songs—more melody, less bombast—take maximum advantage of the musical interplay possible with electronic percussion and studio wizardry. Hendryx evidently still believes that any line worth singing is worth singing half a dozen times, but the well-arranged, muscular backing tracks keep moving, so things don't wind down—even when she drills a lyric into the ground. "If Looks Could Kill (D.O.A.)" is a return to Hendryx's soul roots; Keith Richards guests on "Rock This House," providing trademark rhythm riffing that fits just right.

Sounding in spots very much like Peter Gabriel's **So** album, **Female Trouble**—dedicated to Winnie Mandela—is another unpredictable jumble of styles (synth-dance, rock, Prince-like funk, etc.), songwriters, producers (mainly Hendryx, Dan Hartman and the System) and guest musicians. Hendryx's irrepressible full-throttle approach makes this an invigorating blast, a tough-minded party record about sex *and* sexual politics.   [iar]

HENRY COW
The Henry Cow Legend (Virgin) 1973 (Red) 1979
Unrest (Red) 1974
Concerts (nr/Caroline) 1976
Western Culture (nr/Recommended) 1978
HENRY COW/SLAPP HAPPY
Desperate Straights (Red) 1975
In Praise of Learning (Red) 1975
ART BEARS
Hopes and Fears (Random Radar) 1978
Winter Songs (Ralph) 1979
The World as It Is Today (nr/Re) 1981
Winter Songs/The World as It Is Today [CD] (nr/Recommended) 1987

With its rock-and-reeds lineup and audible debt to both European and American classical music, Henry Cow ostensibly took its original cues from the first few lineups of King Crimson. But whereas Crimso's borrowings from jazz were shallow at best and its symphonic aspirations safely melodic, Henry Cow—trailblazers of British progressive rock—dug deeper. A lot of their unison melodies qualify as solid modern-jazz composition, and their tunes range from heavily chromatic to atonal. The band is also remembered for spawning Fred Frith, one of the few leading musicians of that era to emerge with his integrity and enthusiasm intact.

The Henry Cow Legend (just **Henry Cow** when released in the US), remains their best album, mostly because it avoids the problems that marred later records. Reedmen Geoff Leigh (later replaced by Lindsay Cooper) and Tim Hodgkinson mesh with Frith's guitar to produce rich, carefully ordered textures using material written mainly by Frith and Hodgkinson. Meanwhile, drummer Chris Cutler pioneers a unique style, a light jazz-derived sound that seems offhandedly diffident most of the time but is capable of heating up with the music. Except for three pieces by Frith and one by bassist John Greaves, **Unrest** concentrates on group improvisation. The idea of having this ensemble thrash to its heart's content may have seemed tempting at the time (remember the time), but the results are less impressive than the band's more ordered music.

Henry Cow then melded with likeminded labelmates Slapp Happy for two joint albums. **In Praise of Learning** comes up with a sound only hinted at on **Legend**: Henry Cow with lyrics. With the now-familiar front cover sock turned flaming red, the record's political orientation is unambiguously leftist. The sound, mainly composed and fronted by Slapp Happyite Dagmar Krause's Teutonic-accented pipes, leaves this proggie feeling antsy, over-lectured and not at all amused. **Henry Cow Concerts** contracts the lineup back to **Unrest**-plus-Krause; its two records sport heavy doses of free-form improvs (phooey) along with composed numbers (including a tune by Robert Wyatt on which he duets with Krause). Despite uneven recording, **Concerts** has its zesty moments.

Cow retrenched for **Western Culture**: no vocals, no improvisation. Hodgkinson wrote one side and Cooper (composing for the first time) the other. This is classic Cow, but updated with a highly aggressive edge and a renewed appreciation for the delicate textural balances that made the first two albums so tastefully evocative. Oddly but fittingly, **Western Culture** finishes what the first two albums began, and Henry Cow's last album is the only one to clearly rank with its first.

What started out to be another Henry Cow album got sidetracked when the band broke up; as the Art Bears, however, Cutler, Frith and Krause released the outcome as **Hopes and Fears**, staying together to make two more albums (both later reissued on a single CD). Frith subsequently went on to become an elder statesman of the rock avant-garde. He and Cutler made the badly recorded **Live in Prague and Washington**; Cutler also founded Recommended Records, which has been instrumental in the recording, release and distribution of a wide range of modern music from many countries. Cooper and Hodgkinson have each made solo records and continue to do so. Cooper's most recent projects were a tape-only release, **The Small Screen: Music for Television**, and an LP, **Music for Other Occasions**.   [mf]

See also *Fred Frith, John Greaves, Massacre, Anthony More, Skeleton Crew, David Thomas.*

HE SAID
See *Dome.*

HETCH HETCHY

See *Oh-OK*.

HEY! ELASTICA

In On the Off Beat (nr/Virgin) 1984

Bright, eclectic dance pop produced (mostly) by Martin Rushent. The London band embraces '40s big-band harmony styles as well as '80s synth moves; throughout, a happy beat and inventive arrangements keep things hopping at a joyous, near-frantic pace. Swell fun!   [iar]

NICK HEYWARD

See *Haircut One Hundred*.

JOHN HIATT

Hangin' Around the Observatory (Epic) 1974
Overcoats (Epic) 1975
Slug Line (MCA) 1979
Two Bit Monsters (MCA) 1980
All of a Sudden (Geffen) 1982
Riding with the King (Geffen) 1983
Warming Up to the Ice Age (Geffen) 1985
Bring the Family (A&M) 1987 ●
Slow Turning (A&M) 1988 ●

After two mild (if promising) singer/songwriter records, Midwesterner John Hiatt exploded on the scene in 1979, a fiercely original soul-inflected rock character likened to Elvis Costello, Graham Parker and Joe Jackson, but wholly his own man. His six albums testify to his exceptional and remarkably underappreciated talent, both as a much-covered songwriter and as an emotional, intense performer.

Slug Line is Hiatt's rawest and most powerful LP, with appropriately rudimentary production highlighting dynamic playing on a full set of angry songs. Drawing with genuine conviction on both reggae and fiery R&B styles, Hiatt invests "Madonna Road," "You're My Love Interest," "The Negroes Were Dancing" and other tracks with bitterness, insightful intelligence and occasional tenderness, making it a stunning work by an exciting artist.

Two Bit Monsters essentially repeats **Slug Line**'s style, but with less bite. Several tunes ("Back to Normal," "Good Girl, Bad World," "String Pull Job") are comparably impressive, but the album is less focused and nearly haphazard. Hiatt's venom sears through, but it's not his best work.

Tony Visconti produced **All of a Sudden**,

sympathetically if incongruously displaying the songs in a complex, highly arranged setting that works to good advantage most of the time. Amid a nod to rockabilly ("Doll Hospital") and a dose of Motown ("Getting Excited"), excellent songs like "Something Happens" and "I Look for Love" get filtered once through Hiatt's expanding musical sensibilities and then through Visconti's synthrocking Bowieness, making it a strange collision of seemingly irreconcilable styles.

Hiatt's bumpy career subsequently brought him into contact with Nick Lowe and Lowe's manager, Jake Riviera. The former produced and led the backing band on one side of **Riding with the King**; the latter loaned an eye-popping motorcycle for the front cover photo. The record's other side was produced by Scott Matthews and Ron Nagle; Matthews and Hiatt are the only musicians on those tracks. Although it may be down to the allotment of material, Lowe comes up the loser; on his side, Hiatt affects a languid swamp sound that doesn't convey much excitement. He comes alive only for such Matthews/Nagle-produced tracks as "Death by Misadventure," "Say It with Flowers" and "I Don't Even Try," prime songs given modest but appealing treatment.

Veteran mush-rock producer Norbert Putnam got the nod for **Warming Up to the Ice Age**. On the first track, "The Usual," he smothers Hiatt in raucous heavy metal guitars and arena-scale drums; fortunately, that's not the only sound on this weird record, which also contains a great soul duet with Elvis Costello ("Living a Little, Laughing a Little"), an emotion-laden ballad ("When We Ran") and other typically on-the-mark slices of Hiatt's cynical viewpoint ("She Said the Same Things to Me," "Number One Honest Game"). The mix is consistently too rock-oriented—these aren't dance tracks, for crying out loud!—but Hiatt's subtle vocals keep things in balance.

Hiatt's career was going nowhere fast and his personal life was no picnic, either. Luckily, for his next outing (and label), Hiatt hit on a far more rewarding format. Alone in an LA studio for four days with just Lowe, guitarist Ry Cooder (with whom Hiatt has often played), veteran session drummer Jim Keltner and a hands-off producer, he cut an extraordinary album of uncommon simplicity and candor. Ruggedly real and honest in extremis, **Bring the Family** has bottomless emotional depth and sonic spaces the size of sinkholes. The well-played music only serves to focus attention on that gritty, passionate voice, serving up new melodies and words reflecting the maturation and authority Hiatt's hard travelling has earned him.

[iar]

HILARY
Kinetic EP (Backstreet-MCA) 1983

Dunno who Hilary is but, in partnership with producer Stephen Hague, she came up with one wacky disc here. "Kinetic" takes a strong, happy synth-dance beat and then layers on a repetitive riff that's exactly one note too short, making the entire five-minute escapade as distracting as a leaky faucet. Taking a different approach, "Drop Your Pants" is musically saner and equally catchy, but the lyrics offer virtually every coy (and not-so-coy) sexual metaphor imaginable in a (hopefully) tongue-in-cheek bit of libidinous silliness. The other side is less notable, but this 12-inch remains a bizarre and memorable one-off from a singular talent. [iar]

HOLGER HILLER
A Bunch of Foulness in the Pit (nr/Cherry Red) 1984
Hyperprism (Jap. Wave) 1985
Oben im Eck (nr/Mute) 1986 ●

Virtually the only English on Hiller's first album (released originally by the German Ata Tak label) is the translated title; otherwise, you're on your linguistic own. Hardly the horrorshow the billing might have you imagine, the former Palais Schaumburg member conveys bemusement and tension rather than squalor or desperation, using overlaid (and not always musically related) instrumental lines (mostly keyboards and, if my dictionary guessed correctly, percussion), detached vocals, plus found sounds and assorted blips and squeaks. While the effect is not exactly pleasant—although a few songs, notably "Jonny (du Lump)," are—it is riveting, and Hiller is masterly at aurally painting a scene in living color.

Hiller's collaborators on **Oben im Eck**, a revised version of **Hyperprism** (retitled for a track which appears on it in two versions), include keyboardist Izumi Kobayashi and vocalist Kaori Kano, as well as ex-Associate Billy MacKenzie. Sampling keyboards have opened new creative worlds for sonic experimentalists like Hiller, allowing him to elec-

tronically manipulate sounds that were not so long ago uncontrollable and available only on tape. Although parts of the LP have an offbeat Japanese flavor, sections that are noisy or childlike take a much more neo-European approach, suggesting such sonic adventurers as Foetus or Renaldo and the Loaf. Ostensibly a set of songs, the album's rambling and colorful collections of sounds have little cohesion; even the multilingual lyrics (one song's written by Tom Verlaine) add scant structure to this dadaist picnic.

[iar]

PETER HIMMELMAN
This Father's Day (Orange) 1986 (Island) 1986
Gematria (Island) 1987 ●
SUSSMAN LAWRENCE
Hail to the Modern Hero! (Bigger Than Life) 1980 (Regency) 1980
Pop City (Orange) 1984

Minneapolis quintet Sussman Lawrence works very hard to sound like early Elvis Costello on their first outing, although singer/guitarist Peter Himmelman's vocals tend to favor Phil Lynott more. The songs, which are clearly derivative of Costello and Joe Jackson, are still sharp enough to be entertaining. Absurdist pop culture lyrics add some originality; smart playing and solid production also give this dubious venture its limited validity.

Pop City—a double-album with 21 songs in a number of styles—is far less imitative and proves this likable band to be highly skilled and creative, smoothly skipping across genres (often several times per song) to play everything—jazz-R&B-rock-pop—with abundant good spirits and a commitment to nothing but making simply enjoyable music. (Only reservation: some of the lyrics are clumsy and/or trite.)

Sussman Lawrence vanished when Himmelman opted to continue his career under his own name—remarkably, the other four band members remained as his sidemen. **This Father's Day**, a doleful and sensitive singer/songwriter record (with some polite rock arrangements) dedicated to Himmelman's late father, was recorded on 8-track and originally released on the band's label. After a video (for "Eleventh Confession") became an MTV hit, Island reissued it. Free of the imitative amateurness of early efforts, Himmelman's love, passion and intelligence come to the fore in a strong display of craft and talent.

Gematria, recorded in just three days, is an uplifting explosion of joyful ensemble playing that shows how tight and sympathetic these guys are. Himmelman's lowercase lyrics are fairly meaningless (and worse, pretentious in spots) but his music has spirit, power and clarity that far outweigh such concerns. [iar]

HIPSWAY

Hipsway (Columbia) 1986 ●

This stylish and boring Scottish soul-funk quartet includes ex-Altered Images bassist John McElhone. (His brother, another former Image, manages the band.) Not unlike several other current Scottish bands, Hipsway takes its cues from various black American artists, mixing dance rhythms, percussive guitar and smooth vocals, but winds up mostly sounding like INXS. "The Broken Years" is annoyingly herky-jerky; "The Honeythief" is nearly as distracting for the same reasons. Grahame Skinner has an appropriately husky voice, but is not an especially involving singer; the backing is clever and varied, but never captivating. [tr]

ROBYN HITCHCOCK

Black Snake Diamond Role (nr/Armageddon) 1981 (Relativity) 1987 ●
Groovy Decay (nr/Albion) 1982 ●
I Often Dream of Trains (nr/Midnight Music) 1984 ●
Groovy Decoy (Glass Fish-Relativity) 1986 ●
Invisible Hitchcock (Glass Fish-Relativity) 1986 ●

ROBYN HITCHCOCK AND THE EGYPTIANS

Fegmania! (Slash) 1985 ●
Gotta Let This Hen Out! (Relativity) 1985 ●
Exploding in Silence EP (Relativity) 1986 ●
Element of Light (Glass Fish-Relativity) 1986 ●
Globe of Frogs (A&M) 1988 ●

Robyn Hitchcock's entire body of work—both as leader of the Soft Boys and as a solo performer—remains one of the great undiscovered treasures of modern pop music. His melodic, emotional compositions place him in a songwriting peerage that includes Elvis Costello, XTC's Andy Partridge and very few others. Psychedelic pop of the '60s provides the touchstone for his sound, but Hitchcock blends his own ideas with those of

John Lennon, Syd Barrett, the Doors and Byrds to create music that advances the tradition rather than merely recapitulating it.

Black Snake Diamond Role, his first solo salvo, opens with two jaunty music hall ditties but quickly descends to Hitchcock's typical deranged concerns. He offers a sardonic knock at authority in "Do Policemen Sing?" (which features a chorus like a frenzied hail of blows) and a melodic, cracked-crystal ballad, "Acid Bird," whose mood and production could stand proud next to "Eight Miles High." Alternate takes on emotion—"Meat" (all brash) and "Love" (all heart)—finish off each side.

Groovy Decay, produced by Steve Hillage, has a smoother sound that somewhat undermines the dark emotion and irony that are Hitchcock's greatest strengths. Still, great songs gleam through the mix. "Fifty Two Stations" stunningly captures the alternation of rage, resignation and hope that follows the failure of love, while "St. Petersburg" views only the black side. "Grooving on an Inner Plane" blends an arch rap-styled vocal into a fluid groove (Sara Lee is the album's bassist) with stirring results. In a surprising move four years later, Hitchcock did it his way by putting out the revisionist **Groovy Decoy**. With almost an identical set of songs, the entirely reordered **Decoy** uses only four of **Decay**'s recordings, substituting simple but effective demos produced (and played on) by onetime Soft Boys bassist Matthew Seligman for the rest. The results are a bit rudimentary, but finally give the excellent collection of songs (including "America" and "The Cars She Used to Drive") their due.

After nearly two years of self-imposed retirement, Hitchcock returned in 1984 with a surprising, mostly acoustic album, **I Often Dream of Trains**. Performing all instruments and vocals himself, he echoed the solo work of his models—Barrett in the amiably slapdash production and Lennon on an aching ballad, "Flavour of Night." The album features Hitchcock's usual balance of bitterness and weirdness in unusual settings, rounded off with piano nocturnes at the start and finish. Two bizarre a cappella close-harmony essays—"Uncorrected Personality Traits" (about difficult children when they grow up) and "Furry Green Atom Bowl" (about life on earth)—make this one of the stranger outings in a career dedicated to strangeness.

Fegmania!, which features several old Soft Boy cronies in a new band, the Egyptians, shows Hitchcock polishing the best aspects of his craft to a new sheen, achieving a mature merger of lyric with melody (particularly on the morbidly catchy "My Wife & My Dead Wife" and the beautiful emotional study, "Glass") which sacrifices none of the urgency that brings his best songs to life. He has also continued to hone his sound, adding instruments to create a rich, ringing production that highlights his superb guitar textures and Andy Metcalfe's moody bass lines amid a variety of settings.

Gotta Let This Hen Out! is an essential live album recorded April '85 at London's Marquee. Sampling all of his albums for items like "Brenda's Iron Sledge," "Heaven," "My Wife and My Dead Wife," and tossing in the acerbic "Listening to the Higsons" (a non-LP 45), Hitchcock and the three Egyptians—Metcalfe, Morris Windsor and Roger Jackson—do a fine job of putting the songs across in crisp, energetic fashion. A great introduction for neophytes and a treat for fans. (**Exploding in Silence**, available on picture disc, contains six live cuts, only half of them from the album.)

Except for a creeping trace of self-conscious weirdness-for-its-own-sake in the lyrics, the exceptionally melodic **Element of Light** is another terrific addition to Hitchcock's oeuvre. The descending drama of "If You Were a Priest," the arcing delicacy of "Winchester" and "Airscape," as well as the moody restraint of "Raymond Chandler Evening" put the well-rehearsed Egyptians (especially Metcalfe on fretless bass) to fine use, while still leaving Hitchcock's plain but appealing voice a clear field in which to operate. Most of the record is unmistakably Hitchcock, although it does include two eerie Lennon re-creations: "Somewhere Apart" and "Ted, Woody and Junior."

Recycling a Soft Boys LP title, **Invisible Hitchcock** is a compilation of assorted outtakes dating from 1981-5. A few songs (like "Grooving on an Inner Plane") had previously surfaced in different versions, but most are heard here for the first time. The simple recording quality and mostly non-electric performances with various assortments of sidemen are entirely adequate, if not strictly consistent. **Invisible** may not be crucial but it is certainly illuminating, and a handful of rough gems ("All I Wanna Do Is Fall in Love," "Trash," "Give Me a Spanner, Ralph," "I Got a Message for You") make it a worthwhile purchase.

Thanks to the power of college radio and the music press, Hitchcock's growing popularity brought him a contract with A&M, which released his American major-label debut. Unfortunately, Hitchcock's obscurely lucid liner notes on **Globe of Frogs** are more fascinating than the album, which neglects tuneful songwriting in favor of big beat exercises that would mask insubstantial content with busy production. "Flesh Number One (Beatle Dennis)" and "Chinese Bones"— beautiful pop confections featuring R.E.M. guitarist Pete Buck—keep things from sinking, but "Balloon Man" and the title track, while both likably silly, underscore Hitchcock's annoying tendency to be selfconsciously absurdist.

Hitchcock isn't for everyone. His songs can be repetitious and lean heavily toward darkness. But the intelligence and emotion of his work, together with his devotion to electric guitar as the heart of his music, make him one of the most rewarding performers around. [mp/iar]

HITMEN
Aim for the Feet (Columbia) 1980
Torn Together (Columbia) 1981

London's Hitmen—not the unrelated Australian group, a contemporaneous outgrowth of Radio Birdman, also called the Hitmen—debuted with a DIY debut single ("She's All Mine" b/w "Slay Me with Your 45") of razor-sharp rhythm'n'pop which meshed terse but tasty guitar and keyboards over snappy bass and drums, topped by Ben Watkins' Graham Parker-cum-David Bowie vocals. Yet on **Aim for the Feet**, re-recorded versions of those songs fall flat; it takes repeated listenings to discover that they— along with a passel of other tunes as good and better—have fallen victim to colorless, punchless production.

With producer Rhett Davies at the helm on **Torn Together**, the quintet fares far better, crafting a succession of cleverly arranged and smartly played hooks that grow more impressive (not to mention catchier) with each hearing. The format incorporates more modern, Ultravoxian elements while avoiding the inherent pitfalls—until Side Two, that is, which is alternately arty and bathetic instead of hewing to the earlier, earthier approach.

Ex-Hitmen guitarist Pete Glenister turned up recently recording and touring with Bojangles, Terence Trent D'Arby's band. [jg]

See also *Brilliant, New Asia.*

JOOLS HOLLAND

Jools Holland and His Millionaires (IRS) 1981
Jools Holland Meets Rock'a'Boogie Billy (IRS) 1984

This flamboyant pianist—a cigar-chomping hustler able to energize even the most blasé audience—provided much of the zest on Squeeze's first three albums. For his solo debut, Jools adopted a less contemporary stance, playing old-fashioned bar-room romps with energy and panache. Produced by Glyn Johns, the record contains one classic oldie ("Bumble Boogie") and rollicking originals, some co-written with Squeeze's Chris Difford.

Leaving his Millionaires behind, **Rock'a' Boogie Billy** reunites Holland with once-and-future Squeeze drummer Gilson Lavis; otherwise, the self-produced album was recorded solo "at the back room of Holland's home (which accounts for the authentic sound)." The eight tracks, including four Difford collaborations and the old "Flip, Flop & Fly," offer more rustic uptempo friskiness soaked with American barrelhouse and ragtime atmosphere—imagine a young Jerry Lee Lewis in prime condition with no religious hangups. Turn it up and hoist a few!

When Squeeze reformed in 1985, Holland was back in the piano seat. [iar]

HOLLY AND THE ITALIANS

The Right to Be Italian (Virgin-Epic) 1981

HOLLY BETH VINCENT

Holly and the Italians (Virgin-Epic) 1982

Chicago-born singer/guitarist Holly B. Vincent formed her band in Los Angeles, but it took a 1979 move to England to secure a recording deal. An early single released there ("Tell That Girl to Shut Up") established her tough pop-rock style and briefly captured the full attention of the British press and public. The band's first/last album was hindered by numerous problems (like firing the producer halfway through and starting from scratch with another, losing the drummer in midstream and having to find a replacement) and wasn't finished until over a year later, but it was well worth the wait. Richard Gottehrer's production fits the melodic rock songs perfectly, melding the hybrid LA/London

sound—with glimpses of the Ramones, Blondie and Cheap Trick—into a powerful and original creation. The songs (mostly Vincent's) concern troubled romance, successful romance, teenage rebellion and kitsch culture; her convincing delivery gives them import, and the catchy phrases and solid rock foundation make it a masterful record by an important young talent.

The Right to Be Italian wasn't a commercial success and Holly broke up the band, opting instead for a solo career. The stunning resultant LP, produced by Mike Thorne, has a misleading title and bears little resemblance to its predecessor. **Holly and the Italians** plays up her voice and songs, providing ample room for far-reaching emotional expression; the striking, atmospheric music is based on violin and keyboards as much as guitar. (The American release has one different cut and much better sequencing.) Although Vincent took some flak for recording a totally overhauled version of the Buffalo Springfield's "For What It's Worth," she does manage to make something new and different out of the well-known tune. Elsewhere, sensitive, moody originals like "Samurai and Courtesan" and "Uptown" contrast with upbeat rockers like "We Danced" and "Honalu," all displaying a unique viewpoint in subtly evocative lyrics. Even more than its predecessor, this is an incredible album by an enormously gifted singer, writer and performer.

Vincent has not made a record under her own name since, although she did duet with Joey Ramone on a 45 of "I Got You Babe" and served a brief, unrecorded stint in the Waitresses. In 1988, Britain's Transvision Vamp made a run at international stardom with "Tell That Girl to Shut Up." [iar]

HOLLYWOOD BEYOND

If (Warner Bros.) 1987 ●

Birmingham, England singer/songwriter Mark Rogers, under the name Hollywood Beyond, gave it his best shot on If, an energetic, soulful techno-rock record produced by Bernard Edwards, Mike Thorne, Stephen Hague and others. Rogers' voice isn't altogether distinctive, but he croons and belts ably enough to be heard. The music likewise bends towards facelessness, but If's slickness, verve and variety keep it from being boring. Overambitious and premature, perhaps, but not at all bad. [iar]

HOMOSEXUALS

The Homosexuals' Record (nr/Recommended) 1984

A posthumous compilation of late-'70s singles and rough mixes, this 16-song 45-rpm album has technical shortcomings but lots of justifying character and rock energy. While the vocalist displays incipient David Thomas screech potential, the almost-catchy songs are well-constructed Brit-punk—early-Buzzcocks-meets-Vibrators—with more intelligence and sense than blind aggression; unexpected production fillips add to the fun.

[iar]

HONEYMOON KILLERS

Honeymoon Killers from Mars (Fur) 1984
Love American Style (Fur) 1985
Let It Breed (Fur) 1986
Turn Me On (Buy Our) 1988

Calling the Honeymoon Killers' debut disc a bad album is about as informative as calling **Catch a Fire** a reggae record: it's just a generic description. This New York four-piece (not to be confused with a Belgian band named after the same 1970 psychotronic cinema classic) is firmly rooted in the aesthetics of the splatter drive-in, where badness is just the starting point. The fake voodoo music, recorded in "four track horror fidelity," is abrasive and primitive—like the Cramps with fewer commercial instincts and an even sicker sense of humor. More a curio than anything anyone would ever want to listen to, the album is at least an entertaining curio. Think of it as aural pain in the service of black humor. Or think of it as obnoxious incompetence—you'll be neither alone nor unjustified. But miss it, and you'll never get to hear the world's worst version of "Who Do You Love." A soundtrack to your worst nightmares.

After half of the band split, guitarist Jerry and bassist Lisa recruited drummer Sally for **Love American Style**, another crunching descent into lighthearted aural warfare, recorded at CBGB in such a way as to suggest the sound of a bottomless pit. The squeals, screams, beats and roars hung on vari-speed rockabilly that strolls around like a dissipated hog caller don't always engage, but it's perfect accompaniment for late-night movie viewing with the TV sound off. Don't miss the ultimate garage grunge version of "Batman."

Let It Breed ends with a version of the Cult's (original Long Island version) "Godzilla" that falls right in with the album's horror motif. "Day of the Dead" eulogizes that classic series; "Brain Dead Bird Brain" suggests a future project for some current film student to contemplate. Trimming the musical insanity a tad, the Killers try a few numbers that are relatively straightforward without giving up any of their intensity. Investing more in vocals, the women chime in with Jerry for a neat X/Cramps-like effect; they also exchange bass and drum chores on the brief "Zoo Train."

The Killers expanded to a quartet with the addition of ex-Pussy Galore guitarist Cristina and became an even noisier proposition, as evidenced on **Turn Me On**. Songs like "Choppin' Mall" (basically a reworking of the pre-Who High Numbers' already derivative "I'm the Face"), "Octopussy," "Flophausen" and "Fingerlicken' Spring Chicken" demonstrate abundant junk-cinema wit; the music shows continued development and structural strength. Watch out, Roger Corman—the Honeymoon Killers will jack up yo' mama! [jl/iar]

HOODOO GURUS

Stoneage Romeos (Big Time-A&M) 1984 ●
Mars Needs Guitars! (Big Time-Elektra) 1985 ●
Blow Your Cool! (Big Time-Elektra) 1987 ●

Australia has produced few bands as crazily entertaining as Sydney's Hoodoo Gurus. Who else would dedicate their debut album to, among other pop culture giants, American TV sit-com stars Larry Storch and Arnold [the pig] Ziffel? That their music is an invigorating combination of cow-punk, garage-rock and demi-psychedelia only makes it better fun. "(Let's All) Turn On" is as good as any Lyres song; "In the Echo Chamber" has the mad abandon of prime Cramps; "I Want You Back" is winsome teen-angst power pop with a deadly hook; "I Was a Kamikaze Pilot" resembles the Fleshtones and displays a brilliant sense of absurd humor. (Think about that title again for a second if you didn't get it.) **Stoneage Romeos** is a great record.

Mars Needs Guitars! boasts a hip title, spiffy cover art, characteristically kitschy thank-yous and a top-notch opening tune in "Bittersweet." But while the band's spirit is as willing as ever, an ill-considered mix and several clumsy arrangements hamper the rough'n'ready delivery, losing the melodies in the impressive rave-up playing. Promising numbers like the title track, "Like Wow—Wipeout" and the countrified "Hayride to Hell" don't come off the way they should; the Gurus can definitely make better albums than this.

The improved **Blow Your Cool!** still isn't quite it, despite lively electric sound, plenty of offhand wit, crisp, energetic playing and hardy melodies. Increased emphasis on vocal harmonies distinguishes Side One; backup by the Bangles, blending nicely with songwriter Dave Faulkner's appealing voice on "What's My Scene" and "Good Times," helps put those tunes over the top. The fine "I Was the One" takes a similar tack without them. Lest anyone misjudge the Gurus' intentions, the record quickly turns (and stays) a lot tougher. Wild geographically-minded cave stompers like "Where Nowhere Is," "Hell for Leather," "In the Middle of the Land" and "On My Street" are happily hard-nosed and noisy; "Party Machine," which closes the LP, is virtually a tribute to the Flesh-tones. [iar]

HOOTERS

Amore (Antenna) 1983
Nervous Night (Columbia) 1985 ●
One Way Home (Columbia) 1987 ●

With roots in dull '70s pop band Baby Grand, the Hooters were a popular local Philadelphia outfit with misguided reggae/ska aspirations when they recorded **Amore**, an independent album of mundane quasi-intelligent would-be arena rock, evidencing no wit and little creativity. Then guitarist Eric Bazilian and keyboardist Rob Hyman did an extracurricular gig as the main musicians on Cyndi Lauper's first LP and the Hooters' fortunes changed.

Some of **Amore**'s songs were re-cut for **Nervous Night**, an appallingly successful record produced by Rick Chertoff, who also led Lauper to multi-platinumism. The moronic "All You Zombies" is as clumsy as it gets; mandolin and melodica (the ostensible "hooter" of the band's name) provide a discernible musical identity but make most of the anthemized tunes sound the same. The rousing "And We Danced" and "Blood from a Stone" (later covered to far better effect by Red Rockers) are as close to good as this gets; a version of Love's "She Comes in Colors" is welcome but hardly excuses the slickly soul-less fare that surrounds it.

There are fewer obvious gaffes on **One Way Home**, which mines the same basic vein, offering a reggae tempo (on the title track) and a heartland cliché or ten for would-be contemporary appeal. Amid the romantic anthems, the Hooters strive for relevance with "Satellite," courageously poking humorless fun at televangelists. [iar]

HORIZONTAL BRIAN

Vertical (Gold Mountain) 1983

This wonderful British quartet plays lyrically observant melodic rock, much in the same vein as Stackridge did in oldentide. Bassist Tony Phillips sings his own songs in an engaging, unprepossessing voice, humorously satirizing the shortcomings of parenthood ("Playing with the Babies"), obsession with the colonies ("Everybody Wants to Be an American"), death ("Buried in Your Best Suit") and more. Although not as sharp as the words, the music is dandy. [iar]

HOUSEMARTINS

Flag Day EP (nr/Go! Discs) 1985
Sheep EP (nr/Go! Discs) 1986
Happy Hour EP (nr/Go! Discs) 1986
London 0 Hull 4 (Go! Discs-Elektra) 1986 ●
Think for a Minute EP (nr/Go! Discs) 1986
Caravan of Love EP (nr/Go! Discs) 1986
The People Who Grinned Themselves to
    Death (Go! Discs-Elektra) 1987 ●
Now That's What I Call Quite Good! (nr/Go!
    Discs) 1988

As the cover of their first EP boasts, this quartet from Hull (actually, only drummer Hugh Whittaker's from the city; the rest wound up there for various reasons) are quite good, creating distinctive, finely-crafted pop songs. **Flag Day** is an outstanding debut, four polished tunes that are memorable and intelligent. No fey pop wimps here. The melancholy title track laments the economic deterioration of Great Britain; the punchy and percussive "Stand at Ease" offers an unusual view of militarism. "You" is bright, bouncy pop with spectacular harmonies; "Coal Train to Hatfield Main" is a country stomp. Paul Heaton's vocals shine throughout, providing an integral part of the Housemartins' overall charm.

They followed with **Sheep**: three fine pop songs plus an extraordinary a cappella cover of Curtis Mayfield's "People Get Ready" and an uplifting gospel song (with choir). As the sleeve states, "The Housemartins are my bestest band." **Happy Hour** propelled the Housemartins headfirst into the top of the UK charts (no mean feat for a band on an independent label) and earned them an American record contract. Exuberant guitar pop at its best, the title song is a humorous dig at the yuppie lifestyle.

They followed the success of **Happy Hour** with their brilliant debut album **London 0 Hull 4** (a play on an age-old soccer rivalry), a dozen perfect pop jewels (including "Sheep" and "Flag Day") which firmly established the band's position as the crown princes of the three-minute pop classic. From the lusty bounce of "Happy Hour" to the gospel tones of "Lean on Me," the Housemartins are lyrically literate and musically precise.

Think for a Minute continues the band's ascent to stardom. Five flawless tracks, including the title song (remixed from **London 0 Hull 4**) and a delightful excursion into rap music entitled "Rap Around the Clock."

Caravan of Love (the title track is an Isley/Jasper/Isley song) confirms the quartet's spiritual side and aptitude for gospel stylings with five songs of praise done a cappella. Considering Heaton's voice, this is as natural and comfortable an inclination as their usual pop trappings.

Personnel and musical changes marred the band's second album, **The People Who Grinned Themselves to Death**. Heaton's lyrics, once pointed and exact, have become obtuse and, in some instances ("Me and the Farmer," "I Can't Put My Finger on It"), downright inane. The title track, "You Better Be Doubtful" and the solemn "Johannesburg" provide some good moments, but the majority of songs lack the immediate impact of previous Housemartins records. (The LP's US version contains a bonus 45 of "Caravan of Love" b/w "The Day I Met Jesus.") It's clear from this album the band's pop throne might be in jeopardy—a supposition turned fact when they disbanded months after its release.

Now That's What I Call Quite Good! is a posthumous double LP of odds and ends which spans the band's entire career. [ag]

HOUSE OF FREAKS
House of Freaks (Rhino) 1987 ●

Anyone skeptical of a two-piece rock'n' roll band should immediately check out Richmond, Virginia-to-Los Angeles transplants Bryan Harvey and Johnny Hott. What makes House of Freaks work is not the novelty of the guitar'n'drums lineup, but Harvey's guitar and vocals, which jump out at you with all the urgency and stripped-down emotionalism of **Plastic Ono Band/Imagine**-era John Lennon. Add to that Hott's industrial-strength drumming and Harvey's terrific songs that draw on American folklore and mythology from the days of the slave trade up through the atomic era for a winning combination of punch and intelligence. The CD adds two bonus tracks. [ds]

HOUSE OF SCHOCK
House of Schock (Capitol) 1988 ●

Erstwhile Go-Go's drummer Schock sings and co-wrote the songs on her new band's debut album with her partner, bassist Vance DeGeneres; the backing trio surprisingly includes a drummer who takes her place on half the tracks. Richard Gottehrer's deft production provides the record's bright, appealing sound, but Schock's limited voice and songs, both equally inoffensive, are hardly significant or memorable. [iar]

See also *Zasu Pitts Memorial Orchestra*.

CHRIS HOUSTON WITH THE SEX MACHINE
See *Forgotten Rebels*.

PENELOPE HOUSTON
See *Avengers*.

ROWLAND S. HOWARD
See *Barracudas, Birthday Party, Crime and the City Solution, Lydia Lunch, Nikki Sudden, These Immortal Souls*.

HOWARD AND TIM'S PAID VACATION
See *Windbreakers*.

HUANG CHUNG
See *Wang Chung*.

MICK HUCKNALL
See *Simply Red*.

H.R.

See *Bad Brains.*

HUGO LARGO

Drum (Relativity) 1987 (Opal) 1988 ●

Responding to the predominance of noisemongers on the New York downtown hipster scene, rock critic-turned-Glenn Branca sideman Tim Sommer took a turn for the ethereally haunting and formed Hugo Largo: two bassists, an electric violinist and indescribable vocalist Mimi Goese. The ironically-titled sublime seven-song mini-album, produced in part by Michael Stipe, builds a remarkable bridge between new age airiness and sturdy new wave experimentation. While Goese's voice dives and glides as if airborne, the three instruments (plus a touch of guitar) play at a measured tempo that belies their power; lyrics are diverted into evocative, mesmerizing sounds. Although the originals are substantially engaging, an almost unrecognizable rendition of Ray Davies' "Fancy" provides a beautiful highlight.

The 1988 reissue contains two extra tracks.   [iar]

HUMAN LEAGUE

Dignity of Labour Pts. 1–4 EP (nr/Fast
  Product) 1979
Reproduction (nr/Virgin) 1979 (Virgin)
  1988 ●
Travelogue (Virgin Int'l) 1980 (Virgin)
  1988 ●
Dare (A&M) 1981 ●
Fascination! EP (A&M) 1983
Hysteria (A&M) 1984
Crash (Virgin-A&M) 1986 ●

LEAGUE UNLIMITED ORCHESTRA

Love and Dancing (A&M) 1982

PHILIP OAKEY & GIORGIO MORODER

Philip Oakey & Giorgio Moroder
  (Virgin-A&M) 1985

It took a near-fatal lineup overhaul, two developmental albums and a fortuitous partnership with the right producer to put the Human League in a position to create the record that would make them, for a time, the unchallenged world champs of synthesizer pop. Interestingly, the group that topped the charts in 1982 with "Don't You Want Me" bears almost no resemblance to the dour trio

that recorded "Being Boiled" for Fast Product in 1978.

The first two albums were the work of Sheffield's Phil Oakey, Ian Craig Marsh, Martyn Ware (all synth/vocals) and Philip Adrian Wright, who handled visual chores. **Reproduction** suffers from a cold, simplistic approach—high-tech primitivism—given added monotony by deadpan vocals. Amid all the glum sonic novelties was one track, "Empire State Human," which indicated incipient pop sense and brought the League some success on the British charts.

Travelogue is much better, broadening the palette to include a wide variety of subtle synthesizer shadings, from the arcane to the sublime, and introducing vastly-improved material. Lyrical subjects concern science-fiction and kitsch culture, two facets of the League's personality literally illustrated in concert by Wright's projections. Although still emotionally ambivalent, **Travelogue**, warmer and more fun than its predecessor, suggested a possibly rewarding direction for the band to pursue.

And pursue it they did. After a schism left Oakey and Wright in the Human League and Marsh and Ware as the British Electric Foundation, the band was revamped with four new members and a rededication to danceable pop music. That intent, along with producer Martin Rushent—whose skills dovetailed with almost all of the band's shortcomings (almost all—there's no cure for Oakey's amelodic crooning)—ultimately led to such interplanetary hits as "Don't You Want Me" and "Love Action (I Believe in Love)." The irresistible mix of state-of-the-art technology and old-fashioned pop-single formulae set millions of toes tapping, although the **Dare** LP contains much headier and heavier stuff as well. With incredible ambience and subtle tension, "Seconds"—about the Kennedy assassination—is, in fact, the LP's unheralded best track. A great record, and not just for its popular songs.

The trailblazing (for white rockers, that is) remix album, **Love and Dancing**, pays titularly homage of sorts to Barry White and contains Rushent's revamped versions of seven cuts from **Dare**, plus one extra tune. Some of the record bears listening to; other parts, however, are either repetitively dull or noisily annoying.

Subsequently proven incapable of delivering a timely follow-up to sustain their new-found mega-stardom, the Human League had to make do with stop-gap singles, two of which were compiled on the **Fascination!** EP. "Mirror Man" is pedestrian but catchy; "(Keep Feeling) Fascination" (which appears here in its original form and an extended remix), however, is ruined by awful sick-cow vibrato on the synthetic horns.

Three years after **Dare**, following a pitched battle with their commercial insecurities, the League finally came up with **Hysteria**. Following a traumatic split with Rushent, the band itself produced the LP with Chris Thomas and Hugh Padgham, wisely omitting the prior 45s in favor of new songs, some of which are quite good. Stretching styles to encompass a subtler, tender side, the ballads ("Louise," "Life on Your Own") provide the record's most engaging moments, although they exacerbate Oakey's vocal limitations. Taking an ill-advised political turn, "The Lebanon" offers simpleminded drama with a pop hook; "Don't You Know I Want You" is an almost-clever attempt to acknowledge and recycle the sound (and title) of their biggest hit.

During another Human League hibernation, Oakey collaborated with Giorgio Moroder, first on the entertaining *Electric Dreams* film soundtrack, then on a joint album. Giorgio wrote the music and produced; Phil added lyrics and sang; Arthur Barrow and Richie Zito provided the backing tracks on, respectively, synth and guitar. With a bouncy, upbeat sound, it's an unchallenging bit of fun that could easily be mistaken for a jollified League record were it not for Moroder's lighthanded, deft arrangements and percolating tunes. "Good-bye Bad Times" and a reprise of "Together in Electric Dreams" stand out, but the rest is almost as immediately enjoyable.

In a desperate maneuver to locate a musical personality to call their own, however briefly, the Human League enlisted the stunningly successful pop-funk team of Jimmy Jam and Terry Lewis to produce and co-write the absurdly misbegotten **Crash**. The imprudent collaboration produced a collection of musical nightmares: preening soul ballads ("Human," "Love Is All That Matters") that Oakey isn't up to singing, fraudulent funk workouts ("Swang," "Jam," "I Need Your Loving") that only underscore the band's emotional sterility, and inadequate dance-rock ("Money," "Love on the Run") that trails the field's cutting edge by a few years. Like the cover's intentionally out-of-focus photograph, this halfhearted effort falls well short of nominal quality standards.

[iar]

See also *British Electric Foundation, Heaven 17, Shake.*

HUMANS
Happy Hour (IRS) 1981

LA's Humans were a pop quintet which produced funny and bitter story-songs—like a rocking, stinging version of the Modern Lovers. They made one great single, "I Live in the City," delivered in frantic machine-gun fashion; sadly, that song is not on their album, which was produced by David Kahne. **Happy Hour** is an unsettling attack on the repugnant but fascinating Southern California lifestyle, eerily punctuated by John Anderson's gothic guitar and Sterling Storm's shrill, sarcastic vocals. Like the soundtrack of a horror movie, this is for fans of the pop bizarre. [sg]

HUMAN SEXUAL RESPONSE
Figure 14 (Eat-Passport) 1980
In a Roman Mood (Passport) 1981

A most promising (but ultimately unsuccessful) band from Boston, the seven-person HSR (including four vocalists!) explored sexual identities, both physical and mental, on **Figure 14**, as on the wonderful "What Does Sex Mean to Me?" Elsewhere, there's a healthy irreverence towards the famous and the neurotic, with sex never quite out of the picture. Leanings in the direction of art rock, led by singer Larry Bangor's Tom Verlaine-style vocals, occasionally get HSR in trouble, coming off too cute.

In a Roman Mood is darker and more oblique than **Figure 14**, showcasing the band's growing lyrical complexity regarding human beings and what they expect from each other. Again their nervous rhythms—over an entire LP—don't produce anything outstanding. Human Sexual Response makes background music for difficult relationships.

The band broke up in 1982 and spawned several offshoots. A one-off reunion show took place on Halloween 1984. [gf]

HUMAN SWITCHBOARD
Human Switchboard Live (no label) 1980
Who's Landing in My Hangar? (Faulty
    Products) 1981
Coffee Break [tape] (ROIR) 1982

BOB PFEIFER

After Words (Passport) 1987 ●

Transplant the early Velvet Underground to the present tense, trade that band's kinkier concerns for conventional male-female issues, and you've got Kent, Ohio's Human Switchboard in a nutshell. Repeated disclaimers aside, leader Bob Pfeifer sings in a dry, ironic style suggestive of young Lou Reed, and Myrna Marcarian's wobbly organ-playing adds an amateurish tint that evokes **White Light/White Heat**.

On **Who's Landing in My Hangar?**, the band's sole studio LP, Pfeifer creates a neurotic, high-strung persona that makes for gripping listening. Two uptempo cuts, "Book on Looks" and "(I Used to) Believe in You," celebrate the ups and downs of romance, while the LP's high point, "Refrigerator Door," carefully weaves an intriguing web of personal details. It all seems embarrassingly confessional, which is a pretty neat trick.

The Switchboard's other two releases are live recordings that overlap material extensively with **Hangar**. Both are interesting, if redundant. The 1980 disc, an authorized-bootleg release, features Marcarian's haunting rendition of "Downtown." **Coffee Break** is from a November 1981 Cleveland radio broadcast.

Time mellows even a sourpuss like Pfeifer, it seems. Without the Switchboard behind him (though ex-members of the defunct group appear on **After Words**), he's looser, more willing to play off the rhythms, which themselves are less constricted than before. Pfeifer's still got an obvious affinity for Lou Reed's plain-spoken approach to interpersonal tales, offering diary-like accounts in "She Always Smiled" and "I'm Better for You." In "Knock-Knock," he finally succumbs to the urge to do a straight Reed imitation. Otherwise, worthwhile.

Career footnote: soon after the release of **After Words**, Pfeifer took an a&r job with a major record company and moved from Hoboken, New Jersey (where he had gravitated in the mid-'80s) to Los Angeles. [jy]

HUMPE-HUMPE

See *Ideal*.

IAN HUNTER

Short Back n' Sides (Chrysalis) 1981

Ian Hunter emerged as an early patron saint of punk, quite a feat considering that the movement was allegedly based on the rejection of his generation of old wave musicians. Hunter's popularity with the young rebels stemmed primarily from his salad years as leader of Mott the Hoople and was based on attitude as much as music. In the late '60s and early '70s, Hunter and band were down-to-earth, streetwise blokes who voiced a sense of disillusionment and failure instead of indulging in the fantasy and self-aggrandizement typical of so many big-league rockers. Punks of the later '70s saw themselves as fighting against the same climate of unreality and vanity. Specifics: Beginning with Mott's debut, **Mott the Hoople**, you can hear the tight, driving guitar of Mick Ralphs, later appropriated in whole by the Clash, Pistols and Generation X. **Mott**'s "Violence" and **The Hoople**'s "Crash Street Kids" both forecast with uncanny accuracy the emergence of a new generation of disaffected, angry kids.

Hunter produced Generation X's second LP, **Valley of the Dolls**. The late Guy Stevens, who assembled Mott and produced their first four LPs, produced the Clash's **London Calling** and came to be viewed as a seminal rock figure.

Mick Jones joined with long-time Hunter-mate Mick Ronson to produce Ian's sixth solo effort, **Short Back n' Sides**, an ambitious, unfocused LP that covers more styles than a single record should. Still, Hunter continues to be the straight-shooter that originally endeared him to his "kids." [jy]

HUNTERS AND COLLECTORS

Hunters and Collectors (Aus. White Label) 1982
Hunters and Collectors (Oz-A&M) 1983
The Fireman's Curse (nr/Virgin) 1983
The Jaws of Life (Slash) 1984
Human Frailty (IRS) 1986 ●
Living Daylight EP (IRS) 1987 ●
Fate (IRS) 1988 ●

Melbourne's Hunters and Collectors offer one of Australia's answers to the Fall, an unremittingly bleak and powerful ensemble capable of horrendous noise, gripping drama and slithery funk. They do all three on both eponymous albums, which are almost entirely different records. The Australian release is a self-produced double 12-inch with only three tracks common to the UK/US single disc of the same name, which Mike Howlett produced. (And remixed "Talking to a Stranger.") Utterly oblique lyrics (and a credit to the band as a whole for "lyrics, music, artwork, management") typify this enigmatic album. Fans of challenging, noisy rock and rhythm should enjoy, if not understand, this; real enthusiasts would do well to seek out both versions.

It took a while to locate another American label courageous enough to take the band on, but eventually Slash saw their way clear to releasing **The Jaws of Life**, recorded in Germany with Conny Plank. Thanks to normal cover info, it becomes possible to compliment bassist John Archer and drummer Doug Falconer for their dominant rhythm work, suggest that guitarist Mark Seymour let someone else attempt to sing next time and praise keyboard player Geoff Crosby for the nifty cover assemblage.

Human Frailty was the band's long-delayed IRS debut (a 1983 deal had fallen through with the label at the eleventh hour). One immediately notices the more mainstream sound (or at least as close as they can get to one and still retain some of their trademarks). The unorthodox horn section (trumpet, trombone and French horn) plays conventional parts, and there's a lot more in the way of background vocals. Fans of the band's early work simply won't believe that several cuts, especially the Top 40-flavored "Throw Your Arms Around Me," are actually the work of the band credited on the album cover. While **Human Frailty** doesn't lack in quality per se, Hunters and Collectors have certainly done more interesting music than this.

"Inside a Fireball," which opens the five-track **Living Daylight** EP, indicates that all is well; while not as art-noisy as early work, the record at least has the punch and bite its predecessor lacks. It also contains remixed versions of "The Slab" and "Carry Me" from **The Jaws of Life**. (The entire EP is appended to the **Human Frailty** CD.) [iar/dgs]

HÜSKER DÜ

Land Speed Record (New Alliance) 1981
Everything Falls Apart (Reflex) 1982
Metal Circus EP (SST) 1983 ●
Zen Arcade (SST) 1984 ●
New Day Rising (SST) 1985 ●
Flip Your Wig (SST) 1985 ●
Candy Apple Grey (Warner Bros.) 1986 ●
Warehouse: Songs and Stories (Warner Bros.) 1987 ●

Hüsker Dü emerged from the punk rock scene; vast improvements in songwriting over the years may have changed the shape of their music, but they never lost their firm attachment to bracing, loud guitar rock. Although failing to achieve the mainstream success of R.E.M. or even the Replacements, the often exhilarating Minneapolis trio was hugely popular and influential in certain circles, maintaining its vision, integrity and dedication to independent music to the end. With Bob Mould's impassioned talk-shout-singing and masterful guitar overlaid with feedback and amplifier distortion, Greg Norton's straight-ahead driving bass and Grant Hart's only slightly less demented singing and excessive drumming, the Hüskers piled on the pop hooks in their songs to the point of explosion, creating a startling rush of momentum. These three fashionless guys put on some of the planet's most exciting shows.

The live **Land Speed Record**, however, isn't one of them. Basically a tour document from a year in which they covered a lot of land and took a lot of speed, it's a cheap recording that only hints at any juice the performance may have contained. In those days, the group was naturally sloppy, and this disc captures the mess but not the overkill power.

Everything Falls Apart, in fact, puts everything back together. While the band hadn't totally mastered the studio, this is a great improvement over the live record. And it offers the first taste of pop-oriented things to come: a cover of Donovan's "Sunshine Superman."

Metal Circus marks a giant leap forward. With this disc, Hüsker Dü began to reach for a broader audience. The often misconstrued title refers not to heavy metal (an area of exploration for many hardcore bands), but to the flat gray solidity of alloys, which fairly describes the record. **Metal Circus** is a collection of anthems, slow and fast, with twisted, abrasive guitar licks and twisted lyrics. The rousing Mission of Burma-ish "It's Not Funny Anymore" is the most potent track, but "Diane" is the most haunting, a Hart-penned power dirge about rape and murder. When he screams the title over and over, it sounds like "dying." A monster song from a heavy record.

After **Metal Circus**, Hüsker Dü released a 7-inch statement of purpose, the totally gonzoid cover of "Eight Miles High." The single brings together Mould's love of jangly '60s pop with the band's adrenaline charge. Punk covers of '60s songs generally devolve into camp, but this one retains the flavor of the original without compromising the sonic blitz.

Zen Arcade, an ambitious double-record concept album about the strange adventures of a kid leaving home, covers more ground than Greyhound and is successful a surprisingly high percentage of the time. The band plays acoustic, psychedelic and unabashedly poppy songs; when it's good, the material is among their best. A straight rocker, "Turn on the News," deserves to be a classic. Unfortunately, there's also some over-reaching and self-indulgent dross. As on **Sandinista!**, it isn't really filler because too much work obviously went in; still, backwards tape loops and extended drones dilute the effect.

By contrast, **New Day Rising** is as tight as a duck's behind, and that's waterproof. The band flails the hell out of the kind of loping melodies currently ringing out of the New South. The album is LOUD, intense, funny, accessible and downright catchy. From the opening cut, in which Mould just screams "new day rising" over and over above a rising tide of triumphant sound, to the elliptical closer, "Plans I Make," they do the Dü with nary a false step. Seldom have hooks been this powerful, nor full-throttle punk this melodic.

The Hüskers' final independent label release, **Flip Your Wig**, is positively brilliant—14 unforgettable pop tunes played like armageddon were nigh. The production is taut and claustrophobic, pushing the busy, anechoic drums right into your head, competing with Mould's precise stun-assault guitar wash and vocals. Besides the compressed, efficient Top 40 sound of "Makes No Sense at All" (one of 1985's best 45s), the LP boasts such classic fare as the loving, fragile "Green Eyes," the boppy, bubblegummy "Hate Paper Doll" and the somberly psychedelic (complete with backwards guitar) of "Don't Know Yet," which closes things out in appropriately enigmatic fashion.

Following the Replacements to Warner Bros., Hüsker Dü self-produced **Candy Apple Grey** with an equally unselfconscious lack of commercial consideration, sacrificing nary a dB of energy nor an ounce of spirit. (They did, however, cut back to a mere ten songs.) Too many cuts start with the same brief Hart-beat, but the charged, varied music and never-better reflective, adult lyrics on Mould's six compositions provide a seductive wallop. "Sorry Somehow" (with surprising Deep Purple organ), "Don't Want to Know If You Are Lonely" and "Dead Set on Destruction" are typically staggering rock numbers; "I Don't Know for Sure" sounds good but resembles "Makes No Sense at All" a tad too much. Two all-acoustic numbers ("Too Far Down" and "Hardly Getting Over It") demonstrate the band's flexibility and a casual disregard for punk convention. While more diverse, **Candy Apple Grey** ultimately falls a bit short of **Flip Your Wig** in intensity and impact.

It took wrangling with (and concessions to) Warner Bros., but the group was able to prevail and release the ambitious two-disc **Warehouse: Songs and Stories**, on which Hart and Mould co-produced and evenly split the songwriting. Neither self-indulgently sprawling nor start-to-finish essential, this 20-song collection breaks no new ground and is short on variety but still quite enjoyable—the thick sound is in itself sensually satisfying. With fine tracks strewn randomly throughout, the album's strongest side is its third (with the hypnotically swirling "It's Not Peculiar," the folky "No Reservations" and the late-'60sish "Tell You Why Tomorrow"); other notable cuts are "She Floated Away," a rocking sea chantey, "Standing in the Rain" and "Ice Cold Ice."

In early 1988, it was announced that Hart had been fired and then that Hüsker Dü had decided to break up. At last word, Hart was releasing a solo record and Mould was looking for musicians with whom to form a new band. [jl/iar]

PARTHENON HUXLEY
Sunny Nights (Columbia) 1988 ●

Not his real name; the Parthenon bit may be a tip of the hat to his high school days in Greece. On this debut LP, Huxley engages in thoughtful whimsy ("Between the sacred and the profane/Runs a crooked yellow line/you dance from lane to lane . . . "). The music is power pop that's equally skewed, though not equally effective; its cleverness tends to overpower melodies that seem to deserve better. (He co-produced with David Kahne.) Promising all the same. [jg]

HUXTON CREEPERS
12 Days to Paris (Big Time) 1986
Creep to the Beat (Polydor) 1988 ●

This quartet from Melbourne, Australia plays gritty Stonesish rock and harmony-laden Byrdsy folk-rock on their first American LP, which might easily be mistaken for the work of an American "heartland" band. The Huxton Creepers could use a more mellifluous singer than Rob Craw—gruffness when he strains is a problem—but his guitar interplay with Paul Thomas, supported by a fluid, strong rhythm section, makes **12 Days** an unfailingly engaging record. Guest Hammond (on one song—a second, indicated on the back cover, was somehow omitted from the US LP!) by ex-Procol Harum organist Chris Copping is more eyebrow-raising than ear-opening. [iar]

HYBRID KIDS
Hybrid Kids (nr/Cherry Red) 1979
Claws (nr/Cherry Red) 1980
MORGAN FISHER
Ivories (nr/Strike Back) 1985

What happens when Jah Wobble meets country clods the Wurzels for a rave-up on Kate Bush's greatest hit? You get Jah Wurzel's version of "Wuthering Heights," zonked-out reggae with quizzical vocals in a back-country accent, that's what. Actually, this is Morgan Fisher, ex-Mott the Hoople keyboardist, pretending (with a dab of help from uncredited friends—he himself is billed as "producer/director") to be a baker's dozen different acts having a go at their fave tunes. What purports to be British Standard Unit takes a pretty amusing off-the-wall industrial-synth whack at "D'Ya Think I'm Sexy," but most of the rest of **Hybrid Kids** tends to be gratuitously high in the ozone, or tediously puerile (or both). Nice version of Sun Ra's "Enlightment" [sic], allegedly by Combo Satori, all the same. [jg]

PAUL HYDE AND THE PAYOLAS
See *Payolas*.

HYPSTRZ
Hypstrz Live EP (Bogus-Twin/Tone) 1979
Hypstrization (Voxx) 1980

This Minneapolis quartet plays ragged, revved-up covers of 15 golden oldies on the live **Hypstrization**. Stripping down garage-punk classics—"96 Tears," "Slow Death," "Midnight Hour," "Riot on Sunset Strip," "Little Girl," etc.—they emerge as pre-hardcore punks who happened onto their musical roots and decided not to update them. This is energetically entertaining, although two sides of soundalike performances are more than enough.

The earlier 7-inch EP features just four songs, including the ultimate garage-band motherlode, "Hey Joe."

Following the end of the Hypstrz, the two Batson brothers, Ernest and Bill, formed a new quartet called the Mofos and continued in a slightly more modern vein. [iar]

ICEHOUSE

Icehouse (Chrysalis) 1981 ●
Primitive Man (Chrysalis) 1982 ●
Fresco EP (Chrysalis) 1983
Sidewalk (Chrysalis) 1984
Measure for Measure (Chrysalis) 1986 ●
Man of Colours (Chrysalis) 1987 ●

FLOWERS

Icehouse (Aus. Regular) 1980

For the record, Icehouse began as Flowers. For its first US/UK album, the Sydney, Australia band renamed itself after the title of the Flowers LP, subtracted one cut, remixed and resequenced it.

Icehouse's debut LP effectively mates emotional tension with the streamlined efficiency of modern synthesizer outfits. "Icehouse" and "Can't Help Myself," in particular, exploit the contrast between smooth surfaces and frontman Iva Davies' anxious singing. Despite inconsistent material, this is a promising start.

Unfortunately, Davies let it all go to his head on **Primitive Man**, hiding the underrated band and declaring allegiance to empty stylishness. By emphasizing the elegance in his artful compositions and restricting his passions to poses, Davies ends up with slick, pretty product that neither demands nor encourages listener involvement. (It does, however, contain the global hit single, "Hey Little Girl," a remarkable Roxy Music simulation.)

That song, two others from **Primitive Man**, plus two new tracks of forgettable roaring rock comprise the **Fresco** EP, evidently issued to capitalize on the band's sudden commercial emergence.

Sidewalk is a tedious two-voiced exercise: fake Bryan Ferry (hey—doing it once may be cute, but two albums in a row is lame!) and histrionic guitar rock; occasionally the two are blended together in a misbegotten vision of Roxy Metal. Melt this sucker down.

While retaining the mannered Ferry imitation in spots, **Measure for Measure** adds an equally artificial version of David Bowie (c. **Lodger**) and drops **Sidewalk**'s over-energized sand trap. "No Promises" is the atmospheric pop hit (one of three cuts on which ex-Japan drummer Steve Jansen plays; Eno receives an all-LP credit for backing vocals, treated piano and keyboards), but other songs are more memorable. (Most are less.) Smooth, crafty and pointless.

The unfocused but blatantly commercial **Man of Colours** tries a little of this—ersatz Roxy, imitation Bowie—and a little of that—semi-fake Hall and Oates (Oates co-wrote and sings on "Electric Blue," which sounds like an INXS discard), a halfhearted stab at Billy Idol's neighborhood, etc. Davies' voice briefly resembles Barry Manilow's on the mega-hit single, "Crazy" (which also appears in two needless bonus remixes on the CD), a hollow slab of romantic melodrama.

[jy/iar]

ICE-T

Rhyme Pays (Sire) 1987 ●
Power (Sire) 1988 ●

Those who believe New York is the only locus for credible or popular hip-hop performers should hear Los Angeles rapper Ice-T's convincing argument to the contrary on **Rhyme Pays**. (Moviegoers may have also caught him doing the title track of Dennis Hopper's *Colors.*) Working to bare-bones scratch tracks programmed and produced by New York dj Afrika Islam, Ice puts a little flair into the presentation, using a cloying singsong, various vocal styles and other theatrical gimmicks to make detailed tales of sex, parties, wealth, criminal activity and jail more absorbing and distinguished than they might otherwise be. Solid and sharp.   [iar]

ICICLE WORKS

The Icicle Works (Arista) 1984
The Small Price of a Bicycle (Chrysalis) 1985
Seven Singles Deep (nr/Beggars Banquet) 1986 ●
If You Want to Defeat Your Enemy Sing His Song (Beggars Banquet-RCA) 1987 ●

"Whisper to a Scream (Birds Fly)," which leads off this Liverpool trio's debut album, is a brilliant pop single filled with sparkling guitars, a hook-laden chorus and Chris Sharrock's surprisingly powerful, creative drumming. Unfortunately, the LP (and Icicle Works' career) ran downhill from there, with only brief interludes of nearly similar inspired creativity.

The Small Price of a Bicycle, which appeared and disappeared in the US without fanfare, has its moments of listenable (if ponderous) guitar-pop, but is marred by singer-guitarist-songwriter Robert Ian McNabb's self-important lyrics and weak melodies.

His regrettable vocal resemblance to Neil Diamond and Anthony Newley notwithstanding, McNabb sounds confident and mature on **Defeat Your Enemy**, an album of increased sophistication and ambition. The spectacular "Understanding Jane," an excitingly terse piece of singalong rock, is made even more conspicuous by the relatively leaden tracks which surround it. (Memo to McNabb: spend a bit more time on song titles: "When You Were Mine" and "Walking with a Mountain" were already taken.)

Seven Singles Deep is an A-sides compilation; the cassette adds seven bonus tracks; the CD (entitled **The Icicle Works**) contains the basic seven and a different selection of six more. The tape of **Defeat Your Enemy** adds two; the CD four.   [iar]

ICONS OF FILTH

Onward Christian Soldiers (nr/Mortarhate) 1984

Shouted vocals and medium-speed raw guitar punk provide London's Icons of Filth with their musical formula; generally well-put, lengthy political lyrics make the band's

activist statements on such typical topics as class society, vivisection and nuclear war. ("You're better active today than radioactive tomorrow" may not be catchy, but it is sane.) A far cry from Woody Guthrie perhaps, and not exactly high on the light entertainment scale, but a positive effort to reclaim some of rock's once-lofty ideals.   [iar]

IDEAL

Ideal (Ger. Innovative Communications) 1980
Der Ernst des Lebens (Ger. Eitel Optimal) 1981
Bi Nuu (Ger. Eitel Optimal) 1983

HUMPE-HUMPE

Humpe-Humpe (Warner Bros.) 1985

Odd pop from an innovative and intelligent German quartet. Ideal plays kinetic, herky-jerky guitar-based rock sung in her native tongue by Anete Humpe, a rough but convincing vocalist. Given the Teutonic predilection for electronics and progressive music, Ideal's Anglo-American-styled approach—on Tangerine Dreamer Klaus Schulze's label no less—is quite unexpected. Although the band is not too structurally bizarre on the almost-rudimentary first LP, the record does display incipient invention, with all sorts of delightful bits thrown in to keep things hopping.

On the Conny Plank-produced **Der Ernst des Lebens (The Seriousness of Life)**, however, the polished sound makes the record seem superficially less idiosyncratic, although drippy organ and surprises like cello and extraneous audio effects provide considerable evidence to the contrary. The songs concern some pretty interesting subjects as well—e.g., "Sex in the Desert," "Tension" and "Shoot." With Humpe letting one of her male bandmates sing a good portion of the tunes, they subtly absorb rockabilly, reggae and other influences into the stew.

Bi Nuu exposes Ideal's singing and songwriting shortcomings and is inferior to the prior LPs. In an attempt to keep things happening, the band incorporates more Carib-beats and even jazzy stylings, as well as studio gimmickry, but all for naught—this brief album has precious little life in it.

Following the end of Ideal, Anete and her younger sister Inga formed a band which, with producer Roma Baran (a Laurie Anderson associate) as catalyst, transmuted into Humpe-Humpe. Baran wound up splitting the studio chores on **Humpe-Humpe** with Plank, Gareth Jones and the Humpes; somehow, they collectively came up with something like a modern-age electronic Eurovision record. The sisters sing their compositions in English and German with agreeable harmonic skill, if not much raw vocal talent. The album neglects to include any musician credits, but it sounds like synthesizers are doing it all. Anderson's ghost is audibly present in the gimmicky effects and self-amused tone, but the commercial pop basis puts an utterly different bias on the proceedings. A neat, offbeat pop record. [iar]

BILLY IDOL

Don't Stop EP (Chrysalis) 1981
Billy Idol (Chrysalis) 1982 ●
Rebel Yell (Chrysalis) 1983 ●
Whiplash Smile (Chrysalis) 1986 ●
Vital Idol (Chrysalis) 1987 ●
Idol Songs: 11 of the Best (nr/Chrysalis) 1988 ●

After Generation X's demise, Billy Idol packed his bags and moved to New York, got himself managed by former Kiss svengali Bill Aucoin and began recording with local players and producer/drummer Keith Forsey, Giorgio Moroder's protégé. But the first results of that union—a four-song EP—had only an awkward but entertaining cover of "Mony Mony" and a phenomenal five-minute remake of Gen X's "Dancing with Myself" to recommend it.

Billy Idol (and a series of generally noxious videos) made William Broad a huge star while providing erstwhile fans of his original band with an ideological dilemma: was he new wave's ultimate Frankenstein mutation or an arena-metal fraud masquerading as a punk? In any case, the record—a marriage of Moroder's trademark *Midnight Express* sequencer sound and a throbbing rock beat—proved to be a lode of memorable hits ("White Wedding," "Hot in the City," "Love Calling"). Steve Stevens' caricatured Ronson/Thunders guitar wildness noisily matches Idol's macho postures and sneering vocals; the powerfully-built modern rock band has subtlety *and* near-metal strength. An album to despise while you hum along.

With only writing partner Stevens held over from the first record, Idol kept the same producer and formula on **Rebel Yell**, another collection of hits that run hot ("Rebel Yell," "Blue Highway"), cool ("Eyes Without a Face," "Catch My Fall") and both ("Flesh for Fantasy"). Refined and carefully groomed for platinum success, it's an undeniably good rock'n'roll record that is also reprehensible for its phoniness and calculation.

Whiplash Smile repeats the recipe: Forsey, Stevens and a duotone program of hard/soft songs. Characteristically, the staggering guitar riffarola of "Worlds Forgotten Boy" runs directly into the engagingly modest, sweet-voiced technobilly of "To Be a Lover." The problem here is that there's no wind in Idol's sails: he takes it easy and relies too heavily on his partner's pyrotechnics. Unlike Idol's previous records, his vocals here lack the gism that made his hits soar with enthusiasm and energy. With Idol out of contention and only second-rate material (the notable "To Be a Lover" is a non-original) in attendance, Stevens easily steals the spotlight; all of the record's best moments are his.

Vital Idol, available in the UK for two years before its American release, is a remix/greatest hits LP: extended versions (none under five minutes) of such Idolisms as "White Wedding," "Mony Mony," "Catch My Fall," "Dancing with Myself" and "Flesh for Fantasy." **Idol Songs**, also released first in the UK, offers a more straightforward greatest hits package, presenting the umpteenth appearance of "Dancing with Myself" as well as "Eyes Without a Face," "White Wedding" and "Rebel Yell." [iar]

IGGY AND THE STOOGES

See *Iggy Pop.*

IKE YARD

Night After Night EP (Bel. Crépuscule) 1981
A Fact a Second (Factory America) 1982

Ike Yard—not a person, but a New York-based quartet—mixes vocals not unlike the zombie mutterings of a bum in the subway (and barely more intelligible) with spurts of electronic noise to create minimalist "music" with a funny sort of force. The emphasis is on percussion and rhythm, although there are traces of distinct pitch, courtesy assorted drones and grunts. By and large, the sounds resemble audio vérité—street noises, howling winds, guns, clanging doors—more so on **A Fact a Second**, the preceding EP being more musical.

Ike Yard's Stuart Arbright subsequently went on to more commercial endeavors, such as Dominatrix. [jg]

See also *Dominatrix.*

LOS ILLEGALS

Internal Exile (A&M) 1983

On paper, this looked great—an East Los Angeles Mexican-American rock quintet with a strong political consciousness and tremendous local following getting a major label deal. On vinyl, however, what comes across is characterless (except for a bit of Latin percussion) rock'n'roll with clumsy but righteous lyrics, some in Spanish. Los Illegals don't give away anything in terms of skill, energy or integrity, but it's hard to get excited about their Anyband guitar-laden rock and torpid songwriting. Mick Ronson co-produced.   [iar]

ILLUSTRATED MAN

Illustrated Man EP (Capitol) 1984

I'm not sure if I-Man's brief and miserable existence quite qualified it as a supergroup: Hugo Burnham (ex-Gang of Four), Roger Mason (a Gary Numan sideman), Robert Dean (ex-Japan) and Australian singer/bassist Philip Foxman. I hope not, because this overbearing, overproduced, soul-free dance-funk hardly reflects well on any of the participants. Actually, if they had lost Foxman—his voice *was* the band's worst feature—Illustrated Man might have had a future. Instead, this is just corporate bandwagon-jumping of no merit.   [iar]

INCA BABIES

Jugular EP (nr/Black Lagoon) 1984
Rumble (nr/Black Lagoon) 1985
Surfing in Locustland EP (nr/Black Lagoon) 1985
This Train (nr/Black Lagoon) 1986
Opium Den (Black Lagoon-Fundamental) 1987
Evil Hour (Communion) 1988 ●

There's not much to say about England's Inca Babies beyond noting that they make every conceivable effort to be the Birthday Party. Each member emulates his BP counterpart, with a pounding rhythm section and apocalyptic guitar, but the Inca Babies lack the original's power and completely miss the dark humor. Even the song titles on the early records have that familiar ring: "16 Tons of Fink," "Cactus Mouth Informer," "Luecotomy Meat Boss." Real tribute-band circuit stuff.

Adding a member for **Opium Den**, Inca Babies toned down the Birthday Party-isms and enhanced their presentation with raw psychedelia and some dirty (if not dilettantish) country-blues. Lead singer Harry S combines his Nick Cave imitation with a gratuitous and phony Southern accent (the American South, that is). Still, **Opium Den** shows that the band is capable of producing work with their own signature on it, or at least drawing from more than one influence. Lyrics are provided, an ill-advised move.

[dgs]

INDIVIDUALS

Aquamarine EP (Infidelity) 1981
Fields (Plexus) 1982

This New York quartet bears some resemblance to bands like the (early) dB's, whose Gene Holder produced both records; musically, however, the Individuals' arty pretentiousness makes them sound like a poor copy of the Cure or a less-aggressive Gang of Four.

Aquamarine's five numbers are spartan in both arrangement and melody. Despite characteristically sprightly guitars and simple drum figures, style supplants substance, and there's nothing much lurking behind the hip artifice.

Fields has more fully realized sound, with good vocal harmonies and studio effects; still, the songs are unmemorable and the performances rather tepid. The one number that does stand out, "Dancing with My Eighty Wives," is rather senseless, but mixes real songwriting acumen with an interesting arrangement—and a definite group identity for a change.

Individuals guitarist/singer Glenn Morrow followed his muse into Rage to Live; Janet (bass/vocals) and Doug (drums) Wygal formed a band that bears their surname; guitarist Jon Klages went on to play solo and with Richard Lloyd.   [iar]

See also *Rage to Live.*

INDOOR LIFE

Indoor Life (Fr. Celluloid) 1981
Indoor Life (Relativity) 1983

Indoor Life formed in San Francisco but later emigrated to New York City. On their first album, they field a five-piece lineup that includes trombone, tapes and synthesizer. The music—while generally structured into song form—also contains heaps of silly noises and improvised bleeps and squawks. The lyrics (in English, French and German) are promising, but not all are supported by melodies. Overall, Indoor Life seem to be an artful, pretentious collective of progressive intellectuals bent on making accessible cleverness for their own satisfaction. Maybe you'll like it, too.

Recorded as a trio, the second album is better organized but no less self-indulgent, drawing out simple song ideas into overly long, repetitive excursions. Jorge Socarras has a pleasant, flexible voice; his two cohorts (synths and guitars) evince much technical prowess, but these monotonous creations are only intermittently entertaining and rarely captivating.   [iar]

INMATES
First Offence (Polydor) 1979
Shot in the Dark (Polydor) 1980
True Live Stories (Fr. Lolita) 1983
Five (Fr. Lolita) 1985

Britain's Inmates had a big American radio hit in 1979 with a cover of the Standells' "Dirty Water"; overall, their records sound like a cross between early Stones and early Dave Edmunds. Drawing on realistic-sounding originals plus well-chosen oldies, the Inmates don't offer anything new, but make good, primal rock'n'roll. **First Offence** contains "Dirty Water" as well as Jimmy McCracklin's "The Walk" and Don Covay's "Three Time Loser" (one of several tracks employing the Rumour brass section). Thanks, no doubt, to common icons, there are audible similarities to everyone from Creedence Clearwater to Robert Gordon.

Shot in the Dark dredges up the old Jagger/Richards gem, "So Much in Love," the Music Machine's "Talk Talk" and some real obscurities to repeat the formula. Fun, but too faceless to make any difference.

Continuing on with a new lineup that features original Eddie and the Hot Rods vocalist Barrie Masters, the 1983 live album on Lolita reprises both the Inmates' best-known tracks ("Dirty Water," "The Walk") and the Hot Rods' (Bob Seger's "Get Out of Denver").   [iar]

INNER CITY UNIT
Pass Out (nr/Riddle) 1980
The Maximum Effect (nr/Avatar) 1981
Punkadelic (nr/Flicknife) 1982
New Anatomy (nr/Demi Monde) 1985

If you can accept the notion that Hawkwind was the original punk-psychedelic-heavy-metal-dada fusion band, then it makes

sense that saxophonist Nik Turner should be behind Inner City Unit, a devolving London five-piece whose music is so far over the edge that it almost defies comprehension. Taking mind-expanding drugs is theoretically essential to appreciation here, but the frantic rock-with-horns of numbers like "Watching the Grass Grow" and "Cars Eat with Autoface" (on **Pass Out**) update the Hawkwind legend with style and energy that anyone can enjoy.   [iar]

INSECT SURFERS
Wavelength (Wasp) 1980
Sonar Safari EP (Wasp) 1983

Audacious production values, good pop songs in a number of flavors and skillful (but not slick) playing make **Wavelength**'s eight songs, by one of Washington, DC's better bands, a real pleasure. Nothing too serious here, just a batch of tuneful rock'n'roll numbers with lots of character, thanks to rudimentary synthesizer fills and solid guitar and vocals. Taking their name a bit more to heart, the EP tags some different bases, from bizarre beach music ("Sound of the Surf") to Nazz's "Open My Eyes" to instrumentals with '60sish organ and guitar stylings.   [iar]

INSIDERS
Ghost on the Beach (Epic) 1987

Chicago's Insiders try to sound a bit like the Everly Brothers replacing Tom Petty as frontman for the Heartbreakers. They do a pretty fair job of it, too, and even throw in a cover of Don and Phil's "The Price of Love" to make sure you get the idea. Their own songs are also reasonably serviceable—just don't expect anything really new or innovative.   [ds]

INTIMATE STRANGERS
See *Raise the Dragon*.

INVADERS
Test Card (nr/Polydor) 1980

Take pomp-rock, shorten its sights (unpump the pomp a bit), inject a bit of youth, alternate male and female vocals and what have you got? The Invaders (from West Yorkshire—not to be confused with two American bands of the same name), who still manage to have all the snap and appeal of week-old pastry. Too much of their "Rock Methodology" and not enough playfulness makes the Invaders a dull band.   [jg]

INXS

INXS (Aus. Deluxe) 1980 (Atco) 1984 ●
Underneath the Colours (Aus. Deluxe) 1981
   (Atco) 1984
Shabooh Shoobah (Atco) 1982 ●
Inxsive (Aus. Deluxe) 1982
Dekadance EP (Atco) 1983
The Swing (Atco) 1984 ●
Listen Like Thieves (Atlantic) 1985 ●
Kick (Atlantic) 1987 ●

It took these six Australians (three of them brothers) a long time to develop into something America wanted to hear; **INXS** is dull rock that sounds like a less-musical Joe Jackson or a no-soul Graham Parker. **Underneath the Colours**—like its predecessor, issued in the US only after the band had become successful—has much better audio quality (although they neglected to integrate the drums into the mix) and shifts the focus among keyboards, sax and guitar in a vain effort to vitalize the underwhelming songs.

Shabooh Shoobah, with good loud production by Mark Opitz (and one Farriss brother mysteriously missing from the credits), was the first INXS album to be released in the US and UK. Despite major strides in several areas, on the whole it's still not a happening record. A few outstanding numbers do display growth in personality and style: "The One Thing" sews a bunch of riffs together into an energetic, dense fabric, while "Soul Mistake" generates a foreboding mood and "Don't Change" gets up a good head of textured rock steam.

Following an Australian label change, the group's previous record company issued **Inxsive**, a compilation that includes outtakes and obscurities as well as hits.

Four songs from **Shabooh Shoobah** (three extended remixes plus a wholly new version of a fourth) comprise the club-oriented **Dekadance** EP. If not specifically better, the six-minute edit of "The One Thing" is certainly longer.

The Swing proved to be the first INXS LP of any real significance, moving the group clearly into the mainstream of modern dance-rock with the inclusion of the suavely insistent "Original Sin," produced by Nile Rodgers. (The record was otherwise done under the direction of Nick Launay.) "Burn

for You" is another highlight, using a female backing chorus to affect an amusing resemblance to Roxy Music. On the other hand, "I Send a Message" finally reveals INXS' enormous potential to annoy: a basically tuneless song synth-funked into repetitive and grating obnoxiousness. Elsewhere, **The Swing** offers strong beats, mannered vocals and a unified, au courant sound.

Listen Like Thieves, produced by Chris Thomas, is crisp, lively rock, with as little vocal posturing as Michael Hutchence seems capable of, and substantial aggressive guitar work where required. The title tune, "What You Need" and "This Time" all have solid melodies, strong rhythms and decisive hooks. "Shine Like It Does" attempts to generate a folk-rock sensibility with moderate success; other tracks are, at worst, negligible.

With Hutchence launching an acting career (in the atrocious *Dogs in Space*) and emerging as a pin-up sex god for teenagers, INXS made the completely vapid **Kick**, again using Chris Thomas to work up the notably mediocre material. (Needless to add, it became their biggest seller.) The inappropriate and unconvincing meta-political consciousness of a few lyrics doesn't improve what is essentially tuneless video-dance-rock; the contrived dress-up poses on the sleeve indicate what really makes INXS run. Ludicrous soul pretensions only underscore just how phony INXS is. Easily the worst of their recent albums, **Kick** does contain one consolation: a plodding version of the Australo-punk classic, "The Loved One," originally done around 1967 by Melbourne's groovy Loved Ones and first covered by INXS on a 1981 single.   [iar]

IPPU-DO

Normal (Jap. Epic-Sony) 1979
Real (Jap. Epic-Sony) 1980
Radio Fantasy (nr/Epic) 1981
Lunatic Menu (nr/Epic) 1982
Some-Times (Jap. Epic-Sony) 1982
Live and Zen (Jap. Epic-Sony) 1985

MASAMI TSUCHIYA

Rice Music (nr/Epic) 1982

Led by guitarist Masami Tsuchiya, an androgynous, Bowiesque character, this Japanese trio stepped into the commercial void created by Yellow Magic Orchestra's increased inactivity as a group. It's hard to make out what the songs are really about since most have only a chorus or bridge in English, but they seem simpleminded enough lyrically—themes of romantic fantasy, travel and technology evidently dominate. Tsuchiya's voice is high but gutsy and always in control (even when yelling)—he's got his shtick down pat, and his guitar playing fits as well. Ippu-Do alternates between modernized arrangements of '50s and early '60s vocal pop-rock melodies and steaming, heart-pounding rock'n' roll, sometimes in the same song. They also use reggae syncopation and synthesizers, so all bases are covered—except originality. (**Lunatic Menu** and **Some-Times** are anthologies of the other LPs.)

It sounds like these fellas, especially Tsuchiya, possess the ability to go further but just aren't sure how. Tsuchiya gives it a try on his solo LP with lots of help from YMO's Riuichi Sakamoto, though several tracks include members of Japan (the *English* band) and Bill Nelson on e-bow guitar. Most successful when he tries to mildly funkify Japanese music, with further cross-fertilization, Tsuchiya could be a real innovator.

By 1985's live album, Ippu-Do was just a duo, aided by two ex-members of Japan (with whom Tsuchiya had toured and recorded) plus bass ace Percy Jones. Despite its recent vintage, the album portrays the band treading musical water with jagged, arty treatments of old material (the group's and Tsuchiya's), plus a version of the Zombies' "Time of the Season." Despite stylistic growth, Ippu-Do needs new—not old—content to make it meaningful. [jg]

GREGORY ISAACS

In Person (nr/Trojan) 1975 + 1983
All I Have Is Love (nr/Trojan) 1976 + 1983
The Best of Gregory Isaacs Vol. 1 (Jam. GG) 1977
Cool Ruler (nr/Front Line) 1978
Soon Forward (nr/Front Line) 1979
Showcase EP (Taxi) 1980
The Lonely Lover (nr/Pre) 1980
Extra Classic (Shanachie) 1981
The Best of Gregory Isaacs Vol. 2 (Jam. GG) 1981
The Early Years (nr/Trojan) 1981
More Gregory (Mango) 1981
The Sensational Gregory Isaacs (nr/Vista) 1982
Lover's Rock (nr/Pre) 1982
Night Nurse (Mango) 1982
Mr. Isaacs (Shanachie) 1982
Crucial Cuts (nr/Virgin) 1983
Out Deh! (Mango) 1983
Reggae Greats (Live) (Island) 1984

Live at the Academy Brixton (nr/Rough Trade) 1984
Private Beach Party (RAS) 1985 ●
Talk Don't Bother Me (nr/Skengdon) 1987
Watchmen of the City (Rohit) 1987
Come Along (World Enterprise) 1987

The Cool Ruler, Gregory Isaacs, is one of the best-loved and most durable reggae singers. Highly prolific (he writes nearly all his material) and business-savvy (he runs his own Jamaican label, African Museum), Isaacs' voice is still the key to his success. His delivery is marked by a combination of ice and fire rare even among soul singers—an urgent longing, tempered with cool control. Although comparable to Al Green or Marvin Gaye, Isaacs is a completely unique stylist. His repertoire is equal parts lovers rock and Rasta protest; the link is his seductive delivery. Whether he's urging romance or reform, the call to action will give you goosebumps.

Like many popular reggae performers, however, Isaacs' recording career is a confusing configuration of producers and labels that proves difficult to untangle. For his early work, he relied on a number of producers. **Sensational**, for instance, has one side produced by Rupie Edwards and one by Ossie Hibbert, resulting in a mix of hits ("Black and White," "Mr. Know It All") and duds. **Extra Classic** compiles his work with Pete Weston and Lee Perry, as well as his first self-produced sessions. While also spotty, the record offers early proof of Isaacs' authority and strength as a songwriter.

Isaacs' career began to move under the guidance of producer Alvin Ranglin. Their collaboration is chronicled on the two excellent **Best Of** collections. Though available only as Jamaican imports, these consistently strong LPs are worth finding, and crucial for fans. Another Ranglin/Isaacs session, **In Person** (which includes the UK hit, "Love Is Overdue") is available on Trojan, along with an LP produced by Sidney Crooks, **All I Have Is Love**. Both are of mixed quality, but Trojan took the best from each and combined them with a third batch (produced by Winston "Niney" Holness) for **The Early Years**, good all the way through.

For his next career phase, Isaacs chose to produce himself. Despite weak covers of the Temptations' "Get Ready" and Billy & Vera's "Storybook Children," **Mr. Isaacs** has bold, assured singing, and at least one classic, "Slave Master."

Virgin's Front Line label then released two inconsistent albums, subsequently culling the best tracks for an edition of the **Crucial Cuts** series; still, it's pretty weak. The outstanding **Soon Forward**, however, launched his collaboration with Sly Dunbar and Robbie Shakespeare. The title song of that record also appears on the **Showcase** EP, released on Sly and Robbie's Taxi label, which adds a version of Bob Marley's "Slave Driver." Although tight and lively from start to finish, the record allows Isaacs' personality to be somewhat overshadowed by the duo's fine playing. Besides his work with Sly and Robbie, Isaacs began an association with Roots Radics, another fine Jamaican session band, that would last several LPs.

The Lonely Lover and **More Gregory** contain his finest middle-period work. Both feature excellent backing (divided between the Radics and Dunbar/Shakespeare) and a steady stream of high-quality material. Best of all, Isaacs is singing at the peak of his form. **More**, in particular, firmly establishes his loverboy persona in an easygoing groove that lasts for all ten cuts.

By contrast, Isaacs' work on Island is marred by inconsistency. Both **Night Nurse** and **Out Deh!** boast first-rate singing and playing, but the material is erratic, frequently weak—more a series of gestures than songs. To compensate, perhaps, two live albums were released around the same time. The song selection—an essential greatest hits—is similar on both, but the Brixton set has the edge, featuring a horn section and a more enthusiastic performance.

A short period of inactivity was broken in 1985 by the release of **Private Beach Party**. In a clear effort to lighten the load, Isaacs enlisted the help of an outside producer, Augustus Clarke, and several songwriters. The result is his best album in years—a fresh, diverse package.

Crowded off the charts by successful dance-hall dj's, Issacs has been less visible lately. But he's remained prolific, and recorded LPs of his own material with a variety of producers for a few small labels. While none of these releases are particularly distinct, each of them demonstrates nicely how Gregory Issacs' smooth and sexy formula is as dependable as Smokey Robinson's, and how his professionalism and talent have withstood the test of time.   [bk]

CHRIS ISAAK
Silvertone (Warner Bros.) 1985
Chris Isaak (Warner Bros.) 1987 ●

The look of a sensitive young Elvis . . . moody, atmospheric tunes . . . sweet, brooding vocals . . . heaps of twangy guitar. Chris Isaak has his shtick down cold, that's for sure. Happily, this retro package offers more than self-conscious imagery. At his best, Isaak summons up the deep hurt of a classic blues or the soaring spirits of footloose rockabilly. On **Silvertone**, consult the swinging "Livin' for Your Lover" or "Western Stars," a lazy, loping piece of sagebrush hokum. On **Chris Isaak**, try the quietly menacing "You Owe Me Some Kind of Love" or "Blue Hotel," the woeful sound of a tortured soul crying for help. No wonder Isaak's been compared to Roy Orbison.   [jy]

MARK ISHAM
See *Marianne Faithfull.*

ISM
A Diet for the Worms (S.I.N.) 1983
Constantinople EP (Broken) 1985

A Diet for the Worms is hysterically funny New York hardcore with a tasteless baby-being-delivered cover and gutbusting numbers like "Shitlist," "Vegetarian at a Barbeque," "Life Ain't No Bowl of Brady Bunch" and the classic "John Hinckley Jr. (What Has Jodie Done to You?)." The band (not to be confused with Elliott Sharp's avant outfit, also active around New York in the early '80s) plays at easily followable speed and has a reasonably articulate bellower in Jism, who gives the longwinded lyrics (mostly his) appropriate exercise. A good, scatological laugh for the vulgar at heart.

On **Constantinople**, Jism and his band connect with their roots, slam-dunking songs by the Residents *and* the Fugs with reverent but rowdy enthusiasm. Rather than hardcore, Ism here plays restrained rock with piano and relative subtlety. Judging by this EP, Ism is developing a novel time warp, mixing various breeds of outrage into a hybrid all its own.   [iar]

IT BITES
The Big Lad in the Windmill (Virgin-Geffen) 1986
Once Around the World EP (Virgin-Geffen) 1988

Hailing from Cumbria, a remote northern county of England, It Bites plays energetic, carefully-produced (by Alan Shacklock) chart-pop that adds considerable off-beat spunk to the easy-listening sounds of peppy outfits like Haircut One Hundred. **The Big Lad in the Windmill** has the merry attitude (if not the extraordinary talent) of early 10cc: unexpected styles and noises abound in a shiny rush of giddy melodicism. While hardly ground-breaking, this provincial quartet is agreeably paranormal. [iar]

IT'S IMMATERIAL
Life's Hard and Then You Die
  (Siren-Virgin-A&M) 1986 ●

More bizarreness from the Liverpool art college set. In this case, a duo of Manchester-born Johns plus myriad friends (including the Christians, whose Henry Priestman was an Itsy before forming his current group) cook up a fascinating musical hybrid that touches variously on synth-pop, atmospheric art-rock, recitation and a unique brand of English country music. It may remind you of early OMD, Pete Townshend, Talking Heads, even Ronnie Lane's post-Faces gypsy-rock aggregation Slim Chance—which is to say that there's a lot going into this mix. In fact, if the band lacks anything, it's identity. [ds]

See also *Christians.*

DEBORA IYALL
See *Romeo Void.*

J J J J J J J J J

DAVID J.(AY)

See *Bauhaus, Jazz Butcher, Love and Rockets.*

JOE JACKSON

Look Sharp! (A&M) 1979 ●
I'm the Man (A&M) 1979 ●
Beat Crazy (A&M) 1980 ●
Jumpin' Jive (A&M) 1981 ●
Night and Day (A&M) 1982 ●
Mike's Murder (A&M) 1983
Body and Soul (A&M) 1984 ●
Big World (A&M) 1986 ●
Will Power (A&M) 1987 ●
Live 1980/86 (A&M) 1988 ●

Joe Jackson's debut LP, **Look Sharp!**, was hot stuff indeed, spawning the wry hit "Is She Really Going Out with Him?" and making him the first member of England's angry young triumvirate (Jackson, Parker, Costello) to really sell records in America. Tough and wiry, Jackson's songs mixed an edgy sensibility with a self-deprecating wit that put him in a class apart from his more serious peers.

The follow-up, **I'm the Man**, was an extension of **Look Sharp!**. Material ranges from the banal vindictiveness of "On Your Radio" to the haunting approximation of genius, "It's Different for Girls." While much of the material dates from **Look Sharp!**, the production is less crisp and the record lacks its predecessor's impact.

A conscious reaction to the pop of his first two albums, **Beat Crazy**—Jackson's final LP with his original tight-knit band—drifts with an eerie sense of objectivity. Jackson puts it bluntly in the liner notes: "This album represents a desperate attempt to make some sense

of Rock and Roll. Deep in our hearts, we knew it was doomed to failure. The question remains: Why did we try?"

With the Joe Jackson Band dissolved, Joe took a musical detour, recording **Jumpin' Jive**, an attack of cool jazz vocals over mock big-band swing. Obviously enjoying himself (for once), Jackson romps his way through "Is You Is or Is You Ain't My Baby" and suchlike. Jackson's production is warm and loving, and though **Jumpin' Jive** was a clear respite from the official progress of his music, the album is enormous fun and holds up.

Night and Day proved to be Jackson's most successful outing since **Look Sharp!**, although the urban/Latin flavor bears not the slightest resemblance to the white-hot sound of his early days. The Latin rhythms seem somehow less honest even than the buoyant bop of **Jumpin' Jive**, yet Jackson is obviously sincere.

Jackson's next departure proved to be a hypothetical film soundtrack. Months after the album—billed as the music from *Mike's Murder*—appeared, the movie still hadn't, and rumors began to circulate that various problems were causing the delay, among them the decision not to use Jackson's songs in the film. **Mike's Murder** is a record adrift, created but not used for a specific purpose. In any case, it's a very weak showing—Jackson at his least confident—notable mostly for "Memphis," whose organ line and rhythm are lifted straight from Steve Winwood's "Gimme Some Loving."

Jackson survived that debacle to make **Body and Soul**, an ambitious attempt to simplify and repersonalize the recording process as much as possible. With a distant, light sound—quite in contrast to the stuffy closeness of most contemporary records—and

'50s jazz stylings tinged by an ongoing affection for Latin music, the record has plenty of atmosphere, and contains some of his strongest, most mature songwriting. Unlike his previous time-tunnel trip, **Body and Soul** eschews period re-creation (except on the cover) in favor of a wistful ambience indicative of Jackson's distaste for much modern music.

The three-sided **Big World** was recorded live directly to a digital stereo master with a small band at a three-day New York concert engagement staged especially for that purpose in January 1986. With no post-production tinkering of any sort, the 15 new songs—some about current world political affairs, others about societal issues—are reproduced on two discs as accurately as possible. Stylistically, **Big World** is a return to stripped-down lightly-seasoned jazzy rock. A little self-important (the rampantly multi-lingual booklet smacks of grandstanding) and creatively inconsistent, but an impressively ambitious effort.

Redolent with unrestrained pomposity, the ironically-titled **Will Power** is an instrumental album (on which he plays some of the piano) that mixes Jackson's least interesting film-score composition style with the "overture for two pianos" which turned into the title track. The type-free cover and the inside photo of the suffering artist, sitting dejectedly alone in a huge studio, merely indicate the imagined depths of this trivial self-indulgence. While Jackson may be impressed by his ability to convince an orchestra to play his melodramatically panoramic music, it's unlikely anyone else will find this exercise especially rewarding.

The conceptually masterful live album is divided into four different creative eras; each side presents a different incarnation of the Joe Jackson Experience. Side One, recorded in Manchester and Holland in 1980, features material from the first three albums, played with his original backing trio. Side Two (1983), recorded with a keyboard-laden quintet in Sydney, Australia, is billed as "The Night and Day Tour" but contains only "Cancer" from that album. Instead, it draws further from the same three records, offering the second (this time a cappella) rendition of "Is She Really Going Out with Him?" on the LP. Side Three (1984), recorded in Sydney and Melbourne during the horn-heavy "Body and Soul Tour," again includes that song, only this time in an acoustic version;

Side Four (1986) hails from Canada and Japan and features a straight electric rock quartet doing selections (including "Breaking Us in Two," "It's Different for Girls" and "Jumpin' Jive") from various albums.

[jw/iar]

JACOBITES
See *Nikki Sudden.*

JAGS
Evening Standards (Island) 1980
No Tie Like a Present (Island) 1981

This English one-hit-wonder's one hit, "Back of My Hand," sounded remarkably like Elvis Costello. (Once other bands had repeated that feat, the Jags faded into obscurity.) Surprisingly, their first album, **Evening Standards**, contained other interesting examples of enthusiastic rock-pop, and indicated possible staying power.

Despite a lineup change, new producer and an amusing title, the Jags' follow-up, **No Tie Like a Present**, failed to get them back in the public's ear. Not a bad band by any means, the Jags promised great things and delivered far less. [iar]

JAH LION
See *Lee Perry.*

JAM
In the City (Polydor) 1977
This Is the Modern World (Polydor) 1977
All Mod Cons (Polydor) 1978 ●
Setting Sons (Polydor) 1979 ●
Sound Affects (Polydor) 1980
The Jam EP (Polydor) 1982
The Gift (Polydor) 1982
The Bitterest Pill EP (Polydor) 1982
Beat Surrender EP (Polydor) 1982
Dig the New Breed (Polydor) 1982
Snap! (Polydor) 1983
Compact Snap! [CD] (Polydor) 1984

How ironic that the band from the class of '77 that seemed to stand least for the tenets of punk at the outset should wind up the one that remained truest to them over the long haul. The Jam's refusal to compromise their ideals and integrity during a six-year career tends to polarize reactions to them. In the end, once-common complaints about unoriginality and Paul Weller's lack of vocal prowess are overshadowed by their accomplishments as songwriters, musicians and commentators, but mostly by the Jam's living proof that a band's commercial success need not divorce it utterly from its fans *or* sense of purpose. The trio's parting at the end of 1982 can be looked at as symbolic of victory (a courageous decision not to become pointless dinosaurs in the UK, where they were virtually superstars) or failure (they were never able to achieve more than modest success in America, despite plenty of effort on the part of both the Jam and their label) or just as an indication that Weller's ever-changing moods had led him away from the Jam's rock'n'soul aesthetic toward more "stylish" pursuits. Regardless, the Jam left behind a recorded legacy as important as any the new wave produced.

Black mohair suits, smart white shirts, skinny ties, stylish razor-cut hair, Rickenbacker guitars—on **In the City** the Jam were the new mods, emerging from a sea of spiky-haired leather-and-chain-clad punks. They may have looked different, but their energy level gave no ground, as Weller's jagged, choppy double-tracked guitar led the attack over Bruce Foxton's busy, melodic bass lines and Rick Buckler's stiff-backed drumming. The songs themselves are as taut and well-manicured as the group, but match the explosiveness and attitude of the punks easily enough to establish an indisputable kinship to bands like the Sex Pistols and Clash. (It was no surprise when the Pistols swiped the riff for "Holidays in the Sun" from Weller's "In the City.")

If the songs and playing of **In the City** are derivative—especially of **The Who Sings My Generation** and '60s Motown—there's no arguing that the Jam was speaking to a generation for whom it was all new. Also, the main points—youth regaining pop culture from the grasp of conservative people with old-fashioned ideas, the individual vs. the crowd—were well taken by the group's growing British following.

This Is the Modern World, recorded just months after **In the City** was released, is a cleaner-produced version of its predecessor, breaking little new ground. The songs themselves are hit-and-miss, with "This Is the Modern World," "Standards" and "All Around the World" (a brilliant single, included only on the US version of the LP) the obvious standouts.

Since they had by then spawned dozens of neo-mod soundalikes, the Jam needed a change of direction, and on **All Mod Cons**,

Weller rose to the challenge. Prior inconsistency is replaced by an album that explores new avenues with almost complete success, while never straying too far from the band's roots. Weller's writing showed him to have blossomed into a major-league tunesmith, as well as a lyricist possessing a keen eye for detail and a refreshing sense of the vagaries of his own position. While retaining a great deal of the Who influence, the Jam also began to incorporate other sources. (Especially Ray Davies, which resulted not only in a hit version of the Kinks' "David Watts" but also in the biting social commentary of "Mr. Clean.") "In the Crowd" gives Weller a chance to open up as a guitarist and proves that he's more than just a Townshend copyist. **All Mod Cons** is a brilliant record.

Setting Sons takes five songs from a scrapped concept album about three friends who meet after much of England has been destroyed by atomic war and combines them with four even bleaker tracks, then lightens up by ending the LP with a version of the uplifting "Heatwave." The album is the Jam's most somber—not that any of their records are big on humor—but it is also their most effective. Weller's songs stick, and the beauty of his melodies provides stark contrast to the blackness of his lyrical vision.

Perhaps as a conscious change from the heaviness of **Setting Sons**, **Sound Affects** is more danceable and, for the most part, less pointed, although songs like "That's Entertainment" are hardly cheerful. The rage is still there, but it's channeled into fiery playing and singing, loosening up somewhat on the lyrics.

The Jam EP—five songs previously released on singles—served mostly as an interim measure between LPs, but includes essential tracks like "Absolute Beginners" and "Funeral Pyre."

The Gift explores a lot of new territory on songs like "Trans-Global Express" and "Precious," where a strong funk/Latin rhythm fueled by loads of percusssion is heavily in evidence. The album takes a lot of chances and doesn't always succeed; some of the rhythmic experiments sound forced, others fall victim to overly dense, ponderous production. **The Gift** has its moments, notably "Happy Together," "Ghosts" and the Motownish single, "Town Called Malice." It also offers some evidence as to why Weller may have felt the band had exhausted its possibilities.

The Bitterest Pill (named for an emotional song with one of Weller's best vocals) shows the band forging still further into the realm of R&B. Although not recorded as such, the five tracks form a cohesive work.

Beat Surrender, containing the Jam's last studio visit together, was released as a British double-45 and an American 12-inch. The driving title track is absolutely smashing, and the four accompanying tracks are swell as well, including a lively rendition of Curtis Mayfield's "Move on Up." The record is additionally noteworthy for its audible indications of Weller's subsequent direction with the Style Council.

Dig the New Breed, issued after the band's split had been announced, is an honest, retrospective live album (complete with bum notes) recorded at gigs during various stages of the Jam's career—a powerful parting shot. **Snap!** is an awesome two-disc career retrospective which was later abridged (!) and issued on CD as **Compact Snap!**.

[ds/iar]

See also *Bruce Foxton, Style Council, Tracie.*

JAMES

Village Fire EP (nr/Factory) 1985
Stutter (Blanco y Negro-Sire) 1986
Strip-mine (Blanco y Negro-Sire) 1988 ●

Winsome and demure, Manchester's James proffer a folksy, intricate version of pop with top-notch percussion and vocals that range from baritone to falsetto, often in the same verse. **Village Fire** collects the five tracks on James' first two singles, presenting a diverse range, from folk enhanced with numerous layers of acoustic guitar to revved-up funk and keen-edged punk.

Stutter, produced by Lenny Kaye, proved to be a rather surprising first album for the quartet. Unlike their singles, the LP adheres strictly to one particular style of music—a heavily orchestrated brand of acoustic folk. The vocals and harmonies are characteristically impeccable, yet there's little to make these songs truly exceptional. In focusing their scope, James has inadvertently obscured some of their better attributes. The potential for greatness exists in tracks like "Skullduggery," "So Many Ways," "Why So Close" (an amazing remix from **Village Fire**) and "Just Hip"; unfortunately, this seamless presentation does little to realize it.

James' second album was released in mid-1988.

[ag]

JANES ADDICTION

Janes Addiction (XXX) 1987
Nothing's Shocking (Warner Bros.) 1988 ●

These obnoxious Los Angeles glam-punk poseurs recorded most of their debut album (pressed on clear vinyl) right at home, on-stage at the Roxy. Perry Farrell sings in a womanly aggressive warble—he's obviously listened to his Siouxsie and the Banshees records more than once—as his three bandmates pound out competent but unoriginal post-'70s guitar rock. "My Time" and the dramatic "Jane Says," both played with acoustic guitar, show that JA is indeed capable of mild musical achievement in a sub-Mott the Hoople mode, but most of the record—especially "Sympathy" ("for the Devil") and Lou Reed's "Rock and Roll"—sounds like an Aerosmith cover band. Farrell's habit of lamely interjecting the word "motherfucker" into his lyrics merely frosts the album's maggotry.

[iar]

JAPAN

Adolescent Sex (Ariola-Hansa) 1978 + 1982
Obscure Alternatives (Ariola-Hansa) 1978 + 1982
Quiet Life (nr/Ariola-Hansa) 1979
Gentlemen Take Polaroids (nr/Virgin) 1980 ●
Tin Drum (nr/Virgin) 1981 ●
Assemblage (nr/Hansa) 1981 (nr/Fame) 1985
Japan (Virgin-Epic) 1982
Oil on Canvas (nr/Virgin) 1983 ●
Exorcising Ghosts (nr/Virgin) 1984 ●

MICK KARN

Titles (nr/Virgin) 1982
Dreams of Reason Produce Monsters (nr/Virgin) 1987

In one of rock's most remarkable examples of bootstrapping, South London's Japan pulled themselves up from lowly beginnings, as a ludicrously over-dressed glam-punk-pose band who (badly) emulated the New York Dolls and Alice Cooper, to finish, five years later, as one of the most sophisticated art-rock-pose outfits, earning the respect of their peers and branching out into such fields as sculpture and photography.

Adolescent Sex introduces Japan in all its guitar-rock misery, playing such Bowie-influenced tripe as "Wish You Were Black" with less style than a sense of urgency. **Obscure Alternatives** adds more keyboards but still relies on Rob Dean's buzzing guitars and David Sylvian's sneery vocals for its sound.

(Ill-advised digressions into reggae and funk are strictly dilettantism and sound like it.) The songs are fairly unmelodic, the production nondescript. With a quick listen, you might mistake this for a junior-league Stones imitation.

Japan entered the modern world with **Quiet Life**. The choice of John Punter—who had worked with Roxy Music and Bryan Ferry—to be their producer was significant, as the band's sights had shifted from gutter-glam to sophisticated decadence. A cover of the Velvet Underground's "All Tomorrow's Parties" allows Japan—and especially Sylvian, sporting a totally revised singing voice—to show off their new suave reserve, relying on sequencers, Mick Karn's proto-funk basswork and generally understated aplomb. Around this time, Japan also released a marvelous single of Smokey Robinson's "I Second That Emotion."

With the band's new direction clearly not requiring his presence, guitarist Dean took a powder; Japan recorded the excellent **Gentlemen Take Polaroids** as a quartet. Sylvian's debonair Ferryisms—more shyly quiet than dissipated—are met by Karn's astonishing fretless bass work, Richard Barbieri's wide-ranging keyboard work (incorporating Oriental and other traditions) and Steve Jansen's inventive drumming, creating a unique sound—technically exquisite and musically adventurous—with lots of atmosphere but a very light touch. Sylvian's songs are, however, very hard to hold, as many lack a backbone and seem to waft along with little structure.

Tin Drum presents Japan at peak form, playing subtle creations with intricate rhythms and tightly controlled dynamics. Spare but strong drumming (abetted by Karn's rubbery bass) provides needed propulsion, and the breadth of influences—from Middle Eastern to funk—color the music a number of fascinating shades. Having almost totally escaped pop constraints, Japan's sound here—except for a few tunes (especially "Ghosts") that strongly resemble latter-day Roxy Music—is a willowy fabric of interwoven threads.

Assemblage, as the title might indicate, is a collection of songs, from the band's pre-Virgin period, including "Adolescent Sex," "Quiet Life," "I Second That Emotion" and "All Tomorrow's Parties." (The cassette version adds remixes, an extra studio track and three otherwise unreleased live recordings.) In a new effort to interest America, Epic issued **Japan**, which is actually **Tin Drum**, minus two tracks, plus three from **Gentlemen Take Polaroids**.

Oil on Canvas is a crystalline live set featuring Ippu-Do guitarist Masami Tsuchiya as an adjunct member. The two records offer a good cross-section of the band's repertoire and also introduces some new material that never made it onto any of their studio records. When Japan's long-rumored dissolution finally came to pass, Virgin issued **Exorcising Ghosts**, a two-record anthology of their later work.

Karn's **Titles**, recorded while the band still appeared to be an ongoing proposition, is essentially a showcase for his proficient bass stylings and grasp of woodwinds and keyboards—all very impressive but rather vague and pointless. His guests include Jansen and Barbieri, Ricky Wilde (!) and others. Karn subsequently formed the short-lived Dalis Car with Peter Murphy of Bauhaus.   [iar]

See also *Dalis Car, Ippu-Do, Ryuichi Sakamoto, David Sylvian.*

JASON AND THE SCORCHERS

Reckless Country Soul EP (Praxis) 1982
Fervor EP (Praxis) 1983 (EMI America) 1984
Lost & Found (EMI America) 1985
Still Standing (EMI America) 1986

In 1981, as the legend goes, Jason Ringenberg left his daddy's Illinois hog farm for the bright lights of Nashville and promptly stumbled upon guitarist Warner Hodges and bassist Jeff Johnson in a gutter. With drummer Perry Baggs, they became Jason and the Nashville Scorchers, and recorded a bunch of tunes on a 4-track during a drunken night in the studio. The resulting **Reckless Country Soul** EP, a 7-inch released by a local indie label, is rough-hewn and half-realized, but enough to help the band earn a rep as the best country-metal-thrash band in the state of Tennessee.

Rigorous touring and a rep for wild shows helped spread the Scorchers' noisy mutant gospel. They play tighter and nastier on the 12-inch **Fervor**, displaying Ringenberg's knack for clever songwriting. The band signed to a major label, dropped Nashville from their name, and saw their second EP reissued with the addition of a smoking version of Bob Dylan's "Absolutely Sweet Marie."

Lost & Found puts the Scorchers in the forefront of an ever-growing country-punk genre, only they've got the roots others lack:

Hodges' folks toured with Johnny Cash, Baggs' dad sang gospel and Johnson was reared in the Blue Ridge Mountains. More than just a pedigree to brag about, the band's genuine hick beginnings make them a lot less inhibited and more apt to cross from cool to corny, punk to heavy metal without fretting much about it. There's great tension between Ringenberg's two sides—bible-quoting, straitlaced country boy and yelping, flailing, demon-possessed madman—and the cigarette-chomping, white-noise-mongering Hodges. On **Lost & Found**, Jason and the Scorchers burn like nothing since General Sherman's troops marched through Georgia.

Still Standing was produced by Tom Werman (Cheap Trick, Mötley Crüe, Poison), who captured the Scorchers' melodic power without overdoing it or pushing any obvious commercial concessions down their throats. The folky "Good Things Come to Those Who Wait" and the equally optimistic "Crashin' Down" are as pretty, memorable and uplifting as anything they've done; "Shotgun Blues" and "Ghost Town" give Hodges plenty of encouragement to unleash his wildest electric dreams. A charging cover of "19th Nervous Breakdown" acknowledges the band's clear debt to the Stones and proves that Jason and his boys know just how to treat a piece of classic rock.   [ep/iar]

JAZZ BUTCHER
A Bath in Bacon (nr/Glass) 1982
A Scandal in Bohemia (nr/Glass) 1984
The Gift of Music (nr/Glass) 1984 ●
Sex and Travel (nr/Glass) 1985
Bloody Nonsense (Big Time) 1986
Big Questions (The Gift of Music Vol. 2)
    (nr/Glass) 1987 ●
Fishcotheque (Creation-Relativity) 1988 ●
JAZZ BUTCHER AND HIS
SIKKORSKIS FROM HELL
Hamburg (Ger. Rebel) 1985
Hard EP (nr/Glass) 1986
JAZZ BUTCHER VS. MAX EIDER
Conspiracy EP (nr/Glass) 1986
JAZZ BUTCHER CONSPIRACY
Distressed Gentlefolk (Big Time) 1986 ●
MAX EIDER
The Best Kisser in the World (Big Time) 1987

In six years, the Jazz Butcher has undergone more transformations than most bands do in several lifetimes. Led by the Jazz Butcher (aka Butch) himself, it is, regardless

of incarnation, his lyrical witticisms and humorous critiques around which the groups' music revolves.

The debut LP, **A Bath in Bacon**, is for all intents and purposes a one-man show. Butch plays a startling array of instruments from guitar to xylophone and employs a legion of session musicians to help create an album that encompasses an awesome variety of styles. Good ideas abound in songs like "Love Zombie," "Sex Engine Thing" and "Gray Flannelette"; there's just some uncertainty as to where they're going.

The second album was recorded by a stable quartet that included ex-Bauhaus bassist David J. Almost exclusively in a folky pop-punk format, the songs are better-developed and reach logical conclusions. Among the gems are a hysterical anti-macho anthem "Real Men" ("Some things never change/ Notice how they never sit together on buses?") and "Southern Mark Smith."

The Gift of Music is a collection of single sides, an excellent package that affirms the band's folk-punk commitment. Of special note is an early up-tempo version of "Southern Mark Smith" and the pop gospel "Rain."

Sex and Travel is the Jazz Butcher's crowning achievement. The eight near-perfect tracks run the gamut from funk to folk to country-western and punk. Butch's lyrics aim high; subject matter, more than anything else, determines the style of each song. "President Reagan's Birthday Present" addresses the problems of America, Russia and nuclear arms with a healthy chunk of dance funk. "Holiday" uses a typewriter backing track and cabaret stylings to make light of the staid British persona; the frantic adrenaline punk of "Red Pets" tackles preconceptions about Russians ("Everyone says they lift weights/ Except for me, I think they're great"). All this, plus two great pop tunes: "Big Saturday" and "Only a Rumour."

With a new bassist replacing David J (off to rejoin several old bandmates in Love and Rockets), the rechristened Jazz Butcher and His Sikkorskis from Hell issued the live **Hamburg** LP and an EP, **Hard**, which picks up where **Sex and Travel** left off, adding blues and merseybeat to the Jazz Butcher's seemingly bottomless bag of musical tricks. **Bloody Nonsense** is an American collection that includes some of the above-mentioned tracks.

Leaving the rest of the band by the wayside, Butch and guitarist Max Eider released a four-song 12-inch, **Conspiracy**, as the Jazz Butcher vs. Max Eider. The best things on it are the title track, a clever play on rap music, and the hilarious homage "Peter Lorre."

With Butch and Max as the nucleus, a newly formed Jazz Butcher Conspiracy recorded **Distressed Gentlefolk**. A Jazz Butcher record by any other name, this album employs the usual diversity we've come to expect—folk ("Still in the Kitchen"), funk ("Big Bad Thing"), country-western ("Falling in Love") and pop ("Angels," "Nothing Special")—as well as Butch's ever-incisive wit, which is in rare form on the track "Domestic Animal."

Shortly after **Distressed Gentlefolk**, Eider resigned his Butchership for a solo career. The aptly-titled **The Best Kisser in the World** is a beautifully romantic record consisting of soft rock ballads and jazzy torch songs. Max's vocals almost replicate Butch's exactly; only lyrical content provides a decisive difference. If the Jazz Butcher has a sane serious alter-ego, Max Eider is it.

A two-person Jazz Butcher—Butch and Kizzy O'Callaghan—released the fifth proper LP, **Fishcotheque**, in 1988 proving the Jazz Butcher to be as resilient as he is prolific. Reorganization has had no effect whatsoever on Butch's abilities, and this album rivals **Sex and Travel** in its brilliance. "Next Move Sideways," "Living in a Village" and "Chickentown" are sterling classics.

Big Questions is an assortment of tracks (including "Groovin' in a Bus Lane," "Rebecca Wants Her Bike Back" and "Olof Palme") drawn from previous releases by the Jazz Butcher, Sikkorskis from Hell, Jazz Butcher vs. Max Eider and the Jazz Butcher Conspiracy. Limited quantities of the original pressing contained a live 7-inch EP.

[ag]

JAZZY 5
See *Afrika Bambaataa.*

JAZZY JEFF
On Fire (Jive) 1985

D.J. JAZZY JEFF & THE FRESH PRINCE
Rock the House (Jive) 1986
He's the D.J., I'm the Rapper (Jive) 1988

The first Jazzy Jeff offers solid rap action with a strong, clear delivery, significantly cliché-reduced rhymes and a variety of socially-responsible concerns on his debut album, **On Fire**. He warns about "King Heroin (Don't Mess with Heroin)," shows a real soft spot with "My Mother (Yes I Love Her)" and asks that dj to "Mix So I Can Go Crazy" and "Rock It (Rock It)." Electric guitar, inventive percussion and clever mix gimmickry (by Bryan "Chuck" New and Phil Nicholas of the Willesden Dodgers) give this a fairly familiar sound, but Jazzy Jeff is an above-average rapper.

Although both use the same handle, the same producer and are (were) both on the Jive label, the Jazzy Jeff turntable master who is teamed up with an MC named the Fresh Prince is an entirely different person than the rapper who recorded **On Fire**. (*That* JJ is now reportedly billing himself as the Original Jazzy Jeff.) However it came to pass, the upshot is that this clean-cut young duo (Jeff Townes and Will Smith) from Philadelphia is a big success, scoring big with mild-mannered pop-oriented weenie-rap.

He's the D.J. (which quickly went gold) is a weedy commercially-minded two-record set that leans more towards preppiedom than hip-hop. One disc contains scratch mixes (and a live recording), the other a batch of lighthearted raps like "Parents Just Don't Understand," a comic complaint about middle-class fashion oppression, and "A Nightmare on My Street," which tells a tale about Freddy Krueger, complete with audio bites from a *Nightmare on Elm Street* film. Slight but likable. [tr]

JEAN PAUL SARTRE EXPERIENCE
The Jean Paul Sartre Experience EP (NZ Flying Nun) 1986
Love Songs (NZ Flying Nun) 1987
Love Songs (Communion) 1987 ●

Mankind may be condemned to experience the limitations of its own will with nothing beyond nothingness staring down from the sky but, as long as a copy of a Jean Paul Sartre Experience record exists, there will always be something out there . . . for your stereo. There will be gentle and warm guitar chords, boy-next-door vocals and delicately produced melodies. The JPSE may be nothing more than a simple janglepop band but they're one of the globe's best janglepop bands and their music tingles and shimmers with damning simplicity.

No big budgets behind this band, born in

a Christchurch (New Zealand) suburb in 1984. A grant paid for the first EP's recording, yet the sounds of their shoestring put slick megabudget crap to shame. On "Fish in the Sea," an ounce of water sloshes from one tiny cup to another as a tingling triangle plings delicately. A hand knocking on a block of wood punctuates "Walking Wild in Your Firetime" like a tom-tom in a hazy beatnik coffeehouse, as a soft voice sings "I've got weapons and I've got hope and I've got guns and I've got rope . . . and I don't know what I feel" before xylophone tangs out a repeat of the tune. The result is plain-wrap majesty: simple, uncluttered, satisfying.

Their second vinyl outing isn't as good: too many **Love Songs** sound the same. The album concentrates on song-craft rather than texture, making the lightweight nature of their genre very obvious. From the whisper-breath blues of "All the Way Down" through the sweet-soul-tinged "Let There Be Love" and on to the herky-jerky sparse funk of "Crap Rap," Sartre wind their way through eight love songs about relationships and one about rain.

Fortunately, the US album of the same name is actually their first EP with only four of the tracks from the Oz LP. It would have been nice if the funk and wiggle-guitar of "Let That Good Thing Grow" could have been included in place of the slow, sleepy harmonies of "Grey Parade," but otherwise this US album is truly the best-of. Highly recommended. ['e]

JELLYBEAN
Wotupski!?! EP (EMI America) 1984
Just Visiting This Planet (Chrysalis) 1987 •

New York mixer/producer (Madonna, Jocelyn Brown, Hall & Oates, etc.) John "Jellybean" Benitez stepped out under his own name for the first time on the five-song **Wotupski!?!** mini-album. The only problem is he doesn't play or sing on it. Nor did he write any of the material. Benitez did, however, produce it, bringing together such powerful friends as Nile Rodgers, Madonna, John Robie and Dan Hartman to create one long instrumental and a batch of dance numbers. Best track: an otherwise unrecorded Madonna composition, "Sidewalk Talk."

Three years later, the Great Delegator returned to the creative world with a full-length hands-off album, **Just Visiting This Planet**. Besides producing and some arrang-

ing, just what did the diminutive doyen get saddled with this time? Drum programming on seven of the eight light and infectious dance songs, background vocals on three, synthesizers on two; he actually takes credit for writing one. As strange an approach as Jellybean takes, he certainly can't be faulted for assembling a spectacular cast and assigning the lead vocals to a talented trio: Adele Bertei, Elisa Fiorillo and Steven Danté. Leave your brain at the door and get down!
[iar]

JESUS AND MARY CHAIN
Just Like Honey EP (nr/Blanco y Negro) 1985
Psychocandy (Reprise) 1985 •
Some Candy Talking EP (nr/Blanco y Negro) 1986
Darklands EP (nr/Blanco y Negro) 1987
Darklands (Blanco y Negro-Warner Bros.) 1987 •
Sidewalking EP (Blanco y Negro-Warner Bros.) 1988
Barbed Wire Kisses (B-sides and More) (Blanco y Negro-Warner Bros.) 1988 •

By blithely combining power-pop melodies with industrial-strength noise and low-brow lyrical perversity, the Jesus and Mary Chain—Glasgow brothers Jim and William Reid, bassist Douglas Hart and rotating drummers—created a sound that can't quite be described as new, but does stand miles apart from anything that's been done before and has inspired much imitation. **Psychocandy** generated a storm of discussion, with critics comparing them to everyone from the Velvet Underground and Chad & Jeremy to the Ramones and Sonic Youth. Awash in feedback and fuzz, tunes and drones, wit and vulgarity, **Psychocandy** is the perfect soundtrack to these high-pressure multiphasic times—music for the tense claustrophobia of rush-hour subways. The band's three exceptional pre-LP singles ("Never Understand," "You Trip Me Up," "Just Like Honey") are only the most immediately striking of the 14 cuts; such others as "Inside Me," "Cut Dead" and "Sowing Seeds" further illustrate the Chain's variety, imagination and ability to enthrall. (The American CD helpfully appends a post-LP single, "Some Candy Talking.")

Typical of the Reids' determined anti-conformism, **Darklands** all but eliminates the characteristic crazed sound of the first LP, leaving skeletal guitar-pop songs—menacingly restrained and drenched in echo—colored only occasionally with familiar washes of fuzz guitar. Displaying a notable mid-'60s Dylan influence (check the verses of "Deep One Perfect Morning") and delivering their best song yet, "Happy When It Rains," the album predictably put off fickle fans and critics disappointed by the stylistic regression. Nonetheless, "April Skies," "Down On Me," "Darklands," "Nine Million Rainy Days" and "Fall" ("I'm as dead as a Christmas tree . . . ") stand proudly as exceptional and truly original pop fare for the '80s.

One of J&M's fetishes is to release singles in as many different formats as possible. As a result, there are numerous 12-inch and 10-inch EPs (some of which are listed above), double-pack 7-inch singles and CD EPs which add live tracks, acoustic demos, outtakes and other ephemera. A batch of those, with the addition of a cool T. Rexy new single, "Sidewalking," comprise **Barbed Wire Kisses**: 16 (20 on the CD and cassette) arcane tales from the Chain's darkside. Not a cohesive album and far from consistently excellent, it offers a helpful recapitulation of what the group does in its spare time. Targets include the Beach Boys (the demented slaughter of "Kill Surf City" *and* a semi-reverent version of "Surfin USA") and Bo Diddley (a devolved rendition of "Who Do You Love" and, on the tape/CD, a similar-sounding tribute, "Bo Diddley Is Jesus"). Not a quick fix for fanatics lacking a complete collection, **Barbed Wire Kisses** merely points the direction in which the obscurities lie.   [iar]

JET BLACK BERRIES
Sundown on Venus (Pink Dust) 1984
Desperate Fires (Pink Dust) 1986

NEW MATH
They Walk Among You EP (415) 1982
Gardens (Brain Eater) 1984

Under their original New Math handle this ominously entertaining five-man psychedelic outfit from Rochester, New York is alternately dirgelike and urgent on **They Walk Among You**, a five-song 12-inch that delivers ponderously intoned poetic lyrics over thick rock backing. Heavyweight bass and drums support reasonably normal guitar and pulsing organ for a complex blend of sounds that defies easy description. "Invocation" pays stately homage to the devil and would probably please Roky Erickson; the magnificent

title track recalls (if no one else does) Atomic Rooster's "Death Walks Behind You."

Gardens offers seven new imprecations and tales of madness. The music is grander, more open and less malevolent; New Math reins in the rhythmic power a wee bit and moves the organ drone and lead vocals to the fore. The effect may not be the one desired, however, as the band sounds more accessible but less striking this way. Still, it's the work of a talented, unique group with sicko ideas.

Without undergoing any personnel changes, the quintet became the Jet Black Berries and issued **Sundown on Venus**, an offbeat concept album that attempts to meld two familiar cultural idioms—science-fiction and Westerns—and almost carries it off. The music is polite California cowpunk (think Green on Red or Dream Syndicate, occasionally colored by faint Gary Numan synth noises); the lyrics describe showdowns between bad hombres and masked men in space suits. (A brief run-through of Ersel Hickey's obscure classic "Bluebirds" neither aids nor undercuts the effort.) Unfortunately, the Berries don't bother to develop their imaginative notion musically, letting what might have been a fascinating record drift into mediocrity. The cassette release adds six bonus tracks—also included as a one-sided disc in original pressings of the LP—of similar rock, a surprising slice of Garry Glitter singalong pop, the old group's dirge-pound rock and even another version of "They Walk Among You."

Produced with likable simplicity and directness, **Desperate Fires** is a taut album of Western-leaning rock-pop that hardly resembles the group's early work, but makes a convincing case for the validity of this new direction. Kevin Patrick's voice suits the material; unassuming songs like "Kid Alaska," "The Flesh Element" and the rockabilly "Sweet Revenge" pack a wicked kick.   [iar]

JETS
Jets (nr/EMI) 1981 (nr/Fame) 1982
100% Cotton (nr/EMI) 1982

The three Cotton boys (rockabilly Ramones?) are far from the worst English nouveau rockabilly band you're likely to encounter, although they don't go out of their way to leave a lasting impression. The debut consists primarily of well-worn oldies like "My Baby Left Me" and "Honey Hush." **100% Cotton** constitutes a distinct improvement, with sharper playing, more original material and a shiny, gritless sound courtesy of Shakin' Stevens producer, Stuart Coleman. The birds-of-a-feather rule applies here, at least. [jy]

JFA

Blatant Localism EP (Placebo) 1981 •
Valley of the Yakes (Placebo) 1983 •
JFA (Placebo) 1984
Mad Garden EP (Placebo) 1984
Live (Placebo) 1985 •

These Phoenix, Arizona skate-punks—the name was originally an acronym for Jodie Foster's Army—are major figures on the Southwest hardcore scene. Besides touring extensively and releasing lots of records, their Placebo label is the most active outlet in the area, and has issued discs by a number of non-mainstream bands.

Blatant Localism is a 7-inch whose six songs race along cohesively at warp speed with vocals that mostly defy comprehension. There's an eponymous number explaining the group's name, a relatively prolix exposition on "Beach Blanket Bong-Out" and a four-second display of counting. (I used a stopwatch, that's how.) **Valley of the Yakes** stretches 15 songs out to fill a 12-inch, slowing things down in spots, but not doing much to increase vocal articulation. Still, a crisp, well-played slice of hardcore with real drive and commitment, plus two great, normal-sounding, reverb-splattered surf-guitar instrumentals: "Walk Don't Run" and "Baja." (One CD contains both records.)

JFA exposes increased sophistication and wit, starting with a backwards snippet called "Deltitnu" and continuing by tempering the thrash with variety, understatement and other interesting digressions. In a fit of major cleverness, JFA crash the Ventures into the Dead Kennedys for "Pipetruck" and allegedly cover both David Bowie and George Clinton during the course of the album. (JFA's funky-butt turn on "Standin on the Verge" is nifty.) A bit unfocused, but much more than a simple hardcore record. Standout track: "The Day Walt Disney Died."

Mad Garden, a four-song 12-inch with a wrestling cover and a new bassist in the lineup, encompasses more-or-less straight speedrock plus one milder (non-surf) instrumental with keyboards. The live album was recorded in 1984, at gigs in New York and Pittsburgh. [iar]

JILTED JOHN

True Love Stories (nr/EMI Int'l) 1978

In between releasing early punk records by Slaughter and the Dogs, the Nosebleeds and Ed Banger, Manchester's Rabid label found time to have an enormous chart hit with the novelty shtick of Jilted John, sung in an acne-riddled wideboy voice by Graham Fellows. Gordon the Moron, Julie and other assorted fictitious characters all joined John in this semi-narrative tale of teen angst, set to pop music dopier than anything Herman's Hermits ever imagined. More ridiculous: the unavoidable catchiness of the whole affair. An embarrassingly likable record.

Although John evaporated quickly, Fellows has released at least one subsequent album under his own name. [iar]

JOBOXERS

Like Gangbusters (RCA) 1983

Responsible for a brief Dead End Kids clothes fad in Great Britain, the JoBoxers melded Dig Wayne, a black singer from New York, with the (non-Vic Godard) remnants of Subway Sect to play bouncy, catchy R&B tinged with big-band jazz. **Like Gangbusters** contains a couple of swell singles ("Boxerbeat," "Just Got Lucky") but is otherwise formulaic and uninspired. [iar]

RICHARD JOBSON

See *Armoury Show.*

JOE POP-O-PIE

See *Pop-O-Pies.*

DAVID JOHANSEN

David Johansen (Blue Sky) 1978
In Style (Blue Sky) 1979
Here Comes the Night (Blue Sky) 1981
Live It Up (Blue Sky) 1982
Sweet Revenge (Passport) 1984

BUSTER POINDEXTER

Buster Poindexter (RCA) 1987 •

Having escaped his sordid if magnificent reputation as prime instigator of the New York Dolls, singer David Johansen has managed to earn himself a solid American following. While keeping a firm grip on the soul and rock'n'roll values that originally inspired the Dolls, Johansen has crafted a uniquely urban style that suits his roughthroated singing as well as his Lower East Side personality.

David Jo's solo debut was a very successful launch, containing most of the songs for which he came to be known. "Funky but Chic," "Donna," "Frenchette" and "Cool Metro" are played in grand post-CBGB fashion by some of the Bowery's best vets. Better than bar-band but decidedly unslick, **David Johansen** perfectly transforms an insolent punk into a rock'n'roll adult.

Without destroying his urban soul, **In Style** makes an effort to clean and dress up Johansen's sound. Adding synthesized strings and horns, attempting overambitious stylistic experiments and relying on decidedly sophomore-slump material, **In Style's** two good tracks ("She" and "Melody") are lost in the morass. The failure of **In Style** undoubtedly inspired the misdirected **Here Comes the Night**, an ill-conceived stab at making Johansen simultaneously into a heavy metal shouter and a sensitive, poetic artist. A lot of very talented people had their hands in this project, but weak songs and the lack of cohesion make it a disaster.

Fortunately, **Live It Up** put Johansen's career right back on course. With his longstanding reputation as a great performer and empirical evidence of a well-received live promotional-only record made for radio in 1978, it was a judicious tactic to cut a live album for regular release. Benefiting from carefully chosen classic tunes and Johansen's extraordinary skill as a song interpreter, **Live It Up** is a great party record by a great singer. Johansen comes alive!

Relieved of his CBS-affiliated record contract, Johansen concentrated on performing (appearing regularly in New York as his suave alter-ego, Buster Poindexter) for over a year before returning to the vinyl jungle with **Sweet Revenge**. Sharing the bulk of the songwriting and production with keyboard player Joe Delia and joined in a half-dozen studios by a large collection of sidemen, Johansen disconnects from the R&B rootsiness that, to some extent at least, had always characterized his work, replacing it with strong, synth-heavy rock that would be regrettable were it not for distinctive vocals and witty songwriting. Some of the record flops, but "Heard the News," complete with ersatz Spanish newscaster, blends Latin American political commentary with one of the catchiest melodies of his career. "King of Babylon" is a clever novelty item.

Johansen finally hit the big time when he allowed his part-time persona, adult jazz/blues smoothie Buster Poindexter, to take over his career. Aided by a New York club residency and regular television appearances (on *Saturday Night Live*), Buster's debut album with the horn-heavy non-rock Banshees of Blue (led by Joe Delia) did the trick. The generally lighthearted romp through cabaret and swing styles of the '30s and '40s recalls both Spike Jones and Cab Calloway, blending sweet nostalgia with gruff crooning. Given the inconsistent, scattershot program (a schmaltzy ballad, one terrible rocker, another cover of "House of the Rising Sun" done as a torch song, a few other misdirected duds), the choice of a sprightly Latin dance number, "Hot Hot Hot," as a single was a stroke of genius: it did the chart trick and guaranteed Buster's continued existence. Granted, this is some strange place for the onetime glam-outrage leader to end up, and other modern rockers (Roger Ruskin Spear and Vic Godard, to name two) have mined the same terrain with far more élan, but none of that diminishes the record's throw-away value. [iar]

JOHNNY G

G Sharp/G Natural (nr/Beggars Banquet) 1979
G-Beat (nr/Beggars Banquet) 1980
Water into Wine (nr/Beggars Banquet) 1982

Erstwhile one-man band and pub-rocker Johnny G takes after early Nick Lowe, with a similar sense of humor and absurdity, an alarming variety of musical idioms and a seemingly effortless ability to make sounds fit together in a consistently pleasant manner. But this eccentric's his own man, and his records, while jumping wildly from reggae to R&B, folk music to dub, country blues to cocktail-lounge mush, all have a unique trademark quality. With unerring wit and overall good humor (even on the gloomy songs) Johnny G is perpetually surprising, and never fails to be solidly entertaining.

His early recordings—sarcastic (and, as a result, largely misunderstood) singles like "Call Me Bwana!" and "Hippys Graveyard"—were followed by an EP and finally a first album, **G Sharp/G Natural**, which touches on (among other areas) maudlin pop and jovial jug-band. The album features such luminary sidemen as Steve Lillywhite (who plays bass and didn't produce), the entire cast of skiffle band Brett Marvin and the Thunderbolts and even Mark Hollis, brother of Ed Hollis (who did produce the LP) and now lead singer of Talk Talk. Enough history? This record, while fun, is not essential to the Johnny G story. Proceed directly to his superior second effort.

Recorded with only two sidemen, **G-Beat** has such charming odes as "Rubber Lover," "Suzy (Was a Girl from Greenford)" and "Night After Night (The Last Drink)," all given varied and inventive treatments that hide the low-budget recording circumstances. Using only voice, guitar, minimal drums, keyboards and (mostly acoustic) bass, **G-Beat** accomplishes some great things that must be heard to be appreciated. The LP comes with a bonus: an entire second album, **G-Beat 2 (Leave Me Alone)**, of singles, outtakes and alternate versions that provide a concise background listen for the converted.

After the underproduced (but effective) **G-Beat**, **Water into Wine** sounds state-of-the-art, with a cast of ex-pub luminaries playing on it and Bob Andrews (ex-Rumour) producing. It's a much finer record, with sensitively arranged tracks like "Carving Up the Concrete" and a totally bizarre slide-guitar blues version of King Crimson's "21st Century Schizoid Man." **Water into Wine** *also* includes a bonus LP, **Pure Beaujolais**— half live, half outtakes and unreleased singles. Both discs are great fun with something for everyone. I like the "Johnny G Fan Club Song," a totally over-the-top tribute sung by then-labelmate Ivor Biggun.   [iar]

JOHNNY HATES JAZZ
Turn Back the Clock (Virgin) 1987 ●

Why is it that the most offbeat or imaginative thing about the recent well-scrubbed crop of bland British chart-pop stars is their band names? The notable item in this Anglo-American pablum trio's biography is that Calvin Hayes' father is legendary '60s pop producer Mickie Most. **Turn Back the Clock** alternately sounds like a witless half-speed ABC and an overdone update of Gilbert O'-Sullivan with none of his charm. (The CD appends three 12-inch mixes.)   [iar]

EVAN JOHNS AND THE H-BOMBS
See *Eugene Chadbourne*.

JESSE JOHNSON
See *Jesse Johnson's Revue*.

LINTON KWESI JOHNSON
Forces of Victory (Mango) 1979
Bass Culture (Mango) 1980
LKJ in Dub (nr/Island) 1980
Reggae Greats (Mango) 1984
Making History (Mango) 1984
In Concert with the Dub Band (Shanachie) 1985

POET AND THE ROOTS
Dread Beat an' Blood (Heartbeat) 1978

More a poet and social critic (as the name Poet and the Roots suggests), Johnson bridged the gap between reggae and punk, infusing the music with powerful political content and an urge for freedom rooted in his experience as a black man living in Brixton.

Dread Beat an' Blood was a call to arms, a dark commemoration of police harassment and social repression of blacks told in a forceful but strangely spiteless manner. Speaking his poems over absolutely flawless throbbing reggae, Johnson uses the patois of the streets to speak to his audience, calling for brotherhood and vigilance. The clean, supple, vibrant music and incisive, pointed words make it a powerful and memorable political statement. Highly recommended.

Forces of Victory continues Johnson's call to action. Again supported by feverish reggae, Johnson's voice gains greater range and expressiveness while his poetry speaks of dire truths, and sounds increasingly complex, compact and expert. Muscular, dramatic stuff.

Bass Culture expands Johnson's style, including more humor and even a shy, touching love song. The music is sparer and more coherent, and Dennis Bovell's co-production slickens the sound just enough to remove its rough edges. Johnson is no less determined on his political numbers, but it's nice to know there are other things on his mind as well.

LKJ in Dub is a tribute to Bovell's engineering talents; while it has little to do with the Linton Kwesi Johnson canon, it's an interesting and successful example of dub technique.

In the four-year sabbatical that followed, only the sturdy **Reggae Greats** compilation was released. Johnson and Bovell then reunited for **Making History**, a "comeback" album as vital as any they had made together.

The two-disc **In Concert** documents Johnson's strength and onstage presence. Though hardly perfunctory (the performances are all first-rate), it's still a greatest-hits-live package, and shouldn't deter listeners from acquiring any or all of the studio LPs.

[sg/bk]

MATT JOHNSON
See *the The*.

WILKO JOHNSON
See *Solid Senders*.

JOHNSONS
Break Tomorrow's Day. (Fever-Restless) 1986

Albums with song titles like "Sylvia Plath" and "The Affirmation" should generally be avoided, but this Philadelphia trio's first record, nicely co-produced by Glenn Morrow (Rage to Live) and John Wicks (Records), easily allays such fears with winning harmony-vocal guitar rock that is disarmingly unpretentious. As it turns out, "Sylvia Plath" is an offbeat fan letter written by the late Cleveland legend Peter Laughner; an oddity, but a worthwhile effort. Bassist Adam Miller and guitarist Mike Morrison sing with full-throated conviction and back it up with hard-edged, textured playing; drummer Dana Penny gives the songs an extra kick with controlled dynamics. [iar]

JESSE JOHNSON'S REVUE
Jesse Johnson's Revue (A&M) 1985 ●
JESSE JOHNSON
Shockadelica (A&M) 1986 ●
Every Shade of Love (A&M) 1988 ●

Former Time guitarist Johnson reckons himself another pretender to Prince's throne. His first solo album, **Jesse Johnson's Revue**, reeks of conscious imitation, from the chronic pink color scheme to the band's carefully shaped mustaches. The self-produced music likewise favors a mixture of his former band and Prince's **Purple Rain**; not unpleasant, occasionally catchy ("I Want My Girl"), but no threat to the reigning monarch.

Although Prince's influence is still evident on **Shockadelica** (check "A Better Way"), Johnson's obvious talent and stylistic dexterity diminishes the significance of such comparisons. The accomplishment of leading a ten-piece band (seven instrumentalists and two female vocalists) and ending up with clear, well-organized sound is impressive in and of itself. The LP features a funky duet with Sly Stone ("Crazay") and a diverse, appealing set of danceable songs with a surprising ending: Johnson sings a message of hope on the touching "Black in America," accompanied only by acoustic guitars, synthetic strings and a small chorus.

Dispensing with his band (a drummer, saxophonist and female vocalist are credited) for a harder-edged solo effort, Johnson uses **Every Shade of Love** to show off his Hendrix-influenced guitar work. The eight tracks revolve around skittish strumming as much as surging keyboards, and those tracks that dig bottomless holes with endless one-chord vamps lose listener interest in short order. The delightful title tune and "I'm Just Wanting You" are notable exceptions.

One other way in which Johnson has followed in Prince's footsteps is by taking on numerous outside writing/production projects. Besides a pair of bands JJ handles top to bottom (Ta Mara and the Seen, dá Krash), he has done piecework for Vanity, Debbie Allen, Clarence Clemons and others. [iar]

JOLT
The Jolt (nr/Polydor) 1978

Little wonder the Jolt were written off as a Scottish Jam clone. This trio had—what a coincidence!—the same label, producer, image, name (almost) and sound. The Jolt's album shows they could work up a good sweat, but the material is strictly two-dimensional, not a patch on even Weller's most derivative early stuff. [jg]

JON & THE NIGHTRIDERS
Surf Beat '80 (Voxx) 1980
Recorded Live at Hollywood's Famous Whisky A Go-Go (Voxx) 1981
Splashback! EP (Invasion) 1982
Charge of the Nightriders (Enigma) 1983

Although probably still in nursery school when guitar instrumentals filled the American record charts, John Blair and his three cohorts brilliantly re-create the innocence and excitement of that long-lost genre. With resplendent, ringing tones, vibrato and mountains of reverb, **Surf Beat '80** pays homage with 14 numbers, including a few soundalike originals and a selection of covers that proves the band's dedication to—and familiarity with—their forebears. All of the tracks sound the same, but that's the idea. Great!

The live LP reprises some of the studio record's items, but incorporates new material and spot-on renditions of additional familiar classics like "Pipeline" and "Hawaii Five-0." **Splashback!**, produced by the legendary Shel Talmy (to no particular effect, other than perhaps spiritual), features a six-minute medley that touches on 11 instantly recognizable melodies in one seamless nostalgia romp.

[iar]

GRACE JONES

Portfolio (Island) 1977 ●
Fame (Island) 1978
Muse (Island) 1979
Warm Leatherette (Island) 1980 ●
Nightclubbing (Island) 1981 ●
Living My Life (Island) 1982 ●
Island Life (Island) 1985 ●
Slave to the Rhythm (Manhattan Island) 1985 ●
Inside Story (Manhattan) 1986 ●

At the outset of her singing career, model (later actress) Grace Jones was a musical product in the truest sense of the word, more or less invented by artist Jean-Paul Goude. When new wave became the dance-club staple of the '80s, Grace—whose previous records were strictly disco—sailed into the genre on an airbrush jetstream, performing slickly produced covers of mainstream modern material on loan from Chrissie Hynde, Bryan Ferry, et al., while mixing in a safe dose of thumped-up funk.

Warm Leatherette (named for the pioneering Normal/Daniel Miller new wave electro single, which she courageously covers) was the first Jones disc to embrace this formula; **Nightclubbing** followed suit, utilizing songs by Iggy and Sting. The balance of this LP features a slightly more fluid vocal style than the monotone that rules the previous album.

Living My Life shows Grace maturing, escaping the restrictive machinations that had controlled her. The material allows more personality to show through, and songs like "My Jamaican Guy" and "Nipple to the Bottle" show the Sly-and-Robbie reggae rhythm team to be more into the music at this point. **Island Life** recaps her career to that point, compiling such tracks as "La Vie en Rose," "Pull Up to the Bumper" and "Love Is the Drug," adding "Slave to the Rhythm," a new single taken from a subsequent album which was released almost immediately thereafter.

Some bizarre business dealings must have led to the one-off alliance of Island and Manhattan Records to jointly issue **Slave to the Rhythm**. Trevor Horn produced this outrageous, astonishing so-called biography, including inter-track recitations, recollections and interview bites, and creating theatrically massive orchestrations. The songs—written by a collective of Horn, Bruce Woolley and others—aren't intrinsically strong or interesting, but the ZTT Big Beat Colossus does such a job filling the grooves with beats, strings, horns, vocals, keyboards and god knows what else that the material counts for relatively little. But by the same token, Grace's vocal contribution to this audio love fest seems disconcertingly expendable in light of her spiritual presence.

Returning to the real world for a relatively routine (but still Grace-ious) outing, Jones wrote **Inside Story** with Bruce Woolley and produced it with Nile Rodgers; her collaborators also played most of the LP's music. The lyrics contemplate such offbeat-going-on-dada topics as "Hollywood Liar," "Victor Should Have Been a Jazz Musician" and "Chan Hitchhikes to Shanghai," while the music dully retreads various familiar late-'80s high-tech sounds. Grace's voice is typically fine, but this is not one of her more invigorating records.

[jw/iar]

HOWARD JONES

Human's Lib (Elektra) 1984 ●
The 12-Inch Album (nr/WEA) 1984
Dream into Action (Elektra) 1985 ●
Action Replay EP (Elektra) 1986
One to One (Elektra) 1986 ●

Starting out as something of an '80s answer to early Marc Bolan, Howard Jones is a cleaned-up ex-hippie embracing humanist principles and possessing acute pop sensibilities. Times being what they are, he doesn't play acoustic guitar with a bongo drummer on the side, he controls an array of sophisticated electronic keyboards, singing earnest, reflective lyrics of personal awareness and individualist philosophy. **Human's Lib**, produced mainly by Rupert Hine, boasts a few warm techno-pop standouts—"New Song," "Pearl in the Shell" and "What Is Love"—which stop just short of over-perkiness or saccharine platitudes.

Dream into Action, which employs more outside musicians (horns, vocalists, a cellist) to vary the sound, serves up another dose of engaging nouveau-pop ("Things Can Only Get Better," "Life in One Day," "Like to Get to Know You Well"). The album does, unfortunately, contain an extremely duff howler—"Bounce Right Back"—which I first mistook for one of Falco's onerous rants. **The 12-Inch Album** compiles six hits in their remixed forms.

Taking advantage of Jones' massive American popularity, Elektra issued **Action Replay**, a collection of five alternate versions and remixes of songs from **Dream into Action** and other sources, plus the previously unreleased "Always Asking Questions."

For **One to One**, producer Arif Mardin put Jones in the studio with a full complement of backup musicians, thereby focusing attention on him as writer/singer. The conservative cover portrait reflects an overall stylistic retrenchment: the once-colorful elf has become part of a mainstream adult pop machine. He hasn't sold out—nothing about HoJo was ever that outré to begin with—but the change leaves the soul-inflected **One to One** noticeably short on Jones' irresistible twinky charm. [iar]

MARTI JONES
Unsophisticated Time (A&M) 1985
Match Game (A&M) 1986 ●
Used Guitars (A&M) 1988 ●
COLOR ME GONE
Color Me Gone EP (A&M) 1984

Color Me Gone's one EP introduced a nice, reedy vocalist in guitar-playing Marti Jones; rich arrangements and clear production allowed her to draw everything out of the six agreeable songs. Without really holding to any one style, the North Carolina quartet flirts with radio rock, neo-ethnic Americana, country (in that mode, the downcast "Hurtin' You" is the best thing here) and '60sish folk-rock, winding up pleasant but unmemorable.

Jones' solo debut—brilliantly produced by Don Dixon, who also plays most of the instruments on it—draws strength from a very astute selection of neo-pop tunes. She covers songs by the dB's, Bongos, Costello and Dixon in a clear voice on this delightfully unprepossessing album.

Match Game follows roughly the same pattern, adding songs by David Bowie ("Soul Love") and Marshall Crenshaw ("Whenever You're on My Mind") to the prior album's returning writing collective. Given a comfortable setting by Dixon's sparkling studio work, Marti shines on tracks played by such prestigious supporters as Crenshaw, Mitch Easter, Richard Barone, Gary Barnacle, Paul Carrack, T-Bone Burnett and Darlene Love.

Used Guitars—the third chapter in a by-now-familiar book—again features Dixon as producer, songwriter and instrumentalist. The cast this time includes Janis Ian, the Woods, Crenshaw, Easter, John Hiatt (two of the songs are his) and Graham Parker, who pitched in with one. [iar]

STEVE JONES
Mercy (Gold Mountain-MCA) 1987 ●

The ex-Pistol guitarist, known for his chunky chords and rough'n'randy attitude, caught followers off guard with **Mercy**, a solo debut that allows low-key, sentimental moments—like the title track, the hopelessly sappy "Love Letters" and others—to mingle with the rock numbers. Although Jones is no vocalist, he gamely sing-speaks his way through the record, assisted only by two drummers and a pair of keyboardists. "Drugs Suck" reveals a healthy attitude (even though it's a terrible track); **Mercy** isn't Jones' best post-Pistols work, but it's by no means his worst. [iar]

See also *Duran Duran, Iggy Pop, Professionals.*

JOSEF K
The Only Fun in Town (nr/Postcard) 1981
Heaven Sent EP (nr/Supreme Int'l Editions) 1987
Young and Stupid/Endless Soul (nr/Supreme Int'l Editions) 1987

A leading light in Scotland's neo-pop revival, Josef K attempted an uneasy marriage of pop form and psychedelic sensibilities on a string of melancholic singles, all contained on their one original album. Singer Paul Haig is the only member identified by name, and his presence is certainly the strongest here. There is a fragility in Josef K's gentle but foreboding work, produced in darkest wall-of-molasses sound, that suggests an intensity of thought comparable to Joy Division's. (Some of Haig's subsequent solo work sounds a lot like New Order.) But the album never reaches the level of animation found in the singles, and it was neither surprising nor inappropriate when the group broke up shortly after its release. Dank but intriguing.

Heaven Sent and **Young and Stupid/ Endless Soul** are both posthumous affairs, consisting of singles and John Peel sessions. Ironically, these two records contain the band's best material. "Heaven Sent," "Radio Drill Time" and "Heart of Song" are nothing short of pure pop brilliance, surprisingly unaffected by the passage of time. Josef K were the definitive Scottish neo-pop masters, and their legacy lives on in many of the groups currently emerging from that land. [sg/ag]

See also *Paul Haig.*

JOY DIVISION

An Ideal for Living EP (nr/Enigma) 1978
(nr/Anonymous) 1978
Unknown Pleasures (Factory) 1979 ●
Closer (Factory) 1980 ●
Still (nr/Factory) 1981
The Peel Sessions EP (nr/Strange Fruit) 1986 ●
The Peel Sessions EP (nr/Strange Fruit) 1987
Substance 1977–1980 (Qwest) 1988 ●

Coming from the industrial desolation of Manchester, Joy Division expressed, in uncompromising terms, the angst of the great wrong place in which we live, and their updating/refinement of heavy metal music combined with singer Ian Curtis' tormented lyrics and Martin Hannett's crystalline production to make a qualitative leap onto totally original ground. The band came to an end when Curtis hung himself—hours before they were to do their first American tour, thus (though it may be cynical to say so) proving the strength of his convictions. The surviving trio, with one new member, continued, finding far more commercial success as New Order.

Unknown Pleasures contrasts the message of decay and bemused acceptance of life's paradoxes with the energy and excitement of a band set loose in a studio for the first time. Hannett glazes the chilling, despondent music with a Teutonic sheen, fusing medium and message into a dark, holistic brilliance. The grim songs are punctuated by the sounds of ambulance sirens and breaking glass, picturing a world speeding toward incomprehensible chaos. Very highly recommended.

Closer has a sound that is emptier and more distant, with emphasis on strangely distorted synthesizer and a dislocated Curtis, who meanders through a world that robs him of joy and hope. A refinement of the Joy Division ethos produces a purgatory of sound. A stunning, deeply personal album.

After Curtis' death, much of the extant Joy Division work not already included on an album was gathered for **Still,** a two-record set consisting of studio outtakes (including a version of the Velvet Underground's "Sister Ray") and a live disc. Being a compilation, **Still** lacks the coherent intensity of the other two albums, but features a good representation of the various facets of Joy Division's intimate, desperate music.

There are two **Peel Sessions** EPs: one from January 1979, the other from November of that year. The latter—in a copper-colored cover—contains a brilliant rendition of the classic "Love Will Tear Us Apart" as well as "24 Hours" and two others; the former is available on CD.   [sg]

See also *New Order.*

BRUCE JOYNER AND THE PLANTATIONS
See *Unknowns.*

PHIL JUDD
See *Swingers.*

JULUKA
Scatterlings (Warner Bros.) 1982
Stand Your Ground (Warner Bros.) 1985

JOHNNY CLEGG & SAVUKA
Third World Child (Capitol) 1987
Shadow Man (Capitol) 1988 ●

In a well-intentioned gesture of political unity, singer/guitarist Johnny Clegg (an Englishman raised in Zimbabwe and South Africa) joined forces with Sipho Mchunu, a black South African street musician, to form Juluka, a failed experiment in combining rock with Zulu chants and the *mbaqanga* sound of the South African township. The results, heard on both of the interracial group's records, are a mush of sweet, laid-back California style harmonies over a loping backbeat, with mild anti-apartheid sentiments.

Clegg's work with his new band Savuka (which retains two members from Juluka) is even more Western-oriented. The slicker production of **Third World Child** relieves it of the simple, unassuming emotionality of township music. The self-conscious, breast-beating lyrics of the title track and "Berlin Wall" suggests that Clegg's gunning for the Nobel peace prize while attempting to forge a calculated commercial sound. Too bad Paul Simon beat him to the bank.   [rg]

JUNE BRIDES

There Are Eight Million Stories . . . (nr/Pink Label) 1985
The Peel Sessions EP (nr/Strange Fruit) 1987

The London-based Brides play tuneful, madly strummed guitar-pop with trumpet, viola and occasionally striking lyrics. On their seven-song mini-album, singer/guitarist Phil makes the best of a demi-musical voice, while the others race along in almost coherent, loose fashion. Minor but enjoyable.

The **Peel Sessions** EP was recorded in October 1985.   [iar]

JUST WATER

The Riff (Branded) 1977

These Who-influenced Brooklynites made their homebrew LP a year before causing some international excitement with their rocked-up single of "Singing in the Rain," which almost became the first new wave indie hit in the US. **The Riff** displays solid yet subtle guitars'n'drums rock, but is shackled by clumsy lyrics and poor vocals. Talented but unrealized, Just Water broke up around 1979.   [iar]

K K K K K K K K

HENRY KAISER
Studio Solo (Metalanguage) 1981
It's a Wonderful Life (Metalanguage) 1984
Devil in the Drain (SST) 1987
Those Who Know the Past Are Doomed to
  Repeat It (SST) 1988

FRED FRITH & HENRY KAISER
With Friends Like These (Metalanguage) 1979
Who Needs Enemies? (Metalanguage) 1983
With Enemies Like These, Who Needs
  Friends? [CD] (SST) 1987

FRENCH, FRITH, KAISER, THOMPSON
Live, Love, Larf & Loaf (Rhino) 1987 ●

CRAZY BACKWARDS ALPHABET
Crazy Backwards Alphabet (SST) 1987

If you're in the market for a brilliant post-modern guitar hero, you could do a whole lot worse than Henry Kaiser. This Bay Area diver/filmmaker/musician has appeared on more than 50 records since the early '70s, ranging from total improvisations to jazz to experimental and progressive rock. While augmenting his flawless techniques with a wide array of electronic effects, Kaiser has familiarized himself with the ethnic musics of Southeast Asia, India and Japan, while recently citing Glenn Phillips and Jerry Garcia as his personal guitar faves.

Studio Solo and **It's a Wonderful Life** are solo LPs that find Kaiser building dazzling architechtonic solos, from ghostly and ghastly textures to cartoonlike goofs to disjointed bluegrass, blues and jazz constructions. The key to Kaiser's strategy is never to play the same thing twice, making his records and solos endlessly listenable.

Kaiser adds a Synclavier to the mix on **Devil in the Drain**, allowing him to record impossible lines and create otherworldly textures. The title track is built around a hilarious text by children's writer Daniel Pinkwater. Kaiser returns to his roots on **Those Who Know the Past**, which includes a sidelong version of the Grateful Dead classic "Dark Star" (integrating other Dead hits) as well as the theme from *The Andy Griffith Show.*

With Enemies Like These, Who Needs Friends? contains heretofore unreleased improvised live performances by Kaiser and former Henry Cow guitarist Fred Frith, along with some gems from their two previous duo albums. The two plonk, bang and drone around on guitars, keyboards, violin and a particularly volatile (electronic) set of Linndrums.

Kaiser returns to '70s progressive rock on **Crazy Backwards Alphabet**, his not-entirely-successful linkage with amazing drummer John French (formerly Drumbo of Captain Beefheart's Magic Band), the hockey-influenced Swedish drummer/vocalist Michael Maksymenko and ex-Dixie Dregs bassist Andy West. Gnarly instrumentals are unfortunately forced to share space with distracting vocals.

Live, Love, Larf & Loaf is a much more pleasant supergrouping in which Kaiser, French and Frith (on bass) are joined by British folk-rock guitar wiz Richard Thompson. The LP combines excellent post-Beefheart compositions by French with Thompson's acid-etched Anglo-mysticism and a remarkable Okinawan pop song, "Hai Sai Oji-San." Eclecticism at its finest.   [rg]

HARRY KAKOULLI
Even When I'm Not (nr/Oval) 1981

Following his involuntary departure from Squeeze, bassist Harry Kakoulli recorded this likeminded set of dignified pop tunes. It's an adequate record, although his compositions lack the clarity and crackle that typify the best work of head Squeezers Difford and Tilbrook. [jy]

KANE GANG
The Bad and Lowdown World of the Kane Gang (London) 1985 ●
Miracle (Echo Chamber-Kitchenware-London-Capitol) 1987 ●

The Newcastle-area Kane Gang are a bit of an oddity, consisting as it does of two vocalists—not a harmony duo—plus an instrumentalist who plays (or programs) much of the rest. The trio does get some help here and there on drums and horns; veteran Pete Wingfield handles keyboards and production (some of each on the first album, all keyboards and co-production with the band on the second). What's *really* weird is the difference in results between the two records.

The Kane Gang's debut shows exciting breadth and promise, which it comes tantalizingly close to realizing on nearly every track. The Gang (whose name is an homage to *Citizen Kane*) are neither purists nor trendies, and move comfortably through a variety of R&B sub-styles, distinctly blue-eyed but needing no apology. (Except, that is, for the vocals on—nay, the very choice of—"Respect Yourself." Despite a soulful shot-in-the-arm from English session-singing queen P.P. Arnold, these extremely white boys only embarrass themselves by attempting to mimic the Staple Singers.) The songs fall just short of superb and their musical identity needs fine tuning, but it's a heckuva swell platter. (The US edition is simply called **Lowdown**.)

Miracle, on the other hand, is anything but miraculous. The Kanes have mixmastered their style to resemble all the other slick and faceless white soulsters. Only one track has any grit and spit, but it's short and buried deep on Side Two. The album's most memorable, tuneful track wasn't written by the group, but by LA pop-soul hacks. **Miracle** is mostly processed cheese, even the group's modest American hit, "Motortown." [jg]

BILLY KARLOFF & THE EXTREMES
Let Your Fingers Do the Talking (Warner Bros.) 1981

In 1977, Billy Karloff & the Goats regularly gigged at the Roxy, London's fabled punk venue, and made an obscure album

called **The Maniac**. Having been enjoined from using the name Billy Karloff & the Supremes, a later incarnation (including ex-Tom Robinson Band drummer Dolph Taylor) ultimately became the Extremes. For reasons unknown, this unreconstructed Sham 69-like punk band wound up with an American label deal and recorded a glossily-produced batch of sarcastic shouters. No big deal. [iar]

MICK KARN
See *Dalis Car, Japan*.

KAS PRODUCT
Try Out (Fr. RCA) 1982
By Pass (Fr. RCA) 1983

KaS Product was a French synth/vocal duo in the Suicide/Soft Cell mode, although that comparison is a bit generous, quality-wise. Singing in a frigid, aloof voice, Mona Sayol sounds very impressed with herself; the effect is overwrought, precious and pretentious.

"Loony-Bin" (from **By Pass**) is one of the few numbers that stick, but the exaggerated vocals ruin it after awhile. Former Birthday Party guitarist Rowland S. Howard played with this crew on a semi-regular basis, but it's not easy to envision how he would have fit in. (The group had released a pair of French independent-label EPs prior to the first album.) [dgs]

KATRINA AND THE WAVES
Walking on Sunshine (Can. Attic) 1983
Katrina and the Waves 2 (Can. Attic) 1984
Katrina and the Waves (Capitol) 1985
Waves (Capitol) 1985 ●

WAVES
Shock Horror! (nr/Aftermath) 1983

Further extending the influence and legend of the Soft Boys, guitarist Kimberley Rew found a wonderfully sympathetic outlet for his ace songwriting in this Anglo-American quartet whose other major asset is singer/guitarist Katrina Leskanich, a Kansas native with a great, flexible, strong voice equally suited for full-tilt pop harmonies and belt-it-out rock'n'roll. The band melds a remarkable hybrid of styles, personalities and ethnic backgrounds.

Walking on Sunshine contains such absolutely brilliant songs as "Going Down to Liverpool" (cleverly covered by the Bangles, who can spot a tune worth singing) and the infectious title track. Guarantee: hear this record once and you'll find yourself humming at least one track from it a week later. It flows magnificently from start to end, and subsumes individual accomplishments into a true group effort. A greatest hits album the first time out. (Actually, the second—Rew included two tracks with the selfsame Waves on his 1982 LP, **The Bible of Bop**.)

KATW 2 takes a harder-rocking bent, downplaying the tunefulness slightly to highlight jumping numbers like "She Likes to Groove," the nutty "Maniac House" and a powerful, Janis Joplin-like blues, "Cry for Me." Pointing up the band's only weakness, the lyrics to "Mexico" (written by bassist Vince de la Cruz) don't achieve much in the way of profundity; the soaring vocals and ethnic-flavored Cars-like simplicity, however, make that a strictly academic problem. Other great tracks: "Red Wine and Whisky" and "The Game of Love." Not as glorious as the debut, but a boss record nonetheless.

Katrina and the Waves consists entirely of songs from the first two albums, but they've all been re-recorded or remixed. In most cases, it's an improvement, exposing untapped realms of both pop and power, but the second "Going Down to Liverpool" is a cock-up, obliterating the atmosphere and the hooky melody of the original in an absurdly overheated arrangement. With that one caveat, **Katrina and the Waves** is otherwise a rare and delightful triumph.

Evidencing mild signs of commercial self-consciousness, **Waves** isn't as charming, although several of the tunes boast all the attributes that make the band so appealing. Foamy Hammond organ, prominent in spots, matches Leskanich's newly soul-ized singing to push the group towards a Stax sound. The songs aren't as memorable, but are solid enough to make this a reasonably pleasing, not strikingly great, record.

Shock Horror! is a low-budget 1983 release that contains early versions of eight songs, only two of which have since surfaced on the band's albums. "Strolling on Air," cut with a former bassist, is an especially rich find; the other tunes (except for an MC5-ish raver, "Atomic Rock'n'Roll") are typically engaging but not particularly well-recorded. Interesting and certainly no embarrassment.

[iar]

See also *Kimberley Rew*.

LENNY KAYE CONNECTION
I've Got a Right (Giorno Poetry Systems) 1984

Rock critic, guitarist, Patti Smith musical cohort, producer, New York scene veteran, **Nuggets** albums compiler, Jim Carroll sideman—Lenny Kaye has done a bit of everything, distinguishing himself in most areas. He also led a band under his own name and released this solo album. Kaye may fumble a few lyrics in an attempt to express schmaltzy emotions, but his obvious sincerity makes up for the occasional prosaic excess. The title track is brilliant pop with an infectious hook and anthemic sound; "Luke the Drifter" is a memorable old-fashioned cowboy ballad updated with a pumping rock beat. A swell record from a swell guy. [iar]

TOMMY KEENE
Strange Alliance (Avenue) 1982
Back Again (Try . . .) EP (Dolphin) 1984
Places That Are Gone EP (Dolphin) 1984
Songs from the Film (Geffen) 1986
Run Now EP (Geffen) 1986

As the jacket blurb on **Strange Alliance** attests, Keene's music does bear some superficial resemblance to the Only Ones and early U2, though without their depth or charisma. (Audible influences also include the Beatles and the Byrds.) Keene's first album contains eight immediately likable, if melancholic, tunes, every one a winner. Keene's reedy voice, chiming, arpeggiated guitar chords and occasional piano make for a lightweight but appealing blend. (A later pressing adds a subsequent single. On virtually all of his records, he's accompanied on bass and drums by two former bandmates from Washington, DC's Razz.)

Back Again (Try . . .) offers two cool covers, recorded live at the Rat in Boston, and two studio originals. Roxy Music's "All I Want Is You"—why didn't anyone think of doing that sooner?—and the Stones' "When the Whip Comes Down" show Keene's rock'n'roll abilities, while the title track and "Safe in the Light" are in more of a Tom Petty power pop vein, and quite striking at that. **Places That Are Gone** mixes five originals with Alex Chilton's "Hey! Little Child." All of the memorable melodies are underscored by strong vocal harmonies, yet the delivery retains a gutsy, even abrasive, edge.

Finally signed to a major label, Keene hooked up with producer Geoff Emerick

(Badfinger, Split Enz, Nick Heyward) to make **Songs from the Film**, a further refinement of his virtues with occasionally more substantial lyrics. The standout is a different version of "Places That Are Gone," but the new compositions are good and sturdy in their own right. The sole non-original is a weirdly "normal" version of Lou Reed's "Kill Your Sons."

Run Now adds another enjoyable chapter to the Keene canon, despite the occasional impression of lyrical unease, in both what he says and the way that he says it ("I Don't Feel Right at All"). The closest to a dud is the commercial title track, which is not offensive, just inconsequential. (That number was produced by Bob Clearmountain; the rest was overseen by the team of T-Bone Burnett and Don Dixon.) The EP's closer is a good live version of "Kill Your Sons."

[jg/iar]

KLARK KENT
See *Stewart Copeland.*

NIK KERSHAW
Human Racing (MCA) 1983
The Riddle (MCA) 1984
Radio Musicola (nr/MCA) 1986 ●

Nik Kershaw's first album introduced a pre-fab pop star with one great song ("Wouldn't It Be Good") and a predilection—not to mention surprising facility—for imitating Stevie Wonder's voice (try "Faces" if you don't believe it) while producing bland and pale electro-dance funk. **Human Racing**, however, was just a hint of the Ipswich-bred Kershaw's sizable talent, much more of which surfaces on **The Riddle**. The title track and the mildly self-critical "Wide Boy" at least double his batting percentage, and the encore inclusion of "Wouldn't It Be Good" on the US edition makes it even stronger.

[tr]

KEYS
The Keys Album (nr/A&M) 1981

This overlooked gem of a pop album was criminally ignored in England and never released in the States. The four Keys may wear their influences (mainly the Beatles and their producer, Joe Jackson) a bit too much on their sleeves—several of the songs sound unfortunately like outtakes from Joe's **Look**

Sharp!—but their knack for pretty melodies, close harmonies and intelligent lyrics make the overall sound original and fresh. And any band that can write such sparklers as "If It's Not Too Much" and "I Don't Wanna Cry" can be forgiven a few minor flaws.　　[ks]

KID CREOLE AND THE COCONUTS
Off the Coast of Me (ZE) 1980
Fresh Fruit in Foreign Places (ZE-Sire) 1981
Wise Guy (ZE-Sire) 1982
Tropical Gangsters (nr/ZE-Island) 1982
Doppelganger (ZE-Sire) 1983
Cre-Ole: The Best of Kid Creole and the Coconuts (ZE-Sire) 1984
In Praise of Older Women and Other Crimes (Sire) 1985
I, Too, Have Seen the Woods (Sire) 1987 ●

COCONUTS
Don't Take My Coconuts (EMI America) 1983

In an interview, black Bronxite August "Kid Creole" Darnell—writer, singer, producer—once alluded to not being able to play reggae as well as Bob Marley or salsa as well as Tito Puente, but possibly being able to combine the two styles better than anyone else. Darnell's internationalist fusion may indeed be one of the freshest new sounds of the '80s, drawing together strains of Latin, reggae, calypso, disco, rap and rock into a unique sound. Add to his vision and smarts an amiable partner in "Sugar Coated" Andy Hernandez (aka Coati Mundi, a solo artist in his own right), the singing, dancing Coconuts and a medley of talented sidepeople of every race and sex, and you have one of the most unusual, influential and formidable bands around.

On **Off the Coast of Me**, Darnell and company introduce their unusual sound (more Latin-tinged here than on any subsequent LP). Although the material isn't strong enough to make this more than adequate, its uniqueness and danceability, along with the Kid's occasionally risqué wordplay, are enough to suggest the band's potential. If Darnell's mindset isn't apparent from the music, the lyrics to "Darrio . . ." make clear the course he intends to follow, abandoning Studio 54 to "check out Mr. James White!"

Launching a conceptual album trilogy, **Fresh Fruit in Foreign Places** stands as Kid Creole's tour de force, a musical odyssey in which the Kid and the Coconuts set off from

New York in search of the elusive Mimi. The flavor of the music changes with each stop on the journey, providing a perfect setting for the band to display its mastery of intercontinental bop. Each cut is an adventure, and the album works as well as any rock concept LP ever has. A major achievement.

After the perfect realization of **Fresh Fruit**, nearly anything would have seemed like a bit of letdown. **Wise Guy** (entitled **Tropical Gangsters** outside the US) follows the concept, but much more loosely. The material is far less adventurous, with **Fresh Fruit**'s wonderful diversity toned down in favor of a straighter dance music approach. As a commercial move it worked, at least in Europe, where two tracks ("Stool Pigeon" and "I'm a Wonderful Thing, Baby") became hit singles and elevated Darnell to stardom.

Doppelganger is posited as the continuation of "the saga": in this installment, the Kid is cloned by King Nignat's evil scientist. The songs don't all move the story along in narrative fashion—they sound more like the disjunct score of a Broadway musical—but that's fine, since each stands as a marvelous example of Darnell's multifarious brilliance. Mixing '40s be-bop with Carib-beat, reggae, country, funk, salsa and something like highlife, the record sparkles with a cover of "If You Wanna Be Happy" (a 1966 American hit for the Jimmy Castor bunch as "Hey Leroy") as well as such original frolics as "The Lifeboat Party" and "Bongo Eddie's Lament." "Survivors" laments the death of rockers from Frankie Lymon to Sid Vicious, partially in Spanish.

The less spectacular **In Praise of Older Women** is still another (ca)rousing success, a collection of wittily written, sublimely arranged, energetically performed songs. "Endicott" (cleverly verbose), "Caroline Was a Drop-Out" (a nasty character study), "Particul'y Int'rested" (exaggerated, showy torch song)—to name but three—all reflect the Kid's wonderful attitude and outlook. With Coati Mundi and the Coconuts, plus a stageful of sidemen, King ("self-appointed in Feb. this year") Creole demonstrates his stylistic transcendence by making every track different but identifiable; no longer a mere genre dabbler, he's developed the Kid Creole format.

On **I, Too, Have Seen the Woods**, Darnell seems to be treading water a bit within that format. Although he introduces female singer Haitia Fuller to share lead vocals with

him, her overall impact is fairly negligible. As always, there are some very good tunes (especially "Dancin' at the Bains Douches" and "Call It a Day"); Darnell's words are typically clever and insightful. On the whole, though, the music seems more repetitive of past Kid Creole styles, especially Hernandez's "El Hijo," a near carbon copy of his early '80s dance hit "Me No Popeye") and less innovative this time around. (Hopefully, this wasn't a result of Darnell's recent appearance on a Barry Manilow LP!) Still good, but they can do (and have done) better. Let's hope format doesn't become formula.

The Coconuts' solo album, produced by Darnell to resemble a stage revue (complete with crowd sounds and stage introductions), is rife with innuendo and apparent internecine squabbling. Darnell sings the introductory title track without the three ladies; the inclusion of "If I Only Had a Brain" (from *Wizard of Oz*) might be someone's idea of an editorial comment. Otherwise, it's a typically rich, clever Darnell dance-funk-Carib-salsa-tango stew, and the Coconuts' smooth harmony vocals are as appealing as ever.

[ds/iar]

See also *Coati Mundi.*

STEVE KILBEY
See *Church.*

KILBURN AND THE HIGH ROADS
Handsome (nr/Dawn) 1975 (nr/Pye) 1977
Wotabunch! (nr/Warner Bros.) 1978
Upminster Kids (nr/PRT) 1983

Although it was still two years before new wave, the London music scene of 1975 wasn't all Queen and the Rolling Stones; pub-rock bands were making fresh and exciting music, laying the groundwork for more radical outfits to follow. Some included musicians whose skills came in very handy when the dam broke in 1977; Kilburn and the High Roads, named after a highway sign, included Ian Dury, saxman Davey Payne (a future Blockhead) and Keith Lucas, who changed his name and helped found the group 999. During a commercially frustrating career that lasted from 1970 to 1976, the Kilburns were cult-popular and influential. Their records serve as neat reminders of a wonderful band.

An album cut in 1974 was shelved due to record company politics; the band's debut was in fact their second recording. (That first LP, **Wotabunch!**, was dredged up and finally released once Dury's solo career took off.) The subsequently-recorded **Handsome** contains much of the same material (co-written by Dury with pianist Russell Hardy) that the group had used the first time. Got that?

Handsome is musically low-key, featuring Dury's clever cockney wordplay and a bit of high-powered blowing from Payne, but it leans overly toward understatement, touching on rockin' '50s styles and dapper '40s lounge subtlety to make it a generally debonair record not above some raving. **Upminster Kids** is a reissue of **Handsome** with several tracks deleted. [iar]

See also *Ian Dury*.

KILLING JOKE

Almost Red EP (nr/Malicious Damage) 1979
(nr/Island) 1981
Killing Joke (EG) 1980 ●
what's THIS for . . . ! (EG) 1981 ●
Revelations (Malicious Damage-EG) 1982 ●
Birds of a Feather EP (Malicious Damage-EG) 1982
"Ha" EP (Malicious Damage-EG) 1982
Fire Dances (EG) 1983 ●
Night Time (EG) 1985 ●
Brighter Than a Thousand Suns (EG-Virgin) 1987 ●
Outside the Gate (EG-Virgin) 1988 ●

London's Killing Joke are practitioners of intellectual dance-thrash-rock with a penchant for apocalypse. Originally something like Birthday Party but more restrained and rhythmic, singer/keyboardist Jaz Coleman, bassist Youth (Martin Glover) and guitarist Geordie launched the tumultuous group which has made quite a few intense, angry records of striking strength and fringe weirdness.

Killing Joke is an imaginative interface between heavy metal and new wave. With a few synthesizer incursions, the music fields a basic guitar/bass/drums attack, filtered through distortion and tone modulation. Pounding and pulsating at breakneck speed with occasional funk or reggae overtones, the songs ("Wardance," "Tomorrow's World," "Bloodsport") are cold but compelling doomsday anthems.

what's THIS for . . . ! brings funk to ambient music, implying feeling sublimated in a chaotic world. The retreat from empathy and communication doesn't prevent inventive guitar work that hides steady, rhythmic alterations against repetitious, thumping drums—the postmodern dance.

Revelations returns to the brutal stride of **Killing Joke**, racing atonally towards total collapse, social and otherwise. Conny Plank's production hinders the sound, trying to normalize the enchanting wrongness of the group. Perhaps expecting the end of the world, Coleman and Geordie vanished to Iceland before this album was released and worked with bands there, notably Theyr. Far from being effete pop stars, the quixotic Killing Joke makes a habit of putting money where mouth is.

Birds of a Feather, the first release after the band's traumatic reorganization, showcases a more accessible Killing Joke, less shrill and more tuneful, yet retaining all of the manic depression. The 10-inch **"Ha"** was recorded live in Toronto, proving that this is a trend, not a fluke. Both boast excellent production by the band and Conny Plank.

Fire Dances continues in this manner, but with further sonic refinement. "Rejuvenation," "Frenzy" and "Feast of Blaze" all rank with Killing Joke's very best; **Fire Dances** is a frighteningly solid album. After a sabbatical of nearly two years, **Night Time** was released in 1985. Still concentrating on sharpening their overbearing presence by incorporating some space amidst the fury, it contains "Love Like Blood," their catchiest number yet, and a successful single.

Following another two-year layoff, they returned in 1987 with **Brighter Than a Thousand Suns**, which tones down the trademark guitar thunder in favor of synths, a big dance-floor beat and more of the melodicism explored on "Love Like Blood." Fans of the nihilism of their earlier efforts will have to be patient and attentive for this one. "Sanity" is one of their biggest singles ever; several other cuts are just as good. Although more palatable than previous, the album still packs too much of a wallop to warrant any real sell-out accusations.

Killing Joke's work has rarely strayed far from the general formula of scorching guitar blur, pounding rhythms and apocalyptic lyrics. However, operating within this framework, they've been able to hone their music to combine the early noise assault with a maturing melodic sense for a marriage of beauty and the beast few can successfully imitate. [sg/dgs]

See also *Brilliant*.

KING

Steps in Time (Epic) 1984
Bitter Sweet (Epic) 1985

PAUL KING

Joy (Epic) 1987 ●

From the ashes of the Reluctant Stereo-types, a promising rock-ska band, Coventry singer Paul King decided to go for the gold ring with a crass chart-geared quartet he thoughtfully named after himself. Launched in 1983, King The Group perfected a noxious, unmelodic pseudo-funk concoction, dressed themselves in colorful uniforms and unleashed **Steps in Time** to an inexplicably favorable response: "Love and Pride" and "Won't You Hold My Hand Now" became legit hits. Produced (and drummed on) by Richard James Burgess, the album is filled with alarmingly stupid lyrics, fickle stylistic dabbling, arena-rock attributes and art-school pretensions. Awful.

Bitter Sweet is precisely more of the same. (In fact, the American edition blithely includes "Won't You Hold My Hand Now" for the second time!) Ex-Member Adrian Lillywhite plays the drums, resulting in some improvement in that area, but King The Singer's overbearing, tuneless vocals continue to dominate the band's unpleasant sound. The best thing about this LP is its lyric sheet, which offers no end of unintended giggles.

The inevitable solo career began with **Joy**, an all-American mock-white-soul album masterminded by one of the acknowledged titans of that dubious genre, Dan Hartman. Dispensing with glam-pop gimmickry, Hartman produced the record with commercial savvy, giving a prominent role to the Uptown Horns and session singers. King wisely curbs his past excesses and gets by on what he has: a mediocre but well-controlled sub-Paul Young voice. The songs are nothing, but at least they're not annoying. [iar]

DEE DEE KING

See *Ramones*.

KINGBEES

The Kingbees (RSO) 1980
The Big Rock (RSO) 1981

Prefiguring the Stray Cats, the Kingbees were one of the first neo-rockabilly bands to augment nostalgia with an original approach. The West Coast trio's sound on these two albums is sinewy and unpretentious, thanks primarily to frontman Jamie James' economical guitar and no-nonsense vocals. What's more, the material is a first-rate blend of his originals and well-chosen songs by Charlie Rich, Buddy Holly, Carl Perkins, et al. So how come the Kingbees aren't stars?   [jy]

KING CRIMSON

Discipline (Warner Bros.) 1981 ●
Beat (Warner Bros.) 1982 ●
Three of a Perfect Pair (Warner Bros.) 1984 ●
The Compact King Crimson (EG) 1987 ●

King Crimson, centered around guitarist extraordinaire Robert Fripp, is a seminal band of our time. Formed originally in 1969, the band had, from the outset, pivotal influence on both heavy metal and art-rock. Ever-principled, Fripp refused to let Crimson become a dinosaur and broke up the band in 1974, retreating from the tour-album-tour grind to do solo and session work as a self-styled "mobile compact unit." One of his endeavors, the dance-rock oriented League of Gentlemen, spurred Fripp to reincarnate King Crimson at the start of the 1980s. Consisting of guitarist/vocalist Adrian Belew, Chapman Stick/bassist Tony Levin and drummer Bill Bruford (the only pre-split vet other than Fripp), the current (at least recent) Crimson is a cutting-edge patchwork of modern influences: dance music, art-rock, mysticism, minimalism.

Discipline introduces the new cast of characters and displays their attempt at cerebral dance rock; Fripp is at least as interested in touching the mind as the heart. Not really songs, these pieces are unfolding musical sculptures, played with precision and rare imagination, a mostly-successful synthesis of ambition, simplicity and Kraftwerkian clarity, made with dance clubs in mind.

Beat achieves Fripp's long-sought union of mind, soul and body, centering around the anniversary of Jack Kerouac's *On the Road*. An ode to the beat generation, the album elucidates Crimson's past and purpose, melding Frippertronic tape techniques in equal partnership with Belew's manic physicality. Picking up foreign rhythms and electronic overdubs, the players push their instruments into a new form, akin to fusion and art-rock, but miles beyond either, and beyond description as well.

Three of a Perfect Pair is the most disjunct album in recent memory, even from a band that has prided itself on carefully matched contradictions. Side One sports four of Adrian Belew's poorer songs and a self-derivative instrumental; Side Two is nearly all-instrumental, nearly free-form, nearly brilliant. As a bonus, the LP ends with "Larks' Tongues in Aspic Part III," the latest and possibly last in a distinguished series of rhythmically skewed tours de force. Apparently the Frippressive "discipline" that forged the critically acclaimed pop/art synthesis of the first two latter-day Crimson albums is not a permanent condition.

The Compact King Crimson mixes old and new—tracks by the latest incarnation and items from the original band's earliest albums. [sg/mf]

See also *Bears, Adrian Belew, Robert Fripp, Fripp & Eno, Fripp + Summers.*

KING KURT
Ooh Wallah Wallah (nr/Stiff) 1983
Road to Rack & Ruin (Ralph) 1985
Second Album (nr/Stiff) 1986

This bunch of British goofballs picks up exactly where "Stranded in the Jungle" and "Alley Oop" left off—mixing big-band rockabilly with a crazed, comic book mentality and lots of drums. Dave Edmunds produced their first boisterous LP, which raucously proffers such non-classics as "Bo Diddley Goes East" and "Destination Zulu Land." A bit too formulaic for mega-fun, but a good smirky laugh nonetheless.

KK's **Second Album**, known semi-officially as **Big Cock**, thanks to the surly-looking rooster on the cover, is great, a wildly out-of-control ride through a half-dozen areas of lighthearted rock'n'roll fun. Side One kicks off with an energetic, distinguished version of Eddie Cochran's "Nervous Breakdown" and ends with an uncredited voice that sounds suspiciously like Nigel Planer (of *The Young Ones*) lost in a jazzy novelty number called "Billy." "Horatio" recalls the much-missed Tenpole Tudor; "Pumpin' Pistons" leers like a drunk in a strip joint; the horrific thought of there being a "Momma Kurt" is enough to power this greasy R&B number along. Keep up the bad work, lads. (The disc is available in either black or red vinyl; the tape has two extra tunes.)

Road to Rack & Ruin is an American mini-album culled from tracks on the first LP plus a couple that wound up on the second. [iar]

KINGSNAKES
How Tuff (Fr. New Rose) 1983
Kingsnakes (Midnight) 1986

Ex-Flamin Groovies drummer Danny Mihm's band, which otherwise includes Europeans, plays in a universal language: smoking, uncomplicated barrelhouse rock'n' roll. The uncredited original songs aren't exactly precedent-setters, but the hard-rocking piano-and-guitar energy here tells you everything you might need to know, and then some. If there had been more bands like this back in 1976, punk might never have happened. [iar]

RICHARD H. KIRK
See *Cabaret Voltaire.*

KNITTERS
See *X.*

KNOX
See *U.K. Subs, Vibrators.*

KONK
Konk Party EP (nr/Rough Trade) 1982
    (Celluloid) 1983
Yo (nr/Crépuscule-Island) 1983
Your Life EP (Sleeping Bag) 1984
Konk Jams (Dog Brothers) 1988

Slick and supple New York big-band funk: Konk's seven-piece lineup includes three horn players and a vocalist who doubles on conga drum. The sound leans toward Latin, with scads of percussion and sharp arrangements, plus some subtle dub effects thrown in for good measure. Clocking in at over 23 minutes, the four songs on the **Konk Party** EP are indeed for partying, and probably best heard on a mammoth boombox. **Your Life** is a four-mix 12-inch.

Konk laid low for a while, resurfacing in a big way with the inclusion of "Love Attack" on the soundtrack (and album) of *Bright Lights, Big City.* (Konk had in a sense launched its film career several years earlier when hornman Richard Edson started acting in pictures like *Stranger Than Paradise* and *Platoon.*) **Konk Jams** is a collection of extended remixes (some with vocals) that downplay the funk and the brass for a powerful reliance on rhythm and amusing audio gimmickry. **Jams** is a dynamic club record that proves Konk's ongoing vitality and development. [iar]

KOOL MOE DEE

Kool Moe Dee (Rooftop-Jive) 1987
How Ya Like Me Now (Rooftop-Jive) 1987 ●

Popular New York rapper Mohandas Dewese, a former third of the Treacherous Three, puts his positive social messages (plus the usual braggadocio) to medium-weight rhythm tracks, many of them enhanced by loping synth-bass lines, electronic horns and other musical ingredients. Without succumbing to effeteness or abandoning the rapper's traditional concupiscent party-hearty ethos, the versatile vocalist's records earn their mainstream appeal by tempering the music and taking a firm stand against violence and sexual irresponsibility.

The first album's "Go See the Doctor" offers a slangy but detailed warning about sexual transmission of disease; "Little Jon" characterizes a young hoodlum as a loser not a hero; "Monster Crack" warns kids against messing with that drug. **How Ya Like Me Now** experiments with one-chord funk vamps instead of mere beats, and quotes James Brown, Paul Simon and others, but Kool's raps aren't as captivating as before and the cuts tend to drag. "No Respect," recited to an adaptation of Aretha's "Respect," tells a powerful cautionary tale of a street hustler's downfall and joins the self-serving title track as a highlight. [iar]

PETER KOPPES

See *Church*.

KRAFTWERK

Kraftwerk 1 (Ger. Philips) 1971
Kraftwerk 2 (Ger. Philips) 1972
Kraftwerk (nr/Vertigo) 1972
Ralf and Florian (Vertigo) 1973
Autobahn (Vertigo) 1974 (Warner Bros.) 1984
   (Elektra) 1988 ●
Radio Activity (Capitol) 1975 ●
Exceller 8 (nr/Vertigo) 1975
Trans-Europe Express (Capitol) 1977 ●
The Man Machine (Capitol) 1978 ●
Elektro Kinetik (nr/Vertigo) 1981
Computer World (Warner Bros.) 1981
   (Elektra) 1988 ●
Techno Pop (nr/EMI) 1983
Electric Cafe (Warner Bros.) 1986 (Elektra)
   1988 ●

Kraftwerk (German for "power station") began in the electronic metal trend that erupted in Germany in the early 1970s. The four-piece synthesizer group has shown amazing resiliency, tightening its electro-pop formula to fit smoothly into art-rock and later disco. Kraftwerk essentially created the sonic blueprint from which the British new romantic and techno-pop movements arose.

Autobahn is built around an epic version of the title track, a bizarre hit single that broke the band as a commercial property in numerous countries. Enchanting in its simplicity, hypnotic in its construction, the song introduces the repetition typical of all Kraftwerk music, but the record's other pieces are less inspired synthesizer noodling.

Radio Activity coincided with a change of image that sliced away beards and hair and converted Kraftwerk from aging hippies into modern sonic engineers; greater use of repetition and purposeful self-limitation is evident, though there is no breakthrough.

The robotic **Trans-Europe Express** placed mechanistic aspects of the music up front, in a brilliant epiphany of style. Rhythms and themes recur throughout, with little emotion expressed in the vocals; lyrics emphasize the dehumanization suggested by the production and delivery. Recommended.

The Man Machine further builds on the developments of **Trans-Europe Express**, with the one humanizing effect—background music—yielding to *Star Wars* noises. More work with manipulated vocals—especially on the title track and "We Are the Robots"— takes the automaton stance to the limit. Despite the science fiction themes and heavy musical repetition, the album has inventive, catchy compositions and an eerie warmth. Highly recommended.

Computer World broke years of silence, bringing Kraftwerk into a world that had largely embraced and vindicated their social and musical visions. Technically advanced machinery yields sharper, brighter music, but otherwise Kraftwerk haven't tampered with their style, except to shift their thematic content from science-fiction to industrial documentary. Excellent synthesizer pop.

The musics Kraftwerk helped launch— British post-rock industrial sounds and rhythm-is-everything dance grooves—come full circle on Side One of the long-awaited **Electric Cafe**. The virtually interchangeable

"Technopop" and "Musique Non-Stop" take sparse, simple, unvarying percussion tracks and add bits of treated vocals, synthetic noises and quasi-instrumental effects. On the reverse are three straightforward (albeit numbingly repetitive) songs that use actual melodies, singing and lyrics. While the second side is certainly listenable, even Kraftwerk fans will find this brief album disappointingly short on ideas and content.

There are German-language versions of many, if not all, of Kraftwerk's albums. There have also been several compilations released in the UK. In 1988, the group signed with American Elektra, which promised to reissue many of their out-of-print records.

[sg/iar]

KRAUT
An Adjustment to Society (Cabbage) 1982
Whetting the Scythe (Cabbage) 1984

On their first album, Kraut proved themselves to be one of New York's best hardcore bands, able to maintain awesomely dense but distinct slabs of post-Pistols guitar chords while galloping along at unbelievable speed. Ex-Pistol Steve Jones added guitar to the fray, but the spotlight remains firmly fixed on Doug Holland, one of punk's best-ever string smashers. The lyrics are only a bit above the usual monosyllabic protest, but who listens to them anyway?

Kraut's second release, a nine-song mini-album, finds them abandoning punk for demi-metal, using doubled guitar leads and charging, articulated power at more moderate tempos to fight the arena headbangers on their own turf. It's a partially successful variant, easier to follow than their hyperdrive punk. Kraut has the chops, the intelligence and (occasionally) the songs to make something really unique; for the time being, however, they're just one of the loud'n'fast crowd.

[jg/iar]

ED KUEPPER
See *Laughing Clowns.*

KURSAAL FLYERS
Chocs Away (nr/UK) 1975
The Great Artiste (nr/UK) 1975
Golden Mile (nr/CBS) 1976
Five Live Kursaals (nr/CBS) 1977

In for a Spin: The Best of the Kursaal Flyers (nr/Edsel) 1985

Another seminal pub-rock outfit, the Kursaals are of more interest for what the individuals did after the group split than for their recordings while together. Drummer Will Birch went on to found the Records (with guitarist John Wicks, who was a Kursaal Flyer briefly at the end of the band's existence) and produce records for various people. Graeme Douglas, whom Wicks replaced, joined Eddie and the Hot Rods, and wrote many of their best songs.

The Kursaals' first two LPs are thinly-produced countryish rock'n'roll, bolstered considerably by Birch's witty lyrics. **The Great Artiste** does contain what may be the earliest recorded cover of a Nick Lowe composition, "Television," later done to better effect by Dave Edmunds.

With Mike Batt producing, the group tried something completely different on **Golden Mile**, an eclectic musical travelogue through rock'n'roll's root styles from swing to Spector to ska to '60s pop-rock. The album is a little-known treasure, similar in concept to the Turtles' equally-ignored and enjoyable **Battle of the Bands**.

By the time of **Five Live**, the Kursaals had almost totally weeded out their country strain and, showing the influence of the punk revolution going on around them, got into music with a more driving beat. The band's last hurrah, the "Television Generation" single, is great, proof positive that the band had seen the new light. What else could they do but break up? [ds]

See also *Eddie and the Hot Rods, Records.*

DAVE KUSWORTH
See *Nikki Sudden.*

FELA ANIKULAPO KUTI
Fela's London Scene (nr/EMI) 1970
Fela Ransome-Kuti and Africa '70 with Ginger Baker: Live! (Signpost) 1972
Gentlemen (nr/Creole) 1979
Everything Scatter (nr/Creole) 1979
Black-President (Capitol) 1981
Original Sufferhead (Capitol) 1982
Army Arrangement (Remix) (Celluloid) 1985 ●
Shuffering and Shmiling (Celluloid) 1985 ●
Army Arrangement (Celluloid) 1985 ●

No Agreement (Celluloid) 1985
Upside Down (Celluloid) 1986
2,000 Black (Celluloid) 1986
Mr. Follow Follow (Celluloid) 1986
Volume One and Two (Celluloid) 1987
Teacher Don't Teach Me Nonsense
  (Polygram) 1987

FELA AND AFRIKA 70
Shakara (nr/EMI) 1972
Zombie (Mercury) 1977 (Celluloid) 1985 ●

FELA ANIKULAPO KUTI AND EGYPT 80
Live in Amsterdam (Capitol) 1984

FELA ANIKULAPO KUTI AND ROY AYERS
Music of Many Colours (Celluloid) 1986

One of the world's true musical revolutionaries, Fela Ransome-Kuti's life and work embody most of the contradictions inherent in any major collusion of Western and African styles of thought and art. Born in Lagos, Nigeria in 1938 to an affluent Christian family and educated in London, Fela was just another minor highlife bandleader until he received funk's call via Sierra Leonese James Brown imitator Geraldo Pino in 1966. By weaving funk rhythms into highlife, Fela developed Afro-beat, a mesmerizingly potent style he has spent years refining.

Most of Fela's recorded pieces take up to an entire side of an LP, beginning slowly, with a lengthy electric piano and/or saxophone introduction (Fela plays both instruments) before breaking into exuberant horn fanfares, followed by call-and-response vocals between Fela and chorus and interlocking polyrhythmic percussion patterns.

During a 1968 Los Angeles stint with his group Koola Lobitas, Fela was introduced to American black radical politics. Fela's stock rose considerably when EMI released **Fela's London Scene** in 1970, leading to a friendship and collaboration with ex-Cream drummer Ginger Baker. (Their **Live!** album provides a fairly tame example.) Nigerian authorities tormented the bandleader after

his triumphant return from London in the early '70s, for as Fela's fame grew, so did his influence. (Fortunately, Kuti's name translates as "He who emanates greatness, who has death inside his quiver and who cannot be killed by human entity.") Castigatory songs about government corruption (on **Black-President**'s "I.T.T. (International Thief Thief)," military fascism ("Zombie," on the album of the same name) and national apathy ("Army Arrangement," ditto), sung by a rich marijuana smoker with a couple of dozen wives who isolated himself in a concrete fortress called the Shrine, challenged the local authorities in a manner they couldn't ignore.

Since 1974, Fela has been arrested several times for various crimes; during a particularly vigorous 1981 crackdown, a beating by soliders left him temporarily incapable of playing saxophone. His most recent incarceration came in 1984, on the eve of his first major American tour. Arrested on a trumped-up money-smuggling rap, he was released from his five-year sentence after two years, thanks to intercession by Amnesty International.

Celluloid began re-releasing some of Fela's many records in 1985. **Upside Down** dates from 1976; **No Agreement** from 1977. But the most controversial of these was Bill Laswell's remix of **Army Arrangement**, on which he added tracks by keyboardist Bernie Worrell, drummer Sly Dunbar and talking drummer Aiyb Dieng. This reportedly displeased Fela greatly, and one need only compare the remix with the rough yet stirring original to understand why. Roy Ayers joins Fela on **Music of Many Colors** (originally released on Phonodisk in 1980), eliciting the vibraphonist's meatiest playing ever. **Zombie** is one of the classics of the Celluloid batch.

Polygram cashed in on Fela's successful and long-delayed 1987 American tour by releasing one of his hits from the show. **Teacher Don't Teach Me Nonsense** movingly demonstrates that the wild master hasn't lost his chops.   [rg]

L L L L L L L L L

LADYSMITH BLACK MAMBAZO

Induku Zethu (Shanachie) 1984
Ulwandle Oluncgwele (Shanachie) 1985
Inala (Shanachie) 1986
Shaka Zulu (Warner Bros.) 1987 ●
Umthombo Wamanzi (Shanachie) 1988 ●

Led by Joseph Shabala, who formed the group almost 20 years ago, Ladysmith Black Mambazo is one of South Africa's most popular ensembles. For sheer vocal ecstasy, few groups can equal its lush, comforting and sophisticated choral harmonies sung in the open *mbube* style. Simultaneously sorrowful and optimistic, the music originated in South African dormitories housing immigrant workers who'd left their townships and families for employment in the area's diamond and gold mines.

Employing between 7 and 12 singers, *mbube* is characterized by a cappella harmonies and short phrases either sung in unison or against an overlapping call-and-response pattern. Reflecting on matters both familial and spiritual, the music is tied closely to the group's Zulu culture. They generally sing in Zulu; the occasional English-language songs are a pleasant shock.

Noted ethno-music appropriator Paul Simon got wind of Black Mambazo and, despite the African National Congress' cultural boycott of South Africa, recorded part of **Graceland** with them in Johannesburg and London. (He also featured the group on two subsequent tours.) Simon produced their most recent collection, **Shaka Zulu**. All that American attention led to the group's remarkable commercial exploitation by 7-Up, which adapted "Beautiful Rain" from that album for a TV spot.

On **Unthombo Wamanzi**, Black Mambazo changes its strategy slightly, emphasizing ensemble work rather than call-and-response structures or a leader singing over backing voices; this accentuates their irregular punctuations and stop-start rhythms. As with previous records, it provides an almost overwhelming atmosphere of emotional power and grace. The unadorned human voice has rarely sounded so godlike.   [rg]

LAMBRETTAS

Beat Boys in the Jet Age (MCA) 1980
Ambience (nr/Rocket) 1981

Sad. This Sussex foursome had most of the pop smarts of fellow neo-mods Secret Affair and none of their arrogance, but evidently believed too strongly in the up-the-movement sentiments of **Beat Boys**' title song ("so sure in what we do") not to be blown away when the fad faded. The first LP is mostly free of pretense, with some great hooks in among a batch of good songs (including two hit singles, "Da-a-a-ance" and a cover of "Poison Ivy"). They even reveal a sense of humor.

Ambience, however, shows the Lambrettas to be utterly lost. The tunes aren't nearly as catchy and there's obvious confusion as to which stylistic fork in the road to follow. (The uncredited synth dribbles and sax come courtesy of Wesley Magoogan, subsequently a member of the Beat.) The lyrics, while reasonably intelligent, just aren't smart enough to get serious and still be taken seriously.

[jg]

LANDSCAPE

Landscape (nr/RCA) 1980
From the Tea-rooms of Mars . . . to the
     Hell-holes of Uranus (RCA) 1981
Manhattan Boogie-Woogie (RCA) 1982

RICHARD JAMES BURGESS

Richard James Burgess EP (Capitol) 1984

A high-tech synthesizer group led by Richard Burgess, producer of Visage, King and Spandau Ballet and onetime soft-rocker (as a member of Easy Street). In Landscape, Burgess sang and handled synthetic and acoustic drums, while his four collaborators played bass, keyboards, trombone and woodwinds, all employing both electronic and traditional instruments. Their work is slick and polished, perfect for sophisticated dance parties, but the songs retain a lyrical cleverness that prevents total bland-out. Not quite an '80s version of 10cc, Landscape played rhythmic rock, but with a heavy dose of jazzy fusion.

From the Tea-Rooms of Mars has a witty paean to Japanese industry ("Shake the West Awake") and a tongue-in-cheek tribute to the film *Psycho* ("Norman Bates"). **Manhattan Boogie-Woogie** is more directly disco-oriented, with a driving beat and popping bass, but also manages clever bits like "It's Not My Real Name" ("I got it from a book . . . ") There was always something detached and artificial about Landscape—as though they were slumming in contemporary music and would rather be doing something more artistic—but they did make enjoyable records that work on a number of different levels.

Burgess' self-produced solo record—six long numbers with a large collection of sidemen (one Landscape bandmate) adding synthesizer and guitars—is sophisticated and tedious commercial dance music of little interest. (Feminists might want to hear the noxious "Thank You Ladies" for some immediate hackle-raising.) [iar]

ANITA LANE

See *Nick Cave.*

ROBIN LANE AND THE CHARTBUSTERS

Robin Lane and the Chartbusters (Warner Bros.) 1980
5 Live (Warner Bros.) 1980
Imitation Life (Warner Bros.) 1981

Based in Boston, Robin Lane and the Chartbusters boasted a pedigree of sorts: she appeared on Neil Young's **Everybody Knows This Is Nowhere**; guitarist Leroy Radcliffe was a former Modern Lover; other band members were veterans of the New England music scene.

The chiming guitars that kick off "When Things Go Wrong," the first track on the band's debut, immediately identified Lane as a godsend to oft-neglected folk-rock fans. Throughout the LP, they mix the stylistic grace of the Byrds with the folksy directness of early Fairport Convention. Where many kindred spirits fall into a poised monotony, Lane varies the mood from track to track. "Waitin' in Line" mixes blues with 12-string licks, while "Many Years Ago" and "Don't Wait Till Tomorrow" builds up a head of steam that lends special urgency to Lane's middle-range vocals.

5 Live is what the title says: five live tracks. Since the Chartbusters were much more ragged onstage than in the studio, this one is strictly for the faithful.

Imitation Life ups the ante considerably, creating an atmosphere of tension so heavy it's almost tangible. The band plays more roughly, especially drummer Tim Jackson, and Lane sings like a driven woman, whether the subject is lust ("No Control") or her deepening Christianity ("Solid Rock"). Producer Gary Lyons makes the sound sizzle without resorting to gimmickry. Rather than life, the LP imitates a bomb about to explode. [jy]

CLIVE LANGER AND THE BOXES

I Want the Whole World EP (nr/Radar) 1979
Splash (nr/F-Beat) 1980

The big disappointment of Clive Langer's solo career is that he doesn't give it top priority. Presumably freed from financial pressures by co-producing numerous hit records for Madness and others, the talented singer/guitarist—judging by his lack of "product"—seems to take only passing interest in making records of his own.

As chief songwriter for the late Deaf School, Langer successfully mated the music hall tradition with highly melodic rock'n' roll, topped off with anxious lyrics about modern-day pressures—i.e., a cross between the Kinks and Roxy Music. His solo works are more personal, and lean decidedly to the Ray Davies school, partly because Langer's weary singing has a similar charm.

The five tunes on **I Want the Whole World** are nearly perfect vignettes of anger, tenderness and regret, performed with casual ingenuousness. Though less effective, **Splash** has its moments, including the charming "Had a Nice Night" and the embarrassingly abject "Splash (A Tear Goes Rolling Down)." Elvis Costello produced two of the tracks.

Clive Langer seems like a guy you wouldn't mind inviting to your house for dinner.   [jy]

LAST

L.A. Explosion! (Bomp) 1979
Fade to Black EP (Bomp) 1982
Painting Smiles on a Dead Man (Fr. Lolita) 1983
Confession (SST) 1988 ●

Although heavily indebted to the sounds of the '60s (they touch freely on surf-rock, psychedelia, folk-rock, etc.) Los Angeles' Last—formed in 1976 and led by three Nolte brothers—play with modern-day punk intensity. **L.A. Explosion** is a near-perfect debut, marred only by flat production. The performances are stunning, with Vitus Mataré's authentic Vox/Farfisa organ riffs adding color to the melodic guitar leads and Joe Nolte's distinctive vocals. Every track holds up, especially the hypnotic rocker "She Don't Know Why I'm Here" and a surf-inspired ode to lost youth, "Every Summer Day."

The 12-inch **Fade to Black** EP shows that the Last are indeed a group worth taking seriously. The four tracks are darker and moodier, yet the melodies are so enticing it's a crime this stuff can't find a commercial opening.

Amidst personnel changes, and facing an uncertain future, the Last released a French-only second album, consisting of recordings done between 1981 and '82. **Painting Smiles on a Dead Man** is another winner, moving the organ up front and showcasing vocals that are at once more confident and demanding. Although one of Los Angeles' most gifted groups, the Last split up in 1985.

A new Last—Joe and Mike Nolte, plus three newcomers—resurfaced unexpectedly in 1988 with a neat album produced by All leader Bill Stevenson. (David Nolte—now in Wednesday Week—had been in a very early version of Stevenson's Descendents.) Energized '60s power pop remains the Last's stock in trade, and they've lost none of their pep or melodiousness. The Noltes' new songs have a resigned, cynical edge ("And They Laugh," "Going Gone," "Everywhere You Turn"), but the music belies that with ringing Byrdsy guitars, mild keyboards and appealing harmonies.

Historical footnotes: Alex Gibson designed the sleeve of a 1978 Last single. Mataré became a well-known record producer (Divine Weeks, Angst, Leaving Trains, etc.) around LA.   [cpl/iar]

BILL LASWELL

Baselines (Celluloid-Elektra-Musician) 1983 ●
Hear No Evil (Venture-Virgin) 1988 ●

Erstwhile Material mainman Laswell released his first solo album right around the time people began to realize that his talents extend beyond excellent bass playing into the conceptual stratosphere. **Baselines'** gut-bucket funk foundation and experienced experimentalism provides a convincing résumé for his subsequent work as producer to the stars (Mick Jagger, Yellowman, Herbie Hancock, Motorhead, Afrika Bambaataa, etc.). Guests here include fellow/former Materialists Michael Beinhorn (a frequent co-writer on the LP) and Martin Bisi, percussionist Ronald Shannon Jackson, the ubiquitous Fred Frith and avant-noisemaster extraordinaire David Moss.

Following group albums with Massacre and duo recordings with John Zorn and bass saxist Peter Brotzmann, Laswell essayed another disc under his own name in 1988. Joined by violinist Shankar, guitarist Nicky Skopelitis and a small group of equally sophisticated players, he wrote and produced **Hear No Evil**, an album of hauntingly beautiful instrumentals with resonances of exotic cultures adding depth to the simple compositions. Lovely.   [mf/iar]

See also *Golden Palominos, Massacre, Material.*

LAUGHING CLOWNS

Laughing Clowns EP (Aus. Missing Link) 1979
Sometimes . . . the Fire Dance EP (Aus. Prince Melon) 1980
3 EP (Aus. Prince Melon) 1981
Mr. Uddich Schmuddich Goes to Town (Aus. Prince Melon) 1982
Laughing Clowns (nr/Red Flame) 1982
Laughter Around the Table (nr/Red Flame) 1983
Law of Nature (nr/Hot) 1984
History of Rock n' Roll Volume One (Aus. Hot) 1985
Ghosts of an Ideal Wife (Aus. Hot) 1985

ED KUEPPER

Electrical Storm (Aus. Hot) 1986
Rooms of the Magnificent (nr/Hot) 1986

After the Saints broke up in 1978 (and before Chris Bailey reformed it) guitarist/songwriter Ed Kuepper returned to Sydney to form a band with a couple of early Saints' alumni. The resultant quintet, dubbed Laughing Clowns, included sax and acoustic piano and cut a strange but remarkably bracing debut EP in 1979. The piano both meshes its timbral resonance with Kuepper's guitar chording and co-states melodies with the sax, as well as—at one point—providing an unnervingly calm chordal anchor while the drums run wild. Considering the source, it's a somewhat astonishing, eloquently intense statement of disillusionment and frustration, the romantic and musical clichés of supper club/movie jazz gone berserk.

Oddly enough, the manic energy and tunefulness seemed to dissipate—over the course of two additional EPs—in favor of despair, ennui, cynicism (or just sarcasm?) and decidedly less lustrous music, in both text and texture. The addition of a trumpeter on **3** does provide a spark, only to be neutralized by satirically discordant riffing. By this point, the moments of musical anarchy seem less passionate than perverse.

On **Mr. Uddich Schmuddich Goes to Town**, a shift in the lineup brought in a new saxman and bassist (playing acoustic stand-up) and dropped the pianist. The tracks are more succinct, and the overall impression is that of consolidation and retrenchment.

The Red Flame **Laughing Clowns** is a compilation that includes both Prince Melon EPs plus three tracks from the album.

By **Laughter Around the Table**, the Clowns' sound had coalesced into something resembling the Cure gone avant-jazz. The sax playing states melody lines and provides some credible solos, but the overall effect, with one exception, is too willfully abrasive and reaches beyond its musical grasp, especially the drumming.

The arrangements on **Law of Nature** continue to step on Kuepper's melodies—they're never harmonically brought out to their fullest. Also, the occasional awkwardness or disjointedness of his bitter lyrics is unintentionally emphasized by this kind of non-production, a frustrating undercutting of Kuepper's compositional efforts.

By the time they cut **History of Rock n' Roll Volume One**, though, all the gears meshed. The Clowns turn out music perversely unillustrative of the title, but with its own dark force and rich, occasionally abrasive textures: swaggering, punching horns, sedate, melodic piano, scratchy, tinny guitar and sliding, stretching acoustic bass, all underpinned by frenetic but authoritative drums. Bravo!

Unfortunately, that apotheosis didn't last. **Ghosts** is more controlled than **Law of Nature**, clarity-wise as well as compositionally, but as before it's awkward; the lapses of the drums and sax seem unnecessarily (if unintentionally) overemphasized. The songs seem to making gestures in the direction of more "normal" structure and style without any commitment to that (or any other) direction.

Gone solo, Kuepper gave up the sound he'd obviously struggled to attain over the years in favor of more conventional rock/folk/pop elements—**Rooms** even has a rather Dylanesque track—without surrendering his right to be caustic. It's the sort of music that ought to have gained him far more attention everywhere, especially in the Northern Hemisphere. [jg]

PETER LAUGHNER

Peter Laughner (Koolie) 1982

Laughner, who died in 1977, was in the first incarnation of Pere Ubu, playing guitar, bass and piano on the band's groundbreaking early self-released singles. Also a rock critic, Laughner worked with other Cleveland musicians, some of whom went on to form the Dead Boys. His album is a posthumous compilation of live work (c. 1975) and home demos recorded with acoustic guitar; a fondly created musical memory of an unrecognized but prescient creative force.

[iar]

CYNDI LAUPER

She's So Unusual (Portrait) 1984 ●
True Colours (Portrait) 1986 ●

She's So Unusual certainly didn't sound like a multi-platinum piece of music on first (or even second) listen, but that just goes to show you. Originally recognized as the only memorable member of New York's unlamented Blue Angel, Lauper's big voice grew to scarifying proportions under the sympathetic production of Rick Chertoff, sup-

320

ported by the able playing of Eric Bazilian and Rob Hyman, leaders of Philadelphia's then-obscure Hooters. Lauper's songwriting was just getting started, so the album draws on outside material—a potentially disastrous minefield—which proved superb, from the Brains' "Money Changes Everything" (much better in Lauper's live 45 version than on the album's somewhat turgid rendition) to Prince's unforgettable "When You Were Mine" and, of course, Robert Hazard's "Girls Just Want to Have Fun." With talent, easy confidence and self-deflating humor, the colorful Lauper won countless hearts, injecting much-needed warmth and graciousness into the mega-pop world.

The inevitable letdown of the long-come **True Colours** is fairly serious as Lauper, who co-produced and co-wrote most of the material, takes bad spills on both fronts. While "Maybe He'll Know" and "True Colors" are wholeheartedly wonderful, "Change of Heart" and a cover of Marvin Gaye's "What's Going On" are sabotaged by over-zealous sound (especially the bombastic drumming) on the former and bland dullness on the latter. A pair of sweet love songs—"Boy Blue" and "The Faraway Nearby"—skirt substantial appeal but wind up in the dumper, falling short as songs and productions. Considering what a unique and remarkable singer Lauper is, the squandering of her gifts on this uninspired, half-baked throwaway is tragic.   [iar]

See also *Blue Angel, Hooters.*

CHRISTINE LAVIN

Future Fossils (Philo) 1984 ●
Beau Woes and Other Problems of Modern
    Life (Philo) 1986 ●
Another Woman's Man (Philo) 1987 ●

One of the leading lights in the '80s "folk" revival, Christine Lavin applies an incisive, self-aware wit and a confidently absurdist view of modern relationships and life in the big city (New York) to acoustic music. Sung in a clear, sweet voice (think of very early Joni Mitchell), her songs address microcosmic issues more than matters of war or world extinction. As a result, there's something disconcertingly yuppiesque about Lavin's adult work; that doesn't ruin the fun, but it does draw a clear distinction between tradition-minded folk music and wry intellectual observations presented in a folk music setting.

Future Fossils, a spare live-in-the-studio effort with little accompaniment save Lavin's guitar, takes itself seriously once too often ("The Dakota," about John Lennon; "Damaged Goods") but otherwise offers such cleverness as "Don't Ever Call Your Sweetheart by His Name," "Cold Pizza for Breakfast," "Artificial Means" (about sex aids) and "Regretting What I Said . . . (A Musical Apology)." A promising introduction.

Although the credits on **Beau Woes** suggest a Phil Spector-scale production, what turns out to be delicate accompaniment politely serves Lavin's creations, adding a little swing, without intruding. Indicative of her broad scope, the obvious ("Biological Time Bomb," "Roses from the Wrong Man" and "Summer Weddings") is joined by the offbeat, e.g., "Air Conditioner," "Ballad of a Ballgame" (complete with harp and several dozen backup vocalists) and the regal jealousy of "Prince Charles." Demonstrating an active musical imagination to match her clever words, Lavin grafts together two oldies—"All I Have to Do Is Dream" and "A Summer Song"—to brilliant and beautiful effect.

The seven songs on **Another Woman's Man** were actually recorded—with an electric bassist and percussionist—before the other two records but not issued until 1987. The writing here lacks her razor-sharp wit and tends towards maudlin sentiment ("If You Want Space, Go to Utah" is typical), but Lavin's music remains warm and pure, her vocals strong and sure.   [iar]

LAWNDALE

Beyond Barbecue (SST) 1986
Sasquatch Rock (SST) 1987

As part of an effort to change its image and expand its scope beyond the confines of punk, SST signed this instrumental quartet from Lawndale (the Southern California town where the label is based) and released two albums of their winning guitar twang. Reclaiming the '60s West Coast beach sound from such notable practitioners as New York's Raybeats, Lawndale plays original compositions (plus occasional offbeat borrowings, like "Interstellar Caravan," credited to Pink Floyd *and* Duke Ellington) with unaffected enthusiasm and spunk. The only indication of the band's distinct '80s orientation is song titles like "The Story of Vanna White," "The Days of Pup & Taco," "March of the Melted Army Men" and "Sasquatch Rock." The second album has a less-specific period feel and exchanges Mosrite clarity for ambitious clutter (adding fuzzbox, harmonica and even a fleeting "Robert Plant vocal" on "Take Five," which quotes "Whole Lotta Love"), but both promise a refreshing dip into delightful, if well-charted, waters.

[iar]

LEAGUE OF CRAFTY GUITARISTS
See *Robert Fripp.*

LEAGUE OF GENTLEMEN
See *Robert Fripp.*

LEAGUE UNLIMITED ORCHESTRA
See *Human League.*

LEAVING TRAINS
Well Down Blue Highway
  (Bemisbrain-Enigma) 1984
Kill Tunes (SST) 1986
Fuck (SST) 1987

Co-produced by Rain Parader David Roback and featuring a guest drummer from Gun Club and a keyboard player from Green on Red, their debut album makes it clear that California's Leaving Trains, a Pacific Palisades trio, is well-connected in the nuevo-rock/folk/blues community. Unlike many new bands, they don't sound like R.E.M. and are neither psychedelic, country, or otherwise '60s-derived, which makes **Well Down Blue Highway** individual, but hard to characterize. Falling James' introspective songs and unaffected, clumsy vocals form the basis of the sound and personality, eschewing complexity, hooks and smoothness in favor of a dry, blunt, rock'n'roll delivery. The album isn't immediately engaging, but reveals its quality over the course of repeated playings.

With **Kill Tunes**, the Trains distance themselves even further from the LA paisley underground by opting for bopping, punk-edged rock'n'roll. The LP is particularly inspired by the early Saints ("Private Affair" from **Eternally Yours** is covered) as it manages to continuously shift gears, from shit-kicking 4/4 like "She's Looking at You" and "Black" to lighter ballads ("Light Rain" and "Kinette"), with an appropriate mixture of humor ("A Drunker Version of You" is a blast), anger, sadness and restlessness. An ex-

cellent expression of modern American rock'n'roll.

Fuck debuts a new lineup (with Falling James the quartet's only holdover), and is even more of a slam-bang affair. The songs come in one-minute blasts like "How Can I Explode?"—no frills, just start "em up and let "er rip. **Fuck**'s overall manic tone makes it half the album **Kill Tunes** is, but so long as you can get mounted on this wild bronco, the ride's an exciting one. After such catharsis, the LP ends with a nine-and-a-half-minute dirge called "What the President Meant to Say," offering listeners plenty of time to recuperate.

[iar/jr]

KEITH LEBLANC
See *ABC, Adrian Sherwood.*

JACK LEE
Jack Lee's Greatest Hits Vol. 1 (Maiden
  America) 1981

Lee was one-third of California new wave watershed the Nerves, but gained national prominence when his song, "Hanging on the Telephone," was recorded by Blondie and became a British hit single. A few years later, in the hopes of parlaying that score into a solid career, Lee released a musical résumé of his 11 best songs. With backing by the other two ex-Nerves (Pete Case, then of the Plimsouls, and Paul Collins of the Beat) and the Rubber City Rebels, Lee sings his lightweight pop creations with little élan; the material itself is additionally not all hit quality. Don't wait up for **Vol. 2**.

[iar]

TIM LEE
See *Windbreakers.*

THOMAS LEER AND ROBERT RENTAL
The Bridge (nr/Industrial) 1979

THOMAS LEER
4 Movements EP (nr/Cherry Red) 1981
Contradictions (nr/Cherry Red) 1982
Letter from America (Cachalot) 1982
Scale of Ten (nr/Arista) 1985

Thomas Leer's method of recording is as unique as his work: he locks himself in his home studio alone with his synthesizers and tape machines and emerges months later with a record. Apart from pop trends, Leer has turned out some of the most creative and human synthesizer work on vinyl.

The Bridge, done in tandem with Robert Rental, is Leer's foray into Germanic technique, consisting of dark electro-pop songs underlined by repetitious sound patterns and punctuated by appliance noises. Despite the music's hard edge, some tunes—notably "Monochrome Day's"—are masterpieces of the form. Uneven but entertaining.

With **4 Movements** and **Contradictions**, Leer maps out his own special turf: credible white electro-soul. The unselfconscious work bears signs of natural progression rather than conspicuous affectation. The four songs on **4 Movements** and seven numbers on the two 12-inch 45s of **Contradictions** prove beyond doubt that synthesizer music can have energy and warmth, especially on **4 Movements'** stunners, "Don't" and "Letter from America."

Letter from America compiles the contents of **Contradictions** and **4 Movements** in toto as a two-record set. [sg]

LEMON KITTENS
See *Danielle Dax.*

LEOPARDS
Kansas City Slickers (Moon) 1977

On first listen, you'd swear this early indie album from Kansas City, Kansas is **Muswell Hill**-era Kinks—and on second and third listen, as well. This talented foursome not only perfectly re-creates the Kinks' klassic sound (complete with a spot-on Ray Davies vocal impression), they also turn out originals that subtly rewrite various Kinks tunes without ever resorting to obvious lifts. The Kinks Rutle-ized! [iar]

LEROI BROTHERS
Check This Action (Amazing) 1982
   (nr/Demon) 1984
Forget About the Danger Think of the Fun EP
   (Columbia) 1984
Lucky Lucky Me (Profile) 1985
Protection from Enemies (nr/Demon) 1986
Open All Night (Profile) 1986 •

It goes without saying that none of the five musicians in Austin, Texas' rhythm'n'rockin' Leroi Brothers are related or named Leroi. The six greasy slices of exuberant, unreconstructed rock'n'roll songs on **Forget About the Danger** also need little explanation—they burn with the spirit of Jerry Lee Lewis. "Treat Her Right," "Ain't I'm a Dog" (love that crazy syntax!) and "D.W.I." state the Brothers' case with conviction and excitement.

With Evan Johns sitting in in place of guitarist Don Leady, **Lucky Lucky Me** is even better—a full menu of high-energy tunes played for keeps. "Fight Fire with Fire," the zydeco-tinged "The Back Door" and a quick history lesson, "Elvis in the Army," are among the best cuts.

The following year, a revised four-man lineup (singer Joe Doerr is gone, leaving his brother Steve in charge; Johns has returned to his own career, replaced by Rick Rawls) whipped off the seemingly effortless **Open All Night**, a splendid slice of tasty archetypal Texas R&B that shimmies and howls with understated eloquence from start to finish. Fans of Dave Edmunds are strongly advised not to miss this one.

The Lerois' independent-label debut, **Check This Action**, is also well worth hearing, and easier to find as a Demon import. [iar]

LET'S ACTIVE
Afoot EP (IRS) 1983
Cypress (IRS) 1984
Big Plans for Everybody (IRS) 1986 •
Every Dog Has His Day (IRS) 1988 •

Cursed by chronic cuteness, North Carolina's Let's Active is probably the most misunderstood of the South's new pop bands. Though dogged by a rosy-cheeked nicest-guys-of-wimp-pop image, they can be downright moody. Led by wunderkind producer/multi-instrumentalist Mitch Easter, the trio began in 1981, but emerged nationally in the wake of R.E.M., whose first two discs Easter co-produced in his now-fabled Drive-In garage studio. Joining that band's label, Let's Active released a six-song EP, **Afoot**, bringing new meaning to such overused pop adjectives as crisp, bright and ringing. All the songs, even those with melancholy lyrics, emerged hook-filled, boppy and ultra-hummable.

But things were not as they seemed. Although perceived as the engineer of the now-sound-of-today in American guitar pop, Easter's own tastes run towards the electronic gadgetry of techno-rock. Also, his two original partners—bassist Faye Hunter and drummer Sara Romweber—were viewed as sidepeople, notwithstanding Easter's egalitarian efforts to counter that impression. In real life, the trio were not just simple, cheerful popsters. Both Easter's love of "sounds" and the band's inner conflicts were explored on **Cypress,** making it deeper and more enduring, though not as immediately winning as **Afoot.** Denser, rambling textural pieces—some wistful, even angry—came to the fore. Few records sound so multi-dimensional, and Let's Active has, for that reason, been tagged psychedelic—they make sounds you can almost touch.

Both Romweber and Hunter subsequently left the band. Easter did shows with other players (including Windbreaker Tim Lee), recording **Big Plans for Everybody** piecemeal with four people, including Hunter and two seemingly permanent sidepeople, Angie Carlson (guitar, keyboards) and Eric Marshall (drums). Far less twinky and hardly cute, **Big Plans** is disturbingly downcast, a doleful version of pop music that isn't about sad things, but still leaves you feeling that way. The album connects emotionally, with offbeat songs that really make an impression. [ep/iar]

See also *Snatches of Pink, Windbreakers.*

KEITH LEVENE'S VIOLENT OPPOSITION
Looking for Something EP (Taang!) 1987

Best known for his five-year membership in Public Image Ltd. (which ended in 1983 when he was wiped off the finished mix of **This Is What You Want,** resulting in the dubious distribution of an alternate edition, **Commercial Zone**), guitarist Levene was also an original Clashman, but left after a handful of gigs. (He also played with Ken Lockie in Cowboys International.)

Levene hasn't been all that visible in recent years, so his second solo EP (the obscure first was issued on Iridescence around 1986)—a four-song 12-inch recorded with members of the Red Hot Chili Peppers, Fishbone and Thelonious Monster—comes as something of a surprise, and not an overly good one. "Taang! Ting" proves that he's still fascinated by reggae and noise, but "I'm Looking for Something" and an impressive copycat version of Hendrix's "If Six Was Nine" smack of deep creative aimlessness. [iar]

See also *Cowboys International, Jah Wobble.*

LEVI AND THE ROCKATS
See *Rockats.*

GRAHAM LEWIS
See *Dome, Wire.*

LEW LEWIS REFORMER
Save the Wail (nr/Stiff) 1979

With a dab more arrogance and perhaps a touch more vocal assertiveness on Lewis' part, there'd be no disputing this LP's place on the shelf next to Dr. Feelgood and the first J. Geils Band LP. Lewis (who worked with the Feelgoods very early on and joined up with guitarist Wilko Johnson after this solo excursion) lacks no authority on blues harp, handily living up to the aspiration announced in the title (as does Rick Taylor's guitar). Gavin Povey (of the Edge and other groups) adds pianistic lubrication to a program that includes astute covers (especially James Brown and—yes!—Status Quo) as well as sharp originals. [jg]

LIJADU SISTERS
Horizons Unlimited (nr/Afrodisia) 1983
Double Trouble (Shanachie) 1984

True eccentrics, the Lijadu twins were among the great unexpected pleasures to arrive via the West's mid-'80s affair with African music. Influenced equally by Fela Anikulapo Kuti's funk-mutated Afro-beat and juju, the Lijadus lay down their sweetly-sung unison vocals over drums that do the talking, and guitars and pianos that provide rhythmic bedrock. Unlike Fela, however, the Lijadus leave politics to politicians, and confine their Yoruban lyrics to such subjects as heart and home, kin and country. [rg]

LILIPUT
Liliput (nr/Rough Trade) 1982
Some Songs (nr/Rough Trade) 1983

Formerly known as Kleenex, with a batch of 45s under that name, the three Swiss women in Liliput play a now-popular form of anti-rock characterized by choppy rhythms, harsh melodies and atonal vocals. Amazingly, they exhibit such upbeat enthusiasm in their attack that the music acquires a prickly charm. Hard on the ears, though. [jy]

324

LIME SPIDERS

Slave Girl EP (Big Time) 1986
The Cave Comes Alive! (Virgin) 1987
Volatile (Virgin) 1988 ●

The excellent retro-rock that fills the Lime Spiders' aptly-titled debut album, **The Cave Comes Alive!**, gleefully plunders various '60s punk vaults. Rather than imitating any specific genre, this quartet from Sydney, Australia synthesizes their own version of that musical era with searing guitars, Tony Bambach's exceptional bass work, occasional churning organ, rave-up drumming and Mick Blood's hardy singing. Sketchy but unaffected production allows the group to color their songs (plus a swell cover of Cream's "NSU" and a couple of more obscure non-originals) in different shades of black leather, dayglo green and deep purple.

Slave Girl is a compilation of early Australian 45s.   [tr]

ERIK LINDGREN

See *Birdsongs of the Mesozoic, Space Negros.*

ARTO LINDSAY/AMBITIOUS LOVERS

Envy (Editions EG) 1984

AMBITIOUS LOVERS

Greed (Virgin) 1988 ●

Lindsay, an American who grew up in Brazil, came to New York in the mid-'70s intent on becoming an artist. Only later did he adopt music as his medium and develop a unique percussive style of singing and playing guitar—generally around the beat, seldom on it—and no melodies, thank you. His guitar is untuned; his voice strains to deliver its quota of sounds. (Lindsay's two main vocal influences are James Brown and the sound of people screwing.) In assembling the Ambitious Lovers, Lindsay balances the electronic expertise of Peter Scherer with Brazilian percussionists and injects himself as the catalyst, with help from chum Mark Miller of the Toy Killers.

On their debut outing, Lindsay and five Lovers recapitulate his career—the tight, anti-melodic structures of DNA, the charging funk-noise of the Golden Palominos—yet deliver something new as well. "Let's Be Adult" is an unabashed dancefloor move and, on "Dora," Lindsay turns crooner, caressing a soulful melody anyone could hum. The catch is that it's in Portuguese—oh, that Arto! Lindsay's words are tantalizingly oblique, but there's nothing oblique about his record's lusty cry for recognition.

Only Lindsay and keyboardist Scherer remain in the two-man Ambitious Lovers who recorded **Greed**, although John Zorn, Vernon Reid and Naná Vasconcelos are among those making musical contributions. Still frequently spattered with nutty noises, the album is surprisingly accessible; Arto's singing (again in English and Portuguese) rarely requires listener indulgence. So if "King" contains some impressive chicken squawk guitar and a houseful of Latin percussion instruments, the song being conveyed is reasonably mainstream. Whether **Greed** is viewed as a commercial compromise or a more subtly subversive undertaking than the first LP, the mixture of normalcy and extremism provides it with fascinating dynamic tension.   [mf/iar]

See also *DNA, Golden Palominos, Lounge Lizards, Love of Life Orchestra.*

LINES

Therapy (nr/Red-Fresh) 1981
Ultramarine (nr/Red) 1983

A quest for creativity or self-indulgence of the highest order? Four Londoners construct rudimentary songs (actually just riffs, they're so skeletal) over repetitive drum rhythms with spare bass, guitar, vocal and trumpet accompaniment. Some are outré adventures (like a ragaesque track that sounds as though it was performed by bees), others more conventional, though the fragile vocals are mostly blurred by echo. "Searching . . . for some jewel of the mind we hope that we'll never find." *Please,* look elsewhere.   [jg]

JAH LION

See *Lee Perry.*

LIQUID LIQUID

Liquid Liquid EP (99) 1981
Successive Reflexes EP (99) 1981
Optimo EP (99) 1983

Along with labelmates ESG, Liquid Liquid exemplified the minimalist funk movement that swept New York's music underground in 1981. The band's impressive five-song debut (one side recorded live) fuses metalphones with congas, marimba and other percussive gadgetry to create hypnotic urban-tribal funk. Except for the vocals, that goal is realized. **Successive Reflexes** also works, although full-scale production values alter the previously skeletal sound.

Optimo—four more songs on another 12-inch—continues the rhythmic intensity, and is specially notable for "Cavern," an insidious and lengthy bass/drums groove that was later adopted as the musical basis for Grandmaster Flash & Melle Mel's "White Lines (Don't Don't Do It)." [gf/iar]

LITTLE BO BITCH
Little Bo Bitch (nr/Cobra) 1979
LONELY BOYS
The Lonely Boys (Harvest) 1979

A rare instance of an American improvement on a British album. Although this fresh-faced band's name and LP title was originally Little Bo Bitch, their US label wisely insisted on changing both. Overlooked in the imbroglio, unfortunately, was the record itself: competent non-wuss power pop with some amusing and memorable tunes, among them "Annoying All the Neighbours" which happily recalls the Members' early rabble-rousing. Andy Arthurs' production makes it all sound good. An album worth picking up in a bargain bin. [iar]

LITTLE BOB STORY
High Time (Fr. Crypto) 1976
Off the Rails (nr/Chiswick) 1977
Little Bob Story (Fr. Crypto) 1978
Come On See Me (Fr. RCA) 1978
Live (Fr. RCA) 1979
Light of My Town (Fr. RCA) 1980

France's Little Bob Story play a spectacular blend of R&B, rock'n'roll and blues, mixing up well-chosen classics and credible originals (all in English) for a hot'n'sweaty Stones-influenced good time. Although plainly tradition-minded, they somehow became involved in the London punk scene just as it was getting underway in 1976, cutting singles and a 1977 album for Chiswick, the first British indie label.

High Time, recorded as a quartet, features smokin' versions of "Lucille" (Chuck Berry), "I'm Crying" (Animals), "It's All Over Now, Baby Blue" (Bob Dylan) and "You'll Be Mine" (Willie Dixon) as well as five numbers written by singer Bob Piazza, a

Gallic fireplug with a touch of Rod Stewart in his voice.

Off the Rails, produced in England by Sean Tyla, adds a second guitarist to the lineup, and consists almost entirely of original material. **Little Bob Story** is a collection of singles, including "Don't Let Me Be Misunderstood" and "Tobacco Road," both of which predate the debut LP.

The excellent live album was recorded in London but includes a Springsteen cover ("Seaside Bar Song"); on **Light of My Town**, a new keyboard player and guitarist, plus guest saxophonist John Earl, make for increased sophistication (but no loss in excitement) on a full slate of originals. [iar]

LIVE SKULL
Live Skull EP (Massive) 1984 ●
Bringing Home the Bait (Homestead) 1985
Cloud One (Homestead) 1986
Don't Get Any on You (Homestead) 1987
Dusted (Homestead) 1987 ●

Droning and dragging rusty guitar streaks and deep stormy basslines as dark as bus exhaust, Live Skull combine great grating sheets of guitar shimmer with deliberately monotonous vocals to create swirlingly intense tunes that you couldn't hum or sing along with if a loaded gun were aimed at your head. As part of the New York avant-noisy scene that includes Sonic Youth, Lydia Lunch and the Swans, Live Skull records come complete with creepy lyrics, circular melodies and nod-out drum beats designed to lull your ears into their macabre world.

The guitars-bass-drums-vocals quartet has undergone numerous personnel shifts. Original drummer James Lo was replaced by Rich Hutchins from Ruin; Bostonian Thalia Zedek, who had previously applied her feminist rant'n'roll vocals in Uzi (and, before that, Dangerous Birds), was added to the lineup before **Dusted**. Still, their vision has remained relatively constant.

The quartet plays slow, grinding hypnorock on **Live Skull**; there *are* vocals buried in the mix but you won't notice them much—the relentless wash of semi-organized guitar noise is clearly the band's focal point. The promising **Bringing Home the Bait** features more prominent vocals and livelier tempos; some tracks move along at a good tear. Guitar textures vary from an atonal din to Killing Joke-style ringing quasi-metal; parts of "Skin Job" sound exactly like Hüsker Dü.

Vocals, whether by bassist Marnie Greenholz or guitarists Mark C. and Tom Paine, are all appropriately snarly. Their later work (including the 12-inch "Pusherman" single, a mutant version of a Curtis Mayfield song) is denser and more complex.

The live Live Skull album, **Don't Get Any on You**, was recorded at the end of 1986 in New York prior to Zedek's arrival. [dgs/'e]

LIVING COLOUR
Vivid (Epic) 1988 ●

Led by guitarist and chief composer Vernon Reid (also a music critic and leader of the Black Rock Coalition, the New York music activist organization), Living Colour promises more than it delivers on **Vivid**. The essentially hard-rock album is eyebrow-raising to bigots because the black quartet doesn't match stereotypical preconceptions of "black music"; ironically, one of the few funky moments is contained in a version of Talking Heads' "Memories Can't Wait." If the record's lacking in the catchy tune/riff department, at least the lyrics are far more substantial than most rock'n'roll of this weight, especially the topical ("Cult of the Personality" and "Open Letter to a Landlord") and humorous ("No I'm not gonna rob/beat/rape you, so why you want to give me that Funny Vibe?"). Reid's guitar cuts loose just once (très flash, though); Mick Jagger's guest production of two tracks makes no difference. [jg/iar]

LIZARD
Lizard (Jap. King) 1979

Strangler bassist Jean-Jacques Burnel produced this Tokyo band's first LP in London, and gave it a not-surprisingly bottom-heavy sound. But the comparisons don't end there: Lizard plays synth-laced dance music with simple rhythms and weird vocals (in Japanese). Politically aware, playful, squiggly and dense, Lizard's complex hybrid typifies the fascinating Japanese response to Anglo-American new wave. [iar]

L.L. COOL J
Radio (Def Jam-Columbia) 1985 ●
Bigger and Deffer (Def Jam-Columbia)
1987 ●

Following his electrifying appearance in *Krush Groove* (the film which essentially chronicles the birth of the Def Jam label), young New York rapper L(adies) L(ove) Cool J(ames T. Smith) released **Radio**, a great full-length album ("reduced by Rick Rubin") that promptly went gold. From the monster boombox that gleams on the cover to grooves like "I Can't Live Without My Radio" and "You Can't Dance," L.L. touches all the right cultural totems, delivering his sharp-tongued lines with adolescent urgency and a deliciously snotty attitude. The rhythm tracks are stripped-down and aggressive; raps on familiar subjects sidestep clichés and are clever enough to warrant repeated listening.

The multi-platinum success of L.L.'s second album (billed as **BAD**) proves that his continuing popularity isn't tied to svengali Rubin. **Bigger and Deffer**, produced by L.L. and "the L.A. Posse," draws on redoubtable innovation to diversify itself out of the rap mold. L.L. waxes nostalgic on "Go Cut Creator Go," which uses Chuck Berry guitar edits, and "The Do Wop," an imaginative '50s/'80s hybrid. "I Need Love" is a touchingly romantic ballad with smoothly melodic instrumental backing; "Ahh, Let's Get Ill" makes considerable use of a backing chorus to set off the rapid-fire rap. Meanwhile, back at the same-old-thing ranch, "I'm Bad" picks up on a piece of "The Theme from *Shaft*," "Kanday" touches on classic James Brown and "Get Down" throws the kitchen sink into the hyperactive mix.

Judging by these two impressive records, L.L. Cool J is unquestionably a major talent, a witty and intuitive original who can't be contained by the stylistic strictures that hamstring his less inventive peers. [iar]

RICHARD LLOYD
Alchemy (Elektra) 1979
Field of Fire (Mistlur-Moving Target) 1985 ●
Real Time (Celluloid) 1987 ●

The former Television guitarist's first solo album is a gem. Assisted by assorted New York scene veterans, Lloyd spins a beautiful, understated web that proves him to be a successful songwriter, a limited but engaging vocalist and a relaxed team player who never hogs the spotlight. The material (especially the wonderful title track and a brilliant ballad, "Misty Eyes") pursues the melodic, sensitive side of late-period Television, ceding all the rough edges and manic intensity to Tom Verlaine.

Six years and several lifetimes later, Lloyd returned from oblivion with an all-new album, recorded in Stockholm with local musicians and first released overseas by a Swedish label. Amazingly, **Field of Fire** is another direct hit: loud, energetic rock with sturdy melodies, intelligent lyrics and confident playing. In spots, Lloyd's singing is too raw-throated to be pleasant, but the material holds up regardless, and the fine guitar work is a fair trade-off. **Field of Fire** bears no resemblance whatsoever to **Alchemy**, but is just as relevant, enjoyable and welcome.

Lloyd recorded the live **Real Time** album in the comfort of TV's old haunt, CBGB, with a bass/drums/guitar trio. The song selection draws from both solo records, adding a few new ones—adapting their diversity without incident—and dredging up the ancient "Fire Engine" for a bracing opening salvo. Clear production highlights Lloyd's upbeat and articulate singing as well as the thoughtful and passionate guitar work. (With the inclusion of three extra songs at the end, the CD runs almost an hour.)   [iar]

LMNOP

LMNOP [tape] (Baby Sue) 1982 + 1984
LMNOP LMNOP [tape] (Baby Sue) 1984
LMNO3 [tape] (Baby Sue) 1985
Elemen Opee Elpee (Baby Sue) 1986
Pony [tape] (Baby Sue) 1988

One-man Atlanta power pop auteur Stephen Fievet *is* LMNOP, although the drummer of a transient performing lineup does back him on **Elemen Opee Elpee**. (Two non-participants are also pictured.) The ambitious twinkster, who also draws and publishes a quarterly Baby Sue magazine and numerous pamphlets, writes stupendous melodies with substantial lyrics and sturdy hooks, and loads up the perky arrangements with rich guitar tracks, adorable vocal harmonies and febrile invention. Except for an occasional descent into corny puns or gratuitous vulgarity (**LMNO3**'s "Sitting on Uranus" scores in both departments), LMNOP/Fievet offers quintessential electro-pop packed with intelligence and enthusiasm.

The first cassette offers early versions of songs (e.g., "Breakfast Cereal," "Hide in Fiction's Hands," "Sandwich Time for the Smaller Children") Fievet re-recorded for inclusion on the two most recent releases. Despite rudimentary sound quality (drums especially suffer), it's a fine starting point.

Following two more cassette albums, LMNOP finally reached vinyl. The unfailingly perky **Elemen Opee Elpee** contains charming and provocative contemplations on mendacity ("Please Believe Me"), conformity ("The Big Ride"), world peace ("Breakfast Cereal") and the study of anthropology ("Comparitive Analysis"), all sparked by crisp production and flawless playing. Anyone fond of Shoes, Advertising, Milk'n' Cookies, Sneakers, Three O'Clock, etc., should find the record a most agreeable treat.

Leading off with the brilliant "Idea," the **Pony** tape (issued on vinyl only in France, by New Rose) contains such idiosyncratic outpourings as "Suggestion for Rock Culture in the 90s" and "Automobile History." Not all the songs are of the same quality as on the first album, but LMNOP fans will hardly be disappointed.   [iar]

(LOS) LOBOS

See *Los Lobos*.

LOCAL HEROES SW9
Drip Dry Zone (nr/Oval) 1980
LOCAL HEROES SW9/KEVIN ARMSTRONG
New Opium/How the West Was Won (nr/Oval) 1981

Unlike the Gang of Four, this English trio (which included future Soft Boy Matthew Seligman) offered radical political perspectives that are neither simplistically axiomatic nor delivered amid musical fireworks. The Heroes' brand of dialectical materialism largely avoids slogans; while its more fluid rhythm'n'pop derives from a similar basis, odd bits of pop and tricky turns here and there replace the Gang's jagged-edge approach.

The first album, **Drip Dry Zone**, is more accessible if less ambitious than the second, which is actually half the Heroes and half a solo outing by guitarist Kevin Armstrong. His side is less precise, more indulgent and meandering, but once acclimated to his tracks' reggaefied lope, you may well find that he's not as spaced out as he seems, but is as engrossing as his group. (After the Local Heroes ended, Armstrong continued to work with Thomas Dolby, who had briefly been a member.)   [jg]

KEN LOCKIE

See *Cowboys International.*

LODGE

See *John Greaves.*

LORA LOGIC

See *Essential Logic.*

LOLITA POP

Lolita Pop (Virgin) 1987 ●

Harmless white-bread techno-rock from the land that brought you Abba. Vocalist Karin Wistrand's faint accent adds personality to her singing, which otherwise suggests a meeker cousin of Natalie Merchant; her four bandmates play a varied mix of dance-rock, melodic pop and catchy synthesizer bop. Accomplished and likable if not especially novel, **Lolita Pop** boasts memorable tracks in "Rain of Days" and the Banglesque "Bang Your Head."   [rj]

LONDON

Animal Games (nr/MCA) 1978

Signed to an unhip label, London cut one lone LP without a proper producer, yet still earned posthumous notoriety when drummer Jon Moss, following stints in the Damned and other bands, surfaced in Culture Club. For London's part, maybe a producer could have sorted out the confusion that dominates **Animal Games**—an angry Pistols/Who wallop on one hand and a strong pop sensibility on the other, plus a vocalist who makes Hugh Cornwell sound like Paul McCartney. Still, two slashing yet tuneful tracks suggest the exciting sound that might have been.   [jg]

LONE JUSTICE

Lone Justice (Geffen) 1985 ●
Shelter (Geffen) 1986 ●

It isn't that Lone Justice's first album is bad (it's not) but the ballyhoo that preceded the LA quartet's debut raised expectations that these frisky countrified rock tunes (Linda Ronstadt on speed, perhaps, or Dolly Parton backed by the Blasters) couldn't possibly satisfy. Maria McKee is an impressive young singer—an energetic, throaty powerhouse with a Southern twang and a slight Patsy Cline catch—and the band is solid

enough, but **Lone Justice**, produced by Jimmy Iovine, doesn't come anywhere near extraordinary. Chief songwriter McKee's "A Good Heart," ridden to the top of the charts in late 1985 by Feargal Sharkey, is far more memorable than anything she penned for her own first record.

Little Steven (a guest on the first album) co-produced **Shelter** with Iovine and Lone Justice, helping the almost-entirely-overhauled group (here a loud, vibrant sextet with ex-Patti Smith Grouper Bruce Brody on keyboards) to nail down a dynamic sound that's something like the articulate passion of an old Van Morrison record, pumped up by McKee's gospelly fervor and walloping modern drums. Van Zandt also co-wrote some of the songs, which show a much subtler author at work. The first album's religious content is supplanted here by heartfelt emotions about love, faith and morality. Without burying her beliefs, McKee universalizes them in ways that don't require listeners to share anything beyond humanity and sensitivity.   [iar]

LONELY BOYS

See *Little Bo Bitch.*

ROY LONEY AND THE PHANTOM MOVERS

Out After Dark (Solid Smoke) 1979
Phantom Tracks (Solid Smoke) 1980
Contents Under Pressure (War Bride) 1981
Having a Rock'n'Roll Party (War Bride) 1982
Fast & Loose (Double Dare) 1983
The Scientific Bombs Away (Aus. Aim) 1988

Singer/guitarist Roy Loney assembled the Phantom Movers four years after he split from the Flamin Groovies in 1975. While the Groovies without Loney turned to merseybeat, Byrds covers and other '60s soundalikes, **Out After Dark** finds him rekindling the pure American rock'n'roll spirit that originally inspired them. Abetted by two ex-Groovies (drummer Danny Mihm and guitarist James Ferrell), Loney's band excels at straightforward, unsophisticated party music made strictly for fun. Loney's return is made more impressive by his singing, which lost nothing during his layoff.

Phantom Tracks consists of smokin' live tracks and new studio cuts that aren't terribly different from the material on **Out After Dark**. The only change worth noting is that about half of the **Phantom Tracks** are out-

and-out rockabilly; **Out After Dark**, while rooted in rockabilly, is contemporary-sounding rock'n'roll.

Contents Under Pressure, recorded after both Mihm and Ferrell had been replaced, goes off in a number of directions: Yardbirds-type rave-ups, rockabilly, ska, heavy metal and even corporate mush. A total failure.

As the name implies, **Having a Rock'n' Roll Party** is a return to what Loney does best, and the results are accordingly a big improvement over the previous outing. The band even dips into the Groovies' catalogue for "Gonna Rock Tonight" and "Dr. Boogie." Also released in France, **Fast & Loose** features various lineups and includes a version of the Groovies' "Teenage Head."

After a long absence, Loney returned in 1988 with his best record yet, **The Scientific Bombs Away**. What stands out in this jolt of pure manic rock'n'roll is the uniformly strong material and performances, from the hiccupped neo-rockabilly of "Bad News Travels Fast," "Bip Bop Boom" and "Boy Man!" to the modern rock'n'roll of "Ruin Your Shoes," "Your Best Friend's Number" and "Nobody" to c-razy novelty numbers like "Here Comes Curly" and "Nervous Slim." Not for normals, to be sure, these songs will make you laugh while they rock the socks off your feet.   [ds]

LONG RYDERS

10-5-60 EP (PVC) 1983 ●
Native Sons (Frontier) 1984 ●
State of Our Union (Island) 1985
Two Fisted Tales (Island) 1987 ●

TOM STEVENS

Points of View EP (Pulse) 1982

Born in the South but assembled in California, the Long Ryders (who broke up around the end of 1987) color mild '60s revivalism with country stylings (steel guitar, autoharp, mandolin, etc.) on the five-song **10-5-60** EP, produced by Earle Mankey. Pleasant but too easygoing to be earthshaking, the foursome took care of that business on **Native Sons**, a stirring dose of memorable and unpretentious country-rock that incorporates **Highway 61** Dylan, paisley pop, Kingston Trio balladry and wild rock'n'roll. A guest vocal appearance by Gene Clark legitimizes the Long Ryders' spiritual update of the Byrds' pioneering hybrid.

The major-label **State of Our Union**,

however, is a big disappointment, an occasionally corny collection of weak melodies, inane lyrics and misguided arrangements. The Ryders seem to have been fooled by their own image. "Looking for Lewis and Clark" is sung in a pathetically bad monotone; other tunes which attempt to align the band with American populist sentiment are only slightly better. As produced in England by Will Birch, it sounds good in spots, but heavy-handedness is clearly no asset.

The Long Ryders found solid footing again with the less selfconscious **Two Fisted Tales**, an enjoyable album nicely produced in a variety of appealing styles by Ed Stasium. The writing is back up to snuff and the natural-sounding presentation makes the group's ethical culture far more palatable. One-song studio visits each by the Bangles and David Hidalgo (Los Lobos) are unneeded but unobtrusive—these boys can handle the job nicely by themselves.

On his early solo EP, bassist Tom Stevens (joined by two sidemen) plays guitar and sings half a dozen original melodic pop songs that wouldn't fit the band's format but are quite appealing on their own.   [iar]

See also *Danny & Dusty.*

LORDS OF THE NEW CHURCH

Lords of the New Church (IRS) 1982
Is Nothing Sacred? (IRS) 1983
The Method to Our Madness (IRS) 1984
Killer Lords (IRS) 1985
Live at the Spit (nr/Illegal) 1988

Formed by ex-Dead Boy Stiv Bator (following a solo turn and the developmental Wanderers, which must be where he left "s" from his surname) with ex-Damned/Tanz der Youth guitarist Brian James, ex-Sham 69/Wanderers bassist Dave Tregunna and ex-Barracudas drummer Nicky Turner—what a pedigree!—the Lords emerged with a fully realized debut album that draws on their individual and collective strengths. Dense and powerful, with Bator's sneering whine setting the tone and attitude, the Lords combine '60s punk with '80s apocalyptics to create an original sound that updates the Stooges for a post-punk world without taming their outrage. Only a few awful, indulgent lyrics (one song attempts a tribute to the New York Dolls by merely stringing song titles together) detract from the record's dark power.

Many took exception to the first LP's claustrophobic, murky production; **Is Nothing Sacred?** substitutes a livelier, crisper swirl, with keyboards and horns contrasting the band's throaty roar. Thus armed, the Lords unfortunately ran out of material after the first song. Following the excellent "Dance with Me" (take that, Bauhaus!), it's straight down the songwriting slope, stopping off only briefly to ram through the Grass Roots' venerable "Live for Today" with no audible purpose. As a soundtrack for a gothic punk horror movie, the Lords' second album gets the ambience right, but that's all.

The third album hits a fair compromise, modulating both the volume and the velocity to lighten the mood and cut the stylishness. As a result, **The Method to Our Madness** resembles a cross between **Raw Power** and **Rebel Yell**. It's the band's least distinctive but most popular-sounding record, with "Murder Style," "Method to My Madness" (featuring a funny spoken interjection by IRS owner Miles Copeland) and a pretty ballad, "When Blood Runs Cold," to recommend it. By sacrificing their mystery and danger, the Lords of the New Church are revealed as nice guys after all.

The **Killer Lords** compilation includes not only remixes of essential album tracks but a hysterically nasty mugging of Madonna's "Like a Virgin," a solid and straight reading of John Fogerty's "Hey Tonight," and ex-Advert Tim Smith's duff but amusing "Lord's Prayer." [iar]

LORRIES

See *Red Lorry Yellow Lorry*.

LOS LOBOS

. . . and a Time to Dance (Slash) 1983
How Will the Wolf Survive? (Slash-Warner Bros.) 1984 ●
By the Light of the Moon (Slash-Warner Bros.) 1987 ●

VARIOUS ARTISTS

La Bamba (Slash-Warner Bros.) 1987 ●

Lacking serious competition and buoyed by the enormous success of *La Bamba,* Los Lobos are the leading Mexican-American rock band of the '80s; it wouldn't matter if there were contenders for that honor, however—these four East Los Angelenos (plus ex-Blaster saxman Steve Berlin, who joined in time for the second record) are peerless masters of their music. They smoothly incorporate vastly divergent styles—early rock'n' roll, jazz, rockabilly, *norteño,* Tex-Mex folk music—into a colorful patchwork of joyous noise, beautifully displayed on the seven-song **Time to Dance**. From a sharp cover of Ritchie Valens' "Come on, Let's Go" to the infectious, accordion-powered "Let's Say Goodnight," singer/guitarist David Hidalgo leads a spicy romp (in two languages) back and forth across musical borders few can traverse with such ease.

How Will the Wolf Survive? is an occasionally more serious venture, delving into heavy blues ("Don't Worry Baby") and tender social commentary ("Will the Wolf Survive?," subsequently a country hit for Waylon Jennings) as well as finding time for a jolly square dance ("Corrida #1") and an airy instrumental ("Lil' King of Everything"). Hidalgo's plaintive tenor and the group's subtlety and skill make the album immediately likable; depth and variety ensure its enduring pleasure.

Poised on the brink of major stardom, Los Lobos stopped to make a limp mainstream album, **By the Light of the Moon**. Under the usually reliable production direction of T-Bone Burnett, the maturing band sheds its richly complex musical personality for a hodgepodge of assimilationist easy-listening crap and ill-advised stylistic dilettantism. "Prenda del Alma," a traditional Spanish ballad, seems horribly out of place; the gritty "Shakin' Shakin' Shakes," co-written by T-Bone and guitarist Cesar Rosas, belongs on a Blasters or George Thorogood record; "Set Me Free (Rosa Lee)" is a brassy mess with synth drums. Only "My Baby's Gone," a fine Chicago blues, suggests life in the grooves, but it's too little to salvage the record.

The obvious choice to recreate the music for *La Bamba,* a moronic bio-pic about Ritchie Valens' brief life and career, Los Lobos faithfully and enthusiastically re-recorded the highlights of his slim repertoire and vaulted effortlessly into the pop stratosphere. The skadillion-selling **La Bamba** soundtrack album contains their renditions of "La Bamba," "Come on, Let's Go," "We Belong Together," "Donna," and four more; Brian Setzer (aping Eddie Cochran) and Marshall Crenshaw (finally succumbing to the temptation to play Buddy Holly) each contribute a track as well. [iar]

LOUNGE LIZARDS
The Lounge Lizards (EG) 1981
Live from the Drunken Boat (Europa) 1983
Live 79/81 [tape] (ROIR) 1985
Live in Tokyo Big Heart (Island) 1986
No Pain for Cakes (Island) 1987 ●
TEO MACERO/LONDON PHILHARMONIC ORCHESTRA/LOUNGE LIZARDS
Fusion (Europa) 1984
EVAN LURIE
Happy? Here? Now? (Bel. Crépuscule) 1985
JOHN LURIE
Stranger Than Paradise (Enigma) 1986 ●
Down by Law (Invitation-Capitol) 1988

Despite some interesting personnel in their initial lineup and a memorable debut album, New York's Lounge Lizards will never be remembered as anything more than an interesting footnote in rock's history. This has less to do with the "fake jazz" label they took for themselves than with the purely social nature of their rock connection: they played jazz-as-exotica to a hip downtown rock-club audience.

Nonetheless, **The Lounge Lizards** remains a minor masterpiece for the way it remains true to its Monk-derived jazz (including two covers of Thelonious Sphere himself) by subverting it still further with Arto Lindsay's atonal guitar playing. Whatever Lindsay may lack as a conventional guitarist, he makes up with an innate rhythmic savvy that never fails to entertain and engage. Ex-Feelies drummer Anton Fier, as a rock player learning the jazz ropes, approaches his kit a bit cerebrally, but ironic detachment was never far from the Lizards' agenda. Saxman John Lurie's compositions here turn out to have been his best, alternating a loving, melodic lilt with film noir-ish exhilaration.

By the time of **Live from the Drunken Boat**, the Lurie brothers (John and pianist Evan) were playing with a different and less interesting band; the results are slight and forgettable. The Lizards joined their producer, Teo Macero (veteran producer/arranger of many a distinguished jazz record), as he indulged his post-romantic orchestral fantasies with the London Philharmonic on **Fusion**, an uninteresting '50s "third stream" symphonic jazz composition.

The **Live 79/81** cassette features sharp performances from New York (including their first gig), Cleveland, London and Berlin. The core of the debut lineup (the Luries, Fier and bassist Steve Piccolo) remains intact, but two other guitarists besides Lindsay divvy up the tracks. Nine originals, plus covers of Thelonious Monk's "Epistrophy" and Earle Hagen's classic "Harlem Nocturne."

John Lurie went on to star in and score Jim Jarmusch's film *Stranger Than Paradise*, the album of which devotes a side to an unrelated Lurie dance piece called "The Resurrection of Albert Ayler." His next multimedia collaboration with Jarmusch was *Down by Law:* Lurie co-starred in the picture and composed the score, which he then released as an album. **Down by Law** contains his soundtrack music for that film—played by most of the Lounge Lizards and even alumnus Arto Lindsay—as well as music done for a Betty Gordon film entitled *Variety*. Evan recorded a solo piano record. Lindsay and Fier, who left the Lizards after the first album, formed the Golden Palominos and have done many other interesting projects as well. In mid-'86, the Lounge Lizards (i.e., the Luries) were signed to Island.

A new incarnation of the Lounge Lizards—the Luries bolstered by another saxophonist (Roy Nathanson) and a trombonist (Curtis Fowlkes), plus a rhythm section and guitarist Marc Ribot—has actually made it intact through two releases. While the one-show **Live in Tokyo** continues in the Lizards' almost-jazz tradition, the in-studio **No Pain for Cakes** opens up their frame of reference to include influences like Erik Satie and Kurt Weill. And the group breaks the word barrier with John Lurie's distinctive voice on "Bob and Nico" and the anecdotal "Where Were You." What won't these crazy cats do next? [mf/dgs/si]

See also *Golden Palominos, Arto Lindsay.*

BUDDY LOVE
Buddy Love (Davco) 1983

Smart, varied, funny and memorable power pop and light rock from Long Island, New York. The unctuously-dressed pseudonymous Buddy Love and his now-defunct combo play everything from a Gary Glitter cover version to truly touching ultra-melodic originals that mine a wide variety of pop and rock sources. **Buddy Love** is an unassuming—but great—record. [iar]

LOVE AND ROCKETS

Seventh Dream of Teenage Heaven
(nr/Beggars Banquet) 1985 (Beggars
Banquet-RCA) 1988 ●
Express (Beggars Banquet-Big Time) 1986 ●
Earth-Sun-Moon (Beggars Banquet-Big Time)
1987 ●

The group that refused to die! Love and Rockets, named after the Hernandez brothers' underground comic, reunites three-fourths of Bauhaus, which was supposed to have broken up in 1983. First, guitarist Daniel Ash and drummer Kevin Haskins formed Tones on Tail. Then bassist David J., following his stint with the Jazz Butcher, joined them, whereupon they ditched the only non-Bauhaus alumnus and transmuted into Love and Rockets.

The absence of doom crooner Peter Murphy allows his three former bandmates to avoid any trace of his poseur pretensions on **Seventh Dream of Teenage Heaven**, an odd, unnervingly varied album. There's folk-rock, funk, ominous rock and a number that resembles the Moody Blues crossed with Bow Wow Wow—a huge, boomy drum sound smothered with what sounds like a mellotron and close harmony vocals. "Saudade," a similar (albeit instrumental) piece, blends aspects of New Order and the Dream Academy. The faintly Beatlesque, pretty "Haunted When the Minutes Drag" suggests an '80s take on Donovan in a droney acoustic mode. Neat record—wonder what it all means. (The British CD adds three tracks.) The belated American issue adds "Inside the Outside" and contains a remix of "Dog-End of a Day Gone By."

There's less stylistic dilettantism on the fine **Express**, although disparate variety is still among the trio's hallmarks. To wit, "All in My Mind" appears on one side as evanescent folk-rock and on the other as a dirgey sigh with echoed snare drum accents. "Kundalini Express" updates the old train gambit with modern ideas; "Yin and Yang the Flower Pot Man" puts another Moody Bluesy melody to a galloping beat; "Love Me" has dubwise backing and whispered vocals. Love and Rockets seem to be charting out their terrain ever more clearly, concentrating on genres that work for them. (The US edition adds the band's version of "Ball of Confusion.")

After two good records, the self-produced **Earth-Sun-Moon** is an enigmatic bummer, a dull and often murky digression which buries its few promising ideas in echo and over-dubbed guitar tracks. Ash's flaky lyrics don't help, either. "Welcome Tomorrow" is nonsensical; "The Telephone Is Empty" makes about as much sense as one might imagine from the title; the boppy "Lazy" is simplistic drivel ("A kid like you/had to send me away/left me on my back/I had a heart attack"). The album's funniest track is a Jethro Tull parody, "No New Tale to Tell." **Earth-Sun-Moon** has the earmarks of a record cut reluctantly and/or without benefit of ideas. A shame. (The CD adds a "slow version" of the LP's lead-off track, "Mirror People.") [iar]

LOVE DELEGATION

See *Fleshtones*.

DAMIEN LOVELOCK

See *Celibate Rifles*.

LOVE OF LIFE ORCHESTRA

Extended Niceties EP (Infidelity) 1980
Geneva (Infidelity) 1980

Love of Life Orchestra was created by Peter Gordon (sax, keyboards, composition) and David Van Tieghem, a talented, smart-aleck avant-garde percussionist with ties to new music composer Steve Reich. Both have gone on to greater fame as elder statesmen of the downtown music scene in New York, but these early works stand as an important developmental chapter.

Extended Niceties debuted LOLO's avant-disco in fine form. "Beginning of the Heartbreak"/"Don't, Don't" is quite powerful, pushed along by a vividly colored piano and the distinctive, kinetic rhythm guitars of guests Arto Lindsay and David Byrne.

Geneva succumbs to blandness as Lindsay and Byrne are supplanted by less-inspired full-timers and Gordon attempts to spread his clichéd writing over a longplayer. Exceptions: "Revolution Is Personal" and "Lament," which offers the rarity of a truly interesting drum solo. [mf]

See also *Peter Gordon, David Van Tieghem*.

LOVE TRACTOR

Love Tractor (DB) 1982 ●
Around the Bend (DB) 1983 ●
'Til the Cows Come Home EP (DB-Landslide)
1984

Wheel of Pleasure (DB) 1985
This Ain't No Outerspace Ship (Big Time) 1987 •

Like the Raybeats and others, Georgia's Love Tractor sticks (not quite exclusively) to instrumental rock'n'roll, with reference points in the non-vocal golden rock era of two decades ago. Unlike the Raybeats, they're not so style-conscious, so you get far fewer sly references to the Ventures and other camp heroes, and more outright flirtation with fusion and cocktail lounge muzaks. Though the material is inconsistent, **Love Tractor** never lacks poise.

The quartet exhibits new polish on **Around the Bend**, seeking to avoid stagnation by adding vocals on a few tracks. Not very memorable ones, though. The diverting **'Til the Cows Come Home** EP fails to answer questions about Tractor's future path, since it's a compilation of odds and ends. A 1988 DB CD contains both **Love Tractor** and **Around the Bend**.

Produced (and played on) by ex-Raybeat Pat Irwin, **Outerspace Ship** sees the lads plunging wholeheartedly into vocals, with chirpy singing (led by guitarist Michael Richmond) that's a natural extension of their twinkly guitars. Breezy rockers like "Beatle Boots" and "Cartoon Kiddies" are charming enough but such ephemera ultimately seems like a dubious achievement. When it's done, you'll feel like you've pigged out on cotton candy. Weird cover: a semi-funky take on the Gap Band's "Party Train." [jy]

See also *Method Actors*.

LENE LOVICH

Stateless (Stiff-Epic) 1979 •
Flex (Stiff-Epic) 1980
New Toy EP (Stiff-Epic) 1981
No-Man's-Land (Stiff-Epic) 1982

Lene Lovich helped pave the way for female vocalists to use as many vocal eccentricities as their male counterparts, to be unafraid to play a solo instrument (Lovich's is sax), and—as important as anything else—to feel free to adopt and project personae that are obviously feminine yet neither super vampish nor mellow/submissive.

During her erratic and sporadic career, the Detroit native has made a batch of good tracks, but has yet to deliver a whole satisfying LP. This seems to stem from the fact that she and husband/guitarist/songwriting partner Les Chappell are not exactly prolific; even with choice selection of other people's

material (including songs given to her expressly by Thomas Dolby and Fingerprintz's Jimme O'Neill) she has released only three full albums in a decade.

Stateless, her debut LP, sports a pair of great singles: "Lucky Number" and "Say When." But despite her distinctive chirp'n' yodel vocals, the keyboard-dominated arrangements and the blend of great old American pop-rock with spooky occult and Balkan overtones, she needed more consistent material. Better production also might have helped; the US version has a reshuffled song order and a much-needed remix.

Flex has a more modern studio sound and uses synthesizers, adding more varied vocal colors (and emphasizing the distinctive deep male backing voices). The songs are more consistent, yet even the standouts, original and otherwise, don't match those on **Stateless**. The expansion of Lovich's religio-mystical worldview only partially compensates.

New Toy, a foretaste of **No-Man's-Land**, is a single expanded to EP length; only the title track is truly worthy of any attention. Surprisingly, although two of the songs appear in slightly altered versions on the subsequent LP, "New Toy" itself doesn't. Lacking it, **No-Man's-Land** is another half-good LP, with Lovich's appropriation of "It's You, Only You" (from Holland's Meteors) again demonstrating her ability to bring out melody and create her own airy, eerie atmosphere. Lovich has not released an album since. [jg]

See also *Sinceros*.

NICK LOWE

Jesus of Cool (nr/Radar) 1978
Pure Pop for Now People (Columbia) 1978
Labour of Lust (Columbia) 1979
Nick the Knife (Columbia) 1982
The Abominable Showman (Columbia) 1983
16 All-Time Lowes (nr/Demon) 1984 •
Nicks Knack (nr/Demon) 1986 •
Pinker and Prouder Than Previous (Columbia) 1988 •

NICK LOWE AND HIS COWBOY OUTFIT

Nick Lowe and His Cowboy Outfit (Columbia) 1984
The Rose of England (Columbia) 1985

Once a teen dream with London-area pop group Kippington Lodge, then a pub-rocker with Brinsley Schwarz, Nick Lowe burst into new wave as a pop mastermind who could give you anything you wanted, and to heck with social significance. The cover of his first solo album graphically displays his kaleidoscopic versatility in six different poses/personae, all fairly sleazy. Lowe's tunes, though, are invariably well-crafted, charming (within a '60s pop context) and offbeat enough to hold attention.

For its US release, the wildly diverse **Jesus of Cool** was retitled **Pure Pop for Now People** by corporate wimps. Besides a well-scrambled track order, **Pure Pop** substitutes the smooth "They Called It Rock" for **Jesus'** stompy "Shake and Pop" (in fact, the same song with a different arrangement) and adds "Rollers Show," a parodic tribute to the Bay City Rollers. The US album also inserts Lowe's studio recording of "Heart of the City" (the B-side of Stiff's first-ever release) in place of the searing live version on the British record. (The same live recording, but with a Dave Edmunds vocal replacing Lowe's, appears on Edmunds' **Tracks on Wax 4**.)

Labour of Lust is a calmer collection, sticking mostly to medium-tempo rockers played by the dependable Rockpile (Lowe, Edmunds, drummer Terry Williams and guitarist Billy Bremner). Instead of stylistic variety, Lowe concentrates on love songs, both silly ("Switch Board Susan," "American Squirm") and sincere ("Without Love," "You Make Me"). The album also contains his first (and so far only) US hit single, "Cruel to Be Kind."

Following **Labour of Lust**, Lowe put his solo career on hold to assist Edmunds and play in Rockpile. He resumed with **Nick the Knife**, not surprisingly filled with more foot-tapping love songs. His emotional palette had broadened to include unhappy ("My Heart Hurts," "Too Many Teardrops," "Raining Raining") as well as happy ("Queen of Sheba," "Couldn't Love You Any More Than I Do") subject matter. And of course there are the obvious musical/lyrical borrowings Lowe-watchers enjoy getting incensed about.

The Abominable Showman is fast out of the starting gate with "We Want Action" and "Raging Eyes." After that, Lowe turns surprisingly serious on tracks like "Time Wounds All Heels" and "Wish You Were Here." The album closes on a curious (for Lowe) note: "How Do You Talk to an Angel" even has strings.

He returned to form on **Nick Lowe and His Cowboy Outfit** (which actually features almost the same band as on the preceding album). Once again, Nick essays a variety of pop styles, from Tex-Mex ("Half a Boy and Half a Man") to '50s instrumental ("Awesome"). Don't take the LP title too seriously; on a good day, Lowe takes nothing seriously.

Maintaining the same lineup but cobbling together a far better set of tunes, Lowe made **The Rose of England** with a lot more evident effort. While the variety is impressive, the lack of consistent quality mainly comes down to specific songs. Winners: Costello's "Indoor Fireworks" (predating its appearance on **King of America**), John Hiatt's "She Don't Love Nobody" and Lowe's own "Lucky Dog," "The Rose of England" and "(Hope to God) I'm Right." A new treatment of "I Knew the Bride," produced and performed by Huey Lewis and band, is unsettlingly anxious but reasonably entertaining; a few other items are throwaways or sappy ballads. **The Rose of England** offers some of the deepest, most reassuring music Lowe's done in ages.

16 All-Time Lowes is a compilation of his early solo work, from "So It Goes" and "Heart of the City" through "When I Write the Book." Of special interest: precise musician credits for each track. Statisticians (and those who feel Lowe's quality level has been steadily waning) should note that almost half of these songs appeared on his first album. **Nicks Knack** is a complementary collection of another 16 tracks, including Rockpile's "Now and Always," a rare B-side ("Basing Street") and a balanced selection of mostly second-string material from all of Lowe's pre-Cowboy Outfit albums.

Pinker and Prouder Than Previous was recorded in pieces during 1986 and '87 in London and Texas, with a host of familiar friends, including John Hiatt, Paul Carrack, Terry Williams, Martin Belmont and even ex-bandmate Edmunds, who produced one song. Reclaiming the straightforward one-take-sound R&B/pop magic he has imparted to many protégés, Lowe comes out pub-rocking here, positively glowing with casual aplomb. Besides the familiar helpings of spicy rock'n'roll and smooth pop, he dishes out a bit of greasy roadhouse R&B, some maudlin but touching balladeering, even spots of cajun and demi-reggae, without a hint of selfconsciousness or effort. (The echoes of Rockpile are everywhere.) Minor criticisms: the sequencing doesn't really work, the abrupt fades are disconcerting and a few of the tunes (e.g., Graham Parker's "Black Lincoln Continental") don't rate. [si/iar]

See also *Dave Edmunds, Rockpile.*

LOW NUMBERS

Twist Again with the Low Numbers (Rhino) 1978

The Low Numbers were an ad hoc studio invention attempting a conceptual exercise in Brit-pop nostalgia. The songs on this full-length in-joke—eight originals plus a quartet of very hip covers (has anyone else ever recorded Pete Townshend's never-legally-released "Early Morning Cold Taxi"?)—may lack polish, but tongue-in-cheek lyrics and '60s-styled music makes it good low-rent entertainment for Anglophile smart-alecks. [iar]

THE LUCY SHOW

The Lucy Show EP (nr/Piggy Bank) 1984
. . . undone (A&M) 1985
Mania (Big Time) 1986 ●

This British quartet plays rich, mellifluous songs which owe more than a little to the Comsat Angels and early Cure. On **. . . undone**, a fine debut, they weave nice webs of layered guitar, subtly accentuated with piano and occasional synth, but the dynamics and textures range from A to B. Despite several memorable songs, especially the opening "Ephemeral (This Is No Heaven)," the Lucy Show don't give the impression their hearts are in it.

Some of them definitely didn't have their hearts in it. **Mania** finds the group reduced to a duo of Mark Bandola (vocals, guitar, keyboards) and Rob Vandeven (vocals, bass) with some sidemen. The sonic palette is nicely augmented and the tempos varied with effective results; producer John Leckie (XTC, Bill Nelson, Simple Minds, the Fall) brings the drums up to add more punch to the atmospherics and songs don't meander around the way they tend to on the previous LP. Although there are no major changes, the subtle improvements on **Mania** make the Lucys a band to watch. [dgs]

LUNA TWIST

Luna Twist (nr/Statik) 1983

Commercial modern rock from Belgium: Luna Twist is essentially interchangeable with Wang Chung, the Fixx and a hundred others. The only notable break in the routine here comes from extraneous sounds, including free-form sax riffs, sequencer bursts, jet noises and vocal shrieks, which merely serve as distractions. Like their equally indistinguishable competition, Luna Twist's songs are fine, their musicianship faultless and the whole exercise thoroughly redundant. [iar]

LYDIA LUNCH

Queen of Siam (ZE) 1980 (nr/Widowspeak) 1985 (Widowspeak) 1988
13.13 (Ruby) 1982 (Widowspeak) 1988
The Agony Is the Ecstacy EP (nr/4AD) 1982
In Limbo EP (nr/Doublevision) 1984 (nr/Widowspeak) 1986
The Uncensored Lydia Lunch [tape] (nr/Widowspeak) 1985
Hysterie (nr/Widowspeak) 1986 (CD Presents) 1986
Honeymoon in Red (Widowspeak) 1987

LYDIA LUNCH/MICHAEL GIRA

Hard Rock [tape] (Ecstatic Peace) 1984

LYDIA LUNCH AND LUCY HAMILTON

The Drowning of Lucy Hamilton (nr/Widowspeak) 1985

Lydia Lunch's career since deep-sixing Teenage Jesus and the Jerks has been an unpredictable path governed by boredom, sarcasm, romance, perversity and whatever musicians or collaborators are convenient at the time. **Queen of Siam** proves, at the very least, that she can do more than just scream (although her version of the Classics IV hit, "Spooky," shows she ain't exactly Beverly Sills, either). Half of the album consists of muted, somber variations on her Teenage Jesus fear-and-suffering dirges, but the real surprises are songs like "Lady Scarface," in which the big band arrangements (by *Flintstones*-theme composer Billy Ver Planck) turn Lunch's wry asides into a Billie Holliday nightmare.

On the heels of **Queen of Siam**'s release, Lunch formed 8-Eyed Spy with, among others, ex-Contortions bassist George Scott, drummer Jim Sclavunos and saxophonist Pat Irwin, who had worked on Lunch's solo album. The lifespan of the group set a pattern for Lydia's ventures: assemble a band, work with it for a while, disband it when she got "bored"; six months later some vinyl would appear. (One conglomeration, an alleged blues abortion called the Devil Dogs, didn't last long enough to be documented.)

13.13., concocted with a trio of ex-Weirdos, was hypothetically an attempt at new psychedelia; actually it revived the grind-and-caterwaul of Teenage Jesus as filtered through **Metal Box**-era PiL, all deviant guitar and rolling rhythms. Like her previous stuff, it manages to be simultaneously fascinating and annoying.

Lunch hung out in Europe for a while with Nick Cave and the Birthday Party, a sympathetic association reflected in a number of recordings. **The Agony Is the Ecstacy** (a record which she splits—one side each—with the Party) captures an impromptu London gig featuring Banshees bassist Steve Severin on feedback guitar and is easily one of the most extreme Lunches to date. On the other hand, a 12-inch single done with Party guitarist Rowland S. Howard of "Some Velvet Morning" (an old Lee Hazelwood song—Nancy Sinatra has been a longtime touchstone for Lydia) recalls the softer moments of **Queen of Siam**.

In Limbo is a six-track disc with a supporting crew that includes Thurston Moore of Sonic Youth and former Contortion/Bush Tetra Pat Place. With snail's-pace tempos, Moore's shards of acrid, harsh guitar and Lunch's trademark ululations, it's typically rough going, but recommended for anyone who has trouble contending with an entire album's worth of her clamor. **The Drowning of Lucy Hamilton** is the soundtrack to a film (*The Right Side of My Brain*) starring Jim (Foetus) Thirlwell and Henry Rollins. Lucy Hamilton herself is actually Lydia's collaborator on the record, which consists of eerie instrumentals orchestrated with piano, honking bass clarinet and guitars that sound like they're being played with ice picks and hedge clippers. Something rather different for Lunch, and less like background music than most soundtracks. **The Uncensored** tape is all spoken-word; Lydia shares another spoken-word release, the cassette-only **Hard Rock**, with Michael Gira of the Swans.

Hysterie is an ambitious ten-year two-disc career-spanning compilation, starting with Teenage Jesus, recapitulating 8-Eyed Spy and the little-known Beirut Slump, and winding up with three recent collaborations (die Haut, a pre-These Immortal Souls group and something called Sort Sol).

There's an interesting story to **Honeymoon in Red**, which was recorded with members of the Birthday Party, Thurston Moore and Genevieve McGuckin (now in These Immortal Souls) in 1982 and '83 as a Birthday Party album. When that band split up shortly thereafter, the record was shelved. After being tinkered around with for several years, it was finally remixed by Clint (Foetus) Ruin and released on Lydia's label. (The only BPers whose names appear on the record are Howard and the late Tracy Pew; Nick Cave and Harvey are credited pseudonymously.) Lunch and the Party are/were obvious soulmates, but her input here is too often predominant; her penchant for slow tempos dilutes the band's brutal strength. Not a great album by any means, but of definite interest to fans of those involved.

Besides her recording career, Lunch has appeared in underground films and collaborated with Exene Cervenka (of X) on a book of poetry. Throughout, she continues to project the most negative charisma since Johnny Rotten.   [rnp/dgs]

EVAN LURIE, JOHN LURIE
See *Lounge Lizards*.

LURKERS
Fulham Fallout (nr/Beggars Banquet) 1978
God's Lonely Men (nr/Beggars Banquet) 1979
Greatest Hit (nr/Beggars Banquet) 1980
Final Vinyl EP (nr/Clay) 1984

PETE STRIDE AND JOHN PLAIN
New Guitars in Town (nr/Beggars Banquet) 1980

Despite the occasional glimmer of greatness, the Lurkers were never much more than a lightweight, second-string punk band, playing simple numbers in a plodding manner over repetitive drum figures. The tantalizing bits suggested a much better band lurking (sorry) inside; the post-split record by southpaw guitarist Pete Stride and part-time Lurker Honest John Plain (otherwise in the Boys) proves that the group was not without talent, but simply lacked the ability to express itself successfully.

Fulham Fallout has the advantage of crystal-clear sound (thanks to producer Mick Glossop) and a few impressive songs ("Ain't Got a Clue," "Shadow"), but suffers from tedium and general punky cloddishness. **God's Lonely Men** seems to employ only one beat; the overbearing rhythm section's dense, muffled pounding gives the record an air of mock metal. Two poppier tracks hint at better things ahead musically, but time had run out for the Lurkers.

Greatest Hit, subtitled **Last Will and Testament ...**, gathers up 12 numbers from the two LPs and adds a half-dozen single sides. Surprisingly enough, it's much better than either of the preceding albums, and has enough fun times to make it a worthwhile investment in low-brow punk. Not essential, but good enough.

The relationship between the Boys and the Lurkers began sometime before the latter broke up—guitarist John Plain appears on two of the **Greatest Hit** tracks, including one called "New Guitar in Town"—so it took only a melding of the two bands to provide backing for the collaborative effort by Stride and Plain. **New Guitars in Town** starts off with a Spectoresque version of Sonny Bono's "Laugh at Me" and gets better from there. Rather than a flashy collection of solos as the title suggests, the two stringleaders show off their singing and songwriting more than guitar pyrotechnics, which remain decidedly in the background. All in all, a delicious collection of rollicking pop-rock, played with spit and spirit.   [iar]

LUXURIA
See *Howard Devoto.*

LYRES
The Lyres EP (Ace of Hearts) 1981
On Fyre (Ace of Hearts) 1984 ●
The Box Set (Fr. New Rose) 1986
Lyres Lyres (Ace of Hearts) 1986 ●
Live at Cantones (Pryct) 1987
A Promise Is a Promise (Ace of Hearts) 1988 ●

After the demise of DMZ—one of Boston's most exciting retro-rock-punk bands—singer/organist Jeff "Mono Mann" Conolly assembled the Lyres to play authentic '60s garage music in the '80s. Once an imitator of his heroes, Conolly has become their equal, and the Lyres' debut 12-inch EP showcases a tough, spirited brand of rock'n'roll that sets the standard to which all other contemporary nostalgic grungophiles must be compared.

On Fyre is simply the genre's apotheosis,

an articulate explosion of colorful organ playing, surging guitars and precisely inexact singing. Drawing on just the right selection of songwriters (Ray and Dave Davies each get tapped once; another esoteric cover revives a song originally recorded by ex-Beatle drummer Pete Best) and adding his own brilliant creations (especially the urgent "Help You Ann," powered by phenomenal tremolo guitar), Conolly leads the Lyres on a nostalgic trip that is utterly relevant to the here and now. The CD, issued several years later, adds eight bonus tunes.

A few moments into the excellent **Lyres Lyres**, Conolly quotes the riff from the Grass Roots' "Let's Live for Today" in "Not Looking Back." There aren't any further citations of that caliber, but the entire record rocks with a mixture of Animalized R&B, touching and melodic barrelhouse pop and raving old-style punk. Danny McCormack's guitar work is spectacular; Conolly's voice has never sounded better. Among the covers this time are a pair by veteran Dutch rocker Wally Tax, an idol of Conolly's; others may be even less familiar to loyal Casey Kasem fans.

Live at Cantones is a compilation of assorted live radio broadcasts that suffers from inconsistent, often inadequate, sound quality.

Never the most prolific group, the Lyres let two years elapse before releasing a new studio album. Just prior to **A Promise Is a Promise**, recorded by the Lyres' thirteenth incarnation (according to Pete Frame's detailed family tree on the gatefold), a three-song 12-inch surfaced, containing "Here's a Heart," a neat merseybeat oldie featuring Stiv Bators, and "Touch," recorded in Holland with Wally Tax. Both of those appear on the flatly-recorded LP, which marks a real departure for the group. "Every Man for Himself" flirts with funk; "Feel Good" is a soulful rocker with a vocal that resembles Percy Faith; "Worried About Nothing" has the rueful tone of acoustic Neil Young. Dispensing with most of the dated stylization for about as modern a sound as a group with prominent Vox organ can get, the energy-spewing album drags in spots but blasts off in others. The CD adds seven live tracks.
                                              [cpl/iar]
See also *Barrence Whitfield and the Savages.*

M M M M M M

M

New York*London*Paris*Munich (Sire) 1979
The Official Secrets Act (Sire) 1980
Famous Last Words (Sire) 1982
High Life Music EP (nr/Swahili-Albion) 1983

M (Robin Scott) may stand in Top 40 history as a glorious one-hit wonder but, oh, what a hit! Easily the highlight of his first LP, "Pop Muzik" combines the moronic appeal of a brilliant semi-electronic novelty record with the sturdy danceability of a hot disco mix. Give this Englishman credit for partially inventing hip-hop and modern electro-pop in one fell swoop. Other cuts on the LP, such as "Cowboys and Indians" and "That's the Way the Money Goes," are just as silly but less immediate, leaving the listener free to observe how much Scott can sing like Bowie.

He shifts gears on **The Official Secrets Act**, playing superficial foolishness against an underlying current of fear; "Join the Party," "Working for the Corporation," "Your Country Needs You" and "Official Secrets" conjure up murky images of a threatening world. Scott clearly derives pleasure from inventing unexpected melodies and bending his tunes with quirky production touches.

On **Famous Last Words** Scott confirms his status as a doodler; no two tunes are alike. Everything's a little odd, but never unpleasantly so. In short, this third LP possesses only the limited value of cleverness in a vacuum. One longs for less calculation, and references beyond the studio.

In 1981, Scott collaborated on an album with Yellow Magic Orchestra keyboardist Ryuichi Sakamoto.   [jy]

See also *Ryuichi Sakamoto.*

SIPHO MABUSE

Sipho Mabuse (Virgin) 1987 ●

British new wave pioneer Martin Rushent co-produced and remixed veteran Soweto singer/drummer Mabuse's first American album, recorded in both Johannesburg and London. Mabuse sings mostly in English on the strongly westernized songs, which blend African percussion styles and sounds with rock guitar, popping fretless bass, funk horns and other dance-ready attributes. "Shikisha" and "Ti Nyanga (African Doctor)" both feature backing by a female vocal group and are the most colorfully appealing tracks here; "Burn Out" (previously issued in the US as a 12-inch from a 1985 import LP), with no African character whatever, is just plain terrible.   [iar]

KIRSTY MACCOLL

Desperate Character (nr/Polydor) 1981

Daughter of folk-music giant Ewan MacColl, singer/songwriter Kirsty cut one great two-sided 45 for Stiff ("They Don't Know"—later an international hit when covered by Tracey Ullman—b/w "Turn My Motor On") that went nowhere, and then scored a major UK hit of her own with the twangy "There's a Guy Works Down the Chip Shop Swears He's Elvis" (included on **Desperate Character** in two versions). For the album, ace sidemen like Billy Bremner, Lew Lewis and Gavin Povey helped her whip up a lively rock/country/pop stew that resembles a female-singer version of Rockpile. With nary a bad track in the bunch, **Desperate Character** cries out for a follow-up.

Still no second LP, but the story continues in 1984, when Kirsty married producer

339

Steve Lillywhite. The first musical fruits of this union appeared in early '85—she released a Stiff single of Billy Bragg's "A New England," drastically overhauling the once-spare tune into a pop extravaganza that earned her another hit. Ullman, meanwhile, included another MacColl tune on her second album. Since then, Kirsty has been busy as a guest vocalist on records by numerous groups, including the Pogues. [iar]

See also *Pogues, Tracey Ullman.*

TEO MACERO

See *Lounge Lizards.*

ANDY MACKAY

See *Roxy Music.*

MADNESS

One Step Beyond . . . (Sire) 1979
Work Rest & Play EP (nr/Stiff) 1980
Absolutely (Sire) 1980
7 (nr/Stiff) 1981
Complete Madness (nr/Stiff) 1982 ●
Madness Present the Rise and Fall (nr/Stiff) 1982
Madness (Geffen) 1983
Keep Moving (Geffen) 1984
Mad Not Mad (Geffen) 1985 ●
Utter Madness (nr/Zarjazz) 1986 ●
The Peel Sessions EP (nr/Strange Fruit) 1987

THE MADNESS

The Madness (nr/Zarjazz-Virgin) 1988 ●

The world needs more bands like Madness. One of the original London perpetrators of the ska revival, they grew from a silly novelty group into full-scale international superstars, beloved by seemingly everyone in Europe, from tot to pensioner. Though diversity in contemporary music is generally laudable, the factionalism it sometimes engenders isn't; Madness' ability to appeal to different audiences suggests that pop needn't always polarize listeners into incompatible camps.

Produced by Clive Langer and Alan Winstanley, Madness' records tend to sound the same, which testifies more to their lighthearted, bubbly style of execution than any actual uniformity of material. The band's inspirations originally came (less later on) primarily from ska and the music hall—i.e., sing-along music—though you're likely to find classic rock'n'roll, Arabic overtones, utterly insipid jokes, easy-listening pop, incisive

observations on society (not unlike Ray Davies) and just about everything else.

Highlights of **One Step Beyond** include "Night Boat to Cairo," "Chipmunks Are Go!" and Prince Buster's "Madness." (The subsequent **Work Rest & Play** 7-inch EP has four cuts, including "Night Boat.") **Absolutely** features the giddy "Baggy Trousers" and "Return of the Los Palmas 7." **7** contains "Grey Day," an uncharacteristically somber ballad, and "The Opium Eaters," a tinkly movie-music instrumental.

Complete Madness is highly recommended because it collects the band's many hits, but in reality any Madness LP guarantees lively and—dare it be said?—wholesome fun.

Displaying added maturity and creative breadth, **The Rise and Fall** is another fine crowd-pleaser, with such likable fare as "Tomorrow's Just Another Day" and "Our House," a virtual sociology primer on English family life.

The nutty boys finally did themselves a favor and signed in the US with Geffen Records, who managed to scare up a hit single for the band in the form of "Our House." That track is also included on **Madness**, a compilation of previously-released UK tracks dating back to 1979. (**Madness** contains about half of **The Rise and Fall** in addition to oldies like "Night Boat to Cairo" and the tender "It Must Be Love.") Good stuff.

What followed was a period of tumult: Madness left Stiff, keyboardist Mike Barson left Madness and the band set up their own Zarjazz label. **Keep Moving,** their final LP as a septet, offers a full platter of typically tuneful, thoughtful, lightweight pop songs covering familiar ground, musically and lyrically. "Wings of a Dove" incorporates a gospel choir; "Michael Caine" uses a cute pop-culture gimmick to sell an otherwise weak number. The growing vocal skills of Carl Smyth and Graham McPherson have made them the band's most recognizable trait; the others' seemingly effortless playing is easy to take for granted.

Although it has its moments, **Mad Not Mad** is an uneasy, odd record, sounding a bit like Bryan Ferry in more than one spot ("Yesterday's Men," "Coldest Day"), offering a quizzical look at America ("Uncle Sam") and covering Scritti Politti's beautiful "Sweetest Girl" with little élan. With Barson gone, keyboards are played by Steve Nieve and Roy Davies; a lot of guest musicians add strings, horns and backing vocals. Not unpleasant, but unsettlingly out of the Madness mainstream.

Having achieved far more success in eight years than these north Londoners ever imagined, Madness announced its breakup in September 1986, but late '87 brought the return of a slimmed-down foursome rechristened *The* Madness and a self-titled new album. In the interim, they issued another compilation, **Utter Madness**, containing all of their UK hits ("Wings of a Dove," "Our House," "Michael Caine") from 1982 to 1986. The CD adds "Seven Year Scratch (Hits Megamix)." Madness' John Peel EP dates from their first year together, 1979.   [jy/iar]

MADONNA

Madonna (Sire) 1983 ●
The First Album (nr/Sire) 1985
Like a Virgin (Sire) 1985 ●
True Blue (Sire) 1986 ●
Who's That Girl (Sire) 1987 ●
You Can Dance (Sire) 1987 ●

Forget for a moment, if you can, all the personality, press and image that attends these albums and consider their contents. The first (reissued in the UK with an alternate cover as **The First Album**) consolidates simpleminded singles ("Lucky Star," "Borderline," "Holiday") and five other lengthy numbers for a bouncy program of dance music that owes a lot to the remnants of disco. The album is a bit slick; Madonna's lack of a discernible style keeps it from being a creatively significant debut. Three producers (Reggie Lucas, Jellybean Benitez and Mark Kamins) give her different sonic settings, but in every case the beat and the voice—alternately soulful and coquettish—are the focal points.

Like a Virgin (a British reissue adds the alluring "Into the Groove," recorded for the soundtrack of Madonna the Actor's film debut, *Desperately Seeking Susan*) is a far more impressive affair, a full-blown self-invention that covers all the bases and made Ms. Ciccone a culture-rending global star. Nile Rodgers' outrageous production packs the songs with hooks and gimmicks, finishing each off with a fine sonic shine. "Material Girl," "Like a Virgin," "Over and Over," "Dress You Up" and others (incidentally, Madonna the Songwriter was involved in the composition of but one of those tunes) all served to build her character, fill dancefloors

and remain in pop fans' memories indefinitely. Regardless of opinions about Madonna the Star, **Like a Virgin** is a first-rate record.

True Blue, on the other hand, isn't very good at all. Mega-successful, yes, but the clichéd electro-dance production (Madonna, Patrick Leonard and Stephen Bray) and half-baked songwriting keeps it from serious creative contention. Madonna sings up a storm, but her dedication to musical variety makes for hit-or-miss records, and **True Blue** rarely connects. Only "Open Your Heart," with an unforgettably hooky chorus, the atmospheric "Live to Tell," on which she resembles Joni Mitchell, and the corny '50s-like title track are any good. Maudlin rubbish ("Papa Don't Preach"), mindless dancearama ("Where's the Party") and an embarrassingly amateurish cinematic salute ("White Heat") are among the album's missteps.

Who's That Girl, although virtually billed as such, isn't a Madonna album. The soundtrack of her best-forgotten 1987 film contains tracks by Coati Mundi, Scritti Politti, Club Nouveau and others; Madonna contributes a quartet of new tunes, although only the delightful "Who's That Girl" is worth hearing.

Flexing her dance-club muscles, Madonna then issued **You Can Dance**, a career-spanning retrospective of various producers' mundane remixes. "Holiday," "Everybody," "Physical Attraction," "Over and Over," "Into the Groove" and "Where's the Party" all get the treatment; the record also contains "Spotlight," a previously unissued throwaway. The CD adds three more remixes for a full program of moving and (into the) grooving.   [iar]

See also *Breakfast Club.*

MAGAZINE

Real Life (Virgin) 1978
Secondhand Daylight (Virgin) 1979
The Correct Use of Soap (Virgin) 1980
Sweetheart Contract EP (nr/Virgin) 1980
Play. (IRS) 1980
Magic, Murder and the Weather (IRS) 1981
After the Fact. (IRS) 1982
Rays & Hail 1978–1981 [CD] (Virgin) 1987

Singer/writer Howard Devoto left the Buzzcocks in an effort to move beyond punk and power pop and take rock music to new levels of complexity and sophistication without losing the recently regained energy of the form. To this end, he formed Magazine with then-unknowns John McGeoch (guitar/sax), Barry Adamson (bass), Dave Formula (keyboards) and drummer Martin Jackson (replaced after just one LP). They advanced a music of many styles and moods with lyrics full of obfuscation and a lush, many-faceted sound, still maintaining the rudimentary passion *au courant* in the music of 1978. Devoto disbanded Magazine in 1981 to pursue a solo career.

Produced by John Leckie, **Real Life** sports an eerie Grand Guignol sound throughout its nine punchy pop tunes, including the Devoto/Shelley-composed hit, "Shot by Both Sides." Adamson's driving bass and Formula's electronics dominate the presentation, while Devoto paints a deranged world of betrayal and suspicion, mixing urban alienation with such material as Tibetan mysticism and the Kennedy assassination. But beneath the dark veneer is humor and top-notch music.

Secondhand Daylight, produced by Colin Thurston, benefits from the change in drummers—John Doyle's style is more fluid and less chunky than his predecessor. Devoto's simplified lyrics focus on insurmountable emotional distances between people, aurally realized with dislocated, keyboard-heavy music.

The Correct Use of Soap is more upbeat, returning to **Real Life**'s popness (without the manic depression), and shows Magazine to be a mature and cohesive band. The mix adds an element of funk, and Devoto shows a Costello-like flair for playful lyrics. The album includes some of Magazine's best songs, including "Sweetheart Contract," "Philadelphia" and "A Song from Under the Floorboards." Highly recommended. (The subsequent 12-inch appends three 1980 live performances, including "Shot by Both Sides" and "Twenty Years Ago," to the title track.)

Play. records an Australian concert, but a great performance is marred by production that distances Devoto's vocals from the music. Although guitarist Robin Simon, John McGeoch's replacement, fails to integrate fully, the band is relaxed and in control, and the album continues in **Soap**'s joyously sardonic vein. "Give Me Everything" and "Twenty Years Ago," both otherwise non-LP tunes, are included.

Magic, Murder and the Weather is controlled by Dave Formula's keyboards, with Devoto taking a turn for the grotesque, as on the casual ditty called "The Honeymoon Killers." The prevalent moods are sarcasm and resignation, making Devoto's decision to break up the band almost simultaneously with the record's release a small surprise.

The posthumous **After the Fact.** collection was released in two drastically different forms, with only five tracks in common. The British edition contains a trio of familiar singles and seven album tracks—a nice retrospective, but nothing extraordinary. The American version contains B-sides ("My Mind Ain't So Open," a 1978 item incorrectly noted as having been released in 1977, "Goldfinger," "I Love You, You Big Dummy," "TV Baby" and "The Book") as well as some of the same album extractions. **Rays & Hail**, a 68-minute CD-only compilation which almost completely absorbs the prior UK compilation, draws on all of the band's albums, adding the original single version of "Shot by Both Sides." [sg]

See also *Armoury Show, Howard Devoto.*

MAGNOLIAS
Concrete Pillbox (Twin/Tone) 1986
For Rent (Twin/Tone) 1988 ●

Like a Frankenstein monster assembled to synthesize the sounds of Minneapolis, this young local quartet spews back aspects of the town's three best rock bands (you figure 'em out) with gusto on **Concrete Pillbox**, which they co-produced with Grant Hart of Hüsker Dü. (Note the familiar drum sound.) Some of singer/guitarist John Freeman's songs show melodic and structural promise; a bit of power pop (and a faint Cheap Trick influence) emerges in the group's aggressive playing. (But the cover of Jon Richman's "She Cracked" should land them back in an asylum for misguided souls.)

Replacements' soundman Monty Wilkes co-produced the sloppy **For Rent**, a looser but better-developed collection that features a new bassist and a snare-happy mix. Shedding imitation for a loudly textured (with folky glimmers) personality more their own, the Magnolias seem well on the way to developing into contenders. Send for a great producer and turn these boys loose. [iar]

FRED MAHER
See *Robert Quine.*

MALARIA!

White Water EP (Bel. Crépuscule) 1981
Emotion (Bel. Crépuscule) 1982
New York Passage EP (Cachalot) 1982
. . . Revisited [tape] (ROIR) 1983

Aggressively noisy and discordant, these five German women manage to make a surprisingly tedious, uninvolving racket—it's not even repulsive, just numbing. All in the name of art, mind you. And the problem on **White Water** isn't their German lyrics—they sound the same on the English side of **New York Passage**, recorded in NYC.

Emotion, the band's sole studio album, is far better organized and nearly acceptable, in a rugged, dissonant kind of way. The music is a varied mass of synthesizers, rhythms and sound effects; the German and English lyrics—blurted, chanted and yelled—confront such generalities as money, jealousy, power, death and passion. A virtual philosophy course on vinyl. Not easy listening, but powerful medicine with real impact.

Revisited—a live tape recorded in 1983 at two American club dates—suffers from mighty indistinct sound and an unnervingly loose sense of rhythm. (The vocals alternate languages, but that hardly matters.) Nonetheless, the relentless drive has an incantatory power, and other bands certainly have made far more horrific and less organized noise.   [jg/iar]

STEPHEN MALLINDER

See *Cabaret Voltaire.*

MANDINGO GRIOT SOCIETY

Mandingo Griot Society (Flying Fish) 1978
Mighty Rhythm (Flying Fish) 1981

MANDINGO FEATURING FODAY MUSA SUSO

Watto Sitta (Celluloid) 1985 ●

FODAY MUSA SUSO

Mansa Bendung (Flying Fish) 1986

The Mandingo people of West Africa pass their folklore down through the *griots,* singers who tell stories and praise for pay, accompanied by the kora, a 21-string instrument that sounds like an oddly-tuned guitar. The group Mandingo (formerly the Mandingo Griot Society) fuses traditional kora plunking with jazz, blues and reggae tinges, supporting kora master Foday Musa Suso's tingly lines with Fender bass and a healthy percussion arsenal. Trumpeter Don Cherry is a featured soloist on the first LP; **Watto Sitta** is technically enhanced by producer Bill Laswell's electronic drums and guest musician Herbie Hancock. On it, the group sounds like it's been put through a processor, emerging as Laswellian pitter-patter with a plain-wrap *griot* edge.   [rg]

EARLE MANKEY

See *Concrete Blonde, Sparks.*

TONY MANSFIELD

See *New Musik.*

MAN SIZED ACTION

Claustrophobia (Reflex) 1983
Five Story Garage (Homestead) 1984

To be the coolest band in Minneapolis nowadays you need a little more vision and talent than the gallant Man Sized Action could muster. But to be a cool band anywhere, all you need is this unpretentious lot's commitment to a few good ideas. Man Sized Action opened up punk structures with distorted, ringing guitar, some off-kilter rhythms and emotionally *sung* lyrics. Like Hüsker Dü, they applied a neanderthal, propulsive attack to fundamentally poppy songs. .

The lo-fi **Claustrophobia**, produced by Hüsker Düde Bob Mould, sets up powerful grooves, but never escapes its murky dynamic. Particularly on "My Life," Tippy's singing wall of guitar and Kelly Linehan's supporting bass hint at the band's ability to create beautifully textured sounds without sacrificing power or bracing crudeness.

Five Story Garage adds better production, better songs and a second guitarist. The quintet generates a surge of momentum which threatens to explode its punky pop hooks, making the album fast, powerful and surprisingly accessible. If the Hüskers bring more inspiration to this territory, Man Sized Action brought a cooler name and unquestionable integrity, plus the faith that there can be loud, uncompromising music outside of hardcore.   [jl]

ZEKE MANYIKA

See *Orange Juice.*

PHIL MANZANERA

Diamond Head (Atco) 1975
K-Scope (EG-Polydor) 1978 (EG) 1982

Primitive Guitars (Editions EG) 1982
Guitarissimo 75–82 (EG) 1987 ●

QUIET SUN
Mainstream (Antilles) 1975

PHIL MANZANERA/801
801 Live (EG-Polydor) 1976 (EG) 1982 ●
Listen Now! (nr/Polydor) 1977 (EG) 1982

WETTON/MANZANERA
Wetton/Manzanera (Geffen) 1987

Although not quite the founding guitarist in Roxy Music, Phil Manzanera was one of its three enduring pillars, and his radically unique instrumental ideas were as much a part of the band's early stylistic groundbreaking as Bryan Ferry's equally unprecedented vocals.

Before joining Roxy (as sound mixer; he took over on guitar in early '72), the debonair Briton who was raised in Latin America spent a couple of years in Quiet Sun, a progressive outfit that had broken up but reformed temporarily in 1975 to cut a debut album. **Mainstream** is a jazzy, Soft Machine-like outing enlivened by Manzanera's distortion-crazed solos and slices of other bizarreness (thanks, in part, to Eno's participation) cutting through the sophisticated instrumental arrangements. Best song title: "Mummy was an asteroid, daddy was a small non-stick kitchen utensil." The following year, drummer Charles Hayward went on to form This Heat.

Prior to the Quiet Sun reunion, Manzanera stepped out of Roxy for his pleasurable solo debut, the look-what-I-can-do **Diamond Head**. Joining him on this exploration of diverse styles are Roxy cohorts (Eno, Paul Thompson, Andy Mackay, John Wetton, Eddie Jobson), Quiet Sun (the whole group on one track) and the redoubtable Robert Wyatt, who sings lead—in Spanish—on "Frontera." Manzanera scarcely opens his mouth on the half-instrumental record, leaving Eno the mic for the wonderful "Big Day" and "Miss Shapiro," both of which strongly resemble **Here Come the Warm Jets**.

Manzanera's next significant side project (neglecting, of course, his contributions to records by Nico, Eno, Ferry, John Cale, Mackay, Split Enz and others) was 801. Originally assembled for a handful of concerts to fill a 1976 period of Roxy inactivity, the first 801 consisted of Manzanera, Eno, bassist Bill MacCormick from Quiet Sun, drummer Simon Phillips and two others. Recorded in London, **801 Live** draws material from **Dia-** mond Head, Here Come the Warm Jets and Mainstream, adding the Beatles' "Tomorrow Never Knows" and the Kinks' "You Really Got Me." A spectacular example of cross-culturalization that should be of serious interest to Roxy fans.

Two years later, a studio album, employing almost the entire performing cast and then some, returned 801 to life. **Listen Now!** consists of new Manzanera compositions and is actually not unlike a solo record, but his partnership with MacCormick justifies the group designation. Unfortunately, much of the record is conservative and dull, an overly smooth and sophisticated collection (maybe it's Kevin Godley's influence) that rarely ignites. The long pieces—mostly vocalized by Simon Ainley and a collection of back-up singers—are radio-ready but barely sentient.

During another Roxy hiatus, Manzanera created the livelier solo-billed **K-Scope** in collaboration with many of 801's players. Clever lyrics sung by Tim Finn (ex-Split Enz) and saxes by Mel Collins (ex-King Crimson) are matched by Manzanera's invigorated (and invigorating) guitar work and Phillips' kinetic drumming. There's calm restraint (like "Cuban Crisis" and the endless "Walking Through Heaven's Door") amid the rock drive and dance-happy energy, but that contrast only gives the delightful record even deeper appeal.

To celebrate his tenth anniversary as a professional musician, Manzanera released **Primitive Guitars**, a solo instrumental album that shows numerous sides of his virtuosity. Guided by chronological and geographical themes that defy instant comprehension, the album stretches the sound of guitar all over the map (much of it to Latin lands) in a challenging zigzag of styles and approaches. Except for one bass part, Phil plays everything on the LP, which suffers not a jot by the isolation. As a fascinating self-defined retrospective of Manzanera's musical development, **Primitive Guitars** may be lost on some of his followers, while certainly connecting with others.

The lengthy (over 54 minutes on vinyl!) **Guitarissimo** "collocation" organizes tracks from Manzanera's solo records and both 801 outings into four thematic sections. Careful annotation and thoughtful sequencing make up for the compromise sonic quality: try the CD with four bonus tracks.

Proving that even unassailably tasteful

artists can take a dive, Manzanera made an unfortunate album with onetime bandmate John Wetton, following the latter's superstar sojourn in Asia. **Wetton/Manzanera** is depressing commercial tripe seemingly geared to relaunch Wetton's career from Asia's coattails. Strangely, "Keep on Loving Yourself" is about self-respect, something this project pointedly lacks.   [iar]

THOMAS MAPFUMO

Gwindingwi Rine Shumba (nr./Earthworks)
  1980 + 1986
Ndangariro (Carthage) 1983
Mabasa (nr/Earthworks) 1984
Mr. Music (nr/Earthworks) 1985
The Chimurenga Singles 1976–1980
  (Shanachie) 1984
Chimurenga for Justice (Shanachie) 1985

From nightclub singer to political firebrand, Thomas Mapfumo's career has elevated him to near-sainthood in his native Zimbabwe. **The Chimurenga Singles**, recorded with the Acid (as in bitter) Band, carries an interesting disclaimer: "The quality of these tracks leaves much to be desired, but remember they were made under war conditions." Influenced by Voice of Zimbabwe radio broadcasts, Mapfumo participated in the country's liberation struggle, and was jailed for his troubles. The singles deal in political innuendo and are sung in the native Shona language. The sound is rushed, as if time were of the essence; as the cymbals hyperventilate and the guitars skitter along (in imitation of thumb piano), Mapfumo sings serious and subtle songs of revolution.

His later recordings, made with Blacks Unlimited, are more languid and even include some love songs. The grooves are lazier, but the guitar retains a rapid-fire hunt-and-peck quality. The wonderful **Chimurenga for Justice**, for instance, blends a surprisingly uninflected loping reggae beat with a peppy African sound and even an American soul-influenced approach on half a dozen richly-performed songs about struggle and praise. Trumpets provide sweet counterpoint to Mapfumo's husky singing and his female backing duo.   [rg/iar]

MARC AND THE MAMBAS

See *Marc Almond.*

MARCH VIOLETS

Natural History (nr/Rebirth) 1984
Electric Shades (Relativity) 1985

Although they've been together for more than five years, the March Violets have never actually recorded an album as such—both LPs are compilations of singles. They cite Beefheart as one of their main inspirations, but there's about as much audio evidence of that here as there is of Bach. What is detectable is surging, guitar-based rock somewhere between U2 and the Cult. Generally running over five minutes each, most of the songs are longer than they need to be.

The Violets have had two different lead singers, and it makes a major difference in the quality of their sound. Original vocalist Simon D. (who left to form the Batfish Boys) has an unpleasant snarl; upon his departure, rhythm guitarist Cleo (no surnames in this band) took over, and her voice is truly lovely and tuneful, with a wide emotional range. Not only does she make the band sound warmer and more melodic, she's visually attractive enough to be an asset in the cruel commercial world. The Violets supported Siouxsie on a 1986 US tour.   [dgs]

OLLIE MARLAND & JAH WOBBLE

See *Jah Wobble.*

ZIGGY MARLEY/MELODY MAKERS

Hey World! (EMI) 1986
Conscious Party (Virgin) 1988 ●

Still in their teens, Ziggy Marley and the Melody Makers are poised on the verge of international stardom like no other reggae act before them. This is partly due to genes—Ziggy resembles his late father and, more significantly, sounds uncannily like him. Such instant identification has enabled the group (which includes three other Marley progeny) to easily step into the commercial vacuum left by the elder Marley's death.

But theirs is no Julian Lennon-like simulation. (In fact, the Melody Makers' first LP, which utilizes a traditional Wailers-like sound, is undistinguished.) The group depends on the present as much as the past, and their potential for success lies in their contemporary presentation. Symbolically *and* literally, the Melody Makers represent reggae's new generation.

Conscious Party bears this out, from its

aura of optimism (in songs like "Tomorrow People," "New Love" and "We Propose") to its thoroughly modern sound. Produced by Talking Heads Chris Frantz and Tina Weymouth, and featuring a superb crew of international backup musicians, the record is smart and professional like a Heads album (and more consistent than either Tom Tom Club LP). If the Melody Makers' songwriting doesn't compare with Dad's, it's at least competent and promising. The LP isn't at all rootsy, but it's fresh, appealing and sincere: reggae for the Benetton generation.   [bk]

PAUL MAROTTA
Agit-Prop Piano (Do Speak) 1983
STYRENES
Girl Crazy (Mustard) 1982

On his solo album, Marotta—a very early leading light in the Cleveland underground scene—plays acoustic piano in a thickly overlapping, improvised mesh of ambient sound that can be considered either as serious avant-garde music or a hypnotic drone for trancing out. The two long pieces, much like Glenn Branca's work on guitars, go nowhere, but do something aurally seductive while getting there.

As a fascinating retrospective of a weird old band, the Styrenes' album (which Marotta produced, co-wrote and plays on every track) is worth seeking out for its odd combination of styles and sounds. Best of all, it contains the crazed 1975 "Drano in Your Veins," one of America's first indie new wave records.   [iar]

MARQUEE MOON
Strangers in the Monkey Biz (Ger. Diadem) 1986

One of Berlin's top bands, Marquee Moon may once have sounded like Television, from whose classic song they took their name, but they bear no such resemblance now. They're like Anglo-pop with a posey lead singer and a dash of Dead Boys malevolence (or maybe, as on "Marionette," the guitar-era Cure meets Love It to Death-era Alice Cooper). The production, by Jimmi Quidd of New York's Dots, gives them plenty of snap, crackle and pop; after the catchy opening track ("Here Today and Gone Tomorrow"), though, the songs are enjoyable but less than gripping.   [tr]

MARTHA AND THE MUFFINS
Metro Music (Virgin Int'l) 1979
Trance and Dance (nr/DinDisc) 1980
This Is the Ice Age (nr/DinDisc) 1981
Danseparc (RCA) 1982
M+M
Mystery Walk (RCA) 1984

Martha and the Muffins were originally clever amateurs who had fun fooling around with music in Toronto. However, the subtly catchy "Echo Beach" made them chart stars in the UK and brought their days of leisure to an abrupt halt. A minor miracle of this slick age, Metro Music captures a mild-mannered, unpretentious group at its most charming, before stress and selfconsciousness took their toll. Vocalist Martha Johnson has a sometimes awkward but always personable style of singing on "Echo Beach," "Indecision" and "Paint by Number Heart"; it's as if she walked into a studio to tell what happened to her that day rather than to perform. Sax player Andy Haas adds jazzier, more exotic flavorings (à la Roxy Music's Andy Mackay), while a confident rhythm section preserves the hard foundation. Some might call Metro Music wimpy, but a more sensitive observer would judge it the result of introverts trying to rock, and—on their own terms—succeeding handily.

The more mature Trance and Dance treads less appealing waters. The title track and "Was Ezo" retain the haunting quality of "Echo Beach," but other songs seem a little glib and too willing to be cute. Martha and the Muffins sound as if they're having less fun than before; second vocalist Martha Ladly (composer of "Was Ezo") left the group after this LP.

The band painted itself into a corner with This Is the Ice Age. "Women Around the World at Work," a catchy stab at mainstream pop-singledom, lacks the innocence that was their strong point. Much of the LP suffers from arid artiness—they're too cool for pop but can't settle comfortably into another groove. Sax player Andy Haas left after this LP.

Thus reduced to a quartet, Martha and the Muffins ventured down funky Broadway on Danseparc, adding a throbbing beat to the blend. As a detour, the title track is fine, and the guest sax provides a bit of continuity, but in other spots, Johnson's self-important singing grates and Mark Gane's overdrive guitar can't overcome the repetitious, overbearing pounding. The tunes that have a jazzy pop sensibility are good, but the battle between humming and bumping is clearly lost to the forces of motion. On a positive note, the album ends with a beautifully textured languid instrumental, "Whatever Happened to Radio Valve Road?"

Mystery Walk presents the penultimately reductive group of Martha and Mark—billed as M+M—paradoxically playing prosaic social-conscience funk on "Black Stations/White Stations" and rediscovering delicate, attractive melodicism (best exemplified by "Cooling the Medium") Throughout, the record mixes a less-aggressive intellectual dancefloor sound and enticingly atmospheric, jazz-tinged pop. An excellent return to form.   [jy/iar]

PATRICK D. MARTIN
Patrick D. Martin EP (IRS) 1981

This American 12-inch was gathered from a batch of British singles; the mysterious Mr. Martin plays bright electro-pop that sounds like a simplified "Pop Muzik," but he sings in a heavy accent that eliminates any trace of mechanical coolness. "Computer Datin' " is the standout track.   [iar]

MARTINI RANCH
Holy Cow (Sire) 1988 •

California musician Andrew Todd and Texas-born actor/filmmaker Bill Paxton (director of Barnes & Barnes' classic "Fish Heads" video) comprise Martini Ranch, a wickedly inventive, visually-oriented pop-culture nuthouse of a band based in Los Angeles. **Holy Cow** variously resembles the B-52's (whose Cindy Wilson guests here), Devo (Mark Mothersbaugh and Alan Myers contribute vocally and instrumentally; Bob Casale produced one song) and Oingo Boingo. Judge Reinhold whistles on one tune; Bud Cort vocalizes on another; ex-Missing Person Patrick O'Hearn and Mark Isham also put in appearances. Kinetic, silly, witty, infectious and intelligent.   [iar]

HUGH MASEKELA
Techno Bush (Jive Afrika) 1984
Waiting for the Rain (Jive Afrika) 1985
Tomorrow (Warner Bros.) 1987

Trumpeter Masekela, in self-imposed exile from South Africa for more than two decades (he now lives and records in Goborone, Botswana) is a onetime jazz traditionalist who rediscovered his musical and political roots during the '70s. On **Techno Bush**, the *mbaqanga* rhythms of the South African townships, played by his longtime group Kalahari, support trumpet playing that percolates in staccato ecstasy. Like most secular township music, Masekela's songs combine the political and the pastoral. **Waiting for the Rain** is a more westernized version of **Techno Bush**, though it includes a cover of Fela Kuti's first major hit, "Lady." Masekela's politics are still much in evidence, but he appears to be striving for an even wider audience.

The trend continues on **Tomorrow**, which includes the internationally popular single about Nelson Mandela, "Bring Him Back Home." Employing a number of slickish producers, **Tomorrow** arrived on the heels of Masekela's "discovery" by Paul Simon, with whom Masekela toured on the American's **Graceland** jaunt.   [rg]

MASSACRE
Killing Time (OAO-Celluloid) 1982 •

Bill Laswell (bass) and Fred Maher (drums) of Material came together with avant-garde veteran Fred Frith (guitar) in this radical power trio. The distinctively skewed melodies of the album's composed half—mostly on the first side, a brilliant procession of techniques and ideas—bear the Frith hallmark. Propelled by the virtuoso rhythm section, Frith plays with unprecedented urgency—no cold cerebration here. The improvisations are tough and sinewy too, benefiting from Frith's experience in Henry Cow. Highlights: the bouncy title cut and "Corridor," a manic exercise in machine-gun feedback.   [mf]

See also *Fred Frith, Bill Laswell, Material, Skeleton Crew.*

JAMES MASTRO
See *Bongos.*

MATCHING MOLE
See *Robert Wyatt.*

MATERIAL
Temporary Music 1 EP (Red) 1979
Temporary Music 2 EP (Red) 1981

Temporary Music (Fr. Celluloid) 1981 ●
American Songs EP (Fr. Celluloid) 1981
Busting Out EP (ZE-Island) 1981
Memory Serves (Celluloid-Elektra-Musician)
    1981 ●
One Down (Celluloid-Elektra) 1982 ●
Red Tracks (Red) 1986

Originally formed to back Daevid Allen when the erstwhile Gong leader first toured the US, Material began as a small core of New York-based musicians around which an endless string of interesting one-shot gigging and recording bands formed. Although bassist/producer Bill Laswell is the only remaining musician to carry the Material flag, the original triumvirate with Michael Beinhorn (synthesizer, tapes, vocals) and Fred Maher (drums) made a virtue of eclecticism, effectively blending funk, rock, experimentalism and jazz into a subtle, credible fusion music all their own.

Not that they managed it right away. **Temporary Music 1**, produced by Giorgio Gomelsky, shows a promising progressive-rock band toying with funk and quickly miring itself in extraneous noise. But the funk-rock fusion takes hold on the sequel, as Stockhausen (figuratively) meets Moroder, and that approach didn't let them down thereafter. The **Temporary Music** album reissues the two EPs on one disc, as does **Red Tracks**.

American Songs, which features an intriguing appearance by guitarist Robert Quine on two new items, is just interesting enough not to be expendable.

Memory Serves is Material's most jazz-tinged album, with its complement of prominent jazz players on cut after relentless cut. Guitarist Fred Frith is also featured, starting an intermittently ongoing alliance. The procession of textures is dazzling, the funk cuts like a knife and the hornwork is disciplined within tight structures. As "black" classical and dance music refined with a rock sensibility, **Memory Serves** is a highly original crossover.

One Down extends the experiment to urban pop music with almost equal success, aided by Nile Rodgers, Nona Hendryx, Frith, Oliver Lake and many others. However, it lacks the edge of **Memory Serves**, and Maher's departure is probably the reason. Saxophonist Archie Shepp, black-power spokesman and angry young man of '60s jazz, puts in a politically interesting but musically low-key appearance on Hugh Hopper's "Memories."

Material's extraordinarily skillful rhythm section has been involved with many other projects. They formed Massacre as a trio with Frith; Maher has also worked with Richard Hell and Lou Reed, among many others. Laswell played with a lot of new musicians but has more recently become one of America's hottest producers, working with everyone from Yellowman to Mick Jagger.   [mf]

See also *Afrika Bambaataa, Golden Palominos, Nona Hendryx, Bill Laswell, Massacre, Robert Quine.*

MAZARATI
Mazarati (Paisley Park) 1986

Another product of Prince's musical factory, Minneapolis' Mazarati were favored with a record contract, the attentions of the Revolution's bassist as songwriter and producer, a paisley'n'jewelry fashion consult and one honest-to-god Prince song ("100 MPH"). Unfortunately, the band itself hasn't got an ounce of personality, and this album drifts along interminably through eight laboriously smooth rock-funk numbers.
[iar]

RICHARD MAZDA
Hands of Fate (IRS) 1983

The producer of many cool people's records (e.g., the Fleshtones, Fall, Wall of Voodoo, Tom Robinson), Mazda's own music consists of slick soul-funk that bears more than a passing resemblance to ABC's first album. ("Big Sound" all but quotes the lyrics of "Look of Love.") Guest appearances by many of his studio charges get lost in the smooth, bass-popping sound; Mazda may be a multifarious musician (mostly keyboards and guitar) and an ace producer, but he's not much of a singer or songwriter. A flawless exercise in search of a talent to focus it on.
[iar]

MC5
Kick Out the Jams (Elektra) 1969 + 1983
Back in the USA (Atlantic) 1970
High Time (Atlantic) 1971
Babes in Arms [tape] (ROIR) 1983

The MC5's enduring relevance lies less in the Detroit quintet's music—the in-concert **Kick Out the Jams** sounds closer to early-'70s heavy metal than anything else—and more in the political attitudes behind that music; "Kick Out the Jams" and "Motor City Is Burning" are obvious harbingers of "Anarchy in the UK." Unfortunately for the 5, their utopian beliefs didn't translate to vinyl with the intensity of, say, the first Clash album. **Kick Out the Jams** has plenty of high-energy rock, with science-fiction noise ("Rocket Reducer No. 62" and "Starship," co-credited to Sun Ra) thrown in for class. But will the revolution be recorded by Elektra Records?

Evidently not. The next MC5 album, produced by Jon Landau (prior to his earthshaking alliance with Bruce Springsteen), finds them downplaying the rabble-rousing in favor of claustrophobically taut under-three-minute odes to "High School," "Teenage Lust" and "Shakin' Street" ("where all the kids meet"). The LP also contains performances of "Tutti Frutti" and the Chuck Berry title cut, with its refrain of "I'm so glad I'm living in the USA." Sarcasm? A timely return to the roots? Probably both. At least the concise songs are easier to like than the first LP's hippie-era sprawl.

Having lost their audience between the first two albums, the MC5 felt free to put down the best playing of their recording career on the totally ignored **High Time**. Song lengths are back up, but the band stretches out comfortably on "Sister Anne," "Over and Over" and the jazzy "Skunk (Sonically Speaking)."

The **Babes in Arms** tape is a belated appendix to the catalogue. It consists of early 45 sides done for indie labels, alternate takes and remixes (some scarcely different from the originals) from their albums, plus one otherwise unreleased cut.

Did the MC5's circular saga prove the invincibility of pure pop? In any case, their records and legend remain an oft-cited influence on the nose-thumbing irreverence and chaotic energy of punk groups.   [si]

See also *Mick Farren, New Order, Patti Smith.*

MALCOLM McLAREN

Duck Rock (Island) 1983 ●
D'ya Like Scratchin' EP (Island) 1984
Fans (Island) 1984 ●
Swamp Thing (Island) 1985

Besides being an imperialistic cultural plunderer (a non-judgmental designation), Malcolm McLaren is one of contemporary rock's true visionaries. His role in the formation and promotion of the Sex Pistols has been construed as everything from inspired instigator to Machiavellian manipulator, and his solo career has been as righteously criticized as it's been influential. The ever-provocative McLaren tends to bring out the moral indignation in people.

It's hard to say just what McLaren does as an artist. He's more an assembler than a creator, piecing together artifacts from various musical cultures in such a way that, at the end of the day, his own input seems invisible. And yet his perspective as hip outsider has continued to provide a link between his Anglo-American audience and Third World forms. If McLaren's a musical tourist, these records are his home movies.

Duck Rock, produced by Trevor Horn and featuring the rapping Worlds Famous Supreme Team, is a vanguard album in the new music/rap crossover movement. It offers vignettes of hip-hop, Appalachian music (McLaren shows no real racial preference in his thievery), African music and *merengue*. Instead of assimilating the forms and reconstructing them, McLaren puts his actual source material on vinyl (and then his name to it). The most striking cut, "Buffalo Gals," sets a square dance call over a hip-hop scratch track. **D'ya Like Scratchin'** plucks three songs from the album and funks with the mix, adding two versions of a new tune as well.

Not one to stand still, McLaren succeeds against all odds in combining hip-hop with opera on **Fans**. The synthesis seems a highly unlikely one and it is, but McLaren mainly uses opera for its recitative form and story lines (namely *Carmen, Madam Butterfly* and *Turandot*). And, damn it, the thing works more often than not.

The aptly-named **Swamp Thing** is a murky and bizarre creature growing out of McLaren's 1982-4 scrap heap of various sessions. The title track perverts "Wild Thing" into a nightmarish but enjoyable mess. "Duck Rock Cheer" is so unlike the original that you'd never connect the two, save for minor overlapping of mix components; "Duck Rockers/Promises" sounds only slightly more familiar. "Buffalo Love" has even less to do with "Buffalo Gals," offering instead a smooth disco creation breathily sung by an unidentified woman. "B.I. Bikki" combines McLarenize exercise exhortations with opera and all sorts of extraneous rubbish; "Eiffel Tower" turns the Bow Wow Wow song inside out to interesting effect. As aggravating as he often is, McLaren's work is invariably fascinating and provocative.

[jl/iar]

See also *Bow Wow Wow, New York Dolls, Sex Pistols.*

MC LYTE

Lyte as a Rock (First Priority-Atlantic) 1988 ●

This sassy young rapper from Brooklyn—no-nonsense star of hip-hop's burgeoning distaff side—waxes funny, moral and toughly self-reliant on the musically inventive and entertaining **Lyte as a Rock**. Not only is her assessment of the sexual battlefield a refreshing change of pace, the chip on Lyte's shoulder yields hysterical and vicious putdowns. Aided by sharp production, minor appropriations from Ray Charles, Helen Reddy and the Four Seasons, Lyte fills her LP with a number of strong cuts, like the introductory "Lyte vs. Vanna White" and the hit "I Cram to Understand U."

In one of the most imaginative cross-cultural moments of 1988, Lyte appears in the video for Sinéad O'Connor's "I Want Your (Hands on Me)." What's next? [iar]

MDC

Millions of Dead Cops (R Radical) 1982
Multi-Death Corporation EP (R Radical) 1983
Smoke Signals (R Radical) 1986
Millions of Damn Christians: This Blood's for
    You (R Radical) 1987 ●
More Dead Cops (Boner) 1988 ●

Originally from Austin, Texas, this explosive hardcore quartet (aka Multi-Death Corporation, Millions of Dead Children and Millions of Damn Christians) now works out of San Francisco. The combination of totally political lyrics and precise breakneck rock makes **Millions of Dead Cops** a powerful means by which to deliver messages like "John Wayne Was a Nazi" (originally recorded and released on 45 when MDC was known as the Stains) and "I Hate Work." Best title: "Corporate Cheeseburger." After the first pressing sold out, the LP was remastered and reissued.

Smoke Signals offers a mature lyrical outlook and challenging post-hardcore arrangements, which organize thrash sounds into a tightly structured musical framework. Gordon Fraser's throaty guitar and the deft rhythm section set the scene for Davey's

clearly-enunciated soapbox announcements like "No More Cops," "South Africa Is Free," "Missile Destroyed Civilization" and the vegetarian "Country Squawk." Turning to cultural concerns, MDC also offers the flavorful "Tofutti," the sarcastic "Skateboards to Hell" and "King of Thrash." An exceptionally good record.

The non-'core **Millions of Damn Christians** (aka **This Blood's for You**) starts out as an attack on religion, but quickly broadens the free-fire zone to include flat-out indictments of Reagan ("Bye Bye Ronnie," "Guns for Nicaragua," "Who's the Terrorist Now?"), other bureaucrats ("Henry Kissmyassinger," Cream's "Politician"), agricultural imperialism ("Chock Full of Shit"), intolerant punks ("S.K.I.N.H.E.A.D.") and junkies ("Your Death Wish Is Sick"). The music is likewise expansive: MDC uses acoustic guitar, melody, guitar solos and other good things. A fine development from a deeply committed and talented quartet.

More Dead Cops 1981–1987 is a repackage of the group's three 7-inch releases, with additional tracks from compilations, etc.

[iar]

MEATMEN

Crippled Children Suck (Touch and Go) 1981
Blood Sausage EP (Touch and Go) 1982
We're the Meatmen . . . and You Suck!
    (Touch and Go) 1983
War of the Superbikes (Homestead) 1985 ●
Rock'n'Roll Juggernaut (Caroline) 1986

TESCO VEE

Dutch Hercules EP (Touch and Go) 1984

Obnoxious, crude, offensive, blasphemous, tiresome and funny, Washington, DC's Meatmen are one band you'll never be able to explain to your parents (or even the vast majority of your peers). The rude punk parodists stomp into the sensitive issues of society with a coarseness that makes dead baby jokes seem polite. Their problem is that, without any reference points, the gratuitous irreverence lacks shock value and becomes merely tedious.

Despite its brilliant cover art and title, **We're the Meatmen . . . and You Suck!** (originally pressed on white vinyl) runs aground in a sea of unoriginality. The puerile forays into morbidity ("One Down Three to Go," about the Beatles), homophobia ("Tooling for Anus"), misogyny ("I'm Glad I'm Not a Girl") and racism ("Blow Me Jah") are too familiar and predictable to be really outrageous. A little more wit would make the Meatmen a more engaging (if hateable) cartoon. One side of the album is live; the other is a reissue of the earlier **Blood Sausage** 7-inch.

Singer Tesco Vee's solo record, on which he's joined by guitarists Lyle Preslar and Brian Baker of Minor Threat (both of whom subsequently followed Vee home and joined the Meatmen), stands on more solid musical ground. Apparently mellowing with age, he limits the objects of his attacks to lesbians, blacks, post-punkers and rock stars. The satire works better because Vee offers himself as an object of parody. A reference point! The only useless cut is the side-long disco version of "Crapper's Delight," which pales before the far more clever rap attacks of the Beastie Boys and Red Hot Chili Peppers.

With a new five-jerk lineup, **War of the Superbikes** focuses and refines the band's miserable charm, retooling the punk onslaught into a strong, sharp-edged rock sound and presenting a mixed material grill, from utterly inoffensive (the title track and "Abba God and Me") to typically juvenile (the flamencoed "Kisses in the Sunset," "Cadaver Class" and "What's This Shit Called Love," which opens as a demented Elvis Presley parody). Just what the doctor ordered! Bonus: spoken-word tripe hidden at the end of each side.

James Cooper replaced Baker on **Rock'n' Roll Juggernaut**, leaving the Meatmen a musically undistinguished rock machine, playing tight but plain guitar raunch. Amid bursts of worthless comedy shtick, Vee's lyrics keep the faith, leering salaciously while attacking foreigners ("French People Suck," "Dichstrudel"), American proles ("True Grit") and health nuts ("Nature Boy") with the unenthusiastic knee-jerk bravado of morons yelling out car windows at women. Yawn.   [jl/iar]

MEAT PUPPETS

Meat Puppets (Thermidor-SST) 1981 ●
Meat Puppets II (SST) 1983 ●
Up on the Sun (SST) 1985 ●
Out My Way EP (SST) 1986
Mirage (SST) 1987 ●
Huevos (SST) 1987 ●

This Arizona trio has made a career out of defying expectations. The two Kirkwood brothers, Curt (guitar/vocals) and Cris

(bass/vocals), along with drummer Derrick Bostrom, burst onto the scene with a convincing above-average thrash sound on their first album. On **Meat Puppets II**, however, they return playing radical country-punk. A startlingly strong set of stylistic contrasts—loud and soft, fast and slow—all supporting moving, poetic lyrics, the songs are melodic and memorable, Curt's high'n'lonesome singing even more effective in its shoddiness. One of the best albums ever to blend Joe Strummer with Hank Williams, **Meat Puppets II** avoids clichés of any sort in its brilliant evocation of the wide open world of the Southwest. Make no mistake—this is not a hardcore album with some corny twang, it's a fully-realized work in a unique hybrid style.

Up on the Sun removes the Puppets further from punk, but doesn't adequately replace the rock'n'roll energy. Curt's growing mastery of delicate guitar weaves—the Arizona's answer to Jerry Garcia, perhaps—provides the Puppets' new focus; the hoedown coda of "Enchanted Pork Fist" owes as much to modern jazz as cowboy rock. The title track is a lovely, contemplative folk song with an airy vocal and a skipping guitar riff that repeats throughout. In a lighter moment, Curt and Cris whistle their way through "Maiden's Milk"; waxing serious, "Creator" offers a poetic contemplation on god and nature.

The Puppets sound far more involved and enthused on the superior six-track **Out My Way**, again quite unlike anything in their prior repertoire. An utterly crazed rave-up of "Good Golly Miss Molly" merely caps off an ineffable, diverse collection of occasionally funky, occasionally psychedelic, occasionally countrified rock tunes.

Mirage harks back to the sonic translucence of **Up on the Sun**, forcing Bostrom's muscular drumming to find a way to maintain its reserve while kicking up a subtle storm. Curt's intricate finger-picking and plectrum work leads the relaxed stroll on "Mirage," "Leaves," "Get on Down" and "I Am a Machine." The bluegrass-styled "Confusion Fog" shows a different side of the Pups, as does the rocking "Liquefied," an incongruous souvenir of the band's early sound with acid-trip lyrics and distorted rhythm guitar. The only discordant ingredient on this technically accomplished record is Curt's uncertain, often tuneless singing.

As legend has it, the genesis of **Huevos** began with a magazine interview in which

Curt announced his adoration of ZZ Top guitarist Billy Gibbons. Gibbons' reply sent Kirkwood into a writing frenzy, and the album—which begins with the Top soundalike "Paradise"—was recorded in one marathon 72-hour stretch. The mildly commercialized sound (read: rhythm guitar and a thick Les Paul tone) led hardline fans to call it a sellout, but that's hardly the case. A generally upbeat outing, the only discouraging words can be heard in "Dry Rain" and the self-deprecating "I Can't Be Counted On." Otherwise, Curt celebrates "Fruit," "Sexy Music" and even "Bad Love"; "Automatic Mojo" hits the ZZ Top button again with squiggly riffs popping out behind the hoarse harmony vocals. [iar]

MEDIUM MEDIUM

Medium Medium EP (Cachalot) 1981
The Glitterhouse (Cachalot) 1981

This Nottingham quartet, which plays powerful bass-heavy funk, debuted with a single in '78, appeared on a compilation album in '79 and signed with Cherry Red in 1980. Their eponymous EP is one of the best (not to mention earliest) modern Brit-funk records, featuring two versions of the hypnotic "Hungry, So Angry," the tension-filled "Further Than Funk Dream" and "Nadsat Dream," all sung by John Lewis in an angst-filled emotive style that, along with the taut, bubbling rhythm section, distinguishes the band.

Unfortunately, **The Glitterhouse**, released later the same year and containing both "Hungry, So Angry" and "Further Than Funk Dream," offers nothing else of equal caliber. The remaining material uses too much aural gimmickry and tends to meander aimlessly without ever matching the urgent groove of the EP. [ds]

MEGADETH

Killing Is My Business . . . and Business Is Good! (Combat) 1985
Peace Sells . . . but Who's Buying? (Capitol) 1986 ●
So Far, So Good . . . So What! (Capitol) 1988 ●

After leaving Metallica, guitarist/songwriter Dave Mustaine formed Megadeth to better realize his vision of a band that would play a faster, louder and more intricate brand of metal with far more realistic and relevant lyrics (when you can make them out) than the usual metal macho bravado.

The quartet's first album meets most of those goals. The precise, complex (but clearly articulated) hyperspeed guitar power almost sails into jazz waters; Mustaine's rock vocals dispense with typical tremulous screeching for listenable roughness. Only the lyrics are business as usual: even a retitled overhaul of "These Boots Are Made for Walking" adds vulgarity to maximize headbanger appeal. Other songs—about death, sex and religion—witlessly tread well-worn ground. Still, Megadeth's galloping high-tech sound (check "Rattlehead" and "Mechanix")—soon to influence numerous young rock/metal bands—is clearly taking shape.

Peace Sells continues Megadeth's macabre assault on the senses. Like a metal version of Dante's Inferno, the LP offers various visions of hell on earth—murder, adultery, alienation, imprisonment and (d)evil cults. Quite frankly, the music's scarier than the lyrics, since Mustaine's strangled vocals are barely audible in the mix; the music, on the other hand, hurtles forward with undeniable and relentless power. Oldsters will be left stunned by the incredible version of Willie Dixon's (via Beck and Stewart) "I Ain't Superstitious," rewritten in trademark Megadeth style.

Recorded with a new guitarist and drummer, **So Far, So Good . . . So What!** includes a tribute to Metallica's late bassist Cliff Burton ("In My Darkest Hour"), a driving-while-drunk song ("502"), an instrumental that starts acoustically before hitting typical Mega-drive ("Into the Lungs of Hell"), an unnecessary (and lyrically inaccurate) cover of "Anarchy in the UK" with ex-Pistol Steve Jones in tow and the obligatory PMRC putdown ("Hook in Mouth"). Though Mustaine's vocals are improving and the new guys fit in fine, it's a bit of a letdown after **Peace Sells**.

Megadeth is also featured on the soundtracks to two recent Penelope Spheeris films: *Dudes* (a new, improved version of "These Boots Are Made for Walking") and *Decline of Western Civilization Part II: The Metal Years* (a hot live take of "In My Darkest Hour"). The group performs in the latter and Mustaine is also interviewed on camera. Both segments show why the group is a cut above the current metal crop. [ds]

MEKONS

The Quality of Mercy Is Not Strnen (nr/Virgin) 1979

Devils Rats and Piggies a Special Message
from Godzilla (nr/Red Rhino) 1980
It Falleth Like Gentle Rain from Heaven—The
Mekons Story (nr/CNT) 1982
The English Dancing Master EP (nr/CNT)
1983
Fear and Whiskey (nr/Sin) 1985
Crime and Punishment EP (nr/Sin) 1986
The Edge of the World (nr/Sin) 1986
Slightly South of the Border EP (nr/Sin) 1986
Honky Tonkin' (Sin-Twin/Tone) 1987
New York [tape] (ROIR) 1987
So Good It Hurts (Twin/Tone) 1988 ●
The Peel Sessions EP (nr/Strange Fruit) 1988

The Mekons (not to be confused with the
Manchester Mekon—both take their name
from TV's *Dr. Who*), like the Gang of Four,
hail from Leeds and work some of the same
fragmented guitar funk terrain on their first
album, an early post-punk landmark. Unfortunately, the screamed vocals obscure both
the music and the lyrics: minimalism is one
thing, but rank amateurism another. On the
second album (more commonly known as
The Mekons), the group moves into danceable synth-pop, with protest lyrics attacking
bourgeois culture, the army and hollow lives.
The Mekons Story is a retrospective album
of old tracks and outtakes, punctuated by
inter-track narration. The Mekons ceased
performing in 1980 and quit recording as
well after that 1982 release.

A large new incarnation (still helmed by
singer/guitarist/producer Jon Langford,
who divides his time between this group and
the Three Johns) returned the Mekons to
prominence and much international critical
adulation in 1985 with **Fear and Whiskey**, a
ragged album with sturdily memorable tunes
that mix equal parts of electrified rustic country dance music and cow-rock. Fiddle, piano
and harmonica join the guitars and drums for
a sound that is reasonably comparable to a
less loopy, more rocking version of John
Otway. Sin's label mimics Sun's; the sounds
are likewise Americanized and, characteristically for the new Mekons, a cover of Hank
Williams' "Lost Highway" closes the LP on
an appropriate note. Nothing (well, only
some things, perhaps) could be further from
the Mekons' early noise days. **Crime and
Punishment** offers four songs (including the
Robyn Hitchcock-like "Chop That Child in
Half" and Merle Haggard's "Deep End")
from a John Peel session.

Following the four-song 10-inch **Slightly
South of the Border**, **Honky Tonkin'** (named
for the Hank Williams lyric quoted on the

back cover) finds a cast of dozens (actually
one dozen) working its way stylistically toward the Pogues' drunkenly revisionist folk-
fundamentalism. A case of the sillies
("Sympathy for the Mekons") competes with
responsible topicality ("The Trimdon
Grange Explosion," "Kidnapped," "If They
Hang You," which eulogizes Dashiell Ham-
mett for refusing to name names at the
HUAC hearings) and conspicuous literacy
("Hole in the Ground," "Charlie Cake
Park"). The notes for each song cite relevant
books, movies or artworks for those un-
daunted by intellectualism. The genially appealing music, a well-organized wash of fiddles, accordion, guitars and simple drums,
makes few demands but keeps the folky standards high.

US tours by the octet in 1986 and 1987
yielded the live tracks (and assorted audio
ephemera, like commentary on various subjects by band members) compiled on **New
York**. The material is mostly drawn from
recent albums, although a version of the
Band's "The Shape I'm In" and a handful of
otherwise unreleased items are also included.
Motley but charming, it's a casually enlight-
ening trek.

So Good It Hurts has its share of fiddle
tunes but also expands the band's stylistic
repertoire to embrace reggae, straight rock
and calypso. The results suggest certain portions of the Clash's later career, as well as the
Boomtown Rats and other musical adventurers. The slickest, most accessible album in the
Mekons' long career, it holds fast to a po-
litely-delivered but tough-minded political
consciousness (Richard Nixon is mentioned
in more than one song), pausing to include
the Stones' "Heart of Stone." Although unsettling in its normalcy, **So Good It Hurts** is
a stimulating new chapter in this unfinished
saga. [gf/iar]

MELODY MAKERS
See *Ziggy Marley.*

MEMBERS
At the Chelsea Nightclub (Virgin Int'l) 1979
1980—The Choice Is Yours (nr/Virgin) 1980
Radio EP (Arista) 1982
Uprhythm, Downbeat (Arista) 1982
Going West (nr/Albion) 1983

At the Chelsea Nightclub finds the Members using punk as a jumping-off point, but
that doesn't tell the whole musical story. In-

cipient instrumental smarts and simple tunes nailed down by infectious, above-average riffs countered the rough-edged delivery and Nicky Tesco's one-of-the-lads vocals. The themes—mainly variations on the suburban kid in the city getting streetwise fast—are framed in mischievous yet endearing (even corny) humor. The album's added bonus is that it contains one of the first, and even now best, white punk ventures into reggae (including, on the US pressing, the subsequent "Offshore Banking Business" single). Thoroughly entertaining.

The second album, however, signaled the advent of a downswing from which the band never really recovered. The material seems thin—a cover of ex-Pink Fairy Larry Wallis' "Police Car" is far and away the most memorable track—and any spark and grit the band might have mustered is sterilized by Rupert Hine's production. (The first LP was produced by Steve, the brother of the Members' drummer, Adrian Lillywhite.)

Working with Martin Rushent, the Members' comeback—after a layoff which some mistook for a breakup—sounded for real, first on the teaser EP (one extra track on the US version) and then more substantially on the third LP. Besides the crisp, full sound, the quintet had grown to a septet with a pair of horns, and the music integrated funk and rap in addition to reggae. No longer humorous, lyrics instead alternate social critiques/rallying cries with personal traumas, at which they prove less adept, but the music is more powerful and danceable than ever. Inspired touch: reggaefication of Kraftwerk's "The Model." (About a year after **Uprhythm, Downbeat**'s release in America, it was finally issued—as **Going West**—in the UK. The cassette version has extra tracks.)   [jg]

MEMBRANES

Muscles EP (nr/Rondelet) 1982
Pin Stripe Hype EP (nr/Rondelet) 1982
Crack House EP (nr/Criminal Damage) 1983
Death to Trad Rock EP (nr/Criminal Damage) 1985
The Gift of Life (nr/Creation) 1985
Giant (nr/Constrictor) 1986
Everything's Brilliant EP (nr/In Tape) 1986
Songs of Love and Fury (Homestead) 1986
Time-Warp 1991 (Long Live Trad Rock) EP (Homestead) 1987
Back Catalogue: Peter Sellers Versus the Virgin Mary (nr/Vinyl Drip) 1987
Kiss Ass Godhead (Homestead) 1988

Stalwarts of the British independent recording scene, Blackpool's Membranes have essayed numerous styles with countless line-ups. They began as a quirky, not-too-loud quartet, playing simple tunes with offbeat lyrics and melodica for unexpected coloration. **Back Catalogue** reprises 15 early efforts, including a rare 1980 flexi-disc, the contents of two four-song EPs (the 12-inch **Muscles**, **Pin Stripe Hype**) and three re-recordings of the same material. The six-song **Crack House**, done as a bass/guitar/drums trio, finds the Membranes nearing their creative peak, shooting out jagged, tense jazz-tinged punk—ugly, abrasive, ambitious and gripping—as well as more accessible droney rock.

Death to Trad Rock builds the guitar chaos to an unnerving plateau on four lengthy songs that also feature bassist John Robb's manic vocals and, on "Myths and Legends," a guest violinist. With Robb switching over to guitar, however, **The Gift of Life** sails right over the edge in a tumult of screaming, banging and incoherent music. The goofy "I Am Fisheye" chant offers a briefly amusing alternative, but this seemingly tossed-off album deserves tossing. Jon (Three Johns/Mekons) Langford adds guitar on the title track; a saxophonist only adds to the din. **Giant** is a compilation.

Produced by Langford, the "Everything's Brilliant" 12-inch (two versions plus three B-sides) returns the Membranes to the realm of responsible musicmaking, moving a clear, gothic drum sound and give-a-shit sloppy vocals to the fore and relegating guitars to a subsidiary role at non-distorto volume levels. **Songs of Love and Fury**, with another new bassist and Nick Brown (a guest contributor soon to become a permanent member) adding guitar and violin, takes a further step backwards, almost eliminating electric guitars entirely. Not that far in sound from the band's earliest work, songs like "Kennedy '63," "Day My Universe Changed" and "Phoney T.V. Repairman" mix a flat, trippy '60s approach with the lyrical attitude of Mark E. Smith. A little hard to fathom at first, **Love and Fury**—the band's first US release—reveals itself gradually to be one of the Membranes' best records.

Time-Warp is entirely different, a highly-produced and carefully-performed collection of six folk-rock originals that sound like something the Animals might have done after "Sky Pilot." Synthesizers, drum programs and sound effects add to the bewildering fray. Robb's vocals are reverbed and mixed into a semblance of melodiousness; while not a great record, it certainly is an unexpected one. Incidentally, artist Simon Clegg deserves kudos for his unfailingly brilliant artwork on all of the Membranes' covers and sleeves.

Steve Albini (ex-Big Black) co-produced **Kiss Ass Godhead** with the Membranes; songs like "Bulbous Love Child" "Long Live the Hooligan!" and "Cheap Male Aggression" are as chaotically loud and abrasive as one might expect. [iar]

MEN & VOLTS
Rhythms & Blues EP (Eat) 1982
*Hootersville (Eat) 1983
Tramps in Bloom (Fr. New Rose) 1984
(Iridescence) 1985
The Mule (Shimmy-Disc) 1987

With the arcane musical instincts of Captain Beefheart and the dada poetic mindset of Tom Waits, the well-educated Men & Volts (based in the Boston area, although mainstay/lyricist David Greenberger lives in upstate NY) debuted with the challenging and bizarre **Rhythms & Blues**. Employing horns and difficult tempos, the quartet offers the same four songs—including "Rotten Truth," a disturbing number superficially about cats—pressed on both sides.

*Hootersville (the cover is a map detail; the asterisk marks a locale) is a very full album bursting with unpredictable music that veers from complex and noisy to charmingly rustic and even pastoral. The lyrics on songs like "Pickwick Papers," "Big Ball of String" and "No Shower No Shave" similarly traverse a wide range of topics and are often amusingly absurdist. Stimulating and entertaining.

Dropping the brass and revealing a new folk-based orientation, **Tramps in Bloom** keeps the guitar-built music rudimentary, allowing simply witty paeans to "New York," "Someone Else's Money" and "The History of the Moon" to speak for themselves. At times sounding like the Band, elsewhere resembling the Grateful Dead, Men & Volts make no effort to dress up their artless songs, and it's just as well. Remaining offhandedly unprofessional (not unaccomplished) is no mean feat.

Sounding even more like the Dead, **The Mule** has cloudy sound (so much for direct mastering to metal), noticeably more ambitious arrangements (although nothing you'd

call fancy) and serious, sensitive evocations of loneliness ("Records Go 'Round"), aging ("You and Me, Pushin' Up Daisies") and several intriguing characters ("The Loveless," "One Holiday Too Many"). Not a spectacular record, but one with old-fashioned attributes that won't leave you wondering where to park your brain. [iar]

MENTAL AS ANYTHING
Mental as Anything Play at Your Party EP
(Aus. Regular) 1978
Get Wet (Aus. Regular) 1979
Mental as Anything (nr/Virgin) 1980
Expresso Bongo (Aus. Regular) 1980
Cats and Dogs (Aus. Regular) 1981
If You Leave Me, Can I Come Too? (A&M)
1982
Creatures of Leisure (Oz-A&M) 1983
Fundamental (Columbia) 1986
Mouth to Mouth (Columbia) 1988 ●

A kind of Australian Rockpile with a case of the vaudeville giggles, Sydney's Mental as Anything first surfaced Down Under in 1978 with an EP containing a sly, skiffle-like drinking song called "The Nips Are Getting Bigger" (featured on **Get Wet**, **Mental as Anything**—the equivalent UK release—and the US debut **If You Leave Me**) which accurately summarizes their pub-rock earthiness and randy humor. **Get Wet** is certainly a good-natured introduction to a band unafraid to write a love song to a foreign country based on travel ads ("Egypt") or pitch a cheesy instrumental bit with Sam the Sham organ as a "Possible Theme for a Future TV Drama Series."

Combining one song from **Get Wet** and the best of the Australian-only **Cats and Dogs**, the Anglo-American compilation **If You Leave Me, Can I Come Too?** is more of the same—the band's (un)usual mix of cheek and underlying lyrical sincerity captured in the poignant "Mr. Normal" drawl of singer/guitarist Martin Plaza. The album also features a track produced by Elvis Costello ("I Didn't Mean to Be Mean") in which the rest of the band—guitarist Reg Mombassa, organist Greedy Smith, bassist Peter O'Doherty and drummer Wayne Delisle—work up a good Attractions-like head of steam.

Creatures of Leisure reveals an overwhelmingly downcast band, singing wistful lyrics about romantic discord ("Bitter to Swallow," "Float Away") and a general lack of gumption ("Nothing's Going Right Today," "Spirit Got Lost"). Even the music is depressed, playing in the same countryish style with barely a trace of enthusiasm. These boys are down, and can't help but lay their burden down in the grooves. Without wallowing in self-pity or indulging in any overt declarations of misery, **Creatures of Leisure** is an enormously sad record.

A much better frame of mind prevails on **Fundamental**. Songs like "I Just Wanna Be Happy" and "Live It Up" offer optimistic lyrics about getting past hard times and bad feelings. Other subjects temper that attitude: in "Hold On," O'Doherty admits a case of the guilts about a ladyfriend, while Plaza marvels about public transportation in "Bus Ride." As produced by Richard Gottehrer, the Mentals' music has hit a certain stride that discourages zaniness (a shame), but their sound—still an Australian answer to Nick Lowe—is never less than bouncily appealing.

The emotional barometer holds steady on **Mouth to Mouth**, another Gottehrer production. Employing plain and pleasant music that could use a bit of a recharge, Plaza delivers harsh words to an ex in "Don't Tell Me Now" and "Thinking Out Loud"; Smith welcomes an old friend in "My Door Is Always Open to You" and offers a hopeful suggestion (in the very Nick Lowe-ish "Let's Go to Paradise"). O'Doherty expresses his pleasure about an ongoing relationship in "I'm Glad." There isn't an unlikable moment anywhere on the record, but the Mentals seem in danger of drifting into musical senility unless they find some collective personality and start showing a little more enthusiasm.

[df/iar]

MEN THEY COULDN'T HANG

Night of a Thousand Candles (nr/Imp) 1985
Greenback Dollar EP (nr/Demon) 1986
How Green Is the Valley (nr/MCA) 1987

One of the current rock bands not too unlike the Pogues, this electrified quintet doesn't put a specific ethnic cant to its trad-folkified originals, but does employ similar instruments (e.g., tin whistle, Uillean pipes) and was partially produced by Philip Chevron of MacGowan's clan. Comparisons aside, **Night of a Thousand Candles** (which, incidentally, covers an Eric Bogle song, as have the Pogues) is a fine record, from the tenderness of "Hush Little Baby" to the brutality of "Johnny Come Home." Throughout, MTCH show abundant spirit and a real flair for tossing the occasional odd component into the songwriting stew.   [iar]

MEN WITHOUT HATS

Folk of the 80's EP (Can. Trend) 1980 (Stiff) 1981
The Safety Dance (nr/Statik) 1982 •
Rhythm of Youth (Backstreet-MCA) 1982
Folk of the 80's (Part III) (MCA) 1984
Pop Goes the World (Mercury) 1987 •

From an almost-unknown Stiff EP to a million-selling debut album, Montreal's Men Without Hats made their incredible one-step ascent without drastically revising their sound. Although **Folk of the 80's** is somewhat rudimentary, Ivan Doroschuk's remarkably obnoxious singing is already in full flower and the songs display his characteristically skewed lyrical perceptions and aggressively bouncy tunes.

Reprising the EP's "Antarctica" while adding an unlikely and aggravating hit single, "The Safety Dance," and the eminently likable "I Got the Message," **Rhythm of Youth** (roughly the same record as **The Safety Dance**) is slicker but otherwise pretty similar to the band's first release in every aspect save sales volume. Ivan's yelping and theatrical bellowing cries out for the swift application of duct tape to his mouth; still, the band's earnest individuality makes the album hard to truly dislike. The 1984 follow-up leaves the formula unchanged, and songs like "Where Do the Boys Go?" and "Messiahs Die Young" are reasonably sprightly and entertaining; other parts drag mercilessly as Ivan's inflated self-image is delivered pompously to vinyl.

Chastened by the second album's commercial disappointment, Ivan took a lengthy powder, returning three years later with the best single of his career, "Pop Goes the World," done for the soundtrack of *Date with an Angel*. Unfortunately, the rest of what surrounds that insidious techno-pop ditty on the album of the same name is only pleasantly dull. But give the group—now an artificial quartet of Ivan, his brother Stefan "in the guise of Johnny the guitarist," a bassist named Jenny and noncorporeal drummer J. Bonhomme —the strangest guest of the week award for getting Jethro Tull leader Ian Anderson to add a spot of flute on one song.

[iar]

MERCY SEAT

See *Violent Femmes*.

356

MERTON PARKAS

Face in the Crowd (nr/Beggars Banquet) 1979
The Singles EP (nr/Beggars Banquet) 1983

If the Merton Parkas had called their LP **Just Another Face in the Neo-Mod Crowd**, no review of it would be needed. This utterly unmemorable group had nondescript vocals, tame playing (guitar and piano so polite as to be biteless even at high volume) and dull songs (a cover of "Tears of a Clown" not excepted). They do deserve two points for the name, a pun combining the band's London neighborhood and the essential outer garment of Mod garb. Ha, ha. The group finally earned posthumous notoriety when keyboardist Mick Talbot became Paul Weller's partner in the Style Council.   [jg]

METAL BOYS

See *Metal Urbain.*

METALLICA

Kill 'Em All (Megaforce) 1983 (Elektra)
     1987 ●
Garage Days Revisited EP (nr/Phonogram)
     1984
Ride The Lightning (Megaforce) 1984
     (Megaforce-Elektra) 1984 ●
Whiplash EP (Megaforce) 1985
Master of Puppets (Elektra) 1986 ●
The $5.98 E.P. Garage Days Re-Revisited EP
     (Elektra) 1987 ●

At the forefront of heavy metal's new independent (in sound and label affiliation) wave, California's Metallica originally contained Dave Mustaine, but he had left to form Megadeth by the time **Kill 'Em All** was recorded in mid-'83. Shrugging off many of the genre's traditional sonic clichés to retain only the power, velocity and blazing guitars, the quartet's debut contains impressive instrumental tracks with insignificant vocals by skatepunk James Hetfield. Bracingly unusual (although hardly radical), tracks like "The Four Horsemen" show off lead guitarist Kirk Hammett's technical prowess as well as the mighty Cliff Burton/Lars Ulrich rhythm section. (The 1987 reissue adds a pair of metalband covers originally released on the import-only **Garage Days Revisited**, some copies of which contained four songs—others were pressed with five.)

Ride the Lightning has worse vocals and better guitar playing: lyrics about life and death add little to the literature, but Ham-mett's proficiency is indeed something at which to marvel. The band's overly limited self-production and half-baked riffs and melodies ("For Whom the Bell Tolls" is a notable exception) undercut the onslaught a bit, but the LP remains a convincing powerhouse for fans.

Despite radio's general boycott of underground metal, Metallica managed to get **Master of Puppets**, generally acknowledged to be their best record, into the Top 30. Multi-tracked harmony solos, tautly controlled rhythms and simple vocal arrangements make songs about insanity ("Welcome Home (Sanitarium)" and "The Things That Should Not Be"), the futility of war ("Disposable Heroes") and cocaine addiction ("Master of Puppets") burn white-hot with excitement.

Metallica's future was cast in doubt in September 1986 when a bus crash in Sweden killed Burton. But they recruited new bassist Jason Newsted (ex-Flotsam and Jetsam) and returned in late '87 with **The $5.98 E.P. Garage Days Re-Revisited**, an intriguingly-conceived package of five cover versions recorded casually in LA during rehearsal jams. The bands favored with Metallicazation include Budgie, Killing Joke and the Misfits. Despite the fascinating selection, however, the hurried execution reduces everything to soundalike dullness.   [iar/rj]

METAL URBAIN

Les Hommes Mort (Fr. Celluloid) 1980
L'Age d'Or (Fr. Fan Club) 1985

METAL BOYS

Tokyo Airport (Fr. Celluloid) 1979

Shouted vocals (in French), distorted slash'n'twang punk guitars, ticking percussion—that's what characterizes Metal Urbain, fiery young Gauls who were France's most extreme "progressive" punks at the time. This is harsh and forbidding music, but the group's ultimate place in history will be assured more than anything by their having cut, in 1978, the first single in the extensive Rough Trade catalog.

The Metal Boys were an early splinter of Metal Urbain: they modify the formula to include more (fragmentary) English lyrics and electronic processing. The overall effect sounds considered and industrial—if just as intimidating—in its approach to the texturing of noise. *Formidable.*   [jg]

METEORS

Teenage Heart (PVC) 1979
Hungry (Hol. EMI) 1980

This Dutch sextet is kind of raunchy for such a modern combo: Hugo Sinzheimer's vocals are like Bowie in truck-driver drag, and the band could be Lene Lovich's backup with more guitar and motorcycle jackets. In fact, Lovich picked the lover's pledge, "It's You, Only You," from **Teenage Heart** and recorded it for her own **No-Man's-Land**. Then again, the Meteors also offer an anthem of lust frustrated, "(One Hand) on the Wheel," whose UK title and the chorus are "My Balls Ache." Lots of punch and melodic smarts, but overly juvenile when they turn to swagger'n'shock tactics.

The Meteors shed some of their musical rough edges on **Hungry** in favor of more sophisticated arrangements facilitated, no doubt, by Conny Plank's production. Though the material isn't as immediately appealing as on their first LP, it's more consistent, and the lyrics (save a couple of missteps) indicate growth, with less gratuitous sleaze and even occasional eloquence limning the underside of life. [jg]

METHOD ACTORS

Rhythms of You (nr/Armageddon) 1981
Dancing Underneath EP (DB) 1981
Little Figures (nr/Armageddon) 1981 (Press) 1982
Live in a Room! EP (Press) 1983
Luxury (Press) 1983

The Method Actors hail from the Dixie avant-pop capital of Athens, Georgia, where they made their concert debut on Halloween, 1979. Like Pylon, they dealt in minimalist dance/trance rock. They also made a lot of noise for just two guys. The seven-track 10-inch **Rhythms of You** is a crisp, aggressive capsulization of the Actors' act, a danceable Wire in the stark contrast between David Gamble's thundering drums and Vic Varney's perky chicken-scratch guitar (and bass). "No Condition" is particularly riveting, its psycho-Ramones drive heightened by Varney's choogling guitar and the pair's vocals, one a droll singspeak and the other a madhouse wail.

Dancing Underneath is a 12-inch variation of the first EP, subtracting three tracks but adding the new "E-Y-E," which recalls the experimental dub funk of Public Image's **Metal Box**, thanks to Gamble's hard, shift-ing syncopation and Varney's disorienting overdubbed guitar conversation.

In England, where the Method Actors received ecstatic press, **Little Figures** was originally released as a double album. Songs like "Commotion," a locomotive number with a catchy bass figure and quasi-Eastern guitar interjections (à la Keith Levene), and "Bleeding," with clipped-bass funk rhythm and dub vocal effects, reinforce the PiL comparison. But the Actors add the exotic clang of steel drums to "Halloween"; "I'm in the Mood for Love" (a Varney original) has an eerie poppish melody underlined only by bass guitar before breaking into a hammy "Volga Boatmen" chorus. The American version of **Little Figures**, a one-record distillation with ten of the original 17 cuts, is recommended for the slightly less adventurous. (This version, to complicate discographical matters, was subsequently released in the UK as well.)

Although the Actors first made their reputation as live performers, **Live in a Room!**—recorded at Atlanta's 688 Club—is a disappointing documentary of them on stage. (It must be noted that this is not the original band: Gamble had been replaced by ex-Swimming Pool Q Robert Schmid.) The addition of saxman Stan Satin and occasional guitarist/bassist Michael Richmond (on loan from Love Tractor) fills out their sound without weighing it down. Unfortunately, bootleg-style sound quality dulls the group's manic edge.

Retaining the maximum strength lineup featured on the live record, the Method Actors' next (and final) release was as a quartet. **Luxury** includes a bizarre rocking rendition of the Velvet Underground's "All Tomorrow's Parties" as well as Varney's songs (some co-written with others). Satin's aimless (and ceaseless) sax is an unwelcome addition to the sound, while Varney's falsetto vocals provide ludicrous counterpoint to the rugged beat music. [df/iar]

ANTHONY MEYNELL & SQUIRE

See *Squire.*

M.I.A./GENOCIDE

Last Rites for M.I.A. and Genocide (Smoke 7) 1981

M.I.A.

Murder in a Foreign Place (Alternative Tentacles) 1984

Notes from the Underground (National Trust)
1985
After the Fact (Flipside) 1987

Although Las Vegas may be an entertainment capital, its gambling tourists typically prefer Wayne Newton or Bill Cosby to the Sex Pistols. As a result, Vegas' only great punk band gave up before their career could get off the ground. Were it not for their half of a posthumous release, the prematurely titled **Last Rites**, M.I.A. would have remained an unknown, gifted punk band. **Last Rites** sold well, especially after its outstanding opener, "Tell Me Why" (not the Beatles' tune), was included on **American Youth Report**, an excellent West Coast punk/hardcore compilation. Finding themselves wanted, M.I.A. reformed for good, relocating to the more supportive Southern California punk community.

Last Rites contains a side each by M.I.A. and New Jersey's Genocide. (The less said about *them* the better.) Although M.I.A. come across as naive, uncomplicated, almost willfully unimaginative 1-2-3-4-off-we-go punk, the record drips with the excitement that many such records of that time had. The roaring guitar sounds like a Marshall amp on 12 (one higher than Spinal Tap) and the hooks are as instant as oatmeal—just add *steaming* water. Mike Conley's singing is unusually clear, easy to decipher and pop-melodic. The subject of "Gas Crisis" may be out of date, but on the pulverizing two-chord verse of "I Hate Hippies," Conley's ironic tongue is so far in his cheek it's almost coming out his ear: "Cause they're dumb/I'm smart/They're weak/I'm strong/I'm right/and they're fucking wrong." Hilarious!

The songs on **Murder in a Foreign Place** aren't overly political; the music resembles early Brit-punk (Generation X, Sham 69) in spots. By tempering fierce enthusiasm with clear organization (although the mix buries Conley), relatively leisurely tempos and musical coherence, M.I.A. rises well above the crowd.

The much-improved **Notes from the Underground** leaves hardcore behind for a pretty fair Damned/TSOL-influenced punk LP with occasional acoustic guitar and even sax (on an anti-apartheid song). The hooks are occasionally a little too obvious, but "Another Day," "Write Myself a Letter" and "Shadows of My Life" are first-rate punk-pop. Nick Adams' wall of guitar dominates each of the ten tracks.

After the Fact is one of the best US punk records of the last few years, mostly because it mixes in many post-punk influences, and innovates where other punks cling to tradition. The two guitars rarely play similar parts, there are dynamics and mood settings, contemplative sound ("Whisper in the Wind") and even a Killing Jokey tribal backbeat ("When It's Over"). The production on **After the Fact** is far superior to M.I.A.'s past efforts, with real bottom, kick, drive and guts. Just check out the cover of "California Dreaming" or the effortless "Edge of Forever" for proof that punk can be a fresh aural pleasure, even in the late-'80s. M.I.A. ultimately paid the same price that the original TSOL and the original Effigies did when they went against the grain and tried to take punk to its next step: they split up in early 1988.
[jr]

MICRODISNEY

Everybody's Fantastic (nr/Rough Trade) 1983
We Hate You South African Bastards! EP
  (nr/Rough Trade) 1984
Microdisney in the World EP (nr/Rough
  Trade) 1985
The Clock Comes Down the Stairs (Big Time)
  1985
Crooked Mile (Virgin) 1986 ●
39 Minutes (nr/Virgin) 1988 ●

Originally a duo from Cork, Microdisney combine heavily orchestrated smooth pop with potent songwriting. A sublimely seductive paradox, the music goes down easy but invariably returns to haunt the intellect. After moving to London and recruiting three more members, Cathal Coughlan (vocals/lyrics) and Sean O'Hagan (guitar/music) recorded **Everybody's Fantastic**, 13 gently atmospheric songs that touch the heart and the mind with resonant guitar and Coughlan's passionate brogue. Starkly romantic ("Dolly," "I'll Be a Gentleman") and ardently political ("Come on Over and Cry," "Before the Famine"), the record commands attention.

Virtually nonexistent commercial response to their first LP prompted the release of **We Hate You South African Bastards!**, a mini-album compilation of early singles and demos recorded as a duo that assured Microdisney's surivival while making an unequivocal statement against apartheid. Their next release was a four-song 12-inch of new material, **In the World**.

The Clock Comes Down the Stairs suffers from improved production: Coughlan's vocals, curiously relieved of their Irish accent, are set deep within a mix of overwhelming instrumentation. "Birthday Girl," "Horse Overboard" and "Past" are pleasant enough, but verge on a generic sound. Gone are Coughlan's heartfelt protests and O'Hagan's sharp melodic chords, making this complacent background muzak—a far cry from the compelling impact of **We Hate You**. (The tape has five extra songs.)

The drawbacks so prevalent on **The Clock Comes Down the Stairs** reassert themselves on **Crooked Mile**. Lenny Kaye's typically lush production renders this LP as nothing more than a collection of languid, dismissible pop symphonies. One exception, however, is the passionate "Give Me All of Your Clothes"—the first possible sign that Microdisney may be getting just a bit tired of churning out this kind of useless fodder.

[ag]

MICRONOTZ
Smash! (Fresh Sounds) 1983
The Beast That Devoured Itself (Fresh Sounds) 1985
40 Fingers (Homestead) 1986

MORTAL MICRONOTZ
The Mortal Micronotz (Fresh Sounds) 1982
Live Recording of the Video Soundtrack EP
  (Fresh Sounds) 1984

This quartet—teenagers at the outset, their minds filled with the world—must have felt constricted in the confines of Lawrence, Kansas, where not having long hair and loving heavy metal is evidently enough to make you the odd kid out. The sound on the Mortal Micronotz album is a little tinny, but these guys have your standard '70s Ameripunk moves down cold—sort of a sub-Dead Boys, but tighter. Dean Lubensky is actually an okay singer, making the adolescent alienation lyrics sound more believable than they read. He also handles lyrics given to the band by homeboy William S. Burroughs with similar aplomb. Added treat: a good'n'noisy version of "Let It All Hang Out," which the Hombres first released when these guys were still in diapers.

Their name truncated and Burroughs nowhere in sight, the Micronotz show no sign of losing any of their rock'n'roll energy on **Smash!**, a 45 rpm album that includes Iggy's "I Got a Right" plus seven originals. Lu-

bensky's vocals are mighty rough, John Harper's guitar playing pretty swift and the song subjects a bit more mature; a convincing record with a personality (of sorts) all its own. Production could have been a lot clearer, though.

The band's next release (under the old name) was a 33 1/3 rpm 7-inch EP containing five live renditions. Lubensky then left and was replaced by Jay Hauptli in time for **The Beast That Devoured Itself**, another raggedly entertaining punked-out collection that generally rises above all of the genre's typical limitations.

The bracingly good **40 Fingers** is a triumphant stylistic distillation, a powerful and varied dose of mature post-thrash intelligence that in spots resembles Hüsker Dü. Without losing any of their adolescent strength, the Micronotz are playing better than ever, and Hauptli's coarse vocals have gained a melodic validity, vastly improved by Harper's harmonies. (At times they sound a tad like the Ramones.) A cover of Simon and Garfunkel's "Scarborough Fair" serves as a showcase for the band's newfound abilities.

[jg/iar]

LOS MICROWAVES
Life After Breakfast (Posh Boy) 1981
DAVID MICROWAVE
David Microwave EP (Posh Boy) 1980
BABY BUDDHA
Music for Teenage Sex (Posh Boy) 1981

Los Microwaves—David Javelosa (aka David Microwave), Meg Brazil and Todd Rosa—were a San Francisco trio in which synthesizers predominated. Although they issued 45s as early as 1979, their debut album came out in 1981, by which time leader Javelosa (who's done other production/playing jobs since) had done a five-song, 12-inch EP on his own, using musicians outside his band.

Life After Breakfast shows promise, employing machines to make music that is arty but not obtuse; the vocals (shared by Brazil and Javelosa) don't display the same restraint, too often wandering off into dissonant unpleasantness. On the whole, while the album has its moments, too much draggy material and annoying passages ankle it.

Javelosa's solo effort is much better, offering straightforward (for synths, that is) pop music with swirling keyboards (including familiar-sounding organ), acoustic drums and engaging vocals. The record shows polish, but retains a slightly amateurish sense, making it paradoxically complex and simple at the same time.

Baby Buddha, which involves Javelosa and some of Los otro Microwaves, is a concept piece—one side of his originals, the remainder irreverently synthed-up covers of such standards as "My Generation," "Stand by Your Man" and "All Shook Up." Although portions are both funny and fun, too much of it is merely an overly weird in-joke.　　　　　　　　　　　　　　　　　　　[iar]

MIDDLE CLASS
Homeland (Pulse) 1982

Wrapped in a truly gorgeous jacket, **Homeland** is arty California folk-rock co-produced by the ubiquitous Paul Cutler. Its unpleasant starkness derives mainly from Jeff Atta's colorless (and tuneless) declamatory vocals, but also from the jagged, interwoven guitars that fill the songs and Matt Simon's (later the Pontiac Brothers' singer) drumming, which hurries things along like a waiter in a snooty restaurant.　　　　　[iar]

MIDNIGHT OIL
Midnight Oil (Aus. Powderworks) 1978
Head Injuries (Aus. Powderworks) 1979
Bird Noises EP (Aus. Powderworks) 1980
Place Without a Postcard (Aus. CBS) 1981
10,9,8,7,6,5,4,3,2,1 (Columbia) 1983 ●
Red Sails in the Sunset (Columbia) 1985
Diesel and Dust (Columbia) 1987 ●

A quintet that originally found a following in the rowdy surf crowd frequenting Sydney-area bars, Australia's Midnight Oil went on to become a national phenomenon, and its music grew far beyond its hard-rock roots. But that categorization never quite fit in the first place; hearing their watershed **10,9,8,7, 6,5,4,3,2,1** and then reviewing their previous output, the natural query of "how did they make that leap" becomes "what took them so long?"

Oil's iconoclasm is the primary answer. Lead singer Peter Garrett both symbolizes and embodies it: well over six feet tall and bald as a cue ball, he gave up a law career to sing rock'n'roll. His angst/anger-ridden vocals have nothing in common with the standard styles of hard-rock singers, nor do the band's lyrics share any of the genre's fixation

on refried love themes. The songs are frequently political, yet just as often are couched in extremely personal terms, be they about romance (rarely), self-doubt, hopes and fears and so on. And despite its share of semi-normal hard-rock, complete with blistering guitar solos, the eponymous debut album also includes strange notions about chord progressions and arrangements that would eventually flower: "Dust" is a bluesy riff stated on two basses an octave apart, backed by organ and drums.

No doubt the group's insistence on democratic songwriting and generally doing things its own way had something to do with their refusing a major-league deal for five years. Unfortunately, that also meant a lack of money for studio experimentation, and most of their independent-label work sounds like demos, lacking the firm command of a proper producer.

Democracy also retarded the band in working out the complexities of songs and arrangements, including adapting the music to odd lyrical meter (and/or vice versa). **Head Injuries** makes some progress on that front, and the songwriting—still largely done by various teams in the group—seems to have matured. Several listenings reveal a clutch of songs able to transcend the limitations of their presentation, assisted by Garrett's impassioned vocals and the group's overall intensity. What seem at first to be arranging gaffes eventually take on an air of almost integral idiosyncrasy. The EP continues that development and also features an anomalous but delightful Shadows-like instrumental, "Wedding Cake Island."

Place Without a Postcard should've been a brilliant breakthrough; instead, it's muscle-bound, all worked up and uncertain where to go first. The few simple strokes are the most effective—in fact, "Someone Else to Blame" is a crackler—but most of it's at war with itself. Also, the sound achieved with veteran producer Glyn Johns in England is demo-thin. But the experimentation yielded valuable lessons, and James Moginie, the group's most prolific composer, also began to jell his distinctive guitar sound, as well as creatively exploring keyboards. The stage was set for the group's international introduction.

The strong political views expressed on **10,9,8,7,6,5,4,3,2,1** may have been a sticking point outside the band's homeland, but they're frequently more personally expressed than, say, the Clash's and, when not, they're

361

more articulate. In any case, Australian *Rolling Stone* named **10,9,8,7,6,5,4,3,2,1** album of the year, and why not? Increased use of synthesizer handsomely complements the quintet's most cohesive songwriting and arranging; while no two tracks are more than vaguely similar, they're all completely unified. Some credit must also go to Nick Launay (co-producer, with the band), who obtained a crisp, if slightly odd, sound. From the desperate hopefulness of "Outside World" to the marvelously rampaging, near-hysterical riffarama of "Only the Strong," to the danceable but authentically fist-shaking "Power and the Passion," it's a masterpiece.

On **Red Sails in the Sunset** (again with Launay), the Oils indulge in too much experimentation at once (though more successfully than **Place Without a Postcard**). The LP opens with two relatively simple tracks, "When the Generals Talk" (more clichéd than the band's usual political statements, but a stirring mix of hard rock and—new for the Oils—funk) and "Best of Both Worlds," one of their best straight-ahead rockers ever. From there on, excessive musical complexity, plus some topics that are simply beyond the pale of non-Australians, make it heavy going. Some tracks (notably "Sleep" and "Minute to Midnight") do unfold eventually, but others remain steadfastly impenetrable.

Diesel and Dust isn't brilliant, but it's damned good. The production (the band with Warne Livesey) is snappier than ever. The tunes aren't quite up to the Oils' best, but the passion for the issues at hand comes across loud and clear. Actually, the passion comes across even when the issues don't; few Americans who made "Beds are Burning" the Oils' first US hit single had any idea it was about Aboriginal land rights. **Diesel** also finds the Oils doing some healthy consolidation of strengths. They're not beyond a bit of self-recycling (e.g., **Diesel**'s "Bullroarer" partially reprocesses **Red Sails**' "Sleep"), but that's an easy trade for such dandy goods as "The Dead Heart," sung from an Aborigine's point of view. [jg]

MIGHTY LEMON DROPS

Happy Head (Sire) 1986
Out of Hand (Sire) 1987
World Without End (Sire-Reprise) 1988 ●

Imagine the neo-psychedelia of early Echo and the Bunnymen played with a ringing Rickenbacker as the lead instrument and a less mannered (and less interesting) vocalist and you're on your way to understanding the sound of **Happy Head**. That's not to take anything away from the intensity or dynamic mood shifts Wolverhampton's Lemon Drops (until 1986 known as the Sherbet Monsters) can achieve, but it's hard to hear the album without making the connection. That said, there's at least a side's worth of first-rate songs here, and the uncluttered, stripped-down approach is distinctive enough to recommend it to anyone who likes this sort of thing. (Historical aside: guitarist Dave Newton formed the Mighty Lemon Drops following a 1984 debut album with his previous band, the Wild Flowers.)

Out of Hand, an eight-cut hodgepodge comprising energetic but unrevelatory live versions of three of **Happy Head**'s better songs and some new tunes that add string synthesizers and Eastern flavoring (shades of "The Cutter"!) to the brew, is for fans only. It has the feel of product put out to coincide with a tour or some such.

World Without End shows a group that's matured past obvious comparisons. The sound is fuller and warmer than before, the arrangements more sophisticated. Singer Paul Marsh, if not riveting, exudes confidence. The downside is the loss of some of **Happy Head**'s manic energy, but the band's growing legion of fans doesn't seem to mind. The CD adds "Shine." [ds]

MIGHTY WAH!
See *Wah!*.

MILK 'N' COOKIES
See *Ian North*.

MILKSHAKES

Talking 'bout Milkshakes (nr/Milkshakes)
    1983 + 1986
14 Rhythm & Beat Greats (nr/Big Beat) 1983
After School Session (nr/Upright) 1983
Milkshakes IV: The Men with the Golden
    Guitars (Milkshakes) 1983
The Milkshakes in Germany (nr/Wall City)
    1984
The Milkshakes Sing and Play 20 Rock and
    Roll Hits of the 50's and 60's (nr/Big
    Beat) 1984
Nothing Can Stop These Men (nr/Milkshakes)
    1984

Brand New Cadillac EP (nr/Big Beat) 1984
Showcase (Brain Eater) 1984
They Came They Saw They Conquered (Pink Dust-Enigma) 1984
Thee Knights of Trashe (nr/Milkshakes) 1984
Ambassadors of Love (nr/Big Beat) 1984
The 107 Tapes (nr/Media Burn) 1985
The Milkshakes Revenge (nr/Hangman) 1985
Live from Chatham (nr/Hangman) 1987

MILKSHAKES & PRISONERS
The Last Night at the M.I.C. Club (nr/Empire) 1986
Milkshakes vs. Prisoners (nr/Media Burn) 1986

THE BILLY CHILDISH
The 1982 Cassetes (nr/Hangman) 1987

Once a Canterbury punk band called the Pop Rivits, as the (also "Thee") Milkshakes, this foursome—led by guitarist Billy Childish—quickly became leaders (if only for their monumental output) of the British trash/garage revivalist movement when they switched over to a wonderful, demented guitar-based brew of '60s beat, demi-punk, Link Wray, Chan Romero, R&B and Crampabilly. They've since released *numerous* records touching on various concepts on assorted labels, occasionally jointly with the likeminded Prisoners.

Milkshakes IV is a monaural set of instrumental originals; **20 Rock and Roll Hits** is a brilliant collection of covers. **They Came They Saw** offers another bopping set of originals; **Live from Chatham**, about 40 percent covers, was recorded in late '83. Judging from what little I've heard, the Milkshakes offer no danger of disappointment: jump in anywhere and have a party! (One to avoid, however, is Childish's horrible—and misspelled—home-brew acoustic solo LP. Ingenuously, the cover bears the true-enough warning, "You most likely won't like this record!")   [tr]

DANIEL MILLER
See *Silicon Teens.*

ROGER MILLER
See *Mission of Burma.*

TED MILTON
See *Blurt.*

MILTOWN STOWAWAYS
Tension Melee (NZ Unsung) 1983

Funky bass, choppy guitar, smooth horns and strangled vocals make this New Zealand sextet a challenging musical proposition. The political lyrics are strongly worded, but not preachy or prosaic. This album isn't exactly my idea of a good time, but indicative of great skill and abundant imagination. When it works, it's impressive.   [iar]

MINIMAL COMPACT
Minimal Compact EP (Bel. Crammed Discs) 1981
One by One (Bel. Crammed Discs) 1983
Deadly Weapons (Bel. Crammed Discs) 1984
Next One Is Real EP (Crammed Discs-Wax Trax) 1984
Raging Souls (Bel. Crammed Discs) 1986
Lowlands Flight (Bel. Crammed Discs) 1987
The Figure One Cuts (Bel. Crammed Discs) 1987

Not so much a rock band as a pan-cultural chamber ensemble with rock instumentation, the members of Minimal Compact are (mostly) Israelis who didn't see much of a future in their homeland, emigrated to France and signed with Belgium's Crammed Discs. Their music is tasteful and intelligent but avoids selfconscious artsiness, and they've worked with some connoisseur favorites: Tuxedomoon's Peter Principle, Wire's Colin Newman and John Fryer (Cocteau Twins) have all produced them. They served as Newman's backup band on his **Commercial Suicide** LP; some of their sleeves were designed by Eno collaborator Russell Mills. Minimal Compact's records consistently display an ability to switch gears between atmospheric, British-style art-rock, Middle Eastern-flavored folk and Beatlesque pop, while also retaining the ability to rock out with a danceable beat.

Minimal Compact's first American release was an expanded EP. **The Next One Is Real** contains five songs (including two mixes of the title track) and is a relatively commercial effort, containing hard funk played masterfully by a band whose usual approach is considerably gentler. Both **Lowlands Flight** (part of Crammed's Made to Measure series, and written in part for a Dutch dance troupe) and **The Figure One Cuts** show quieter moments and greater versatility; those familiar with **Commercial Suicide** will recognize the guitar textures and delicate arrangements that gave that LP its unique sound. Minimal Compact may be very refined and mature, but they're never boring. [dgs]

MINIMAL MAN
The Shroud Of (Subterranean) 1981
Safari (CD Presents) 1984
Minimal Man EP (Fundamental Music) 1985
Slave Lullabyes (Fundamental Music) 1986
Sex with God (Ger. Dossier) 1986

This San Francisco anti-music group is the brainchild of Patrick Miller, who screams largely incomprehensible lyrics over plodding instrumentals punctuated by wild, dissonant screeches that bleat painfully at varying intervals. On **The Shroud Of**, Minimal Man is a trio (drummer, bassist doubling on sax and flute, Miller on synths and vocals) plus seven guest instrumentalists who increase the chaos and noise level, making it a veritable nightmare in wax.

For the relatively restrained **Safari**, Miller relies on three sidemen to create a well-organized ominous roar of bass, drums and guitar; his own vocals and keyboards are intense and unsettling, but much more listenable. Minimal Man may not provide much in the way of routine entertainment, but Miller is nonetheless a challenging artist of dark talent and vision. [iar]

MINISTRY
With Sympathy (Arista) 1983 ●
Work for Love (nr/Arista) 1983
'Twitch' (Sire) 1986
Halloween Remix EP (Wax Trax) 1987

Chicago singer/writer/keyboard player/producer Alain Jourgensen is the essence of modern-dancing Ministry. On **With Sympathy (Work for Love**, the British edition, resequences the record and replaces one track), he and a drummer (joined by various sessioneers and co-produced by Psychedelic Fur Vince Ely) play sophomoric yuppie-funk, filled with numbing repetition, brutish singing and scanty, derivative ideas. Most heinously, "I Wanted to Tell Her" chants the title lyric like a litany, as does "Work for Love," while adding moronic lyrics to the numbing two-chord vamp. If second-rate dance retreads with none-too-bright words sound appealing, Ministry will suit you just fine. I'm afraid, however, neither sympathy nor love is among my feelings about this band.

'Twitch', largely produced by Adrian Sherwood, employs a far different sound, a murky swamp in which vocals take a backseat to enormous, Cabaret Voltaire-style rhythm onslaughts. It's a welcome change: although the results still aren't to my taste, I imagine there are intelligent people who relish this kind of stuff. 'Twitch' isn't half as obnoxious or grating as Ministry's previous records. [iar]

MINK DEVILLE
Mink DeVille (Capitol) 1977
Return to Magenta (Capitol) 1978
Le Chat Bleu (Capitol) 1980
Coup de Grâce (Atlantic) 1981
Savoir Faire (Capitol) 1981 ●
Where Angels Fear to Tread (Atlantic) 1983
Sportin' Life (Atlantic) 1985

WILLY DEVILLE
Miracle (A&M) 1987 ●

Around 1976-7, Willy DeVille and pals could, on a good night, be the coolest cats on the New York underground scene, despite occasional stylistic sidetracking. After being "discovered," producer Jack Nitzsche got them on the lean, tough R&B beam for a first LP that sweats and smokes through and through as a classic of such fully and lovingly assimilated music should.

Unfortunately, **Return to Magenta** is more of the same but less; on the first LP, the cover of Moon Martin's "Cadillac Walk" was one of many highlights, but here Martin's inferior "Rolene" is pretty much it. **Le Chat Bleu**'s arrival was welcome mainly because it ended Willy's prolonged absence from recording, but it confirmed that stagnation had set in. The band was, by then, a couple of Minks plus sessionmen; it seemed Willy was looking to become the soul crooner of his dreams without providing the songs to fuel ours (despite some collaborative songwriting with Doc Pomus, hitsmith for Joe Turner, Dion, the Drifters, etc.). **Savoir Faire** collects tracks from those three albums.

Evidence that DeVille had lost touch with the trash/sleaze aesthetic (not to mention Louie X. Erlanger's lowdown guitar) is even plainer on **Coup de Grâce**. Despite a new, young band and a reunion with Nitzsche (Mink saxist Steve Douglas had produced the third LP), the magic is still largely absent. Tracks like "Maybe Tomorrow" offer traces of the old bite almost as a concession.

Where Angels Fear to Tread, produced by the hitmaking team of Ron and Howard Albert (who ruined a Gang of Four album that same year), is a fine record of new DeVille originals, starting with the soulful and sweet "Each Word's a Beat of My Heart." An uncluttered and uncomplicated tribute to DeVille's forebears—Sam Cooke, Phil Spector, the Drifters, Joe Tex, James Brown—it also forays into Spanish Harlem and other wondrously nostalgic time warps. DeVille's songwriting and singing have returned to top strength, and the record burns with sincerity and warmth. Simply, elegantly excellent.

Sportin' Life maintains those standards with a set of brand-new oldies that effortlessly transport you back to the era of sweet soul music. "Something Beautiful Dying" (note the Righteous Brothers reference) is tenderly melancholic; "Little by Little" tries barrelhouse rockabilly; "Italian Shoes" is classic bad dude strutting. Apt production and a sharp backing band make this first rate.

Inexplicably selected to write and sing the theme song for *The Princess Bride,* DeVille astonishingly earned an Academy Award nomination for "Storybook Love," the schmaltzy cut which ends **Miracle**. While the pale and inconsistent record is nowhere near Willy's best work, his seasoned voice is as strong and colorful as ever. The snappy "Angel Eyes," romantic "Nightfalls" and Van Morrison's "Could You Would You?" are among the album's merits. Mark Knopfler, who played all the guitar here, produced the LP cleanly but without color, forgetting the smoky ambience essential to DeVille's music.   [jg/iar]

MINNY POPS
Drastic Measures, Drastic Movement (Hol.
   Plurex) 1979 + 1982
Sparks in a Dark Room (Bel. Factory Benelux)
   1982
SMALTS
Werktitels EP (Hol. Plurex) 1982
POSTE RESTANTE
Poste Restante (Hol. Plurex) 1983

Even in 1979, Minny Pops didn't seem drastic in the purest sense but rather deliberately, almost clinically extreme. The Dutch foursome's most salient characteristic on record is dissonance, even sheer noise—valid artistic devices in the proper hands, but it takes vision and inspiration, of which the Pops

seem to possess little. Whether they're having a go at industrial clang or setting pop clichés and oldies in jarringly alien musical contexts, even their best comes up short of what others (e.g., Throbbing Gristle, Half Japanese) have achieved in the same area. No doubt they've applied themselves diligently to make this music, but the net result lacks spark and invention. Minny Pops' first LP, released on the band's Plurex label, Holland's most important and active indie, was reissued in 1982 with the addition of a bonus 45.

Glimmerings of something better flicker on the Smalts EP. The syncopated percussion and keyboards/synth noises, including an arresting accordion/harmonium-type sound, are like a soundtrack in search of a movie, but effective within its limits. Smalts was, in fact, two members of Minny Pops exploring new avenues in preparation for creating the musical setting for a stage production entitled *Poste Restante.* The resulting LP of that name involved the whole band, plus others; although they didn't write all the material, Minny Pops perform everything except some vocals (mostly declaimed, not sung). Out of context, and entirely in Dutch, whatever meaning it has is limited to the vaguely unified feel and the knowledge that it's ostensibly a drama about travel.   [jg]

MINOR THREAT
Bottled Violence EP (Dischord) 1981
In My Eyes EP (Dischord) 1982
Out of Step (Dischord) 1983
Minor Threat (Dischord) 1984
EMBRACE
Embrace (Dischord) 1987

Between Minor Threat and the Bad Brains, our nation's capital once had a hopping hardcore scene. The quartet played fast, impassioned music that defined the genre while never succumbing to its shortcomings—Minor Threat had both a sense of melody and a sense of purpose. "Straight Edge" was among the first hardcore songs to call for abstinence from drugs and booze, and their self-titled theme song acknowledged both the aspirations and realities of political punk rock.

The posthumously released **Minor Threat** compiles the band's two 7-inch EPs. The 12 selections effectively define hardcore, with powerhouse sound, adrenalized rush and Ian MacKaye's talented vocals. "Filler," "I Don't Wanna Hear It" and "Minor Threat" are some of *the* classics of the genre; if you haven't heard them, you have never—repeat, never—heard hardcore. One of the most intense, ungodly-force-of-technology records ever launched.

Out of Step, the group's only true LP, shows Minor Threat coming out of adolescence and slowing down to merely quick tempos where they have more room to move. If less a direct rush than the early EPs, the tradeoff is a good one: dynamics and crashing hooks come to the fore, replacing the old burn with a punk musicianship up there with only the Ruts (a prime influence) for crack precision. **Out of Step** is a whale of an LP, one that made their ensuing demise (the pressures of being the most revered and hardline message-oriented hardcore band taking its toll) that much more of a tragedy. Not surprisingly, nothing has come close to matching their ability, drive and emotional level since.

Sometime after Minor Threat's 1983 breakup, MacKaye joined forces with the three musicians from the also disbanded DC hardcore band Faith (ironically, Faith's singer was Alex MacKaye, so he was effectively replacing his younger brother!) to form Embrace. After a brief existence, Embrace also disappeared seemingly without a trace but a 1987 LP of their 1985 recordings was released, making it apparent that they should have stuck around a bit longer. If not equal to Minor Threat's one-of-a-kind sonic excellence, Embrace are strong and muscular, an effective backdrop for MacKaye's lead vocals. The confrontational lyricist rages through "Money" and "No More Pain" like a hellfire preacher, condemning a corrupt and greedy culture. Overenunciating, shouting, cajoling and screaming at the top of his lungs, this is an impressive performance by a seemingly possessed man, transforming an okay mid-tempo punk LP into a great one.

[jl/jr]

See also *Meatmen.*

MINUTEMEN

Paranoid Time EP (SST) 1980
The Punch Line (SST) 1981 ●
Bean-Spill EP (Thermidor) 1982
What Makes a Man Start Fires? (SST) 1983
Buzz or Howl Under the Influence of Heat (SST) 1983
Double Nickels on the Dime (SST) 1984 ●
The Politics of Time (New Alliance) 1984

Tour-Spiel EP (Reflex) 1985
My First Bells 1980–1983 [tape] (SST) 1985
Project: Mersh EP (SST) 1985
3-Way Tie (for Last) (SST) 1985 ●
Ballot Result (SST) 1987 ●

MINUTEFLAG

Minuteflag EP (SST) 1986

San Pedro, California's greatest musical export clearly understood the concept of brevity. The trio's albums and EPs pack an astonishing number of songs, most of which (on the early releases, at least) clock in at under a minute. In that brief time, they took apart rock, jazz and funk and put the pieces back together in a jagged collage. Although the Minutemen refused to write verses and choruses, based on their belief that rock'n' roll as we know it is a lethargic dinosaur, each of their songs is a satisfying composition.

The Minutemen saga began in 1980 as a four-piece called the Reactionaries that played regular length songs. Later that year, they slimmed down (numerically speaking) and adopted their new name and radical modus operandi. They stuck to that twisted idea of dada with a groove until the end, and with one out-of-chronology exception, their records kept getting more ambitious *and* better.

The 7-inch **Paranoid Time** EP offers dogmatic politics redeemed by idiosyncratic Wire-type songs. Each abbreviated blurt of rhythm serves as a backdrop for the rants of bassist Mike Watt and guitarist D. Boon. The best is the apocalyptic "Paranoid Chant," in which Boon screams, "I don't even worry about crime anymore."

The Punch Line is more complex, musically and lyrically. The band loosens up with more funk, off-kilter rhythms and enigmatic twists in which songs seem to fall apart but don't quite. As proof of the musicians' seriousness, the 12-inch 45 includes an insert entitled *Fundamentals of Design,* which waxes philosophic about "The Order of Harmony," "The Order of Balance" and "The Order of Rhythm." Actually, the record is evidence enough, as it reveals three imaginative musicians capable of playing music that holds together without a center. A subsequent 7-inch, **Bean-Spill,** contains five songs (total running time six minutes) and a vulgar genitalia drawing by Raymond Pettibon on the label, over the legend "(We need the money)."

What Makes a Man Start Fires? throws jazz and blues elements into the blender, and features the Minutemen's first semi-dramatic song ending—that is, the first on which they do something other than just stop playing. The songs tend toward near-epic length—only one of 18 is under a minute. On this album, the Minutemen show their instrumental depth, shifting effortlessly from one fragmentary clash of styles to another. The eight-song **Buzz or Howl** is the trio's most poetic record, and the one on which they try the least to make the pieces add up, with the loosest improvisations and Boon and Watt screaming their lyrics.

Double Nickels on the Dime slaps 45 numbers onto four sides of vinyl. The unifying concept is driving in a car, but the record is really held together by the band's unflagging commitment to idiosyncrasy. The quirky songs are about Michael Jackson, Minutemen history, WW III and virtually everything else under the sun. Each is different and somehow good. With this much room to work, the Minutemen don't attempt to bludgeon listeners with lyrics, and deliver terse gems like "If we heard mortar shells we'd cuss more in our songs and cut down the guitar solos."

As if their abundant output left unjustifiable gaps, the trio issued **The Politics of Time**, a collection of unused tracks that vary widely in recording and performance quality. The 7-inch **Tour-Spiel** consists of four covers: Van Halen's "Ain't Talkin' 'Bout Love," Blue Oyster Cult's "The Red & the Black," Creedence Clearwater Revival's "Green River" and the Meat Puppets' "Lost." Like their other records, no matter what shape they take, this sounds above all like the Minutemen.

My First Bells is a retrospective cassette—62 cuts!—collecting the contents of the first four releases listed above, plus singles and compilation contributions from the same era. Essential.

Project: Mersh (the title is a sardonic reference to commercialism—"I got it! We'll have them write hit songs," says Boon's cover painting) consists of six lengthy tracks, including Watt's autobiographical "Tour-Spiel" as well as the endlessly looped, psychedelicized "More Spiel" and a cover of Steppenwolf's "Hey Lawdy Mama." Half employ guest trumpet; one even has synth. Typically brilliant and intelligent? Yes. Better presented and more accessible? Somewhat. A compromise of any sort? Hardly. A fine record.

Taking time out from both bands' busy schedules, the Minutemen and Black Flag recorded a one-day-studio-party EP in March 1985 under the spliced name of Minuteflag. In an odd tontine, the participants reportedly agreed not to issue the results until at least one of the bands had broken up. They could have waited: the four rambling song-jams are long on bonhomie but short on cohesion. **Minuteflag** is an ill-advised outing that was undoubtedly fun to record but unwise to release.

3-Way Tie (for Last) ironically appeared the same week (in December 1985) Boon's tragic death in an Arizona car crash ended the Minutemen. Indicating now-moot artistic independence or divergence, the sides are marked "D." and "Mike." Boon's collection combines three of his tunes (including the gripping Vietnam veteran tribute, "The Price of Paradise," and a Nicaragua protest, "The Big Stick") with straight readings of the Meat Puppets' "Lost" (again) and John Fogerty's "Have You Ever Seen the Rain," plus a composition by Watt and then-Black Flag bassist Kira. Watt's more diverse ten-track side has two by Boon, a spoken word piece named "Spoken Word Piece," four more co-written with Kira, Roky Erickson's "Bermuda" and another killer take on the Cult's "The Red & the Black."

The Minutemen had included a mail-in ballot with **3-Way Tie**, offering fans the opportunity to select their favorite songs for inclusion on a planned triple-live set. The idea was to do all of the selections in concert for the mooted album, provisionally titled **Three Dudes, Six Sides, Half Studio, Half Live**. Despite Boon's death, the votes were tabulated and the **Ballot Result** was assembled from extant material and released anyway. Drawing on various radio broadcasts, audience and board performance tapes, studio outtakes and rehearsals (with three LP tracks serving as needed ringers), the two discs bulge with almost three dozen representations of the group's best-loved material. The audio quality varies, but the trio's vitality and invention never wavers. A fine epilogue.

Watt and Hurley continued on, forming fIREHOSE with Ed (Crawford) fROMOHIO, a diehard Minutemen fan who sought them out and badgered them into forming a new group. Watt also formed the two-bass Dos with Kira. [jl/iar]

See also *Dos, fIREHOSE, Saccharine Trust.*

MIRACLE LEGION

A Simple Thing [tape] (Incas) 1984
The Backyard EP (Incas) 1985 (Rough Trade) 1987
Surprise Surprise Surprise (Rough Trade) 1987
Glad (Rough Trade) 1988

Criticized for their uncanny resemblance to R.E.M., Connecticut's Miracle Legion cannot be so easily dismissed as rote imitators. There's no denying the obvious similarities (vocals and guitar); thanks to musical creativity, however, Miracle Legion manages to stake out their own territory.

Savvy production techniques and aggressive playing make **The Backyard** a landmark. Mark Mulcahy's whining vocals tend to grate after a few listens, but not enough to sully the sheer brilliance of the title track, "Stephen Are You There," "Closer to the Wall" and "Butterflies." **Surprise Surprise Surprise** lacks the honest abandon of **The Backyard**, an essential ingredient to Miracle Legion's appeal. In spite of improved musicianship and vocals, it's a disappointment.

The new studio work on **Glad** (a side of the LP was recorded live in New York with a one-song guest appearance by the entirety of Pere Ubu!) is a welcome relief from the restraint of **Surprise**. The three songs literally bristle with renewed heartfelt emotion. The formerly enigmatic lyrics now conjure up a vast array of crystalline images on "A Heart Disease Called Love" and "Hey, Lucky." Glad? Definitely! [ag]

MIRACLE WORKERS

Inside Out (Voxx) 1985

Time-tripping garage raunch from Portland, Oregon. The quintet keeps their songs short, their guitars distorted, their beats simple and their blurted vocals appropriately snotty. Greg Shaw shows his typical period production finesse on **Inside Out**, which is perfectly adequate for the genre but undistinguished. [iar]

MI-SEX

Graffiti Crimes (Aus. CBS) 1979
Computer Games (Epic) 1980
Space Race (Epic) 1980
Shanghaied (Aus. CBS) 1981
Where Do They Go? (Epic) 1984

Credit must go to this New Zealand band for its international hit single, "Computer Games," which preceded the glut of similar-sounding British chart entrants by a year or more. Unfortunately, it was Mi-Sex's only shining hour.

The band's first LP, **Graffiti Crimes**, had been released in Australia before the single was recorded; the song was added and the LP retitled for release in the US and UK. Problem: the earlier material that fills the album sounds nothing like "Computer Games" and lacks both electronic catchiness and overall punch, making it a misleading disappointment for those hooked by the single.

Despite the sci-fi graphics and an attempt to become a genuine techno-rock band as opposed to dabblers, **Space Race** is an equally forgettable follow-up, offering nothing remotely commercial. **Shanghaied**, released only in Australia, sounds more confident and less selfconsciously clonelike, but is still only pleasantly mediocre, and does nothing to dispel the band's one-hit onus.

Where Do They Go?, compiled from several antipodean releases, allows Mi-Sex to regain its dignity, if not chart position. A blend of reggae, commercial rock and lightheartedness that could pass for a rougher, less glib Men at Work, the unmemorable album is at least engaging. [iar]

MISFITS

Beware the Misfits EP (nr/Cherry Red) 1980
Three Hits from Hell EP (Plan 9) 1980
The Misfits Walk Among Us (Ruby) 1982 + 1988
Evilive EP (Plan 9) 1982
Evilive (Plan 9) 1985
Wolf's Blood (Plan 9) 1983
Earth A.D. (Plan 9) 1983
Legacy of Brutality (Plan 9) 1985
Misfits [CD] (Plan 9) 1987

Although considered part of the hardcore punk scene, New Jersey's Misfits date back to the first CBGB and London punk surge. Drawing their sound from the Ramones and the Damned and their look from horror movies and Kiss, the Misfits began by releasing a string of singles on their Plan 9 label. Two of the better maxi-singles—"Bullet" and "Horror Business"—are compiled on the English **Beware** EP and epitomize what makes the Misfits great: a combination of hooky power-chording, weird, horrific lyrics and singer Glenn Danzig's distinctive basso roar. (For a musical genre in which tone and articulation don't count for much, Danzig's power and control are awesome.)

After years as a strictly underground force, the Misfits seized on the emergence of hardcore in the '80s and grafted horror-punk onto slam-thrash. As a result, **Walk Among Us** practically wallows in psychotronic shock imagery, with songs like "Mommy, Can I Go Out and Kill Tonight?" and "Astro Zombies." Unfortunately aligning themselves with the speedrock crowd, the 'Fits replaced the leisurely whomp-whack of their early singles with a faster, stiffer beat that robs many of the songs of their innate tunefulness. The **Evilive** EP (later expanded and reissued as a full-length album) is a 7-inch which catches the boys on good 1981 nights in New York and San Francisco, drawing mostly from **Walk Among Us**. One cut includes guest vocals by Black Flag's Henry Rollins.

Wolf's Blood finds the Misfits at the point of self-parody; performances are competent enough, but the music has deteriorated to generic hardcore/speed-metal, loaded with gratuitous lyrical references to death, blood, ghouls, etc. (A German edition adds the 45, "Die Die My Darling"; a subsequent American cassette issue appends the single's three songs to **Earth A.D.**, the band's final studio album.)

Aficionados should dig up **Legacy of Brutality**, a posthumous collection of outtakes and alternate versions, including "Halloween" and Danzig's "Who Killed Marilyn?" solo single. The record is somewhat uneven, but does preserve a few of the Misfits' finest moments, including "Angelfuck" and "She." The **Misfits** CD is a 20-cut retrospective of the group's work.

Danzig subsequently released a solo record and formed Samhain, a more metallic trio that has issued several albums. His current group is called Danzig.   [rnp/dgs]

See also *Undead*.

MISSING PERSONS

Missing Persons EP (Capitol) 1982
Spring Session M (Capitol) 1982
Rhyme & Reason (Capitol) 1984
Color in Your Life (Capitol) 1986
The Best of Missing Persons (Capitol) 1987 ●

DALE

Riot in English (Paisley Park) 1988 ●

PATRICK O'HEARN

Ancient Dreams (Private Music) 1985
Between Two Worlds (Private Music) 1987
Rivers Gonna Rise (Private Music) 1988

Notwithstanding singer Dale Bozzio's outrageous auto-sexploitation and the overall commercial-record-industry-hype packaging that permeated the group, Missing Persons were one positive manifestation of the '80s accommodation between new and old in rock. Designed to shift product, but retaining high musical standards and an adventurous outlook, Missing Persons fell between genres, simultaneously offending and intriguing intelligent sensibilities.

Originally built on the core of Bozzio, her then-husband—drummer/keyboardist Terry (once a Zappa employee and a member of would-be supergroup U.K.)—plus ex-Zappa guitarist Warren Cuccurullo, Missing Persons changed their name from U.S. Drag and were given a boost by producer Ken Scott who recorded and released their debut EP; it became a hit when picked up by Capitol. In the latter form, it contained both "Words" and "Destination Unknown," idiosyncratic songs that also turned up on the first LP.

Spring Session M (an anagram of the band's name) is slick, clever modern rock, using synthesizers and guitars in a hybrid style that has come to be very familiar in the '80s. What sets Missing Persons apart from other state-of-the-arters, however, is Bozzio's non-clichéd singing—tough/smart with a bemused, occasionally philosophical outlook, and a characteristic hiccup hitch that recalls Lene Lovich's early vocal gymnastics. Especially for a debut album, Bozzio's voice exudes confidence to spare, and enough personality to invest the band's novel tunes with an appropriate attitude as required.

Continue to suspend your disbelief for a few lines more: although it takes a while to become accustomed, **Rhyme & Reason** is an equally fine record. The lyrics of "Give," in what weirdly became a minor pop music trend, amount to an ethical exhortation to selflessness, attached to dynamic rock backing. Elsewhere, "Right Now" and "Surrender Your Heart" address romance with a little sensitivity, attractive melodies and sophisticated, full-blooded instrumentation. Bozzio sings with less affectation but consistent skill and subtlety. At its worst, the album offers appealing vacuity. Ignore the trappings and enjoy the music.

Bernard Edwards produced **Color in Your Life**, pumping up the volume with horns and funk rhythms on the Motown-based "Flash of Love" and "I Can't Think About Dancin'," one of the few rock songs to use the word "pretentious." Elsewhere, the dancebeat of "Boy I Say to You" sells this once-provocative band extremely short. While the inviting title track could fit on any of the band's albums, the cloying keyboards and messy arrangements here compete with Bozzio's vocals to no one's benefit. The misconceived stylistic overhaul proved a total disaster; despite a couple of worthwhile tunes, this LP is a must to avoid.

With that, Missing Persons split up, something Dale and Terry had already done. Capitol issued a comprehensive retrospective and Dale signed on the dotted line with Prince's label. Her first solo record is a joint project with producer Robert Brookins, who wrote most of the songs and played drums and keyboards on a lot of them. Although Prince's instrumental sound permeates the LP, it is nowhere so evident as on his contribution, "So Strong." The unarguably commercial dance music on **Riot in English** plays up the flexibility of Dale's voice, but the prefab cookie-cutter material and arrangements come as quite a disappointment after the stylistic invention of her former group.

Missing Persons' bassist/keyboard player O'Hearn (another Zappa alumnus and member of the 1980 Group 87 with Mark Isham and Terry Bozzio) has made three nicely textured instrumenal albums with assists from various ex-bandmates. [iar]

MISSION OF BURMA
Signals, Calls, and Marches EP (Ace of
   Hearts) 1981
VS. (Ace of Hearts) 1982
The Horrible Truth About Burma (Ace of
   Hearts) 1985
Mission of Burma EP (Taang!) 1987 ●
Forget (Taang!) 1987 ●
Mission of Burma [CD] (Rykodisc) 1988

ROGER MILLER
No Man Is Hurting Me (Ace of Hearts) 1986
Groping Hands EP (Ace of Hearts) 1987
The Big Industry (Ace of Hearts) 1987 +
   1988

During its existence, Boston's Mission of Burma was one of the most important American bands surviving outside the major-label record industry. Their thrilling and challenging vocal rock is both intellectually and emotionally engaging. Staking out bracing postpop guitar turf with hard edges and sharp corners, Burma's records never leave melody or structure behind; they just meander around it sometimes.

The debut EP has two sides (musically speaking): aggressive/strident in some spots, inviting/attractive elsewhere. Standing out among the six tracks is one tremendous song, "That's When I Reach for My Revolver," as well as a powerful but pretty instrumental, "All World Cowboy Romance."

VS. is more unremittingly intense, a loud, vibrant assault that never becomes unpleasant. While the lineup (guitar, bass, drums, tape manipulation) doesn't inherently stake out any original stylistic ground, Burma never proffers clichés; every track has individual character. On first listen, these records sound very British; on further investigation, they're all American.

Because of hearing problems the astonishingly loud band had caused, guitarist Roger Miller left Burma, turned to piano and devoted himself to Birdsongs of the Mesozoic, taking time out to make solo records as well. Tapeman Martin Swope joined him in Birdsongs. Drummer Peter Prescott formed Volcano Suns who, as the pseudonymous Din, have also backed Dredd Foole on two albums.

But on record at least, the Mission of Burma saga was far from over. The posthumous **Horrible Truth** compiles live performances from four US cities on the band's final (1983) tour. Besides a merciless rendition of the Stooges' "1970" and nine dynamic minutes of Pere Ubu's "Heart of Darkness," the album offers eight originals in several stylistic veins. Some of the tracks are intense and captivating, while others are sloppy, lacking the focused punch of their best work.

The all-fun **Mission of Burma** EP consists of five loud studio cuts, recorded between '79 and '82. (Two songs overlap the live LP.) "Peking Spring" is an obsessive dark mantra with cool choral chanting; the title track builds a powerful drone over a bewildering drum pattern; "Dumbells," although not much of a song, has an amazing overdriven guitar sound. (The cassette and CD both contain five bonus cuts.)

Under a photo of an empty stage, the inner sleeve of **Forget** begs "can we stop now . . . please . . . " The unannotated album of previously unreleased songs, given basic studio treatment (rehearsals?), offers little reason why Burma should have continued. Obviously not the band's premier material nor ideal recording circumstances, the loud and muscular songs seem undeveloped, samey. The most exciting moments are breaks in which Miller and Swope work their rowdy magic. Fans won't be disappointed—these are by no means trivial scraps—but the preceding EP seems to have contained the band's best outtakes.

Finally, there's an 80-minute-plus CD-only compilation: tracks from all three Ace of Hearts records, the A-side of Burma's first single and two previously unreleased items. The sound, as might be imagined, is astonishing. [iar]

See also *Birdsongs of the Mesozoic, Dredd Foole and the Din, Space Negros, Volcano Suns.*

MISSION (UK)

Gods Own Medicine (Mercury) 1986 ●
The First Chapter (Mercury) 1987 ●
Children (Mercury) 1988 ●

Leeds natives Wayne Hussey (guitar, vox) and Craig Adams (bass) left the gothic Sisters of Mercy to form their own group, the Mission. (The American "UK" was appended because a Philadelphia R&B band was already using the name.) Joined by ex-Red Lorry Yellow Lorry drummer Mick Brown and a guitarist drafted from Artery, the group planted one foot in the British neo-hippie camp and the other in that doomily pretentious land of pompous stupidity populated by the Cult and their ilk.

The dull and insipid guitar/keyboard/string bombast of **Gods Own Medicine** proceeds from a horrible amalgam of Led Zeppelin, Yes and Echo and the Bunnymen. Several tracks were huge British hits, but listening to the LP fails to reveal any exceptional qualities "Garden of Delight" or "Stay with Me" might have that would explain their popularity. Hussey's ponderous and toneless intonation ruins the songs' scant intrinsic merit; thick-sounding production (by Tim Palmer and the band) finishes the job. The CD has two extra cuts.

As if anyone cared, an odds-and-sods collection was issued to bring listeners up to date with non-LP items. **The First Chapter**, which is actually less of an audio trial than **Gods Own Medicine**, presents the Mission's debut 45, "Serpents Kiss," as well as an extended remix of "Garden of Delight" and unwarranted covers—"Tomorrow Never Knows" (Beatles), "Wishing Well" (Free), "Dancing Barefoot" (Patti Smith) and "Like a Hurricane" (Neil Young)—that only point up the band's songwriting incapacity. Despite the borrowed title, "Over the Hills and Far Away" is an original.

John Paul Jones evidently didn't hold that bit of pilferage against the Mission: he produced their semi-listenable second album, **Children**. Hussey's pseudo-poetic lyrics are pure middle-brow malarkey and his singing is still a problem, but the measured music benefits from the organization and air of Jones' firm dynamic grip, economically applied guitar lines and occasionally neat fripperies, like the sitar on "Beyond the Pale." Not recommended, but not altogether horrible. (But they'd better quell those Simple Minds/U2/Echo tendencies right now—and forget about becoming the new Led Zeppelin as well.) [iar]

MR. PARTRIDGE
See *XTC.*

KEITH MITCHELL
See *Opal.*

M+M
See *Martha and the Muffins.*

MOBERLYS
The Moberlys (Safety First) 1979

JIM BASNIGHT AND THE MOBERLYS
Jim Basnight and the Moberlys EP (Precedent) 1984

What distinguished this Seattle foursome from the post-Knack plague of power pop bands is the effervescent snap of singer/guitarist Jim Basnight's songs and cheery crackle of the band's twin-guitar interplay. On their eponymous (and posthumous) album, lacking the low-budget home studio finesse of kindred souls Shoes, the Moberlys compensate for the rough sound of this half-live waxing with shiny harmonies and a bright, rhythmic step.

Five years later, with a new bassist and drummer, Basnight (who had lived in New York for a while) released a brilliant, well-produced 12-inch EP (reprising a prior 7-inch single from the year before) that rocks with real guitar power, great vocals and infectious pop hooks. There's one white-hot screamer and three slices of stunning, non-wimpy catchiness that evade easy influence-pegging. Clearly in the same class as Chris Stamey and Richard Barone, Basnight is a startlingly talented power-pop titan who deserves far greater acclaim and popularity than he has yet been accorded.   [df/iar]

MODERN ENGLISH

Mesh & Lace (nr/4AD) 1981
After the Snow (Sire) 1982
Gathering Dust EP (nr/4AD) 1983
Ricochet Days (Sire) 1984
Stop Start (Sire) 1986

Colchester's Modern English undertook a drastic change of direction after its debut, an oppressively pretentious (sarcastic?) load of monotonous droning and shouting by a precious art band. **After the Snow**, on the other hand, is a flawed but rewarding batch of hard-edged, melodic dance songs, a style to which the group subsequently adhered. Instead of the muddy production that favored only the drummer on **Mesh & Lace**, the second record has both sparkling sound and overtly normal musical intentions. Not everything on **After the Snow** is as striking as the wonderful "I Melt with You," but as a first step on a new musical path, it's quite an improvement.

Ricochet Days, an attempt to reconcile the band's abiding commitment to artistic expression with the lure of growing American stardom, is rather equivocal, offering several finely wrought slices of catchiness ("Hands Across the Sea," "Rainbow's End") as well as slightly more obscure efforts. Greater intricacy nicely tints all the material; pristine production by longstanding collaborator Hugh Jones adds to their appeal. Still, Modern English remains precariously perched on a fence between making a musical statement and aiming for commercial easy street. That decision can't be postponed indefinitely.

With the release of **Stop Start**, it's obvious which way Modern English is leaning. It may be a bit early to write them off as boring has-been sell-outs (like, for instance, Simple Minds), but they're certainly not going anywhere particularly challenging. Bad sign: the refrain of "Ink and Paper," co-written by the band and erstwhile Rubinoo (!) Tommy Dunbar, is too reminiscent of "Born to Run" to be a coincidence. Put these guys on the endangered species list.

Gathering Dust consists of five non-LP tracks from Modern English's pre-pop era, originally released in 1980 and 1981. Atmospheric, dense, aggressive and abrasive.
                                                    [iar]

See also *This Mortal Coil.*

MODERN EON

Fiction Tales (nr/DinDisc) 1981

Liverpudlians of the early Echo school, Modern Eon plays cold rock music that pushes anxiety as much as rhythm. Although not an easy album to like, **Fiction Tales** does convey originality and stylishness as well as flashes of accessibility; occasional use of odd instrumentation and a good drummer make this more than just a routine genre exercise.
                                                    [iar]

MODERN LOVERS

See *Jonathan Richman and the Modern Lovers.*

MODERN MAN

Concrete Scheme (nr/MAM) 1980

Produced by fellow Scot Midge Ure, Modern Man is much like a second-string Rich Kids. The vocals are like Ure's but a tad stiffer, the plangent guitars can also snarl— even the melodies are similar. Withal, not too poor, for a side, but on the flip the quintet's catchiness, brevity and solid (if borrowed) musical identity seems to evaporate.   [jg]

MODERN ROMANCE

Adventures in Clubland (Atlantic) 1981
Trick of the Light (Atlantic) 1983
Party Tonight (nr/Ronco) 1983
Burn It! (nr/RCA) 1985

Formerly doing business as minor-league punk parodists the (Leyton) Buzzards, Geoffrey Deane and David Jaymes switched styles radically without altering their outlook and became a UK chart sensation. **Adventures in Clubland** is fake disco-salsa, with enough beat to satisfy the most demanding feet and enough smirking to prove they don't believe a second of it. For proof, sample "Bring on the Funkateers" or "Ay Ay Ay Ay Moosey." Regardless—or perhaps because— of the insincerity, this is good fun.

A subsequent split left Jaymes in sole command but hardly shorthanded, and he took the band for another joyride on **Trick of the Light**, hitting an infectious happy-feet high on "Best Years of Our Lives," rhumbaing through "High Life," swinging in bigband land on "Don't Stop That Crazy Rhythm" and so on well into the night. (Well, for 40 minutes at least.) Again, a good time is assured for all.

Party Tonight is an everything-you'd-ever-want-to-hear-by-Modern Romance compilation. [jy/iar]

MO-DETTES
The Story So Far (nr/Deram) 1980

Four women—an American, a Swiss and two Britons—made up the London-based Mo-dettes. Not as poppy as the Go-Go's or as radical as the Slits, the Mo-dettes worked a middle ground, offering feminist consciousness but avoiding polemics and overseriousness. This competent album has its charming moments, but also suffers from a plainness that makes the lesser songs tedious and the better ones not as convincing as they might have been. What the Mo-dettes needed was a really clever producer. [iar]

MOFUNGO
Elementary Particles EP (Living Legends) 1980
End of the World [tape] (Mofungo) 1982
Out of Line (Zoar) 1983
Frederick Douglass (Coyote-Twin/Tone) 1985
Messenger Dogs of the Gods
  (Lost-Twin/Tone) 1986
End of the World, Part 2 (Lost-Twin/Tone) 1987
Bugged (SST) 1988

Mofungo's frayed vocals, twitchy rhythms and snarling saxes are an acquired taste, but on **Out of Line** the New York quartet does an excellent job of saving discordance from descending to chaos. The urgent attack of "Wage Slave," "FBI Informer (He Sold His Soul)" and others never lacks the credibility that eludes many fancier bands. Hard on the nerves, though.

Frederick Douglass furthers Mofungo's drive into annoyingly random sounds and pointedly political lyrics. Guitars and producer Elliott Sharp's occasional saxual contributions wander off in the most haphazard directions; the rhythm section isn't exactly session-level tight, but at least Phil Dray (or maybe Chris Nelson, who is also credited with drums) and Robert Sietsema keep a semblance of the beat going between them. Pretentious and unlistenable.

Dray's departure (and vocalist Heather Drake's temporary arrival) prior to **Messenger Dogs of the Gods** was accompanied, evidently, by a total sonic rethink, leaving Mofungo a rhythmically loaded, occasionally jagged-edged (Sharp's free-form blowing can still rattle the walls) folk-rock group. Palatable, even pretty in spots, the album includes such American classics as "Big Rock Candy Mountain" and Woody Guthrie's "Deportees," alongside original instrumentals and topical songs like "Johnny Didn't Come Marching Home," "The Typist's Plea" and "George Washington Carver/Sojourner Truth." Humorless but estimably well-intentioned.

While the independently-minded blend of folk and rock on **End of the World, Part 2** shows ongoing improvement, the album's lyrics evidently merit a helpful paragraph of footnotes on the back cover. The vocals strongly suggest a less melodic Tom Verlaine, while the music travels various stylistic avenues without ever straying far from musical convention. [jy/iar]

See also *(The) Scene Is Now*.

MONKS OF DOOM
See *Camper Van Beethoven*.

MONOCHROME SET
Strange Boutique (DinDisc) 1980
Love Zombies (nr/DinDisc) 1980
Eligible Bachelors (nr/Cherry Red) 1982
Volume, Contrast, Brilliance (nr/Cherry Red) 1983
Jacob's Ladder EP (nr/Blanco y Negro) 1985
The Lost Weekend (nr/Blanco y Negro) 1985
Fin (nr/El-Cherry Red) 1985
Color Transmission [CD] (Virgin) 1988

Beginning with a series of arty rock singles, this London quartet (aided by producer Bob Sargeant on keyboards) took a sharp swing toward lightweight pop when they hit LP form. **Strange Boutique** mixes uncommon source material (polkas, etc.) into cabaret material (à la **Village Green** Kinks). Fortunately, the highly controlled results are untainted by seriousness, and even without much to say, the quartet says it well.

Love Zombies expands the cabaret stylings while limiting the bizarre material, producing a smoother and more accessible sound. The melodies are stronger, with Bid's vocals brought up to spotlight lyrics that take sharp, light jabs at emotional traps and social mores.

With a new drummer in the lineup, **Eligible Bachelors** strips the music down to essential elements—clean, bouncy melodies and gently satirical verse, performed with deceptive facility. Songs like "March of the Eligible Bachelors," "The Jet Set Junta" and "The Great Barrier Riff" typify the band's wittily intelligent verse.

Another lineup revision ensued, making Bid and bassist Andy Warren (like founding guitarist Lester Square, a veteran of the early Adam and the Ants) the only remaining originals. Leading off with the suave pop of "Jacob's Ladder," **The Lost Weekend**, produced by John Porter, has such a light touch that it threatens to float away. Nostalgic recollections from the '30s, '50s and '60s color most of the songs, variously suggesting "When I'm 64" crossed with recent XTC and a bikini beach movie soundtrack. Clever and entertaining, although only the second side makes for truly compelling listening.

Volume, Contrast, Brilliance compiles early singles and significant album tracks. **Fin** is a compilation of live recordings dating from 1979 to 1985. The American **Color Transmission** CD repackages the entire contents of **Strange Boutique** and **Love Zombies**. [sg/iar]

MONSOON

Third Eye (nr/Mobile Suit Corp.) 1983

A different pop concept to say the least, but one that works marvelously. Producer/writer/instrumentalist Steve Coe, along with his collaborator, Martin Smith, creates (with some outside assistance, mostly on percussion) raga-rock along the lines of George Harrison's Beatle excursions ("Within You, Without You," especially). Delivered in a very lovely voice by Anglo-Indian actress Sheila Chandra, alternately languid and kinetic songs (English lyrics and pop structures, hybrid instrumentation) like "Wings of the Dawn (Prem Kavita)" and "Shakti (The Meaning of Within)" meld intriguing sounds to memorable melodies, making **Third Eye** a wondrous, if insufferably gimmicky pop achievement. [iar]

See also *Sheila Chandra*.

MOOD

Passion in Dark Rooms EP (RCA) 1983

Disposable synth-rock. This British trio's five songs, originally released on singles, comprise a tedious 12-inch that is far more technological than original. (For Culture Club collectors: Roy Hay guested and Steve Levine produced.) [iar]

MOODISTS

Engine Shudder (nr/Red Flame) 1983
Thirsty's Calling (nr/Red Flame) 1984
Double Life EP (nr/Red Flame) 1985

Originally from Australia, the Moodists are graduates of the thump'n'grind school of gothic punk. Combining dense metallic bass and razor-sharp guitar riffs with singer Dave Graney's demonic growl, the band is capable of a most unholy din. Although dark and ominous, the music can at times be surprisingly melodic.

The seven-song **Engine Shudder** is not the Moodists at their most effective. The tracks are devoid of coherence and slip readily into redundancy. Only "Gone Dead" hints at a promising future, thanks to Graney's layered vocals and Chris Walsh's bass work.

Thirsty's Calling is a remarkable improvement. The addition of a second discordant guitar and judicious production makes this music for nightmares. Setting vocals and guitars further back in the mix, the rhythm section comes into its own on "That's Frankie's Negative" and the standout, "Machine Machine." Grimly primal, this music—in no uncertain terms—breathes life into pop's forbidding alter-ego, a region where many dare to tread, but few prove this successful.

The Moodists' reign of terror continues on the six-song EP. Bass and voice are upfront this time, giving the tracks full-bodied menace. "Double Life," "Six Dead Birds" and "Can't Lose Her" are wonderfully desperate songs and by far the Moodists' best to date. Following the EP, the band underwent personnel and label changes, returning in '86 with the "Justice and Money Too" single—light, bluesy pop augmented with strings and piano. They may have lost their venom, but not the ability to craft stunning tunes. [ag]

R. STEVIE MOORE

Phonography (Vital) 1976 (HP Music) 1978
Four from Phonography (HP Music) 1978
Stance EP (HP Music) 1978
Delicate Tension (HP Music) 1978
Everything You Always Wanted to Know
    About R. Stevie Moore but Were Afraid
    to Ask (Fr. New Rose) 1984
What's the Point?!! (Cuneiform) 1984
Verve (nr/Hamster) 1985
Glad Music (Fr. New Rose) 1986
Teenage Spectacular (Fr. New Rose) 1987

The son of a top Nashville session bassist, R. Stevie Moore began doing his own one-man home recordings in the early '70s. Over the course of years spent perfecting his technical and conceptual skills, Moore's individualistic, wry pop and musique concrète excursions have developed into an awesome —and seemingly bottomless—well of talent just waiting to be unleashed on the masses. In recent years, Moore (now living in New Jersey) has self-released cassettes of his work via mail order; the two 1984 albums draw (in part) their contents from those tapes. Suffice to say, if you like what you hear on the discs, there's plenty more of equal quality where that came from.

Phonography (issued twice with different artwork) consists of his very early efforts, done between 1974 and 1976. Some of it is fairly rudimentary, but the Bonzo Dog Band-like "Goodbye Piano" displays Moore's incipient brilliance, and a massed-guitars rendition of the *Andy Griffith Show* theme is classic.

Stance is a three-song 12-inch, running time around 15 minutes. Recorded in '76 and '77, top-to-bottom improvement is obvious, from the moody, mostly instrumental "Ist or Mas"—an interpretation of awakening (theme for a ballet perhaps?)—to "Manufacturers," a rollicking jazzy rocker.

Delicate Tension is excellent: great songs of astonishing variety, all tied together by his idiosyncratic, gentle perceptions of life and smooth, versatile voice. There are hints of Zappa, Rundgren, Townshend, McCartney and countless others; Moore's limitations, if indeed he has any, have yet to be encountered.

Moore's tape club's issue is staggering in sheer volume, variety and consistency of quality. (His catalogue includes well over 150 titles!) More like eclectic radio shows than straight collections of music, he includes anything and everything on the tapes, and they collectively provide an in-depth self-portrait of a truly prodigious talent.

Everything You Always Wanted to Know is a two-record compilation of tracks—with historical liner notes (in English) by Robert Christgau—sampling a decade's worth of recording from Moore's preceding discs and tapes. Although disjointed in spite of Moore's skillful efforts to compile it in some rational fashion, it provides proof positive of the man's remarkable gift to do virtually any type of music and do it well. More concise and better conceived, the one-disc **What's the Point?!!** provides an ideal introduction to Moore, with such gems as "Part of the Problem," "Puttin' Up the Groceries" and "Bloody Knuckles."

Released by a small UK label, the **Verve** compilation quickly became a rarity; **Glad Music**, a proper studio album recorded in late 1985, reprises "Part of the Problem" and adds a dozen more examples of Moore at the top of his creative powers. There's real C&W played with mock-seriousness ("I Love You So Much It Hurts"), an unnervingly precise synth-flavored version of the Association's "Along Comes Mary" and witty, hand-clapping rock'n'roll ("Shakin' in the Sixties"). Delightful!

Teenage Spectacular includes covers of Dr. Hook ("The Cover of Rolling Stone," half of it performed a cappella) and Dr. Dylan (the anti-boxing classic "Who Killed Davey Moore?" given an ironically upbeat folk reading) amidst the original pop musings, witty balladeering and brief mind-altering tape experiments ("Non Sequitur I–V"). The simple musical constructions on guitars, keyboards and drums reveal traces of Moore's many influences—from the Beatles to Todd Rundgren to the Bonzo Dog Band to XTC and back again—and huge chunks of his monumental creative grasp. "On the Spot" is satiric big band bar-room sleaze in the key of G sharp; "Blues for Cathy Taylor" is a delightful love song of a different sort; "Baby on Board" castigates childless drivers with those yellow stickers on their car windows.

The American record industry's failure to recognize and promote the unique gifts of this giant talent is a case of criminal neglect. [iar]

JOHNNY MOPED

Cycledelic (nr/Chiswick) 1978

Johnny Moped's ludicrously silly falsetto rendition of Chuck Berry's "Little Queenie" sets the tone for this album by a seemingly drunken bunch of grungy simpletons whose band genealogy (detailed on the record sleeve) involves some members of the Damned. [iar]

ANTHONY MORE

Pieces from the Cloudland Ballroom (Ger. Polydor) 1971
Secrets of the Blue Bag (Ger. Polydor) 1972
Reed, Whistle and Sticks (Ger. Polydor) 1972

Flying Doesn't Help (nr/Quango) 1979
World Service (nr/Do It) 1981
The Only Choice (nr/Parlophone) 1984

Anthony More (aka Moore) was a founding member of progressive trio Slapp Happy in the early '70s; following that band's merger with Henry Cow, More went his own way, producing solo records at erratic intervals. His three most recent releases are stunning, fully-realized works of a highly idiosyncratic innovator who combines art and rock into a far-reaching, weird and wonderful set of styles, from the atonal to the hook-laden. More imparts all his songs with a nonconformist's perspective that defies easy comprehension.

Flying Doesn't Help displays More's melodic stance, with such beautiful and haunting creations as "Judy Get Down" and "Lucia"; his wit surfaces in sardonic pieces like "Caught Being in Love" and "Girl It's Your Time." Building dense sonic forests filled with jagged splinters and dry, incongruously delicate vocals, the results fall somewhere between Peter Gabriel, John Cale, David Bowie and Kevin Ayers. An extraordinary record that reveals itself a little further each time it's played.

World Service (which, unlike **Flying**, offers musician credits) takes a decidedly less attractive route, better displaying the anti-music aspect of More's work; dour singing and bitter lyrics make it a challenging record that's as brilliant but not as easily enjoyed as the first. "Broke'n Idol," despite glum intent, contains the record's strongest melody. In contrast, "Fat Fly" is unrelentingly bleak; the light relief is provided by atonal background guitar. **World Service** isn't unpleasant; rather, it explores different ground with the same caustic eye and inventive mind.

With ex-Fingerprintz guitarist Jimme O'-Neill in tow and ex-Slapp Happy bandmate Dagmar Krause providing backing vocals, More lightens the mood considerably on **The Only Choice**. He incorporates African rhythms on a few cuts, found sounds on others, and presents a lyrical mix of wry observations on ills of the modern world ("Industrial Drums," "Find One Voice") plus fascinating outlooks on communication and relationships (and not simply romantic ones). The often-understated music is consistently likable but a bit less invigorating than his best. Nonetheless, More's varied talents, craft and incisiveness combine to make it a rewarding album. [iar]

MORELLS
Shake and Push (Borrowed) 1982

How's this for an intriguing assortment of musicians: a middle-aged couple (he, once of Arthur "Sweet Soul Music" Conley's band, on bass and guitar; she on keyboards; both sing), a phenomenal guitarist who'd be stiff competition for Dave Edmunds and Brian Setzer if he were based in a city larger than Springfield, Missouri and—on occasional sax—a fellow whose main occupation is producing unconventional country star Boxcar Willie. Guitarist D. Clinton Thompson and bassist Lou Whitney (producer of the first Del-Lords LP) have been together in a variety of lineups; the former's superb "Driving Guitars" 45 rescued a swell Ventures tune from obscurity. In the Skeletons and Original Symptoms, the pair has mined the vaults of rock, R&B and country arcanity for some ought-to-have-been classics (and the inspiration to pen their own instant winners).

The Morells can easily slay most of the revivalists, and **Shake and Push** proves it with a casualness that's all the more ingratiating. A dozen bars into the second track, if you ain't slobbering on the LP jacket wondering where you're gonna find a deeluxe greaseburger place like "Red's," then you just ain't American. [jg]

GIORGIO MORODER & PHILIP OAKEY
See *Human League.*

MORRISSEY
See *Smiths.*

MORTAL MICRONOTZ
See *Micronotz.*

MOSQUITOS
That Was Then, This Is Now! EP (Valhalla) 1985

New York's Mosquitos were toiling in relative obscurity when the quintet released this likable 12-inch of Beatlesque '60s mersey-styled pop. Sort of a junior Smithereens with less songwriting aptitude, the Mosquitos invested the five catchy originals with tuneful spunk, attractive harmonies and rocking charm. Although the reformed Monkees subsequently turned the disc's remarkably apropos title track into a Top 20 national hit, the Mosquitos have not been heard from since. [iar]

ELTON MOTELLO
Victim of Time (Can. Attic) 1979
Pop Art (Passport) 1980

Best known for an obnoxious 1978 single ("Jet Boy Jet Girl") that coupled the backing track of Plastic Bertrand's "Ça Plane Pour Moi" with smarmy lyrics about fellatio, Elton Motello, an Englishman who had worked in the studio with the Belgian Bert, escaped that juvenility and became a half-baked quirky pop-rocker. Each album—the first, a collection of singles and other items recorded during 1977 and 1978; the second, a fully conceived and executed band effort—has worthwhile tracks that flatter the artist (if not his minor songwriting talent).

Victim of Time leads off with seven minutes of "Jet Boy Jet Girl," but also boasts a funny ode to a drunken father ("He's a Rebel") and great versions of "Pipeline" and the Small Faces' "Sha La La La Lee" (again using Bertrand's backing track). The Ramonesy rock is functional and, when he's not sinking to topics like "Teen Pimp" and "Artificial Incemination" [sic], Motello's jovial manner makes the record entertaining. Proceed, but with caution.

Pop Art is a wholly different affair—synth-pop that aspires to be weird for weird's sake, but with occasional success. The best track is a totally syncopated version of the Who's "I Can't Explain"; other numbers work New Musik/M dance-pop terrain to good effect. [iar]

MOTELS
Motels (Capitol) 1979 ●
Careful (Capitol) 1980 ●
All Four One (Capitol) 1982
Little Robbers (Capitol) 1983
State of Shock (Capitol) 1985 ●

MARTHA DAVIS
Policy (Capitol) 1987 ●

Rising up from Los Angeles' early new wave underground to become MOR stars, the Motels abandoned the world that launched them as soon as it was feasible to do so. At first committed to calculated oddness, they found success making bland, almost colorless sophisti-pop records. Both **Motels** and **Careful** present the group's music on a take-it-or-leave-it basis, presumably on the assumption that it would be uncool to attempt persuasion. Martha Davis croons with just a trace of husky sensuality, prevented from getting too involved by relentlessly quirky material and jagged backing. **Motels** includes "Anticipating" and "Porn Reggae," icy songs about sex; **Careful** features "Danger," which flirts with emotion without succumbing.

All Four One was produced by Val Garay (Linda Ronstadt, Kim Carnes) who simultaneously pulled the Motels away from the rock fringe and, to his credit, made a crumbling low-commercial-potential outfit into stars. Though much of the material is still irritatingly affected, you can bet everyone noticed that the LP's big hit, "Only the Lonely," is an old-fashioned romantic ballad.

Despite the addition of ex-Stooges keyboardist Scott Thurston to the lineup (which already included onetime Iggy drummer Brian Glascock), **Little Robbers** continues the profitable process of selling the Motels as a mainstream torch song enterprise. "Suddenly Last Summer" and other cuts are so atmospheric that you'll just want to take a nap. At this point, the Motels are essentially a one-woman show—Davis might as well junk the band and go solo.

She did, but not before Richie Zito bombastically overproduced the band's dreadful swan song, **State of Shock**. The huge drum sound and zealous commercial aspirations bury the album's few seductive tunes in noisy miscalculation. Zito repeated that ill-advised formula on Davis' **Policy**, vying against her hardy vocals with layers of loud rock guitar and echo-laden percussion, yielding something akin to Heart. "Just Like You" features Clarence Clemmons [sic]; "What Money Might Buy" has a Charlie Sexton solo. Sad. [jy/iar]

See also *Pop*.

MOTHMEN
Pay Attention (nr/On-U Sounds) 1981
One Black Dot (nr/Do It) 1982

Sort of psychedelic and sort of danceable (in a soulless way), the Mothmen just plod along with all-too-few interesting touches. Bob Harding's plaintive vocals are the most distinctive thing here, but they're not enough. If this were 1969, this quintet would be my bet for turning into Yes. [ds]

377

MOTOR BOYS MOTOR

Motor Boys Motor (nr/Albion) 1982

Strange sense of humor: the cover and enclosed poster is a freak-show photo of a black man's face with lots of little snakes coming out of his mouth. The foursome (two guitars, bass, drums) do a song called "Here Comes the Flintstones." They should have done the show's actual theme—this ditty ain't happening. Nothing much here is, despite the energetic punk-cum-boogie musical mode and Beefheartian overtones. Interesting, but doesn't come near justifying its existence. (Half of MBM later organized the Screaming Blue Messiahs and put a song called "I Wanna Be a Flintstone" on their second album.) [jg]

See also *Screaming Blue Messiahs.*

MOTORHEAD

Motorhead (nr/Chiswick) 1977
Overkill (nr/Bronze) 1979
Bomber (nr/Bronze) 1979
On Parole (nr/UA) 1979
Motorhead EP (nr/Big Beat) 1980
The Golden Years EP (nr/Bronze) 1980
Ace of Spades (Mercury) 1980
No Sleep 'til Hammersmith (Mercury) 1981
Iron Fist (Mercury) 1982 (nr/Raw Power) 1987
Another Perfect Day (Mercury) 1983 (nr/Raw Power) 1988
What's Words Worth? (nr/Big Beat) 1983
No Remorse (Bronze) 1984 (nr/Raw Power) 1987
Orgasmatron (GWR-Profile) 1986 ●
Rock 'n' Roll (GWR-Profile) 1987 ●

MOTORHEAD AND GIRLSCHOOL

St. Valentine's Day Massacre EP (nr/Bronze) 1980

WURZEL

Bess EP (nr/GWR) 1987

The early pigeonholing of Motorhead as punks may have stemmed from their loud'n' fast playing, their leather jackets, engagements opening for the Damned and their early releases on a UK indie label, but then, as now, the band was engaged in its own hard-rockin' rebellion—slashing guitar, flailing drums and Lemmy playing bass like a lead and rhythm instrument, singing as though he were in the process of being strangled. Inspired moronism? You bet, just like "Louie, Louie," which the band covered for a minor hit in 1978!

Motorhead's very existence opposed the safe, sterile, flabby ritual "heavy music" had become (not to mention the rest of what had been passing for rock'n'roll), and prefigured the new wave of rawer British metal bands (Iron Maiden, Saxon, et al.) in the early '80s. (Not to mention the thrash bands of recent years. Motorhead themselves say they don't listen to, don't like and don't see the resemblance to themselves in the thrash-metal groups.) All told, Motorhead's primal urgency clearly recalled their spiritual forebears: the Amboy Dukes/Bob Seger System/ MC5 Detroit axis.

After being fired from Hawkwind, bassist Ian (Lemmy) Kilmister hooked up with two ex-Pink Fairies (also Hawkwind chums): Larry Wallis and Lucas Fox. Producer Dave Edmunds allegedly fled their recording session, covering his ears; Fox was dumped then and there and his replacement, Phil "Philthy Animal" Taylor, overdubbed some of the drum parts. UA let Motorhead's contract expire, and didn't see fit to release the results until 1980, as **On Parole**. In any case, Lemmy sought to beef up the sound by bringing in guitarist "Fast" Eddie Clarke (like Jimi Hendrix, a former employee of Curtis Knight), at which point Wallis took a powder.

In their second attempt at a debut album, Speedy Keen (of Thunderclap Newman, in days of yore), who'd mis-mixed the Heartbreakers' **L.A.M.F.** LP, successfully captured Motorhead's sturm and klang. Cut after cut, it's phenomenal: the remakes of two Hawkwind tracks, "Motorhead" and "Lost Johnny" (the latter co-written by Mick Farren), "White Line Fever," "Iron Horse/Born to Lose" and more, all with a force and fury unequalled until the 1981 live LP (and tons better than versions on the UA LP). A 1980 EP of outtakes from those Chiswick sessions features one original, Wallis' "On Parole," and oldies by John Mayall and ZZ Top. In '83, Chiswick's live **What's Words Worth?** revealed the band in an early '78 show—uneven, although some of the cover tunes, like "Leavin' Here" and "Train Kept a-Rollin' " strike some pretty good sparks.

Moving from Chiswick to Bronze, and from Keen to ex-Stones producer Jimmy Miller, the trio put out a trio of solid LPs, each with its own merits and classic Motorhead tracks. **Overkill**'s title track, "Stay Clean" and that ultimate putdown, "No Class," are balanced by the atypically slow, deliberate "Capricorn." **Bomber** has its title track and "Dead Men Tell No Tales" as highlights. **Ace of Spades** also has a great title track and "(We Are) The Road Crew." Vic Maile produced the last of those LPs, achieving more sonic fullness and texture than Miller had, though **Overkill**'s material is the best of the three.

Motorhead and labelmates Girlschool ganged up on the 1959 Johnny Kidd & the Pirates hit "Please Don't Touch" (backed with each group murdering a fave song by the other, and packaged on 7-inch and 10-inch as the **St. Valentine's Day Massacre** EP) and had a hit. Then **No Sleep** went into the UK album charts at number one. What a killer—Maile did a super job of balancing ambience and clarity—you don't exactly hear it this distinctly at a hundred skazillion dB, while jumping up and down and playing air guitar, do ya? It was all any Motorfan could've asked.

Fast Eddie ran the console for **Iron Fist**, with the help of engineer Will Reid Dick. The results are relatively lackluster, in material as well as sound. Eddie was not happy with the direction of the band, and while the others were busy combining with the Plasmatics as they had with Girlschool (less successful artistically and commercially, on "Stand by Your Man"), he decided to split. (He formed the bluesy, Zep-ish Fastway, ultimately a dead end.) Ex-Thin Lizzy guitarist Brian Robertson immediately replaced him. **Another Perfect Day** was a good change of pace. Considering how unsuited Robertson figured to be, it works surprisingly well. But it just wasn't Motorhead, and after a tour-shortening illness, he left.

No sooner was he replaced by two unknowns, Phil Campbell and Mick "Wurzel" Burston, than Taylor decided he wanted out, too. In stepped Pete Gill (ex-Saxon, and before that the Glitter Band, as in Gary!). The next release, **No Remorse**, was no stopgap, though. They didn't get the rights to the Chiswick tracks, but otherwise the two-record set is a model best-of collection: a wise, balanced choice of LP and EP cuts, non-LP single sides, four smokin' new numbers, annotation (and commentary by Lemmy) on all tracks, complete lyrics, a smart, detailed band history (by *Kerrang!*'s Malcolm Dome) and some cute pics. It does include "Please Don't Touch," "Louie, Louie," "Leavin' Here" (the best version of the *five* the band has cut over the years, from the snappy

Golden Years live EP) and that instant classic, "Killed by Death." ("If you squeeze my lizard, I'll put my snake on you.") Sheer Shakespeare in a Chevy.

Orgasmatron was produced by New York art-jazz-funk downtown bass player Bill Laswell with Jason Corsaro. Làswell's involvement got lots of critics to pay attention, and they got to hear a decent Motorhead record, but hardly their best. On the LP's opener ("Deaf Forever") and closer ("Orgasmatron") the sound is a striking juggernaut but, generally, it seems a bit sonically squashed.

The very next LP, **Rock 'n' Roll**, produced by the band and Guy Bidmead (who'd engineered **Orgasmatron**), has more sonic depth, a bit of slide guitar and backing-vocal *harmonies*! Also Phil Taylor, who had a change of heart and was allowed to step back in after Gill departed. Better than **Orgasmatron**, though not quite classic—which still leaves it miles beyond most of the competition. (It also includes "Eat the Rich," done for the film of the same name in which Lemmy has—gasp!—an acting role! It might also be noted that Lemmy appears—for no good reason—in Michael Moorcock's *Entropy Tango* novel.)

Wurzel's EP is not bad: a "Sleepwalk"-esque instrumental, a Jeff Beck-ish hyper-waltz and a couple of Motorhead Jr.-type numbers. [jg]

MOTORS

Motors 1 (Virgin) 1977
Approved by the Motors (Virgin) 1978
Tenement Steps (Virgin) 1980
Greatest Hit (nr/Virgin) 1981

Formed by two ex-members of Ducks Deluxe—Andy McMaster and Nick Garvey, both singers/songwriters/multi-instrumentalists—plus two younger pub vets—Bram Tchaikovsky and Ricky Slaughter—the Motors seemed like a hit machine from the outset. On record, they made grandiose rock-pop—wide-screen, brilliantly arranged and energetically performed—drawing on their longtime experience and solid talents. Thus armed, the Motors became a full-blown chart contender with nary a gimmick or pretty face (far from it) to use for teen appeal.

Motors 1, produced by Robert John Lange, is a fresh, exciting record, light-years more subtle and three-dimensional than the rock'n'roll retreads the band's members had been playing prior to the Motors. The engrossing and muscular "Dancing the Night Away"—all six minutes of it—leads off the LP but is unmatched by anything that follows. **Approved By** is a better effort, containing the fruits of the Motors' attack on the singles chart ("Airport" and "Forget About You" both went Top 20 in the UK) and exhibiting all of the band's strengths: catchy melodies, inventive arrangements and exciting, energetic use of rock instrumentation.

The Motors effectively disbanded after the second album, having tired of touring (and possibly each other). Garvey and McMaster continued working together using the group name, eventually engaging Jimmy Iovine to produce their next album in New York. **Tenement Steps**, the unfortunate result of far too much time spent in the studio, is an appalling, overblown mess, reeking of self-indulgence and artistic confusion. The chorus of the best-known track, "Love and Loneliness," sounds exactly like Steve Still's "Love the One You're With"—and that's as good as this record gets.

Greatest Hit has all of the above-mentioned songs as well as the rest of the Motors' best work. Neophytes would do well to start (and end) here.   [iar]

See also *Nick Garvey, Bram Tchaikovsky.*

JUDY MOWATT

Black Woman (Shanachie) 1979
Only a Woman (Shanachie) 1982
Working Wonders (Shanachie) 1985
Love Is Overdue (Shanachie) 1987

Partly because Rastafarianism is intrinsically patriarchal, the number of important women reggae performers can still be counted in single digits. Singing behind Bob Marley, the I-Threes (Marcia Griffiths, Rita Marley and Judy Mowatt) were, for a long time, the only visible female presence in roots music. While they've all enjoyed successful solo careers, Mowatt has made the most significant strides, writing and producing her own material.

On **Black Woman**, she covers three Wailers songs and dedicates an original to Marley. The album amply displays her talents as a composer as well as performer, and brought her international acclaim. The quiet militancy of **Only a Woman** is offset by an engaging vocal style—strong and clean—that recalls American R&B. By the time **Working Wonders** was released, she was being called

the queen of reggae by the press. Featuring a variety of producers and material, the LP suffers from its crossover efforts, but Mowatt's singing is more assured than ever.

By contrast, **Love Is Overdue** is nearly ruined by Mowatt's attempt to reach the mainstream. Produced by TSOP alumnus Dexter Wansel, Side One's first four tracks (including covers of "Try a Little Tenderness" and UB40's "Sing Our Own Song") are lightweight pop-soul, bland and forgettable. Luckily, Mowatt salvages the rest of the LP by singing, writing and producing the sprightly reggae she does best.   [bk]

ALISON MOYET

Alf (Columbia) 1984 ●
Raindancing (Columbia) 1987 ●

Alison Moyet's soulful vocals were the best thing about Yazoo, her oddly successful partnership with ex-Depeche Moder Vince Clarke. He went on to form another duo, Erasure, with a male singer who sounds a lot like Moyet; she launched a commercially rewarding mainstream solo career. On **Alf**, her amazing pipes are supported by smooth synth-and-drums dance music created by full-service producers Tony Swain and Steve Jolley, who co-wrote the material and played on it as well. Moyet's consistently great singing and her producers' impersonal backing leave songwriting the only variable, and that's unfortunately what it is. Other than "All Cried Out," the coyly tasteless "Love Resurrection" and Lamont Dozier's magnificent "Invisible," there aren't many tunes in the winning column. What made Yazoo work was great writing; judging by **Alf**, maybe Moyet's symbiotic partnership with Clarke wasn't such a weird idea after all.

Producer Jimmy Iovine stayed out of the other aspects of the creative process on **Raindancing**, leaving Moyet to take greater responsibility for the material. Although sincere enough, her lyrics about romantic challenges don't amount to much; the mostly collaborative music is plain but sturdy, allowing Moyet's rich voice to do the work. Standouts are "Glorious Love," "Is This Love?" and a wonderful oldie, "Weak in the Presence of Beauty." The low point is the stiflingly schmaltzy "Sleep Like Breathing."
                                                    [iar]

MUNCHENER FREIHEIT

Umsteiger (Ger. CBS) 1982
Licht (Ger. CBS) 1983

Herzschlag Einter Stadt (Ger. CBS) 1984
Von Anfang An (Ger. CBS) 1986
Traumziel (Ger. CBS) 1986
Fantasie (Ger. CBS) 1988

FREIHEIT
Romancing in the Dark (Ger. CBS) 1987

Munchener Freiheit (Munich Freedom) started as a two-guitar quartet on **Umsteiger (Transfer)**. Displaying a definite knack for power pop with exceedingly good Beatlesque harmonies, they also go in for some tracks with slightly eccentric arrangements. At points they reach genuine offbeatness, fitting for a band led by an ex-member of fringe space rockers Amon Duül II, namely singing guitarist Stefan Zauner. It's a bit of an unsatisfying mix, but the high points are, well, kind of like eating Ring Dings: empty calories, but awfully tasty. (Despite Zauner's Anglo-pop voice, the record's all in German, including a version of Dylan's "It's All Over Now, Baby Blue.")

They subsequently jettisoned the musical weirdness altogether. On **Licht**, with Zauner moving over to keyboards, the overall sound is more commercial and pop-oriented. That it comes shrink-wrapped with a combination sweat-band/visor (!) should suggest the record's intended appeal. Again, there's the same kind of swell pop-rock, but some veers dangerously close to pap.

By **Herzschlag Einter Stadt**, possibly the group's best album, the lineup was stabilized as a quintet with two keyboardists including Zauner, by this point primarily the singer and chief songwriter. He'd also been the producer, with former bassist Freddie Erdmann but, starting with **Herzschlag**, the records were overseen by Armand Volker. This proved to be a formula for success—the quintet are now quite big pop stars—but the slickness that went into it became increasingly annoying. (Here, it's just insidiously ingratiating.)

Von Anfang An (From the Beginning On) conveniently summed up Munchener Freiheit's output for their hit parade fans, with non-LP single tracks and the most commercial (not necessarily the best) of the previous LPs, including live, alternate and remixed versions. **Traumziel** has a surprisingly mature sound and, while some of it lapses into blandness, the rest is enjoyable ear candy. Curiously dropping the first half of their name, Freiheit issued **Traumziel** in an English-language version, **Romancing in the Dark**, with three remakes from previous LPs slotted in. **Traumziel** actually hangs together better, and understanding the lyrics hardly makes a big difference.

Gradual stylistic modernization, adding in dance-rock elements and so on, was so effective that, by **Fantasie**, most of the original charm—even of Zauner's voice—has been cancelled out. Commercial but dull.
[jg]

COATI MUNDI
The Former Twelve Year Old Genius (nr/Virgin) 1983

Coati Mundi—aka Kid Creole sidekick "Sugar Coated" Andy Hernandez—has done a lot of odd musical projects in his time (including a production job for Germany's Palais Schaumburg!). The singing vibraphone and keyboard player's solo album is no less idiosyncratic in lyrical outlook, if not content. In addition to the clever title reference to Stevie Wonder, the irrepressibly funny Hernandez also parodies "Grand Master Flush and the Fluffy Five" and "Kurtis Bluff" on the rap jape "Everybody's on an Ego Trip." While the album cleverly—and occasionally buoyantly—mixes soul, salsa and disco, it also suffers from Hernandez's simply trying too hard.
[jy]

PETER MURPHY
See *Dalis Car.*

MURPHY'S LAW
Murphy's Law (Rock Hotel-Profile) 1986

New York's Murphy's Law—popular skate punks from Astoria, Queens—take a wisely unserious approach to thrash on their fine debut album, pressed on green vinyl. The quartet varies the tempos every which way—the LP only intermittently utilizes hardcore burn velocity—holding fast to a rollicking punk spirit without conforming to its stylistic regulations. The clearly-produced record's title track has a winning "arf-arf" chorus; "Sit Home and Rot" addresses the urgent topic of couch potatodom without apology; other numbers ratify such essential life functions as "Fun," "Crucial Bar-B-Q" and "Beer." Throughout, the violent energy, good playing and Jimmy Gestapo's spirited vocals make **Murphy's Law** a near-brilliant mistake.
[iar]

PAULINE MURRAY AND THE INVISIBLE GIRLS

Pauline Murray and the Invisible Girls (nr/Illusive) 1980
Searching for Heaven EP (nr/Illusive) 1981

PAULINE MURRAY

Hong Kong EP (nr/Polestar) 1987

Fresh out of Penetration, the early punk band in which she was lead vocalist, Pauline Murray joined forces with producer Martin Hannett's occasional agglomeration, the Invisible Girls which, in this particular 1980 incarnation, included Buzzcocks drummer John Maher. The album features subtle pop that is closer in spirit and execution to British folk-rock than to the Beatles or Sex Pistols. Murray's singing is too bright and lively to handle the more downbeat material, but the band's ability to pattern exciting sounds around her brings out her voice's inherent passion, while the soft but dense rock creates a mood of chilling agitation.

Searching for Heaven repeats the album's accomplishments but varies notably on "Animal Crazy," which introduces a dislocated disco beat that turns it into an interesting dance music variant.

Murray has continued to record on her own, releasing several singles and a 1987 EP. [sg]

MUSIC REVELATION ENSEMBLE

See *James Blood Ulmer*.

MUTABARUKA

Check It (Alligator) 1983
Outcry (Shanachie) 1984
The Mystery Unfolds (Shanachie) 1986

VARIOUS ARTISTS

Word Soun' 'ave Power (Heartbeat) 1983
Dub Poets Dub (Heartbeat) 1983

As a dub poet, Mutabaruka (born in Jamaica as Allan Hope) inevitably inspires comparisons to Linton Kwesi Johnson, but where LKJ's poems are often ironic and his delivery knife sharp, Mutabaruka's work is more direct, thick with dread. Unlike Dennis Bovell's gorgeous formal arrangements on Johnson's LPs, Mutabaruka is more spontaneous. His poems dictate the musical direction—the rhythms jerk the band along. Suffice to say both artists derive from the same traditions of Jamaican poetry and music; if you like one, chances are you'll like the other.

Mutabaruka's first two albums are equally strong. **Check It**, a bold debut, contains three early singles: "Naw Give Up," "Everytime I Hear de Soun'" and "Hard Time Loving." **Outcry** continues the poet's verbal attack, while showing the influence of his dramatic concert appearances. (He performs in manacles.) Music and lyrics sound more linked than on the prior LP, and the band seems to be working with the poet rather than just backing him up.

On his third release, **The Mystery Unfolds**, Mutabaruka's lyrics are presented in a variety of musical settings. The LP is an ambitious mixed bag: there are a cappella tracks and ones with full accompaniment, audio effects and special guest vocalists (including Marcia Griffiths and Ini Kamose). Overall, this album is assured and versatile, widening the performer's range as well as his appeal.

Mutabaruka has also produced other West Indian poets, with two significant compilations (**Word Soun' 'ave Power** and **Woman Talk**) to his credit. The first also spawned the excellent **Dub Poets Dub**, a companion LP of instrumental tracks. [bk]

MUTANTS

The Mutants (MSI-Quality) 1982

Many bands have used this name; these particular Mutants had been active in the San Francisco area for years before releasing this LP. Ex-art students, the septet's personnel hadn't changed much from their early days, but there had been a lot of maturing, from a peppy, loose-limbed Mott the Hoople/Rolling Stones sound to a tighter, poppier, modish style even more suitable to the sci-fi lyrics. The tunes are consistently pleasing, with Frederic Fox playing the dandified Philip Marlow of the cosmic lounge circuit against a chirpy female chorus, and many of the lyrics, for all their jokey fantasy, unexpectedly hit home with more zap than Space Invaders. [jg]

MX-80 SOUND

EP (BRBQ) 1976 (Gulcher) 1977
Hard Attack (nr/Island) 1977
Out of the Tunnel (Ralph) 1980
Crowd Control (Ralph) 1981

This weird post-metal art band originally from Bloomington, Indiana centers their sound around Bruce Anderson's slashing, trebly guitar riffing and Rich Stim's deadpan, often indecipherable mumble. As a five-piece (with two drummers, no less), they twice released a 7-inch EP (subtitled "Hard pop from the Hoosiers") on local labels, impressing Island Records enough to sign them. But the resulting **Hard Attack** never came out in the States and attracted little attention aside from some critical raves. A move to San Francisco (shedding one drummer in the process) brought them to the attention of that city's Ralph Records, home of the Residents and other offbeat types.

Out of the Tunnel may well be MX-80's high-tide mark, particularly on the concurrent single, "Someday We'll Be King" b/w "White Night"; on these two sides, their formula of convoluted, breakneck melodies, cross-fed musical genres and Anderson's white-hot soloing nears critical mass. Unfortunately, the follow-up, **Crowd Control**, proved virtually unlistenable—a messy, depressing collection of metallic dirges best characterized by their atonal slaughter of the theme from Brian DePalma's film, *Sisters*.

[rnp]

N N N N N N N

NAILS

Hotel for Women EP (City Beat-Jimboco-PVC) 1981
Mood Swing (RCA) 1984
Dangerous Dreams (RCA) 1986

Formed as the Ravers in Boulder, Colorado, the Nails moved to New York in the late '70s and established themselves on the local club circuit. Although recorded as a sextet, the most notable item on the four-song **Hotel for Women** is the bizarre minimalism of "88 Lines About 44 Women," a sardonic personal romantic history recited in quirky couplets backed by a dinky electronic drone.

The album features a fleshed-out version of that number, as well as a swell remake of the Hombres' classic "Let It All Hang Out" and seven new murky, moody songs that bring rhythm to the fore and vaguely recall Wall of Voodoo without the Southwestern flavor. [iar]

NAKED EYES

Burning Bridges (nr/EMI) 1983
Naked Eyes (EMI America) 1983
Fuel for the Fire (EMI America) 1984

CLIMIE FISHER

Everything (Capitol) 1988 ●

Following closely in the wake of the far less wholesome Soft Cell, this vocalist-and-synthesist duo (Pete Byrne and Rob Fisher) from Bath had the good sense to (a) have hitmaker Tony Mansfield produce them and (b) cover a classic pop tune, Bacharach/David's "Always Something There to Remind Me." Thus armed, the pair's assault on America was enormously successful. **Naked Eyes** (almost the same LP as **Burning Bridges**) contains the duo's second hit single, "Promises, Promises," and another good number, "Voices in My Head." **Fuel for the Fire** has "(What) in the Name of Love" to recommend it, but little else.

When the two Naked Eyes set off in different directions, Fisher did session work before forming another pop duo with Londoner Simon Climie, a singing songwriter with an effeminate Rod Stewart voice. The bland and predictable **Everything** is an overproduced and characterless all-commercial pop outing. [iar]

NAKED PREY

Naked Prey (Down There-Enigma) 1984
Under the Blue Marlin (Frontier) 1986
40 Miles from Nowhere (Frontier) 1987

Van Christian was at one time Green on Red's drummer; back home in Tucson, Arizona, he switched to vocals and guitar and formed Naked Prey. The quartet plays rough-edged country rock with similarities to Green on Red (as well as Dream Syndicate and others). Although the seven-song debut's powerful sound is strictly modern, "Flesh on the Wall" bears a striking resemblance to the Hombres' 1967 "Let It All Hang Out," and some of David Seger's sociopathic guitar solos recall that era's acid-drenched shows at the Fillmore. An unassuming, occasionally exciting record.

With a new drummer, label and producer (Paul B. Cutler), Naked Prey revved up their folk-distorto-rock on **Under the Blue Marlin** which appropriately contains a Stooges song (from **Funhouse**). Christian's colorful singing and Seger's guitar work remain the group's virtues, as Prey's songs don't make much of an impression. The same problem plagues the thematically linked **40 Miles from Nowhere**: despite killer guitar (including slide) and relentless energy, unimaginative melodies and lyrics derail the effort. (Christian's deteriorating voice is another trouble spot.) For future reference, a pair of covers—Jagger/Richards' "Silver Train" and a funereal version of "Wichita Lineman" (get the drift?)—proves what these boys might do with substantial material. [iar]

NAKED RAYGUN

Basement Screams EP (Ruthless) 1983
Throb Throb (Homestead) 1985 ●
All Rise (Homestead) 1986 ●
Jettison (Caroline) 1988 ●

Chicago's Naked Raygun is one of those encouraging new punk bands that bloomed in the Midwest long after thrash had apparently isolated the punk aesthetic in its own circumscribed ghetto, where it would never again challenge the musical values of regular folk. Lump Raygun in with Hüsker Dü, Man Sized Action, Big Black and Breaking Circus and you'll be oversimplifying, but you'll have your finger on a movement of sorts. All of these bands expanded the boundaries and cast aside some of the trappings of punk to bring it back into contact with the mainstream. If none of them ever attained huge success, all at least appealed to adventurous people who don't have mohawks.

Naked Raygun (like most of the other bands mentioned) has an unabashed love for the naive arty experimentation of Wire and the Buzzcocks. **Basement Screams** is a hodgepodge of underproduced, underconceived songs with a lot of Misfits-type paramilitary chanting; energetic and articulate but not directly compelling. **Throb Throb**'s songs are much better, its drive more urgent and John Haggerty's piercing guitar lines a sonically expansive, sharp force. Even at low volume, the album is loud. The best track, "I Don't Know," is a grippingly melodic art-punk anthem that turns on singer/plumber Jeff Pezzati's anti-idol wail, "What poor gods we do make." A potent, impressive album.

All Rise keeps up the all-out assault level, with dynamic co-production by Iain Burgess making the guitars roar with speaker-shredding distortion. Pezzati's subtly vindictive lyrics (e.g., "Mr. Gridlock" and "The Strip") voice their critiques in an oblique, ironic fashion generally outside the capabilities of

punk auteurs. **All Rise** may be a bit short on melodies (something hinted at in "Knock Me Down"), but Raygun is obviously getting better all the time.

Raygun continue to achieve excellence on their third LP, **Jettison**. Quite different from previous releases, the music's considerably slower speed (only the most notable change) gives almost breathtaking impact to their already forceful sound. "Hammer Head," "Soldier's Requiem," "When the Walls Come Down" and the utterly brilliant "Walk in Cold" are staggering in their intensity. The CD adds four songs: three live cuts and "Vanilla Blue," originally issued as a single. [jl/iar/ag]

WAZMO NARIZ

The E.P. (Fiction) 1979
Things Aren't Right (Illegal-IRS) 1979
Tell Me How to Live (Big) 1980

On record, Chicago's Wazmo Nariz (Larry Grennan) mixes witty double entendres and a semi-jaundiced, semi-naive view of the mysteries of sex with solid songwriting and unusual vocal gyrations, backed by an excellent band. The result is offbeat Midwestern pop: "Tele-tele-telephone" (an independent single eventually reissued in the UK by Stiff) and "Checking Out the Checkout Girl," contained on **Things Aren't Right**. (The album has no overlap with the preceding four-song 7-inch EP.)

Tell Me How to Live varies Nariz's style with parodies (the Presleyesque "Don't Say Always, If You Mean Never") and anthems ("Welcome to the Eighties, Ladies"). Despite a wealth of talent and wild humor, Nariz fell between niches—too bizarre to be pop, too pop to be avant-garde—and the band dissolved amid financial worries and critical apathy. [sg]

NASMAK

Indecent Exposure 1 [tape] (Hol. Plurex) 1981
Indecent Exposure 2 [tape] (Hol. Plurex) 1981
Indecent Exposure 3 [tape] (Hol. Plurex) 1982
Indecent Exposure 4 [tape] (Hol. Plurex) 1982
Indecent Exposure 5 [tape] (Hol. Plurex) 1982
Indecent Exposure 6 [tape] (Hol. Plurex) 1982
4our Clicks (Hol. Plurex) 1982
Heart Ache Blow Up EP (Hol. Plurex) 1982

NASMAK/PLUS INSTRUMENTS

Nasmak/Plus Instruments (Hol. Plurex) 1980

This prolific Dutch group started off as a punky quintet with a flair for melodrama and deliberately offbeat quirks, yet was intent on breaking serious artistic ground even then, as the joint Nasmak and Plus Instruments album shows.

The declaration of artistic commitment evidently resulted in the exit of one member and, subsequently, the six **Indecent Exposure** cassettes, subtitled "The Smell Remains." Nearly an hour apiece, they show occasional flashes of genuine creativity, but each bogs down in its own self-indulgence. Any resemblance to the Residents is superficial at best; Nasmak lacks the wit and spark of the Unfab Four and seems incapable of humor, even when that's their intent.

The melodrama remains in the lyrics, as does a punk-derived penchant for stark, punchy bass/drums riffs with spare but nasty guitar and gruff English vocals. Nasmak's defining characteristic is the way they write songs and then work at denuding them of melody, replacing much of it with sonic spaces and disc(h)ord(s). Intriguing, but still seeking an apt musical voice. The two 1982 discs are the best to sample, since they are leaner and more disciplined, if still a touch misguided. [jg]

NAZ NOMAD AND THE NIGHTMARES

See *Damned.*

NEATS

The monkey's head in the corner of the room. (Ace of Hearts) 1982
Neats (Ace of Hearts) 1983
Crash at Crush (Coyote-Twin/Tone) 1987

Boston's Neats started out playing unself-conscious nouveau folk-rock. Sidestepping nostalgia, the quartet's simple, low-key style would sound perfect in the discothèque scene of some '60s Sunset Strip teen-scene movie, but there is also something clearly modern in the straightforward guitar/bass/drums blend. Eric Martin's dramatic voice gives the seven tunes on the 1982 **Monkey's Head** mini-album their strength. Although the material is serviceable, none of it is striking; a really memorable number would have made this a great debut.

Neats sports an extraordinary white and black pop/op-art cover and nine new tunes, but little evidence of development other than the addition of organ (which makes them resemble a droning California paisley neo-

psychedelic band). The album has good, dense sound and solidly mesmerizing, if rushed, playing, but lacks the exemplary songs (or even findable melodies) to give it shape or form.

The Neats returned to vinyl four years later a much different proposition, even if the lineup is 75 percent intact. (Only bassist Dave Lee, who ironically resembles Eddie Van Halen, is new.) With the song "Big Loud Sound" and a raunchy remake of "The Monkey's Head" as watchwords, the pounding big-beat swamp-rock comes as a shock from this once modestly amplified group. Raspy guitar distortion (intentional and otherwise—the shitty production adds its own fuzziness) dominates, with Martin's raw-voiced singing gallantly vying for attention. While bluesy passages suggest a cross between Creedence and old Gun Club, other cuts take an aboveground rock'n'roll approach and resemble something like Scruffy the Cat. (Throughout, Terry Hanley's mongoloid tom-tom drumming recalls the Cramps.) Although **Crash at Crush** doesn't quite work, the Neats' new musical direction holds definite promise. [iar]

NECESSARIES

Big Sky (nr/Sire) 1981
Event Horizon (nr/Sire) 1982

These two albums are almost the same; the original release was withdrawn, given a partial overhaul, a new title and a relaunch. Although the band was from New York, and included ex-Modern Lover bassist Ernie Brooks, both LPs are UK-only. (Chris Spedding was a member, but had split by the time of these recordings.)

The Necessaries' high-power pop puts the best attributes of rock (crazed, distorted guitars, loud drums) to the service of melodious, intelligent songwriting. Like the early Motors or Records, the Necessaries start with catchy, solid tunes and then give 'em full electric treatment. Rough but sensitive, **Big Sky/Event Horizon** is an impressive outing from a criminally neglected band.

Brooks went on to play with numerous bands around New York; keyboardist Arthur Russell became a radically original new music cellist; singer/guitarist Ed Tomney wound up in Rage to Live; drummer Jesse Chamberlain continued to work with Spedding and others. [iar]

See also *Rage to Live.*

NECROS

Necros EP (Dischord-Touch and Go) 1981
Conquest for Death (Touch and Go) 1983
Tangled Up (Restless) 1987 ●

NECROS/WHITE FLAG

Jail Jello EP (Gasatanka) 1986

This Ohio punk quartet's crunching thrash metal is devastating—and not just in its speed and power, although those qualities are present in brutal abundance. The tough part about listening to the Necros is the awkward, ungainly chord sequences they drag you through. As soon as they gather a head of steam, the band dives into a deliberate tune-defeating change for the mosh section. But the harsh result keeps a fresh edge on the energy, preventing the thrash from blurring into generic noise. Although **Conquest for Death** is pigeonhole hardcore, the Necros have enough creative verve and imagination to make it exciting. (The earlier EP—nine surprisingly clear-sounding pre-hardcore punk slices on a 7-inch 45—shows a young early lineup, including Touch and Go's Corey Rusk on bass, to be starting out with a commitment to song structure and careful playing.)

Tangled Up comes wrapped in a spiffy Big Daddy Roth cover painting of Rat Fink; the Necros (only two original members remain) temper their hardcore instincts for bristling, burly guitar rock—an easily accessible and likable punk sound. There are still a few obligatory mosh parts so skins know where to change their mode of dance, but, for the most part, songs blaze straight through without a breather. Stalwart Barry Henssler sings routine lyrics in a strong and listenable voice against the answering refrains as Andy Wendler's power chords sizzle with distortion in a frenzy of well-focused energy. (Credit the band and their manager for the noteworthy production.)

The joint EP with White Flag contains three songs by each, recorded in support of Dead Kennedys leader Jello Biafra during his censorship-related legal troubles. [jl/iar]

NEGATIVLAND

Negativland (Seeland) 1980
Points (Seeland) 1981
A Big 10-8 Place (Seeland) 1983
Jamcon '84 [tape] (Seeland) 1984
Escape from Noise (SST) 1987

One member of California's Negativland works in a day-care center; another writes computer programs. That pretty well sums up the group's conceptual spectrum. Negativland raids the sonic junkyards of suburban culture to create disjointed, pointedly inorganic aural sculptures that seem to start where John Cage left off. They frequently juice up the found sounds with keyboards and percussion, but that only serves to emphasize the tenuous nature of that crazy stuff we like to call pop music.

Negativland, each copy of which is uniquely and attractively packaged with a different kind of wallpaper, isn't really music and it isn't merely sound effects. Lots of different things blip by, while voices allude to subjects that one never really gets a grip on. Evocative yet very elusive.

Points adds more music to the mix. Beginning in rather a childish mood, it turns increasingly darker and more despairing, finally fading out into a monotonous industrial hum.

A Big 10-8 Place is a musical exploration of the band's Contra Costa County home (just over the hills from Berkeley). As much a loving tribute as a scathing indictment of suburbia's soulless façade, the record is a richly detailed, remarkably complex combination of the inorganic (electronics and industrial atmospherics) and the human (voices discuss whatever).

Escape from Noise attempts to answer a musical question—"Is there any escape from noise?"—*and* parody a perfect pop product. Amid a wide variety of sonic constructions and actual songs, you'll find "Christianity Is Stupid" (allegedly the impetus for a Minnesota teenager's parricide), a little girl with hiccups singing "Over the Rainbow," and calculatedly negligible guest appearances by Jello Biafra, Jerry Garcia, the Residents, Fred Frith and Mark Mothersbaugh. Definitely outside. [rg]

NEIGHBORHOODS

Fire Is Coming (Mustang) 1984
" . . . the high hard one . . . " (Restless) 1986
Reptile Men (Emergo) 1987

This veteran Boston trio's appeal is immediate: they sound good. Nothing fancy or intricate, just good tunes, good vocals, good rock'n'roll drive and feel. Leader David Minehan (guitars, singing, songs) ain't exactly a lyrical Einstein, but he's no stoop either.

The group started out playing strong

power pop (a 1980 single, "Prettiest Girl," remains a local classic) in the wake of British neo-mods. The eight-song **Fire Is Coming** is a get-your-feet-wet proposition, relative to the albums; a likable pointer to the future. The production is a bit thin, but you can tell what the horns on the very first track (ambitious idea) were meant to sound like. The cover of "If I Had a Hammer" was a great idea, enthusiastically (if unimaginatively) executed.

The two full-length LPs show maturation; both are full of instantly memorable tunes, though the first still has some sincere but clichéd lyrics. The production on **high hard one** is plain but crisp; **Reptile Men**'s sound is fuller and punchier. The Who influence (the EP's horns were an inchoate hint) is more early Who on **hard one**, middle Who on **Reptile Men** (the silly part is the use of "Tommy" and "Pure and Easy" as song titles, but the rest reflects an unslavish **Who's Next** influence). The first LP recalls early Gen X and a stripped-down U2, the second (Whoisms aside) really starts sounding like the Neighborhoods. Solid rock'n'roll.   [jg]

BILL NELSON

Northern Dream (nr/Smile) 1971 (nr/Butt) 1981
Quit Dreaming and Get on the Beam (nr/Mercury) 1981
Sounding the Ritual Echo (nr/Mercury) 1981 (nr/Cocteau) 1985
Das Kabinett (The Cabinet of Dr. Caligari) (nr/Cocteau) 1981 + 1985
The Love That Whirls (Diary of a Thinking Heart) (PVC) 1982
La Belle et la Bête (PVC) 1982
Flaming Desire and Other Passions EP (PVC) 1982
Chimera EP (nr/Mercury) 1983
Savage Gestures for Charms Sake (nr/Cocteau) 1983
Vistamix (Portrait) 1984
Trial by Intimacy (The Book of Splendours) (nr/Cocteau) 1984
2fold Aspect of Everything (nr/Cocteau) 1985
The Summer of God's Piano (nr/Cocteau) 1985
Getting the Holy Ghost Across (Portrait) 1986
On a Blue Wing (Portrait) 1986
The Chamber of Dreams (Cocteau) 1987
Chance Encounters in the Garden of Lights (Enigma) 1988 ●

BILL NELSON'S RED NOISE

Sound-on-Sound (Harvest) 1979 (Cocteau) 1985
Revolt into Style EP (nr/Cocteau) 1983

ORCHESTRA ARCANA

Iconography (nr/Cocteau) 1986

From hippie folk singer to awesome rock guitarist to high-tech art-adventurer, Bill Nelson's musical career—now spanning the better part of two decades—has consistently shown style, character and exemplary attention to quality, as well as unrestrained indulgent excess. Beginning with a homemade solo album released by a local Yorkshire record store, through a six-album stint leading Be-Bop Deluxe, then the short-lived experimental Red Noise and finally as a wholly independent solo act (again), Nelson has made lots of brilliant music, and has also worked with some of the most interesting purveyors of modern sounds, producing and playing on numerous records.

Northern Dream is a lovely amateur work, mixing some electric lead guitar with a melodic folk sense—sort of early Neil Young with an English accent. Very impressive, given the circumstances, and not without genuine merit. **Northern Dream** led to the glam-inflected Be-Bop Deluxe and a major-label contract; that band succumbed to audience expectations and business problems, becoming an unfortunate symbol of guitar showboating and retarded creative development.

Nelson launched Red Noise after the dissolution of Be-Bop, which had forced him into the confining role of guitar pyrotechnician. Retaining Be-Bop's keyboard player but outlawing guitar solos, Nelson attacked the future with gusto, drawing together lyrical modernism and subtly infiltrated synthetic sounds. Only the songs are the weak link—despite good ideas, some are half-formed and not up to his usual standards. **Sound-on-Sound** has its moments, but is essentially a work in progress.

Also in progress during Red Noise's brief existence was Nelson's solo work. Although not issued until 1981, **Quit Dreaming and Get on the Beam** was recorded, piecemeal, at various times and places in early 1979. Unaccompanied save for his brother Ian on sax (and all of Red Noise on one cut), Nelson relieved the selfconsciousness of Red Noise's technocracy with more varied subjects and styles. There are more keyboards, but his avoidance of guitar is less forced, and there's even an old-fashioned solo on one number. Although a little disjointed, **Quit Dreaming** is a mature record of real substance and style. Included in the first ten thousand copies was a bonus LP, **Sounding the Ritual Echo (Atmospheres for Dreaming)**, which consists of synthesizer/tape instrumental fragments; interesting if unfocused. The 15 pieces sound like audio sketches for later works.

Das Kabinett (The Cabinet of Doctor Caligari) was written and recorded as the score for a stage presentation by the Yorkshire Actors Company. Released on Nelson's own label, the record consists of 18 instrumental pieces, each designed to accompany a particular scene in the story. Although musically stunning, it's a hard concept for rock fans used to song structure (and words) to grasp.

The Love That Whirls—which also included a bonus record, **La Belle et la Bête (Beauty and the Beast)**, the score for another dramatic production by the same company—was Nelson's finest work to that point. Preponderantly synthesized and showcasing great songs, it finds him dabbling in a variety of styles—Oriental, techno-pop, dance rock, artsy—all with confidence and success. His most accessible work outside of Be-Bop, it was Nelson's long-overdue breakthrough, opening many eyes and ears to his talents. (**Das Kabinett** and **La Belle et la Bête** were reissued in 1985 as a double-album set.)

The 12-inch **Flaming Desire** EP consists of an extended version of the title song (an LP track) and five leftovers from the **Love That Whirls** sessions, some also available on UK 45s.

Chimera is an important release, documenting Nelson's acknowledged influence by Japan's Yellow Magic Orchestra, most notably drummer Yukihiro Takahashi, who plays on four of the six tracks. Also joining the previously hermetic artist is Japan (the group) bassist Mick Karn and others, making tracks like "Acceleration" and "Glow World" invigorated and dynamic. Again playing a lot of guitar, Nelson is in fine form, singing better than ever and writing strong, fascinating songs in a number of different modes. (All of **Chimera** wound up on the American **Vistamix**, joined by four prior creations, including "Flaming Desire" and "Empire of the Senses.")

Nelson's next major new album was **Getting the Holy Ghost Across**, ten fully-produced numbers ranging in length from under one minute to nearly nine. The sound is vintage Nelson—percolating rhythms, layered synths and guitars, passionately cool vocals—and the songs are warmly accessible, with proper lyrics and likable melodies; the wiggly synths and hornwork on "Heart and Soul" even forge a faint link to funk. Perhaps marking the length of time that had passed since Be-Bop, "The Hidden Flame" throws a fiery guitar solo amid the keyboards.

On a Blue Wing is another chapter in Nelson's demi-commercialism, with tasteful lyrics in service of engaging pop music that is not attributable to any specific instrument. (Actually, bass—most of it played by Iain Denby—is the most easily distinguishable sonic element.) Bracketed by a pair of instrumentals, songs like "Contemplation," "Heart and Soul" and "The Hidden Flame" employ simple rhythms and chord structures, but nicely reflect the gentleness and textural nuance of Nelson's work. Nelson's writing has ceased to explore new ground, but he continues to mine the same field with success.

Savage Gestures for Charms Sake is a lovely but inessential collection of one-man studio instrumentals. The sumptuously-packaged **Trial by Intimacy** is a boxed set containing four individually-titled records (**The Summer of God's Piano**, also released on its own, **A Catalogue of Obsessions**, **Pavillions of the Heart and Soul, Chamber of Dreams**), all previously unreleased solo instrumentals: ambient pieces, improvisations, experiments, incidental mood music and odds and ends.

The **2fold Aspect of Everything** is a two-disc (**Eaux d'Artifice** and **Confessions of a Four-Track Mind**) compilation of obscurities: B-sides, remixes, demos and other non-LP matter. The Orchestra Arcana album, **Iconography** (which Nelson conceived, wrote, arranged and produced), is another batch of trivial home-studio instrumental doodles with found-sound and spoken-word additions.

Nelson made another monumental addition to his canon in 1988 with **Chance Encounters in the Garden of Lights**, a huge set of meditative instrumentals on two discs, **The Book of Inward Conversation** and **The Angel at the Western Window**: 41 short pieces in all. You want more? Get the double cassette (49 selections) or the jumbo double-CD (63 items!). [iar]

See also *A Flock of Seagulls, Ippu-Do, Skids, Yukihiro Takahashi, Units.*

NENA

Nena (Ger. CBS) 1983
99 Luftballons (Epic) 1984 ●
It's All in the Game (Epic) 1985

German pop sensation Nena hit it big internationally in 1984 with a nuclear protest song, "99 Luftballons." Boasting the attractive voice of Gabriela "Nena" Kerner and a jolly modern sound, Nena's catchy songs tend towards bubblegum simplicity, but are undeniably engaging, whether sung in English or German. **Nena**, the band's homeland debut, is monolingual, but does contain "99 Luftballons" as well as the equally wonderful "Nur Geträumt" and "Leuctturm," all melodic and bouncy hits that mix rock strength with pure pop arrangements. However, the record is inconsistent, and has a lot of draggy songs that don't make any lasting impression.

The first Anglo-American album translates the hits and other cuts (offering "99 Red Balloons" as well as the German-language original, smoothly converting "Nur Geträumt" into "Just a Dream") while also preserving several more of the original LP's tracks unchanged and appending new material (from a second German LP) to flesh out a stronger, but still flawed, program.

Although no serious stylistic changes were made in the interim, **It's All in the Game** (sung entirely in English, translated by Lisa Dalbello) is fairly irrelevant, lacking any great songs that would vindicate this forgettable collection. Guest sax work by David Sanborn is innocuous; an overall resemblance to mid-period Abba suggests where this lot might be headed—if they have a future.

[iar]

See also *Stripes.*

NERVUS REX

Nervus Rex (Dreamland) 1980

One of the few artistic successes on producer Mike Chapman's short-lived Dreamland label, **Nervus Rex** epitomizes the bubblegum side of new wave pioneered by Blondie. The pace is brisk and the touch light on predictable yet pleasing throwaways like "Go Go Girl" and "The Incredible Crawling Eye." As a perfect point of reference, the New York band includes a lively cover of Shocking Blue's giddy early '70s hit,

"Venus." (I wonder what it would sound like if Bananarama gave that same song a disco-fied try. . . .) Flimsy but fun.

Guitarist/singer Lauren Agnelli went on to form a neo-beat folknik group, the Washington Squares. [jy]

See also *Washington Squares.*

NEUROTICS

See *Newtown Neurotics.*

NEW AGE STEPPERS

New Age Steppers (nr/On-U Sound) 1980
    (nr/Statik) 1982
Action Battlefield (nr/On-U Sound-Statik) 1981
Crucial 90 [tape] (nr/Statik) 1981
Threat to Creation (nr/Cherry Red) 1981
Foundation Steppers (nr/On-U Sound) 1983
Victory Horns (nr/On-U Sound) 1983

Producer Adrian Sherwood is the only constant in this ever-changing jam session that has included members of the Slits, Public Image, Rip Rig + Panic, Raincoats and the Pop Group and in a wild melting pot of synthesized post-rock and reggae, transmuted through dub studio techniques. In practical terms, it amounts to variations on a theme or, more accurately, a rhythm. Everything is built on top of a slow, steady reggae base, but what's heaped on varies from electronic no-wave noise to pretty, melodic singing. It's weird, but occasionally very nice, and consistently unpredictable.

New Age Steppers varies widely, from entrancing to repulsive, with lots of synthesizer babble and overlong dub mixes. A few of the songs stand out, but it's an effect they're reaching for, not hit singles, so you take the whole package, not bits and pieces. Intriguing, if not entirely successful.

Action Battlefield (repackaged, along with the first LP, on the cassette-only **Crucial 90**) is much better—more organized and song-oriented. Ari of the Slits sings lead on all the tracks; her voice, while not exactly pleasant, adds a comforting personality and continuity. Not as weird or chaotic as its predecessor, **Action Battlefield** is strange but appealing.

Which is not true of **Threat to Creation**, recorded jointly with reggae band Creation Rebel. The LP has almost no vocals, little structure and no discernible direction. When it doesn't consist of understated meanderings, it's self-indulgent art-noise that could please only the most indiscriminate fan. Keith Levine [sic] performs half of the guitar chores.   [iar]

See also *Adrian Sherwood.*

NEW ASIA

Gates (nr/Situation 2) 1982

Of more discographical than musical interest, **Gates** is a passel of grating, noisy tracks from a recording project (not a band) led by Ian Little, a Phil Manzanera protégé who has become a noted and successful producer. Other participants include Manzanera and former Hitmen Ben Watkins and Pete Glenister.   [jg]

See also *Brilliant.*

NEWCLEUS

Jam on Revenge (Sunnyview) 1984
Space Is the Place (Sunnyview) 1985

A couple of songs from **Jam on Revenge** were successful, so it would be unfair to call the youthful Newcleus a one-hit wonder. But the only track that's worth talking about is "Jam on It," a hip-hop celebration of the joys of juvenilia. Innocent but not gooey, the song takes rap off the street and cleans it up for mass consumption without emasculating it. The clincher is a lightweight synthesized bass lick that's the bounciest bottom (excuse me) since Chic's "Good Times." Over this, treated voices tweet nonsense syllables and the kids just have a good time. Unfortunately, the band never regained the magic of this rap classic, so the 12-inch of "Jam on It" remains the definitive Newcleus purchase.
                                              [jl]

COLIN NEWMAN

A-Z (nr/Beggars Banquet) 1980
provisionally entitled the singing fish (nr/4AD) 1981 ●
Not to (nr/4AD) 1982 ●
Commercial Suicide (Crammed Discs-Enigma) 1986 ●
It Seems (Crammed Discs-Restless) 1988 ●

A-Z was actually meant to be Wire's fourth album, but EMI didn't see it that way. As a consequence, it became a Newman solo LP, demonstrating that he was indeed the prime creative force in the group, but also suggesting that perhaps ex-partners Lewis and Gilbert might have stemmed the excesses of producer Mike Thorne, who (as he'd done with Wire) both runs the console and adds keyboards. On **A-Z** (as before) he helps create spacious, sensuous soundscapes, but often overcrowds them with keyboards. Newman delivers his willfully oblique lyrics with a strangely detached urgency; the overall effect at times suggests being drugged and locked in a room with an inquisitor shouting senseless questions. **A-Z**'s triumph is that it shows how even simple pop-rock devices can be rearranged and/or modified to devastating effect.

Newman experiments on **the singing fish** by building up textures and melodies with an interesting assortment of instruments (all played and produced by him) in a dozen different ways ("Fish 1," etc.). It isn't the tuneless or monotonous "art" you'd expect from this sort of no-vocals venture either—it's thinking man's muzak which, unlike ambient Eno-isms, doesn't dissipate before your ears upon careful attention. Newman is at once more clinical *and* more playful than ever before.

Not to is a return to the instrumental format of **A-Z**, with a significant change: Thorne is absent. Wire drummer Robert Gotobed and Desmond Simmons remain (with Simmons' guitar/arranging role expanding) and Simon Gillham picks up the bass, giving it an identity of its own. Wire and **A-Z** leftovers are interspersed between newer songs, and the feeling suggests what post-**Pink Flag** Wire might have been without Thorne: minimalist threads rather than sheets of sound; thorny, sometimes atonal, dissonant and rhythmically disjointed, but somehow more personally engaging. Newman himself seems vulnerable—bitter, wistful, showing less lyrical self-assurance, like Ray Davies' art-rock cousin. (In 1988, UK 4AD issued a CD containing both **Not to** and its immediate predecessor.)

Four years later, that vulnerability is again exposed on **Commercial Suicide**. ("I'm still here, waiting for mercy," he sings.) As potent a creator as Newman is, he seems to function best with outside creative input and tension in the situation. That's ideally been provided by Lewis and Gilbert and, to lesser extents, Thorne and Simmons. For this LP, Malka Spigel and Sean Bonnar of Minimal Compact (one of several bands he's produced) individually co-wrote four of the nine tracks, which aren't quite up to their predecessors. It's more than worthwhile—quiet, thoughtful, delicate, artistic, melancholic, hopeful—but it lacks the ineffable edge that makes Newman optimally effective in the re-formed Wire, even on that group's dreamy **A Bell Is a Cup** LP.

It Seems is by the same crew, plus engi-neer/musician/co-producer Gilles Martin, with guest appearances by Gotobed and sev-eral horn and reed players. The fuller, more expressive arrangements and general honing of focus suggest they've gotten to know each other better, and it is a distinct improvement. Much of the LP is as conventional and "nor-mal" (in terms of musical and lyrical struc-ture) as Newman's ever been, and as pretty. It still could be more consistent and, al-though Bonnar and Spigel between them co-write half the ten tracks, the best two are by Newman alone. If you like his other work, you won't want to miss either of these recent discs. [jg]

See also *Desmond Simmons.*

NEW MATH
See *Jet Black Berries.*

NEW MODEL ARMY
Venegance (nr/Abstract) 1984
No Rest for the Wicked (Capitol) 1985
Better Than Them EP (nr/EMI) 1985
The Ghost of Cain (Capitol) 1986
New Model Army (Capitol) 1987
Radio Sessions 83–84 (nr/Abstract) 1988

A trio vigorously lauded by supporters as the new Clash, New Model Army are long on principle and maintain a fervent, unyielding political stance. Taking their primary inspi-ration from early punk roots, though less ab-rasive and more melodic, NMA breathe life into the genre, providing a most effective me-dium for singer/guitarist Slade the Leveller (né Sullivan) to deliver his politcally charged messages. The eight angry, vehement cuts on **Venegance** rely equally on Stuart Morrow's acrobatic bass lines and Slade's accusatory cockney rants. Although the intensity wanes towards the end, it's an arresting debut.

Morrow left prior to the release of **No Rest for the Wicked**. Despite his presence on it, the LP lacks the determined ferocity of its predecessor. Some potentially great songs ("My Country," "Grandmother's Foot-steps," "No Rest") are forceful enough to have belonged on **Venegance**; other tracks swap enthusiasm for overindulgence and suffer as a result. "Better Than Them," a

surprising acoustic foray, meanders intermi-nably; the preachy "Shot 18" is simply ridic-ulous. Without appropriate musical backing, Slade's harsh protests lose their impact, lean-ing dangerously towards hollow sloganeer-ing.

The **Better Than Them** EP—a double-pack 45 of the titular LP track plus three new items—ventures deeper into acoustic terri-tory and shows the Army at ease in these surroundings, but sacrifices the remainder of their vitality in the process. The new songs have the heartfelt honesty that was becoming questionable on **No Rest for the Wicked**.

The Ghost of Cain presents a revitalized (remobilized?) New Model Army, due in large part to the international success of the single "51st State" (a phrase quickly becom-ing *the* British protectionist cliché of the '80s) which is included here. They've stabil-ized as a three-piece unit, and refueled the fires of their convictions, making this record a welcome return to form.

The self-titled fourth album (part studio recordings, part live material) stays the course, with "White Coats" and a live ver-sion of "51st State" as the standouts. [ag]

NEW MUSIK
Straight Lines EP (Epic) 1980
From A to B (nr/GTO) 1980
Anywhere (nr/GTO) 1981
Sanctuary (Epic) 1981
Warp (nr/Epic) 1982

New Musik's Tony Mansfield (writer, producer, vocalist, keyboardist) has never been overly enamored of trendy trap-pings of music or image, which is why his band, never fashionable, had only minor UK hits. (As a freelance producer, however, Mansfield has had no such trouble.) None-theless, in attempting to recast and/or redis-cover pop-rock through modern technology, New Musik helped launch the style as a com-mercial force in America, where its debut single, "Straight Lines"—predating Gary Numan's US hit with "Cars"—nearly crossed over from the dance clubs to the mass market as an import. (The 10-inch EP also includes its follow-up and both B-sides.)

New Musik's full but spacious sound is immediately appealing: vocals, acoustic gui-tars, synths and other keyboards ply melodi-ous ditties impeccably deployed and inge-niously enhanced at the mixing console. What's most telling about this new musik is that it's sensuous but not sensual, energetic but not violent, calling up a sort of bittersweet, melancholic feeling, but never redolent of the gloom-doom syndrome. Which makes the band either a breath of fresh air or an overly polite and sterile waste of time.

Yet, surprisingly enough, the lyrics are almost all about loneliness, alienation and humanity's inability to cope with the modern world—but worded simply, and exclusively in terms of ideals (safety, identity, luxury), abstractions (lines, numbers, motion) and/or metaphors (often to do with the ocean and travel). Though hardly immortal poesy, when put in context by the music, core phrases can be most evocative.

From A to B contains three strong singles (one, "This World of Water," is brilliant) unmatched by those on **Anywhere**, but otherwise there's little difference in quality or style between the two. **Sanctuary** takes the best of both, making it a near-apotheosis of ear candy. **Warp**, however, sounds transitional: band involvement in the studio had apparently increased, adding a new rhythmic component with no effective niche. More acute (and pessimistic) lyrics are accompanied by a paucity of new melodic ideas.

Mansfield's subsequent life as a pop producer has yielded hits for Naked Eyes, the B-52's, Captain Sensible and others.   [jg]

NEW ORDER

Movement (Factory) 1981 ●
1981–1982 EP (Factory) 1982
Power, Corruption and Lies (Factory) 1983
   (Qwest) 1985 ●
Low-life (Qwest) 1985 ●
Brotherhood (Qwest) 1986 ●
The Peel Sessions EP (nr/Strange Fruit)
   1986 ●
Substance 1987 (Qwest) 1987 ●
The Peel Sessions EP (nr/Strange Fruit) 1987

Following the bizarre 1980 death of Ian Curtis and the remarkable success of "Love Will Tear Us Apart," the three remaining members of Joy Division transmuted into New Order, adding guitar/synth player Gillian Gilbert before recording **Movement**. Largely accomplishing what Joy Division set out to do, New Order has sold millions of records and earned boundless critical enthusiasm playing a heady and uncompromising mix of dreamy meanderings and unforgettable techno-dance music, taking off from that memorable swan song, alleviating some of

Curtis' lyrical suffering while retaining the depth and unique musical personality he outlined.

Movement, produced by Martin Hannett, wisely sidesteps the Joy Division comparisons by downplaying the vocals and emphasizing electronics; it may lack the former band's sheer sharpness of vision, but maintains a fascination with decay and paradox, showcasing excellent guitar and synthesizer work.

The **1981–1982** EP consists of five songs taken from British 45s, and presents New Order's pop-styled work, especially the magnificent "Temptation" and "Procession." Coincidentally, New Order was already showing remarkable facility for making uncommon—but highly popular—singles, issuing a huge UK smash, "Blue Monday." (Long unavailable on album, the song was later added to the cassette version of **Power, Corruption and Lies**. In 1988, the song was newly remixed and successfully reissued on 12-inch in America.)

New Order's second album is an utter masterpiece, from the cryptic (but decipherable if you work hard at it) artwork to the eight lengthy tracks of state-of-the-creative-art electronic dance music. Blending moody strains of pseudo-strings with seemingly misplaced guitar bits and coldly kinetic rhythms, plus artless but engaging vocals and syncopated effects, deceptively simple tracks like "Age of Consent" and "Leave Me Alone" convey intense sensations that you can't easily shake. An emotionally and physically moving record by one of the era's most important bands. The CD adds two tracks.

Oddy enough, New Order was formally introduced to America through the auspices of Quincy Jones, whose Qwest label put out **Low-life** and reissued **Power, Corruption and Lies**. One of the finest LP's of 1985, **Low-life** starts out with an ironic folk-form ballad, "Love Vigilantes," that is utterly unlike anything the band has ever tried but scores brilliantly. "The Perfect Kiss" is very poppy, with lush synth strains and perfectly inappropriate froglike (!) sound effects. The other six tracks are almost as appealing, tentatively exploring other stylistic areas without abandoning the essence of New Order's format.

The lightheaded and seemingly half-hearted **Brotherhood** retreads the characteristic sound of **Low-life** but largely lacks the first-rate songwriting that gives purpose and significance to the proficient synthesizer/guitar musical machine. Only "Weirdo," the downcast "All Day Long" and the magnificent "Bizarre Love Triangle" intertwine the delicately rising and falling electro-beat tides with melodies that fix themselves firmly in your head; the rest shimmer with the same near-folk veneer but are just not as memorable.

Fashioning their own version of a career retrospective, the enigmatic and retiring quartet gathered six years' worth of 12-inch singles (some appearing in special new mixes) on two discs under the title **Substance 1987**. If one needs a reminder of New Order's unique genius, this album has it all: "Blue Monday," "Perfect Kiss," "Shellshock," "Confusion," "Bizarre Love Triangle" and seven more. (The CD adds another dozen cuts.)

New Order's first **Peel Sessions** 12-inch (the initial release in the UK series) was recorded in June 1982 and contains four songs; the second hails from January 1981.

[sg/iar]

See also *Paul Haig.*

NEW ORDER
The New Order (Fr. Isadora) 1977
NEW RACE
The First and the Last (nr/Statik) 1982
DESTROY ALL MONSTERS/
SONIC'S RENDEZVOUS BAND
Ron Asheton/Sonic's Rendezvous Band (Fr. Revenge) 1987

Early American punk fanzines had little to write about, which is probably why New Order (the first one) got a lot of press. But just because the group featured Ron Asheton (Stooges guitarist), Scott Thurston (Stooges keyboardist and future Motel) and Dennis Thompson (MC5 drummer) didn't mean its music had to be worthwhile. **The New Order** is full of misplaced guitar breaks, heavy metal sludge and little or no passion. Some things look great on paper, but on vinyl this one stinks.

New Race, a 1981 one-Australian-tour aggregate of Asheton, Thompson and three former members of Sydney punk band Radio Birdman (including guitarist Deniz Tek—who grew up in Ann Arbor, Michigan—and singer Rob Younger), fares a lot better on an album recorded live and then studio-improved by an added guitarist on two numbers and a backing vocalist on three. Production,

sound and playing are all real good (except for the intros and the applause, you may not think it's a concert album at all) and the energy level is impressive. The material includes the MC5's "Looking at You" (given a blistering seven-minute-plus rave-up), several Birdman tracks and one (ugh!) topical number, "November 22, 1963," written by Asheton and Niagara, his singing bandmate in Destroy All Monsters. **The First and the Last**, while not an essential historic document, remains a powerfully charged rock'n' roll album with some searing moments.

The joint album melds a side of Asheton's band, Destroy All Monsters—four songs originally issued on singles around 1978-9—with a side of ex-MC5er Fred Sonic Smith's band, which includes ex-Stooge Scott Asheton. Two of Sonic's four tunes were cut live in 1977; the rest come from a 1978 single. None of the music merits much consideration, although Sonic's works up a helluva head of steam onstage. [cpl/iar]

NEWTOWN NEUROTICS
Beggars Can Be Choosers (nr/Razor) 1983
NEUROTICS
Repercussions (nr/Jungle) 1986
Is Your Washroom Breeding Bolsheviks (nr/Jungle) 1988
Never Thought EP (nr/Jungle) 1988
NEUROTICS ET AL
Kickstarting a Backfiring Nation (nr/Jungle) 1987

The Newtown Neurotics began in the late '70s in Harlow, just north of London, as a brave trio who still thought punk could be something other than a spent force. Singer/guitarist Steve Drewett must have been inspired by early punk's willingness to discuss politics, as his socialist-flavored lyrics—which are never overbearing—have been grouped with those of Easterhouse, Billy Bragg, Three Johns and Housemartins.

For rockin' humdingers influenced by a synthesis of everything cool in early punk—Ramones to the Clash to mid-period Undertones—**Beggars Can Be Choosers** is a blast from the past; punk with extraordinarily happy get-up-and-go that's both fun-sounding and sharp-edged. Drewett's social commentary is at its best, from the "sexual double standards" in "No Respect" to his version of the Members' "Solitary Confinement," redone with a clever twist as "Living with Unemployment." Punk-reggae is even handled competently (far better than the earliest efforts of the Clash or Stiff Little Fingers!) on "Newtown People."

By '86, the Neurotics had dropped their Newtown and had come up with a different sound. The (mostly) moderate tempos, restrained guitar and other refinements (such as the addition of blaring Stax horns) on the engaging **Repercussions** showed the Neurotics could broaden their appeal without changing their message. "This Fragile Life" condemns the Falklands War through the story of a young woman widowed by it; "(Fanatical) Sects" takes the piss out of religious extremists. But the bulk of the record concerns the families of striking miners, to whom the LP is dedicated.

Is Your Washroom Breeding Bolsheviks continues this progress. The rock-soul-mod hybrid has advanced to a point where the Neurotics sometimes sound like a Motown group, with more wild brass and keyboards. (Ex-Member Chris Payne chips in.) "An Inch Away," a breathless number about women victimized by domestic violence, shows that Drewett can still pair sadness and hard-pop with great success; "Local News" proves they can also crank up the attack on demand.

In a novel sidestep, the brilliant-sounding **Kickstarting a Backfiring Nation** was recorded live—with no overdubs—in the studio before an actual audience of paying punters. Selections draw from the first two LPs, plus the Flamin Groovies' "Shake Some Action" redone as "Take Strike Action," again for the miners. The record also contains poetic contributions, recorded live the same evening, by Atilla the Stockbroker, the Big J, Porky the Poet and Peter Campbell. Their rants identify them as offspring of John Cooper Clarke; the subject matter is entirely commensurate with the Neurotics' and fills out this fine package.

The **Never Thought** 12-inch contains five live tracks on the flipside.   [jr]

NEW YORK DOLLS

New York Dolls (Mercury) 1973 ●
In Too Much Too Soon (Mercury) 1974 ●
New York Dolls (Mercury) 1977
Lipstick Killers [tape] (ROIR) 1981
Red Patent Leather (Fr. Fan Club) 1984
Best of the New York Dolls (nr/Mercury) 1985

Night of the Living Dolls (Mercury) 1986
Personality Crisis EP (nr/Kamera) 1986

DAVID & SYLVAIN

Tokyo Dolls Live! (Fr. Fan Club) 1986

The New York Dolls had the style, attitude, rawness and audacity to reinterpret the notion of punk as it had existed in the '60s and to create a decidedly '70s over-the-edge new reality prior to punk. Although they made only two proper albums and were a meaningless relic by the time the Sex Pistols played their first gig, the Dolls singlehandedly began the local New York scene that later spawned the Ramones, Blondie, Television, Talking Heads and others. A classic case of the whole being greater than the sum of its parts, the Dolls were much more than just a band. Their audiences emulated them and formed groups. Detractors' venom inspired countless teenage rebels. Their signing to a major label set an example of commercial feasibility; their subsequent failure to shift product turned the record industry anti-punk for years.

After building a reputation on seedy late-night New York stages, the Dolls' awful magnetism netted them a label contract. Todd Rundgren took the production reins, and delivered a great-sounding document with all the chaos intact. A genuine rock classic, **New York Dolls** contains "Personality Crisis," "Looking for a Kiss," "Trash" and other wondrous slices of gutter poetry punctuated by David Johansen's slangy howl and Johnny Thunders' sneering guitar. No home should be without one.

The legendary Shadow Morton produced the second album; though the results don't match Rundgren's, the Dolls come roaring through nonetheless. There are fewer originals, but the songs they covered have never been the same. "Stranded in the Jungle," "Showdown," "Bad Detective" and "Don't Start Me Talking," reflecting the band's live repertoire at the time, affirm the Dolls' R&B roots.

Johansen and Thunders (and, to a lesser degree, guitarist Syl Sylvain) have gone on to notable solo careers; bassist Artie Kane and drummer Jerry Nolan went through various local bands before disappearing entirely. (A minor footnote: In 1983, Fan Club released **The Legend of the Corpse Grinders**, capturing a band that included Kane for a year. Another LP called **Children of the Dolls** compiles assorted post-Dolls 45s.) In 1977,

Mercury repackaged both albums together with new artwork and liner notes by Tony Parsons.

Except for the appearance of original drummer Billy Murcia (whose overdose death in London, noted in Bowie's "Time," considerably helped build the Dolls' legend), the cassette-only collection of 1972 demos released as **Lipstick Killers** is of archival value only, underscoring the enormity of Rundgren's accomplishment on the first record.

More archaeology: **Red Patent Leather** captures the fading Dolls on a New York stage in 1975 during a brief era when a pre-Pistols Malcolm McLaren managed them. The set includes a bunch of otherwise unvinylized numbers (e.g., "Daddy Rolling Stone," "Something Else," "Pirate Love") but is not exactly a peak performance. The Johansen/Sylvain record, recorded a few months later in Tokyo on a post-breakup contractual obligations tour, is a bootleg-quality live album by the remains of the band (Thunders and Kane are absent; Tony Machine is on Nolan's stool). Strangely, the cover of this blue-vinyl item makes an unabashed bid to be mistaken for a David Sylvian (of the group Japan) release.

Indicative of the Dolls' enduring relevance to young people, both English and American Mercury have issued compilation albums. **Night of the Living Dolls** manages to uncover a heretofore unreleased take of Morton's "Give Her a Great Big Kiss," a tune the Dolls used to play. [iar]

See also *Heartbreakers, David Johansen, Sylvain Sylvain, Johnny Thunders*.

NICO

Chelsea Girl (Verve) 1967 ●
The Marble Index (Elektra) 1969
Desertshore (Reprise) 1971
The End (Island) 1974
Drama of Exile (nr/Aura) 1981
Do or Die! Nico—in Europe—1982 Diary [tape] (ROIR) 1982
The Blue Angel (nr/Aura) 1985 ●
Behind the Iron Curtain (nr/Dojo) 1986 ●
Live in Japan (nr/Dojo) 1986
(Live) Heroes EP (Performance) 1986

NICO + THE FACTION

Camera Obscura (Beggars Banquet-PVC) 1985

KEVIN AYERS/JOHN CALE/ENO/NICO

June 1, 1974 (Island) 1974

A fashion model and bit player in Fellini's *La Dolce Vita,* the German-born Nico (Christa Paffgen) was plunged into the maelstrom of rock when Andy Warhol introduced her to the Velvet Underground, which she then joined. **Chelsea Girl,** her maiden voyage on a solo musical career, is of interest mainly for its links to the band Nico had just left. Five songs were written (but not recorded) by Velvet Undergrounders; three others were written or co-written by a very young Jackson Browne. The material, however, is sabotaged by tepid arrangements and weak production. Highlight: the hypnotic "It Was a Pleasure Then," on which Nico's sepulchral voice is accompanied only by feedback guitar (undoubtedly played by Lou Reed).

The Marble Index was a substantial improvement. Producer John Cale took Nico's disturbing poetry and set it to even more disturbing music; the result is one of the scariest records ever made. Unlike **Chelsea Girl,** in which Nico tried to adapt to an outmoded chanteuse tradition, **The Marble Index** blasts her off to her own universe. Regardless of whether more credit is due her or Cale, the album is powerfully effective. The Nico-Cale collaboration continued on **Desertshore.** Here the disjunctive imagery is set to slightly less gothic arrangements than before, proving Nico's chanting (she doesn't "sing" any more than she writes "songs") can be as chilling a cappella as it is accompanied by a horror-movie soundtrack.

Three years later—Nico's not exactly a studio hound—she and Cale turned up with Roxy Music guitarist Phil Manzanera and Brian Eno on synthesizer for **The End.** The title track is the Doors epic, which Nico had also just previously recorded on the all-star **June 1, 1974** album. With one exception, the rest of **The End** is original material, putting the emphasis on Nico's voice and eerie, foot-pumped harmonium rather than on distracting sound effects. The exception, "Das Lied der Deutschen" (or "Deutschland über Alles"), is enough to make you run out and buy war bonds.

Seven years later, Nico re-emerged without Cale but with a conventional rock band on **Drama of Exile.** This jarring blend hurts everyone involved; adding insult to injury, bassist/producer Philippe Quilichini filters

Nico's voice for a tinny effect. Her psychotic writing is still fascinating, and certainly preferable to aimless versions of the Lou Reed's "Waiting for the Man" and David Bowie's "Heroes."

In 1985, joined by two sidemen and Cale as producer, Nico resurfaced with the odd but exciting **Camera Obscura**. This modernization program includes both the nearly vocal-less title track's meandering semi-random improvisation and an attractively somber version of "My Funny Valentine," with stops in between for fascinating blends of Nico's unique singing and post-noise industrial music. **Camera Obscura** raises Nico's artistic average this decade to a respectable 50 percent.

Do or Die!, recorded live throughout Europe with various bands (the Blue Orchids, Samarkand) backing her, is a lengthy sampler of Nico's work minus the production flourishes of her studio albums. The fascinating and innately bizarre **(Live) Heroes** mini-album draws on some of the same shows—adding two tracks done with the Invisible Girls—for such things as "My Funny Valentine," "Heroes" and five others. Another concert set, the two-LP **Iron Curtain** was recorded in 1985 in Warsaw, Budapest and Prague with a band that included Eric Random. **The Blue Angel** is a retrospective compilation that even includes Velvet Underground material.

Nico died in July 1988 on the island of Ibiza. She suffered a cerebral hemmorhage after falling off a bicycle. She was 49.

[si/iar]

STEVE NIEVE

Keyboard Jungle (nr/Demon) 1983 ●
Playboy (nr/Demon) 1987

Nieve first stepped out of Elvis Costello's Attractions for **Keyboard Jungle**, a cute set of miniatures crafted at the keyboard of a Steinway. Contents: fake film and classical music, none of it taken (or given) particularly seriously. Quite agreeable.

The cover of **Playboy** shows Nieve, dressed to the nines, looking a bit like Bryan Ferry; the solo acoustic piano record mixes suave originals with unique (di)versions of standards, just like Ferry's first solo efforts. The material in receipt here of Nieve's straightfaced (and, therefore, hysterically funny) cocktail-lounge treatment includes Sting's derivative and trivial "Russians,"

Bowie's overwrought "Life on Mars," 10cc's weepy "I'm Not in Love" and the Specials' nearly-tuneless "Ghost Town." (X and Wham! also get their comeuppance in Nieve's graceful hands.) The 11 other short pieces display the artist's wit, compositional talent and abundant instrumental agility.

[jy/iar]

NIGHTINGALES

The Nightingales EP (nr/Cherry Red) 1982
Pigs on Purpose (nr/Cherry Red) 1982
Hysterics (nr/Ink-Red Flame) 1983
The Crunch EP (nr/Vindaloo) 1984
Just a Job (nr/Vindaloo) 1984
In the Good Old Country Way (nr/Vindaloo) 1986
The Peel Sessions EP (nr/Strange Fruit) 1988

Trebly guitar scrubs and busy drumming, both at a hyper pace, support the snide, self-mocking, self-pitying, annoyed, despairing, sarcastically scathing and generally intelligent (if not always intelligible) tirades of one Robert Lloyd. (Dry wit, too.) The boy has a lot of mind to give the world a piece of. (Prior to the Nightingales, Lloyd led the late-'70s punk Prefects; he later organized the Vindaloo label.)

On the Nightingales' first EP, the melodies are memorable if minimal, and the playing seems just a touch out of control. **Pigs on Purpose** shows a bit more instrumental skill (despite bad mastering) and an increased variety of tempos and textures. The Fall would seem to be a major influence, not only in the abrasive, paradoxically unobtrusive guitar work but Lloyd's singing/ranting, which owes something to Mark E. Smith's vocal and lyrical style.

Hysterics marks a label change and much improved production; tone colors are expanded with the use of banjo, trombone and viola. The Nightingales also demonstrate a greater assortment of styles: bass parts borrowed from reggae, an inside-out Bo Diddley beat on "Ponces All" and a flirtation with country-western in "The Happy Medium." **The Crunch** EP features the contrast of tightly-controlled chaos *and* some of Lloyd's more melodic vocals. Released during a period of numerous personnel shifts (they were briefly a sextet), the Nightingales manage to avoid sounding transitional; there's plenty of drive and power on these tracks. Highly recommended.

Country Way wisely isn't an attempt to

make a straightforward country album. Many bands lacking a real identity might make such an error, but the "Gales are able to embellish their own sound with country and bluegrass elements. Lyrics are more smart-ass than ever (see "Part Time Moral England" and "I Spit in Your Gravy"); the playing gets downright hot on "The Headache Collector." Highly recommended, even—or maybe especially—for those who hate country-western.

Just a Job is a compilation of **The Crunch**, non-LP singles and a track from **Hysterics**. [jg/dgs]

NIHILISTICS

Nihilistics EP (Visionary) 1982
Nihilistics (Brain Eater) 1983

Nihilistics are a stupid, obnoxious hardcore band from Long Island, New York. Their lyrics are predictable banalities and their attitudinizing is irritating. That's the bad news. The good news is that the album is pretty good (even if the preceding five-song 7-inch is much better). However full of it their ideas may be, the band members at least believe in them, and advance them with all the passion of the errantly self-righteous. Emotional commitment does count for something, even if that commitment is to a credo like "Take it from me man . . . fuck the human race." (At least it suggests comprehension of the band's moniker.) People hate hardcore precisely for stuff like this, but the Nihilistics go far enough to almost make it work. [jl]

NILS

Sell Out Young! EP (Can. Psyche Industry) 1985
The Nils EP (Can. Siegfried) 1986
The Nils (Rock Hotel-Profile) 1987 ●

Inspired into existence a decade ago by the Sex Pistols, this young Montreal guitar quartet, led by brothers Alex and Carlos Soria, plays energetic and competent punkergized rock with rich vocals on their Chris Spedding-produced debut album. (Ivan Doroschuk of Men Without Hats financed and produced the first Canadian EP; the second was actually recorded earlier but unreleased until 1986. **The Nils** is only a semi-official title; the record is also known as **The Red EP**.)

Their debut album, **The Nils**, has the

same kind of fearless commercial sensibility and melodic intuition as 1978 Generation X or 1987 Soul Asylum: songs like "When the Love Puts on a Sad Face," "Bandito Callin' " and the Hüsker Dü-like "Young Man in Transit" don't reach those bands' highs but show just as much effort and ingenuous spirit. [iar]

NINE BELOW ZERO

Live at the Marquee (nr/A&M) 1980
Don't Point Your Finger (A&M) 1981
Third Degree (nr/A&M) 1982

The underrated Nine Below Zero had progressed from being a cautious but promising R&B cover band to performing fresh, confident originals at the time it broke up in 1982. Releasing a live album as a debut is a mite unusual, but **Live at the Marquee** clearly captures NBZ's tightness and enthusiasm. The material draws mostly on such old tunes as the Four Tops' "I Can't Help Myself" and Sam the Sham's "Woolly Bully," given powerful readings by these Londoners.

Don't Point Your Finger, produced by old pro Glyn Johns, is a transitional album. Though the majority of songs are originals, most written by singer/guitarist (and founder) Dennis Greaves, they sound authentically old.

Nine Below Zero updated its sound on **Third Degree** with wonderful results. Greaves successfully cuts his beloved R&B roots with elements of traditional rock'n'roll, pop and even a touch of reggae ("Easy Street SE 17"), all infused with a healthy shot of punky energy ("Eleven Plus Eleven," "Tearful Eye," "True Love Is a Crime" and the terrific "Wipe Away Your Kiss.") [ks]

See also *Truth*.

999

999 (nr/UA) 1978
Separates (nr/UA) 1978
High Energy Plan (PVC) 1979
Biggest Prize in Sport (Polydor) 1980
Biggest Tour in Sport EP (Polydor) 1980
Singles Album (nr/UA) 1980
Concrete (Polydor) 1981
13th Floor Madness (nr/Albion) 1983
Face to Face (nr/Labritain) 1985
In Case of Emergency (nr/Dojo) 1986
Lust Power and Money (nr/ABC) 1987

Despite a large recorded output and an avoidance of typecasting, 999 never amounted to anything more than an undistinguished and dispensable band of moderate ability. Variously posing as mutant bubblegum, rocky art-school cleverness, heavy metal and quirky pop, 999's problem has always been a lack of adequate talent to invest their music with real originality; to be fair, they *have* managed a few good sides along the way and also deserve credit for endurance and persistence.

999 introduced the band, dressed in kicky, colorful clothes and working with pop producer Andy Arthurs, yet it's not a pop album. The music is harmless but charmless, although the vocals are occasionally winning, as on "Me and My Desire" and the whiny "Emergency."

For their second effort, 999 enlisted soon-to-be-a-superstar producer Martin Rushent, and **Separates** does have a lot more going for it. The band's playing is harder and tighter, with better focus, although the semi-hit "Homicide" benefits more from a clever arrangement than intrinsic quality. Other good tunes include the taut "Feelin' Alright with the Crew" and an all-out rocker, "High Energy Plan." Still minor, but improving. (**High Energy Plan** is an American revision, with two tracks deleted and two 45 cuts added.)

Biggest Prize in Sport teamed 999 (temporarily a five-piece, having added a second drummer to aid the injured Pablo Labritain) with producer Vic Maile, resulting in a disc that is trebly and lifeless, except for the poppy title track, which sounds like a cockney Ramones.

Hoping to stir up some domestic interest, 999's American record company issued a six-song mini-album, **Biggest Tour in Sport**, recorded live in 1980 in the States. The sound's good and hot; selections include "Homicide," "Emergency" and "Feelin' Alright with the Crew."

Not to be outdone, their English label whipped up a collection—in chronological order—of 999's singles, starting with "I'm Alive" (1977) and running through "Waiting" (1978), including both sides of each—15 tracks in all. If you need to find out about 999, **Singles Album** is the record to have, containing all their esssential (i.e., good) material.

Concrete could almost be mistaken for an Inmates record, thanks to two pointless covers ("Li'l Red Riding Hood," "Fortune Teller") and a mundane, characterless guitar-rock sound.

13th Floor Madness was slagged off in the press as soft disco, but the self-released **Face to Face** is a pleasant surprise, offering melodic rock with a certain charm (despite occasional gaffes and lapses of wit). The band's original lineup, still together after all these years, is not exactly getting better by leaps and bounds, but the songs here are their most likable in a long time—a few could even be characterized as memorable—and bits of invention keep them moving along.

Following the release of another compilation (**In Case of Emergency**), 999 released an all-new live-in-London album, recorded in April 1987. The band's lineup is essentially intact (only the bassist is new); the program includes the ancient ("Hit Me," "Homicide," "Feelin' Alright with the Crew") and the relatively recent ("White Trash" and "Lust Power and Money"). The performance is dull but the sound is good. (One hopes there was more audience present than what's audible.) [iar]

NITECAPS

Go to the Line (Sire) 1982

The Nitecaps (including onetime New York Dolls roadie/bassist Peter Jordan) were a multi-racial quartet—sort of an American counterpart to Graham Parker's Rumour—spearheaded by erstwhile Voidoid (known then as X-sessive), Jahn Xavier. On **Go to the Line**, with the fab Uptown Horns and production by Langer and Winstanley, this babyfaced imp reveals himself to be not only a mean guitarist, but a throaty growler with a voice that crosses Joe Jackson and Otis Redding. R&B like this rarely sounds so strong or credible. The only misstep is a Zombies/Easybeats medley; the rest (originals, aside from an arcane, super-cool oldie) is solid, foot-stompin' fun. Nitecaps guitarist Al Maddy later joined the Dots. [jg]

NITS

Tent (Hol. Epic) 1979
New Flat (Hol. CBS) 1980
Work (Hol. CBS) 1981
Omsk (Hol. CBS) 1983
Kilo EP (Hol. CBS) 1983
Adieu, Sweet Bahnhof (Hol. CBS) 1984
Henk (Hol. CBS) 1986
In the Dutch Mountains (Hol. CBS) 1987

R.J. STIPS

U.P. (Hol. CBS) 1981

The obvious derivativeness on the Nits' early albums could have been written off as cut-rate local filtration/reassembly of the real thing from Britain and America (Beatles, Talking Heads, etc.). In retrospect, however, those records can be seen as learning experiences of a world-class band now deserving international attention.

Comparisons to tongue-in-cheek pop synthesists like 10cc and fellow Dutchmen Gruppo Sportivo leave the early Nits on the short end of the stick; they come off as cute and clever, but in a too-tidy, sterile way, especially on **Tent**. On **New Flat**, the occasional arty touch provides a welcome contrast, and the melodies are snappy enough not to be dismissed out of hand. The music on **Work**, however, is too thin to carry the selfconsciously arty lyrics. Some promise is revealed on **New Flat** and **Tent** by Hans Hofstede's growing aptitude at creating little emotional postcards.

Omsk and **Kilo** show the Nits beginning to find their voices; it must be at least partly attributed to the addition of keyboardist Robert Jan Stips. Previously known for producing Gruppo Sportivo albums, he produced part of **Tent** and all of **New Flat**. His own LP is a curious blend of pop-rock and jazz syncopations, in a unique style that starts out intriguing but turns irritating. All the same, he does bolster the Nits' brighter, poppier side and shades the darker, moodier aspect most often explored by Hofstede. On **Omsk** and **Kilo**, Hofstede unveils a style not unlike Elvis Costello (but more vulnerable and less venomous); Stips' keyboard-dominated settings are affecting, even haunting.

Adieu, Sweet Bahnhof reflects the group's odd international sensibility. None of the Nits' lyrics have ever been in Dutch; a song on the LP refers to Holland, but it's sung half in English, half in Turkish. Is there some national inferiority complex at work here? In any case, this is a more musically confident and aggressive, yet less affecting, record than its immediate predecessors. There are still clumsy phrasings and syntactical mistakes (in songs by Stips and Michiel Peters, not Hofstede), which would be more easily forgiven/ignored if the melodies were stronger. This album seems to be a move sideways, a retrenchment, a sort of public ironing out of the kinks, though the really good tracks (like those featuring Hofstede's Lennonish Costelloisms) do make it a respectable opus.

Henk is another story altogether. Firstly, there's the mystery of the title (weirder since Hofstede changed his name from Hans to Henk after the **Work** LP). Peters is gone. Hofstede now writes all the lyrics, while he, Stips and agile drummer Rob Kloet share equal credit for the music. Other than a spot of banjo (!) and one track's worth of guitar, there are no fretted instruments to be heard—it's all voices, keyboards and drums. And it's great—oddball pop-rock of the first order. The imaginative range of electronic sounds and textures can be breathtaking, as on "Cabins" and "Under a Canoe." The melodies are attractive. The words are often abstract but always evocative. The Nits now sound like . . . the Nits.

In the Dutch Mountains—the title track no doubt inspired by Cees Nooteboom's acclaimed quasi-fantasy novel—is also impressive. The Nits again sound like the Nits, but substantially different Nits. Intended to resemble a live show, it was recorded "in their own rehearsal room, an old gym in Amsterdam . . . straight to two-track digital tape with no dubbing or mixing after the actual recording." New bassist Joke Geraets plays only a stand-up acoustic; Hofstede's back to playing guitar. The occasional guests are three female backing vocalists and a steel guitar player. Hofstede's lyrical approach is—as on **Henk**—offbeat, but also consistently personal (even at one point confessional). Surreal juxtapositions of prosaic imagery suggest travels through his dreams. The cleverly contrapuntal music and rhythms use a tonal/timbral palette that is more subdued (yet equally effective in its way) than **Henk**. And this is nearly a live album! Brilliant.   [jg]

MOJO NIXON AND SKID ROPER

Mojo Nixon and Skid Roper (RBI-Enigma) 1986
Frenzy (Restless) 1986 ●
Get Out of My Way! (Restless) 1986 ●
Bo-Day-Shus!!! (Enigma) 1987 ●

OK, you figure it out. Mojo Nixon and his sidekick, Skid Roper, first gain attention with a love-letter ditty to then-MTV veejay Martha Quinn subtly entitled "Stuffin' Martha's Muffin." In addition to bluntly proclaiming his desire to get intimate with the perky Ms. Quinn, the call-and-response vocals in the bridge take on the whole institution: "MTV/get away from me . . . I say, Music Television/should be covered in jism." Several years later, there's Mojo doing spots on MTV, talking about post-punk philosophers while hanging from a jungle gym and serving as a roving reporter on the beach for Spring Weekend.

Sold out? Quite the opposite. **Mojo Nixon and Skid Roper** is a bit on the tame side—songs with titles like "Jesus at McDonald's' ' and "Art Fag Shuffle" should be great, but are merely clever. Mojo finds his true voice on **Frenzy**. The musical accompaniment to Nixon's often hysterical socio-political commentary is mostly a frisky down-home mixture of blues, R&B and rockabilly. Roper's contributions consist of things like washboard, harmonica, mandolin, etc. Besides "Stuffin' Martha's Muffin," **Frenzy** offers Nixon's appraisal of such topics as gigging ("Where the Hell's My Money"), fatherhood ("I'm Living with the Three-Foot Anti-Christ") and savings & loans ("I Hate Banks"). Add to that his hilarious checkout line tabloid spoof, "The Amazing Bigfoot Diet," and a fleeting harmonica-driven version of "In-a-Gadda-da-Vida," and this LP should appeal to anyone with a funny bone.

Get Out of My Way! is a seven-track mini-LP reprising "Stuffin' " and "Jesus at McDonald's," plus a few of Mojo's very own Christmas songs. All of these tracks are included on the **Frenzy** CD.

Bo-Day-Shus!!! is every bit as much a hoot, with the epic "Elvis Is Everywhere" (finally revealing the identity of the much-feared anti-Elvis!) and a topical ode to the just-say-no crowd, "I Ain't Gonna Piss in No Jar." (It's a shame Nancy Reagan and Ed Meese will never hear it.) Other little slices of Americana include "B.B.Q.U.S.A.," "Wash Dishes No More" and "I'm Gonna Dig Up Howlin' Wolf." Folks, Nixon is the man this country needs—Mojo ain't no Dick. [dgs]

NO DIRECTION

No Direction (No Direction) 1984

On what is likely to be the only independent album ever released by a Sioux Falls, South Dakota punk band, No Direction play earnest political protest numbers with a lot more spirit than technique. Far removed from any stylistic trendiness (or, for that matter, trends), this trio is simply basic and that's a strength. The 16 songs have energy

but a spare sound with open spaces that would benefit enormously from bigger amps and a skilled producer. Impressive mostly for its heart and lack of guile, **No Direction** is a record possessing many of the attributes other punkers lack. [iar]

NOMEANSNO

Mama (Can. no label) 1984
Sex Mad (Can. Psyche Industry) 1986
    (Alternative Tentacles) 1987
The Day Everything Became Nothing EP
    (Alternative Tentacles) 1988

With some of the same type of slash'n' burn egghead energy as Couch Flambeau, this trio from Victoria, British Columbia pours out punky collegiate weirdness on **Sex Mad**, their first American album, revised from its original Canadian release. Songs like "Self Pity" and "Dead Bob," not to mention an appropriately titled instrumental, "Obsessed," reveal Nomeansno's conscientious bizarritude and feverish proto-musical attack.

The credits on **The Day Everything Became Nothing** mention Rob and John Wright, who collectively cover bass, guitar, drums, keyboards and vocals; "another guy does a bunch of other stuff." The 12-inch's six songs offer more dadaesque invention with concertedly intense and pointed music. The unstructured prose of the title track is supported by pounding drums alternating with bursts of guitar noise; "Beauty and the Beast" syncopates the rhythms for a disorienting effect that suggests funk and negates it in the same line. Impressive. [iar]

KLAUS NOMI

Klaus Nomi (nr/RCA) 1982
Simple Man (nr/RCA) 1982
Encore! (nr/RCA) 1983

One of the 1980s' most profoundly bizarre characters to emerge through rock music, the late Klaus Nomi specialized in unexpected mixes of vocal styles in anomalous settings. His awesome falsetto and dramatic tenor were equally applied to classical music and rock'n'roll, producing startling records that ramble wildly from high-pitched operatic vocals accompanied by a synthesized orchestra to ultra-stylized pop and warped interpretations of rock oldies. Nomi's records stretch from hauntingly beautiful (Purcell's stunning "Cold Song") to hysterically funny (a somber reading of "Can't Help

401

Falling in Love," a languid dissection of "The Twist") to straightforward Sparks-like big band rock ("Simple Man"). His final album, a compilation that also includes a live performance, is the one to get, an utterly unique creation that defies you not to fall under its wonderful spell.   [iar]

NON

See *Boyd Rice.*

NORMAL

See *Robert Rental and the Normal, Silicon Teens.*

IAN NORTH

Neo (nr/Aura) 1979
My Girlfriend's Dead (Cachalot) 1980
Rape of Orchids (Neo) 1982

MILK 'N' COOKIES

Milk 'n' Cookies (nr/Island) 1977

The multifarious North (singer, guitarist, synthesist, producer and songwriter) was the leader of Long Island's finest contribution to wimp rock, Milk 'n' Cookies, who were playing dingy New York bars in their cute baseball uniforms when a visiting tycoon took them to England in hopes of making them a hit machine in the Anglo-pop sweepstakes. The band's sole LP—recorded in 1975 but released two years later—is full of catchy melodies, twee lyrics and energetic fizz-pop guitar hooks. Awfully early for the power pop revival, it never was very popular; however, fans of bands like Shoes and Sparks might appreciate its preciously naive charms.

North's subsequent solo career has taken several turns. Living in England for a while, he led a new wave band called Neo which collapsed after recording an unreleased album. North salvaged and revised various studio efforts (with two different lineups) to piece together **Neo**, actually a pretty good record. The overall timbre is modern rock with melody and bitterness; some of the songs are excellent. The problem is North's pretentiously unnatural deep voice.

Returning to New York, he began recording by himself, producing two discs at home on simple equipment, using synthesizers as a major sonic component (the only one on **Rape of Orchids**). **My Girlfriend's Dead** contains some good songs played dully; **Rape of Orchids**, a four-song 12-inch, is sub-Gary Numan tedium.   [iar]

NOVEMBER GROUP

November Group EP (Modern Method) 1981
Persistent Memories EP (Brain Eater) 1983
Work That Dream EP (A&M) 1985

Boston's November Group starts with a powerful rhythm section, and then adds Kearney Kirby's synthesizers, sporadic guitar and Ann Prim's stern vocals to make slick, modern dance music utterly devoid of warmth. The first record is unnervingly more suited to marching than dancing or listening. **Persistent Memories** shows more diversity and less formula, and introduces a promising factory number, "Put Your Back to It." The far more accomplished **Work That Dream**, recorded by Kirby and Prim in Frankfurt with German musicians, takes another intriguing swipe at "Put Your Back to It." The other tunes are less distinguished, but all are functional for club play.   [iar]

GARY NUMAN

The Pleasure Principle (Atco) 1979
Telekon (Atco) 1980
Living Ornaments '79 (nr/Beggars Banquet) 1981
Living Ornaments '80 (nr/Beggars Banquet) 1981
Dance (Atco) 1981
I, Assassin (Atco) 1982
New Man Numan (nr/TV) 1982
Warriors (nr/Beggars Banquet) 1983
Berserker (nr/Numa) 1984
White Noise—Live (nr/Numa) 1985
The Fury (nr/Numa) 1985 ●
Strange Charm (nr/Numa) 1986 ●
Exhibition (nr/Beggars Banquet) 1987

TUBEWAY ARMY

Tubeway Army (nr/Beggars Banquet) 1978 (nr/Fame) 1983
First Album (Atco) 1981
The Peel Sessions EP (nr/Strange Fruit) 1987

GARY NUMAN & TUBEWAY ARMY

Replicas (Atco) 1979
The Plan 1978 (nr/Beggars Banquet) 1984

Gary Numan (né Webb) originally rose to prominence with a frigid synthesizer dance hit, "Are Friends Electric?" His basic sound—subsequently very influential in the dance music and new romantic spheres—began with precise, antiseptic synth handling much of the instrumental work, and topped it with lobotomized deadpan vocals singing science-fiction lyrics, a combination that is sometimes abrasive but more frequently engaging.

Tubeway Army (released in America three years later as **First Album**) features primitive electronics and production that showed some flair, though guitars dominate and compositions are locked into the three-minute post-punk structure. **Replicas**, on which synth is the dominant instrument, includes "Are Friends Electric?" and reached the top of the British charts. A composite of material from J.G. Ballard novels, Germanic iciness and '60s pop, the album forged a style that was stunningly new at the time but now sounds hopelessly dated.

The Pleasure Principle, Numan's first release under his own name, contains the international hit "Cars" and continued Numan's maturing love affair with the synthesizer. His interest in technology showed itself to be increasing in both the lyrics and the music. **Telekon** brought guitar noticeably back into the mix. The songs raised Numan's despondent romanticism to new heights (depths?), permeated by doom and synthetic syncopation.

Living Ornaments '79 and **Living Ornaments '80**, which capture Numan's tours of those years, were issued separately as well as in a special boxed set. (All three were, by plan, quickly deleted.) Performances give energy to the songs, and Numan's live voice is frequently more impassioned than his studio persona's. The 1979 LP features synthesizer pyrotechnics by Ultravox's Billie Currie that are unmatched on the 1980 recording.

Dance was Numan's first outing following the disbanding of his backup group and his retirement from touring. It exposes a flair for ironic lyrics and a most undanceable set of dance tunes, downplaying the beat and showing new interest in melodics. Unfortunately, **I, Assassin** suggests that Numan had hit a stylistic quandary, as it tended back toward his hits but lost his style in the wake of new fashion. Whereas **Pleasure Principle** was the vanguard of the future, the equally professional **I, Assassin** borders on nostalgia.

Subsequently stumped for a way to revive his flagging career, Numan made the roundly dismissed, almost laughable **Warriors**. He was much better served by the TV best-of and, surprisingly, a collection of pre-synthesizer riff-rockers dating from 1978 that had previously languished unreleased. The dozen guitar-based demos on **The Plan** are punky but clear and nonaggressive, providing an unassuming setting for Gazza's characteristically robotic voice and ridiculous lyrics, free of the formulaic setting that typified his early hits, some of which clearly had their beginnings in this material. (A number of the songs turned up, re-recorded with more keyboards, on **Tubeway Army**.) Funny stuff that holds up quite well and proves he hasn't always been a bozo.

Except for a neat 1985 single ("Change Your Mind") done with Shakatak keyboardist Bill Sharpe, Numan has spent the past four years in the pop doldrums (with no indication that he ever intends to mount a serious return). Nonetheless, abiding interest in Numan's old records prompted the 1987 release of a comprehensive two-disc, 25-cut (studio and live) career summary, **Exhibition**. Completists may also feel compelled to shell out for **The Peel Sessions** EP, recorded in January 1979.   [sg/iar]

See also *Dramatis*.

NUNS

The Nuns (Posh Boy-Bomp) 1980
Rumania (PVC) 1986

For a brief moment in the late '70s, it seemed as if the Nuns might be the catalyst for a successful new wave/punk scene in San Francisco. Their early days earned media praise and they owned a rabid local cult following, but time quickly passed them by. Aggressive musicianship and demanding vocals—especially Jennifer Miro's ice-cold, intense singing—make the first album (which the group had to reform to record) well worth hearing. Lyrically, the Nuns spoke to the decadent side of life as well as anyone, with such tales as "Wild," "Child Molester" and "Suicide Child."

The Nuns inexplicably reformed again, with much the same lineup, for another, more innocuous, album six years later. Miro and Jeff Olener share the vocals on **Rumania**, a sophisticated dance record that generally resembles a tasteful version of Berlin (the group). Although he's evidently serious, Olener's idiotic melodramatics suggest Fred Schneider as a sarcastic lounge sleaze, while the far more talented Miro melds nicely with the lightweight synthesizer concoctions. Enjoy her solo turns here, but pitch the rest.
                      [cpl/iar]

See also *Rank and File*.

N.Y.C. PEECH BOYS

Life Is Something Special (Island) 1983

With a colorful Keith Haring graphic on the cover, the interracial Peech Boys (starring singer/guitarist Bernard Fowler, who's since sung with Philip Glass and others, and keyboardist Michael de Benedictus, co-producer with Larry Levan) emerged from the downtown club scene, cross-cultural loyalties obvious. A funk band with rock instincts, or a rock band adapting itself to urban dance music? Whatever the modus operandi, this album stands as an enjoyable pioneering hybrid, early proof that the two sounds cannot only coexist peacefully, but can mingle creatively.   [iar]

JUDY NYLON AND CRUCIAL

Pal Judy (nr/On-U Sound) 1982

SNATCH

Snatch EP (nr/Fetish) 1980

Snatch (nr/Pandemonium) 1983

Abandoning New York for London, no-waver Judy Nylon teamed with Pat Palladin to form Snatch, ultimately making the German-inspired sound collage "R.A.F." with Brian Eno, which appeared on the B-side of his "King's Lead Hat" 45. The **Snatch** EP features Nylon and Palladin teaming up for a pseudo-Tom Waits blues drone called "Shopping for Clothes" and the softly electronic ballad, "Joey," as well as "Red Army," which imitates the technique and style of "R.A.F." Clever and inventive, the work has gentle strength, bitter humor and a thoroughly jaundiced worldview.

Pal Judy, which she co-produced with Adrian Sherwood, grafts Snatch's blues poetics and electronic compositional structures onto fairly straightforward rock music. The result—a moody, adeptly created and performed record suggestive of Patti Smith—smacks of modernized cocktail-lounge music (in the best tradition of that genre). Nylon's originals are acrid and funny in their scope, but the record is stolen by her laconic, opiated rendition of "Jailhouse Rock."   [sg]

See also *Johnny Thunders*.

O O O O O O

PHILIP OAKEY & GIORGIO MORODER

See *Human League.*

EBENEZER OBEY

Je Ka Jo (nr/Virgin) 1983
Miliki Plus (nr/Virgin) 1983
Juju Jubilee (Shanachie) 1985

Along with King Sunny Adé, Chief Commander Ebenezer Obey dominates the juju music genre, that beautiful, spiritual and eminently danceable combination of traditional chants, hymns, African highlife, rock and country-western. An easy way to think of juju is as inverted Western pop: interlocking guitars function as rhythm instruments while numerous drummers take on the melodic responsibilites. Born in Lagos in 1942, Obey joined his first professional band, the Fatai Rolling Dollars, in 1958. By 1963 he had formed his own group, and has since released over 90 singles and albums.

Obey calls his personal style the *miliki* (enjoyment) sound. Beginning where noted juju entertainer I.K. Diaro left off, Obey has drawn in such Western elements as multiple guitars and a Hawaiian steel guitar soloist, adding them to the traditional rhythmic fundament. Songs tend to reflect Obey's strong Christian beliefs as well as the common problems (often economic) of everyday life.

No record could do justice to the endlessly intense melodic and rhythmic variations heard during one of Obey's all-night concerts. (His touring band is 15 members strong.) Most juju albums contain side-long songs, but even those rarely put across the scope of a single number. **Je Ka Jo** and **Miliki Plus** are similar to Obey's many Nigerian records; **Jubilee** is a sampler package—edited versions of eight tunes—which displays Obey's progression from grassroots juju to ever-more-sophisticated compositions. Unfortunately, it suffers from a severe case of enjoyment interruptus.   [rg]

RIC OCASEK

See *Cars.*

HAZEL O'CONNOR

Breaking Glass (A&M) 1980
Sons and Lovers (A&M) 1980
Glass Houses (nr/Albion) 1980
Cover Plus (nr/Albion) 1981
Smile (nr/RCA) 1984

Something of a jane-of-all-trades (including, during one dog-days period, a soft-core porn flick), Coventry-born O'Connor first came to prominence as protagonist of the film *Breaking Glass,* a British new wave variation on *A Star Is Born,* and on the soundtrack LP, which consists wholly of her songs. O'Connor tailored them to the plot—to a frustrating extent, their "onstage" performance by O'Connor's rock heroine *was* the plot—and they are stagey, overstated, even cornball. Her few savvy lyrics are buried amid exhortatory sloganeering, almost hippieish (rather than punky) in its fuzzy mystical tinge. The backing is dominated by sax supported by keyboards, with muted guitar and assorted psychedelic touches.

This set the stage for the style O'Connor sought on **Sons and Lovers**; released from theatrical demands and having accrued her own ongoing band, she still honed the same musical style (and kept the soapbox handy when her store of failed romance lyrics ran down). **Sons and Lovers** marches along (literally) at an even headier and less varied pace; her vocal style nearly caricatures itself, not unlike Siouxsie Sioux doing an endless, mechanical stutter. Underneath this, the credible band (including her guitar-playing brother Neil, formerly of the Flys, and saxman Wesley Magoogan, later of the Beat) struggles to enhance her promising melodies even as it runs roughshod over them.

Tony Visconti, who'd surrendered the producer's chair to Nigel Gray for **Sons and Lovers**, returned for **Cover Plus**, on which he successfully moderates O'Connor's more extreme tendencies. At long last, not every song is an anthem; the title track was a Top 10 UK hit by virtue of a good melody given the poppier treatment it merited. Yet strangely enough, O'Connor seems a little lost, as if excessive idiosyncrasy were essential to her identity. [jg]

SINÉAD O'CONNOR
The Lion and the Cobra (Ensign-Chrysalis) 1987 ●

It's been a while since a newcomer has burst onto the scene with quite as much impact as this Dublin lass. Visually arresting, with big Bambi eyes—and, oh yeah, a shaved head—this seemingly autonomous artist has been compared to just about every contemporary female rocker you can name, but the most frequent and perhaps appropriate referent is Kate Bush. Also discovered at a young age by a guitar hero of the day (the Edge rather than David Gilmour), O'Connor rocks a bit harder, but shares Bush's ability to switch gears between the delicate and the pompous or the direct and the ambiguous. Perhaps even more reliant on affected vocals, O'Connor can wail, shriek, whisper, croon, snarl and bellow with the best of them.

The self-produced **Lion and the Cobra** combines bits of hard rock, funk, '70s-style spaciness and Celtic traditionalism with (probably deliberately) vague lyrics which manage to at least *sound* poetic. She doesn't display much sophistication in the way of musical skills—the songs are pretty basic—but her creativity and expressiveness are quite impressive. It wouldn't hurt if she did lighten up a bit, but it's rare to hear such a young artist (20 when the LP was recorded) so clearly in control; if the six-and-a-half-

minute "Troy" sounds slow and laborious, she probably wanted it that way. And if she wouldn't have gotten less attention if she had hair, more power to her. [dgs]

See also *U2*.

OCTOBER FACTION
The October Faction (SST) 1985
The Second Factionalization (SST) 1986

Greg Ginn's October Faction is an occasional and meaningless (not occasionally meaningless) Black Flag spin-off that has so far yielded two slabs of self-indulgence. **October Faction** (silver cover and label) was recorded live in San Francisco in 1984 and features guitarist Joe Baiza, Chuck Dukowski, Tom Troccoli and even Henry Rollins wailing away on seven tuneless songs that are only sporadically interesting.

The miserable second record (copper cover and label) has much the same lineup but doesn't bother cutting the formless guitar-rock improvisations into individual pieces. Instead, it contains only an appalling Baiza-Ginn guitar duel, "Sam," and "Pocohontas," which runs for 20 minutes on one side and continues for 13 more on the back. I've heard interesting rehearsal tapes and jam sessions, but this ain't one of 'em. No third chapter, please. [iar]

OFFS
First Record (CD Presents) 1984

This punk-identified San Francisco quartet-plus-horns ensemble, possessed of both art and boogie aspirations, won a place in rock'n'roll history with the single, "Everyone's a Bigot," one of the best songs from the almost uniformly fine **Let Them Eat Jellybeans** compilation. A rolling sax riff and naive but sincere lyrics gave the song a compelling sense of urgency as well as a credible dance quotient. The Offs' LP, however, takes the band into fake jazz and reggae pastures and sacrifices that single's directness. The journeyman grooves, punctuated by corny horn parts, do nothing to launch the lyrics over their unrealized pretensions. The album offers cool, atmospheric music, but that's the best thing one can say about it. [jl]

PATRICK O'HEARN
See *Missing Persons*.

OH-OK
Furthermore What EP (DB) 1983
HETCH HETCHY
Make Djibouti (Texas Hotel) 1988

After hearing so many art bands buried in their own sense of self-importance, it's refreshing to bask in the modesty of Athens' Oh-OK. Like R.E.M. (with whom they share a family tie), the humble four put their elliptical ideas over as much by being good guys as anything else. The songs on **Furthermore What** offer dreamy melodies, ringing guitars (this *is* the New South) and quirky, minimal arrangements that hover just outside the pop realm. David McNair's angular drumming and Lynda (sister of Michael) Stipe's pumping bass give the music drive; Linda Hopper's breathy singing and Matthew Sweet's Athenian economical guitar space things out up top. This kind of modesty rarely ascends to greatness, but Oh-OK is distinctly a fresh pleasure. Hopper later put out an EP on DB with a band called Holiday.

Although her name is now Lynda L. Limmer, the Hetch Hetchy singer with a sometimes harsh loud-soft-loud style is the selfsame Stipe sister. (Indeed, Michael produced this debut album by the trio.) From the lightly laughing clarinet that opens "Retarded Camel" through chunks of darkly deep guitar and lots of smooth new music electronic keyboards, the melodic group—named after a valley in Yosemite National Park—creates the kind of lightly arty pop-rock that college radio eats for breakfast, lunch and dessert. [jl/'e]

See also *Matthew Sweet.*

OIL TASTERS
Oil Tasters (Thermidor) 1982

Armed with an inspired ugly name, this avant-jazz-rock trio (sax/organ, drums, bass/vocals) has abundant kitsch intelligence, which provides witty, dadaist lyrics for sharp songs like "What's in Your Mouth" and "(I Don't Want to Be an) Encyclopedia Salesman." The music's a bit grating and only slightly melodic, but exciting in its own abrasive way. Rather than assaulting music, the Oil Tasters kick at sounds with curiosity and enthusiasm, creating an unpleasant but listenable breed of weirdness. [iar]

OINGO BOINGO
Oingo Boingo EP (IRS) 1980
Only a Lad (A&M) 1981 ●
Nothing to Fear (A&M) 1982 ●
Good for Your Soul (A&M) 1983 ●
Dead Man's Party (MCA) 1985 ●
Boi-ngo (MCA) 1987 ●
DANNY ELFMAN
So-lo (MCA) 1984

This eight-piece LA outfit (with a three-man horn section) works very hard at being America's answer to XTC in a transparently Devoesque manner, but the studied wackiness/quirkiness sounds awfully forced and usually manages to hide solid cleverness behind overproduction and hamminess.

The EP, all 10 inches of it, is the band's most succinct engagement. The four cuts belie the size of the lineup—a trio might have made these long slices of mild perversity. The album that followed, however, plays up OB's flaws, letting contrived bits diminish the impact of demi-clever lyrics and thoroughly competent music. The only track that stands out is "On the Outside," and it succeeds because it sounds normal. Despite obvious talent, **Only a Lad** is a waste.

Taking a turn toward synth-funk (as either a commercial ploy or an amused art statement), **Nothing to Fear** is more likable, yet still sounds phony. A couple of the tunes, especially the title cut, are forceful enough to be exciting. When not pushing pressurized dance rock, Oingo Boingo revert to their previously established lighter style, and the horns play it subtle rather than brassy. Better, but still a derivative disappointment.

Electronic music veteran Robert Margouleff produced **Good for Your Soul** and trimmed some of the usual excess, giving Oingo Boingo a streamlined and powerfully-driven attack. The timely "Wake Up! (It's 1984)" and "Who Do You Want to Be" are among the most invigorating and engaging things the band has ever done. There's still significant quantities of chaff, but on this outing the wise-guy dance-rock largely works.

Singer, chief songwriter and Oingo Boingo leader Danny Elfman made **So-lo** with five members of the band, but it offers a slightly different, more synthesized outlook. "Gratitude" is a brilliant construct combining Elfman's best melody and absurd vocals in one wacky tour de force; other tracks (a ballad, a rave-up, etc.) are more like Oingo Boingo's work. Displaying Wall of Voodoo B-movie aspirations, Elfman (who's since become a very successful film and TV music creator) unfortunately lacks the focus or vision to counteract his grandiose, theatrical instincts.

Dispersing rumors of defunction, Oingo Boingo returned with their least obnoxious record yet. **Dead Man's Party** benefits from one captivating soundtrack single ("Weird Science") and a couple of other strong songs (including "Stay," a soulful "Help Me" and the Devoesque title track).

Did Spike Jones mix **Boi-ngo** or what? Instruments fly out of the speakers at crazy angles as if this were a stereo effects demonstration record. The absurdly busy arrangements make the songs take a back seat to the studio showboating as each guitar chord, horn toot and drumbeat calls attention to itself. Elfman is really in control here, and his mastery of this hyperkinetic niche (at times it sounds like two coordinated recordings being played simultaneously) is an awesome individual accomplishment. The LP jitterbugs, bounces and slides from start to finish, leaving listeners either happily exhausted or utterly exasperated. [iar]

OK JIVE
Life at the Blue Chonjo Sky Day & Night Club (nr/Epic) 1982

These expatriate South Africans managed to come up with a unique sound on their album, despite having borrowed an awful lot of it from African and Caribbean pop. Characterized by tight, choppy ultra-rhythmic interplay between two guitarists and a female lead singer's initially charming (but ultimately monotonous) voice, the group's perky ethnic dance music lacks enough dynamic material to make it work for a whole album. In short, the sound is pleasing, but the songs are boring. Pity they didn't include their first (Joe Jackson-produced) single, "On Route," which not only sounds great, but goes somewhere, too. [ds]

SONNY OKOSUN
Liberation (Shanachie) 1984
Which Way Nigeria? (Jive Afrika) 1984

A decade younger than Fela Kuti, Nigeria's Sonny Okosun grew up on the Beatles and Elvis Presley rather than the country-western twang that influenced Sunny Adé, or the funk explosion that gripped Fela. He and his group blend highlife, reggae, funk and various African beats into an international style, an Afro-rock that dovetails nicely into his politics.

On **Liberation**, "Tell Them" spiritedly invokes (in English) martyred freedom-fighters around the world; other songs mix Yoruba and English. **Which Way Nigeria?** is more of the same, and also quite good. The horn-happy sound is both accessible and eminently danceable, and has served him well through a career that spans over a dozen albums. Since scoring a major political hit in 1976, with "Fire in Soweto," Okosun's music has taken a softer turn. [rg]

100 FLOWERS
100 Flowers (Happy Squid) 1983
Drawing Fire EP (Happy Squid) 1984

You wouldn't know it to listen to their records, but Los Angeles' 100 Flowers started as a joke, a black-humored parody of the punk scene. As the Urinals, they recorded a pair of 1979 7-inch EPs and a single for Happy Squid, then got serious, changed their name and got *real* serious. In their new incarnation, the trio plays arty, poetic music that is kinetic in spite of its murkiness.

100 Flowers owes a debt to the Fall, although its sound is all-American. Dispensing with such concepts as verses and choruses, the group favors subterranean funk grooves and drones; the effect is impressive if limited and wears thin over the course of the record. The **Drawing Fire** EP has the benefit of stronger material. With songs that build but never cop out with climaxes and releases, this is how R.E.M. might sound if it were a punk band. [jl]

101ERS
Elgin Avenue Breakdown (nr/Andalucia) 1981

Before there was a Clash, Joe Strummer was in a gritty, R&B-styled London pub band. The 101ers broke up after a short career, issuing only one incredible 45, "Keys to Your Heart" (included here), while in business. This album, released five years after the fact, combines three 1975-6 demo sessions and a live performance captured on cassette. It's an essential artifact for Clashologists, spreading hints of things to come all over the place; as an energetic slice of simple, raucous rock'n'roll, it's worth every penny as well.

[iar]

ONE THE JUGGLER
Django's Coming EP (nr/Regard) 1983
Nearly a Sin (Regard-RCA) 1984

Mixing Bowie's **Ziggy Stardust** era with doses of T. Rex and Mott the Hoople, One the Juggler update acoustic-based glam-rock into the '80s, with occasional success. "Passion Killer" is a tune Adam Ant should have written, as acoustic guitars collide with poseur vocals and throaty sax in a cool and catchy explosion. "Damage Is Done" *really* sounds like old Bowie/Mott the Hoople. The rest of the record is mixed, with some of the derivation more ludicrous and pointless than clever and agreeable. **Nearly a Sin** is nearly good. [iar]

ONLY ONES

The Only Ones (nr/CBS) 1978
Even Serpents Shine (nr/CBS) 1979
Special View (Epic) 1979
Baby's Got a Gun (Epic) 1980
Remains (Fr. Closer) 1984
Alone in the Night (nr/Dojo) 1986

Singer Peter Perrett and ex-Spooky Tooth drummer Mike Kellie comprised the prominent half of the Only Ones. The quartet drew on Perrett's romanticism and artfully decadent stylings and Kellie's musical skills and long experience. This contrast of youth and seasoned professionalism helped gain the Only Ones quick prominence, but only one song, "Another Girl, Another Planet," earned them any lasting acclaim.

The Only Ones (including that ace song) is the best of their three original albums. Perrett's languid vocals and songs provide the character and focus, while the band's skills carry it off handsomely. **Even Serpents Shine** varies little from its predecessor and contains some captivating material, but lacks anything as great as "Another Girl, Another Planet." **Special View** picks tracks off both albums and adds the two sides of the band's self-released 1977 debut single—a fair condensation of the band's work to date.

Although finally realizing simultaneous release in the US and the UK with the Colin Thurston-produced **Baby's Got a Gun**, the Only Ones' commercial success was still too slight to sustain them; after three albums of at least adequate quality, they called it quits in 1981. [iar]

OPAL

Happy Nightmare Baby (SST) 1987

KENDRA SMITH/DAVID ROBACK/KEITH MITCHELL

Fell from the Sun EP (Serpent-Enigma) 1984

After he left the Rain Parade, guitarist David Roback and ex-Dream Syndicate bassist Kendra Smith formed a quartet known as Clay Allison (obscurely named after a character in a TV movie) with drummer Keith Mitchell and guitarist Juan Gomez. The group issued a single, but dropped a member and shed the moniker before adding two new songs to flesh out **Fell from the Sun**. On it, Smith's vocals perfectly meld with the subtle mood music—a pleasant drone with translucent elegance that resembles the Velvet Underground at their most restrained. Lovely and touching.

Clinging to neo-psychedelia after many of their original Los Angeles scene compatriots had abandoned the fad, Roback and Smith (switching to guitar) formed the five-piece Opal. **Happy Nightmare Baby** has its share of nostalgic organ-colored drone contemplations, but adds an unexpected and amusing item to the repertoire: a stripped-down T. Rex imitation ("Rocket Machine") that drifts towards Television. Criticisms: Smith's laconic singing can become arduous, some of the instrumental work is self-indulgent nonsense and the pace is too slow. Qualities: the songs are there, the ambience is affecting and the performances offer enough texture and dynamics to make Opal's debut album ultimately satisfying. [iar]

ORANGE JUICE

You Can't Hide Your Love Forever
(nr/Polydor) 1982
Rip It Up (nr/Polydor) 1982
Texas Fever EP (nr/Polydor) 1984
The Orange Juice (nr/Polydor) 1984
In a Nutshell (nr/Polydor) 1985

ZEKE MANYIKA

Call and Respond (nr/Polydor) 1985

Glasgow's insufferably coy Orange Juice, leaders of the Scottish neo-pop revolution, typified a UK trend toward clean, innocent looks that unfortunately spilled over into the music. Emphasizing their "unspoiled" raggedness, the band began with clumsy tunes about insecurity and romantic rejection. Singer Edwyn Collins mumbles and croons like a slowed-down Ray Davies. **You Can't Hide Your Love Forever** is supposed to be charming, but isn't.

Surprisingly, **Rip It Up** (not named after the Little Richard tune) explores the first album's ingenuousness in greater depth with thought-provoking results. Though young love remains the theme, tension has replaced cuteness; on the title track, "Louise, Louise" and others, Collins responds angrily to being treated like a chump. He's still a bit of a narcissistic vocalist, but **Rip It Up**'s more realistic approach is appealing and rewarding.

Escalating musical differences and other internal conflicts caused the band to split prior to the release of **Texas Fever**, leaving Collins and drummer Zeke Manyika to carry on as a duo. Salvaged from the original band's final sessions, the **Texas Fever** EP further refines the standards set on **Rip It Up**. There's an implicit Western theme, but most of the songs have a quirky, exotic Afro-funk feel, fleshed out with stellar guitar work by Collins and Malcolm Ross (later of Aztec Camera). Their talents make "Punch Drunk," "A Place in My Heart" and "Sad Lament" memorable.

Collins and Manyika teamed with producer pal Dennis Bovell for **The Orange Juice (The Third Album)**, which contains some of Edwyn's strongest songs: the sadly biographical "Lean Period," the melodically haunting "What Presence?!" and "Artisans," a garage-styled rave-up.

Embittered by their commercial failure, Zeke and Edwyn called it quits. **In a Nutshell** is a posthumous compilation that contains the very best of this often overlooked band, from their early days on Postcard ("Falling and Laughing," "Poor Old Soul") through the last days on Polydor (tracks from the third LP). Collins and Manyika continue to be musically active. On his own and with singer Paul Quinn, the former has released several fine singles; fronting his band Dr. Love, the latter has issued some excellent 45s as well as the wonderful **Call and Respond** album. [jy/ag]

WILLIAM ORBIT
Orbit (IRS) 1987
Strange Cargo (No Speak-IRS) 1988
TORCH SONG
Wish Thing (IRS) 1984
Exhibit A (IRS) 1987

Torch Song debuted as a trio on **Wish Thing**, an ethereal set of instrumentally subtle synth-dance tracks, given most of their character by Laurie Mayer's delicate voice and the gimmicky production. "Don't Look Now" and "Sweet Thing" are appealing, airy concoctions; a demento version of "Ode to

Billy Joe" seems calculated to shock and/or offend but is nonetheless amusing. Intriguing.

Three years later, reduced to a duo, Torch Song ("featuring William Orbit") issued a second record consisting of four cuts (including "Don't Look Now" and "Sweet Thing") remixed from **Wish Thing**, plus five new ones that also benefit from Mayer's wan singing. Inconclusive but equally appealing, **Exhibit A** has another weird cover version: an atmospheric deconstruction of Blind Faith's "Can't Find My Way Home."

Multi-instrumentalist Orbit then dropped the Torch Song name, found a new singing partner in Peta Nikolich and recorded **Orbit**. (Mayer is still his co-writer, but she performs on only one song.) A disappointingly conservative—except for the mock-Spanish horns—cover of the Psychedelic Furs' "Love My Way" leads off the album, which never gets much more adventurous than that. Despite an assortment of genres, most of the music is short on individual character; Nikolich is a capable singer without a strong enough personality to carry the weight. "Feel Like Jumping," a mildly revisionist reggae cover (Jackie Mittoo), is the weak album's lively highlight.

Building on his soundtrack work, Orbit released **Strange Cargo**, a one-man-band collection of unrelated instrumental pieces recorded between 1984 and 1987. Mostly urgent and kinetic, with colorful sound effects, the unresolved semi-songs are mood-heavy and suggest a number of visual idioms, including action-adventure, comedy, espionage and mystery. [iar]

ORCHESTRA ARCANA
See *Bill Nelson.*

ORCHESTRAL MANOEUVRES IN THE DARK
Orchestral Manoeuvres in the Dark
   (nr/DinDisc) 1980 (Virgin) 1987 ●
Organisation (nr/DinDisc) 1980 (Virgin)
   1987 ●
O.M.D. (Virgin-Epic) 1981
Architecture & Morality (Virgin-Epic) 1981 ●
Dazzle Ships (Virgin-Epic) 1983 ●
Junk Culture (Virgin-A&M) 1984 ●
Crush (Virgin-A&M) 1985 ●
The Pacific Age (Virgin-A&M) 1986 ●
The Best of OMD (Virgin-A&M) 1988 ●

Moving from electronic tape experiments to highly polished synthesizer pop and beyond, Liverpudlians Andy McCluskey (bass/vocals/keyboards) and synthesist Paul Humphreys (with other full-time members, including—very significantly—a corporeal acoustic drummer) are among the most successful practitioners of electro-pop, as first demonstrated by a delightful string of singles. Abandoning their formula after two albums, however, OMD proved capable of far more ambitious creations not tied to the apron strings of technology.

Orchestral Manoeuvres in the Dark exhibits stylish electro-pop comparable to Ultravox's music. Aided by Dalek I's Andy Gill, McCluskey and Humphreys build the songs up from computer-generated rhythms and, while the album does not create any new forms, it polishes the synthesizer song into a full-bodied medium. Thanks to a knack for melodies and hooks, notable attractions are the catchy "Electricity" and "Messages."

Organisation (which originally included an excellent bonus single of early tape experiments and live tracks) introduces drummer Malcolm Holmes and ethereal synthesizer techniques that suit the depressive subject matter of "Enola Gay" and the like. It also pays attention to ensure variation in the tunes, a problem that mars the first LP. With nods to John Foxx and David Bowie, OMD overlays melodies to dramatic effect; the performances are excellent.

O.M.D. is an American compilation of songs from the two British albums, including both catchy OMD standards, "Enola Gay" and "Electricity." Recommended.

Architecture & Morality struggles with new techniques, and includes two magnificent, ethereal hit singles: "Souvenir" and "Joan of Arc." OMD is again experimenting with sound and much of the album sounds more naturalistic than electronic. An intriguing and highly inventive use of the technology.

The conceptual **Dazzle Ships** overreaches by a mile, succumbing to excessive found-tape gimmickry in lieu of adequate songwriting. It does contain the striking "Genetic Engineering" (which integrates a Speak and Spell toy to make a point) and "Radio Waves," as well as some amazing sounds and a powerful atmosphere to recommend it. Impressive but not satisfying.

Junk Culture is much stronger, pulling away further from sparkling pop while re-taining smart melodies in far denser and newly dance-based styles. "Tesla Girls" employs scratch production to great effect while fixing on science as a clever lyrical base (shades of Sparks); the rhythm-heavy "Locomotion" and the more fanciful "Talking Loud and Clear" are likewise ace tracks.

Despite its easygoing ambience and a shortage of really memorable songs, **Crush**—OMD's least stylized, most mainstream album—isn't half-bad. "So in Love" and "Secret" are the obvious romantic singles, but the record has more serious moments as well· the topical "88 Seconds in Greensboro," "Women III" (an ambiguous consideration of feminism) and "Bloc Bloc Bloc," wherein McCluskey sings some truly stupid lyrics with only a trace of embarrassment.

OMD's international commercial breakthrough began with **Crush** but exploded when "If You Leave," a dull ballad from the *Pretty in Pink* soundtrack, became a Top 10 American single.

That song was thankfully omitted from OMD's subsequent album, **The Pacific Age**, but so was anything that might have prevented the record from being dull, ponderous and self-important. (Typical of the band's well-meaning absurdity is "Southern," an instrumental bed over which excerpts of Martin Luther King speeches are played.) OMD's expansion from a duo to a sextet—the three recent additions play horns, guitars and more keyboards—has cost the group focus and clarity, its singleminded creative vision. Except for the smoothly contrived hit "(Forever) Live and Die" and the catchy "We Love You," this dilettantish mess is less a set of songs than a meaningless collection of sounds.

The Best of OMD is the ideal remedy for **The Pacific Age**. Not only does it concisely recapitulate the band's artistic development—via 14 A-sides, from clever synth-based pop ("Electricity," "Enola Gay," "Souvenir") to well-realized audio experiments ("Tesla Girls," "Locomotion") to increasingly bland chart fodder ("So in Love," "If You Leave")—but it ends with a promisingly pert new single, "Dreaming." The CD adds two bonus tracks.   [sg/iar]

ORDINAIRES

The Ordinaires (Ger. Dossier) 1985 (Zoar) 1987

Like many of the all-instrumental big-band ensembles on New York's semi-underground scene, the Ordinaires' debut album was released only in Germany. On **The Ordinaires**, nine men and women—covering guitars, horns, woodwinds, strings and percussion—make a sound like nothing you've ever heard before, combining assorted styles and eras with equanimity. Polytonality rules here with a twisted but firm hand, guiding the convoluted pieces through strident (never discordant) passages that are filled with sharp turns, sudden volume shifts and abrupt tempo changes. Advanced without being obnoxiously arty, this is an album to curl your hair and spark your imagination. Amazing!

[iar]

ORIGINAL MIRRORS

Original Mirrors (Arista) 1980
Heart-Twango & Raw-Beat (nr/Mercury) 1981

After Deaf School bit the dust, that band's Steve Allen, a strong crooner in the Bryan Ferry mold, started his own band with ex-Big in Japan guitarist Ian Broudie (now a successful producer). It didn't work out well at all. The Original Mirrors seemed entranced by the kind of pop-opera bombast that characterized Deaf School at their worst; self-discipline was never a high priority. For every rockin' moment that crystallizes passion into something comprehensible, there are ten others of sprawling excess.

[jy]

ORIGINAL SINS

Big Soul (Bar/None) 1987

Big Soul is an instant classic, contemporary garage grunge stripped of nostalgia and ready for consumption. Led by diminutive howler J.T. (John Terlesky), the Pennsylvanians recreate the down and dirty excitement of the Standells and the Seeds on "Not Gonna Be All Right" and "Can't Feel a Thing," with Dan McKinney's cheesy organ adding the appropriate icing. Less aggressive tunes like "Why Don't You Smile, Joanie" maintain the no-nonsense spirit, peeling away tough posturing to get at searing emotions that are never far from the surface.

[jy]

BEN ORR

See *Cars*.

JOHN OTWAY AND WILD WILLY BARRETT

John Otway & Wild Willy Barrett
  (nr/Extracked) 1977 (nr/Polydor) 1977
Deep & Meaningless (nr/Polydor) 1978
Way/Bar (nr/Polydor) 1980
Deep Thought (Stiff) 1980
I Did It Otway EP (Stiff America) 1981
I Did It Otway (Can. Stiff Canada) 1981
Gone with the Bin (nr/Polydor) 1981
Head Butts EP (nr/Empire) 1982

JOHN OTWAY

Where Did I Go Right? (nr/Polydor) 1979
All Balls and No Willy (nr/Empire) 1982
John Otway's Gleatest Hits (nr/Strike Back) 1986

This charming nutter from Aylesbury, best heard in the company of his multi-instrumental sidekick/musical interpreter Barrett, is tough to evaluate on vinyl. The more help he has making records apart from Barrett, the more lost he gets. He is somewhat mercurial too, scraping bottom on those thankfully rare occasions when he takes himself seriously. And so much of what he's about just doesn't translate to disc—though seeing him even once enhances listening to even the relatively duff tracks.

Otway renders (once or twice per LP) someone else's material—from "Green Green Grass of Home" to Alfred Noyes' "The Highwayman"—with daffily inspired abandon. He can write hysterically infectious ditties ("Really Free") or likably folky and sentimental tunes, though these can be a little drippy. There's little pattern for rule-of-thumb judgment, save that Barrett-less he comes off bland (**Where Did I Go Right?**) or energetic but less effective (**All Balls and No Willy**).

The most consistent records are the first album and **Way/Bar** (or **Deep Thought**, which is half the latter plus assorted cuts). The **Gone with the Bin** compilation is a neat if incomplete summation of Otway's ragged but right repertoire.

Prospective aficionados are alternatively referred to the **I Did It Otway** EP (four of the cuts not on previous albums) or its expanded Canadian equivalent, which contains ten songs and boasts a red version of the cover artwork.

An even better mixture of new and old Otway is offered on the recent **Gleatest Hits** album. (The title is a cheap Japanese dialect joke.) The record trundles out some of his familiar classics ("Really Free," "Beware of the Flowers Cause I'm Sure They're Gonna Get You, Yeah," "Headbutts" and "Green Green Grass of Home") as well as some excellent new original material ("Middle of Winter," "Montreal") and an uproarious cover version of Bachman-Turner Overdrive's "You Ain't Seen Nothing Yet." [jg/iar]

OUR DAUGHTERS WEDDING
Digital Cowboys EP (EMI America) 1981
Moving Windows (EMI America) 1982

This snappy San Francisco-relocated-to-New York electro-pop trio's indie single "Lawnchairs" became a dancefloor favorite, combining a good beat with lyrics of bemused paranoia ("lawnchairs are everywhere"). **Digital Cowboys** makes the mistake of trying to redo "Lawnchairs" with a real drummer and badly rephrased vocals. An innocuous one-hit wonder. [rnp]

OUTCASTS
Self Conscious Over You (nr/Good Vibrations) 1979
Blood and Thunder (Fr. New Rose) 1983
Seven Deadly Sins EP (Fr. New Rose) 1984

Once reckoned the most popular punk outfit in Belfast, the Outcasts never quite developed their assets as did the rivals that passed them by. On the quartet's first LP, they faintly suggest a young, punky Slade, but they're not intensely raucous enough, nor are their songs—save for the title tune—catchy or cogent enough to make them memorable. [jg]

OUTLOUD
Out Loud (Warner Bros.) 1987 •

Instead of making a third solo album, ex-Chicster Nile Rodgers—who's become such a busy producer that he's excused from regular album creation schedules—formed a stylistic crossover band with Philippe Saisse (keyboards, vocals) and Felicia Collins (guitar, vocals). Armed with more hi-tech equipment than the Pentagon, the trio synthesizes, samples and strums its way through this airy, digitally-recorded LP of sophisticated rock/soul songs. A mild funk bump occasionally surfaces beneath the shimmering pop veneer, but generally the perky rhythms don't come near breaking a sweat. The romantically-geared songs (all three write) are ideal for radio and club play, replacing typical contemporary pounding with a refined, skipping beat. "Circle of Love/Music Lover," a wonderful and authentic-sounding tribute which breaks the mold and ends the LP on a high note, combines an old S. Stewart tune with a new N. Rodgers one for a joyful re-creation of Sly Stone's uniquely uplifting dance stand. [iar]

OUTSETS
Outsets EP (Plexus) 1983

Led by guitarist Ivan Julian (ex-Richard Hell's Voidoids and later briefly in Shriekback), this trio's EP is a clear and strong exercise—half funky-butt dance grooves, half slow rockers—with particularly interesting axework and a lot of spunk. The four songs produced by Garland Jeffreys aren't brilliant, but Julian's singing and playing provide them with a distinctive and attractive flavor. [iar]

OUTTA PLACE
We're Outta Place (Midnight) 1984
Outta Too!! (Midnight) 1987

On their first record, the garage-rock quintet billed as "New York's own cave teens" plays seven songs (including "Louie, Louie" and their namesake) in overload distorto-mono that ignores all modern recording conventions in favor of conveying sheer rock'n'roll energy neat, replete with organ and crazed shrieks. Great! [iar]

P P P P P P P P

AUGUSTUS PABLO

This Is Augustus Pablo (Jam. Tropical) 1973
   (Heartbeat) 1986
Ital Dub (nr/Trojan) 1975
King Tubbys Meets Rockers Uptown (Jam.
   Clocktower) 1976 (Shanachie) 1984
Original Rockers (Shanachie) 1979
Africa Must Be Free Dub (Ras) 1979
Rockers Meets King Tubby in a Firehouse
   (Shanachie) 1981
East of the River Nile (Shanachie) 1981
Earth's Rightful Ruler (Shanachie) 1983
Thriller (nr/Vista) 1983 (nr/Echo) 1985
King David's Melody (Alligator) 1983
Rising Sun (Shanachie) 1986
Rebel Rock Reggae (Heartbeat)
   1987 ●
Rockers Comes East (Message-Shanachie)
   1987

A true reggae original, dubmeister Augustus Pablo is as closely identified with his instrument—the melodica—as most jazz musicians are with theirs. Pablo (Horace Swaby) was a Kingston pianist when he borrowed a melodica and learned to play it. The simple instrument's unusual sound caught the ears of local record producers, who hired him to give their dub treatments some exotic color. Soon he was composing, arranging and producing his own instrumental tracks; now the reedy, vaguely Middle Eastern sound of Pablo's melodica is immediately recognizable—a plaintive cry in the dub landscape.

Pablo's earliest available recordings are mainly session work. Both **Ital Dub** and **King Tubbys Meets Rockers Uptown** (widely considered a dub classic) are as much showcases for King Tubby's mixing as for Pablo's playing. His own debut, **This Is Augustus Pablo**, is much better, distinguished by strong presence and lively playing. So is **Original Rockers**, a collection of singles he doctored. The selection is diverse, and Pablo's production (particularly the drum sound) is bright and snappy. For the uninitiated, either of these two offers a perfect starting point.

His recent work is, to some extent, of a piece, with little variety and few distinguishing characteristics. **Africa Must Be Free Dub** is an adequate companion to an LP made by singer Hugh Mundell, a young Pablo protégé who was murdered. **Rockers Meets King Tubby in a Firehouse**, while compelling, features less melodica than usual. **East of the River Nile** is quintessential Pablo, and perhaps his most consistent LP. **Earth's Rightful Ruler** includes a real rarity—a vocal—along with a new version of Pablo's first record, "Java." **King David's Melody**, a singles collection, has the evenness of sound and style of an album. It's a bit sleepy, but lovely all the same.

Pablo's '86 release, **Rising Sun**, marked a change in direction. Mixed by Scientist, the overall sound is less distinctive than Pablo's other work. Many of the tunes are up-tempo and disappointing, even though some of the playing—particularly on "Pipers of Zion"—is superb.

But it proved to be a transitional album rather than a glimpse of things to come. On **Rockers Come East**, Pablo returns to the dreamy sound that is his trademark, using lots of synthesizer bits to supplement his melodica. The synthetics are subtle, however, so the dub remains warm and compelling. More richly textured than ever, the music on the LP ranks with Pablo's best, and shows the maestro at mid-career to be at the top of his form. [bk]

PAINTED WILLIE

Mind Bowling (SST) 1985
Live from Van Nuys EP (SST) 1986
Upsidedowntown (SST) 1987

More noisy guitar excitement from SST: this non-punky Los Angeles trio shows a certain wit and lyrical perception on **Mind Bowling**. Although the music sounds like a sanitized junior version of Motorhead, songs about Chia Pets, sex without love and an obscure monkey species share an uncommon view of the world that elevates the tiresome vamps a bit. The inclusion of the classic "Little Red Book" only points up the band's lack of songwriting aptitude.

The energetic live mini-album features that song plus "Cover Girl" from **Mind Bowling**; there's the next-LP preview of "Upside Down Town" plus three other "tunes." These guys (especially guitarist Vic Makauskas) can play well enough, but their material lacks melody, focus and structure—once again, Burt Bacharach steals their thunder without even showing up!

Upsidedowntown has spiffy cover art and more taut riff-rock songs, this time on such less intriguing topics as "My Seed," "Personality and Style" (13 minutes of it!) and "Totem Pole." The playing keeps getting stronger, but the Willies should put out an APB for a songwriter. [iar]

PALAIS SCHAUMBURG

Das Single Kabinett EP (Ger. ZickZack) 1981
Palais Schaumburg (nr/Kamera) 1982
Lupa (Ger. Phonogram) 1982
Parlez-Vous Schaumburg? (Ger. Phonogram) 1984

Palais Schaumburg is an eccentric, intelligent pop band of frequently shifting personnel from Hamburg, Germany. While their eclectic records display obvious oddball/new wave influences, they seem to have also listened to their share of jazz and 20th-century European composers. **Das Single Kabinett** is a six-track mini-LP of stripped-down, danceable electro-pop, with vocals and synthesizer work owing more than a little to the Residents. The concluding "Aschenbecher" features tight ensemble playing and complex chords, proving the band knows what it's doing. No run-of-the-mill egghead weirdness here.

Palais Schaumburg, their first LP, is a strong collection of smartly-arranged dance tracks, with sounds and harmonies that get more bizarre as the album progresses. Their only record released in England and the last before lead singer Holger Hiller left the group, it is highly recommended.

Produced by Kid Creole associate Andy (Coati Mundi) Hernandez, **Lupa** shows a major change in the band's sound, as prominent vibes and horns mix with odd synth textures to yield a clear jazz feel. Throughout it all, they exhibit a Pere Ubu-cum-XTC quirkiness, and at times sound like a hip German Weather Report. Whether or not that's something the world needs, **Lupa** is an interesting, unique album.

Making another about-face, they released **Parlez-Vous Schaumburg?**. Incorporating some Latin tinges, a punchy horn section and ersatz big-band soundtrack arrangements (on a Fairlight, no doubt), it is—idiosyncrasies notwithstanding—their most accessible record, at times sounding like Shriekback's experimental side. [dgs]

See also *Holger Hiller*.

PALE FOUNTAINS

Pacific Street (nr/Virgin) 1984
. . . from across the kitchen table (nr/Virgin) 1984

Although they have precious little to say, this Scottish quartet takes an incredibly long time to get it out. Overdramatic to the point of absurdity, much of the Fountains' music falls somewhere between fake jazz and soul, with occasional digressions into pop and folk.

Pacific Street has few redeeming qualities other than Mick Head's soulful crooning and the imaginative use of super-amplified acoustic guitar. The eight weighty songs borrow from a wide variety of stylistic sources, failing to elaborate on any. The only fully-developed idea is the pop tune "Reach."

The Fountains manage to pull off more than one good number on their second LP. "Shelter" is a reckless rocker, as is the boisterous "27 Ways to Get Back Home" and the breezy "Jean's Not Happening." Elsewhere, the same indulgences that made **Pacific Street** intolerable reassert themselves. It's plain to see that acoustic pop/folk is the band's strong suit—they should abandon pretentious soul and jazz forays. [ag]

ROBERT PALMER

Clues (Island) 1980 ●
Maybe It's Live (Island) 1982
Pride (Island) 1983 ●

415

Riptide (Island) 1985 ●
Heavy Nova (EMI Manhattan) 1988 ●

It's not surprising that this stylish rock dilettante—whose '70s dabblings included excursions into R&B, funk, reggae and Little Feat-backed rock'n'roll—should catch up with post-punk in the '80s. What is remarkable is that on **Clues**, his sixth solo LP, he manages to come up with two tracks as sublime as "Johnny and Mary" and "Looking for Clues," which are heady, intricate and danceable at the same time. Also commendable is the job he does on a couple of collaborations with Gary Numan, injecting more life into them than one would think possible. Still, **Clues** retains an irritating stylistic disparity (heavy metal track/Beatles cover), as if Palmer were afraid his going wholeheartedly into anything new might alienate his audience.

Two years on, Palmer's dilemma is even more apparent on **Maybe It's Live**, a sidestep tentative down to its title and half-live/half-studio format. Combining inferior concert versions of old material, blah new stuff and another collaboration with Numan, the LP continues Palmer's indecisive course.

Without any big-name collaborators, Palmer again delivers a weirdly mixed bag on **Pride**, venturing into electro-disco with the herky-jerky, overbearing "You Are in My System," while affecting a charming calypso flavor in other spots. There's also a reprise of the unsettling undercurrents of "Johnny and Mary" on "Want You More." Palmer's voice is such that the less he tries, the better he sounds: when the going gets hot, his singing becomes overwhelming and irritating.

Palmer's next move was into the vile but hitbound Power Station, a temporary all-star band with two Durannies, produced by Bernard Edwards. When the group opted to tour, however, Palmer bailed out, retaining Edwards and Tony Thompson from the brief collaboration to finish **Riptide**, a bombastic funk record with such tripe as "Addicted to Love," a song whose main value lies in its parody potential.   [ds/iar]

See also *Power Station*.

PANDORAS

The Pandoras EP (Moxie) 1984
It's About Time (Voxx) 1984 ●
Stop Pretending (Rhino) 1986

The unashamedly '60s-obsessed Pandoras (led by singer/writer/guitarist Paula Pierce) are revivalists in the best sense of the word, recapturing the gleeful amateurism of vintage garage-punk-pop while adding their own cheerfully slutty persona to the mix. Following an energetic 7-inch EP, the LA band made its longplaying debut on **It's About Time** (produced by kindred spirit Greg Shaw), which makes a virtue of its shoestring primitivism. With some crackerjack tunes awash in Pierce's fuzztones and Gwynne Kelly's appropriately trashy organ, it's as good a '60s punk record as any contemporary combo is likely to make. (The CD adds five bonus tracks, including three songs from the prior EP.)

Pierce ditched the rest of the band soon after the debut LP (though the other three original members continued performing under the Pandoras name for a while) and recorded **Stop Pretending** with a new lineup. While maintaining her '60s fixation and playing up the brash-hussy stance, **Stop Pretending** features stronger playing and a harder-rocking edge (there's no reason why "In and Out of My Life in a Day" shouldn't have been a hit), suggesting that the Pandoras aren't as hopelessly mired in historical fetishism as one might assume.

Although the Pandoras were signed to Elektra and indeed recorded an album (entitled **Come Inside**), the band and label went their separate ways and the unreleased LP was scrapped. The Pandoras subsequently signed to Restless and went to work on another album.   [hd]

TAV FALCO'S PANTHER BURNS

Behind the Magnolia Curtain (Rough Trade) 1981
Blow Your Top EP (Animal) 1982
Sugar Ditch Revisited EP (Frenzi) 1985
Now! [tape] (Frenzi) 1985
Shake Rag EP (Fr. New Rose) 1986
The World We Knew (Fr. New Rose) 1987
Red Devil (Fr. New Rose) 1988

For folks who prize unspoiled simplicity in rock'n'roll, and especially in rockabilly, Tav Falco's Panther Burns may be the ultimate band. His voice drenched in echo, Falco goes through a familiar repertoire of Presley-derived whoops, mutters and coos, while an amateurish backing ensemble that often includes Alex Chilton grinds away laboriously like high-school rockers struggling through their first rehearsal. The deliberately slowed-down tempo and brazen sloppiness invest **Behind the Magnolia Curtain** with an intriguing conceptual purity, but the rawness turns prolonged exposure into a painful experience.

The four songs on **Blow Your Top** provide more of the same frayed recklessness. Thanks to cleaner sound and playing that verges on being professional, this set almost has commercial potential. (See "Love Is My Business" for proof.) There's still plenty of ground separating Falco's sweaty hysteria and the well-oiled appeal of the Stray Cats, though.

Falco recorded **Sugar Ditch Revisited** at Sam Phillips' Memphis studio with "Lx" Chilton and a few other Panther Burnsmen; the six tracks are well-played, well-sung, well-recorded, under control and somewhat underwhelming. The countrybilly spirit and sincerity is there, but the performances start and stop without ever really heating up, and the absence of chaos leaves the simple (if esoterically sourced) material to stand alone, which—until the frisky finale, "Tina, the Go Go Queen"—it doesn't do all that well.

The **Now!** cassette, issued by Falco's label, contains seven numbers (including ten minutes of "Jump Suit") taped absolutely live in Memphis in 1984. New Rose subsequently included that material as a bonus disc in original pressings of the killer 12-inch **Shake Rag E.P.**: studio recordings with Jim Dickinson that include one original (the stomping "Cuban Rebel Girl," also on the live tape/disc) and three typically swell obscurities.

Chilton's revitalized production and playing on **The World We Knew** helps make it one of Falco's all-time best showings. Using a rotating collection of sidemen, the carefully annotated songs—a scholarly combination of R&B, Sun rockabilly, blues and other wondrous musical inventions ("desert skulk fugue; decorticated cycle tune; the Stuttgart, Arkansas sound," to quote the liner notes)—get a thorough and affectionate workout that remains surehanded without ever slipping down off the rustic funk meter. (There are no originals on this non-didactic history course.) Everyone concerned sounds as though they're having a blast, and that feeling comes right through the speakers.

The 10-inch **Red Devil** signals a measured return to the uncontrolled wildness of early Panther Burns' records. Falco lays some truly soulful hollerin' over noisy electric guitars and a thumping backbeat on tracks produced individually (not to mention artlessly) by Chilton, Dickinson and others. **Red Devil**—ten songs and an abundance of hellacious energy—features esoterica by Chuck Berry, Lee Hazelwood and others, adding the songwriting talents of Dickinson and even Tav himself to the party.   [jy/tr]

PARACHUTE CLUB
The Parachute Club (RCA) 1983
At the Feet of the Moon (RCA) 1984

On their first LP, this fine Canadian septet—a soulful, low-tech match for labelmates M+M—displays a strong rhythmic consciousness (timbales and congas rather than synth thwack). Boasting a phenomenal singer (Lorraine Segato) and produced on the first LP by M+M/Eno collaborator Daniel Lanois, the Club gets positively inspirational on the joyous "Rise Up," while also addressing specific topics like nuclear war, sexism and hunger with intelligent lyrics and inventive, colorful music. Folk of the '80s, indeed!

At the Feet of the Moon, produced by ex-Materialist Michael Beinhorn, bounces to a funkier beat, with muscular drumming, strong bass and substantial electronic intrusion. (There's a truncated Beinhorn remix of "Rise Up" pasted on the second side—it's out of place but welcome.) Segato's voice, while equally magnificent, gets less prominence; coupled with more functional/less unique music, this record isn't nearly as captivating as its predecessor.   [iar]

PARASITES OF THE WESTERN WORLD
The Parasites of the Western World (Criminal) 1978
Substrata (Match Box) 1980
PATRICK BURKE
Silence and Timing (Criminal) 1981

Down from Portland, Oregon came the two-man Parasites, spreading electronic weirdness throughout the land. Patrick Burke and Terry Censky play just about everything but the kitchen sink; they're aided by an occasional guitarist and drummer on their two combo albums, but it's mainly them.

The first LP is full of dense (but not monotonous) semi-electronic rock pieces. Some have words, but most are evocative, cinematic instrumentals that are good and loud—none of that wimpy ambient crap! As a treat, they run through the song that might have inspired them—the Beatles' "Flying."

Substrata leans toward more routine rock—vocals, guitar, less weirdness—and tries hard to be mainstream; its amateurish predecessor is much more entertaining.

Burke's solo record—one of those no-body-helped jobs—differs greatly from the Parasites' releases. Using more technology, **Silence and Timing** works to display his songs in a sleek, modern setting.   [iar]

GRAHAM PARKER AND THE RUMOUR

Howlin Wind (Mercury) 1976
Heat Treatment (Mercury) 1976
Live at Marble Arch (nr/Vertigo) 1976
Stick to Me (Mercury) 1977
The Pink Parker EP (Mercury) 1977
The Parkerilla (Mercury) 1978
Squeezing Out Sparks (Arista) 1979 ●
Live Sparks (Arista) 1979
The Up Escalator (Arista) 1980 ●
High Times (nr/Vertigo) 1980
Pourin' It All Out: The Mercury Years
(Mercury) 1986

GRAHAM PARKER

Another Grey Area (Arista) 1982 ●
The Real Macaw (Arista) 1983
Anger: Classic Performances (Arista) 1985
The Mona Lisa's Sister (RCA) 1988 ●

GRAHAM PARKER AND THE SHOT

Steady Nerves (Elektra) 1985 ●

Before Elvis Costello and Joe Jackson, there was Graham Parker, redefining the singer/songwriter category for mid-'70s rock'n'roll audiences suspicious of the James Taylors and Carly Simons. With his raspy, Van Morrison-influenced vocals and soul-on-fire tunes, this diminutive Englishman burst on the scene just before the punk explosion and showed how to make music personal without sacrificing power.

Produced by Nick Lowe, **Howlin Wind** is a classic debut album, full of fine ideas fleshed out with ragged enthusiasm. Parker acknowledges his roots throughout, singing original R&B boppers ("White Honey" and "Lady Doctor") with sly wit and masterfully reconstructing rockabilly on the angry "Back to Schooldays," complete with guest twangin' by Dave Edmunds (who later recorded the song himself on **Get It**). Evidencing an equally powerful sensitive side, Parker checks in with the reflective "Between You and Me" and "Don't Ask Me Questions," the latter a chilling wail of anguish.

On **Howlin Wind** (and all subsequent LPs through **The Up Escalator**), Parker received

formidable backing from the Rumour: Brinsley Schwarz (guitar) and Bob Andrews (keyboards), both ex-Brinsley Schwarz band members; Martin Belmont (guitar), ex-Ducks Deluxe; Stephen Goulding (drums) and Andrew Bodnar (bass), both ex-Bontemps Roulez. Often compared to Dylan's erstwhile '60s cohorts, the Rumour displays the same self-assurance and finesse as the Band, but rocks harder. Despite a checkered recording career on its own, the Rumour was always a stellar support group.

Heat Treatment is essentially a continuation of **Howlin Wind**; although it has two fewer songs, each is punchier than the earlier LP. For spirited soul, there's "Hotel Chambermaid" and "Back Door Love." Parker's serious tunes are also more intense: "Turned Up Too Late" delivers a devastating romantic rejection; the anthemic "Fools' Gold," one of his finest achievements, affirms the need to search for the best, however elusive—it's unaffected and inspiring.

The oft-bootlegged **Live at Marble Arch** promo LP (produced by Nick Lowe) contains live renditions of tracks from these first two discs; original copies are impossible to locate, but counterfeits were widely circulated in both England and America.

With the vastly improved music scene as a catalyst, Parker evidently felt the need to assert himself more strongly on **Stick to Me**, but the resulting overstatement and stylistic diversity couldn't be contained comfortably on one LP. Nonetheless, taken individually, many tracks are undeniably compelling. The title cut is Parker's soaring declaration of dedication in the face of a hostile world; he unleashes exhilarating nastiness in Ann Peebles' "I'm Gonna Tear Your Playhouse Down." But one need only look at Side Two to sense the confusion: it begins and ends with raucous throwaways designed to compensate for the massive epics in the center. No amount of party fun, however, could clear the air after the overblown theatrics of the seven-minute "Heat in Harlem." Parker is sabotaged by his own indecision.

In classic contract-fulfilling tradition, Parker cranked out a two-record set, **The Parkerilla**: three live sides plus a second studio version of "Don't Ask Me Questions." Adequate but musically unnecessary, it did the legal trick, and Parker was free to switch to a different American label. The sour-grapes "Mercury Poisoning" (1979) was his first release on Arista, which declined to put its name to the promo-only gray 12-inch one-sided single, now also a rare collectors' item.

Squeezing Out Sparks resolved Parker's stylistic dilemma. It's his toughest, leanest and most lyrically sophisticated LP; in a way a sad loss of innocence. Eschewing the lighter soul elements of his earlier work, Parker adopts a harsh, nearly humorless tone that suggests cynicism instead of anger. (Regardless, critics generally loved it and sales were decidedly improved over previous efforts.) "Discovering Japan" and "Nobody Hurts You" are sizzling, passionate rockers; for better or worse, the album's centerpiece is "You Can't Be Too Strong," an anti-abortion ballad full of disturbing imagery and emphatic phrasing. In his eagerness to forge a coherent style, Parker neglects to vary the emotional tone.

A novel promo album featuring live versions of every **Sparks** song in the same running order as on the studio version, plus two other live cuts, was issued to radio as **Live Sparks**, further strengthening the band's concert reputation.

Parker somehow lost his sense of purpose on **The Up Escalator**. Although retaining the intense, driven approach of **Squeezing Out Sparks**, the material on this album falls short, possessing fury without context, which results in unsatisfying overkill. Individually, "No Holding Back," "Devil's Sidewalk" and "Love Without Greed" crackle nicely; collectively, they produce a hollow roar. Those looking to assign blame will notice the increasing influence of the king of rock melodrama, Bruce Springsteen, who even joins in vocally on the bloated "Endless Night." Also, the departure of Bob Andrews must have added to the changing situation.

The rest of the Rumour followed Andrews through the exit prior to **Another Grey Area**, which actually constitutes a minor comeback, avoiding the noisier extremes of **The Up Escalator**. A band of New York session musicians provides precise though unspectacular accompaniment; Parker co-produced with Jack Douglas. Interestingly, the harder-rocking tracks are the least effective: "Big Fat Zero" and "You Hit the Spot" seem little more than halfhearted gestures. In contrast, ballads like "Temporary Beauty," "Dark Side of the Bright Lights" and "Crying for Attention" have a graceful and unforced ring of sincerity never before heard on a Parker LP. Though **Another Grey Area** seldom overwhelms, it does indicate that, after six studio albums, Parker is still willing to take chances.

The Real Macaw, however, is a chance he probably shouldn't have taken. Songs like "You Can't Take Love for Granted" and "Life Gets Better" reach Parker's required level of intensity, but the production and playing do not. David Kershenbaum gives Parker the kind of sparse, colorless setting he used to create for Joe Jackson; the musicianship is unnecessarily understated. The end product: a disc that is watered-down and should have been harder.

Steady Nerves rights the balance, blending the pop veneer of **The Real Macaw** with a tougher band attack. Reunited with firebrand guitarist Brinsley Schwarz, Parker turns in a bracing series of characteristically pithy performances, from the cheerfully raunchy "When You Do That to Me" to the gorgeously romantic "Wake Up (Next to You)" to "Break Them Down," a classic Parker fist-waver. A solid album that bodes well. (The CD has an extra song, "Too Much Time to Think.")

Parker soon left Elektra and, following an abortive alliance with Atlantic that never actually resulted in a new record, signed to RCA and, three years after **Steady Nerves**, released **The Mona Lisa's Sister**. With excellent backing by the extraordinary Schwarz (who co-produced with Parker), Bodnar, ex-Rockpile drummer Terry Williams and keyboardist James Hallawell, Parker revs up his sharp tongue and sketchy melodicism for another collection of smooth songs that has its ups ("OK Hieronymous") and downs ("Get Started. Start a Fire"). Brittle sound tends to undercut Parker's soulful strut (especially on "I'm Just Your Man" and a lovely reading of Sam Cooke's "Cupid"); "The Girl Isn't Ready" and "Don't Let It Break You Down," however, gain edgy tension from the same audio characteristic. Although hardly one of his best, **The Mona Lisa's Sister** confirms Parker's continued artistic vitality.

High Times and **Pourin' It All Out** are (English and American, respectively) greatest hits packages of songs cut with the Rumour. **Anger** collects tracks from Parker's Arista-era albums.   [jy/iar]

See also *Rumour*.

PARROTS

The Parrots EP (nr/Desert Island-Attrix) 1980

A quartet that made promising noises on the **Vaultage 78** compilation of Brighton bands fizzles on its EP. Intelligent lyrics and a nascent pop sensibility are couched in ska and reggae rhythms, but a lack of character and drive, especially in the vocals, renders it little more than inoffensively bland.   [jg]

PASSAGE

Pindrop (nr/Object) 1980
For All and None (nr/Night & Day-Virgin) 1981
Degenerates (nr/Cherry Red) 1982
Enflame (nr/Cherry Red) 1983
Through the Passage (nr/Cherry Red) 1983

Keyboardist/vocalist/composer/producer Dick Witts *was* the Passage, regardless of lineup shifts (at first a quartet, later a trio). A former percussionist with a noted classical orchestra, Witts and his fellow Mancunians made records that defy pigeonholing, evoking comparisons to Keith Emerson and Weather Report on one hand and Wire, Gang of Four and Joy Division on the other. The reviewer who sat them smack between early Soft Machine and the Fall may have come the closest of all.

Unlike the Softs, Witts uses a goodly assortment of keyboards—strictly for delivering and coloring the music, without obligatory solos. And while the Passage can boast no brilliant Robert Wyatt parallel at the traps, the drums are also an effective part of the music (as when fluttering like a heartbeat). Witts is no strident caterwauler like Mark E. Smith, and if his socio-politically oriented lyrics do reduce complexities to catchphrases, they also promptly expand upon them—generally avoiding egregious didacticism or exhortation—articulately and strikingly. Witts frequently uses sensationalism, but as an effective device, not just for shock value.

The songs are often surprisingly memorable. The later work shows improved clarity and cogency, and tracks like "XOYO" (from **Degenerates**) couple the usual unlikely lyrics with surprisingly conventional, even commercial, hooks.

Through the Passage is, sadly, a disappointing compilation. It does include "Devils and Angels" and "Taboos," two worthy 45s never before on LP, but the other selections haven't got the collective intensity of any of the original albums.   [jg]

PASSIONNEL

See *Alex Gibson.*

PASSION PUPPETS

Beyond the Pale (Stiff-MCA) 1984

The Passion Puppets play reasonably concise melodic guitar rock with a strong rhythmic component. The sound is consistently attractive—nearing U2 or the Alarm in spots—but there are no distinguishing features or memorable songs on their bland album.   [tr]

PASSIONS

Michael and Miranda (nr/Fiction) 1980
Thirty Thousand Feet Over China (nr/Polydor) 1981
Sanctuary (nr/Polydor) 1982

Introduced on **Michael and Miranda**, the Passions—most of whom had been in a London punk band called the Derelicts—appeared to be part of the post-punk movement, characterized by spare arrangements, stark vocals and fairly unmelodic—though lyrically interesting—songs. Subjects like unhappy love ("Oh No, It's You") and frustrated attempts at relationships and communication ("Palava"), along with "Obsession," "Suspicion," fear ("Man on the Tube") and neuroses ("Absentee"), make the world of **Michael and Miranda** a particularly anxious one.

Thirty Thousand Feet Over China is less bleak, though still tainted with anger, deceit and suspicion. With a new producer, Nigel Gray, and a new bass player, the Passions sound smoother and more melodic (as on "Someone Special," "Runaway" and the nicely poppy "Bachelor Girls"). Lyrics are as sharp and offbeat as ever—check the clever, almost tongue-in-cheek "I'm in Love with a German Film Star."

Between **Thirty Thousand Feet** and **Sanctuary**, the Passions released a single, "Africa Mine," arguably their best song. It's a pretty, haunting, bitter and impassioned condemnation of colonialist exploitation but could really be applied to greed by any name. "Africa Mine" foreshadowed the sound of **Sanctuary**, which is smooth without being bland, sophisticated without being smug, and pretty without being soppy. Barbara Gogan shows growing confidence as a singer; her new expressiveness and the addition of a synthesizer serve to fill in and soften what used to be rough edges. The soaring title track is especially memorable.

Historical footnotes: Barbara Gogan's sister Susan, who had been in the Derelicts (but not the Passions), later surfaced as the mastermind of a bizarre record under the name pragVEC. Before the Passions, guitarist Clive Timperley had been in the 101ers.

[ks]

PASTELS
Up for a Bit with the Pastels (Big Time) 1987
Comin' Through EP (nr/Glass) 1987
Suck On (nr/Creation) 1988 ●

Thoroughly wistful and eternally childlike, Scotland's Pastels exemplify a much maligned style of UK music often referred to by the press there as "indie anorak pop." Characterized by an amateurish devotion to '60s pop conventions and wide-eyed naiveté, it is as lovable as it is easily copied. The Pastels have the distinction of being more influential than imitative, making them one of the better outfits working in this well-trod arena.

The Pastels' debut, **Up for a Bit**, followed a five-year string of wonderful singles. Ten polished guitar tracks stamped with Steven Pastel's near atonal vocals, the LP falls just short of fulfilling the 45s' promise, and overproduction is the culprit. "Crawl Babies," "Automatically Yours" and "I'm Alright with You" are winning tracks; however, checking the excesses would have made this a much better album.

Comin' Through restores many of the rough edges lost on the LP, giving these four tracks a refreshing boldness. The rockabilly-laced "Sit on It Mother" is the fiercest this band is likely to get and displays the intuitive versatility which separates the Pastels from the rest of the anorak pack. [ag]

PAYOLA$
Introducing Payolas EP (IRS) 1980
In a Place Like This (IRS) 1981
No Stranger to Danger (A&M) 1982
Hammer on a Drum (A&M) 1983

PAUL HYDE AND THE PAYOLAS
Here's the World for Ya (A&M) 1985

ROCK AND HYDE
Under the Volcano (Capitol) 1987 ●

Vancouver, British Columbia was the site of one of Canada's most volatile early punk explosions, but only a couple of bands managed to spread their fame much beyond the city limits. The Payolas were one of those, and temporarily managed to retain some of the scene's fire after signing to an American label.

The gatefold 7-inch EP—four songs, two of them redone for the first album—records an early four-piece lineup, produced by guitarist Bob Rock to sound like a high-voltage cross between the New York Dolls, the Clash and the Ramones.

An impressive debut, **In a Place Like This** is political (but not preachy), offering sophisticated punk with reggae seasoning, which makes it again reminiscent of the Clash without being derivative. Musical variety, lyrical quality and youthful power add to the album's strong impact.

No Stranger to Danger, expertly produced by Mick Ronson (who had not previously distinguished himself in that role), shows enormous progress—from an able but inexperienced adolescent band to a skilled and creative heir to Mott the Hoople. (If that connection doesn't register, consider that Ronson was a late member of Mott and subsequently worked extensively with Ian Hunter.) The judicious addition of contemporary keyboards, vastly improved singing and a more-melody/less-thrash outlook make every track a treat. In a nice touch, it's dedicated to the late Alex Harvey.

Sticking with Ronno, **Hammer on a Drum** takes a large step away from the youth and energy of the band's beginnings. Singer Paul Hyde selectively affects a near-perfect vocal imitation of Ian Hunter (who also appears on the record, furthering the Mott relationship). It's slick and engaging, but sorely lacking in believable personality. It may not be fair to expect any group to remain true to its (perceived) principles, but getting this fogeyish so fast is neither commendable nor flattering.

Here's the World for Ya, produced by big-time mainstreamer David Foster, is even worse. Typical of this boring and bland synth-rock record, the band is careful to thank members of Rush and Loverboy.

Ditching the band name, Rock (guitar, keyboards and bass) and Hyde (vocals, guitar), joined by ex-Payola Chris Taylor (drums, keyboards) and several other part-timers, returned with an excellent duo album. Producer Bruce Fairbairn receives a pointed (consider the preceding two records) thanks for "[letting] us be ourselves (we can all look in the mirror in the morning now)." Spanning a number of styles—all of which show imagination, pop and rock smarts and enthusiasm—the album is adult and intelligent. One of those rare multi-faceted records that reveals itself differently each time, **Under the Volcano** more than makes up for the long dry spell. [iar]

PENETRATION

Moving Targets (nr/Virgin) 1978
Coming Up for Air (Virgin Int'l) 1979
Race Against Time (nr/Clifdayn) 1979

Originally inspired into existence by Patti Smith and the Sex Pistols, Penetration emerged from northern England (Durham, near Newcastle) in 1977 with a great punk single, "Don't Dictate." Led by singer Pauline Murray, the band's brash amateurism had been converted into competent musicianship by the time of **Moving Targets**, released at first on glow-in-the-dark gimmick vinyl that was far noisier than illuminating. Playing mostly originals (written by Murray in collaboration with bandmates), but including Smith's "Free Money" and the Buzzcocks' "Nostalgia," Penetration's debut LP mixes expansive creations and direct punk-outs, all done with flair and originality. Unlike other LPs by young bands of this era, **Moving Targets** still sounds surprisingly fresh years later.

Coming Up for Air, produced poorly by Steve Lillywhite, isn't nearly as good, despite some swell tracks. Where the first record was almost consistently exciting, only "Shout Above the Noise," "On Reflection" and "Lifeline" have the same melodic, dramatic intensity. The band had evidently run out of good songs, and the muffled sound only exacerbates the mishmash.

An officially-sanctioned bootleg, **Race Against Time**, consists of a side of demos and a live side. The studio work predates the band's album sessions and is pretty boring; the live material, recorded in Newcastle mostly in 1979, is energetic and well-played. [iar]

See also *Pauline Murray and the Invisible Girls.*

PERE UBU

The Modern Dance (Blank) 1978 (Rough Trade) 1981 ●
Datapanik in the Year Zero EP (nr/Radar) 1978
Dub Housing (Chrysalis) 1978
New Picnic Time (Rough Trade) 1979
The Art of Walking (Rough Trade) 1981
390 Degrees of Simulated Stereo (Rough Trade) 1981
Song of the Bailing Man (Rough Trade) 1982
Terminal Tower: An Archival Collection (Twin/Tone) 1985 ●
The Tenement Year (Enigma) 1988 ●

Originally from Cleveland, Pere Ubu combined disorienting—often dissonant—rock and urban blues in a stunningly original and outlandish mix, but never lost an urgent, joyous party atmosphere. Lead singer David Thomas' plebian warble is the most noticeable feature of their sound, coloring all of Ubu's proceedings in a bizarre light; casual listeners might, as a result, overlook the band's powerful, polished musicianship. One of the most innovative American musical forces, Pere Ubu is to Devo what Arnold Schoenberg was to Irving Berlin.

The Modern Dance includes two songs remade from early 45s Pere Ubu had released on their Hearthan label (when Thomas was calling himself Crocus Behemoth and the late Peter Laughner was one of the sextet's guitarists). Focusing on themes of alienation and adolescent angst, the album cuts a precarious middle ground between art-rock and Midwestern garage pop. **Datapanik in the Year Zero** is more successful, collecting five of the original Hearthan tracks, including the dynamic, paranoiac "30 Seconds Over Tokyo." Dark, challenging material.

Dub Housing takes a quantum leap in production and material. Eerie guitar and keyboard work by, respectively, Tom Herman and Allen Ravenstine rivets Thomas' otherworldly vocals to a dark vision at once surreal and lodged in claustrophobic real life. Ubu's music is uncompromising music and their songwriting solid, especially on the obsessive drone, "Codex." Highly recommended.

New Picnic Time shifts toward brighter, more open sound and a deformed blues ethic. Still bearing an air of disaster, Thomas' lyrics develop story-songs that increasingly focus on common elements of everyday life, drawing more in line with his strong religious beliefs. The factors combine into a bizarre music reminiscent of Captain Beefheart.

The Art of Walking features increasing interest in musical development, tending toward ambient use of sound to create new aural landscapes, as well as more creative use of dissonance.

390 Degrees of Simulated Stereo overviews Pere Ubu's development through a collection of live recordings, featuring their best songs from the 1976–1979 era, including "30

Seconds Over Tokyo," "My Dark Ages" and "Heart of Darkness." Recommended.

The addition of Anton Fier (Feelies, Lounge Lizards) and Mayo Thompson (Red Crayola) to Pere Ubu brings the group firmly into the art-rock fold on **Song of the Bailing Man**. With clean production and spare sound, Pere Ubu abandoned the chaotic inspiration that charged their earlier work, replacing it with an unaccustomed restraint that sounds out of place.

Terminal Tower is, as billed, an archival collection with lyrics and abundant liner notes. Many of these 11 essential Ubu tracks—from "Heart of Darkness" and "The Final Solution" to "Not Happy" and "Lonesome Cowboy Dave"—are otherwise hard to find; two are alternate mixes.

Pere Ubu formally reformed in late 1987, but all that actually meant was a name change and the return of original Ubu drummer Scott Krauss to the lineup of Thomas' most recent solo support band, the Wooden Birds. In July 1988, Thomas, Krauss, bassist Tony Maimone, synthesist Allen Ravenstine, drummer Chris Cutler and guitarist Jim Jones released an all-new album, **The Tenement Year**, containing the first new Ubu music since 1982's **Bailing Man**.   [sg/iar]

See also *Red Crayola, David Thomas, Tripod Jimmie.*

LEE PERRY

Roast Fish Collie Weed and Corn Bread (Jam. Upsetters) c. 1976
Scratch on the Wire (nr/Island) 1979
The Return of Pipecock Jackxon (Hol. Black Star Liner) 1980
The Upsetter Collection (nr/Trojan) 1981
Mystic Miracle Star (Heartbeat) 1982
History, Mystery and Prophecy (Mango) 1984
Reggae Greats (Mango) 1984
Battle of Armagideon (Millionaire Liquidator) (nr/Trojan) 1986
Time Boom X De Devil Dead (nr/Syncopate) 1987

LEE PERRY AND THE UPSETTERS

Super Ape (Mango) 1976
Scratch and Co.: Chapter One the Upsetters (Clocktower) c. 1982
The Upsetter Box (nr/Trojan) 1985
Some of the Best (Heartbeat) 1986 ●
The Upsetter Compact Set [CD] (nr/Trojan) 1988

JAH LION

Colombia Colly (Mango) 1976

VARIOUS ARTISTS

Heart of the Ark Vols. 1 & 2 (nr/Seven Leaves) 1982
Megaton Dub Vols. 1 & 2 (nr/Seven Leaves) 1982
Give Me Power (nr/Trojan) 1988

Certainly eccentric, possibly mad, Lee "Scratch" Perry is reggae's most influential producer, with a career that spans the entire history of the music. He started at Coxsone Dodd's Studio One label, first as a talent scout, then as producer. Moving on to other labels, he recorded hit after hit for Jamaican artists, assembling the original Wailers and producing their earliest—some say best—tracks. Perry has also done extensive solo work, composing, arranging and singing his own records. With the help of a studio band, the Upsetters (named for one of his aliases), Perry has forged a style that's idiosyncratic and revolutionary—full of shifting, echoey rhythms and weird sound effects. His characteristic sound is unique—extended grooves layered like fog, with odd vocals and percussion shimmering in the dense mist.

Perry became an Island house producer in the '70s and a major influence on new wave bands with an affinity for reggae. (The Clash covered "Police and Thieves," a tune he co-wrote with Junior Murvin, on their first LP; Perry later did some production for the band.)

Perry's early work as both producer and performer is well chronicled. **Some of the Best** contains many fine recordings, including "People Funny Boy" and others that make plain American R&B's essential link to reggae. **The Upsetter Collection** has "Return of Django," a UK hit, and the Gatherers' "Words of My Mouth," the rhythm track of which Perry has used again and again. **Chapter One** features a dub of Junior Byles' "Curly Locks," Ricky and Bunny's "Bush Wed Corn Trash" and others co-produced with Brad Osbourne. All three compilations are lively, vital and consistent.

Perry's Island releases are also notable. **Colombia Colly** (billing him as Jah Lion) is one of the best, showing him in stylistic transition and getting weirder, with a cover of Peggy Lee's "Fever" and one cut that features a creaking door. **Super Ape**, from the same year, is more conventional, a dub LP that emphasizes the Upsetters' playing. Perry's personality is evident, though subdued. The number of engineers credited on

History, Mystery and Prophecy, Perry's last Island LP, suggests the label might have been attempting to smooth out the roughness. The sound is too clean, static and unexciting.

Perry's Island years also yielded two almost identical compilations—**Scratch on the Wire** and **ReggaeGreats**. Both feature "Police and Thieves," as well as "Roast Fish and Cornbread" and "Soul Fire" (from the brilliant Jamaican-only **Roast Fish Collie Weed and Corn Bread** LP), but neither is essential.

His other LPs vary in quality. **The Return of Pipecock Jackxon** derives from Dutch sessions during which Perry reportedly experimented with LSD and destroyed the studio. Needless to say, it's brilliant. So is **Mystic Miracle Star**, which he made with the Majestics. Surprisingly straightforward, with few sound effects, it's still filled with his characteristic production signatures. Less impressive are the two so-so volumes of **Heart of the Ark** (compilations of Perry-produced singers); worse, the two **Megaton Dub** volumes are so lackluster that one authority wondered in print whether Perry had actually produced them.

Two notable '85 releases: on "Judgment in a Babylon," a startling Jamaican 12-inch, Perry accuses Island Records boss Chris Blackwell of being a vampire who killed Bob Marley. Although libelous and crazy, it must be heard. In a more historical vein, **The Upsetter Box** makes three classic out-of-print LPs (**African Blood**, **Rhythm Shower** and **Double 7**) available again. Pricey but worthwhile, the set features appearances by U-Roy, I-Roy and others, and marks Perry's return to Trojan.

His next release for the label, **Battle of Armagideon**, is a collection of new tracks recorded in London. A return to form of sorts, the LP is full of his characteristically dense production (which sounds thoroughly contemporary) and lots of cryptic, stream-of-consciousness lyrics. (On one song, "I Am a Madman," he even celebrates his lunatic persona.) Perry's time in London also resulted in **Time Boom X De Devil Dead**, a collaboration with British dubmeister Adrian Sherwood. Influenced by Perry in the past, co-producer Sherwood provides a steadying hand, so the music is consistent, even if Perry's personality—he does all the singing—seems restrained. While perhaps lacking the eccentric edge of Perry's own work, the LP is still weird and wonderful, a sample

of some of the best avant-garde groove music being made today.

Going backward at the same time he proceeds forward, in 1988 Trojan released **Give Me Power**, another compilation of tracks Perry wrote and produced for other artists. Superbly sequenced and annotated, it's one of the best and most representative collections of the producer's past work. Don't miss it. [bk]

MARK PERRY
See *Alternative TV*.

PET SHOP BOYS
Please (EMI America) 1986 ●
Disco (EMI America) 1986 ●
Pet Shop Boys, actually. (EMI Manhattan) 1987 + 1988 ●

Chapter 53 in the Most Unlikely Chart-Topping Bands of All Time Book: Pet Shop Boys, the London duo of ex-*Smash Hits* journalist Neil Tennant and Chris Lowe, have disproven the longstanding belief that rock-crit bands (other than the Pretenders, that is), by definition, are incapable of holding mass appeal. **Please** is a slick set of anonymous easy-listening disco tracks, brilliantly, soullessly produced (mostly by Stephen Hague), with ridiculous, overbearingly smug lyrics recited by Tennant, who speak-sings suspiciously like a young Al Stewart. The in-joke references and self-amused esoterica strewn throughout songs like "West End Girls" and "Opportunities (Let's Make Lots of Money)" should have precluded their general popularity, but evidently the laxative-smooth synth backing has some utilitarian value for some people. Ghastly, depressing and offensive.

The archly-titled **Disco** remix album employs an assortment of American dubmeisters (Shep Pettibone, Arthur Baker, the Latin Rascals and others) for extended if unimproved versions of those two songs, plus "In the Night" (the B-side of "Opportunities") and other selections from **Please**: the dreamy "Love Comes Quickly" (botched by the inappropriate ticking sequencers) and the sarcastic "Suburbia," subtitled here "The Full Horror" and loaded with barking dogs and other ambient ephemera. A crackling snare drum on "West End Girls" is likewise an extraneous annoyance. While it's nice that the pair can acknowledge the crassness of their motives, how much better does that make the music sound?

The uncertain attitudinal incoherence of **Please** is traded for a decisive formula on **actually**, a crafty album of naked '80s yuppiedom. The Pet Shop Boys being young, British and snide, however, one must hear songs like "Shopping" and "Rent" as incisive social satire. Uh-huh. To be fair, their melodic sense shows remarkable improvement, and the well-arranged record (played on Fairlights) draws as much from **Abbey Road** as Kraftwerk. Tennant's voice has lost none of its creepy unctuousness—and songs like the abominable "One More Chance" are virtual rewrites of past hits—but "It's a Sin" has a brilliant refrain and Dusty Springfield's guest vocals on "What Have I Done to Deserve This?" salvage the tune handily.

The **actually** album was reissued (in the US only) in early 1988, adding a second disc (or CD) with two versions of "Always on My Mind" (the Willie Nelson hit) and "Do I Have To?" [iar]

BOB PFEIFER

See *Human Switchboard*.

PHANTOM LIMBS

Romance (Trotter) 1983
Train of Thought (CD Presents) 1986

If Bob Dylan were presently 18 years old and raised on a mixture of the Violent Femmes, Devo, the dB's and Stray Cats, he might sound like this excellent, offbeat trio based in San Francisco. On **Romance**, guitarist Jefferson Keenan's unmusical adolescent voice sings lyrics that casually mention Kierkegaard, paint detailed portraits of maladjustment and do a considerable amount of soul-bearing; the music is a well-played hodgepodge of folk-rock, rockabilly and ragtime. This much personality can be hard to take, but the jolly music keeps things light, and the intelligence obvious in the lyrics makes these guys sound like fascinating people.

Keenan's artless adenoids are again the trio's featured organ on **Train of Thought**, a distinctly Femmesy semi-acoustic rock record that boasts intriguing arrangements, excellent playing and delicately interwoven electric guitar instead of rampant stylistic variety. Although less personally revealing than those on **Romance**, songs like "Saw the

Woman in Half," "Psychology Today" and the jazzy "Formaldehyde" reaffirm the odd slant of Keenan's lyrical interests. A mention of "sitting around like sophomores do, arguing ethics" may help explain exactly where he's coming from. Another very good record from this talented band. [iar]

PHANTOM, ROCKER & SLICK

See *Stray Cats*.

BINKY PHILIPS

Binky Philips EP (Caroline) 1987

Sixteen years after his band, the Planets, first opened for the New York Dolls, this Manhattan scene veteran finally made his first record. Whew! Amazingly, he seems none the worse for wear. The five songs cut live at CBGB sound pretty darned fresh: an infectiously rockin' plea for peace (between lovers? friends? countries?), a power pop love song (slight but durable), a nasty slice of early Elvis Costello-meets-Pete Townshend (or, how to say goodbye to an ex-lover with no physical violence but still be guilty of assault and battery), a regretful farewell that's sort of a wailin' hard-rock hoedown and a sardonic expression—in loud, modern guitar-funkatiousness—of the hoary dictum, "Nothing's Free." It all hangs together by virtue of Philips' strong guitar playing and savvy (if a bit hoarse) vocals, and the tight, punchy rhythms of his cohorts, ex-Gang of Four/League of Gentlemen bassist Sarah Lee (who left prior to the record's release) and ex-Susan drummer Mick Leyland. [tr]

PHONES

Changing Minds (Twin/Tone) 1983
Blind Impulse (Twin/Tone) 1984

On their first album, these Minneapolis bar-banders play cagey, roughed-up Anglo-pop with popping bass, manifold rhythms, literate lyrics and a vaguely resigned tone that colors the proceedings a darker, more adult hue than the style generally dictates. Although full of obvious invention and skill, it's an inconclusive debut that suggests more than it delivers.

On **Blind Impulse**—dropping one guitarist to become a quartet—the Phones grow more artistic and oblique while still maintaining a rootsy sound via powerful rock guitar. In spots, they resemble erstwhile labelmates the Suburbs; elsewhere, a synth-flecked funk feel creeps in to further complicate matters. The panoply of styles on this worthwhile album results in a bit of confusion that still needs to be focused. (A strong producer might be the ticket.) [iar]

PHOTOS
The Photos (Epic) 1980

Post-Blondie popsters in punk clothing, the Photos were a competent male trio backing Wendy Wu's distinctive visage and Ronnie Spectorish voice. Unfortunately, Wu and her Worcestershire compatriots lacked the presence and sheer sauciness to compensate for inane lyrics and likable but forgettable tunes. There are some smart touches—like the punk-cum-strings reworking of Bacharach/David's "I Just Don't Know What to Do with Myself." Early UK pressings included a bonus disc of the Photos' developmental Blackmail Tapes, proving that the band could actually work up a sweat while remaining amiably dull. [jg]

PHRANC
Folksinger (Rhino) 1985

Looking like a buzz-cut Matt Dillon on the cover of her first album, California's Phranc (a self-described lesbian Jewish folksinger) is an otherwise tradition-minded descendant of such '60s protest singers as Bob Dylan, Phil Ochs, Joan Baez and Tom Paxton. Her topical songs, performed with simple beauty on acoustic guitar, address various subjects and personalities of current interest, from women athletes to Marvel's comic book about the Pope to "Female Mudwrestling" to Los Angeles' celebrity coroner, Thomas Noguchi. Taking one too many cues from Dylan, there's an unnecessary reading of his chilling "Lonesome Death of Hattie Carroll" and several similar originals. Phranc's not a timeless melodicist, but her wry lyrical observations and attractive singing make Folksinger a fine effort. [iar]

PIANOSAURUS
Groovy Neighborhood (Rounder) 1987 ●

High concept on a low budget: New York-region trio Pianosaurus plays Alex Garvin's charmingly lighthearted pop songs entirely on toy instruments for a tikki-takki effect that only adds to their winsome adora-

bility. Plinking away on itsy-bitsy pianos, cheapie organs, kiddie guitars, baby drum kits and plastic horns with sincerity and enthusiasm, Pianosaurus proves that big-people equipment isn't necessary for big-people music. (Renditions of Chuck Berry's "Memphis" and John Lee Hooker's "Dimples" indicate that the gambit can work on well-known songs without any diminution of delight.) Peter Holsapple of the dB's produced this warm and wonderful debut.

[iar]

CHARLIE PICKETT AND THE EGGS
Live at the Button (Open) 1982 (Safety Net) 1988
Cowboy Junkie Au-Go-Go EP (Open) 1984 (Safety Net) 1988

CHARLIE PICKETT
Route 33 (Twin/Tone) 1986

CHARLIE PICKETT & THE MC3
The Wilderness (Safety Net) 1988 ●

Pickett may have led *the* new wave bar band; on the Eggs' records, these Floridians throw original tunes in with covers of wildly varying notoriety, shake it all up and pour out fiery stuff. That Pickett's own tunes often compare favorably to those he chose to cover makes their scarcity on the live LP disappointing, and using three tunes by the Pirates (during and after Johnny Kidd) and three written or adopted by the Flamin Groovies on one album is a bit much, even if Pickett's slide work and the nasty ensemble nearly makes numbers like "Slow Death" sound newly minted. (Other borrowings come from Manfred Mann and Lou Reed.)

For their long-awaited second vinyl outing, the Eggs took to the studio and cut five songs, including "Overtown," a great number about the Miami riots of the early '80s, and "Marlboro Town," a dopey "Louie Louie" adaptation that was a local hit two decades ago for its author, Charlie's cousin Mark Markham. (Markham also penned "If This Is Love, Can I Get My Money Back?" which is included on the live LP and was also recorded and issued as a 1982 single.) Even without the special charge they get onstage, the Eggs reel off true-blue high-energy rockers, further establishing guitarist John Salton as a first-rate student of Thunders, Fogerty and Sky Saxon (not to mention a dead-great slide player). It's hard to believe this band isn't as big a global legend as it deserves to be.

Eggless, but joined by such sympathetic grunge talents as ex-Panther Burns guitarist Jim Duckworth and Maureen Tucker, Charlie is still burning with unquenchable rock'n'roll fire on **Route 33**. The material is almost entirely Pickett's; Minneapolis legend Chris Osgood produced it to resemble an old Stones album from a real ethnic American perspective. A little bit blues, a little bit country, but strictly bullshit-free, the album is a straightforward electric charge from a real heartlands original.

The Wilderness finds Pickett howling and rocking at top form with a new backing band. The Magic City (Miami, that is) Three includes ex-Egg Salton, whose blistering blues-based guitar excitement provides fiery encouragement for Pickett's plain and emotional singing which, at times, recalls Neil Young's mournful country wail. Covers of a 12-bar blues and a gospel song, both penned by Son House, and an electrifying new rendition of "If This Is Love" settle in nicely alongside such new originals as "Religion or Pleasure" and the cowboy saga, "Destry Rides Again."

The CD of **The Wilderness** contains **Cowboy Junkie Au-Go-Go**. That record was also re-released in an expanded edition that appends the contents of Pickett's first two singles and a track from a compilation cassette.

[jg/iar]

JEFFREY LEE PIERCE
See *Gun Club*.

PIGBAG
Dr. Heckle and Mr. Jive (Stiff) 1982
Lend an Ear (nr/Y) 1983
Pigbag Live (nr/Y) 1983
Favourite Things (nr/Y) 1983
Discology: The Best of Pigbag [CD] (nr/Kaz) 1987

Britain's Pigbag played only instrumentals, as befits a sextet with a four-piece brass-and-reed section. The music is mostly up-tempo, Latin-tinged jazz-funk and good fun for the length of a single; "Papa's Got a Brand New Pigbag," included on the first album, was a big dancefloor hit. Stretched out over an album, though, the band's writing limitations become stultifyingly clear.

Dr. Heckle and Mr. Jive contains three variations on the "Papa" formula and a couple of slower cuts that reveal a band with

plenty of technical know-how and nothing to say. Following a second studio album and a poorly-received live set, Pigbag called it a day. **Favourite Things** and the CD-only **Discology** are retrospectives, the latter containing "Papa's Got a Brand New Pigbag" in both its album and 12-inch remix versions.

[si]

PIL
See *Public Image Ltd.*

PINK INDUSTRY
Forty-Five EP (nr/Zulu) 1982
Low Technology (nr/Zulu) 1983
Who Told You, You Were Naked (nr/Zulu) 1983
New Beginnings (nr/Zulu) 1985
Pink Industry (nr/Cathexis) 1988

With many of their Liverpool compatriots (Echo, Frankie, Pete Burns) gone on to worldwide fame and fortune, these two stalwarts—singer Jayne Casey and bassist/keyboardist Ambrose Reynolds (actually a onetime member of Frankie Goes to Hollywood), adding a guitarist after the first album—continued to evade commercial success as Pink Industry (following the dissolution of Casey's Pink Military). Far from being simply credible by association, PI makes highly pleasing music that is original, fragile, attractive, ethereal and haunting.

The eponymous album is a posthumous collection of rarities and remixes that was released following an unexpected spurt of UK interest in the band. [iar]

PINK MILITARY
Blood and Lipstick EP (nr/Eric's) 1979
Do Animals Believe in God? (nr/Eric's) 1980

A minor chapter in the explosion of new Liverpool bands, Pink Military was formed by Jayne Casey after Big in Japan folded in 1978. The group's one album, recorded after two years and numerous lineup changes, is an eclectically derivative (yet amusing) hodgepodge that is neither stunningly original nor disgustingly clichéd. [sg]

PIRANHAS
The Piranhas (nr/Sire) 1980

The Piranhas hailed from England's south coast—a charming, idiosyncratic quintet with thick accents, funny lyrics and a jaundiced attitude that led to such neurotic numbers as "Getting Beaten Up," "I Don't Want My Body" and "Green Don't Suit Me." The music is mostly good-natured ska—in the general direction of early Madness or Bad Manners—though a number of the tracks fall well outside the genre, some recalling spy-movie soundtracks from the '60s. The Piranhas are likable, and smart enough to be a lot more than mere fun.

[iar]

PIXIES

Come on Pilgrim (nr/4AD) 1987 (4AD-Rough Trade) 1988 ●
Surfer Rosa (4AD-Rough Trade) 1988 ●

The Pixies hail from such diverse locales as Ohio, the Philippines, California and Boston, where the foursome actually assembled in 1986. Following their neighbors Throwing Muses onto Britain's 4AD label, the Pixies debuted with **Come on Pilgrim**, an eight-song explosion (recorded roughly as a demo) of gritty art passion: strummed and scratched acoustic and electric guitars, vocals sung and shrieked in English and Spanish, rhythms that race, rest and drift. The fuzzy chaos alternates noisy pop melodicism with primal anarchy; fervid singer Black (Charles) Francis' lyrics, when audible, skew towards surprising, occasionally shocking terrain. Difficult and intriguing.

Writer/ex-Big Black leader Steve Albini produced the cleverly-titled **Surfer Rosa**, giving the Pixies a virulent, slashing guitar sound and organizing drummer David Lovering and bassist Mrs. John Murphy into a stronger, surer rhythm unit. A sturdy grasp on melody and the importance of good—not necessarily pleasant—vocals (Francis and Murphy) make songs like "Bone Machine," "Gigantic," "Vamos" (reclaimed from **Pilgrim**) and the crazed B-52's noise parody of "Tony's Theme" into gripping rock that equally invites dancing and bewildered head shaking. (The CD of **Surfer Rosa** includes **Come on Pilgrim**.) With so much of what was once the rock underground drifting towards shamefaced respectability and mainstream acceptance, the Pixies reclaim the land of the disenfranchised with a lively, thoughtful new outlook and unique sounds for these disturbing times.

[iar]

HONEST JOHN PLAIN

See *Lurkers.*

DER PLAN

Normalette Surprise (Optional) 1981
Die Letze Rache (Ger. Ata Tak) 1983
Japlan (Jap. Ata Tak) 1985

The only American release by this Düsseldorf *neu deutsche welle* band pairs three bonus songs on one side with a full-length album on the other. Whimsical and dissonant, in spots very much like the Residents, der Plan incorporates toylike instrumental sounds, tape cut-ups, sing-song vocals, TV theme music and Spike Jones sound effects to create a diverting excursion into the weird and wonderful. Must be heard to be believed. (There are other records in the group's catalogue.)

[tr]

PLANET PATROL

Planet Patrol (Tommy Boy) 1983

Modern hip-hop meets classic soul: Arthur Baker and John Robie supply the songs, music(ians) and production, while the five members of Planet Patrol add skillful Motownish vocals that especially recall the Temptations in their prime. The four originals are soulful and exciting, with synth percussion and scratch-mix tricks interweaving with the inspiring singing. On two interesting covers—Gary Glitter's "I Didn't Know I Loved You (Till I Saw You Rock and Roll)" and Todd Rundgren's "It Wouldn't Have Made Any Difference"—the stylistic traffic jam gets mighty bizarre, but the tracks still work.

[iar]

PLAN 9

Frustration (Voxx) 1982 ●
Dealing with the Dead (Midnight) 1984
Plan 9 (Fr. New Rose) 1984
I've Just Killed a Man I Don't Want to See Any Meat (Midnight) 1985
Keep Your Cool and Read the Rules (Pink Dust) 1985 ●
Anytime Anyplace Anywhere EP (Pink Dust) 1986
Sea Hunt (Enigma) 1987 ●

BRIAN T. & PLAN 9

"Hideaway" (Midnight) 1984

Outside of its art college, Rhode Island hasn't exactly been a watershed for modern rock music. But the state has a group to be proud of in Plan 9, whose **Frustration** is exciting garage psychedelia. The swirling, mesmerizing effect of four (!) guitars recalls the best of the late '60s and gives able support to Eric Stumpo's emotional vocals. There are no original songs here, just covers of obscure period gems like "I Can Only Give You Everything."

The French-only **Plan 9** is an assortment of 1981-4 studio recordings (plus a live cut) by various lineups, including a poppy five-piece fronted by singer/guitarist Brian Thomas. (Three songs—two of which overlap the LP—by that formulation also appear on the "Hideaway" maxi-single.) Surprisingly, these recordings manage to hang together as an album.

Dealing with the Dead features eight originals, played with a '60s sound so convincing you'll swear you can smell incense burning. Stumpo's vocals are great, a whiny growl cross-breeding Michael J. Pollard and John Kay; the massed guitars and Deborah DeMarco's atmospheric keyboards increase the sense of déjà entendu even further. Far more convincing than a lot of other similar-minded outfits, Plan 9 knows just how to launch a magic carpet ride to the center of your mind. Diabolical.

I've Just Killed a Man is a steamy live album recorded as a six-piece in Boston, Washington, DC, New Haven and back home in Providence. A trio of ace covers, including the MC5's "Looking at You," and a guest appearance by head Lyre Jeff Conolly on "I'm Gone" add extra excitement to the spirited fun.

Keep Your Cool covers lots of stylistic ground, including the film noir ambience of "Street of Painted Lips" sung by Deborah D, an unclassifiable rollicking instrumental ("King 9 Will Not Return") and various stripes of '60s rock, running the stylistic gamut from Spirit to Steppenwolf. Although some are a little undeveloped, the band's songs are solid; the two covers are righteously arcane.

Anytime Anyplace Anywhere is a five-song EP of new material, including the title tune and "Green Animals."

A revised seven-person lineup on **Sea Hunt** cuts the guitar army down to three and adds a female sax player. The LP removes Plan 9 from revivalism, leaving in the resulting vacuum a rather plain-sounding rock band with a predilection for guitar solos. **Sea Hunt** is by no means bad, but the lack of focus creates an imbalance that Stumpo's unexciting originals doesn't resolve. The dreamy title track drifts along aimlessly for almost 14 instrumental minutes; it's followed by the Ramonesque 11-second "Human Mertzes." Faced with a choice of the lady or the tiger, Plan 9 fluffs it. [cpl/iar]

PLASMATICS

New Hope for the Wretched (Stiff America) 1980
Beyond the Valley of 1984 (Stiff America) 1981 ●
Metal Priestess EP (Stiff America) 1981 ●

New Hope for the Wretched, "produced" by Jimmy Miller, represents the Plasmatics' first stage—mere artless gimmickry—as conceived by the group's manager and lyricist, ex-porn entrepreneur Rod Swenson. Former sex-show queen Wendy O. Williams hoarsely talks/shouts/heavy-breathes lyrics jumbling the psychotronic film aesthetic (sex, violence, gratuitous grotesqueries) accompanied by a band playing with no subtlety whatever at punk speed and volume, reprising the "best" bits of the "Matics' preceding proto-hardcore indie singles (e.g., Williams buzzsawing a guitar in half). Entertaining for its sheer crassness perhaps, though hardly listenable.

Beyond the Valley of 1984, though, is quite listenable, if only intermittently memorable. Swenson's lyrics aspire to nightmares of apocalypse and superhuman lust and degradation. The music is likewise heavier, but clearer and not without flashes of finesse: punchy drums (courtesy of guest Neal Smith, once in Alice Cooper), good guitar squeals from Swenson's main writing collaborator, Richie Stotts, and even a culture-shock backing-vocals appearance by the girl-group Angels. (The CD, released many moons later on the PVC label, appends **Metal Priestess**.)

Metal Priestess—25 minutes at a sub-LP price—is the best buy of the lot: smokin' live versions of two of **Beyond the Valley**'s best, not to mention proof that Williams *can* sweetly carry a tune, as grim as it is ("Lunacy"). The record also notably captures the Plasmatics before the completion of their heavy metal metamorphosis. (See the band's major-label sortie, **Coup d'Etat**, and Williams' solo albums for those grisly details.)

Stotts went on to front various New York bands, including King Flux and the Richie Stotts Experience; Jean Beauvoir began a solo career and became a successful producer. [jg]

See also *Jean Beauvoir*.

PLASTIC BERTRAND

Plastic Bertrand AN1 (nr/Sire) 1978
Ça Plane pour Moi (Sire) 1978
J'te Fais un Plan (Bel. RKM) 1979
L'Album (Can. Attic) 1980
Greatest Hits (Can. Attic) 1981
Plastiquez Vos Baffles (Can. Attic) 1982

One of the first punk gag records and still one of the greatest, "Ça Plane pour Moi" was a major European hit in late '77 and early '78, launching the career of blond Belgian pretty boy Roger Jouret, aka Plastic Bertrand. Scuttlebutt at the time claimed Bertrand was the invention of some anonymous French studio pranksters; in fact, Jouret had already played drums in an earlier Belgian punk trio called Hubble Bubble (whose one LP was notable for a trashy cover of the Kinks' "I'm Not Like Everybody Else"). Together with producer/songwriter Lou Deprijck, he created the persona of Plastic Bertrand, a jolly satire on the safety-pin image and jackhammer crunch of punk.

"Ça Plane pour Moi" ("This Life's for Me") is truly great dumbness—Bertrand singing verbose, seemingly nonsensical French lyrics over a classic three-chord Ramones roar with Spectorish saxes and a winning falsetto "oooh-weee-oooh" on the chorus. Ça Plane pour Moi (the US title of Plastic Bertrand AN1, released first in Belgium, then in England) also contains more of the hilarious same—a spirited remake of the Small Faces' "Sha La La La Lee" and "Wha! Wha!," wherein Bertrand does barnyard animal imitations.

J'te Fais un Plan has two limp reggae entries actually recorded in Jamaica (the title song and "Hit 78") and a sugary-sweet ballad ("Affection") dedicated to Jonathan Richman. More interesting is the ten-minute electro-disco "Tout Petit la Planète," a blatant Kraftwerk cop tarted up with a nagging hook and a rich synthesizer sound—predating by two years the synth-pop confections of the Human League and OMD.

L'Album is for the true P-Bert devotee, its more tightly formulaic new wave pop distinguished only by a catchy vanilla-funk rap track, "Stop ou Encore," which bears a passing similarity to Blondie's "Rapture." Greatest Hits collects his big European successes with a pair of bonus live tracks.   [df]

See also Elton Motello.

PLASTICLAND

Pop! Op Drops EP (Scadillac) 1982
Color Appreciation (Fr. Lolita) 1984
Plasticland (Pink Dust) 1985
Wonder Wonderful Wonderland (Pink Dust) 1985 ●
Salon (Pink Dust) 1987 ●

Following several 7-inch EPs and 45s on their own label, this time-warped psychedelic quartet from Milwaukee (the successor to a legendary band called Arousing Polaris) began issuing wonderful albums of original acid-paisley retro-rock. Both the pink-vinyl Plasticland (with a Pretty Things' tune joining such evocative band creations as "Euphoric Trapdoor Shoes," "Rattail Comb" and "Driving Accident Prone") and Wonder Wonderful Wonderland (featuring such giddy items as "Grassland of Reeds and Things," "Processes of the Silverness" and "Fairytale Hysteria") are charming, whimsical, stylish, exciting, witty and utterly entertaining.

Color Appreciation—actually the band's first album release—is the French equivalent to Plasticland with two track substitutions; both editions contain all four songs from Pop! Op Drops. Adding two bonus cuts, the cassette of Plasticland contains the whole kit and kaboodle: 17 slices of droning delight.

Salon puts an even less selfconscious twist on things (although the faint British component in Glenn Rehse's accent argues against that) and shows an easy command of swinging London art-school power pop psychedelia. Armed with a mellotron and other relevant instruments, Plasticland infuses delicious flashes of Manfred Mann, frilly-shirt-era Who and Stones, Yardbirds and Magical Mystery Tour into their creations, making Salon an incisive nostalgia exercise that transcends its basis to stand on its own merits. A remarkably good time. [iar]

PLASTICS

Welcome Plastics (nr/Island) 1981
Plastics (Island) 1981

HAJIME TACHIBANA

H (Jap. Yen-Alfa) 1982
Hm (Ralph) 1984
Taiyo-Sun (Jap. School) 1985

The Plastics released three albums in their native Japan, and at least one of those is significantly better than their sole Western release, Welcome. (Plastics is the US equivalent.) An art-pop quintet comprising four men and a female singer, Plastics' cues come from American pop culture of the '60s in general and the B-52's in particular. Jumpy and clever, nervous and kitschy, they take

Western ideals of technology and commercialism and give them an Asian flavor. A great, original band; as noted, however, this is not their best record.

Following Plastics' breakup at the end of 1981, Tachibana put down his guitar in favor of exploring jazz sax, resulting in **H**, a diverting album which is wacky but not silly—his commitment to this musical path is no less sincere for its synthesis with what he helped develop in Plastics.

Three years on, his saxisms on **Hm** are artier and less lightheartedly playful—but not too much of either; **Hm** is still fun. Primitive drums (or were they copped from a '40s B-movie conga line production number?) are often used to underpin "outside" jazz sax charts and solos, interlarded with quieter numbers minus bass and drums in which pretty melodies are stated. Odd but ingratiating. [iar/jg]

PLAYHOUSE
Gazebo Princess (Twin/Tone) 1987

Soul Asylum's Dave Pirner co-produced **Gazebo Princess**, this uncommon Minneapolis trio's rawboned mini-album debut. Skittish, disorienting syncopation supports guitarist Eric Haugesag's distorted power'n'jazz chords and throaty vocals in a punk-folk-jazz hybrid that derives equally from Killing Joke, the Minutemen and Love. Melodic but no less challenging than the flintier tracks that surround them, "My Eyes" and "Rule No. 1" are standouts that indicate the extent of Playhouse's potential. [iar]

PLIMSOULS
Zero Hour EP (Beat) 1980
The Plimsouls (Planet) 1981
Everywhere at Once (Geffen) 1983

PETER CASE
Peter Case (Geffen) 1986

LA's Plimsouls were one of numerous bands which were sucked up by record-label power pop madness in the Knack's wake. Following a short independent recording career, they signed a big deal and made one fine LP that didn't sell. That was very nearly the end of that.

Heaps of promise are already evident on the cheap-sounding **Zero Hour** 12-inch EP. Fronted by sharp-voiced Peter Case (formerly Paul Collins' bandmate in the Nerves), the Plimsouls toss out enough cutting harmonies and nifty guitar licks to recall **Beatles**

VI, although their spirit is totally fresh and beyond nostalgia, the aggression modern.

That promise is fulfilled on **The Plimsouls**, their first major-label LP, which trims only the raggedest edges to showcase vibrant, hummable tunes like "Now." The Plimsouls' affection for '60s soul also gets a tumble via the use of a horn section and a hot cover of "Mini-Skirt Minnie."

The band's relationship with Planet soured soon after the LP stiffed, and the Plimsouls left the label to make a wonderful independent 12-inch called "A Million Miles Away." In a show of enormous resilience (both commercial and individual), the Plimsouls subsequently joined the Geffen roster and produced **Everywhere at Once**, re-recording that memorable single alongside a batch of similarly strong new ones, all bubbling with undiminished fire and melody. Lyrics, however, show signs of frustration: "How Long Will It Take?," "My Life Ain't Easy," "Play the Breaks." But the Plimsouls were never to hit the big time, and soon faded away.

Produced by J. Henry (T Bone) Burnett and Mitchell Froom, Case's solo debut is a portrait of the artist as a literate young troubadour, baggy suit and all. Putting the Plimsouls' rock-band sound aside in favor of diverse, lean arrangements, the team focuses squarely on the material (some of it co-written by Burnett; the Pogues' "Pair of Brown Eyes" is included) and Case's soul-on-fire vocals. The emotional kick of the best tunes—the rocked-up folk of "More Than Curious" and "I Shook His Hand," plus the bluesy "Old Blue Car"—point to greatness around the corner. However, other tunes (the contrived "Small Town Spree," arranged by Van Dyke Parks, the sub-Mellencamp "Horse & Crow") indicate the need for a good editor. Hang in there, Pete. [jy/iar]

PLUGZ
Electrify Me (Plugz) 1979
Better Luck (Fatima) 1981

Guitarist/singer Tito Larriva—later in Cruzados—led this early LA band. The Plugz play sharp and punky rock'n'roll with a strong sense of pop structure on the varied **Electrify Me**. The title track is mildly reggaefied; there's also a cover (in Spanish) of "La Bamba" as well as some folky things, all sticking close to the band's essentially unadventurous core.

The more mainstream **Better Luck** ups

the band's folk and country sides for a blend of Rank and File (whom they predated) and Tom Petty, displaying a promising rock talent enervated to the point of tedium. (The Plugz subsequently contributed three very divergent songs to the *Repo Man* soundtrack.)   [tr]

See also *Cruzados.*

POET AND THE ROOTS

See *Linton Kwesi Johnson.*

POGUES

Red Roses for Me (nr/Stiff) 1984
(Stiff-Enigma) 1986 ●
Rum Sodomy & the Lash (Stiff-MCA) 1985 ●
Poguetry in Motion EP (Stiff-MCA) 1986
If I Should Fall from Grace with God (Island)
1987 ●

VARIOUS ARTISTS

Straight to Hell (Hell-Enigma) 1987 ●

The London-based Pogues (originally known as Pogue Mahone—Gaelic for "kiss my ass") are a motley Anglo-Irish agglomeration (at last count a nine-piece) of erstwhile punk rockers (singer/songwriter Shane MacGowan was in the late and unlamented Nips; guitarist Philip Chevron led Dublin's estimable Radiators from Space) and knockabout folkies. Their repertoire mixes traditional Irish, English and Australian folk songs with an increasing majority of MacGowan's stylistically antiquated originals. Although early supporters of the group conveniently overlooked the existence of genuine folk artists in Great Britain who play traditional music with more knowledge and credibility, the Pogues have managed to transcend such beginnings to hone themselves into a unique and original creation.

The first two albums are exploratory, but both have their fine moments. Concertina, banjo, pipes, guitar, bass, minimal drums, mandolin and the like in the hands of post-rock rebels make for an intriguing blend of old-fashioned and newfangled. Recorded as a drape-jacketed six-piece, **Red Roses for Me** (the American cassette of which adds three cuts) mixes traditional balladry ("Poor Paddy," "Greenland Whale Fisheries") with Shane's derivative but promising creations ("Boys from the County Hell," "Dark Streets of London").

Red Roses' rudimentary acoustic instrumentation gave way to relative sophistication on the more varied **Rum Sodomy & the Lash** (produced by Elvis Costello), which evidences growing stylistic ambition as well. MacGowan, a besotted Tom Waits-like figure with an obvious Brendan Behan/James Joyce jones, shows increased confidence and talent as a songwriter on numbers like "The Old Main Drag" and "A Pair of Brown Eyes," notable examples of his gritty, realistic tales of life's urban downside.

Miles better than either of those, however, is **Poguetry in Motion**: an EP of three new MacGowan songs and a reel. Mixing zydeco with Gaelic soul, "London Girl" is a rousing singalong, an urban travelogue that sounds like the hit of Kevin Rowland's dreams; "A Rainy Night in Soho" plays a hauntingly beautiful Van Morrison-like waltz on piano, with tasteful horns and strings; "The Body of an American" is a drinking song that most closely resembles the Pogues' primal busker sound, with Uilleann pipes, martial drums and jolly tin whistle.

Along with Costello and Joe Strummer, the Pogues fell in with director Alex Cox, contributing a pair of tracks to *Sid and Nancy,* appearing in the motley *Straight to Hell* and providing the bulk of its soundtrack. Surrounded by contributions by the (Declan) MacManus Gang, Strummer and others, the Pogues offer atmospheric Latinisms like "Rabinga" and Ennio Morricone's "The Good, the Bad and the Ugly," as well as more European creations like "If I Should Fall from Grace with God" (a preview of their next album) and the traditional "Danny Boy," recorded as a reunion with ex-bassist Cait O'Riordan.

If I Should Fall from Grace with God is an excitingly strong album which opens new vistas for the Pogues. Almost all of the material is by the band; amidst winningly unreconstructed folk designs ("The Broad Majestic Shannon," "Medley," the title tune) is a jazz/swing instrumental ("Metropolis") and the oddly accented "Turkish Song of the Damned." But the record's easy standout is another example of the melancholic urban balladeering introduced on **Poguetry in Motion**: "Fairytale of New York," a fragile piano'n'strings lullaby with guest vocals by Kirsty MacColl, wife of the album's producer, Steve Lillywhite, and daughter of folk titan Ewan MacColl, whose songs the Pogues have covered.   [iar]

BUSTER POINDEXTER

See *David Johansen.*

POINTED STICKS

Perfect Youth (Can. Quintessence) 1980

Fellow Vancouverite Bob Rock of the Payolas produced this modestly appealing pop punk. But one of Pointed Sticks' earlier 45s ("What Do You Want Me to Do?" b/w "Somebody's Mom") boded far better. The faint stirrings of imaginative pop on Side Two don't go far enough, either, and Nick Jones' mischievous Everly Brothers-ish voice can't carry it alone. [jg]

POISON GIRLS

Chappaquiddick Bridge (nr/Crass) 1981
Total Exposure (nr/Xntrix) 1981
Where's the Pleasure (nr/Xntrix) 1982
I'm Not a Real Woman EP (nr/Xntrix) 1983
7 Year Scratch (nr/Xntrix) 1984
Songs of Praise (CD Presents) 1985

The Poison Girls—a middle-aged woman who wittily calls herself Vi Subversa plus a male backing band—are highly politicized musical agitators employing rock (minimalist at the start, highly diverse and sophisticated of late) as their means for registering social and sexual protest. Lyrics are clever and subtle, making points with intelligence rather than sloganeering.

Chappaquiddick Bridge is a studio recording with a bonus flexi-disc bluntly entitled "Statement." Leaving the Crass camp for their own label, **Total Exposure**—pressed on clear vinyl and fitted in a transparent plastic sleeve—is a live album with some of the same songs. But the earlier LP offers an easier entry point, due to a somewhat varied approach that doesn't carry over in concert.

With their musical skills much improved, **Where's the Pleasure** balances intellectual integrity with audio listenability and achieves a measure of success on musical merit alone. Largely ignoring the governmental politics of the first two discs, **Where's the Pleasure** deals almost solely with sexual matters, using music that's more refined and vocals that are crystal clear. Subversa's weary, whisky-and-tobacco-stained voice is a husky but serviceable instrument that perfectly suits the material and lends a tragic, poetic air to the record.

Even more accessible is the wonderful **I'm Not a Real Woman** EP—four varied songs that utterly abandon punk for a rock-cabaret sound, Celtic folk singing and poetic recitation. At her funniest, Subversa employs a Noel Coward-like delivery to offer her sharp lyrics.

Songs of Praise is even more skillful and attractive. Vi is in fine voice, having proven to be a talented and unique singer; the band stretches further into areas of sublime, suave rock and funk scarcely imaginable at the group's outset. Lyrics are likewise subtler and more intriguing, setting this album somewhere between Marianne Faithfull, John Cale and Ian Dury. [iar]

POLECATS

Polecats Are Go! (nr/Vertigo) 1981
Make a Circuit with Me (Mercury) 1983

This young, stylish London trio virtually disappeared after releasing **Polecats Are Go!**, a gem of a rockabilly revival album. Producer Dave Edmunds applies the same polish he brought to the Stray Cats, and these 'Cats truly sparkle. Piano, saxophone and careful vocal harmonies ice the usual neo-rockabilly cake of trebly guitars, acoustic bass and driving drums. A bizarrely-conceived stab at David Bowie's "John, I'm Only Dancing" doesn't quite come off; otherwise, this mix of oldies and originals parties like crazy.

The Polecats' American label passed on releasing the band's original LP, and instead patched together a seven-cut disc from singles (the glossy title track, a version of T. Rex's "Jeepster" and the aforementioned Bowie tune) and album tracks. The band was gone by then, but it was a nice gesture. [si]

POLICE

Outlandos d'Amour (A&M) 1978 ●
Regatta de Blanc (A&M) 1979 ●
Zenyatta Mondatta (A&M) 1980 ●
Ghost in the Machine (A&M) 1981 ●
Synchronicity (A&M) 1983 ●
Every Breath You Take/The Singles (A&M) 1986 ●

VARIOUS ARTISTS

Brimstone & Treacle (A&M) 1982

Though neither bassist/singer Sting nor veteran guitarist Andy Summers would have gone in this direction individually, they became intrinsic to drummer Stewart Copeland's notion of being new wavers in 1977, when it was still pretty new. As a band, the three worked in earnest to stake out their own musical turf, even probing a few of rock's boundaries. Their considerable abilities eventually yielded the Police sound: rock and reggae interlocked in proportions varying from number to number, further spiced with musical influences like Summers' quasi-classical harmonic overtones and Sting's reggae-into-jazz vocalisms.

Outlandos d'Amour is the brisk, brash initial Police barrage of bright, featherweight tunes (like "Roxanne," "Born in the 50's," "Can't Stand Losing You") and deceptively clever riffs and rhythms. It's pithy, infectious and seductive, sometimes all at once. Only a silly joke in dubious taste and Sting's pair of "let's own up" diatribes are irksome, but those can be ignored—musically, they aren't bad anyway.

Sting came up short of material on **Regatta de Blanc** and only one of Copeland's attempts at taking up the slack is truly spot-on, funny and catchy. All the same, "Message in a Bottle" is an all-around gem, and if Sting's other material isn't stellar, the performances are: effective vocal emoting and instrumentally sparkling tours de force like the title track (which also shows the virtue of space in music). The sound was further enhanced for **Zenyatta Mondatta**, and that same instrumental excellence brightens much of the record, but *too* much of the album relies on just that. The more direct cuts are too cute for words (hence "De Do Do Do . . . ") but, like bubblegum (the music and the candy), they stick to you.

Ghost in the Machine was critically considered the milestone marking the threesome's arrival as Major Artistes, but this critic begs to differ. Aside from a half-step forward (mainly Sting's saxual experimentation) the record shows the Police taking several giant leaps in the direction of the rock mainstream at the expense of at least half the songs (which are, in and of themselves, okay to pretty good).

Synchronicity (or at least "Every Breath You Take") pitched the Police into the ranks of commercial rock superstars, but most of the record simply can't be taken seriously by anyone but a chowderhead and/or indiscriminate fan. The "humor" is flat, the "experiments" with jazz shadings and electronic touches more yawn-provoking than mood-evoking; in the end, it seems just an overgrown platinum molehill. Sting's "love me—I'm the sexy, intellectual and vulnerable

man of the '80s" off-the-record image is hard to divorce from his songs, especially when he whines about being "The King of Pain." And Iron Maiden has churned out epics as gripping as "Synchronicity II." The Police have clearly become the bloated dinosaur they once complained about. But "Every Breath You Take" *is* every bit a classic, a surf-music rhythm line utterly transmogrified, relentlessly driving Sting's declaration of love-hate-obsession. So skip the LP and get the 45, which even edits out the song's draggier bits. (The posthumous singles compilation named for that huge hit features a dozen Police standards, including a 1986 remake of "Don't Stand So Close to Me" in lieu of the 1980 original.)

As a movie, *Brimstone and Treacle* has lots of mystical mood, with Sting effective as a rogue busy smudging the line between good and evil. The soundtrack album consists of one Go-Go's track, a Squeeze item, two choral pieces and some miscellaneous music by Sting, with and without his two compatriots, successful only on the evocative title instrumental and the band's resurrection (from Sting's early days in Last Exit) of the smoldering "I Burn for You." [jg]

See also *Stewart Copelannd, Fripp + Summers, Sting, Andy Summers.*

POLKACIDE

Polkacide (Subterranean) 1986

Accordion, horns, yelps and general lunacy? Yep, it must be San Francisco's Polkacide, the post-punk art concept (a sometimes bassist is in Tragic Mulatto) that dresses funny and whacks out convincing and generally reverent polkas with occasional vocals. **Polkacide** contains such nerve-rattling winners as "Baruska" (with a noise guitar solo), the venerable "Who Stole the Keeshka?" (interesting phonetic spelling there) and "In Heaven There Is No Beer." Hardly rock, but certainly a refreshing change of pace.

[iar]

POLYPHONIC SIZE

Live for Each Moment/Vivre pour Chaque Instant (Fr. New Rose) 1982
Mother's Little Helper EP (Enigma) 1982
Walking Everywhere (Fr. New Rose) 1984
The Overnight Day (Fr. New Rose) 1987

Polyphonic Size is Belgian; their first album was produced by Strangler Jean-

Jacques Burnel, who also contributed bass and vocals. Unlike Burnel's other work outside the Stranglers (his first solo LP, production for Japan's Lizard), this has none of his usual aggression. Instead he delicately captures Polyphonic Size's lovely synthesizer art-pop. Sung primarily in French by a man and a woman backed by simple (not rudimentary—carefully constructed and subtle) electronics, this resembles Orchestral Manoeuvres' lighter work. Excepting some perky numbers that lean toward Japanese synthesists like Plastics, a low-key approach—gentle, almost tender singing and languid tempos—makes **Live for Each Moment** as relaxing as a hot bath, but without the ennui, thanks to a resolute commitment to pop song structures. A very pretty record.

The **Mother's Little Helper** 12-inch singles assemblage has five tracks, including a humorous electronic re-interpretation (not unlike the Flying Lizards) of the Rolling Stones classic after which it is named.

A new four-piece lineup, working with producer Nigel Gray (Police, Siouxsie and the Banshees) on **Walking Everywhere** and **The Overnight Day**, has kept Polyphonic Size moving towards mild, commercialized pop fare—a less quirky Plastic Bertrand or perhaps a Flemish answer to Nena. The wispy male and female vocals (in French and lightly accented English) and the understated music keep the records unfailingly pleasant, but a shade too skimpy on character to make Polyphonic Size a bigger international commercial property. [iar]

POLYROCK

Polyrock (RCA) 1980
Changing Hearts (RCA) 1981
Above the Fruited Plain EP (PVC) 1982
No Love Lost [tape] (ROIR) 1986

Formed in 1978, Polyrock was one of New York's first groups to explore post-disco/new-sensibility dance music. The band led by ex-Model Citizens singer/guitarist Billy Robertson gained unquestionable artistic credibility through the patronage of Philip Glass, who (with Kurt Munkacsi) produced their two albums. The first combines minimalist repetition with electro-pop and smart, aware songs, then strips it all down to skin and bone for extremely singleminded dance music. Fascinating in its extremity.

Changing Hearts follows the same basic pattern but loosens up the sound, occasionally breaking away from austere dance music for a taste of straightforward pop, including a reworking of the Beatles' "Rain." Otherwise, Billy and Tommy Robertson write some of the most vulnerable songs this side of David Byrne, with solid (if lean) performances and production.

Following Tommy's departure (which left Polyrock a notably improved five-piece), his brother produced **Above the Fruited Plain**, five tracks with more character and melody than any of the group's previous releases. **No Love Lost** is a posthumous collection of 1980 and 1983 live performances, plus unreleased studio demos done as recently as 1984. [sg/iar]

PONTIAC BROTHERS

Big Black River (Fr. Lolita) 1985
Doll Hut (Frontier) 1985
Fiesta en la Biblioteca (Frontier) 1986
Be Married Song EP (Frontier) 1987
Johnson (Frontier) 1988 ●

Even their record company describes the Pontiac Brothers as Stones-influenced, a rare case of restraint in advertising. The Orange County, California band has never denied it; indeed, they originally got together in 1983 to play Stones tunes. (Guitarist Ward Dotson had previously been a mainstay in the Gun Club; the other Brothers are California scene veterans with numerous credits.)

Big Black River, their first album, was released only in France, which might reinforce prejudices about French taste in rock. Singer Matt Simon pushes his Mick Jagger impression beyond what it's worth; the original songs are uninspired pastiches of the Rolling Stones and '60s punk in general; the production can charitably be called shitty.

The Pontiacs re-recorded half of **Big Black River** for **Doll Hut**. Their US debut has a more polished sound, though still decidedly Jagged vocals. The new Dotson/ Simon material shows promise: "Out in the Rain" sets a poignantly wasted lyric against well-juggled musical clichés, while "Keep the Promise"—with acoustic guitar, a first—is passionate if murky. (The cassette reflects the band's fondness for performing vintage covers by including a version of the MC5's "Tonight.")

Simon finally downplayed his Jagger tendencies on **Fiesta en la Biblioteca**, also the first Pontiac Brothers album as a quartet (after going through two rhythm guitarists).

There's some welcome variety in tempos, arrangements and sentiments. (The cassette adds a Bad Company song, "Movin' On.") The album's wistful "Be Married Song"—a rare Dotson lead vocal—was redone in an electric arrangement on a 12-inch EP, which also contains "Doll Hut" (from **Fiesta**), the fine non-LP "Brenda's Mom" and a bracing rendition of AC/DC's "Dirty Deeds (Done Dirt Cheap)."

The Pontiacs' *chef d'oeuvre* to date is **Johnson** (co-produced by Randy Burns), which starts with a roar ("Ain't What I Call Home") and scarcely lets up in intensity. The inevitable Stones substratum remains—guest pianist Ian McLagan adds British authenticity—but the band has grown its own shaggy personality. Replacements fans will enjoy the frustrated vitriol of "Creep" (another Dotson vocal) and "Real Job," which Simon delivers in a Westerbergian howl. (The cassette and CD add Paul McCartney's "Magneto & Titanium Man.") Identifying with the underdog without getting misty-eyed about it, the Pontiac Brothers are ragged but right.   [si]

POP

The Pop (Automatic) 1977
Go! (Arista) 1979
Hearts and Knives EP (Rhino) 1981

Essentially a routine hard-rock/power pop outfit, this LA group acquired hipness through an actively pro-local scene stance as well as attitudes shared with more overtly rebellious colleagues. The do-it-yourself debut LP shows them equally adept at pounding out fierce rockers and lovingly constructing softer, more melodic tracks, with occasionally eccentric production touches, linking both in the anthemic "Down on the Boulevard." As good as the Raspberries' **Starting Over** but more urgent, and less studiedly nostalgic or obviously derivative.

Go!, produced by Earle Mankey, shows how the band moved with the times, modifying British modern pop notions to suit themselves. Not quite as humor-conscious (for better and worse) as XTC, the Pop employ a strangely detached intensity that gives a fillip to each track. There isn't any one brilliant number (although "Under the Microscope" comes close), yet **Go!** is entertaining straight through.

Two years later, without the guitar and arranging talents of Tim McGovern (who had joined the pre-stardom Motels) or the

support of a major label, the remaining foursome sound somewhat chastened for not having played it safer—and they do. **Hearts and Knives** presents a blander version of their former selves: pleasant, lightweight originals and a lame Stones cover that's limply out of character.

Pop singer/guitarist Roger Prescott recently surfaced in a band called Train Wreck Ghost, which he formed with ex-Plimsouls guitarist Eddie Munoz following the latter's brief stint in the dB's.   [jg]

IGGY POP

The Idiot (RCA) 1977
Lust for Life (RCA) 1977
TV Eye Live (RCA) 1978
New Values (Arista) 1979
Soldier (Arista) 1980
Party (Arista) 1981
Zombie Birdhouse (Animal) 1982
I Got a Right (Invasion) 1983 (Enigma) 1985
Choice Cuts (RCA) 1984
Blah-Blah-Blah (A&M) 1986 ●
Instinct (A&M) 1988 ●

STOOGES

The Stooges (Elektra) 1969 + 1977 + 1982 ●
Fun House (Elektra) 1970 + 1977 + 1982 ●
No Fun (nr/Elektra) 1980

IGGY AND THE STOOGES

Raw Power (Columbia) 1973 + 1981
Metallic K.O. (Import) 1976
Rubber Legs EP (Fr. Fan Club) 1987
Raw Power EP (Fr. Revenge) 1988
Death Trip EP (Fr. Revenge) 1988
Gimme Danger EP (Fr. Revenge) 1988
Metallic 2 X K.O. (Fr. Skydog) 1988 ●

IGGY POP & JAMES WILLIAMSON

Kill City (Bomp) 1978 ●

Iggy Pop (James Jewel Osterberg) embodied everything punk stood for when it exploded in England in the mid-'70s, but he had begun performing in Middle America nearly a *decade* earlier. In the late '80s, he is still a vital and active performer, serving up much the same arrogant honesty that first put him in the punk pantheon.

The Stooges (the debut LP by Iggy's self-willed band) sounds like nothing else released in 1969. Moronic lyrics and three-chord "tunes" clearly anticipate the lowest-common-denominator populism of '70s punk.

Tempos are a bit draggy, but all the ingredients for what followed are present. One of the most superficially artless records ever made.

By contrast, **Fun House** knowingly sucks the listener into its raucous vortex. This ingeniously constructed album starts out menacingly ("Down on the Street") and builds relentlessly to its apocalyptic conclusion ("L.A. Blues"). Iggy's singing—much more expressive than on **The Stooges**—veers from sullen petulance to primal scream on songs of adolescent solipsism. **Fun House** comes as close as any one record ever will to encapsulating what rock is, was and always will be about. Inspired touch: Steven Mackay's saxophone. (**No Fun**, issued between reissues of the two original Stooges albums, consists of tracks from both.)

Raw Power is another masterpiece, featuring the stinging lead guitar of James Williamson in a reorganized Stooges. With Williamson as co-author, Iggy's songs are more musical (i.e., a sense of structure emerged) in their sex-and-death conflation ("Gimme Danger," "Death Trip"). The title track and "Search and Destroy" are only two of **Raw Power**'s tunes to achieve classic status for staring into the abyss. Heavy metal in every sense, the album marked the end of the Stooges as a band concept—Iggy hereafter received solo billing—and, effectively, the first stage of Iggy's career.

Metallic K.O. is a semi-notorious, semilegal document of the Stooges' final concert, in 1974. The band staggers toward entropy as Iggy maliciously baits the crowd, which responds in kind. There are only six songs, but more than your money's worth of bile. Highlight: a version of "Louie Louie" you've never heard before. The two-disc 1988 edition adds three previously unreleased songs from the same gig and a pair of studio demos. Also from that show comes **Gimme Danger**: the "new" material and the track from the original LP for which it is titled.

As a solo artist, Iggy resurfaced under the influence of David Bowie, **The Idiot**'s producer and co-writer. Instead of flailing all over the place, Iggy conserves his energy on numbers like the surprisingly funky "Sister Midnight" and the menacing "Funtime." The album's tone is generally subdued ("Baby," "Nightclubbing," "Dum Dum Boys"), lumbering along in medium gear. It's disturbingly effective, but of mixed parentage.

Iggy reasserted himself on the rapid follow-up, **Lust for Life**. More upbeat than its predecessor, the album swaggers along to Iggy's confident delivery of the title track, "Success," the powerful "Turn Blue" and other self-analytic tunes. Jim Morrison's unmistakable influence is noticeable on a few vocals, but the clear-eyed vision is Iggy's own.

Kill City was salvaged from the period between the Stooges' breakup and Iggy's Bowie-inspired redemption. The songs plod, the sound is bad and the vocals—recorded on weekend leaves from the hospital where Iggy was residing at the time—are buried. The strung-out music has a morbid voyeuristic appeal if you enjoy wallowing in other people's degradation; otherwise, avoid this nasty stuff. (After **Kill City** had gone out of print, **I Got a Right** reissued half of it, adding a side of 1973-4 rehearsal tapes—including a version of the title tune—that are rough but intense and worthwhile.)

The dreadful **TV Eye Live** was a contract-breaker and sounds like it. Half of the tracks—recorded on 1977 US tours—include Bowie on keyboards. Those sound bad; the others sound worse. Iggy is uninspired throughout. Forget this quickie.

Reuniting with Williamson, Iggy signed to Arista and released **New Values**, a no-nonsense collection of hard rockers. His increasingly sophisticated lyrics abound in mordant humor ("I'm Bored," "Five Foot One," "New Values"). **Soldier** features a supergroup of sorts (Glen Matlock, Ivan Kral, Steve New, Barry Andrews, Klaus Kruger) riffing along to Iggy's mostly bitter rants. **Party** continues in this vein, vacillating between self-deprecation ("Eggs on Plate") and obnoxiousness ("Rock and Roll Party," "Sincerity," etc.). Two non-original oldies— "Sea of Love" and "Time Won't Let Me"— also get perfunctory treatment.

After the aesthetic dead-end of the Arista albums, **Zombie Birdhouse** marks a welcome shift in strategy. No longer singing so much as rap-chanting, Iggy turns surprisingly cerebral for a crazy blend of sociological ("The Villagers") and philosophical ("Eat or Be Eaten") discourse, pseudo-folk ("The Ballad of Cookie McBride") and topical documentary ("Watching the News"). Spare musical accompaniment underscores the album's ascetic nature. He's come a long way since the Stooges, but **Zombie Birdhouse** reveals that Iggy is far from reaching the end of his creative tether.

Following Bowie's 1983 hit version of the pair's collaborative "China Girl" (originally from **The Idiot**), Iggy's two RCA albums were culled for the hoped-for-fast-buck **Choice Cuts**, the cover of which helpfully notes the inclusion of that song and prominently mentions Bowie's songwriting and production credits.

Their creative partnership thus re-established, Iggy took some time off before recording **Blah-Blah-Blah** in Switzerland with Bowie. The individual musical changes both have undergone (with further diversion by the considerable involvement of ex-Pistol Steve Jones) make it a strange and sometimes mainstream-sounding maelstrom of styles, but the lyrics—thoughtful personal reflections on various topics—provide at least intellectual cohesiveness. The commanding "Cry for Love," "Fire Girl," "Winners & Losers" and a wonderful cover of '50s Australian rocker Johnny O'Keefe's "Real Wild Child (Wild One)" are more than worthy of Iggy's ready-to-wear legend.

In late 1987, a bunch of semi-legal archival Stooges records began drifting out of France. The best of the bunch is **Rubber Legs**, a rehearsal tape which reveals James Williamson in all his glory on such songs as "Head On" and "Cock in My Pocket" (both included on the subsequently-recorded **Metallic K.O.**), as well as the even-rarer title track. In addition to a studio take on the song after which it is titled, the five-cut **Raw Power** contains such oddities as acoustic Iggy/Williamson versions of "Purple Haze" and "Waiting for My Man" and an old radio commercial. **Death Trip** is a must to avoid, with atrocious sound, some track duplication ("Rubber Legs," "Head On") and an endless cover of Dylan's "Ballad of Hollis Brown."

Iggy's newest album, **Instinct**, was produced by Bill Laswell and features the guitar work of Steve Jones, who also co-wrote half the songs. [si/iar]

See also *New Order*.

POP GROUP
Y (nr/Radar) 1979
For How Much Longer Do We Tolerate Mass Murder? (Y-Rough Trade) 1980
We Are Time (nr/Y-Rough Trade) 1980

These abrasive, militant British punks rage against racism, oppression, hunger and anything else that's a world problem; as usual, there's no solution, only anger. This seminal Bristol band synthesizes Beefheartian structures and tribal dance beats to create a didactic soundtrack that barely lets you breathe. Their two primary albums are alternately brilliant and intolerable, with exhortatory songs like "Feed the Hungry," "Rob a Bank" and "Communicate." **We Are Time** collects outtakes, live tracks and other assorted items.

Despite the limitations of their own records, the Pop Group made their influence strongly felt, both as credible minimalists ahead of their time and via its members' subsequent musical ventures. Bassist Simon Underwood helped found Pigbag; multi-instrumentalist Gareth Sager formed Rip Rig + Panic; singer Mark Stewart is well-known under his own name. [gf]

See also *Pigbag, Rip Rig + Panic, Mark Stewart and the Maffia*.

POP-O-PIES
The White EP (415) 1982
Joe's Second Record EP (Subterranean) 1984

JOE POP-O-PIE
Joe's Third Record (Subterranean) 1986

It seems fitting that a New Jersey resident should have to travel to San Francisco to record a Grateful Dead satire. On **The White EP**, Joe Pop-O-Pie and his cohorts offer two devolved versions (rap and punk) of "Truckin'," along with four other supposed sidesplitters like "Timothy Leary Lives" and "The Catholics Are Attacking." Unfortunately, while the group shows multilateral musical aptitude and a certain lyrical wit, the EP ceases to be funny after one or two spins.

The six-song **Joe's Second Record**, believe it or not, takes yet a third swipe at that Dead chestnut. Otherwise, Joe raps ("Industrial Rap") and even waxes political ("A Political Song"), showing off both his wit and his wisdom.

Joe's Third Record—a full album at last—clearly announces "There are no 'Truckin' 's on this record." Instead, Joe and his pickup Pies turn to "Sugar Magnolia," as well as "I Am the Walrus" ("recorded 1st take live with no overdubs and includes all the mistakes"). Although parts of the record run backwards, the music itself is plenty disorienting; Kirk Heydt's amazingly hyperkinetic noise guitar work is an extremist delight that almost elbows Joe's plainspoken wit ("Bummed Out Guy," "Shut Up and Listen") and ragged singing off the record. A cool slice of strangeness. [iar]

POP WILL EAT ITSELF
Poppiecock EP (nr/Chapter 22) 1986
Poppiecock (nr/Chapter 22) 1986
The Covers EP (nr/Chapter 22) 1987
Box Frenzy (Rough Trade) 1987 ●
Now For a Feast! (Rough Trade) 1988

In the grand British tradition of selling a band on self-hype and a look, with the music added on as an afterthought, Pop Will Eat Itself became the guiding lights of England's "grebo" (slimy-looking lowlifes playing retrograde raunch) movement of 1986-7, probably because nobody else wanted to. PWEI has so far made a career out of hopping on the latest musical bandwagon (so long as it doesn't require dressing up or sounding like Duran Duran). They may lack originality, but more than compensate for it with good dirty fun.

The ten cuts (expanding a previous five-song EP of the same name) of hooliganism on **Poppiecock** owe more than a little to early Damned records (not to mention several pints of lager). Just draw a mental picture of longhairs in torn jeans thrashing away on guitars, playing songs with titles like "The Black Country Chainstore Massacreee," "There's a Psychopath in My Soup" and the seminal "Oh Grebo I Think I Love You" and you can't help but get a pretty accurate synopsis.

The Covers EP is just that—four good, raunchy rave-ups of an interesting selection of tunes, highlighted by Sigue Sigue Sputnik's "Love Missile F1-11" (vastly superior to both the original and the different take on **Box Frenzy**) and Hawkwind's classic "Orgone Accumulator." **Box Frenzy**, their first US release, goes for both of 1987's top trends, hip-hop and sampling. This time around, they're basically a British answer to the Beastie Boys—their rapping is laughably awkward but they do get the self-promotion part down just fine. The sampling is funny, too, with everyone from LL Cool J to Nat King Cole making unauthorized guest appearances. The approach on **Poppiecock** seems more up their alley, but **Box Frenzy** is still a good time.

Now For a Feast! compiles **Poppiecock**, three covers and the "Sweet Sweet Pie" 45 for a solid pre-**Frenzy** recapitulation. (The cassette adds two for a fuller course.)

PWEI are unpretentious, marginally talented bullshitters at heart, which is something rock music can actually use these days. [dgs]

PORK DUKES
Pork Dukes (nr/Wood) 1978 (nr/Butt) 1979
Pig Out of Hell (nr/Music Galore) c. 1981

Whoever these four no-good rotters masquerading behind pseudonyms were, they had good reason to hide. Except for musings by such children of the revolution as the Meatmen, the pink-vinyl **Pork Dukes** is the most vulgar, offensive, rude, disgusting, infantile, noxious load of puerile rubbish ever released commercially. In its defense, for those who can stomach it, the music is competent and the lyrics pretty funny. One can only pray this was done for laughs. . . . [iar]

POSITIVE NOISE
Heart of Darkness (nr/Statik) 1981
Change of Heart (Sire) 1982
Distant Fires (nr/Statik) 1985

The title of Positive Noise's second album signifies the drastic change that had taken place after the group's debut LP as a result of the departure of Ross Middleton, the band's singer/leader/lyricist who left in mid-1981 to form Leisure Process with saxophonist Gary Barnacle. The Scottish band began as a five-piece (including two other Middleton brothers) and in late 1980 recorded **Heart of Darkness**, which is pretty dire—a badly produced mishmash of art-funk, Skids-like cheering, PiL noise and assorted pretentious nonsense. It suffers from indecisive direction as much as a lack of originality.

For **Change of Heart**, guitarist Russell Blackstock also assumed the vocal chores, and Positive Noise transmuted into a slick electronic dance machine, churning out precise rhythms with anxious, semi-melodic vocals. Gone is the audio clumsiness and uncertain footing of the first LP; Positive Noise's niche is definitely in club music. They put out some excellent subsequent singles and a new album in 1985. [iar]

POSTE RESTANTE
See *Minny Pops.*

WILL POWERS
Dancing for Mental Health (Island) 1983

I've encountered many a strange record in my day, and the rock web seems capable of stretching to include virtually any bizarre concept anyone cares to bring to it, but this album clearly exists in a weird league all its own. Simply outlined, it consists of New York photographer Lynn Goldsmith reciting motivational self-improvement exhortations and emotional psychodrama, mostly in (synthetically altered) seemingly male voices, over busy dance music co-written variously by Sting, Steve Winwood, Tom Bailey, Nile Rodgers and Todd Rundgren and performed by an uncredited crew, all ostensibly produced by Goldsmith who, to my knowledge, has no previous musical experience. A phenomenal exercise of super-ego, this is both a Great Artistic Achievement and an unbelievably smug heap of horse puckey.   [iar]

POWER STATION
The Power Station (Capitol) 1985 ●

This short-lived supergroup (whose name would be "Kraftwerk" in German) agglomerates Andy and John Taylor—then the guitar/bass axis of Duran Duran—with ex-Chic drummer Tony Thompson and singer Robert Palmer. (Plus Bernard Edwards as producer.) On paper, a promising idea—especially in light of the Durannies' funk pretensions and Simon Le Bon's vocal inadequacies—but, on vinyl, a miserable, boring explosion of overbearing drums pounding (you thought the drums were mixed high on **Let's Dance**?) through tuneless, formless "songs." While Power Station's slickly functional dance-funk is just minor on the softer numbers, the ultimate realization of the concept, "Some Like It Hot," offers a numbingly industrial take on electro-funk made truly execrable by Palmer's contemptible singing. But that's *nothing* compared to the excruciating jam/destruction of Marc Bolan's classic "Bang a Gong (Get It On)," matching an appalling lack of originality (why didn't they also swing through "Johnny B. Goode" while they were getting to know one another?) with utter disdain for and desecration of the song's melody, tempo and boppy charm. Repugnant.

When the band that swore it would not tour hit the road, it was without Palmer, replaced for disputed reasons by the even-less-

talented Michael Des Barres, adding another chapter to his Chequered Past.   [iar]

PRAGVEC
No-Cowboys (nr/Spec) 1981

Bizarre, kitschy doodlings in a semi-pop mode by a London band loosely formed around four members, including singer/guitarist Susan Gogan, sister of the Passions' Barbara Gogan. Pleasant if you don't pay too much attention.   [iar]

PREFAB SPROUT
Prefab Sprout EP (nr/Kitchenware) 1983
Swoon (Kitchenware-Epic) 1984
Steve McQueen (nr/Kitchenware) 1985
Two Wheels Good (Kitchenware-Epic) 1985 ●
From Langley Park to Memphis (Kitchenware-Epic) 1988 ●

Smart and sophisticated garden-pop-jazz. Imagine Aztec Camera meets Steely Dan with absurdist lyrical inventions and close-formation female backing vocals—that's Prefab Sprout, essentially the creation of Newcastle singer/songwriter Paddy McAloon. Performed by a trio joined by a guest drummer, the debut EP and **Swoon** (no overlapping tracks) reveal a unique and ingenious wit—the album's "Cue Fanfare" is about chess champ Bobby Fischer—supported by light and mellifluous music in a number of refined styles. Remarkable and enticing.

Steve McQueen (issued in the US as **Two Wheels Good**) was produced with a fine hand by Thomas Dolby, who also plays on it as the group's fifth member. A significant advancement over **Swoon**, the adult gossamer pop includes the remarkably airy "When Love Breaks Down" (guest produced by Phil Thornally, indicating the band's strong stylistic backbone), the obscure but lovely "Appetite" and the mesmerizing "Goodbye Lucille #1." "Blueberry Pies" sounds like a lost Sade tune; "Horsin' Around" is as cavalier as its title. Brilliant!

On the airy **Langley Park to Memphis**, the quartet gets minor assistance from Pete Townshend (inaudible acoustic guitar on one track), Stevie Wonder and gospel's Andrae Crouch Singers; Dolby produced and played keyboards on four tracks. Notwithstanding one energized exception ("The Golden Calf," which bizarrely resembles Cheap Trick), the easy listening lounge music—deco-era strings, movie-music horns, stage-whisper vocals, restrained tempos—is boring and uninvolving, burying McAloon's offbeat lyrics in too deeply mellow an audio disguise.

[iar]

PRESSURE BOYS

Jump! Jump! Jump! (A-Root-Da-Doot-Doo) 1983
Rangledoon (AR3D) 1984
Krandlebanum Monumentus (AR3D) 1987

Chalk up another one for Mitch Easter, who co-produced **Jump! Jump! Jump!** at his world-famous Drive-In Studio. You might be expecting power pop, but North Carolina's P-Boys instead deliver hot'n'sweaty horn-inflected ska-beat rock. The sextet's gangbusting, headlong enthusiasm recalls the early Specials (without the accents or trebly sound) but songs like "Tina Goes to the Supermarket" undercut any seriousness that might have been intended. Easter acquits himself admirably on this atypical production fare, making a record likely to pump your speakers free of their cabinets.

The less stylized **Krandlebanum Monumentus** contains a second rendition of "Tina" as well as such offbeat weirdities as "Terrible Brain," "Trombonehead" and "A Chew and a Swallow." Three horns still lead the kinetic attack, but the Pressuremen no longer hie to bluebeat, choosing a straighter rock direction (a bit like Oingo Boingo) that shows off their tightness but leaves a less-lasting impression.

[iar]

PRESSURE COMPANY

See *Cabaret Voltaire.*

PRETENDERS

Pretenders (Real-Sire) 1980 ●
Extended Play EP (Real-Sire) 1981
Pretenders II (Real-Sire) 1981 ●
Learning to Crawl (Real-Sire) 1984 ●
Get Close (Real-Sire) 1986 ●
The Singles (Real-Sire) 1987 ●

Although bands fronted by ex-music critics have generally been doomed to culty oblivion, the Pretenders—formed in London by Ohio-born Chrissie Hynde—became huge around the world. Surviving the tragic deaths of guitarist James Honeyman Scott in 1982

and bassist Pete Farndon (after leaving the group) a year later, Hynde has pressed on, overcoming disaster with incredible strength and resilience. At this point, the Pretenders seem capable of existing and succeeding as long as Hynde cares to exercise her unique talents as a songwriter and vocalist.

After several brilliant singles (starting with an unforgettable Nick Lowe-produced Kinks cover, "Stop Your Sobbing"), the long-awaited **Pretenders** proved that the 45s were only the beginning. The band's several strengths—Hynde's husky voice and sexually forthright persona, drummer Martin Chambers' intricately syncopated (but never effete) rock rhythms, Honeyman Scott's blazing, inventive guitar work—give numbers like "Tattooed Love Boys," "Mystery Achievement," "Kid," "Brass in Pocket" and "Stop Your Sobbing" (the last three were pre-LP singles) instantly identifiable character and obvious rock excitement.

Mind-boggling success caught the Pretenders short of material, and producing a follow-up proved no small challenge. Eighteen months of touring left little time for writing or recording; the stopgap EP compiles both sides of two singles and a live version of "Precious." The record's fine as a placeholder, but was rendered redundant when both A-sides turned up on the second album.

Pretenders II would have been a real stiff, creatively speaking, were it not for those self-same 45 cuts ("Message of Love" and "Talk of the Town"), the latter being one of the best things the band has ever done. Only a handful of the other ten tunes match the first album's quality, with selfconsciousness and repetition marring Hynde's writing and performance. An air of uncertainty—whether to play up the overstated arena-scaled side or explore restrained ballads and more complex, subtle arrangements—stymied them, and resulted in a confusion of conflicting directions.

Scott's death and Farndon's departure, coupled with Hynde's pregnancy, kept the band out of action for most of 1982. They released only one 45: "Back on the Chain Gang" b/w "My City Was Gone," with Billy Bremner guesting on guitar and future Big Countryman Tony Butler on bass. The band's paltry output the following year was also one single, the wistful, sentimental "2000 Miles."

Learning to Crawl could have been a petrified, self-pitying record, but that's hardly the case. In a remarkable return to prime form, a revitalized Hynde and Chambers lead two new Pretenders through a collection of characteristic songs, including all three aforementioned single sides and such new grippers as "Middle of the Road" and "Time the Avenger," which are equal to anything Hynde had previously written or recorded. The only thing lacking is Chambers' percussive complexity, replaced here by sturdy beats that are nothing special. But free of the misjudgment that ankled the second album, the Pretenders again prove both their mettle and their talent.

Unrelated to the music, but typical of the inescapable private life drama that seems intrinsic to the band, Hynde then took time off to marry Simple Minds' singer Jim Kerr and tend two children, forcing another long wait between records. When the Pretenders returned to action in 1986 with the disappointing **Get Close**, Chambers (and everyone else, save for guitarist Robbie McIntosh) was gone, although he does appear on an ill-advised cover of Jimi Hendrix's "Room Full of Mirrors." Although the new lineup includes ex-Haircut One Hundred drummer Blair Cunningham, the record relies on session players (including Bernie Worrell, Carlos Alomar and Simon Phillips) and contains only two sentimental love songs ("Don't Get Me Wrong" and "My Baby") and Meg Keene's haunting ballad ("Hymn to Her")—all released as singles—to recommend it.

That trio, plus a dozen more classics and near-greats, comprise what is unquestionably the best Pretenders album of all. One can overlook **The Singles**' shockingly shoddy packaging; this is a true best-of career distillation (all the A-sides from 1979 to 1986) with one bonus track: Hynde's winning duet with UB40 on a reggaefied "I Got You Babe."   [iar]

PRETTY POISON

Laced EP (Svengali) 1983
Catch Me I'm Falling (Virgin) 1988 ●

You've got to hand it to these hardy Camden, New Jersey natives. Pretty Poison, possibly the only group ever to cover a Tuxedomoon composition (which they did on a flexidisc included with one of several rare self-released singles), kept going through the '80s without recognition long enough to somehow wind up scoring an honest-to-god Top 10 soundtrack single in 1987.

The 12-inch **Laced** EP shows off all of the band's strengths, from the massed percussion of "Let Freedom Ring" to the catchy electro-pop of "Expiration." Keyboardist Whey Cooler (ouch) leads the varied synth-dance-rhythm-rock, providing solid support for big-voiced singer Jade Starling. More resourceful than inventive, Pretty Poison stakes a strong case for national exposure.

"Catch Me I'm Falling," recorded for a quickly forgotten Jon Cryer film called *Hiding Out*, did the trick—a bouncy, insistent dance hit with stuttering production that clicked, thanks to numerous soundalikes polluting the airwaves around the same time. Caught off guard by their runaway success, it took PP a while to pull an album together, using an assortment of producers. Indeed, a few of the songs (including "Let Freedom Ring" and "Nighttime") on **Catch Me I'm Falling** are remakes of old indie releases, a sign of material shortage. In any case, the album of predictable, utilitarian high-tech dancercise is no better or worse than the single that induced it.   [iar]

PRIMITIVE CALCULATORS

Primitive Calculators (Aus. no label) 1978 + 1987

Inspired by New York City's Suicide, this avant-rant quartet made stripped-down, noisy and intense music with guitars, harshly-pounding electric keyboards and deliberately unmelodic vocals. Their overall sound was similar to "Ugly American"-era Big Black. Although the Calculators never released another record after leaving Melbourne in the vain pursuit of fame and fortune in Europe, they were highly popular and influential among underground Australian musicians, causing their lone album to be reissued in 1987 with a 7-inch single as a bonus disc. Guitarist Stuart Grant and bassist David Light have since surfaced (back in Australia) in the Bum Steers.   ['e]

PRIMITIVES

Thru the Flowers EP (nr/Lazy) 1987
Lovely (RCA) 1988 ●

Coventry, England's Primitives are in the forefront of a genre of British independent pop that first became popular around 1986 in the wake of the Jesus and Mary Chain. Characterized by naive (in this instance, female) vocals over a backing track of politely distorted guitar, drums and the occasional synthesizer, the style can be either grating or endearing. Though few dissimilarities exist between the purveyors of this style, the Primitives' songs *are* memorable, thanks to competent musicianship and judicious changes of pace.

Essentially a duo but constituted here as a quartet, the young group's wonderful first album, **Lovely**, followed an exceptional string of UK singles, only two of which ("Thru the Flowers" and "Stop Killing Me") are recounted on it. (The American version adds a third, the pure-pop "Crash.") The album touches on a variety of musical formats—from abject California bubblegum pop ("Thru the Flowers," "Crash," "Stop Killing Me") to early Blondiesque punk ("Nothing Left") and '60's mock-Indian psychedelia ("Shadow"). With **Lovely**, Primitives Tracey and Paul have defined the genre while crafting an album of instantly accessible pop standards. A stunning debut.

[ag]

PRIMITONS

Primitons (Throbbing Lobster) 1985
Happy All the Time (What Goes On) 1987

The two prime movers in Birmingham's Primitons are drummer/accordionist Leif Bondarenko and singer/guitarist/organist Mots Roden, a Swede who somehow wound up living in Alabama. Following a long stint in Jim Bob and the Leisure Suits (a promising but gimmicky local adaptation of new wave), the pair formed the all-pop Primitons with singer/guitarist Brad Dorset and non-performing lyricist Stephanie Truelove Wright.

Joined by a guest vocalist, the trio recorded a sturdy and attractive seven-song debut, produced with Mitch Easter. **Primitons** is a pop record, but with the same sort of gravity and lyrical depth as the Windbreakers. "All My Friends" offers a rich R.E.M.-influenced rush; "She Sleeps" puts a gothic tale of death and grieving to simple music strengthened by high, lonesome singing; "You'll Never Know" is an ominous whisper about nuclear destruction.

Bassist Don Tinsley replaced Dorset; the trio (plus Wright) issued an ambitious and spectacular Anglo-pop 12-inch, "Don't Go Away," which covers the Left Banke's "Something on My Mind" as one of its two B-sides. **Happy All the Time**, which boasts "Don't Go Away" and other similarly well-

executed numbers, is a winning collection and shows what a fine band the Primitons are. Layers of guitars and vocals are the main ingredients; subtlety and diversity are a bonus; talented songwriting and offbeat lyrics provide the solid foundation. Tim Lee guests.

[iar]

PRINCE

For You (Warner Bros.) 1978 ●
Prince (Warner Bros.) 1979 ●
Dirty Mind (Warner Bros.) 1980 ●
Controversy (Warner Bros.) 1981 ●
1999 (Warner Bros.) 1982 ●
Sign "o" the Times (Paisley Park) 1987 ●
The Black Album (unreleased)
Lovesexy (Paisley Park) 1988 ●

PRINCE AND THE REVOLUTION

Purple Rain (Warner Bros.) 1984 ●
Around the World in a Day (Paisley Park) 1985 ●
Parade (Paisley Park) 1986 ●

Prince's impact on the direction and sound of '80s pop music can't be overstated. By the mid-'70s, race segregation had become nearly as rigid a musical barrier as it was at the outset of rock'n'roll in the '50s, but Prince's brilliant stylistic cross-fertilization has been a major agent in its slow dissolution. He continually demonstrates a phenomenal grasp of forms, styles and production techniques *and* has the ability to create stunning syntheses of them. True, he's shown a lyrical penchant for excessive and/or tasteless sexuality, but he's also responsible for some of the most playful, open and un-hung-up sexiness in pop music, especially in his later work. Prince is the biggest figure in '80s pop music whom musicians at opposite ends of the rock and soul spectrum will admit liking and paying attention to.

Prince has expanded his dominant position in the music world by franchising himself through a widening spectrum of artists, including the Time (and that group's offshoot, the Jimmy Jam/Terry Lewis writing and production team), Sheena Easton, Sheila E., the Bangles, Vanity, Wendy and Lisa, etc. He's become a bottomless source of toss-stones, spreading ripples across a huge area. That all this came from one man is even more impressive when you stop to consider that his first five albums have hardly a note he didn't write, produce or perform.

The upstart 19-year-old's first album, **For You**, operates within the conventions of soul

443

music—even of disco—without sounding like a tired string of clichés or succumbing to corporate overkill. The assertive sexuality (e.g., "Soft and Wet") isn't the LP's big surprise, which he saves for last—something like a cross between MFSB and the Delfonics trying to condense the Cream songbook into one number. **Prince**'s soul is also slick, its rock less crunchy. His libido advertisements range from mock-coy to wham-bam, from straightforward to confusing ("I wanna be your lover . . . your brother . . . your mother and your sister too") to confused ("It's mainly a physical thing . . . [but] I think it's love"). **Prince** is a bit more entertaining than **For You**, but both are a touch too clinical.

Dirty Mind and **Controversy** began to attract the attention of the new wave crowd. To oversimplify, the two LPs blend Blondie, Bootsy and Blowfly; while other artists bared their souls, Prince preferred to bare his genitals. Ultimately, **Dirty Mind** comes off as a flawed triumph, **Controversy** as a miscalculation. The former's crotch-mindedness is offset by ingenuous ingenuity. The sly lyrics, good tunes, strong production and his super falsetto all make for a winning combination; a song like "When You Were Mine" (later covered to great effect by Cyndi Lauper) declared that he was a tunesmith to be reckoned with. **Controversy**, though, shows too much flash with too little substance—Prince is straining too hard for approval from his new audience and the touch-all-bases agenda yields "Ronnie, Talk to Russia," "Annie Christian" and "Jack U Off," all on one LP side.

The largely dance-oriented **1999**, however, is his first real tour de force. Prince exercises even greater skill than before, and when he couples that with some restraint, the results are incredibly gratifying. (The first side alone has three of his best-ever cuts: "1999," "Little Red Corvette" and "Delirious.") Gratuitous sexuality and stylistic indulgences that overstretch tracks make the double-album set less than an unmitigated success; all the same, sometimes his talent is so dazzling that you don't notice (or care about) his excesses.

Purple Rain is the first Prince album to use a band in the studio, and his first movie music; however much those factors influenced the outcome, it also clearly topped its predecessors. Superior focus and control enable him to move effortlessly from the party-down ebullience of "Let's Go Crazy" to the spare, delicate anguish of "When

Doves Cry" to the commandingly Hendrixian guitar balladry of the title track.

From back-to-back killers, though, he went to back-to-back turkeys: **Around the World in a Day** and **Parade**. But no matter what he gets into on these records, each has at least one ace track and another just a notch below. Prince's father helped him write three of the tunes on **Around the World**, but don't blame Dad—the blatherings on sex and religion, and the neo-psychedelic/flower-power tripe in which it's couched, are all Prince's doing. All the same, "Raspberry Beret" is an uncanny recycling of the Small Faces and the bouncy "Pop Life" (which allegedly incorporates a tape of the crowd that booed him offstage when he opened for the Stones) offers politely witty lyrics. **Parade**'s strangeness isn't as bad as the worst of **World**, though it's a wonder the soundtrack of Prince's laughably bad second film, *Under the Cherry Moon,* was any good at all. Some of it is weird—stripped-down funk that just doesn't work—but the spartan "Kiss" is an instant classic. Right on its heels comes "Anotherloverholenyohead," which isn't—*can't* be—as good, but is still pretty stimulating.

The time for the Revolution had evidently come and gone, so Prince decided to strike out on his own again. The split was apparently amicable; Wendy and Lisa (guitar, keyboards, vocals) appear on his next LP (while also making one of their own). **Sign "o" the Times** is a two-disc bag of goodies, filled with different flavors and colors. The title track is the most minimal of his minimalist singles (even compared to "Kiss"), an offbeat reality-minded protest record that's hardly there. It shouldn't work, but it does, like crazy. Sheena Easton and Sheila E. join in for "U Got the Look," a throwback to the "old" Prince sound and over-the-top sexual aggression ("let's get to rammin' ") and a strong track in spite of itself. Otherwise, there's some of everything—rap, funk, pop, James Brown tributes, rock'n'roll, etc. Highlights include "If I Was Your Girlfriend," which redefines a relationship in a surprisingly mature way; "Strange Relationship," a nonplused admisson of emotional sado-masochism; and the sleeper ending Side Three, "I Could Never Take the Place of Your Man," a "When You Were Mine" melody with an older and wiser message. A double album eminently worthy of the vinyl.

In a disagreement with Warner Bros. ostensibly over release scheduling, Prince withdrew a completed record known as **The**

Black Album, which wound up widely bootlegged on cassette. It's not a great album, but it's pretty damned neat. Except for the pretty (X-rated) ballad, "When 2 R in Love," each track offers a slightly different kind of (usually scatological) funk. The sneer of "Le Grind," a leering call to orgy to the beat, is grating but, like the rest, is so well done it succeeds anyway. "Bob George" is fabulously nasty, off-the-wall black (in many senses) humor; "2 Nigs United 4 West Compton" is a sort of tribute (?!?) to guys like Jimmy Smith and Brother Jack McDuff; "Cincy C" is a hot, sexy groove. Lots of synthetic sounds, not the least of which is the obvious electronic alteration of Prince's voice. This LP would've received no airplay, but it's a gas.

Prince must have known **The Black Album** wouldn't really pass muster at the label: he already had **Lovesexy** ready. (Its cover caused a different retail furor.) With backing by the group Madhouse (minus its drummer, replaced by Sheila E.), it's a fine record. "Alphabet St." brightly continues that minimalist single string. "Anna Stesia" is a wonderfully weird intertwining of love, sex and religion that works where it failed before; the title track is a funny/affecting affirmation of real and exciting romance that *doesn't* have to be immediately consummated (even though "race cars burn rubber in my pants"!). The only song carried over from **The Black Album** is "When 2 R in Love." Prince is on a creative roll; and the sky's the limit.   [jg]

See also *Andre Cymone, Morris Day, Sheila E., Jesse Johnson's Revue, Mazarati, Time, Wendy and Lisa.*

PRINCE CHARLES AND THE CITY BEAT BAND

Gang War (Solid Platinum) 1981
Stone Killers [tape] (ROIR) 1983 (nr/Virgin) 1984
Combat Zone (nr/Virgin) 1984

Boston funk flautist Charles Alexander leads the City Beat Band through eight long Gap Band-styled party grooves on **Stone Killers** (released first in America on cassette and then in England on vinyl). The music is infectious and unassailably danceable; the semi-rap lyrics vary from juvenile and obnoxious—"Big Chested Girls"—to simplistic and funny—"Cash (Cash Money)." **Combat Zone** is a more ambitious LP. Several real songs mix an aggressive blend of Mayfield/

Chicago soul and modern stylings; elsewhere, Alexander parties hearty and even tries a notable scratch-funk revision of "Jailhouse Rock."   [iar]

PETER PRINCIPLE

See *Tuxedomoon.*

PROCESS AND THE DOO-RAGS

Too Sharp (Columbia) 1985

Having found considerable leering success with the sexploitative Mary Jane Girls, Rick James continues his musical outreach program with this humorously-named male vocal quintet. They sing, while James handles virtually everything else, listing his name (as writer, producer, arranger and performer) a dozen times on the back cover. Except for the familiarity of the lyrical conceits ("Serious Freak," "Dance the Way You Want," etc.), it's an enjoyable detour, an agreeably modern soul record disguised as hot dance-funk.   [iar]

PROCLAIMERS

This Is the Story (Chrysalis) 1987

One of the neo-folk movement's most rewarding eruptions is the Proclaimers, a pair of sharp-tongued Scottish twins (Craig and Charlie Reid) who not only acknowledge their thick accents, they sing about 'em (in "Throw the 'R' Away"), strumming acoustic guitars and tapping on bongos for accompaniment. Oldtimers will be forgiven for thinking the duo sounds like Lonnie Donegan, the Glaswegian whose skiffle records served to popularize American folk music in the UK three decades ago. By telling it straight and artlessly, **This Is the Story** stands out, embracing and updating ancient traditions without selfconsciousness or phony posing. Those who like Billy Bragg's sound but find his politics an impediment are recommended to the Proclaimers for a largely non-topical dose of similarly spare melodicism.   [iar]

PROFESSIONALS

I Didn't See It Coming (nr/Virgin) 1981

Following the breakup of the Sex Pistols, Paul Cook and Steve Jones—aka the Professionals—stuck together, finishing some final tracks under the Pistols' name, backing people like Joan Jett and Johnny Thunders and doing lots of production work. **I Didn't See**

It Coming, however, is their only joint post-Pistols album. With Paul Meyers (bass) and Ray McVeigh (guitar), the trademark Cook/Jones rock crunch stretches over wide terrain, on songs that are neither trusty punk oldies nor retreads thereof. The album's not consistently good, but "The Magnificent" (a song seemingly aimed at John Lydon, complete with parodic Public Image guitar), "Payola" and the anthemic "Kick Down the Doors" are among the tracks that bear repeated spins.

Cook and Jones can be seen in several movies, including the Pistols' *Great Rock'n' Roll Swindle* and *Ladies and Gentlemen, the Fabulous Stains*. Jones went on to record a solo album and work with Iggy Pop, Andy Taylor and others; Cook wound up in a band called Chiefs of Relief. [iar]

See also *Chiefs of Relief, Steve Jones.*

PROLETARIAT

Soma Holiday (Non U-Radiobeat) 1983
Indifference (Homestead) 1986

Powerful full-frontal assault guitar rock from a politically committed Boston quartet. **Soma Holiday** ventures nebulous (and brief) opinions on 18 topics (famine, farm subsidies, soldiering, McCarthyism, etc.); the rock'n' roll is decidedly more focused, raging and roaring with conviction. Richard Brown's vocals aren't nearly as good as Frank Michaels' overdrive guitar, still **Soma Holiday** is a cool-sounding, reasonably intelligent protest record that offers a viable, equally intense alternative to hardcore. [iar]

PROPAGANDA

Calling on Moscow EP (Epic) 1980

Originally called the Passengers, this British quartet was deemed by their US label to be apt representatives of the acceptable sound of new wave, so—*voilà!*—a 10-inch EP containing four tracks of forgettable, mildly humorous rock'n'roll. Whee. [jg]

PROPAGANDA

A Secret Wish (ZTT-Island) 1985 ●
Wishful Thinking (nr/ZTT-Island) 1985

Germany's Propaganda—two men and two women—play intricate, almost orchestral synth-based rock of little inherent excitement. As encouraged by Trevor Horn and Paul Morley, each divergent track is a huge stylized production number, but none offers much in the way of listening pleasure. The band's character—when any is present—derives mainly from gimmickry (gory English S&M lyrics on "Duel," Art of Noise-styled mix hysterics on its invigorating instrumental doppelgänger, "Jewel"). **A Secret Wish** includes contributions from Steve Howe, David Sylvian, Glenn Gregory and others, but you'd never notice from listening. **Wishful Thinking** is an album of remixes and reworkings of previously released material. [tr]

PSEUDO ECHO

Autumnal Park (Aus. RCA) 1986
Love an Adventure (RCA) 1986

The distance between Australia and the world's musical capitals occasionally leads to time-zone wrinkles like Pseudo Echo, a Melbourne quartet whose functional dance-rock sound would have fit nicely alongside Duran Duran or other emergent hair-synth-guitar bands five years earlier. The Pseuds' other weird move was hitching their wagon to turn-of-the-decade American disco, cutting a pablumized Sparks-like version of "Funkytown." For whatever it's worth, that goofy hybrid appears on **Love an Adventure**, the US edition of which incorporates three tracks—including the memorable Ultravoxy "Listening"—from the Australian-only **Autumnal Park** debut LP. [iar]

PSYCHEDELIC FURS

The Psychedelic Furs (Columbia) 1980 ●
Talk Talk Talk (Columbia) 1981 ●
Forever Now (Columbia) 1982 ●
Mirror Moves (Columbia) 1984 ●
Midnight to Midnight (Columbia) 1987 ●

The Furs, whose lineup has varied substantially around a core of three (singer Richard Butler, his bassist brother Tim and guitarist John Ashton), came onto the London scene well after the initial punk explosion, but debuted with an album that mixed a drone-laden wall of noise (two guitars, sax and/or keyboards) and an odd adaptation of the quieter Bowie **Low**-style sound. The impact is shallow, due less to the profusion of producers than to the lyrics rasped by Butler in his bored, asthmatic drawl.

Talk Talk Talk, produced by Steve Lillywhite, displays surprising melodiousness in a newly crystallized style which amalgamates the Velvet Underground, **Highway 61**-era

Dylan and even **Revolver**-era Beatles, all given a fresh face and a driving beat. The wall of noise is sculpted to bring the components into sharp relief; Butler tosses off memorable imagery with mock-casual aplomb. The catchy opening track, "Pretty in Pink," served as the titular inspiration for a 1986 film and soundtrack album of the same name.

Butler writes to his strengths on **Forever Now**. Though the Furs had lost two key members, the others' increased sophistication—shored up by wisely-chosen session help (somber cello, horns, Flo & Eddie)—is orchestrated by Todd Rundgren in a major production coup, best exemplified by the brilliant single, "Love My Way."

In collaboration with producer and pro tem drummer Keith Forsey, the Furs turned decisively commercial on **Mirror Moves**, which is distinguished by a full side of memorable rockers written and played in the group's by-now-inimitable style. "The Ghost in You," "Here Come Cowboys," "Heaven" and "Heartbeat" may not be profound or timeless, but they do show perspicacity and exceptionally well-ordered playing and production.

Midnight to Midnight gets off to a fine start with "Heartbreak Beat," a deceptively restrained rocker lyrically reflecting Butler's relocation to New York, but then founders amid listenable but low-impact songs that sound overly self-derivative. The Furs may have grown into a reliable "new music" hit machine but, on this record at least, are running on empty.

Note: The first three LPs have different track sequences in their US and UK releases. Also, two tracks were substituted for a controversial cut on the first LP and one was altered and retitled on the third. [jg/iar]

PSYCHIC TV

Force the Hand of Chance (nr/Some Bizzare) 1982
Dreams Less Sweet (nr/Some Bizzare) 1983
N.Y. Scum Haters (nr/Temple) 1984
Berlin Atonal Vol. 2 (Ger. Atonal) 1984
25 December 1984—A Pagan Day
  (nr/Temple) 1985
Those Who Do Not (Ice. Gramm) 1985
Themes II (nr/Temple) 1985
Mouth of the Night (nr/Temple) 1985
Live in Paris (nr/Temple) 1986
Live in Tokyo (nr/Temple) 1986
Live in Heaven (nr/Temple) 1987

Live in Glasgow (nr/Temple) 1987
Live in Suisse (nr/Temple) 1987
Live in Gottingen (nr/Temple) 1987
Live in Toronto (nr/Temple) 1987
Live in Reykjavik (nr/Temple) 1987
Themes III (nr/Temple) 1987
The Yellow Album (nr/Temple) 1988
Allegory and Self (nr/Temple) 1988

PSYCHIC TV/Z'EV

Berlin Atonal Vol. 1 (Ger. Atonal) 1984

An album that appears to be devoted to an obscure faith known as "The Temple ov Psychick Youth" might be accepted on face value—after all, various cults have produced albums of devotional music to spread their gospel among rock fans. However, when the musicians behind the project are two ex-members of Throbbing Gristle (Genesis P-Orridge and Peter Christopherson), aided by a onetime Alternative TV-er (Alex Fergusson), it becomes much harder to judge where religious sincerity ends and elaborate put-on begins. Adding to the confusion, Stevo, who runs Some Bizzare (the label that originally abetted the group), is quoted on the back cover of their first album: "A naive person can open his eyes in life, but someone with his eyes open can never end up naive." Just who's kidding who here?

Force the Hand of Chance, regardless of its sincerity or utter lack thereof, is an amazing package: two records (one purported to be the partial soundtrack of a four-hour videocassette), a poster/booklet, pictured costumes, symbology and mail-order merchandise offerings. Musically, the main disc is a weird assortment of quiet ballads, screeching white noise, simple pop and more, with lyrics by P-Orridge that drift over terrain not all in keeping with the mystical concept. At times, form far outweighs function and some songs become merely effect without substance; others stand up nicely on their own regardless of the accompanying baggage. The adjunct record, **Psychick TV Themes**, uses real and imagined ethnic instruments from various exotic cultures to produce instrumentals that range from crazed to cool, intense to ephemeral—something like Eno's ambience filtered through a Spike Jones sensibility.

Dreams Less Sweet is another remarkable record, no less appealing for its equally abundant bizarrity. From the sweet vocal pop of "Hymn 23" or "White Nights" to pan-ethnic soundscapes and soundtracks that employ everything from English horn to Tibetan thigh-bone (as well as a lot of found sounds), PTV display an ineffable mastery of avant-garde dadaism as well as traditional musicmaking. Like tuning into a radio station overrun by university-educated acid-freaks, **Dreams Less Sweet** provides a thoroughly unpredictable and unsettling, yet utterly profound experience. The LP originally contained a bonus 12-inch entitled **The Full Pack**. (The cover photograph, while seemingly innocuous, is an astonishingly vulgar visual double entendre. Shades of **Lovesexy**.)

PTV has since continued to release disturbing live albums, featuring different lineups around the P-Orridge-Christopherson-Fergusson core. **Berlin Atonal Vol. 1**, recorded at a festival in December 1983, matches a grisly side of speaker-shredding, grinding, excruciating chaos by PTV with a side by American percussionist Z'ev. The limited edition (5,000) **N.Y. Scum Haters**—an all-PTV onslaught, captured at New York's Danceteria in November 1983—is better organized and recorded, more varied and sporadically more musical. There's still a lot of fearsome noise, but there's also some respite from the mania. **Berlin Atonal Vol. 2** is shared with a band called La Loora. **Mouth of the Night** is music to accompany a dance company.

In late '86, PTV began releasing a series of albums—all vintage concert recordings, each titled after the location of the performance—on the 23rd of each month. PTV has also released a pseudonymous record as Jack the Tab. [iar]

See also *Coil*.

PUBLIC ENEMY

Yo! Bum Rush the Show (Def Jam-Columbia) 1987 ●
It Takes a Nation of Millions to Hold Us Back (Def Jam-Columbia) 1988 ●

There are a lot of things about Public Enemy not to like. Besides the normal amount of braggadocio and self-promotion inherent in most rap, these radical black nationalists from New York's Long Island offer graphic accounts, if not outright glorification, of urban violence, a major selling point to critics who never ride the F train to Brooklyn. Their shows have gained notoriety for riotous crowds, and it could be argued that their sidemen on the stage with toy Uzi ma-

chine guns appeal to the mob's uglier side. The trio's logo is a silhouette of a man seen through the scope of a gun; they are ardent supporters of noted racist and anti-Semite Louis Farrakhan.

On the other hand, Public Enemy's first album is a brilliant combination of white-hot, hard-edged guitar thumping (supplied largely by Vernon Reid) and odd, off-kilter sampled sounds of all descriptions, topped with in-your-face raps by Chuck D and Flavor Flav, whose style is both rhythmic and conversational. **Yo! Bum Rush the Show** takes the musical innovations made in the rap genre by the likes of Run-DMC several steps further and is probably one of the best rap LPs ever made. But Public Enemy's attitude towards inner-city terror is seriously wack. [dgs]

PUBLIC IMAGE LTD.

Public Image (nr/Virgin) 1978 ●
Metal Box (nr/Virgin) 1979
Second Edition (Island) 1980 ●
Paris in the Spring (nr/Virgin) 1980
The Flowers of Romance (Warner Bros.) 1981
Live in Tokyo (nr/Virgin) 1983 (Elektra) 1986 ●
This Is What You Want . . . This Is What You Get (Elektra) 1984
Commercial Zone (PiL) 1984
Album/Cassette/Compact Disc (Elektra) 1986 ●
Happy? (Virgin) 1987 ●

The Sex Pistols were a tough act to follow, even for Johnny Rotten. After that band's entropic dissolution, Rotten reclaimed his civilian surname, Lydon, and started Public Image Ltd., supposedly more a way of life than a mere band, "rock" or otherwise.

PiL's opening salvo, **Public Image** (aka **First Issue**) couldn't seem to make up its mind between more-or-less straight rock (the unnaturally likable guitar drive of "Public Image") and musical endurance tests. "Annalisa" could be a Led Zeppelin backing track, but other cuts ("Theme," "Fodderstompf") are excruciating and/or self-indulgent. PiL knew they wanted to annoy, but were still working out the best way to do it.

They found the form on **Metal Box**, a brilliant statement, from original packaging—three 12-inch 45s in an embossed circular tin—to performance. Jah Wobble's overpowering bass sets up throbbing lines around which Keith Levene's guitar and keyboards flick in and out. Lydon wails, chants and moans impressionistic lyrics. A disturbing and captivating milestone. The limited-edition **Metal Box** wasn't cheap to produce, and so was reissued as **Second Edition**: the same music on two LPs in a gatefold sleeve. **Second Edition** benefits from printed lyrics and funhouse photos, but has inferior sound— this is *tactile* music—and a running order that makes less sense.

The live **Paris in the Spring** offers no new material, and may even have been released primarily to stifle a bootleg from the same concert. The band plays well, with drummer Martin Atkins—later known as Brian Brain—more noticeable than on **Metal Box**. But the Parisian audience is barely perceptible. All cover type (title, songs, etc.) is in French. Get the joke?

PiL shows a healthy desire not to repeat itself on **The Flowers of Romance**. With Wobble gone, Lydon relies on other resources; compared to this, **Metal Box** could be played in supermarkets. Lacking a bass, the "band" centers its "songs" around drum patterns and little else. Lydon's romantic imagery dabbles in ghostly apparitions ("Under the House") and Middle East chic ("Four Enclosed Walls"). He also serves up customary rants against hangers-on ("Banging the Door"), women ("Track 8") and Britain ("Go Back," "Francis Massacre"). But the music is so severe as to lend credence to a record executive's statement that **The Flowers of Romance** is one of the most uncommercial records ever made—at least within a "pop" context.

Never a comradely bunch, PiL seemed to unravel beyond repair when Levene left in 1983. But the band had just scored a surprise comeback demi-hit with "(This Is Not a) Love Song," so Lydon rounded up some unknown New Jersey accompanists and went to Japan. Only two of the ten tracks on **Live in Tokyo** are new songs; the faceless recruits are shoved in the back of the sonic mix; the album stretches about 45 minutes of material over two 12-inch 45s without **Metal Box**'s punch. Forget this one.

PiL had started work on **This Is What You Want** before Levene's departure. His guitar parts were wiped off the finished product, leaving them spiked only by Lydon's glum caterwauling. Levene saw to the release of his own version of the session tapes under the name **Commercial Zone**; the music here is considerably more interesting—perhaps even lively. By taking PiL seriously as a career, Lydon committed heresy against punk anomie. But at least he's still excruciating.

The same can't be said for the eminently listenable **Album** (or **Cassette** or **Compact Disc**, depending on your format of choice), which is either the worst sell-out of Lydon's career or the first popular-oriented PiL album ever. Dispensing with noise, free-form aggression and anti-music production, a stack of uncredited musicians play powerful, highly organized, prickly but accessible rock (and, on the brilliant "Rise," demi-pop) while Lydon masterfully bleats in near-tuneful harmony on top. The studio sound (courtesy Lydon and Bill Laswell) is live and virile; the seven tersely-titled songs ("FFF," "Home," "Ease") are as intelligent and captivating as any in PiL's past. **Album**. Great.

Happy? (co-produced by Gary Langan), hindered only by not-quite-as-good material, continues PiL's productive gambit of playing self-amused footsie with the rock audience. Despite conscious concessions to formal structures and traditions, the record maintains an unbending undercurrent of off-center subversion, manifested in skewed melodies, bizarrely contrapuntal instrumental figures and dub-styled percussion. Joined by a wonderful, tight band—guitarists Lu Edmonds (ex-Damned et al.) and John McGeoch (ex-Magazine, Siouxsie and the Banshees, Armoury Show), drummer Bruce Smith (Rip Rig + Panic, Float Up CP) and New York bassist Allan Dias—Lydon (or Rotten, depending on his fluctuating preference) is in peak form, creating captivating dance rock ("Seattle," "Hard Times," "The Body," "Fat Chance Hotel") that holds back the bile and intentional aggravation in favor of first-rate musicianship and invention.

[si/iar]

See also *Afrika Bambaataa, Brian Brain, Keith Levene, Jah Wobble.*

PUNISHMENT OF LUXURY

Laughing Academy (nr/UA) 1979

In its (few) better moments, Newcastle's Punilux resembled a cross between Roxy Music and a drunken edition of early XTC. The rest of this album is synth-sweetened heavy metal riffing from a minor talent turned sophomoric and sour. Favorite line: "Vanity has bum ways." [mf]

PURPLE ELECTRICITY

See *Red Cross.*

PURPLE HEARTS

Beat That! (nr/Fiction) 1980

While this LP shows them to be too derivative to be taken seriously, Purple Hearts were still one of the most sincere (or at least convincing) neo-mod bands. At points they closely approximate '65/'66 Who and Stones (and even endow a '66 Bowie single with more credibility than the original). Almost analogous to early Badfinger. [jg]

JIMMY PURSEY

Imagination Camouflage (nr/Polydor) 1980
Alien Orphan (nr/Epic) 1982

JAMES T. PURSEY

Revenge Is Not the Password (nr/Turbo) 1983
The Lord Divides (nr/Eskimo Green) 1983

As a solo artist, the earnest Sham 69 mouthpiece took a turn for the artier, leaving behind some of his plain-spoken charm as well as much of his obstreperousness in favor of more emotional and creative depth and range. Slide guitar, sax and even synthesizers broaden the instrumental palette of **Imagination Camouflage**; while none of the songs are excellent, they're almost all good. (Renegades from Generation X aided in composition and performance.)

Unfortunately, **Alien Orphan** goes almost too far. Leaving behind the stagey rock of its predecessor for a goulash of electro-rock-funk-jazz often held together by fluid, graceful bass riffing (guitar and keyboard are used only as embroidery), Pursey seems to have forgotten the notion of songs as songs, not elaborate aural concoctions. Still, it's swell background music—a meticulously constructed soundscape—and other than the parts that *do* try to be poignant or obvious, most of it does connect eventually, one way or another.

Revenge is similarly varied in its stylistic concept: eight spare semi-songs which wander off in different directions as if the idea of consistency had never occurred to the artist. Pursey is not the cleverest lyricist or suavest composer in the world, but his heart has always been in the right place and it's hard to denigrate sincerity. Although the album

doesn't hold up at all, a few of Pursey's unpredictable forays are odd enough to work.

[jg/iar]

PUSSY GALORE

Feel Good About Your Body EP (Shove) 1985
Groovy Hate Fuck (Shove) 1986
Pussy Gold 5000 EP (Buy Our) 1987
Right Now! (Caroline) 1987 ●
Groovy Hate Fuck (nr/Vinyl Drip) 1987

The aesthetic dilemma presented by intentionally offensive and/or consciously anti-musical groups is probably best settled by a critical rumble in the alley. There's certainly no rational way to discuss the potential merits of a record like this Washington, DC aim-to-offend quartet's four-song 7-inch debut or the eight-song 12-inch **Groovy Hate Fuck**, a raucous one-take no-rehearsal guitar-army tossoff. Setting the question of their atrocious non-musicianship aside, puerile compositions like "Teen Pussy Power," "Cunt Tease" and "Dead Meat" are nothing more than smears of self-satisfied juvenilia. You're *supposed* to be repulsed by Pussy Galore, but that certainly doesn't make this pathetic effluvia worth hearing. Cheap thrills for vulgar sissies.

Relocating to New York and adding a fifth member, the band issued two limited-edition cassettes at the end of 1986: an infamous home-brew version of **Exile on Main Street** (in its entirety) and a live set called **1 Yr. Live**.

Pussy Gold 5000, five-songs on a 12-inch, has improved—not good, but better—playing and sound. (On the studio tracks, that is. The live "No Count" is as wretched as ever.) It's still trash, but not quite as rank as before.

Following further personnel changes (one member defected to the much more likable Honeymoon Killers), Pussy Galore wound up a quartet: three guitarists (they've never had a bassist) and a metal-pounding percussionist. The full-length **Right Now!** album, co-produced (without credit) by the group, Big Black's Steve Albini and Bongwater's Kramer, has 19 songs of almost interesting garage raunch. The LP brings Pussy Galore into the realm of artistic consideration but reveals them as a fairly bad noise band. (The CD adds six previously-released tracks.)

The 1987 **Groovy Hate Fuck** import album is a compilation of the first three records. [iar]

PYLON

Gyrate (DB) 1980
Pylon!! EP (nr/Armageddon) 1980
Chomp (DB) 1983

This influential and highly-rated Athens, Georgia combo came on like a cross between the B-52's and Gang of Four. Atop thin, almost brittle, metallic guitar, bass and nononsense driving drums—which all mesh into stark but inviting dance rhythms—Vanessa Briscoe artlessly shouts/talks/gargles celebrations of life and innocent warnings/wonderings about restrictions on freedom. Though limited in material—the first two records contain about four really good songs all told; the rest are merely okay or repetitive—Pylon is fraught with possibilities for development. The 10-inch **Pylon!!** EP has two of their best, including the dance-club staple, "Cool."

Promise notwithstanding, **Chomp**, produced by Chris Stamey and Gene Holder (both then of the dB's), was the quartet's swan song. More ambitious in scope, Pylon incorporates a psychedelic drone in spots and sometimes sounds less anxious and strident than before. The album includes both melodic (!) sides of a great preceding single ("Crazy" b/w "M Train") and other cool slices ("Beep," "Gyrate") of floor-shaking art.

One of the most revered bands from the new South, Pylon did a reunion show in mid-'88 and is making moves toward a permanent return to action.   [jg/iar]

Q Q Q Q Q Q

Q-FEEL

Q-Feel (Jive) 1983

These tiresomely upbeat British techno-poppers recall the giddy chirp of Pilot, getting down to their appointed dance-music chores with mucho polish and absolutely no soul. The popular club single contained here, "Dancing in Heaven (Orbital Be-Bop)," is a descendant of "Pop Muzik," lacking only that song's charm and originality.   [iar]

QUANDO QUANGO

Pigs + Battleships (nr/Factory) 1985

A masterful assortment of big-beat grooves helped make Quando Quango, an Anglo-Dutch quartet, popular on dancefloors (if not record stores) on both sides of the Atlantic. Latin and jazz-tinged funk shares the spotlight with reggaefied disco; orchestration is primarily busy percussion beneath bass, keyboards and horns, with mostly tuneless, chanted vocals of lyrics that aren't exactly poetry. Playing and production are uniformly sharp, but Quando Quango would be best served with 12-inch dance mixes; an entire LP's worth becomes redundant and forgettable.   [dgs]

QUESTION MEN

We Could Be Wrong (Samsa) 1983

Although bands who name their record label after a Kafka character are immediately suspect, the casual cover photo of **We Could Be Wrong** rules out any grand pretensions this unique San Francisco quartet (which contains some former Units) might harbor. An uncommon lineup—bass, drums, sax and keyboards—provides a fascinating jazzy rock sound which underscores the songs. The title track, unlike its surroundings, is bouncy, likable and routine; otherwise, an uneasiness derives from the hollow, rhythmically complex arrangements and amelodic sax excursions. A slowly pulsing version of the Beatles' "Getting Better" pushes the mood a bit more upbeat, but is not likely to be mistaken for the original. Fans of offbeat rock will find the talented and inquisitive Question Men well worth a listen.   [iar]

QUICK

Mondo Deco (Mercury) 1976
Alpha/Beta EP (Quick Fan Club) 1978

After losing his grip on the Runaways, Kim Fowley discovered the Young Republicans, five male Californians he rechristened the Quick. They aspired to be an adolescent version of Sparks, playing melodic, Anglophilic tunes verging on bubblegum (like, but not as good as, Milk 'n' Cookies). Guitarist/songwriter Steven Hufsteter was pretty much the man in charge, and his limited talents shunted the Quick into a fairly tight mold; **Mondo Deco** is now more of an amusing artifact than it seemed at the time.

Alpha/Beta, a 10-inch souvenir of the group's unsuccessful attempt to court Elektra Records in 1977, came out early the following year through the band's fan club and showed they could draw on far more power than had previously been indicated. They're still basically Anglo/effete but, even on a version of "Somewhere Over the Rainbow," the Quick could manage real punch.   [iar/jg]

See also *Cruzados, Three O'Clock.*

QUIET SUN

See *Phil Manzanera.*

QUINCY

Quincy (Columbia) 1980

Abetted in their escape from the Bowery circuit by CBGB's owner, signed to a major label and produced by the talented Tim Friese-Greene, Quincy tried to make pleasant but predictable fare like "Critics' Choice" and "Roamin' Catholic" work in a crisp, slightly Carsish, neo-pop setting, but were too faceless to merit any daylight notice.

[iar]

ROBERT QUINE/FRED MAHER

Basic (EG) 1984

New York guitar master Quine (Voidoids/Lou Reed) and ex-Material drummer Maher recorded a mesmerizing no-frills celebration of the sound of the electric guitar. Over the pro forma mechanized rhythm patterns suggested by the title, the pair lay down their riffs and then Quine embroiders them—magically. Don't look for memorable tunes or even clever tricks—this is a player's album, amazingly pure, though not so simple. Warning: Quine and Maher are credited jointly with guitars, bass and drum programs, so don't assume that Quine plays all the guitar.

[mf]

See also *Jody Harris and Robert Quine, Richard Hell, Lou Reed.*

R R R R R R R R

MAXIM RAD
Times Ain't That Bad (Fr. Dreyfus) 1980

Odd fella, this Rad; not all of the strange verbal juxtapositions can be ascribed to gaps in his fuzzy grasp of English (I mean, "White Action, African Lemons"?). Rad seems to *want* to be outré and often is, though he's more compelling when direct. He gets a surprising amount of mileage out of a simple rock'n'roll/R&B format, thanks to darting, dirty-twanging guitar and hyperactive, fretless bass lines. Rad's vocal style offers hints of Tom Verlaine and Richard Hell, alongside Van Morrison and Jackson Browne. After a breakdown like this, you could be excused for thinking Rad's just plain confused; what makes him worth hearing is that, on the contrary, he's pretty darn engaging.   [jg]

RADIATORS FROM SPACE
TV Tube Heart (nr/Chiswick) 1977
RADIATORS
Ghostown (nr/Chiswick) 1979

London independent label Chiswick discovered these early Irish punk frontiersmen in Dublin; although never a commercial success, the Radiators from Space proved to be a wonderful musical find. Their recording career, which actually predated the debut vinyl of such first wavers as the Clash and Elvis Costello, evinces talent and intelligence far beyond many forgotten bands of that generation.

TV Tube Heart may not have been revolutionary, but energetic delivery of clever and melodic songs about such soon-to-become-hackneyed topics as the music press and club denizens make it a much better survivor of its era than many now hopelessly dated artifacts. From the outset, Radiators from Space showed themselves to be a better breed of punk.

Ghostown, produced by Tony Visconti, is nearly a power pop record with some unsettling flaws damaging another batch of good tunes. One item is almost identical to later Boomtown Rats (although who recorded it first is unclear); there's also a trite '50s homage that seems out of place. **Ghostown** does have its moments, though, and several tracks have the same wonderful feel as the second Fingerprintz LP. Obviously a band with great untapped potential, the Radiators were a surprisingly sophisticated bunch whose records are worth hearing.

In 1985, leader Philip Chevron surfaced in consort with Elvis Costello as a producer and performer; he then joined the Pogues.   [iar]

See also *Pogues.*

RADIO BIRDMAN
Burn My Eye EP (Aus. Trafalgar) 1976
Radios Appear (Sire) 1978
Living Eyes (Aus. WEA) 1981
VISITORS
Visitors (AR3D) 1982

The Saints' international success sent American and English labels scurrying to Australia. Sydney's Radio Birdman is what they brought back. The sextet (who could have used a capable producer on their one international LP) owed a lot to the Stooges and their predecessors; the band went so far as to co-write a song with Ron Asheton and record Roky Erickson's venerable "You're Gonna Miss Me." (The connection was Birdman guitarist Deniz Tek, who had grown up in Ann Arbor, Michigan.) Rounding off **Ra-**

dios **Appear** (an overhauled version of the band's first Australian indie LP) with a sendup/tribute to *Hawaii Five-O* ("Aloha Steve & Danno"), Radio Birdman did make its contribution. Over the years, their importance as Aussie punk pioneers—through ex-members' work with the likes of New Race (Tek and singer Rob Younger), the New Christs (Younger), Lime Spiders (bassist Warwick Gilbert) and the Screaming Tribesmen (guitarist Chris Masuak) and as a positive and seminal scene influence—has come to be better understood.

Living Eyes was recorded in Wales in 1978 but remained unreleased for three years, as Birdman had broken up soon after its completion. The Visitors was a band led by Tek and drummer Ron Keeley. [iar]

See also *New Order, Screaming Tribesmen.*

RADIO STARS
Songs for Swinging Lovers (nr/Chiswick) 1977
The Holiday Album (nr/Chiswick) 1978
Two Minutes, Mister Smith (nr/Moonlight) 1982

Britain's Radio Stars generally had more good ideas than they knew what to do with. On their two original albums they play fast-moving pop/rock with heavy overtones and a penchant for bizarre lyrical matter. On **Songs for Swinging Lovers** (even the cover is a poorly executed great idea), they come on like a 1977 version of singer Andy Ellison's legendary '60s psychedelic pop outfit, John's Children; faster and louder, but still decidedly off-center. Bassist Martin Gordon, fresh from a stint in Sparks (a band many compared to John's Children), supplies the odd ditties, covering such topics as rotting corpses, rapists and macaroni'n'mice casseroles. He even adds a jingle for the group's label, "Buy Chiswick Records." If Gordon's way with a tune were always up to his words, the band might have lived up to its name. But the quality of the material is too inconsistent to sustain interest for a whole album—there's too much dull, repetitive riffing.

The Holiday Album suffers from much the same malady as its predecessor: too many throwaways. For that reason, **Two Minutes, Mister Smith**, a posthumous compilation of singles and choice album tracks, is *the* Radio Stars album to own. The group's heights were almost all achieved on singles, especially the brilliant "From a Rabbit," a kitchen-sink pop production number of the highest order, included here. [ds]

RAGE TO LIVE
Rage to Live (Bar/None) 1986

The dissolution of New York's Individuals produced a number of positive local outgrowths. Doug and Janet Wygal formed a group under their family name and later recruited ex-dB Gene Holder for it; Glenn Morrow launched Bar/None Records, brought out They Might Be Giants' records and formed the inordinately likable Rage to Live with ex-Necessaries leader Ed Tomney. Morrow's limited voice proves no serious impediment to enjoying the album's well-written, exuberantly played melodies. Almost a sampler of contemporary New York/Hoboken stylings, Morrow's songs lean from mild soul to twangy cow-pop to a Marshall Crenshaw-like gossamer; the quartet plays 'em clean and sweet. Very nice. [iar]

RAINCOATS
The Raincoats (nr/Rough Trade) 1979
Odyshape (Rough Trade) 1981
The Kitchen Tapes [tape] (ROIR) 1983
Animal Rhapsody EP (nr/Rough Trade) 1983
Moving (nr/Rough Trade) 1984

The Raincoats introduced four English women parked on the fringes of conventional pop music. Or are they just an avant-garde edition of the Roches? The harmonies are there and the lyrics are esoteric and philosophical, eschewing predictable sentiments, but the music comes together only in spurts. A cover version of "Lola" plays havoc with that song's gender enigma. The rest of the songs just play havoc.

On **Odyshape**, the scope of the band's sound expands; the mingling of snappy acoustic and jangly electric guitars provides saner contrast to the violin shrieks. There's even a poignant song about a girl who's "Only Loved at Night." But the Raincoats are still no easy listen.

The Kitchen Tapes captures a December 1982 New York show, on which the Raincoats are supported by three demi-monde musicians. The playing, while still a bit low on the virtuosity index, shows refinement and development. In spots, the Raincoats spin a shimmery curtain of lovely sound; elsewhere, pan-cultural percussion supports fascinating vocal arrangements. But their potential for cacophony (better organized than before, but boisterous nonetheless) will keep you alternately straining to hear and jamming your fingers in your ears. **Moving** reprises some of the material from the live cassette; the four-song **Animal Rhapsody** EP in turn reprises two from the LP.   [gf/iar]

RAIN PARADE

Emergency Third Rail Power Trip (Enigma) 1983
Explosions in the Glass Palace EP (Enigma) 1984
Beyond the Sunset (Restless) 1985
Crashing Dream (Island) 1986

Like most of the bands implicated in the West Coast psychedelic revival (paisley underground, if you will), Rain Parade has a better ear for style than for substance. Most of the genre's bands tend to make very deft, subtle music but have nothing to say; Rain Parade at least knows the nuances of form better than anyone else. And if the Velvet Underground-meets-the Lemon Pipers pop sound tells more about who they like than who they are, at least the Paraders have good taste.

Emergency Third Rail Power Trip is a gentle record with neatly-crafted songs and mildly trippy textures. However, the retreat into style discourages listener identification and, while the songs make good background music, as foreground they're a snore. **Explosions in the Glass Palace** is a somewhat misleading title: there are, in fact, no explosions on this EP. But the sound is filled out and less generic. The record has a dreamlike quality to it—where the band once sounded lethargic, it now waxes hypnotic. The psychedelic touches, rather than offering a running historical narrative filled with inside jokes, give the pop structures some depth. Not a glandular jolt, but a nice quiet listen.

Crashing Dream, Rain Parade's major label debut, has one simply beautiful song ("Depending on You"). Another ("Mystic Green") sounds uncannily like the Records, while "Don't Feel Bad" hybridizes two Beatles songs (you figure out which ones). The album's flimsy but attractive, competent technique in search of a spine and a direction. **Beyond the Sunset** is a live album recorded in Japan.   [jl/iar]

See also *Opal, Windbreakers.*

RAISE THE DRAGON

Deliverance EP (IRS) 1984

INTIMATE STRANGERS

Charm (IRS) 1986

At his smoothest, Raise the Dragon's Richard Spellman sings like a debonair blend of David Bowie and Bryan Ferry (loud, his voice is quite less appealing); Sean Lyons provides attractive, fragile guitar threads. With backing from five sessionmen, including ex-Rumour bassist Andrew Bodnar, and production by Art of Noise's Anne Dudley, the crafty pair spin both lovely, melodic tunes ("The Blue Hour") and tedious light dance-rockers ("Deliverance" and "Raise the Dragon") on **Deliverance**. But an ill-advised cover of "Hold On (I'm Coming)" is laughable.

Returning two years later as Intimate Strangers, Spellman and Lyons released **Charm**, which contains two remixes and one peppy re-recording of their first EP's best songs and seven new creations in roughly the same plangent dance vein. Nicely done, but easily forgotten.   [iar]

PHILIP RAMBOW

Shooting Gallery (Capitol) 1979
Jungle Law (nr/EMI) 1981

Yet another singer who owes a considerable debt to Van Morrison, former Winkies leader Philip Rambow never fulfilled the promise of his appealing hot-coals-in-mouth singing style. On **Shooting Gallery** the Canadian is casual rather than driven—bouncy numbers like "Don't Call Me Tonto" and "The Sound and the Fury" could be downgraded fairly easily to fluff pop.

Jungle Law turns the heat up considerably, boasting sharper musicianship, memorable material and impassioned singing. The tunes seem drawn from life, especially "Snakes and Ladders" and "Beyond the Naked and the Dead." Phil Rambow may not be capable of matching the white-hot histrionics of Elvis Costello or Graham Parker, but **Jungle Law** proves he can make a direct, emotionally credible record.   [jy]

RAMONES

Ramones (Sire) 1976 ●
Leave Home (Sire) 1977 ●
Rocket to Russia (Sire) 1977
Road to Ruin (Sire) 1978
It's Alive (nr/Sire) 1979

End of the Century (Sire) 1980
Pleasant Dreams (Sire) 1981
Subterranean Jungle (Sire) 1983
Too Tough to Die (Sire) 1984
Animal Boy (Sire) 1986 ●
Halfway to Sanity (Sire) 1987 ●
Ramones Mania (Sire) 1988 ●

VARIOUS ARTISTS
Rock'n'Roll High School (Sire) 1979

With just four chords and one manic tempo, the New York's Ramones blasted open the clogged arteries of mid-'70s rock, reanimating the music. Their genius was to recapture the short/simple aesthetic from which pop had strayed, adding their own caustic sense of trash-culture humor and minimalist rhythm guitar sound. The result not only spearheaded the original new wave/punk movement, but also drew the blueprint for subsequent hardcore punk bands, most of whom unfortunately neglected the essential pop element.

Ramones almost defies critical comment. The 14 songs, averaging barely over two minutes each, start and stop like a lurching assembly line. Joey Ramone's monotone is the perfect complement to Johnny and Dee Dee's precise guitar/bass pulse. Since the no-frills production sacrifices clarity for impact, printed lyrics on the inner sleeve help even as they mock another pretentious convention—although the four-or-five-line texts of "Now I Wanna Sniff Some Glue," "I Don't Wanna Walk Around with You" and "Loudmouth" are an anti-art of their own. Like all cultural watersheds, **Ramones** was embraced by a discerning few and slagged off as a bad joke by the uncomprehending majority. It is now inarguably a classic.

The slightly glossier **Leave Home** is cut from the same cloth: another Ramones' dozen (14 hits) and under a half-hour in length. The band's warped Top 40 aspirations emerge on "I Remember You" and "Swallow My Pride," sandwiched between such anthems as "Gimme Gimme Shock Treatment" and "Pinhead." Like "Let's Dance" on **Ramones**, "California Sun" relates the band to the pandemic moronity that has always informed the best rock'n'roll.

Rocket to Russia is the culmination of the Ramones' primal approach. Virtually all 14 tracks (including ideal golden oldies "Do You Wanna Dance?" and "Surfin' Bird") are well-honed in execution, arrangement and songwriting wit. Clean production streamlines toe-tappers like "Cretin Hop," "Teenage Lobotomy" and "Rockaway Beach," and emphasizes Joey's increasingly expressive singing on two ballads, "I Don't Care" and "I Wanna Be Well." The LP also contains the Ramones' naive first attempt at a hit single, "Sheena Is a Punk Rocker."

"Sheena" only scraped the charts, and drummer Tommy Ramone (né Erdelyi) left, to be replaced by ex-Voidoid (and ex-Dust!) Marky Ramone (né Marc Bell). The Ramones had spewed out well over 40 tracks (including a couple of B-sides) inside of two years. They next emerged with **Road to Ruin**, an understandably downbeat collection. Desperate to join the mainstream, the band lengthened its material, even breaking the three-minute barrier on "I Wanted Everything" and "Questioningly," a touching love song. Despite the perky "I Wanna Be Sedated," pretty "Don't Come Close" and oldie "Needles and Pins," **Road to Ruin** is a bit lackluster; earlier rave-ups, unlike "I'm Against It" and "Go Mental," never sounded forced. A rethink seemed in order.

Meanwhile, the band lent their musical and dramatic talents to the movie *Rock'n' Roll High School.* The soundtrack album includes two new compositions (one the theme song), an 11-minute live medley of previously-recorded tunes, plus the Ramones backing the Paley Brothers ("C'mon Let's Go") and co-star P.J. Soles (on a different version of "Rock'n'Roll High School"). Appropriate songs by various artists fill out the record. Anyone whose appetite for live Ramones was whetted by the film soundtrack should seek out **It's Alive**, a two-disc London concert recording (with Tommy drumming) that pretty much reprises their first three albums.

End of the Century features intimidating production by the legendary Phil Spector. The band responds with a good brace of songs whose polish and (relative) wordiness show them outgrowing punk. Dubious bonus: Joey warbling "Baby, I Love You." On **Pleasant Dreams**, the Ramones move away from their pioneering minimalism and into heavy metal territory, although distinctive lyrics insured they hadn't lost their grasp of teenage angst.

Subterranean Jungle put the Ramones back to where they once belonged: junky '60s pop adjusted for current tastes. That means not only a couple of acid-age oldies ("Time Has Come Today," "Little Bit o' Soul") but original tunes with male protagonists hung up on girls and themselves. It also means easing off the breakneck rhythm that was once Ramones dogma. **Subterranean Jungle** is an underrated item in the band's canon.

On **Too Tough to Die**—with Richie Ramone as the new drummer and Tommy Erdelyi returning as co-producer—the Ramones got serious about stealing back some thunder from the hardcore punk scene they'd inspired. The sound is more ferocious than ever, and they dip back into quick-hit song lengths. Some by-now predictable macho sentiments (the title track, "I'm Not Afraid of Life") are offset by the token dose of sensitivity ("Howling at the Moon," guest-produced by Eurythmician Dave Stewart). But the Eddie Cochranesque "No Go" that closes the album shows they haven't lost their sense of humor.

The Ramones' big release in what was for them an otherwise quiet 1985 was "Bonzo Goes to Bitburg," a UK-only 45 assailing Ronald Reagan for the itinerary of his German vacation. That song, retitled "My Brain Is Hanging Upside Down," turned up on **Animal Boy**. Produced by ex-Plasmatic Jean Beauvoir, the Ramones resemble a straight rock band as never before (mostly in the drum sound and articulated rhythm guitar). The animal-theme record has typically entertaining entries (Richie's "Somebody Put Something in My Drink," a wistful ballad called "She Belongs to Me"); Dee Dee (the LP's main songwriter) affects a quasi-British accent to sing "Love Kills," a Pistols-styled tribute to Sid'n'Nancy just in time for Alex Cox's film. Meanwhile, the nostalgically terse "Eat That Rat" is the Ramones' closest brush with punk in years.

The years of stylistic foundering ended on **Halfway to Sanity**, a bracing and confident-sounding dose of Ramones fundamentalism. The dozen cuts mix basic guitar riffs ("I Know Better Now," "Bop 'Til You Drop") and effervescent pop ("Go Lil' Camaro Go," with guest vocals by Debby Harry, "A Real Cool Time"), adding some of the most intriguingly thoughtful lyrics ("I Wanna Live," "Garden of Serenity") in the band's career. This encouraging and long-due return to top form also benefits from gutsy rock production by the band and Wild Kingdom guitarist Daniel Rey. (The UK CD adds the bubblegum classic "Indian Giver" and "Life Goes On.")

Also in 1987, "Dee Dee King" (with the aid of Rich Reinhardt, who had just relinquished the band's drum chores to Marc Bell) released a solo record, the inexcusably stupid rap-rock 12-inch, "Funky Man."

The long-overdue **Ramones Mania** compilation packs 30 cuts onto two digitally remastered discs (some of the tracks sound ace; others don't fare so well), adding detailed annotation and Billy Altman's voluminous liner notes. Although the song selection is straightforward, the running order is entirely non-chronological; a British B-side ("Indian Giver"), a previously unvinylized movie mix of "Rock'n'Roll High School" and a couple of 45 versions make it mildly attractive to collectors. Despite such dubious inclusions as "Commando," "Wart Hog" and "Momma's Boy," **Ramones Mania** isn't a bad textbook for Ramones 101.   [si/iar]

See also *Holly and the Italians, Rattlers.*

RANDY RAMPAGE
Randy Rampage EP (Can. Friend's) 1982

Early D.O.A. bassist Rampage—with assists from ex-D.O.A. drummer Chuck Biscuits and former members of California's Dils and Avengers—shows he can almost approximate solid, even (gasp) "musical" punk rock, if he'd just tighten up his wig (and get a producer).   [jg]

LEE RANALDO
See *Sonic Youth.*

ERIC RANDOM
That's What I Like About Me EP (nr/New Hormones) 1981
Earthbound Ghost Need (nr/New Hormones) 1982

ERIC RANDOM & THE BEDLAMITES
Time-Splice (nr/Doublevision) 1985
Ishmael (nr/Fon) 1987

Experimental multi-instrumentalist (and Cabaret Voltaire associate) Random dabbles in a wide variety of styles, hopping around from art-noise to reggae to jazz to non-Western idioms. But instead of merely regurgitating these genres, Random gives them unusual arrangements, adding odd and eerie synths, guitar, percussion, etc.

That's What I Like About Me is a four-track 12-inch whose sound owes much to early Cab Volt; over a cheap little rhythm box and simple bass riffs, Random layers a plethora of synth washes, treated vocals and other assorted sounds. The one live cut shows no loss of sonic capabilities that might be expected from such a techno-noodler.

Time-Splice (on Cab Volt's label) features much cleaner production and sharper playing than on Random's first album, **Earthbound Ghost Need** (title derived from William Burroughs' *Naked Lunch*), which includes a version of Ravel's *Bolero* that would have left *10*'s Bo Derek in a much different mood. Production, arrangements and styles seem to take priority over songwriting, but Random is a talented artist.

[dgs]

RANK AND FILE

Sundown (Slash-Warner Bros.) 1982
Long Gone Dead (Slash-Warner Bros.) 1984
Rank and File (Rhino) 1987 ●

Rank and File first came together in Austin, Texas, although three of the four original members were Californians who had played in San Diego's Dils and San Francisco's Nuns. The distance from those early punk outfits is more than geographical: Rank and File was formed to play delicately crafted cowboy rock. (Imagine if Marshall Crenshaw had been raised on a straight diet of Hank Williams.) David Kahne's production of **Sundown** gives a squeaky clean sound to the tuneful and tasty pop numbers that also benefit from pretty harmonies and confident playing. Effortlessly enjoyable.

But, alas, too good to last. **Long Gone Dead** retains only half the band—brothers Chip and Tony Kinman (the main creative force on **Sundown**, writing almost all the songs)—joined by such temps as Tom Petty drummer Stan Lynch. It's hard to pin down the problem: **Long Gone Dead** has all the right ingredients but only a skimpy bit of **Sundown**'s evocative magnificence. Perhaps it's Jeff Eyrich's production, which is fussier than Kahne's and partially obscures the Kinmans' melody-laden writing and rich vocals. Lacking the first LP's lost and lonesome prairie feel, **Long Gone Dead** is appealing but disappointing.

Hanging onto **Long Gone Dead** guitarist Jeff Ross, the Kinmans added a permanent drummer and kept going, but didn't release another album for three years. The loud run-of-the-mill rock production on **Rank and File** doesn't totally obscure the melodies and

Tony's fine voice, but the band's wandering personality all but evaporates in the guitar solos, bass riffs and overeager drumming.

[iar]

See also *True Believers*.

RANKING ROGER

See *(English) Beat, General Public*.

RATIONAL YOUTH

Cold War Night Life (Can. YUL) 1982
Heredity (Capitol) 1985

Although this Canadian synthesizer trio occasionally lapses into lyrical pomposity, for the most part, Rational Youth serves up fresh sounds and workable songs that show lots of promise. A bit like early Human League (but not grim), **Cold War Night Life** is a well-produced LP from talented technicians with minds *and* hearts. **Heredity** blends in more guitar for increased commercial appeal, but maintains a certain down-to-earth spunkiness that distinguishes Rational Youth from other post-Duran tech-pop bands. Flash of fame footnote: the group was later featured—on the soundtrack and in a concert scene—in a Canadian Kiefer Sutherland movie called *Crazy Moon*. [iar]

RATTLERS

Rattled! (PVC) 1985

Led by Joey Ramone's soundalike younger brother Mickey Leigh, New York's Rattlers take a less stylized but equally sincere approach to essential '60s pop on **Rattled!**, a swell LP of zesty originals and cool covers partially produced by ex-Ramone Tommy Erdelyi. The quartet uses a touch of keyboards and neat vocal harmonies to dress up simply-drawn tunes like the melodic "I Won't Be Your Victim," the beat-era "Pure + Simple" and imaginary monster-movie theme song "On the Beach." An ace version of obscure '60s punk classic "Little Black Egg" (originally by the Nightcrawlers, but also covered by Bebe Buell and the Chant) is worth the price of admission, but the rest of the LP won't disappoint. [iar]

See also *Lester Bangs*.

RAUNCH HANDS

El Rauncho Grande EP (Relativity) 1985
Learn to Whap-a-Dang with the Raunch
    Hands (Relativity) 1986

In their mid-'80s heyday (such as it was), New York's Raunch Hands were retro-rock representatives of that presumed golden age of sleaze, the mid-'50s to mid-'60s. Thus **El Rauncho Grande** offers neo-rockabilly, neo-R&B and even neo-Mex, all filtered through the band's beer-heightened (lowered?) sensibilities. **Learn to Whap-a-Dang** is less quaint than the EP, and its denser band sound helps the Raunch Hands barrel through their own R&B: Raucous & Bawdy. Mike Chandler isn't much of a singer, but attitude counts for a lot here, and Mike Tchang's occasional sax is a definite plus. Too bad their originals (about half of each record) can't match the '50s obscurities for sheer mindlessness—not counting **Whap-a-Dang**'s "Kangaroo Juice," an "original" stolen from Eddie Cochran. [si]

RAVE-UPS

Class Tramp EP (Fun Stuff) 1984
Town + Country (Fun Stuff) 1985
The Book of Your Regrets (Epic) 1988 ●

At the time they were being touted as the next big thing to break out of the LA club scene, the Rave-Ups were working as mailroom clerks and warehouse grunts at A&M Records. Although launched by singer/guitarist Jimmer Podrasky in Pittsburgh, the group on the 1984 EP was a quartet he assembled in California. **Class Tramp** is a mighty impressive debut, a hook-laden six-song rocking pop collection that reveals Podrasky as an inventive, commercially-minded songwriter with a wealth of ideas and a fresh lyrical perspective. Richly multi-tracked guitars, crisp rhythms and easy-to-like vocals buttress original tunes that deftly sidestep power pop and other pigeonholes.

Podrasky and drummer Timothy Jimenez acquired a new bassist and guitarist before recording the refined *and* ruralized **Town + Country**, a good (not great) record that gives away some of the EP's '60sish pluck to take an energetic crack at unstylized Southwestern twang and winds up sounding a shade or two less distinguished than before. Pedal-steel master Sneaky Pete Kleinow plays on two tracks. The record still manages a fair amount of variety: "Remember (Newman's Lovesong)" is almost a bluegrass breakdown done as a rock song, while "Positively Lost Me" (one of two songs the band performed in *Pretty in Pink*) tells of a broken relationship with only a mild country touch.

The lighthearted Beach Boys car-song parody of "In My Gremlin" harks back to **Class Tramp**; Dylan's "You Ain't Goin' Nowhere" becomes an uptempo rocker.

Indeed, the Rave-Ups couldn't find the record industry's on-ramp for a long while, and it was three years before Epic issued **The Book of Your Regrets**. Guitarist Terry Wilson takes a more prominent role here, co-writing most of the material with Podrasky and expanding his instrumental contribution to include mandolin, keyboards and harmonica. While retaining a glimmer of the previous LP's country inflection, this well-produced (by David Leonard) record leans towards the textured, harmony-laden sound of West Coasters like Translator, Peter Case and Wire Train. Consistently invigorating and remarkably original, **The Book of Your Regrets** signals the Rave-Ups' unyielding vitality and creative resources. [iar]

RAW POWER

Screams from the Gutter (Toxic Shock) 1985
Wop Hour EP (Toxic Shock) 1986
After Your Brain (Toxic Shock) 1987

In an interesting bit of Euro-American hardcore fraternity, the debut album by this Italian punk band—five guys from Reggio—was recorded in Indiana and issued by a California label. On **Screams from the Gutter**, Raw Power play genre creations like "Hate," "Nihilist," "Bastard" and "My Boss" with fiery punk venom, helpfully singing them in English. (The cassette adds the contents of **Wop Hour**, a subsequent four-song 7-inch.)

After Your Brain offers far better production and more instrumental refinement, but Raw Power still burns up the grooves on 13 new cuts like "You Are Fired," "We Shall Overcome," "Shut Up" and "What For." Mauro's careful diction makes him clearer and more understandable than many American vocalists; the two guitarists (one of them a new arrival in the band) work hard to avoid sounding routine. A powerful piece of work. [iar]

RAYBEATS

Roping Wild Bears EP (nr/Don't Fall off the Mountain) 1981
Guitar Beat (PVC) 1981
"It's Only a Movie!" (Shanachie) 1983

With so many late-'70s musicians possessing a strong sense of rock'n'roll history in addition to their overriding interest in style, the emergence of groups like the instrumental Raybeats was inevitable. Pat Irwin, Jody Harris and Don Christensen, refugees from the New York City no-wave avant-garde, had been in such outfits as the Contortions and 8-Eyed Spy. Together (with a procession of bassists including, on **Guitar Beat**, Danny Amis), they made frothy rock dance pieces, recalling the tightly structured formats of the Ventures, Duane Eddy and the Shadows. The simple melodies are defined by sparkling guitars, junky organ and wailing sax—a golden opportunity for most educated bands to condescend. But the Raybeats never did. They obviously enjoyed what they were playing, and that made their records absolutely lovable.

The **Wild Bears** EP offers four songs (including the Shadows' "Rise and Fall of Flingel Bunt") on a 12-inch. The UK and US versions of the peppy **Guitar Beat**, ably produced by Martin Rushent, differ by two tracks. **"It's Only a Movie!"** introduces electronic instruments (and ceramic destruction on "Doin' the Dishes") to remind listeners of the band's actual time frame, but also includes appropriately dated covers: Henry Mancini's "Banzai Pipeline" and Booker T's "Jelly Bread." [jy/iar]

See also *Jody Harris.*

RAYMEN
Going Down to Death Valley (Ger. Rebel) 1985
Desert Drive (Ger. Rebel) 1986
Tonight the Raymen: From the Trashcan to the Ballroom (Blue Turtle) 1988

Imagine a band playing Cramps-type stuff, somewhere out in the heartland. Now imagine that heartland's in Germany, and you'll have some idea of how bizarre the Raymen are. The guitar-bass-drums-singer dementobilly combo hails from Dortmund, which has been described as the Gary, Indiana of West Germany; maybe they're not as inspired as the Cramps or Shockabilly, but fun anyhow.

The first LP is charmingly wacked-out and trashy. One leader of the hit parade is "I'm a Hillbilly Werewolf," which Hank Ray sings with as much sincerity as anyone could muster for such a song. (His heavily echoed baritone typically hits the right notes at least two-thirds of the time.) The title track is the Raymen's idea of traditional cowboy country

music (where they're usually most effective), and includes suitably strange slide guitar. Axeman Martin Toulouse uses feedback, slide, fuzz-box and twang-bar to excellent noisemaking effect throughout the LP (if anything, not often enough). A so-horrible-it's-grand rendition of "Locomotion" completes the picture.

Desert Drive isn't as good. The new rhythm section is an improvement, but the material doesn't hold up. Toulouse puts down his slide and doesn't go wild as often. Ray is most fun when he's frantically stuttering and echoing every word into complete unintelligibility, which doesn't happen much here.

The third album continues both trends. There's more music (17 tracks on two 45 rpm discs) but less frenzy from Ray and less craziness from Toulouse (if it's him—guitar is credited to Junior Ray). When he does let it all hang out, as on "Saturn Doll," it sounds like it could well be our man. There's still some of the crew's trademark wigginess, but only on half the tracks; they do take the time to bludgeon the Contours' "Do You Love Me" into complete submission, though.
[jg]

REAL KIDS
Real Kids (Red Star) 1978
Outta Place (Star-Rhythm) 1982
All Kindsa Jerks Live (Fr. New Rose) 1983
Hit You Hard (Fr. New Rose) 1983
TAXI BOYS
Taxi Boys EP (Star-Rhythm) 1981
Taxi Boys EP (Bomp) 1981
REAL KIDS/TAXI BOYS
Girls! Girls! Girls! (Fr. Lolita) 1983
JOHN FELICE & THE LOWDOWNS
Nothing Pretty (Ace of Hearts) 1988

The Real Kids were one of Boston's earliest new wave bands; their debut album is full of dynamite tracks that take the trashier aspect of the Rolling Stones and couple it with the high-power guitar approach of the Ramones. Frontman (and onetime Modern Lover) John Felice not only provides tough guitar and distinctive lead vocals, but also has a knack for writing clear, infectious melodies. Spin "All Kindsa Girls," "She's Alright" or "My Baby's Book" for proof.

Poor sales of the first Real Kids LP led to Felice becoming a Ramones roadie, but he subsequently returned to Boston and formed the Taxi Boys, whose two EPs (each with a different lineup) carry on the Real Kids tradition with high-energy '60s garage-band rock. The production of the records might be crude, but Felice is in fine form on both. (The Bomp release is a 12-inch, the earlier one a 7-inch pressed on pink vinyl.)

Reactivating the Real Kids with a new and improved lineup, Felice then made the dandy **Outta Place**. Harder yet still pop-oriented, with stellar production by Andy Paley, the record is strengthened by consistently good material and plenty of rock'n'roll spirit. After releasing the album in France, that country's New Rose label kept the Real Kids' recording career going, issuing another sharp studio LP, **Hit You Hard**, and the live-in-Paris **All Kindsa Jerks Live**, which recaps Felice's song catalogue onstage with fiery enthusiasm. The Lolita release is a Real Kids/Taxi Boys compilation.

After five years of national invisibility, Felice returned, unrepentant and embittered, with a rocking new trio and the **Nothing Pretty** album. Although his casual writing and punchy guitar playing is in fine shape, uncertain singing undercuts the songs' impact somewhat; Felice's attitude is likewise a little worse for wear. The title track rues the loss of innocence; "I'll Never Sing That Song Again" describes a view of life as a musician that is both cynical and poignant; "Nowadaze Kids" tells the other side of the story, castigating modern audiences for lacking the rock'n'roll spirit that inspires him. Fans who fear that he's becoming too disgusted to carry on should take note of the LP's final cut, "Can't Play It Safe." [cpl/iar]

RECORDS

Shades in Bed (nr/Virgin) 1979
The Records (Virgin) 1979
Crashes (Virgin) 1980
Music on Both Sides (Virgin Int'l) 1982

Like the Motors, the Records were reborn pub-rockers, who made a giant leap into the present by leaving their history behind and starting afresh with finely honed pop craftsmanship and the full-scale record company support they had never previously enjoyed. While the Motors went for grandiose production numbers, the Records—led by ex-Kursaal Flyer drummer Will Birch—made sharp, tuneful confections that offered maximum hooks-per-groove in a classic Anglo-pop style not unlike the Hollies, with

similarly brilliant harmonies and ringing guitars.

Shades in Bed (resequenced, retitled **The Records** and dressed in a completely different cover for America) is a wonderful LP, featuring song after song of pure pop with clever lyrics and winning melodies. Almost every track could have been a single; "Starry Eyes" and "Teenarama" were actually released, which left "Girls That Don't Exist," "Affection Rejected" and "Girl" as untested chart material. The English album included a bonus 12-inch, **High Heels** (an untitled 7-inch in the US), of the Records' renditions of four classic tracks, including the Kinks' "See My Friends" and Spirit's "1984."

Crashes, produced mainly by Craig Leon, showcased a revised lineup, Jude Cole having taken Huw Gower's guitar slot. (Gower resurfaced a continent away in David Johansen's band around 1982.) Nothing here can match the first LP's charm except for two tracks produced by Mick Glossop—"Man with a Girl Proof Heart," written while Birch was still a Kursaal Flyer, and "Hearts in Her Eyes," which was done better by the Searchers later that year. At best a weak rehash of the first LP, **Crashes** is passable, but hardly a great follow-up.

After a two-year recording gap, **Music on Both Sides** introduced a new five-piece lineup, with guitarist Dave Whelan and singer Chris Gent joining the surviving core of Birch, bassist Phil Brown and guitarist John Wicks. Birch produced this muddled but generally pleasant album, which sounds like **Rubber Soul** with a crappy rock singer. Not a great parting shot, although less annoyingly precious than their early work.

[iar]

See also *Huw Gower.*

RED BOX

The Circle & the Square (Sire) 1986 ●

This fascinating British twosome takes an offbeat and rewarding direction on their first album, folding American Indian (covering Buffy Sainte-Marie in the process) and other ethnic folk influences into sophisticated modern pop creations for an unpredictable and indescribable pan-ethnic mélange. Unlike arid studio-based partnerships, Simon Toulson Clarke (vocals, acoustic guitar) and Julian Close (programming, flute, sax) make warm and varied music, much of it employing a vocal chorus which adds African color.

The evocative lyrics bring a global political intelligence to the songs, making them not only appealing but affecting as well. Something like a less stern Peter Gabriel LP, this imaginative and engaging record is simply astonishing. [iar]

RED CRAYOLA

Parable of Arable Land (International Artists) 1967 + 1980 (nr/Radar) 1978
God Bless the Red Crayola and All Who Sail on Her (IA) 1968 + 1980 (nr/Radar) 1979
Soldier-Talk (nr/Radar) 1979
Three Songs on a Trip to the U.S.A. EP (nr/Recommended) 1984

ART & LANGUAGE AND THE RED CRAYOLA

Corrected Slogans (Music Language) 1976 (nr/Recommended) 1982
Kangaroo? (Rough Trade) 1981

RED CRAYOLA WITH ART & LANGUAGE

Black Snakes (Sw. Rec-Rec) 1983

MAYO THOMPSON

Corky's Debt to His Father (nr/Glass) 1986

Red Crayola first surfaced on Texas' International Artists label during the psychedelic era of the mid-'60s, with **Parable of Arable Land** and **God Bless the Red Crayola and All Who Sail on Her**. Rather unusual even for that time, the group faded into limbo until turning up to do sessions in 1976 with the Art & Language organization, which yielded the demos collected on **Corrected Slogans**; the album parallels somewhat the serious/silly music of Robert Wyatt. Largely acoustic in nature, **Corrected Slogans** has extremely simple songs, operatic vocals and complex lyrics that are satirical and/or political. It qualifies as rock only by association.

Radar Records, exhilarated by the critical success of Pere Ubu's dada punk, reissued **Parable of Arable Land** in 1978 and **God Bless** in 1979. Mayo Thompson and partner Jesse Chamberlain reformed Red Crayola to make **Soldier-Talk**, aided by Lora Logic and the entirety of Pere Ubu. Uniting Red Crayola's flower-power garage music with modernistic, fragmented arrangements and a fierce, broken beat, the album centers on cynical military themes. A challenging work.

Kangaroo?, reuniting Red Crayola with Art & Language, tones down the chaos for a musical discussion of Soviet Communist ideals and history, including a gentle, poignant instrumental, "1917." More in the style of avant-garde theater music than rock, the LP is like Brecht out of Vivian Stanshall, with impressive results. **Black Snakes** has more of Thompson's dramatic vocals and features Ubu's Allen Ravenstine on sax and synth. The cornerstone tracks are "The Sloths," a prolix acid fable, the puerile "Ratman, the Weightwatcher" and "A Portrait of V.I. Lenin in the Style of Jackson Pollock." [sg/iar]

RED CROSS

Red Cross EP (Posh Boy) 1980
Born Innocent (Smoke 7) 1982

REDD KROSS

Teen Babes from Monsanto (Gasatanka) 1984
Born Innocent (Frontier) 1986
Neurotica (Big Time) 1987 ●

VARIOUS ARTISTS

The Siren (Posh Boy) 1980
Desperate Teenage Lovedolls (Gasatanka) 1984
Lovedolls Superstar (SST) 1986

SKY "SUNLIGHT" SAXON AND PURPLE ELECTRICITY

Private Party (Voxx) 1986

TATER TOTZ

Alien Sleestacks from Brazil (Gasatanka-Giant) 1988

Originally known as the Tourists, Red Cross was formed in Hawthorne, California (home of the Beach Boys) by brothers Steve and Jeff McDonald and high school chums Ron Reyes (later of Black Flag) and Greg Hetson (a future Circle Jerk). Through various lineups, adventures and setbacks, the McDonalds have kept their group going and growing, turning Redd Kross into the bemused focus of an increasing national cult.

Red Cross' recorded debut (later reissued as a stand-alone 12-inch EP) was on **The Siren**, a three-band sampler LP. Although bassist Steve was barely 13 at the time, the six tracks sound surprisingly self-assured. The culturally resonant snot-punk-rock-pop selections include "Annette's Got the Hits" (which proved to be an LA radio staple), "I Hate My School" and the B-52'sish "Standing in Front of Poseur" (a hip clothing store).

After Hetson and Reyes left, the McDonalds formed a new band and released 1982's **Born Innocent**. (It was subsequently re-released under their post-legal-intervention name.) The LP celebrates such wonderful pop anti-idols as "Linda Blair," "Charlie" (Manson) and Patty Hearst; although unmentioned on the sleeve and label (for fear he would come after them for royalties) the LP actually includes a cover of Manson's "Cease to Exist." The muddy sound and sloppy, uninspired playing make **Born Innocent** dull in spots, but Jeff's wild-eyed singing and the overall junk-is-good aesthetic make it a record of—and for—its time.

Ex-Black Flag singer Dez Cadena had already come and gone through Redd Kross by the time Geza X produced the seven-song **Teen Babes from Monsanto**. Running strictly on wicked irreverence, the McDonalds and drummer Dave Peterson turn the spotlight on various musical victims, and the Redd Kross living jukebox bangs out loud and convincing covers of Kiss ("Deuce"), the Stones ("Citadel"), Stooges ("Ann"), Bowie ("Savior Machine") and others, leaving "Linda Blair 1984" the sole original. A record of the ultimate bratty garage band in its element.

With Redd Kross providing most of the music, the McDonalds appeared in *Desperate Teenage Lovedolls,* a no-budget Super-8 psychotronic Z-movie made by LA scenesters. The soundtrack album—tracks by Black Flag and a few minor bands as well as various interlocking permutations of Redd Kross and White Flag—is well-produced and for the most part a real offhand treat. "Legend," by Redd Kross with their manager, Joanna Spockolla McDonald (we're all McDonalds in this life), singing, is typical of the rocking pop that keeps the record hopping. Redd Kross offered the same service for the soundtrack album of the sequel, *Lovedolls Superstar,* which includes a brilliant rendition of "Sunshine Day," an obscure *Brady Bunch* chestnut.

Drummer Roy McDonald (no relation) and guitarist Robert Hecker fill out the lineup card on **Neurotica**, the band's national underground breakout record. The LP reclaims "Ballad of a Love Doll" from the first film's score and adds such fuzzed-out folk-pop acid trips as "Peach Kelli Pop," "Janus, Jeanie, and George Harrison," "Frosted Flake" and "Ghandi Is Dead (I'm the Cartoon Man)." With harmony-heavy arrangements that occasionally suggest Shoes, Redd

Kross has never sounded better—a full-fledged mind-boggling outing that confirms their potential and makes the next record something to anticipate. (The CD appends "Tatum O'Tot," a hint of what was in store.)

Joined by various collaborators, Special Guest Tater Danny Bonaduce (David Cassidy's kid brother on *The Partridge Family*) and such Accessory Tots as Michael Quercio of Three O'Clock, Steve and Jeff launched their motley but funny side band, the Tater Totz, on **Alien Sleestacks from Brazil**, subtitled "Unfinished Music Volume 3." Besides perpetrating such cover atrocities as "Give Peace a Chance," "I've Just Seen a Face," "Sing This All Together," "We Will Rock You" and "Tomorrow Never Knows," the record offers a seemingly endless and vicious version of Yoko Ono's "Don't Worry Kyoko."

Hooking up with a genuine '60s acid-rock casualty, the McDonalds and a drummer, under the name Purple Electricity, played a show with ex-Seeds leader Sky Saxon. **Private Party**, recorded at LA's Cavern Club in March '86, is a muffled bootleg-quality piece of tripe that includes Saxon originals and sketchy covers (like "Dazed and Confused") retitled and credited to him.   [iar]

RED GUITARS

Slow to Fade (nr/Self Drive) 1984 ●
Tales of the Expected (nr/Virgin) 1986

On their major-label debut, Hull's Red Guitars sound briefly like Cockney Rebel (from whom they borrow the refrain of "Sweetwater Ranch"), as well as Lloyd Cole, Bowie, Aztec Camera and Dream Academy. The quintet's light songs are pretty flimsy; guitarist Robert Holmes' vocals are likewise second-rate. While delicate and varied, arrangements and production alone can't make up for **Tales of the Expected**'s inherent lack of *raison d'être*.   [iar]

RED HOT CHILI PEPPERS

The Red Hot Chili Peppers (Enigma-EMI America) 1984
Freaky Styley (EMI America) 1985
The Uplift Mofo Party Plan (EMI Manhattan) 1987 ●
The Abbey Road EP (EMI Manhattan) 1988

Awesomely powerful and remorselessly sarcastic, this California quartet melds floor-shaking rock-funk to wickedly clever songs like "True Men Don't Kill Coyotes," "Baby Appeal" and "Get Up and Jump" on their debut album. The Chili Peppers, who aren't above a little self-obsessed boasting or earnest political protest, play a thoroughly entertaining mutation of George Clinton, Was (Not Was), Peter Wolf, Sly Stone, Kurtis Blow, Sonic Youth and Wall of Voodoo. Shake it, but make sure you pay attention at the same time!

Founding guitarist Hillel Slovak, who had missed the Peppers' debut LP during a stint with What Is This, returned to the fold in time for the second outing. (Slovak died, reportedly of an overdose, in June 1988.) Sagely engaging Clinton to produce, the Peppers made **Freaky Styley** more outrageous but easier to swallow as utilitarian dance-rock as well. A version of Sly Stone's "If You Want Me to Stay" shows they can play it straight; "Yertle the Turtle," based on Dr. Seuss, proves their dadaist sensibilities remain in full force. Other bits of rhythmicized doggerel—"Catholic School Girls Rule," "Thirty Dirty Birds," "Blackeyed Blonde"—keep tongue in cheek and mind in the gutter. **Freaky Styley** is a ton of raunchy, funky fun.

Bob Dylan's "Subterranean Homesick Blues" gets a weirdly re-tempoed electro-rap overhaul on **The Uplift Mofo Party Plan**, a busy, casual-sounding album that divides rock and funk down the middle. On some guitar-heavy tracks ("No Chump Love Sucker," "Fight Like a Brave," "Me and My Friends"), Flea's popping bass is the only connection with the group's characteristic sound; elsewhere, familiarly repetitive rhythm grooves reaffirm the Peppers' primal commitment to butt-shaking. In "Organic Anti-Beat Box Band," the self-described Fax City 4 issue their offbeat statement of (cross) purpose: "We represent the Hollywood kids . . . you just might slam dance."   [iar]

See also *What Is This.*

RED LORRY YELLOW LORRY
Talk About the Weather (nr/Red Rhino) 1985
Paint Your Wagon (nr/Red Rhino) 1986 ●
Smashed Hits (Red Rhino-Fundamental) 1987 ●
Nothing Wrong (Beggars Banquet-RCA) 1988 ●

LORRIES
Crawling Mantra EP (Homestead) 1987

If you loved Joy Division, you'll like the Lorries (a nickname which briefly became

official), who similarly inhabit a bleak world in which swirling guitar figures and pretentious, gloomy lyrics are the only comforts. While Joy Division was the unchallenged champ of these nether regions, Leeds' Lorries work the territory with enough savvy and intelligence (not to mention a cool supressed-acid-rock guitar sound) to make it work. **Talk About the Weather** ultimately succumbs to its own murky tunelessness, but not without a fight.

After that LP, they recorded a great single, "Chance." With distorted organ drone and a rushed tempo, it sounded as if the band had located its own true voice. However, **Paint Your Wagon** borrows enough from Ian Curtis and Joy Division that you'd think it had been released by Factory (c. 1981), especially on cuts like "Head All Fire" and "Save My Soul." A disappointing follow-up to such a promising debut.

The back cover of **Smashed Hits**, a singles compilation, is covered with flattering bits from newspaper clippings, and the tracks really do live up to most of the praise. Most of the band's finest moments are included, such as "Hollow Eyes," "Generation" and "Chance." The guitar work is so good that it covers up the weak points, especially the vocal Curtisisms and the kickless, rudimentary rhythm section. They've changed their name back and forth between Red Lorry Yellow Lorry and the Lorries a few times recently, releasing one mini-LP as the latter.   [jl/dgs]

RED NOISE
See *Bill Nelson.*

RED ROCKERS
Condition Red (415) 1981
Good as Gold (415-Columbia) 1983
Schizophrenic Circus (415-Columbia) 1984

New Orleans' Red Rockers not only sound a bit like early Clash on their debut album, they match political conviction word for word, through songs like "Guns of Revolution," "White Law" and "Dead Heroes." But the Rockers lack the Clash's wit, and humorlessness makes the record more preachy than passionate.

Thus armed with no great expectations, **Good as Gold** came as something of a surprise, starting with the first track. Gone was the raging rhetoric, replaced by a startlingly pretty pop song, "China," filled with articulate, ringing guitars and John Griffith's newly smoothed-up vocals. With ex-Stiff Little Fingers drummer Jim Reilly in the lineup, Red Rockers switched to melodic pop-rock, much like 415 labelmates Translator but with more emphasis on electric drive and generally less-exceptional songwriting.

Good as Gold is consistently good and "China" deservedly became a hit single, but the band failed to really catch on commercially, and returned with an equally bewildering follow-up, **Schizophrenic Circus**. Seemingly an attempt to become America's Alarm, the LP—produced by Rick Chertoff—goes nouveau-country and encompasses both the anthemic, folky "Blood from a Stone" (covering the Hooters) and a totally unnecessary remake of "Eve of Destruction." Danger sign: too little original material of any significant quality. [iar]

REDS

The Reds (A&M) 1979
10-Inch Record EP (A&M) 1979
Stronger Silence (Ambition) 1981
Fatal Slide (Can. Stony Plain) 1982

The Reds perfected a hard-hitting, theatrical style that makes the music jump off the record and pin you to the wall. Suggesting an educated alternative to the Stooges, or a double-time interpretation of the Doors, this Philadelphia quartet played only at peak intensity, much like a dumb heavy metal band. However, the Reds don't exaggerate the flourishes or crescendos; instead, they move on rapidly to the next explosion, punk style. This breakneck hybrid is topped off with the tormented vocals of Rick Schaffer, who never seems fully in control of himself.

The Reds' A&M outing suffers from overstatement: too much sound and fury, not enough power. (The 10-inch EP contains two album tracks plus a version of the Doors' "Break on Through" and another non-LP tune.) The more recent efforts harden the attack to simulate the effect of getting hit with a tossed brick, while highlighting the clean, surprisingly graceful musicianship. **Stronger Silence** features "The Danger" and "Driving Me Crazy"; **Fatal Slide** includes "Five Year Plan" and "Gone Too Far." [jy]

REDSKINS

Neither Washington nor Moscow (nr/Decca) 1986
The Peel Sessions EP (nr/Strange Fruit) 1987

Along with the Style Council, Test Dept. and Billy Bragg, the Redskins are at the forefront of British rock's Socialist movement. Led by guitarist Chris Dean (whose alter-ego, X. Moore, is a former *New Musical Express* scribe), the trio augments an R&B-influenced sound with keyboards and a horn section, covering much the same musical terrain on **Neither Washington nor Moscow** as the first Dexys album, only marred by erratic production and mastering. Most of the songs are simple and catchy, and almost all the titles end in exclamation points! More important to the comrades than tunes, however, are lyrics—each song is a call to arms for the oppressed to rise up. Though doctrinaire, the Redskins are dead honest, committed to what they're doing and make some good music. There aren't many bands around these days with those qualities.

The **Peel Sessions** EP was recorded live in the studio in October 1982 and contains such activist tunes as "Unionize" and "The Peasant Army." [dgs]

REDUCERS

The Reducers (Rave On) 1984
Let's Go (Rave On) 1984
Cruise to Nowhere (Rave On) 1985

Quick—name a great band from Connecticut. Well, you need be stumped no longer. Just keep the Reducers in mind. This New London quartet has absorbed all sorts of styles—from Chuck Berry to Anglo-pop, glam-rock to punk—and return them all in a solid hybrid of tunes, blazing guitars and speedy tempos. On **The Reducers**, they sing of "Black Plastic Shoes," "Better Homes and Gardens" and "Information Overload," painting a picture of alienation in the boonies ("Out of Step"). Polite but energetic, **The Reducers** introduces a band with ideas and spunk.

The title track on the better-produced **Let's Go** is a great number about getting out, with a catchy, urgent chorus; the rest of the LP (which includes a raving cover of the beat classic "Hippy Hippy Shake") is equally enthusiastic and has more acute lyrics. (On "Bums I Used to Know" they play a churning R&B vamp while chiding themselves for "this honky imitation of the blues.") The Reducers may not be fashionable—no synthesizers or even cowpunk aspirations—but they have the spirit and the sense to keep changing and working. Their albums have an integrity

466

and sincerity that more than compensates for any lack of stylishness.

The Reducers released a 1988 album with Roger C. Reale, a Connecticut singer and bassist whose 1978 indie LP featured two young sidemen: Hilly Michaels and G.E. Smith. [iar]

LOU REED

Lou Reed (RCA) 1972
Transformer (RCA) 1972 + 1981 ●
Berlin (RCA) 1973 + 1981 ●
Rock n Roll Animal (RCA) 1974 + 1981 ●
Sally Can't Dance (RCA) 1974
Lou Reed Live (RCA) 1975 + 1981
Metal Machine Music (RCA) 1975
Coney Island Baby (RCA) 1976 + 1980
Rock and Roll Heart (Arista) 1976
Walk on the Wild Side: The Best of Lou
    Reed (RCA) 1977 ●
Street Hassle (Arista) 1978
Live Take No Prisoners (Arista) 1978
The Bells (Arista) 1979
Growing Up in Public (Arista) 1980
Rock and Roll Diary 1967—1980 (Arista)
    1980
The Blue Mask (RCA) 1982
Legendary Hearts (RCA) 1983
Live in Italy (nr/RCA) 1984
New Sensations (RCA) 1984 ●
City Lights: Classic Performances (Arista)
    1985
Mistrial (RCA) 1986 ●

Since he formed the Velvet Underground in 1966, Lou Reed's career has spanned several major rock upheavals, but he has always managed to be a leader not a follower, despite an iconoclastic resistance to fashion. A highly principled free-thinker, Reed has provided inspiration, direction and songs for bands with a taste for the seamier side of the rock sensibility.

Reed's influence began with the Velvet Underground's predilection for forbidden fruit—drugs, bizarre sex, suicide—in its lyrics, and raging chaos in its music. How could punk (much less the Jesus and Mary Chain) have ever occurred without "Sister Ray" or "Heroin" as touchstones? In his solo work, Reed has casually strayed far into heavy metal territory and experimental noise, as well as restrained, seemingly normal rock, but always with a rebellious attitude, probing honesty and unselfconscious abandon. He has always managed to remain relevant, serv-

ing as a guide for all sorts of unconventional music makers.

Lou Reed, recorded in England with session players like Steve Howe and Rick Wakeman (both of Yes!), includes previously unreleased Velvet Underground material (some of which turned up much later on **VU**) and the first incarnation of "Berlin." Effortlessly alternating nihilism with ironic wistfulness, the music is surprisingly lean and no-nonsense, getting Reed's solo career off the ground with a flourish.

The existence of a New York café society in the early '70s led to an alliance between Reed and David Bowie, who co-produced **Transformer** with his sideman, Mick Ronson. Joining the legion of androgynous glamrockers, Reed penned "Walk on the Wild Side," a chronicle of the Warhol crowd that—issued as a single—became a genuine subversive hit (and, many years later, a television jingle!). Although **Transformer**'s music is a bit too campy, the LP is nonetheless a classic.

Fresh from his work with Alice Cooper, Bob Ezrin produced **Berlin**, using such players as Jack Bruce and Steve Winwood. While lyrically intense and haunting, the music is understated, almost plain. But Reed's tragic tales—like "Caroline Says" and "Sad Song"—pack an intense emotional charge. **Berlin**, in spite of itself, is one of his best, although not recommended for depressives or would-be suicides.

Rock n Roll Animal captures Reed on-stage in New York with an unbelievably bombastic heavy metal band powered by guitarists Steve Hunter and Dick Wagner. Playing a collection of elongated hits ("Sweet Jane," "Rock'n'Roll," "Heroin") at stun volume, Reed proves he can sound as neanderthal as any arena band of the day, but his songs and singing make it powerful.

Sally Can't Dance attempts a mainstream sound with boring songs that lack fire; although a commercial success, it's one of Reed's most forgettable efforts, marking the beginning of a bad period in his career. To mark time, his next release was **Lou Reed Live** (more **Rock n Roll Animal**), followed by the truly deviant **Metal Machine Music**, four sides of unlistenable noise (a description, not a value judgment) that angered and disappointed all but the most devout Reed fans. If he was simply looking to goad people and puncture perceptions, **Metal Machine Music** was a rousing success.

Coney Island Baby and **Rock and Roll Heart** proffer the same unambitious restraint as **Sally Can't Dance**; the new wrinkle is Reed's revelatory lyrics. After years of describing a depraved life-style with a hint of defensive pride, Reed began to open up and admit personal pain and doubts. A new creative vista mired in a musical rut.

Street Hassle shows Reed somewhat revitalized—or at least moved to action—by the onslaught of his young punk apostles. More aggressive sound and new-found vocal strength power songs like "Real Good Time Together" and the scathing "I Wanna Be Black." The band is exciting, and every path pursued bears fruit.

Another live album, **Take No Prisoners**—recorded at New York's Bottom Line—gives Reed a chance to try his hand at being a standup comedian. The four sides include only two or three songs each: the band vamps endlessly as Reed banters with the crowd, offering sharp opinions and cutting comments on a variety of subjects. Although not a great musical accomplishment, it's one of the funniest and most entertaining live albums of all time.

Reed continued to expose his sensitive side on **The Bells** and **Growing Up in Public**, using driving rock and delicate melodicism to back thoughtful lyrics and impassioned singing. A triumphant success, **The Blue Mask** uses almost no instrumental overdubs to get a spontaneous feel from a basic backing trio (including ex-Richard Hell guitarist Robert Quine) and features some of Reed's strongest writing in years. The portraits he paints are miserable characters living outside society; it's not clear whether or not they're fictional.

Walk on the Wild Side, **Rock and Roll Diary** and **City Lights** are compilations—the first of his RCA albums and the second (which has excellent liner notes) mixing Velvet Underground material (almost two sides' worth) with a spotty bunch of tracks from both RCA and Arista records. **City Lights** draws only from the Arista releases. There are other English and European retrospectives as well.

Reed found new acclaim with the band he enlisted for **The Blue Mask**; adding drummer Fred Maher to the core of Quine and bassist Fernando Saunders completed a perfect touring/recording unit that Reed lost no time in exploiting. **Legendary Hearts** could just as well have been credited to the Lou Reed Band—every song is fully developed and confidently delivered in a manner suggesting a tight, well-rehearsed unit. It ranks with any Reed record all the way back to the Velvets in substance and stands out as his strongest work in style, using the group as a powerful lens that magnifies his themes and obsessions down to the finest detail. Picking an ideal moment to sum up his career to date, Reed recorded **Live in Italy** with the same band—two albums of material divided almost evenly between Velvets-era and solo work.

It seemed almost too good to continue. For his next record, Reed decided to play all the guitar himself, yet **New Sensations** is anything but self-indulgent. Forsaking the two-guitar sound just throws Saunders' distinctive fretless bass playing and Reed's spare arrangements into higher relief, and they merit the attention. As do the songs, which prove that a middle-aged rock songwriter can have plenty to offer.

Mistrial is an essentially styleless observation of the times in which we live, simply played as variable-strength rock with Lou on guitar and Saunders (with a little outside assistance) doing the rest. Reed's 1986 concerns are television ("Video Violence"), the state of world affairs ("The Original Wrapper," in which a credible funk track sets the stage for Reed to demonstrate his abilities as an urban wordsmith), emotional violence ("Don't Hurt a Woman," "Spit It Out") and personal realities ("Mama's Got a Lover" and a moving, memorably beautiful pair that close the album: "I Remember You" and "Tell It to Your Heart"). Although many of the melodies are too spare and casual to make any enduring impression, lyrics are obviously what's important here; by this point, Reed's albums have a higher purpose than mere toe-tapping or bus-stop humming.   [iar/mf]

REELS

The Reels (Polydor) 1979
Quasimodo's Dream (Aus. Polygram) 1981
Beautiful (Aus. K-Tel) 1982

Singer David Mason sounds like a deep-echo Elvis Costello with a nagging cough. The songs have a wacky Madness edge and the band leaps into them with the speeding ska fury of classic 2-Tone. The suspicion that you've heard it all before does not diminish the eccentric, energetic joy of **The Reels**, the only US/UK release by this Australian quintet. The Reels' resounding lack of success in this hemisphere can probably be attributed to murky production too idiosyncratic for American radio and the fact that various English bands had already done this sort of thing better. [df]

RE-FLEX
The Politics of Dancing (Capitol) 1983

I can't tell them apart from the Fixx or INXS or any other like-minded outfit with "x" in their name, but England's Re-Flex display a knack for penning strong melodies and playing walloping dance grooves, best excmplificd on the title track and "Hurt." The quartet's debut LP was ably produced by John Punter. [tr]

REGINA
Curiosity (Atlantic) 1986 ●

Longtime New York scenester Regina Richards finally hit it big by dropping her last name, allowing crazy things to be done with her hair and cutting a formulaic LP of post-Madonna rock and dance originals. The singing guitarist left the underground far behind on the ultra-commercial Curiosity, which credits four people for the simple (and not at all original) cover concept and a fifth for Artist's Image Development. (Does anyone remember when talent had something to do with it?) The Supremes-into-Bananarama "Baby Love" (co-written by Madonna collaborator Stephen Bray, who produced and played on the track) was a Top 10 hit, but nothing else on the album comes close to it. [iar]

BLAINE L. REININGER
See *Tuxedomoon.*

REIVERS
Saturday (DB-Capitol) 1987
ZEITGEIST
Translate Slowly (DB) 1985

Out of Austin, Texas—the rowdy college town that Stevie Ray Vaughan and the Butthole Surfers call home—comes an impressive debut from Zeitgeist, two guys and two girls making moody, melodic and occasionally stunning folk-rock with a deep debt to the '60s, although there's plenty of modern angst and a rootsy feel more western than country. On Translate Slowly, John Croslin and Kim Longacre work up a Byrdsy guitar

drone and evocative vocal interplay that either lulls with a tepid sonic wash ("Cowboys") or explodes with brooding fury ("Things Don't Change") and hot-breath passion ("Araby"). Croslin's dry-as-dust vocals mix equal measures of desire and distance, but harmonies soar on a remake of Willie Nelson's "Blue Eyes Crying in the Rain."

Forced to abandon the Zeitgeist name by a minimalist Minneapolis sextet that had it first, the quartet chose an equally inappropriate new handle. (Capitol stickered the second LP with the band's former name; DB returned the favor by stickering copies of Translate Slowly with a mention of the new one.) Both sides of the Don Dixon-produced Saturday begin with hard-edged Pylonesque syncopation, but otherwise the LP consists of unpretentious guitar pop suggesting 10,000 Maniacs with less idiosyncracy. The band's personality hinges on appealing vocals; ironically, a nutty instrumental ("Karate Party") is one of the record's standouts. The ability to change gears from delicate melodicism ("Electra") to driving rock ("Wait for Time," "Secretariat") is a definite asset. [kh/iar]

RELUCTANT STEREOTYPES
The Label (nr/WEA) 1980

This Birmingham outfit played likable reggaefied rock/pop much like another band of the same city and era, the Beat. Similarities include pointed-but-subtle lyrics that avoid clichés while covering political topics, prominent horn work, boppy dance rhythms and high musical standards. Differences include a more free-form, less-soulful approach and stricter adherence to reggae rhythms on most tunes. Comparisons aside, The Label is an ace record by a skillful, inventive band. [iar]

See also *King.*

R.E.M.
Chronic Town EP (IRS) 1982 ●
Murmur (IRS) 1983 ●
Reckoning (IRS) 1984 ●
Fables of the Reconstruction (IRS) 1985 ●
Lifes Rich Pageant (IRS) 1986 ●
Dead Letter Office (IRS) 1987 ●
Document (IRS) 1987 ●

Who would ever have expected an American musical revolution to be launched from

Athens, Georgia? R.E.M.'s rough-hewn guitar pop, introduced in 1981 by a stunning independent single ("Radio Free Europe"), has put them in the vanguard of a wide-reaching musical movement that relies on homegrown, populist rootsiness rather than any transatlantic inspiration. Blending Pete Buck's Byrdsian guitar playing with Michael Stipe's hazy, sometimes melancholic (but never miserable) vocals and impressionistic lyrics, plus a strong, supple rhythm section (Bill Berry and Mike Mills), R.E.M. plays memorable songs with unprepossessing simplicity and emotional depth. As hip acceptance has given way to full-fledged stardom, R.E.M. has grown less exciting but remained intelligent and committed to artistic expression (not only theirs).

The five-song **Chronic Town** EP, co-produced by Mitch Easter, continues the sound (if not all the rushed excitement) of the single, and boasts the remarkable "1,000,000" and the equally memorable "Carnival of Sorts (Boxcars)."

Murmur is a masterpiece, containing all the essential components of truly great serious pop music. On "Catapult," "Pilgrimage" and a reprise of "Radio Free Europe," Stipe inscrutably (but evocatively) mumbles his vocals with unmistakable passion, while the band spins haunting webs of guitar rock that are heavy with atmosphere. A completely satisfying collection, **Murmur** served as a guidepost for many of the bands who chose to follow R.E.M. back to the New South for inspiration.

Doomed to disappoint by comparison to the debut, **Reckoning** is not quite as consistent, although it contains enough equally great music to maintain R.E.M.'s reputation for excellence. "Harborcoat," "So. Central Rain (I'm Sorry)," "(Don't Go Back to) Rockville" and "Pretty Persuasion" are all wonderful, and display not only clearer production (Easter and Don Dixon) but a less hurried pace and more articulate singing.

Fables of the Reconstruction (aka **Reconstruction of the Fables**), produced in London by Joe Boyd, finds R.E.M. largely neglecting catchy melodicism and driving rhythms for reflective, languidly meandering numbers that lack focal points and seem to start and finish with the structured inexorability of a light switch. A number of the songs are flat-out boring, and the album in toto is vague and colorless, although not entirely useless. "Can't Get There from Here," "Driver 8"

and the raucous "Auctioneer (Another Engine)" do have familiar R.E.M. attributes.

A shortage of rewarding musical ideas and an air of flagging enthusiasm on the politically-minded and far too restrained **Lifes Rich Pageant** makes it a remote and generally ignorable chapter in R.E.M.'s inexorable march towards the big time. Excepting a totally ace cover of the Clique's psychedelic obscurity, "Superman," sung in a delicious near-whine by Mike Mills, the rushed "Hyena" and the languid "Fall on Me," the record is instrumentally dull and almost entirely uninvolving.

With Stipe opting for a brave new world of enunciation on **Document**, Scott Litt's dynamic co-production pushes the songs back into the world of the living, with a bright, loud sound and an infusion of much-needed rock energy. Without sacrificing sensitivity, Buck plays up a storm, pushed into high gear by Berry's walloping big beat. The entire first side is brilliant, from the maniacally intense "Finest Worksong" to the stomping horn-flecked nostalgia of "Exhuming McCarthy," a goofball cover of Wire's "Strange" and the wordily name-dropping nonsense of "It's the End of the World as We Know It (and I Feel Fine)." The back of the LP is half as good, which is to say the sound is swell but the songs aren't. Nonetheless, millions misunderstood the stinging irony of "The One I Love" and made it a huge hit single.

Dead Letter Office, a curious and amusing back-pages collection, reveals R.E.M.'s proclivity for recording covers (it contains material by Pylon, Roger Miller, the Velvet Underground and Aerosmith) and a goofy sense of humor not often heard on their albums. Buck's liner notes explain the origins of all 15 LP outtakes, pisstakes and oddities, including "Walter's Theme," written to be a restaurant commercial. The CD has a bonus: the contents of **Chronic Town**.   [iar]

See also *Fleshtones.*

RENALDO AND THE LOAF

Songs for Swinging Larvae (Ralph) 1979
Arabic Yodelling (Ralph) 1983
Streve and Sneff [tape] (Ralph) 1984
The Elbow Is Taboo (Ralph) 1987

RESIDENTS & RENALDO AND THE LOAF

Title in Limbo (Ralph) 1983

Only the Residents' label would deign to sign a duo as deeply weird as Renaldo and the Loaf—in real life two Englishmen named David Janssen and Brian Poole (the latter *not* of '60s swingers the Tremeloes). Their bizarre studio-doctored vocals, cut-and-paste arrangements, jerky robot rhythms and alien instrumentation (among the pair's noisemakers: scalpel, metal comb, hacksaw blade, pickle jar, biscuit tins) suggest that Renaldo and the Loaf was evolved in the Residents' image. Unfortunately, **Songs for Swinging Larvae** has all the madness and none of the coherence of the Residents' nutty concepts, its offbeat wit stampeded instead by rampant disorienting eclecticism. Guaranteed to clear the room of your choice.

Arabic Yodelling is roughly more of the same, a collection of Rube Goldberg home-brewed insanity recorded over a two-year period. A bit less weird for weird's sake (although hardly in danger of mass appeal), it keeps the blindly whimsical faith the Residents themselves have partially outgrown. **Title in Limbo**, the group's joint effort with their American soul brothers, however, is not at all enticing. **Streve and Sneff** is an American reissue of a pre-**Larvae** cassette the band had previously distributed on their own.

The general worldwide overuse of electronic sampling instruments may partially explain the delightful alternate-reality sound of **The Elbow Is Taboo**; then again, perhaps Renaldo and the Loaf have simply advanced past musical infantilism. The songs are indeed songs; they may contain obscure, unexpected sounds and bizarre vocals, but little of it seriously impedes the spare, charming folksiness. "A Street Called Straight," a most agreeable mélange, employs dulcimer and bouzouki as well as a keyboard; the title track shuffles along on a devolved reggae beat with mandolin as a prime instrument; the vocalless "Dance for Somnambulists" mixes in glockenspiel and guitars. Crazy, man, crazy! [df/iar]

ROBERT RENTAL AND THE NORMAL

Live at the West Runton Pavilion (Rough Trade) 1981

Emerging from the do-it-yourself school of synthesizer playing, Robert Rental teamed up with the Normal (aka Daniel Miller, head of Mute Records) for this one-off show, reproduced on a one-sided album. The compendium of noises involved bears relation to music only by inference, though it *is* an im-

pressive display of live electronics, tape loops and devices, similar in scope and approach to avant-garde electronic events of the '60s. Rental and the Normal are firmly rooted in rock, however, and this half-record proffers more ideas per minute than can be found anywhere, except the more esoteric recordings of Cabaret Voltaire. [sg]
See also *Thomas Leer and Robert Rental.*

REPLACEMENTS

Sorry Ma, Forgot to Take Out the Trash (Twin/Tone) 1981
The Replacements Stink EP (Twin/Tone) 1982 + 1986
Hootenanny (Twin/Tone) 1983 ●
Let It Be (Twin/Tone) 1984 ●
The Shit Hits the Fans [tape] (Twin/Tone) 1985
Tim (Sire) 1985 ●
Boink!! (nr/Glass) 1986
Pleased to Meet Me (Sire) 1987 ●

Folks say that Minneapolis' Replacements are the best rock'n'roll band in the world, and when it all clicks—volume, rawness, speed (pace *and* ingested substances), energy and passion—they're right. But lots of times, when the band can't be bothered to play their own songs or finish whatever they're in the midst of, when they really just want to be difficult, they're possibly the worst.

The original foursome got written off a lot as sloppy, but only by those who chose not to see beyond the chaos. Chris Mars drums like he's possessed; Tommy Stinson is a spoiled teen (he was 12 when the band started) but thumps a mean bassline; buffoonish original guitarist Bob Stinson might wear a dress (or less) onstage but can alternate between ripping metal leads and achingly tender melody lines that prove he's got a heart (if not a brain). And Paul Westerberg—too terrified to sing his soft songs—hides behind the band's noise. The Mats (short for Placemats) are one of those classic rock'n'roll combos whose music, looks and personalities fit together perfectly, the stuff of which legends are made. The lore surrounding them is already pretty thick.

The musical evidence of their creative importance was there on the first album, 18 songs following the usual loud/fast rules with titles like "Shut Up," "Kick Your Door Down" and "Shiftless When Idle." But they showed depth on a slow, bluesy ode to J.

Thunders, "Johnny's Gonna Die." The **Stink** EP went for pure driving thrash and produced some gems, including "Dope Smokin Moron," "Kids Don't Follow" and "God Damn Job." But it landed them in the hardcore bins, even though the music and lyrics are much sharper than most, mixing equal parts arrogance and self-deprecating humor.

When **Hootenanny** combined blues, power pop, folk, country, straight-ahead rock, surf (or, more accurately, ski) and punk in a way few hardcore bands could even imagine, people started taking notice. **Stink**'s "Fuck School" gave way to "Color Me Impressed," a soaring rock number about drunkenness and trendinista parties, proving a wisdom beyond their years, and sounding pretty incongruous next to "Run It," a paean to beating red lights. Westerberg reached into his bag of solo heartstoppers for a naked (yet never sappy) confession of loneliness, "Within Your Reach."

With **Let It Be**, the Mats became "stars," at least on the independent club/college radio circuit. The LP is more focused than anything else they'd done, boldly carrying out what they'd only tried on **Hootenanny**. They blended rock-pop and country shuffle on "I Will Dare" and raved-up on novelty rockers like the lyrical vérité of "Tommy Gets His Tonsils Out" and "Gary's Got a Boner." Westerberg's loneliness gave way to total emptiness on the harrowing "Unsatisfied."

Critics trampled each other in a rush to claim discovery rights, Sire signed them and Twin/Tone celebrated with a cassette-only live tape—stolen from some kid bootlegging an Oklahoma show—which showed the feckless Mats at their most messed-up, playing (at least starting to play) a motley collection of their favorite covers, from R.E.M. to the Stones, Thin Lizzy to X.

Although there's no consensus on the issue, the Replacements made the transition to major-labeldom with their artistic integrity intact. It looked for a while as if Alex Chilton would get the nod, but ex-Ramone Tommy Erdelyi ended up producing **Tim** (great title, that), retaining all of the raggedness and devil-may-care rock'n'roll spirit that make the Replacements great. Westerberg's tunes here are among his best ever, from a melancholy bar ballad ("Here Comes a Regular") to an obnoxiously mean-spirited anti-stewardess slur, "Waitress in the Sky." His raging insecurity shines through on

"Hold My Life" ("because I just might lose it . . . ") and the anthemic "Bastards of Young." "Left of the Dial" celebrates alternative radio, while "Kiss Me on the Bus" considers the romantic possibilities of public transportation. A stupendous record.

Boink!! is an eight-song UK condensation of their pre-**Let It Be** catalogue, with the added bonus of an otherwise unreleased Chilton-produced cut, "Nowhere Is My Home."

When it became apparent that Bob Stinson was in danger of succumbing permanently to the band's treacherous lifestyle, the Mats fired him and proceeded to record the incredible **Pleased to Meet Me** as a trio. With Jim Dickinson producing and Westerberg doing all the guitar work, the group stirred up another batch of their patented blend: virile, witty rockers ("Valentine," "Red Red Wine," "I.O.U."), tender ballads ("Nightclub Jitters," "Skyway"). There's a rollicking number about "Alex Chilton," a bizarre but fabulous stab at commercial radio acceptance ("Can't Hardly Wait") in which the Memphis Horns echo a deliciously nagging guitar riff over a wicked backbeat, and "The Ledge," a tense suicide vignette musically rewritten from **Hootenanny**'s "Willpower." On tour following the LP's release, the group unveiled a new guitarist, Slim Dunlop (ex-Curtiss A), and a far less obstreperous onstage attitude.

Although four Replacements albums are out on CD, not one of them includes a bonus track. Bastards. [ep/iar]

RESCUE
Messages EP (A&M) 1984

Cleverly produced by Tony Mansfield, this American quintet sounds decidedly British on **Messages**' five nifty dance-rock tunes. Although nothing else matches up to it, the title track—with powerful drumming and a weedy synth figure—points up the band's strengths: crafty, original songwriting and a likable singer in guitarist Paul McGovern. [iar]

RESIDENTS
Meet the Residents (Ralph) 1974 + 1977 + 1985
The Residents Present the Third Reich 'n Roll (Ralph) 1975 + 1979 [CD] (ESD) 1987
Fingerprince (Ralph) 1976 [CD] (ESD) 1987

Duck Stab EP (Ralph) 1978 + 1987
Duck Stab/Buster & Glen (Ralph) 1978 + 1987 ●
Not Available (Ralph) 1978 ●
Eskimo (Ralph) 1979 [CD] (ESD) 1987
Nibbles (nr/Virgin) 1979
Diskomo/Goosebump EP (Ralph) 1980
The Residents Commercial Album (Ralph) 1980 ●
Mark of the Mole (Ralph) 1981
The Tunes of Two Cities (Ralph) 1982
Intermission EP (Ralph) 1982
The Residents' Mole Show (no label) 1983
Residue of the Residents (Ralph) 1983
George & James (Ralph) 1984
Whatever Happened to Vileness Fats? (Ralph) 1984
Assorted Secrets [tape] (Ralph) 1984
Ralph Before 84: Volume One (nr/Korova) 1984
The Census Taker (Episode) 1985
The Big Bubble (Black Shroud-Ralph) 1985
PAL TV LP (nr/Doublevision) 1985
Heaven? [CD] (Rykodisc) 1986
Hell! [CD] (Rykodisc) 1986
Stars and Hank Forever (Ralph) 1986 ●
13th Anniversary Show—Live in Japan (Ralph) 1986
Hit the Road Jack EP (Ralph) 1987
Live in Holland (Hol. Torso) 1987 [CD] (ESD) 1988
God in Three Persons [CD] (Rykodisc) 1988 (Ryko Analogue) 1988

RESIDENTS & RENALDO AND THE LOAF

Title in Limbo (Ralph) 1983

What's a Resident? Epithets abound, but anent actual identities, anyone who knows ain't talking. Cinéastes transplanted—so the story goes—from Shreveport, Louisiana to the San Francisco area who also dabble in musical experiments, the foursome (trio? duo? *solo*?—one guy does almost all the singing, aside from guest vocalists) has woven a remarkable cloak of secrecy. Aside from the avowed purpose of avoiding misleading and potentially divisive individual credits, this creates an attention-getting mystique which, when the limited speculation on same has been exhausted, leaves absolutely nothing to contemplate but the music itself.

The Residents led Ralph Records from cottage industry to self-sufficient label, able to sell artistically ambitious *oeuvres* without selling themselves out. They're also paradigmatic of limited technical and compositional ability marshalled, along with wit and imagination, in the service of works seeking to trample sacrosanct icons and rock's boundaries.

It's evidently not in them to write distinctive melodies that don't sound utterly bizarre. When they try, the results invariably sound like someone else's—albeit distinctly distorted or perverted—which is probably one reason why the dissection and reassembly of various bits of rock tradition was their early forte. Also, the Residents' approach owes great debts to the early groundbreaking of both Frank Zappa and Captain Beefheart. (It was at one time rumored that the storied N. Senada, a poet/saxist who allegedly collaborated with the Residents during his brief sojourn in the Bay Area, was actually Beefheart.) All that said, the Residents are superior synthesists, and the derivations of their work can't deny the entertainingly provocative nature of their best achievements.

The first four efforts by the then-unnamed group were album-length tapes, including one which was sent (with no name on it) to a record company in the hopes of a deal and sent back to the quartet's return address, care of "Residents." Hence the moniker.

N. Senada's contribution, the concept of phonetic (re)organization, was adapted by the Residents on their vinyl LP debut, **Meet the Residents** which, after alleged legal threats by the Beatles' record label, was reissued in '77 with graphics not so savagely parodic of the similarly named Beatles LP (and with improved sound). The record is alternately a goofy sophomoric giggle and a striking, off-the-wall twist of musical mind. The Residents had arrived, but weren't yet sure quite where they were.

On **The Residents Present the Third Reich 'n Roll** the band transforms hooky bits from '60s Top 40 hits into two ridiculous, funny, scary and just plain jaw-dropping-weird side-long suites, "Swastikas on Parade" and "Hitler Was a Vegetarian," intended as "revenge" for the brainwashing of American youth into acceptance of rock's trivialization (or something like that). The LP was reissued with partially censored graphics in '79 (the original cover showed a carrot-toting Nazi officer who bore a distinct resemblance to Dick Clark) and on CD in '87, with the addition of two brilliant early 45s (and their B-sides): "Satisfaction," which makes Devo's subsequent try sound like the 1910 Fruitgum Co., and the Beatles perversion, "Beyond the Valley of a Day in the Life".

Originally recorded in 1976 as **Tourniquet of Roses**, the project was shortened by Ralph from its three-side length and released as a single album, **Fingerprince**. While echoing the first LP's contrast of very short tracks with one lengthy one, **Fingerprince** finds the group operating in considerably higher gear: imagine a meeting of Frank Zappa and Steely Dan in a very avant mood, with the results processed through a computer programmed by a paranoid schizophrenic with a sense of humor. (The late Snakefinger, who had played outrageous guitar on their early tapes and "Satisfaction," also guests here.) In 1987, the record's CD release restored the missing side for the first presentation of the complete 53-minute version. (The deleted material had previously been made available on a limited-edition EP, **Babyfingers**.)

Duck Stab was originally released as an EP—the group at its most consistently accessible—but was enlarged to album size by the **Buster & Glen** half (also succinctly catchy and humorous). A 1987 reissue of the album dropped **Buster and Glen** from the title; the CD of the same name appends **Goosebump** (the B-side suite of the **Diskomo** 12-inch) and a swell lyric book.

Duck Stab was evidently cut as a lightweight diversion from the sessions for the more crucial conceptual masterwork, **Eskimo**. That project may have gotten out of control, since its release was postponed a year. Instead, out popped **Not Available**, supposedly recorded just after **Meet the Residents**—and, according to "the theory of obscurity," never intended for release. Hooey? If new, it's the culmination of various ideas the band had cultivated; if genuinely old, a lasting influence on Residentiala to come. I'd say the latter, since most everything said to have been recorded after it seems more refined in execution, if not so grand in sweep. Can you imagine a vast epic in five sections told with the recitative cadence of nursery rhymes (a Residents vocal trademark) but sounding as though played by E.T. and family?

With help from ex-Mothers keyboardist Don Preston and drummer Chris Cutler (of Henry Cow/Art Bears fame), **Eskimo's** broad, electronically spacey sonic contours form a backdrop for what the Residents would have you believe is a re-creation of Eskimo life and culture (instrumental, but

with printed narration on the jacket to explain the "stories.") It's brilliant and—yep—chilling, their most (but not totally) serious undertaking yet, evocative if not quite authentic. Some of its sections were reprogrammed as "Diskomo" and coupled on an EP with a Residential look in on Mother Goose. The **Eskimo** CD appends the Residents' four contributions to Ralph's 1979 **Subterranean Modern** compilation.

The Residents then went incredibly unserious and recorded an album of 40 one-minute songs, some with anonymous celebrity assistance. (Fred Frith is credited; Lene Lovich and XTC's Andy Partridge, among others, aren't.) **The Residents Commercial Album** is a gimmick, and the inspiration brought to bear on its challenge of brevity is hit-and-miss, with too many tracks mere fragments.

The Mole trilogy began auspiciously with **Mark of the Mole**, a murkily limned, yet engrossing story of the Moles, forced out of their home into sharing one with the Chubs, and the ensuing conflict between the "underground" and slick complacency. A thin story, but musically harrowing. Unfortunately, **The Tunes of Two Cities** suggested that the Residents had painted themselves into a corner. The narrative isn't advanced and, although its context is fleshed out, it's simply not enough. The Residents seek to convey the cultural contrast in musical terms, alternating the Moles' abrasive, industrial grind with the Chubs' offbeat yet unctuous cocktail jazz. Neither the device nor its execution, notwithstanding some swell sax work by Norman Salant, can justify a whole album.

This should have been a sign that the Residents' camp was in disarray. Despite the temporary acquisition of hotshot LA management, the Residents began to reel, first from internal dissension and later from several desertions by members of the Ralph brain trust.

The 1983 live **Mole Show** LP is the Residents' own authorized bootleg of the show's groundbreaking presentation at LA's Roxy Theatre in late '82. (The band also toured Europe and released live albums there as well.) It scopes down the two extant installments and adapts them for live performance. This makes it hard to follow unless you're already well-versed in the two LPs, and it's aurally limited in the way you'd expect a live record of complicated studio music to be.

That said, it's surprisingly good—and the Residents do find a charming way of squirming out of having presented an unfinished work. But it's still an evasion. **Intermission** is exactly as billed—"extraneous" music from the show—and the first Residents record unable to stand on its own.

Residue collects Resident leftovers, rarities and unreleased versions. It, too, sidesteps the Mole issue, but is at least exciting and entertaining (if a bit uneven and unintegrated), relying notably on the group's patented warpage of rock clichés. That's more than can be said of their collaboration with likeminded English weirdos Renaldo and the Loaf. Just who's at fault isn't clear (it can't all be Renaldo), but the record is far less than the sum of its parts. Only one track ("Monkey & Bunny") is truly worthy of the Residents; the rest deserves to be forgotten.

Not content with one incomplete ambitious venture, the Residents then launched another: the American Composers Series, an attempt to lionize their favorite songwriters by interpreting their work. The first volume of the projected 16-year (!) undertaking, **George & James**, matches up a side each of George Gershwin and James Brown (live at the Apollo, no less—with crowd sounds) and is an excellent, typically bizarre success. **Stars and Hank**, the series' second volume, has some worthwhile material, but isn't up to the creative level of **George & James**. Its examination of Hank Williams on Side One is hit (amusing) and miss (silly); the flip's funhouse-mirror treatment of John Philip Sousa's marches could've been done as effectively in a third of the time. That's a case of the format dictating the execution, something they've wisely never allowed to happen before.

Soundtrack albums—one of a Residents short film ('84) and the other of a Hollywood feature ('85)—are hardly the records you'd expect to offer hope for a bright Residential future, but that's just what they do. The long-rumored *Vileness Fats* was intended to be a full-length music video back in 1972 (!), but was later abandoned. It's hard to believe the music was recorded that long ago; the songs may date from then, but the recordings on **Whatever Happened to Vileness Fats?** sound of more recent vintage. And it's a good, if not major, addition to the group's canon. Even better is the certifiably recent **The Census Taker**, which subverts more soundtrack music genres than you can shake a stick at in

brilliant Residential fashion. Could this be the band's mode of entry into the real world?

Next came **The Big Bubble**. The contradictory "Part Four of the Mole Trilogy" self-description suggests that the Residents don't know how to kill off the monster they've created. That much of the album is entertaining is beside the point. We've mainly heard this before, and positing it as the politically-charged record by the miscegenated offspring of Moles and Chubs doesn't justify its billing. The Unfab Four (or Three, or—by now, most likely—One) are (is?) doing too much tail-chasing.

The neat **Live in Japan** draws on diverse corners of the group's output, from their 1984 single of James Brown's "It's a Man's Man's Man's World" (which isn't on **George and James**) all the way back to "Smelly Tongues" from their very first LP. They do two songs from their collaborations with Snakefinger, and even the one decent number from their ill-begotten hook-up with Renaldo and the Loaf. Several tracks from **The Commercial Album** are exhumed and reworked with great success.

The UK-only **PAL TV** offers excerpts from **Vileness Fats** and selections from a Dutch performance of *The Mole Show*. **Heaven?** and **Hell!**, two lengthy CD-only compilations, offer plenty of good music, but no rhyme or reason in the selection other than a general division into "beautiful" (**Heaven?**) and "ugly" (**Hell!**). A randomly sampling CD player equipped with a complete Residents catalogue could have done just as good a job choosing material as these discs do.

Hit the Road Jack—the Percy Mayfield classic popularized by Ray Charles—gets an uncharacteristically accessible Residential once-over in a "special almost dance mix" on a 12-inch that also contains one track each from three recent albums.

The ambitious and unprecedented **God in Three Persons** (did anyone mention that pesky old Mole trilogy?) starts out with a dramatic singing, by "song stylist" Laurie Amat, of the album's credits, including an abridged music publishing ID, and proceeds to expose an hour-long scenario—with surprisingly natural narration and singing, supported by relatively restrained keyboard music—concerning the yin and yang of pain and pleasure, reality and illusion. A more direct manipulation of conventional music than any other Residents record save **The**

Census Taker, God in Three Persons indicates how the group can work its subversive magic in seemingly innocuous musical settings. The remarkable candor with which the piece addresses lust—we're talking *plain speaking* here—is but one of this striking work's atypical attributes. After being issued on CD, **God in Three Persons** also came out as a double-album.

As we always knew they would, the Residents finally reached network television, through a likely door—the one that leads into *Pee-wee's Playhouse.* Following artist Gary Panter (who used to do Ralph record covers) into his nutty corner of the CBS Saturday morning lineup, the Residents supplied the music for the infamous Zizzybalubah episode. On another media front, the group has frequently appeared as guest protagonists in *Those Annoying Post Bros.,* a comic book series by Matt Howarth, creator of the *Mole Trilogy* mini-comics. [jg]

See also *Snakefinger.*

MARTIN REV

Martin Rev (Infidelity) 1980
Clouds of Glory (Fr. New Rose) 1985

The keyboard half of pioneering New York psycho-electronic duo Suicide proves only slightly more melodic on his eccentric eponymous solo outing—all keyboards and rhythm machines, with only the occasional grunting vocal. The rich layering of synthesizer effects—at least compared to the brute minimalism of Suicide—is close to the articulate electronic orchestration of the Ric Ocasek-produced **Suicide** album (also released in 1980). The simple floating melody and disco rhythm-box ping of "Mari" also suggest the mantric pop quality of Suicide's near-hit 12-inch single, "Dream Baby Dream." More typical of **Martin Rev**, though, is the hellish pumping of "Nineteen 86" and "Jomo" 's industrial racket; the only thing missing is Suicide singer Alan Vega's mad bark.

Half a decade later, Rev returned with the likeminded **Clouds of Glory**, pressed on red vinyl. Musical styles may have finally caught up with this minimalist electro-rhythm pioneer, but he sticks resolutely true to course here, dispensing with vocals and layering weird sound effects over sturdy sequencer lines. The gently attractive "Whisper" would have made a very pretty song were Rev to give it lyrics. [df/iar]

See also *Suicide.*

KIMBERLEY REW

The Bible of Bop (Press) 1982

Like ex-bandmate Robyn Hitchcock, Kimberley Rew survived the end of the Soft Boys to produce further forays into melodious '60s folk-rock and psychedelia, as the eight tracks (seven previously released) on this 45-rpm mini-LP prove. Working with the dB's, ex-Soft Boys and Waves, Rew doesn't pursue weirdness as avidly as Hitchcock does, but the singer/guitarist/keyboardist has a neat winner with **The Bible of Bop.** Rew's next venture was a full-time career with the rock-popping Katrina and the Waves. [iar]

REZILLOS

Can't Stand the Rezillos (Sire) 1978
Mission Accomplished . . . but the Beat Goes On (nr/Sire) 1979

REVILLOS

Rev Up (nr/Snatzo-DinDisc) 1980
Attack (nr/Superville) 1983

Scotland's Rezillos were a blast of fresh air compared to the more serious bands of new wave's first charge. The ex-art students were partial to an overhauled '60s look (e.g., foil mini-skirts, pop-art fabrics) and songs with titles like "Flying Saucer Attack" and "Top of the Pops." **Can't Stand the Rezillos** is an action-packed document of their pop/camp approach. Thrashings of the Dave Clark 5's "Glad All Over" and Gerry & the Pacemakers' "I Like It" surround "(My Baby Does) Good Sculptures," a typically loopy original.

The band flew apart not long after their album debut, leaving the live **Mission Accomplished** as an unsatisfactory memorial. Besides duplicating six tunes from **Can't Stand,** the record is plagued by near-bootleg-quality sound. Otherwise the performance is a rave-up from start to finish, with five new originals and versions of the Kinks' "I Need You," Cannibal & the Headhunters' "Land of 1000 Dances" and even Sweet's "Ballroom Blitz."

Fortunately, singers Fay Fife and Eugene Reynolds regrouped with new musicians as the Revillos, and took the Rezillos' promise even further. **Rev Up** is filled with pastiches of '60s genres—"Bobby Come Back to Me," "On the Beach," "Secret of the Shadow," "Motorbike Beat"—and the obligatory non-originals—"Cool Jerk," "Hungry for Love,"

"Hippy Hippy Sheik" [*sic*]. The only foul touch is retitling the Rock-a-Teens' "Woo-Hoo" as "Yeah Yeah" and pawning it off as an original. But **Rev Up** is hilarious.   [si]

See also *Shake*.

RHYTHM & NOISE

Contents Under Notice (Ralph) 1984
Chasms Accord (Ralph) 1985

The experimental, largely unstructured sounds on **Contents Under Notice** fall roughly under the umbrella of the band's name, but just barely. One side consists of various-length sonic mood pieces ("Lull," "Vagues," "Looms," etc.); the other is filled with "Monomenon," a long hypothetical score of indescribable audio goings-on. It incorporates industrial sounds, other audio vérité, synthesizers, tape manipulations and god knows what else. In its raucous, multi-layered complexity, the piece asymptotically approaches sheer white noise din. Maybe this is what Martians with insomnia listen to.

The troubling anti-new age ambience on **Chasms Accord** could serve as the soundtrack to any number of offbeat films. Cut up into 13 segments with wonderful titles like "Lingering Fingers," "Bent Metal Forest" and "Delve," the LP—which acknowledges the assistance of Z'ev, Diamanda Galas and others—is high on drama and low on intentional ugliness, making it a vivid and apropos match for the stress of modern life.   [iar]

BOYD RICE

Boyd Rice (nr/Mute) 1981

NON

Physical Evidence (nr/Mute) 1982
Blood and Flame (nr/Mute) 1987

BOYD RICE/FRANK TOVEY

Easy Listening for the Hard of Hearing
(nr/Mute) 1984

The first album by California conceptualist Rice (one of the first "musicians" to use turntables as a creative tool) was recorded in the mid-'70s, contains no information (save on the label) other than the artist's name embossed on the all-black cover and is "playable at any speed." The droning noise slices are not ascribable to any specific instruments and seem to consist of short tape loops layered over one another to create repetitive but varying textures (like Frippertronics, but without the guitar) that slow down and speed up on their own. Unlistenable.

Physical Evidence by Non (i.e., Rice) is a collection of pieces, some of them recorded live, reflecting his work over the years subsequent to those on the first LP.

Easy Listening, while fairly routine for the eccentric Rice, takes Frank Tovey—aka Fad Gadget, himself no stranger to found sounds—off on a conceptual trip far from his usual recording format. "All sounds either collected or generated . . . by non-musical appliances"—in other words, this ain't music at all, rather repetitive, rhythmically ordered noises, mostly on the order of church bells and other things that can be struck. Not radical enough to compare with Einstürzende Neubauten and not in the slightest bit charming (like, say, Renaldo and the Loaf), the LP, which was recorded in 1981, is structurally impressive but aggravating in the extreme.   [iar]

RICH KIDS

Ghosts of Princes in Towers (nr/EMI) 1978
(nr/Fame) 1983

After being squeezed out of the Sex Pistols, bassist/singer Glen Matlock formed the Rich Kids with guitarist Midge Ure and drummer Rusty Egan (both of whom later collaborated on Visage, with Ure eventually going on to join Ultravox), plus one Steve New. During their tempestuous year-long alliance, the Rich Kids managed only one album, ludicrously misproduced into a muffled mess by Mick Ronson. Despite abysmal sound, the band's talent emerges, and **Ghosts** is an extraordinary album of daring experimental rock/pop that has two utterly brilliant pieces (the title track and "Marching Men") plus a few others nearly as good. While the predominant guitar work is occasionally mundane, there are enough novel ideas and convincing songs to make this uniquely flavored project survive the audio bloodbath and emerge victorious.   [iar]

See also *Ultravox, Visage*.

JONATHAN RICHMAN AND THE MODERN LOVERS

Jonathan Richman & the Modern Lovers
(Beserkley) 1977 (Rhino) 1986
Rock'n'Roll with the Modern Lovers
(Beserkley) 1977 (Rhino) 1986
Back in Your Life (Beserkley) 1979 (Rhino)
1986
The Jonathan Richman Songbook
(nr/Beserkley) 1980

Jonathan Sings! (Sire) 1983
Rockin' and Romance (Twin/Tone) 1985
It's Time for Jonathan Richman and the
  Modern Lovers (Upside) 1986 ●
Modern Lovers 88 (Rounder) 1987 ●
The Beserkley Years: The Best of Jonathan
  Richman and the Modern Lovers [CD]
  (Rhino) 1987

MODERN LOVERS

The Modern Lovers (Beserkley) 1976 (Rhino)
  1986
Live (Beserkley) 1977
The Original Modern Lovers (Bomp) 1981

At the outset of his career, Jonathan
Richman was considered a radical trail-
blazer, precociously exploring minimalist
rock years before such behavior became popular (or even acceptable). Not only was his
unique approach enormously influential on
later bands, early members of the Modern
Lovers went on to become successful in such
groups as Talking Heads and the Cars. Over
the course of his recordings, however, Richman's predilection for childlike whimsy replaced the angst-ridden emotionalism of his
first songs, and he eventually lost his flock by
refusing to remain the same character he had
been a decade earlier.

The first Modern Lovers album was cobbled together by Beserkley supremo Matthew
King Kaufman out of demos, the bulk of
which had been produced by John Cale in
1971 when it looked as if the band would be
signed to Warner Bros. Despite the fragmentary nature of its parts, **The Modern Lovers**
is surprisingly coherent and contains all of
Richman's classic creations: "Roadrunner,"
"Pablo Picasso," "Girl Friend," "She
Cracked," etc. The stark, simple performances highlight an adenoidal New England
voice that lacks everything technical but
nothing emotional. One of the truly great art-
rock albums of all time.

Although released shortly after **The
Modern Lovers**, **Jonathan Richman & the
Modern Lovers** was recorded five years later
with a totally different band, and has little in
common with the first LP. Not realizing the
time frame, many people took this as a sign
of artistic inconsistency, and were put off by
such silliness as "Abominable Snowman in
the Market" and "Hey There Little Insect."
The record is, in fact, pretty great, blending
guilelessness with such heart-wrenching
pieces of honesty as "Important in Your
Life." Enough of Richman's early approach

carries over to temper the giddy romps, and
it's a thoroughly charming, low-key album.

Rock'n'Roll takes Richman even further
away from seriousness. Mixing traditional
folk songs and lullabies with originals that
would do Mister Rogers proud ("Ice Cream
Man," "Rockin' Rockin' Leprechaun"), the
ironically-titled album stretched the ability
of his adult fans to join in the fun. Abiding
wittiness—like "Dodge Veg-O-Matic"—
hedges the album's stylistic bet, but many
were left wondering just where Richman was
heading.

Live, recorded in England, is full of the
flakiest songs in his repertoire—featherweight and best suited for very young people.
The Jonathan Richman Songbook is a compilation, as is **The Beserkley Years**, a fine CD-
only collection of 18 classic tracks, both studio and live.

Back in Your Life was recorded (after a
long layoff) with two different bands, the regular Modern Lovers and a vocals/string
bass/glockenspiel ensemble. The songs are
totally over the top, as fanciful and ridiculous
as possible. There's nothing remotely connected to the original Modern Lovers'
rock'n'roll work; comparisons to Groucho
Marx's musical ventures are more relevant.
Impossible to hate, this record merely defies
honest enthusiasm.

Four years later, the same is fortunately
not the case on **Jonathan Sings!**, an utterly
wonderful LP showcasing a fully revitalized
Richman with an altogether new outlook.
Audibly bursting with love, Richman eloquently (in his own ingenuously clumsy way)
sings of "That Summer Feeling," exclaims
"You're the One for Me" and rejoices at having "Somebody to Hold Me." Elsewhere, he
defends the innate wisdom of infants in "Not
Yet Three," offers a new look at world travel
("Give Paris One More Chance") and even
extolls the joys of "This Kind of Music." The
new Modern Lovers—two women and three
men—have a strong but understated presence that keeps Richman exciting without
getting in his way. Simply put, **Jonathan
Sings!** is one of the most uplifting albums in
memory, and Richman's best since his debut.

Jonathan's stayed on the right track (with
an exception) ever since, issuing one charming album after the next. **Rockin' and Romance** (retaining two Modern Lovers from
Sings) is a spartan, casually-produced (to the
point of sonic obscurity) affair, but songs
about "The Beach," "Vincent Van Gogh"

(number two in Richman's Great Painters series), baseball ("Walter Johnson," "The Fenway"), travel ("Bermuda") and other winning topics are all filled with his remarkable wit and intelligence. Who else could write a paean to bluejeans that discusses the relative merits of various brands without being mistaken for a commercial? Slight demerits for the shoddy sound quality, but no complaints whatsoever about the music.

It's Time For reunites Richman with erstwhile Modern Lover guitarist Asa Brebner. The audio fidelity is better; an accordionist, producer Andy Paley's guitar work and Richman's sax tooting make for an unusual, busier-than-ordinary (relatively speaking) rock sound. "Yo Jo Jo" is a crazed instrumental rave-up, the most electric thing he's done in this decade. Richman's lyrical concerns are more general than in the recent past: for every "Double Chocolate Malted" (which has a strangely cranky tone to it) or "Corner Store," there are two songs (e.g., "It's You," "When I Dance," "Just About Seventeen," "This Love of Mine") that are less specific and to a degree less captivating. A confusing (or is that confused?) album, **It's Time For** has the aura of a transitional project.

Never fear. Accompanied by a second guitarist and a drummer, Richman grabbed his oft-neglected saxophone and cut the magical **Modern Lovers 88**, an all-too-brief set of semi-electric rock tunes that hark back in composition and presentation to **Jonathan Richman & the Modern Lovers**. The woolly "Dancin Late at Night" and the romantic "Gail Loves Me" display a budding Holly orientation that bears more exploration; "New Kind of Neighborhood" resembles Dion; "California Desert Party," "Everything's Gotta Be Right" and "Circle I" (a delightful ode to vegetables) convert the essential ingredients of '50s R&B into airy but exciting dance-rock as only the Modern Lovers can.

The demos dredged up for **The Original Modern Lovers** date from 1973 and were produced by Kim Fowley. The LP includes two versions of "Roadrunner," plus "Astral Plane," "Girlfren" and "She Cracked," as well as some otherwise unreeorded numbers. Despite thin sound it offers slightly different approaches than what surfaced on the first album. Shoddy but relevant.   [iar]

See also *Cars, Robin Lane and the Chart-busters, Necessaries, Real Kids, Talking Heads.*

STAN RIDGWAY

The Big Heat EP (nr/Illegal) 1985
The Big Heat (IRS) 1986

It's no coincidence that the lyrics on **The Big Heat** album (the EP is a pre-LP teaser) are printed on the inner sleeve in prose format; ex-Wall of Voodoo singer Ridgway's a pulp novelist at heart. Delivered with his exaggerated side-of-the-mouth delivery and instrumentation that reaches for maximum film noir ambience, the songs recount amazing stories of crime, war and bizarre characters in a highly engaging and uncommon fashion. **The Big Heat** is a rare record—one that will have you as interested in the lyrical action as its substantial musical attributes.
[iar]

ZOOGZ RIFT

Idiots on the Miniature Golf Course (Snout) 1979 (SST) 1987
Amputees in Limbo (SST) 1984 ●
Ipecac (SST) 1985
Interim Resurgence (SST) 1985
Island of Living Puke (SST) 1986
Looser Than Clams . . . a Historical Retrospective (SST) 1986
Water (SST) 1987
Water II: At Safe Distance (SST) 1987
Nonentity (Water III: Fan Black Dada) (SST) 1988

As imaginative and stimulating as he is irritating and vitriolic, former New Jerseyite and present Californian Zoogz Rift is an iconoclastic original, a reactionary whose paranoia too frequently detracts from his music's experimental pizzazz and considerable exotic charm. This might be explained by his primary intellectual inspirations: Salvador Dali's dadaist strategies and Ayn Rand's objective realism. Rift is (too) often compared musically to Frank Zappa and Captain Beefheart; while this may have applied to his earlier recordings, the past few years have found Rift toiling prolifically in a fertile field all his own.

Idiots on the Miniature Golf Course, by Zoogz Rift's Micro Mastodons, features songwriting and percussion by Rift's longtime associate Richie Häss. Dedicated to Don Van Vliet, this collection of private surrealistic humor, overambitiously complex writing and self-consciously zany performances sets the tone for much of what was to follow. Another featured player on this collection is John Van Zelm Trubee, who has stuck it out with Rift on and off over the years, and is infamous in his own right for the classic novelty single, "A Blind Man's Penis," and his own albums (e.g., **The Communists Are Coming to Kill Us!**) with the Ugly Janitors of America.

Ipecac and **Amputees in Limbo** form a paranoid pair whose emotional timbre is evident in titles like "My Daddy Works for the Secret Marines," "Art Band" ("You're nothing but a fart band"), "I Was the Only Boy at the Teen Girls Slumber Party" and "You Fucked Up." Rift's Amazing Shitheads, as his band of the time was called, was an uncompromising group of competent yahoos in acerbic synch with their leader.

On **Interim Resurgence** and the charmingly-titled **Island of Living Puke**, Rift begins to lighten up slightly. Amusing self-analysis ("Nightclub Sequence") and cosmic etherea ("X-Ray Girls") share space with his usual spleen ventilation.

Looser Than Clams is an, ahem, "greatest hits" LP that serves as an intermission prior to Rift's H20 trilogy. By **Water**, his musical talents have far surpassed his ranting, although his misanthropy continues unabated. **Water II** is tighter yet, with synthesizers and samplers coming to the fore. And finally, **Nonentity** (the final installment in the **Water** trilogy) may well be Rift's sweetest sugar plum to date, with off-kilter instrumentals showing off his idiosyncratic guitar playing to finest advantage, and allowing the group to simmer eccentrically in the breeze.   [rg]

WILL RIGBY
See *dB's.*

RIKKI AND THE LAST DAYS OF EARTH
Rikki and the Last Days of Earth (nr/DJM) 1978
RIKKI SYLVAN
The Silent Hours (nr/Kaleidoscope) 1981

Rikki and the Last Days of Earth made a couple of 45s and one roundly ignored album; Sylvan's subsequent solo venture doesn't do much to improve his credibility. Vocals that fall between Gary Numan and David Sylvian, predictable technocratic

songs ("I Am a Video," "Into the Void") and arty but generally bland rock with occasionally prominent synthesizer make **The Silent Hours** a derivative, dull exercise.   [iar]

MARC RILEY WITH THE CREEPERS
Creeping at Maida Vale EP (nr/In Tape) 1984
Cull (nr/In Tape) 1984
Gross Out (nr/In Tape) 1984
Shadow Figures EP (nr/In Tape) 1984
Fancy Meeting God! (nr/In Tape) 1985
Four A's from Maida Vale EP (nr/In Tape) 1985
Warts 'n' All (nr/In Tape) 1985
CREEPERS
Miserable Sinners (In Tape-Last Time Round) 1986
Rock'n'Roll Liquorice Flavour (Red Rhino-Fundamental) 1987 ●

Guitarist/keyboardist Riley was booted out of the Fall in 1982, reportedly over an unseemly penchant for pop. His prolific output as a solo artist and bandleader, however, only slightly deserves such categorization. Although Riley shares his former group's taste for deadpan vocals and distorted guitar and keyboard sounds, freed of Mark Smith's clutches he exhibits more melodic, structured songwriting and has one foot firmly rooted in the garage punk tradition.

All three EPs are taken from sessions for John Peel's radio program and feature one of Riley's favorite lyrical gambits—taking the piss out of other groups. **Creeping at Maida Vale** is a great little record, with four strong songs, including "Location Bangladesh," a clever stab at bands who travel the world for exotic video locales. **Four A's**, equally enjoyable, contains "Bard of Woking," aimed at the people's-poet pretensions of one Style Councillor. The **Cull** compilation fills one side with **Creeping** and the other with reprises of prior, vaguely Velvets-ish singles.

Gross Out, while not breaking any new musical ground, does contain one of Riley's finest moments, "Gross." **Fancy Meeting God!** is an energetic, sometimes catchy and often hilarious LP, which unfortunately loses a little zip towards the end. Had it been edited together with **Gross Out**'s highlights, the sum would have been much greater than the parts.

Warts 'n' All is a fun greatest-hits run-through recorded live in Amsterdam. As entertaining for Riley's between-song banter as it is for great songs (including Eno's pre-ambience "Baby's on Fire"), it can serve as a very good introduction to the uninitiated.

Miserable Sinners and Rock'n'Roll Liquorice Flavour both drop Riley's name (even though he's still obviously the leader) and employ Mekon/Three John Jon Langford in the producer's chair. It is on these two LPs that the Creepers are at their peak. The sound on Miserable Sinners is a dense swirl of guitars, but the real change is in the lyrical approach, which has gone from satiric funmaking to introspective and self-referencing. "I strive to be original/have my own sound/I don't run my VU records/into the ground," sings Riley.

Rock'n'Roll Liquorice Flavour follows suit with clever but serious self-examination, again tipping a hat to influences (and including a brilliant cover of the Pretty Things' '64 classic, "Rosalyn"). The Tom Waits-like piano ballad "Sweet Retreat" states "You don't have to listen to Swordfishtrombone [sic] . . . but it helps." The LP has a down-home feel—not unlike the Mekons—on several tracks, giving it more textural and stylistic variety than its predecessors. (The artsy, spoken "Derbyshire" almost sounds like Sonic Youth.) It's only reasonable that the group should break up—amidst strange stories of internal fights, both physical and artistic—after releasing their finest record. Do keep your eyes on what becomes of Riley, who has been one of rock's great hidden treasures for most of the decade. [dgs]

RIP RIG + PANIC
God (nr/Uh Huh-Virgin) 1981
I Am Cold (nr/Virgin) 1982
Attitude (nr/Virgin) 1983
MARK SPRINGER
Piano (nr/Illuminated) 1984

One of the Pop Group's numerous offshoots, Rip Rig + Panic was a jazz-funk fusion band that left art-punk behind musically but retained an irreverent sensibility. Named after a Roland Kirk LP, the band appropriately featured saxophone/piano free-for-alls. They were not as anarchic as their jazz inspirations, though; repetitive bass licks (Sean Oliver) and stable percussion (Bruce Smith) are great aids for more right-wing listeners.

The band's most appealing aspect is its high-spiritedness. Beyond absurd titles, Rip Rig + Panic leap around stylistically from (short) track to track. Tranquil piano (Mark Springer) solos and silly chats provide respite from screeching sax (Gareth Sager), Arabic and Far Eastern touches and hard-edged vocals (Neneh Cherry and, on God, ex-Slit Ari Upp). Attitude, the band's most accessible album, comes closest to normal songs, while maintaining a zany eclecticism. Far from forbidding, Rip Rig + Panic keep the show rolling with deft musicianship and oddball humor. In late 1983, they reorganized as Float Up CP. [si]

See also Float Up CP.

BRIAN RITCHIE
See Violent Femmes.

TOM ROBINSON BAND
Power in the Darkness (Harvest) 1978
TRB Two (Harvest) 1979
Tom Robinson Band (nr/Fame) 1982
TOM ROBINSON
North by Northwest (IRS) 1982
Cabaret '79 (nr/Panic) 1982
Atmospherics EP (nr/Panic) 1983
Hope and Glory (Geffen) 1984
Still Loving You (nr/Castaway) 1986
Midnight at the Fringe (nr/Dojo) 1987
The Collection 1977–1987 (nr/EMI) 1987 ●
SECTOR 27
Sector 27 (IRS) 1980

In 1975, Tom Robinson escaped from the ashes of Cafe Society, a lightweight London outfit produced by Ray Davies, to become a highly visible rock bandleader, championing various radical causes through music. Signed to EMI in the wake of that label's disastrous liaison with the Sex Pistols, Robinson's avowed homosexuality and uncompromising political stance made him an extremely controversial figure. Luckily, a brilliant (and surprisingly non-topical) first single, "2-4-6-8 Motorway," and a riveting album made the band internationally successful, affording the singing bassist the opportunity to be a real rock activist—spearheading Rock Against Racism and other organizations—rather than merely a complainer. But a myopic outlook and limited musical range drew Robinson into a morass of sloganeering and overbearing self-righteousness (especially onstage) that forced a major career rethink after only two LPs.

Power in the Darkness contains track after track of impassioned, heartfelt political anger, funneled through articulate lyrics and Danny Kustow's roaring guitar figures. The memorable songs seethe with honest conviction and convert rock energy into anthemic power. (The American release originally contained a bonus seven-song disc, compiling live tracks from an English EP and both sides of the "Motorway" single.)

TRB Two was produced by Todd Rundgren and basically encores the style and content of its predecessor, but with a more mainstream sound and fewer rough edges (not really an improvement). Robinson's alternate approach—slower numbers played at a bouncy shuffle perfect for in-concert sing-alongs—*does* improve with Todd's treatment. This brace of polemics isn't as striking as Robinson's first, but fans of **Power in the Darkness** won't find anything obviously missing here (except perhaps drummer Dolph Taylor and keyboardist Mark Ambler, who had both been replaced).

After the TRB collapsed under its own weighty baggage, Robinson formed Sector 27; its focus was more on personal relationships than politics. With a new lineup—notably including a bassist, which allowed Robinson to concentrate on singing—the restrained album has some winning songs, although none with the immediacy of his previous outings.

North by Northwest—recorded in Hamburg with only producer Richard Mazda and a drummer—is Robinson's most mature and subtle album. Featuring material co-written with Peter Gabriel and a cover of a Lewis Furey song, Robinson explores various sophisticated settings and succeeds in making a pleasantly slight record, marred only by an agonized (and agonizing) song of love lost, "Now Martin's Gone."

Cabaret '79 is a live recording made shortly after the original TRB's dissolution; it includes Robinson's confrontational signature tune, "Glad to Be Gay," as well as a reading of Noel Coward's "Mad About the Boy," which resulted in some legal problems between Robinson and Coward's estate. **Tom Robinson Band** is a useful compilation (with notes by the artist) of the band's best tracks, drawing on singles and EPs for items like "Don't Take No for an Answer," "Glad to Be Gay" and "Motorway."

Turning over a new page, Robinson then began a successful era of plainly commercial rock, captured on the **Atmospherics** EP (parts of which were incorporated onto the subsequent LP) and **Hope and Glory**. He's certainly capable of writing and recording skillfully routine music; it just doesn't make for very interesting listening: "War Baby" and a terrible version of Steely Dan's "Rikki Don't Lose That Number" were inexplicable hits. Robinson's sincerity and commitment are obvious, but mediocre singing and bland arrangements keep **Hope and Glory** from being anything but ordinary.   [iar]

TABU LEY ROCHEREAU
Tabu Ley (Shanachie) 1984
TABU LEY ROCHEREAU WITH FRANCO
Omona Wapi (Shanachie) 1984

Singer Tabu Ley Rochereau and guitar hero Franco are, respectively, the leading celebrities in their musical style. *Soukous* ("having a good time") is a shimmering, perky and ridiculously danceable pan-African sound. On **Tabu Ley**, the sexy soul singer adds a horn section, organ and backing vocalists to the sweet melodies, acoustic guitars and Afro-Cuban rhythms that define Congolese music. With comfortable naiveté, Rochereau sings (in both Zairean and French) of making love and money. **Omona Wapi** ditches a lot of the excess baggage, emphasizing instead—along with Rochereau's sweet vocals—three interlocking guitarists led by Franco's ululating lines.   [rg]

ROCK AND HYDE
See *Payolas*.

ROCKATS
Live at the Ritz (Island) 1981
Make That Move EP (RCA) 1983
LEVI AND THE ROCKATS
Louisiana Hayride (Posh Boy) 1981
LEVI
The Fun Sessions EP (PVC) 1983

The Rockats, hybrid English/American rockabilly specialists, were formed by singer Levi Dexter, whose appreciation of '50s American rock infused the band with a real traditionalist ethic. They made only one record together before splintering; bassist Smutty Smiff subsequently kept the Rockats' name alive. **Louisiana Hayride**, recorded live in Shreveport, Louisiana in 1979, bristles with feeling, but lacks something in recording quality, especially as regards the mix. And if there was an audience at that gig, no one bothered telling them to clap.

Live at the Ritz, cut in New York over a year later, is a much slicker affair—a premonition of the Stray Cats but without a magnetic personality like Brian Setzer. With Levi gone and a new lineup in place, the playing's fine, the sound quality is great and the tunes all sound like Johnny Cash should be singing 'em. (One of the new members—guitarist Tim Scott—went on a few years later to make an EP of unpleasant dance-rock under his own name.)

Make That Move, with a new guitarist and drummer in the quintet, attempts to effect a stylistic escape. Produced by Mike Thorne, one side isn't rockabilly at all, instead using keyboards to build an energetic but characterless soup. On the flip, the overbearing "Go Cat Wild" contains more drums than all of the Stray Cats' records put together. Only the title song and "Never So Clever" recapture the band's original sound with a glimmer of the old spirit.

Dexter, for his part, sticks to the straight and narrow on **The Fun Sessions**. Sharing production with Richard Gottehrer and employing a basic 'billy trio, he hiccoups his way through five cool tracks exploding with understated energy. Not innovative by any means, but I'll take his earnest copies over the Rockats' boring originals any day.

[iar]

See also *Tim Scott.*

ROCKPILE
Seconds of Pleasure (Columbia) 1980 ●

Rockpile's sole moment in the spotlight is at least as exhilarating as anything Nick Lowe or Dave Edmunds has done on his own. As usual, this is rock'n'roll with the accent on "roll." Obvious influences include the Everly Brothers ("Now and Always") and Chuck Berry (his own "What a Thrill"). The blues "A Knife and a Fork" and the medium-tempo "When I Write the Book" are rare respites. **Seconds of Pleasure** has the extra bonus of guitarist Billy Bremner singing the rollickin' "Heart" and "You Ain't Nothin' but Fine." Throughout, the band delivers the hard-partying, good-time music we've come to expect from Lowe and Edmunds, together or (now, sadly) apart.

The LP originally included a 7-inch single, **Nick Lowe & Dave Edmunds Sing the Everly Brothers**, with their renditions of "Take a Message to Mary," "When Will I Be Loved" and two more classics. [si]

See also *Billy Bremner, Dave Edmunds, Nick Lowe.*

NILE RODGERS
Adventures in the Land of the Good Groove (Mirage) 1983
B-Movie Matinee (Warner Bros.) 1985 ●

Guitarist Nile Rodgers co-produced David Bowie's best—uh, best-*sounding*—album. So does the runaway success of **Let's Dance** mean Rodgers is a musical mastermind? Chic's string of hits (the group's own as well as productions for others) suggests the answer is yes; Rodgers' first solo LP, however, begs to differ. Nile proves he can make a fair-to-middling one-man Chic (no mean feat), but a visionary he's not—unless you define vision as smug sexism. The neatest touch on the record is the mass of chorus vocals sung with a drum machine "at P.S. 111 playground right after school," according to the sleeve notes. A pity the song ("Yum-Yum") is the album's most offensive meditation on the desirability of "poontang."

Complete with 3-D cover (but no glasses), **B-Movie Matinee** reflects Rodgers' cinematic tastes, offering such promising referents as "Plan-9," "Doll Squad" and "The Face in the Window." Unfortunately, while the music is unassailable (especially Jimmy Bralower's precision drumming and Rodgers' snappy guitar work), the thankfully smug-free lyrics aren't half as good as the titles. Nonetheless, a state-of-the-art dance record. (And the dreamy ballad, "Wavelength," is lovely.) [mf/iar]

See also *Outloud.*

HENRY ROLLINS
Hot Animal Machine (Texas Hotel) 1987 ●
Big Ugly Mouth (Texas Hotel) 1987

HENRIETTA COLLINS & THE WIFEBEATING CHILDHATERS
Drive by Shooting EP (Texas Hotel) 1987

ROLLINS BAND
Life Time (Texas Hotel) 1988
Do It (Texas Hotel) 1988

Since the dissolution of Black Flag in 1986, singer/lyricist Henry Rollins has pursued a dual existence as a poet (by the time Black Flag broke up, he was already a seasoned veteran of the spoken-word tour circuit) and leader of his own band. While Greg Ginn's post-Flag projects have taken a decidedly acid-metal turn, Rollins has thankfully stayed on course to produce powerful, driven rock, not unlike **Loose Nut**-era Black Flag.

His first solo effort, **Hot Animal Machine** (recorded in the UK in late '86), with cover art by Mark Mothersbaugh, gets off to an explosive start with "Black and White" before sailing into a paranoia-tinged trio ("Followed Around," "Lost and Found," "There's a Man Outside") that keeps up the frenzied pace. The LP occasionally lapses into silliness ("A Man and a Woman," the bluesy, cliché-riddled "Crazy Lover"), but provides some neat covers (Suicide's "Ghost Rider" and the Velvets' "Move Right In").

Drive by Shooting (credited to Henrietta Collins & the Wifebeating Childhaters—band members are rechristened with female monikers—Henry Rollins gets guest billing), recorded during the **Hot Animal Machine** sessions, kicks off with with the title track, a novelty number about Los Angeles gang warfare, replete with surf/car song appropriations (guitar line courtesy of "Wipeout"). The EP also boasts a solid rendition of Wire's "Ex-Lion Tamer" and a pretty funny (albeit tasteless) send-up of Queen's "We Will Rock You" called "I Have Come To Kill You." To prove his fallibility, Rollins includes two total throwaways: "Hey Henrietta" and "Men Are Pigs."

Big Ugly Mouth was culled from various speaking engagements around the country. In an uncharacteristic display of humility and sensitivity, he discourses on a variety of subjects including social and racial injustice, child abuse and sexual harassment. In a more humorous vein, he tackles masturbation, birthdays and advertising—just for starters. Sharp, witty and entertaining.

Life Time is the first LP by the newly formed Rollins Band. Only guitarist Chris Haskett remains from the former lineup; the new rhythm section comes, oddly enough, from Greg Ginn's Gone. Alienation is the unifying lyrical theme on this record: "Burned Beyond Recognition," "What Am I Doing Here?" and "There's Nothing Like Finding Someone When You're Lonely to Make You Want to Be All Alone" should get the point across. A typical lyric: "I hate the world that I think hates me/Punch holes in the wall you know that hurts me/I feel dark and cold and alone, it burns me/Wish someone would come and touch me." Musically, it's Rollins' most adventurous project. Straightforward rock stylings give way to more experimental song structures, jazz-inflected bass lines and tricky time changes without compromising the sheer force.

In addition to his musical exploits, Henry Rollins has published six volumes of poetry, available through the Illiterati Press.   [rj]

ROLL-UPS
Low Dives for Highballs (nr/Bridge House) 1979

These popsters from South London anomalously emerged in the midst of the mod revival, on a mod label no less. They go in a lot of different directions but are saved by spunky individuality that lets them build a niche of their own. Lea Hart (almost all the songwriting) sings like a cocky cockney crossed with a dollop of—it's true!—Donald Fagen, and melds his guitar to Jeff Peters' in dual-axe moves Brian May didn't have in mind when he wrote the book. Add an assortment of non-electronic keyboards, and you've got a swell pop recipe for songs ranging from a 10cc-ish look at adulterous "Blackmail" to shock-horror destruction as epic as any punk's. (Hart later tried a solo career, formed Ya Ya for a major label LP which is best forgotten and, most recently, hooked up with Fast Eddie Clarke of Motorhead in a new outfit.)   [jg]

ROMAN HOLLIDAY
Roman Holliday EP (Jive) 1983
Cookin' on the Roof (Jive) 1983
Fire Me Up (Jive) 1984

Typical of the ability of English pop to absorb virtually any musical style so long as the band dresses colorfully, the seven-man Roman Holliday succeeded for a minute by playing fired-up jumpin' jive in sailor caps. The five-song EP, an American teaser compiled from UK singles, is great fun, containing "Stand By," "Motor Mania" and "Don't Try to Stop It." Dead catchy and brilliantly produced by Peter Collins, if utterly disposable.

Cookin' on the Roof expands the EP to ten numbers but with no accompanying increase in entertainment. The new tracks are largely over-stylized and under-ingenious.

Music this derivative and gimmicky requires pinpoint accuracy in hitting just the right balance of new and old; the filler isn't bad, just dispensable in light of their better efforts.

Following a top-to-bottom rethink by the band, **Fire Me Up** sounds nothing like its predecessor. Looking like rockabilly sharpies and soft-pedaling the horns and jazz in favor of synths and modern rock'n'roll, Roman Holliday's bland new direction is strictly yesterday's news. Useless. And "One Foot Back in Your Door," the Mutt Lange-written single which leads off the LP, is really bad bombast.   [iar]

ROMANTICS

The Romantics (Nemperor) 1980 •
National Breakout (Nemperor) 1980
Strictly Personal (Nemperor) 1981
In Heat (Nemperor) 1983 •
Rhythm Romance (Nemperor) 1985 •

Once upon a time, Detroit's Romantics were the band the Knack always wanted to be, hammering out a few essential chords while the singer wailed out inconsequential lyrics, usually about girls. They played fast, loose and tough but, unlike the Knack, weren't obnoxious. This is the kind of band that would have been happy jamming to "Louie, Louie" or "La Bamba" all night if they hadn't been able to devise their own alternatives.

The Romantics' self-titled debut and **National Breakout** capture that era beautifully. Silly red leather suits notwithstanding, **The Romantics** shows the boys at their most raucous, crashing through "What I Like About You" (their best-ever track) and other dance-floor pips. The optimistically-titled second LP continues in the "Twist and Shout" vein, highlighted by "Tomboy" and "Stone Pony."

Strictly Personal, the panicky response to disappointing sales, finds the Romantics switching from powerful pop to soulless arena-rock. All broad, exaggerated gestures and no charm. Sad. **In Heat** wiped away the tears, elevating the band into the Top 10 with the execrable "Talking in Your Sleep" and the far more likable "One in a Million." Having hit the heights, drummer/singer Jimmy Marinos left the group; the others hung in to make **Rhythm Romance**, another likably dumb batch of pop songs culminating in a credibly rootsy version of "Poison Ivy."
                                                    [jy/iar]

ROMEO VOID

It's a Condition (415) 1981
Never Say Never (415-Columbia) 1982
Benefactor (415-Columbia) 1982
Instincts (415-Columbia) 1984

DEBORA IYALL

Strange Language (415-Columbia) 1986

Walloping big-beat riffs with snaky sax and darkly intelligent lyrics characterize this San Francisco area dance/think combo. Native American artist-and-poet-turned-vocalist Debora Iyall uses her smoky, conversational voice to wax reflective on love and lust in these modern times; consistent with the band's name, she sings not only of situations where love is absent, but also of when it *should* be absent.

It's a Condition introduced Romeo Void's unique blend of jazz, funk, rock and confrontational poetry in its formative stages, the music a bit tentative and unfocused, especially in contrast with Iyall's hard-edged lyrics. **Never Say Never**, a four-song EP co-produced by Ric Ocasek, gained the group significant airplay and sales, leading to the link between San Francisco independent 415 and the CBS megalith. It's consequently no surprise that a truncated version of "Never Say Never" opens up **Benefactor**; as it turns out, that song proved to be more of a stylistic mold than might be considered healthy.

The most fully-realized record of the bunch, **Instincts** boasts rich, full-blooded production, top-notch playing and reprises of various stylistic avenues. "Just Too Easy" resembles "Never Say Never" and pairs Ben Bossi's ace sax work with Iyall's sardonic, spoken monologue; "A Girl in Trouble (Is a Temporary Thing)" touches a poppier, more melodic side; "Six Days and One" reverts to a spare, mainly rhythmic approach. Mixing strength with beauty, Romeo Void makes very special dance music for the mind.

A strange blend of unlikely people creating rather unsurprising music, Iyall's solo album was produced by Pat Irwin, once a Lydia Lunch collaborator in 8-Eyed Spy and later a Raybeat. The cast includes Irwin (clarinet, sax, guitar, synth), Richard Sohl (pianist in the original Patti Smith Group) and others; Ben Bossi (sax) and Aaron Smith (drums) of Romeo Void also participate. Iyall obviously takes her poetry seriously; unfortunately, Irwin (co-writer of six tunes here) leads the musicians through underwhelming, blandly faceless rock backing that pointedly lacks Romeo Void's atmospherics. [rnp/iar]

KRISTI ROSE AND THE MIDNIGHT WALKERS

Some People (Rounder) 1986

High-voltage country-western rock from New York: powerhouse singer Rose, backed by a loud trio that boasts ex-Television bassist Fred Smith, belts out twangy Nashville-styled originals and a couple of classics on this energetic debut. Rose's bracing voice takes after Wanda Jackson and is the most notable ingredient here; the Midnight Walkers wander between polite country backing and near-punk aggression. The Uptown Horns help out on a couple of tracks. [iar]

KEVIN ROWLAND

See *Dexy's Midnight Runners.*

ROXY MUSIC

Roxy Music (Reprise) 1972 (Atco) 1977 ●
For Your Pleasure . . . (Warner Bros.) 1973
  (Atco) 1977 ●
Stranded (Atco) 1973 ●
Country Life (Atco) 1974 ●
Siren (Atco) 1975 ●
Viva! (Atco) 1976 ●
Greatest Hits (Atco) 1977
Manifesto (Atco) 1979 ●
Flesh + Blood (Atco) 1980 ●
The First Seven Albums (nr/EG-Polydor) 1981
Avalon (Warner Bros.) 1982 ●
The High Road EP (Warner Bros.) 1983
The Atlantic Years 1973–1980 (Atco) 1983 ●

ROXY MUSIC/BRYAN FERRY
Street Life (nr/EG) 1986 ●

ANDY MACKAY

In Search of Eddie Riff (nr/Island) 1974
Resolving Contradictions (nr/Bronze) 1978

Arguably the most influential rock group of the '70s, Roxy Music's impact has become more obvious in the years since the original punk return-to-the-basics ethos gave way to a growing interest in style and fashion and art. The "new romantic" movement and the synth fops would have had no historical traditions to follow were it not for the pioneering efforts of Bryan Ferry, Brian Eno, Phil Manzanera, Andy Mackay, Paul Thompson and their various cohorts. Even though Roxy

Music grew pale and rather timid in its later years, the recorded work (not to mention the countless side projects that all the various members have produced or participated in) stands as a seminal wellspring of nonconformity and successful art-pop experimentation.

With the release of their first LP, London's fledgling Roxy Music revolutionized rock—trashing concepts of melodic conservatism, ignoring the prevalence of blues-based and otherwise derivative idioms and denying the need for technical virtuosity, either vocally or instrumentally. The flamboyantly bedecked poseurs presaged such low couture iconoclasts as the New York Dolls and all that followed them; the music mixed all sorts of elements into a newly filtered original sound that set the stylish pace. The tracks—classics like "Re-make/Re-model," "2 H.B.," "If There Is Something" and (on later versions) "Virginia Plain"—are amateurish but highly developed, blunders of brilliance that took some getting used to. The use of kitsch graphics on this landmark LP also proved to be often imitated.

For Your Pleasure refines and magnifies Roxy's style with equally amazing material like "Do the Strand," "Editions of You" and "In Every Dream Home a Heartache." Another classic record. **Stranded**, the first LP after the departure of Brian Eno, introduces violinist Eddie Jobson to the fold and pursues a more subtle sound, favoring slower and quieter songs, such as "Mother of Pearl," "Sunset" and "Psalm," while still finding room to rock on the whirlingly chaotic "Street Life."

Roxy's best LP, **Country Life**, ran into trouble over its revealing cover photo—some American copies were shrink-wrapped in opaque green plastic; later the cover was changed to remove the bra'n'panties-clad models and leave only the foliage. Regardless, the ten tracks are exemplary and of consistent strength—almost a greatest-hits album of new material. Highly recommended.

Siren was the final studio album of Roxy's first era. There are some great tracks ("Love Is the Drug," "Both Ends Burning," "Sentimental Fool"), but an overabundance of forgettable numbers substantially diminishes its value. Roxy then went on sabbatical, with only the one-disc live document (**Viva!**) and the essential **Greatest Hits** collection issued during the two-year gap.

Reactivating Roxy Music, Ferry, Manzanera and Mackay made three group LPs with various part-time sidemen, but it wasn't the same. Although there are a few brilliant tracks (like "Dance Away," "Over You," "Angel Eyes," etc.) on each of the albums, the overly refined low-key approach bears only passing resemblance to the unpredictable rock weirdness of their best work. (An otherwise needless compilation, **The Atlantic Years**, consolidates the best of **Manifesto** and **Flesh + Blood** onto one disc, adding two earlier cuts from **Greatest Hits**.) Fortunately, these records neither embarrass nor contradict the Roxy legacy; this period (subsequently proving to be the group's last and, in America at least, most successful) is separate and, though not equal, at least estimable.

Addenda: In 1981, the band's English management and label repackaged all of Roxy Music's studio albums to that point—seven in all—as a boxed set; add in **Avalon**, and you've got the works. Mixing selections from the band with Ferry's solo career, **Street Life** offers 20 tracks on two discs. **The High Road**, recorded live in Glasgow, offers four oddly-chosen tunes and a running time approaching half an hour as a ten-person lineup walks through Neil Young's "Like a Hurricane," John Lennon's "Jealous Guy" and two Ferry tunes. The playing is, of course, great and the sound magnificent—only the band's crucial personality is absent.

Roxy Music finally called it a career after 1983. Ferry resumed his solo work again with a new album in mid-'85; Manzanera and Mackay formed a new trio called the Explorers and have each recorded solo albums.

As big a long-term disappointment as Ferry's and Manzanera's extra-Roxy careers have been, Andy Mackay's individual efforts reached the blandness plateau first, way ahead of the pack. His first showcase, **In Search of Eddie Riff**, is a mildly diverting mostly-instrumental outing enlivened only by a sweaty saxual interpretation of Richard Wagner's "Ride of the Valkyries" and several more-traditional covers. Otherwise, it's merely a display of his technical abilities.

His next big project was to write and produce two albums' worth of pop music for *Rock Follies,* a neat '70s British TV show about a female singing trio. They're neat, but clearly work for hire. By the time of the Asian-oriented **Resolving Contradictions**, Mackay had banished any trace of wit: the record is a snooze. However, on a literary front, Mackay wrote a useful 1981 text on the development of electronic music.   [iar]

See also *Brian Eno, Explorers, Bryan Ferry, Phil Manzanera, Savage Progress, Yukihiro Takahashi.*

ROYAL COURT OF CHINA
Off the Beat'n Path (Desperation) 1986
The Royal Court of China (A&M) 1987 ●

Nashville's Royal Court of China (formerly known as the Enemy) play it hot and sloppy on their independent-label debut, a vivacious seven-song mini-album that fills out Joe Blanton's songs with swirls of wild-eyed guitar to counterbalance his dramatic singing. The quartet's ripping cover of the Yardbirds' "Heart Full of Soul" indicates one influence on their garage-rocking Southeastern pop, but only one of several. A fine informal introduction to a promising band with a cool sound.

As if the group's meaningless name weren't misleading enough, the artwork on their 1987 album furthers the stylistic obfuscation. **The Royal Court of China**, which RCC produced, shows impressive instrumental and studio facility, but cuts back on the youthful energy a tad too much. While there's no shortage of melodies or guitars, some of the songs fade towards repetitive anonymity, veering into an undistinguished Byrds-country sound. The Royal Court may have escaped the bar band wilderness for a brighter, smoother future, but they need to find something more compelling to replace the immediacy they've lost.   [iar]

ROYAL CRESCENT MOB
Land of Sugar (nr/Play It Again Sam) 1986
Omerta (Moving Target-Celluloid) 1987 ●

This multi-racial quartet from Columbus, Ohio takes punk-funk to its logical extreme, combining a strongarm/goodfoot rhythm section with a guitarist weaned on both James Brown (whose "Payback" they cover) and the Stooges, and a passionate harmonica-blowing singer (David Ellison) who doesn't hide the color of his skin. The results on **Omerta** are pretty excellent: the casually-recorded vamps display an irreverent sense of humor and rock like crazy, drawing on two lifetimes of musical tradition for a blast of unstereotyped dance noise. Whether rocking up the Ohio Players' "Fire" or revving on an original like "Get on the Bus," the Mob plays it tight and lets things fall apart with equal aplomb.   [iar]

RUBBER CITY REBELS
From Akron (Clone) 1977
Rubber City Rebels (Capitol) 1980
FIRETONES
Trouble EP (Warner Sisters) 1983

Although Devo, Rachel Sweet, Chrissie Hynde and the Waitresses all fared well on major labels, the Rubber City Rebels proved it was possible to come from Akron, Ohio and still find total commercial oblivion. The Rebels' stock in trade was blazing guitar and funny lyrics that recalled the first Dictators' album. **From Akron**, a local self-release, was shared with the Bizarros; the Rebels' side contains such ghastly/funny send-ups as "Child Eaters" and "Brain Job."

Leaving Akron for Los Angeles, the Rebels became known, got signed and were produced by ex-Knacker Doug Fieger. With loud instrumental skill and a finely developed sense of the absurd, **Rubber City Rebels** is a knockout record, mixing wonderfully snotty originals like "Young and Dumb" and a re-recorded "Child Eaters" with great covers—Jack Lee's touching "Paper Dolls" and the Sex Pistols' "No Feelings." A truly enjoyable dose of rock satire for the terminally stupid. I love it.

After the Rebels split up, leader Rod Firestone formed the Firetones and released the **Trouble** EP—four songs duplicated on both sides of a 12-inch. Unlike his former band, all the humor here is on the sleeve; the melodic guitar tunes offer rock excitement but not much rib tickling.   [iar]

RUBBER RODEO
Rubber Rodeo EP (Eat) 1982
Scenic Views (Mercury) 1984 ●
Heartbreak Highway (Mercury) 1986

Armed with the slogan "It don't mean a thang if it ain't got that twang" inscribed in the vinyl, the six-song **Rubber Rodeo** 12-inch helped announce/advance the development of country-punk. The band hailed from Rhode Island, but that didn't stop it from dressing in Nashville finery and forging a mix of synthesizer, fiddle, organ, pedal steel guitar and drums that's different and fun. The originals (especially "How the West Was Won") are bouncily tuneful and heartfelt; a cover version of Dolly Parton's "Jolene"

comes off a bit like Heart without the arena pomp. Weird but worth it.

Following a three-song 12-inch most notable for its inclusion of the theme from "The Good, the Bad and the Ugly," Rubber Rodeo signed to a major label and recorded a debut album under the supervision of Hugh Jones (Echo and the Bunnymen, Damned). Unfortunately, along the way to **Scenic Views**, Rubber Rodeo misplaced their personality and emerged a plain-sounding dance-rock group (mild pedal steel coloration notwithstanding). Only the vocals—by Trish Milliken and Bob Holmes, sometimes together—serve to distinguish it from any routine MTV outfit. "The Hardest Thing," which recalls the band's early Great Plains ambience, is the LP's strongest song.

Heartbreak Highway (produced by Ken Scott) is much better, but still leaves one wishing the band's records were more colorful and gimmicky. Rubber Rodeo's urban cowpoke image remains stronger than its musical personality, although some of the songs (most notably the title track, "Maybe Next Year," a radical cover of the grotesquely sappy "Everybody's Talkin'" and an instrumental called "The Civil War") have a redeemingly jaunty air of good-humored kitsch.   [iar]

RUBINOOS
The Rubinoos (Beserkley) 1977
Back to the Drawing Board (Beserkley) 1979
Party of Two EP (Warner Bros.) 1983

The adolescent Rubinoos' inclusion on Beserkley's highly selective roster may have been related to the fact that guitarist T.V. Dunbar had a brother in Earthquake, the label's charter band. Or it may simply have been that someone noticed they were a great, fresh-sounding pop band with talent far beyond their tender years. A clear, no-frills approach, solid original songs and convincing vocals (from Jon Rubin, the group's namesake) made them eminently likable, and earned the band a moderate national hit with Tommy James' "I Think We're Alone Now." Their first album, which included the single, also boasted a great white-soul tune called "Hard to Get" and a lightly raucous rave-up, "Rock and Roll Is Dead." Although a bit bland, **The Rubinoos** doesn't have one bad song, half-baked performance or dumb lyric. Slight but fun.

Their second album, aptly named for the

band's near brush with the big time, found them a bit more mature but less self-assured. Except for one superb Raspberries soundalike, "I Wanna Be Your Boyfriend," the record seems too anxious to please, and suffers from noticeable timidity and fewer memorable songs.

Reduced to a duo of Rubin and Dunbar, the Rubinoos drifted back into view four years later with **Party of Two**, a disposable EP of five slick pop songs produced and played by Todd Rundgren and Utopia. All the right components are in place—melodies, harmonies, meaningless lyrics, etc.—but there's no youthful spark left to ignite any serious excitement. [iar]

RUDIMENTARY PENI

Rudimentary Peni EP (nr/Outer Himalayan) 1981
Farce EP (nr/Crass) 1982
Death Church (nr/Corpus Christi) 1983

This London hardcore trio from the Crass family was forced to dissolve by illness. The eponymous EP is pretty rough going: the band is fairly tight but tuneless. Nick Blinko's screeching vocals obscure heartfelt lyrics and more than one track is ruined by wrong-speed mastering. A wider variety of rhythms than most of their ilk offer suggested promise, however, and the second EP corrects most of the problems. Things come together on **Death Church**, as venomous lyrics rip through loud and clear (as they should, given titles like "Vampire State Building" and "Alice Crucifies the Paedophiles"). While the songs are not exactly hook-laden, this is quite melodic for the genre. Tempos run from moderate metal through Pistols-style thrash to hyper-drive blur. An intelligent, exciting and highly recommended album. [dgs]

RUEFREX

Flowers for All Occasions (MCA) 1986
Political Wings EP (nr/Flicknife) 1987

Ireland's Ruefrex (whose first release was an EP on the estimable Good Vibrations label) is one of the growing legion of nouveau guitar bands whose existence proves how influential (and inimitable) U2 really is. **Flowers for All Occasions** is a forgettable album, produced by Mick Glossop, which fits nicely alongside the earnest and overblown pomp of the Alarm, Zerra I, the Waterboys, etc. The

drums sound annoyingly huge, and lead vocalist Allan Clarke is a breast-beating Richard Jobson type. On the rare occasion songs display some subtlety, you know just when the big climax will occur—they have energy, but no idea how to use it. To make things worse, "Even in the Dark Hours" proves that '70s-length guitar solos aren't totally dead. Avoid this one.

Political Wings, five new songs recorded live in the studio and produced by drummer/lyricist Paul Burgess. As poor as the ugly industrial funk is, it's no match for the self-righteous lyrics. [dgs/iar]

RUMOUR

Max (Mercury) 1977
Frogs Sprouts Clogs and Krauts (Arista) 1979
Purity of Essence (Hannibal) 1980

It's tempting to compare the Rumour's relationship with Graham Parker to the Band's with Bob Dylan: Highly respected but unsuccessful bar band (Brinsley Schwarz and Ducks Deluxe versus the Hawks) hooks up with talented singer/songwriter (Parker versus Dylan) to create some of the decade's best music ('70s versus '60s). Of course Parker is not Dylan, and **Max**, the Rumour's first LP on their own, is not **Big Pink**, although they would obviously have loved it to be. Often enough, the Rumour (Brinsley Schwarz, Bob Andrews, Martin Belmont, Andrew Bodnar, Steve Goulding) captures the *sound* of the Band, minus Robertson's lyrical profundity. What's really strange is that the Rumour is far more natural and interesting as a minor-league Band (on great tracks like "Hard Enough to Show," "Mess with Love" and a sublime Band-like arrangement of Duke Ellington's standard "Do Nothing 'Til You Hear from Me") than when attempting to forge their own identity on the subsequent albums. **Max** may not be terribly original but it is utterly enjoyable.

Frogs, on the other hand, seems to be an attempt to recast the Rumour in a vein that conforms more with Stiff's offbeat image. As a clever pop-oriented band, they succeed mainly in *sounding* stiff, with only a couple of songs ("Emotional Traffic," "All Fall Down") standing out from other failed experiments.

Purity of Essence succeeds in recapturing some of the looseness of **Max**. The band had been reduced to a quartet with the departure of Bob Andrews, whose voice—the group's best—and keyboards are missed. Even so, the album has its moments, although they mostly come on non-original material. While lacking a real frontman and strong material of its own, the Rumour is talented enough to make enjoyable (if not hit) records.

The Rumour also backed Garland Jeffreys on his **Rock & Roll Adult** live LP and have worked—as a whole or individually—on other projects since parting ways with Graham Parker after **The Up Escalator**. In 1985, Brinsley Schwarz rejoined Parker. Belmont was later part of Nick Lowe's ensemble. [ds]

RUNAWAYS

The Runaways (Mercury) 1976
Queens of Noise (Mercury) 1977
Live in Japan (nr/Mercury) 1977
Waitin' for the Night (Mercury) 1977
And Now . . . the Runaways (nr/Cherry Red) 1979
Flaming Schoolgirls (nr/Cherry Red) 1980
Little Lost Girls (Rhino) 1981
The Best of the Runaways (Mercury) 1982 ●
I Love Playing with Fire (nr/Laker-Cherry Red) 1982

Opinion is still divided on the Runaways' place in the musical universe. To many, they were the first all-girl (instrument-playing) rock band to matter, spiritual godmothers to the Go-Go's and Bangles, and seminal punk rockers to boot. Others see them as nothing more than a pre-packaged peepshow whose heavy metal-cum-glitter approach was dated from the very start.

Here are the facts: LA teenagers Joan Jett (whose love of T. Rex and Suzi Quatro inspired her to learn guitar) and drummer Sandy West decided to form a band with encouragement (and eventual management) from Kim Fowley. The band that recorded **The Runaways** was a combination of raw garage-band playing and brassy, high-school-bad-girl sexuality typified by their unofficial anthem, "Cherry Bomb."

By the time **Queens of Noise** (a decided improvement over the debut) was released, trouble was fomenting; although Cherie Currie was the "official" lead singer, Jett wound up taking the microphone on six of the ten songs. Things came to a head when, after a tour of Japan (documented on the **Live in Japan** album), Currie and bassist Jackie Fox quit the band. Vicki Blue was hired as a new

bassist, and Jett took over the reins for good.

Except in Japan, the Runaways never made any real commercial inroads. Many saw them as inept puppets—merely another Fowley hype—and refused to take the music seriously. **Waitin' for the Night** did nothing to alter that. The album came out just as modern-day punk was emerging, and Jett (if not the rest of the band) readily latched onto the scene to the extent that Steve Jones of the Sex Pistols contributed one song ("Black Leather") to **And Now . . . The Runaways**. But West and guitarist Lita Ford wanted to go in a more heavy metal direction, and the album would prove to be their last.

Posthumous notes: **Flaming Schoolgirls** is a substandard compilation of live tracks and studio outtakes, while **Little Lost Girls** is actually **And Now . . . The Runaways** re-released as a picture disc. **The Best of the Runaways** and **I Love Playing with Fire** are further recaps of various material. As for the band members, Lita Ford has become a huge metal star under her own name; West and Blue have been active but out of the national spotlight; Laurie McAllister (who held down the bass spot in the waning months) ended up in another all-girl Fowley project, the Orchids. After failed attempts at making it both as a solo act and with her sister Marie, Currie married Toto guitarist Steve Lukather. And we all know where Joan Jett's love of rock'n' roll got her. [rnp]

RUN—DMC

Run—D.M.C. (Profile) 1984 ●
King of Rock (Profile) 1985 ●
Raising Hell (Profile) 1986 ●
Tougher Than Leather (Profile) 1988 ●

This three-man rap band from Hollis, Queens was the first to succeed in doing what no other black artist (with the exception of Grandmaster Flash, briefly) had done before: make white people listen to rap in large numbers. Having established themselves with their core New York audience via several smart and witty singles ("Sucker M.C.'s" and "It's Like That"), the pioneering step that lifted them into a league all their own was "Rock Box," included on the first album. Melding a simple bass riff to the thunderous rhythm tracks that provided the entire accompaniment for their early raps, the song's coup de grâce is blazing rock guitar, played by Eddie Martinez (for a while an adjunct member of Blondie). The perfect combination—verbal acuity and theatrical drama matched by an inexorable pounding beat *and* the power of electric guitar—made the single huge, setting the stage for a whole meeting of the races that has helped chip away the barriers that kept "black music" and "white music" segregated all through the '70s.

Run—D.M.C. contains all their early hits and is an utterly essential record, and not just for rap fans. Even though the repetitious rhythms get tiring if you're not in the dancing mood, the funny, perceptive interwoven raps remain captivating centers of attention, and just trying to catch everything the pair of MCs fire off can become a full-time hobby. **King of Rock** takes some chances—like a reggae/rap blend—while repeating the functional formula of "Rock Box" on the title track, which simply inverts the riff and recasts the rap. Currently peerless in their field, Run (Joe Simmons), DMC (Darryl McDaniels) and ace dj/musician Jam Master Jay (Jason Mizell) were already showing enormous potential, and this was only the beginning.

Producer (with Russell Simmons) Rick Rubin adds his characteristic rock-funk touches to **Raising Hell**—like the "My Sharona" riff in the Beastie Boyish "It's Tricky" and the chart-topping hybrid cover of Aerosmith's rap-like "Walk This Way" (with Steve Tyler and Joe Perry contributing). On the downside, most of the rhymes are nothing special, making the commendable racial consciousness of "Proud to Be Black" stand in strong contrast to the litany of typical "I'm Run/He's DMC" script, the commercial culturalisms contained in "My Adidas" and the predictable words to "Dumb Girl." Overly spartan backing—simple beats (some of which sound positively acoustic) and Jay's percussive turntable action—hurt some of the tracks (especially since the group's proven itself equal to more active and complex arrangements); in addition, the daring duo's sharp verbal gymnastics don't really get started until the second side. More familiar than inherently exciting, **Raising Hell** could still use some more heat. Regardless, the record sold millions, elevating Run—DMC (alongside LL Cool J and the Beastie Boys) to the top echelons of the pop world.

Preceding (and apparently scantily related to) the film it's named after, **Tougher Than Leather** is a self-assured three-dimensional superstar record with a dense, rock-influenced sound that's become as distinguishable as their trademark verbal jousting. Utilizing the rap gimmick of stealing bits from classic records and building original songs around them, the trio grabs the Monkees' "Mary, Mary" and turns it into a hysterical putdown, while the Temptations' "Papa Was a Rollin' Stone" becomes "Papa Crazy," the same paternal disenchantment given a modern chop job. (Flashes of James Brown, Malcolm X, Led Zep—even old Run—DMC—crop up as well.) At the record's strangest, Run, DMC and Jay (affecting snooty accents) rap over a mock-Dixieland band. Throughout, the witty writing, deft delivery and riotously crowded production makes **Tougher Than Leather** a progressive and peerless statement of the art that neither excludes nor panders to any audience segment. [iar]

RUTS

The Crack (Virgin Int'l) 1979
Grin & Bear It (nr/Virgin) 1980
The Peel Sessions EP (nr/Strange Fruit) 1986
The Ruts Live (nr/Dojo) 1987
Live and Loud (nr/Link) 1987

RUTS D.C.

Animal Now (nr/Virgin) 1981
Rhythm Collision Vol. 1 (nr/Bohemian) 1982
[tape] (ROIR) 1987

On **The Crack**, the Ruts meld the Pistols' instrumental attack with leader Malcolm Owen's Strummeresque bellow; while less inspired than either of those bands, the Ruts started out with far more finesse (including nimble bass). True to their early association with reggae collective Misty in Roots (sponsor of their first 45), the Ruts often incorporated reggae riffs—adeptly, not heavy-handedly, and without missing a single roughshod 4/4 stride. Simple, straightforward political lyrics are heartfelt but not strident.

The late-'80 **Grin & Bear It** is odds'n'sods and sounds it, but the LP does contain an assortment of minor gems (including their pre-Virgin debut 45, live sides, etc.), highlighted by brilliant career-high-point single "Staring at the Rude Boys." In short, a fitting tribute (as intended) to Owen, dead of an OD four months previously.

As Ruts D.C. (for da capo) the remaining three made saxist/keyboardist Gary Barnacle a full member. On **Animal Now**, personal themes of self-doubt and angst ("Despondency," anyone?) get equal airing with the

491

usual attacks on hypocrisy and social manipulation. It's often gripping, but undercut by a tendency to infuse intrusive jazz-funk touches.

Minus Barnacle (who departed for session work and Leisure Process), the trio—along with the Mad Professor, a reggae producer—cut **Rhythm Collision**, an LP of funk-inflected reggae in ready-made dub form, akin in concept to Dennis Bovell's **I Wah Dub**. It's a sharp, sometimes powerful, sometimes catchy piece of work, with saxist Dave Winthrop (ex-Secret Affair) and one Mitt (harmonica) supplying additional shades to the dark-hued mood. In 1987, the long-deleted record was reissued on cassette (attributed jointly to the Ruts and Professor) as **Rhythm Collision Dub Volume 1**.

Although Ruts D.C. stopped working in 1983, three archival releases have recently appeared. Joy Division and the Ruts were BBC dj John Peel's two favorite bands, so it's fitting they've both been remembered in the **Peel Sessions** EP series. The Ruts' artifact from May 1979 unfortunately doesn't debut any long-lost material, and the versions sound too similar to the Virgin recording on **The Crack** to get worked up about it, but it nevertheless documents a great band.

Live and **Live and Loud**, on the other hand, fail to document *anything*. Though both are legal releases, they both sound like bootlegs; the muddy, plodding sound falls far short of capturing what was an explosive live band. In particular, **Live and Loud** gets the concert right, but used the wrong tape: the live track recorded at the Marquee on the UK edition of **The Crack** sounds great, but the same concert, as presented here, is of dodgy quality. Until a true live artifact can be excavated and released, these two are for scholars only.   [jg/jr]

S S S S S S S

SACCHARINE TRUST
Paganicons (SST) 1981
Surviving You, Always (SST) 1984
Worldbroken (SST) 1985
We Became Snakes (SST) 1986

JOE BAIZA & THE UNIVERSAL CONGRESS OF
Universal Congress Of (SST) 1987

UNIVERSAL CONGRESS OF
Prosperous and Qualified (SST) 1988

A different breed of hardcore, this Southern California quartet doesn't try to create a blizzard of noise—they go at it more artfully, but with equally ear-wrenching results. On **Paganicons**, singer Joaquin Milhouse Brewer tunelessly barks lyrics (as in "We Don't Need Freedom" and "A Human Certainty") that aren't bad in a pretentious mock-intellectual vein; the music is loudly abrasive, but with spaces and dynamics largely uncommon to the genre.

From Brewer's back cover credit of "vocals and sermons" to his complex, provocative lyrics (despite numerous misspellings on the lyric sheet), Saccharine Trust—armed with a new rhythm section—takes an abrupt religious turn on **Surviving You, Always**. "Yhwh on Acid," "Lot's Seed," "Remnants" and "Our Discovery" all contain biblical imagery and religious references, but in a context that obscures and reorients the themes well beyond easy recognition and comprehension. Musically, Sac Trust uses the punk idiom like avant-jazz, liberating the vocals to function semi-independently as blurt poetry, while the band goes through tight formation riffs that are carefully structured but not really within traditional song form. Sophisticated, and engrossing once you get past the daunting attack.

Proceeding further into the experimental realms generally reserved for the "new music" folks, Saccharine Trust attempted something *really* unusual with **Worldbroken**. The LP was not only recorded live, it was improvised on the spot! Joined by ex-Minutemen bassist Mike Watt, Brewer and two surviving sidemen rise to the challenge, producing a loose but controlled-sounding jam record (no punks here) that reveals its total extemporaneousness only in the rambling narrative of Brewer's lyrics.

On the jazzy **We Became Snakes**, a five-piece lineup (with sax and a new bassist) returns to the old-fashioned way: write 'em, rehearse 'em and *then* record 'em. Watt produced the record, which again reflects Brewer's religious fixation. The sonic formula includes syncopated rhythm vamps, lots of riffy solos on sax and guitar and dramatic vocal recitations. Imaginative and far-reaching, if not exactly enjoyable or accessible.

Guitarist Baiza's first solo record contains two endless studio jams, *sans* vocals. "Certain Way" covers the entire first side and part of the second; whether you'll actually turn the record over to hear how it finishes depends entirely on your ability to remain awake during 19 enervating minutes of four guys dicking around formlessly in the studio. Baiza's band's next outing, **Prosperous and Qualified**, is much better—a jazzy, spacious rock record that contains actual songs, credible sax riffing (by Steve Moss) and other good stuff.   [iar]

See also *October Faction*.

SADE
Diamond Life (Portrait) 1984 ●
Promise (Portrait) 1985 ●
Stronger Than Pride (Portrait) 1988 ●

The '80s British trend towards mild jazz/Latin-inflected pop music (Carmel, Everything but the Girl) found its first globally successful proponent in Sade. A stunningly beautiful Nigerian raised in England, Sade Adu writes (the lyrics are hers alone, the music mostly co-written with Stuart Matthewman, the sax/guitar player in her trio) and performs mellifluous, thoughtful tunes with aplomb and jazz leanings that seem to derive from a wholly different era. Despite the music's obvious stylization, Sade's almost colorless voice exudes little personality; her strength is a cool timbre that conveys dispassionate wisdom.

Somehow avoiding both nostalgia and schmaltz, **Diamond Life** is an anomaly: nothing about it would turn off Andy Williams fans, but selfconsciousness legitimizes it to the rock audience. "Hang on to Your Love," "Sally," "Smooth Operator" and "Your Love Is King" are the standouts, evoking chic nightclub society of the '60s. (In fact, the first of those tracks includes the very noticeable sound of glasses clinking.) The perfect soundtrack to your Laurence Harvey dreams, amd a very alluring pop record.

Sade's follow-up, **Promise**, is slightly drier and less cozy, but the nine songs are every bit as good. Economical arrangements make every carefully-placed rim shot and guitar twang count on such excellent songs as "Is It a Crime" and "Sweetest Taboo." Her long-awaited third album came out in mid-1988. [iar]

SAD LOVERS & GIANTS

Epic Garden Music (nr/Midnight Music) 1982 ●
Feeding the Flame (nr/Midnight Music) 1983 ●
In the Breeze (nr/Midnight Music) 1984
Total Sound (nr/Midnight Music) 1986
The Mirror Test (nr/Midnight Music) 1987 ●

The quintet, which originally came from Watford—near London, but evidently insulated from that city's turbulent trendiness—resembles a cross between R.E.M. and a garage-spawned analogue of **Dark Side of the Moon**. Tristan Garel-Funk plays jangly guitar, almost all of it arpeggio chorded (à la Byrds/Searchers), and David Woods adds texture and melody with sax and keyboards, eventually growing more sophisticated in sound and shading, if not technique. The songs canter at new wave uptempo or a more brooding mid-speed, but the music is moody and contemplative. Vocals by one Garce Allard aren't trendily emotive, instead possessing the kind of quiet gravity that makes overstatement unnecessary, even with lyrics of hurt or anger.

Epic Garden Music is pretty much what its self-satiric title suggests, but also boasts several excellent crystallizations of the group's style. **Feeding the Flame**, after an abrasive opening, is much quieter, a less immediate and ultimately more distressing record. **In the Breeze** consists of alternate versions of some tracks plus a few unreleased rough gems; it's almost as essential as the first LP, although the three songs the two discs share are presented in earlier, rawer takes here.

The group dissolved around the end of '83, but resumed activity in 1985. On **The Mirror Test**, Allard and original drummer Nigel Pollard are joined by a completely new guitar/bass/keyboards axis, not to mention new songwriting partners for Allard. Sad Lovers are a smoother crew this time around and, although the LP does resemble the band's previous sound, the music is pleasant without being quite so memorable; the lyrics are generally less poignant. Yet each listening does reveal more, as with all of their records. (The CD adds four bonus tracks.) [jg]

SAFETY LAST

Safety Last EP (Twin/Tone) 1981
Struck by Love (Twin/Tone) 1983

This wonderful rockabilly quartet left Minneapolis for New Mexico in the late '70s; returning home, they made a couple of records that are joyous explosions of unstylized, exuberant (mostly original) rock'n'roll and swing tunes that jump like nuts and display the pure musical strength of underamplified guitar, bass, drums and a spot of piano.

The trebly six-song (including two sturdy instrumentals) EP is a crackling energy jolt from start to finish. Exchanging two members, thereby acquiring both male and female lead vocals, the full-length album is positively brilliant—originals that sound like classics and oldies that sound brand new. No tattoos or pompadours, just talent and pep. Perfect. [iar]

GREG SAGE

See *Wipers.*

SAINTS

(I'm) Stranded (Sire) 1977
Eternally Yours (Sire) 1978
Prehistoric Sounds (nr/Harvest) 1978
Paralytic Tonight Dublin Tomorrow EP (Fr. New Rose) 1979
Prehistoric Songs (Fr. Harvest) 1981
The Monkey Puzzle (Fr. New Rose) 1981
Out in the Jungle . . . (nr/Flicknife) 1982
A Little Madness to Be Free (Fr. New Rose) 1984 ●
Live in a Mud Hut (Fr. New Rose) 1985
Best of the Saints (nr/Razor) 1986
All Fools Day (TVT) 1987 ●
Prodigal Son (Aus. Mushroom) 1988

CHRIS BAILEY

Casablanca (Fr. New Rose) 1983
What We Did on Our Holidays (Fr. New Rose) 1984

Every decade's snotty kids are the same, as Brisbane, Australia's Saints handily prove. These so-called modern punks emerged in '77 with a raw, driving sound recalling the Pretty Things of the early '60s. On **(I'm) Stranded**, Chris Bailey sings with the same irritable snarl that band's Phil May had back when he was considered competition for Mick Jagger. The rest of the Saints (guitarist Ed Kuepper, drummer Ivor Hay and bassist Kym Bradshaw) respond in kind, issuing sheets of rough, gray rock'n'roll noise, including the title track, a pioneering international punk hit.

Eternally Yours refines the attack without diminishing the impact, boasting tighter playing and even a horn section. Highlights include "Know Your Product," a cynical outburst, and "Run Down," the kind of put-down bands like this have to do well to maintain credibility. With consistency and tasteful variety (handling sharp acoustic ballads as well as the standard burners), the LP is deservedly regarded as a punk classic, and even yielded a UK Top 40 single, the searing "This Perfect Day."

On **Prehistoric Sounds**, the Saints abandoned punk (for good) in favor of a brooding, bluesy, R&B-flavored style they've been expanding on since, best characterized by the melancholy and hypnotic "All Times Through Paradise." Though a bit of a downer compred to the meteoric energy of the first two LPs, and containing claustrophobic bits of paranoia like "Brisbane (Security City)," a succinct condemnation of boring-town inertia, and "The Prisoner," the album has a strange, soothing effect. Unfortunately, it was the last LP by the original lineup.

Chris Bailey re-emerged in 1979 with an all-new band of Saints, and debuted the group on the French-only **Paralytic Tonight Dublin Tomorrow** EP, the first-ever release on the now mighty New Rose label. There's hornwork on several of the five tracks, but the rip-roaring energy drive finds these Saints working into something like punked-up Chicago blues.

Prehistoric Songs collects highlights from the preceding albums, along with various singles. Hearing a bunch of their ragged cover versions in succession can be unsettling, but it's also thrilling, in a sick way, to witness "River Deep, Mountain High," "Kissin' Cousins," "Lipstick on Your Collar" and Otis Redding's "Security" being put through the meatgrinder. Not for the fainthearted or tradition-minded.

The Monkey Puzzle continues to develop the new Saints' tone. Although this lineup is not nearly as abrasive as the original band, the devotion to rootsy no-nonsense rock'n' roll remains undiminished. See the buoyant cover of "Dizzy Miss Lizzy" for details.

Out in the Jungle finds Bailey at his most polished, handling brooding ballads and horn-laden rockers with impressive aplomb. Although still a superlative growler, much of the exhilarating edge of previous Saints classics has been unduly muted by professionalism. Brian James, then in the Lords of the New Church, guests on guitar.

Bailey recorded his first solo album, **Casablanca**, in Paris; accompanying himself only on simple guitar (acoustic/electric, double-tracked in spots) he sings like a folk/blues troubador. The songs are mixed in quality—from a straight reading of Jimmy Reed's "(Take Out Some) Insurance on Me Baby" to the pretty "Wait Till Tomorrow"—and, lacking domineering rock power to drive them, have a tendency to drift a bit. Nonetheless, some of the songs are quite strong, and gain urgency from the stark, unprepossessing presentation.

What We Did on Our Holidays followed: half acoustic solo, half backed by a full band. With the exception of one original ("Wait Till Tomorrow" again, retitled "Ghost

Ships"), this album is all covers: folk/blues on the acoustic side and Sam Cooke, Marvin Gaye, Wilson Pickett, etc. on the electric side. A good workout for Bailey's rich voice, which is obviously growing deeper with age.

Bursting with fresh enthusiasm, Bailey then reassembled the Saints, and made two studio albums that are the crowning achievement of a long career. **A Little Madness to Be Free** reveals him to be a consummate arranger, as violins, cellos, trumpets, you-name-it fill the record without cluttering up the sound. "Ghost Ships," "Down the Drain" and "The Hour" are lush, yet powerfully dramatic.

All Fools Day, the Saints' first US release in nine years, is more of the same formula, only even better. Recorded in Wales at the famous Rockfield Studios with Hugh Jones producing, the LP even features the return of original drummer Ivor Hay and a batch of the strongest Saints material ever, particularly on Side One. With more strings, horns and soul/blues influences than ever, it's a brilliant and inspired work.

Live in a Mud Hut is an official bootleg of sorts, taken from a 1984 European tour. The recording quality is fair, but the LP is best avoided by all but fans who already own the studio versions. The performances range from flat to buzzed, but the biggest problem is the lack of a horn section or any other embellishments.

Best of the Saints is hardly a best-of at all, as its track selection almost mirrors that of the previous greatest hits anthology, **Prehistoric Songs**. However, as the early Saints LPs are largely out of print, it can serve as a useful introduction.   [jy/iar/jr]

See also *Laughing Clowns*.

RYUICHI SAKAMOTO

The 1,000 Knives of Ryuichi Sakamoto (Hol. Plurex) 1982
B-2 Unit (nr/Alfa-Island) 1980
Merry Christmas, Mr. Lawrence (MCA) 1983
Esperanto (Jap. Midi) 1985
Futurista (Jap. Midi) 1985
Illustrated Musical Encyclopaedia (nr/10) 1986
Media Bahn Live (Jap. Midi) 1986
Adventures of Chatran (Jap. Midi) 1986
Miraiha Yaro (Jap. Midi) 1986
Koneko Monogatari (Jap. Midi) 1986
Honneamise (Jap. Midi) 1987
Neo Geo (Epic) 1988 ●

RYUICHI SAKAMOTO & THE KAKUTOUGI SESSION
Summer Nerves (Jap. CBS-Sony) 1979
RYUICHI SAKAMOTO WITH ROBIN SCOTT
Left Handed Dream (Epic) 1981
RYUICHI SAKAMOTO FEATURING THOMAS DOLBY
Field Work EP (nr/10) 1986
RYUICHI SAKAMOTO, DAVID BYRNE AND CONG SU
The Last Emperor (Virgin Movie Music) 1988 ●

Japanese session keyboardist Sakamoto first worked with both of his Yellow Magic Orchestra-mates-to-be on his modest yet promising solo debut (**1,000 Knives**, which was originally released in Japan in 1978). While with YMO, he made **B-2 Unit** with the help of British reggae musician/producer Dennis Bovell and XTC's Andy Partridge. Though not throwing up as many sparks with them as might have been expected, it clearly shows him to be an adventuresome oddball rather than a studio hack.

On **Left Handed Dream**, he effectively draws out and integrates his collaborators (ex-M Scott and Adrian Belew, as well as both YMO cohorts), who in turn get the best out of him. The LP varies from slippery, fractured funk to a duel between a grim, darkly atmospheric drone and assorted percussion; it consistently scintillates, though sometimes in a curiously offhanded way.

Merry Christmas, Mr. Lawrence is the soundtrack to a film starring Tom Conti, David Bowie and Sakamoto himself. He performed the entire evocative synth score alone (save a vocal of dubious worth by David Sylvian in an alternative version of the main theme). Sakamoto more recently acted in *The Last Emperor*, also contributing half of the suitably atmospheric Oscar-winning score's LP. The disc's only memorable music is Sakamoto's main theme (with its surprisingly European feel), which he explores through much of his side.

Esperanto is an abridged version of his end of a dance performance collaboration with New York choreographer Melissa Fenley. **Adventures of Chatran** and **Koneko Monogatari** are also movie scores, the latter for one of Japan's biggest-ever box-office flicks; **Honneamise** is his score for an animated sci-fi film.

Illustrated Musical Encyclopedia (originally released in 1984 in Japan, as **Ongakuzukan**) opens with "Field Work," a low-key dance-rock joint venture with Thomas Dolby; it's immediately likable but unrelated to the rest of the record in feel if not theory. The LP's title states an idea Sakamoto has toyed with since **1,000 Knives**: combining pieces of Eastern and Western musics so they're not readily identifiable, yet complement each other as part of an organic whole. He sometimes crosses the line into pretentious piano muzak when meddling with European "classical" music, but it's a mostly worthwhile attempt, although it requires patience to absorb the subtler angles. (He explores all this more ambitiously—and successfully—on **Neo Geo**.)

Media Bahn is a double live LP of his tour promoting **Futurista**. He's aided on it by percussionist David Van Tieghem and NYC Peech Boys vocalist Bernard Fowler. **Miraiha Yaro** is a collaboration with his wife, Akiko Yano (lyrics), Fowler and guitarist Arto Lindsay; this grab-bag is as varied as **Left Handed Dream**, though not as exciting or distinctive.

Neo Geo is his biggest all-star affair, boasting Van Tieghem, drumming by jazz star Tony Williams and reggae heavyweight Sly Dunbar, bassists Bootsy Collins and Bill Laswell (also Sakamoto's co-producer/writing partner here), and (on one track) a strangely simpatico Iggy Pop vocalizing his own thoughtfully dramatic lyrics. Sakamoto spends the rest of the album carrying forth the **Illustrated Musical Encyclopedia** experiments, which get most exciting when he tries weird intertwinings of Japanese music and rock/funk. The LP's highlights are among Sakamoto's best work.   [jg]

See also *Virginia Astley*.

NORMAN SALANT

Saxaphone Demonstrations (Alive) 1981
Sax Talk (CD Presents) 1984
Sax Talk EP (CD Presents) 1984

San Francisco saxman Salant has played with everyone from the Residents to Romeo Void. On **Saxaphone** [*sic*] **Demonstrations**, he multi-tracks himself into full-throated majesty on "4 saxaphone demonstrations in the new wave" and "4 saxaphone ramifications of sex and love." Original, inventive,

bracing, alternately abrasive and beautiful—a magic blend of modernism and tradition that is really neither rock nor jazz nor any other typical horn genre.

Sax Talk is a full-length album with backing by a stack of notable Bay Area musicians. A bit more restrained, it's nonetheless an engaging and excellent collection of instrumental excursions—some fairly beat-heavy for dancing—in a number of different styles. The title track, co-written with bassist Stephen Ashman, also appears on a 12-inch in two remixes, along with two versions of another LP track and "Heavenly Choir," a mellifluous wall of sax.   [iar]

See also *Zasu Pitts Memorial Orchestra, Residents*.

WALTER SALAS-HUMARA
See *Silos*.

SALEM 66

Salem 66 EP (Homestead) 1984
A Ripping Spin (Homestead) 1985
Frequency & Urgency (Homestead) 1987
Your Soul Is Mine, Fork It Over [CD]
 (Homestead) 1987
Natural Disasters, National Treasures
 (Homestead) 1988 ●
Something's Rockin' in Denmark (Homestead)
 1988

The three Massachusetts women in Salem 66 make generally delicate electric guitar music that embraces folk more than rock traditions. Their six-song EP—produced by Neighborhoods guitarist David Minehan—has plenty of poetic ambience and some surprisingly complex arrangements, but consistent jangly-cum-trebly sound makes it hard to stay engrossed, and occasional bum notes also interrupt the mood. And while Judy Grunwald and Beth Kaplan can each sing, their harmonies aren't great. There's talent here—it just needs more development.

With the arrival of guitarist Robert Wilson Rodriguez, the Salems expanded to a quartet in time for **A Ripping Spin**, a full-length LP again produced by Minehan. The songs and playing are better, but the vocals are still hit-or-miss. Kaplan takes a decidedly indecisive approach to the issue; Grunwald's gurgly warble can also be a trial. The brief "Fragile" shows their swell potential, but other tunes are less mellifluous.

Drummer Susan Merriam and guitarist

Wilson left before **Frequency & Urgency** and were replaced by two new members. **Your Soul Is Mine** is a CD-only compilation.

[iar]

SALVATION ARMY

See *Three O'Clock*.

SAQQARA DOGS

World Crunch EP (Pathfinder) 1986
Thirst (Pathfinder) 1987 ●

BOND BERGLAND

Unearth (Pathfinder) 1986

The Saqqara Dogs' effective drug-trance music combines onetime Factrix leader Bond Bergland's Pink Floydish psychedelic guitars with Hearn Gadbois' Middle Eastern and Indian drumming and Sync66's (aka Chris Cunningham, ex-James White and the Blacks) Chapman Stick manipulations (as well as guitar, other bass, cello and organ). I find it happily reminiscent of British ethnocultists the Suns of Arqa; perhaps the two tribes are distantly related.

The nine-minute "Greenwich Mean Time" highlights the four-track **World Crunch**. **Thirst** contains richly-textured alien soundtracks with such pagan titles as "Gregorian Stomp," "Grave of Love" and "Splatter Dance." The record is marred only by a couple of Bergland vocals (typical lyrics: "Bye bye black sheep/Sacrificial lamb steak, terminated/Landscapegoat").

Bergland's solo LP, **Unearth** (recorded in 1985, prior to the band's formation), unfortunately contains more of the same. Gadbois' ritualistic drumming is eliminated in favor of more atmospherically inclined guitars and electronic percussion. Not awful, just not as swell as the Dogs. [rg]

SAVAGE PROGRESS

Celebration (nr/10-Virgin) 1984

Led by bassist/songwriter Rik Kenton— one of the two bassists on the first Roxy Music album over a decade earlier—Savage Progress plays dance-rock with much the same loose and funky feel as the Thompson Twins. The quartet incorporates glints of various Third World musics, adding character to the otherwise plain melodies and banal lyrics. Vocalist Glynnis sings like a member of Bananarama; the band (whose lineup fields bass, keyboards and percussion) is facile and flexible, making easy transitions from the calypso of "Falling" to the eerie Arabia of "My Soul Unwraps Tonight" to the Bow Wow Wow-styled "Heart Begin to Beat." By not allowing themselves to become too involved in any of these flavors, Savage Progress remains light and likable, but they will need stronger songs to keep from being just a well-produced shell of appealing styles. [iar]

SAVAGE REPUBLIC

Tragic Figures (Independent Project) 1982 + 1987 ●
Trudge EP (Bel. Play It Again Sam) 1986
Ceremonial (Independent Project) 1986 ●
Live Trek '85–'86 (Nate Starkman & Son) 1987
Jamahiriya (Fundamental Music) 1988 ●

17 PYGMIES

Hatikva EP (Resistance) 1983 (It. Viva) 1988
Jedda by the Sea (Ger. Rough Trade) 1984
Captured in Ice (Resistance) 1985
Welcome (Great Jones) 1988 ●

Originally named Africa Corps, Los Angeles' Savage Republic got its start at UCLA, where Jeff Long, Bruce Licher, Mark Erskine and Jackson Del Rey (Philip Drucker) were attending school. The basic lineup of bass, bass, drums and percussion (plus some outside assistants) yielded an arty, industrial ensemble which serenaded cement walls with lightly droning grates of monotone guitar, exotic percussion and noisy, ranted vocals. The band changed their name to avoid confusion with the East Coast Afrika Korps (and the implied affiliation with the Nazi-punk fad of the time) a week before releasing their debut album, **Tragic Figures**. (The unique look of their early records was the result of a school project that gave Licher access to an antique letterpress.)

A combination of industrial drone with deep machine-like swaths of dragging bass, Halloween horror-movie screams and some of the most delightfully tribal and tropical percussion found on disc, **Tragic Figures** also introduced a tourch of Arabic cat slink that would show up more prominently in later work. When Robert Loveless joined, the quintet's sound turned from frantically abrasive to almost meditatively cool.

Drucker and Loveless launched a side band, 17 Pygmies, to delve into lighter, more melodic music than Savage Republic. Retaining the group's tribal percussion and Arabic feel, they added electronic keyboards for

498

Hatikva, an EP which crosses Emerson, Lake & Palmer's "The Sheriff," a spaghetti Western soundtrack and a Caribbean rhythm fest. Only a thousand copies were originally pressed, but it was recently reissued by an Italian label.

In the midst of recording a second album at the end of 1983, Savage Republic split up; Drucker and Loveless, under the 17 Pygmies name, completed the record, which was released as **Jedda by the Sea**. The Pygmies went on to record **Captured in Ice**, an even more pop-oriented album which features lilting electronic keyboards, clearly sung female vocals, new wave "oooohh-oooohh"'s, sometimes crisp, dance-club drumming and synthesizers.

Licher and Erskine reformed Savage Republic. The ambient, almost meditative **Trudge** EP came out in Belgium only. A crawling, building excursion into the avant Arabic surf textures the band had been exploring live, it lopes through a kind of Western movie soundtrack with some limited vocalizations but no lyrics. The abrasive edge that was engraved in the music from their industrial days is gone, leaving only the racing adrenaline that accompanied it, the clank and clatter of clay-pot percussion accents. At times, there's a processional majesty that hints at what Savage Republic's completion of the **Jedda** tracks might have sounded like.

Almost the same week as **Trudge** was released, the Republic came out with **Ceremonial** in the US. With Loveless back in the band, the album showcases a pop and melodic side with gentle male and Pygmy-like female vocals and only a hint of the Savage's banana Republic feel. There are even keyboards, mandolin, wind chimes and a dulcimer hidden in the (almost) lush and relaxed grooves. (**Tragic Figures** and **Ceremonial** were later issued on one CD.)

Live Trek (1985–1986) is most like **Trudge** in texture, reworking the material from their earliest industrial days to excise the abrasion. It would make a good introduction for anyone who has not heard the band.

Jamahiriya continues to fuse their past into their future with a sound that reflects and melds all of their evolutions onto one disc. Jackson Del Rey is back in the band, but Loveless is gone. The CD version of the disc includes three additional instrumental remixes of songs that are on the vinyl in vocal versions.

Meanwhile, 17 Pygmies have been signed to Island. **Welcome** reportedly includes numerous guest artists and spoken word stuff.
[ʼe]

TENOR SAW
Fever (Jam. Blue Mountain) 1985
Tenor Saw/Coca Tea Clash (nr/Witty) 1986
Tenor Saw Meets Don Angelo: The Golden Hen EP (nr/Uptempo) 1986

One of the best new reggae singers, Tenor Saw released several 12-inch singles in 1985 (notably "Ring the Alarm" and "Roll Is Called"), and has appeared on albums paired with other singers. Unfortunately, his first full-fledged LP, **Fever**, is a middling effort. The playing is fine and Saw's immediately distinctive voice is rich, but the material is weak. On the best tracks ("Pumpkin Belly" and "Eenie Meenie Minie Mo") he does some weird vocal improvisation against synthetic bass lines; the rest of the record is bland and typical.
[bk]

SKY SAXON
See *Red Cross*.

SCARS
Author! Author! (nr/Pre-Charisma) 1981
Author! Author! EP (Stiff) 1981

If this Scottish band's post-psychedelia didn't lean so far toward pomp-rock, its highly melodic writing would be vastly more infectious. Ho-hum words and a disconcerting tendency to sound like early-'70s Alice Cooper don't help; fully fleshed-out production of a colorful guitar-based sound and the band's own bravura do. The EP features three from the album plus an extra song that shows the Scars' best side.
[mf]

(THE) SCENE IS NOW
Burn All Your Records (Lost) 1985
Total Jive (Lost-Twin/Tone) 1986
Tonight We Ride (Lost-Twin/Tone) 1988

Defectors from Mofungo formed this New York/Hoboken axis quartet, also produced (in part) by Elliott Sharp. TSIN takes a more easygoing approach to music and lyrical subject matter than their former band, maintaining a firm grip on melody and keeping the sound light and attractive. While some of the songs are topical, they avoid overbearing seriousness or obnoxious pontification. **Total Jive** takes a few listens to

499

reveal its summery urban charms but, once found, the LP becomes a low-key delight. [iar]

ARMAND SCHAUBROECK STEALS

A Lot of People Would Like to See Armand
 Schaubroeck . . . DEAD (Mirror) 1975
"I Came to Visit, but Decided to Stay."
 (Mirror) 1977
Live at the Holiday Inn (Mirror) 1978
Shakin' Shakin' (Mirror) 1978
Ratfucker (Mirror) 1978

To describe Armand Schaubroeck as over the top hardly does him justice. This incredible independent-recording oddball began his musical career in the mid-'60s, after a prison stay (he was convicted of grand larceny). Although his subsequent livelihood has centered around a well-known music store he owns and operates in upstate New York, he has found time to make a large *oeuvre* of albums and singles that spring from his bitterness and cynicism. Yet Schaubroeck is no raving looney—his records are intense but they're sane, and ambitiously conceived and executed. And while his musical and songwriting skills have grown by leaps and bounds over the years, he has never mellowed—his fifth album is more intense and gritty than any of his others, save the first.

A Lot of People Would Like to See Armand Schaubroeck . . . DEAD, the cover of which pictures the artist with a bullet hole in his forehead, is a three-record extravaganza in quadrophonic sound (!) that tells the story of Schaubroeck's incarceration in 22 scenes combining songs and dialogue. While powerful and impressive, the subject and treatment is far too personal to be of general interest, and the length makes complete listening a real challenge. This catharsis may have been necessary for him, but it's more an accomplishment than an entertainment.

Religion is the general subject of Schaubroeck's second effort. His vicious cover picture and many of the record's lyrics criticize various aspects of the church, but he couches it all in subdued, sophisticated music that's superficially attractive. While cleverly sardonic, the laconic treatment wants for more unleashed aggression.

Live at the Holiday Inn features six songs on two discs. Armed with an eight-piece band and facing a seemingly enthusiastic audience, Schaubroeck performs selections from his first LP, giving the songs (written,

actually, in the late '60s) the benefit of improved singing and stronger musical backing. The band hits a repetitive groove while Armand improvises and draws out the vocal portions ad infinitum. A powerful document.

Shakin' Shakin' adds a rockabilly twinge for several tunes; lyrics about winning and losing at love make the record's stance almost appealing. There's still bitterness, but Armand sounds more upbeat than usual. Unfortunately, despite great sound quality and solid playing, the album's bland.

With **Ratfucker**, Schaubroeck created the masterpiece he'd been building towards. Were it not for the indelicate title and similarly strong language throughout, this concept album about death and depravity might have finally found him a major audience. Schaubroeck—as Lou Reed has also done, especially on **The Blue Mask**—posits himself as an assortment of wretched characters—a flesh peddler, a hired killer, an abuser of women—and sneers his way to disconcerting believability against a musical backdrop of excellent uptempo rock and funk. Cinematic and convincing, obscuring the line between art and life, **Ratfucker** uses horns and a background chorus to complement the characters' singing, talking and growling. In painting images of villains who wear their sickness like a badge, Schaubroeck delivers a rough, stunning tour de force. [iar]

PETER SCHILLING

Major Tom (Coming Home) EP (Elektra) 1983
Error in the System (Elektra) 1983
Things to Come (Elektra) 1985

Back when German music was affectionately referred to as "krautrock," it seemed as if spacey progressive experimentalism was the only kind of music Teutonic youth could play. Since that era, the nation's stylistic scope has widened considerably and been exported to global popularity as well. So there's something nostalgic and heartwarming about the sci-fidom of Peter Schilling's left-field hit single, "Major Tom (Coming Home)," which essentially copies the story of David Bowie's "Space Oddity" into a modern electro-pop setting. The 12-inch offers the single four ways: English, German, instrumental and an eight-minute John Luongo remix. The song sounds best *auf deutsch*.

Error in the System contains "Major Tom (Coming Home)" sung in English, a plodding, otiose instrumental called "Major

Tom Part II" and a German version of "Silent Night, Holy Night" (with new lyrics), as well as fake reggae and a bunch of needless "Major Tom" soundalikes. Throughout, Schilling's almost accentless multi-tracked vocals are blandly sweet, and the metronome-powered electro-bubblegum pleasant if shallow. A full album of this synthetic weightlessness is more than enough; briefer doses aren't at all painful.

Things to Come proves the narrow limits of Schilling's appeal. At best, a few songs echo his hit; otherwise, it's a tedious and unoriginal bore. [iar]

IRMIN SCHMIDT
See *Can.*

FRED SCHNEIDER AND THE SHAKE SOCIETY
See *B-52's.*

SCHOOLLY D
Schoolly-D (Schoolly-D) 1986
Saturday Night!—The Album (Schoolly-D) 1987 (Jive) 1987
The Adventures of Schoolly-D [CD] (Rykodisc) 1987
Smoke Some Kill (Jive) 1988 ●

Philadelphia rapper Schoolly D (Jesse Weaver) has made his reputation by dispassionately reporting on the grittier aspects of urban life, offering dilettantes (and others) the tantalizingly threatening thrill absent from the upbeat messages of more socially acceptable groups. While some have expressed doubts about the entertainment value of rhymes that endorse gun possession and discuss street violence without any negative context, Schoolly argues that people take his lyrics too seriously. Uncompromising, self-sufficient and independent of the trends of musical convention, he raps about drugs, sex, gangs and guns, making records that are an unromanticized corollary of Martin Scorsese's films.

Ably supported by dj Code Money and uncomplicated rhythm tracks, Schoolly released two albums on his own label before Jive picked up on him, re-issuing **Saturday Night!** with three added tracks. **The Adventures of Schoolly-D** combines the contents of both records (in their original configurations) and adds an extra cut. The first LP contains "PSK—What Does It Mean?" (Parkside Killers, a local gang), "Gucci Time" and "I Don't Like Rock'n'Roll," a scratch-happy warning to long-haired freaks: "be on your guard."

The more ambitious and unsettling **Saturday Night!** has "We Get Ill" (the Beastie Boys were allegedly greatly influenced by seeing Schoolly perform), "Do It Do It" (complete with children's chorus singing "Who's afraid of the big bad wolf?"), "It's Krack" and the title track; the revised edition adds "Housing the Joint" (which quotes Sly Stone), "Parkside 5-2" and "Dis Groove Is Bad."

Smoke Some Kill contains such rugged numbers as "Same White Bitch (Got You Strung Out on Cane)," "Mr. Big Dick" and "No More Rock'n'Roll." [iar]

BRINSLEY SCHWARZ
Brinsley Schwarz (Capitol) 1970
Despite It All (Capitol) 1970
Silver Pistol (UA) 1972 (nr/Edsel) 1986
Nervous on the Road (UA) 1972
· Please Don't Ever Change (nr/UA) 1973
New Favourites (nr/UA) 1974
Original Golden Greats (nr/UA) 1974
Fifteen Thoughts (nr/UA) 1978

Many pub-rock bands of the early '70s served as launching pads for English musicians whose fame and fortune increased enormously with the advent of new wave. Along with Ducks Deluxe, Brinsley Schwarz easily takes the cake as a hotbed of talents just waiting for the right moment to burst forth. Although largely unheralded (and commercially ignored) at the time, its five members—Nick Lowe, Ian Gomm, Brinsley Schwarz, Bob Andrews and Billy Rankin—have surely proven their skill and importance many times over since the band dissolved in 1975.

Lowe's solo career and membership in Rockpile, not to mention his voluminous production credits, have made him a constant presence, a revered elder in the Church of Cool. Gomm's solo albums are more in keeping with the Brinsleys' laid-back, easy-listening countrified pop. Confirmed sidemen Schwarz and Andrews both served in the Rumour (with and without Graham Parker) and have each produced and played alongside many other spotlight stars as well. Rankin played in a band called Tiger and has drummed on loads of records by likeminded rockers. (He and Schwarz also joined future Rumour member Martin Belmont in the last incarnation of Ducks Deluxe.)

The music on Brinsley Schwarz's albums seems at once totally removed and perfectly in keeping with the individuals' later escapades; little hints of the future keep cropping up amid the genial, American-flavored rock and mild pop. Dave Edmunds later recorded "Ju Ju Man" (a cover included on **Silver Pistol**) on **Get It**, backed by Lowe, Rankin and Andrews. The first appearance of Lowe's "(What's So Funny 'Bout) Peace, Love and Understanding" is on **New Favourites**; it's since become a classic item in Elvis Costello's repertoire. Lowe's brush with American chart success, "Cruel to Be Kind," was co-written with Gomm and doesn't sound very different from some of the Brinsleys' richer pop numbers. Much of the Rumour's crisp Van Morrison swing is present in tracks like "Surrender to the Rhythm" (**Nervous on the Road**). You get the point.

In a nutshell, while some of the music on these albums is either dull or wimpy beyond belief—and check those embarrassing hippie pictures!—they contain enough wonderful stuff to make Brinsley Schwarz's records well worth discovering. Of discographical interest: the first two LPs are also available as an American twin set (**Brinsley Schwarz**) released in 1978. **Original Golden Greats** and **Fifteen Thoughts** (kudos to the latter's art director) are compilations of tracks from the band's entire career; there's some duplication, but both have gems not otherwise found on any album. Brinsley Schwarz also contributed five cuts to the 1972 live compilation, **Greasy Truckers Party**.   [iar]

See also *Ducks Deluxe, Nick Lowe, Graham Parker, Rockpile, Rumour.*

SCIENTISTS

Scientists EP (Aus. White Rider) 1980
The Scientists (Aus. YPRX) 1981
Blood Red River EP (Aus. Au-go-go) 1983
This Heart Doesn't Run on Blood, This Heart Doesn't Run on Love EP (Aus. Au-go-go) 1984
Demolition Derby (Bel. Soundwork) 1985
Atom Bomb Baby (nr/Au-go-go) 1985
You Get What You Deserve (nr/Karbon) 1985
Heading for a Trauma (nr/Au-go-go) 1985
Rubber Never Sleeps [tape] (Aus. Au-go-go) 1985
Weird Love (Big Time) 1986
The Human Jukebox (nr/Karbon) 1987

Perth, Australia; May 1978. An unrecorded band named the Invaders (which included bassist Boris Sujdovic, guitarist Rod Radalj, and guitarist/lead vocalist Kim Salmon) joins forces with drummer James Baker, changes their name to the Scientists and releases "Frantic Romantic," a bright little pop single. A four track EP and a delightfully gritty LP of hard pop follow. But music life in Perth (on the far west coast of Australia, 2,500 miles of outback away from anyplace else) becomes frustrating. Baker leaves for Sydney where he meets up with fellow Perth renegade Dave Faulkner (who had been in a band named the Gurus and was then in an unnamed ensemble with fellow Perth-escapee Radalj). Baker joins the new Faulkner/Radalj group and they name it Le Hoodoo Gurus.

Time: September 1981. Kim Salmon also gives up on Perth and relocates to Sydney, where he and Sujdovic create a new Scientists with a manic swamp-grunge sound. Full of dirty feedback and great swaths of nod-out guitar, **Blood Red River** pays homage to Suicide with pounding basslines and echo-chamber-overkill vocals, while hinting at the hypnotic fusion of '60s hookah smoke and screechingly overheated guitar that bubbles through **This Heart** and on into **Weird Love** to become the Scientists sound. From screaming blues-rooted mania laid over repeating circles of bass and twists of cacophony lead guitar, through the frenetic Cramps-meet-Birthday Party dirges of the Belgian-only **Demolition Derby**, each release nudges the band's sound a step further through a path of deep, dark, nod-out blasts until 1985 when, ever in search of someplace else, the Scientists left Australia for London, where their story begins to fall apart.

Except for the very Cramps-y "You Only Live Twice" single (a cover of the James Bond theme), the next three Scientists releases are pure archive material. **You Get What You Deserve** is an English release combining **Atom Bomb** and **Demolition Derby** with the B-side from "You Only Live Twice" as a bonus cut. **Trauma** is a compilation of pre-**Blood** singles and rarities with the **Demolition Derby** tracks (again). The tape-only **Rubber Never Sleeps** digs even further into Scientists vaults to include live material from two of their their pre-Hoodoo Gurus lineups, as well as 1982/1983 live tracks. Although the poundingly intense **Weird Love** (the only Scientists record released in the US) was newly recorded live in London (February 1986), it again portrays the band's music as history by consisting entirely of old "hits."

By the 1987 release of **The Human Jukebox**, only Salmon and Tony Thewlis remained from the Australian band. A dreary album lacking the searing frenzy that gave the Scientists their impact, **Jukebox**'s repetition comes off as industrial rather than mesmerizing; Salmon's vocals are flat and droney as if he'd taken lessons from a reject from Lou Reed High. ['e]

ROBIN SCOTT
See *M, Ryuichi Sakamoto.*

TIM SCOTT
Swear EP (Sire) 1983
The High Lonesome Sound (Geffen) 1987 ●

Ex-Rockat guitarist Scott pounds out some of the dumbest dance-rock ever on the five-song **Swear**, produced by Richard Gottehrer. Joined by ex-Holly and the Italians bassist Mark Sidgwick and future Beat Rodeo drummer Lewis King (with one guest vocal by Jane Wiedlin), Scott's inadequacy as a singer and writer are made abundantly clear on the moronic title song and "Good as Gold"; elsewhere, he's just a bland and forgettable rocker.

So much for stylistic consistency: **The High Lonesome Sound** is unconvincing predigested commercial country and cowpunk. Mitchell Froom produced and played the keyboards; Elvis Presley sideman Jerry Scheff is the bassist; David Hidalgo of Los Lobos adds accordion and backup vocals; the redoubtable James Burton even takes a nice dobro solo on "Release." Give Scott points for improved vocals and bland inoffensiveness, but that's about all. Which bandwagon is next? [iar]

SCRAPING FOETUS OFF THE WHEEL
See *Foetus.*

SCRATCH ACID
Scratch Acid (Rabid Cat) 1984
Just Keep Eating. (Rabid Cat) 1986
Berserker EP (Touch and Go) 1987

Give this Austin, Texas quartet credit for an evocative band name and a remarkably unsettling outlook. The eight intense songs on the 12-inch **Scratch Acid** live up to their abrasive promise, powerfully and painfully muscling around just on the edge of listenability, with only sometime-Big Boy/Jerry's Kid Rey Washam's strong drumming to anchor walls of guitar noise and ex-Toxic Shocker David Yow's hysterical shriek-singing. In spots, relative restraint and organization prevail and the record succeeds in conveying something; elsewhere, an overdose of PiL/Bauhaus/Birthday Party takes hold and you get nothing but chaotic, raw angst that is simply no fun at all. Some of the inspired lyrics ("Cannibal," "Monsters") are classic *Mondo Cane* material, but a more palatable sonic setting would have increased their impact.

Without sacrificing a jot of their psycho weirdness, Scratch Acid show a mite more focus and control on the full-length **Just Keep Eating**. The music is just as virulent and loud, but Yow's increased effort to be understood gives an extra kick to the demented lyrics of songs like "Eyeball," "Unlike a Baptist" and "Crazy Dan," the longwinded chronicle of a crazed murderer. Fun stuff!

Lacking the far-reaching conceptual imagination of their Austin neighbors, the Butthole Surfers, Scratch Acid keep the presentation simple while reaching deep into the lyrical cesspool on the **Berserker** EP's six well-produced songs. Yow's raging, hysterical delivery goes nicely with the punk wash of "Mary Had a Little Drug Problem" and a perverted character study called "Moron's Moron," but the words are their most amusing element. Likewise, the festering dermal ugliness of "Skin Drips" (accompanied by a bluesy swing) and the ironic near-hardcore of "This Is Bliss" do their best work on the lyric sheet. Throughout the 12-inch EP, debauchery, vulgarity and viciousness intertwine for a truly seedy experience. [iar]

SCREAMING BLUE MESSIAHS
Good and Gone EP (nr/Big Beat) 1984
Twin Cadillac Valentine EP (nr/WEA) 1985
Gun-shy (Elektra) 1986 ●
The Peel Sessions EP (nr/Strange Fruit) 1987
Bikini Red (Elektra) 1987 ●

One part Scottish, two parts English, this fierce trio (led by two ex-members of Motor

Boys Motor) is well-named. Not averse to howling until blue in the face, they could very well be the prophesied saviors of static '80s pop. The Messiahs take their jaundiced love of Americana and render it into an unrecognizable hybrid of psychobilly, R&B, garage grunge and lethal punk energy.

Blistering would be a euphemistic description for **Good and Gone**—singer/songwriter/guitarist Bill Carter shrieks and wails his way through these six tracks in a merciless attack. The crudely worded "Someone To Talk To" (supposedly culled from a Marine drill chant), "Happy Home" and a cover of Hank Williams' "You're Gonna Change" give the Messiahs a roguish sort of appeal. Daring, foolhardy and just plain good fun. (The Peel EP dates from July of that same year and captures the band in its primal glory.)

On the title track of **Twin Cadillac Valentine**, the jagged edges have been smoothed down and the tune wanders amid sterile production. The three other tracks are raucous live versions of previously issued songs and provide the EP's only real signs of life.

Gun-shy contains "Twin Cadillac Valentine" and generally suffers from the same restraint. Occasional glimpses of the old form seep through, but never gain the momentum needed to sustain the effort. (Vic Maile and Howard Gray produced separately.)

Overproduction couldn't restrain a band this volatile, and **Bikini Red** is the triumphant outcome. An American tour after the release of **Gun-shy** apparently intensified the trio's love of America, because it's a consistently recurring theme throughout this entire album, produced by Vic Maile. The title song, "I Wanna Be a Flintstone," "I Can Speak American," "Jesus Chrysler Drives a Dodge" and "55—the Law" all derive from singularly American ideals and are the strongest tracks on this LP. **Bikini Red** is a joyous powder keg of a record that makes the transgressions on **Gun-shy** easy to forgive.
[ag]

SCREAMING MEEMEES

If This Is Paradise, I'll Take the Bag (NZ Propeller) 1983

For all the offbeat get-up, packaging and names, this Auckland foursome plays relatively conventional pop-rock (though some of it with a fashionably quirky sound). Strengths: tunefully boyish vocals, melodies

that pull you in a after a few listens and a lack of fuss and worry—even when the Meemees *are*, according to the lyrics, worried—that's refreshingly ingenuous but not cutesy. The ringing guitars recall the sound of Stuart Adamson when he was in the Skids but again minus the tension. Added bits of keyboards help fill out the sound. A dash more substance and these guys—very popular at home—could graduate to world class. [jg]

SCREAMING TREES
See *Beat Happening*.

SCREAMING TRIBESMEN
EP (Aus. no label) 1982
Move a Little Closer EP (What Goes On) 1984
Date with a Vampyre EP (What Goes On) 1985
Top of the Town EP (Aus. Rattlesnake) 1986
Bones + Flowers (Aus. Survival) 1987 (Ryko Analogue) 1988 ●

There's nothing tribal about the sound of these Aussies; neither their vocal nor guitar styles scream. Instead their music is full of pop-song harmonies, including "oohh" and "ahh" background singing, jangle chords and repeated refrains. From their start as a post-Ramones punky ensemble (on the first four-track EP) through **Bones + Flowers**, they've gone through an assortment of members and sonic textures but all of their releases have been exercises in good old (or bad old, depending on your viewpoint) pop-rock. **Move a Little Closer**, a US compilation of the band's first two Citadel singles ("Igloo" and "A Stand Alone") could easily mix and match with a stack of mod-revival albums while the squealier and grungier guitar chords of **Date with a Vampyre** (also four songs) nudge their sound closer to garage territory.

Top of the Town contains six songs by a new lineup that reveals an ongoing transition away from grunge and towards more mainstream pop-rock. "You Better Run" is the most impressive track, and a fair precursor to the excellent **Bones + Flowers**. The album launches the Tribesmen into a new international league, offering richly-played rock-melody songwriting (by guitarist/pianist/producer Chris "Klondike" Masuak and singer/guitarist Mick Medew) that's got all the needed attributes for major stardom.

Standouts: a new version of "Igloo," the wittily '60sish "Our Time at Last," the peppy Anglo-popping "Dream Away" and the Rockpiling "Living Vampire." The CD has two bonus tracks. ['e/iar]

!SCREAMIN' SIRENS!
!Fiesta! (Enigma) 1984
ROSIE FLORES
Rosie Flores (Reprise) 1987

Ah, the wonders of showbiz. As lead guitarist and singer for the !Screamin' Sirens!, Rosie Flores (previously of San Diego's Rosie and the Screamers) performed her share of perky throwaway power pop, the kind of junk that fairly exploded out of the woodwork in the wake of Blondie's late-'70s success. At other times, the four Sirens served up transparently fake country-rock or the entertaining bogus funk of "Mr. T Luv Boogie."

Lo and behold, three years after the half-hearted !Fiesta!, Flores turns up as a "real" country artist, doing that old Bakersfield boogie on a fine solo album produced by Pete Anderson of Dwight Yoakam fame. Billy Bremner is her guitarist; Los Lobos' David Hidalgo contributes rippling accordion on "Midnight to Moonlight," a Flores tune first heard on !Fiesta!. [jy]

SCRITTI POLITTI
Works in Progress EP (nr/St. Pancras-Rough Trade) 1979
4 A-Sides EP (nr/St. Pancras-Rough Trade) 1979
Songs to Remember (nr/Rough Trade) 1982
Cupid & Psyche 85 (Warner Bros.) 1985 ●
Provision (Warner Bros.) 1988 ●

Originally an arty conceptual trio from Leeds, Scritti Politti underwent a number of drastic developmental changes on the way to becoming, ultimately, just a vehicle for Welsh-born singer Green Gartside. By the time Scritti Politti released its long-awaited first album in 1982, Green had pulled the band through a phase of haunting synth-pop ("The Sweetest Girl") and into a souled-out revamp of early T. Rex, minus Bolan's unique sword-and-sorcery outlook. Songs to Remember is an unassumingly warm and charming set, with boppy beats, quirky tunes and abundant catchy goodwill. While Green's obvious songwriting mastery and affecting voice make every song appealing, a few—"Asylums in Jerusalem," "Faithless" and "The Sweetest Girl"—are absolutely wonderful.

Subsequently shedding the pretense of a band, Green moved himself to New York, where he turned to high-sheen soul music as his life's work. With venerable producer Arif Mardin, Material drummer Fred Maher and other heavyweights, the entirety of Green's output for the following two years turned up on a 1984 12-inch, establishing him as a truly brilliant pop craftsman. "Wood Beez (Pray Like Aretha Franklin)" and "Absolute" are stunning, in terms of both traditional musical excellence and up-to-date modern stylings and sound.

Green consolidated his triumph by including both songs on Cupid & Psyche 85, only the second Scritti Politti album in six years. Recorded and produced in the main with Maher and keyboardist David Gamson but featuring numerous other musicians, the painstakingly well-crafted record is unfailingly pleasant. Nonetheless, only "The Word Girl" approaches the engaging excellence of the two singles.

Provision retains the core group with Gamson and Maher, but adds a few unexpected guests, including singer Roger Troutman and Miles Davis (!). The CD adds extra tracks. [jw/iar]

SCRUFFY THE CAT
High Octane Revival EP (Relativity) 1986
Tiny Days (Relativity) 1987 ●
Boom Boom Boom Bingo EP (Relativity) 1987

Boston combo plays good-natured countryish rock with a romantic streak—sometimes a bit too ephemeral for its own good, but always unpretentiously enjoyable. Frontman Charlie Chesterman sings the surprisingly witty lyrics (all five Scruffys write) in an earnestly bemused drawl, and the band plays in an amiably rollicking—if not particularly individual—style that's well-suited to their modest musical goals.

Both the six-song High Octane Revival (produced by Dave Minehan of the Neighborhoods) and Tiny Days (produced by ex-Waitress Chris Butler) are consistent funfests, with such winning numbers as the former's "Tiger, Tiger" and "40 Days & 40 Nights" and the latter's "Shadow Boy" and "My Fate Was Sealed with a Kiss." Multi-instrumentalist Stona Fitch left after Tiny Days, but the loss isn't evident on the inconclusive **Boom Boom Boom Bingo**, two new studio tracks (including the wonderful busted-heart kiss-off "You Dirty Rat") plus three live tunes, among them a decent cover of Del Shannon's "Runaway." [hd]

SECRET
The Secret (nr/Oval-A&M) 1979

A British duo, aided here by three added musicians, the Secret pursued roughly the same muse as Sparks, playing quirky, up-tempo inventions with witty lyrics and intricate arrangements. Lacking any real character, though, their album succeeds in tweaking the intellect and making toes twitch, but falls short of substantial impact on either front. [iar]

SECRET AFFAIR
Glory Boys (Sire) 1979
Behind Closed Doors (Sire) 1980
Business as Usual (nr/I Spy-Arista) 1982
The Peel Sessions EP (nr/Strange Fruit) 1988

Secret Affair were the mod revival's top dogs because they forged a distinctive sound that didn't simply pick up where the Jam (or Who) left off. Ian Page's mellifluous vocals and Dave Cairns' plangent guitars spearheaded the band's enthusiastic drive, hampered only by occasionally stiff drumming; the consistently above-average tunes of **Glory Boys** get an extra fillip by the sporadic addition of horns. What grates, though, is the pushy, overstated rhetoric, especially in light of the would-be movement's brief, faddish existence.

The instrumental attack on **Behind Closed Doors** is tighter and the lyrics—though still pretentious—arty on a more personal level. At least half of the songs are excellent. By the time of **Business as Usual**, though, the Affair was a big fish in an evaporated neo-mod pond. The group could hardly maintain its self-important image, and with it went the creative spark. The album, while smoother than ever before, is as journeyman-like as its title suggests. [jg]

SECRETS*
The Secrets (Why Fi) 1982

This Midwest American quartet (whose name, for some reason, has an asterisk) made its debut in 1979 with a single released on a Kansas City, Missouri independent label.

Three years later, the band's LP, co-produced by Tom Petty sideman Stan Lynch, leads off with "It's Your Heart Tonight," that 45's A-side. A bit older and more stylish perhaps, the new-lineup Secrets still play brilliant power pop, with instantly memorable songs, sparkling vocal harmonies and crisp rock'n'roll instrumentation. Ten could-be-hits on one disc. [iar]

(U.S.) SECRET SERVICE
(U.S.) Secret Service EP (Moonlight) 1980

These are the members of Sneakers who didn't follow Chris Stamey to New York, plus other Winston-Salem, North Carolina pals. The record is pleasant power pop, more "professional" than Sneakers and consequently lacking most of that band's ingratiating twinkiness (although they're still too cute to be true hard-rockers). The EP includes one goodie ("Backseat Sinner") and three other tunes that are only fair. [jg]

SECTION 25
The Key of Dreams (Bel. Factory Benelux) 1982
Always Now (nr/Factory) 1982
From the Hip (nr/Factory) 1984
The Peel Sessions EP (nr/Strange Fruit) 1988

Blackpool's Section 25 followed in the Joy Division tradition, anchoring their songs to basso depresso vocals and upfront drums, backed by synthesizers and guitar. Though lacking that band's intensity, they did nicely reproduce the atmosphere. The self-produced **Key of Dreams** presents nine examinations of paranoia and anxiety, using lurking glissandi, curious touches of Doorsish piano and Oriental philosophy. **Always Now** works away from imitation, giving greater emphasis to musical technique outside the parameters of rock. Producer Martin Hannett thickens the sound, bringing new body to Section 25's work. (The package is also worth mentioning: a marbleized inner sleeve in a heavy-weight top-opening bright yellow envelope.)

From the Hip takes after New Order a bit and explores two alternate paths—pastoral mood pieces featuring soothing ambient synthesizer and faint guitar, and driving electronic dance music with a light touch—both of which succeed to great effect. It's their best album (and "Reflection" could be a hit single)—a distinguished example of where modern synthesizer music is going. [sg/iar]

SECTOR 27

See *Tom Robinson Band.*

SELECTER

Too Much Pressure (Chrysalis) 1980
Celebrate the Bullet (Chrysalis) 1981

The Selecter—an interracial, multinational seven-piece—emerged from the same Coventry scene that gave birth to the Specials; founder Neol Davis was in on the creation of 2-Tone, the label which in turn ignited the entire neo-ska movement in England. The company's first release was a Specials 45; its flipside was an instrumental credited to and entitled "The Selecter" which had, in fact, been recorded by Davis and Specials drummer John Bradbury some months earlier. When the A-side became a hit, interest in the Selecter also grew, and Davis was obliged to recruit musicians and start up the group. With the gifted Pauline Black handling most of the lead vocals, the Selecter sounded like no other band in the genre; they employed the same upbeat rhythms, but added a much poppier and individual touch, much of it due to Black's style and influence.

Too Much Pressure is bursting with great songs like "On My Radio," "Three Minute Hero," "Time Hard" and the title track. Davis wrote much of the material, but contributions from other sources—within and without the lineup—add further variety. As the playing hops along, with a horn section added in spots, Pauline Black, shining with enormous vocal talent, continually provides the spark.

Celebrate the Bullet has little of the first LP's brilliance; although the performances don't lack anything tangible, the songwriting is vastly less inspired and none of the anti-trendy cleverness so vital to the previous album's uniqueness can be discerned. The Selecter dissolved soon after; Black did several solo singles and some acting.   [iar]

SEMINAL RATS

Omnipotent (Aus. Mr. Spaceman) 1986
   (What Goes On) 1987
Barbeques, Hospitals & Lear Jets EP (Aus.
   Mr. Spaceman) 1988

An Australian response to every noisy scum-sucking band that ever crawled out of the Detroit hardrock scene, early Rolling Stones' records in hand. The Seminal Rats make primal, '70s-rooted three chord punk with chanted vocals, loud hard guitar, more and even more guitar. **Omnipotent,** a seven-song introduction to the quintet, contains such gritty numbers as "Rat Race" and "Part Time Girl."   ['e]

SENDERS

Seven Song Super Single (Max's Kansas City) 1980

Although the Senders never broke out of the New York club circuit, they left behind this delightful, too brief memento. The rambunctious blend of originals and oldies (Little Richard, Howlin' Wolf, et al.) disproves the conventional wisdom that classicism has to be stuffy; the energy level here matches that of the Ramones in their prime. Bands will continue in R&B and rockabilly no matter what the wave, but few will match the verve of the Senders.   [jy]

WILL SERGEANT

See *Echo and the Bunnymen.*

SERIOUS YOUNG INSECTS

Housebreaking (Aus. Native Tongue) 1982

At times, this (Melbourne) Australian trio, originally a five-piece, resembles the Police—intricate, subtle rhythms smoothly interwoven with fluid guitar and bass lines—but these guys (as the band's handle might indicate) have more whimsical ideas than that. There's a song called "I Want Cake" which is simply the title chanted, mantra-like, over a pulsing dance instrumental. Other tunes—"Parents Go Mental," "Why Can't I Control My Body?"—play up an XTC-like side, although there are evident traces of the Jam and others as well. The Insects' playing is excellent and their tunes well-developed. **Housebreaking** is a strange record and well worth finding.   [iar]

BRIAN SETZER

See *Stray Cats.*

17 PYGMIES

See *Savage Republic.*

SEVERED HEADS

Since the Accident (nr/Ink) 1983
Dead Eyes Opened EP (Can. Nettwerk)
   1985 ●

Come Visit the Big Bigot (Can. Nettwerk)
1986 ●
Bad Mood Guy (Can. Nettwerk) 1987 ●
Greater Reward (Can. Nettwerk) 1988 ●

This cheerfully obscure Australian chaos group manipulates tapes, found sounds and assorted electronic gear to squeak and plonk their way through synthetically rhythmatized fogs of craziness on their two albums issued in North America. **Come Visit the Big Bigot** has flashes of cogency (for instance, "Army") amid a general hubbub that might have been created by Martians armed only with Eno's **Here Come the Warm Jets** for a template. Not exactly a noise combo, Severed Heads generally stay on the safe side of unpleasant, but jumble up so many contradictory sounds on their tracks that focusing on any particular thread of a song is no mean feat. (The **Big Bigot** CD contains the entirety of **Dead Eyes Opened**, a prior five-track EP.)

Bad Mood Guy takes a slightly less polyphasic approach, centering the tracks with stable tempos and reasonably sturdy song structures, keeping the distracting gimmicks back in the mix until needed. Something like a lightweight Cabaret Voltaire or a hyperactive dj collective spinning five records simultaneously, this Severed Heads outing is as close to normalcy as they're likely to get. My advice: jump in here if you're so tempted, and swim your way upstream against the chronological tide until you hit a wall.

[iar]

SEX GANG CHILDREN
Song and Legend (nr/Illuminated) 1983
Beasts (nr/Illuminated) 1983
Live in London and Glasgow (nr/Corpus
Christi) 1983
Ecstasy and Vendetta Over New York [tape]
(ROIR) 1984
Re-enter the Abyss (nr/Dojo) 1985
Nightland (nr/Arkham House) 1986
Live (nr/Arkham House) 1987

ANDI SEX GANG
Blind! (nr/Illuminated) 1985

Alongside Specimen and others, Sex Gang Children came out of the Batcave movement, a largely meaningless collection of British bands dedicated to dressing up like old Alice Cooper, clinging to a raunchy post-Bowie outlook, writing lyrics that virtually define pretentious pseudo-literary bullshit and adopting names guaranteed to keep radio censors on their toes. Certainly not the worst of the horrid lot, the Sex Gang Children at their outset bore an obnoxious and uncanny resemblance to Adam and the Ants, but lacked that group's originality or talent. The band's *best* feature is a vague sense of song structure. So unless war whoops, overactive echo, pounding percussion and songs about "German Nun," "Kill Machine," "Cannibal Queen" and "Shout and Scream" (all on **Song and Legend**) sound enticing, skip Sex Gang Children for now and wait until they grow up.

Beasts is a singles compilation of singles which slightly overlaps the first LP. **Ecstasy and Vendetta** captures the Sex Gang Children flailing away onstage in the Big Apple at the end of 1983. About half the material comes from the first studio album; the performance is blurry, overwrought and horrible. [iar]

SEX PISTOLS
Never Mind the Bollocks, Here's the Sex
Pistols (Warner Bros.) 1977 ●
The Great Rock'n'Roll Swindle (nr/Virgin)
1979 ●
Some Product Carri On (nr/Virgin) 1979
Flogging a Dead Horse (nr/Virgin) 1980
The Heyday [tape] (nr/Factory) 1980
The Mini Album EP (nr/Chaos) 1985 (Restless)
1988 ●
The Original Pistols Live (nr/Receiver) 1985
(nr/Dojo) 1986
After the Storm (nr/Receiver) 1985
Live Worldwide (nr/Konexion) 1985
Best of the Sex Pistols Live (nr/Bondage)
1985
Anarchy in the UK Live (nr/UK) 1985
Never Trust a Hippy (nr/Hippy) 1985
Where Were You in '77 (nr/77) 1985
Power of the Pistols (nr/77) 1985
We Have Cum for Your Children (Wanted:
The Goodman Tapes) (Skyclad) 1988 ●
Better Live Than Dead (Restless) 1988 ●
The Swindle Continues (Restless) 1988 ●

Although their importance—both to the direction of contemporary music and more generally to pop culture—can hardly be overstated, the Sex Pistols did not make their stand primarily on albums. In fact, the massive discography notwithstanding, the Pistols made only one actual studio album during their 14-month existence (November 1976 to January 1978). In a textbook McLuhanesque example of the media being the message, the quartet's impact did not result from vast commercial success; against the general rock tide, most of their revolutionary work was released on 7-inch singles. (Six of which were posthumously packaged in a boxed set for collectors.)

Fulfilling an essential and immaculate role as martyrs on the new wave altar by logically self-destructing (and politely waiting until no one was paying much attention before descending into typical wasted rock-stardom) rather than falling prey to standard rock'n'roll conventions, the Pistols and manager/provocateur Malcolm McLaren challenged every aspect and precept of modern music-making, thereby inspiring countless groups to follow their cue onto stages around the world. A confrontational, nihilistic public image and rabidly nihilistic socio-political lyrics set the tone that continues to guide punk bands. On top of everything, the Pistols made totally unassailable and essential electric music that sounds just as exciting and powerful today as it did over a decade (!) ago.

Populated by such classics as "Anarchy in the UK," "God Save the Queen" and "No Feelings," **Never Mind the Bollocks, Here's the Sex Pistols** is a wonderful rock music record. Prototypical punk without compromise, it includes almost everything you need to hear by the Sex Pistols. Oddly, at the time of its release, the LP was a disappointment in light of sky-high expectations. Four of the tracks had already been released as singles; many others had circulated on well-known album-in-progress bootlegs, like the legendary **Spunk**. Now, of course, as the best recorded evidence of the Pistols' existence, it almost defies criticism. Paul Cook, Steve Jones, Johnny Rotten (Lydon) and Sid Vicious (plus Glen Matlock, the original musical architect and author, who was sacked early on, allegedly for liking the Beatles) combined to produce a unique moment in rock history and **Bollocks** is the evidence. (The American release has one extra track, a different running sequence and altered artwork.)

The Great Rock'n'Roll Swindle, the soundtrack to an amazing bio-pic about the band, posthumously banged together into semi-coherent form by Julien Temple from a number of aborted film projects, exists in three forms: a one-disc album of highlights and two slightly different full-length two-disc collections. In any case, it's a semi-connected batch of songs by various bands (not just the Pistols) that's just full of surprises, fun and strange goings-on. There are regular Pistols tracks—some with vocals by Sid, Steve Jones and Eddie Tudorpole taking the departed and uncooperative Rotten's place—as well as live performances, studio outtakes, symphonic renditions, a surprisingly great disco medley, McLaren's first vocal foray and much more. A bit lighthearted (and light-headed), but with loads of sharp music. The single-record extract has most of the prime material, but either full dose is highly recommended.

Some Product Carri On is for diehards only, scraping the barrel for radio interviews and commercials—audio vérité for idiots whose interest in the Pistols has more to do with sociopathic fascination than pop culture. However gratuitous and unnecessary as it may be, the album shows careful assembly and is wickedly funny in spots—good for one embarrassing listen then straight into the trash compactor.

While **Some Product** is completely expendable, **Flogging a Dead Horse**—wretched back-cover scatology aside—provides the commendable service of compiling seven ace 45s (both sides of each) into one handy Pistols primer. From "Anarchy in the UK" to "The Great Rock'n'Roll Swindle," all of their greatest moments are delivered. If you don't have a complete set, this record catches you right up; for newcomers, the LP is a must-have. **The Heyday** is a cassette-only collection of interviews with Lydon, Cook, Jones and Vicious.

In 1985, a veritable flood of new Sex Pistols records—legal, dubious and plainly unauthorized—hit British record shops. **The Mini Album** (issued in the US three years later) consists of a half-dozen early album outtakes (July '76, with Matlock), probably from the same studio supply as those issued on **Spunk**. **The Original Pistols Live**, with liner notes by producer Dave Goodman, records a 1976 gig with moderate fidelity and a lively mix. **Live Worldwide** is a compendium of a dozen cuts, presumably from various shows.

The low-fi/high-energy **Better Live Than Dead** documents another pre-Sid concert with selections from the Pistols' non-original repertoire—"Substitute," "Stepping Stone," "No Fun"—alongside their own classic compositions. Fascinating and reasonably well-mastered, **We Have Cum for Your Children** is a motley but meaningful packet of oddities and endities: the notorious "Filth and the

Fury" Bill Grundy television interview (1 December 1976), radio spots, live and for-broadcast recordings and an intriguing assortment of studio rehearsals and outtakes. Although it contains "Pretty Vacant," "Submission," "EMI" (mistitled, perhaps intentionally, "Unlimited Supply") in versions that are, or at least closely resemble, the ones on **Spunk**, the LP's main value lies in clear recordings of the otherwise unavailable "Revolution in the Classroom," "Suburban Kid" and the Cook'n'Jones "Here We Go Again."

Jointly billed to the Sex Pistols and Ex-Pistols, **The Swindle Continues** is a similar (and overlapping) studio compilation with a side of first-album rehearsals, demos and outtakes (with one actual B-side, "No Fun," as a ringer) and a side of post-split items, mostly by Cook and Jones. There's the fabulous "Silly Thing" (a '79 B-side with Jones doing lead vocals), an absurd acoustic version of "Anarchy in the UK" from a French single, a hysterical disco-mix medley-of-hits called "Sex on 45" and much less. The sound is a shade below good and the total lack of credits a large annoyance, but the LP title precludes any such carping. Ever had the feeling you've been conned? [iar]

See also *Chequered Past, Chiefs of Relief, Steve Jones, Malcolm McLaren, Public Image Ltd., Professionals, Rich Kids, Sid Vicious.*

SHAGGS

Philosophy of the World (Third World) 1969
    (Red Rooster) 1980 ●
Shaggs' Own Thing (Red Rooster) 1982

There's always room for dada in rock, and New Hampshire's three Wiggins sisters virtually define ingenuous amateurism on their first album, a home-brew oddity originally released in 1969. This startling treatise tears down every skill-related barrier that generally precludes musically unskilled children from making records and boasts that perennial candidate for worst song of all time, "My Pal Foot Foot." **Philosophy of the World** is truly inspired awfulness: incompetent drumming totally unrelated to the song under attack, two not-quite-tuned guitars and clumsy vocals offering Hallmark card platitudes. In toto, a triumph!

After reissuing the first album, NRBQ's Red Rooster label saw to the Shaggs' creation of another batch of tunes, this time making

a concerted effort to achieve a semblance of musical acceptability. To that end, another Wiggins was brought in to play bass, the selection of material encompasses some non-originals, and both the sound and playing is several hundred times improved. (The benchmark is a swell remake of "My Pal Foot Foot.") **Shaggs' Own Thing** gives up a lot in terms of ear-wrenching misery, achieving instead a simple Jonathan Richman-like sweetness—a piece of true rock primitivism.
[iar]

SHAKE

Shake EP (nr/Sire) 1979

When the Rezillos split into vocal and instrumental factions, the latter became Shake. A trio led by guitarist Jo Callis (who'd penned 90 percent of the Rezillos' originals), Shake over-reacted to their ex-bandmates' frivolity by playing their loud'n'fastisms deadpan on this 10-incher. Second mistake: Callis let the other two write. Third mistake: dull sound. Smart move: breaking up. Smarter move (for Callis): joining the Human League. [jg]

SHAKIN' PYRAMIDS

Skin 'Em Up (nr/Cuba Libre-Virgin) 1981
The Shakin' Pyramids and Lonnie Donegan
    EP (nr/Cuba Libre-Virgin) 1981
Celts and Cobras (nr/Cuba Libre-Virgin) 1982
Shakin' Pyramids (Rock'n'Roll) 1983

Few neo-rockabilly combos are as down-home folksy as Glasgow, Scotland's Shakin' Pyramids. This trio not only avoids electricity, they barely condone musical instruments, having started out as a pair of busking acoustic guitarists and a singer/harmonica player.

The corrupting touch of fame lured them into adding electric guitar, acoustic bass and a spot of drums to **Skin 'Em Up**. The album pounds furiously, putting your average megawatt metal band to shame. Songs—mostly non-originals—zip by at a blinding rate; the record's only flaw is its brief running time. Then again, if brevity be the soul of this music, the Shakin' Pyramids are a rockabilly Ramones.

Probably the first credible skiffle recording made in a generation, the 7-inch EP with Lonnie Donegan (Scottish-born skiffle king who popularized "Rock Island Line" in 1955 and is best known for "Does Your Chewing

Gum Lose Its Flavor on the Bedpost Overnight") offers four old songs (including "Wabash Cannonball") and one original in a joyous traditional setting.

Like the Ramones, the Pyramids have a growth problem. **Celts and Cobras** offers a higher percentage of their own songs, but on it they're accompanied by piano, accordion, electric bass and even—gack!—a string section. More dismaying is the band's descent into schlock-pop consciousness: instead of Eddie Cochran and Link Davis tunes, we get the Everly Brothers and Gene Pitney. The band still rocks, but they'd better figure out where they're going.

The American release (whose cover pictures and sleeve lists them as a quartet) distills the two albums, featuring mainly originals. [si/iar]

SHAKIN' STREET
Vampire Rock (Fr. CBS) 1978
Shakin' Street (Columbia) 1980

Led by singer Fabienne Shine and her songwriting partner, guitarist Eric Lewy, Shakin' Street emerged from obscurity in France thanks to American producer/manager Sandy Pearlman, who procured an international recording deal for the band. **Vampire Rock**, recorded in London but released only in France, is an impressive, raucous and wild rocker, with English lyrics that touch a number of bases, from sharp to silly. Shine's accented singing, which at times recalls Grace Slick, is a powerful asset; the twin-guitar roar sounds almost uncontrollable.

Taken under Pearlman's wing, the band recorded its second album in America, with ex-Dictator (and future metal star) Ross the Boss replacing one of the guitarists. Playing simple, direct hard-rock-cum-metal, the album offers little original, save for a strong song recut from **Vampire Rock** ("No Time to Lose") and one truly great number, "Susie Wong," which supports a haunting melody with subtly arranged electric/acoustic instrumentation. [iar]

SHAMEN
Drop (Communion) 1987 ●
What's Going Down EP (Communion) 1988 ●
Strange Daydreams (It. Materiali Sonori) 1988

Groovy acid-rock from Scotland: Aberdeen's Shamen trip back to the spacey side of 1967 Britain with scrappy production, tremolo guitars, whining mellotrons and echoed vocals, suggesting **Sellout**-era Who, early Pink Floyd, the Move, Tomorrow and others without specifically quoting anyone. Except for a few songs that lean towards less colorful folk-rock and aren't as bewitching, **Drop** is adventurous and entertaining stuff that easily outclasses most neo-psychedelic wannabes with abundant invention and élan. In a brilliant piece of unintentional subversion, a Scottish brewery—completely missing the song's lyrical intent—chose the LP's "Happy Days," an ironic protest against the Falklands War, for use in a massive TV ad campaign. [iar]

SHAM 69
Tell Us the Truth (Sire) 1978
That's Life (nr/Polydor) 1978
The Adventures of Hersham Boys (nr/Polydor) 1979
The Game (nr/Polydor) 1980
The First, Best and Last (nr/Polydor) 1980
Live and Loud (nr/Link) 1987
Live and Loud, Volume 2 (nr/Link) 1988
Volunteer (nr/Legacy) 1988

The archetypal working class ramalama dole-queue band, deliverers of socio-political bromides over blazing guitars, Hersham's Sham 69 had a bad case of arrested development. Their populist slogans were ultimately chanted like football cheers and taken seriously only by the enormous British Sham army. Arguably their best single, "Hurry Up Harry" is about the importance of "going down 'a pub." Lead singer/lyricist Jimmy Pursey was earnest enough, and the band simple and basic: although their records are of no lasting import, Sham became the most popular UK punk band of their time, scoring seven UK Top 50 singles.

The first LP sidesteps the issue of decent production by having one side with none at all and the other recorded live. The sound, oddly enough, isn't so much derived from the Clash and Pistols as it is from the Dolls, Heartbreakers and Ramones. (It's hard to judge how much of that is by design and how much is due to sheer incompetence.) More than any of those, Pursey's cockney yelling tabbed him as the anykid who could, but it's also true that almost any kid could have written the LP in his sleep.

That's Life offers more of the same, while enlarging on an idea heard briefly on **Tell Us the Truth**: inserting narrative slice-of-life dialogues (kid vs. parents, boy and girl, boy and girl's boyfriend, etc.) between songs. Pursey lets on that he has bigger ambitions, as he plays the cockney wideboy imitating Bob Dylan on one cut. All told, a funny punk LP which features "Hurry Up Harry" and the anthemic "Angels with Dirty Faces," both singles hits.

Pursey worked up some "poetic" lyrics for **Hersham Boys**; this, plus the increased use of keyboards (played by Pursey's co-producer, Peter Wilson) meant that Sham was nearing the stage of early Boomtown Rats, complete with a surprising cover of the Yardbirds' classic "You're a Better Man Than I." Their first break with the punk scene, but no less aggressive. (Discographical point: Polydor US imported copies of the LP, stickered them with an American list price and distributed a few as if it were an American release.)

By **The Game**, Sham's playing and lyrics had sharpened to the point of respectability, with the strongest material (the single "Give the Dog a Bone" in particular) of all their LPs. However, having perfected their narrow craft, there was nothing to do but disband, which they did soon after. The **First, Best and Last** compilation does include some non-LP singles (but not their first, from '77, on Step Forward) plus a limited-edition bonus live EP.

Live and Loud, a scorching live album recorded in 1979 and released eight years later, dwarfs Sham's studio catalog. Featuring their best, most mature (**Hersham Boys/ The Game**) lineup, the LP is an ideal distillation of material from the first three albums, played with fire and confidence. It's odd that the truly essential Sham LP—their finest moment and the only record that could put to rest their reputation as a sloppy, by-the-numbers punk circus—would emerge so late in the game.

Immense UK sales of **Live and Loud** led to **Volume 2** (though redundant, it's more of the same quality) and the 1987 reformation of the group. Unfortunately, from their two singles so far, the new Sham is a heavy-metal/rap group, a fifth-rate Beastie Boys —and an awfully banal one at that.

[jg/jr]

See also *Angelic Upstarts, Cockney Rejects, Jimmy Pursey, Wanderers*.

SHANGO

See *Afrika Bambaataa*.

FEARGAL SHARKEY

Feargal Sharkey (Virgin-A&M) 1985 ●
Wish (Virgin) 1988 ●

Following a slow start—three singles, only one of which ("Never Never," with Vince Clarke's Assembly) was any good—Sharkey's ascent from ex-Undertone to chart-topping singing sensation was accomplished with relative alacrity, thanks in large part to producer Dave Stewart of Eurythmics. Sharkey's first solo album is an uneasy pairing of his distinctive vocals and tame, mainstream-ish arrangements of material from diverse sources. "A Good Heart" (written by Lone Justice's Maria McKee, but unrecorded by her own band) is a sturdy piece of slightly soulful pop; "You Little Thief" (by Benmont Tench of Tom Petty's Heartbreakers) is similarly memorable. "Love and Hate" resembles late-period Undertones, while the Sharkey version of the venerable "It's All Over Now" is simply a mistake.

Sharkey takes another giant step away from his past with **Wish**. The high-gloss West Coast album—production, guitar and keyboards by Danny Kortchmar; songs mostly co-written with Kootch, Waddy Wachtel and Mark Goldenberg—has characterless backing tracks that could serve any number of lame singers. The stark contrast of Sharkey's strange voice with such bland commercialism results in an utterly listenable soul-pop-rock record with only one strong character trait. A guest turn by Keith Richards on Ben Tench's "More Love" is wasted; except for the rousing "Out of My System," the routinely romantic songs, while competent, are entirely forgettable.   [iar]

SHEENA AND THE ROKKETS

Sheena and the Rokkets (Jap. Alfa) 1979
Sheena and the Rokkets (A&M) 1980

An ingenious Japanese techno-pop quartet with a female singer and a taste for Anglo-American rock'n'roll of the '60s. The Rokkets' Japanese debut contains over-the-top readings of "The Batman Theme," James Brown's "I Got You" and a truly nutty version of "You Really Got Me," as well as impressive originals like "Radio Junk" and "Rocket Factory." A perfectly wonderful blend of cultures and musical sensibilities, sung in Japanese and fractured English.

The American release, reprising five songs, is a very different record. Some tunes, cut originally in Japanese, were redone with English vocals; others sound like the results of completely new sessions. Overall, it lacks the carefree zaniness that imbues the Japanese album with its bubbling infectiousness. More serious, less entertaining.

After spending most of a decade out of sight and mind, Sheena and the Rokkets turned up playing in (at least) New York City in early 1988. [iar]

SHEILA E.

Sheila E. in The Glamorous Life (Warner Bros.) 1984 ●
Sheila E. in Romance 1600 (Paisley Park) 1985 ●
Sheila E. (Paisley Park) 1987 ●

Multi-talented Sheila Escovedo—drummer, percussionist, singer, composer, producer, actress (well . . .)—made quite an entrance under Prince's wing on **Glamorous Life**. The frenetic nine-minute title tune, filled with rhythms, hooks and insidious lyrics, is the record's best-known item, but the other five tracks display other equally appealing sides of Ms. E's musical personality. Probably due to his non-involvement in the songwriting, Prince's touch is light, his influence relatively subtle.

One could not easily miss the first album's erotic content, but **Romance 1600** is far hornier, with coy titles like "Bedtime Story" and "Toy Box" driving the point home. Otherwise, the album centers around the overextended "A Love Bizarre." Sheila and Prince (guitar, bass, vocals) stretch this minor tune to over 12 minutes, leaving all but the most mechano-minded drifting off the dance floor and out the door. If you're listening at home, forget it! Luckily, Side Two is tons better—"Yellow" and "Romance 1600" go a long way towards redeeming the excessive mess.

Sheila's overheated libido is still breathing heavy on her eponymous third album, but at least the song titles are more presentable in polite company. A more reserved outing than the first two records, **Sheila E.** has a slow ballad, Prince-influenced funk-rock workouts, straight rock (where her power drumming drives like a racer) and an Escovedo family affair, the mostly instrumental "Soul Salsa," which features five relatives. [iar] See also *Prince*.

PETE SHELLEY

Sky Yen (nr/Groovy) 1979
Homosapien (Genetic-Arista) 1982
XL1 (Genetic-Arista) 1983
Heaven and the Sea (Mercury) 1986 ●

As creative linchpin of the Buzzcocks, Pete Shelley perfected a pop style based on intellectualizing his emotional responses, often to humorous effect. But, as with the group, he is strongest making singles, apparently hard-pressed to sustain his energy throughout an entire album.

Shelley's first solo LP, **Sky Yen**, was actually recorded in 1974, long before the Buzzcocks, and demonstrates an early interest in Germanic electronic music. An exercise in simpleminded drone electronics conducted on a single oscillator rather than full-fledged electronic instruments, the album is a collectors' item of minor interest.

The post-Buzzcocks **Homosapien**, including the hit single of the same name, is a dance album in which Shelley takes the reins and eliminates guitars and drums as the axis of his songs. The turn to electronics doesn't signal a surrender to them, though; the songs, not the technique, remain paramount. Shelley seems to draw influence from a wide group of sources (such as the Doors and Marc Bolan), and the album cleverly sidesteps the trap of monotony that sometimes afflicted the Buzzcocks. (There are differences between the UK and US versions: the latter replaces "Pusher Man," "It's Hard Enough Knowing" and "Keats' Song" with "Love in Vain," "Witness the Change" and "In Love with Somebody Else." Fine. The more Shelley the better.)

Shelley reintroduced guitar on **XL1** and downplayed the electronics to create more direct, urgent dance music. "Telephone Operator" is equal to "Homosapien"; the LP also contains other solid examples of clearheaded songwriting—"If You Ask Me (I Won't Say No)" and "You Know Better Than I Know," for instance—that allow strong rhythms to predominate without obscuring the abundant musicality. The tape version in both countries is different: the American adds dub mixes of "Homosapien" and another track; the English an extra LP's worth of remixes.

Heaven and the Sea serves up more of

Shelley's reflective soul-searching, but without much relish. Except for the percussion-laden "No Moon," the songs are fairly routine and Stephen Hague's mundane production does little to distinguish any. Shelley is becoming a specialized taste—fans will appreciate this record as much as any of his prior solo releases, unbelievers won't be especially affected.   [sg/iar]

ADRIAN SHERWOOD
DUB SYNDICATE
One Way System [tape] (ROIR) 1983
Tunes from the Missing Channel (On-U
    Sound) 1985
KEITH LEBLANC
Major Malfunction (World) 1986
GARY CLAIL'S TACKHEAD
SOUND SYSTEM
Tackhead Tape Time (Upside) 1987

Working with illustrious sidemen on both sides of the Atlantic, English producer Adrian Sherwood has labored throughout the '80s to hybridize such rhythmically-oriented studio styles as reggae, dub, hip-hop and dance music into something radically different than what's expected from any of those.

Following his work with New Age Steppers, the prolific Sherwood moved on to the loosely constituted Dub Syndicate. The ad hoc cast on the **One Way System** compilation cassette includes members of Aswad, Roots Radics and Creation Rebel; the languid, instrumental reggae is more repetitive and unnaturally elongated than invigorating. The subsequent Dub Syndicate album on Sherwood's On-U Sound label has Keith Levene and others providing fodder for his wild studio assemblies.

Besides a creative partnership with Mark Stewart and the Maffia, Sherwood's current focus is Tackhead, a quartet with three American sessioneers, all former members of Sugar Hill's house band: Keith LeBlanc (drums), Skip McDonald (guitar) and Doug Wimbish (bass). On their own, they created **Major Malfunction**, credited to LeBlanc; paired with British rapper Gary Clail, the beat-crazy experimentalists recorded **Tackhead Tape Time**, a wildly invigorating hodgepodge of pounding rhythms, musical adventures, bracing tape manipulations, spoken word contributions and various kitchen-sink additions.   [iar]

See also *New Age Steppers, Judy Nylon and Crucial, Mark Stewart and the Maffia.*

SHIRTS
The Shirts (Capitol) 1978
Street Light Shine (Capitol) 1979
Inner Sleeve (Capitol) 1980

These six Brooklynites were playing Top 40 covers in local bars until they happened onto the Bowery club circuit in 1975. Abandoning the boroughs for a career in Manhattan with original material, the Shirts became a popular if unhip fixture, and eventually wound up making three albums of totally bland hoping-for-the-mainstream rock. Singer Annie Golden has had some individual success—in the movie of *Hair,* with a solo single in 1984 and on Broadway—but the band is little more than a bad memory. Each of the albums has an enjoyable song or two, but there's nothing remarkable about any of them.   [iar]

SHOCKABILLY
The Dawn of Shockabilly EP (nr/Rough
    Trade) 1982
Earth vs. Shockabilly (nr/Rough Trade) 1983
Greatest Hits EP (Red) 1983
Colosseum (nr/Rough Trade) 1984
Vietnam (Fundamental Music) 1984
Heaven (Fundamental Music) 1985

Crazed rockabilly-tinged remakes of "Psychotic Reaction" and two Yardbirds classics isn't a bad idea, especially if gonzo guitar and drums like those on **The Dawn of Shockabilly** are brought to bear on 'em. Taking the same tack on "A Hard Day's Night" and a country oldie, adding silly organ also makes a funny kind of sense. But guitarist Eugene Chadbourne's nonsense vocals (stupidly muffled, or in silly cartoon character styles, with at least two or three different voices per track) ruin the whole thing. Eugene shouldn't be careful with his axe, but with his mouth.

Greatest Hits takes one track each from the two preceding English records and adds a quartet of stunning live cuts, including the amphetaminized "Bluegrass Breakdown" and a nearly unrecognizable version of the Doors' "People Are Strange." **Vietnam** is a relatively grand affair, with a huge tour-diary poster and material by Arthur Lee, John Fogerty, John Lee Hooker and the Beatles mercilessly savaged by Chadbourne and his two henchmen.

Heaven takes the terrible trio further into the realms of the truly weird. Only three covers (Bolan, Lennon and a mystery), but such inspired originals as Eugene's "How Can You Kill Me, I'm Already Dead" and "She Was a Living Breathing Piece of Dirt" more than make up the difference. On that (bum) note, Shockabilly ceased to exist.

Occasionally listenable, often more stupid than funny, Shockabilly was, if nothing else, absolutely unique. [jg/iar]

See also *Eugene Chadbourne*.

SHOES

Un dans Versailles (no label) 1975
Black Vinyl Shoes (Black Vinyl) 1977 (PVC) 1978
Present Tense (Elektra) 1979
Tongue Twister (Elektra) 1981
Boomerang (Elektra) 1982
Silhouette (nr/Demon) 1984
Shoes Best [CD] (Black Vinyl) 1987 [tape] (Black Vinyl) 1988

The brilliant power pop outfit from Zion, Illinois began by recording at home on a 4-track, which resulted in a self-released LP that attracted national attention and, eventually, a major-label contract. John and Jeff Murphy, Gary Klebe and drummer Skip Meyer blend electric guitar—loud, distorted, multi-tracked—with breathy, winsome vocals to create melodic rock made most impressive by the presence of three equally talented singer/songwriters.

Black Vinyl Shoes was recorded in a living room; the intricately layered guitars and vocals make that hard to believe. The songs, telling tender tales of failed romance, are catchy and instantly likable. The band also put the record in an impressive package and distributed it as a vinyl demo; in fact, it's one of the finest home-brewed releases ever, and is a much more valid piece of music than many productions by well-known bands with far greater technical resources. After the small initial pressing sold out, the album was licensed to PVC and reissued with wholly different artwork.

(**Black Vinyl** is actually not Shoes' first album. A prior longplayer was recorded by the Murphy brothers with a previous drummer and privately issued in a minute pressing quantity. Charming but a bit rough, it sounds like a less-developed attempt at what was to come. Shoes also recorded—but never released—an album's worth of excellent

tunes in 1976 under the working title **Bazooka**.)

After signing to Elektra, Shoes recorded **Present Tense** in a full-scale English 24-track studio with a professional producer, but ended up sounding pretty much the same as before, only with much greater audio fidelity. Given the chance to experiment and open up their sound, Shoes opted to hold fast—lots of vocals, lots of melody, lots of fuzzed-out guitars. Another triumphant LP that probably could have been made at home without losing any appreciable amount of charm or appeal—it's Shoes' talent, not studio technology, that matters here.

Tongue Twister succcessfully maintains the quality level of **Present Tense**, but Shoes are clearly standing still creatively. Their style is honed as far as it's going to go, and they're sticking with it. **Boomerang**, recorded near the band's home base without a strong outside producer, suffers from inconsistent song quality and an overanxious feeling, no doubt brought on by the band's failure to catch on commercially. (Early pressings of **Boomerang** included a 12-inch live EP, **Shoes on Ice**, recorded at the Zion Ice Arena in 1981, offering six of the band's best tunes as proof of their ability to play them well live.)

Parting company with their label, Shoes retired to the studio they had built in Illinois and continued writing and recording. A trio of Murphy, Murphy and Klebe made the next Shoes album, **Silhouette**, released only in Europe via various licensing arrangements. The sound (incorporating more keyboards and subtler dabs of guitar) is typically exquisite, and the songs (four by each member) are fine examples of the band's seemingly effortless pop suss. A fine, relaxed return that reasserts Shoes' considerable talent.

Reacquiring the rights to their three Elektra albums, Shoes issued their own 22 track CD-only non-chronological career retrospective, later putting it on cassette as well. The collection includes one previously unreleased item, a live cut from **On Ice** and a new song from an as-yet unreleased album provisionally entitled **Stolen Wishes**. (P.S. I wrote the liner notes.) [iar]

SHOP ASSISTANTS

Shop Assistants EP (nr/Subway Organisation) 1985
Safety Net EP (nr/53rd & 3rd) 1986

Shop Assistants (nr/Blue Guitar-Chrysalis)
1986

Along with the Jesus and Mary Chain, Edinburgh's Shop Assistants are part of a trend away from the terribly twee pop coming out of Scotland six or seven years ago. Four lasses and a lad (including two drummers), Shop Assistants are raw, catchy and utterly without pretense. Their two EPs combine some of J&M's white-noise pop with Buzzcocks-influenced buoyancy, and—when necessary—tuneful delicacy (see **Safety Net**'s "Somewhere in China"). The four-song debut is promising; **Safety Net** is nothing short of brilliant.

The band's first album reprises two songs from each of the preceding releases; while it's by no means a bad record taken by itself, there aren't any ideas on it that weren't already covered on the EPs. While **Shop Assistants** is good, straightforward, tuneful rock'n'roll (and a real good party album), there are simply too many tracks that blend into one another. In 1987, lead singer Alex (a woman) split to form the extremely similar Motorcycle Boy, not to be confused with the American band of the same name. [dgs]

SHRIEKBACK
Tench EP (Y America) 1982
Care (Warner Bros.) 1983
Jam Science (nr/Arista) 1984
Knowledge, Power, Truth and Sex EP (Ger.
Arista) 1984
The Infinite (nr/Kaz) 1984
Oil and Gold (Island) 1985 ●
Big Night Music (Island) 1986 ●
The Best of Shriekback: The Infinite [CD]
(nr/Kaz) 1987
The Best of Shriekback Volume Two:
Evolution [CD] (nr/Kaz) 1988
Go Bang! (Island) 1988 ●
The Peel Sessions EP (nr/Strange Fruit) 1988

Barry Andrews was a founder of XTC and later the organist in Robert Fripp's League of Gentlemen. David Allen was coincidentally replaced in Gang of Four by League bassist Sara Lee. Together with guitarist/vocalist Carl Marsh and a drum machine, Andrews and Allen formed Shriekback, a cagey dance band with solid rhythms and insidiously weird vocals. The playing is top-notch, a slithering swamp snake that oozes cool malevolence on **Tench**'s six tracks. Shriekback abounds in originality and creativity, if not warmth. Despite changes in personnel, Andrews has remained the band's core, preserving its spirit of prickly iconoclasm and imaginative exploration.

Care is an intelligent, well-produced, spirited debut, demonstrating what every XTC fan knew all along—Andrews is one of rock's most original and musical keyboard players. Over Allen's slinky, oblique bass lines, he provides subtle shadings and clever doodles that move in and out of the mix, making this perfect for both dancing and scrutiny. Most bands with this much talent would be content to showcase their chops, but Shriekback can write a good song, too, especially the haunting "Lined Up," a unique funk concoction that sets an impossible standard for inferior but likeminded bands.

Jam Science doesn't quite match **Care** for sheer invention, but is nonetheless a solid, confident LP. More prominent use of drum machines, female backing vocals and string synths give the record a slick Euro-disco feel. (Released by UK Arista, this LP should not be confused with an unauthorized release of the same name on Dutch Y, which contains most of the same songs but in unfinished form. The German EP, with four of the proper album's tracks, is legit.)

Oil and Gold goes for a much harder sound, with booming, sometimes overpowering guitar and drums (most evident on "Nemesis," a big club hit and the only pop song ever to make good lyrical use of the word "parthenogenesis") When they do go for the more ethereal colors found on **Care**, the results are pretty boring ("This Big Hush," "Faded Flowers"). After the LP was released, Marsh left the group, and was replaced, for one American tour, by former Voidoid guitarist Ivan Julian.

The garrulous liner notes on the next album explain it in some detail. "Shriekback celebrate the blessed dark—the place where they were always most at home. Songs to sing in your sleep . . . the shape and rhythm of two different kind of nights—nights of heat and weirdness . . . and nights incandescent with moonlight and dreams. **Big Night Music** is entirely free of digital heartbeats of every kind." Except for a few familiar-sounding entries, this radical departure resembles nothing in the Shriekback's previous repertoire and thus requires a real commitment to get over the shock of hearing evanescent continental delicacy and understated piano music instead of pounding dance-rock bizarritude. But do it—your efforts will be well rewarded with beauty, grace and originality. Dave Allen left after this album, making Andrews the only remaining original member.

The first of two British CD-only compilations offers a solid introduction to the band's early period, excerpting **Tench** and **Care**, with some other things. The second volume is more eclectic, containing tracks from Shriekback's Arista releases, **Oil and Gold**, 12-inch versions of three singles and another song from **Care**.

With guest star Doug Wimbish playing a lot of the bass, Andrews and stalwart drummer Martyn Barker—joined by guitarist Mike Cozzi, who first appeared on **Big Night Music**, and two backup singers—returned to musical daylight on **Go Bang!**, a winning LP produced by Richard James Burgess. While the ominous undercurrent in Andrews' voice remains one of the band's best features, the kinetic arrangements (including electronic horns) are almost playful, largely picking up where **Oil and Gold** left off.

For a time, Shriekback was very big on remixes. Many of their singles offer non-album versions plus additional alternative mixes. Several of these (along with some originals) are available on **The Infinite**, a compilation drawing from **Tench** and **Care**. [iar/dgs]

SHRINK
Shrink EP (nr/Oval-A&M) 1979

Charlie Gillett, aside from being one of the most astute writers to chronicle rock'n' roll's development, was also clever enough to first spot the talents of, among others, Lene Lovich and Holly Vincent. His own Oval label, however, also had *this* clod. Shrink's prior single (written by the Secret, labelmates who also produced this EP) was okay glam-rock, but 20 minutes of his dull rock-cum-guitar-noise heroics alternating with quiet, studiously eccentric mush on this 10-inch disc is intolerable. Talk about studied weirdness—the cover photo shows his stage persona, a bizarrely-clad character with half a head of hair and the rest of his noggin and face sprayed with metallic paint, toting a Flying V guitar. Keep the cover for a laugh and pitch the record. [jg]

JANE SIBERRY
No Borders Here (Open Air) 1983
The Speckless Sky (Duke Street-Open Air) 1985 ●
The Walking (Duke Street-Reprise) 1987 ●

This talented, thrush-voiced Canadian has inspired comparisons with iconoclastic female artistes as diverse as Kate Bush, the Roches and Laurie Anderson, but Siberry is a refreshing original. On **No Borders Here**, her witty, literal compositions (consistently well-served by imaginative, near-cinematic arrangements and production, as on the epic "Mimi on the Beach") marked her as sort of Great White North hope for the moribund singer/songwriter genre. The subsequent **Speckless Sky** is even better, with impressive tracks like "One More Colour," "Vladimir, Vladimir" and "Map of the World (Part II)."

The Walking is a bit too airy for its own good, neglecting Siberry's knack for rousing melodies in favor of low-key atmospherics. Still, Siberry obviously possesses the goods to score major points (both artistically and commercially) in the future. [hd]

SIC F*CKS
Sic F*cks EP (Sozyamuda) 1982

After building a worldwide reputation for unserious total-outrage rock, the uncommercially-named but innocuous Sic F*cks broke up, leaving New York nightlife in a bored panic. Fortunately, after a year of sporadic existence, the F*cks reformed and finally committed themselves—to vinyl—with a five-song 12-inch, produced by ex-Dictator Andy Shernoff. The sound could be clearer, but for the delivery of such mind-boggling material as "Spanish Bar Mitzvah," "Rock or Die" and "Chop Up Your Mother" (they're only kidding), mere technical considerations hardly matter. Not as good as the band was live, but a fond reminder of a true mania. [iar]

SIDEWAY LOOK
Sideway Look (nr/Virgin) 1984

This Scottish quintet writes solid nouveau pop songs and plays them with a mix of guitars and keyboards (did I mention accordion?). The arrangements haul in everything—from controlled guitar feedback to mellow horns—which makes the album highly varied in sound, but Brian Smith's posey vocals—a dramatic Bowie/Eric Burdon delivery—occasionally seem out of place. Smoothly capable on everything from mild soul to straightforward guitar-based dance rock (and managing to drop hints of everyone from Big Country to Haircut One

Hundred), Sideway Look look ready to have a hit, but it might be in any one of their styles.

[iar]

SIGUE SIGUE SPUTNIK
Flaunt It (Manhattan) 1986 ●

In this cynical and suspicious era, criminals—including politicians, preachers, murderers and swindlers of all persuasions—have found it easy to get away with the most amazing transgressions by being up-front about their sins. Nothing succeeds these days like the appearance of sincerity: most people, it seems, prefer a known felon to a possible liar. No matter how indefensible one's actions may be, a confident pre-emptive announcement or tearful apology evidently wipes away all evil.

Spurred no doubt by former Generation X bandmate Billy Idol's solo stardom (and possibly the successful no-music-necessary starmaking machinery of Frankie Goes to Hollywood), Tony James formed this colorful and sweeping multi-media hype as a post-everything adaptation of Malcolm McLaren's great rock'n'roll swindle. But instead of trying to manipulate the record industry and music-consuming public with cagey behind-the-scenes machinations, Sigue Sigue Sputnik confronted the challenge of turning a quick (and huge) buck with total frankness, acknowledging the naked crassness of their intentions at every turn. The sextet has proven exceedingly adept at outrageous stylemongering, attracting press coverage (much of it highly unfavorable), self-marketing and favorable deal-making. Creating and selling records, however, is another matter.

Prior to the release of **Flaunt It**, SSS debuted with a three-version 12-inch of "Love Missile F1-11"—a ticking bass sequencer with a simple vocal, shards of guitar and piles of unpredictable sound effects, goosed with wild production tricks into a mixed trashcan of trivia that's amusing enough but bears only the scantest relationship to music. The album, also produced by Giorgio Moroder, proffers another version of "Love Missile," following it with an utterly useless program of near-identical assemblages and other likeminded tripe. (A large debt to Suicide is tangentially acknowledged by occasional cries of "Rocket USA.") Despite spectacular Japanese-styled art and the distinction of being the first rock record to contain paid audio advertisements, **Flaunt It** doesn't got it.

[iar]

SILENCERS
A Letter from St. Paul (RCA) 1987 ●

You can't keep a good Scot out of the recording studio. After his commercially frustrating experience with Fingerprintz, Jimme O'Neill reunited with guitarist Cha Burns, formed the Silencers and went further—commercially—than his old group ever did. Not that this band purveys pop pastry: **A Letter from St. Paul** addresses neuroses both personal and political, set to churning guitar-based rhythms. The music's hypnotic, the lyrics compelling. "We decided we wanted to write only about serious subjects without sounding anxious," O'Neill said. Without sounding derivative of U2, the Silencers appeal to the same psychological demographic—only minus the naiveté. [si]

SILENT RUNNING
Emotional Warfare (EMI America) 1984
Walk on Fire (Atlantic) 1987 ●

If Belfast bands are generally esteemed for their passionate intensity, someone forgot to tell these losers. **Emotional Warfare** (the American title of what was originally released as **Shades of Liberty**) contains slick humdrum dance-rock with only Peter Gamble's Bonoesque bellow to suggest, not generate, any enthusiasm. The pounding "Emotional Warfare" is as good as it gets, and that's not very. The eager-for-airplay **Walk on Fire** reduces Silent Running to a quartet (the keyboardist left) and sounds like a dull hybrid of the Fixx and Bad Company.

[iar]

SILICON TEENS
Music for Parties (Sire) 1979

Whether people realize it or not, Daniel Miller has probably been as responsible as anybody (save Robert Moog) for the rise of synthesizers in modern rock, via his Mute Records, a groundbreaking single (as the Normal) and production work for Depeche Mode and many others. The illusory Silicon Teens (despite the personnel list on the sleeve) is a pseudonymous Miller studio project, offering 14 percolating synth versions (with vocals) of such rock'n'roll classics as "Memphis, Tennessee," "Judy in Disguise," "You Really Got Me"—you get the idea. There are several originals as well, but the title says it best: a good time is guaranteed for all. The approach here is more conservative and reverent than David Cunningham's more devolutionary Flying Lizards, but the two concepts are not that far apart. (And I'm not sure who did it first.) [iar]

See also *Robert Rental and the Normal.*

SILOS
About Her Steps. (Record Collect) 1985 ●
Cuba (Record Collect) 1987 ●
Tennessee Fire EP (Record Collect) 1987
WALTER SALAS-HUMARA
Lagartija (Record Collect) 1988 ●

This New York combo's style is basically an idiosyncratic urban-bohemian variation on country-rock, with sly melodies, deceptively simple lyrics and the attractively laconic vocals of frontmen Walter Salas-Humara and Bob Rupe (formerly one of Florida's Bobs, who had an EP and LP on Safety Net). The eight short songs that comprise **About Her Steps**. have a laid-back charm, with the jangly "Shine It Down," the steel-guitar-drenched "4 Wanted Signs" and the slow, haunting "Start the Clock" standing out.

Cuba forges a more distinctive band persona on tracks as diverse as the incendiary "Tennessee Fire," the poignant "She Lives Up the Street," the jauntily hippieish "Mary's Getting Married" and the regretful, acoustic "Going Round." This last song makes good use of a string quartet; the rest of **Cuba** finds Mary Rowell's violin emerging as an integral element in the Silos' sound.

The **Tennessee Fire** 12-inch contains the album versions of the title track and "Start the Clock," plus two unremarkable previously-unreleased numbers. Salas-Humara's well-crafted and appealing solo album (not very different from the group's sound) has contributions from Rupe and includes "About Her Steps." and "Cuba," neither of which have been recorded by the Silos. [hd]

JIMMY SILVA AND THE EMPTY SET
See *Young Fresh Fellows.*

DESMOND SIMMONS
Alone on Penguin Island (nr/Dome) 1981

On his own record (which Simmons singlehandedly wrote and performed), this Colin Newman cohort fell in with the austere minimalism of Newman's (then former) Wire colleagues, Graham Lewis and B.C. Gilbert, who produced **Penguin Island**. Simmons is more song-oriented than they are, but seemingly mistook reduction for redaction; despite some good songs here, they've been cut to the bone, made somewhat alien and abstract. A few even sound as though they were recorded underwater. All the same, a moving, high, lonesome quality does come across, as on the melodica-dominated instrumental title track. Patience is rewarded, but you may feel he made you work too hard. [jg]

SIMON F
Gun (Chrysalis) 1986
Never Never Land (Reprise) 1987 ●

Singing keyboardist Simon F was half of a mid-'80s British flash-in-the-pan flop called Intaferon; ex-partner Simon G is one of the guitarists on his first solo album. **Gun** leads off with its best offering, a histrionic version of the Hoodoo Gurus' memorable "I Want You Back" that boasts a blinding Steve Stevens solo, and heads downhill from there. Despite an annoying synthesizer squeal, the mock-Bowie pop of "Baby Pain" isn't bad; everything else on this half-baked, unoriginal synth-dance LP is.

Never Never Land begins with "New York Girl," which blends ticking sequencers, surging guitar chords and a wall of backing vocals: the resemblance to Billy Idol's early records is unmistakable. But so is the marked difference in vocalists. Elsewhere, Simon fails to lay a glove on funk, botches the Beach Boy allusion on "American Dream," makes assorted absurd lyrical assertions and generally bores his way through two sides of this insipid and illogical attempt to squeeze talent out of recording studio walls. [iar]

SIMPLE MINDS
Life in a Day (PVC) 1979 (Virgin) 1987 ●
Real to Real Cacophony (nr/Arista) 1980
    (nr/Virgin) 1982 (Virgin) 1988 ●
Empires and Dance (nr/Arista) 1980
    (nr/Virgin) 1982 ●
Sons and Fascination/Sister Feelings Call
    (nr/Virgin) 1981 ●
Sister Feelings Call (Virgin) 1987 ●
Celebration (nr/Arista) 1982 (nr/Virgin) 1982
Themes for Great Cities (Stiff) 1982
New Gold Dream (81-82-83-84) (Virgin-A&M)
    1982 ●

Sparkle in the Rain (Virgin-A&M) 1984 ●
Once Upon a Time (Virgin-A&M) 1985 ●
Live in the City of Light (Virgin-A&M)
    1987 ●

Scotland's Simple Minds once took a lot of (mostly) undeserved criticism for being arty and pretentious, but in their early days, their mix of serious/philosophical lyrics with danceable rhythms supporting oblique musical structures did make them something of an acquired taste. Often dense, occasionally discordant and gloomy, Simple Minds' music also stretches to commercial pop, an area they've pursued with increasing enthusiasm and success of late.

Life in a Day largely recalls Roxy Music, but also touches lightly on several forms, including pop, psychedelia and an adventurous tense/terse style they explored on subsequent albums. "Sad Affair" is modish; "All for You" has disturbing overtones of the Doors and early Jefferson Airplane; "No Cure" sounds like the Buzzcocks-meet-the-Who; "Chelsea Girl" is delightful '60s pop, complete with full orchestration.

With **Real to Real Cacophony**, the band lives up (or down) to the album's clever title. Excepting a couple of standouts like "Carnival (Shelter in a Suitcase)" and the haunting instrumental "Film Theme" (Simple Minds are one of the few bands that can and do create worthwhile instrumentals with real skill), **Real to Real Cacophony** is just like the band in the title song; "Real to real cacophony/Echo, echo on endlessly."

The minute the needle sets down on **Empires and Dance**'s "I Travel," it's obvious that Simple Minds have reorganized and changed direction; while not completely successful, the album is extremely atmospheric and promising, including some good dance tunes and a few more quasi-psychedelic ones ("Kant-Kino" and "Room"). **Celebration** is a compilation of tracks from the first three albums.

Sons and Fascination/Sister Feelings Call—two discrete albums originally released as one packaged work, then reissued separately (the latter more than once)—is Simple Minds' first really good record. While still experimental, the group sounds more comfortable in the semi-funky, semi-dancey, semi-electronic groove introduced on the prior **Empires and Dance**. "The American," "20th Century Promised Land" (from **Sons and Fascination**) and "Love Song" are all top-drawer examples of modern dance music;

"Theme for Great Cities" is another fine instrumental.

Picking up its title from that composition, **Themes for Great Cities** (subtitled "Definitive Collection 79–81") takes the best material from albums not then released in America—**Real to Real Cacophony, Empires and Dance** and **Sons and Fascination/Sister Feelings Call**—and presents the band much more strongly than the individual records originally did. (One notable omission: "20th Century Promised Land.")

New Gold Dream (81-82-83-84) takes another great step forward. The songs are stronger and the sound shows a definite thawing, mellowing trend, while retaining its majestic power. "Promised You a Miracle" (soulful and dramatic dance tune), "Glittering Prize" (warm, pretty ballad) and the panoramic title track stand out. A memorable, mature record marked by compassion and sensitivity.

Working with producer Steve Lillywhite, **Sparkle in the Rain** is another fine, affecting record with textured, intricate rhythmic rock and Jim Kerr's personable singing. Simple Minds sound firmly in control of their sound, equally capable of grand gestures and subtle nuance. The first side is great, featuring four of their best songs: "Speed Your Love to Me," "Book of Brilliant Things," "Up on the Catwalk" and "Waterfront." The flipside is less exhilarating, but does include a cover of Lou Reed's "Street Hassle." Drummer Brian McGee had left the group, and was replaced on the LP by three different players, one of whom—Mel Gaynor—wound up a permanent member.

At this point, Simple Minds' story gets complicated. Jim Kerr married Chrissie Hynde in 1984. The following year, the band had its first chart-topping hit with "Don't You (Forget About Me)." Bassist Derek Forbes quit to go solo and was replaced by John Giblin. They appeared at Live Aid. Jim and Chrissie had a baby. And their first post-stardom LP is the most appalling sell-out in recent memory. Produced by Jimmy Iovine and Bob Clearmountain, **Once Upon a Time** is virtually unlistenable, a perversion of the group's sound specifically and unpleasantly geared for American radio. To be fair, none of the tracks sound like the *Breakfast Club* theme (Kerr having too much integrity to allow that), but "Sanctify Yourself," "Alive and Kicking," "Oh Jungleland" (great title), etc. overcompensate for the band's onetime obscurity and are surprisingly wretched, transparent stabs at the Sound of Today's Album Rock Radio, bearing only passing resemblance to Simple Minds' prior work.

The sumptuous and sonically excellent live double album was recorded in Paris in 1986, a triumphant celebration of the band's enormous success. Augmented by a backing vocalist, percussionist, violinist and computer programmer, Simple Minds play the recent hits, reaching back before **New Gold Dream** only once, in a three-song medley on Side Four that runs together "Love Song" (from **Sons and Fascination**), Little Steven's "Sun City" and Sly and the Family Stone's "Dance to the Music." [ks/iar]

SIMPLY RED
Picture Book (Elektra) 1985 ●
Men and Women (Elektra) 1987 ●
MICK HUCKNALL
The Early Years (nr/TJM) 1987

From the American soul-funk school of Manchester musical thought comes the multi-racial Simply Red: raspy redhead Mick Hucknall (ex-Frantic Elevators), a rhythm section that had been in Durutti Column and three others, including a trumpet player. Mixing original tunes with an eclectic pair of covers, **Picture Book** sounds like much of contemporary UK soul: a slick, earnest imitation that often goes astray. The LP contains the group's first big hits—the Valentine Brothers' well-meaning but awfully clumsy "Moneys Too Tight (To Mention)" (sample rhyme: "They're talking about Reaganomics/Lord, down in the Congress") and the limp "Holding Back the Years"—as well as Talking Heads' "Heaven," which gets a throughly sleepy treatment. On **Picture Book**, Simply Red is simply dull.

Produced by the late Alex Sadkin, **Men and Women** jazzes matters up a bit. Most of the record falls into the polite dance groove of its predecessor, and smokey ballads aimed at the adult audience are irredeemable. But glimmers of excitement in the unrestrained joy of "I Won't Feel Bad" and the sensual bump of Sly Stone's "Let Me Have It All" suggest there may indeed be life after stardom for this lot.

The Early Years consists of pre-Simply Red tracks issued to cash in on the band's huge success. [tr]

SINCEROS
The Sound of Sunbathing (Columbia) 1979
Pet Rock (Columbia) 1981

Having played together (under a different name) in the mid-'70s, the Sinceros' first break was that the group's rhythm half backed Lene Lovich on **Stateless** and toured with her; they carried some of her bizarritude back with them onto **The Sound of Sunbathing**. Basically a vehicle for guitarist/singer Mark Kjeldsen, the band's other historical claim is that Sinceros keyboardist (and ex-Vibrator) Don Snow replaced Paul Carrack in Squeeze.

The debut LP has two great tracks—a quirky bit of silliness called "Take Me to Your Leader" and a Joe Jackson soundalike, "Little White Lie." Otherwise, it's an amiable pop record with little character. The even lower-key **Pet Rock**, produced by Gus Dudgeon, removes any trace of oddness and fails to deliver the cleverness that would have redeemed it. ("Memory Lane," however, does transcend the album.) [iar]

SINGLE BULLET THEORY
Single Bullet Theory EP (Artifacts) 1977
Single Bullet Theory (Nemperor) 1982

Early new wave rumblings from below the Mason-Dixon line: Richmond, Virginia's SBT filled their independent 12-inch with four energetic, two-minute Yardbirds/Kinks-influenced pop songs. Unfortunately, they run between four and six minutes each. The band's combination of power and finesse is impressive, though, as is their sense of humor on the best track, "Rocker's Night Out (Punk for a Day)"—they just lacked a good editor. Although it sounds pretty mainstream now, consider the time and place.

SBT subsequently got a track on the 1980 **Sharp Cuts** compilation; their persistence finally paid off by landing a deal with the CBS-affiliated Nemperor label. Their debut album, released at the end of 1982, is crisp power pop with strong vocals and precise playing. Nothing new, but pleasant enough.

Having taken their turn at the gold ring and failing to catch it, Single Bullet Theory toured with Adam Ant and then dropped out of sight. [ds]

SIOUXSIE AND THE BANSHEES
The Scream (Polydor) 1978 (Geffen) 1984
Join Hands (nr/Polydor) 1979 (Geffen) 1984

Kaleidoscope (PVC) 1980 (Geffen) 1984
Juju (PVC) 1981 (Geffen) 1984
Arabian Knights EP (PVC) 1981
Once Upon a Time/The Singles (PVC) 1981
   (Geffen) 1984
A Kiss in the Dreamhouse (nr/Polydor) 1982
   (Geffen) 1984
Nocturne (Geffen) 1983
Hyaena (Geffen) 1984 ●
The Thorn EP (nr/Wonderland-Polydor) 1984
Tinderbox (Geffen) 1986 ●
Through the Looking Glass (Geffen) 1987 ●
The Peel Sessions EP (nr/Strange Fruit)
   1987 ●

In 1976, Siouxsie Sioux (née Susan Dallion) and Steve Severin were part of the clique of steady Sex Pistols fans known as the Bromley Contingent. As Siouxsie and the Banshees, the nascent punk rock stars debuted at the 100 Club's legendary 1976 punk festival; aided by future Ant guitarist Marco Pirroni and the undiscovered Sid Vicious on drums, the motley crew bashed through a lengthy free-form rendition of "The Lord's Prayer," stopping only when they became bored.

From such uncertain beginnings, Siouxsie and the Banshees quickly evolved into a highly popular band, regularly appearing on the British charts despite the group's brooding, abrasive style. **The Scream** capsulized the first-generation sound of the Banshees: Siouxsie's icy, sometimes tuneless wail swooping over the brutish rhythms of bassist Severin and drummer Kenny Morris and the metal-shard roar of John McKay's guitar. The songs are relentlessly grim, albeit often sardonic (as in "Carcass" and their version of the Beatles' "Helter Skelter"). The only break in style is "Hong Kong Garden," an almost upbeat song that, as a 45, punched its way into the UK Top 10. (The **Peel Sessions** EP, done at the end of '77, contains renditions of "Love in a Void," "Mirage," "Metal Postcard" and "Suburban Relapse," all of which predate the group's first record release.)

The Scream seems positively cheerful in light of its follow-up, **Join Hands**, a plodding, depressive album notable only for the commission of their "Lord's Prayer" butchery to vinyl. Two days into a tour to promote the album, Morris and McKay abruptly walked out of the band. Guitarist Robert Smith from opening act the Cure and ex-Big in Japan/Slits drummer Budgie were drafted to complete the tour. Budgie subsequently

signed on as a permanent Banshee and the group proceeded to record **Kaleidoscope** without a guitarist to call their own. (Guest stars John McGeoch of Magazine and ex-Pistol Steve Jones alternated guitar duties on the LP.) **Kaleidoscope** marked a bilateral move away from the group's original wall of noise; many of the songs are softer and more melodic (e.g., "Happy House" and the flower-powery "Christine"), and there is an increased use of framing concepts ("Red Light" is built around the whirr-click of a camera auto-winder). Shortly afterward, McGeoch officially joined the band and they toured America for the first time.

Finally a full-fledged band again, the Banshees released **Juju**, their strongest and most satisfying record to date. Siouxsie's voice had developed into a surprisingly subtle instrument, and the technical prowess added by Budgie and McGeoch brought power and complexity to songs like "Spellbound" and "Arabian Knights."

Also released in 1981, **Once Upon a Time** assembled all of the band's singles (including the otherwise non-LP "Staircase (Mystery)" and "Israel") on one record. The American **Arabian Knights** EP reprises the contents of a British 12-inch plus one extra tune.

A Kiss in the Dreamhouse finds the Banshees veering back into the more experimental terrain of **Kaleidoscope**, letting their jarring, near-pop style pass through some pretty strange permutations (like the deviant neo-bop of "Cocoon" and the medieval recorder stylings of "Green Fingers.")

Nocturne is a two-LP live set recorded (with no overdubs) at the Royal Albert Hall in late 1983. Robert Smith is the featured guitarist on a full-course selection from the band's repertoire, stretching back to "Switch" and "Israel," but also drawing heavily from **Dreamhouse**. Awesome.

With Smith again rounding out the lineup, **Hyaena** starts off with the utterly magnificent "Dazzle," a haunting blend of industrial-strength drumming and symphonic backing, with some of Siouxsie's best singing ever. The album is much more melodic, light and inviting than any of the band's others, going so far as to touch on an earlier extra-curricular excursion into jazzy stylings ("Take Me Back") and allowing piano to dominate "Swimming Horses." The Beatles' "Dear Prudence," a big 1983 single for the Banshees, also helps leaven the traditional dark intensity.

Smith was subsequently forced to flee, as being a full-time member of two major groups had taken its toll on his health. Former Clock DVA guitarist John Carruthers replaced him. Already maintaining a rather low 1985 profile, the Banshees were set back a bit further when Siouxsie broke her kneecap during a show.

At a point where some were ready to write the band off as aging, lazy veterans, they came back in early '86 with **Tinderbox**, one of their strongest LPs in years. Carruthers fits in well, his rich playing stylistically similar to both Smith's and McGeoch's; the rhythm section is as steady as ever. The big plus is punk's original princess herself—Siouxsie's voice has never been so warm and tuneful as it is on tracks like "The Sweetest Chill," "Cannons" and the great single, "Cities in Dust."

Through the Looking Glass—an eclectically entertaining album of covers—works best on the numbers which receive the most radical revamps. Crisp hornwork and a nononsense vocal performance focus Iggy's "The Passenger"; orchestral lushness and rock power beautify "This Wheel's on Fire." Kraftwerk's spare "Hall of Mirrors" is converted into an alluring dance drone; "Trust in Me," originally sung by a snake in Disney's *Jungle Book,* becomes a delirious tropical seduction. But seemingly arbitrary—mostly symbolic—choices of oldies by the Doors, Roxy Music, Sparks, John Cale and Television receive little creative comment and fall flat. But all in all, this digression into the Banshees' musical roots is worth pursuing.

Not bad for a band whose initial intent at that 1976 debut was to annoy the crowd enough to get thrown off the stage.   [tr]

See also *Creatures, Glove.*

SISTERS OF MERCY

Alice EP (Brain Eater) 1983
The Reptile House EP (Brain Eater) 1983
First and Last and Always (Elektra) 1985 ●
Floodland (Elektra) 1987 ●
Dominion EP (nr/Merciful Release) 1988

SISTERHOOD

Gift EP (nr/Merciful Release) 1986

Leeds' originally all-male Sisters, named after an order of cut-the-crap Catholic nuns, began by playing what they jokingly called heavy metal, which it sort of was; an odd feat, considering that the only "drummer" the band's ever had is Doktor Avalanche, a rhythm generator. Andrew Eldritch is the band's focus: chief lyricist, co-producer of virtually every track (briefly at first with Psychedelic Fur John Ashton, then with Dave Allen of Associates/Cure fame), graphics designer and lead singer, in a deep, aptly gothic voice.

Although their pre-LP body of work amounted to several albums' worth of tracks, only two songs were ultimately used **First and Last and Always**. As with most of their early work, the 12-inch **Alice EP**, particularly its excellent title track, suffers from sub-par sound. The sound got better and the group's identity began to come into its own by **Reptile House**. (You might say it grew claws.) With the issue of the brilliant "Temple of Love" (available only as a single), the Sisters extended their reach to include *danceable* doom-rock.

The first album at last attains the group's long-sought clarity and sophistication and, ergo, is nearly sublime in its pristine bleakness. (Well, Side One anyway; the flipside ain't too poor, neither.) Somewhat distanced from the original metal idea, incorporation of power-poppish guitars and dancey rhythms does nothing to place the Sisters within either category; their sonic integrity somehow remains intact. Eldritch's vocals—Jim Morrison meets David Bowie and slowed down to half-speed—are as gloriously gloomy as ever.

Eldritch had cultivated a posture for the band, while advancing an anti-fashionist philosophy. A live German bootleg gives some indication of where he's coming from: mainly reworkings of oldies, the Sisters draw on the canons of Dolly Parton and Hot Chocolate as well as the Stooges and Stones. Regrettably, the other members of the group became, as Eldritch (only partly tongue-in-cheek) put it, "distorted little creatures with black teeth . . . set on making a career." Guitarist Wayne Hussey (who'd come to the Sisters from an early edition of Dead or Alive) and bassist Craig Adams formed the pose-heavy Mission (UK). Co-founding guitarist Gary Marx seems to have sunk without trace.

There was in fact some legal wrangling over the split, making it uncertain who had the legal rights to the band's name. While this was being sorted out, Eldritch cut the **Gift** EP as the Sisterhood. He doesn't sing on it (presumaby also for litigial reasons), but substituted tape collages and speaking by other folks, including Alan (Suicide) Vega.

Not too hummable, but effective in conveying some serious concerns, notably the sinister dehumanization inherent in acts of terrorism.

Ex-Gun Club bassist Patricia Morrison, who'd guested on **Gift**, became Eldritch's only fellow Sister (so to speak) when the legal coast was clear. For **First and Last and Always**, Eldritch wrote the material half with Hussey and half with Marx; could he equal that alone?

He came through on **Floodland** as though he'd been writing every song by himself since the beginning. American producer/songwriter Jim Steinman oversaw two key tracks, "This Corrosion" and "Dominion," and that worked out fine too, great Sisterly Grand Guignol-rock. Much of the rest is not so theatrical, but lyrics printed on the sleeve make it easier to discern the deliberation, the nuances, the juxtaposition of terse, concrete observations amid poetic, abstract feelings struggling to emerge (even by use of incomplete phrases). Overall, it's a richer LP than the first, the tracks more maturely constructed and lyrically engrossing.

Dominion is an album track, two okay instrumentals and a strong version of Hot Chocolate's "Emma," which the old Sisters used to play onstage.

Collectors should also be aware of a live album, mainly from two 1984 German shows, released that year in an extremely limited edition. [jg]

See also *Mission (UK)*.

SKAFISH
Skafish (Illegal-IRS) 1980
Conversation (IRS) 1983

Indiana's Jim Skafish is one of the oddest eggs ever to wander into the shopping mall of rock music. Visually androgynous and, well, unattractive, Skafish builds his songs on neurotic angles of romance, suicide and growing up different that are most pessimistic. Yet, by couching them in sprightly tunes delivered with great geniality, he creates an unnerving dynamic. His band is skilled and supple; his first album, despite all its personality flaws, is clear and fascinating rather than grim or depressing.

Skafish lunges off in a different direction on the disappointing **Conversation**, which starts with "Secret Lover," a mundane disco track notable only for his voice's jarring unsuitability to the genre. With the exception of two loud rockers and a few blandouts, the rest of the record follows stylistic suit. What's worse, the lyrics aren't even very interesting. [iar]

SKEETERS
See *Fetchin Bones*.

SKELETON CREW
Learn to Talk (Rift) 1984
The Country of Blinds (Rift) 1986

Its three-man lineup quickly trimmed to a less-extravagant two, Skeleton Crew regaled audiences in America, Europe and Japan with a unique and functional mix of rhythmically twisted rock, electric and acoustic noise, wittily interpolated taped voice fragments and "fake folk music." Most of the latter had a distinctly East European flavor, though one New York gig consisted entirely of folk music from around the world. Guitarist Fred Frith alternated conventional and homemade guitars, six-string bass, violin and keyboards while occasionally singing in a high-pitched voice. Tom Cora busied himself on cello as well as four-string bass and devices; both worked kickdrums with their feet as their fingers flew. They had enough material for maybe three good albums, but the fine **Learn to Talk** will serve for posterity.

Joined by singer/keyboardist Zeena Parkins, the Skeleton Crew issued a second album a couple of years later; Frith and Cora have pursued countless other projects independently. The latter has worked alone (**Live at the Western Front**) and jointly, with Dave Moss and Ferdinand of France's Etron Fou Leloublan. [mf]

See also *Fred Frith*.

SKIDS
Wide Open EP (nr/Virgin) 1978
Scared to Dance (Virgin) 1979
Days in Europa (nr/Virgin) 1979
The Absolute Game (nr/Virgin) 1980
Joy (nr/Virgin) 1981
Fanfare (nr/Virgin) 1982
Dunfermline [CD] (Virgin) 1988

The Skids' rise and fall revolved almost wholly around Richard Jobson—singer, writer, creative dilettante. Emerging from Scotland as a promising punkish quartet playing literate and challenging rock music with anthemic proclivities, under Jobson's leadership the Skids became more and more pretentious and less and less a band, finally evaporating into the mist after a miserable fourth LP, recorded as a duo. The first three albums, however, offer a precious body of inspiring and unique rock'n'roll with obvious Scottish blood. In hindsight, it's easy to see what role guitarist Stuart Adamson (now a star in his own right with Big Country) played in defining the Skids' sound.

Wide Open, a four-song 12-inch on red vinyl, contains two inspired successes in "The Saints Are Coming" and "Of One Skin," both of which also appear on the similarly excellent **Scared to Dance**. Using loud guitar and semi-martial drumming for its basis, Jobson's hearty singing sounds like an 18th century general leading his merry troops down from the hills into glorious battle. Two other standouts on the LP ("Into the Valley" and "Hope and Glory") maintain the style but are different enough to keep things exciting. (The US release substitutes two tracks and has an altered song order.)

Bill Nelson produced the Skids' (with a new drummer and bassist) second album, **Days in Europa**, but the match-up proved problematic. In polishing and refining the band's sound even a little, he smoothed off the vital edge. There's less gusto in the grooves, although some songs (like "Working for the Yankee Dollar," "Charade" and "Animation") shine through regardless.

While the lineup remained stable for **The Absolute Game**, a new producer took over the helm. Mick Glossop did a good job presenting Jobson's widening vision amidst semi-grandiose arrangements, but the blooming Jobson ego had led the band a long way from its early forthrightness. Parts of **The Absolute Game** are just arty pretense, but the inclusion of substantial, engaging material makes it a reasonable addition to the collection. **Strength Through Joy**, a bonus album of finished studio outtakes, came with early pressings—interesting, but not essential.

After a few more changes in the lineup, only Jobson and bassist-cum-multi-instrumentalist Russell Webb remained Skids. Joined by an all-star guest cast of ten, they made **Joy**, a failed concept album about Scotland. To call it bad is curt but realistic.

Fanfare, released after the sinking group finally (mercifully) ceased, is an excellent compilation of singles and album tracks that serves as the perfect introduction to the Skids' magic. Six years later, the **Dunferm-** line CD appeared, reprising **Fanfare** (though deleting one cut) and adding seven more, only one ("Scared to Dance") of which is truly consequential.

Afterlife: Adamson formed Big Country and furthered the Skids' pan-ethnic experimentation in service of arena metal; Jobson, after several wanky albums of pretentious poesy, formed the Armoury Show, and has followed his former bandmate back into the rock'n'roll fray.   [iar]

See also *Armoury Show, Big Country, Zones.*

SKIN

See *Swans.*

SKINNY PUPPY

Chainsaw EP (Can. Nettwerk) 1983
Remission EP (Can. Nettwerk) 1984
Bites (Can. Nettwerk) 1986 ●
Mind: The Perpetual Intercourse (Capitol) 1986 ●
Cleanse Fold and Manipulate (Capitol) 1987 ●

One of the more interesting bands to come from north of the border in quite a while, Vancouver's Skinny Puppy was formed by multi-instrumentalist cEVIN Key (that's how he spells it) and singer/lyricist Dave Oglivie (aka Nivek Ogre). They have produced a large body of dark electronic music, drawing on such obvious influences as Cabaret Voltaire, Chrome, Suicide and Throbbing Gristle. Orchestration is predominantly distorted, non-melodic vocals and very creative use of synths and tapes. The problem has been that Skinny Puppy has often worked harder at creating a mood or a sound than writing songs, and that they have borrowed just a little too freely at times from their favorite bands.

There isn't much evident progress from **Bites** to **Mind: The Perpetual Intercourse** (how's that for a title?); both are filled with mildly gloomy but danceable tracks, virtually indistinguishable from early Cabaret Voltaire, both instrumentally and vocally. Production is a little better (at least the sound is a bit clearer) on **Mind**. The **Bites** CD also includes all the cuts from the **Remission** EP.

There's a third Puppy on **Cleanse Fold and Manipulate**, one D. Rudolph Goettel, adding assorted electronics and sampling. He helps open up the sound, which is more finely honed, although precious few new musical ideas are evident. A lyric sheet also contains no surprises—just your basic foreboding visions of a skewered world. Skinny Puppy (who are outspoken anti-vivisectionists) may not be quite as evil or demented as they seem to fancy themselves, but **Cleanse Fold and Manipulate** does show promise for their future. [dgs]

SKUNKS

The Skunks (Republic) 1982

This Texas trio (not the British band of the same name) was led by bassist/singer Jesse Sublett, whose previous group included future Go-Go Kathy Valentine. An earlier incarnation of the Skunks stuck a couple of neat tracks on an Austin compilation LP; the band on **The Skunks** includes a pair of brothers who were previously two-thirds of that city's Terminal Mind. But enough history.

Produced by Earle Mankey, **The Skunks** is better-than-average melodic rock that draws on Southwestern musical traditions to give it special character, but isn't ethnic enough to be confused with the more colorful outpourings of Tex-Mex. The trio shares songwriting duties with consistently solid results; a novel reworking of the Yardbirds' "For Your Love" suggests an adventurous streak as well. [iar]

SLAMMIN' WATUSIS

Slammin' Watusis (Epic) 1988 ●

And slam they do! When this breathless midwestern quintet thanks the Damned (in the liner notes), they aren't kidding: their ripsnorting platter has the careening, free-for-all edge of those zany punk pioneers. It's buzzy fun with a message: "Won't Sell Out" champions integrity, while "It's Alright to Show You CARE" proves the Watusis aren't blank generation poseurs. Special kudos to Fast Frank Raven's sizzlin' sax. [jy]

SLAPP HAPPY

See *Henry Cow.*

SLAUGHTER AND THE DOGS

Do It Dog Style (nr/Decca) 1978
Slaughter and the Dogs EP (nr/TJM) c. 1979
Live Slaughter Rabid Dogs (nr/Rabid) 1979
Live at the Factory (nr/Thrush) 1982
The Way We Were (nr/Thrush) 1983

SLAUGHTER

Bite Back (DJM) 1980

This Manchester punk group released the first 45 on that city's pioneering independent label, Rabid Records, and were regular giggers at London's famed Roxy Club. (They appear in the punk documentary Don Letts filmed there.) Unfortunately, Slaughter and the Dogs were more timely than talented, and **Bite Back**, their lone internationally-issued LP (by which time they had dropped part of their name), is totally undistinguished guitar-based rock noise, produced by ex-Mott the Hoople drummer Dale Griffin. [iar]

SLICKEE BOYS

Hot and Cool EP (Dacoit) 1976
Separated Vegetables (Dacoit) 1977 (Limp) 1980
Mersey, Mersey Me EP (Limp) 1978
Third EP (Limp) 1979
Here to Stay (Ger. Line) 1982
Cybernetic Dreams of Pi (Twin/Tone) 1983
Uh Oh . . . No Breaks! (Twin/Tone) 1985
Fashionably Late (Fr. New Rose) 1988

Washington, DC's Slickee Boys have been scene stalwarts for a decade; they've developed over the years from a punky rock'n'roll band with an affection for classic English forebears into a far more individualistic and distinctly American band with their own ideas. **Hot and Cool** is a 7-inch EP with one original (by leader/guitarist Kim Kane) joining arcane covers like the Yardbirds' "Psycho Daisies" and "Brand New Cadillac."

The German-only **Here to Stay** recapitulates the contents of that EP, the two which followed, plus a couple of independent singles. Guileless, earnest, occasionally embarrassing, bizarre in its selection of covers (from Talking Heads to the Grass Roots), often exciting in its basic enthusiasm, **Here to Stay** is an unprepossessing, entertaining collection of homemade records by a developing band.

On **Cybernetic Dreams of Pi** the Slickee Boys play brawny, good-natured power pop. Songs like "When I Go to the Beach" (jolly surf parody), "Pushin' My Luck" and a breezy version of Status Quo's ancient "Pictures of Matchstick Men" may be a bit glib, but are loads of fun nonetheless. **Uh Oh . . . No Breaks!** finds the quintet plundering their own vaults for material to re-record. No matter: all 13 tracks display the same vim and charm of their first record, but scads more skill and smarts. Melodies, hooks and energy to spare, variety and clever lyrics—these boys may not be the *dernier mot,* but they *are* worthwhile.

After 12 years, the Slickee Boys are still going strong, even if they again have to go abroad to get a record released. **Fashionably Late** is another winner—the rock'n'rolling spunk of the original Flamin Groovies crossed with the seasoned flair and solidity of the Fabulous Thunderbirds. Although a bit less varied than usual (Side 1 concentrates on driving music; Side 2 is lighter and more melodic), this is another easy-to-like outing from a natural energy resource that will, thank goodness, never be fashionable.

[iar/jy]

SLITS

Cut (Antilles) 1979
Retrospective (nr/Y-Rough Trade) 1980
Return of the Giant Slits (nr/CBS) 1981
The Peel Sessions EP (nr/Strange Fruit) 1987

Lurching into existence during the original 1977 explosion of pre-commercial London punk, the all-female Slits wrested the anyone-can-make-a-band-so-why-not-do-it-yourself ethos away from the traditionally no-women-allowed rock brotherhood and unselfconsciously paraded their stunningly amateur rock noise with support from bands like the Clash. While on the road as part of a punk package tour, the Slits were immortalized in all their primitive glory in *The Punk Rock Movie.* Looking back at the group's tentative beginnings now, it's clear that while the Slits may have been truly awful, they weren't much worse than many of their male contemporaries, and undoubtedly a damn sight better and smarter than some.

It was probably fortunate, however, that several years elapsed before the Slits got around to recording a debut album; by the time they reached the studio, Viv Albertine, Ari Upp and Tessa, joined by drummer Budgie (later of Siouxsie and the Banshees) had become reasonably competent players. Spare and rudimentary, but bursting with novel ideas and rampant originality, **Cut**—produced brilliantly by Dennis Bovell—forges a powerful white-reggae hybrid that serves as a solid underpinning for Ari Upp's wobbly, semi-melodic vocals.

"Retrospective" (so-called; the LP actually has no title) is a coverless authorized bootleg consisting of early (pre-reggae) studio doodles and live tracks that should really have stayed in the can (or wherever).

Return of the Giant Slits, released originally with a bonus 45 featuring an extra track and an interview with the band (both appended to the cassette version) turned toward African, rather than Jamaican rhythms, and attempted to make the Slits slightly more commercially accessible. The Peel session was done in 1977. [iar]

See also *New Age Steppers.*

SLOW CHILDREN

Slow Children (Ensign) 1981
Mad About Town (Ensign) 1982

Although originally a full-sized Los Angeles club band (which at one time included future Bangle Michael Steele), by the time of their two LPs, Slow Children had diminished to a duo: Pal Shazar (vocals) and Andrew Chinich (vocals/guitar). (The records were done with the aid of producers/players Jules Shear and Stephen Hague and others, including Translator drummer David Scheff.)

Signed after relocating to England, Slow Children's first album was available in the UK almost a year before a revised version appeared in America. **Slow Children** includes their dance semi-hit, "Spring in Fialta," a heavy but skittish beat layered with anxious synth noises and Shazar's dramatic vocals. The album isn't otherwise much like that track, but one constant factor is intellectually bright lyrics that seem too good for the music.

Mad About Town has a strong second side, with energetic tunes supporting more smart words; the first side, however, is distinctly underwhelming, failing to anchor ideas with grabby musical settings. By and large, Slow Children's records are more suited to reading than listening. [iar]

SLY & ROBBIE
See *Sly Dunbar.*

SMALTS
See *Minny Pops.*

KENDRA SMITH
See *Opal.*

PATTI SMITH

Horses (Arista) 1975 ●

PATTI SMITH GROUP

Radio Ethiopia (Arista) 1976 ●
Easter (Arista) 1978 ●
Wave (Arista) 1979 ●
Dream of Life (Arista) 1988 ●

Patti Smith was already an established poet and playwright on the New York underground literary scene when she expanded her repertoire to include rock criticism (her work appeared in *Creem, Crawdaddy* and *Rolling Stone*) and public performance, first reading her poetry and then singing with minimalist musical accompaniment provided by Lenny Kaye, professional rock writer and (then) amateur guitarist. Sharing Tom Verlaine's fascination with 19th century decadent literati like Rimbaud, Baudelaire and Verlaine (the original), Smith drifted into the New York rock underground, becoming an enormously popular performer/figure. A debut single ("Piss Factory") was privately released, featuring Smith, Kaye and pianist Richard Sohl. By the time Smith signed to Arista in 1975, Ivan Kral had joined her group, sharing guitar and bass chores with Kaye, and drummer Jay Dee Daugherty had been lured away from Lance Loud's Mumps.

Horses, produced by John Cale, broke a lot of stylistic ground, thanks to Smith's wild singing and disconcerting lyrics, but it also showcased inspired amateurism in the playing and an emotional intensity that recalled the Velvet Underground at its most powerful. Too idiosyncratic to be generally influential, **Horses** is a brilliant explosion of talent by a challenging, unique artist pioneering a sound not yet fashionable or, by general standards, even acceptable.

With **Radio Ethiopia**, the Patti Smith Group made an effort to drop **Horses'** clumsiness in favor of a more refined, organic sound and grander artistic pretensions. Smith plays a lot of guitar on the album, and producer Jack Douglas renders the proceedings with great seriousness. Tracks like "Ask the Angels" and "Pumping (My Heart)" have a nearly routine rock sound, made special largely by Smith's untrained but expressive voice and, of course, her highly individual songwriting.

Bruce Brody replaced Richard Sohl for **Easter**, and Jimmy Iovine produced the album, which contains the band's big hit single, "Because the Night," co-written by Bruce Springsteen. Having proven that they could play as well as most bands, the PSG set out to make something of their sound; Iovine did a fine job. By this point a much more mature singer, Smith sounds confident and striking and the band keeps pace.

After the success of **Easter**, **Wave** stumbles, evidently due to overconfidence. Todd Rundgren's production seems to have been an error in judgment. Smith's lyrics are at their most self-indulgent; although songs like "Dancing Barefoot" and "Frederick" are accessible and memorable, much of the record is unfocused, half-baked and insufferable. A misguided cover of the Byrds' "Do You Want to Be (A Rock 'n' Roll Star)" rings phony and hollow.

Smith took an extended career breather after **Wave**. In September '79 she bailed out, moved to Detroit, married ex-MC5/Sonic's Rendezvous Band guitarist Fred Smith and raised children. The Smiths stayed far from the spotlight until the summer of 1988, when a long-mooted new album, **Dream of Life**, was finally released. Fred and Patti co-wrote the songs; Fred and Jimmy Iovine co-produced the record, on which the music is played by Fred and old cohorts Sohl and Daugherty.   [iar]

See also *Lenny Kaye Connection*.

SMITHEREENS

Girls About Town EP (D-Tone) 1982
Beauty and Sadness EP (Little Ricky) 1983
   (Enigma) 1988
Especially for You (Enigma) 1987 ●
The Smithereens EP [CD] (Restless-Enigma)
   1987
Green Thoughts (Enigma-Capitol) 1988 ●

You like pop music? You want to hear three potential number one singles played as if the future of the world depended on making them impossibly winsome, memorable and rapturous without sacrificing any rock'n' roll energy or guts? Then get **Beauty and Sadness**, a 12-inch EP by New Jersey's Smithereens, and prepare to have your heartstrings and your hamstrings tugged mercilessly. These four guys may not be pretty, but singer/guitarist Pat DiNizio knows exactly what it takes to write great pop songs, and his bandmates prove they know what to do with 'em on "Beauty and Sadness," "Some Other Guy" and "Tracey's World." As a bonus, they rock'n'bop on "Much Too Much" and reprise the title tune as an instrumental. Topnotch. (The prior **Girls About Town** is a charming but rudimentary four-song concept single, including three originals with "girl" in the titles and a cover of the Beach Boys' "Girl Don't Tell Me.")

After signing to Enigma, the Smithereens wound up placing a song ("Blood and Roses") on a film soundtrack. The picture was a flop, but the song garnered airplay and brought the Smithereens national attention. Their Don Dixon-produced album, **Especially for You**, benefitted from the exposure and momentum, and wound up a successful chart happening. Fortunately, it's also a wonderful record, an unfancy set of memorable songs—"Alone at Midnight," "Strangers When We Meet," "Time and Time Again"— that reflect both DiNizio's sour view of romance and the quartet's sincere fandom for a number of great bands of the '60s—the Beatles, Searchers, Who and Kinks. (Suzanne Vega, with whom DiNizio had worked in an office, guests on "In a Lonely Place.")

The Smithereens is a live CD-only EP, recorded in New York City in late '86. The six-song selection (including a perfect cover of the Who's "The Seeker" along with originals from the album and 12-inch) is flawless, the performance crisp and exciting. Smithereens drummer (and record collector) Dennis Diken's witty and informative liner notes are exemplary. (The other American collectors' item is a picture disc of **Especially for You**.)

Green Thoughts (the titular reference is to jealousy) neatly dodges the sophomore jinx, delivering another set of terrific DiNizio songs, played with the same unpretentious guitar-driven excellence. "House We Used to Live In," "Drown in My Own Tears," the countryish "Something New" and the paranoid (and proud of it) title track are especially good, but the entire record is instantly likable and hard to shake. (Producer Don Dixon and Del Shannon are among the small group of guests.)   [iar]

See also *Young Fresh Fellows*.

SMITHS

The Smiths (Rough Trade-Sire) 1984 ●
Hatful of Hollow (nr/Rough Trade) 1984 ●
Meat Is Murder (Rough Trade-Sire) 1985 ●
The Queen Is Dead (Rough Trade-Sire) 1986 ●
The World Won't Listen (nr/Rough Trade) 1987 ●
Louder Than Bombs (Rough Trade-Sire) 1987 ●

Strangeways, Here We Come (Rough Trade-Sire) 1987 ●
"Rank" (Rough Trade-Sire) 1988 ●

MORRISSEY

Viva Hate (Sire-Reprise) 1988 ●

You'd be perfectly within your rights to hate the Smiths. No other pop music act since Jonathan Richman has raised blatant self-absorption to such a high level. The Smiths' ability to turn shameless solipsism into incalculable mega-stardom, however, is their entirely unique accomplishment. Mancunian singer/lyricist (Stephen) Morrissey and company stand for the traditional values of selfishness, self-pity and the unbearable anguish of love. His melancholy romantic sensibility makes Elizabeth Barrett Browning sound like Nelson Algren.

The key to the Smiths' enormous success is that the no-nonsense band—under the direction of brilliant guitarist/songwriter Johnny Marr—offsets Morrissey's flightiness with bright and catchy music. Supported by a deft rhythm section, Marr's spare, hooky guitar creates a seriously compelling underground pop sound with a simplicity more telling than all of the singer's unwanted confessions.

The Smiths boasts ten near-perfect tunes (the US edition adds "This Charming Man"), over which Morrissey sings—in his wavery, defenseless voice—about the bittersweet agonies of coming out of the closest. He overindulges to the point of sounding almost like a parody of a lounge singer, but goes far enough to make it more daring than forced. With lines alternately funny ("Hand in glove/The sun shines out of our behinds") and clunky ("Does the body rule the mind/Or does the mind rule the body/I dunno"), the album dares you to resist it and then makes it very difficult to do so.

The UK-only **Hatful of Hollow** is a generous collection of singles and early live-on-the-radio takes which doubles **The Smiths'** best cuts and betters its lesser material. It also adds the tremolo-crazy single "How Soon Is Now?," which takes the heaviest art-rock dance groove since U2's "Pride (In the Name of Love)" and throws the lines "I am the son/and the heir/Of a shyness that is criminally vulgar" in its path. Quite a formidable obstacle, but the groove wins out. The Smiths in a nutshell.

Meat Is Murder is both less frilly and less appealing than prior efforts. Morrissey is nearly as dry as the rest of the band, and the whole thing sounds two-dimensional. And while anyone at all disposed toward tragic romanticism can accept some of his indulgences in that direction, who can forgive the vegetarian self-righteousness (that's right) of the title track? (The US edition adds "How Soon Is Now?" to the program.)

The most dangerous gift for the chronically self-obsessed is a devoted audience, and **The Queen Is Dead** shows just how far Morrissey could take his outrageous neurotic fantasies. "Never Had No One Ever" is ostensibly a paean to virginal celibacy; "Frankly, Mr. Shankly" questions the benefits of stardom; "Bigmouth Strikes Again" (" . . . now I know how Joan of Arc felt," uh-huh), "There Is a Light That Never Goes Out" and "The Boy with the Thorn in His Side" obliquely address an assortment of insecurities. The band is typically brilliant and subtle, although Marr's guitar playing takes a relatively inconspicuous lead role.

The World Won't Listen is a second British-only compilation of singles (A's and B's) and obscurities, covering 1985–86, including "That Joke Isn't Funny Anymore," "Shakespeare's Sister," "Shoplifters of the World Unite" and "Panic." The album contains one otherwise-unreleased item, "You Just Haven't Earned It Yet, Baby."

Louder Than Bombs, a two-record set also issued in the US, contains many of the same tracks (deleting those which appeared on **The Queen Is Dead** and two others), adding items from as far back as 1983. The album contains such Smiths essentials as "Hand in Glove," "Heaven Knows I'm Miserable Now," "William, It Was Really Nothing" and "Please Please Please Let Me Get What I Want," plus a pair of radio broadcast cuts. Five numbers feature ex-Aztec Camera guitarist Craig Gannon, who was briefly a Smith; "Ask" has backing vocals by Kirsty MacColl. Amazingly, the band's stylistic consistency and musical excellence never falter, leaving the impression that these two dozen songs could have been recorded in one lengthy session. Remarkable.

Marr and Morrissey parted company in late 1987, putting an end to the Smiths with a disappointing final album, **Strangeways, Here We Come**. In spots, Marr's guitar takes a harder tone than ever before. Drummer Mike Joyce and bassist Andy Rourke also come on stronger than usual; strings and saxophone contribute to the crowded melodic

din. Morrissey's lyrics are half-baked and artless, turning especially annoying when they substitute naked anger and disgust ("Paint a Vulgar Picture," "Unhappy Birthday") for clever snideness. The delicate "Girlfriend in a Coma" and the shimmering "Stop Me if You Think You've Heard This One Before" are the album's best tracks, and they aren't exceptional additions to the canon.

Marr went off to record with Bryan Ferry, Paul McCartney and Talking Heads; Morrissey launched a solo career. **Viva Hate** features Durutti Column guitarist/backbone Vini Reilly and bassist/co-writer Stephen Street (co-producer of **Strangeways** and a past Durutti guest), as well as a drummer and string section (containing Durutti Column part-timer John Metcalfe on viola). The bland LP mainly serves to provide striking proof of how special and irreplaceable his partnership with Marr was. Morrissey brings his usual lyrical angst and wobbly singsong to the project, but the colorless music offers nothing beyond smoothly orchestrated static. The minimally-arranged and epic-length "Late Night, Maudlin Street" is the closest thing to a good track, but it's too simple to make a lasting impression. "Suedehead" attempts to mimic the Smiths with moderate selfconscious success, but little inherent creativity. **Viva Hate** drops Morrissey from masterful pop star to bland solo artist in one easy step. The tape and CD add "Hairdresser on Fire."

Later in 1988, a posthumous live Smiths album, recorded in London, was released.
[jl/iar]

T.V. SMITH'S EXPLORERS
The Last Words of the Great Explorer (Kaleidoscope-Epic) 1981
T.V. SMITH
Channel 5 (nr/Expulsion) 1983

Tim Smith was the leader of the Adverts, who clung on long enough to make two albums. After they expired, Smith formed the Explorers—originally a trio, but expanded to a five-piece (including an ex-Doctors of Madness bassist) by the time of their first album. A far cry from the Adverts' stripped-down guitar drone, **The Last Words** uses synthesizer and slick musicianship to mold an engaging dance album that benefits from Smith's strong voice and inventive songwriting. There are touches of Sparks, the Only Ones, Duran Duran (figuratively speaking; DD came after) and others, making it a great record from a gifted performer.

Channel 5 finds Smith going it alone on a tiny indie label, with only ex-Adverts keyboard man Tim Cross, a bassist and a drum machine helping out. The LP reverts to Smith's early no-nonsense, no-frills sound (if not exactly Adverts-styled punk), with his guitar leading the charge. A pleasant little record, with unusually strong songs, cute production and Smith's burgeoning social conscience ("On Your Video," "War Fever"). Clever lyrics make the spry "A Token of My Love" the best track on this entertaining (if sobering) record.

Sales were probably nonexistent, since T.V. hasn't attempted another record since. He was, however, spotted around London clubs in 1987 playing with his new band, the Cheap. [iar/jr]

SNAKEFINGER
Chewing Hides the Sound (Ralph) 1980
Greener Postures (Ralph) 1981
Manual of Errors (Ralph) 1982
Against the Grain (Ralph) 1983
SNAKEFINGER'S VESTAL VIRGINS
Live in Chicago [tape] (Ralph) 1986
Night of Desirable Objects (Ralph) 1986 ●

Although his musical career began in the early '60s and he recorded two albums with pub-rockers Chilli Willi and the Red Hot Peppers in the early '70s, guitarist Phil "Snakefinger" Lithman is best known for his association with the Residents and his resultant Ralph Records solo career. On songs like "Sinister Exaggerator" and their savage reworking of "Satisfaction," Snakefinger's deranged slidework and upside-down solos—trickily playing the wrong notes in the right places—adds an immediately recognizable deviant edge. He died of a heart ailment in July 1987; the work he left behind typifies both imagination and technical excellence.

Snakefinger's first solo outing was "The Spot," a cutely weird little single that ended up on **Chewing Hides the Sound**. But his first two albums pointed up Snakey's major weakness as a solo artist: even with copious musical and technical input from the Residents, he just isn't that weird (for a Ralph act, that is). Skeletal arrangements and over-reliance on clichéd rhythm-box beats don't help, either. Nonetheless, swell subsequent singles

("Man in the Dark Sedan" and Kraftwerk's "The Model") became modest (but deserving) underground hits.

Around the time of **Greener Postures**, Snakefinger hit the club circuit with a backing band variously known as Bast and the Dead Residents. The presence of steady company (including Beefheart alumnus Eric Feldman) makes **Manual of Errors** an improved listening experience; juxtaposed against (relatively) straight rock backing, Snakefinger's innate weirdness comes across as even more subversive.

Against the Grain is a thoughtful compilation of his Ralph work to date, providing the perfect entry to this unique guitarist's demi-warped world. Everything you'd want to hear is here—from "The Spot" through "Beatnik Party"—plus a great unreleased track, "I Love You Too Much to Respect You."

Armed with his new backing group, the Vestal Virgins (again led by keyboardist Feldman), Snakefinger recorded **Night of Desirable Objects** and the cassette-only **Live in Chicago**, which have no songs in common. The excellently-produced record is quite good, comprising complex jazz instrumentals, a believable English fiddle ballad, unadorned a cappella gospel and typical (for Snakey) originals like "There's No Justice in Life" (which might serve as a blueprint for Oingo Boingo) and the organic "I Gave Myself to You." The live tape gives up something in audio sophistication and audio variety, but offers showy and extended new versions of such oldies as "Save Me from Dali," "Beatnik Party," "The Model" and Ennio Morricone's "Magic & Ecstasy." [rnp/iar]

SNATCH
See *Judy Nylon*.

SNATCHES OF PINK
Send in the Clowns (Dog Gone) 1987

They're from Chapel Hill, North Carolina. Sara Romweber (ex-Let's Active) plays drums. They're on a label run by R.E.M. manager Jefferson Holt. Think you've got 'em pegged? Wrong! This loud trio is a tasty blend of Stones raunch and punk insistence, well-crafted tunes delivered with jackhammer finesse. Singer Andy McMillan is a young good-old-boy with an aching twang stuck in his throat, spurred to spill his guts by Michael Rank's barbed guitars. Need a party starter? Try "One's with the Black." A good'un. [jy]

SNEAKERS

Sneakers EP (Carnivorous) 1976
In the Red EP (Car) 1978

The 7-inch **Sneakers** EP—six songs engineered by Don Dixon—marked the first vinyl appearance of a seminal but little-heard band containing North Carolina rock scene VIP's Chris Stamey, Will Rigby and Mitch Easter. To get the folklore out of the way, Stamey and Rigby later founded the dB's; Stamey went on to a solo career; Don Dixon became a busy producer (working with R.E.M., among many others); Easter is also a well-known producer, fronts Let's Active and operates Mitch's Drive-In Studio, one of the hotbeds of new American rock.

The 12-inch **In the Red**, made after Stamey had relocated to New York, was really a reunion of sorts. Instigators Stamey and Easter combine their Angloid pop/rock with brooding, quasi-baroque clavinet, the saunter of a Parisian *boulevardier,* even some avant-gardish desperation, all with an air of sophistication received in innocence.

[jg/iar]

See also *dB's, Let's Active, Chris Stamey.*

SIGMUND SNOPEK III

See *Violent Femmes.*

SOCIAL DISTORTION

Mommy's Little Monster (13th Floor) 1983
Prison Bound (Restless) 1988 ●

Formed around the turn of the decade by singer/guitarist Mike Ness (more a punk pinup than Billy Idol ever was), Social Distortion established themselves as a top-rank Southern California punk group in 1982 with the "1945" 45. In an era known more for West Coast hardcore (Black Flag, TSOL, Circle Jerks, Fear) this Fullerton band covered the Stones (the B-side is a *red*-hot "Under My Thumb") and Creedence in their live shows. **Mommy's Little Monster** is a near-perfect example of melodious, riffing punk, just oozing rock'n'roll suss. From the piledriving opener, "I Just Want to Give You the Creeps," to the swaggering "It Wasn't a Pretty Picture" to "Another State of Mind,"

Monster is a two-guitar punk-pop classic.

Five years later, Social Distortion are among the last practitioners of this form, and **Prison Bound** adds a new twist. Acoustic guitars abound and Ness has obviously been listening to Johnny Cash; at least half of the LP is tinged with a country feel. "Indulgence" and "Like an Outlaw" (with cowboy yells and snapping whips) are like parts of a soundtrack for a heroic but sad Western we'll never see; there's also another Stones cover, "Backstreet Girl." **Prison Bound** lacks the all-out dynamics of **Monster** (the loss of the original rhythm section of bassist Brent Liles and singing drummer Derrick O'Brien hurts), but it's still a maturely paced, knowing follow-up not just for punks. [jr]

SOFT BOYS

A Can of Bees (nr/Two Crabs) 1979
(nr/Aura) 1980
Underwater Moonlight (nr/Armageddon) 1980
Two Halves for the Price of One (nr/Armageddon) 1981
Invisible Hits (nr/Midnight Music) 1983
Live at the Portland Arms [tape] (nr/Midnight Music) 1983 (nr/Glass Fish) 1987
Wading Through a Ventilator EP (nr/De Lorean) 1984

From Cambridge they came, in 1976: a brilliant songwriter leading a two-guitar band that revered the Byrds, the Beatles and, most of all, Syd Barrett's Pink Floyd. Some called it the start of a psychedelic revival; the Soft Boys' verve and wild-eyed sincerity made it more of a post-psychedelic awakening.

The Boys' earliest non-45 recording was their last to be released and contains three otherwise unissued cuts. Featuring an early lineup, **Wading Through a Ventilator** shows a promising weirdness that sets it apart from what most everyone else was doing in 1977, but reveals singer/guitarist Robyn Hitchcock as a still-embryonic songwriter. He got off a few good ones on **A Can of Bees**, by which time guitarist Kimberly Rew had joined the band, but the rest declines disappointingly into grating medium-metal power pop.

That same year (1979), the Soft Boys recorded an uncharacteristically all-acoustic live tape—later sold by mail to buyers of **Invisible Hits** as **Live at the Portland Arms** and subsequently reissued and generally distributed on disc—which contains the most bizarre assortment of cover versions imaginable. But then cover versions were always one of the band's strong suits, from Hitchcock's intense reading of John Lennon's "Cold Turkey" on **Can of Bees** to his hilarious ravings on "That's When Your Heartaches Begin" (on the tape). Also of historic interest are two Syd Barrett numbers: "Vegetable Man" on a British maxi-single and the Canadian (Attic label) issue of **Underwater Moonlight** and "Astronomy Domine" on **Two Halves for the Price of One**. That album is actually two, with individually titled sides and cover art. **Lope at the Hive** was recorded at London's Hope and Anchor; **Only the Stones Remain** contains otherwise unreleased oddities mixed in both chronology and quality.

The core of the Soft Boys canon, however, are **Invisible Hits** (actually recorded in '78 and '79) and **Underwater Moonlight**. Some form of insanity prevented the timely release of the former; it shows Hitchcock at his best—maturely immature and crazily serious—as he races from hearty lust ("Let Me Put It Next to You") to vulnerable harangue ("Empty Girl," "Blues in the Dark"). Few other albums capture the humor, pathos, anger and grotesquerie of man/woman so well.

Underwater Moonlight is one of the new wave's finest half-dozen albums and unquestionably its most unjustly underrated one. "I Wanna Destroy You" is a rant against war and intolerance; "Insanely Jealous" builds to a frenzy—twice; "I Got the Hots" contains some of the funniest erotic lines ever written. This album has everything—melody, power, wit, laughs and heart, not to mention a great guitar sound.

Hitchcock remains one of the '80s most unique songwriters. He later reunited with the original Soft Boys rhythm section of Andy Metcalfe (also in the reformed Squeeze) and Morris Windsor for some of his solo recordings; Rew went on to form Katrina and the Waves. [mf]

See also *Robyn Hitchcock, Katrina and the Waves, Kimberley Rew.*

SOFT CELL

Non-Stop Erotic Cabaret (Sire) 1981 ●
Non-Stop Ecstatic Dancing EP (Sire) 1982
The Art of Falling Apart (Sire) 1983
Soul Inside EP (Sire) 1983

This Last Night in Sodom (Sire) 1984
The Singles (nr/Some Bizzare) 1987

Singer Marc Almond and keyboardist David Ball performed a minor miracle in 1981, taking an obscure soul song and turning it into a most atypical synthesizer tune, coming up in the process with a worldwide smash hit that rode *Billboard*'s chart for almost a year. "Tainted Love" (recorded originally by Gloria Jones) is as passionate and desperately sleazy as Kraftwerk is cool and clean. The Almond/Ball originals on **Non-Stop Erotic Cabaret** don't always cut so deeply, but all offer nice, decadent fun. Among them: "Sex Dwarf," highlighted by a nagging synthesizer riff, and "Say Hello, Wave Goodbye," blatant though stirring sentimentality. Almond's breathy, insinuating vocals and Ball's surprisingly varied electronic and acoustic keyboards (kudos to producer Mike Thorne) never stand pat.

Non-Stop Ecstatic Dancing, half an hour (six tracks) of dance mixes, intends primarily to divert and manages to overcome its basic filler role. Highlights include a languid version of "Where Did Our Love Go?" and the unforgettably neurotic "Insecure . . . Me?"

It's too bad Almond and Ball didn't part ways before descending into the embarrassing self-parody of **The Art of Falling Apart**. With Ball's keyboards growing progressively cooler, Almond tries ever more desperately to invoke a sleazy atmosphere and just ends up sounding silly. The nadir—indeed, the worst Soft Cell effort of all time—is the pitiful ten-minute Jimi Hendrix medley of "Hey Joe," "Purple Haze" and "Voodoo Chile (Slight Return)" that comes on a bonus 12-inch 45. It's like a five-year-old trying to read Shakespeare. **Soul Inside** is a collection of odds and ends, including a version of "You Only Live Twice (007 Theme)," two remixes and a live radio session.

This Last Night in Sodom contains further fruitless flailing, as titles like "The Best Way to Kill" and "Mr. Self Destruct" attest. After this, Soft Cell broke up once and for all. Outside of one solo album, little has been heard from Ball; Almond has released a number of records. [jy]

See also *Marc Almond, Dave Ball.*

SOLID SENDERS

Solid Senders (nr/Virgin) 1978

After leaving Dr. Feelgood, guitarist Wilko Johnson formed a likeminded quartet which lasted only long enough to record this one album. (Johnson subsequently made solo records and formed a 1982 band with Lew Lewis.) Based in R&B, but with other evident influences (reggae, blues, pop), **Solid Senders**—a studio disc plus a bonus live 12-inch—downplays Johnson's frenetic guitar brilliance in favor of a group approach, which leaves sonic room for John Potter's keyboards to share the spotlight. Old-fashioned, but extremely lively. [iar]

SONIC'S RENDEZVOUS BAND
See *New Order.*

SONIC YOUTH
Sonic Youth EP (Neutral) 1981 (SST) 1987
Confusion Is Sex (Neutral) 1983 (SST) 1987 •
Kill Yr. Idols EP (Ger. Zensor) 1983
Sonic Death Sonic Youth Live [tape] (Ecstatic Peace) 1984 (SST) 1988 •
Bad Moon Rising (Homestead) 1985 •
Death Valley 69 EP (Homestead) 1985
EVOL (SST) 1986 •
Sister (SST) 1987 •

LEE RANALDO
From Here to Infinity (SST) 1987

CICCONE YOUTH
The Whitey Album (Blast First) 1988

Latter-day rock'n'roll revolutionaries have shown a marked tendency toward swift burnout. They reveal their raw vision to the world; the world—being the philistine place that it is—turns away; the musicians move on. Sonic Youth, unlike so many of the noise bands that formed in New York in the early part of this decade, has had the fortitude to stick it out and develop its ideas beyond the original stances. As a result, the band has gotten better and better, and can now articulate its rough sounds with chilling beauty.

The debut EP proves that a reliance on artsy posturing can get boring in an awful hurry. Rigidly defined beats and disembodied poetic vocals eviscerate Sonic Youth's principal weapon—jangling, ringing, dissonant guitar noise. This disc is no fun.

Confusion Is Sex gives the guitars freer rein, and the result is a happily anarchic and intense mess. The tortuous "She's in a Bad Mood" captures its subject matter like few songs before it, and a crude cover of Iggy's "I Wanna Be Your Dog" proves that the artistes can rock. The record alternates between pulse and drone; its quiet spaces quickly get cluttered with weirdly-tuned percussive guitars, often bowed or struck with a drumstick.

Kill Yr. Idols reprises two tunes from **Confusion Is Sex** and adds three similarly twisted tracks. Like **Confusion**, this EP is dark and haunting, particularly on "Early American," where the guitars ring like macabre bells.

Bad Moon Rising brings Sonic Youth into the light, and shows an enormous developmental leap. The sounds are still harsh—feedback, distortion and dissonance—but the group uses them to create a variety of effects and moods. Like many records made in 1984 and 1985, the album is a statement about America and, while avoiding the ennoblement of the mythological common man, does capture both the beauty and creepiness of the frontier west of the Bowery. "Death Valley 69," recorded with Lydia Lunch, sounds like X on a bad trip, and puts the band's screaming guitars into a straight rocker. The rest of the disc is more painterly and less propulsive; the band gets its explosiveness from the quiet sections, where interwoven guitar parts hint at jarring disorder. (Creedence fans can be reassured that Sonic Youth does not cover the song from which the record takes its name.) The **Death Valley 69** EP, its title track a reprise from the LP, also culls one track each from the previous three discs, adding the heretofore unissued anarchy of "Satan Is Boring."

The material on **EVOL** is presented in more basic song structures, giving the band more accessibility and versatility than ever before without diluting their brutal strength one iota. Command of their resources is so great that they can make rackety shards of atonal guitars sound almost catchy on tracks like "Green Light," while "Shadow of a Doubt" and the end of "Expressway to Yr Skull" (listed as "Madonna, Sean and Me" on the back cover) both take raw, jagged sounds and blend them into a peaceful stillness. **EVOL** is a very impressive album wherein Sonic Youth makes the step from great noise band to great band. The CD adds "Bubblegum" from the "Starpower" 12-inch.

EVOL is a tough one to follow, but **Sister** proves well up to the task. Reportedly recorded on all vacuum tube equipment (mixing board and all), the album has a very warm, immediate feel, and the tonalities aren't so strange as to alienate the general public. Not that it's all polished up—far from it—but the emphasis is more on rocking out than on bizarre guitar tunings or defining East Village art. Sonic Youth is simply one of the very best American bands of the decade. The CD adds "Master Dik."

Guitarist Lee Ranaldo's solo outing, **From Here to Infinity** is a challenging adventure in listening. Sonically akin to **Metal Machine Music**, with plenty of fuzzy drones and repetitious sounds of various descriptions, each short track (most under a minute) ends with a lock groove (the cassette version achieves the same effect by inserting extended pauses between numbers), so they can actually be very long tracks if you want. Pressed on grey marbleized vinyl; the sleeve explains that it is a variable-speed 45. Difficult but rewarding.

Ciccone Youth, Sonic Youth's parodic and loopy part-time side project with Mike Watt of fIREHOSE, issued a single in 1986 and announced an album in 1988.

There have also been legitimate limited edition live Sonic Youth albums and cassettes, as well as bootlegs.   [jl/dgs]

SORE THROAT
Sooner Than You Think (nr/Hurricane) 1979

Interesting although mediocre, Sore Throat started as a punk band, yet quickly developed sophisticated, precocious attributes—using horns and dance rhythms long before they came into vogue. Sore Throat's lone album displays the sextet's broad range—from slow ballad to high-energy rocker—as well as a plain set of songs, but, unfortunately, no particularly absorbing moments. More impressive for its prescience than content. File under Promising but a Few Years Early.   [iar]

SORROWS
Teenage Heartbreak (Pavillion) 1980
Love Too Late (Pavillion) 1981

The mid-'70s New York club scene had a large population of Anglo-pop bands, playing Merseybeat root music as accurately as possible. The Sorrows were formed in 1977 from the remains of the Poppees, a minor member of the skinny tie brigade; two years later the Sorrows had a major-league record deal.

Teenage Heartbreak, a dozen melodic originals, isn't bad, blending all the right ingredients with enough aggression to shun wimpiness. In another time and place, the Sorrows might have been a non-salacious Knack.

The coup on **Love Too Late** is the production credit—Shel Talmy, the man behind all the early Kinks/Who records. Disappointingly (although the same thing happened when Talmy produced surf-rockers Jon and the Nightriders), the sound is not exceptional, and the record is basically similar to the group's first outing.   [iar]

SOUL ASYLUM
Say What You Will . . . (Twin/Tone) 1984
Made to Be Broken (Twin/Tone) 1986 ●
Time's Incinerator [tape] (Twin/Tone) 1986
While You Were Out (Twin/Tone) 1986
Hang Time (Twin/Tone-A&M) 1988 ●
Clam Dip & Other Delights EP (nr/What Goes On) 1988

Emerging from the Minneapolis hardcore circuit (where the young quartet was originally known as Loud Fast Rules), Soul Asylum quickly set about earning the right to be considered in the same league as that city's two leading ex-punk outfits, the Replacements and Hüsker Dü. **Say What You Will**, produced by the latter's Bob Mould, closes off their punk phase and introduces an instinct for rhythmic complexity, an awareness of country music and deft vocal interplay, albeit in nascent and only semi-perceptible (at the time) fashion. Dave Pirner's hoarse singing leaves something to be desired here, but the intimation that he possesses real songwriting talent—especially in the wry, often self-deprecatingly depressive lyrics—is encouraging.

The confident, emotionally compressed sound and material on **Made to Be Broken** is light years better: rich dual vocals by guitarists Pirner and Dan Murphy, supported by Grant Young's precise, varied drumming and a wash of loudly but subtly interwoven guitars make the tuneful power of "Tied to the Tracks," "Ship of Fools," the countryish "Made to Be Broken" and "New Feelings" staggeringly original and memorable. Additionally, "Never Really Been" reveals the group's ability to convey the same wit and energy on touching (mostly) acoustic guitar ballads; Murphy displays his own songwriting ability on "Can't Go Back." The onomatopoetic "Whoa!" explodes in a breathtaking syncopated fury of incoherent shrieking and stands as one of Soul Asylum's funniest, most accomplished adventures. An astonishing, original and durable record that states the band's case most convincingly.

One of the highlights of **Time's Incinerator**—a tape-only 1980–86 compilation of outtakes, covers, concert cuts and other nonsense—is a live version of James Brown's "Hot Pants" sung by bassist Karl Mueller. Otherwise, there are a few ace studio tracks, a lot of justifiable discards and some wild bits of onstage craziness. Unessential, but a worthwhile place-keeper between albums.

While You Were Out (Sides 5 and 6 in the band's consecutively-numbered *oeuvre*) is a disappointment that doesn't do the songs adequate justice. Chris Osgood's production is messy and uneven; the performances sound hurried and the arrangements unfinished. As evidenced on "Carry On," "No Man's Land," "The Judge," "Closer to the Stars"— complex songs filled with melody, energy and intelligence—Pirner's writing (not to mention vocals) just keeps getting better. Murphy's "Miracle Mile" is also a highlight, but the delivery here lacks the clarity and elaboration they deserve.

Thanks to a pact between A&M and Twin/Tone, **Hang Time** elevated Soul Asylum to a new career plateau and landed them in a New York studio with the production team of Ed Stasium (Ramones, Julian Cope, Living Colour, etc.) and Lenny Kaye (James, Suzanne Vega). Bolstered by unprecedented sonic excellence and the luxury of time to flesh out and refine their material, Soul Asylum entered the big leagues with a riff-rocking bang. The first two tracks—"Down on Up to Me" and "Little Too Clean"—surprisingly suggest a regression to the '70s chart fare of their youth, but the record abruptly rights itself with the throaty roar of "Sometime to Return" and doesn't again falter. Highlights of a consistently impressive platter are "Ode," "Marionette," Murphy's "Cartoon" (containing such typically succinct lines as "if you're cryin' in your beer you're gonna drown"), the poignant "Endless Farewell" (a wistful ballad on which Pirner plays piano) and the explosively Clashlike "Standing in the Doorway." (The CD adds "Put the Bone In," a vulgar canine double entendre played on acoustic guitars as a **Beggars Banquet**-styled goof, which was—as claimed—the B-side of Terry Jacks' gold-selling 1974 hit single, "Seasons in the Sun.")

The 12-inch **Clam Dip EP** was scheduled

to precede **Hang Time** (hence the latter's numbering as sides 9 and 10), but things didn't work out that way, and the enjoyable mixture of favorite cover versions (Janis Joplin-by-way-of-Slade's "Move Over," Foreigner's "Juke Box Hero" and "Chains," a terrific Minneapolis new wave obscurity) and originals (including a topical labor song, "P-9," written and originally recorded to benefit a striking local) was delayed for months, surfacing first on an English label. But while the title and cover—a nude Mueller up to his waist in party dip—parody an old Herb Alpert (the "A" in A&M) album, the contents assuredly don't.   [iar]

SOULSONIC FORCE
See *Afrika Bambaataa*.

SOUND
Jeopardy (nr/Korova) 1980
Live Instinct EP (Hol. WEA) 1981
From the Lions Mouth (nr/Korova) 1981
All Fall Down (nr/Korova) 1982
Shock of Daylight EP (A&M) 1984
Heads and Hearts (nr/Statik) 1985
In the Hothouse (nr/Statik) 1985
Thunder Up (Can. Nettwerk) 1987 ●

It's hard to understand why this London quartet never found commercial success. At their best, the Sound's excellent neo-pop bears favorable comparison to the Psychedelic Furs and Echo and the Bunnymen. **Jeopardy** has a stark, beautiful quality, with the material given direct exposure rather than a production bath. Adrian Borland's vocals are sincere and gripping; the musical attack is both subtle and aggressive.

The inconsequential **Live Instinct** contains four songs recorded onstage in London, including renditions of their 1979 debut single ("Cold Beat") and a few **Jeopardy** songs. The recorded performances add little to the studio versions. **From the Lions Mouth** builds on **Jeopardy**'s firm foundation with a fuller sound that faintly recalls U2. Produced by Hugh Jones (around the same time he did Echo's **Heaven Up Here**), it's bright, dramatic and sometimes (e.g., "Fire," "Sense of Purpose," "Winning") powerful. A riveting LP, and the group's best.

Warned by their label that they'd be dropped if they didn't start sounding more commercial, **All Fall Down** is the defiant reply—a stark, barren landscape of harsh tones and dark passages. The black, clashing music makes the LP an acquired taste, an ambitious, admirable exploration of the downside, a challenging and unique record. Not surprisingly, the record company sent the band packing.

Shock of Daylight—a six-song mini-album produced by Pat Collier—is a strong return, building melodic, dramatic songs on a gutsy bass/drums drive, overlaying guitar, keyboards and even brass to create an attractively textured and varied sound. **Heads and Hearts** is even better, a quilt of bright colors woven with simple care. Though it lacks the knockout punch they'd shown in the past ("Winning" or **Shock of Daylight**'s "Golden Soldiers," for example), the record's modesty and continuous flow make it a thoroughly engaging listen, a memorable LP whose sum is greater than its parts.

In the Hothouse is a double live thriller from London's Marquee, with all the claustrophobic ambience of the club's packed space coming through on the recording. Live records this immediate sounding are hard to find. With the bulk of the material chosen from **Heads and Hearts** and **Lions Mouth**, this is a superb introduction for the curious.

Thunder Up is a middle ground between **All Fall Down**'s emotional warfare and the later, more sensuous pop. Punching right in with one of their most exciting tracks, "Acceleration Group," the LP is a rollercoaster ride through desolation ("Shot Up and Shut Down"), titillation ("Kinetic"), cynicism ("Prove Me Wrong") and profound beauty ("You've Got a Way"). Though the contrast can be jarring, unpredictability is a strength, a bold up/down, hot/cold, built-up/knocked-down record most bands would not attempt. It was to be their last such uncompromising work; the group finally called it quits in early '88. [cpl/iar/jr]

SOUND BARRIER
See *Tot Taylor and His Orchestra.*

SOUP DRAGONS
Hang-Ten! EP (nr/Raw TV Products) 1986
Hang-Ten! (Sire) 1987
This Is Our Art (Sire) 1988 ●

This young foursome from Edinburgh, Scotland garnered a lot of initial interest because of their striking musical resemblance to the Buzzcocks. Singer Sean Dickson's fal-

setto whine, in front of the speedy grind of his and Jim McCulloch's guitars, made the Soup Dragons the very reincarnation of those punk-pop pioneers. An admirable point of reference, to say the least.

The four-song **Hang-Ten!** EP followed two well-received UK singles. The blistering title track can be aptly described as punk-surf-pop—the Beach Boys sifted through the Buzzcocks, if you will. The other songs run about the same speed, and are just as outstanding.

The American **Hang-Ten!** album collects the UK EP, three songs from a previous single ("Whole Wide World"), and three songs from a later single ("Head Gone Astray"). All reaffirm the band's reverence for the Buzzcocks tradition.

This Is Our Art (subtitled "Useless, boring, impotent, elitist and very, very beautiful.") is, however, a shocking and totally unexpected album. The new Soup Dragons (in terms of direction, not membership) are devoid of any Buzzcocks references, mutating instead into a bizarre assortment of styles: '60's garage psychedelia ("Great Empty Space"), hard rock (the Black Sabbath sounding "Passion Protein") and Scottish funk ("King of the Castle"), to mention just a few. It's an amazing range, yet there's something insincere about these songs, which seemingly don't know when to end. Memo to the Dragons: don't overcompensate to shake the Buzzcocks tag. [ag]

SOURIS DEGLINGUEE
La Souris Deglinguee (Fr. New Rose) 1981

This Parisian punk quartet had a Vietnamese lyricist/guitarist; their songs (all sung in French) concern topics like rebellion, racism and political freedom. A swell translation of American and English rock idioms, they combined the best musical aspects of early Clash, New York Dolls, Eddie and the Hot Rods and the Stray Cats. Now defunct, la Souris Deglinguee ("The Collapsing Mouse," or thereabouts) made great, energetic rock that's forceful and fun. They were easily good enough to compete internationally, but never became known outside their homeland. [iar]

SOUTHERN DEATH CULT
See *Cult.*

SPACE NEGROS

Maximum Contrast from Moment to Moment
EP (Sounds Interesting) 1979
The Space Negros Go Commercial EP (Arf
Arf) 1980 + 1984
Tell White Lies EP (Arf Arf) 1981
Have a Lousy Xmas EP (Jingle Jungle-Arf Arf)
1981
The Space Negros Do Generic Ethnic Muzak
Versions of All Your Favorite Underground
Punk/Psychedelic Songs from the Sixties
(Arf Arf) 1987

FAMILY FUN

Record (Eat) 1981

Before there was a Mission of Burma, two
of that group's future founders played in this
minor Boston group, along with keyboard-
ist/producer Erik Lindgren, a future member
of Birdsongs of the Mesozoic. The 7-inch
Maximum Contrast contains six offbeat offerings of experimental synth'n'tape tricks,
perhaps done under the influence of German
and British progressives of the '70s. That
same year, the original Space Negros fell
apart; **Go Commercial** (shades of the Residents), another 7-inch with eight songs, is
actually a Lindgren solo record. His upbeat
pop songs—sort of a synth-happy R. Stevie
Moore—are witty and sophisticated; the B-
side includes a cover of the Yardbirds' "Happenings Ten Years Time Ago." The original
EP's rendition of that classic took a Kraftwerkian electro-pop approach; a 1984 reissue
of the record replaced it with a heavy metal
guitar rendition.

Tell White Lies is a two-sided flexidisc
compiling Lindgren recordings going back as
far as 1975. **Have a Lousy Xmas** offers a
topical foursome of laughable ill cheer originals (e.g., "Jingle Hell") played by Lindgren
with Space Negro alumnus Roger Miller and
others.

The windily-titled album, recorded between 1981 and 1985 with a large number of
instrumental contributors, consists entirely
of exotically idiomatic (raga, bluegrass, Balkan, etc.) easy-listening instrumental interpretations of songs originally popularized by
such venerable musical organizations as the
Seeds, Who, Easybeats, Balloon Farm,
Smoke, 13th Floor Elevators, Hotlegs and
Tomorrow. Not as conceptually explosive as
the Residents, perhaps, but utterly original
and delightful.

Flipper may have a gripe against Public
Image for lifting their concept of a generic

record sleeve, but Family Fun—a Lindgren-
led quartet—has them both beat. The cover
of their 1981 EP (one side of four electro-pop
tunes with Sara Goodman providing folkie
vocals over the slightly off-kilter backing and
a side of instrumental "EZ Listening Music")
mimics the no-name products in grocery
stores by carrying only the word "REC-
ORD" stenciled over "Net Wt. 4.9 Oz. (45
RPM.) 135 g."   [iar]

SPANDAU BALLET

Journeys to Glory (Chrysalis) 1981 ●
Diamond (Chrysalis) 1982
True (Chrysalis) 1983 ●
Parade (Reformation-Chrysalis) 1984
The Singles Collection (Chrysalis) 1985 ●
The 12-Inch Mixes (nr/Chrysalis) 1986
Through the Barricades (Epic) 1986 ●

Viewed at the start by some as adventurous and trendsetting, the ludicrous garb and
chic disco of London's Spandau Ballet were
both dubious new wave developments, but
spawned much replication. Head poseur
Tony Hadley and his four cohorts found
great club success with a heavily rhythmic
brand of distant funk-rock dolled up with
synthesizers and stentorian singing. Produced by Richard James Burgess, **Journeys
to Glory** contains one great dance hit (actually, one tightly-compressed riff: "To Cut a
Long Story Short," their first single) and a
batch of retread variations thereon. With the
addition of horns and other reformulated
moves, **Diamond**—issued in the UK as a set
of four 12-inch singles as well as a regular
single album—also produced a few more estimable British chart smashes ("Chant No. 1,"
"Paint Me Down"). Possessing only limited
talent themselves, Spandau opened the
floodgates to a wave of superior electro-dance
bands who had little trouble creatively eclipsing them.

Spandau then abandoned synthesizers
and high-tension funk for schmaltzy pop
with American soul pretensions. Working
with the production team of Tony Swain and
Steve Jolley, the fivesome cut **True** and **Parade**, the first yielding several attractive
blends of energy, melody, warmth and stylishness ("Communication," "Lifeline") as
well as some of the sappiest MOR in memory
("True," which became an enormous hit).
Generally less wimped-out, **Parade** nonetheless continues the bland chart fare, with the
stylistic divergence best represented by

"Revenge for Love" (good) and "Only When You Leave" (egregiously mellow).

Amidst a legal tumult between Spandau and Chrysalis, the label issued a worthwhile collection of the band's singles, followed by a compilation of remixes.

Through the Barricades, easily the worst Spandau Ballet LP yet, dumps the Perry Como snooze for an overheated American album-rock sound that echoes Eric Carmen, REO Speedwagon (or is it Styx?) and Billy Joel. Gary Langan's co-production (with the group) has all the earmarks of a desperate last-ditch grab at reclaiming US airplay. Guitarist Gary Kemp's songs are worthless; the echo on Hadley's melodramatic warbling (backed in maximally clichéd fashion by a female trio) only makes the whole affair more laughable. Say goodnight, boys.   [iar]

SPARKS

Halfnelson (Bearsville) 1971
Sparks (Bearsville) 1971
A Woofer in Tweeter's Clothing (Bearsville) 1972
Kimono My House (Island) 1974
Propaganda (Island) 1974
Indiscreet (Island) 1975
Big Beat (Columbia) 1976
Introducing Sparks (Columbia) 1977
No. 1 in Heaven (Elektra) 1979
Best of Sparks (nr/Island) 1979
Terminal Jive (nr/Virgin) 1979
Whomp That Sucker (Why-Fi-RCA) 1981
Angst in My Pants (Atlantic) 1982
Sparks in Outer Space (Atlantic) 1983
Pulling Rabbits Out of a Hat (Atlantic) 1984
Music That You Can Dance To (Curb-MCA) 1986
Interior Design (Rhino) 1988 ●

Ron and Russell Mael—two enormously talented wiseacres from Los Angeles—have influenced numerous bands through their own records and outside projects; it's possible to trace many contemporary musical trends back to the pair's prescient and trailblazing efforts. Although their lengthy recording career has the consistency of chunky peanut butter, some of their albums are truly wonderful in a number of stylistic modes. Sparks remain unpredictably capable of greatness each time they enter the studio.

As an art-rock quintet called Halfnelson, Sparks made their earliest, misanthropic efforts to appeal to the neurotic nouveau pop

segment of 1971 America via a debut album produced by Todd Rundgren. First released as **Halfnelson** (by Halfnelson), it was promptly withdrawn, repackaged and reissued as **Sparks** (by Sparks). That original band—sort of Marlene Dietrich meets the Stooges—included Earle Mankey, who went on to become a producer (and recording artist) of some note, and his brother Jim, who later formed the chartbound Concrete Blonde. The album is a subtle and brilliant exposition of unique talent, displaying the Maels' remarkable facility for bizarre, dadaist lyrics and Russell's scarifying falsetto. The triumphant **A Woofer in Tweeter's Clothing** refined, energized and improved on the first LP; it's a demented blueprint of incomprehensible weirdness. Many hated them, few heard them, but none who did forgot them on the basis of this utterly individual effort. (The first two LPs were subsequently packaged together and reissued in Britain.)

Moving to London and recruiting an all-new set of sidemen, keyboardist Ron and singer Russell hooked up with producer Muff Winwood and made a series of singles (many included on the first two Island albums) that turned them into enormously popular glam-pop teen idols. Mixing prolix and profoundly funny wordplay with killer hooks and a solid guitar-and-piano-based sound, Sparks were the forerunners (and, to some extent, instigators) of the skinny tie Anglo-pop revival that swept America a few years later. Two brilliant albums (**Kimono My House** and **Propaganda**) worked that irresistible formula, but the gimmickry wore thin; **Indiscreet**, produced pompously by Tony Visconti, has some terribly boring, unbelievably overblown numbers amidst the succinct pop smashes. Sparks were outgrowing bubblegum.

Their lock on the top of Britain's charts ended, the Maels fired their band and returned to America to begin a very bad career patch, starting with **Big Beat**. They benefit from a bit of leftover momentum (and perhaps material) from their previous work, but it's basically a poor homecoming. (The band for this record included head Tuff Dart Jeff Salen on guitar, ex-Milk 'n' Cookies bassist Sal Maida and drummer Hilly Michaels.) The far worse **Introducing**, recorded with LA session men, is Sparks' creative nadir.

The group's complex saga then began to involve Giorgio Moroder, who produced **No. 1 in Heaven**, converting the one-time pure-guitar-poppers into a driving Euro-disco synthesizer machine, pounding out repetitive drum-laden dance grooves. Only semi-successful, musically speaking, it does deserve credit for predating the entry of countless other rock groups onto the high-tech dance-floor. **Terminal Jive**, the only Sparks album not released in the US, tempers the funk but suffers a serious personality loss, the result of the Maels' co-writing too much of the material with others.

Leaving the disco behind, Sparks next began an alliance with a Moroder associate, German producer Mack. They recorded **Whomp That Sucker** in Munich with their first steady band since **Indiscreet**: David Kendrick, Leslie Bohem and Bob Haag (who also work on their own as Gleaming Spires). The songs reclaim some of Sparks' early pop wit, but with new maturity and dignity. A definite improvement, it's still a transitional record, leading the Maels out of the creative woods with some ace numbers, but they're still not at peak power.

Angst in My Pants, however, is that promise fulfilled, a top-notch collection of tunes with offbeat humor, winning melodies and excellent arrangements, displaying the benefits of touring with a band. It's the first new Sparks album that belongs alongside **Woofer** and **Kimono**. The self-produced **In Outer Space** features Jane Wiedlin (then in the Go-Go's) duetting with Russell on two songs, and is a mixed creative success due to songs that drag and a shortage of stunning lyrics. The equally inconclusive **Pulling Rabbits Out of a Hat** has better material but less personality and again only a handful of standout tracks.

Hooking up with yet another record label (but keeping the band intact), Sparks next made **Music That You Can Dance To**, an aggressively loud high-energy dance record—dynamic keyboards, mock-symphonic arrangements and Bohem's bass play a large part—that has its moments (the title track, "Change," "The Scene") and its mistakes (a painful version of Stevie Wonder's "Fingertips"). Clever lyrics help, as does the Maels' inventive self-production.

Ron and Russell have (together) done numerous projects for other artists, including production and collaborative songwriting (or just lyrics). Their clientele has included Telex, Lio and the Go-Go's.   [iar]

See also *Bijou, Concrete Blonde, Gleaming Spires, Telex.*

SPEAR OF DESTINY

Grapes of Wrath (nr/Burning Rome-Epic) 1983
One Eyed Jacks (nr/Burning Rome-Epic) 1984
World Service (nr/Burning Rome-Epic) 1985
Outland (Virgin) 1987 ●
The Epic Years (nr/Epic) 1987

Following the stormy existence of Theatre of Hate, singer/guitarist Kirk Brandon and bassist Stan Stammers launched Spear of Destiny. **Grapes of Wrath**, produced by Nick Launay, unveils a straightforward guitar/bass/drums quartet; Andy Mackay-like saxophone work provides the sole distinguishing tonal component. Brandon's songs are a drag—spare, dirgey things with hopeless quasi-Scottish melodies and self-important, insignificant lyrics. Slight Nick Cave tendencies don't add enough extremism to salvage these effortlessly ignorable tracks.

One Eyed Jacks introduces a different, larger lineup (including ex-Tom Robinson Band drummer Dolph Taylor); the superior results lean alternately towards Big Country and Adam Ant. A basically inept vocalist with nothing in the way of a natural instrument, Brandon sings everything like he's rousing the troops for a final assault, a tactic that overpowers the flimsy tunes. Lacking a feel for full-blown majesty (like Richard Jobson), he's too zealous for his own good.

Co-produced by SOD and Rusty Egan, **World Service** is again hindered by Brandon's horrifically bad singing. He repeatedly misses notes on "Rocket Ship" and makes the lyrics on "Come Back" sound almost unpronounceable. The operatic melody of the title track exposes all of his aural inadequacies at once. Soulful backing by a stellar vocal trio on three songs only underscores the problem.

On the occasion of the band's departure from the label, **The Epic Years** recapitulates those three albums and contemporaneous singles.

Outland unites Brandon with ex-Ant guitarist Marco Peroni [sic], the Barnacle brothers rhythm section and producer Zeus B. Held. It's not such a bad record. The advent of goth-metal groups like the Cult, Sisters of Mercy and the Mission makes marble-mouthed Brandon seem a far less offensive character than ever before; perhaps he's also improved a bit. (Naaah.) While nowhere near a desert island disc, **Outland** is a reasonable current example of rough'n'ready semi-political rock by a sincere, if limited, individual. [iar]

SPECIALS

The Specials (2-Tone) 1979 ●
More Specials (2-Tone) 1980
Ghost Town EP (2-Tone) 1981
The Peel Sessions EP (nr/Strange Fruit) 1987

SPECIAL A.K.A.

The Special A.K.A. Live! EP (nr/2-Tone) 1980
In the Studio (2-Tone) 1984

STAN CAMPBELL

Stan Campbell (Elektra) 1987 ●

Coventry's Specials spearheaded the ska revival in 1979, with leader/keyboard player Jerry Dammers also serving as head of 2-Tone, the band's trendsetting label, which altered pop culture by releasing records by Madness, the Beat, Selecter and Bodysnatchers.

Produced by Elvis Costello, the Specials' debut LP also boasted the assistance of an elder statesman of bluebeat, trombonist Rico Rodriguez, an original member of the Skatalites. With the double lead vocals of Terry Hall and Neville Staples, guitarists Lynval Golding and Roddy Radiation and an impeccable rhythm section composed of John Bradbury and Sir Horace Gentleman, the Specials were widely acclaimed as the most exciting band to emerge in 1979, and their impact continued well into the '80s.

The Specials contains such classic 2-Tone (as the sound came to be called) numbers as "Doesn't Make It Alright," "Too Much Too Young," "A Message to You Rudy" and (on the American edition) the hit single "Gangsters." Mixing socially and politically aware lyrics with infectious dance rhythms, **The Specials** served as a virtual blueprint for many bands to follow. A few months later, under their full Special A.K.A. handle, the band released a hot 7-inch EP—recorded live in London and Coventry—that includes "The Guns of Navarone" and a side-long medley of covers dubbed "Skinhead Symphony."

Unfortunately, their momentum foundered with the release of **More Specials**. The group abandoned the fresh sound of their debut in favor of a more turgid experimental approach. (**More** does, however, contain some prime material: "Enjoy Yourself" and, in the US, "Rat Race.") Rumors of internal strife abounded, and though the Specials managed to release the angry **Ghost Town** 12-inch—which went straight to number one in riot-torn Britain—the original band soon succumbed to infighting. Hall, Staples and Golding split off to form the Fun Boy Three, and other members drifted off as well.

By then it was clear that the Specials name was merely a vehicle for Dammers' projects, but it was three (reportedly arduous) years before he completed the "group's" ' third album, ironically titled **In the Studio**. Working with several steady associates (notably vocalists Stan Campbell and ex-Bodysnatcher Rhoda Dakar, in addition to loyal drummer John Bradbury) plus a large pool of sessioneers, Dammers filled the album with disarmingly varied, largely unstylized (nothing you would really call ska) essays on serious political topics ("Racist Friend," "Free Nelson Mandela," "Alcohol") leavened by the lighthearted "(What I Like Most About You Is Your) Girlfriend." Striking but troubled, the music's easygoing bounce belies the overweening polemicism.

In 1987, ex-Special Campbell released a bland soul/reggae-flavored commercial solo album. A vocal resemblance to Michael McDonald (Doobie Brothers) is only one of Stan's problems; his dull originals and underdone cover versions ("Don't Let Me Be Misunderstood," "Crawfish" and "Strange Fruit") are the others. [jw/iar]

See also *Colour Field, Fun Boy Three, Selecter.*

SPECIMEN

Batastrophe EP (Sire) 1983

Specimen was a leading exponent of the Batcave glam-punk non-movement; this demi-album (an American compilation of UK singles, all on the London label) blends T. Rex, Adam Ant, Ziggy Bowie, Gary Glitter and Tommy Steele into a reasonably innocuous breed of loud chart-pop played for all the inherent B-movie melodrama possible. "The Beauty of Poisin" and "Returning from a Journey" are both catchy tunes with big beats; the other four are swell, but not as memorable. Meanwhile, ponder this: is the EP title meant to be pronounced like *catastrophe*? [iar]

CHRIS SPEDDING

Chris Spedding (nr/RAK) 1976
Hurt (nr/RAK) 1977

Guitar Graffiti (nr/RAK) 1979
I'm Not Like Everybody Else (nr/RAK) 1980
Friday the 13th (Passport) 1981
Mean and Moody (nr/See for Miles) 1985
Enemy Within (Fr. New Rose) 1986 ●

One of Britain's top session guitarists of the '70s (even participating in records by the furry Wombles!), Chris Spedding has had a truly aberrant solo career. A veteran of numerous outfits starting in the '60s, Spedding made several LPs under his own name before joining Andy Fraser's post-Free band, Sharks, who made two hard-rocking LPs in 1973 and '74. (Spedding also played on one of Sharks vocalist Snips' subsequent solo outings.) After that band split, Spedding released a succession of LPs that combine exquisite rock guitar with lackluster vocals and songs so vapid as to be virtually nonexistent. The "highlight" of **Chris Spedding** is a novelty item called "Guitar Jamboree" which features Spedding aping various guitar heros in a show of chameleonlike virtuosity.

We pick up the story later in 1976, however, when Spedding teamed up with the then-unrecorded Vibrators for a great single, "Pogo Dancing," the first punk dance record. **Hurt**, Spedding's next LP, is a more solid follow-up, thanks to Chris Thomas' crisp production. The material is generally better, and there's one outstanding number, the ominous "Lone Rider."

Guitar Graffiti finds Spedding meandering again, producing a crass attempt to cash in on his new wave credibility (legitimately established through his seminal alliances with the Sex Pistols and the Cramps, for whom he produced demos, and the Vibrators). The worthwhile track is "Hey, Miss Betty," the only one produced by Thomas; the song is a rocking homage to '50s bondage queen Betty Page.

In 1979, Spedding surprised everyone by joining the Necessaries, a New York band that included former Modern Lover Ernie Brooks. Though he kept a low profile—refusing featured billing within the group—the combination of his dark pop ditties and leader Ed Tomney's preppie sensibility never melded. Spedding added brilliant leads to Tomney's material, but his songwriting still lacked coherency, and in some instances he abandoned guitar for keyboards. Spedding split without fanfare after less than a year (he was gone by the time the Necessaries made their LP in 1981), returning to England to record **I'm Not Like Everybody Else**,

an album of his Necessaries-era material.

In 1981, PVC released **Friday the 13th**, a live set with Spedding joined by former Sharks/occasional Talking Head bassist Busta Cherry Jones and New York drummer Tony Machine. Featuring a selection of songs from all the above-listed albums, **Friday the 13th** was released primarily as an ersatz retrospective of his RAK material. Showing off Spedding's guitar work in the context of some extended soloing, it's the best of the lot.

Spedding does a fairly good Dave Edmunds turn on **Enemy Within**, mixing a few rock'n'roll classics ("Love's Made a Fool of You," "Shakin' All Over") with unprepossessing originals, filling them all with twangy guitar work and serviceable vocals that somehow resemble Mark Knopfler. "Hologram," co-written with Marshall Crenshaw, is a highlight of this likable record.   [tr/iar]

See also *Necessaries, Vibrators*.

SPHERICAL OBJECTS

Past and Parcel (nr/Object Music) 1978
Elliptical Optimism (nr/Object Music) 1979
Further Ellipses (nr/Object Music) 1980
No Man's Land (nr/Object Music) 1981

This Manchester group was centered around Steve Solamar, a terrible singer with an intensely personal viewpoint. His songs concern typical subject matter, but utter lack of self-consciousness invests his writing with more openness and introspection than you're probably hoping to hear.

The five Objects of **Past and Parcel** play simple rock that's lightweight but pleasant; Solamar's overbearing vocals spoil it. **Elliptical Optimism** has the same lineup and a more textured sound, featuring organ (prominently) and trumpet (occasionally). The songs are instrumentally inventive, while the vocals are less abrasive but no more interesting.

Further Ellipses takes a danceable turn, playing it smooth and rhythmic with more horns and synthesizer and less guitar. Solamar's singing continues to resemble David Thomas' but sounds too forced to be believably weird. The musical development is impressive, the songs are good, but the same old problem persists.

No Man's Land, which announces itself to be the final Spherical Objects album, has a different lineup from the previous three and sounds it. Gone are the keyboards and horns, replaced by rudimentary guitar/bass/drums plus patches of Solamar's wailing harmonica. There are some very pretty songs that are slowed down to add emotion, but overall the initial impression isn't as strong as **Further Ellipses**. A strange way to go out, **No Man's Land** is a record that slowly reveals itself to be quite lovely in spots.   [iar]

SPITBALLS

Spitballs (Beserkley) 1978

Not a band, but a wonderful novelty album done at the height of the Beserkley label's prominence and activity. **Spitballs** employed everyone on the label's roster—the Modern Lovers, Greg Kihn Band, Earthquake, Rubinoos and Sean Tyla—to record (in various permutations) 15 rollicking cover versions of songs from the '60s. The resulting LP is a joyous celebration of the participants' roots, a thoroughly enjoyable collection of great songs performed with affection and élan. Samples of the repertoire: "The Batman Theme," "Chapel of Love," "Boris the Spider" and "Bad Moon Rising."   [iar]

SPIZZ

Spizz History (nr/Rough Trade) 1982

ATHLETICO SPIZZ 80

Do a Runner (A&M) 1980

SPIZZLES

Spikey Dream Flowers (A&M) 1981

SPIZZOIL

The Peel Sessions EP (nr/Strange Fruit) 1987

Whatever vocalist Spizz's incarnation—as Spizzoil, Spizzenergi, Spizzles, Athletico Spizz 80—he'll always be best remembered for one genuine novelty hit, 1979's "Where's Captain Kirk?" The charm and wit of that single was nowhere to be found on the subsequent **Do a Runner**, which was mired in the band's predilection for science fiction imagery. If it seems tough to conceive an album of time warps, time machines and almost nine minutes of "Airships," imagine how tough it would be repeat that formula; **Spikey Dream Flowers** offers robots, deadly war games and incessant runaway guitar with no place to go.

Spizz History compiles tracks from various Spizz eras. It includes "Where's Captain Kirk?" as well as "Soldier Soldier," a version of Roxy Music's "Virginia Plain" and a 1982

single, "Megacity," to recommend it; otherwise Spizz needs to recharge his batteries.

The **Peel Sessions** EP memorializes Spizzoil, recorded in the summer of '78. [gf]

SPK

Information Overload Unit (Ger. Normal) 1980
Leichenschrei (Thermidor) 1982
The Last Attempt at Paradise [tape] (Fresh Sounds) 1982
Auto-Da-Fe (Ger. Walter Ulbricht) 1983
Machine Age Voodoo (Elektra) 1984
Digitalis Ambigua, Gold and Poison (Can. Nettwerk) 1987 ●

This Australian band—Graeme Revell and vocalist Sinan—has variously explained their acronym as Surgical Penis Klinik, System Planning Korporation and Sozialistisches Patienten Kollektiv. Their music has likewise varied from industrial metal noise to sophisticated and moderately restrained dance-rock, but always with strange attributes.

The first two albums are pretty rugged going—the three favorite instruments seem to be drum machine, feedback and a synth set to produce only white noise. Fans of Throbbing Gristle and early Cabaret Voltaire might be interested, as would anybody with hard-to-eject party guests. **The Last Attempt at Paradise** cassette is a live recording done in Lawrence, Kansas in April 1982. No song titles are indicated; the two musicians' names are enigmatically given as Oblivion and Jack Pinker.

Auto-Da-Fe is so devoid of information (no track listing even) that it makes New Order records seem encyclopedic by comparison. SPK's approach is somewhat softened relative to prior work; while hardly poppy, synth melodies and dance beats in a style resembling D.A.F. are present. Lyrics are often vulgar and/or morbid, but the results aren't half as shocking as they seem to imagine. **Machine Age Voodoo** might be mistaken for a more adventurous Blondie with Kraftwerkian tendencies; an interesting hybrid of mainstream disco and experimental electronic aggression.

SPK subsequently gained notoriety for their performance practices. One London gig ended in a riot when officials stopped them ten minutes into the show for violating fire regulations. (They were featuring onstage welding at the time.)

Gold and Poison, a bland dance record with Cab Volt-esque sound effects, introduces a second female vocalist to the proceedings without making any noticeable difference. The band's strongest emotional characteristic is Revell's obnoxious smugness, which comes across loud and clear. What a drag.   [iar/dgs]

SPLIT ENZ

Mental Notes (Aus. Mushroom) 1975
Mental Notes (Chrysalis) 1976
Dizrhythmia (Chrysalis) 1977
Frenzy (Aus. Mushroom) 1979 (A&M) 1982
The Beginning of the Enz (Aus. Mushroom) 1979
The Beginning of the Enz (nr/Chrysalis) 1981
True Colours (A&M) 1980 ●
Waiata (A&M) 1981
Time and Tide (A&M) 1982
Enz of an Era—Greatest Hits 1975–1982 (Aus. A&M) 1982
Conflicting Emotions (A&M) 1983 ●
See Ya Round (Aus. Mushroom) 1984
The Living Enz (Aus. Mushroom) 1985
History Never Repeats: The Best of Split Enz (A&M) 1987 ●

TIM FINN

Escapade (Oz-A&M) 1983
Big Canoe (nr/Virgin) 1986 (Virgin) 1988 ●

New Zealand's Split Enz began their recording career in pleasantly uncommercial fashion, writing gently eccentric tunes that echoed the softer side of **Foxtrot**-era Genesis. Consisting of demos, Mushroom's **The Beginning of the Enz** chronicles those earliest days and finds Tim Finn's bittersweet singing style starting to work its magic.

For **Mental Notes**—their first proper album—the Enz took shape as a sprawling seven-piece, including spoons player Noel Crombie. They had grown overtly weird and flamboyant, with many tunes resembling little, distorted symphonies. The effects don't always work, simply because flakiness carried past a certain point can't be taken seriously on any level. The Genesis parallel holds here as well.

By the time Roxy Music's Phil Manzanera produced the second **Mental Notes**, the Enz were ready for the world beyond Oz. Bizarre carnival costumes and distorted upsweep hairdos served as colorful attention-grabbers. Tim Finn's wistful voice adds a sweet patina to disoriented and lyrically offbeat outings like "Stranger Than Fiction"

and the morbid "The Woman Who Loves You."

Dizrhythmia made a distinct lurch toward the mainstream, thanks primarily to the departure of co-leader/guitarist Phil Judd, replaced by Tim's brother Neil. With Tim in full command, the melodically intricate material went from coldly quirky to genuinely appealing, even cute. Highlights: the dizzy "Bold as Brass" and "Crosswords," at once bristling and ornate.

Financial woes subsequently forced the band to work on a diminished budget. With Neil Finn contributing songs and vocals as well as guitar, the Enz cut **Frenzy**, poppier still and less elusive than before. It's hampered by cheap sound, but "I See Red" creates a delightfully tuneful whirlwind, and "Mind Over Matter" re-creates the warmly majestic quality of the best of **Dizrhythmia**. The US/UK version of the LP differs from Mushroom's by half.

The second LP to be called **Beginning of the Enz** is a distillation of tracks from Chrysalis' **Mental Notes** and **Dizrhythmia**.

The Enz staged a full assault on America with **True Colours**. They had become a cuddly pop band with sweet vocals, crackerjack melodies and hardly any strangeness. Fortunately, the material is genuinely first-rate, including the bouncily contagious "I Got You" and "I Hope I Never," a plainly melodramatic number suitable for Barbra Streisand. (As a marketing ploy, the LP was pressed on laser-etched plastic and packaged in variously-colored covers.)

Although **Waiata** (issued in Australia under the Aborigine title **Corroboree**) has gorgeously haunting tracks like "Iris" and "History Never Repeats," as well as adorable ones like "Clumsy," there's a hint of blandness around the edges. The Enz show no desire to surprise here, and seem on the verge of becoming a hipper Bee Gees.

Happily, **Time and Tide** restores the passion, adding a new sense of wonder to the palatable melodies. "Dirty Creature" (of habit), "Hello Sandy Allen" and "Make Sense of It" all merit inclusion in the Enz hall of fame, blending a gentle beauty with vaguely unsettling otherworldliness.

Conflicting Emotions is the band's effective swan song, and it's hard to imagine a grander exit. Keeping the ethereal melodies intact, the Enz finally build up the physical side of the music to equal strength. The playing is tough and direct like never before;

"Bullet Brain and Cactus Head," "I Wake Up Every Night" and others drive hard without obscuring the wholesome moralism of the lyrics. The message? Try to lead a good life. Who could quarrel with that?

The final Enz studio LP, **See Ya Round** is an unusually mild affair, hard to remember once it's over. However, it's of historical note as Neil Finn's warmup for his massive success with Crowded House. Big bro' Tim has flown the coop, leaving Neil in charge, with a golden opportunity to make his own mistakes and get the art affectations out of his system once and for all. Which he apparently did: compare the pale version of "I Walk Away" here with the full-bodied reading on the first Crowded House LP.

The Living Enz is a decent two-disc live set from a band not widely known for its stage performances.

History Never Repeats, a lovingly assembled posthumous compilation, has swell liner notes and such Enz necessities as "I See Red," "History Never Repeats," "I Got You" and "I Hope I Never."

Singer Tim Finn successfully carved out an identity distinct from the band with **Escapade**, his first solo album. On his own, he's milder, sweeter and more conventional (though still worth the time). The precedent for **Escapade** can be found in the romantic grandeur of **True Colours**' "I Hope I Never." One track here, the moving "Not for Nothing," is a bona fide lump-in-the-throat masterpiece.

Apparently, the meager sales of **Escapade** were a major setback to Finn's solo career. Released in Europe in '86, **Big Canoe** only came out domestically after brother Neil went big-time with Crowded House—and then as a budget LP. Anyway, it's a middling effort, with overproduction and mega-arrangements (a classic Split Enz weakness) dulling the emotional edge of Finn's bittersweet crooning. He's still boss on "Don't Bury My Heart," a haunting ballad, and the lightheaded rocker "Water into Wine."

[jy]

See also *Crowded House, Swingers.*

SPLODGENESSABOUNDS

Splodgenessabounds (nr/Deram) 1981
In Search of Seven Golden Gussets
(nr/Razor) 1982

A fiercely tasteless joke band, led by singer Max Splodge. The rest of the crew on the eponymous debut sports names like Miles Runt Flat and Pat Thetic Von Dale Chiptooth Noble. The record includes an order form for such delectables as "moulded bum logo badge" and is generally concerned with various bodily functions and scatological maladies (not to be confused with scat melodies!), with only the scantest trace of humor. Except for some clever song titles, this is utterly worthless tripe.   [iar]

TREVA SPONTAINE
See *Graphic.*

SPOOKS
See *Curtiss A.*

MARK SPRINGER
See *Rip Rig + Panic.*

SQUEEZE
Squeeze (A&M) 1978
Cool for Cats (A&M) 1979
6 Squeeze Songs Crammed into One
   Ten-Inch Record EP (A&M) 1979
Argybargy (A&M) 1980 ●
East Side Story (A&M) 1981 ●
Sweets from a Stranger (A&M) 1982 ●
Singles—45's and Under (A&M) 1982 ●
Cosi Fan Tutti Frutti (A&M) 1985 ●
Babylon and On (A&M) 1987 ●

DIFFORD & TILBROOK
Difford & Tilbrook (A&M) 1984 ●

Squeeze's songwriting team of Glenn Tilbrook (melody) and Chris Difford (words) has been compared favorably to Lennon and McCartney; that's not only a reflection of their abilities but also an indication of how little real craftsmanship is found in rock'n' roll these days. Like their supposed models, Difford and Tilbrook are blessed with enormous talent which has often enabled them to get by on less than full expense of effort. What has often passed for ingenuity in Squeeze has, in fact, been little more than glibness.

A classic premature debut, **Squeeze** finds the five lads barreling through inconsistent material, a situation exacerbated by John Cale's cluttered production. However, "Take Me I'm Yours" and "Bang Bang" (both produced by the band) show spirit and potential.

Squeeze entered adolescence with **Cool**

for Cats. Primary vocalist Tilbrook, a sweet triller, and the gruffer Difford show greater confidence at the mic; together, they create arresting, odd harmonies to go with their bent pop tunes. Wonderful cuts abound, including "Slap and Tickle," a sleazy synth rocker, "Cool for Cats," a modern pub-rock romp, and "Up the Junction," three minutes of working-class heartbreak that outdoes McCartney for pathos. 6 Squeeze Songs, a well-chosen mini-greatest hits, was an effort to establish the band in the US.

Squeeze grew up on Argybargy. Tilbrook and Difford had found their style and were settling into it, creating finely etched pop music with increasing intricacy. "If I Didn't Love You" is wryly awkward; "Farfisa Beat," is a delightful throwaway; "Pulling Mussels (from the Shell)" teaches a herky-jerky lesson in catchy cleverness. Any lack of commitment is outweighed by the witty humor, variety and freshness of the material.

If the Beatles parallel holds, East Side Story is Squeeze's White Album. Produced by Elvis Costello and Roger Bechirian (apart from one cut by Dave Edmunds), the jumble of 14 songs touches on everything from soul to country to psychedelia. Each tune qualifies individually as a glittering little gem, but the album lacks coherence; still, it's a dazzling tour de force. Highlights include "Someone Else's Heart," a Difford excursion into sentiment that recalls the Zombies, "Mumbo Jumbo," reflecting Costello's influence, and "Messed Around," a slick piece of fake rockabilly.

The band pulled back slightly from the elaborate excesses of East Side Story for Sweets from a Stranger, without any loss of class. "When the Hangover Strikes" conducts a leisurely trip into Cole Porter land, while "I've Returned" soars on the strength of an exuberant Tilbrook vocal and ringing guitars. But again, the record has little coherence or musical vision.

Because Squeeze concentrated on making albums rather than singles after Cool for Cats, their singles compilation, released soon after the band's dissolution was announced, serves little purpose, pleasant though it may be. The choice of things like "Is That Love" and "Black Coffee in Bed"—one of Difford and Tilbrook's worst ever—for singles seems totally arbitrary. Thus, there's no sense of occasion. Even "Annie Get Your Gun," the one new track, isn't very good.

As it was their decision to disband

Squeeze and continue writing and performing together, Difford and Tilbrook surprised no one by releasing an album that, except for being funkier and even more boring, basically sounds no different from the band's lesser efforts. Joined by the rest of a Squeezelike lineup (drums/bass/keyboards) plus occasional horns and strings, the dull duo try to come on like Hall and Oates, but lack the cynical instincts to make a slick veneer interesting. "Action Speaks Faster," "Love's Crashing Waves" and "Picking Up the Pieces" are merely turgid, overproduced and lifelessly smooth.

After two years of unsatisfying divorce, Tilbrook and Difford reconvened Squeeze with original pianoman Jools (now Julian) Holland, drummer Gilson Lavis and a new bassist, Keith Wilkinson. But things didn't fall into place. The Laurie Latham-produced Cosi Fan Tutti Frutti is a bland collection that generally repeats the Difford & Tilbrook laxo-soul approach to much the same (non-) effect. The utterly depressive "Last Time Forever," while sonically impressive, is a regrettably somber development for this once-giddy band.

The new Squeeze righted itself on Babylon and On, a confident and likable return to the band's pre-breakup sound and form. "Tough Love," "Footprints" and especially "The Prisoner" affirm Squeeze's aptitude for agreeable pop. However, dubious stabs at soul and funk (like "Hourglass" and the annoying "853-5937") fall flat and Tilbrook's sitar playing on the insipid "Some Americans" is absurd. (Genealogical alert: second keyboardist Andy Metcalfe is indeed Robyn Hitchcock's bassist as well.)   [jy/iar]

See also Paul Carrack, Jools Holland, Harry Kakoulli, Sinceros.

SQU!RE

... Get Smart! (nr/Hi-Lo) 1983
The Singles Album (nr/Hi-Lo) 1985

ANTHONY MEYNELL & SQU!RE

Hits from 3000 Years Ago (nr/Hi-Lo) 1981 + 1984

Woking neo-mods Squire never got a major-label LP contract, so leader Meynell gets top billing on Hits from 3000 Years Ago, presumably since he put it out himself, wrote all 14 tracks (11 demos, the rest live, all played by Squire) and sings almost all of them. The band is remarkable for avoiding image-mongering and "us vs. them" polemics; they love the music, plain and simple. Most of this really sounds as though it was recorded around 1965.

Get Smart! presents a dozen sprightly new love songs sung and played by Meynell, his drummer brother and guest horn and keyboard players. The glorious pop stylings eschew replication of any specific genres, instead holding to an ingenuous squeaky-clean approach that, by default, recalls the Beatles, Turtles and Herman's Hermits. Hummable and charming. [jg/iar]

SQUIRREL BAIT

Squirrel Bait (Homestead) 1985 ●
Skag Heaven (Homestead) 1987 ●

Now that they're gone, Louisville, Kentucky's Squirrel Bait unfortunately may be remembered only by a slew of myopic, ignorant Hüsker Dü comparisons, for that was the only precedent most critics could find for this kind of manic, crackling, power-pop destruction. Singer Peter Searcy's anguished delivery is like a frightened Paul Westerberg, ten years younger, on 18 cups of coffee (and twice as animal brutish), the terrified scream of a boy being chased by an axe-murderer. With a total lack of refinement or restraint, David Grubbs and Brian McMahan's distorted guitars threaten to blow the felt right out of your speakers. A sonic overload of immense proportions with monster hooks.

The self-titled debut may be a bit too thrashy for those unused to such fast speeds, but "Sun God" into "When I Fall" pack a total power wallop. The far better, more midtempo **Skag Heaven** manages to keep this intensity and great songs coming throughout, right from the opening shocker "Kid Dynamite." An eye-opening, blasting, sweaty, over-the-edge satori not for the timid. Unfortunately, the group packed it in before its release (the members scattered to various colleges), thereby diminishing **Skag Heaven**'s impact and relegating Squirrel Bait to a footnote in the US indie hall of famous obscurities.

Both records are available on a single compact disc. [jr]

CHRIS STAMEY

It's a Wonderful Life (DB) 1983
Instant Excitement EP (Coyote) 1984
It's Alright (Coyote-A&M) 1987 ●

CHRIS STAMEY GROUP

Christmas Time (Coyote) 1986

One of the guiding lights and progenitors of the Southeast's nouveau-pop explosion, Chris Stamey led North Carolina's pioneering Sneakers before moving to New York, recording ultra-pop records on his own label, playing with Alex Chilton and forming the dB's. Recorded while Stamey was still a dB, **It's a Wonderful Life** (subtitled, on the back cover in reverse type, "It's a Miserable Life") takes him far afield from the offbeat Big Star sound for which he is best known. Joined by longstanding compatriots Ted Lyons and Mitch Easter, Stamey plays mesmerizingly moody and somber tunes ("Winter of Love," "Depth of Field," "Oh Yeah!") and aggressive demi-pop ("Never Enters My Mind"). Elsewhere, he warps the lyrics of "Tobacco Road" over a nearly all-drums background ("Get a Job"), offers cynical humor about urban life in a jarring, percussive setting ("Brush Fire in Hoboken") and plays a quiet piano piece with tape effects (the aptly named "Still Life #3"). The only relatively straightforward pop song is the bitter "Face of the Crowd." Overall, a strange and unsettling album, filled with fascinating adventures and subcurrents of profound unhappiness.

Following his decision to opt out of the dB's—on the eve of their first American album—Stamey instead made his own **Instant Excitement**, an odd but more upbeat hodgepodge which encompasses a homely reading of John Lennon's "Instant Karma," an idyllic love song ("When We're Alone"), a frisky country-rocker and an instrumental opus, "Ghost Story." Produced by Don Dixon, the songs are somewhat more typical of Stamey's original outlook and played with little attempt to impose a style in the studio. Eclectic and a little casually halfbaked, but likable and, in spots, utterly touching.

The delightful **Christmas Time** minialbum introduces Stamey's new combo (actually the same people credited on **Instant Excitement**) and marks a brief reunion with his old one, the dB's, who get cover credit as "special guests." Reviving a long-lost tradition, the original songs are all seasonal— "The Only Law That Santa Claus Understood," "You're What I Want (For Christmas)," "Snow Is Falling," even a new acoustic version of the unexpectedly appropriate "It's a Wonderful Life." The attractive title track sounds a lot like Brian Wilson's reflective mode.

Stamey recorded and toured extensively with the Golden Palominos and then settled down to make **It's Alright**, the most emotionally lucid pop-rock album of his career, with a snazzy collection of old and new friends. Alex Chilton, Richard Lloyd, Anton Fier, Mitch Easter, Faye Hunter, Bernie Worrell and Marshall Crenshaw are among the players. The songs vary from boppy ("Cara Lee") to somber ("The Seduction") to loud ("Incredible Happiness") to idyllic ("27 Years in a Single Day") but Stamey's dry, plaintive voice invests it all equally with peerless sincerity and familiar melodic appeal.   [iar]

STARGAZERS

Watch This Space (nr/Epic) 1982

If your idea of fun encompasses be-bopping pseudo-swingtime, then the nostalgic Stargazers—one of London's '80s throwbacks—may be for you. Five young men dressed in powder-blue Buddy Holly jackets adorn the LP's front cover; the music inside combines elements of early '50s rock in the Bill Haley mode with the shoutalong big band jive of Cab Calloway. It's fine if you're into such campy silliness; however, if either the Stray Cats or Joe Jackson's **Jumpin' Jive** digression leaves you cold don't make this date.   [iar]

STARJETS

Starjets (Portrait) 1979

Spunky if unoriginal, this Belfast quartet showed some promise, but not enough to really count. The album consists of simple punky rock, with added melody and restraint (plus some clever touches, like Beach Boys harmonies), but not as poppy as the Undertones. The lyrics rerun predictable subject matter—school, camaraderie, war, stardom—and the music's not strong enough to divert on its own merits. Likable but lost. Some Starjets later wound up in the Adventures.   [iar]

START

Look Around (Fresh Sounds) 1983

Lawrence, Kansas has been the site of interesting commingling of young bands and aging literati. Start's album boasts the presence of Allen Ginsberg, who wrote the lyrics for and sings (a bizarre treat) one number.

Look Around is low-key but charming—'60s Midwest pop given an '80s sensibility. Some of the songs are overtly socio-political (especially Ginsberg's), but the sound is so authentically old-fashioned you half expect the rhetoric to be anti-Nixon.   [iar]

WALTER STEDING

Walter Steding (Red Star) 1980
Dancing in Heaven (Animal) 1982

The idea of an avant-garde punk violinist may be intriguing; as one of the genre's few proponents, Walter Steding is not. Aside from Robert Fripp's enlivening, energetic appearance on "Hound Dog," the first side of this New Yorker's 1980 debut LP offers little more than self-conscious preppie punque. The second half is mainly aimless processed fiddle scraping. Producer Chris Stein provides superficial technical polish, but one can only wonder why he bothered.

For his second outing (on Stein's label, this time) Steding recruited a larger band and several part-time helpers. Despite an apparently sincere resolve to master pop forms, he still has little to say and even less wherewithal to say it.   [mf]

STEEL PULSE

Handsworth Revolution (Mango) 1978 •
Tribute to the Martyrs (Mango) 1979 •
Caught You (Mango) 1980 •
Reggae Fever (Mango) 1980
True Democracy (Elektra) 1982 •
Reggae Sunsplash '81 (Elektra) 1982
Earth Crisis (Elektra) 1983 •
Reggae Greats (Mango) 1984 •
Babylon the Bandit (Elektra) 1986 •
State of . . . Emergency (Loot-MCA) 1988 •

In the mid-'70s, this young black sextet from Birmingham, England—inspired into existence by Bob Marley's **Catch a Fire**—found an affinity with the righteous rebellion of white new wavers and built its early reputation largely by touring British punk venues (as documented on live anthology records from Manchester's Electric Circus and London's Hope and Anchor). Steel Pulse's crossover appeal derives in large part from its young, modern thoughtfulness, but even more so from the group's incredible strength as one of the very best self-contained reggae units in the world.

Steel Pulse's virtues include a gorgeous, multi-textured musical palette, especially on the first album and much of **Caught You**, intelligent lyrics (most notably on **Handsworth Revolution**, but also on **Tribute to the Martyrs**), a wondrous, sinuously propulsive beat and sweet lead vocals by Selwyn "Bumbo" Brown, who also has a nice quasi-scat style. Criticisms: the music, while always ear-enriching and heartfelt, lacks consistently memorable tunes. An increasing tendency toward preachy, trite lyrics on **Caught You** and **Reggae Fever** is a surprising disappointment, since songwriting guitarist David Hinds has already shown he can do better.

If **Caught You** (retitled **Reggae Fever** in America) is Steel Pulse at its most pop-oriented, **True Democracy** has the band reaching for the most common denominator. Steel Pulse's best falls between the two extremes. Which brings us to **Earth Crisis**, where tasty use of synth and sharp production make it their finest, most consistent album since **Tribute to the Martyrs**. As for the documentary festival album, **Reggae Sunsplash '81**, Steel Pulse has an entire side, but never quite shakes a frustrating stiffness and artificiality. Pass it up. **Reggae Greats** is a compilation.

With the release of **Babylon the Bandit**, however, it was clear that the band's professed ideals were no longer jibing with their attempts to crack the (American) market. Protest lyrics swathed in slick, upwardly mobile production were pretty hard to take seriously, and the LP sank like a stone.

The group then left Elektra and, three years later, returned on MCA with **State of Emergency**. Although still fairly high-tech, the LP isn't as aggressively slick as its predecessor, and is saved by the determined performances of uneven songs. The fiery energy that marked the group's early work still manages to come through. [jg/bk]

STEPMOTHERS

Stepmothers EP (Posh Boy) 1981
You Were Never My Age (Posh Boy) 1981

Given their energy and general demeanor, Southern California's Stepmothers might have been mistaken for a hardcore band except that musicianship and melody were the quartet's watchwords. Led by ace guitarist and producer Jay Lansford and singer Steve Jones, who sounds like an American Billy Idol, the five-song EP has good tunes and some hot guitar solos mixed in with energetic speedrock.

You Were Never My Age reprises three

of those tracks and adds five more Jones and/or Lansford compositions, as well as "To Sir with Love" and Kim Fowley's "All the Kids on the Street," all performed with abundant talent and steamy excitement. "If I Were You," with a Jeff Beck-like riff and catchy, shoutalong chorus, is a fine example of what the Stepmothers were about.

Ex-Simpletone Lansford subsequently worked in the studio with CH3 and Agent Orange. [iar]

STETSASONIC

On Fire (Tommy Boy) 1986
Sally EP (Tommy Boy) 1988
In Full Gear (Tommy Boy) 1988 ●

New York's six-piece Stetsasonic gangs up a trio of rappers (Daddy-O, Delite and Fruitkwan) with a keyboardist/drummer/scratcher (DBC) and two mixers (Prince Paul and Wise). The sound of **On Fire** is hard and spare: one-at-a-time raps over rhythm tracks (including human beat box noises) with sporadic bits of music added. Topics are likewise familiar ("My Rhyme," "Faye," "Bust That Groove"), but Stetsasonic has a decisive sound that takes advantage of the varied voices and winds up possessing an indescribable impact.

As a precursor to Stet's second album, the **Sally** 12-inch contains two versions of the title tune (which faintly resembles—without quoting—Wilson Pickett and Sly Stone) and three mixes of "DBC Let the Music Play," which surprisingly almost uses a rock drumbeat for its bed. [iar]

TOM STEVENS

See *Long Ryders.*

MARK STEWART AND THE MAFFIA

Learning to Cope with Cowardice (nr/Plexus) 1983
Mark Stewart + Maffia (Upside) 1986 ●

MARK STEWART

As the Veneer of Democracy Starts to Fade (nr/Mute) 1985
Mark Stewart (nr/Mute) 1987 ●

Teamed with dubmeister Adrian Sherwood, ex-Pop Grouper Stewart produces what could best be described as avant-garde reggae on **Learning to Cope with Cowardice**. Making a wide left turn past Sly and Robbie, the disc is dark and forbidding, with a plethora of ghostly, off-center sounds floating in and out of nowhere, rarely paying heed to musical convention. At times, things get gimmicky enough to resemble a demo disc for effects units, but **Cowardice** is a rewarding album with political consciousness.

Stewart's convictions push further to the fore on his second album, **As the Veneer of Democracy Starts to Fade**. This time abandoning reggae for a disorienting marriage of big-beat drums and dissonant electronics that is not unlike early Cabaret Voltaire, several tracks feature taped authoritarian voices that you probably thought only existed in your nightmares.

Mark Stewart + Maffia, Stewart's debut US release, is a compilation culled from those first two LPs (plus one non-LP cut). Well worth it for those who'd rather not shell out the money for a pair of imports. The next offering is just called **Mark Stewart**, although the Mafia members (spelling changed for some reason) are all present. The reggae is replaced by funk and stripped-down metal; while Stewart and Sherwood's aural experiments work well in this context, running out of ideas doesn't deter them from letting a track go on for seven or eight minutes. The lyrics are uncharacteristically innocuous—some are even kind of smug. The CD contains a bunch of extra remixes of cuts that went on too long in the first place. Stewart is a very talented artist (who should be mandatory listening for anyone who thinks using synthesizers only means sounding like the Human League), but those wishing to sample his work should go for the US compilation and leave this one alone. [dgs]

STICKMEN

This Is the Master Brew (Red) 1982
Get Onboard EP (Red) 1983

One of the two major demento-funk avant-noise ensembles to emerge from Philadelphia (Bunnydrums are the other), the five Stickmen ramble from Residential silliness to Contorted crypto-disco, jabbing at your ears, daring you to dance/comprehend/listen/run. Horns honk and squeal, drums pound and rattle, guitars spit and sting; vocals are equally mellifluous. This is chaos with class. [iar]

STIFF LITTLE FINGERS

Inflammable Material (Rough Trade) 1979
Nobody's Heroes (Chrysalis) 1980
Hanx! (Chrysalis) 1980
Go for It (Chrysalis) 1981
Now Then . . . (nr/Chrysalis) 1982
All the Best (nr/Chrysalis) 1983
The Peel Sessions EP (nr/Strange Fruit) 1986
Live and Loud (nr/Link) 1988
No Sleep 'Til Belfast [CD] (nr/Kaz) 1988

Belfast political punks Stiff Little Fingers began as exciting (if narrow-minded) sloganeers, led by raw-voiced singer/guitarist Jake Burns. SLF's debut (the Rough Trade label's first LP release) includes such classic protest punk as "Suspect Device," "Alternative Ulster" and "Wasted Life." The LP is generally regarded as a classic punk LP; its UK chart success was the spark that set off a second wave of new bands like the Ruts and Undertones.

By **Nobody's Heroes**, they had changed labels, acquired a new drummer and developed a bit more subtlety in their music and lyrics. The title track and "Gotta Getaway" are the highlights, but "Wait and See" audaciously thumbs a collective nose at the band's detractors and a roughed-up version of the Specials' "Doesn't Make It Alright" showed SLF to be developing interests outside punk's limited ken. Although slicker, more sedate and barely half as fiery as **Inflammable Material**, it's a solid LP. A live set, **Hanx!**, served as a premature greatest hits collection, containing powerful renditions of their best material in a well-recorded concert environment, before an enthusiastic audience.

Go for It broke Stiff Little Fingers' mold. They emerged a much different sounding band. Burns' voice is smoother and less anguished; the music, while no less energetic or committed, is more diverse and sophisticated. The title track, a memorable martial guitar instrumental, shows how far they'd come, bearing scant resemblance to their early rabble-rousing roughness. Other numbers draw on reggae stylings for variety; "Silver Lining" even utilizes prominent brass.

Now Then, their least popular but most lasting LP, continues the exploration of more accessible musical turf and is full of solid rock songs that pair energy and melody with clever guitar play. With new drummer Dolphin Taylor (ex-Tom Robinson Band) in the lineup, SLF sounds better than ever. Their political consciousness remains undiminished, but subtler and stronger lyrics effectively replace inchoate rage with on-target criticism.

Following the group's dissolution, the

retrospective double singles LP **All the Best** was released, containing 30 tracks that chronologically review their progression from raw rage to sharp power-pop. Burns later released several solo singles.

Five years later, SLF unexpectedly reformed for two UK tours (December '87 and March '88), both of which were immediate sellouts. The crowd's excited roar is the real star of **Live and Loud**, a double LP from a December London gig. After a house-on-fire version of "Alternative Ulster," SLF proves sloppier and slower than when they left off, and the choice of material clearly aims to please, with not one selection from **Now Then**. Nevertheless, the LP documents a triumphant, if brief, comeback of a once-great band ironically at the height of its popularity. The 74-minute **No Sleep 'Til Belfast** CD, taped at the same show, is essentially the same record. [iar/jr]

STING

The Dream of the Blue Turtles (A&M)
1985 ●
Bring on the Night (A&M) 1986 ●
. . . Nothing Like the Sun (A&M) 1987 ●

In 1985, with the Police on hiatus and heading for an unannounced *fin,* Sting produced a multi-platinum solo debut, **The Dream of the Blue Turtles**. Enlisting a seasoned band of top-notch black American players (Branford Marsalis, Omar Hakim, Kenny Kirkland and Darryl Jones), Sting attempted to distance himself from the common vulgarity of mere rock music by introducing jazz trappings to a new batch of songs, including "If You Love Somebody Set Them Free," "Love Is the Seventh Wave," "Fortress Around Your Heart" and the unbelievably stupid "Russians." Despite the illustrious company and the switch from bass to guitar, Sting alone is little different than Sting in the Police: his smug pretensions still dominate, and his like-it-or-not voice is still his voice.

The four sides of **Bring on the Night**—recorded at several 1985 European concerts with the same sidemen—prove Sting can work the same gimmick live. Mainly drawing on **Blue Turtles**, the LP also revamps old Police songs like "Driven to Tears," "I Burn for You" and "Demolition Man," giving them airy refinement and a measured gait. The sound quality is spectacular, the instrumental arrangements and performances dull

but unassailably accomplished. Sting's liner notes even reveal a glimmer of self-effacing humility.

The same can't be said for the effete intellectual masturbation of **Nothing Like the Sun**. (The title is possibly a punny reference to Sting's late mother—the LP is dedicated to her.) Even as the nouveau sophisticate sings "History Will Teach Us Nothing," his pedantic instincts and bulging ego inform the lyrics at every turn with political dilettantism, literary namedropping and prolix pseudo-profundities. Aided by a new collection of virtuosos and famous guests (Andy Summers, Gil Evans, Eric Clapton, Mark Knopfler and Rubén Blades, credited on one track with "Spanish"), Sting stretches a dozen delicate songs over two short discs, coming down off his horse long enough to show Jimi Hendrix fans a numbingly dull way to perform "Little Wing." A tedious, bankrupt and vacuous cavern of a record. [iar]

STINKY TOYS

Stinky Toys (nr/Polydor) 1977

The concept of a French punk band with a female singer seemed remarkably promising when Stinky Toys first began gigging around London in late 1976. A year later, this record came as a major disappointment, consisting as it does of uninspired sub-Rolling Stones rock'n'boogie with terrible vocals by Elli Medeiros. [iar]

R.J. STIPS

See *Nits.*

STOOGES

See *Iggy Pop.*

RICHARD STRANGE

The Live Rise of Richard Strange (ZE-PVC)
1980
The Phenomenal Rise of Richard Strange
(nr/Virgin) 1981
Going—Gone (Ger. Side) 1987
(nr/Nightshift) 1988

This former Doctor of Madness made two albums of a thematic work similar in concept to the rise and fall of a demagogue chronicled by the Kinks in **Preservation Act 2**, but less meticulously plotted and more thoughtful in content. Only the vocals on

Live Rise were recorded onstage at Hurrah in New York; the backing tracks had been cut previously and played back for the performance.

Aside from the obvious sound/production quality upgrade, the second (all-studio) version drops three numbers and adds five to flesh out the concept, and sports beefier back-up (stronger guitar plus some super sax work courtesy of ex-Secret Affair Dave Winthrop.) Strange emerges as a significant artist in the vein of Ziggy-era Bowie, but tougher and minus the androgyny.

The record that marked Strange's return after a number of years is more than welcome, and more than worthwhile. Originally issued in Germany and then remixed and released in the UK, Going—Gone was evidently recorded over quite some time in half a dozen studios; five of the ten tracks were produced by Dave Allen (Cure, Sisters of Mercy, etc.). James T. Ford co-wrote all but two tracks, co-produced (with Strange) a pair and handled "electronic hardware" on all but one. The 53 minutes of music ranges from mid-Eastern intrigue ("Damascus") to Poe-ish theatrics ("Fall of the House of 'U' ") to sentimental pop ("Dominoes") to ominous, churning dance-rock ("Fear Is the Engine"). The inner sleeve bears, with no elaboration, the legend "recalled to life." No kidding.

[jg]

STRANGLERS

IV Rattus Norvegicus (A&M) 1977 •
No More Heroes (A&M) 1977
Black and White (A&M) 1978 •
The Stranglers EP (Jap. UA) 1979
Live (X Cert) (nr/UA) 1979 •
The Raven (nr/UA) 1979 (EMI America) 1985
IV (IRS) 1980 •
The Meninblack (Stiff) 1981
La Folie (nr/Liberty) 1981
The Collection 1977–1982 (nr/Liberty) 1982 •
Feline (Epic) 1982
Great Lost (Jap. UA) 1983
Great Lost Continued (Jap. UA) 1983
Aural Sculpture (Epic) 1984
Off the Beaten Track (nr/Liberty) 1986
Dreamtime (Epic) 1987 •
All Live and All of the Night (Epic) 1988 •

HUGH CORNWELL + ROBERT WILLIAMS

Nosferatu (nr/Liberty) 1979

J.J. BURNEL

Euroman Cometh (nr/UA) 1979

D. GREENFIELD & J.J. BURNEL

Fire & Water (Ecoutez Vos Murs) (nr/Epic) 1983

HUGH CORNWELL

Wolf (Virgin) 1988 •

Formed in 1975, the Stranglers became enormously popular in Britain and Europe when they burst on the scene in 1977 with one of the first new wave albums, preceding both the Clash and the Sex Pistols to the shops by several months. Eleven years and no personnel changes later, the Stranglers are still going strong, churning out periodic hit singles and reasonably credible albums.

The first album was produced by Martin Rushent (who continued to work with them through 1979's live LP). Rattus Norvegicus includes both sides of the awesome debut single, "London Lady" and "(Get a) Grip (On Yourself)," as well as other blunt gonad-grabbers like "Hanging Around" and "Sometimes." The violently emotional lyrics and bitterly spat vocals are supported by Jean-Jacques Burnel's almost impossibly deep-throated bass grunts and Hugh Cornwell's slashing guitar, with contrasting jolly organ sounds by Dave Greenfield providing the only relief from otherwise relentless aggression. A great album.

No More Heroes continues in the same vein, but drops whatever hint of restraint may have been in force the first time around. Rude words and adult themes abound, with no punches pulled, from the blatant sexism of "Bring on the Nubiles" to the sarcastic attack on racism ("I Feel Like a Wog") to the suicide of a friend ("Dagenham Dave"). Despite the increased virulence, the music is even better than on the debut, introducing pop stylings that would later become a more common aspect of the Stranglers' character. No More Heroes is easily their best album.

Tricked out with gray-swirl vinyl and a limited edition bonus 45 (three tunes, including a wonderful gruff version of "Walk on By"), Black and White lacks only good songs. Except for "Nice 'n' Sleazy," most of the tracks are merely inferior rehashes of earlier work, making the LP easily forgettable.

Four gigs in '77 and '78 provided the basis for Live (X Cert). The material is all familiar, but the high-tension ambience and some choice bits of Cornwell-versus-the-audience banter make it an effective dual-function live/greatest hits album.

Borrowing a gimmick from the Rolling Stones, original copies of **The Raven** sported a 3-D cover panel. Inside, a political consciousness (first unveiled on **Black and White**) flowered, permeating songs like "Nuclear Device," "Shah Shah a Go Go" and "Genetix." Freed from the relative mundanity of exploring interpersonal relationships, the basis of most of the Stranglers' previous lyrics, **The Raven** adopts a global perspective, including the scathing put-down entitled "Dead Loss Angeles." Meanwhile, "Duchess" pioneered another new direction—catchy, level-headed melodic pop totally outside the group's general sound.

Having lacked an American label for two years, the Stranglers signed with IRS, who assembled **IV**, a mongrel consisting of half of **The Raven** and some non-LP singles, plus one totally new track, "Vietnamerica."

The Meninblack—previewed on **The Raven** (and **IV**) by a song of that name—is a hypothetical soundtrack/concept album concerning aliens with godlike powers that is at heart an attack on organized religion. There's a fair amount of non-vocal instrumental content, lots of synthesizers and other keyboards, tricky special effects and little of the Stranglers' usual thrust. Although radically different, **Meninblack** is a departure for nowhere.

Without abandoning their melodic pop explorations, the Stranglers returned to topicality and forthrightness on their next LP. **La Folie** offers a striking juxtaposition of attractive backing and scathing lyrics. Subtle, effective, mature and energetic.

Following a change in British labels, a catalogue compilation called **The Collection** appeared in 1982, including almost everything you'd want from the preceding albums, plus a couple of bonus sides from singles. A great introduction for neophytes and a record that should be of interest to anyone not owning absolutely everything the band has done.

A worldwide deal with Epic allowed the Stranglers to free themselves of past musical baggage and gave them a consistent American release schedule. The first fruit of that arrangement, **Feline**, is restrained and dignified, but also lackluster and boring. (The US edition adds the appropriately low-key 1981 single, "Golden Brown.")

Aural Sculpture is far better, containing several strong tracks: "Skin Deep," melodic rippling-organ pop that recalls "Duchess," and "Ice Queen," a simpleminded allusion to cinematic irony that has lots of neat hooks and a pleasing chorus, punctuated by brassy brass. Additionally, "Uptown" melds powerful acoustic guitar to a fractured melody and comes out like a Pete Shelley song that wasn't. Although not fully satisfying, **Aural Sculpture** has enough quality merchandise to make it a worthwhile purchase.

Another (albeit slower) byproduct of their label switch was **Off the Beaten Track**, a compilation of pre-Epic B-sides and other collectible tracks.

The Stranglers' steady march towards total blandness continues on **Dreamtime**, an unfocused time-filler that randomly touches areas that resemble Ultravox, Fleetwood Mac, Shoes, Glenn Miller and Johnny Cash with an overall lack of enthusiasm. Unfailingly accomplished, but bereft of ideas or concept, **Dreamtime** is a soporific, characterless nightmare. There's hardly an identifiable trace of the once-great band in these grooves.

The subsequent live album—recorded at three gigs in 1985 and 1987—underscores the Stranglers' paradox. Despite their recent wimpo work, onstage—banging out such classics as "London Lady," "Nice 'n' Sleazy" and "No More Heroes" with a horn section—they can convincingly revive the grungy electric power we used to know and love. The lengthy **All Live** draws heavily from recent albums; fortunately, these concert renditions improve on the songs, providing them with a little context. (Still, the notion of the Stranglers performing with acoustic guitars is not easy to accept.) Capping things off is a hearty but economical UK-hit-single studio version of the Kinks' song which the LP title paraphrases.

Solo work: Burnel's gravel-bottom bass and guttural vocals played a crucial role on the group's early, maximum-aggression records. For his own 1979 album, Burnel made a self-indulgent political statement, complete with historical maps, slogans and polemic songs like "Euromess" and "Deutschland Nicht über Alles." Using a rhythm box and playing almost all the instruments himself, Burnel invests the pedantic **Euroman Cometh** with neither musical direction nor engaging ideas, making it about as much fun as sitting through a poly sci lecture.

Teaming with bandmate Dave Greenfield, Burnel's second album "forms the mu-

553

sical basis for the film 'Ecoutez Vos Murs' by Vincent Coudanne." **Fire & Water** takes two approaches—typical soundtrack ambience, relying on doomy keyboard effects, and songs, some with vocals. "Rain & Dole & Tea" is sung in Phil Spector fashion by a multi-tracked female vocalist; "Nuclear Power (Yes Please)" actually quotes Albert Einstein in a remarkably clumsy science lesson; "Detective Privée" is a sensuously murmured French number. It's not heinously awful, but few are likely to give it repeated spins.

For *his* first extracurricular outing, Cornwell co-wrote, co-produced and co-performed an album with American drummer Robert Williams. The collaborative compositions on **Nosferatu** offer substantive lyrics, but the atonal performances sound even more dour than the early Stranglers. Two members of Devo put in guest appearances, and there are some Devo-like effects worked in but, if not for an incongruous cover of Cream's "White Room," there wouldn't be any light relief at all. While it's nice that the pair (with some assistance from Ian Underwood) has the instrumental prowess to do it all themselves, **Nosferatu** requires more from the listener than it deserves (or returns).

[iar]

See also *Lizard, Polyphonic Size, Taxi Girl, Robert Williams.*

STRAWBERRY SWITCHBLADE

Strawberry Switchblade (nr/Korova) 1985

Glaswegian glamourdolls (matching polka-dot dresses, colorful hair streamers, blood-red lipstick) Jill Bryson and Rose McDowell do all the vocals, songwriting and guitar work; seven sessionmen (and an orchestra) provide the bubblegummy electropop backing that makes lightweight creations such as "Since Yesterday" and "Secrets" so unavoidably charming and catchy. Capping a brief but colorful career, the duo went their separate ways in June of 1986.   [tr]

STRAW DOGS

See *F.U.'s.*

STRAY CATS

Stray Cats (nr/Arista) 1981
Gonna Ball (nr/Arista) 1981
Built for Speed (EMI America) 1982 ●

Rant n' Rave with the Stray Cats (EMI America) 1983
Rock Therapy (EMI America) 1986

PHANTOM, ROCKER & SLICK

Phantom, Rocker & Slick (EMI America) 1985
Cover Girl (EMI America) 1986

BRIAN SETZER

The Knife Feels Like Justice (EMI America) 1986
Live Nude Guitars (EMI Manhattan) 1988 ●

Disenchanted with modern new wave, Brian Setzer bagged his trendy New York group, the Bloodless Pharaohs, formed a rockabilly trio, and abandoned Long Island for London. There, the Stray Cats wowed 'em with exotic American appeal, spearheading a rockabilly revival that naturally became absorbed into new wave. Is there a moral here?

Unlike some neo-rockabillies, the Stray Cats don't care about painstaking reconstructions of moldy old recordings. They diddle around with non-originals, while Setzer's own early songs tackle topical events ("Storm the Embassy," "Rumble in Brighton"). Setzer's extended guitar soloing sometimes seems descended from jazz rather than rockabilly, but there's no faulting his skill or the group's spirit.

Gonna Ball, released about nine months after **Stray Cats**, finds the band moving into R&B turf. Musical veterans like Ian Stewart and Lee Allen help fill out the sound; a strong producer, like Dave Edmunds on the first album, would have helped even more. Setzer is a better guitarist than singer, and some of **Gonna Ball**'s songs resemble the music rockabilly was revolting against.

Combining the best of both British albums and adding one new cut, **Built for Speed** is a good introduction to the band. The US, generally not known for humoring nostalgic musical throwbacks, sent it into the Top 5. The Stray Cats must have been doing something right.

If chart success is the yardstick, they continued to do that something on **Rant n' Rave**, the trio's first identical and simultaneous US/UK release, and also their last record together. Again produced by Dave Edmunds, the effervescent rock'n'roll teen rebellion of "(She's) Sexy + 17" leads the stylistic parade (with one exception—the beautiful soul ballad, "I Won't Stand in Your Way," with vocal backing by Fourteen Karat Soul) and the rest of the record falls neatly in line, recalling Eddie Cochran, Carl Perkins and the whole rockabilly-into-early-rock'n' roll era. Sure it's formulaic and derivative as hell, but timelessly enthralling and truly entertaining as well.

The Stray Cats broke up in late 1984; while his bandmates teamed up with guitarist Earl Slick and issued a run-of-the-mill rock album the following year, Brian Setzer worked with the Honey Drippers and released a strong, varied solo album in early 1986 that further illustrates his multi-dimensional talent. The record encompasses unembellished frontier rock ("The Knife Feels Like Justice"), wistful balladry ("Boulevard of Broken Dreams"), Cochranesque rock'n' roll ("Radiation Ranch"), soulful power pop (the autobiographical "Chains Around Your Heart"), rock bluegrass ("Barbwire Fence") and lots more. With tasteful restraint, Setzer checks his wilder instincts, avoiding showy guitar work, verbal grandstanding or self-parody; maturity and subtlety are the two most unexpected welcome components of **The Knife Feels Like Justice**.

In 1986, Phantom and Rocker made **Cover Girl**, an improved—credit producer Pete Solley and generally better original material—but equally pointless and bland second album with Slick. Then, prompted by a contract they wanted out of, the threesome quickly cut a Stray Cats reunion LP, **Rock Therapy**, and redeemed themselves handily. With Setzer back at their helm, the rhythm section sounds good as new; amazingly, the fine record picks up exactly where **Rant n' Rave** left off. Setzer's old-fashioned originals blend seamlessly with fine borrowings from appropriate sources (Buddy Holly, Chuck Berry, Gene Vincent, Charlie Feathers) and contributions from his bandmates. (The only misstep is "Broken Man," his clumsy attempt to write and play bluegrass.) The spare self-production gives the record a comfortably loose feel; the exuberant air of playing for fun, free of commercial considerations, adds a magical dimension.   [si/iar]

PETE STRIDE/JOHN PLAIN
See *Lurkers*.

STRIPES
The Stripes (Ger. CBS) 1980
German post-Blondie rock of the most rudimentary variety, the Stripes take better

to updated Gidgetude than fake petulance, telling virtually the same joke 13 times with only minor variations (notwithstanding the two American-written tunes, one by Hall and Oates, no less). Kicker: the quartet's singer and prime asset went on to earn much greater fame a few years later in a far-superior band bearing her (nick)name, Nena.   [jg]

JOE STRUMMER
Walker (Virgin Movie Music) 1987 •
VARIOUS ARTISTS
Permanent Record (Epic) 1988 •
Having discovered that the Clash without Mick Jones was not a viable proposition, and that Big Audio Dynamite wasn't big enough for the both of them, Joe Strummer turned instead to solo film soundtrack work. In 1986, Strummer began working for director Alex Cox, creating "Love Kills" (the theme song for *Sid and Nancy*), starring in *Straight to Hell* (1987) and contributing to its soundtrack.

Strummer also did a credible job scoring and producing the mock-Latin music for Cox's *Walker*. Strummer sings the narrative "Unknown Immortal" and "Tennessee Rain" in likably rustic folk fashion, adding mostly spare, relaxing acoustic instrumentals that use *guitarron,* marimba, horns and piano to evoke the Central American locale.

The soundtrack album of *Permanent Record,* a 1988 (non-Cox) flick about teen suicide, features an assortment of bands (Stranglers, Godfathers, Lou Reed) on one side. Joe Strummer & the Latino Rockabilly War (a small band including Zander Schloss, who also worked on **Walker**) fill the rest with four energetic vocal songs (funk/folk-rock/R&B) and an instrumental theme, proving that the old Clashman hasn't lost his touch.   [iar]

STUMP
Mud on a Colon EP (nr/Ron Johnson) 1985
Quirk Out EP (nr/Stuff) 1986
The Peel Sessions EP (nr/Strange Fruit) 1987
A Fierce Pancake (Ensign-Chrysalis) 1988 •
This wacky British quartet plays Beefheart-inspired avant-pop with good-naturedly surreal lyrics. The low-budget **Mud on a Colon** is shambolic and unfocused, with little to distinguish it from scads of less-talented UK indie combos. But the subsequent **Quirk Out**, smartly produced by Hugh Jones, is a delight, channeling the band's

boundless energy into a more disciplined and rewarding direction. Highlights include the hiccupy Yank-bashing caricature "Buffalo," the quasi-vulgar litany-of-bodily-functions "Everything in Its Place" and the uncharacteristically melodic, introspective "Our Fathers."

A Fierce Pancake (the US version reprises "Buffalo") strips away still more surface kookiness, revealing some memorable melodies and genuinely inventive instrumental work (particularly from guitarist Chris Salmon). And, while vocalist Mick Lynch's absurdist lyrics are as full of puns and non sequiturs as ever, they're also cogent statements—as in "Chaos," which bemoans Britain's sinking-ship economy via a metaphorical sea chantey, and "Bone," which builds a convincing case against human evolution.

[hd]

STYLE COUNCIL

A Paris EP (nr/Polydor) 1983
Introducing the Style Council EP (Polydor) 1983 ●
Café Bleu (nr/Polydor) 1984
My Ever Changing Moods (Geffen) 1984
Our Favourite Shop (nr/Polydor) 1985
Internationalists (Geffen) 1985
The Lodgers EP (nr/Polydor) 1985
Home & Abroad (Geffen) 1986 ●
The Cost of Loving (Polydor) 1987 ●
Confessions of a Pop Group (Polydor) 1988 ●

After six years spent growing up in public with the Jam, Paul Weller felt the need to function within a more relaxed, less restrictive framework. That in mind, he enlisted the services of former Merton Parkas/Dexys keyboard player Mick Talbot to form the Style Council, with all other needed instruments to be supplied by guests. Promising that the band would be nothing if not unpredictable, the duo then proceeded to issue a single, "Speak Like a Child," that sounded much like where the Jam left off. Another single, the funky "Money-Go-Round," preceded the four-song A Paris EP, the sleeve of which shows the pair carefully posed with the Eiffel Tower in the background, looking like a Giorgio Armani ad. Highlighted by the catchy "Long Hot Summer," the material is light, breezy summertime soul, owing as much to Weller's pretensions of some sort of continental flair as it does to obvious referents like Curtis Mayfield.

The American Introducing the Style Council combined both singles with the contents of the UK EP, although some of the numbers were remixed. Not released in England, it sold better there as an import than it did in the country of its issue.

Café Bleu and My Ever Changing Moods are equivalent LPs with slightly different tracks. (The US version replaces two minor cuts with the UK hit, "A Solid Bond in Your Heart.") A scrambled assortment of soul, bebop, cocktail jazz, rap and whatever else Weller could think of, it's simply too schizophrenic to be a good album, although it does show integrity—this band is unlikely to be guided by public demand. "Headstart for Happiness" and "The Paris Match" (this time featuring Everything but the Girl) are improved versions of previously-released material; "My Ever Changing Moods" gave Weller the first US Top 30 single of his career.

The Style Council's second album was also released in alternate trans-Atlantic forms. Internationalists has a different cover than Our Favourite Shop and omits the latter's title song. Though still rather varied, the album is much more coherent than its predecessor. There are still clinkers: "The Stand Up Comic's Instructions" is clever but awkward, and the rhumba-shuffle of "All Gone Away" would sound at home in a dentist's office. However, tracks like "Walls Come Tumbling Down!," "Come to Milton Keynes" and "Boy Who Cried Wolf" more than tip the scales in the record's favor. As ever, it's undeniable that Weller means every word, but the continuing trend towards a crystalline, antiseptic sound is unfortunate.

It was obvious that the *Absolute Beginners* film was not going to be released without a contribution from Weller, so the band rewrote "With Everything to Lose" from the second album (itself already a direct lift from "Long Hot Summer") and came up with "Have You Ever Had It Blue." Shortly thereafter, the Style Council issued a live album, Home & Abroad, a squeaky-clean, all-too-accurate collection of songs drawn from both albums as well as singles. (The UK CD adds two tracks.) Considering that the Style Council often put live version on their flipsides (see The Lodgers EP), this set seems to be mostly for those who absolutely must own everything Weller puts his name to.

By the time The Cost of Loving was released, both Weller's demi-god status in

Britain and the Style Council's significance had plunged. The LP—originally issued (limited quantities) in the UK as a set of two 12-inch 45s—is nothing more than a collection of redundant, forgettable jazz/soul trifles, played very professionally but bloodlessly, with arrangements that resemble Chicago (the band) more than anything else. The first album of Weller's career to fall completely on its face comes after a lengthy drought of particularly meritorious undertakings. Ousted by Morrissey as young England's favorite male pop icon, his creativity seems to be waning. Can a Jam reunion be far off? [dgs]

POLY STYRENE
See *X-Ray Spex.*

STYRENES
See *Paul Marotta.*

SUBTONES
Boys Want Fun (Ger. Teldec) 1986

Germany's biggest " '60s band" is a Berlin trio which blends Who, Kinks, Hollies and perhaps a dash of Searchers into a seamless sound that could have come straight off a British '60s anthology. (Although the Subtones admittedly have sonic technology on their side.) **Boys Want Fun** is cute and has a big beat, even if the lyrics are a bit sappy. A super-schmaltz track and an overextended live version of the Who's "Circles" are the only turkeys, but conveniently they're both side-closers. [jg]

SUBURBAN LAWNS
Suburban Lawns (IRS) 1981
Baby EP (IRS) 1983
SU TISSUE
Salon de Musique (Adversity) 1982

This eccentric California quintet made a minor splash in 1979 with an independent single, "Gidget Goes to Hell," a spirited, twisted variation on the '60s *Gidget* movies. But the group's jittery industrial pop comes off highly ordinary on **Suburban Lawns**, a sub-Devo mesh of hiccupping vocals, angular tunes with tiresome stop-start rhythms and a high, weedy guitar/organ sound.

Reduced to the quartet of Su Tissue, Frankie Ennui, Chuck Roast and a bizarrely named bassist, the Lawns returned with a much better outlook on **Baby**. Richard Mazda produced the five songs, including the alluring "Flavor Crystals" and a batch of muscular syncopated dance creations that evade rhythmic pursuit.

Following the group's dissolution, Tissue recorded a solo album of piano and voice and played a small but memorably mousey part, as Peggy Dillman, in the movie *Something Wild.* [df/iar]

SUBURBAN STUDS
Slam (nr/Pogo) 1978

Laboring through these 17 tracks of mostly stereotypical punk thrash, you might begin to suspect the Studs were a put-up job. Yet buried in the midst of **Slam** is a diamond in the rough: "I Hate School" sounds like a hybrid of the Sex Pistols and the Heartbreakers having a rave-up. Then you begin to notice other flashes of dumb cunning . . . [jg]

SUBURBS
The Suburbs EP (Twin/Tone) 1978
In Combo (Twin/Tone) 1980
Credit in Heaven (Twin/Tone) 1981
Dream Hog EP (Twin/Tone) 1982 (Mercury) 1983
Love Is the Law (Mercury) 1983
Suburbs (A&M) 1986

One of Minneapolis' major musical resources, the Suburbs maintained the same lineup from their vinyl debut (and the first single on the extraordinary Twin/Tone label), via a 1978 nine-song 7-inch red vinyl EP of above-average punkish rock'n'roll, to the band's 1987 dissolution.

With their first album, the Suburbs began displaying signs of incipient greatness; singer Beej Chaney's ominous, neurotic calm providing perfect counterpoint for the band's enthusiastic playing; guitarist B.C. Allen adding tension with scrabbly rhythm and violent lead. The songs unpredictably explore real-world subjects like "Hobnobbin with the Executives" and "Cig Machine."

After demonstrating what they could do on **In Combo**, the Suburbs proved how well they could do it with the double-album, **Credit in Heaven**, a slickly-delivered opus that refines the band's approach and fairly bubbles over with creative concepts, great playing and bizarre songs. The Chaney comparisons to Bryan Ferry—cool in the eye of the storm—are amplified by his blasé delivery, but the music—powered by Hugo Klaers' ultra-busy drumming—is something else, blending cool funk with nervous disco and jazzy aplomb. A highly recommended stunner, regardless of religious persuasion.

Things heated up for the Suburbs in '82, when they started attracting significant club play for a 12-inch of the song "Waiting." They included that track on the **Dream Hog** EP (in original and extended remix form), along with two sharp new white-funk tunes (one of them about dance music) plus a restrained near-ballad. When they signed to Mercury, the label reissued it before sending the 'Burbs into the studio to cut a new album.

The result of that maneuver, **Love Is the Law**, is easily their best vinyl chapter, a powerful and personality-laden set of songs that incorporate more rock than usual, as well as horns and some of their most offbeat lyrics ever. "Rattle My Bones" is brilliantly demento bebop; the superb "Love Is the Law" has the most memorable hook in the repertoire; "Hell A" took one of its verses from a Los Angeles phone booth scrawl. **Love Is the Law** is a great, great album.

Making the probably inevitable Prince connection via the production guidance of Robert Brent (better known as Revolution drummer Bobby Z), the Suburbs came roaring back three long years later with another powerful record, albeit one whose character is less firmly held in its musical approach than its lyrics. Gone is the antsy, skittish urgency of yore; **Suburbs** is utterly listenable (but not overwhelmingly unique), with equally subtle nods to both the band's traditional crypto-funk and Prince's happy-feet dance rock. Thankfully, Chaney and keyboardist Chan Poling's nastily humorous lyrics—notably on "Every Night's a Friday Night" (. . . in hell), "America Sings the Blues" and "Superlove"—are as clever as ever.

That, unfortunately, was the end of the Suburbs. [iar]

SUBWAY SECT

See *Vic Godard & the Subway Sect, JoBoxers*.

NIKKI SUDDEN

Waiting on Egypt (nr/Abstract) 1982 + 1986
The Bible Belt (nr/Flicknife) 1983

JACOBITES: NIKKI SUDDEN & DAVE KUSWORTH

Jacobites (nr/Glass) 1984 ●
Shame for the Angels EP (nr/Pawn Hearts) 1985
Robespierre's Velvet Basement (nr/Glass) 1985 ●
Pin Your Heart to Me EP (nr/Glass) 1985
Lost in a Sea of Scarves (Ger. What's So Funny About) 1985
When the Rain Comes EP (nr/Glass) 1986
The Ragged School (Twin/Tone) 1986
Fortune of Fame (nr/Glass) 1988 ●

NIKKI SUDDEN AND THE JACOBITES

Texas (nr/Creation) 1986
The Last Bandit EP (nr/Creation) 1986
Dead Men Tell No Tales (nr/Creation) 1987

NIKKI SUDDEN & ROWLAND S. HOWARD

Kiss You Kidnapped Charabanc (Creation-Relativity) 1987

DAVE KUSWORTH

The Bounty Hunters (Swordfish-Texas Hotel) 1987

BOUNTY HUNTERS

Wives, Weddings and Roses (Kaleidoscope Sound-Texas Hotel) 1988

After dissolving Swell Maps, singer/guitarist Nikki Sudden released two solo albums, **Waiting on Egypt** and **The Bible Belt**, which basically offered more of what that band had been doing. But then he formed the Jacobites—a core trio of Sudden, guitarist Dave Kusworth and ex-Swell Maps drummer Epic Soundtracks (Sudden's brother), plus assorted friends—and began to sing an altogether different tune. With Kusworth co-writing the songs, Sudden promptly rid himself of all references to his previous career.

The Jacobites' records all have a similar romantic format: seductive acoustic guitar, a thumping muffled rhythm section and Sudden's whining, Dylanesque vocals. (Imagine a folky Johnny Thunders growing up in the English countryside and learning to play guitar by listening to "Knockin' on Heaven's Door.") The group pillages idols like the Stones, Neil Young and Dylan with such loving devotion—as on "Fortune of Fame" (**Shame for the Angels**), "Where Rivers End" (**Robespierre's Velvet Basement**) and others—that their motives transcend any appearance of carbon-copy revivalism.

Lost in a Sea of Scarves contains out-takes from Robespierre's Velvet Basement, which was to have been a double album. The Ragged School is an American compilation of Jacobites tracks from most of the preceding records.

Switching his label affiliation to Creation and parting company with Kusworth, Sudden released Texas, relying on his brother and bassist Duncan Sibbald for primary assistance. A violinst and ex-Birthday Party guitarist Rowland S. Howard make notable appearances, giving Sudden's languid, atmospheric Southwesternisms the extra color they need to prevent sameness. (Two notable style-busting exceptions are the Velvetsy "Glass Eye" and "Such a Little Girl," both winning piles of melodic distortion.) The Last Bandit EP pairs two album tracks with two others.

Having finished Texas, Sudden returned to the studio a month later to begin work on the spare Dead Men Tell No Tales, which has almost no percussion and very little accompaniment of any sort for his guitar, bouzouki and dulcimer strumming. Howard and Sibbald again put in appearances and the cover still credits the Jacobites, but it's basically a solo album, and an underwhelming one at that. Only "Girl with the Wooden Leg" makes a powerful impression, as Howard's crazed guitar noises contrast with Sudden's maudlin balladeering.

Howard takes a more prominent role on Kiss You Kidnapped Charabanc, another largely drum-free record that drifts along aimlessly at quarter-speed. Nikki does the singing and Rowland provides most of the instrumentation; the duo split the songwriting. (The following year, German Rough Trade combined Kiss You Kidnapped Charabanc and Dead Men Tell No Tales into a single CD release.) By this point, it's obvious that Sudden is too productive for his own good: the improvisations and drawn-out songs are uneven and inconsistently worth releasing. Album after album of roughly the same contents, despite different emphases and alternate player permutations, leave one with the impression that Sudden can't tell the difference between quality and nonsense, and is in desperate need of the guiding hand of a producer, or at least someone else to hold the studio keys. He's unquestionably talented, but not as much as he evidently reckons.

Kusworth lay low for a while after leaving the Jacobites in mid-'86, spending his time recording a solo album (also credited to the Bounty Hunters, the quartet he leads) which was released the following year. Marriage is on Dave's mind on The Bounty Hunters, as several of the songs—which interlock to form a long, vague romantic narrative—make reference to weddings, rings, wives and other such symptoms of betrothal. Showing an affinity for the folky side of Johnny Thunders, Kusworth's thin voice is no dynamic instrument, but it serves the material, as do the energetic arrangements of acoustic guitar and electric rock rhythms.   [ag/iar]

See also *Barracudas.*

SUGARCUBES

life's too good (Elektra) 1988 ●

Not since the Jesus and Mary Chain made their initial assault a few years back has a band come out of nowhere to generate as much excitement and acclaim as Iceland's Sugarcubes. Drumming (by Siggi, ex-Theyr) and guitar work point to such influences as Joy Division and Siouxsie and the Banshees and, in more delicate moments (such as "Birthday," their debut single), bits of the Cocteau Twins. They also make very interesting use of an electronically mutated trumpet and sound effects. But the Sugarcubes' main instrument is the amazing voice of lead singer Björk. A petite young woman who could easily pass for about 16, her range of pitch is only surpassed by her range of emotions: one moment she's a little girl soprano, the very next she's growling like a crazed animal about to go for the kill. Trumpeter Einar Örn handles some of the vocals with awkwardly accented English (an occasional flipside or remix is in the native tongue), but Björk's background vocals usually steal the show on those tracks.

What she sings is noteworthy as well: Freud would have a field day with the childhood/sexual metaphors of the lyrics, most of which are more interesting than those from bands whose first language is English. life's too good is no letdown from the initial 45s (both are on the LP), with 11 cuts that retain a signature sound but avoid redundancy. Iceland is a country whose little-known rock scene has produced a number of rather interesting, if not earth-shattering bands. This one is the real thing.

"Birthday" and "Cold Sweat" were also issued as CD singles. The CD of the album adds six extra tracks—some in Icelandic—

including an incredible alternate version of "Deus." [dgs]

SUICIDAL TENDENCIES

Suicidal Tendencies (Frontier) 1983 ●
Join the Army (Caroline) 1987 ●
How Will I Laugh Tomorrow When I Can't
  Even Smile Today (Epic) 1988 ●

Every once in a while, a band previously lost in genre mire emerges from the crowd ineffably different and better than their competition. Suicidal Tendencies—a Venice, California quartet voted Worst and Best New Band in *Flipside* magazine's 1982/83 readers' poll—could have been just another hardcore band, but they're not. The first LP benefits enormously from clear production (by Glen E. Friedman), tight, careful playing—fast and blurry in spots, but never indistinct—and singer/lyricist Mike Muir, whose intelligence and forceful personality invest songs like "Fascist Pig" and "Suicide's an Alternative" with wit and wisdom. Suicidal Tendencies' other strength is a facility for sudden tempo shifts, a gambit best used on the great "Institutionalized," a half-sung, half-recited alienation number which powerfully encapsulates all the punk sociology of *Repo Man* and *Suburbia* in four minutes. Don't miss this one.

While the first album sold unbelievable quantities for an independent release, Suicidal Tendencies—armed with an enormous, vehement national following—took their time organizing a new lineup and recording their next record. Following the general hardcore drift towards metal, Muir, stalwart bassist/co-writer Louiche Mayorga and two new bandmembers straddle styles on the Motorhead-ish **Join the Army**, embracing ominous war-pigs power and blistering crap-guitar solos, but cutting it with sudden shifts into hyperspeed (or halfspeed for moshing), punk vocals and a continuing dedication to skate-punk culture. The sound isn't great, but the playing and energy, plus Muir's exceptionally strong singing, makes the LP worthy of the band's exalted status. [iar]

SUICIDE

Suicide (Red Star) 1977 + 1981
24 Minutes Over Brussels (nr/Bronze) 1978
1/2 Alive [tape] (ROIR) 1981
Ghost Riders [tape] (ROIR) 1986

ALAN VEGA AND MARTIN REV

Suicide (ZE) 1980

A mainstay of the New York rock underground since the early 1970s, the two-man Suicide (prefiguring Soft Cell, Blancmange, Tears for Fears, etc.) mixed Alan Vega's blues-styled vocals and Marty Rev's synthesizer, originally a broken-down Farfisa organ they couldn't afford to repair. Escaping the dingy clubs of Manhattan, Suicide went on to cause riots in Europe while on tour supporting Elvis Costello. They provided a soundtrack for Werner Fassbinder's film *In a Year of Thirteen Moons* and always provoked extreme reactions. Often confrontational in nature, they produced an unequalled, obsessively American electronic music that scarcely resembles—but undoubtedly influenced—other singer/keyboard outfits.

Suicide (1977) is a nearly perfect relic of mid-'70s Manhattan attitudes, a portrait of society grinding down to self-destruction. Rev's powerful minimalist repetition catapults Vega's pained and constantly cracking voice through indictments of Vietnam mentality ("Ghost Rider"), broken romance ("Cheree," "Girl") and holocausts both public and personal ("Rocket USA," "Frankie Teardrop"). Stolid and restrained, the record simmers with repressed emotion and excellent, unusual performances. Four years later, the LP was reissued with "I Remember," "Keep Your Dreams" and "96 Tears" added, as well as a flexi-disc of Suicide live in Brussels, taken from a 1978 authorized live bootleg. Recommended, though clearly not for everyone.

Suicide, the confusingly titled Vega/Rev LP, was produced by a fan, the Cars' Ric Ocasek, who smoothed the sound out to an almost socially acceptable level. (These same sessions produced the duo's zenith, 1980's anthemic "Dream Baby Dream," issued as a 12-inch single.) Rev's use of electronics had grown more subtle and complex, while Vega's vocals seem tethered and uneasy. "Harlem" is a stunning mélange of urban despair and tortured musicianship, and is the album's most affecting number.

The tape-only **Half-Alive** pairs one side of live material and one side of studio outtakes. Released soon after Suicide's dissolution, it offers no breakthroughs, but stands simply as a tribute to a fine, underrated band. The live side demonstrates how much fun Suicide was in concert, despite sloppiness and

Vega's antagonism toward audiences. **Ghost Riders**, another live cassette, chronicles the pair's 1981 tenth anniversary gig in Minneapolis with clear sound and a convincing performance. [sg]

See also *Martin Rev, Alan Vega.*

SUICIDE COMMANDOS

Make a Record (Blank) 1978
The Commandos Commit Suicide Dance
    Concert (Twin/Tone) 1979

Minneapolis' Suicide Commandos were a pre-hardcore punk trio with a big local following. Signed in 1977 (along with Pere Ubu) to Phonogram's short-lived but prescient subsidiary, Blank, they proved that New York wasn't the only launching site for new wave groups, and helped further the notion that records need not sound like Pink Floyd to be entertaining. In fact, **Make a Record** is surprisingly good, thanks largely to guitarist Chris Osgood. The live last-gig limited edition concert document contains another dose of convincing rock'n'roll with energy and enthusiasm. [iar]

See also *Beat Rodeo.*

ANDY SUMMERS

XYZ (MCA) 1987 ●
Mysterious Barricades (Private Music)
    1988 ●

As the Police's mostly mute guitarist, Summers—whose long and winding career stretches back to 1963 and includes stints in both the Soft Machine and the Animals, not to mention sessions for Neil Sedaka—was recognized as one of rock's most versatile and venerated sidemen. Additionally, he asserted his independence by cutting two artsy instrumental records with Robert Fripp. But whatever could have possessed him—hubris? jealousy? a bet?—to write lyrics and *sing* on a solo album? **XYZ**'s laughable first line: "Some sex can be better when it's on the phone." Summer's froggy, unmusical croak overshadows his extraordinary musicianship, making him sound far less talented than we know him to be.

Prudently, **Mysterious Barricades** is an all-instrumental album done in continuation of Summers' partnership with co-producer/keyboardist David Hentschel. [iar]

See also *Fripp + Summers.*

SUN AND THE MOON

See *Chameleons (UK).*

SUN CITY GIRLS

Sun City Girls (Placebo) 1984
Grotto of Miracles (Placebo) 1986
Horse Cock Phepner (Placebo) 1987

They may not be girls, but this elusive trio does live in a place known as Sun City, Arizona. (It's a bit northwest of Phoenix.) Like the Meat Puppets, another bizarre band from that part of the world, they seem to have been out in the heat too long. Their hallucinatory debut album contains 17 sketchy tracks (including the brilliantly titled "Your Bible Set off My Smoke Alarm") that range from nerve-wracking noise instrumentals to avant-jazz horn fantasies to actual songs with lyrics and seemingly conscious arrangements. "Uncle Jim" offers a ranting monologue with jazz guitar and sax; "My Painted Tomb" is a raga with toy piano; "Metaphors in a Mixmaster" presents free-form guitar improvisation. Bewildering, aggravating and intriguing.

Grotto of Miracles continues the group's unconventional adventures, carrying them out of the noise grotto into the same sort of airy guitar instrumentals the Puppets favor: well-rehearsed Wes Montgomery threads and textures. (The Girls, however, don't evince any particular taste for local stylistic traditions.) The demented lyrical concepts and offbeat musical accessories (trumpet, cello, antelope bells, chimes, temple blocks, etc.) preclude any overall resemblance between the two groups, but openminded fans of the Puppets should find things of interest here. **Grotto of Miracles** is an ethnic stew that shows enormous creative growth.

After that relatively restrained album, it's back to perverse wild-eyed politicized insanity on **Horse Cock Phepner**. Forget jazzy guitar breakdowns, this record concentrates on tuneless chants and foul-mouthed expositions, performed over backing that varies from promising acoustic folk to conscientiously ugly noise. The maniacally vulgar "Nancy Reagan" is spoken over tribal chanting and drumming; Tuli Kupferberg's "C.I.A. Man" (with new lyrics by the SCG) uses only monotonic piano and a simple drum beat for accompaniment; the lengthy "Without Compare" is a collection of simultaneous conversations, a grisly refrain, a speech about history, an all-play-at-once bridge, a news report and a chaotic fade. Yeuch! Amid such delicacies (and worse—trust me), "Esta Susan en Casa?" provides the neatest alternative: a brief but convincing flash of rock salsa. [iar]

SUNNY JIM BAND
Maximum Pain (Ger. Vertigo) 1980
Jay (Ger. Vertigo) 1982

This quartet consists of two Brits, a Frenchman and a Dutchman based in Cologne who once contracted (but wound up not going) to tour Iron Curtain countries. They play tight, assured, angular rock'n'roll and reggae, with smart-enough arrangements and some above-average lyrical ideas. Unfortunately, like their melodies, the words are too often half-baked, not quite complete or satisfying.

Despite its title, the first album suffers from stiffness, as if they're unwilling to let go. The second LP, produced by Steve Nye (Roxy Music, Japan), loosens them up a bit. Although the hooks are again generally a hair short of the mark, excerpts would make an eyebrow-raising EP. [jg]

SURF M.C.'S
Surf or Die (Profile) 1987 ●

I'm as convinced as anyone about the salutary effects of stylistic miscegenation in music, and I'm all for the geographical spread of local phenomena, but some experiments just don't work out. This wholesome California group attempts to make an amusing gimmick out of rapping about beaches and boards, but their pathetic sub-Beasties stab at urban delivery and East Coast slang has all the uncomprehending conviction of a Steve Allen recitation. It's amazing that Surf or Die was released by a label that most assuredly knows better. [iar]

SURF TRIO
Almost Summer (Voxx) 1986

The Surf Trio thank their idols—Link Wray, Jon and the Nightriders, Brian Wilson, the Ventures and the Ramones—for inspiration on Almost Summer, and those names go a long way towards describing the Oregon quartet's joyful sound. Facility for Ramonesy '60s melody-punk, surf-twang, beach pop and garage-rock makes each track in this sampler of delightful retro styles a different kind of magic. Exemplary and refreshing. [iar]

FODAY MUSA SUSO
See Mandingo Griot Society.

SUSSMAN LAWRENCE
See Peter Himmelman.

BOBBY SUTLIFF
See Windbreakers.

SWA
Your Future if You Have One (SST) 1985
Sex Dr. (SST) 1986
XCIII (SST) 1987

Damaged-era Black Flag bassist Dukowski now leads this LA power-rock quartet which unselfconsciously draws on the sound of the '70s for likable, if unchallenging, original mainstreamisms that stop well short of metal. Former Flag bandmate Greg Ginn produced the hard-driving, intelligent debut album which revolves around Merrill Ward, a singer who can really project.

Sex Dr., produced by Dukowski and company, refines the concept on a batch of new tunes, penned mostly by Ward. The lyrics are generally presentable without saying much; tight group playing lends the music—which favors Steppenwolf a bit—conviction and dignity.

Replacing guitarist Richard Ford with Sylvia Juncosa (who simultaneously leads her own band, To Damascus), SWA took a radically different route on the third LP, which exchanges the precisely focused rock for a noisier, chaotic smear of aggression. Despite spots of MC5-ish excitement ("Optimist," for instance), XCIII is a disappointment, with SWA's best feature—Ward's voice—partially blunted by Dukowski's blurry production and Juncosa's ceaseless garbage riffing. [iar]
See also To Damascus.

SWANS
Filth (Neutral) 1983
Cop (nr/K.422) 1984
Raping a Slave EP (Homestead) 1985
Greed (PVC) 1986
Holy Money (PVC) 1986
Children of God (Caroline) 1987 ●
Love Will Tear Us Apart EP (Caroline) 1988

SKIN

Blood, Women, Roses (nr/Product Inc.) 1987
Shame, Humility, Revenge (nr/Product Inc.) 1988 ●

Play the Velvet Underground's "Sister Ray" at half-speed—go ahead, do it—and you've got Swans plus a sense of humor and the possibility that, if you just adjust the speed control, everything will get good. Take away the sense of humor and the speed control, and you've got Swans. In all probability, you've also got either a high threshold for crunching pain or a splitting headache. Well, that's Swans: downtown New York artics, friends of the infinitely more imaginative Sonic Youth. Swans trudge through dragging tempos, 2/2 meters and low frequency mush, all the while howling about alienation and despair. Listening to their records isn't like banging your head against a wall; it's like banging your head against the side of a swimming pool—underwater.

Filth is all that it promises to be: squalor without catharsis (now there's an LP title!) The group is so conceptually strapped to its sludge m.o. that this album is actually more formulaic than Kajagoogoo. **Cop** features new album and song titles, a new label, a trimmed-down lineup and new cover art. What it lacks are new ideas. *Boom.* Crunch. *Boom.* Crunch. Where Sonic Youth makes great music that's painful to listen to, Swans offer pain without reason.

The 1985 **Raping a Slave** EP offers few changes in the actual sounds they incorporate, but makes things more interesting by using them in unexplored ways. A marked improvement over previous discs, and a good lead-in to **Greed**, where everything finally jells. New weapons are added to the Swans' arsenal, along with a variety of seemingly inconceivable approaches: the harrowing "Fool" is almost all piano and (sung!) vocals; several songs feature female background singers (serving more as an instrument than harmony). The closing "Money Is Flesh" has a two-note trumpet part played ad nauseum. Each track is a complete work in itself, enthralling and narcotizing.

Holy Money is more or less a twin to **Greed**, virtually identical in cover art and musical approach (the two LPs sandwich a great single, "Time Is Money (Bastard)"). Instrumentation is back to basic guitar, bass and drums, but the introduction of female vocalist Jarboe on "You Need Me" provides an effective counterpoint to leader Michael Gira's basso profundo. The lineup was in a state of flux; eight different performers appear on this album.

Children of God is Swans' finest moment, a double album of pure, primitive, naked emotion, but not all presented the same way. Sure, some cuts pound the listener into submission, but others (generally those sung by Jarboe), are delicate, gentle ballads, finally giving the more thunderous numbers a point of reference. The lyrics deal with religious obsession, submission and suffering—they are stated simply yet remain open to all sorts of interpretations. A unique and powerful vision.

The 1988 EP contains two renditions of the Joy Division chestnut, as well as alternate versions of two **Children of God** tracks.

Skin is a spinoff band of Gira and Jarboe. Their first release as a duo is **Blood, Women, Roses**, an LP dominated by Jarboe's avant-garde torch songs. The overall tone is one of quiet passion, with mostly acoustic instruments, but the occasional drum thunder will remind the listener of just who these folks are. Highlights include the mostly vocal and percussion "Come Out" and an impressive reading of Gershwin's "The Man I Love." Swans, yes, but they'll always be one of rock's ugliest ducklings.

The compact disc of **Shame, Humility, Revenge**, Skin's second sortie, contains a rendition of "I Want to Be Your Dog."

[jl/dgs]

MATTHEW SWEET

Inside (Columbia) 1986

Interesting list of musical connections for the ex-Oh-OK guitarist's solo debut, produced in NYC, Boston, London and LA by Stephen Hague, Scott Litt, Don Dixon and Dave Allen, among others. Sweet co-wrote three songs with Pal Shazar (ex-Slow Children) plus one each with Jules Shear and Adele Bertei; performers include Aimee Mann ('Til Tuesday), John McGeoch (ex-Magazine, Banshees), two Bangles, Jody Harris, Mike Campbell (Petty's Heartbreakers), Valerie Simpson (Ashford and . . .), Bernie Worrell, Chris Stamey, Fred Maher and Anton Fier—again, among others. (Sweet was part of a 1987 Golden Palominos mini-tour.)

For all of this impressive name-dropping, Sweet plays nearly everything himself on two tracks, and manages to maintain a consistent feel throughout the LP. It's a bit like R.E.M. and early dB's doing sincere power-pop with keyboards. While most of Side Two is simply good, four of the five tracks on Side One are excellent. [jg]

RACHEL SWEET

Fool Around (Stiff-Columbia) 1978
Protect the Innocent (Stiff-Columbia) 1980
. . . And Then He Kissed Me (Columbia) 1981
Blame It on Love (Columbia) 1982

The proverbial little girl with the big voice, Rachel Sweet burst out of Akron, Ohio in her early teens under the watchful eye of producer Liam Sternberg. An integral component (along with Lene Lovich) of the second Stiff Records signing blitz, Sweet recorded an impressive debut on which Sternberg figured prominently as both writer and producer. In its original English release, **Fool Around** is a great-sounding record that has Sweet voicing Sternberg's vision of the hip girl-child. The American version—remixed, re-ordered and with two different tracks—has much less vitality.

Protect the Innocent shows Sweet forsaking Sternberg's new wave-cum-country sensibility, muddling about in search of a focal point. Dolled up in black leather and singing songs that run the gamut from Lou Reed's "New Age" to Elvis' "Baby, Let's Play House" to the Damned's "New Rose," Sweet seems the victim of somebody's half-assed marketing goof.

And Then He Kissed Me is Sweet's third horse change in the middle of a career busy going nowhere, a Spectorish stab at MOR rock. Devoid of the freshness that was her most obvious asset, the LP contains her first genuine American hit, "Everlasting Love," a duet with teen dream Rex Smith.

Blame It on Love shows signs of revitalization. Though it sounds Tom Petty-influenced, Sweet wrote the entire album's worth of catchy material. She may never regain the youthful charm of her debut LP, but at least this LP shows her regaining control over her musical direction. If she can steer away from the temptations of MOR, Sweet could still become a woman to watch.

Unfortunately, Rachelites had little to do for more than five years, as the diminutive powerhouse was not again heard from until early 1988, when John Waters tapped her to record the title song of his film, *Hairspray*. [jw]

SWELL MAPS

A Trip to Marineville (nr/Rather-Rough Trade) 1979
Jane from Occupied Europe (nr/Rather-Rough Trade) 1980
Whatever Happens Next . . . (nr/Rather-Rough Trade) 1981
Collision Time (nr/Rather-Rough Trade) 1982
Train Out of It (nr/Antar) c. 1986

England's Swell Maps proved that a group of intelligent, fearless, versatile people can record five LPs (counting the double **Whatever Happens Next**) and produce little of any value.

A Trip to Marineville, released with a bonus four-song EP, finds our embryonic cartographers dabbling in Pistols-styled punk and more experimental noise-making, using unorthodox implements. Despite their energy and tenacious desire to produce something new, the package simply does not contain enough ideas that work. The following **Jane from Occupied Europe** shows the band's confidence waxing while its will to organize wanes. Since it's the *desire* to organize sound that fills the gap left when avant-gardists throw the rules away, this proved to be Swell Maps' undoing.

By the time of the interminable two-record **Whatever Happens Next**, mainly a collection of homemade cassette demos, Swell Maps were rambling and floundering. **Collision Time** consists of about half of **Jane from Occupied Europe** plus an assortment of singles. The group broke up around 1980 or '81.

Following the success of leader Nikki Sudden in the Jacobites, a belated compilation of singles and outtakes, **Train Out of It**, was issued. Though promising at the outset, Swell Maps succumbed to preciousness and self-indulgence with depressing speed. [mf]

See also *Nikki Sudden.*

SWIMMING POOL Q'S

The Deep End (DB) 1981
The Swimming Pool Q's (A&M) 1984
Blue Tomorrow (A&M) 1986
The Firing Squad for God EP (DB) 1987

The Athens sound of the B-52's and Pylon—a singular fusion of collegiate-ham artiness and post-punk desperation—also typifies the snappy debut by Atlanta's Swimming Pool Q's, but the Q's add a few interesting wrinkles of their own. While "Big Fat Tractor" favors familiar "Rock Lobster" whimsicality, "Rat Bait" is an exhilarating chip off Captain Beefheart's block with jarring rhythm and growling guitar. In "Stick in My Hand," the Q's apply a heavy blues throb and aggro-folk vocal harmonies (guitarist Jeff Calder and organist Anne Richmond Boston) to a story of Southern religious fanaticism. What's more, they have a great sense of black humor, like the comic masochism of "I Like to Take Orders from You."

Acknowledging new responsibilities as major-label artists, the Q's play it more seriously on their second album, blending intelligent, evocative lyrics with a roaring folk-in-to-rock sound. When Boston sings "The Bells Ring," you feel like you're on the Trailways bus with her, escaping from romance with a Walkman turned up full-blast. When Calder sings "Pull Back My Spring," you can tangibly sense the tension. Armed with excellent, semi-regional songs and great flexibility in arranging and singing them, the quintet fills the LP with honest, heartfelt music that has inherent strength not reliant on volume or dance beats.

Blue Tomorrow is even better, evidencing the band's growing confidence and burgeoning songwriting skill. Mike Howlett's production finesse adds the audio definition and power their records previously lacked; the Q's take the opportunity to stretch their stylistic range further afield than ever before. Boston's vocals are exquisite—Linda Ronstadt meets Wanda Jackson and Sandy Denny—and songs like "Now I'm Talking About Now," "Pretty on the Inside" and "More Than One Heaven" show them off to best effect. (For aficionados, a brand new version of "Big Fat Tractor" demonstrates how far they've traveled since that first LP.)

Back on DB Records, the Q's next issued a rocking, Cheap Trickish single, "The Firing Squad for God," joined on a 12-inch by four diverse items recorded between 1982 and '86. Although she designed the cover (and plays pedal steel on "Working in the Nut Plant," the oldest track), Boston is gone from the current lineup, leaving a stronger but less sensitive quartet. [df/iar]

STEVE SWINDELLS
See *Hawkwind*.

SWINGERS
Counting the Beat (Backstreet) 1982
Picking Up Strangers (Aus. Mushroom) 1982
VARIOUS ARTISTS
Starstruck (A&M) 1983
PHIL JUDD
Private Lives (Aus. Mushroom) 1983
The Swinger EP (MCA) 1983

Leading this trio up from Down Under, ex-Split Enz guitarist/composer Phil Judd rejected his earlier, convoluted melodicism for a still-quirky but more compact, abrasive approach, with phenomenal results. Judd's eccentric mental mixmaster spews out the clichés of mid-'60s Anglo-rock (Beatles, Stones, Who, Kinks) wackily updated, unreal and askew. His Dave Davies-as-young-schizo vocals (often abetted by gibberish falsettos) deliver lyrics almost too rock-song banal to believe, surrounded by twangy guitars that resemble so many layers of electrified rubber bands. (The band performed selections from both of their LPs in the 1982 movie *Starstruck*, the soundtrack album of which contains Swingers tracks not found on **Counting the Beat**.)

Following the Swingers, Judd made a solo album, the Australian-only **Private Lives**, partially produced by Al Kooper. Although the cover is nicely surreal, the American EP that draws five songs from it shows no audible vestiges of his once-eccentric outlook, instead offering forgettable missives from the mainstream. Ironically, the album's six superior tracks—deemed unfit for American consumption (and co-produced by Judd)—show the old goofball's still got a few aces up his sleeve. [tr/jy]

SWING OUT SISTER
It's Better to Travel (Mercury) 1987 ●

Although prone to confusion with similarly named/costumed chart bands—like the awful Curiosity Killed the Cat and Johnny Hates Jazz—emerging from England around the same time, this Manchester trio is an entirely better breed. Martin Jackson (Magazine's original drummer and a later member of the Chameleons) and keyboardist Andy Connell, who played in A Certain Ratio, lead SOS down the path of such neo-smoothies as Everything but the Girl, Sade and Carmel: jazzy, horn-colored pop with an '80s techno veneer and an aroma of smokey late-'50s nightclubs. Ex-Working Weeker Corrine

Drewery's cool, dry vocals perfectly suit appealing, upbeat creations like "Breakout," "Fooled by a Smile" and "Twilight World," making them ideal summer fare; Unfortunately, the songwriting is inconsistent: if all the material were of that quality, **It's Better to Travel** would be an out-and-out joy.

[iar]

SYLVAIN SYLVAIN
Sylvain Sylvain (RCA) 1979

SYL SYLVAIN AND THE TEARDROPS
Syl Sylvain and the Teardrops (RCA) 1981
'78 Criminals (Fr. Fan Club) 1985

To hear Syl Sylvain nowadays, you'd never guess he was once a member of the dreaded, subversive New York Dolls. For one thing, he's an absolutely winsome singer, the perfect punk-with-a-heart-of-gold who seems to be striking an "aw, shucks!" pose at the mic. For another, his records are glistening, rocking pop with no hard edges, plenty of ingratiating melodies and lots of pizazz. One of the fun things about Syl is trying to spot all the elements his eclecticism has absorbed. Over the course of these two LPs, he borrows from salsa, Tom Petty, Phil Spector, Gary Lewis and the Playboys and many more.

Sylvain's solo debut features the breathless "14th Street Beat," an ode to the Big Apple; the better-focused follow-up heightens the romantic angle with such tunes as "I Can't Forget Tomorrow," "Just One Kiss" and "It's Love." Pure charm.

'78 Criminals is a compilation of singles Sylvain did with various bands, including the Criminals, following the Dolls' collapse.

[jy]

RIKKI SYLVAN
See *Rikki and the Last Days of Earth*.

DAVID SYLVIAN
Brilliant Trees (nr/Virgin) 1984
Alchemy—An Index of Possibilities [tape] (nr/Virgin) 1985
Words with the Shaman EP (nr/Virgin) 1985
Gone to Earth (Virgin) 1986 ●
Secrets of the Beehive (Virgin) 1987 ●

DAVID SYLVIAN AND HOLGER CZUKAY
Plight & Premonition (Venture-Virgin) 1988 ●

Sylvian's first solo record expands and refines Japan's approach with assistance from bandmates Jansen and Barbieri and such modern-music luminaries as ex-Canman Holger Czukay, YMO's Ryuichi Sakamoto and Eno collaborator Jon Hassell. Japan fans should wholeheartedly enjoy **Brilliant Trees**, which closely resembles some of the band's final efforts.

Once Japan officially terminated, Sylvian (real name: David Batt) continued his solo career, releasing the ambitious **Gone to Earth** with contributions from Jansen, Barbieri and such artsy stars as Bill Nelson and Robert Fripp. Sylvian's voice occasionally resembles Bryan Ferry's, but there's certainly no imitation going on here. While both artists have a commitment to musical sophistication and sonic excellence, Sylvian makes rhythm a very low priority, allowing his compositions to drift along languidly. Indeed, **Gone to Earth** could have been called **Gone to Sleep**—four sides of this lulling politesse are a little much to ask of any listener. No one else makes vocal records that are as delicate and quiet as Sylvian's; the dedication of one entire disc to dreamy instrumentals is both an accomplishment and a hazard.

Sakamoto provided the string arrangements for **Secrets of the Beehive**, a concise and occasionally energized record that is nonetheless suave and spare. Mark Isham's hornwork on several tracks (the sturdily melodic "Orpheus," "Let the Happiness In") further adds appropriate ambience which, after all, is what this music's about.

[iar]

See also *Ryuichi Sakamoto*.

SYSTEMATICS
Rural EP (Aus. M Squared) 1980

This Australian pair seems utterly determined to be outré, but unlike most others with the same goal, they have a talent for the strikingly oddball: synth with all the texture of processed cheese hums a bright little tune while the vocalist rhapsodizes over a female freak ("She's my little revulsion"), a guitar does nimble abstract-jazz figures to accompany the musings of a blithely suicidal mutant (no legs or shoulders). Then there's a number about a mutation-inducing agent designed to remove toes. Cleverly done, and grimly amusing in its way.

[jg]

T T T T T T

HAJIME TACHIBANA
See *Plastics*.

TACKHEAD
See *Adrian Sherwood*.

YUKIHIRO TAKAHASHI
Saravah! (Jap. Toshiba-EMI) 1977
Neuromantic (Alfa) 1981
Murdered by the Music (nr/Statik) 1982
What, Me Worry? (nr/Alfa) 1982
What, Me Worry? EP (Jap. Yen-Alfa) 1982
Time and Place (Jap. Yen-Alfa) 1983
Wild and Moody (nr/Cocteau) 1985
Poissons d'Avril (Jap. Yen-Alfa) 1985

BEATNIKS
The Beatniks (nr/Statik) 1982

The outside projects of Yellow Magic Orchestra drummer/vocalist Takahashi (not to mention his colleague, Ryuichi Sakamoto) suggest that there was something amiss with the band's format during its existence; his solo work is far more amusing than YMO's, even when the other members are involved. (They contributed half an album's worth to his solo LPs and play on lots more; Sakamoto even appears on the pre-YMO **Saravah!** LP.)

Takahashi's albums are far less programmatic and predictable than YMO's. He'll go from a reggae-style version of "Stop in the Name of Love" to a new-romantic soap opera to tongue-in-cheek pop powered by galloping synths to poignant soul-searching to a loopy update of Duane Eddy guitar instrumentals. He gives prominence to guitar (mostly played by YMO pal Kenji Omura, although Bill Nelson's e-bow graces much of **What, Me Worry?** and Phil Manzanera, bringing fellow Roxy Musician Andy

Mackay along for the ride with sax and oboe, is on much of **Neuromantic**).

The two 1982 albums are pleasant surprises, with playing and material that's at once aggressive and arty. **Murdered by the Music** (from 1980 but unreleased in the West for two years) is the more goofy and eclectic. The **What, Me Worry?** EP features three tracks from the LP of the same name—one with Japanese lyrics this time—plus another bright original and a sprightly cover of an old German tune.

Selecting those songs that best combine melody and muscle, **Time and Place** is a strong live set mostly interpreting Takahashi's previous repertoire but also adding some new things (plus a version of Bacharach/David's "The April Fools"). The band giving it all a unified feel is keyboardist Keiichi Suzuki, Bill Nelson, Hajime Tachibana (ex-Plastics) and drummer David Palmer. Interestingly, Takahashi doesn't drum—he sings, plays keyboards and guitar.

Wild and Moody is an LP of pretty songs—mainly romantic, though a little lyrically offbeat—dressed (but not tarted up) in electro-dance clothing. Nothing awesome, but nearly all of it delightful.

Poissons d'Avril (the French idiom meaning "April Fools") is the soundtrack LP of a movie starring Takahashi. (A large poster of "Yuki" is included.) He was apparently seized by an urge to *become* Burt Bacharach; most of it is soundtracky, a surprisingly large amount in the style of the "sophisticated" '60s romantic comedy. Enh.

The Beatniks are a duo of Takahashi and Keiichi Suzuki; they split all of the playing (including some twittery synth) and singing. Suzuki's vocals are better than Takahashi's (which often resemble an overly echoed

567

mumble), but the lyrics, translated into English, are moodier but less cogent than those on Yuki's solo LPs. [jg]

TALKING HEADS

Talking Heads: 77 (Sire) 1977 ●
More Songs About Buildings and Food (Sire) 1978 ●
Fear of Music (Sire) 1979 ●
Remain in Light (Sire) 1980 ●
The Name of This Band Is Talking Heads (Sire) ●
Speaking in Tongues (Sire) 1983 ●
Stop Making Sense (Sire) 1984 ●
Little Creatures (Sire) 1985 ●
True Stories (Sire) 1986 ●
Naked (Sire) 1988 ●

Talking Heads—three conservative-looking refugees from the Rhode Island School of Design—first appeared on the New York Bowery circuit in mid-1975, playing on a CBGB bill headlined by the Ramones. From the outset, it was clear that, although the Heads shared an attitude and commitment to self-expression with the other bands then on the New York scene, they were charting a course all their own. That individuality, coupled with a strong adventurous streak, has resulted in both critical and commercial success for their group albums and some spin-off projects as well.

The impossibly high-strung David Byrne (who has mellowed somewhat over the years) leads the Heads, his neurotic but insightful perceptions focusing the group's sensibility. The core of Talking Heads additionally consists of bassist Tina Weymouth, drummer Chris Frantz (now her husband) and keyboardist/guitarist Jerry Harrison, an ex-Modern Lover who joined the trio in time for their first album. Together, and enlarged at times by temporary adjunct members, the Heads have produced intellectual dance music and artistic pop of different sorts, finding numerous rewarding levels on which to function.

Talking Heads: 77 is an astonishing debut with uncomplicated, almost low-key music supporting tense, bizarre lyrics, sung by Byrne in a wavering voice. He sounds downright uncomfortable admitting rather than proclaiming the words, but that only adds to the edgy appeal of such songs as "The Book I Read," "Psycho Killer" and "Uh-Oh, Love Comes to Town."

The Heads began a relationship with Brian Eno on their second album, essentially taking him on as a temporary fifth member. On **More Songs About Buildings and Food** (and the two succeeding LPs), they worked a sonic overhaul, at first adding elements to the basic framework and then ultimately subsuming the foundation into a wholly new approach. Here, the use of acoustic and electronic percussion fills previous spaces; the inclusion of Al Green's "Take Me to the River" indicated the band's deep interest in "black music" and provided them with their first glimpse of mainstream popularity. The material isn't as startlingly fresh or satisfying as on the first LP, but some of the tracks work fine.

The collaboration with Eno shifted into high gear on **Fear of Music**, moving rhythm to the front on "I Zimbra," and foreshadowing the band's new direction. It's a tentative step—most of the album sounds like a refinement of **More Songs**—but it draws still further away from their spartan origins.

Remain in Light incorporates various outside players (Adrian Belew, Nona Hendryx, a horn section) and makes a fully realized Great Step Forward. Funk and African influences meet electronics and selfconscious intellectual artiness to produce intricate, occasionally stunning tapestries that almost abandon song structure but do make a new kind of sense. "Once in a Lifetime" and "Houses in Motion" are among the group's finest achievements, and the relationship with Eno seems at its peak. But trouble was apparently brewing, and the Heads spent the next year pursuing solo projects, leaving the band on hold and revoking Eno's guest membership.

The Name of This Band is a two-record live album which showcases the group's best material and recapitulates the stages in its development to that point. Sides One (1977) and Two (1979) feature the basic quartet in the early days; Sides Three and Four (1980 and 1981) chronicle the augmented lineup, with Belew, Hendryx, Bernie Worrell, Busta Jones and others adding a brilliant funky flavor. The Heads' second concert record is **Stop Making Sense**, the one-disc soundtrack to their documentary feature film of the same name. Not only are the performances uniformly excellent, but the selection—from "Psycho Killer" to "Once in a Lifetime" to "Burning Down the House"—again neatly recaps the various periods of their career in a concise, cohesive setting.

Speaking in Tongues, a perfectly realized synthesis of budding pop instincts, powerful atmospherics and solid dance tunes, contains some of the Heads' best work, exemplified by "Burning Down the House" and "Girlfriend Is Better." Having experimented with communal music-making, the Heads reclaimed their tight control; while there are numerous guest players, it is the Heads' album all the way. Uncovering new areas of ambition, the group commissioned noted modern artist Robert Rauschenberg to design a novel plastic package for the record (also issued with a Byrne painting on a more traditional sleeve.)

Nine simple songs played with relative restraint and the fewest sidemen they've employed in a long time, **Little Creatures** is ostensibly the Heads' back-to-the-minimalist-roots rock'n'roll album, an escape from pan-culturalism and artistic grandiosity. (It's not.) Byrne's songs are as straightforward and non-Headsy as he can make them; considerations of mundane topics (sex, babies, television) join his typically oblique character studies and essays on being and nothingness. Were the flimsy songs sturdier, the album might have been more creatively successful; as realized, **Little Creatures** merely sounds careless and insignificant. "Road to Nowhere" and "Walk It Down" are the winners in a weak crop.

Although released in conjunction with Byrne's film of the same name, **True Stories** is not its soundtrack, but a new Heads LP. Again artfully exploring the complexities of modern culture in the superficially simple context of unembellished pop music, renaissance genius Byrne selfconsciously masks his awesome sophistication to sing *seemingly* (or so one is expected to understand) trivial ditties. Some are likable ("Love for Sale" and "Wild Wild Life," for instance) enough, but the conceptual attitude that attends its creation makes respecting **True Stories** impossible. Unfortunate though it may be, Talking Heads—with far-flung experimentation and groundbreaking originality under its collective belt—can't possibly sell conviction when slumming in the mundane world of tunesmiths and working musicians.

After two records of jus'-us-rock-folks, the courageous world-beat exploration (or overwhelming pretension, as you will) of **Naked**, recorded in Paris with Steve Lillywhite, seems reassuringly honest, if not especially refreshing. Each song augments the quartet with numerous classy session players

in varying combinations: ex-Smiths guitarist Johnny Marr, reggae keyboardist Wally Badarou, Pogue accordionist James Fearnley, percussionists Abdou M'Boup, Manolo Badrena and Nino Gioia, etc. Horns and mountains of percussion filter a full set of oblique Byrnisms into merrily danceable exotica that's not as challenging as it is uninvolving. The CD adds one song ("Bill"); three tracks appear in longer versions than on the LP. Furthermore, the CD is "graphics-ready," meaning that those in possession of the needed equipment—a CD player with a graphics output and a not-then-available decoder ($500 or so)—can watch the lyrics and real-time instrument list on a television screen while listening. [iar]

See also *David Byrne, Jerry Harrison, Tom Tom Club.*

TALK TALK

Talk Talk EP (EMI America) 1982
The Party's Over (EMI America) 1982 ●
It's My Life (EMI America) 1984 ●
The Colour of Spring (EMI America) 1986 ●
Spirit of Eden (EMI Manhattan) 1988 ●

Talk Talk's debut is slick and professional but lifeless, sounding as though it were programmed by record company execs to be a synth-rock Foreigner. Talk Talk earned some early comparisons to Duran Duran, thanks to the similarity of their double name, a common producer (Colin Thurston) and a similarly superficial veneer. But Talk Talk lacked Duran's panache. Most of the group's songs are full of melodramatic angst and amateurish lyrics (which might have been overlooked had they not foolishly included a lyric sheet). The eponymous EP is a preview of **The Party's Over**: four selections from it.

Things took a turn for the better on **It's My Life**, although Talk Talk still hadn't become an essential component of modern culture. The title track handily wins the 1984 Roxy Music soundalike award; other synth-powered dance tracks like "Dum Dum Girl" reveal Mark Hollis to be a truly mixed-up vocalist. Now that Talk Talk seemed capable of making reasonably interesting (and varied) records, their creative future looked a lot brighter.

Bad bet. **The Colour of Spring** finds producer Tim Friese-Greene collaborating with Hollis as a songwriter and keyboard player, joining Talk Talk's two other members (drummer Lee Harris and bassist Paul Webb) and a lot of other musicians. Except for "Life's What You Make It" and a gritty guitar solo on "I Don't Believe in You," the first side is gruelingly slow and soporific; Side Two is sporadically more energetic, but the languid pacing still makes it an endurance challenge. [ks/iar]

TALL DWARFS
Three Songs EP (NZ Furtive) 1981 (NZ Flying Nun) 1985
Louis Likes His Daily Dip EP (NZ Flying Nun) 1982
Canned Music (NZ Flying Nun) 1983
Slugbucket Hairybreath Monster EP (NZ Flying Nun) 1984
That's the Short and Long of It (NZ Flying Nun) 1985
Throw a Sickie EP (NZ Flying Nun) 1986
Hello Cruel World (nr/Flying Nun) 1987 (Homestead) 1988 ●
Dogma (NZ Flying Nun) 1988

Snow White had it easy. She only had to deal with seven little men who whistled while they worked. New Zealand's Tall Dwarfs not only whistle, they jingle, jangle, gurgle, grumble, grunt, sputter, bang on tables and guitars, play crumhorn, clarinet, clavinet, spoons and shake an angry bee-colony's worth of tambourine. Worse yet, as many as three times the population of White's house turn up for recording sessions: "Nothing's Going to Happen" (from **Three Songs** and **Hello Cruel World**) features 20 different players on everything from bagpipes to *cabasa* (a Cuban percussion instrument).

The core of the group is Alex Bathgate and Chris Knox, formerly of commercial band Toy Love. The inspiration for Tall Dwarfs comes from somewhere between the alienated dementia of the Beatles' "Blue Jay Way" and comic horror movies on late-night TV. Obscene green munchers with purple eyes and unearthly cries mix uneasily on Dwarfs albums with bores who crawl out the doors and other things with pulpy, pulsating innards. The Dwarfs could almost be accused of having a Simon and Garfunkel fixation for all the melodic acoustic guitars used in their early work, but then out spills a mangled masterpiece (such as "Paul's Place" from **Louis Likes His Daily Dip**) where tremolo overkill and Knox's simple, clear singing suggest a lovesick Irishman trapped in a bagpipe. No matter how pretty, the Dwarfs' music is always strange.

Tall Dwarfs don't have a drummer, so

they use creative repetition of all sorts to provide a percussive element, from **Canned Music**'s pitterpat pawbeats and growling monster groans (which appear in "Turning Brown, and Torn in Two") through the harsh guitar saws and scat singing loops of "The Brain That Wouldn't Die." (That number surfaced originally on **Slugbucket Hairybreath Monster**, and was reissued on **Hello Cruel World**, a European sampler of the band's first four releases.)

Most of the group's material was recorded on Knox's home Teac with neither EQ nor expensive microphones. This is strictly primitive—do-it-yourself psychedelicacies with great green gobs of greasy grimy talent and monstrously surreal cover art (drawn by Knox) to match. ['e]

TROY TATE
Ticket to the Dark (nr/Sire) 1984
Liberty (nr/Sire) 1985

Armed with an impressive résumé (Shake, The Teardrop Explodes, Fashion), singer/guitarist Troy Tate released his first solo album in 1984. Working with various musicians from his past associations (including ex-Teardrop David Balfe), Tate uses his attractively husky voice and substantial songwriting skill, as well as deft sound effects and complex arrangements, to put across ten melodic songs that approach modern pop from several different directions. The most memorable tracks on **Ticket to the Dark** are "Safety Net," "Love Is . . . " and "Thomas," but virtually all are well worth hearing. An exceptionally good record. [iar]

TATER TOTZ
See *Red Cross*.

TAXI BOYS
See *Real Kids*.

TAXI GANG
See *Sly Dunbar and Robbie Shakespeare*.

ANDY TAYLOR
See *Duran Duran*.

TOT TAYLOR AND HIS ORCHESTRA
The Girl with Everything EP (nr/GTO) 1981
Playtime (nr/Easy Listeners) 1981

TOT TAYLOR

The Inside Story (nr/Easy Listeners) 1984
Box-Office Poison (nr/London Popular Arts) 1986
Arise, Sir Tot EP (nr/London Popular Arts) 1986
My Blue Period (nr/London Popular Arts) 1987
Menswear (nr/London Popular Arts) 1987
Blue Turns to Grey EP (nr/London Popular Arts) 1988
Jumble Soul (nr/London Popular Arts) 1988
Scrapbook (nr/London Popular Arts) 1988

SOUND BARRIER

The Suburbia Suite (nr/Compact Organization) 1984

Tot Taylor is a Brit-popper who loves Tin Pan Alley. His band, Advertising (pop-rock plus punky perspiration), deceived EMI long enough to cut an LP before being judged non-starters. Tot then convinced another commercial powerhouse to take him on but, after three 45s, GTO decided it had been a big mistake. By then, he'd discovered Mari Wilson (who'd also signed to GTO) and Virna Lindt, so when he and Mari were dumped, he had the starting roster for his own label, the Compact Organization. An empire was born. (GTO, meanwhile, has long since gone out of business.)

Tot had recorded **Playtime** for GTO, and arranged to take all 16 tracks of it with him. The usual rhythm section (including the odd bit of dribbly synth) is frequently augmented by horns and strings. What saves Taylor from seeming an insufferable twit for presuming to emulate Porter, Gershwin, Rodgers and Hart, Kern, etc. is his cleverly unassuming and self-parodic wordplay. Sometimes he spouts gloriously goofy rock ("I Wanna Play the Drums Tonight"—Kevin Ayers meets Sparks), but he also slips in observations on the grayness of the modern day-to-day—we *are* all "Living in Legoland"—for effective commentary.

The Inside Story (which Taylor pretty much plays all himself) is another delightful grab-bag; less playing time than **Playtime**, but otherwise nearly its equal. A wacky pop-rock side is manifested in "The Crimson Challenge" (the chorus is "You may think words are funny but they mean so much to me," plus the syllable "wo" repeated 20 times); he also increasingly indulges his incurable romanticism. Taylor's flaky charm is even equal to his choice of Porter's "All of You" as an album-closer, in a treatment which, believe it or not, sounds more sincere—and truer to the original song—than, say, Mel Torme's.

Next, Tot composed a whole instrumental LP, **The Suburbia Suite**, for the Sound Barrier, and penned Slim Gaillard's number (plus some incidental music) for the film *Absolute Beginners*. Then he cut three new albums in two years! Regrettably, none of them are up to his first two. Sometimes he tries too hard to be witty; other times, songs or arrangements go on too long; still other times, he seems bereft of his former lyrical incisiveness and coherence. All the same, there are treasures to be found in them thar grooves, and some less-immediate tracks will grow on you.

Box Office Poison might appear more impressive if it not for its illustrious predecessors. In fact its musical execution is, if anything, more facile. "Arise, Sir Tot" gently deflates his own delusions of grandeur; "Australia" is a longing toast to a place we haven't destroyed—yet; "Spoil Her" is romantic strategy that's only partly tongue-in-cheek. (The **Arise** EP is a 12-inch with four of the LP tracks on it.)

My Blue Period is Tot's jazz record; members of the John Dankworth and Loose Tubes Orchestras help him construct, well, Aluminum Pan Alley. The aptly named "The Wrong Idea," a strained attempt at cleverness, gets things off on the wrong foot. "The Compromising Life" is a much better notion, and its swell mute trumpet work is a well-executed example of the LP's stylistic intentions. Additionally, "A Girl Did This" ranks with his best, but **Period** just isn't consistent.

On **Menswear**, Tot went to the other extreme for a do-it-yourself approach in his modest home studio. Lyrically and arrangement-wise, he regains top form (16 tight little vignettes) but, melodically, his catchiness quotient is still not one hundred percent. When he's on, however, the LP ranges from good ("Trouble in Store," as in department store) to brilliant ("Waiting for My Egg," a procrastination anthem). The four-cut EP is good but uneven, in style as well as quality, but the return of some rockishness missing since the second LP is a good sign.

Jumble Soul is a 14-cut best-of, collecting some of the first three LPs plus some unalbumized 45s (including the two non-LP GTO A-sides). **The Girl with Everything** is a 7-inch single: the A-side from **Jumble Soul**. It also contains "Modern Wife" (from **Play-**

time); the remainder is instrumental sound-track music looking for a film.   [jg]

See also *Advertising, Mari Wilson.*

BRAM TCHAIKOVSKY

Strange Man, Changed Man (Polydor) 1979
The Russians Are Coming (nr/Radar) 1980
Pressure (Polydor) 1980
Funland (Arista) 1981

Bram Tchaikovsky was a group as well as Peter Brammell's nom de rock, but it was the lack of a similarly strong second creative force to him in the band that proved to be its undoing. The ex-Motors guitarist/bassist/vocalist had the talent to make his band work for a while, but couldn't maintain its quality alone.

Strange Man, Changed Man sounds fresh and punky (if rather trebly)—an energetic mixture of the Byrds, Springsteen and, not surprisingly, the Motors. (Nick Garvey, one of Bram's ex-bandmates, co-produced.) The LP includes three fine singles ("Girl of My Dreams," "I'm the One That's Leaving," "Sarah Smiles"); the rest of the material has also worn remarkably well.

Expanding from a trio to a quartet and doing the production themselves, Bram (the band) came up with a sophomore effort (**The Russians Are Coming**, retitled **Pressure** for the cold-war-minded USA) that improves the sound but has far less consistent songs, with writing divided among various combinations of the members.

Subsequent personnel shifts left Bram (the man) with neither satisfactory writing partners nor an alternate (or harmony) vocalist to shore up his own shortcomings. An attempt to pursue several ill-advised directions makes **Funland** (production again by Garvey) lifeless. The only times Bram's tepid vocals cut loose are on an old Motown tune (the oft-covered "Breaking Down the Walls of Heartache") and an old Motors B-side, "Soul Surrender," which was recorded as an afterthought by Bram, Garvey and deputized drummer Hilly Michaels.   [jg]

THE TEARDROP EXPLODES

Kilimanjaro (Mercury) 1980 (Skyclad) 1988 ●
Wilder (Mercury) 1981 (Skyclad) 1988 ●

Charming despite frequent bouts of pretentiousness, singer/songwriter Julian Cope led Liverpool's great psychedelic hope, The Teardrop Explodes, through two albums before moving on—in the midst of an aborted third—to a solo career. Cope's influences include everyone from Scott Walker to the Doors to Tim Buckley, but Teardrop's sound was better than the sum of its parts. The group's problem was Cope's scattershot approach—his songs are filled with too many amorphous, meaningless and just plain silly images—and his unanswered need for a good editor.

Kilimanjaro is the more focused of the two; next to it, **Wilder** sounds like a debut, as whatever restraining influence the band had on Cope was removed, leaving him to write all of the songs unaided. **Kilimanjaro** was released twice in the UK (the second version added a single, "Reward," and a totally different cover). The American release uses the first cover but switches the sequencing and swaps two cuts. In any form, it's a lush, mesmerizing, appealing album, whose only problem (other than the lyrics) is that the songs tend to float together with little individual character. But the ones that do stand out are terrific: "Poppies in the Field," "Treason," "Reward" and "When I Dream," the last providing a brush with American radio success. Most of the songs have a childlike, dreamy quality.

While better-defined musically, **Wilder** is more confused lyrically, though it still carries the band's unique atmosphere. Cope's flat voice and sometimes turgid lyrics serve as instruments used for sonic value to provide color, especially on "Bent Out of Shape," "Seven Views of Jerusalem" and "The Culture Bunker."   [ks]

See also *Julian Cope, Troy Tate.*

TEARDROPS

Final Vinyl (nr/Illuminated) 1980

Buzzcocks bassist Steve Garvey was a Teardrop; the rest of this Manchester outfit had ties to the Fall and other local legends. **Final Vinyl** is very inconsistent—too much mucking about in the studio ruins the decent tracks with spurious talking and noises—but there is some fine music here that hovers between the Buzzcocks and the Sex Pistols.   [iar]

TEARS FOR FEARS

The Hurting (Mercury) 1983 ●
Songs from the Big Chair (Mercury) 1985 ●

In this highly industrialized age, efficiency remains a highly valued commodity, so there is something socially responsible about the burgeoning population of duos in pop music. Pairs of pale, fashionable youngsters making hugely popular self-contained (often synthesizer-based) records has increased the number of potential bands by at least a factor of two over the more traditional quartet format. Bath's Tears for Fears, one of the better nouveau intellectual pop exponents—the highly listenable variety, not the challenging work-for-your-culture sort—make clever, memorable records with startling, thought-provoking lyrics about alienation, psychological analysis and failed romance. That they avoid formula and repetition is an added bonus.

The Hurting introduces Roland Orzabal and Curt Smith (the band actually includes two low-profile sidemen as well) and their intensely dour, introspective worldview. Orzabal's songs—largely derived from Janovian primal scream theory and other aspects of modern psychology—discuss only somber topics of deep pain and sorrow. Like their titles ("The Hurting," "Mad World," "Start of the Breakdown," "Watch Me Bleed"), the songs are more often depressed than angry. Odd fare for hit records with teenybop appeal to be sure, but occasionally anxious vocals and the eclectic, often remarkable music belie the dark thoughts being conveyed. It's disconcerting to find yourself humming along with such misery, but The Hurting is an excellent, mature record.

Over two years in the making, **Songs from the Big Chair** finds Tears for Fears less miserable, more capable of expressing anger and well on their way to major international stardom. "Head Over Heels" (grand pop), "Everybody Wants to Rule the World" (haunting pop) and "Shout" (measured gruff rock)—all co-written by Orzabal with others in the group—are the best three out of eight. The music is more ambitious and sophisticated, allowing a few numbers to go on too long without generating much of an impact, but the strong entrants are excellent. (The UK tape release adds six tracks.)

In mid-1988, it was reported that the pair was finally (still?) at work on their third album. [iar]

TEENAGE HEAD
Teenage Head (Can. Goon Island) 1979
Frantic City (Can. Attic) 1980
Some Kinda Fun (Can. Attic) 1982

TEENAGE HEADS
Tornado EP (MCA) 1983

This hard-rockin' quartet from Toronto owes more than its name to the Flamin Groovies—their records are full of non-stop crazed rock'n'roll songs about cars, parties, girls, booze and general wanton fun, all imbued with the original Groovies' unreconstructed spirit. With nods to Eddie Cochran, Chuck Berry, Gene Vincent and other rock pioneers, Teenage Head races along, guitars blazing, through numbers like "Ain't Got No Sense," "Kissin' the Carpet," "Teenage Beer Drinking Party" and "Disgusteen." If they were smarter and more sarcastic, T. Head might have more in common with the old Dictators; as it stands, their sound, while hardly original, is perfect for parties held in gymnasiums. The first three records aren't hip, but they are solid, sweaty and convincingly salacious.

Given a pluralizing, name-sanitizing "s" for **Tornado**, their American debut—six new songs that aren't particularly invigorating—the group lowers its hysteria level in an ill-advised stab at maturity and commercial hard-rock acceptability, dropping from Canada's would-be Van Halen to a junior-league Loverboy in one easy step. [iar]

TEENAGE JESUS AND THE JERKS
Teenage Jesus and the Jerks EP (Lust/Unlust) 1979

VARIOUS ARTISTS
No New York (Antilles) 1978

LYDIA LUNCH
Hysterie (nr/Widowspeak) 1986 (CD Presents) 1986

Teenage Jesus pushed the anything-goes/anyone-can-do-it philosophy of punk about as far as it would stretch without breaking. Formed in 1976 by onetime CBGB waitress Lydia Lunch and saxophone/conflict artist James Chance, TJ & the Jerks went beyond minimalism and atonality into what Lunch proudly called "aural terror"; the band cranked up a musical death knell over which she screamed her lyrics of fear, pain and unpleasantness. After Chance quit to form the equally abrasive but funkier Contortions, the Jerks soldiered on as a trio, leaving their sonic bloodbaths on the **No New York** anthology and the two Bob Quine-produced singles ("Orphans" and "Baby Doll") preserved on the 1979 EP. Lydia ranks as one of the most creatively untalented guitarists of all time; her blistering walls of noise, while completely lacking in melody or taste, possessed an unremitting atavistic ferocity akin to latter-day King Crimson. Never a band to waste the audience's time, Teenage Jesus specialized in 20-second songs and ten-minute sets (which witnesses still considered about nine minutes too long.)

The **Hysterie** compilation album contains an entire side of Teenage Jesus & the Jerks: ten tracks from the aforementioned and other contemporaneous releases. Lydia went on to numerous other bands and musical alliances. Drummer Bradley Field popped up briefly as a bongo player for the Contortions; bassist Jim Sclavunos became the *drummer* in two of Lydia's subsequent bands, Beirut Slump and 8 Eyed Spy. Alternate bassist Gordon Stevenson died. [rnp]

See also *James Chance, 8 Eyed Spy, Lydia Lunch.*

TELEPHONE

Telephone (Fr. Columbia-EMI) 1977
Crache Ton Venin (nr/EMI) 1979
Au Coeur de la Nuit (nr/Virgin) 1980
Telephone! EP (nr/Virgin) 1982
Un Autre Monde (nr/Virgin) 1984

Telephone's biggest contribution to rock culture was proving to a stodgy French record industry that a local band could succeed singing teenage protest lyrics in their native tongue. As far as the rest of us are concerned, Telephone's sound is more Stonesy hard-rock than Pistols punk thrash. They are quite good at it, though, investing the crunchy guitar boogie with cutting punk force, while singer Jean-Louis Aubert shoots as much Jaggeresque venom as possible into the soft curves of a romance language.

Both the band's first LP, produced by Mike Thorne, and **Crache Ton Venin**, produced by Martin Rushent in his pre-Human League days, are recommended for their spunk and energetic garage sound. The **Telephone!** EP, produced by Bob Ezrin, has six songs—delivered mostly in lightly accented English—that show development into subtler, more modern territory, e.g., "The Cat," a slinky number sung by female bassist Corinne Marienneau and accented by bawdy trombone.

Glyn Johns produced **Un Autre Monde**, on which Telephone shifts sideways and back. Marienneau gets more chances to sing

(in French) formless numbers that have neither personality nor energy, while Aubert's turns in the spotlight again recall the Glimmer Twins. A boring mess.   [df/iar]

TELEVISION

Marquee Moon (Elektra) 1977 ●
Adventure (Elektra) 1978 ●
The Blow-Up [tape] (ROIR) 1982

Live, they were the ultimate garage band with pretensions—Television's influences were Coltrane and Dylan as well as Roky Erickson—but on record they achieved a polish that added genuine strength. The group evolved from the Neon Boys and initially consisted of Tom Verlaine (guitar/vocals), Richard Lloyd (guitar), Billy Ficca (drums) and Richard Hell (bass). Hell left, later forming the Heartbreakers with Johnny Thunders, and ex-Blondie bassist Fred Smith took over his slot. Thus constituted (and significantly reduced in fringe aggression), Television recorded "Little Johnny Jewel," a privately pressed single which many regard as a turning point for the whole New York scene.

TV signed to Elektra and released **Marquee Moon** in 1977. A tendency to "jam" onstage caused detractors (and, paradoxically, British fans) to refer to them as the Grateful Dead of punk, but it was the distinctive two-guitar interplay (along with Verlaine's nails-on-chalkboard vocals) that set them apart. Verlaine's staccato singing in songs like "Prove It" and "Friction" is impressive, and the long workout on the title track showed a willingness to break away from the solidifying traditions of their more selfconscious contemporaries.

Adventure was, contrary to its title, smoother and more controlled than its predecessor, but did not want for good material. "Glory," "Foxhole" and the beautiful "Days" showed the band to have a firm grip on their songwriting. Television lasted about another year before splintering. A posthumous tape-only compilation of live performances shows the band's rawer side and includes such concert cover staples as "Knockin' on Heaven's Door," "Satisfaction" and the 13th Floor Elevators' classic "Fire Engine" (inexplicably listed as "The Blow Up" and credited to Verlaine, though the song is mentioned by its true name and source in the liner notes). Verlaine and Lloyd have both pursued solo careers; Ficca became a Waitress and other things. Richard Hell released records and fronted bands under his own name after leaving the Heartbreakers.

[jw]

See also *Heartbreakers, Richard Hell, Richard Lloyd, Kristi Rose and the Midnight Walkers, Tom Verlaine, Waitresses, Washington Squares.*

TELEVISION PERSONALITIES

. . . And Don't the Kids Just Love It
(nr/Rough Trade) 1981
Mummy Your Not Watching Me (nr/Whaam!)
1982 (nr/Dreamworld) 1987
They Could Have Been Bigger Than the
Beatles (nr/Whaam!) 1982
(nr/Dreamworld) 1986
Then God Snaps His Fingers (nr/Whaam!)
1983
The Painted Word (nr/Illuminated) 1983
Chocolat-Art (Ger. Pastell-Principe Logique)
1985

Drawing their inspiration from '60s British pop and psychedelia, London's TV Personalities are an amateurish, haphazard band whose records offer nothing in the way of slick musicianship but loads of brilliantly adapted pop-art weirdness. They started out wide-eyed and Jonathan Richman-like but have evolved into (and beyond) rambling, jagged space noise and various stripes of time-warped psychedelia.

The first album is altogether charming in its guileless version of Carnaby Street pop given a modern neurotic outlook. The cover sets the period with a collage that fits together John Steed of *The Avengers* and Twiggy. From a Kinksish tale of boyish admiration ("Geoffrey Ingram") to the lyrically acute "I Know Where Syd Barrett Lives," simply and softly played guitars, bass and drums support coy vocals sung with a strongly adenoidal accent by Daniel Treacy. Haunting melodies and abundant wit make the record bizarre but wonderful, far more eccentric and original than the solemn neo-mod rehashers of the same era.

Moving from succinct pop art and flower power to trippy psychedelia, a mixture of keyboards and low-budget studio effects helps make **Mummy Your Not Watching Me** very different. Although some of the songs follow the pattern of the first album ("Painting by Numbers" and "Lichtenstein Painting"), others meander through mild mind expansion, in homage to Syd Barrett and other ancient acid-rockers. The standout in this vein is "David Hockney's Diaries," which also demonstrates the problems inherent in adorableness trying to be spacey. The shoebox production removes any grandiosity that may have been intended, and what's left sounds mixed up and silly. If it weren't for the redeeming pop tunes, **Mummy** would have been a real disappointment.

Released concurrently with the announcement of the band's dissolution (a temporary situation, as it turned out), **They Could Have Been Bigger Than the Beatles** includes reprises of previously recorded songs as well as a pair of prime numbers— "Painter Man" and "Making Time"—by '60s ultra-mods the Creation, which receive affectionate and respectful (if incompetent) treatment. The album offers 16 tracks of should-have-been-good nostalgic art-rock, but sacrifices a lot of charm with an overly heavy guitar sound. Best cut: "The Boy in the Paisley Shirt."

The Painted Word lists a four-man lineup and actually features a group photo (albeit a dark, fuzzy one) on the front cover. Musically, the TVPs have drifted off into spare, droning psychedelia and ultra-restrained rock that's hauntingly beautiful, like the most delicate moments of the Velvet Underground. The songs are all originals, and effectively convey a melancholic sense of futility, even when superficially addressing relatively jolly topics. Surprisingly serious, but excellent.

Chocolat-Art (sarcastically subtitled "A Special Tribute to James Last") was recorded live as a trio in Germany, and features simple but effective performances of such TVP classics as "Silly Girl," "I Know Where Syd Barrett Lives" (appending "I know where Paul Weller lives—'cause he's a hippie, too") and the stupendous "Look Back in Anger." They're not always quite in tune, but you know they mean well. Parochial music-lovers may understandably lose patience with the group's unabashed amateurishness, but the Television Personalities say what they mean and mean what they say, with integrity and an intangible quality that makes them unique and wonderful. [iar]

TELEX

Looking for Saint Tropez (nr/Sire) 1979
Neurovision (Sire) 1980
Sex (PVC) 1981
Birds and Bees (nr/Interdisc) 1982

This Belgian synth trio specializing in suave Euro-disco is at once a bland dance machine and a reasonably clever techno-pop team. Deadly slow adaptations (with artificial-sounding processed vocals) of "Rock Around the Clock" and Plastic Bertrand's "Ça Plane pour Moi" make **Looking for Saint Tropez** noteworthy; the originals, while faster, are mundane and one-dimensional.

Neurovision takes the same approach, giving Sly Stone's "Dance to the Music" the full Telex treatment amid another batch of boring originals. (If the group's use of synthesizers weren't as dull as technically possible, their records might be a lot better.) **Sex** adds a novel element by employing Ron and Russell Mael of Sparks as lyricists; the collaboration resembles their own band's work with Giorgio Moroder in form, if not content. Unfortunately, Telex's languid creations lack the spunk to keep up with the warped wordplay of "Sigmund Freud's Party," "Exercise Is Good for You" and "Carbon Copy." (**Birds and Bees** replaces three of **Sex**'s tracks with subsequent singles.)

For anyone concerned, Telex has continued to be quietly active throughout the '80s. [iar]

TELL-TALE HEARTS
The Tell-Tale Hearts (Voxx) 1984
The "Now" Sound of the Tell-Tale Hearts EP (Voxx) 1985

The old quote about those who fail to learn the lessons of history has evidently been taken to heart by this nostalgic San Diego quintet. Having absorbed the sounds of such '60s beat and punk innovators as the Animals, Georgie Fame, Them, the Yardbirds, Syndicate of Sound and a dozen others, they regurgitate carefully crafted originals that are hard to distinguish from the real thing. (A fondness for Chicago blues adds an appropriate twist to the band's stylistic arsenal.) Singer Ray Brandes' anguished passion, Bill Calhoun's atmospheric organ and Eric Bacher's spectacular rave-up guitar work all make the debut album a genre (this one, not that one) classic; the better-recorded six-song EP is equally energetic and (superficially speaking) exciting. [iar]

TENPOLE TUDOR
Eddie Old Bob Dick and Gary (Stiff) 1981
Let the Four Winds Blow (Stiff) 1981
Swords of a Thousand Men (Can. Stiff) 1981

This wonderful, over-the-top crew of drunken rowdies is led by the inimitable Eddie Tudorpole, whose wobbly vocals lend the proper air of debauchery to the band's hard-driving arias. **Eddie Old Bob Dick and Gary** contains such classy trash as "Wunderbar," "3 Bells in a Row" and "Swords of a Thousand Men," replete with bizarre concepts, catchy melodies and loopy singing. The great tracks co-exist with some real dogs, but when Tenpole Tudor are on the mark, their good humor and rock energy are undeniably infectious.

Let the Four Winds Blow takes the band (up or down isn't an issue) to a new plateau, working flippant pseudo-country ("Throwing My Baby Out with the Bathwater"), mock-funk ("Local Animal"), even ersatz ballroom schmaltzola ("Tonight Is the Night"). The Canadian-only **Swords of a Thousand Men** picks the best tracks from both LPs and wraps them in the artwork from the second. Not for the uptight or supercilious, but John Otway fans will understand.

Sir Edward has seemingly abandoned his full-time singing career for a series of blindingly funny cameos in such films as *The Great Rock'n'Roll Swindle* (in which he sings "Who Killed Bambi?" into a vacuum cleaner handle), *Sid & Nancy* (a great bit as a hotel clerk), *Walker* (a dramatic role for a change) and *Straight to Hell.* [iar]

TEN TEN
Ordinary Thinking (Generic) 1984
Walk On (Chrysalis) 1986

Ordinary Thinking offers diabolically good melodic rock from a Virginia quartet with a British accent. The memorable tunes are energetically played with attractive, intricate vocals and arrangements that smoothly blend guitars and synthesizers in almost equal doses. Such an excellent independent album undoubtedly helped Ten Ten snag their major label contract; unfortunately, the resultant record, **Walk On**, is terrible, sub-Ultravox tripe that includes a pitiful cover of the Plimsouls' powerful "Million Miles Away." [iar]

10,000 MANIACS
Human Conflict Number Five EP (Mark) 1982 (Christian Burial-Press) 1984
Secrets of the I Ching (Christian Burial-Press) 1983

The Wishing Chair (Elektra) 1985 ●
In My Tribe (Elektra) 1987 ●

Hailing from Jamestown in provincial upstate New York, 10,000 Maniacs play deceptively challenging new pop music. On the early records, singer Natalie Merchant's innocent girl voice skips lightly over gentle melodies, while her five cohorts provide the body of the music—unobtrusive reggaefied grooves. But on closer inspection, all is not so cozy. Warped guitars slice in and out, and Merchant's fragmented lyrics gently evoke images of a decaying society bent on violent self-destruction.

The five-song **Human Conflict Number Five** EP is simple and a little underbaked, but does introduce the Maniacs' early trademarks: Merchant's voice and lilting Caribbean grooves. **Secrets of the I Ching** offers a much deeper look at the band, serving up tastes of Latin and Spanish in the lyrics, and ranging from screeching noise over a pop hook to almost psychedelic power calypso. Both records present difficult ideas without compromise in a most palatable manner.

The band's major label debut codified their sound as never before, essentially dispensing with everything they had tried except for neo-traditional electric folk. Comparisons to Fairport Convention (Joe Boyd produced **The Wishing Chair**) help somewhat, although the sensibility and cultural references are totally different: small-town Americana isn't rural Great Britain. Merchant's reflective, impressionist lyrics and clear, powerful singing shine on new songs like "Can't Ignore the Train" and new versions of three tunes from **Secrets of the I Ching**. Honest, intelligent and enthralling.

Peter Asher's slick production of **In My Tribe**, the band's first release as a quintet, is initially bland and off-putting, but the songs' emotional depth and Merchant's awe-inspiring voice ultimately overcome the record's dispiriting homogeneity. The matter-of-fact child abuse in "What's the Matter Here?" is as troubling as Suzanne Vega's "Luka"; "Cherry Tree" addresses illiteracy with poignant understanding; the cautionary "Gun Shy" is spoken directly at a brother who has newly become a soldier. For contrast, the delighted family vignette of "My Sister Rose" shares joy for its own sake and the cover of Cat Stevens' "Peace Train" offers a utopian alternative to Merchant's more realistic originals. [jl/iar]

TEST DEPT.

Beating the Retreat (nr/Some Bizzare) 1984
The Unacceptable Face of Freedom
(nr/Ministry of Power-Some Bizzare)
1986 ●
A Good Night Out (Ministry of Power-Some
Bizzare-Relativity) 1987 ●
Terra Firma (Play It Again Sam USA)
1988 ●

TEST DEPT. AND THE SOUTH WALES STRIKING MINERS CHOIR

Shoulder to Shoulder (nr/Some Bizzare) 1985

Like that other notable contemporary band of philosophical noisemakers, Einstürzende Neubauten, Test Dept. eschew all musical tradition to play stunning ultra-percussion with an industrial bent. Like their Teutonic soul brothers, this enigmatic British organization uses large metallic objects and power tools to add stark modern realism to the drum overload, but also brings more structure and rhythm to the assault.

Beating the Retreat—two 12-inch EPs comprising a single-length album—adds occasional vocal effects (not singing) that do little to vary the din, which is simply awesome in its intensity and singlemindedness. But several startling tracks take a wholly different approach, offering sparse ambient sound and effects that blithely incorporate real instruments like cello and harp.

Shoulder to Shoulder, proving the band's political commitment and activism, gives half of its running time to the 90-member Welsh choir. In one truly strange exercise, the two seemingly unconnectable forces collaborate on a track.

The Unacceptable Face of Freedom, with an unwieldy fold-out cover Hawkwind would have been proud of, is a powerful record, both in its potent musical attack and ongoing political convictions. Real drums seem to have replaced most of the steel-bashing, and the instrumentation also includes Fairlight-built orchestras, taped voices (speaking and singing), sequencers and bagpipes. Observations about the state of British life are angrier than ever—"Statement" features a miner giving a first-hand account of picket-line police brutality, while recurring military themes in the music drive the point home even harder.

A Good Night Out continues their forceful manifesto, although the execution has progressed from the tribal pounding of early work to ambitious performance art. Much of the LP was recorded live in London and Amsterdam in what was, judging by the cover photo, a huge multi-media extravaganza—some sort of Marxist military opera. Lyrics which continue to spew bitter, sarcastic and intelligent tirades against the domestic policies of the British Empire are more powerful than ever. Pretentious perhaps, but **A Good Night Out** also shows Test Dept.'s abiding commitment to their beliefs—social, political and artistic. [iar/dgs]

TÊTES NOIRES

Têtes Noires (Rapunzel) 1983
American Dream (Rapunzel) 1984
Clay Foot Gods (Rounder) 1987 ●

This Minneapolis sextet shows what can happen when a demented Girl Scout singalong turns into a pop band. Their musical assets are formidable, with three lead singers—ranging from credible to incredible—and a songwriting collective that easily harnesses its riot of pop influences to produce work that demands serious consideration.

Which is not to say that all this coalesced into perfection on **Têtes Noires**. But any record that introduces a band with such spunk (and a drum machine named Barbie) can't be too bad. **American Dream** shows what the Têtes can do as songwriters. Not every line flows—a few are rhythmically jarring (a surprising weakness for a singer-dominated group)—but they've got plenty to say on subjects ranging from world peace to Moonies to gay murder to that ultimate horror, the American family. Anchored by strong bass, the odd instrumental mix begins to hit more often than it misses. And those meshing voices—unified, unique, powerful—could blow the Bangles off the map.

Increasing their instrumental independence by fitting a drummer into the lineup, the talented Têtes recorded **Clay Foot Gods**, a dud produced by two of the Violent Femmes. An insincere air of commercial slickness turns the songs towards unnatural danceability without any corresponding increase in their musical merit. The Têtes have come a long way since the first record's unfettered joy, but now seem to be lost. [mf/iar]

TEX AND THE HORSEHEADS

Tex and the Horseheads (Bemisbrain-Enigma) 1984
Life's So Cool (Enigma) 1985

One of the wilder exponents of cow-punk, Tex and the Horseheads are spiritual kin to the Gun Club. And while they lean toward a very punky image (lead singer Texacala Jones dresses like a female Stiv Bator; on the first album, the bassist's name is Smog Vomit and the drummer is Rock Vodka), their playing is fairly coherent. Mixing mutant blues (even a cover of Jimmy Reed's "Big Boss Man") into the first album's punk-country-rock blender, Tex and the Horseheads have a convincingly strong sound, but are a few pints short on material.

The John Doe-produced **Life's So Cool** is much better, an out-of-control blues-rock riot that more than anything recalls **Exile on Main Street**. It starts with an uncredited quote from the old instrumental "Cat's Squirrel" (see Jethro Tull's first LP for corroboration) and then goes on to such topics as drinking, fornicating and tangling with the law in songs that are substantial and thoughtfully developed. Texacala's singing shows great improvement; exciting guitarist Mike Martt and bassist J. Gregory Boaz also join in with complementary vocals. A very impressive showing with enough bite and spit to satisfy anyone. [iar]

See also *Divine Horsemen*.

THAT PETROL EMOTION

Manic Pop Thrill (nr/Demon) 1986 ●
Babble (Polydor) 1987 ●
The Peel Sessions EP (nr/Strange Fruit) 1987

The talented O'Neill brothers left the ashes of the peerless Undertones behind with few prospects for their musical future. While Feargal Sharkey began his transformation into a boringly mature California pop chanteur, they lay low, quietly scorning the business that had shattered their teenage dreams. After several false starts, they returned with an excellent new quintet that built on their past accomplishments without revisiting them. Damian O'Neill switched to bass to play in the Petrols; big brother Seán (previously known as John) and Derry homeboy Reámann O'Gormáin play guitar; drummer Ciaran McLaughlin and singing Seattle native Steve Mack complete the band, which is politically aware, occasionally abrasive and devoutly independent.

Manic Pop Thrill is an apt title for the angry, articulate rock melodies that span the continuum from sweet balladry to PiL/Fall-like noise. Mack is a fine, controlled shouter in the Keith Relf/Steve Marriott tradition;

the band's combination of slide guitars, Bo Diddley beats, wild harmonica wailing and rave-up energy recalls the early Stones, Yardbirds and Velvet Underground. The utter lack of nostalgia or revivalism here suggests that, even with all the crap that masquerades as music nowadays, some things about rock'n'roll will never die. (The CD adds four tracks.)

Produced by Foetus partner (in Wiseblood) Roli Mosimann, **Babble** puts the issues—mostly concerning religion and Irish nationalism—right up front: "Creeping to the Cross," "Big Decision," "Swamp," "Chester Burnette" and others unleash the group's vehemence and informed radical commentary. Since the lyrics aren't very specific and the singleminded music is ruggedly invigorating, agreement isn't a prerequisite to appreciation. The Petrols could benefit from a little more stylistic consistency (everybody writes, often in very different directions), but the melding of real-life anger with germane musical passion gives **Babble** a visceral quality that is impossible to ignore. [iar]

THE THE
Soul Mining (Epic) 1983 ●
Infected (Epic) 1986 ●
MATT JOHNSON
Burning Blue Soul (nr/4AD) 1981 + 1984

When Matt Johnson—in his guise as the The—is in prime form, his pop creations are excellent (despite an eerie vocal resemblance to Ian Anderson of Jethro Tull). Unfortunately, he also displays horrid tendencies toward studio self-indulgence, making worthless, wanky instrumentals. On **Burning Blue Soul**, Johnson (produced on two tracks by Dome) meanders tiringly through formless "songs" with laughably precious lyrics. **Soul Mining** contains "Uncertain Smile" and "This Is the Day," both attractive, warm and nicely arranged with understated eloquence. But it also has its share of snores.

Johnson reportedly recorded and scrapped an entire album (provisionally entitled **The Pornography of Despair**) before releasing the ambitious and sophisticated **Infected**. The eight metaphorical songs—addressing sexual, social and political issues—use a studio full of notable musicians (Neneh Cherry, Roli Mosimann, Zeke Manyika, Anne Dudley and others) for a wide range of new sounds, some far more energetic than the The's previous work. So while "Heartland" recalls the low-key ambience of **Soul Mining**,

the title track is pounding dance music, with big drums and broad-brush production; "Twilight of a Champion" is '40sish jazz noir that sounds faintly like Foetus. Overall, however, it's surprisingly uninviting. While Johnson strains to say something important on **Infected**, he fails to connect on a most basic musical level. [iar]

THEATRE OF HATE
He Who Dares Wins Live in Leeds (nr/SS) 1982
He Who Dares Wins Live in Berlin (nr/Burning Rome) 1982
Westworld (nr/Burning Rome) 1982
Revolution (nr/Burning Rome) 1984
Live at the Lyceum [tape] (nr/Burning Rome) 1984
Theatre of Hate EP (nr/Stiff) 1985
Original Sin Live (nr/9 Mile) 1985

Although singer/guitarist Kirk Brandon's heart and conscience were obviously in the right place, Theatre of Hate's recorded work—unremittingly morose and often strident—was rarely as good as the band's enthusiastic UK press notices made it out to be.

Mick Jones (then of the Clash) produced the studio LP, **Westworld**, capturing the full extent of Brandon's urgency, especially in the ominous, chilling, "Do You Believe in the Westworld." But, despite a variety of interesting arrangements, the mix is muddy and, while the feeling is strong, his vocals aren't. What good's a conscience if you can't express it understandably? "Do You Believe" is the LP's strongest track, concerning the US, China, Russia, the world and the aftermath of a neutron bomb explosion. Although Brandon sounds understandably agitated, the band resembles punked-up Sergio Leone. The only other track of any note is the haunting "Love Is a Ghost." **He Who Dares Wins** (live in Berlin), produced by manager Terry Razor, has thick, dense sound, but reasonably clear vocals. The muscular rock sound, intense atmosphere and teetering sax give it an edgy excitement.

Brandon shut down the Theatre of Hate in 1982 and formed a new band, Spear of Destiny. The posthumous Stiff EP compiles four early tracks; another live album followed. [ks/iar]

See also *Spear of Destiny*.

THELONIOUS MONSTER
Baby . . . You're Bumming My Life Out in a Supreme Fashion (Epitaph) 1986
Next Saturday Afternoon (Relativity) 1987

Thelonious Monster built its rep on the LA club scene by playing lurching, shambolic club sets (featuring a seven-man, four-guitar lineup), but the thinly-produced **Baby . . . You're Bumming My Life Out in a Supreme Fashion** does little to capture the wacked-out appeal of the Monster's live act. What you get instead is a half-assed grab-bag of styles, some of them effective and others just plain lazy, unified by self-indulgent down-in-the-gutter lyrics and frontman Bob Forrest's whiny personability.

Next Saturday Afternoon is a bit closer to conventional rock'n'roll and is the better for it, unveiling heretofore hidden strengths. The band, now pared down to a quintet (including guitarist Dix Denney, ex-Weirdos, and bassist Rob Graves, ex-45 Grave) has apparently discovered melody, producing musically and lyrically impressive material like "Next," "Anymore" and "Walk on Water." They're not such dopes after all. [hd]

THE SCENE IS NOW

See *(The) Scene Is Now.*

THESE IMMORTAL SOULS

Get Lost (Don't Lie!) (SST) 1987 ●

The members of this band have been around the block a few times. First there was the Birthday Party, from the ashes of which arose Crime and the City Solution, led by ex-Birthday Party guitarist Rowland S. Howard. After two years and three releases, Howard had his differences with singer Simon Bonney and left, taking his bass-playing brother Harry and drummer Epic Soundtracks (ex-Swell Maps/Jacobites) with him. Adding keyboardist Genevieve McGuckin, he formed These Immortal Souls in 1987.

Get Lost (Don't Lie!) is a 30-minute mini-LP that works as well as, if not better than, any Crime and the City Solution record. Howard can't really sing much, but this doesn't require him to: the shady lyricism which underlies all seven tracks would lose its color if sung by someone more conscious of pitch than self. McGuckin has listened to plenty of Ray Manzarek; Soundtracks turns in brilliant performances. Most of the guitar work is acoustic strumming, although Howard does allow himself to cut loose on "'Blood and Sand' She Said." A very impressive marriage of splendor and squalor. [dgs]

THEY MIGHT BE GIANTS

They Might Be Giants (Bar/None) 1986 ●
Don't Let's Start EP (Bar/None) 1987 ●
(She Was a) Hotel Detective EP (Bar/None) 1988

Imagine, if you will, a modern all-pop update of the Bonzo Dog Band crossed with the Mothers of Invention, Residents, XTC, Stackridge and R. Stevie Moore. Contemplate the idea of a NYC-based duo with a highly sophisticated sense of humor which writes, sings and plays guitar, accordion and keyboards. John Flansburgh and John Linnell—They Might Be Giants—might in fact be geniuses; their debut album is one of the greatest musical things ever, a diabolically clever and wildly diverse collection of fully realized masterpieces that could not possibly fail to entertain even the fussiest, hardest-hearted idiot. Literate, accomplished, bursting with ideas, hooks, puns, dadaist absurdities and other neat tricks, TMBG are almost beyond belief. By conservative estimate, roughly 15 of the album's 19 tracks are brilliant. Maybe they'll do better next time out.

The 12-inch "Don't Let's Start" EP (and 3-inch CD) takes one of the LP's best songs and appends the mild peer fun of "We're the Replacements," "The Famous Polka" (it's not but it might as well be) and "When It Rains It Snows." The title track of **Hotel Detective** is another LP cut, remixed; the foot-long EP also contains four swell new songs ("Kiss Me, Son of God," "For Science," "The Biggest One" and "Mr. Klaw") plus a bewildering phone conversation *about* the group. [iar]

THEYR

Mjotvidur Maer (Ice. Eskimo) 1982
The Fourth Reich (nr/Shout) 1982
As Above . . . (Enigma) 1982

Theyr (an approximation of untranslatable characters) has released several albums in their native Iceland; **As Above . . .**, issued in the US and UK, copies the artwork from **Mjotvidur Maer** but has little in common with its content. Musically harsh but never strident, Theyr shares stylistic ground with bands like Killing Joke, the Fall and A Certain Ratio, plus the Residents and urban funksters, but they still have an identity all their own, forged with indifference to any trends going on elsewhere. Distinctly modern, full-blooded and powerful, Theyr's biggest shortcoming is their lyrics, which are awful and pretentious.

Bar conversation footnote: Theyr's drummer, Siggi Baldursson, went on to become a world-famous Sugarcube. [iar]

See also *Sugarcubes*.

THIN WHITE ROPE

Exploring the Axis (Frontier) 1985
Moonhead (Frontier) 1987
Bottom Feeders EP (nr/Zippo) 1987
In the Spanish Cave (Frontier) 1988 ●

Psychedelia has nothing to do with the '60s or day-glo trousers. It is music of an altered state and nobody sees the world with a more altered perspective than Guy Kyser of Davis, California's Thin White Rope. He sings like the leader of the Twilight Zone house band. With a high, tangled voice that quavers between the band's sinewy guitar slithers, he has an exotic clip to his inflection that sometimes chops phrases into stabbing bits.

Thin White Rope exist in the same general Western-roots-influenced-rock genre as Green on Red or True West. On **Exploring the Axis**, that shows up in clean, slippery touches of country guitar work and fuzzy little edges of deeper and darker chords. "Disney Girl" lopes along with Jozef Becker's laid-back drum pulse as squealy shivers of feedback slip between the smooth flows of the melody. "Down in the Desert" marches off the disc with a martial beat and bopping intensity. Throughout the LP, Becker's drumming speeds up to heighten tension but softens when the guitars or lyrics change mood. Laid between his constant changes and the warmth of Rope's guitar (Kyser and Roger Kunkel), the twisted tales almost seem to make sense. (The cassette adds a bonus track, "Macy's Window," which was later included on **Bottom Feeders**.)

Thin White Rope are also mantra-minded, setting up a groove and driving down it until their amps threaten to smoke. That love of repetitive textures fueled by subtle changes begins to show up in **Moonhead**, giving it a smoother and more unified sound. The guitar interplay strongly suggests Television.

On **Spanish Cave**, the hoedown rhythms and acoustic-sounding bass of "Mr. Limpet" and the Dylan-meets-Roky Erickson narrative of "Ahr-Skidar" prove Rope aren't just country wannabes, but a band of the country.

Thin White Rope is also dedicated to rock'n'roll. The **Bottom Feeders** EP (four originals and two cover versions) puts all the dark, bluesy guitar and frog-throated vocal delivery a raunch hand could want in Jimmy Reed's "Ain't That Loving You Baby"; later on, their textures collide with a jackhammer in a loud and searing live rendition of Suicide's "Rocket USA." (The version of "Atomic Imagery" is different from the one on **Axis**.) ['e]

THIS HEAT

This Heat (nr/Piano) 1979 (nr/Recommended) 1983
Deceit (nr/Rough Trade) 1981 (nr/These) 1988
This Heat with Mario Boyer Diekuuroh [tape] (Fr. Tago Mago) 1982
The Peel Sessions EP (nr/Strange Fruit) 1988

In 1976, Charles Hayward of Gong (and Phil Manzanera's Quiet Sun) joined with Charles Bullen and Gareth Williams to form This Heat. Though arising from art-rock and the British school of fusion jazz, This Heat quickly developed into an experimental band largely dependent on tape loops and production tricks.

This Heat covers two years of the band's history, with both live and studio cuts. They use guitar, clarinet, drums and keyboards, permutated with loops, phasing and overdubs, breaking down patterns into only faintly-connected musical moments that include artificial skips and looped end-grooves. Though insolent and withdrawn, the music is adventurous and, in its own peculiar way, engrossing. The punnily titled **Deceit** is more coherent and raucous, yet avoids the dismal drones and cacophony of other "experimental" groups. Free of clichés, the music blends politics and intelligence, steering clear of artifice and trendiness. Austere, brilliant and indescribable.

This Heat with Mario Boyer Diekuuroh, which compiles tapes from 1977/8, features studio sessions with the Ghanian drummer who greatly influenced their perceptions of rhythm.

Renamed Camberwell Now, the group has continued to release albums on the Swiss Recommended label. [sg]

THIS MORTAL COIL

It'll End in Tears (4AD-Valentino) 1984
Filigree and Shadow (nr/4AD) 1986 ●

Not so much a band as a hip British studio party, This Mortal Coil combines the prodigious talents of members of the Cocteau Twins, Modern English, Dead Can Dance, Xmal Deutschland and others in the 4AD label stable to produce atmospheric vignettes, drawing material from such diverse sources as Alex Chilton, Tim Buckley and Colin Newman as well as penning new songs. **It'll End in Tears** mixes a few instrumentals with lush vocal performances; though all rather agreeable, most of it wouldn't disturb a sleeping infant.

Filigree & Shadow is a double album, with most of the work being done by various members of Dif Juz, the Wolfgang Press and Simon Raymonde of the Cocteau Twins. Once again, it neither rocks nor rolls. Tender, light piano and string arrangements predominate; the second side is half over before any drums enter the picture. With very few exceptions (including Wire and Talking Heads covers), this is the aural equivalent of herbal tea and would probably bore your grandparents. [dgs/iar]

DAVID THOMAS AND THE PEDESTRIANS

The Sound of the Sand and Other Songs of the Pedestrians (Rough Trade) 1981
Vocal Performances EP (nr/Rough Trade) 1982
Variations on a Theme (Sixth Int'l) 1983
More Places Forever (Twin/Tone) 1985

DAVID THOMAS & HIS LEGS

Winter Comes Home (nr/Re) 1982

DAVID THOMAS AND THE WOODEN BIRDS

Monster Walks the Winter Lake (Twin/Tone) 1985 ●

Blame the Messenger (Twin/Tone) 1987

A song stylist in the truest sense of the word, David Thomas is one of rock's few *truly* one-of-a-kind artists. But the Pere Ubu vocalist's first solo album came as something of a surprise. His lyrics and unusual compositions bring strangenesss out of the mundane—imparting magic to everyday objects and activities—aided by an eclectic bunch: Richard Thompson, Anton Fier, Chris Cutler, Eddie Thornton, Philip Moxham and others. Each demonstrates hitherto unimagined aspects of their talents, and Thomas' otherworldly voice—animal noises transmuted into human speech—has never been more expressive. A high point of Thomas' avant-garde folk-blues-jazz-rock cultural synthesis.

Variations on a Theme, which prominently features Richard Thompson, again mixes a bit of everything—including country, jazz and blues—into Thomas' own unique style. Only two tracks on this musically sedate, almost "normal"-sounding record recall Pere Ubu's general looniness. Throughout, Thomas demonstrates genuine fascination with his subject matter, as well as an invariably novel perspective. A good follow-up, and one indicative of enormous artistic reach.

Winter Comes Home—which gives front cover billing to ex-Henry Cows Chris Cutler and Lindsay Cooper—mixes intellectual stand-up comedy with winning performances, all recorded live in Munich in 1982. Cooper's bassoon perfectly suits Thomas' tastefully strident vocal excursions. Most notable is the title track, essentially a shaggy-dog story.

Thomas reunited with Ubu bassist Tony Maimone for **More Places Forever**. Along with Cutler's drums and Cooper's one-woman woodwind section, Thomas has all the backdrop he needs to gather us into his little world and cast his spell. He displays his love for things like insects and sunshine, and in "New Broom" follows some dust on its journey. Ubu fans finally get to hear the track for which **Song of the Bailing Man** was titled.

The new band (re)assembled for **Monster Walks the Winter Lake** is almost an Ubu reunion, with Maimone joined by Allen Ravenstine on synths and Paul Hamann producing. The low-key music moves more slowly than usual, with cello and strangely-played accordion often the predominant instruments; the increasingly philosophical lyrics containing recurring monster metaphors. The four-part, 11-minute title track is a real treat.

Blame the Messenger was recorded with much the same lineup that reformed Pere Ubu. One listen confirms that they must have been itching to get back together; the sound and arrangements are more a throwback to the band's earlier recordings than any of Thomas' previous solo work, thanks especially to Ravenstine's electronic keyboards. The lyrical fascination this time is mostly with nature, particularly ironic when juxtaposed with such beautifully unnatural sounds. A great record. [sg/dgs]

See also *Pere Ubu*.

MAYO THOMPSON

See *Red Crayola.*

THOMPSON TWINS

A Product of . . . (nr/T) 1981
Set (nr/T) 1982
In the Name of Love (Arista) 1982 ●
Quick Step & Side Kick (nr/Arista) 1983 ●
Side Kicks (Arista) 1983 ●
Into the Gap (Arista) 1984 ●
Here's to Future Days (Arista) 1985 ●
Close to the Bone (Arista) 1987 ●
The Richard Skinner Sessions EP (nr/Night-
   tracks-Strange Fruit) 1987
Greatest Mixes: Best of the Thompson Twins
   (Arista) 1988 ●

The name notwithstanding, there are no twins and no Thompsons in this globally successful modern pop band. Once an obscure, loose collection of as many as seven London-based players led by singer/synthesist/song-writer Tom Bailey, the Twins pared down to just Bailey, New Zealander Alannah Currie and Joe Leeway and became one of the world's leading purveyors of occasionally adventurous, invariably danceable modern chart fare.

All six musicians credited on **A Product of . . .** manage to play some percussion in addition to their primary instruments—sax, guitar, keyboards, etc. The cleverness and variety of the tracks, however, eliminate any potential monotony that might have resulted from the heavy reliance on rhythm. And although the music is designed to incite maximum motion, there isn't one track that skimps on lyrical, melodic or structural depth. The album isn't uniformly wonderful, but the textures and sounds make it pleasurable and energizing.

Set adds one member (a full-time bassist) but is otherwise not very different—in cast or content—from its predecessor. Exemplified by such great numbers as "In the Name of Love" and "Bouncing," Bailey and his cohorts prove that it is possible to make totally listenable dance music that doesn't beg suspension of critical faculties. Producer Steve Lillywhite and Thomas Dolby also pitch in, making **Set** a very nice record. (The Thompsons' first exposure in America came via **In the Name of Love**, which consists of two tracks from the first LP and eight from the second.)

Building on the popular dance sound of "In the Name of Love" (in fact, deftly quot-ing it on the first track, "Love on Your Side"), the three Twins emerged mature, motivated and commercially focused on their third album, **Quick Step & Side Kick**. Demonstrating varied and skilled songwriting and extraordinary self-contained music-making—the trio plays almost everything you hear on keyboards—the album bounces from start to finish, but no two tracks have much in common other than a good mood and a strong beat. (The American label perversely altered the title and rearranged the tracks a tad. The British cassette includes a bonus side of remixes.)

Consolidating their stardom, **Into the Gap** is a virtual new greatest hits album, containing "Hold Me Now," "Doctor Doctor," "You Take Me Up" and "Sister of Mercy," which were all radio, chart and club staples for many months. The Twins' strength is their avoidance of repetition; the songs vary widely in tempo, style, instrumentation, subject matter and vocal arrangements (all three sing).

By **Here's to Future Days**, co-produced by Bailey and Nile Rodgers, the hit machine was starting to run down a bit. "Lay Your Hands on Me" is brilliant, but "Don't Mess with Doctor Dream" is boring. "King for a Day" is cute but overly familiar; "Tokyo" is corny. And who needed to hear a new version of the Beatles' "Revolution"? **Future Days** is not significantly inferior to the Twins' best albums, but it lacks their freshness and vitality.

In April 1986, at the end of a six-month world tour, Joe Leeway left the band, reportedly to go solo, although the results have yet to surface. Bailey and Currie carried on, releasing the modest and, for the most part, quietly likable **Close to the Bone** (produced by Rupert Hine) the following year. Currie's lyrics (Bailey wrote the music) take a surprisingly reflective approach here, suggesting doubt and anxiety instead of the usual oblique contemplations. "Gold Fever" bitterly attacks someone (wonder who?) for greed, saying "Now it bothers me to think that I used to call you a friend." While spottily derivative (mostly of their own work, but "Long Goodbye" could easily be mistaken for Sting) and notably lacking the group's characteristic energy and rhythmic magic, the record proves that the Thompson factory can turn out quality merchandise even when the creative thinkers are taking a rest.

[iar]

583

TRACEY THORN

See *Everything but the Girl*.

THRASHING DOVES

Bedrock Vice (A&M) 1987 ●

Another entrant in the circus of informed modern pop stylists, London's Thrashing Doves mix and match their varied stylistic borrowings. "Beautiful Imbalance" takes spectacular chart-ready flight; otherwise, Ken Foreman's vocals merely echo Tom Verlaine, Lloyd Cole and Violent Femme Gordon Gano in songs that often seem transparent attempts at imitating various Bob Dylan eras. Colorful but meaningless. Producers on the proficient quartet's minor album include Chris Thomas and Jimmy Iovine.   [iar]

THREE JOHNS

Some History EP (nr/Abstract) 1983
Men Like Monkeys EP (nr/CNT Productions) 1983
A.W.O.L. EP (nr/Abstract) 1984
Do the Square Thing EP (nr/Abstract) 1984
Atom Drum Bop (nr/Abstract) 1984
Death of the European EP (nr/Abstract) 1985
Brainbox (He's a Brainbox) EP (nr/Abstract) 1985
The World by Storm (nr/Abstract) 1986
Live in Chicago (Last Time Round) 1986
Demonocracy: The Singles 1982–1986 (nr/Abstract) 1986

This trio from Leeds—actually comprising three fellows named Jo(h)n—specializes in discordant socio-political guitar punk with trembling falsetto vocals. Their preference for a rhythm machine over a live drummer creates a unique tension in the overall sound.

Some History compiles two singles (from 1982 and 1983) on one 12-inch, and is very much indicative of the trio's approach. Save for a surfacing maniacal edge, **Men Like Monkeys** and **A.W.O.L.** stake out more of the same turf. The singing John's whining vocals would grate in large doses, but brevity—four songs each—keeps these two records from becoming downright annoying.

The Johns plunge headfirst into dance rock on **Do the Square Thing**. Lyrically oblique and riddled with innuendo, the title track is, for these thrashers, an extraordinarily slick piece of extended dance-floor fodder. Surprisingly, it makes a stronger impression than their usual dirges.

Characteristics that might be tiresome if

abused are kept judiciously in check on the Johns' first LP, **Atom Drum Bop**. The vocals don't wander unnecessarily, guitar lines are blindingly sharp and melodic and the production is crystalline. "Teenage Nightingales to Wax," "Firepits," "Do Not Cross the Line" and the odd ballad, "No Place," all help make this the trio's most fully realized endeavor.

The two succeeding four-song EPs both show continued growth towards tuneful pop. Without losing any of their bite, the A-sides offer incisive comments on some pretty heady subject matter: America's destructive influence on continental heritage ("Death of the European") and yuppiesque self-centered apathy ("Brainbox"). The B-sides are more jagged, and just as strong.

The World by Storm, released with a limited edition 7-inch live EP, is highly recommended. The Johns have honed their craft to seeming perfection: it will be difficult for them to improve on tunes like "King Car," "Torches of Liberty," "Demon Drink" and the pre-LP single, "Sold Down the River."

Jon Langford's (guitar/vocals) simultaneous commitment to the Mekons, as well as his high demand as a producer, have temporarily put the Three Johns on hold. **Live in Chicago** and **Demonocracy** are interim releases, the latter a compilation of singles and LP tracks. The live album—the Johns' first American release—dates from June 1985 and contains renditions of such material as "Teenage Nightingales to Wax," "Death of the European" and "The World of the Workers," as well as a brief (and uncredited) version of Madonna's "Like a Virgin." Both albums offer excellent—and different— overviews, and are highly recommended.   [ag]

THREE O'CLOCK

Baroque Hoedown EP (Frontier) 1982
Sixteen Tambourines (Frontier) 1983 ●
Arrive Without Travelling (IRS) 1985
Ever After (IRS) 1986 ●
Vermillion (Paisley Park) 1988 ●

SALVATION ARMY

The Salvation Army (Frontier) 1982

BEFOUR THREE O'CLOCK

Befour Three O'Clock (Frontier) 1985

One of the brightest lights of new American pop psychedelia, LA's Salvation Army debuted with an album that was liable to inspire young bands all around the world to join in the fun. The melodies have the ethereal quality of a young Syd Barrett; the music is a blend of all the most colorful '60s sounds, showing the influence of such groups as the Byrds, Move, Hollies, Music Machine and others.

Following legal action by the real Salvation Army (concerns over musical competition?), the group changed into the Three O' Clock. (Three years later, Frontier cleverly repackaged the original album under the name **Befour Three O'Clock**.) The five songs on **Baroque Hoedown** have poppier vocals and equally engaging music. The addition of ex-Quick/Weirdos drummer Danny Benair also brought the group a harder edge. Don't miss their cover of the Easybeats' "Sorry."

Sixteen Tambourines is even better—an incredible full-length collection of chiming, memorable power pop tunes played and sung as if each track were likely to get played on every radio station coast-to-coast. Slick and inventive production by Earle Mankey delivers the songs (most co-written by guitarist Louis Gutierrez and bassist Michael Quercio) in utterly engaging style. Best numbers: "On My Own," "Jet Fighter," "And So We Run." Absolutely charming and remarkably memorable.

In 1985, the Three O'Clock signed to IRS and released their second album. **Arrive Without Travelling** isn't quite as delightfully twinky as its predecessor, but it does contain enough characteristically lightheaded material ("Her Head's Revolving," "Simon in the Park") to maintain the group's standing as preeminent paisley popsters.

Ever After saw Gutierrez exit the group (he's now in Louis and Clark), to be replaced by Steven Altenberg without any major changes in the group's sound or direction. Shortly after its release, the group parted ways with IRS, spent some time in legal limbo and then signed to Paisley Park. Apparently, Prince had heard and liked them (not too surprising, since **Around the World in a Day** draws on many of the same influences as Three O'Clock's records), though they'd never actually met. With Jason Falkner replacing Altenberg and Ian Ritchie producing, the group recorded **Vermillion**, their most interesting and varied album to date, which includes Prince's (I mean Joey Coco's) "Neon Telephone"—just right for them—a lead vocal apiece by Falkner and keyboardist Mike Mariano (both great!) and

Quercio's six-minute ballad, "Through the Sleepy Town." [cpl/iar/ds]

THROBBING GRISTLE

Second Annual Report (nr/Industrial) 1978 (nr/Fetish) 1979 (nr/Mute) 1983
D.o.A. (nr/Industrial) 1979 (nr/Fetish) 1981 (nr/Mute) 1983
Twenty Jazz Funk Greats (nr/Industrial) 1979 (nr/Fetish) 1981 (nr/Mute) 1983
Heathen Earth (nr/Industrial) 1979 (nr/Fetish) 1981 (nr/Mute) 1983
Throbbing Gristle's Greatest Hits (Rough Trade) 1980
Funeral in Berlin (Ger. Zensor) 1981
24 Hours [tape] (nr/Industrial) 1981
Mission of Dead Souls (nr/Fetish) 1981 (nr/Mute) 1983
Five Albums (nr/Fetish) 1982
Thee Psychick Sacrifice (nr/Illuminated) 1982 (nr/Dojo) 1986
Editions Frankfurt—Berlin (nr/Illuminated) 1983
Once Upon a Time (Live at the Lyceum) (nr/Casual Abandon) 1983
Live at Heaven [tape] (nr/Rough Trade) c. 1985
TG CD1 [CD] (nr/Mute) 1986

Raised on William S. Burroughs and Philip K. Dick, and inhabiting a science-fiction-now world of industrial depression, Britain's prolific Throbbing Gristle produced some of the most confrontational and unpleasantly fascinating music of recent years, ostensibly as a means to radicalize the listener into abandoning bourgeois romanticism for a realistic view of life.

Second Annual Report (the quartet's first release) uses mournful synthesizer drones to paint a grimly powerful vision of post-industrial, mid-depression England.

D.o.A. is brighter in tone and more polished in technique. Less cohesive than the previous album, **D.o.A.** places greater emphasis on live material, found tapes and individual productions by separate members of the band. The music is aggressively anti-melodic, but the spirit is powerful and the surprises plentiful. Recommended for the strong.

Twenty Jazz Funk Greats breaks away from **D.o.A.**'s stark bleakness in an attempted truce between the group's radical attitudes and pop music, removing the cutting edge from their calculated chaos but offering more accessibility.

Heathen Earth is a return to form, adding savagery to the mix, expanding TG leader Genesis P-Orridge's obsession with the profane juxtaposition of everyday symbols and motifs. The music is clean, vicious, sharp and occasionally displays the band's transition to energetic, if still outré, rock.

Greatest Hits, subtitled "Entertainment Through Pain" (an apt description of the band's approach), collects material from the first four albums. Recommended for a solid overview.

Funeral in Berlin and **Mission of Dead Souls** are live albums. The first features all previously unreleased material; the latter is a recording of the band's final show in San Francisco. Those who desire a lot more Throbbing Gristle live should check out **24 Hours**, a collection of two dozen C-60 cassettes packed in a suitcase and containing most of the group's live shows. (Rough Trade reportedly also offered a suitcase set of 33 tapes around the same time. Did anyone actually buy one of these?) In 1983, however, Rough Trade bowed to public pressure and made those 33 cassettes available individually. **Five Albums** is more reasonably sized, a boxed set reissuing all the albums that had previously been on Fetish.

Although the group has been defunct now for years and its members (P-Orridge, Chris Carter, Cosey Fanni Tutti, Peter Christopherson) scattered into the similarly uncommon Chris and Cosey, Psychic TV and Coil, new TG records—most of them live (how can there be anything left?)—are still being released. **TG CD1**, however, contains 42 minutes of previously unissued instrumental studio dribblings from early '79, with reflective '86 liner commentary by the participants. [sg/iar]

See also *Chris and Cosey, Coil, Psychic TV*.

THROWING MUSES

Throwing Muses (nr/4AD) 1986 ●
Chains Changed EP (nr/4AD) 1987
The Fat Skier (Sire) 1987
House Tornado (Sire) 1988 ●

If for no other reason, this Boston/Providence quartet will have earned a place in music history for being the first American band ever signed to the exclusive British 4AD label. An eclectic blend of jerky guitar pop and Kristin Hersh's hiccupping singing, Throwing Muses bears no resemblance to any other group or artist in recent memory.

Their first album is startling; attribute the uniqueness to Hersh's remarkable vocals on "Hate My Way," "Green" and "America (She Can't Say No)." Truly one of a kind. With fewer twists and turns than the songs on the preceding album, the four tracks on **Chains Changed** somehow have even more impact.

College radio airplay and critical acclaim prompted Sire to sign Throwing Muses and release **The Fat Skier**: six songs on one side and a nearly-nine-minute seventh ("Soul Soldier") on the flip. With onetime Violent Femmes producer Mark Van Hecke behind the board (the first two records were produced by Gil Norton), the music appears to be verging on the formulaic; the record is considerably less striking than the band's prior output. It's still distinctive, but an injection of fresh ideas at this point couldn't hurt.

House Tornado amplifies the problems of **The Fat Skier** as songs run into one another with a minimum of musical variety. What was, upon inception, avant-garde has become static and predictable. [ag]

JOHNNY THUNDERS

So Alone (nr/Real) 1978
In Cold Blood (Fr. New Rose) 1983
Diary of a Lover EP (PVC) 1983
New Too Much Junkie Business [tape] (ROIR) 1983
Hurt Me (Fr. New Rose) 1984 ●
Que Sera, Sera (nr/Jungle) 1985 ●
Stations of the Cross [tape] (ROIR) 1987

JOHNNY THUNDERS & PATTI PALLADIN

Copy Cats (nr/Jungle) 1988 ●

For his first solo LP, the legendary New York Dolls/Heartbreakers guitarist enlisted the aid of ex-Pistols Paul Cook and Steve Jones, some of the Hot Rods, the Only Ones and even old-timers Steve Marriott and Phil Lynott. Choosing material representative of all his prior musical phases, and aided immeasurably by co-producer Steve Lillywhite, Thunders turns in reasonably strong performances, perfectly employing his gutter guitar and New York sneer in a number of (musical) veins, including greasy R&B and a tender ballad. Not since the Dolls' two records has he sounded so lucid and involved— **So Alone** is Johnny Thunders at his best.

Thunders didn't release anything else

under his own name for five years after that. The LP-plus-EP **In Cold Blood** returned him to the racks, combining five newly-recorded studio tracks—with just a drummer and guitarist Walter Lure—that don't amount to much with a poor live Boston show taped in 1982. (**Diary of a Lover** consists of those studio cuts plus a subsequent item.) At **Cold Blood**'s best, Thunders pounds out a stinging "Green Onions" that suggests his guitar skills aren't gone yet.

Narrated in New Yawkese by the artist, **New Too Much Junkie Business** offers live, demo and live-in-the-studio recordings from 1982, co-produced by Jimmy Miller, with a variety of players helping out on renditions of everything from the Dolls-era "Jet Boy" and "Great Big Kiss" to numbers that overlap **Diary of a Lover**. Most notable is "Sad Vacation," a tribute to Sid Vicious. That song also appears on the French-only **Hurt Me**, alongside "Eve of Destruction," "It Ain't Me Babe" and renditions of some of Thunders' best songs. (The **Hurt Me** CD contains five bonus tracks.)

Que Sera, Sera boasts a batch of solid new songs, a solid rhythm section (Keith Yon and Tony St. Helene), an illustrious cast of guest stars and a surprisingly easygoing, clearheaded outlook. Variety is a watchword, as Stonesy pseudo-reggae ("Cool Operator"), sneering sexist raunch ("Little Bit of Whore"), restrained reality ("Short Lives," wherein JT denounces the live-fast-die-young credo), familiar Dollsy bebop ("Tie Me Up") and "Endless Party, co-written with David Johansen) and a hot uptempo instrumental ("Billy Boy") mix gaily. In fact, the most wasted thing about this LP is the unnecessary cover shot of Thunders looking like the not-so-living dead.

Punk filmmaker Lech Kowalski shot and recorded a pair of 1982 Mudd Club shows to use in his junkie portrait feature (*Gringo*) but didn't, so the music for an hour of them wound up on another cassette-only release, **Stations of the Cross**. Backed by Lure and drummer Jerry Nolan, plus someone identified only as Talarico, a reasonably cogent J.T. runs through such songs as "So Alone," "In Cold Blood," "Chinese Rocks" and "Too Much Junkie Business," punctuating the lively performances with typically hysterical inter-song patter. Before ending, the tape takes an odd detour: a hotel room conversation, participants unknown, followed by a solo acoustic number.

Copy Cats—a joint effort with ex-Snatch vocalist Pat Palladin (who also produced the LP) and a bunch of friends—contains covers of songs by Dion, the Seeds, Elvis Presley, the Chambers Brothers, Screaming Jay Hawkins and the Shangri-Las, among many others. [iar]

See also *Heartbreakers*.

TIGERS
Savage Music (A&M) 1980

So what if three of these Tigers were former members of old bands like Juicy Lucy and Van der Graaf Generator? The London fivesome sound as credible as the other ska/reggae bands that cropped up in the Specials' wake, and more fun than most: tart lyrics delivered with good humor, catchy reggae making distinctive use of synth as lead instrument, even some energetic, pop-tinged R&B. Hardly immortal, but highly entertaining. [jg]

'TIL TUESDAY
Voices Carry (Epic) 1985 ●
Welcome Home (Epic) 1986 ●

Boston's underground scene has spawned some excellent, adventurous bands, but 'Til Tuesday is not one of them. "Voices Carry," the quartet's one mega-hit, is an adequate (if clumsy) song that utilizes the full extent of ex-Young Snakes singer/bassist Aimee Mann's limited vocal capabilities; the rest of the band's Mike Thorne-produced debut album is surprisingly unstylish, bland and unengaging.

Armed with a Chrissie Hynde-like warble and another clutch of slow-going sensitive torch-rockers, Mann and her three men issued a soundalike follow-up, produced by Rhett Davies. Although the dynamically-mixed sound is technically flawless, the playing is dull and there aren't many melodies you're likely to remember. (The soaring "On Sunday" is as close as it comes.) In addition, Mann's singing is uncertain and her lyrics are a model of earnest collegiate pretentiousness. Just what kind of home would welcome 'Til Tuesday? [iar]

TIMBUK 3
Greetings from Timbuk 3 (IRS) 1986 ●
Eden Alley (IRS) 1988 ●

Pat and Barbara K. MacDonald are best known for their much-misunderstood fluke hit "The Future's So Bright, I Gotta Wear Shades," and for eschewing backup musicians in favor of overdubs on record and pre-recorded rhythm tapes live. But the Austin-based couple is more noteworthy for Pat's songwriting talent than for the mere novelty of their minimalist lineup. Unlike the deceptively breezy "Shades," MacDonald generally writes sardonic slices of life; his pessimism is consistently redeemed by unflagging humanity and perfectly complemented by the drawling, deadpan harmonies. Despite—or because of—the pair's fondness for mechanical percussion, the music has a homey ambience that balances frequent lyrical archness.

Greetings, surely one of the darkest albums ever to have yielded a hit single, collects some rueful snapshots of Americana ("Life Is Hard," "Just Another Movie") alongside enjoyable lighter fare ("Facts About Cats," "Hairstyles and Attitudes") with impressive results. **Eden Alley** trades much of that album's country twang for a more varied recording approach (e.g., "Sample the Dog" does just that). **Eden Alley**'s stylistic eclecticism comes in handy as Pat's mini-morality-plays (the title track, "Dance Fever," "Rev. Jack & His Roamin' Cadillac Church"). Barbara, meanwhile, shines on her two featured cuts, "Welcome to the Human Race" and "Easy."

For Christmas 1987, Timbuk 3 released one of the most effective protest songs in recent memory, the non-LP "All I Want for Christmas." [hd]

TIME

The Time (Warner Bros.) 1981 ●
What Time Is It? (Warner Bros.) 1982 ●
Ice Cream Castle (Warner Bros.) 1984 ●

Prince's first major male extracurricular effort, Minneapolis' Time was an exceptionally fertile launching pad for several careers: vocalist Morris Day, who walked away with the *Purple Rain* film and a successful solo career, Jesse Johnson, who went on to emulate Prince not only with soundalike records but by mentoring a number of other artists as well, and Jimmy Jam and Terry Lewis, who became an awesomely succesful freelance writing-production team, scoring hits for/with Janet Jackson, Cherrelle, Patti Austin, the S.O.S. Band, Force M.D.'s, Human League and many others.

The Time's albums alternate between straight, infectious dance-funk tunes and ex-

tended jams punctuated by all sorts of silly business. Day's personality informs all of the songs, filling them with sharp-dressed sex-machine jive, but occasionally allowing a glimpse of the self-effacing chump who realizes that having an onstage valet to hold the mirror for on-site preening is a satire on that selfsame smugness. **Ice Cream Castle** is the best of the three, six tracks including several killer dance grooves. (The Time performed "Jungle Love" in a memorable *Purple Rain* club sequence.) But they've still mainly got loving on the brain: witness "If the Kid Can't Make You Come" and "My Drawers." To cap off this divergent LP, "Ice Cream Castles" is fine bubblegum funk-pop. [iar]

See also *Morris Day, Jesse Johnson's Revue.*

TIMES

Pop Goes Art! (nr/Whaam!) 1981
This Is London (nr/Artpop!) 1983
I Helped Patrick McGoohan Escape EP
    (nr/Artpop!) 1983
Hello Europe (nr/Artpop!) 1985
Go! with the Times (Ger. Pastell-Principe
    Logique) 1985
Up Against It (nr/Artpop!) 1986

Led by singer/songwriter Edward Ball, these psychedelic poseurs neatly recapture the lightweight pop sounds of swinging England, circa 1967, in a seamlessly integrated genre lift. The low-budget **Pop Goes Art!** includes the marvelously kitsch "I Helped Patrick McGoohan Escape" as well as appropriately-devised creations like "Biff! Bang! Pow!" and the title track.

Although they aren't as fringe weird or inventive as the Television Personalities (whom they originally resembled), when the Times spin out tunes like "Goodbye Piccadilly" and "The Chimes of Big Ben" on **This Is London**, you'll swear it's the paisley-colored '60s all over again. The Times aren't totally unconnected to the present: "Whatever Happened to Thamesbeat" offers a lucid insight into the neo-mod revival with pointed lyrics.

Inspired by British playwright Joe Orton's screenplay commissioned and discarded by the Beatles, Ball and Tony Conway of Mood Six wrote and attempted to mount a one-act theatrical condensation of *Up Against It* in 1984; the following year, they co-directed a complete stage production of Orton's script, incorporating original songs Ball had written for it. **Up Against It** is a studio album of 14 discrete pop tunes in the Times' familiar '60s idiom, reflecting subsequent developments by quoting the Sex Pistols in one number. (Note: other than its Orton basis, this project has absolutely nothing to do with the forthcoming Broadway musical of the same name, scored by Todd Rundgren.)

If you don't mind that the Times are totally derivative and enjoy the style they lift, the group is a great example of nostalgia that succeeds on its own merits. [iar]

TIME ZONE
See *Afrika Bambaataa.*

TIN HUEY
Contents Dislodged During Shipment (Warner Bros.) 1979

This sextet of eccentrics from Akron, Ohio (hometown of Devo—something in the water supply, perhaps?) were more eclectic and musicianly than their local colleagues. The Hueys' stunning should-have-been-a-hit version of the Monkees' "I'm a Believer" (included on the album) was inspired by Robert Wyatt's re-arrangement, and the band owes a nod to Frank Zappa as well. Yet their blend of blues, jazz and progressive rock is hilariously unique, offering up a warped vision of Middle America. For Tin Huey, "weekends in my Lay-zee Boy" (from "Hump Day") might be punctuated by the discovery of a car filled with doll heads ("Puppet Wipes"); a surreal "Chinese Circus" comes to town; they even admit to fantasies of technological megalomania ("I Could Rule the World If I Could Only Get the Parts"—later the title of a mini-LP by the Waitresses).

After Tin Huey's artistically fruitful (but commercially hopeless) one-album career ended, various members went on to pursue other projects, the most notable of which are guitarist Chris Butler's creation, the Waitresses, and multi-horn wizard Ralph Carney's Swollen Monkeys. [jg]

See also *Waitresses.*

TIN TIN
See *Stephen Duffy.*

TIREZ TIREZ
Etudes (nr/Object Music) 1980 (nr/Aura) 1981

Story of the Year (Bel. Crépuscule) 1983
Social Responsibility (Primitive Man) 1987 ●
Against All Flags (Primitive Man) 1988 ●

French *nom* to the contrary, Mikel Rouse originally formed his trio in Kansas City, relocating it home to New York in 1979. **Etudes** borrows far too much from early Talking Heads to be accused of originality. As a singer, Rouse shows promise, but **Etudes** is too rhythmically monotonous to take in one sitting. Following a Belgian LP release, Tirez Tirez signed with Sire (for one 12-inch single) before finding an American label to put out the group's third album. (Rouse also records with a forward-thinking chamber quartet, Broken Consort.)

Except for bass (credit James Bergman), Rouse sings and plays (keyboards, guitars, drum programs) **Social Responsibility** singlehandedly; he wrote all nine songs and co-produced it as well. Not surprisingly, there's a certain sluggish insularity to the music, an audible lack of human interaction. But when Rouse's over-educated structuralism succumbs to the uplifting pop momentum, Tirez makes for attractive, intelligent listening. [jy/iar]

See also *Tuxedomoon.*

SU TISSUE
See *Suburban Lawns.*

TO DAMASCUS
Succumb (Ringent) 1986
Come to Your Senses (Ringent-Restless) 1987

Originally a keyboardist, LA's Sylvia Juncosa switched to guitar and formed To Damascus after leaving Leaving Trains and touring with Kendra Smith and David Roback in Clay Allison. (She's also concurrently a guitarist in SWA.) **Succumb,** her trio's ragged first album, contains undistinguished post-punk. Juncosa's a carefree, marble-mouthed singer and a solid rhythm guitarist but a sloppy soloist with few original ideas; the rhythm section does its part adequately, but no more.

The lyrics on **Come to Your Senses** indicate Juncosa's evocative talent for expressing alienation and disaffection in unusual ways; her organ and piano contributions leaven the much-improved hyperactive guitar smears (if not her dubious singing). The inclusion of acoustic creations with strings and things offer helpful variety but are also limited in appeal by wobbly vocals. A creative focal point and stronger songwriting would have helped, as Ethan James' co-production fills the LP with layers of energizing aggression that are left hanging like burning wallpaper. [iar]

See also *SWA*.

RUSS TOLMAN
See *True West*.

TOM TOM CLUB
Tom Tom Club (Sire) 1981 ●
Close to the Bone (Sire) 1983

Tom Tom Club provides light refreshment for Talking Heads Tina Weymouth (bass) and her husband Chris Frantz (drums). Although their albums appear during lulls in Heads activity, the first gained its own momentum with two popular dance tracks: "Wordy Rappinghood" and "Genius of Love." Weymouth and her three sisters' airy vocals sound delightfully innocent over steady but unthreatening rhythm. **Close to the Bone** continues in the same whimsical and sensitive vein (e.g., "Pleasure of Love"). Both records skirt cloyingness, saved by the Tom Tommers' selfconsciousness. Even former art school students can have fun sometimes. [si]

TONES ON TAIL
Tones on Tail (nr/Situation Two) 1983
'Pop' (Beggars Banquet-PVC) 1984
Night Music [CD] (Beggars Banquet-PVC) 1987

Freed of the inept artistic pretensions of singer Pete Murphy, Bauhaus guitarist Daniel Ash and drummer Kevin Haskins remained together after the split and, with Glenn Campling, formed Tones on Tail, a generally interesting, shortlived experiment in various styles. (When ToT was done in 1984, Ash and Haskins reunited with erstwhile Bauhaus bassist David J. to form Love and Rockets.)

Tones on Tail, a full-length album made up of the group's early (1982-3) singles, careens from languid, whispered rock to jumpy light funk to spare atmospheric soundtracks and offers very little songwriting content—scanty ideas in service of largely pointless studio fiddling. But while '**Pop**' reveals some draggy recidivist Bauhaus tendencies, it also has real songs of modern music that show taste, delicacy and moderate imagination. "Lions," for instance, works an attractively light synth-samba sound while proffering lines like "Lions always hit the heights/'Cause to kill it's always the easy way out." (I said they weren't *completely* cured.) The multi-movement "Real Life" blends acoustic guitar picking with hushed vocals, angry lyrics and weird sound effects—neo-Yes? There's also a song titled "Slender Fungus."

With the admonition "don't rock—wobble," the 72-minute **Night Music** CD compiles 16 previously released items, including most of '**Pop**,' half of **Tones on Tail**, the wonderfully bent dance kineticism of "Go!" and a horrible bootleg-quality live "Heartbreak Hotel." [iar]

See also *Love & Rockets*.

WINSTON TONG
See *Tuxedomoon*.

TOP JIMMY & THE RHYTHM PIGS
Pigus Drunkus Maximus (Down There-Restless) 1987

Chris Morris' LP liner notes characterize Top Jimmy as a legendary live attraction in Los Angeles, a true-blue white bluesman with a wide, star-studded following. (Van Halen wrote and recorded a song about him on **1984**.) Regardless of where the burly singer and his crackerjack band (unrelated to the Texas thrash trio called the Rhythm Pigs) come from, it's easy enough to hear where they're going—straight into the history books, for playing blues and old-fashioned rock'n'roll with more electric panache and gusto than almost anyone else currently on the scene. Covering Merle Haggard, Bob Dylan, Willie Dixon and Jimi Hendrix with unwavering comprehension and equally enthusiastic sweaty abandon, these no-shit barbusters turn their debut LP into a resounding lesson on how it's s'posed to be done. Steve Berlin produced and plays sax; guest star Don Bonebrake (of X) does most of the drumming. [iar]

TORCH SONG
See *William Orbit*.

TOTO COELO/TOTAL COELO

"I Eat Cannibals" EP (Chrysalis) 1982

These Englishwomen (most of them stage or screen actresses) made one great novelty single, "I Eat Cannibals," produced by ace pop hack Barry Blue. In America, the group's name was mysteriously changed to Total Coelo and the song released on a 12-inch, in two versions with an added number. Over a big mock-tribal beat, the five winningly chant the nonsense lyrics, making it a memorable exercise in silliness.

In 1986, one Coeloite surfaced in the Cherry Bombz, a new outfit with Terry Chimes and other ex-members of Hanoi Rocks.   [iar]

TOURÉ KUNDA

Touré Kunda (Fr. Celluloid) 1981 (Celluloid) 1987 ●
Ém'ma Africa (Les Frères Griots) (Fr. Celluloid) 1982 (Celluloid) 1987 ●
Amadou-Tilo (Celluloid) 1984
Casamance au Clair de Lune (Celluloid) 1984 ●
Live Paris—Ziguinchor (Celluloid) 1984 ●
Natalia (Celluloid) 1985 ●
81/82 (Celluloid) 1986 ●
83/84 (Celluloid) 1986 ●
Karadindi (Celluloid) 1988 ●

The international appeal of Senegal's Touré brothers—Ismaila, Sixu Tidiane and Ousmane—must be attributed in large part to their soothingly mellifluous voices, tones that wash over the listener like warm milk. Of course, their sultry and tasteful integration of Afro-urban and Western dance music have something to do with it too. Like traditional griot songs (they themselves belong to the artisan class), many of their lyrics consist of simple reflections on nature and family life. But after first performing on such traditional instruments as balafon and kora, they gradually integrated electric guitars and keyboards into their arrangements.

Their first album, **Touré Kunda**, contains beautiful melodies over reggae and Arabic rhythms, along with unobtrusive hints of rock music. **Ém'ma Africa**, featuring the music of Sixu and Ismaila, has a notable Jamaican influence.

Amadou-Tilo memorializes Amadou Touré, who died (reportedly from exhaustion) in 1983. The group next recorded an acoustic album of traditional songs, **Casamance au Clair de Lune**, before falling under

the sway of Celluloid house producer Bill Laswell and his studio regulars (including former Parliament keyboardist Bernie Worrell, guitarist Nicky Skopelitis and drummer Aiyb Dieng) on **Natalia**.

In 1986, Celluloid released a pair of compilations, **81/82** and **83/84**.   [rg]

TOURISTS

The Tourists (nr/Logo) 1979
Reality Effect (Epic) 1979
Luminous Basement (Epic) 1980
Tourists (nr/RCA Int'l) 1981

In light of Dave Stewart and Annie Lennox's relatively inventive and adventurous subsequent work as Eurythmics, the Tourists were remarkably low on vitality or originality, playing instead a redundant rehash of '60s American acid and folk-rock. Symptomatic of the group's shortcomings, their crowning achievement was scoring a hit with an utterly dull remake of Dusty Springfield's "I Only Want to Be with You."

Lennox, who later proved to be a much more expressive singer, here sings with strength but no character; duets with guitarist Peet Coombes resemble the worst of the Jefferson Airplane. Otherwise, the group recalls It's a Beautiful Day, the Byrds, Mamas and Papas, the Who and others. If the Tourists had had a personality to call their own, they probably wouldn't have known what to do with it, they were so busy aping others. It's a shame, because some bands have successfully absorbed and adapted these same musical prototypes with much greater élan. At their best, the Tourists could only imitate.

The 1981 LP called **Tourists** is a compilation of previous album tracks; the US edition of **Reality Effect** combines the "best" contents of the band's first two British releases.

                                                                      [iar]

See also *Eurythmics*.

FRANK TOVEY

See *Fad Gadget, Boyd Rice*.

TOXIC REASONS

Independence (Risky) 1982
Kill by Remote Control (Sixth Int'l) 1984
Within These Walls (Treason) 1985
Bullets for You (Alternative Tentacles) 1986
Dedication 1979–1988 (Fun House) 1988

Indianapolis, Indiana's most prominent punks prefer not to be tagged as such—they have more populist aspirations—but can't help admitting (in **Independence**'s "Noise Boys") that they were "born to be hardcore." That's an accurate description, though: watchspring-tight buzzsaw guitar at high speed. For variety, they toss in a mauled remake of "Shapes of Things to Come" (from *Wild in the Streets*) and the hesitant reggae of "Ghost Town," the theme of which is not unlike the Specials' song of the same name, but neither lyrics nor music are as fleshed out.

Kill by Remote Control, with a revised lineup, is great, a cogent punk onslaught with articulate protest lyrics and finely tuned dynamic guitar (Rob Lucjak and Bruce Stuckey) rock. Some of the numbers vamp into a tedious overdrive mode, but most of the record uses its full-tilt electricity in service of well-constructed (if not really melodic) songs.

That isn't Richard Butler of the Psychedelic Furs singing on **Within These Walls**, but it sure sounds like him on "Dreamer." The loud, carefully crafted guitar rock here has its punky moments—as when the slow and steady "Too Late" abruptly shifts into high gear—but is overall too eclectic for any one genre classification. ("Guns of September" recalls the Clash's early reggae efforts.) Lucjak and Stuckey remain a white-hot team, especially in service of these more refined (not less energetic) songs with sturdy melodies. An intelligent, all-electric punch that will leave you grinning.

Lucjak then left the quartet and was replaced by Terry Howe. The resulting **Bullets for You** is little more than political speedcore—poorly recorded, rushed, riff-happy, with shouted/answered vocals—that bears only the faintest resemblance to the formerly winning band. The re-recordings of "Too Late" and "Party's Over" (from **Walls**) don't quite eviscerate the songs, but do show up the inferior surrounding material by contrast.
[jg/iar]

TOYAH & FRIPP
See *Robert Fripp*.

TRACIE
Far from the Hurting Kind (A&M) 1984
Paul Weller discovered Tracie Young in 1982 by announcing a talent hunt in Britain's *Smash Hits;* he selected the 17-year-old from the hordes that responded and set about fashioning her into a blue-eyed soul singer in a rebirth of the great pre-fab pop tradition of the early '60s. And, not unlike the idol-making of *Expresso Bongo,* the main component lacking was significant—or at least developed—talent. Tracie has improved since her tentative beginnings, but her airy Weller-produced LP is still tepid and tedious; the songs (including four by the impresario and one by Elvis Costello) are rendered indistinguishable by bland arrangements and Young's colorless singing. At its best, a few Motownish tunes show signs of life but never capture more than a fraction of the excitement they aim for. A noble experiment, perhaps, but not a successful one. [iar]

TRAGIC MULATTO
Judo for the Blind (Alternative Tentacles) 1984
Locos por el Sexo (Alternative Tentacles) 1987
If you aren't totally repelled by the first album's title or indescribably grotesque cover painting, you may find yourself enthralled by Tragic Mulatto's bizarre musical universe. The five members—whose names are given as Fluffy, Blossom, Flossy, Sweetums and A Piece of Eczema—comprise an atypical rock lineup, as they collectively sing and play bass, drums, trumpet and sax. Produced by Dead Kennedy bassist Klaus Flouride (the audio quality could be better), parts sound like jazzy Flipper; an ominous rock rumble with jagged horn noise and dramatic vocals. Some numbers are faster and well-organized to the point where they resemble a '40s big band on bad drugs; others sound like an incompetent jazz band vainly tuning up while someone soundchecks the microphones. TM have a vision all their own, plus the courage of their convictions.

A suspiciously rechristened quartet (ex-Polkacidist Reverend Elvister Shanksly, Flatula Lee Roth, Jazzbo Smith and Richard Skidmark, aka Wife of God) turned up for the salacious second LP (intentionally numbered VIRUS 69), a wild honking noise party that includes such brilliantly titled scat creations as "Swineherd in the Tenderloin," "Underwear Maintenance" (a detailed paean to menstruation) and a sex manual titled "Twerpenstein." Strangely, the music is really good, with enough structural backbone to give the songs non-satirical legitimacy.

Flatula the female vocalist (who triples on sax and tuba) is wonderful, and the taste-is-no-obstacle lyrics are funnier than a coronary. Fans of the vulgar but hysterical are strenuously recommended to bathe in this delectable cesspool.   [iar]

See also *Polkacide*.

TRANSLATOR

Heartbeats and Triggers (415-Columbia) 1982
No Time Like Now (415-Columbia) 1983
Translator (415-Columbia) 1985
Evening of the Harvest (415-Columbia) 1986
Everywhere That I'm Not—A Retrospective
   (415-Columbia) 1986

Formed in Los Angeles in 1979, this talented quartet really got rolling after moving to San Francisco and signing with 415 Records there. Translator's music encompasses elements of traditional folk-rock, adding modern sounds, novel ideas and cool deadpan pop—simply put, diversity makes Translator fine and often fascinating. Singing guitarists Steve Barton and Robert Darlington have a wide stylistic arsenal and each has the ability to write varied songs of quality and endurance. **Heartbeats and Triggers**, produced by David Kahne, is a great debut album with very few weak tracks.

No Time Like Now contains another batch of melodic and rocking tunes played with ringing guitars and attractive harmonies; unfortunately, a lot of the songs don't wash. While "Un-Alone," "Break Down Barriers" and the title track keep the musical faith, "L.A., L.A." is a trite, gimmicky digression and "I Hear You Follow" is too reserved. Others are equally unprepossessing or simply plain. Stick with the first album.

Translator, produced by Ed Stasium, is for the most part a return to form. "Gravity" is as good as anything they've done; other tunes maintain a tasteful, invigorating blend of vocals, rhythm guitars and intelligent songwriting. The biggest problem here is time: for a third album, they're not really going anywhere new creatively, and commercial success still seems well over the horizon.

Perhaps that frustration explains the radically different album that followed: the one-take guitar rock on **Evening of the Harvest** scarcely resembles prior Translator music. To be fair, this isn't your average numbskull arena rubbish, but the muscle comes as an unwelcome shock. Each track includes (individually credited) guitar riffing,

but most retain a trace of the band's melodicism amid the audio clutter.

The quartet broke up in mid-'86. A definitive career summary, **Everywhere That I'm Not**, contains four cuts from the first album, two each from the second and third, three from the fourth and an otherwise non-LP bonus of Jefferson Airplane's "Today." The track selection isn't perfect, but it's still a fair representation of this very special group's work.   [iar]

TRANSMITTERS

And We Call That Leisure Time
   (nr/Heartbeat) 1981
The Peel Sessions EP (nr/Strange Fruit) 1988

One-time Glaxo Babies vocalist Rob Chapman leads the Transmitters, an interesting enigma of riveting lyrics and free-form minimalism on guitar, bass, drums and squawking sax. The Transmitters walk a very fine line between accessibility and weirdness—easy to appreciate but hard to like. Chapman's a talented singer and writer, and the music might be really good if it weren't so one-dimensional. File under "Eager-to-please-Pere Ubu-offspring."   [iar]

TREES

Sleep Convention (MCA) 1982

A one-man synth army from San Diego, California, Dane Conover (here dubbed Trees) offers a wonderful collection of modern musical ideas and clever tunes that efficiently combine up-to-date electronics with old-fashioned rock instruments, tossing in inventive production and intelligent, provocative lyrics. **Sleep Convention** is a stunning debut which shows remarkable originality and talent. That this record died the commercial death is not just incomprehensible, it's criminal.   [iar]

TRIFFIDS

Treeless Plain (nr/Hot-Rough Trade) 1983
Raining Pleasure (nr/Hot-Rough Trade) 1984
Field of Glass (nr/Hot-Rough Trade) 1985
Love in Bright Landscapes (Hol.
   Hot-Megadisc) 1986
Born Sandy Devotional (Hot-Rough Trade)
   1986
In the Pines (nr/Hot-Rough Trade) 1986
The Peel Sessions EP (nr/Strange Fruit) 1987
Calenture (Island) 1987 ●

Although relocated to London since 1984, this quintet originally hails from Perth, Australia. Their musical influences, however, are strictly American. Occasionally augmenting standard rock instrumentation with strings, trumpet and pedal steel, the Triffids manage a spacious country blues-meets-Television sound.

Raining Pleasure is a lightweight, lilting album with some nice songs and more-than-competent playing, but self-righteous lyrics decrying promiscuity and alcohol are pretty much ruinous. The preachy "Property Is Condemned" is almost worthy of a TV evangelist's seal of approval.

Treeless Plain and **Field of Glass** both have more bite—"My Baby Thinks She's a Train" (from the former) sounds like the best song Tom Verlaine never wrote. (Singer/songwriter David McComb's voice bears similarity to both Verlaine and Jim Morrison.) Most of the Triffids' best material is on **Love in Bright Landscapes**, a Dutch compilation.

The production on **Born Sandy Devotional** is bigger and denser than that on prior releases; while it sounds just fine and is a natural progression, one wishes that McComb's maturing songwriting talents would be allowed to stand on their own a bit more. But on the other hand, it's kind of difficult for a six-piece band (with additional backing on strings, keyboards, vibes and vocals) to be minimalist. **In The Pines** strips things back down; it was recorded in a wool-shearing shed in the Aussie outback on a budget of less than $1,200 Australian (more of the budget was spent on beer, wine and vodka than hiring the 8-track gear, according to the liner notes). A lot of it sounds as though it was done live, and such immediacy suits the Triffids well.

Calenture marks the band's US and major label debuts. Once again, McComb's sensitive, personal visions are all but obscured by big league gloss from producer Gil Norton (Throwing Muses), this time the band's personality barely surfaces. There are plenty of good songs here, mind you, they're just hidden. Once the Triffids find an appropriate means of presenting their talents, they'll really be a band to be reckoned with.

True believers should also be aware that the Triffids have pseudonymous releases under the name Lawson Square Infirmary.

[dgs]

TRIO

Trio (nr/Mobile Suit Corporation) 1982
Live im Frühjahr 82 [tape] (Ger. Mercury) 1982
Trio EP (Mercury) 1982
Trio and Error (Mercury) 1983
Bye Bye (Ger. Mercury) 1983

Originally issued in Germany in 1981, Trio's Klaus Voorman-produced debut album was updated to include their European million-seller, "Da Da Da ich lieb dich nicht du liebst mich nicht aha aha aha." (With the lyrics redone in English, the song was popular in dance clubs outside Germany as well.) Compared to the rest of the album, though, the minimalist hit sounds nearly symphonic; **Trio** is basically guitar and drums behind monotonal (but bilingual) vocals. Lyrics are obsessed with lousy relationships and steeped in black humor—sometimes just blackness without the humor. But the band's brutally primitive sound announces itself first.

The cassette-only **Live im Frühjahr 82** essentially reprises the album, emphasizing guitar for a hot sound, and includes between-song raps *auf deutsch*. The 12-inch **Trio EP** consists of five tracks from the album of the same name (including six-plus minutes of the English-language "Da Da Da") plus a later single, "Anna."

After that tentative step, Trio's American label took the plunge with **Trio and Error**, which *also* includes "Da Da Da"; the new material—almost all in English—is a little more musical and only a little less downbeat. But the naiveté is charming.

With **Bye Bye**, Trio departed roughly the same as they entered: simple, witty and sarcastic in two languages. A '50s revivalist spirit informs the crazed guitar work of "Ich lieb den Rock'n'Roll" and a constipated "Tutti Frutti"; for those with longer memories, Trio thoughtfully includes an (almost) reverent version of "Tooralooralooraloo." Full-scale production on "Out in the Streets" renders it the most routine-sounding track Trio ever recorded; others (e.g., the catchy "Immer Noch Einmal") are as deliciously spartan as ever.   [si/iar]

TRIPOD JIMMIE

Long Walk off a Short Pier (Do Speak) 1982
Warning to All Strangers [tape] (no label) 1986

Tripod Jimmie, a trio starring ex-Pere Ubu guitarist Tom Herman, inhabits a world of hypertense vocals and simple, rough, aggressive rock noise—an underground '80s revision of the power trio concept. Recorded "live on the shores of Lake Erie," **Long Walk**'s 11 numbers show traces of Television, Ubu and Talking Heads, all essentially similarly-minded organizations. Powerful and disquieting. [iar]

TOM TROCCOLI'S DOG
Tom Troccoli's Dog (SST) 1985

Black Flag guitarist Greg Ginn produced and played bass for this trio, whose low-key, Neil Youngish album (cover drawn by D. Boon) includes everything from a politely acoustic "Girl from the North Country" to occasionally anarchic meltdowns like "Suicide," "Slow Dancing" and "Davo's Boogie." [iar]

See also *October Faction*.

TROUBLE FUNK
Drop the Bomb (Sugar Hill) 1982
In Times of Trouble (D.E.T.T.) 1983
Saturday Night. Live! from Washington DC
  (Island) 1985
Trouble Over Here Trouble Over There
  (Island) 1987 ●

Trouble Funk belongs to Washington, DC's go-go scene, for years the best-kept secret in "black music." Go-go is a throwback to percussive, endless-groove funk that sacrifices structure, production and slickness for loose feeling and community involvement. The bands—basically fluid rhythm sections with a few added frills—do their thing while the musicians and audience yell a whole lot of nonsense (like "Let's get small, y'all" or "Drop the bomb!") The funk is solidly Southern, with a strong James Brown flavor and tons of sloppy percussion. In no other North American music does the cowbell play such a major role.

Chuck Brown, father of go-go, developed it from drum breakdowns which he used in clubs to link Top 40 covers. Not surprisingly, he found people were grooving more on these bridges than the songs. Go-go has grown concurrently with hip-hop, and offers a spirited group alternative to beatbox isolationalism. The unsophisticated grooves began to break out nationwide in '85, and Trouble Funk were quickly established as one of the genre's leaders. (They were, however,

eclipsed in 1988, when E.U. had a huge smash with "Da'Butt," a number originally created for Spike Lee's *School Daze*.)

Drop the Bomb is a seminal go-go album because it was released by Sugar Hill, home of the uptown rap set. Virtually all prior go-go releases were on Washington's local T.T.E.D. (aka D.E.T.T.) label. Bronx djs used to find the discs and soak the labels off to keep audiences (and competitors) from learning what they were playing; **Drop the Bomb** gave everyone a chance to get go-go. It also produced two classic tracks: the title tune and the monster 12-inch, "Hey Fellas." Both are wet, sticky and great for dancing. Spin them and you're part of the party.

In Times of Trouble is like two separate albums. The two sides of studio material have nowhere near the juice of the debut. The other two contain long live jams that sum up the scene. The band maintains a low-tech groove, and the four lead singers move the jam along with a lot of assistance from the crowd. It's not like the Godfather of Soul's side-long live medleys because Trouble Funk doesn't do songs: just a hot bottom, some rolling percussion, a couple of tag phrases and a lot of audience participation. The ultimate funk spirit of these sides is intoxicating.

Saturday Night continues the fun with six long, generic demi-instrumentals (and a couple of shorter shards) wisely cut live in front of an enthusiastically cooperative crowd. Cue it up and move!

The title of **Trouble Over Here** is prophetic, as T-Funk rides off the rails in a fit of misguided stylistic ambition. With production and performing assistance by Bootsy Collins and Kurtis Blow, the studio grooves are gussied up in defiance of the band's traditional limber unpretentiousness. The familiarly mobilizing rumble'n'shuffle bottom is intact, but the attempt to turn the grooves into songs busies up the business and blunts the infectious impact. [jl/iar]

TRUE BELIEVERS
True Believers (Rounder-EMI America) 1986

Rank and File grad Alejandro Escovedo (guitar/vocals) and his brother Javier spearheaded this unjustly overlooked band and album, which offers a bristling brew of big-beat rock, rockabilly-influenced rhythms and sweaty ol' noise. The stomping "Hard Road," sexy "So Blue About You" and the country tang of "We're Wrong" deliver what

595

they promise, meaning cathartic rock'n'roll that doesn't insult your intelligence. Jim Dickinson (Replacements, Panther Burns) produced. [jy]

TRUE SOUNDS OF LIBERTY

T.S.O.L. EP (Posh Boy) 1981
Dance with Me (Frontier) 1981
Beneath the Shadows (Alternative Tentacles) 1982
Change Today? (Enigma) 1984
Revenge (Enigma) 1986 ●
Thoughts of Yesterday 1981–1982 (Posh Boy) 1987 ●
Hit and Run (Enigma) 1987 ●

CATHEDRAL OF TEARS

Cathedral of Tears EP (Enigma) 1984

True Sounds of Liberty (aka TSOL) exploded out of Long Beach in 1978 to become one of Southern California's premier hardcore bands. Their first vinyl foray, in 1981, is a tough, politically inspired five-song EP that bristles with excitement. Ron Emory's thrashing guitar provides a steady foundation for vocalist Jack Greggors, credited on the sleeve with "mouth and other organs." These fine songs, like "Abolish Government/Silent Majority," are super hot.

Moving from Posh Boy to Frontier, TSOL made other changes as well. For one thing, Greggors changed his name to Alex Morgon; more importantly, the group abandoned politics to join the trendy horror/shock-rock movement. Along with a cover depicting the grim reaper in a boneyard, the lyrical themes of **Dance with Me** are largely those of B-movie scare flicks, and nearly as much fun. While other bands have proven useless at this genre, TSOL succeed because their brutal, razor-edge sound keeps its musical conviction, regardless of the subject matter.

Volatility is a TSOL hallmark. **Beneath the Shadows** introduces a third label, an added keyboard player and a new drummer (plus a "new" vocalist named Jack Delauge taking over for Morgon). Oh, and they also sound totally different. Dropping any remaining connection with hardcore, this newly refined approach takes the group on a neo-psychedelic trip, but with bonus amounts of rock drive and character. A great record from an always surprising band.

Singer Jack Takeyourpick selected another surname (Loyd) and joined Cathedral of Tears, which issued a weirdly commercial six-song mini-album—raunchy guitars, synthesizers and a danceable resemblance to both the Cult and Dead or Alive—in 1984.

The aptly named **Change Today?** unveils another stage in TSOL's ongoing impermanence: a new label and two new members. Stalwart guitarist Ron Emory and bassist Mike Roche are joined by Joe Wood (guitar/vocals) and Mitch Dean (drums). Fielding a whomping near-punk rock sound, the foursome is aggressive, coherent and lucid, singing shapeless songs that pack a wallop but little lasting substance. Not a bad record, but not a primo effort.

Remarkably retaining both lineup and label, TSOL issued **Revenge**, a powerful record that shows the group in no danger of getting old or tired. The mixture of Alice Cooper/Golden Earring-styled '70s arena rock and traditional LA punk (with a dollop of X-into-the Doors on the title track) could have soared with better (or at least more consistent) material, but there's nothing wrong with the self-assured, energetic performances. (Incidentally, **Revenge** includes a new song entitled "Change Today.")

[cpl/iar]

TRUE WEST

True West EP (Bring Out Your Dead) 1983
Hollywood Holiday (Fr. New Rose) 1983
Drifters (PVC) 1984
Hand of Fate (CD Presents) 1986

RUSS TOLMAN

Totem Poles and Glory Holes (Down There-Restless) 1986

True West may have been part of California's psychedelic underground, but the Davis quintet has definitely got a sound and style all its own. Drawing inspiration from Syd Barrett (the band's first release was a single of his "Lucifer Sam," reprised on the EP) and Roky Erickson, they play a frenetic, dense drone with crazed guitars and dramatic vocals.

Co-produced by guitarist Russ Tolman and Dream Syndicater Steve Wynn, **True West** is a rough, marvelous record—five slices of chaos that kick out nostalgia in favor of powerful rock with a dark, threatening ambience. Echo-laden sound gives tunes like "Hollywood Holiday" and "Steps to the Door" an unsettling noise/chaos level that considerably heightens tension. **Hollywood Holiday** contains the entire EP plus three more-sophisticated tracks subsequently recorded with a new rhythm section. (And a spiffy cover snap of James Cagney as well.)

Drummer Jozef Becker left to rejoin Thin White Rope; True West recorded the **Drifters** album with his not-so-good replacement. The nine new songs (reprising "And Then the Rain" from the French LP) showcase Gavin Blair's vocals as much as Tolman's inventive, original guitar work. A strikingly good record that escapes the strictures of neo-psychedelia by incorporating folk-rock ambience, **Drifters** retains just enough raw-edged aggression to keep things from getting unacceptably melodious. "Look Around" is the clear standout, but other numbers— "Shot You Down" and "Hold On," for instance—also marry engaging sound and arrangements to solid songwriting.

After losing Tolman (and with him their edge), True West pressed on as a quartet. Despite compensatory efforts—the country-ish **Hand of Fate** receives valuable guitar assistance from Matt Piucci (Rain Parade) and Chuck Prophet (Green on Red)—Tolman's departure has had a major negative impact on True West. The record is by no means bad, just colorless. A careful, nostalgic cover of the Yardbirds' "Happenings Ten Years' Time Ago" lacks the energy surge needed to justify the effort.

The (intentionally?) shoddy self-production on Tolman's eccentric solo debut covers up any of the guitarist's potential vocal inadequacies in a blur of flat, boomy sound; there's enough echo on the rhythm section to fill the Grand Canyon. (Maybe that's where this was recorded.) Fortunately, Tolman's spirit and songwriting aptitude are strong even if the audio is weak—cheap bootleg ambience only adds to the outlaw fun.   [iar]

TRUTH
Five Live EP (nr/IRS) 1984
Playground (IRS) 1985
Weapons of Love (IRS) 1987 ●

Leaving behind the constricted scope of Nine Below Zero's skinny-tie R&B revivalism, singer/guitarist Dennis Greaves formed the Truth and proceeded to follow the Style Council's lead in updating '60s soul (Hammond organ, doo-wop vocal backing, shingaling rhythms) for an audience unlikely to know or care that much about the originals. After the introductory **Five Live** EP, **Playground** is a fine album of intelligent, tasteful originals played with real character and a

minimum of selfconsciousness. Of special note: "Exception of Love," "I'm in Tune" (an exciting rave-up) and the title track, a straight rocker.

Weapons of Love finds Greaves suffering from burgeoning Robert Palmer delusions and transparent commercial aspirations. The bombastic album veers wildly from one dodgy style (INXS, U2, etc.) to another, with nary a glimmer of originality or dignity. This is the Truth, eh?   [iar]

TRYPES
See *Feelies.*

T.S.O.L.
See *True Sounds of Liberty.*

MASAMI TSUCHIYA
See *Ippu-Do.*

TUBEWAY ARMY
See *Gary Numan.*

MAUREEN TUCKER
Playin' Possum (Trash) 1981
MOE TUCKER
MoeJadKateBarry EP (50 Skidillion Watts) 1987

In 1981, original Velvet Underground drummer Maureen (Moe) Tucker released a one-woman album on her own Trash Records. The frantic guitar playing and cluttered sound on **Playin' Possum** could have come straight from sessions for the first Velvets album, if you can imagine that band playing "Slippin' and Slidin'," "Bo Diddley" and other oldies.

Tucker subsequently joined forces with a label run by rich'n'famous dilettante Penn Jillette and the hardworking Velvet Underground Appreciation Society. Motley as hell but reeking with credibility and unpolished spirit, the wonderful **MoeJadKateBarry** EP (pressed on red vinyl) was recorded in six hours in an actual Florida garage! Jad Fair (vocals) of Half Japanese and two young locals (on bass and guitar) joined in for the 1986 date; the five songs cover VU obscurities ("Guess I'm Falling in Love," "Hey, Mr. Rain," "Why Don't You Smile Now"), a Jimmy Reed blues ("Baby What You Want Me to Do") and an impromptu instrumental, "Jad Is a Fink." In her own simple way,

Tucker has kept the Velvets' legacy alive better than anyone else. [si/iar]

TUFF DARTS

Tuff Darts (Sire) 1978

New York's Tuff Darts will probably be best remembered (if at all) as a résumé item for Robert Gordon, who was the glam-punk band's original singer in 1976. Although he did record as a Dart on the **Live at CBGB's** compilation, Gordon was long gone by the time the band made an album of its own two years later. (The band was on hold for part of that time while guitarist/leader Jeff Salen played with Sparks.)

The Darts—a junior-league rock band with a penchant for gangster clothes—had a total of two good songs, both of which are included on the LP. Otherwise, the record ranges from simply bad to truly wretched, as on the moronic "(Your Love Is Like) Nuclear Waste." [iar]

See also *Robert Gordon*.

TUXEDOMOON

No Tears EP (Time Release) 1978
(nr/CramBoy) 1985
Scream with a View EP (nr/Pre) 1979 (Bel.
CramBoy) 1985
Half Mute (Ralph) 1980 (nr/CramBoy)
1985 ●
Desire (Ralph) 1981 (nr/CramBoy) 1985 ●
Divine (nr/Operation Twilight) 1982
A Thousand Lives by Picture (Ralph) 1983
Holy Wars (Restless) 1985 ●
Ship of Fools (Restless) 1986
You (nr/CramBoy) 1987 ●
Pinheads on the Move (nr/CramBoy) 1987 ●
Suite en Sous-Sol—Time to Lose (Bel.
Crammed Discs) 1987

BLAINE L. REININGER/MIKEL ROUSE

Colorado Suite EP (Bel. Crammed Discs) 1984
Instrumentals 1982–86 (nr/Interior) 1987

WINSTON TONG

Theoretically Chinese (nr/Crépuscule) 1985

PETER PRINCIPLE

Sedimental Journey (Bel. Crammed Discs)
1985

Pioneers in performance-oriented synthesizer music, Tuxedomoon started out in San Francisco at the very beginning of that city's punk upsurge. The mercurial aggregate of musicians and artists later relocated to Belgium and became a leading light in the international post-rock avant-garde. Sidestepping the mistakes of many early synthesizer bands, Tuxmoon leavened their attack with sax and violin and were quick to integrate electronic percussion as a true substitute for real drums.

Prior to their Ralph records, Tuxedomoon had released singles and EPs on their own label. **No Tears**, a four-cut EP, is an early new wave DIY effort, which sounds coyly dated but still exciting at the time of its reissue seven years later. It was immediately obvious that Tuxedomoon were a step apart from many other bands of the era. Winston Tong had been a mime, and brought a theatrical approach to singing; plenty of synths and electronic percussion (when they were still called rhythm boxes) dominate, violin gets some use and two of the songs exceed the five-minute mark. The succeeding **Scream with a View** (also four songs) is noticeably more art-damaged; itemization of instrumentation cites parallel thirds guitar, vocal concept, six-part doo-wahs and CB interference. In retrospect, this release makes obvious the direction in which they were headed.

Half Mute is a balanced assemblage of pop ("What Use?"), futuristic chamber music ("Tritone") and impressionistic sound collages ("James Whale"). **Desire** is a generally unsatisfying follow-up, save for a sneaky parody of "Holiday for Strings" entitled "Holiday for Plywood." **Divine**, the score for a Maurice Béjart ballet, jettisons the synth beat that makes their best work so attractive. **A Thousand Lives by Picture** is a compilation of tracks previously issued on Ralph.

By the time of **Ship of Fools**, only Principle and singer/multi-instrumentalist Steven Brown remained from the original lineup. Trading in clever humor for selfconscious artsiness (always just beneath the surface anyway), the LP falls flat on its face, especially on the second side, where the band proffers "pieces" rather than songs; titles include "A Piano Solo," "Lowlands Tone Poem" and "Music for Piano + Guitar." Flirting with both light jazz and 20th century classical styles without getting much of a grip on either, the music is about as creative as the nomenclature.

You is a squeaky-clean, virtually bloodless record of meandering jazz-rock fusion with lots of mellow trumpet and sax riffs. Yuck. In "Never Ending Story," we're told "This is only the beginning of a long story that will take many more songs to tell." I'm not sure if I've heard it before, but I'll stop you anyway. Side Two introduces a *Twilight Zone*-style three-part yarn, spoken with minimalist backing. Skip it.

Pinheads on the Move is a two-disc compilation dating all the way back to the band's California beginnings (the title song was their first 45) and contains singles, B-sides, rehearsals, live tracks and jingles for radio programs. Most of the material and performances date from 1977–79, and the lengthy liner notes (an excerpt from an Italian book about the band) provide an intensive history lesson.

Tuxedomoon continues to eschew the commercial success they likely could achieve. Tong has done many outside projects, including a solo album, **Theoretically Chinese**, on Crépuscule. Violinist Blaine L. Reininger, Tuxmoon's co-founder, recorded **Colorado Suite** with Mikel Rouse of Tirez Tirez in 1984 as part of Crammed's Made to Measure series. The four-track, 28-minute mini-LP of a performance piece, is similar to Philip Glass in its bright timbre and repetitive motifs, but lacks Glass' technique of introducing changes so subtly that they're barely noticeable. This suite goes for a little while on one riff, then another similar one, then another and so on, often with Reininger's violin counterpoint dominating. Not a winner.

About half of **Sedimental Journey**, bassist Peter Principle's first solo record (also from the Made to Measure collection), is a video film soundtrack. The one-man show is stylistically similar to the off-center pop of the first two Tuxedomoon albums—lots of mild synth dissonance with found voices drifting around. Agreeable enough, but nothing the band hasn't already accomplished.

[rnp/dgs]

See also *Tirez Tirez*.

TV PERSONALITIES

See *Television Personalities*.

TV21

A Thin Red Line (nr/Deram) 1981

This neat Scottish quintet sounds at times variously like Haircut One Hundred, U2 and XTC; variety keeps things hopping throughout **A Thin Red Line**. Although basically guitar-oriented, the lineup includes trumpet and synth/organ; songs are personal and thoughtful. Singer Norman Rodger has a serviceable voice and tries hard; the rest of the

band, when the recording quality does them justice (different studios and sessions make for inconsistent sound), are no slouches either. [iar]

23 SKIDOO

Seven Songs EP (nr/Fetish) 1982
(nr/Illuminated) 1985
Tearing Up the Plans EP (nr/Pineapple-Fetish) 1982
The Culling Is Coming (nr/Operation Twilight) 1983
Urban Gamelan (nr/Illuminated) 1984
Just Like Everybody (nr/Bleeding Chin) 1986

One of England's most daringly experimental post-punk bands, 23 Skidoo are friendly with the members of Cabaret Voltaire; the two outfits once entertained thoughts of merging. But while 23 Skidoo's early avant-dancefloor style was similar to the Cabs', they've always maintained a closer link to both free-form improvisation and non-Western idioms, especially in their recent work.

Seven Songs (which lists eight tracks, has nine and was reissued with 12) is a near-brilliant fusion of funk, tape tricks and African percussion. The band switches gears effortlessly between different-yet-accessible dance tracks like "Vegas el Bandito," the ethnomusicology of "Quiet Pillage" and sound collages ("Mary's Operation"). **Tearing Up the Plans** continues in much the same vein.

On **The Culling Is Coming**, 23 Skidoo gets too obscure for its own good. The first side, recorded live at the WOMAD Festival, is a mish-mash of tape loops, random percussion and primitive horn honks which sound like dying animals and add up to third-rate Stockhausen. Side Two utilizes Balinese gamelans (tuned gongs of a sort) and sounds better thought-out. **Urban Gamelan** is a stronger album, livelier and less esoteric. As the title implies, real gamelans aren't used, but glass jugs and carbon-dioxide cylinders are. 23 Skidoo will never enjoy wide-scale popularity, but they are an earnest, disciplined band which makes uncompromising music.

Just Like Everybody is a compilation.

[dgs]

20/20

20/20 (Portrait) 1979
Look Out! (Portrait) 1981
Sex-Trap (Mainway) 1982

599

Originally from Tulsa, Oklahoma, LA's 20/20 started out cute and unthreatening, their lush vocal harmonies announcing their love for the Beatles, Byrds and Beach Boys. That's not to say that Steve Allen and his cohorts aren't interesting in their own right: on their debut, producer Earle Mankey helps the band convert their influences into a striking present-tense form, adding dabs of electronics to dense arrangements. Songs like "Yellow Pills" and "Remember the Lightning" give the impression of being squeezed into a smaller space than is safe—that contents-under-pressure tension adds an exciting edge.

Recorded without Mankey, **Look Out!** is pleasing, but doesn't sparkle the way **20/20** does. More spacious sound exposes the essential banality of the material and shows up the often formulaic nature of the vocal harmonies.

After a lack of commercial acceptance (and the end of the industry's infatuation with skinny-tied power pop bands) cost them their major-label deal, 20/20 dropped out of national sight, but came back in late '82 as a trio with an independent release that unfortunately isn't very impressive. The band subsequently evaporated; guitarist Chris Silagyi became a record producer. [jy]

TWIST

This Is Your Life (nr/Polydor) 1979

This obscure transitional band has loads of fascinating history, the details of which are thus: guitarist Pete Marsh had been in a schmaltzy duo which evolved into the horribly wimpy Easy Street, a British band signed to Georgia-based Capricorn Records. (Easy Street also included Richard Burgess, who later abandoned easy listening for synthesizer funk, working with Visage, Spandau Ballet and forming Landscape. He's not in this band.) Twist bassist Andy Pask became a member of Landscape while Marsh went on to form pseudo-mystery band Blanket of Secrecy. Drummer Steve Corduner was an ex-member of Nasty Pop.

With guest stars Elvis Costello and Steve Nieve, it's not overly surprising that **This Is Your Life** occasionally resembles **My Aim Is True**. An interesting album with some good songs, it deserved better than it got; despite the uncertain devotion of its members to bouncy rock'n'roll, together they carried it off admirably. [iar]

SEAN TYLA GANG
Yachtless (Beserkley) 1977
Moonproof (Beserkley) 1978
SEAN TYLA
Just Popped Out (Polydor) 1980

From seminal pub-rock bandleader (Ducks Deluxe) to early Stiff signee (his "Texas Chainsaw Massacre Boogie" was the label's fourth release) to the Tyla Gang and a solo career, guitarist Sean Tyla's been around. His three albums (the first two with a steady band of pub compadres) are hard-rocking and honest but not thrilling, despite good playing and Tyla's sincere hoarse vocals. **Yachtless** is the raunchy one, full of lead guitar and aggressive drumming. **Moonproof** takes a subtler attack, introducing acoustic guitar and a more American sound, but no energy loss. **Just Popped Out**, which employs an amazing cast of pub-rock characters (including former members of Ace, Bees Make Honey, Ducks Deluxe, Chilli Willi and the Red Hot Peppers and Man) not to mention Joan Jett and Kenny Laguna, offers bitter, depressed songs given the best studio treatment of Tyla's career. Comparisons to Bob Seger's gritty rock don't exactly say it, but both have a commitment to personal vision and unfancy, straightforward music. [iar]

U U U U U U U

UB40

Signing Off (nr/Graduate) 1980 ●
Present Arms (nr/DEP Int'l) 1981 + 1985
Present Arms in Dub (nr/DEP Int'l) 1981 +
   1985
The Singles Album (nr/Graduate) 1982
UB44 (nr/DEP Int'l) 1982
Live (nr/DEP Int'l) 1983 ●
1980–83 (A&M) 1983
Labour of Love (A&M) 1983 ●
Geffery Morgan (A&M) 1984 ●
The UB40 File (nr/Graduate) 1985 ●
Baggariddim (nr/DEP Int'l) 1985 ●
Little Baggariddim EP (A&M) 1985
Rat in the Kitchen (DEP Int'l-Virgin-A&M)
   1986 ●
UB40 CCCP—Live in Moscow (A&M) 1987 ●
The Best of UB40 Volume One (nr/DEP Int'l)
   1987 ●
UB40 (Dep Int'l-A&M) 1988 ●

This eight-man integrated reggae outfit from Birmingham built its huge following on an independent label (the band's own DEP International) with non-Rastafarian lyrics concerning social issues—not unlike what many new wave bands addressed—and an ineffable pop sensibility. From the get-go, UB40's music has held appeal far beyond the specialized market; they are the most commercially successful self-contained reggae band in the world. Quietly percolating grooves garnished with sultry horn lines and centered around Ali Campbell's cool, Stevie Wonderesque crooning (with and without sweet harmonies) give UB40 an instantly identifiable sound—or formula, as you will.

On the early albums, even the best of the uneven songwriting—as catchy as it does get—sounds samey and is dominated by the group's style. Contrary to the lyrics' urgency,

the music suggests that even when "The Earth Dies Screaming," we'll hear it calmly sipping tea in a hot tub. In the early days, the band's tunesmithing seemed to rise to the occasion only for singles (and often, surprisingly, for B-sides).

The Singles Album is UB40's best English-only LP, even though over half of it had already appeared on **Signing Off**. (For the quantity-minded, the latter does include a bonus disc with another 21 minutes of music.) As a matter of fact, any non-fan possessing a couple of UB 45s might hesitate before buying an album by the group.

Present Arms is notable for more prominent use of toasting (which continued on **UB44**) and little else, aside from two solid singles. **Present Arms in Dub**, though, thoughtfully attempts an alternative to the usual dub style, which is generally just vocalless electronic fiddling of greatly variable quality. Here, UB40 drastically changed the face of its music to the point where some songs are hardly recognizable; it's nearly as though the material were written explicitly for dub treatment. An "A" for effort.

UB44, in addition to minor alterations (more Latin percussion, sparingly applied gurgling synth), displays wider lyrical range and increased verbal acuity, but the only truly striking tune is, naturally, a single ("So Here I Am"). It's not that UB40 have little to offer; it's just that their singles are the brightest spots cut from the same relatively unvarying cloth.

The group's first live album was recorded on tour in Ireland in 1982 and features such tunes as "Food for Thought," "Tyler" and "One in Ten."

In an effort to export some of UB40's success to the States, the group's American label issued **1980–83**, a selection of tracks from **UB44**, **Present Arms** and early singles. Not a bad set, but not the introduction America wanted to hear. What finally did the trick was a novelty of sorts, but one that sidestepped the band's shortcomings as songwriters: **Labour of Love** is an LP of cover versions, drawing on reggae (and reggaefied) hits from a number of diverse authors: Neil Diamond ("Red Red Wine"), Jimmy Cliff ("Many Rivers to Cross"), Delroy Wilson ("Johnny Too Bad") and others. The resultant variety and melodic quality make it UB40's most easily enjoyable album, richly filled with loving tributes played superbly.

Geffery Morgan, entirely new original material, shows a vastly more creative UB40 at work. Inventive production, intriguing rock rhythms, powerful and memorable songwriting and new outlooks all combine to make it a great record that remains rooted in reggae but is much more diverse than the form generally allows. "Riddle Me" and "If It Happens Again" are ace reggae/rock hybrids; "Nkomo a Go Go," with a propulsive dance-rock beat and wailing saxophone, shows the full range of UB40's development. A very impressive step forward from a band who already know the formula for success.

The UB40 File is a repackage of **Signing Off**, with a second disc consisting of all the singles the band cut that year. (It doesn't require a detective to realize that it merely reissues—and not for the first time—everything on their original label.) Unnecessary, except for completists.

Baggariddim consists of three new recordings (the catchy "Don't Break My Heart," "Mi Spliff" and a charmingly reggaefied "I Got You Babe" sung with Chrissie Hynde) on an EP plus a seven-song album of dub mixes—with guest toasters—from **Labour of Love** and **Geffery Morgan**. The one-disc **Little Baggariddim** offers the three new items, plus "I Got You Babe" dub and two additional numbers.

Rat in the Kitchen is another spectacularly accomplished collection of originals that makes it clear that UB40's songwriting has fully matured. Lyrics concern employment and poverty; "Sing Our Own Song" vaguely discusses apartheid. (The LP includes postcards for protesting to P.W. Botha and contributing to Amnesty International.) Although no tracks particularly stand out, **Rat in the Kitchen** bops from start to finish with infectious warmth and top-notch musicianship.

Live in Moscow, a single disc recorded during a historic 1986 Russian tour, draws from various periods in the band's career and includes "If It Happens Again," "Don't Break My Heart," "Cherry Oh Baby," "Johnny Too Bad" and "Please Don't Make Me Cry." Lively performances but thin, barely adequate sound make it more of a milestone in UB40's history than an essential contribution to their catalogue. **The Best of UB40 Volume One** compiles 14 British hits; the CD adds four bonus tracks.

Tragedy struck UB40 in November 1987, when bassist Earl Falconer drove his car into a Birmingham factory wall, killing his brother Ray, the band's co-producer. He was eventually sentenced to prison for causing a death by reckless driving.   [jg/iar]

See also *Pretenders*.

U.K. SUBS

Another Kind of Blues (nr/Gem) 1979
Live Kicks (nr/Stiff) 1980
Brand New Age (nr/Gem) 1980
Crash Course (nr/Gem) 1980
Diminished Responsibility (nr/Gem) 1981
Endangered Species (nr/NEMS) 1982
Best Of (1977–1981) (nr/Abstract) 1982
Flood of Lies (nr/Scarlet-Fall Out) 1983
Demonstration Tapes (nr/Konexion) 1984
Subs Standard (nr/Dojo) 1985
Gross-Out USA (nr/Fall Out) 1985
In Action—Tenth Anniversary (nr/Fall Out) 1986
Left for Dead: Alive in Holland '86 [tape] (ROIR) 1986
Raw Material (nr/Killerwatt) 1986
A.W.O.L. (nr/New Red Archives) 1987
Japan Today (Restless) 1988

CHARLIE HARPER
Stolen Property (nr/Flicknife) 1982

URBAN DOGS
Urban Dogs (nr/Fall Out) 1983

Alongside their contemporaries, London's never-say-die U.K. Subs' 1977 punk sounds old-fashioned, yet Nicky Garratt's wall-of-sound rhythm guitar and Charlie Harper's chanted/sung vocals make for highly enjoyable charged rock'n'rage that owes more to bands like the MC5 than Sex Pistols. Maybe it's the familiarity of their style that makes the quartet more listenable than, say, the early Exploited; whatever the case, the Subs play high-energy, fast-paced punk with a social conscience, and that keeps them one of England's most successful speed-rock outfits.

Brand New Age finds the Subs bemoaning alienation in the modern world (on the title track) and singing their signature tune, "Emotional Blackmail," twice. **Diminished Responsibility** confronts such issues as racism, rioting, gangsters, Paris, prison and urban decay. Harper's songwriting (in collaboration with various members of the band) shows lyrical growth—he's quite capable of incisive lines and spot-on humor—on **Endangered Species**, a fact he almost acknowledges on "Sensitive Boys"; elsewhere, the bleak terrain is littered with better-expressed and subtler observations about the world's ills. Best tune: the touching "Fear of Girls."

Flood of Lies showcases a new lineup and has a great political cartoon of Maggie Thatcher on the cover; the songs are once again more aggressive ("Violent Revolution," "Soldiers of Fortune"), but there's room for some humor as well ("Revenge of the Jelly Devils"). **Gross-Out USA**, the Subs' second live album (after **Crash Course**), recapitulates the band's career in fine raucous form with 16 songs offered start-to-finish, just as they happened. **Left for Dead** does the same feat, adding to the Subs' live album legacy with a tape-only release, recorded with yet another lineup in Holland. The 23 songs overlap only a half-dozen with **Gross-Out**; the performance is typically incendiary and the recording quality not half bad.

Japan Today is the Subs' tenth studio album (but who's counting?), a more controlled and musical assault than usual, recorded by Harper and five sidemen, including ex-Vibrator guitarist Knox. The sound is a bit '70s hard rock, the lyrical stance broader and less clichéd as well. An improvement, but not exactly a high point in contemporary rock'n'roll.

Harper's first solo effort is worth checking out. Unlike the Subs' all-original music, **Stolen Property** oddly consists of traditional garage band standards, such as "Pills," "Louie, Louie," "Hey Joe" and "Waiting for My Man."

The not-so-super session of Harper and Knox (plus a rhythm section) dubbed Urban Dogs plays highly charged riotpunk that sounds like a cross between early Stranglers, early Pistols and early Stooges. Alongside Knox originals (including the Vibrators' classic "Into the Future," here retitled "Sex Kick") and a couple of Harper's own raunchy numbers, there are covers like Iggy's "I Wanna Be Your Dog" and the Dolls' "Human Being," complete with soundalike Thunders licks. The raunch, spirit and electricity run high from start to finish, making **Urban Dogs** everything a great punk record should be. [cpl/iar]

TRACEY ULLMAN

You Broke My Heart in 17 Places (Stiff-MCA) 1983
You Caught Me Out (nr/Stiff) 1984
Forever: The Best of Tracey (nr/Stiff) 1985

A weekly show on American television has made Tracey Ullman a well-known figure, but it's unlikely most viewers are familiar with these records. Her musical career revolved around chameleonlike visual characterizations (pictured on both LP jackets) and good taste in choosing songs to record. She hasn't got any particular talent as a singer, but that didn't prevented the spunky Briton from having hits on both sides of the Atlantic.

On **You Broke My Heart in 17 Places**, with producer Peter Collins and a stack of top sessioneers, Ullman (overdubbed like crazy in spots) covers such campy classics as "Move Over Darling" and "Bobby's Girl," as well as more contemporary winners, like "(I'm Always Touched by Your) Presence Dear" and Kirsty MacColl's "They Don't Know." To some extent a commercially minded snooze, the mix of songs and sounds, relatively free of kitsch and gratuitous nostalgia, makes it a mild treat.

You Caught Me Out is essentially the same album with a dozen different numbers. Besides co-writing the title track, MacColl again has her back catalogue tapped, this time for "Terry," which Ullman stifles; other jukebox selections here include "Where the Boys Are," "Give Him a Great Big Kiss" and, for anomaly's sake, a terrible version of the Waitresses' "I Know What Boys Like."

Except for a compilation LP to keep her in the bins, Ullman's been doing less with vinyl and more with celluloid since. She was quite good alongside Meryl Streep and Sting in *Plenty*. [iar]

JAMES BLOOD ULMER

Tales of Captain Black (Artists House) 1979
Are You Glad to Be in America? (nr/Rough Trade) 1980
Free Lancing (Columbia) 1981
Black Rock (Columbia) 1982
Odyssey (Columbia) 1983
Part Time (nr/Rough Trade) 1984

Got Something Good for You (Ger. Moers)
1986
Live at Caravan of Dreams (Caravan of
Dreams) 1987
America—Do You Remember the Love? (Blue
Note) 1987

MUSIC REVELATION ENSEMBLE
No Wave (Ger. Moers) 1980

Arguably the most innovative electric guitarist since Jimi Hendrix, Ulmer is certainly worthy of that challenge. With mentor Ornette Coleman, Ulmer introduced many to the avant-garde concept of harmolodics with the release of **Tales of Captain Black**, eight songs of hot funk and boiling rhythms. But the production is somewhat flat, and Coleman upstages him. Still, an eye-opening debut.

Are You Glad to Be in America?, featuring his first vocal efforts, is Ulmer's finest album, revealing a staggering understanding of the roots of jazz, dance music, Eastern polyrhythms and harmolodic textures in a lively sound mix. Without Coleman, Blood works with fabled electric bassist Amin Ali and the stunning sax combo of David Murray (tenor) and Oliver Lake (alto); the music fairly crackles.

No Wave is an experimental album recorded with the Music Revelation Ensemble (Ali, Murray, Lake and Ronald Shannon Jackson on drums). It's Ulmer's most inaccessible work, as well as his least focused.

Free Lancing and **Black Rock** are technical masterpieces, making up in precision what they lack in emotion (as compared to **Are You Glad to Be in America?**). Working to expand his audience, Ulmer concentrates more on electric guitar flash, and actual melodies can be discerned from the improvised song structures (improvisation being one of the keys to harmolodics).

Odyssey takes Ulmer in a novel direction: working with just a drummer (Warren Benbow) and violinist (Charles Burnham), he builds mesmerizing but patchy fabrics of busy guitar, traversing kinetic jazz, blues, pop and rock idioms with relaxed power. Singing in an engaging rustic blues voice, Ulmer essays extremely traditional song forms. ("Little Red House" and "Are You Glad to Be in America?" sound like Taj Mahal.) Matching the cheery cover photo, this is easily his most accessible, commercial and likable record. With a firm grip on jazz-rock and progressive music, Ulmer's future possibilities remain boundless.   [gf/iar]

ULTRAVOX
Ultravox! (Island) 1977
Ha!Ha!Ha! (nr/Island) 1977
Systems of Romance (Antilles) 1978
Live Retro EP (nr/Island) 1978
Three into One (nr/Island) 1980
Vienna (Chrysalis) 1980 ●
Rage in Eden (Chrysalis) 1981 ●
New Europeans (Jap. Chrysalis) 1981
Mini-LP EP (Aus. Festival) 1981
Quartet (Chrysalis) 1982 ●
Monument—The Soundtrack EP (nr/Chrysalis)
1983
Lament (Chrysalis) 1984 ●
The Collection (Chrysalis) 1984 ●
U-Vox (nr/Chrysalis) 1986 ●
The Peel Sessions EP (nr/Strange Fruit) 1988

MIDGE URE
The Gift (Chrysalis) 1985

Originally lost in the gap between glam-rock and punk, Ultravox became prime movers of the electro-pop and new romantic movements when they combined synthesizer with the direct and danceable pop music of the new wave.

Ultravox!—produced by Brian Eno, Steve Lillywhite and the group—marries the flamboyance of poseurdom to the cold minimalism of Kraftwerk, with more than a touch of punk's roughness. John Foxx's voice is typically distant, singing lyrics that contain jumbled images expressing passive dislocation (a popular Ultravox theme). While synthesizers are in short supply, the budding Ultravox style can be noted in "Dangerous Rhythm," the oddly passionate "I Want to Be a Machine" and the classic "My Sex."

Ha!Ha!Ha! comes closer to the spirit of punk, filled with tight, straightforward rockers outlining a spirit of alienation and life free of love, companionship and comprehension. Billy Currie's electric violin playing is stunning, and the climactic track, "Hiroshima Mon Amour," introduces full-force synthesizer into Ultravox's music, delineating the boundary between past and future. Recommended.

Systems of Romance, produced by Conny Plank, fuses the band's pop vision with spare, crystalline electronic sound. Focused both lyrically and musically on the fragmentation of experience, the album weaves a sinuous existential mood that suggests dreams and autumn nights. Highly recommended.

Vienna, also produced by Plank, was marked by the departure of Foxx and guitarist Robin Simon (who had replaced founding member Stevie Shears after the second LP); Scottish vocalist/guitarist (ex-Slik/Rich Kids) Midge Ure filled out the new lineup and took over the group. Ultravox's recast sound included a more symphonic use of synthesizer, layered in deep swells for new heights of sonic density. **Vienna** includes Ultravox's best hits: "All Stood Still," "Sleepwalk," "Passing Strangers" and the title track. The new approach proved highly satisfying and successful, spawning a horde of less-inspired imitators collectively referred to as new romantics.

Noting **Vienna**'s success, Island issued **Three into One**, a compilation of songs drawn from the first three albums, including "My Sex" and "Hiroshima Mon Amour."

Rage in Eden, Ultravox's last outing with Plank, finds Ure sliding into operatic vocals and pretentious lyrics, but the music—again displaying complex synthesizer patterns—is superb, with Currie, Ure, bassist Chris Cross and drummer Warren Cann blending brilliantly.

New Europeans is a Japanese compilation of B-sides from the **Vienna** and **Rage in Eden** period, added to A-sides "The Voice" and "New Europeans." Though the flipsides are hardly top-notch, they are interesting, and the mastering/pressing provides exceptional audio quality.

The Australian **Mini-LP** combines two rare tracks from an early flexi-disc ("Quirks" and "Modern Love") with the contents of **Live Retro**, an excellent 7-inch concert EP originally released in 1978. (The **Peel Sessions** EP also chronicles that era, as it was recorded in November 1977.)

Quartet continues in much the same vein as **Rage in Eden**, but producer George Martin thins out the sound too much, reducing the band to a subordinate role as backing for Ure, whose lyrics are infused with religious overtones. Clear but unsatisfying.

Ultravox self-produced **Lament**, proving themselves quite capable of working without outside supervision. The album contains two of their finest singles, "One Small Day" and "Dancing with Tears in My Eyes," amidst a host of other suave and personable excursions. **Lament** further elevates Ultravox's reputation as one of the few groups to capably incorporate synthesizers and other modern conveniences into a truly unique sound.

The live **Monument** also serves as the soundtrack to a concert videocassette of the same name. **The Collection** is a remarkable compilation of the band's singles (1980–1984): 14 cuts, including "Sleepwalk," "We Came to Dance," "All Stood Still" and "One Small Day," all stellar examples of craft and creativity. Not a bad introduction to the group's post-Island work.

Except for a slightly increased guitar focus and the large proportion of instrumentals, Ure's one-man solo album (with a little assistance, mostly on bass and vocals) sounds enough like Ultravox in spots to unsettle his bandmates—it could easily be mistaken for a group effort. (Although few would believe *they* would attempt a laid-back cover of Jethro Tull's "Living in the Past"—downright bizarre, but not as awful as you might imagine.) "If I Was" has a nice refrain but trite lyrics—Ure's uncertainty quickly becomes aggravating—and goes on too long. If nothing else, this mix of familiar synth-rock and adventurous instrumentals proves that Ure will easily survive the end of Ultravox when it comes; perhaps **The Gift** has hastened that eventuality.

Warren Cann quit in mid-1986 and has not been heard from since; the three remaining members deputized Big Country drummer Mark Brzezicki and finished the competent but unassuming **U-Vox** album. All their fire and personality seems to have evaporated. Ure's singing has never been so restrained; the bland overall sound (punctuated with brass on two big production numbers) bears only occasional resemblance to their past work, yet offers nothing especially new to replace it. "Follow Your Heart" is about as good as it gets; in an odd detour, "All Fall Down" is a folky anti-war drinking song with accompaniment by the Chieftans.

[sg/iar]

See also *Faith Global, John Foxx, Visage.*

UNDEAD

Nine Toes Later EP (Stiff) 1982
Never Say Die! (Ger. Rebel) 1986

Guitarist Bobby Steele quit the Misfits in 1980 and formed the Undead, a trio that cut Stiff's very last US release. (Its title refers to the accident that left Steele with a pronounced limp.) **Never Say Die!** combines the EP with two subsequent independent singles into a solid mini-LP (eight songs in under 19 minutes). It's gritty, rocking, catchy and angry but, like the title track, often shows a positive attitude. With a settled lineup, the Undead might have made a super live record; these documents are just as good. [jg]

UNDERTONES

The Undertones (Sire) 1979
Hypnotised (Sire) 1980
Positive Touch (Harvest) 1981
The Love Parade EP (nr/Ardeck) 1982
The Sin of Pride (nr/Ardeck) 1983
All Wrapped Up (Ardeck-Capitol) 1983
Cher o' Bowlies (nr/EMI) 1986 ●
The Peel Sessions EP (nr/Strange Fruit) 1986

The best band ever to come from Northern Ireland, the Undertones took a youthful adoration for the glam-rock era and gave it the stripped-down simplicity and energy of punk to create truly wonderful albums of pop/rock (and, towards the end, soul) with a difference. Their body of work reveals rapid creative growth; each album clearly shows a different stage in their development. The group's 1983 wind-up, as unavoidable as it was disappointing, resulted from a lack of sustained commercial success and the inability to shake the public's first impression of them as an Irish Ramones.

Very young when they began in 1976 Derry, the Undertones started out writing simple, fetching melodies with lyrics about teenagehood and playing them fast and raw on basic guitars, bass and drums. With Feargal Sharkey's unique, piercing tenor out front, songs on the first album ("Jimmy Jimmy," "Here Comes the Summer," "Girls Don't Like It") are spare and efficient pop gems that are as infectious as measles, suggesting a bridge between teenybop and punk. (The US edition has two songs added from an early single; a limited-edition English 10-inch released at the same time contained those two tracks plus a pair from the LP.)

The Undertones broadened their scope for **Hypnotised**, making the sound clearer and more instrumentally distinct while offering uniquely cast lyrics telling stories and describing characters with impressive skill. Outstanding tracks include "My Perfect Cousin," the delicate "Wednesday Week" and the gently self-mocking "More Songs About Chocolate and Girls." Of the four original albums, **Hypnotised** has the best balance of sophistication and innocence.

Positive Touch introduces well-placed horns and piano (by Paul Carrack) to the sound and explores much more ambitious ground, in reflection of the band's personal and musical maturation. While the songs are not all immediately catchy, they are ulti-mately rewarding, displaying numerous new sides and levels to the Undertones. An enormous artistic achievement for a band that had been playing rudimentary four-chord riff numbers a scant two years earlier.

The Love Parade EP—actually a 12-inch single with four songs on the B-side—includes three otherwise unavailable live recordings tied together with weird noises and unfathomable dialogue. Most importantly at the time, it showed the band to be newly rooted in '60s soul psychedelia.

Perhaps overly stung by their commercial problems, the Undertones made their final album with more ambition than concentration. **The Sin of Pride** has its brilliant moments—the soulful "Got to Have You Back" (a soul cover), "Bye Bye Baby Blue," "The Love Parade," "Chain of Love"—but the fear of being thought of as an immature pop band drives them into low-key excursions that drift away tunelessly, and overactive horn charts bury the band's instrumental personality. Also, the sound quality is disturbingly distant.

The English version of **All Wrapped Up**, the Undertones' posthumous singles collection, has two discs and features all 13 of their A-sides plus 17 flips—30 magnificent cuts in all. From "Teenage Kicks" right up through "Chain of Love," it's a stirring reminder of what a truly marvelous band they were. The American version has the same gross cover photo (nude model with cured meats) but drops one disc and 16 of the B-sides. **Cher o' Bowlies**, subtitled "The Pick of the Undertones," is another compilation with some overlap, but rather than concentrating on 45s, the selection of album tracks portrays the group differently. The Peel BBC radio EP, produced by Bob Sargeant in January 1979, offers live versions of "Here Comes the Summer," "Family Entertainment" and two others.

Since the 'Tones broke up, Feargal Sharkey has been the most visible of the five, making one great 1983 single ("Never Never") with Vince Clarke's otherwise stillborn Assembly and then a not-so-great solo 45 ("Listen to Your Father") for Madness' Zarjazz label the following year. He made an additional one-off single, produced by Queen drummer Roger Taylor, before linking up with Eurythmic Dave Stewart and scoring with "A Good Heart." The O'Neill brothers formed That Petrol Emotion, while the other two left the music biz. [iar]

See also *Feargal Sharkey, That Petrol Emotion.*

UNDERWORLD
See *Freur.*

UNITS
Digital Stimulation (415) 1980
Animals They Dream About (unreleased)
New Way to Move EP (Epic) 1983

One of the first American synthesizer-based rock bands, San Francisco's Units started out playing Cabaret Voltaire style cacophony, but quickly developed an educated electro-pop approach. Lyrically, **Digital Stimulation** is rife with irony and black humor; the spontaneous, creative music complements it well. The Units obviously prefer purer electronic sounds to the pseudo-pipe organ noises employed by many other synth bands, but stop before succumbing to the dreaded noodling disease. The upshot is a dozen sharp pop tunes of estimable value.

Typical of the Units' hard-luck recording career, the band made a second album for 415, produced by Bill Nelson. Although it solidified the early test-run of **Digital Stimulation** into a unique and coherent style wrapped around brutal assaults on American thought, the record was never released, due to a falling out between the Units and their label. A loss.

In 1983, following the success of an independently issued 12-inch dance-floor hit ("The Right Man," produced by Michael Cotten of the Tubes), the Units signed with Epic and went to Wales to record, again with Nelson. Incredibly, the resulting album also never saw the light of day, but an EP *was* released, combining "The Right Man" and "A Girl Like You" with three songs from those otherwise discarded sessions and a remix by Ivan Ivan. Solidly appealing and catchy dance-rock.   [sg/iar]

UNIVERSAL CONGRESS OF
See *Saccharine Trust.*

UNKNOWNS
Dream Sequence EP (Bomp-Sire) 1981
The Unknowns (Invasion) 1982

BRUCE JOYNER AND THE PLANTATIONS
Way Down South (Invasion) 1983

Liam Sternberg, Ohio's answer to Phil Spector, produced the six tracks for **Dream Sequence** "in an aircraft hangar." California's Unknowns play pure '60s garage rock with Mosrite guitars (displayed and mentioned on the cover for added authenticity), heaps of echo and tremolo, and incorporate various period genres (surf music, Creedence swamp choogle, psychedelia, punk) into their songs. Where **Dream Sequence** is slick but boring, **The Unknowns** shows them in greater command of their musical vocabulary and adds traces of the Animals, Yardbirds, Blues Project and the Doors to spice things up considerably. A rendition of Buddy Holly's "Rave On" ties up a neat package of heavily stylized nostalgia.

After the Unknowns, Bruce Joyner formed the Plantations. **Way Down South** abandons the literal aspects of the Unknowns' nostalgia for a more direct, unassuming sound that is still colored by weedy organ and other '60s affectations. Some of the 14 varied numbers are catchy and well-constructed; others drag. (Appearances aside, none of the music and only the occasional lyric is particularly reflective of the land below the Mason-Dixon line.) Joyner is moderately talented but needs stronger collaborators.   [iar]

UNTOUCHABLES
Live and Let Dance EP (Twist-Enigma) 1984
Wild Child (Stiff-MCA) 1985
Dance Party EP (Stiff-MCA) 1986

There were numerous promising local R&B-cum-ska outfits on the LA scene at the time, but it was the worthy Untouchables who caught Stiff's attention and wound up with a label deal on both sides of the Atlantic. **Live and Let Dance** introduced the band's energetic dance attack with a half-dozen exciting numbers, starting with the unforgettably catchy "Free Yourself." (One listen and you'll swear you heard it on a 1980 2-Tone single.) The 12-inch also presents solid reggae and ska in the UB40 mold; the live take of "(I'm Not Your) Stepping Stone," however, clarifies their individuality.

Wild Child reprises "Free Yourself," surrounding it with ten other strong tracks, including the similarly effective title track, a cool version of "I Spy (For the FBI)—an obscurity also recorded by John Hiatt—produced by Jerry Dammers, a slice of straight rap-funk ("Freak in the Streets") and a synth-tinged rock tune ("Lovers Again"). Stewart Levine's production could be more full-bodied, but the sextet's enthusiasm and precision keep things rocking from start to finish.

With no new material forthcoming, a 12-inch compilation EP was released. **Dance Party** contains four album track remixes, including "Freak in the Street" (by Don and David Was) and "Free Yourself," plus a tune from the first EP and a new live funk workout. Fine, but what else can you show me? [iar]

URBAN DOGS

See *U.K. Subs.*

URBAN HEROES

Age of Urban Heroes (Hol. Ariola Benelux) 1980
Who Said . . . (nr/Handshake) 1980

These Dutchmen have the ability to make sparks fly from what would otherwise be just homely old R&B-flavored rock'n'roll, adding plenty of poppy touches to the arrangements. But their coarse aggressiveness sometimes overpowers whatever else they have to offer. And they should not have manhandled a great tune like the Equals' "Baby Come Back." [jg]

URBAN VERBS

Urban Verbs (Warner Bros.) 1980
Early Damage (Warner Bros.) 1981

Fascinating but tragically overlooked, Washington, DC's Urban Verbs were an arty quintet whose lead singer was the brother of Talking Heads drummer Chris Frantz. And therein lay the Verbs' problem: while guitarist Robert Goldstein guided the band through striking modern instrumental pieces of depth and quality, Roddy Frantz's urban-alienation lyrics, delivered in a fair approximation of David Byrne's vocal style, typecast the group as second-string imitators. The Verbs' records showed great potential, but this needless flaw prevented them from being taken seriously. [iar]

MIDGE URE

See *Ultravox.*

U-ROY

Dread in a Babylon (Virgin) 1976 + 1983
Natty Rebel (nr/Virgin) 1976 + 1983

Rasta Ambassador (nr/Virgin) 1977
Version Galore (nr/Front Line) 1978
Jah Son of Africa (nr/Front Line) 1979
Crucial Cuts (nr/Virgin) 1983
Music Addict (RAS) 1987 •

Just as dub reggae anticipated funk and rock remixes, toasters—chanting reggae dj's—prefigured rap. U-Roy (Ewart Beckford) was one of Jamaica's first djs to graduate from sound systems to chart success in the late '60s. His signature style is plain and direct: he shrieks and chants over the instrumental tracks of other hits, interrupting and talking back to the vocals. When he first appeared, such musical antics were unprecedented on record, and he became an immediate sensation. While it can't be said that U-Roy invented toasting, he's considered the style's godfather, and an inarguable reggae pioneer.

Because U-Roy isn't very active, his records drift in and out of print. **Version Galore**, which collects many of his first hits, is a must, although far from definitive. Most of his available LPs, in fact, date from the mid-'70s, when he was signed to Virgin and produced by Tony Robinson. Both **Dread in a Babylon** and **Natty Rebel** are excellent samplings of U-Roy's forceful toasting, though the sound and production are smoother, less offbeat and startling than his early work. (**Dread** has the slight edge for featuring the wonderful "Runaway Girl" and "Chalice in the Palace.") **Crucial Cuts** combines some early items with tracks from **Rasta Ambassador** for an odd combination of old and new styles (some hits are re-recordings) that is inconsistent but serviceable.

U-Roy quietly resurfaced in 1987 with **Music Addict**, a collection of contemporary tracks produced with Prince Jazzbo. The LP finds him in fine form, toasting with authority and ease, and it compares favorably with much of his older work. Ironically, the record got lost in the flood of releases by younger and hipper dj's, U-Roy's musical descendants, and attracted little attention. [bk]

U.T.F.O.

"Beats and Rhymes" (Select) 1984
"Roxanne, Roxanne" (Select) 1984
U.T.F.O. (Select) 1985
Skeezer Pleezer (Select) 1986
Lethal (Select) 1987

For a brief period in late winter 1984/5, you couldn't leave your house or turn on your radio in New York without hearing some rapper going on about a girl named Roxanne. There was "Roxanne's Revenge," "The Real Roxanne," "Roxanne You're Through," "Roxanne's Mother," "Roxanne's Brother," "Roxanne's Doctor"—even "Roxanne's a Man." Demonstrating the volatility of the dance music market, Roxanne replaced "y'all" as the word most frequently used in raps, and the term quickly passed into urban slang for an unaccommodating woman. Credit for this fad goes to Brooklyn's U.T.F.O. (Untouchable Force Organization), the trio who started it all with "Roxanne, Roxanne," a playful poke at a good-looking girl with the temerity to resist their suave attentions.

From the beginning, Doctor Ice, the Kangol Kid and the Educated Rapper (later joined by Mix-Master Ice) have led a charmed life. After winning a break-dancing contest, they went on a European tour with Whodini and ultimately found themselves on the *Phil Donahue Show,* which led to an invite to Dustin Hoffman's daughter's birthday party. Before things could get any weirder, they released a 12-inch of the sharp and fast "Beats and Rhymes," oddly, a better rap than its follow-up, "Roxanne, Roxanne" (included on the band's first album). The latter's lyrics aren't exceptionally clever, but U.T.F.O. created such strong personae for themselves and the stuck-up Ms. R., while isolating such a familiar problem (girl says no), that teenagers identified with them in a singular way. What the record may have lacked in raw power, it made up for in character.

The Roxanne fad disappeared, leaving the very talented U.T.F.O. at mortal levels of popularity. Several years later, staying under the Full Force production umbrella, their third LP, **Lethal**, reveals the rapping/singing quartet to be more mature and confident than before, a hard-edged, articulate crew with a strong musical personality and crisp dance grooves. Unfortunately, they haven't come up with any exciting new ideas lately: even the anti-drug title track, a cross-cultural mating ritual with Anthrax, doesn't get off the ground. All told, **Lethal** is far from what its title promises—a lackluster and disappointing collection of old moves and tired routines.   [jl/iar]

See also *Full Force.*

U2
Boy (Island) 1980 ●
October (Island) 1981 ●
War (Island) 1983 ●
Under a Blood Red Sky (Island) 1983 ●
The Unforgettable Fire (Island) 1984 ●
Wide Awake in America EP (Island) 1985 ●
The Joshua Tree (Island) 1987 ●

THE EDGE
Captive (Virgin) 1987 ●

With a unique, passionate sound, individualist lyrical outlook and youthful guilelessness, Dublin's U2 made a big splash quickly. The quartet had released a few praiseworthy singles before **Boy** introduced them to the world at large, via such songs as "I Will Follow," "An Cat Dubh" and "Into the Heart." Powerful and emotional, singer Bono (Paul Hewson) mixes a blend of rock, Gaelic and operatic styles with the occasional yowl or yodel to lead the band's attack; guitarist Dave "the Edge" Evans largely shuns chords in favor of brilliant lead or arpeggio figures that propel and color the songs. Drummer Larry Mullen Jr. and bassist Adam Clayton provide a driving and solid (but sensitive) foundation, completing **Boy**'s musical package, delivered to disc with great skill and invention by producer Steve Lillywhite. An unquestionable masterpiece, **Boy** has a strength, beauty and character that is hard to believe on a debut album made by teenagers.

Although it might have been unreasonable to expect U2 to remain pure and ingenuous indefinitely, **October** seems a bit overblown and oblique by comparison. Already showing signs of becoming a bit of a sensitive *auteur,* Bono's lyrics abandon "Stories for Boys" and adopt "Stranger in a Strange Land." Lillywhite, meanwhile, embellishes the magnificent and direct rock power with found-sound gimmicks, piano and abundantly atmospheric sensuality. **October** does have significant virtues: "Gloria," "I Fall Down" and "Is That All?" rank with the group's best work, and several others fall just short, mostly the result of incomplete songwriting efforts. But, in totality, not a great record.

War, on the other hand, *is* tremendous—an emotional, affecting collection of honest love songs ("Two Hearts Beat as One," "Drowning Man") and political protest ("Sunday Bloody Sunday," "Seconds," "The Refugee") given complex and varied, but unfailingly powerful, treatments. The mix is uncomfortably skewed—towards the drums and, on "New Year's Day," bass—but judicious addition of violin and trumpet supports, rather than detracts from, the band's fire. (Bizarre casting note: the LP's backing vocals are by Kid Creole's Coconuts.)

Taking advantage of U2's growing rep as a commanding live act, **Under a Blood Red Sky** presents them on American and German stages, playing eight dynamic numbers drawn from all three albums, with awesome strength and clarity. Although billed as a mini-LP, the running time exceeds 32 minutes.

Abandoning Steve Lillywhite in the hopes of exploring new audio terrain, U2 made an unusual selection of producer and recorded **The Unforgettable Fire** with Brian Eno and his Canadian collaborator, Daniel Lanois. While the record's lyrical theme—largely a commemoration of Martin Luther King Jr., freedom and individual heroism in general—is both commendable and occasionally articulate, the record's success as an ambitious piece of pop music is more mixed, hitting highs—"Pride (in the Name of Love)," "A Sort of Homecoming," "Wire," the title tune (all on the first side)—as well as an embarrassing low—"Elvis Presley and America." U2's predicament is that their strength is their strength, and the more complex their aspirations, the harder to convey their passion.

One doesn't ordinarily expect to encounter an epiphany on a budget-priced disc of outtakes and ephemera, but **Wide Awake in America**'s absolutely mesmerizing eight-minute live version of "Bad" is among U2's finest recordings, and sent me scurrying back to **The Unforgettable Fire** to hear what else I might have missed. Besides another live track, the EP also contains two worthy-of-release studio cuts: "Three Sunrises" and "Love Comes Tumbling." Even when these guys don't put their best forward, what they've got is still pretty amazing.

The Joshua Tree, again produced, but with less personality this time, by Eno and Lanois, helped elevate U2 into the commercial stratosphere, making them one of rock's all-time biggest—and least creatively compromised—money machines. (Whatever the shortcomings of their records, pandering is not one of them.) The LP begins magnificently, with three classic tracks ("Where the Streets Have No Name," "I Still Haven't Found What I'm Looking For" and "With or Without You") that perfectly crystallize the essence of U2's greatness. Atmosphere, power, melody, instrumental invention *and* rock drive fill each of those songs, yet they are all strikingly different and original. From there, the album is oddly inconsistent. "Bullet the Blue Sky" shows the danger of listening to too many Doors records; the semiacoustic "Running to Stand Still" has mood but no presence; "In God's Country" puts the pieces together just right, with a haunting, countryish refrain; the jaunty "Trip Through Your Wires" is weird but intriguing; "One Tree Hill" sounds like a good track but collapses under Bono's Daltreyesque bellowing and Edge's distorto guitar; "Mothers of the Disappeared" may have commendable intent but it lacks a cogent musical framework. Not as good as it is popular, **The Joshua Tree** indicates both U2's strengths and weaknesses.

The Edge wrote the score for political kidnapping film *Captive,* playing and co-producing it with Michael Brook. The instrumental pieces—a variety of understated acoustic guitar/piano excursions and gripping synthesizer/electric guitar adventures—may not be extraordinary (despite the cool guitar work), but the LP earned enduring significance for featuring the album debut of Sinéad O'Connor, who sings "Heroine (Theme from *Captive*)." [iar]

V V V V V V V

CHERRY VANILLA

Bad Girl (nr/RCA/ 1978
Venus d'Vinyl (nr/RCA) 1979

Onetime David Bowie publicist Vanilla left Staten Island behind to pursue a recording career in Britain, making two inconsistent but surprisingly good albums. Along with guitarist/songwriter Louis Lepore and a loose collection of backup players, Vanilla—a passable singer—works her way through songs woven of her own experiences.

The first album, **Bad Girl**, is a bit on the blunt side—"I Know How to Hook" and "Foxy Bitch" are unfortunately typical—but the follow-up takes a subtler approach and neatly balances cleverly arranged, varied music with sensitive, believable lyrics. While La Vanilla isn't breaking down any musical barriers, her two albums prove her talent as a writer and performer.   [iar]

DAVID VAN TIEGHEM

These Things Happen (Warner Bros.) 1984
Safety in Numbers (Private Music) 1987 ●

In her bid to become the leading terpsichorean patron of avant-rock music, choreographer Twyla Tharp followed projects with David Byrne and Glenn Branca by commissioning a score from Van Tieghem, a multi-instrumentalist mainly known as a drummer in the Love of Life Orchestra and other New York experimental ensembles. Working with many local luminaries, Van Tieghem's music for *Fait Accompli* (released as **These Things Happen**) covers a wide range of styles, from African-tinged rhythms to obscure pop. The interpolation of extraneous bits of found sounds (news, animal noises, etc.) keeps things going when the music threatens to drag, which—given its subordi-

nate role as accompanying earwork—it frequently does.

Excerpts from two subsequent ballet scores and another theatrical project appear on **Safety in Numbers**, as well as a pair of trans-Pacific computer collaborations with Ryuichi Sakamoto. Ultra-modern electronic equipment and ancient acoustic instruments blend harmoniously into an unidentifiable but fascinating sonic stew that favors percussion sounds more than rhythmic adventurism. Much of the album is spare and open, a well-ordered and dynamic backdrop for dances—and dreams.   [iar]

VAPORS

New Clear Days (UA) 1980
Magnets (Liberty) 1981

One of the first in a breed of fresh-faced bands who fit neatly into the UK pop charts and accompanying teenybopper trappings while retaining vague new wave credibility, the Vapors started at the top and quickly sank from view. Their first single, "Turning Japanese," was a coy paean to masturbation and an enormous international hit; the inability to match it made both of the Vapors' subsequent albums big disappointments. They weren't that bad, though.

New Clear Days follows in the veddy British vein originated by Ray Davies and carried on by Paul Weller and Madness. Some of singer David Fenton's songs show a talented, mature tunesmith at work; unfortunately, they all suffer in light of the awesomely catchy jingle that dominates the record, overshadowing the subtler, more thoughtful material.

Magnets also lacks a peer for "Turning Japanese," although "Jimmie Jones" (about

611

Jonestown) nearly meets the challenge. Unfortunately, Fenton's greater aspirations and budding political conscience are severely out of step with the band's unbreakably commercial image. Had they not been doomed by their own devices from day one, the Vapors might have proven well worth following.

[iar]

BEN VAUGHN COMBO
The Many Moods of Ben Vaughn (Restless) 1986
Beautiful Thing (Restless) 1987 ●

BEN VAUGHN
Ben Vaughn Blows Your Mind (Restless) 1988 ●

This no-frills New Jersey rock'n'roll outfit—whose first claim to fame was Marshall Crenshaw's recording (on his **Downtown** LP) of Vaughn's brilliant "I'm Sorry (But So Is Brenda Lee)"—made a highly entertaining debut album. (Unfortunately, the sleepy acoustic/country version of that song on **The Many Moods** is disappointing.)

Vaughn has a clever way with lyrics and titles. Besides penning romantic ditties, he pokes fun at the tyranny of trendies ("Wrong Haircut," "I Dig Your Wig") and defines down-to-earth suburbanism ("Lookin' for a 7-11," "M-M-Motor Vehicle") with implicit satire of statemate Springsteen's epochal bombast. With a trio (bass, drums, accordion) providing raucous support for Vaughn's unstylized vocals and guitar, **The Many Moods** is a highly enjoyable musical diversion.

Beautiful Thing has a fresh, easygoing feel, but too much restraint can be a bad thing; halfway through the first side, this mild record threatens to slide right off the turntable. (Flat-sounding production sorely deficient in highs and lows exaggerates that impression.) The record's other shortcomings are its lack of funny titles ("Jerry Lewis in France" is as good as it gets), the paucity of overtly clever lyrics (two exceptions being "Shingaling with Me" and "Big House with a Yard") and a decided shortage of rave-ups (a crazed polka called "Gimmie, Gimmie, Gimmie" and the peppy guitar instrumental "Desert Boots" notwithstanding). [iar]

TESCO VEE
See *Meatmen.*

ALAN VEGA
Alan Vega (ZE-PVC) 1980
Collision Drive (ZE-Celluloid) 1981
Saturn Strip (ZE-Elektra) 1983
Just a Million Dreams (ZE-Elektra) 1985

As the vocal half of Suicide, singer Alan Vega was an infuriating electronic shaman. On his own, he creates seductive, '50s-inspired music that succeeds with or without rockabilly revivals. **Alan Vega**'s impact is the result of its spare instrumentation—just the singer plus Phil Hawk on guitar and drums—and deceptively simple songs. "Jukebox Babe" transcends a stuttering lyric and solitary riff to engulf its idiom and then the universe. "Lonely" should be the last word (or moan) on that subject. The rest of the album is similarly zen-like, and no less enjoyable for it.

Collision Drive has a three-piece band and broader musical range. Besides the droning rock'n'roll of "Magdalena 82" and "Magdalena 83," "Outlaw" flirts with heavy metal rhythms and textures; "Viet Vet" is an extended narrative reminiscent of the Doors. Vega's moody lyricism has the poet's touch—sometimes heavy-handed but always his own. This recycling is creative.

Continuing Ric Ocasek's association with Suicide, the tall Car produced Vega's third solo album, which mostly abandons the simplicity of his early work in favor of propulsive keyboard-dominated drone-rock, played by Ocasek and a variety of sidemen, including members of Ministry and the Cars' Greg Hawkes. Vega mumbles like an inarticulate offspring of Lou Reed and Jim Morrison, but **Saturn Strip** covers a lot of ground. "Video Babe" reasserts his atmospheric rockabilly sensibility (recall "Jukebox Babe") but with very modern accessories, while an offhand cover of Hot Chocolate's "Every 1's a Winner" closes the LP on an enigmatic, inconclusive note.

Just a Million Dreams finds Vega acquiescing in an almost routine rock milieu. He's not exactly Mr. Mister, but the backing tracks are so filled with typical synth sounds, electronic rhythms and sizzling lead guitar that they provide little or no musical excitement to stimulate vocal hysteria. In fact, it's difficult at times to believe that this bland singer is actually Vega. [si/iar]

See also *Suicide.*

SUZANNE VEGA
Suzanne Vega (A&M) 1985 ●
Marlene on the Wall EP (nr/A&M) 1986
Solitude Standing (A&M) 1987 ●

Like Patti Smith a decade earlier, Suzanne Vega was selected from an "underground" New York scene—in this case, the post-rock folk generation that outgrew new wave for acoustic guitars and sensitively poetic lyrics—and elevated to preeminent status with a major label record deal. Whether or not that makes her more noteworthy than those left struggling in greater obscurity is arguable, but irrelevant to the qualities of her first album. Singing in a cool, wispy voice, and accompanying herself on guitar, Vega resembles a mix of Joni Mitchell with Laurie Anderson and Tim Buckley. Producers Lenny Kaye and Steve Addabbo assembled a number of studio players to support Vega in discreet, restrained fashion; the unobtrusive backing presents her songs clearly and pleasingly. **Suzanne Vega** has some memorable material and generally avoids preciousness or willful obscurity. She's a talented melodicist, and this album suggests lots of potential for development.

Whatever its other merits, **Solitude Standing** will always be known as the album containing the enormous hit single, "Luka." Vega's offbeat first-person tale of a child-abuse victim sends chills up your spine as it raises questions about motivation and intent. Captured with exquisitely clear sound, her quartet's subtle, inventive accompaniment provides texture, dynamics and context for Vega's wan tales of urban alienation, preventing her unchanging voice—soft, dry, seductive—from unduly homogenizing the sound.

[iar]

VELVET ELVIS

Fun and Trouble EP (Hit a Note) 1985
What in the World (Hit a Note) 1986
Velvet Elvis (Enigma) 1988 ●

Mitch Easter produced the confident-sounding 1988 album for this Lexington, Kentucky quartet, corralling their pleasing harmonies (all four sing) and crisp, accomplished musicianship into extremely attractive country-edged pop-rock (that thankfully never resembles R.E.M.). The mix of drummer Sherri McGee's tangy harmonies and the male frontline's Petty/Dylan-influenced lead vocals provides some of the best moments on **Velvet Elvis**; elsewhere, subtle guitar/keyboard interplay laces the confident record with sparkle and character. Except for occasional patches of blandness, this varied collection is a most auspicious debut. [iar]

VELVET UNDERGROUND

The Velvet Underground and Nico (Verve) 1967 + 1985 ●
White Light/White Heat (Verve) 1968 + 1985 ●
The Velvet Underground (MGM) 1969 (Verve) 1985 ●
Loaded (Cotillion) 1970 ●
Live at Max's Kansas City (Cotillion) 1972
Squeeze (nr/Polydor) 1973
1969 Velvet Underground Live (Mercury) 1974
VU (Verve-PolyGram) 1985 ●
Velvet Underground (nr/Polydor) 1986
Another View (Verve) 1986 ●

The Velvet Underground marked a turning point in rock history. After the release of **The Velvet Underground and Nico** the music could never be as innocent, as unselfconscious as before, knowing the power of which it was capable. The band's first album may have come on a bit cute with its Andy Warhol-designed banana cover—indeed, patron Warhol's name (he also "produced") was splashed around like a talisman—but singer/guitarist Lou Reed's tough songs and the band's equally tough playing owed nothing to anybody. In perverse subject matter ("Heroin," "Venus in Furs"), deceptively simple musical forms and anarchic jamming, the Velvets displayed the rebellious traits new wave bands would pick up on ten years later. Singer Nico's four vocals provide textural context and breathing space between Reed's darker visions.

With Nico gone, **White Light/White Heat** is almost unbearably intense. John Cale recites a gruesome little story ("The Gift") over steamy accompaniment, and Reed sings the praises of amphetamines (the title track)—and that's the light entertainment. The second side consists of extended, feedback-wailing guitar solos ("I Heard Her Call My Name") and graphic porno-junkie tales ("Sister Ray"). The album is as morally black as its cover.

Something had to change, and when the Velvet Underground next surfaced, they sounded like a different band. Cale's departure (replaced by Doug Yule) might have played a part, but remaining *auteur* Reed has since shown himself capable of wide mood swings. The music on **The Velvet Underground** is quiet, melodic, gentle even when it turns up the juice ("What Goes On," "Beginning to See the Light") and—who would have believed it?—moving ("Jesus," "I'm Set

613

Free"). Only "Murder Mystery," with its double-tracked chatter, is guilty of self-indulgence.

The group started on a fourth, unreleased album before switching record companies. Sixteen years later, songs from those sessions finally surfaced officially on **VU**. They show the Velvet Underground stoking the rock'n' roll fire that blazed forth on **Loaded**: "Foggy Notion" is a timeless rave-up of classical simplicity (though typically kinky subject matter). Reed recycled half of **VU**'s material on his early solo albums, but it's charming to hear them played forcefully by a functioning band.

By 1970, the Velvet Underground was into a wholesome overdrive. **Loaded** may have seemed superficial in comparison to the preceding albums, but it does include Reed's twin anthems, "Sweet Jane" and "Rock and Roll." Personality conflicts, however, resulted in his leaving the group before the record's release; Yule took some of the vocals and most of the credit. **Loaded**'s sweetness-and-light music was the Velvets' death throes.

With its creative force gone, the band shuffled along for two more years and even released a British album, **Squeeze**, with no original members. For new doses of the real thing, fans had to be content with live recordings of past glories. **Live at Max's Kansas City** is a low-fi document of the Velvets' last hurrah in the Big Apple. The band is tight but mellow; three of the four songs taken from the first album were originally sung by Nico.

The two-record **1969** is more interesting in its extended view of the group and choice of material. As on the Max's LP, the post-Cale band is generally relaxed—a far cry from the musical entropy of the first two albums. The Velvet Underground got its groundbreaking out of the way early.

In 1986, British Polydor released **Velvet Underground**, a five-album boxed set which reissued the first three original LPs and **VU**, adding a bonus record of nine previously unavailable tracks, including an early "Rock and Roll," an instrumental "Guess I'm Falling in Love," a studio take of "We're Gonna Have a Real Good Time Together" and two versions of "Hey Mr. Rain." Sensibly, **Another View** was also issued separately.   [si]

See also *John Cale, Nico, Lou Reed, Maureen Tucker.*

VENUS AND THE RAZORBLADES
Songs from the Sunshine Jungle (Visa) 1978

After Kim Fowley helped assemble the Runaways, he worked on Venus and the Razorblades, a less stable project along the same lines—finding young Los Angeles punks with promise and fashioning them into a band. Including, variously, guitarist Steven T. (with whom Fowley wrote the group's material), 14-year-old female wunderkind Dyan Diamond, Roxy Music bassist Sal Maida (sessions only) and others, Venus and the Razorblades managed a short but unsightly career. This posthumous record, cobbled together from miscellaneous tapes Fowley had produced, is their legacy—well-played, noisy-but-safe melodic punk that owes more to California wholesomeness than Bowery decadence.   [iar]

TOM VERLAINE
Tom Verlaine (Elektra) 1979
Dreamtime (Warner Bros.) 1981
Words from the Front (Warner Bros.) 1982
Cover (Warner Bros.) 1984
Flash Light (IRS) 1987 ●

Television was the satisfying result of a clash between two disparate styles. Leader Tom Verlaine was the dreamer, playing sinuous guitar and singing in the strangled, intense voice of a young poet. Guitarist Richard Lloyd and the rhythm section of Billy Ficca and Fred Smith tended more to classic, bash-it-out rock'n'roll. When Verlaine went solo, many assumed he'd simply float off into the ozone.

Surprisingly, he managed to preserve Television's delicate balance and even add new elements on his first solo LP. Two tortured, driving mini-epics—"The Grip of Love" and "Breakin' in My Heart," a classic from TV's live sets—blend flesh and spirit perfectly. The vividly desperate "Kingdom Come" has the honor of being covered by David Bowie (on **Scary Monsters**)—how's that for an endorsement? There's even a playful nonsense song, "Yonki Time," indicating Verlaine is using his freedom to grow.

Alas, with **Dreamtime**, Verlaine narrows his scope, seeming to retreat into the isolation of the familiar. There are taut, anxious tunes ("Down on the Farm"), lilting ones ("Without a Word") and an abundance of exquisite guitar licks, but it's too predictable. A performer who trades in passion can't afford *not* to surprise.

614

Words from the Front shows more daring, although—like its predecessor—it suffers from inconsistent material. "Postcard from Waterloo" proves that Verlaine can be as romantic as Barry Manilow without sacrificing keenness. "Days on the Mountain" provides perhaps the ultimate in lightheaded ecstasy, with his fluttering guitar skillfully imitating the ascension into heaven.

In some ways, **Cover** constitutes a return to the style of Verlaine's first LP. The songs are short and to the point, without the sometimes florid expansivess of his previous two efforts. On the other hand, brevity doesn't discourage Verlaine from floating into the ozone—he just does it quicker. For every "Lindi-Lu," a fine jerky rocker, there's two like "Swim," a gentle evocation of airheadedness.

Verlaine co-produced **Flash Light**—his first record for IRS—with Fred Smith, achieving an energetic rock sound that exudes new-found confidence. His poetry is characteristically brilliant. In "The Scientist Writes a Letter," a song taking precisely that form, he writes, "It's funny how attractive indifference can be/My sense of failure . . . it's not so important/Electricity means so much more to me." Although Verlaine has developed and refined his music over the years, the urgency of his vocals and guitar (especially on "Cry Mercy Judge") still connects stylistically with his old band. [jy/rj]

VERLAINES

Ten O'Clock in the Afternoon (NZ Flying
   Nun) 1984
Hallelujah All the Way Home (NZ Flying Nun)
   1985
Bird Dog (NZ Flying Nun) 1987 (Homestead)
   1988 ●
Juvenilia (Homestead) 1987

Like their American namesake, this Dunedin, New Zealand trio (one of whose current members previously played in the Chills) produces an acoustic and electric guitar-dominated style of solemn pop. Graeme Downes' anguished voice lends an aura of gloom to music that is punchy, percussive and at times unpredictable.

The Verlaines attempted to define and refine their style on **Halleleujah All the Way Home**, which is too diverse for its own good. The US-only **Juvenilia** is a compilation of singles and remixes. Dour and raw, it's a stunning anthology which brings to light the Verlaines' true talents—multi-range vocals ("Death and the Maiden"), intricate guitar patterns ("Baud to Tears," from **Ten O' Clock**) and impeccable melodies ("You Cheat Yourself of Everything That Moves"). A necessary record!

Bird Dog is a stronger, more realized effort. Augmenting their sound with horns, strings and piano, the Verlaines crafted a truly memorable album. "Makes No Difference," the title track and "Slow Sad Love Song" are just a few of the standouts on this beautiful, thoughtful record.   [ag]

VIBRATORS

Pure Mania (Columbia) 1976
V2 (nr/Epic) 1978
Batteries Included (nr/CBS) 1980
Guilty (nr/Anagram) 1983
Alaska 127 (Can. Dallcorte) 1984
Fifth Amendment (nr/Ram) 1985
Live (nr/FM—Revolver) 1986
Recharged (nr/FM—Revolver) 1988

KNOX

Plutonium Express (nr/Razor) 1983

Like the Stranglers, the Vibrators were considerably older than the other bands comprising the London punk scene in 1977. A rudimentary quartet with a knack for insidiously catchy songs, the Vibrators—after a brief alliance with Chris Spedding, whom they backed on the first punk novelty record, "Pogo Dancing"—established themselves with a stream of clever pop singles that captured the minimalist energy (but not inchoate anger) of their peers.

Pure Mania—with its soon-to-be-a-cliché color-Xerox artwork cover—is a treasure trove of memorable ditties that strip down pop in a parallel to the Ramones' streamlining of it. A brilliant record, cheerful in a loopy way and filled with great fragmentary tunes and innocuously threatening lyrics.

V2, recorded in the Vibrators' briefly adopted home base, Berlin, features new bassist Gary Tibbs (later a Roxy Musician and Ant) and a more ambitious agenda. While some of the material on it is not that different from the debut LP, **V2** is too pretentious and overblown, following too many different cul-de-sacs to hang together.

Although trends quickly passed them by, the Vibrators trundled on until 1980. When they split up, CBS issued the **Batteries Included** retrospective, with such classic tunes as "Judy Says" and "Yeah Yeah Yeah." As both of the Vibes' original LPs have long been deleted, it's an essential class of '77 punk album.

Two years later, the Vibes reformed. **Alaska 127** features the entire original lineup (Knox, Eddie, Pat Collier and John Ellis) playing routine but likable rock that has good sound and a bit of the old melodic acuity, but none of **Pure Mania**'s underground ambience or innocent excitement. Following a live LP, **Recharged**—a baker's dozen new songs, mostly written by Knox—finds only him and Eddie remaining, joined by a new bassist and guitarist.

Knox has recorded solo and done an album with Charlie Harper of the U.K. Subs as the Urban Dogs. Pat Collier has become a successful producer. [iar]

See also *U.K. Subs.*

VICE SQUAD

No Cause for Concern (nr/EMI) 1981
Live in Sheffield [tape] (nr/Live) 1981
Stand Strong Stand Proud (nr/EMI) 1982
Shot Away (nr/Anagram) 1985

It's easy to understand why Vice Squad was one of the most successful early-'80s Brit-punk bands. They made powerful music with bitterly intense lyrics and had—until she departed, following a disagreement over animal rights—a major focal point in lead singer Beki Bondage. **No Cause for Concern** is a passable debut; **Stand Strong Stand Proud** is a first-rate punk effort with a driving, punchy sound and Beki's demanding voice sending chills down the spine. Also, the material is better developed, showing Vice Squad to be evolving without sacrificing their original ideas.

Following Bondage's departure to form Ligotage, the Vice Squad pressed on, but never with the same level of British success. [cpl]

SID VICIOUS

Sid Sings (nr/Virgin) 1979
Love Kills NYC (nr/Konexion) 1985

A classic piece of campy horribleness, **Sid Sings** is a miserable-sounding live record of one of Sid's New York rent-party gigs. The ex-Pistol teams here with ex-Doll Jerry Nolan's band, the Idols, for a pathetic performance of punk standards. Depressing and morbid. **Love Kills NYC** is a similar record,

issued six years later during the blizzard of archival Pistols vinyl. [iar]

HOLLY BETH VINCENT
See *Holly and the Italians.*

VIOLENT FEMMES
Violent Femmes (Slash) 1983 ●
Hallowed Ground (Slash) 1984 ●
The Blind Leading the Naked (Slash) 1986 ●
BRIAN RITCHIE
The Blend (SST) 1987
MERCY SEAT
Mercy Seat (Slash) 1987
SIGMUND SNOPEK III
WisconsInsane (Dali) 1987

The remarkable and original Violent Femmes burst out of Madison, Wisconsin in the early '80s, playing acoustic instruments and singing intense, personal songs with remarkable candor and love. Initially resembling a punk version of the Modern Lovers, the Femmes—Gordon Gano (vocals, guitar, songs), Brian Ritchie (bass) and Victor De Lorenzo (drums)—have proven to be strictly unique. On the skeletal first album, Gano's articulate passion and lyrical maladjustment combine with the charged (but not very loud) playing to convey an incredible sense of desperation and rage. "Blister in the Sun" and "Kiss Off" are typical of the anger seething in the grooves, while "Gone Daddy Gone" and "Please Do Not Go" show a more upbeat side still rooted in extreme individuality and super-ego. The disc's best couplet: "Why can't I get just one fuck?/Guess it's got something to do with luck."

Hallowed Ground takes a much different approach, displaying Gano's religious fervor and connecting with traditional American folk music. (He subsequently launched a side project, Mercy Seat, to perform strictly gospel music. That group issued its first album in 1987.) The cast includes a banjo picker and autoharp strummer, as well as a horn'n'clarinet section; the material encompasses tragic balladry ("Country Death Song"), old-timey spirituals ("Jesus Walking on the Water," "It's Gonna Rain"), mild be-bop ("Sweet Misery Blues") and demented jazz-funk ("Black Girls"). Not as pointed as the first album, it nonetheless showcases an inquisitive and amazing band deeply committed to self-expression, regardless of the consequences.

Surprisingly, the cleverly titled third LP was produced by Talking Head Jerry Harrison with conscious mainstreaming intent. Of course, the Femmes at their most commercial are still pretty radical, although "I Held Her in My Arms" does sound unnervingly like Bruce Springsteen. As if to prove their orneriness, a vituperative attack on "Old Mother Reagan" and the similarly anti-authoritarian "No Killing" demonstrate an undying rebellious spirit. But it's another type of spirit that invests the bluesy "Faith" and the Stonesy "Love and Me Make Three," keeping god in the grooves alongside Marc Dolan, who gets worked over with a misbegotten Headsish version of "Children of the Revolution." The Velvet Underground fares better on "Good Friend," a Femmes original that uncannily echoes Lou Reed.

Ritchie's solo debut ("dedicated to Sun Ra, Son House and my son Silas") shows off his diverse musical interests, from topical blues to avant-garde exotica and beyond. Joined by various players, he sings and handles guitar, banjo, flute, recorder, accordion and other instruments, leaving most of the bass chores to Cynthia Bartell of Têtes Noires. (Ritchie and DeLorenzo had earlier produced her group's **Clay Foot Gods** LP.) Not all of the excursions work equally well, but **The Blend** certainly proves that Ritchie's talents extend far beyond his role in the Femmes.

DeLorenzo co-produced and, with Ritchie, provided most of the instrumental backing on **WisconsInsane**, the latest loopy extravaganza from singing dairy state keyboardist/flautist Sigmund Snopek III. While their contributions to such serio-comical midwest maunderings as "The Rose of Wisconsin," "Thank God This Isn't Cleveland" and "I'm So Tired of Singing About the Sky" tend to be lost in the slick production, the LP is a cute theatrical diversion.

[iar]

See also *Têtes Noires.*

VIPERS

Outta the Nest! (PVC) 1984

Rather than discuss the relevance or validity of the entire garage-rock-cum-psychedelic revival—y'know, the bands who dress up like it's 1967 and play tambourines and fuzzed guitar—I'll just note that New York's Vipers are one of the leading lights of said movement. Suffice to say **Outta the Nest** sounds precisely like your (best/worst) memories of mid-'60s American rock, from the Seeds to the Standells to the Shadows of Knight. The Vipers write good tunes that sound properly dated and play them with equally stylized vim. The production could be better, but that's not the idea. As they sing in the lead-off track, "Nothing's from Today." [iar]

VIRGIN PRUNES

A New Form of Beauty 2 EP (nr/Rough Trade) 1981
A New Form of Beauty 4 "Din Glorious" [tape] (nr/Rough Trade) 1982
. . . If I Die, I Die (nr/Rough Trade) 1982
Over the Rainbow (Fr. Baby) 1985
Our Love Will Last Forever Until the Day It Dies EP (Touch and Go) 1986
The Moon Looked Down and Laughed (Touch and Go) 1986

Dublin weirdos with androgynous names and a predilection for semi-melodic rock and conceptual lyrics, the Virgin Prunes (one of whom is the Edge's brother) released a tape-only album and several 45s before getting around to a proper debut LP. The 10-inch **A New Form of Beauty 2** contains two ominously dark and abrasive assaults plus a quieter abrasive doodle; the cassette features highlights from a Dublin gallery performance, mixing early PiL-style semi-songs with all sorts of taped sounds to very unsettling effect.

Produced by Colin Newman, **If I Die** offers hard-edged but delicate pop ("Ballad of the Man") contrasted by challenging, long-winded opuses with skewed, angular instrumentation and ponderous vocal recitations ("Baudachong," "Caucasian Walk"). A complex band of many minds, the Prunes stake out unique ground, straddling art and mundanity with style and skill. Difficult but fascinating modern music. **Over the Rainbow** is an odds and ends compilation of the group's early days.

The Moon Looked Down and Laughed, rather unimaginatively produced by ex-Soft Cellar Dave Ball, is an unpalatable mishmash of Bowiesque glitter and music-hall camp. Gavin Friday's vocals are overwrought; several songs plod along painfully, going nowhere and taking forever to get there. Jim (Foetus) Thirlwell guests to little effect.

[iar/dgs]

VISAGE

Visage (Polydor) 1980 ●
The Anvil (Polydor) 1982 ●
Fade to Grey—The Singles Collection
    (Polydor) 1983
Beat Boy (Polydor) 1984

Formed around cult-figure fop Steve Strange, Visage began as a part-time group uniting the formidable talents of Ultravox's Midge Ure and Billy Currie, Magazine's Dave Formula and ex-Rich Kid drummer Rusty Egan for the ultimate in dance-oriented new romanticism. **Visage** is filled with rich humor and sound puns in addition to solid musicianship on guitars and synthesizers; how could anyone not crack a smile over the Ennio Morriconesque homage to Clint Eastwood, "Malpaso Man," or the self-mocking "Visa-Age"? Added to the humor, the fine music automatically deflates Strange's colorful pretensions.

Unfortunately, those pretensions dominate **The Anvil**, wherein Strange attempts to wring every mannered drop of angst and meaning out of his lyrics and vocals. Luckily, the rest of Visage perform as strongly as ever, although in a far darker mood than before.

Continuing their strictly dance version of Heaven 17-styled electro-funk, **Beat Boy** finds Visage (comprising, this time, Strange and Egan joined by the Barnacle brothers and Andy Barnett) readier to rock, using plentiful guitar on the endless title track (and elsewhere) to color the inexorable rhythms and repetitious, vapid lyrics. The songs are incredibly (and annoyingly, if you're paying attention) long, but there are still eight of 'em, with a total party time of over 45 minutes.

Fade to Grey is the most concise proof of Visage's merit, compiling nine catchy slices of dance-rock (two remixed for the occasion) and an otherwise unreleased (and utterly unnecessary) cover of Zager & Evans' "In the Year 2525." "Pleasure Boys," "We Move" and "Night Train" are among the best efforts, showing that conciseness can surely be an asset. [sg/iar]

VISITORS

See *Radio Birdman.*

VITAMIN Z

Rites of Passage (Geffen) 1985

On the only memorable track this wimpy synth-rock trio can deliver, singer Geoff Bar-radale does an appallingly close approximation of Marc Almond; the lyrics, however, are so stupid that no one could ever mistake "Burning Flame" for Soft Cell. A strange collection of sidemen played on **Rites of Passage**, including ex-Ant Chris Hughes and ex-Roxy Music guitarist Neil Hubbard, but it's a lost cause: these no-talents are dead in the water. [iar]

VIVABEAT

Party in the War Zone (Charisma) 1980

This one-hit (well, almost one) California guitar-plus-synthesizer sextet sounds like Sparks played at half speed. Their big number, "Man from China," is a foursquare dance track with a catchy riff that is whistled for novel effect. Otherwise, the LP is a stiff. [iar]

VOICE FARM

The World We Live In (Optional) 1982
Voice Farm (Ralph) 1987

On **The World We Live In**, San Francisco's Voice Farm was a trio—two guys who appear on the front cover dressed only in their underpants, and a less-exposed female—employing synthesizers, vocals and acoustic percussion to weave moody instrumentals, some of which are paired with incisive, intelligent (and, in one case, horrifying) lyrics. The band's dynamic range, from hauntingly beautiful to startlingly intense, and stylistic variety—encompassing movie-music vagueness, machine noise and disco bump, as well as direct song forms—surpasses many other all-electronic bands, and makes this a totally fascinating album with nary a dull moment. Producer David Kahne did an ace job as usual, and whoever thought of covering the venerable "Sally Go Round the Roses" also deserves a special commendation.

The radically different **Voice Farm** finds the group reduced to its essential elements: Myke Reilly (keyboards/percussion/voices) and Charly Brown (vocals/keyboards). Aided by an assortment of backing singers and a guitarist, the two are firmly in vocal/song mode, pairing their rhythmic sonic adventures with witty, pointedly satirical lyrics about intriguingly offbeat modern subjects. (A relatively straight cover of the Supremes' "Nowhere to Run" doesn't add anything to the song or the record.) The accomplished assemblages overlay the dance beats with synthesized effects, found sounds, spoken-word tape manipulation and other ear-catching ephemera for a diverting album that has real club-play potential but not much home turntable longevity.   [iar]

VOLCANO SUNS

The Bright Orange Years (Homestead) 1985
All-Night Lotus Party (Homestead) 1986
Bumper Crop (Homestead) 1987 ●

When Mission of Burma ended in 1983, only drummer Peter Prescott continued to play loud rock music. On **The Bright Orange Years**, his trio with bassist Jeff Weigand and guitarist Jon Williams takes energetic folk-rock with sturdy Midwest melodies and overplays it into a punky mixture of Cheap Trick and Hüsker Dü. The record's sound could be sharper, but there's no mistaking the talent in songs like "Jak," "Balancing Act" or "Corn-field," which pitches a noise piano solo into the mixture.

The ghost of Burma looms in Williams' mindblow guitar on **All-Night Lotus Party**, a less tuneful album (credit Prescott's reduced music-writing role) that is nonetheless rewarding. The Suns reach into new regions with "Cans," a crypto-rockabilly rave-up; "Walk Around," a Ramonesy punk rush; "Sounds Like Bucks," a distorted crypto-ballad; and "Dot on the Map," a Wall of Voodoo-styled slice of Americana gone off the deep end.

Prescott reclaimed creative control on the Suns' third album, which also unveiled a new incarnation of the trio. (Williams and Weigand left in March '87.) Although lyrics continue to reflect **Lotus Party**'s fascination with the social and cultural mundanities of rural life, **Bumper Crop** more closely resembles the first LP in song, sound and style.   [iar]

See also *Dredd Foole and the Din.*

W W W W W

WAH!
Nah = Poo—The Art of Bluff (nr/Eternal)
1981
The Maverick Years '80–'81 (nr/Wonderful
World) 1982

MIGHTY WAH!
Hope EP (nr/Eternal) 1983
Come Back EP (nr/Eternal-Beggars Banquet)
1984
A Word to the Wise Guy (nr/Eternal-Beggars
Banquet) 1984
Weekends EP (nr/Eternal-Beggars Banquet)
1984
The Way We Wah (nr/WEA) 1984
The Peel Sessions EP (nr/Strange Fruit)
1986

PETE WYLIE
Sinful (Virgin) 1987 ●

One of the most significant and underappreciated groups of the second Liverpool scene, Wah! (and numerous titular variations thereon) functions as a vehicle for extrovert Pete Wylie. On **Nah = Poo**, Wah! sounds like Emerson, Lake and Palmer with hipper (though equally flamboyant) arrangements. Wylie sings melodramatically on stirring but superficial material like "The Death of Wah!" and "Seven Minutes to Midnight." The man may (as he intimates) be a fraud, but at least he's an entertaining one.

A Word to the Wise Guy—a full album and a bonus single—contains more of Wylie's flighty excursions into soul, pop, funk and anything else he happens across. Although not very consistent, it's an unpredictable and generally likable collection. The 12-inch **Come Back** has two versions of that ace track (also on the LP) plus a couple of other items. **Weekends** contains an alternate version of that album track as well as a demo for it and two other odds and ends from Wylie's sprawling career.

The Way We Wah is a retrospective of Wylie's single successes, from "7000 Names of Wah," "Hope" and "Story of the Blues" to his reading of Johnny Thunders' poignant "Can't Put Your Arms Around a Memory."

Wylie's first-ever American release, the delightful and commercial **Sinful** drops the Wah! front and finally acknowledges his soloness. He takes credit for vocals, guitar, harmonica and "odd bits"; the only other contributor listed is vocalist Josie Jones. Colorful wide-screen production (suggestive of the Motors a bit) frames the peppy melodies ("Break Out the Banners," "If I Love You," the memorable title tune) and unpredictable lyrics ("Train to Piranhaville"), making the ambitious **Sinful** a rewarding, fully realized effort reflecting Wylie's unique perception of pop music and the world.

The Peel Sessions contains four familiar Wah! songs, recorded live for British radio in 1984. [jy/iar]

WAITRESSES
Wasn't Tomorrow Wonderful? (ZE-Polydor)
1982
I Could Rule the World If I Could Only Get
the Parts EP (ZE-Polydor) 1982
Make the Weather EP (nr/Polydor) 1983
Bruiseology (Polydor) 1983

Composer/guitarist Chris Butler invented the Waitresses; fellow Akronite Patty Donahue gave the group/idea its voice. From an original germinal joke (before Butler's spell in the more avant-garde Tin Huey) and appearance on a local Ohio compilation LP, the Waitresses grew into a well-known New York-based sextet (including ex-Television

620

drummer Billy Ficca) churning out danceably funky pop tunes spiked with a few twists (not the least of which is Mars Williams' searing and satirical sax). Furthermore, Donahue's persona—she doesn't sing so much as carry a simultaneous conversation and tune—has been developed into the archetypal young, white, middle-class woman trying to sort out her identity while beset with standard societal conditioning on one hand and specious, voguish "alternatives" (the Sexual Revolution, the Me Generation) on the other. The Waitresses' combination of musical aplomb and lyrical acuity makes the first LP at once funny, sad and universally true.

The American **I Could Rule the World** EP contains a TV sitcom theme ("Square Pegs"), a wonderful Yuletide rap track ("Christmas Wrapping"), a live-for-TV take of an old Hueys-era Butler tune and more. The related English release, **Make the Weather**, is somewhat different, most notably lacking "Christmas Wrapping."

Bruiseology was recorded amidst serious personnel tension. (Donahue subsequently quit, was briefly replaced by Holly Vincent, but later rejoined.) Although Butler penned another batch of witty and wise songs about the exigencies of modern womanhood—perhaps less pointed, but not far removed from those on the first LP—and the playing and production are fine, the formula doesn't wear all that well. The Waitresses have since broken up but the name endured for several years, surfacing sporadically in concert listings. [jg]

DAVE WAKELING
See *(English) Beat, General Public.*

WALL
Personal Troubles & Public Issues (nr/Fresh) 1981
Dirges & Anthems (nr/Polydor) 1982

The Wall hail from the northernmost reaches of England, which may explain the faint but audible Scottish influence on their first album. Essentially a revisionist hardcore band, the Wall play a brand of punk that refuses to toe the genre line, employing different tempos (none of them too fast) and occasionally novel ideas to countermand the restrictions that make so many lesser groups sound alike.

Personal Troubles & Public Issues (one side per subject) is a pretty decent record, with blazing guitars, clear vocals and relatively thoughtful lyrics. Like a heavy metal album, the sound is crisp and well-balanced, but the songs concern much more engaging topics than bats or hell.

Dirges & Anthems, which comes with a three-song bonus single, refines and improves the approach somewhat, toning the guitars down a little and adding a bit of saxophone, acoustic guitar—even a reggae rhythm. The Wall seem to be pursuing an individual direction that only coincided with the thrash brigade for a short while. [iar]

WALL OF VOODOO
Wall of Voodoo EP (Index-IRS) 1980
Dark Continent (IRS) 1981
Call of the West (IRS) 1982 ●
Granma's House (nr/IRS) 1984
Seven Days in Sammystown (IRS) 1985
Happy Planet (IRS) 1987 ●
The Ugly Americans in Australia* (IRS) 1988 ●

Los Angeles' Wall of Voodoo makes junk music that can be extremely entertaining as long as you don't expect too much from it. Working in the same general cinematic groove as Devo, only taking their cues from Westerns and film noir rather than science fiction, Voodoo generate a stiff (though human) sound that furnishes a vivid backdrop to Stanard Ridgway's semi-catatonic vocals. Poised uneasily between machine music and rock'n'roll, Wall of Voodoo embodies the conflict between old and new for the serious-minded: classy Halloween music that's scary, but pleasantly so.

The four-song EP includes a wacked-out version of Johnny Cash's "Ring of Fire." The band displays more polish on **Dark Continent**, with tunes like "Back in Flesh" and "Full of Tension" benefitting from colorfully morose guitar and keyboards.

Call of the West's execution is livelier and more articulate, but just as spooky. It contains the now-classic "Mexican Radio," which crytallizes the band's loopy approach in one memorable number.

Ridgway left Wall of Voodoo in 1983 for a solo career; the band decided to replace him and continue. The 1984 compilation album, **Granma's House**, contains all of Voodoo's best tracks, from "Ring of Fire" to "Mexican Radio."

Unveiling two new members (drummer Joe Nanini having departed as well), Wall of Voodoo returned to action with **Seven Days in Sammystown**, their first new album in three years. Ridgway's absence forced a major rethink of the band's sound and purpose; the record is adequate, but somewhat short of character and thus uncompelling. "Far Side of Crazy" and a dirgey cover of "Dark as the Dungeon," an old folk song about miners, are quite good, but the rest falls short; an attempt to mimic Ridgway (on "Big City") fails.

The vanishing Devo left a wide open field of informed weirdness, but Voodoo failed to grab the opportunity. **Happy Planet** reveals an intact sense of humor left dangling by an utter lack of demented invention which would enliven it. The band works over the Beach Boys' "Do It Again," converting it to their idiom but adding nothing substantial which would make it worth hearing. The rest of the album takes aim at other needy cultural artifacts but lacks the requisite inspired oddness to make the songs truly original.

The Ugly Americans in Australia* is a rambunctious live disc recorded in Melbourne and (here's where the asterisk comes in) Bullhead City, Arizona. Stripped of studio comforts, the quartet (plus keyboard guest) gamely confronts old material like "Far Side of Crazy," "Mexican Radio" and "Ring of Fire" and introduces several newies. (The cassette and CD add two songs: "The Grass Is Greener" and "Pretty Boy Floyd.") [jy/iar]

See also *Stan Ridgway.*

WANDERERS

Only Lovers Left Alive (nr/Polydor) 1981

This brief liaison between members of Sham 69 and ex-Dead Boy Stiv Bators set the stage for the subsequent Lords of the New Church, and resulted in one album. Although begun as a Sham 69 record (with Bators replacing singer Jimmy Pursey), contracts prevented its release as such; under the Wanderers name, it attracted almost no attention.

It deserved a better fate. Presenting legible rock with a strong political bent, **Only Lovers Left Alive** brings together loads of influences that had never been present in either faction's background, and synthesizes a varied, well-produced angry assault that's more radical in stance than music. In any case, the album is noteworthy for including a courageous rockified version of "The Times They Are A-Changin'." [iar]

See also *Lords of the New Church.*

WANG CHUNG

Points on the Curve (Geffen) 1984 ●
To Live and Die in L.A. (Geffen) 1985 ●
Mosaic (Geffen) 1986 ●

HUANG CHUNG

Huang Chung (Arista) 1982

Despite the exotic name, this posh British band plays familiar post-Ultravox pop—with saxophone instead of keyboards and less of a heavy dance beat—on **Huang Chung**. The talented and proficient quartet lacks only an identity and the first-rate songs that might have made it memorable.

Points on the Curve unveils several major changes (chunges?), including the new spelling, a different label and a slimmed-down trio lineup (no more sax), now focused on singer Jack Hues. "Dance Hall Days" has dumb lyrics but a good rhythmic sound and a strong hook; "Wait" has dumb, awkward lyrics ("evidently/there's a difficulty") but a clever arrangement with synthesized strings and chimes for punctuation. Elsewhere, they essay dance-funk and Foreigner-like pomposity. Having banished its facelessness, Wang Chung is revealed in all its mediocrity.

And then there were two. Drummer Darren Costin formed a band called Heroes which released its first LP, **Here We Are**, in 1987. The remaining members of Wang Chung (Hues and multi-instrumentalist Nick Feldman), meanwhile, wrote and recorded the soundtrack for the movie *To Live and Die in L.A.*—a good title song plus lots of expendable atmospheric instrumentals.

That same slender lineup, aided by drummer/producer Peter Wolf, a horn section and a stack of backup singers, created **Mosaic**, another stylish and trivial synth-dance (plus the horrific ballad "Betrayal") pursuit which happened to contain one catchy and clever number, "Let's Go," and the monster hit single/video clip "Everybody Have Fun Tonight." (Which Tom Jones reportedly sang in his act for a while, changing the lyrics to "Everyone Tom Jones tonight!") [iar]

WARSAW PAKT

Needle Time! (nr/Island) 1977

Out of London's exploding early punk scene came this novelty—an album that reached local shops *within 24 hours of the start of its recording!* The band wasn't anything extraordinary—just amateur working class thrash'n'bash—but the speedy creation of the record made quite a stir for a few moments. The record came packed in a mailing envelope covered with stickers and rubber stamps; the insert sheet includes a complete log of the 21 hours it took to finish. Bizarre. [iar]

WASHINGTON SQUARES
Washington Squares (Gold Castle) 1987 ●

Outfitted with uniform berets, conservative suits, black sunglasses and acoustic guitars, these three New Yorkers escaped their post-punk backgrounds to shoulder the untendered responsibility of being the in-crowd's '80s version of Peter, Paul & Mary. The pretentious folk-beatnik pose is inexcusable; the image, however, isn't what makes the harmonies so attractive or the band's evident sincerity so agreeable. (The simpleminded lyrics are another matter entirely; their treatment of two traditional songs isn't very nice, either.) That people who never liked real folk music will embrace this self-conscious imitation because of the knowing wink that accompanies the enthusiastic strumming makes the Squares an affront; the likelihood that this LP may inspire curiosity far beyond the group's limited parameters gives it value and validity. Ex-Television drummer Billy Ficca and producer Mitch Easter (on piano) help out. [iar]

WAS (NOT WAS)
Was (Not Was) (ZE-Island) 1981
Born to Laugh at Tornadoes (ZE-Geffen) 1983
What's Up, Dog? (Chrysalis) 1988 ●

Shattering all illusions of a division between "black music" and "white music," Detroiters David (Weiss) Was and Don (Fagenson) Was use undated soul and funk as a backdrop for making overt and implicit political statements, opening new doors for artists of all colors. The material on their first album leans on familiar elements from sources like Grace Jones and Stevie Wonder, but blends in much humor and cleverness, making virtually every song an original gem, including the disco hits "Out Come the Freaks" and "Tell Me That I'm Dreaming," which includes mutilated found vocals from Ronald Reagan.

Born to Laugh at Tornadoes is a conceptual tour de force, a wacked-out collection of incongruous guest vocalists. Among the stars on parade: Ozzy Osbourne, Mel Torme, Mitch Ryder and Doug Fieger. Also in attendance: Wayne Kramer, Marshall Crenshaw, Kiss' Vinnie Vincent and many others. The songs—Was Bros. originals—typically mix wiseacre/devolution lyrics with muscular soul-funk-rock, making the album enjoyable on at least three levels—powerful dance music, cleverly worded smart-aleckdom and super-session bizarreness.

The historical problem with a lot of dance music has been its rabid dissociation from intellect; more than almost any other group, Was (Not Was) obliterates that gap.

Continuing their fecund cross-fertilization, Was (Not Was) have produced records for numerous artists and worked on all sorts of projects. In 1988, they released a long-awaited new album, with some minor song differences between the US and original UK issue. [sg/iar]

WATERBOYS
The Waterboys EP (Island) 1983
The Waterboys (nr/Ensign) 1983
A Pagan Place (Island) 1984 ●
This Is the Sea (Island) 1985 ●

Mike Scott leads this bombastic Scottish band through hideously pompous over-produced epics that sound vaguely like Bruce Springsteen (horns and backing vocals) crossed with the Alarm (overwrought drama and acoustic guitars) and topped off with a misbegotten impression of Bob Dylan (voice and lyrics). Scott seems to fancy himself the purveyor of some important message, but there's precious little worth receiving from these records. **This Is the Sea**, while hardly down-to-earth, shows Scott developing a bit of non-melodic songwriting skill, even as his production approaches are getting more and more absurd. Some of the tracks are so bizarrely realized that they're memorable in spite of their repulsiveness. If Scott ever decides to cover "MacArthur Park" I suggest we all head for the hills! [iar]

See also *World Party.*

BEN WATT
See *Everything but the Girl.*

623

JOHN WATTS

See *Fischer-Z*.

WAVES

See *Katrina and the Waves, Kimberley Rew*.

WC3

WC3 EP (Fr. CBS) 1981

This French quartet has the '80s version of swinging '60s go-go beat down pat. They season it with atonalities and spooky effects (courtesy of keyboardist and sometime *chanteur* Francoise; there's no guitarist) as well as occasional shifts into unlikely rhythms. Emerging through all of this is the gruff Gallic growl of main vocalist Renaud Isaac, painting verbal pictures (in French) of themes like dancing, violence and boredom. The lyrics are actually quite clever in spots, and the music is catchy in its offbeat way. [jg]

WEDNESDAY WEEK

Betsy's House EP (WarfRat) 1983
What We Had (Enigma) 1987 ●

Named for the Undertones' song but not sounding it, Los Angeles' Wednesday Week—two Callan sisters (drums, guitar/vocals) plus a non-sibling female bassist—play fairly simple rock-pop with some outside assistance on the five-song **Betsy's House** EP. The music is nice but nothing special, while the lyrics are fairly self-aware, addressing the generation gap, uncertain romance, individualism and alienation. Kristi Callan is a winsome singer and an adequate guitarist; the band is talented but at this point slight.

Expanded to a quartet with the addition of a guitar alumnus from the Last, Wednesday Week cut a far more impressive follow-up, produced by Don Dixon. **What We Had** sounds like a cross between early Bangles (with more rock energy and simpler vocal arrangements), Chrissie Hynde and the Smithereens, with a few outstanding songs ("Why," "All That Again") and consistently spirited playing. The tape and CD add a bonus track. [iar]

WEIRDOS

Who? What? When? Where? Why? EP
  (Bomp) 1979
Action Design EP (Rhino) 1980

LA's Weirdos were one of that town's earliest and most popular new wave bands; their first singles (including a 1977 Bomp maxi-single) were routine genre fare. But by '79 they had evolved an intriguing blend of punk, psychobilly and gonzo rock with unsettling lyrics. The six songs on **Who? What? When? Where? Why?** present a wide variety of styles, all reasonably successful in conception and execution.

The band seemed to settle down after that. **Action Design** has only four numbers, and one of them is a needless soundalike version of the Doors' "Break on Through." The other tracks are loud, fast and well-played, with less weirdness and more of a simple rock'n'roll feel. An interesting but inconsistent outfit. [iar]

See also *Thelonious Monster*.

STEFAN WEISSER

See *Z'ev*.

WENDY AND LISA

Wendy and Lisa (Columbia) 1987 ●

On their maiden voyage away from former führer Prince, ex-Revolution guitarist Wendy Melvoin and keyboard player Lisa Coleman delivered a generous helping of smooth, likable tunes. The lyrical department is a little shakier, sometimes veering into bathos—"The Life," "Song About" (guess who). But the compositions show flashes of harmonic and structural daring, and there's no faulting Wendy and Lisa's chops: they play almost all the instruments. Respectable, if not Revolutionary. [si]

JOHANNA WENT

Hyena (Posh Boy) 1982

Hyena offers bizarre big-band no-wave rock rubbish by a stack of players with babbled lyrics by LA performance artist Went. ("Arrangements by the musicians who played them.") Noisy, raucous and unpleasant, soured by relentlessly squawking sax and showing no audible wit or structure, **Hyena** is someone's idea of art, but not mine. [iar]

HOWARD WERTH

Six of One and Half a Dozen of the Other
  (nr/Metabop) 1982

Werth's checkered career has included singing in lovable British folk-pop deviants

Audience, almost joining the Doors as Jim Morrison's replacement and putting out a single on California indie punk label Dangerhouse, backed by local LA talent (including a Wall of Voodoo member-to-be).

Funnily enough, this solo album (Werth issued his prior solo LP in 1975) is no cash-in job; here's a man who's finally found the musical climate he's been waiting for. There's one side of goofy-but-smart originals, his mellifluous, elastic voice a joy to hear telling of an encounter with an astrology nut, the virtues of "Meek Power" and other items of like value. The other side offers oldies of variable obscurity chosen wisely from rock's roots stockpile. The backing—by the likes of Billy Bremner, Carlene Carter and members of the Attractions—is impeccable, as is the shrewd production by Will Birch of the Records. Enough to turn the heads of fans of Dave Edmunds, Nick Lowe, et al.   [jg]

WESTERN EYES
Western Eyes (Trace Elements) 1984

Fascinating, intense rock with a strong beat and provocative, depressed, introspective lyrics. Western Eyes has an uncanny knack for throwing in the right musical effect at just the right spot to heighten the drama and tension. Robert Poss, the mainman of this New York quartet, plays guitar, sings and writes most of the material. The blend of dance rhythms with blazing rave-up guitar noise on discernible tunes makes the album exciting and gutsy; lines like "How many things have I done just to add to my list or impress someone . . ." evince intelligence and talent. A great record.   [iar]

See also Band of Susans.

WESTWORLD
Rockulator (RCA) 1987 ●

Having seen two former Generation X bandmates—Billy Idol and Tony (Sigue Sigue Sputnik) James—score big in the '80s popstakes, guitarist Bob "Derwood" Andrews made a colorful and emptyheaded juvenile stab at British chart fame in this gimmicky comic book trio with American singer Elizabeth Westwood and Welsh drummer Nick Burton. Rockulator melts down parts of Sigue Sigue, Wide Boy Awake, Bow Wow Wow, Haysi Fantayzee and other equally significant sources, seasoning the mélange with sound effects, borrowed bites and assorted production distractions. Cute and ridiculous.   [iar]

JOHN WETTON
See Phil Manzanera, Roxy Music.

WE'VE GOT A FUZZBOX AND WE'RE GONNA USE IT
We've Got a Fuzzbox and We're Gonna Use It EP (nr/Vindaloo) 1986
Bostin' Steve Austin (nr/Vindaloo-WEA) 1986 ●

FUZZBOX
We've Got a Fuzzbox and We're Gonna Use It!! (Vindaloo-Geffen) 1986

These four young misses from Birmingham took over-the-top hairdos, colorful clothes and a devil-may-care amateurish attitude straight into the British Top 30 with their five-song debut EP. (All of the songs are one side of a 12-inch; the flip uses the vinyl only as a medium for scratched-in portraits of the group.) Proud of their lack of instrumental prowess (rightly so—it's a main part of their appeal), WGAFAWGUI simultaneously exploits and satirizes the prurient tabloid mentality on great cuts like "X X Sex" and "She." And isn't "Aaarrrggghhh!!!" a totally inspired title? Musically, the songs are built around rudimentary drums and guitar (yes, they do use their fuzzbox), occasional bass and unbridled enthusiasm. A real breath of fresh air.

The quartet's splendid name was truncated to just Fuzzbox for the retitled American release of Bostin' Steve Austin, which actually has music on both sides. Along with two songs redone from the EP, the well-played record includes the world's worst version of Norman Greenbaum's "Spirit in the Sky" and a bunch of new originals that waffle between Banglish girl-group harmony pop ("What's the Point," "Love Is the Slug," "You Got Me") and chanted dancebeats. In a far more professional setting, Jo's distorto guitar drones along nicely at varying levels; arrangements also feature sax and keyboards. "Preconceptions," which might be a poppy X-Ray Spex number, ends the album on a bewildering note, instructing listeners to "pay less attention to the packaging and listen to the voice!"   [dgs/iar]

WHAT IS THIS
Squeezed EP (San Andreas) 1984
What Is This (MCA) 1985
3 out of 5 Live EP (MCA) 1985

Wild, muscular rock-funk with a demented outlook, LA's What Is This bears more than a passing resemblance to the Red Hot Chili Peppers, but that's no mystery—guitarist Hillel Slovak formed What Is This after leaving the Peppers, whom he rejoined after making **Squeezed**. Chris Hutchinson and Jack Irons ride a fearsome rhythm behemoth, and Alain Johannes and Slovak both provide offbeat songs ("Mind My Have Still I" isn't even the weirdest), unnervingly mental vocals and psycho guitar licks, making **Squeezed** a gut'n'butt-shaking experience you won't soon forget.

Cut as a Slovak-free trio, **What Is This** (produced by Todd Rundgren) is a less invigorating move towards the rhythmic rock mainstream. Some of the excitement remains, but not enough. The subsequent EP adds live versions of three numbers to a pair of album cuts.   [iar]

See also *Red Hot Chili Peppers.*

WHERE'S LISSE?

Where's Lisse? EP (nr/Glass) 1982

Don't be put off by the stupid name. They're a bit scratchy, just barely keeping in step, but when the inchoate instrumental expression of this UK foursome threatens to unravel, they're pulled along by the steadfast, determined (double-tracked) vocals of John Novak. The playing's scruffy, but cut through the rough edging to the heart of it and you'll find lean but proud melodies fighting to escape.   [jg]

WHIRLWIND

Blowin' Up a Storm (nr/Chiswick) 1977
Midnight Blue (nr/Chiswick) 1980

This London quartet (named after a Charlie Rich Sun recording) was one of the first English rockabilly bands to emerge at a time when the music press was looking for the "next big thing" after punk. On its debut, **Blowin' Up a Storm**, Whirlwind—whether by design or simply limited competence—offers up a bare-bones style, with little or no concession to the advancement in recording quality since the originals. The instrumentation is semi-traditional (one lead guitar, one muted-bass-strings rhythm guitar, electric bass and snare drum) and was recorded with no overdubbing, resulting in a sound that can charitably be called "thin." While painstakingly trying to recapture the simplicity of early rockabilly recordings, Whirlwind never manages to re-create the frenzied, fiery abandon that is really what it was all about.

Midnight Blue, recorded over two years later, shows the group past its hang-ups about purity: the sound is filled-out, the drummer plays an entire kit (albeit with amazing clumsiness at times) and pedal-steel guitar even finds its way onto one track. While an improvement over the first LP, **Midnight Blue** still fails to present any clear reason why anybody would want to listen to it, when both the originals and far more imaginative updates like the Stray Cats are available.   [ds]

WHIRLYWIRLD

Whirlywhirld EP (Aus. Missing Link) 1980

On their four-song 12-inch (original copies of which included a bonus 45), Whirlywirld combines guitar, bass, drums and electronics—not synthesizers—to make lots of staccato noise over which Ian "Ollie" Olsen can dispense his own brand of doom and gloom. This sort of amelodic anger has to be compelling to succeed, but Whirlywirld aren't and don't. Surprisingly, when the pioneering Melbourne quartet (considered locally to be Australia's home-spun Suicide) gets relatively conventional on the final track, the savagery of their ska styling does indeed make you sit up and take note.

Keyboardist Olsen, whose pre-Whirlywirld band also boasted future Birthday Party guitarist Rowland S. Howard, scored and served as musical director of the 1987 film *Dogs in Space,* which starred INXS singer Michael Hutchence. A reformed Whirlywirld contributed two songs to the soundtrack, one with Hutchence as their vocalist.   [jg/iar]

JAMES WHITE

See *James Chance.*

WHITE ANIMALS

Nashville Babylon EP (Dread Beat) 1981
Lost Weekend (Dread Beat) 1982
Ecstasy (Dread Beat) 1984

Proof that Jason and the Scorchers aren't the only modern, independent rock band in

Nashville, the White Animals have been active on the scene there for a number of years. These three releases on the band's own label showcase a developing style, from hard-driving rootsy rock'n'roll on **Nashville Babylon** (which features covers of "Tobacco Road" and "For Your Love" as well as four originals) to more refined power pop and odd rock digressions (marred by muddy production) on **Lost Weekend** to a slick, commercial sound on **Ecstasy**, their best record except for nine onerous minutes of "Gloria." The White Animals aren't exactly bursting with personality, but make it up with sincere enthusiasm. [iar]

WHITE DOOR
Windows (Passport) 1983

White Door consists of two synthesists and a singer; with some guests, **Windows** offers lovely pop-with-a-beat. Although the UK band's material and arrangements are not extraordinary for synth-pop, the way in which the fragile, ethereal vocals and durable dance music are blended on the best tracks ("Love Breakdown" is the standout) makes this LP more affecting than affected. [iar]

BARRENCE WHITFIELD AND THE SAVAGES
Barrence Whitfield and the Savages (Mamou) 1984
Dig Yourself (Rounder) 1985
Call of the Wild EP (nr/Rounder Europa-Demon) 1987
Ow! Ow! Ow! (Rounder) 1987 ●

The music young New Jersey native Barry White had in mind was entirely different from the bass soul cooing of his namesake so, when the Boston University student decided to shout gutbucket R&B with a swinging band, he became Barrence Whitfield. On the spectacular first album, backed by a frisky quartet of young, greasy roadhouse rockers (including a couple of ex-Lyres), he stakes his reverent claim to the priceless hipshake legacy of Screaming Jay Hawkins and other venerable titans of primal rock'n'roll. Whitfield is a tremendous vocalist with a bloodcurdling falsetto, the enthusiasm of a drunk amateur and the easy control of a seasoned pro. The Savages—especially saxman Steve LaGrega—keep pace on wacky old numbers like "Bip Bop Bip," "Mama Get the Hammer" and "Georgia Slop," contributing

likely originals to this raw adventure that hardly seems like it was recorded in 1984.

The brief but exhilarating **Dig Yourself** adds a little surface sheen and showband politesse to the proceedings, but still contains a weekend's worth of sweaty, sexy excitement. "Juicy Fruit," "Geronimo's Rock" and "Breadbox" fit all the pieces together in a sweet frenzy, but the remaining tracks are almost as good.

Whitfield recorded **Call of the Wild**, a six-song 12-inch released only in the UK, with an entirely new set of Savages, revamping the sound with piano and organ as well as a slicker, steadier rhythm section. Not as wildly thrilling as either previous record, this takes a tamer posture and reduces the fun accordingly: Ben Vaughn's bluesy but lightweight "Apology Line" indicates Whitfield's moderate direction here. The American **Ow! Ow! Ow!** album expands the EP with four more tracks recorded around the same time. It's likable enough—this man can *sing*—but seriously short in the funkalicious spirit that makes the earlier ones so precious. [iar]

WHODINI
Whodini (Jive) 1983
Escape (Jive) 1984
Back in Black (Jive) 1986 ●
Open Sesame (Jive) 1987 ●

This two-man crew (now a trio) from Brooklyn does something very original and exciting within the context of rap, blending in wit and variety to make entertaining records. On their debut, Jalil Hutchins and Ecstacy worked with three different producers—Thomas Dolby, Conny Plank and the Willesden Dodgers—to come up with an '80s version of "Monster Mash" ("The Haunted House of Rock"), two bouncy history-of-rap/rap-is-good numbers ("Magic's Wand" and "Rap Machine") plus a couple of alternate versions and three more cuts. Although the moderate-tempo big-beat gets a bit numbing, the pair's sharp lyrics and straightforward delivery, plus countless bits of electronic flotsam and jetsam prevent serious tedium.

Escape brought Whodini under the talented studio wing of Run—DMC co-producer Larry Smith, who created a smooth, semi-spare sound and did a lot of the writing as well. With fewer quirky synthesizer accents, the action centers on raps about the urban nightmare ("Escape (I Need a

Break)"), failed romance ("Friends") and New York's 24-hour lifestyle ("Freaks Come Out at Night"), as well as other more egocentric topics. Airy without being simple, **Escape** is appealing and innovative.

With Grandmaster Dee (celebrated on an **Escape** song) officially expanding Whodini to a threesome, **Back in Black** is a blunter record, with less reliance on fancy production and more concentration on varied, organic arrangements. However, while Whodini's music has gotten noticeably stronger, their lyrics are stagnant: all eight cuts cover familiar rap ground with no special outlook and only intermittent cleverness.

The centerpiece of the lively **Open Sesame** teams the trio with the original bad girl of rap, Millie Jackson. (A pre-LP 12-inch offers six different mixes of "Be Yourself," a busy statement against mindless conformity, a message which is reprised, after a fashion, on the LP's "For the Body.") Elsewhere along this moralistic ride, Whodini praises mom ("Early Mother's Day Card"), recommends lusty human devotion as an alternative to drugs ("Hooked on You") and touts personal responsibility ("You Brought It on Yourself"). Behind the board, Smith touches on all of hip-hop's current sonic trendsetters, from LL Cool J to Full Force to Rick Rubin to Run—DMC, making **Open Sesame** an exciting sampler of rap styles. Whodini may not have a sound of their own, but they synthesize what else is around with flair.   [iar]

WIDE BOY AWAKE
Wide Boy Awake EP (RCA) 1983

Ex-Ant bassist Kevin Mooney formed and led London's Wide Boy Awake, an exciting interracial quartet which only released some singles, the first two of which were collected on this eponymous American 12-inch. Hard to classify, the Wide Boys offer clever wordplay and a preponderant funk beat on "Slang Teacher," while square-dancing into wonderful country-tinged pop for "Bona Venture." Elsewhere, they try scratch cajun and dance-rock.   [iar]

JANE WIEDLIN
Jane Wiedlin (IRS) 1985
Fur (EMI Manhattan) 1988 ●

Free of the Go-Go's, guitarist/singer/songwriter Wiedlin's first record is stylistically eclectic to a fault, and stresses goody-

goody lyrical concerns too bluntly. But it's also substantial, attractive and joyously reflects her new-found artistic freedom. "Blue Kiss" is an adorable love lament; "Somebody's Going to Get into This House" is sturdy dance-rock. "Where We Can Go" could have been done by her former band, while the moody "Modern Romance" would better suit the Motels. Wiedlin's not the world's strongest vocalist, but her enthusiasm and sincerity largely compensate.

Wiedlin returned to action in 1988 with her second solo album, **Fur**.   [iar]

WILD WILLY BARRETT
See *John Otway and Wild Willy Barrett.*

SCOTT WILK AND THE WALLS
Scott Wilk and the Walls (Warner Bros.) 1980

Encountering the line between artistic influence and stylistic plagiarism, Scott Wilk grabbed a copy of Elvis Costello's **Armed Forces** and blithely pushed ahead. Parts of his record are uncannily accurate impressions; the cover design and group photo do nothing to reduce the Costello/Attractions allusion. Funny thing, though—the album is really good! If you can ignore its derivative raison d'être, you'll find powerful, well-crafted songs, impressive playing and production and an overriding sense of cohesion. An unexpected but disconcerting thrill.

[iar]

ROBERT WILLIAMS
Buy My Record EP (A&M) 1981
Late One Night (A&M) 1982

Drummer/singer/composer   Williams has played with some real heavyweights in his low-profile career: several years as a member of Captain Beefheart's Magic Band, tours with Bo Donaldson and the Heywoods, an LP with Hugh Cornwell. So it's hardly surprising that the credits on Williams' solo records read like a who's who of modern music. Appearing on these two discs are the likes of Mark and Bob Mothersbaugh of Devo, a couple of Go-Go's, Cornwell, Danny Elfman, ex-Door Robby Krieger, ex-Wing Laurence Juber and a veritable orchestra-full of Beefheart and Zappa sidemen. So much for the illustrious company.

Musically, Williams has absorbed a lot of

different styles and spews them back with alarming variety and an overriding sense of fun. From mock-raga (on a neat remake of "Within You Without You" from **Late One Night**) to straight pop-rock, heavy dance rhythms, reggae and jazz-funk-art-fusion, Williams tries everything and gets away with most of it. The four-song EP is a bit closer to Beefheart with Zappaesque lyrics; the album expands the musical scope and succeeds more in terms of accessible smart-aleck rock.

[iar]

See also *Stranglers.*

JAMES WILLIAMSON
See *Iggy Pop.*

MARTY WILLSON-PIPER
See *Church.*

MARI WILSON
Showpeople (London) 1983
Born Lucky [tape] (nr/Compact Organization) 1983
The Mari Wilson Chat Show [tape] (nr/Compact Organization) 1983

Joined by the Wilsations, crowned with an awesome beehive hairdo and dressed in formal evening wear, England's Mari Wilson attempts to singlehandedly effect a return to the days when singers were known as song stylists and the loudest instruments on a record were trombone and violin. I can't fathom the pose's appeal—this is so far removed from rock as to lose any satirical value and hardly aimed at people desirous of the real article. If the world was in need of a new Peggy Lee, wouldn't the call go out for a real middle-aged schmaltz-spooner?

Anyway, if you don't have a conceptual problem with it, **Showpeople** is a likable, grandly produced (mostly by Tony Mansfield) and bountifully tuneful record. Wilson is an almost-very-good singer with a fair amount of versatility, judging by the mock-rock mixed in with the MOR crooning. The centerpiece and virtual statement of purpose is Wilson's smoky cover of "Cry Me a River," a hit for Julie London in 1957. The British release contains a calender poster; the American edition deducts two songs and shifts the running order.

Born Lucky is a live cassette recorded in 1982. Given the problems of recording an orchestra and vocalist in one take, the sound is a bit cluttered, but Wilson sounds swell, her big voice taking charge of the six numbers, most of them not from the studio album. The **Chat Show** tape is an hour of Mari talking and playing assorted recordings, including outtakes, demos and live cuts.

[iar]

WIND
Guest of the Staphs EP (Cheft) 1984

Cluttered, busy arrangements typify this New York City pop trio, here co-produced by Mitch Easter. Several of the wordy and melodic tunes—with interesting rhythms and rampant guitars and vocals—sound something like Let's Active or the dB's. However, "Delaware 89763" is a '60s rave-up that recalls early Manfred Mann. Throughout, abundant talent and style take center stage, powering the songs along. These guys are really good!

[iar]

WINDBREAKERS
Meet the Windbreakers EP (Big Monkey) 1982
Any Monkey with a Typewriter EP (Big Monkey) 1983
Terminal (Homestead) 1985
Disciples of Agriculture (Fr. Closer) 1985
Run (DB) 1986
A Different Sort . . . (DB) 1987

HOWARD & TIM'S PAID VACATION
I Never Met a Girl I Didn't Like (Midnight) 1985

GONE FISHIN': MATT PIUCCI & TIM LEE
Can't Get Lost When You're Goin' Nowhere (Restless) 1986

TIM LEE
What Time Will Tell (Coyote-Twin/Tone) 1988 ●

BOBBY SUTLIFF
Another Jangly Mess EP (nr/Tambourine) 1986
Only Ghosts Remain (PVC) 1987 ●

Mississippi singer/guitarists Tim Lee and Bobby Sutliff gave their band a terrible name (one hopes the reference is to jackets, not flatulence) but do bring something distinctly unique to the power pop genre, reflecting more of an American than English influence with strange melodic turns and a ragged Southern vocal style. Following the group's introductory salvo, via a 1982 debut 7-inch on their own label, Mitch Easter produced **Any Monkey with a Typewriter**, assisting the trio instrumentally as well. (Richard Barone of the Bongos also appears on the record.) The six-song 12-inch is amateurish but well worth hearing.

Recorded as a duo with Easter and others helping out, **Terminal** is a brilliant, raw pop-rock-folk record with insidious melodies, fuzzed-out guitars, bristly lyrics and unself-conscious sincerity. An appropriately atmospheric version of Television's "Glory"—produced by and played with the Rain Parade—led to Lee's side projects with Paraders Steven Roback (as Distant Cousins) and Matt Piucci (as Gone Fishin').

The engaging **Run** is another collaboration with Easter, who had by then become a virtual (non-writing) bandmember, and long-time associate Randy Everett. A bit less quirky than prior releases, the electrically energized pop could have been mixed more evenly, but that's not a major distraction. Although the coolest song concept is Lee's anxiety-ridden "Braver on the Telephone," Sutliff's "Visa Cards and Antique Mirrors" runs a close second.

Sutliff and Lee then went their separate ways, leaving the latter—no sign of Easter this time—alone to make the final Windbreakers' LP, which he co-produced with Everett. **A Different Sort** offers another striking set of unsettling lyrics, powerful, inventive playing and production, and emotional singing. From the bells on "Knowing Me" through the affecting piano on "We Never Understand" to the pained roughness of "Forget Again," Lee demonstrates his multifarious talents and abundant creativity.

The French-only **Disciples** recaps the Windbreakers' career up through **Terminal**.

The low-budget Paid Vacation LP Lee cut in 1985 with Howard Wuelfing (an ex-Slickee Boy bassist who led the Washington-area Nurses in the late '70s and then worked with Half Japanese) offers sketchy previews of three Windbreakers' songs: "Run" (from **Run**) and "Fit In" and "Forget Again" (from **A Different Sort**). Besides a cover (Tommy Hoehn and Alex Chilton's "She Might Look My Way"), the LP also contains Wuelfing singing his own originals, one of which ("The Week You Were Mine") is quite lovely. Unfortunately, muffled sound and indifferent performances limit the value of this seven-song artifact.

Lee and Piucci recorded the unexciting Gone Fishin' LP together in Mississippi in February 1986. While the arrangements mix things up effectively, the pair co-wrote only two tracks—the rest are individual efforts. The creative collaboration is unproductive: meandering acoustic doodles with electric guitar overdubs, poorly sung rock tunes and dusty pop songs that suffer from the incompatibility of their voices. The nerdy organ on the joint "Lift It Up" suggests a possibly functional period approach that is otherwise ignored on the LP.

Left to his own devices on **What Time Will Tell** (relativity speaking: members of Let's Active, the Bongos and the Wygals all lend a hand), Lee comes up with another winner. His first actual solo album, produced by dB-turned-Wygal Gene Holder, offers sparkling, occasionally beautiful guitar pop and richly resonant lyrics about romance and life (mentioning religion a bunch of times) in the South. Trimming his tendency to experiment, Lee plays his songs (and one by Faye Hunter) with straightforward arrangements and evident craft.

Sutliff's first record after leaving the Windbreakers is a wryly titled British 12-inch magically produced at the Drive-In by Easter, who also plays drums and some guitar. (On his own, Sutliff recorded one cut in Jackson, Mississippi with Tim Lee and a rhythm section.) His pretty voice, piercing guitar solos, understated keyboards and Beatlesque pure-pop sensibility combine to make **Another Jangly Mess** a state-of-the-art exposition on the genre. The equally spectacular **Only Ghosts Remain** repeats the EP's five songs and adds six more (including Richard Thompson's "Small Town Romance") of equal quality, four of which employ Wuelfing as bassist. [iar]

WINKIES

The Winkies (nr/Chrysalis) 1975

Best known for their role as Eno's just-post-Roxy Music tour band, the Winkies included Philip Rambow as well as future sidemen for Phil Manzanera, John Cale and Sean Tyla. Less under-endowed than immature, the sub-Stones pub-rock on this album sounds too presumptuously casual, too unfocused—like demos in a pricey studio, despite Guy Stevens' production—to support

Rambow's lyrical pretensions and nasal Canadian twang. The sole standout is "Trust in Dick," written by Guy Humphreys, a Winkie who became more obscure after the group dissolved. [jg]

See also *Philip Rambow.*

WIPERS

Is This Real? (Park Ave.) 1979
Youth of America (Park Avenue) 1981
Over the Edge (Brain Eater) 1983 (Restless) 1987
Wipers (Enigma) 1985
Land of the Lost (Restless) 1986
Follow Blind (Restless) 1987 ●

GREG SAGE

Straight Ahead (Restless) 1985

Portland, Oregon's Wipers, led by singer/guitarist Greg Sage, are a neat trio playing heavy rock that flirts with hardcore. Their first LP is kind of primitive, allowing high velocity and volume to obscure (but not hide) a competent collection of songs with introspective and intellectual lyrics. Raw and abrasive, but well above the usual.

Youth of America shows refinement and bears some resemblance to early Stranglers but for Sage's weird guitar work on some long instrumental bridges. The title track, a ten-and-a-half-minute monster, is worth noting: a simple, repetitive, colossal anthem, then (as now) the ultimate Wipers' moment.

Over the Edge is as appealing, with some of Sage's most memorable songs. The thick title track, the simmering "Doom Town" and the roaring "So Young" define the Wipers' sound—dense and methodical chunky aggression with heavy, cloudy guitar so full it gains a Hendrix-like flavor. The LP also includes the zippy "Romeo," which adds a weird country twang.

Sage recorded his solo album as a fundraiser of sorts while looking for a new label for the band. When Restless picked up the Wipers, the label released **Straight Ahead** as well. Side One sounds much like the group (which has since performed a few of the selections live), but Side Two is just Sage and his guitar making atmospheric space pieces—haunting and strange consciousness-expansion compositions like "Astro-Cloud." The therapeutic music is so ethereal that it's over before you notice it. An unexpected, intriguing work.

Wipers is a live album which highlights a 1984 tour and includes three excellent tracks

never recorded in the studio, ending with the epic "Youth of America." The sound is honest, the playing true.

Land of the Lost, the Wipers' first new album in three years, shows they didn't get rusty. "Way of Love" and "Nothing Left to Lose" add a certain spark to the charging rockers fed by Sage's fire-breathing guitar. "Just Say," on the other hand, glides on a pretty, lilting guitar line like a quiet waterfall. A strong return.

Follow Blind backsteps a bit, with more hypnotic guitar riffing and much more challenging bass parts. Perhaps the first "moody" Wipers LP, the prominent bass sets up subconscious undercurrents—in much the way Joy Division once did—for Sage to sing over. "Any Time You Find" is what you might get if you plugged Sage's solo atmospherics into the Wipers' repetitive style. Yet another quality LP from one of America's best-kept secrets. [iar/jr]

WIRE

Pink Flag (Harvest) 1977 ●
Chairs Missing (nr/Harvest) 1978 ●
154 (Warner Bros.) 1979 ●
EP (nr/Rough Trade) 1980
Document and Eyewitness (nr/Rough Trade) 1981
And Here It Is . . . Again . . . Wire (nr/Sneaky Pete) 1985
Wire Play Pop (nr/Pink) 1986
Snakedrill EP (nr/Mute) 1986 (Mute-Enigma) 1987 ●
The Ideal Copy (Mute-Enigma) 1987 ●
Ahead EP (Mute-Enigma) 1987 ●
The Peel Sessions EP (nr/Strange Fruit) 1987
A Bell Is a Cup Until It Is Struck (Mute-Enigma) 1988 ●
Kidney Bingos EP (Mute-Restless) 1988 ●
Silk Skin Paws EP (nr/Mute) 1988

In the beginning, this self-taught South London quartet were as much atavistic thrashers as many other bands of the time, yet they were honing a genuinely expressive, "minimalist" style that made them one of the most influential bands of the class of '77, touching everyone from R.E.M. to the Minutemen to Big Black to Sonic Youth. The 21 (count 'em) tracks of **Pink Flag** show Wire still experimenting with their style—angry, abrupt, defiantly odd. Their primitivism was no cover-up for lack of ability, as demonstrated by the excellent pair of conventional rockers, not to mention what just might be the prettiest song ever by a punk band, "Fragile." (Since Wire will not play such old stuff themselves, a New York area band named Ex Lion Tamer faithfully reproduced the LP's songs onstage as Wire's chosen opening act on their 1987 US tour.)

Chairs Missing is more mature, moving decisively beyond any simple punk pigeonhole with much greater scope. As on its predecessor, amid the anger of "Being Sucked in Again," the bile of "I Am the Fly," the neurotic anxiety of "Too Late," even the ironic detachment of "French Film Blurred," sat the pretty if abstruse "Outdoor Miner."

On **154**, producer Mike Thorne became more integral than on the first two LPs, acting almost as a fifth member, using keyboards and studio technique to stylize the sound. That was Wire's development—stylized and smoothed out—although still dissonant; more abstract and detached, with the venom and sardonicism more subtly conveyed. Thus refined, this brilliant groundbreaking band adjudged their experiment complete and broke up, with guitarist Bruce Gilbert and bassist/vocalist Graham Lewis creating Dome and vocalist/guitarist Colin Newman pursuing a solo career.

The 1980 EP is a bizarre 45 rpm 12-inch: one side is titled "Crazy About Love," but the anxiety (among other things) conveyed over a haunting, repeated riff *for more than 15 minutes* suggests something other than the usual meaning of the phrase. The flip is a powerhouse remake of the single "Our Swimmer" plus "Catapult 30" (strange, pulsing doings).

Document and Eyewitness, two live discs (one full-length, the other an eight-song quickie which plays at 45 rpm), owes its raunchy sound as much to Wire's disdain of musical niceties as to dodgy recording. Audience sounds and other incidental noise are left in; for aficionados only. **And Here It Is . . . Again . . . Wire** is a career retrospective containing singles, album tracks and live cuts. **Wire Play Pop** likewise compiles seven old tracks, but limits its scope to Wire's extraordinary, trailblazing A-sides, including "Dot Dash," "I Am the Fly," "Mannequin" and "1-2-X-U."

In 1986, seemingly out of nowhere (well, Mute UK, anyway) popped the **Snakedrill** EP. These were indeed new tracks, but the portent was mixed; the two on the A-side ("'A Serious of Snakes'" and "Drill") are

engrossing, dangerous music, while the pair on the back are interesting without being eyebrow-raising impressive. If they'd gotten back together, they must have felt they had something new to say. But did they? **The Ideal Copy** declared Wire was plugged in again, for real. It's a varied bill of fare, in some ways resembling a more mature **Chairs Missing**, with highlights ranging from the breezily melodic, rhythmically busy "Ahead" to the slow, relentlessly fearsome "Feed Me" (an awesome Graham Lewis vocal) to the topical funk (!) of "Ambitious." Perhaps it's not brilliant—maybe "merely" excellent?

The **Ahead** EP contains two remixes of that track, plus three live cuts, two previously unreleased, including the strange a cappella "Vivid Riot of Red." Those three live (from Berlin) cuts, as well as the entirety of **Snakedrill**, are appended to the CD and cassette of **The Ideal Copy**.

In a sense, **A Bell Is a Cup** is to **The Ideal Copy** what **154** was to **Chairs Missing**; it's a stylized set of dreamscapes and consciousness streams (though it's not as musically sedate as Newman's own **Commercial Suicide**). Some of it has extensive lyrical wordplay, with the accent on *play* (a new attitude for Wire that Newman developed on his own **singing fish** LP); a prime example is "Kidney Bingos," which also happens to be one of the most melodious tracks Wire's ever recorded. Other tracks offer vignettes, yet the subjectivity of view, with its associative images, is continually emphasized. It's arguably Wire's most ruminative album, and while immersion in it won't, as "Silk Skin Paws" suggests, "wring your senses"—that's more a job for **Chairs Missing**—it will twirl your lobes a time or two. An album to live with. (The five-song **Kidney Bingos** EP includes live-in-London takes of "Drill" and "Over Theirs," as well as two versions of the brooding, intense "Pieta," which deserved to be on the LP but would not quite have fit in.) The **Bell** CD adds the four extra items from **Kidney Bingos**, which is also available on a separate 3-inch CD.

The **Silk Skin Paws** EP consists of three numbers from **Bell Is a Cup** in remixed or alternate versions plus the otherwise unreleased "German Shepherds."

Wire's first three albums have been reissued on CDs, all with extra tracks. **Pink Flag** adds "Options R," a non-LP B-side, while **Chairs Missing** has two non-LP Bs

("Go Ahead" and "Former Airline") plus the classic menacingly jaunty non-LP A-side, "Question of Degree." **154** has four otherwise unalbumized tracks: "Song 1," "Get Down 1 & 2," "Let's Panic Later" and "Small Electric Piece." [jg]

See also *Dome, Colin Newman, Desmond Simmons.*

WIRE TRAIN
In a Chamber (415-Columbia) 1983
Between Two Words (415-Columbia) 1985
Ten Women (415-Columbia) 1987 ●

Like former 415 labelmates Translator, San Francisco's Wire Train plays exceptional, character-filled modern folk-pop, using strong songwriting as a basis. (The two groups also shared producer David Kahne, whose brilliant efforts contributed greatly to both's records.) Wire Train achieves its style with a full-blooded guitar attack, echoey vocals and strong, rushed drumming. **In a Chamber** has wonderful, memorable tracks like "Chamber of Hellos" and "I'll Do You"; lesser creations at least *sound* just as good. A great debut album.

Between Two Words, despite Kahne's absence and a version of Dylan's "God on Our Side" that unintentionally trivializes the song's earnest concerns, is equally memorable. Not all of the songs work, but those that do—"Last Perfect Thing," "Skills of Summer," "Love, Love"—exhibit folk-derived melodic beauty and an uneasy emotional perspective that is not easily ignored. The writing/singing/guitar-playing duo of Kevin Hunter and Kurt Herr doesn't display a lot of range or depth, but gives the group an unmistakable, invariably pleasing identity.

Herr was replaced prior to **Ten Women** and his absence from the record is immediately evident. While the crystalline pop production and Hunter's sandy voice give the record a familiar patina, the slower-paced songs are pretty but routine; the guitar interplay lacks any character. The new Wire Train may be viable, but far less meaningful. [iar]

WISEBLOOD
See *Foetus.*

WITCH TRIALS
The Witch Trials EP (Subterranean-Alternative Tentacles) 1981

Jello Biafra of the Dead Kennedys was the brains and voice of this mysterious one-off studio project, recorded in England and released originally in France. With unidentified musicians providing guitar and synthesizer backing—an atmospheric drone on one side, jarring unpleasantness on the other—Biafra recites two dramatic tales of mayhem and chants two more pieces of madness that exhibit his characteristic venom and wit. **Witch Trials** is an interesting detour from the DKs, and Biafra proves to be just as capable and clever in this vein. [iar]

JAH WOBBLE
The Legend Lives On . . . Jah Wobble in "Betrayal" (nr/Virgin) 1980
V.I.E.P. EP (nr/Virgin) 1980
Jah Wobble's Bedroom Album (nr/Lago) 1983
Psalms (nr/Wob) c. 1986
Island Paradise (nr/Wob) c. 1986

DON LETTS, STRATETIME KEITH, STEEL LEG, JAH WOBBLE
Steel Leg v the Electric Dread EP (nr/Virgin) 1978

JAH WOBBLE, JAKI LIEBEZEIT AND HOLGER CZUKAY
How Much Are They EP (nr/Island) 1981

JAH WOBBLE + ANIMAL
A Long, Long Way EP (nr/Island) 1982

JAH WOBBLE—THE EDGE—HOLGER CZUKAY
Snake Charmer EP (Island) 1983

JAH WOBBLE & OLLIE MARLAND
Neon Moon (nr/Island) 1985

After falling out with John Lydon and Keith Levene, bassist Wobble left Public Image Ltd. and launched an on-again-off-again solo/collaborative career. He also played in a group called the Human Condition, and did a brief stint as a London taxi driver.

Wobble's anti-musical playfulness on **The Legend Lives On** is matched only by his horrid vocals. But then again, that's the appeal: the return to the DIY, no-rules punk tradition. Wobble accentuates his reggae pretensions, fiddles with electronics and overdubbing and plays shadowy, threatening bass. If nothing else, Wobble has anti-style. Not to be taken seriously, as he would probably be the first to admit.

V.I.E.P., which sounds like outtakes from the album sessions, reprises the LP's "Blueberry Hill." Twice. "Sea Side Special" is notable for its professionalism and use of brass. But the EP is for completists only.

Far more indicative of Wobble's real talent is the four-song 12-inch made with erstwhile Can members Jaki Liebezeit and Holger Czukay in 1981. Manifesting a dour modern landscape, Wobble's bass buttresses the dark tunes with style and precision that balance his earlier solipsistic sloppiness. Freed from ego, Wobble teeters at last towards art.

Unlike previous Wobble projects, **A Long, Long Way** is sweetly pop-like, treading on Joy Division territory (with assistance from guitarist Dave "Animal" Maltby). Especially interesting is "Romany Trail," which mixes "Peter Gunn" jazz with modern sensibilities. Top-notch.

The Bedroom Album was recorded alone—you guessed it—in the master's chamber, with Animal providing the only outside contact. A cross between a legit solo studio job and the kind of one-man-band who plays on street corners, the LP finds Wobble building unstable and atmospheric polyrhythmic instrumentals over which he intones ponderous lyrics with only the barest glimpses of melody or meter. The lengthy record requires a lot of patience, but is not without undercurrents of charm or appeal.

In collaboration with producer Francois Kevorkian, Czukay, Liebezeit, Animal and U2's guitar star (among others—Wobble certainly appears to make friends easily), he pounds out far slicker dance-rock on **Snake Charmer**, but it's all for nought, as the record is overstaffed and overstuffed, mixing repetitive rhythms with extraneous sounds to achieve audible boredom.

Wobble's 1978 pre-PiL 12-inch with Keith Levene, filmmaker (and future Big Audio Dynamite member) Don Letts and someone called Steel Leg is a bizarre assemblage of dub reggae and noisome doom-funk that has Levene playing drums and guitar while Wobble adds bass, synth and vocals. Whew!   [sg/iar]

WOLFGANG PRESS

The Burden of Mules (nr/4AD) 1983
Scarecrow EP (nr/4AD) 1984
Water EP (nr/4AD) 1985
Sweatbox EP (nr/4AD) 1986
The Legendary Wolfgang Press & Other Tall Stories (nr/4AD) 1986
Standing Up Straight (nr/4AD) 1986 ●
Big Sex EP (nr/4AD) 1987

Ever-changing and always challenging, London's Wolfgang Press is one of the more enigmatic groups on an already enigmatic label. Known better for their stylish Alberto Ricci record covers than their music, the trio comprises Michael Allen (vocals/bass), Mark Cox (keyboards) and Andrew Gray (drums).

The Burden of Mules is dark and cacophonous, an angry, intense slab of post-punk gloom that is best left to to its own (de)vices. **Scarecrow**, however, makes the most of the band's better attributes with spotless production by Cocteau Twin Robin Guthrie. Allen's almost-spoken, heavily accented vocals sputter through a mix of up-front bass, rhythm guitar, synthesizers and creative percussion. Some dreary moments remain, but a send-up of Otis Redding's "Respect" reflects the lightened mood.

Water continues the band's evolution, but in a totally different direction. Over minimalist backing, Allen's vocals turn baladeerish: Frank Sinatra sifted through Joy Division. A track called "My Way" is curiously reminiscent of Burt Bacharach.

Continuing to work with Guthrie, the Wolfgang Press sounds fully mature and more musically adept than ever on **Sweatbox**. The EP strengthens and confirms their fundamental approach: the deconstruction and reconstruction of pop conventions in their own image. Put through the Wolfgang Press breakdown process, Neil Young's "Heart of Gold" becomes "Heart of Stone," in effect creating an original. **Sweatbox** also establishes the group's mastery of moving instrumentals. **The Legendary Wolfgang Press** compiles the three EPs onto one disc, with some songs remixed and/or edited from their original form.

Musically, **Standing Up Straight** is as challenging and inventive as the band's other work, adding industrial and classical instrumentation to the creative arsenal. "Dig a Hole," "Hammer the Halo" and "Rotten Fodder" are the best the Press has to offer—dark and thoroughly uncompromising—on a record which is not for the easily intimidated. Also of interest is the enclosed lyric sheet, a multi-fold affair in which lyrics are presented as artistic design elements.

The Wolfgang Press continue to astound

and delight on the **Big Sex** EP—four tracks that clearly demonstrate just what it is that makes this band so special. "The Wedding" is weighty and primal; "The Great Leveller" is desperate, insistent and the closest the Press will likely come to a real pop tune. The oppressive "That Heat" has wonderful blasts of distorted guitar throughout; "God's Number" is virtually all drums, with the novelty of female soul backing vocals. Daring music for daring times! [ag]

WOODEN BIRDS

See *David Thomas and the Pedestrians.*

WOODENTOPS

Straight Eight Bushwaker EP (Hol. Megadisc) 1986
Well Well Well . . . (Upside) 1986 ●
Giant (Rough Trade-Columbia) 1986 ●
Live Hypno-Beat Live (Upside) 1987 ●
Wooden Foot Cops on the Highway (Rough Trade-Columbia) 1988 ●

In this era of retro-rock, revivals and rip-offs, it's not easy to find truly innovative pop music. That's what makes this quintet from Peckham so special—they literally defy categorization. Led by the exuberant Rolo McGinty, the Woodentops employ only the barest of essentials—vocals, keyboards, acoustic guitars, bass and rudimentary drums.

The first two records chronicle a string of five brilliant singles. The Dutch EP collects six tracks. "Move Me," like many of the Woodentops' songs, builds to a manic crescendo before collapsing into a wall of sound; "Well Well Well" is held together with skittering drums and pulsating keyboard chords; "It Will Come" rushes along in a flurry of guitar, piano and good-natured mayhem. The Woodentops tend to throw caution to the wind on their B-sides, and the three here explore all sorts of new territory. **Well Well Well** adds two more B-sides (from 12-inch singles) and substitutes a longer version of "Well Well Well" that has incredible keyboard and drum breaks. (When that record was subsequently issued on CD, it was retitled **The Unabridged Singles Collection**.)

The Woodentops' long-awaited debut album proved to be more than worth the wait. **Giant** is a bright handful of pop gems hallmarked with the band's special sound.

They've filled out musically with the addition of trumpet, marimba, strings and accordion, and the songs are more structured. But that in no way detracts from their originality. You're not likely to hear more innovative pop than "Hear Me James," "Love Affair with Everyday Livin' " or "Travelling Man." An incredible first album.

Recorded in Los Angeles at the end of 1986, **Live Hypno-Beat Live**, which draws its material from singles and **Giant**, reveals that the Woodentops play three times as fast on-stage as they do in the studio. You'll work up a sweat just listening to this. The CD adds the contents of **Straight Eight Bushwaker**; the cassette also contains an extra pair of live recordings.

Wooden Foot Cops on the Highway finds the band suffering a bit from a lack of fresh ideas and the loss of keyboard player Alice Thompson. Some good songs appear (e.g., "In a Dream" and "What You Give Out"), but there is little distinction between this album and **Giant**. Some bands survive for years (even decades) by making the same album over and over; the Woodentops deserve a better fate. [ag]

WOODS
It's About Time (Twin/Tone) 1987

Like the Georgia Satellites, North Carolina's Woods are terminal fans of early Rod Stewart. (In fact, Satellite singer Dan Baird tarried with the then-Woodpeckers before hitting platinum.) Alas, these guys seem to be running on low-octane gas, only occasionally ("Battleship Chains") summoning up the abandon required to raunch out fully. Other times, poppier stuff like "I Don't Want Her (Anymore)," later covered by Marti Jones, veers dangerously close to wimpland. Major curiosity: "Walk," a thinly veiled rewrite of "Maggie May." [jy]

BRUCE WOOLLEY AND THE CAMERA CLUB
English Garden (nr/CBS) 1979
Bruce Woolley and the Camera Club (Columbia) 1979

FIRMAMENT AND THE ELEMENTS
The Essential EP (Press) 1983

Bruce Woolley came out of the Buggles camp, having co-written several of their songs, including the monumental "Video Killed the Radio Star." That song, as well as

"Clean Clean," is reprised on **English Garden** (which was retitled **Bruce Woolley and the Camera Club** for the US), an LP of light power pop strongly reminiscent of the early Move. Woolley's musical attitudes were doomed to commercial failure, as this music was too lodged in the '60s to make a dent in the futurist '70s, and the record vanished in the flood. The Camera Club, however, can claim fame of a sort in that Thomas Dolby was a member.

Woolley abandoned the past and discovered the future in the '80s. Along with his brother Guy, he formed a weird, somewhat experimental group, Firmament and the Elements. Their intriguing EP contains nice tunes as well as bizarre effects and tape sounds.   [sg/iar]

See also *Grace Jones.*

WORLD AT A GLANCE

World at a Glance (Island) 1988 ●

Some people were just born in the wrong place and time: this New York quartet's first LP reveals a deep desire to be British dance poseurs. As singer David Ilku affects a mild finishing school accent, Michael Lawrence shoots off impressive guitarisms that would sound at home on an Ultravox record; guest keyboardists (including producer Chris Lord Alge) fill in the stylistic gaps. (For credibility's sake, drummer Doug Bowne was a Lounge Lizard.) While inarguably accomplished, **World at a Glance**, with its echoes of Duran Duran, Simple Minds, Japan, Bill Nelson, U2 and others, is utterly redundant.

[tr]

WORLD DOMINATION ENTERPRISES

Let's Play Domination (Product Inc.-Caroline) 1988 ●

The wall-shaking noise/chaos level achieved by this London trio is indeed something marvelous: the astonishing racket of **Let's Play Domination**'s opening salvo ("Message for You People") may send you rushing to the turntable to see if your stylus is accidentally gouging a hole in the platter. Besides sturdily unsettling originals, the album includes a relatively straight rendition of LL Cool J's "I Can't Live Without My Radio" and deranged interpretations of Lipps, Inc.'s "Funkytown" and a U-Roy number. Keith Dobson layers on the scathing

guitar and sings in a plain, serviceable voice; the rhythm section likewise lurches and pounds in a tight phalanx. Not as pop-oriented as the Jesus and Mary Chain or as anti-musical as the Swans, World Domination Enterprises builds its thoughtful tumult with a firm hand.   [iar]

WORLD PARTY

Private Revolution (Chrysalis) 1986 ●

For all intents and purposes, Karl Wallinger *is* World Party on this LP, which he recorded at home after leaving the Waterboys. (He later formed World Party, the group.) He sings, plays guitars and keyboards and uses various samples to create a refreshingly unique musical backdrop that probably owes more to the psychedelicized Beatles than any one other source, yet never actually sounds like them. The music, in fact, serves as a free-flowing pop soundtrack to Wallinger's lyrics which hybridize '60s-hippie and '80s-new age ideas about ecology and self-knowledge. (Thankfully they're not quite as silly as that sounds.) Highlights include a terrific cover of Dylan's "All I Really Want to Do" and a cameo by Sinéad O'Connor. Leave your cynicism at the door and you may find yourself trading in your black leather jacket for love beads. In a word: groovy.

[ds]

WRECKLESS ERIC

Wreckless Eric (nr/Stiff) 1978
The Wonderful World of Wreckless Eric (nr/Stiff) 1978
The Whole Wide World (Stiff) 1979
Big Smash (Stiff-Epic) 1980
The Peel Sessions EP (nr/Strange Fruit) 1988

ERIC GOULDEN

A Roomful of Monkeys (nr/Go! Discs) 1985

On the front of his first LP, the grinning "Wreckless" Eric Goulden wears a badge proclaiming "I'm a mess," and a drop of the needle on the disc confirms it. Led by producer Larry Wallis (himself an ex-Pink Fairy), a motley crew whose previous employers include Ronnie Lane, Marc Bolan and Ian Dury slosh together some mangy guitars, slurpy sax and cheesy organ to surround the strangled, semi-sodden vocals of this lovable scruffy runt from Brighton. All too often, though, catching the bits of perception and knowing desperation requires clearing the sonic mud, not to mention deciphering Eric's drawl.

All, that is, except on the brilliant "Whole Wide World," produced and mostly played by Nick Lowe. As if noticing that Lowe's well-defined pop sense seemed to bring out Eric's best, a series of producers then tried to clean up and dress up his sound. The next album's roster was only slightly less rag-tag (Hollywood Brats holdovers and ex-Man man Malcolm Morley), helmed by Pete Solley. This time, though, a balance was obtained between Eric's innate looseness and the clarity and sheer musicality needed to adequately present his tunes. As a result, **The Wonderful World** is a rollicking good time propelled by Eric's trademark guitar chug.

No hits were forthcoming, though, and Stiff apparently decided to clean Eric's act up further, as is evident from the new-material first half of the double set, **Big Smash**. Fresh faces in the band (who also collaborated with him on songwriting) and decidedly more commercial-minded production unfortunately seemed to have sanded off all of the Wreckless edges. (The standout tune, "Good Conversation," is one he wrote alone; it's also the nastiest.)

Clearly establishing his merits once and for all, the other half of **Big Smash** is an irreproachable distillation of the first two LPs and a batch of singles. That disc had previously been issued separately in the US as **The Whole Wide World**, indicating—even to those who might have otherwise dismissed him—Eric's surprising resonance, not to mention his squandered and/or squelched potential.

For collectors of odd discs, the first LP was also issued as a brown-vinyl 10-incher, with two songs fewer.

Returning in 1985 under his own name and fronting a band containing such stalwarts as Norman Watt-Roy and Mickey Gallagher from the Blockheads, Goulden recorded and released his first LP in five years, **A Roomful of Monkeys**. [jg]

WÜRM
Feast (SST) 1985

Würm pre-figured Chuck Dukowski's tenure in Black Flag; he reformed the group temporarily in 1982 and cut a belated LP which SST issued a few years later. **Feast** features the gallingly awful singing of Dead Hippie's Simon Smallwood but, in fairness to him, is pretty dire all by itself. I'm not sure,

but I think it's an imitation of the Crazy World of Arthur Brown. Then again, it might have been more influenced by Atomic Rooster . . . [iar]

WURZEL
See *Motorhead.*

ROBERT WYATT
The End of an Ear (Columbia) 1971 (nr/CBS) 1980
Rock Bottom (Virgin) 1974
Ruth Is Stranger Than Richard (Virgin) 1975
Rock Bottom/Ruth Is Stranger Than Richard (nr/Virgin) 1981
Robert Wyatt (It. Rough Trade) 1981
Nothing Can Stop Us (nr/Rough Trade) 1981 (Gramavision) 1986
The Animals Film (nr/Rough Trade) 1982
Work in Progress EP (nr/Rough Trade) 1984
1982–1984 EP (Rough Trade) 1984
I'm a Believer EP (nr/Virgin) 1984
Old Rottenhat (Gramavision) 1985
The Peel Sessions EP (nr/Strange Fruit) 1987

MATCHING MOLE
Matching Mole (nr/CBS) 1972
Matching Mole's Little Red Record (Columbia) 1973

Having first come to prominence as founding drummer/vocalist with Canterbury's Soft Machine, Bristol-born Robert Wyatt is one of the English art-schools' most notable (and best-loved) musical alumni, retaining that genre's spirit of musical adventurousness but never at the expense of his humanity. In the unselfconscious experimentalism of his post-Softs work, and in the political commitment of his more recent material, Wyatt has served as an inspiration for a new generation of socially-conscious British artists.

End of an Ear, Wyatt's first solo LP, was recorded right before he left Soft Machine and basically continues in that group's free-wheeling avant-jazz spirit. Wordless scat-sung originals are bookended by two lengthy versions of Gil Evans' "Las Vegas Tango."

The four-man Matching Mole—the name is a phonetic adaptation of the French translation of "soft machine"—recorded two albums of meandering (and occasionally charming) pieces, mostly instrumentals. The spotty **Matching Mole** is mainly a Wyatt showcase; the more driving **Little Red Record** (produced by Robert Fripp) is a collective effort, but both are weighed down with the sort of aimless noodling that helped give progressive rock a bad name.

Following a crippling fall that left him permanently wheelchair-bound, Wyatt recorded **Rock Bottom**, produced by Pink Floyd's Nick Mason, and the self-produced **Ruth Is Stranger Than Richard**. Both records are idiosyncratic, mixing woozy experimentation ("Little Red Riding Hood Hit the Road," which appears in two utterly different versions on **Rock Bottom**, and **Ruth**'s "Muddy Mouse," a collaboration with Fred Frith) with charmingly pastoral nursery rhymes ("Sea Song," "Alifib," both from **Rock Bottom**). **Ruth** is the better focused of the two, and includes the remarkable "Team Spirit," which hints at the political outlook that dominates Wyatt's later work. **I'm a Believer** and the live **Peel Sessions** also contain material from this period; both feature Wyatt's droll non-LP reading of the Monkees' Neil Diamond-penned classic.

Wyatt lay low for the remainder of the the '70s, finally reemerging at the turn of the decade with a series of four audacious Rough Trade singles. Those eight sides (two of which are performed by artists other than Wyatt) are collected on the Italian **Robert Wyatt**, and form the basis of **Nothing Can Stop Us**. Though basically a compilation with only one original composition, **Nothing Can Stop Us** is a cohesive and incredibly moving statement, with Wyatt's fragile, plaintive vocals breathing new life (and political content) into material as diverse as Chic's "At Last I Am Free," the obscure American gospel tune "Stalin Wasn't Stallin'," the folk song "Caimanera" (aka "Guantanamera") and the disquieting lynchmob protest "Strange Fruit" (most as-sociated with Billie Holliday). Though Wyatt personally adheres to a fairly ruthless strain of Stalinism, you'd never know it from the compassion and empathy that radiate from every groove of this record.

Nothing Can Stop Us was subsequently re-released with the significant inclusion of the Elvis Costello/Clive Langer-penned "Shipbuilding" (produced by Costello, Langer and Alan Winstanley), as subtle and insightful an anti-war song as anyone's ever written. The album's US version, released in 1986, ditches the poet Peter Blackman's reading of his "Stalingrad" and adds "Shipbuilding," plus its British 12-inch B-sides (interpretations of Thelonious Monk's "Round Midnight" and Eubie Blake's "Memories of You") and cover art.

The Animals Film contains Wyatt's appropriately harsh instrumental score for a harrowing documentary chronicling institutionalized human cruelty. The four-song **Work in Progress** is similar in approach to **Nothing Can Stop Us**, with a reworking of Peter Gabriel's "Biko" and Spanish-language folk songs by Victor Jara and Pablo Milanes. The American **1982–1984** combines the contents of **Work in Progress** and the British "Shipbuilding" 12-inch.

The completely self-penned **Old Rottenhat** is a perceptive, beautifully performed and ultimately bleak view of ongoing political struggle, more specific than **Nothing Can Stop Us** but equally emotive. Though many of Wyatt's lyrics veer towards the doctrinaire, his singing is as quietly passionate as ever.   [hd]

PETE WYLIE
See *Wah!*.

X X X X X X X

X
Los Angeles (Slash) 1980 ●
Wild Gift (Slash) 1981 ●
Under the Big Black Sun (Elektra) 1982 ●
More Fun in the New World (Elektra)
  1983 ●
Ain't Love Grand (Elektra) 1985 ●
See How We Are (Elektra) 1987 ●
Live at the Whisky A Go-Go on the Fabulous
  Sunset Strip (Elektra) 1988 ●

KNITTERS
Poor Little Critter on the Road (Slash) 1985

EXENE CERVENKA + WANDA
  COLEMAN
Twin Sisters (Freeway) 1985

Named after the band's hometown, X's debut album is identifiable as a forerunner of hardcore; simple, unrestrained energy often threatens to crush the "realistic" tunes ("Sex and Dying in High Society," "Nausea," etc.), but never does. Certainly, the elements that give X their majesty on later LPs are already present: Billy Zoom's vibrant rockabilly/Chuck Berry guitar licks, D.J. Bonebrake's thundering drums and arresting vocal harmonies by Exene Cervenka and bassist John Doe, strongly reminiscent of early Jefferson Airplane. Doors organist Ray Manzarek produced the first four albums; on **Los Angeles**, the band saluted him by covering "Soul Kitchen."

Wild Gift constitutes a great leap forward, bringing **Los Angeles**' action blur into sharp focus. Zoom's ingeniously simple guitar transcends its influences, and the Doe/Exene harmonies attain a knifelike sharpness. Also, their songs are frequently as incisive as their voices: "We're Desperate," "In This House That I Call Home" and

"White Girl," a spooky ballad, ambitiously peer into unglamorous realities without either diminishing or inflating their subjects. **Wild Gift** was such a success as an independent label release that the band's jump to a big company (where greater success has ironically eluded them) was practically inevitable.

Though **Under the Big Black Sun** primarily refines the techniques of **Wild Gift**, it's no disappointment. Bonebrake's drums just get harder and harder, while Doe and Cervenka continue to expand their prowess as singers and songwriters. "Motel Room in My Bed" revives the sleaze motif of earlier LPs; "The Have Nots" skillfully separates compassion from mawkishness.

The problematic **More Fun in the New World** is the work of a band filled with energy and ideas, but unsure how to apply them. As a result, this thoroughly respectable LP is too much like **Big Black Sun** to be fully satisfying. Sizzling tracks such as "Make the Music Go Bang!" and "I Must Not Think Bad Thoughts" would have worked fine on that previous disc, which is a bad sign for a band accustomed to growing by leaps and bounds. In "True Love Pt. #2," X wonders about its own relationship to American mainstream music without arriving at a clear answer. After the LP, they attempted to make contact with Top 40 by covering "Wild Thing" and fell flat.

An album by the Knitters—a part-time, mostly-acoustic band consisting of X (minus Billy Zoom), Blaster Dave Alvin and a stand-up bassist—proved to be a glimpse into the future when, in early '86, Zoom left X to form his own band and Alvin gave up the Blasters (at least temporarily) to replace him. **Critter on the Road** records a sincere but

639

futile attempt to imitate several varieties of folk and country music, from traditional to swing. The material mixes cleverly cliché-laden originals (and an acoustified version of "The New World" for anyone who didn't realize what a weak song it is) with Merle Haggard and Leadbelly covers; Doe/Exene's wistful "Love Shack" is the record's standout.

Ain't Love Grand, the original lineup's final album together, is a hot (if styleless) rock'n'roll record that cuts the crap to bang out unprepossessing rave-ups like "Burning House of Love." On most songs, lead vocals are taken by Exene or Doe alone; the partial elimination of their harmonies is a distinct improvement, as is Michael Wagener's loud, gimmick-free production style. The biggest boner here, a misbegotten amateurish cover of the Small Faces' "All or Nothing," indicates that X—or at least some portion thereof—has never had a clue about rock music's heritage.

X rebounded from the loss of guitarist Billy Zoom with a vengeance on **See How We Are.** Dumping Wagener's metal flourishes for the less flashy approach of producer Alvin Clark, this polished platter cooks wickedly on desperate rockers like the lead-off "I'm Lost" then tugs at the heartstrings with "You," an old-fashioned love lament even non-fans should appreciate. The standout track, however, is "4th of July," penned by Dave Alvin. A wide-screen tale of terminal alienation that holds out little hope of redemption, "4th of July" matches the epic sweep of "Born to Run."

The two-record **Live at the Whisky A Go Go** makes a good case for the band onstage, showcasing pithy axework by Alvin's successor, Tony Gilkyson (ex-Lone Justice). A studio album of new material would have been more welcome, though. (N.B. This is not the soundtrack of the rarely-seen X feature film *The Unheard Music.*)

Singer Exene Cervenka takes one side of the spoken-word disc **Twin Sisters** to ramble through her poetry. Unless you're enthralled with Ms. C. in the first place, it's pretty heavy sledding, with pretense outweighing the wit. Notable moments: "Peas and Beans," which belittles synth bands, and three penned by her late sister Mary. [jy/iar]

See also *Blasters, Divine Horsemen.*

XDREAMYSTS

Xdreamysts (Hol. Polydor) 1981

This Northern Irish combo moves in the general direction of Elvis Costello (**My Aim Is True** strain), but lightly, gingerly—like Any Trouble or the Keys—and makes even those bands sound fully individual and almost original by comparison. Oddly enough, it's on the slower numbers that songwriting singer/guitarist Uel Walls shows signs of the kind of maturity it would take to emerge from behind's Elvis' shadow. [jg]

XMAL DEUTSCHLAND

Incubus Succubus EP (Ger. ZickZack) 1982
Fetisch (nr/4AD) 1983 ●
Tocsin (nr/4AD) 1984 ●
The Peel Sessions EP (nr/Strange Fruit) 1986
Viva (nr/Phonogram) 1987

The dense, throbbing rock of this German quintet may be too strong for some; on "Incubus Succubus," the title track of a three-song 12-inch, semi-tonic vocalist Anja Huwe bellows and shrieks with dark drama while the band drones and pounds out an unbelievably heavy track behind her, a horror movie cross between Siouxsie and the Banshees and Hawkwind.

The lineup for **Fetisch,** recorded in England, includes Huwe and three other women (guitar, keyboards, drums) plus a male bassist. With a slightly toned-down attack, Xmal Deutschland's drone loses some of its allure, and a full album's worth of onrushing chaos and numbing noise is more tedious than gripping.

Also recorded in London, but this time with mainstream producer Mick Glossop, **Tocsin** tempers the band's ugly side with economy, variety and restraint. They're still loud as hell and sound in spots like Hawkwind but, at this point, they're also at a nexus with Joy Division, using bleak noise to convey a variety of moods. With the subtlety and dynamics that were lacking, **Tocsin** clearly displays Xmal Deutschland to be cogent and invigorating.

The **Peel Sessions** EP was recorded in early 1985. [iar]

See also *This Mortal Coil.*

X-RAY SPEX

Germ Free Adolescents (nr/EMI Int'l) 1978

POLY STYRENE

Translucence (nr/UA) 1980
God's & Godesses EP (nr/Awesome) 1986

One of the most exciting groups of its time, X-Ray Spex was at once an ideal and atypical punk band. While boasting as much raw aggression as any of its peers, X-Ray Spex used a distinctively different means of delivery—augmenting Jak Airport's obligatory buzzsaw guitar with Rudi Thompson's (Lora Logic's replacement) even-more-abrasive sax and giving center stage to Poly Styrene (Marion Elliot), a talented teenager who yowled witty lyrics with all the delicacy of a cat in heat.

X-Ray Spex's one LP collects some of the ace singles that made them such an early punk standout, although it doesn't contain their classic first outing, the wildly polemic "Oh Bondage, Up Yours!" Styrene's songs focus on the artificiality of modern life; hence such titles as "The Day the World Turned Day-Glo" and "Warrior in Woolworths." Whether the tune is a ballad or a crazed rocker, the band surges as if there were no tomorrow. And for them, there wasn't. A masterpiece!

Styrene always seemed one of punk's most dispossessed souls, so perhaps the solo album that followed the band's dissolution should be viewed as a last stab at finding some sense of place in musical terms. A feeling of alienation still prevails: **Translucence** is so smooth and coolly delivered that one could easily miss the dark side in the lyrics. Jazzy cocktail-hour backing combines with Styrene's childlike visions to make the music's effect most elusive.

Styrene subsequently left music completely to join a British Hare Krishna sect, but resurfaced commercially in early 1986 with a delightful, well-adjusted 12-inch EP. Jak Airport arranged two of the four originals comprising **God's & Godesses**; the record's main musicians are Mick Sweeney and Paul Inder. The anti-cult "Trick of the Witch" has hauntingly echoed vocals and a driving rock beat; synthesized log drum and sitar give the jazzy mantra of "Paramatma" fascinating color. "Big Boy Big Toy" attacks the nuclear arms race with humor and urgency. Welcome back, Poly—please make more records! [jy/wk/iar]

See also *Essential Logic.*

XTC

3D EP (nr/Virgin) 1977
White Music (Virgin Int'l) 1978 (Virgin-Epic) 1982 (Virgin-Geffen) 1984 ●
Go 2 (Virgin Int'l) 1978 (Virgin-Epic) 1982 (Virgin-Geffen) 1984 ●
Drums and Wires (Virgin) 1979 (Virgin-Epic) 1982 (Virgin-Geffen) 1984 ●
Black Sea (Virgin-RSO) 1980 (Virgin-Epic) 1982 (Virgin-Geffen) 1984 ●
5 Senses EP (Can. Virgin) 1981
Ball and Chain EP (nr/Virgin) 1982
English Settlement (nr/Virgin) 1982 (Virgin-Epic) 1982 (Virgin-Geffen) 1984
Waxworks/Beeswax (nr/Virgin) 1982 (Virgin-Geffen) 1984
Mummer (Virgin-Geffen) 1983 ●
The Big Express (Virgin-Geffen) 1984 ●
The Compact XTC—The Singles 1978–85 [CD] (nr/Virgin) 1985
Skylarking (Virgin-Geffen) 1986 ●
Dear God EP (Virgin-Geffen) 1987

MR. PARTRIDGE
'Take Away' (nr/Virgin) 1980

DUKES OF STRATOSPHEAR
25 O'Clock EP (nr/Virgin) 1985 ●
Psonic Psunspot (Virgin-Geffen) 1987 ●
Chips from the Chocolate Fireball [CD] (Geffen) 1988

XTC has never been easy to categorize. At first they seemed like one more high-spirited new wave band, gleefully trampling on rock conventions set the day before. On **White Music**, XTC delights in dissonance, unresolved melodic lines and playful lyrics; guitarist Andy Partridge's hiccuping vocals are matched by equally nervous music. Amid hyperactive material like "Radios in Motion" and "Spinning Top," only a version of Bob Dylan's "All Along the Watchtower" shows respect for the past.

The follow-up, **Go 2**, is even further out. The songs, mostly by Partridge, excoriate conformism and other hang-ups in kaleidoscopic imagery; the music is alternately herky-jerky and menacing. (If that sounds too coherent, a bonus 12-inch EP called **Go+** pulverizes five of the album's tracks with dub remixes.)

The band settled down on **Drums and Wires**, proving they could make commercial-sounding music without sacrificing their considerable intelligence. The departure of organist Barry Andrews—replaced by guitarist Dave Gregory—seemed to take some helium out of the arrangements. XTC's funhouse world on **Drums and Wires** is more accessible, but still booby-trapped: "Making Plans for Nigel," "Real by Reel," "Life Begins at the Hop," "Scissor Man," "Complicated Game." As Mr. Partridge, a separately released "solo" album, **'Take Away'/'The Lure of Salvage,'** finds Andy playing more dub games with tracks from **Drums and Wires**. "This used to be some XTC records," the sleeve notes. "It is now a collection of tracks that have been electronically processed/shattered and layered with other sounds or lyrical pieces."

Black Sea refines **Drums and Wires**' approach. Heedless of fashion, XTC builds up the music with multiple strains, undanceable rhythms, intricate interplay and gloriously literate lyrics. The dazzling result is the band's finest achievement up to that point: an album that, like its songs ("Respectable Street," "Generals and Majors," "Towers of London"), unsentimentally employs the past to make new statements.

English Settlement continues in the same vein but succumbs to rococo excess. (Five songs were pruned from the original British two-record set to fit it onto one US disc, although the 1984 Geffen reissue returned it to two.) Partridge evidently feels compelled to match musical sophistication with like words; he unfortunately outdoes himself. His prolix lyrics on offbeat but straightforward topics (war, paranoia, even love) read better than they sing and, as recorded, must be read to be understood. **English Settlement** tilts like an over-frosted wedding cake. That it doesn't quite topple is a tribute to the band.

XTC's most winning material, much of it written by bassist Colin Moulding, invariably turns up on their EPs and 45s. **5 Senses** gathers a few non-LP sides (including "Smokeless Zone" and "Wait Till Your Boat Goes Down") from 1980 and '81. But that EP was soon superseded by **Waxworks—Some Singles 1977–1982**, which cleverly assembles the band's 45s, almost all originally drawn from albums, on one superb LP. The accompanying second disc, **Beeswax—Some B-Sides 1977–1982**, collects their non-LP B-sides— not deathless music, but inventive as always and decidedly unpretentious. The advent of new technology a few years later yielded **The Compact XTC**, an 18-song CD-only singles compilation which picks up all of **Waxworks** and then continues, starting with "Great Fire" and running up through "Wake Up." (There is not, as yet anyway, a corresponding B-sides CD.)

Following drummer Terry Chambers' departure, XTC next found themselves in a precarious position with their British record label, which was reportedly hesitant to release another brilliant but uncommercial album. That hitch delayed the appearance of **Mummer** for quite some time. As far removed as it may be from the quirky pop that originally characterized XTC's music, it's a lovely record, resplendent in a quiet, rural sound and ethos. Co-existing with the invigorating whomp of "Great Fire" and the loud rock and disgusted lyrics of "Funk Pop a Roll," there's Partridge's rustic "Love on a Farmboy's Wages" and Moulding's lazy "Wonderland," offering a perfect summery escape from the pressures and excitement of rock. **Mummer**: Music for Picnics.

Continuing on as a trio, **The Big Express** returned XTC to the world of urban reality: disgruntled songs about life in the big city, celebrating the alternative ("The Everyday Story of Smalltown") but, more surprisingly, again playing full-blast rock rather than bucolic lyricism. "All You Pretty Girls," incorporating a British folk idiom, is as catchy a number as they've ever done; and the record's overall sense of recharged enthusiasm is quite infectious.

Partridge's unfortunate post-release sniping notwithstanding, XTC's collaboration with Todd Rundgren on **Skylarking** yielded an organic album as good as any in their catalogue. The songs are thoughtful, winsome, introspective and melodic; Rundgren's likeminded production (and sequencing) brings them out in a cavalcade that is resonant and memorable. Moulding's best numbers—"Grass," "The Meeting Place" and "Big Day"—address (respectively) sex al fresco, illicit romance and the dangers of marriage; meanwhile, Partridge worries about making ends meet in "Earn Enough for Us" and space junk in "Another Satellite." Adult, provocative and plainly brilliant. (A pre-LP UK 12-inch of "Grass" b/w "Extrovert" and "Dear God" focused unexpected attention on Partridge's startling and controversial song about religious skepticism. Those three numbers were then released as an American EP, adding "Earn Enough for Us." Finally, the album was withdrawn and reissued with "Dear God" replacing "Mermaid Smiled," as it does on the CD.)

Partnered with producer John Leckie, XTC launched a pseudonymous side career in 1985 as the Dukes of Stratosphear. The day-glo watches and peace symbols on the cover of the carefully-appointed satirical **25 O'Clock** mini-album match the six Rutlesque rewrites of '60s classics like "I Had Too Much to Dream Last Night." Unfortunately, the gaily psychedelic put-on is so clever and careful that it is less funny than notable for its accomplishment. The full-length **Psonic Psunspot** downplays the pose with a far lighter parodic touch—the most prominent touchstone is **White Album**-era Beatles—and basically amounts to a very casual XTC album with an intuitive '60s feel rather than a conscious art context. By not striving for specific imitation and merely enjoying the romp, the Dukes have a better time, and so do listeners.

Although **Psonic Psunspot** was issued on CD by itself, the CD entitled **Chips from the Chocolate Fireball** consists of both Dukes' records. [si/iar]

See also *Robert Fripp, Shriekback.*

X-TEENS
. . . big boy's dream EP (Moonlight) 1980
X-Teens (Dolphin) 1983
Love and Politics (Dolphin) 1984

On their first release, these North Carolina popsters (produced by Don Dixon) seem ready to burst with giddy excitement. The songs rush along as bassist Kitty Moses, guitarist Robert Bittle and organist Todd Jones alternately sings their hearts out. Additionally, Jones plays a prominent instrumental role and paints the X-Teens in a number of happy hues.

Their eponymous album, released several years after being recorded, has a less frantic tone, but just as much enthusiasm and witty pop intelligence. Bittle and Jones individually write songs that encompass a lot of stylistic ground, from romantic sophistication to a wackiness that variously resembles XTC and the B-52's. Without adding anything inappropriately slick, Dixon (working here with Mitch Easter) gussies the band up a tad and makes the LP a ton of fun.

More mature and varied, yet no less enticing, **Love and Politics** is the X-Teens' final release; in 1985, they divided in half to form two new groups. The only thing really missing here is the lyrical silliness, downplayed in favor of more straightforward prose. An excellent pure pop album utterly free of guile and bogus commercial compromises. [iar]

XYMOX
See *Clan of Xymox.*

Y Y Y Y Y Y Y

YACHTS

Yachts (Radar-Polydor) 1979
Without Radar (Radar-Polydor) 1980

Liverpool's Yachts were capable of alternating a scaled-down version of pomp-rock (faster, more cheaply tricked out, no instrumental exhibitionism) and '60s-influenced rock with leader Henry Priestman's cheesy organ sound, not unlike an Anglicized Joe "King" Carrasco. And that in the service of humorously melodramatic caricatures of the usual boy/girl lyric fodder: love by letter ("Box 202"), unfair romantic competition ("Yachting Types," "Semaphore Love," etc.). Despite sympathetic production by Richard Gottehrer, Yachts sounds a bit tinny, and the group was unable to equal their mini-classic Stiff debut single ("Suffice to Say"), though the potential to do so is evident.

Not being taken seriously because of funny lyrics may have taken its toll; on Without Radar, the jokes and even the previously solid songwriting sound as thin as Martin Rushent's uncharacteristically poor production. [jg]

See also Christians, It's Immaterial.

YANKEES

High 'n' Inside (Big Sound) 1978

This odd album by rock writer-turned-musician Jon Tiven's band has some really good songs (mostly originals written or co-written by Tiven), guest appearances by Voidoid Ivan Julian, Alex Chilton and Hilly Michaels, and a musical range that covers MOR, power pop, Leon Russellish pseudo-gospel, devolved R&B, off-the-wall Spectorized production and more. High 'n' Inside is unpredictable and uneven, but well worth a listen or three. Tiven and his wife Sally have since concentrated on creating rock songs for movies. [iar]

YAZOO

Upstairs at Eric's (Mute-Sire) 1982 ●
You and Me Both (Mute-Sire) 1983 ●

Yazoo (known as Yaz in the US) was one of England's most interesting synth-pop duets, mostly because of the sharp contrast provided by vocalist Alison Moyet's incredibly rich and soulful voice, a more powerful and emotive sound than one generally expected to hear paired with high-tech instrumentation in those days. Along with ex-Depeche Mode synthesist/songwriter Vince Clarke, Yazoo represented a stylistic breakthrough that proved influential in the development of electronic-based dance music.

Unfortunately, while Upstairs at Eric's is admirable for its experimentalism, it contains just one really striking song (the beautiful ballad, "Only You"), some moderately interesting quirky pop ("Too Pieces," "Bad Connection"), two solid dance numbers ("Don't Go" and "Situation") made tolerable by the band's talent and strengths and one truly awful piece of tape-looping ("I Before E Except After C").

You and Me Both, on the other hand, offers a better selection, from Moyet's defiant and atmospheric "Nobody's Diary" and funky "Sweet Thing" to Clarke's bouncy "Walk Away from Love." There are some serious low-points to be sure, but in general it's a more even and exciting album, further exploring the blend's possibilities.

Given the dynamic tension of the partnership, it was hardly surprising when Moyet and Clarke decided, after two albums, to go their separate ways: he to form the Assembly (later, Erasure) and she to a successful solo career. [ks/iar]

See also *Erasure, Alison Moyet.*

YEAH YEAH NOH

Cottage Industry EP (nr/In Tape) 1984
Weakling Lines EP (nr/In Tape) 1984
Prick Up Your Ears EP (nr/In Tape) 1984
When I Am a Big Girl (nr/In Tape) 1985
Cutting the Heavenly Lawn of Greatness . . . Last Rites for the God of Love (nr/In Tape) 1985
Temple of Convenience EP (nr/In Tape) 1986
Fun on the Lawn Lawn Lawn (nr/Vuggum) 1986
The Peel Sessions EP (nr/Strange Fruit) 1987

Like In Tape labelmates the Creepers, this Leicester quartet (later quintet) displays some Fall influence (albeit less harsh) and makes things easy for record buyers by combining several releases onto a single disc. **When I Am a Big Girl** reprises the first three EPs in their entirety and has such highlights as "Cottage Industry," "Prick Up Your Ears" and "Starling Pillowcase and Why" which, like the rest of the record's songs, are unpolished, raw pop gems with smartass lyrics. Cymbal-less drums and chunky bass lines form a foundation for modest guitar work and Derek Hammond's deadpan baritone. Great fun.

Cutting the Heavenly Lawn of Greatness adds some well-placed psychedelic embellishments and a little (but just a wee bit) more production to the homespun sound. Lyrics are sharp as ever: "Home-Ownersexual" is the clever tale of a bored, dissatisfied housewife; "Stealing in the Name of the Lord" decries religious hypocrisy. Some earlier tracks pop up again in new versions, and the LP also contains the title track from the **Temple of Convenience** EP. Sadly, Yeah Yeah Noh disbanded upon that release but left behind a catalogue of great records, permeated with real DIY spirit, warmth and humor.

Fun on the Lawn Lawn Lawn is a posthumous collection of various sessions for John Peel's radio program. (Yeah Yeah Noh were one of his faves. One entire session, from January 1986, was also released by Strange Fruit.) It includes versions of most of their best tracks ("Home-Ownersexual" is listed as "Another Side of Mrs. Quill") and a few songs that are otherwise unavailable. [dgs]

YELLO

Solid Pleasure (Ralph) 1980 (Mercury) 1987 ●
Claro Que Si (Ralph) 1981 ●
Bostich EP (Stiff) 1982
You Gotta Say Yes to Another Excess (Elektra) 1983 (Mercury) 1987 ●
Yello EP (Elektra) 1983
Stella (Elektra) 1985 (Mercury) 1987 ●
One Second (Mercury) 1987 ●

Switzerland's Yello (Boris Blank, Dieter Meier and Carlos Peron—all non-musicians in the finest Brian Eno tradition) has harnessed the synthesizer to become one of the most important and creative bands working in the medium.

Solid Pleasure is a record of their exploration of the studio and instruments, surging with discovery and innovation. On this LP, Yello are dark experimenters of the highest order, treading fearlessly through a perilous forest of electronics. The music is a confident cross-pollination of lighthearted pop and avant-garde. Inspired.

Claro Que Si continues Yello's adventurous innovation, but applies it to dance music with stunning results. Meier's vocals, though limited in range, slide blissfully against Blank's synthesizer and backing vocals and Peron's tape effects to create a pop/disco album full of evocative, warm tunes, evincing a dynamism rare in this sort of music. And they stay far away from pretensions, too.

Bostich presents new versions of songs from the albums, with an otherwise unavailable track, "She's Got a Gun," added to the US edition. Remakes aren't normally essential listening, but Yello proves they're one of the few bands capable of transfiguring old material rather than rehashing it, and with exquisite intelligence at that.

Signing to Elektra (will wonders never cease?), Yello made **You Gotta Say Yes to Another Excess**, which contains some of their most accessible dance music, although it would be far from accurate to call Yello commercial or mainstream at this point. "I Love You" pushes a pulsing electro-beat and whispered vocals vaguely about driving, throwing in screeching tires to underscore the point. "No More Words" recites the title over herky-jerky rhythms and little else; "Great Mission" is a suave dramatic travelogue. The 23-minute EP that followed contains remixed, extended versions of three LP tracks plus "Bostich."

Stella—revealing a slimmed-down Yello of just Meier and Blank—adopts more of a Euro-disco sound, dropping the reliance on electronics and most of the weirdness to play it relatively straight. Meier's vocals have gone from wondrously strange to cloying; several guest musicians provide vocals, piano, drums and guitar, making this a most routine and non-intriguing release.

Meier and Blank split the chores on **One Second** simply: Boris composed and arranged the music, Dieter wrote and sings the lyrics. Guests include Shirley Bassey and ex-Associate Billy MacKenzie, who provided lyrics for two cuts and vocals for one. Continuing down the conservative path indicated on **Stella**, Yello pushes a reserved, suavely-textured sound that is dance-oriented, but not overpowered by rhythm. Polite Latin styles on a few songs provide character; continental excursions and adult pop fill out the program. A pleasant, debonair waste of time.

[sg/iar]

YELLOW MAGIC ORCHESTRA

Yellow Magic Orchestra (A&M) 1979
Solid State Survivor (Jap. Alfa) 1979
  (nr/Alfa) 1981
Public Pressure (Jap. Alfa) 1980
X00 Multiplies (Jap. Alfa) 1980
  (nr/Alfa-A&M) 1980
X00 Multiplies (A&M) 1980
BGM (A&M) 1981
Technodelic (Alfa) 1981
Service (Jap. Alfa) 1983
After Service (Jap. Alfa) 1983
Naughty Boys (Jap. Alfa) 1983
Naughty Boys Instrumental (Hol. Pickup)
  1985
Sealed (Jap. Alfa) 1985

For the technology-minded Japanese (who, after all, do have their own musical logic and traditions), the rock medium most suited to adaptation rather than bland mimicry has been electronic-oriented pop. By their third LP, YMO represented to Japanese kids a heterodoxy almost equivalent to the Sex Pistols and, in Japan at least, many times their commercial success.

None of the three members were musical neophytes at YMO's outset. While recording his first solo LP, session keyboardist Ryuichi Sakamoto met drummer Yukihiro Takahashi, who'd not only cut his own album but had been a member of the Sadistic Mika Band (Japan's well-known art-rock export

who made three LPs for UK Harvest) and its offshoot, the Sadistics. The pair met bassist/producer Haruomi Hosono, a veteran of two historically important Japanese bands, while he was cutting his *fourth* solo LP. (He's done more since, but unlike his two bandmates, his solo records have never been released in England or America. His mid-'80s **Video Game Music** employs the electronic sounds of arcade games.)

Despite the pedigree, YMO's first LP is merely inane electro-disco, distinguished only by efforts at diddling video-game blips and squonks into songs. **Solid State Survivor** (their second Japanese LP, issued intact but out of chronological sequence in the UK) is a qualitative leap forward: clever instrumentals and excellent electro-rock tunes with terse, sharp English lyrics by Chris Mosdell. Takahashi's flat, inflexible vocals are a mixed blessing—no silly histrionics, but an air of cool detachment that's, at least initially, off-putting.

X00 Multiplies has two more fine tracks in the same vein, but the rest of the original Japanese half-hour 10-incher is given over to mostly unfunny comedy skits (and two humorous tries at Archie Bell and the Drells' "Tighten Up"). In the UK, the LP of the same name adds the aural vid-bits from the first LP, but the US release retains only the title and the two good cuts, the rest being the best part of **Solid State Survivor**. **Public Pressure** is a live album.

BGM and **Technodelic** are both mixed bags. On the plus side, they explore new (for YMO) stylistic areas—"Strawberry Fields" gone synth, Germanic bleep strutting, bleak Anglo synth-rap—but little on either is as distinctive or just plain entertaining as Takahashi's or Sakamoto's solo work. Hosono's production (the first six YMO LPs, as well as discs by Sandii and the Sunsetz, Sheena and the Rokkets and others) has clarity but lacks the snap and depth that would make these two records come alive.

Service is a frustrating record for us non-Nipponese, since it alternates YMO tracks with cuts just as long as the songs by the comedic (?) theatre group S.E.T. It might be annoying to those who *do* speak Japanese, since no matter how good those bits may be, if you want to hear music, you won't appreciate the interruptions. It's doubly irksome because the songs are excellent. Wisely, **Naughty Boys** has equally good songs without the comedy. The melodies on both discs are much more accessible and consistently pleasing than any of the previous YMO LPs, with no noticeable shift in songwriting balance. (Beginning with **Service**, Peter Barakan, who's written lyrics for Takahashi's LPs, supplies them to YMO in place of Mosdell. Also, YMO produced these two albums as a group.)

After Service is a double live set, but the name has more to do with the order of its release than its content, drawing on previous records. **Sealed** is a four-disc boxed set.

[jg]

See also *Ryuichi Sakamoto, Yukihiro Takahashi.*

YELLOWMAN

Mister Yellowman (Shanachie) 1982
Bad Boy Skanking (Shanachie) 1982
Zungguzungguguzungguzeng (Shanachie) 1983
King Yellowman (CBS) 1984
Nobody Move Nobody Get Hurt (Shanachie) 1984
Galong Galong Galong (Shanachie) 1985
Going to the Chapel (Shanachie) 1986
Rambo (Moving Target) 1986 ●
Don't Burn It Down (Shanachie) 1987
Yellow Like Cheese (RAS) 1987 ●

YELLOWMAN/CHARLIE CHAPLIN

The Negril Chill [tape] (ROIR) 1988

Albino reggae toaster Yellowman (Winston Foster) parlayed his unusual looks and talent into overnight success. His music is versatile and engagingly comic in a dancehall style. Like his counterparts in American rap, he's often swaggering, boasting about his toasting and his luck with the ladies. Because his strut is good-natured and backed up by fierce turntable work (his improv and rhythm are extraordinary), he's extremely convincing, and has become quite a sex symbol. Due to his sudden notoriety, however, more than two dozen Yellowman albums flooded the market in the early '80s. Many are so-so live sets, collections of singles and outtakes, Jamaican-only releases, or team-ups with other djs. The listing above contains only his most widely available (in the US) studio LPs.

Mister Yellowman, the album that helped launch his international fame, remains among his best. Nearly every cut is strong, including "Mister Chin," "Two to Six Supermix" and the *My Fair Lady*-inspired "Yellowman Getting Married" (in the morning). While they often come close, none

of his other records equal this consistency and easy versatility.

Zungguzungguguzungguzeng, for instance, isn't even in the same league. For one thing, it's misleading (if not mistitled): seven of ten cuts are actually duets with another dj (Fathead). They make an okay team, but their rapport is mostly in a rub-a-dub style, and the record bogs down as a result. Best is the title tune, a solo toast to the music of Michigan and Smiley's "Diseases"; worst is "Who Can Make the Dance Ram," a reworking of Sammy Davis Jr.'s "Candy Man."

Admirably, CBS tried to encourage Yellowman's versatility when he signed with the label, but the resulting **King Yellowman** is another mixed success. Most of Side One is fine ("What Dat," for instance), but the flip is a mess. Yellowman meets Material for "Disco Reggae," tries to "Reggae Calypso" and finally covers Frankie Ford's pop hit "Sea Cruise." All of these fusion attempts go wildly astray.

Less contrived versatility is evident on his later Shanachie albums. **Nobody Move** is a bit spotty, but the strong cuts are really great. The title track, as well as "Strictly Mi Belly" and "Why You Bad So" are all cookers, guaranteed to make you rock and groove. **Galong** is also worth investigating, for it features an anti-Michael Jackson number called "Beat It"; "Reggae Win a Grammy," Yellowman's report on his trip to the awards ceremony; and "Skank Quadrille," a toast to Bunny Wailer's "Walk the Proud Land."

Going to the Chapel, on the other hand, lags a bit and is less consistent, although a variety of rhythms are featured and the title cut is a wacko cover of the Dixie Cups' "Chapel of Love." Track for track, **Don't Burn It Down** is stronger, full of energy and fire from first cut (the title song, a ganja anthem) to last (the consummately rude "Dry Head Adassa").

As the '80s progress, so does Yellowman's label-hopping. **Rambo**, on a Celluloid subsidiary, is a noble experiment featuring Robert Lyn on piano, Sly Dunbar on drums and Robbie Shakespeare going heavy on the bass synthesizer. The backup is unusually high-tech for a Yellowman record, but he raps up a storm, pushing the music aggressively forward like the character commemorated in the title track. (There's another appropriate cut called "Computerize.")

Yellow Like Cheese marks a return to

rootsy form: less dance-oriented and with sparser musical backup. (Unfortunately, the title cut never lives up to the promise of its name.) **The Negril Chill**, a joint recording with Charlie Chaplin, captures a live show from early 1987. [bk]

YIPES!
Yipes! (Millennium) 1979
A Bit Irrational (Millennium) 1980

Wisconsin's Yipes! first appeared on **Big Hits of Mid-America Vol. 3**, the watershed Twin/Tone compilation. Their two albums are filled with sprightly, hard-edged power pop given distinction by energetic, cliché-free music, witty songs and Pat McCurdy's expressive, gangly vocals. The first includes such neat originals as "Russian Roll" and "The Ballad of Roy Orbison," while the inferior **A Bit Irrational** has "Ballad of Rudolf Kaiser (Einstein)" as well as covers of the Supremes' "Come See About Me" and the Beach Boys' "Darlin'." What makes Yipes! worthwhile is their spirit of good fun, an avoidance of obvious derivativeness and well-conveyed enthusiasm. [iar]

YOBS
See *Boys*.

YO LA TENGO
Ride the Tiger (Coyote-Twin/Tone) 1986
New Wave Hot Dogs (Coyote-Twin/Tone) 1987

Led by Hoboken rock-crit types Ira Kaplan (vocals/guitar) and Georgia Hubley (drums), Yo La Tengo (named for the cry of the Spanish-speaking outfielder) nicely weds the underground noise-rock impulse and the fannish cover-band vibe. Rather than doing the eclectic dilettante bit, Kaplan, Hubley and rotating bandmates work their influences into a surprisingly cohesive and satisfying whole.

Ride the Tiger, produced by ex-Mission of Burma bassist Clint Conley, benefits from Dave Schramm's sterling guitarings which, like Kaplan's reedy (as in Lou) vocals, underline Yo La Tengo's vintage-Velvets connection. The band also covers Ray Davies' "The Big Sky," but it's originals like "Cone of Silence" and "The Forest Green" that make **Ride the Tiger** such a pleasure.

New Wave Hot Dogs suffers a bit from Schramm's absence, but it's more consistent than its predecessor, with distinctive originals ("House Fall Down," "Blocks from Groove St.") and a dead-ringer cover of Lou Reed's "It's Alright (The Way That You Live)." [hd]

PAUL YOUNG
No Parlez (Columbia) 1983 ●
The Secret of Association (Columbia) 1985 ●
Between Two Fires (Columbia) 1986 ●

From the ashes of London neo-soulsters the Q-Tips emerged Paul Young, whose smoky voice, singing a mixture of classics and originals, quickly put him in the British, and later, American charts. The choice of songs on **No Parlez** ranges from the prudent ("Love of the Common People," "Wherever I Lay My Hat (That's My Home)," both of which are magnificent) to the surreal (Joy Division's "Love Will Tear Us Apart," which Young slowly mangles beyond recognition). A few of the new compositions are swell as well. The Royal Family (his band) and the Fabulous Wealthy Tarts (singers) supply sympathetic backing; Laurie Latham's wide-screen production is appropriately lush but never abandons the rock basis that anchored classic Motown records of the '60s. Young's first solo outing is promising: a solid pop album by an especially good singer.

The Secret of Association, Young's follow-up as a big star, shows a far more judicious selection process at work, resulting in an exquisite collection that mixes appropriate covers with originals he co-wrote. Items like "Bite the Hand That Feeds," "I'm Gonna Tear Your Playhouse Down" and especially Daryl Hall's "Everytime You Go Away" showcase Young's carefully controlled vocals and Latham's exceptionally subtle production. Every clearly-articulated sound functions perfectly in the arrangements, resulting in seamless, emotionally resonant pop-soul creations.

Parting company with Latham, an increasingly self-confident Young co-wrote most of the songs and co-produced **Between Two Fires** with keyboardist Ian Kewley and Hugh Padgham. Although lacking the finely-honed impact of **The Secret of Association**, a few tracks (e.g., "Wonderland," "A Certain Passion," "Some People") and the generally high level of appealing quality prove that—in this case, at least—it's possible to tamper with success and not upset the apple cart. [iar]

YOUNG FRESH FELLOWS

The Fabulous Sounds of the Pacific
Northwest (PopLlama) 1984
Topsy Turvy (PopLlama) 1986
The Men Who Loved Music
(PopLlama-Frontier) 1987
Refreshments (PopLlama-Frontier)
1987
Totally Lost (Frontier) 1988 ●

ERNEST ANYWAY AND THE MIGHTY SQUIRRELS

Sing the Hits of Johnny Kidd and the
Pirates/Five Virgins (PopLlama) 1986

JIMMY SILVA AND THE EMPTY SET

Fly Like a Dog (PopLlama) 1987

From the back cover of **Fabulous Sounds**: "A collector's disc of the sounds that we in the Pacific Northwest live and play by—a high-hearted, medium-fi recording of such nostrums as the whistle of a ferryboat, the hoofbeats of the rodeo, the roar of racing hydroplanes and the musical beat of our symphonies and jazz." Nostrums? From the narrated grooves: mild frivolity like "Power Mowers Theme," "Teenage Dogs in Trouble" and "Rock and Roll Pest Control," played by an adaptable, skillful pop trio with folly in their minds and a tune in their hearts. Perfect.

Topsy Turvy only contains songs, but that's no hazard for such bright, well-played numbers as the traveloguish "Searchin' U.S.A." and "You've Got Your Head on Backwards," a "Tobacco Road"-styled beat rave-up borrowed from the estimable Sonics. Armed with a winsome sense of nerdiness (check out the teen angst of "Hang Out Right") and a finely-tuned grasp of Culture 101 ("The New John Agar"), the four Fellows put a humorous spin on everything they touch here, but not in such a jokey way that they can't be taken seriously. Another delightful outing.

The characters assassinated by **The Men Who Loved Music** (entitled **Chicago 19** on the spine: ask for it by name in your local record store) include an assortment of old tube stars (on "TV Dream"), a rueful tune about "Hank, Karen and Elvis" and the white-funking "Amy Grant." But there's nothing cruel about these iconic invocations—it's just the Fellows' way of saying "hey!" The quartet's best LP so far boasts winners in a number of mocking styles, e.g.,

the stomping "Get Outta My Cave" (a perfect song for the Troggs to cover), "I Got My Mojo Working (And I Thought You'd Like to Know)" and the blues-rocking "I Don't Let the Little Things Get Me Down." Despite their growing underground-band-makes-good coolness, they can still admit to selfconscious geekiness on the power-popping "When the Girls Get Here."

The seven-song **Refreshments** mini-LP gathers up rarities: "Back Room of the Bar" (recorded for but omitted from **Topsy Turvy**), "Beer Money" (included on the **Men Who Loved Music** cassette), "Young Fresh Fellows Update Theme" (an obscure 1985 single) and the previously-unissued "Broken Basket."

Singer Scott McCaughey's songs on **Totally Lost** give the Fellows the straightest, least inventively kooky things they've ever done. The LP is by no means bad, merely underwhelming. Despite flashes of familiar lyrical absurdity ("The Universal Trendsetter," "Take My Brain Away," "I'd Say That You Were Upset"), simplification, with a damaging air of haste, eliminates a lot of the band's ebullient personality in favor of guitar-rocking forthrightness. Some of the music preserves the ambitious cross-pollination ("Picky Piggy," "No Help at All," "Little Softy"), but **Totally Lost** as a whole is disappointingly serious and unimaginative. The CD substitutes a longer version of "Totally Lost Theme" and adds "You're Not Supposed to Laugh" and "World Tour '88."

Two related projects: As the Mighty Squirrels (and the New Age Urban Squirrels), the Fellows back Rob (Ernest Anyway) Morgan on a brilliant dual-concept album. One side covers pre-Beatles classics (intentionally overlooking the best-known "Shakin' All Over" and "Please Don't Touch") by Johnny Kidd and the Pirates; the flip attacks representatives of the rest of that decade: e.g., "Hair" and "Spirit in the Sky," which they devolve into cocktail lounge laxative sleaze.

Bay Area singer Jimmy Silva, a longtime associate who has written and recorded with the Fellows, gets the favor returned on his second album, **Fly Like a Dog**. McCaughey contributed to the songwriting; the entire band, alongside Smithereen Dennis Diken, onetime Beau Brummel Sal Valentino and others provide the instrumental backing for Silva's charging rock tunes. (Diken also appears on Silva's first LP.) [iar]

YOUNG MARBLE GIANTS

Colossal Youth (Rough Trade) 1980
Testcard EP (nr/Rough Trade) 1981
The Peel Sessions EP (nr/Strange Fruit) 1988

Singer Alison Statton and the Moxham brothers, Philip (bass) and Stuart (guitar, organ), from Cardiff managed to stay together long enough to produce one oddball album before apathy got the upper hand. Using few overdubs, **Colossal Youth** re-creates the mythical ambience of a beatnik coffeehouse. Statton's gentleness and the soft accompaniment contribute to a hushed mood that's either soporific or enchanting, depending on your point of view (or blood pressure). Minimalism never had such polite advocates before. Statton subsequently formed Weekend; Philip Moxham became the Gist. [jy]

See also *Gist*.

YOUTH AND BEN WATKINS

See *Brilliant*.

YOU'VE GOT FOETUS ON YOUR BREATH

See *Foetus*.

Y PANTS

Beat It Down (Neutral) 1982

The women who comprised this eccentric New York trio played drums, keyboards (nothing fancy or high-tech), bass and ukulele. They also sang—such numbers as "The Shah Song," lyrics like "Don't be afraid to be boring" and adaptations of "Bert" Brecht. Mostly, though, **Beat It Down** consists of skimpy, dada music that is baldly amateurish but charming. The Y Pants offer no stylistic pretensions, merely highly idiosyncratic music for aficionados of the arcane, intelligent and delightful. [iar]

YUNG WU

See *Feelies*.

Z Z Z Z Z Z Z Z

THIERRY ZABOITZEFF
See *Art Zoyd.*

ZANTEES
Out for Kicks (Bomp) 1980
Rhythm Bound (Midnight) 1983
The Zantees EP (Midnight) 1984

The Zantees, a New York-based rock-abilly combo, aren't too serious about their music, which makes **Out for Kicks** delight-fully irreverent. Singing and playing with a spirit money can't buy and synthesizers can't replicate, they easily make the oldies ("I Thought It Over," "Cruisin'," three others) their own; the originals ("Gas Up," "Blonde Bombshell," six others) sound like oldies. A futile gesture, perhaps, but a grand one. Poor recording quality adds atmosphere. (Bassist Rob Norris graduated to the Bongos.)

With a one-take loose sound on **Rhythm Bound**, method singer Billy Miller barks out such ethnic 'billy originals as "Tic Tac Toe" and "Money to Burn." Drummer Miriam Linna also vocalizes on a couple: "I Need a Man" and "I'm Ready." The guitar-picking Statile brothers' proficient chromatic single-string playing provides a dual carburetor rhythm thrust.

The subsequent 12-inch combines two tracks from the second album with a pair of blazing live oldies (one sung each by Miller and Linna). [si/iar]

PETER ZAREMBA'S LOVE DELEGATION
See *Fleshtones.*

ZARKONS
See *Alley Cats.*

ZASU PITTS MEMORIAL ORCHESTRA
Greatest Hits! Volume One EP (Slithering Disc) 1984

STEPHEN ASHMAN
Cooler Than Death (Slithering Disc) 1984

San Francisco bassist Ashman formed the ZP Orchestra just to play classic songs from Motown and other sources casually at parties, but the loosely-constituted soul revue proved mighty popular in those parts. The menu on **Greatest Hits!** includes "To Sir with Love" as well as "Nowhere to Run" and "River Deep Mountain High," all given rev-erent big-band treatment with a rotating 15-strong cast of singers and players. A little too polite and slavish perhaps, but good-hu-mored fun all the same.

The earlier **Cooler Than Death** features almost exclusively original material and only three musicians other than Ashman in com-mon, but the Orchestra still gets cover bill-ing. (Drummer Gina Schock, then still in the Go-Go's, appears on three of the seven tracks.) In this far more ambitious undertak-ing, Ashman plays slithery, rhythmic instru-mentals with inventive horn work, sardonic dance rock, low-key/dramatic soundtrack music, even a noisy piano improvisation. But the pièce de resistance is a brilliant juxtaposi-tion: Katie Guthorn singing George Gersh-win's "Summertime" over the "Peter Gunn Theme." [iar]

ZEITGEIST
See *Reivers.*

ZERRA I
Zerra I (nr/Mercury) 1985

651

ZERRA ONE
The Domino Effect (Mercury) 1986 •

Todd Rundgren has said that, as a producer, he can make bands sound like anything they choose. Little doubt as to what this client asked for on their first album: they emulate a certain (far more talented) quartet of fellow Dubliners. (It's a wonder the guitarist doesn't call himself the Ledge or something.) Zerra I go for a big, bombastic sound (cf. Rundgren's Meat Loaf album), with lyrics full of grandiose imagery. On "Tumbling Down," singer Paul Bell majestically proclaims, "We see it, we hear it, we know, we say." Problem: they don't.

Presumably to overcome confusion as to whether their name is Zerra I or Zerra 1, they started spelling it out on **The Domino Effect**. A trio with revolving drummers (including Pete Thomas, the LP's only real attraction), they offer up nine more anthems in the four-and-a-half-to-six-minute range, with Barry Blue providing even a bigger sound than Todd. Instead of the previous U2-style density, however, the approach is more crystalline, with lots of synths, a big guitar sound and female background vocals not unlike, say, the Psychedelic Furs. Once again, not one song sticks. Three strikes and you're out, guys. [dgs]

Z'EV
Elemental Music (Subterranean) 1982
Production and Decay of Spatial Relations
   (Hol. Backstreet) 1982
The Kremlin Party [tape] (Hol. Kremlin) 1983
My Favorite Things (Subterranean) 1984

STEFAN WEISSER
Contexts & Poextensions EP (Subterranean)
   1981
Editeditions & Contexts EP (Subterranean)
   1982
Life Sentence—An Uns Retrospective [tape]
   (Subterranean) 1982

Z'EV ET AL
Fifty Gates [tape] (Hol. Staalplatz) 1983

Z'EV/PSYCHIC TV
Berlin Atonal Vol. 1 (Ger. Atonal) 1984

Elemental Music, recorded live in San Francisco in early 1981, finds bald percussionist Z'ev (Stefan Weisser) creating an amorphous and utterly atonal wall of pulsating sound on instruments that are neither identified nor aurally identifiable. Although different from what one usually thinks of in

terms of ambient music—this shit gets *loud!*—as a soundscape for the post-industrial wasteland, it's fine in a numbing sort of way. (Z'ev's pioneering noise work prefigures similar experimental efforts by such metallic heavy hitters as Einstürzende Neubauten and Test Dept.)

The Weisser EPs are 7-inchers that can be played at any speed (although it only makes sense at 78, where it sounds like something a cheap cassette recorder might have picked up inside a factory). The **Life Sentence** tape is an expensive limited edition package recorded live in 1980. Z'ev/Weisser has also performed live as a featured musician in Glenn Branca's "Symphony #2," in which he did a lot of Neubautenish smashing together of large metal objects.

My Favorite Things—divided into an "Access" side and a "Memory" side—collects ten live performances, recorded in America and Europe between 1979 and 1983. Z'ev's half of **Berlin Atonal**, an LP he shares with Psychic TV, is a typically exhausting side-long piece ("Titan Night") recorded live in Germany, 3 December 1983. **Fifty Gates** is a cassette with one side of Z'ev and an international side of various artists. There's plenty more, and I can't help wondering how hard it would be for Z'ev to take audience requests . . . [iar]

ZIPPERS
The Zippers EP (Rhino) 1981

Ray Manzarek produced this six-song mini-album for LA's Zippers, a longstanding punk outfit with strong pop tendencies. Although once strictly a tough club band, the tracks here expose a mature, musical quartet with songs and skills aplenty; the mood runs hot *and* cold. A neat record, but deduct points for swiping the Small Faces' "What' cha Gonna Do About It" for an "original," "I'm in Love." [iar]

ZODIAC MINDWARP AND THE LOVE REACTION
High Priest of Love (nr/Food) 1986
Tattooed Beat Messiah (Vertigo) 1987 •

Perhaps hoping to repeat the career feat of ex-*Smash Hits* editor-cum-Pet Shop Boy Neil Tennant, onetime *Flexipop!* art director Mark Manning adopted the grungelicious psychedelic motor-thug persona of Zodiac

Mindwarp, concocted a ridiculous story about being from another planet, assembled a backing band with names like Slam Thunderhide, Trash D Garbage and Cobalt Stargazer, and set about to test the gullibility of the pop world with a great single called "Prime Mover." Brilliantly produced by Liverpool coolsters Dave Balfe (ex-Teardrop Explodes) and Bill Drummond (Zoo label entrepreneur/Echo and the Bunnymen manager), **Tattooed Beat Messiah** (originally released in the UK as **High Priest of Love**) crosses AC/DC with T. Rex: a back-straightening, breath-taking guitar assault, intentionally low-brow wiseacre lyrics and chanted choruses that demand enthusiastic attention. The melodic headbanging metal power could give Motorhead, Judas Priest or Van Halen a youthful run for their money; one can savor the selfconscious stupidity of songs like "Backseat Education" and "Let's Break the Law" either as sophisticated parody or the real thing.   [iar]

ZONES

Under Influence (nr/Arista) 1979

This offshoot of Midge Ure's pre-Rich Kids Scottish pop outfit, Slik, had strong players, two of whom—guitarist Willy Gardner and keyboardist Billy McIsaac—wrote good songs and one of whom (Gardner) had an attractive if limited vocal style, like a young hybrid of Mick Ronson and Dave Edmunds. But what to do with it all? Pop? Hard stuff? Commercial new wave? Reggae-pop? The Zones try a little of everything on **Under Influence** without any forceful, unifying personality, despite passing nods to Mott and the Skids (which two Zones later joined). No bad cuts, but only one rises from enjoyable to exciting.   [jg]

ZOUNDS

The Curse of Zounds (nr/Rough Trade) 1982

Someone must have slipped one of those post-anarcho-syndicalist pamphlets in with these guys' *Beano* comics! This is sturdy, above-average pop-punk with some surprisingly infectious hooks. But the foursome ain't just disaffected youngsters lookin' for a kiss (or any ol' white riot)—they're searching out the meaning of life in the post-industrial capitalist system. As long as you've got the tunes, guys—go for it! Zounds later issued a singles compilation on an Italian label.   [jg]

TAPPER ZUKIE

Man Ah Warrior (nr/Klik) 1974 (Mer) 1977
MPLA (Jam. Klik) 1976 (nr/Front Line) 1978
Tapper Roots (nr/Front Line) 1979
Peace in the Ghetto (nr/Front Line) 1979
In Dub (nr/Front Line) 1979
Black Man (nr/Mobiliser) 1979
Raggy Joey Boy (nr/Mobiliser) 1982
Earth Running (nr/Mobiliser) 1983

Though Tapper (or Tappa) Zukie isn't active in the reggae mainstream, his toasting, which combines staunchly Rasta lyrics with heavy roots accompaniment, has always enjoyed an audience. His rock notoriety was boosted in the late '70s via an association with the Patti Smith Group; **Man Ah Warrior** was reissued by Lenny Kaye on the Mer label. Cuts like "Simpleton Badness," "Viego" (the Jamaican sound system where he got his start) and "A Message to the Pork Eaters" fill the LP with dread, seasoned with irony and humor. Not to be missed.

MPLA is likewise classic and **Tapper Roots** is almost as good. **Peace in the Ghetto**, on the other hand, is lackluster and uninspired; despite the inclusion of the single "Phensic" (retitled "Dangerous Woman"), the rhythms are flabby, the toasting less interesting. Parting company with Virgin/Front Line, Zukie returned to Jamaica.

His work in recent years is decent if inconsistent. **Black Man** is sturdy, as is the first side of **Earth Running**, which features "The General," a tribute to the late General Echo. (Side Two, however, has two unconvincing disco cuts.) **Raggy Joey Boy** has more singing than toasting.   [bk]

SOURCES

For more information on non-mainstream music, the following publications—all available by subscription—are recommended, as are the two retail establishments at the end:

OPTION: This excellent bi-monthly covers a wide range of alternative musics, from underground to exotic. The articles are generally good, there are always plenty of reviews—even the ads are worth perusing. (Lots of mail order sources.) Sonic Options Network, 2345 Westwood Blvd. #2, Los Angeles CA 90064; 213-474-2600.

THE BIG TAKEOVER: Jack Rabid's writing is the backbone of this stimulating and readable fanzine, which has extensive interviews with bands and a lot of provocative record and concert reviews. 249 Eldridge Street, New York NY 10002.

FLIP SIDE: Los Angeles' leading punkzine has been going for over a decade, and remains as unspoiled and enthusiastic now as it ever was. Lots of interviews and a great letter section covers the international scene in addition to California. Box 363, Whittier CA 90608.

ROCKPOOL NEWSLETTER: This venerable bi-weekly trade publication has plenty in it for non-industry types. It's not a fun read, but contains plenty of dope on new releases and the state of the independent label scene. 83 Leonard Street, New York NY 10013; 212-219-0077.

THE CATALOGUE: Also geared towards industry folk, this British monthly is all about independent-label records, and the quality and amount of information should please even the most rabid fan. Airmail subscriptions are pricey, but worthwhile for the right people. 61 Collier Street, London N1 9BE; 01-833-2843.

The New Music Distribution Service publishes a huge annual catalogue of offbeat records from numerous labels. Lots of obscure stuff you won't find in your local store and a fascinating browse. 500 Broadway, New York NY 10012; 212-925-2121.

See Hear is a unique store (open seven days a week, afternoons to early evening) that carries only music magazines—from hip imports to tiny fanzines. They publish a catalogue and do sales by mail. 59 East 7th Street, New York NY 10003; 212-505-9781.

ABOUT THE EDITOR

Ira Robbins co-founded *Trouser Press* magazine in 1974 while completing an electrical engineering degree; he was Publisher and Editorial Director of the New York-based music monthly when it ceased to exist ten years—and 96 issues—later. He has edited and/or contributed to numerous books on rock music, including *The Virgin Rock Yearbook 1983* and *The Rolling Stone Review 1985;* his writing has also appeared in music magazines large and small. A lifelong resident of New York, he has been a rock'n'roll fanatic ever since hearing Del Shannon's "Hats off to Larry" on the radio in 1961.